OF THE UNITED STATES

N

THE ORIGINAL

UNITED STATES

(BY TREATY WITH BRITAIN, 1783)

ANA

SE

303)

S

D, 1845

1810 1813

(SEIZED FROM
SPAIN)

FLORIDA
(BY TREATY WITH SPAIN, 1819)

The political consolidation of
half a continent, 1783 – 1853

THE AMERICAN PAGEANT

A History of the Republic

The American Pageant

A HISTORY OF THE REPUBLIC

THIRD EDITION

THOMAS A. BAILEY
Stanford University

D. C. Heath and Company BOSTON

Preface

LIKE its own ancient redwood trees, the United States today towers gigantic and unique. It is the oldest large-scale democracy, and it continues to thrive under the oldest of written constitutions. It has made substantial contributions —in many cases noteworthy ones—to every phase of human activity. The record is highly impressive and richly colored, yet many Americans, their tastes dulled by superficial familiarity, are inclined to dismiss their history as commonplace and dull. The present book unfolds a narrative which, it is hoped, will help stimulate interest in what must be recognized as a truly magnificent achievement by the American people.

In attempting to write a book that may be read with some sense of pleasure and excitement, I have purposely thrust the human actors forward on the stage and have emphasized the color and drama of the story. My intention in doing so has been not so much to entertain as to create a sympathetic understanding of the problems confronting our statesmen, and to implant a more lively concern for the lessons of the past. A reader who relives our history cannot fail to come away with a deeper appreciation of the hardships and contributions of the men and women who built America.

I have made a conscious effort to avoid burdening the narrative with more detail than seemed necessary for a proper understanding of historical developments. The emphasis is on causes and effects; on underlying trends and movements. American history is here conceived as a broad stream that flows forward, with the most clearly identifiable channel the political one. Attention is concentrated on the main channels, and on the more significant tributaries that flow into them. For further exploration the reader is referred to the rewarding accounts that are listed in the carefully selected bibliographies.

THOMAS A. BAILEY

Stanford University

Preface to the Second Edition

THE hurried march of events, combined with the friendly reception given *The American Pageant*, has necessitated a new edition. The most conspicuous changes are the addition of a new chapter on the Eisenhower era, the extensive revision of the short concluding chapter, and the expansion of the bibliographies. In addition, scores of revisions have been made throughout the book to incorporate certain corrections, to reflect the findings of recent scholarship, and to update statistics. The index has been expanded and entirely reset.

Attention is especially directed to the bibliographical addenda at the end of each chapter under the heading New Titles. The original Select Readings were purposely kept brief, partly because of the existence of the detailed *Harvard Guide to American History*, published in 1954. The appearance of many titles in the past six years suggested the desirability of making the end-of-chapter bibliographies of *The American Pageant* more inclusive. In a sense the *Harvard Guide* has been brought up to date by including all of the more important book titles. The Supplementary Bibliography in the appendix has also been revised and expanded, and a new section entitled The Pick of the Paperbacks has been added.

I am keenly aware of my debt of gratitude to the dozens of friends and critics who made suggestions that I have incorporated in this second edition. Four of my colleagues, Richard S. Cramer, Don E. Fehrenbacher, John J. Johnson, and Otis A. Pease, graciously read and helpfully commented on the new Eisenhower chapter.

THOMAS A. BAILEY

Stanford University

Preface to the Third Edition

The friendly reception accorded *The American Pageant* has necessitated a third edition on this its tenth anniversary of publication. It now appears not only in a hard-cover edition but also in a two-volume soft-cover edition.

The essential features of this new edition are as follows: (1) The inclusion of a new chapter on the Kennedy and early Johnson years, together with illustrations, charts, and tables. (2) A partial rewriting and complete resetting of the last chapter. (3) A consolidation, expansion, and updating of the end-chapter bibliographies, with a conspicuous labeling of all titles now known to be paperbacked. The emphasis is on readable and recent titles which will help to supplement the *Harvard Guide*. (4) An expansion and further refinement of the *Supplementary Bibliography* in the Appendix, with a labeling of titles in paperback. (5) A revision of many of the plates where recent scholarship has necessitated corrections or other substantial material change; alterations, minor or major, have been made on about one-fourth of the original pages. (6) An updating of certain charts and some tabular data to include the most recent census returns and other information, as well as the addition of the two new amendments to the Constitution. (7) An expansion and resetting of the index.

As before, I am indebted to many people for assistance, including colleagues and also students, a number of whom have mailed in helpful and encouraging comments. Dr. Hugh Ross of the College of San Mateo, collaborator in *The American Pageant Guidebook*, did yeoman work in helping to prepare the new bibliographies and in commenting on the new chapter, as did Mr. William R. Meyer of Stanford University.

THOMAS A. BAILEY

Stanford University

First Edition Acknowledgments

My first debt is to the earlier laborers in the vineyard, whose numerous published contributions cannot be fully indicated in the capsuled bibliographies. In addition, numerous friends were generous enough to read and comment on portions of chapters, individual chapters, or groups of chapters relating to their specialties. While here acknowledging my deep indebtedness, I absolve them of all responsibility for my own shortcomings. They are:

Professor Thomas P. Abernethy, of the University of Virginia; Professor Charles A. Allen, of Stanford University; Mr. Francis F. Beirne, of Baltimore; Professor Carl F. Brand, of Stanford University; Dr. Edward H. Brooks, of Stanford University; Professor Robert P. Browder, of the University of Colorado; Professor Ira V. Brown, of Pennsylvania State University; Professor Claude A. Buss, of Stanford University; Professor Dan E. Clark, of the University of Oregon; Professor Leland H. Creer, of the University of Utah; Mr. George Dangerfield, of Carpinteria, California; Professor Wallace E. Davies, of the University of Pennsylvania; Professor Alexander DeConde, of Duke University; Professor Harold C. Deutsch, of the University of Minnesota; Dr. William Diamond, of Washington, D.C.; Professor Brainerd Dyer, of the University of California at Los Angeles; Professor Howard M. Ehrmann, of the University of Michigan; Professor Charles Fairman, of Harvard University; Professor Sidney B. Fay, of Harvard University; Professor Don E. Fehrenbacher, of Stanford University; Professor Harold H. Fisher, of Stanford University; Professor John Hope Franklin, of Howard University; Professor Frank Freidel, of Harvard University; Professor Ralph H. Gabriel, of Yale University; Professor Paul W. Gates, of Cornell University; Professor Norman A. Graebner, of Iowa State College; Professor Wood Gray, of the George Washington University; Professor Fletcher M. Green, of the University of North Carolina; Professor Alfred H. Grommon, of Stanford University; Professor Edward O. Guerrant, of Los Angeles State College; Professor William B. Hesseltine, of the University of Wisconsin; Professor Richard Hofstadter, of Columbia University; Professor Edgar A. Hornig, of San Jose State College; Dr. George F. Howe, of Washington, D.C.; Professor H. Stuart Hughes, of Stanford University; Professor William T. Hutchinson, of the University of Chicago; Professor W. Turrentine Jackson, of the University of California at Davis; Professor Merrill M. Jensen, of the University of Wisconsin; Professor John J. Johnson, of Stanford University; Professor Frank W. Klingberg, of the University of North Carolina; Professor George H. Knoles, of Stanford University; Professor Arnaud B. Leavelle, of Stanford University; Professor Richard W. Leopold, of Northwestern University; Professor Arthur S. Link, of Northwestern University; Dr. Seward W. Livermore, of Washington, D.C.; Professor Ella Lonn, of Goucher College; Professor Ralph H. Lutz, of Stanford University; Dr. Beverly McAnear, of Stanford University; Professor Anatole G. Mazour, of Stanford University; Professor Frederick Merk, of Harvard University; Professor John C. Miller, of Stanford University; the Reverend Robert M. Minto, of Stanford University; Professor Elting E. Morison, of the Massachusetts Institute of Technology; Professor George E. Mowry, of the University of California at Los Angeles; Professor Clair E. Nelsen, of Fresno State College; Professor Curtis P. Nettels, of Cornell University; Dr. Jeannette P. Nichols, of Philadelphia, Pa.; Professor Roy F. Nichols, of the University of Pennsylvania; Professor Charles D. O'Malley, of Stanford University; Professor E. Louise Peffer, of Stanford University; Professor Earl Pomeroy, of the University of Oregon; Dr. Rollie E. Poppino, of Washington, D.C.; President Harry W. Porter, of Fredonia State Teachers College; Professor Julius W. Pratt, of the University of Buffalo; Professor Howard H. Quint, of the University of South Carolina; Professor James F. Ragland, of Long Beach State College; Professor Armin

Rappaport, of the University of California at Berkeley; Professor J. Fred Rippy, of the University of Chicago; Professor Rolland C. Rogers, of Stanford University; Professor Earle D. Ross, of Iowa State College; Professor Theodore Saloutos, of the University of California at Los Angeles; Professor Max H. Savelle, of the University of Washington; Dr. Bernadotte E. Schmitt, of the University of Chicago; Professor Louis M. Sears, of Purdue University; Dr. Charles Seymour, of Yale University; Dr. Daniel M. Smith, of Stanford University; Dr. Charles P. Stacey, of the Canadian Department of National Defense, Ottawa; Professor Kenneth M. Stampp, of the University of California at Berkeley; Professor Carl B. Swisher, of the Johns Hopkins University; Professor Glyndon G. Van Deusen, of the University of Rochester; Professor Albert T. Volwiler, of Ohio University; Professor Wayne S. Vucinich, of Stanford University; Professor Richard L. Watson, Jr., of Duke University; Dr. Charles M. Wiltse, of Washington, D.C.; Professor Oscar O. Winther, of Indiana University; Professor Harvey Wish, of Western Reserve University; and Professor C. Vann Woodward, of the Johns Hopkins University.

The cooperation of hundreds of Stanford students, both in seminars and in undergraduate lecture classes, has been of inestimable value. In addition, ten graduate or undergraduate students read and commented on much or all of the manuscript. They are: William M. Armstrong, John C. Burnham, Stuart G. Cross, Paul H. Gertmenian, Philip J. Houseman, Alice McKinney, Raymond G. O'Connor, Carl Grant Spaeth, John O. Tipple, and Frank F. Walker, Jr.

Dr. Vaughn D. Bornet, now of the Commonwealth Club of California, subjected an earlier draft to an amazingly meticulous reading. Mrs. Margaret Treat, of the Ethel Walker School, Simsbury, Connecticut, painstakingly checked the factual data and contributed many valuable suggestions growing out of her teaching experience and wide reading. Wise counsel regarding their specialties was provided by four colleagues: Professors Edith R. Mirrielees, Joseph E. Williams, Edgar B. Wesley, and Arthur Yvor Winters. The staff of the Stanford Library proved unfailingly helpful, particularly Mrs. Maria Volkov and Mr. Jack Plotkin. Secretarial help of a high order was cheerfully provided by the secretary of the History Department, Mrs. Celeste C. McKee. Special thanks go to Dr. Marie L. Edel, of D. C. Heath and Company, for superb editorial assistance. Mr. Russell H. Lenz, Chief Cartographer of the *Christian Science Monitor*, drew the maps, graphs, charts, and diagrams. They speak for themselves.

Contents

Maps and Charts

BY RUSSELL H. LENZ

xi

THE AMERICAN PAGEANT

A History of the Republic

Sail, sail thy best, ship of Democracy,
Of value is thy freight, 'tis not the Present only,
The Past is also stored in thee,
Thou holdest not the venture of thyself alone, not of
  the Western continent alone,
Earth's résumé entire floats on thy keel, O ship, is
  steadied by thy spars,
With thee Time voyages in trust, the antecedent na-
  tions sink or swim with thee,
With all their ancient struggles, martyrs, heroes, epics,
  wars, thou bear'st the other continents,
Theirs, theirs as much as thine, the destination-port
  triumphant. . . .

WALT WHITMAN

THOU MOTHER WITH THY EQUAL BROOD, 1872

1

New World Beginnings

*. . . For I shall yet live to see it [Virginia] an
Inglishe nation.*

SIR WALTER RALEIGH, 1602

Perspectives

SEVERAL billion years ago that whirling speck of dust known as the earth,
fifth in size among the planets, came into being.

About six thousand years ago—only the day before yesterday geologi-
cally—recorded history began. Certain peoples of the Middle East, developing a primitive culture, gradually emerged from the haze of the past.

Nearly five hundred years ago—only yesterday—the American continents were uncovered. This epochal achievement, one of the most dramatic in the chronicles of mankind, opened breath-taking new vistas, and
these in turn reacted vibrantly upon the Old World.

The two new continents eventually brought forth a score of sovereign
republics. The most influential of this brood—the United States of America
—was born a pygmy and developed into a giant. It was destined to leave
a mighty imprint upon the rest of the world as a result of its refreshingly
liberal ideals, its revolutionary democratic experiment, and its boundless

opportunities for the oppressed and underprivileged of foreign lands. The
enormous productiveness of its assembly-line machines, among numerous
advantages, ultimately caused it to become a decisive weight in the world
balance of power.

The pageant of the American people, fascinating though it is, does not
loom large on the time chart of man's known past. The roots of the United
States reach back into the subsoil of the colonial years more deeply than
is commonly supposed.

3

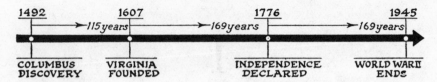

The American republic, which is still relatively young, was from the outset singularly favored. It started from scratch on a vast and virgin continent, which was so sparsely peopled by Indians that they could be eliminated or pushed aside. Such a magnificent opportunity for a great democratic experiment may never come again, for no other huge, fertile, and uninhabited areas are left in the temperate zones of this crowded planet.

The United States, despite its marvelous development, will one day reach its peak, as Greece and Rome did. It may ultimately fall upon evil days, as they did. But whatever uncertainties the future may hold, the past at least is secure, and it will richly repay examination.

Impulses to Discovery

The American continents were slow to yield their virginity. The all-conquering Romans, a half century after the birth of Christ, expanded their empire northwestward as far as Britain. But for nearly fifteen hundred years thereafter the New World lay unknown and unsuspected, awaiting its discoverers. It is true that about the year 1000 A.D. blond-bearded Norsemen from Scandinavia chanced upon the northeastern shoulder of North America, at a place abounding in wild grapes which they named Vinland. But their settlements were soon abandoned, and the discovery was forgotten, except in Scandinavian saga and song.

The United States was to be a child of Europe, not of England alone. One must seek in the Old World that momentous chain of events which

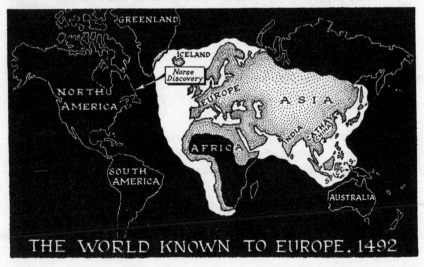

THE WORLD KNOWN TO EUROPE, 1492

led to a drive toward the Far East—and a completely accidental discovery of the New World.

The Christian Crusaders must take high rank among the indirect discoverers of America. Tens of thousands of these European warriors, clad in shining armor, invaded Palestine during the 11th to the 14th centuries. Whatever their true motives, they avowedly were attempting to wrest the Holy Land from the polluting hand of the Moslem infidel. Foiled in their repeated attempts, these Christian soldiers did manage to come into closer contact with the exotic delights of Asia—delights already introduced to Europe on a limited scale. The European "barbarians" learned more fully the value of spices for spoiled and monotonous food; of silk for rough skins; of drugs for aching flesh; of perfumes for unbathed bodies; and of colorful draperies for gloomy castles.

But the luxuries of the Far East were almost prohibitively expensive in Europe. They had to be transported enormous distances from China and India, often on swaying camel back, to the ports of the eastern Mediterranean. Moslem middlemen exacted a heavy toll en route. By the time the strange-smelling goods reached the Italian merchants at Venice and Genoa, they were so costly that both purchasers and profits were narrowly limited. The consumers and distributors of Western Europe were naturally eager to find a less expensive route to the riches of Eastern Asia—one that would also break the monopoly of the Italian cities.

European appetites were further whetted when foot-loose Marco Polo, an Italian adventurer, returned to Europe in 1295, after a sojourn of nearly twenty years in China. Several years later, while a war prisoner, he dictated a classic account of his travels. He too must be regarded as an indirect discoverer of the New World, for his book, with its descriptions of rose-tinted pearls and golden pagodas, stimulated European desires for a cheaper route to the treasures of the Indies.

The urge to find a short-cut waterway to Eastern Asia was strong, but success awaited new horizons and new facilities. Fortunately the Renaissance, which dawned in the 14th Century, shot hopeful rays of light through the mists of the Middle Ages. Better maps reduced superstitious fears of the unknown. The mariner's compass, possibly borrowed from the Arabs, eliminated some of the uncertainties of navigation. The printing press, introduced about 1450, facilitated the spreading of scientific knowledge. An atmosphere of rebirth also accompanied the Renaissance, and created a healthy spirit of optimism, self-reliance, and venturesomeness.

Portuguese Pathfinders

As the kings gradually unhorsed the nobles, the modern national state emerged in Europe from the feudalism of the Middle Ages. This new type of government alone had the unity, power, and resources to shoulder the formidable tasks of discovery, conquest, and colonization.

The first nations to unite were the first to flourish as colonial empire builders—Portugal, Spain, England, France, and the Netherlands. Those countries that did not achieve unity until the 19th Century, notably Germany and Italy, were left with crumbs dropped by the early feasters.

Little Portugal took the lead in discovering what came to be the coveted water route to the Indies. A courageous band of Portuguese navigators, edging cautiously down the coast of Africa, pushed southeasterly in the general direction of Asia. In 1488, four years before Columbus discovered America, Bartholomeu Diaz rounded the southernmost tip of the Dark Continent. Complete success crowned Portuguese efforts when, in 1498, Vasco da Gama reached India. He failed to induce the inhabitants

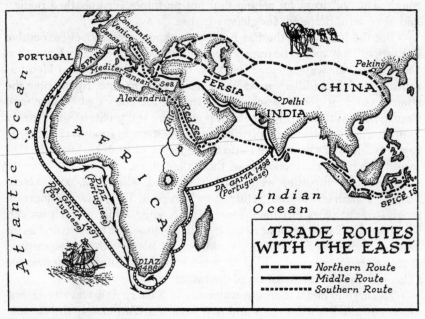

TRADE ROUTES WITH THE EAST
------- Northern Route
———— Middle Route
••••••••••• Southern Route

to part with more than a handful of precious stones and spices, but subsequent voyagers reaped lush profits from this fabulous treasure trove.

Portuguese empire builders ultimately established flourishing trading stations in India, Africa, China, and the East Indies. Immense wealth flowed to European coffers from these ventures. The hold-up prices of Asian products collapsed, and the monopolistic grip of the Italian commercial cities was broken.

Brazil was unveiled in 1500. An India-bound Portuguese navigator, Pedro Cabral, touched upon the giant bulge of South America, eight years after the first voyage of Columbus. Portugal subsequently erected a huge empire in the Brazilian wilderness. But the net return from this New World outpost was but a small fraction of the profits that the Portuguese garnered from exploiting their water route to the treasure chests of the Indies.

A New World Unfolds

The Kingdom of Spain became united—an event freighted with destiny—late in the 15th Century. This achievement resulted primarily from the marriage of two sovereigns, Ferdinand and Isabella, and from the wholesale expulsion of the "infidel" Moslem Moors. The Spaniards, feeling their new strength, were eager to get ahead of their Portuguese rivals in the race for the fabled Indies.

Christopher Columbus, a skilled Italian seaman, now stepped upon the stage of history. A man of vision, energy, resourcefulness, and courage, he finally managed, after heartbreaking delays, to gain the ear of the Spanish rulers. Like all of his informed contemporaries, he was convinced that the world was round. Then why not find the way to East Asia by sailing westward into the darkness of the Atlantic, instead of eastward around Africa?

Success finally rewarded the persistence of Columbus. The Spanish monarchs helped outfit him with three tiny but seaworthy ships, manned by a motley crew. Daringly, he spread his sails. The winds were friendly and progress was rapid, but the superstitious sailors became increasingly mutinous. Nearly six weeks passed and failure seemed imminent when, on October 12, 1492, land was sighted—an island in the Bahamas. A new world thus swam within the vision of civilized man.

The sensational achievement of Columbus has obscured the fact that he was one of the most successful failures of history. Seeking a new water route to the Indies, he was certain he had found it—so certain in fact that he called the near-naked natives "Indians." Actually, he had chanced upon a new route to the New World. In three subsequent voyages to America, from 1493 to 1504, the Great Admiral failed to uncover the riches of the Indies, though finding enough golden trinkets to excite greed. He died in 1506, a cruelly disappointed man.

The discouraging fact gradually dawned that Columbus had merely stumbled upon an enormous barrier to the Indies. For many years thereafter men strove to get through it—or around it. Yet in 1493–1494 the Spanish sovereigns, suspecting that the new territories might contain riches in their own right, staked out a formal claim. Arrangements were officially made, by the Treaty of Tordesillas, to divide with Portugal the "heathen lands" of the New World. The major share went to Spain, but Portugal received compensating territory in the East Indies and also title to Brazil when it was discovered.

France was left out in the cold. Her king, deeply annoyed, growled something about wanting to see the clause in Adam's will that bequeathed the earth to his two rivals. But neither he nor his immediate successors, because of internal turmoil and external war, were in a position to challenge the Spanish-Portuguese monopoly in the Americas. Yet in 1524 France did manage to send out a lone Italian navigator, Giovanni da

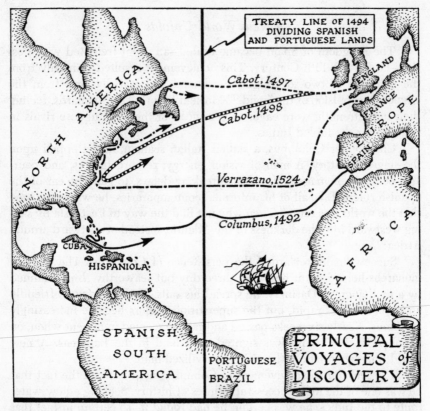

TREATY LINE OF 1494
DIVIDING SPANISH
AND PORTUGUESE LANDS

PRINCIPAL
VOYAGES of
DISCOVERY

Verrazano. By cruising along the coast from North Carolina to New-foundland ("New found land"), he established a shadowy title to that part of North America. The quaint custom then prevailed of merely skirting the edge of a continent and claiming all areas that stretched inland, from ocean to ocean.

England, like France in 1492, was not sufficiently unified to challenge Spain seriously as a colonizer. Yet Henry VII, the tight-fisted Tudor, did outfit a free-lancing Italian navigator by the name of John Cabot. In 1497, and again in 1498, this bold mariner voyaged along the coast of North America between Newfoundland and Chesapeake Bay, while searching for a trans-American route to the Indies. Upon this rather casual voyage rested England's momentous claim to North America, later buttressed by the sword. Henry VII was pleased with Cabot but not lavish; he bestowed a cash reward of £10 upon the lucky discoverer.

The Spanish Conquistadores

As the realization gradually dawned that the American continents were a rich prize in their own right, Spain became the dominant exploring and colonizing power in the 1500's. On her long roster of heroic deeds two spectacular exploits must be headlined. Vasco Nuñez Balboa, as discoverer of the Pacific Ocean, waded into the foaming waves off Panama in 1513. Ferdinand Magellan, starting from Spain in 1519 with five ships, was slain by the natives in the Philippines, but his one remaining vessel completed the first circumnavigation of the globe in 1522.

Exploratory beginnings were made by other adventuresome Spaniards in what was destined to be the United States. In 1513 Juan Ponce de León discovered Florida, which he thought an island. Debauched by high living, he was seeking the mythical Fountain of Youth. He found instead death— from an Indian arrow. Francisco Coronado, in quest of golden cities that turned out to be squalid pueblos, wandered in 1540–1542 with a clanking cavalcade through Arizona and New Mexico as far east as Kansas. The expedition discovered en route two impressive natural phenomena: the Grand Canyon of the Colorado and enormous herds of buffalo (bison).

Hernando de Soto, with six hundred armor-plated men, undertook a fantastic gold-seeking expedition during 1539–1542. Floundering through marshes and pine barrens, from Florida westward, he discovered and crossed the mighty Mississippi north of the Arkansas River. After cruelly misusing the Indians with iron collars and fierce dogs, he at length died of fever and wounds. His remains were secretly buried at night in the Mississippi, lest the Indians abuse the body of their abuser.

All these meanderings had little bearing upon the events that gave birth to the United States, with two noteworthy exceptions. Hernando Cortés, with seven hundred men and eighteen horses (which awed the horseless natives), tore open the coffers of the Mexican Aztecs in 1519–1521. Francisco Pizarro, an iron-fisted conqueror, crushed the Peruvian Incas in 1532, and

PRINCIPAL SPANISH EXPLORATIONS AND CONQUESTS

added another incredible hoard of gold and silver to the loot from Mexico. The Spanish invaders not only robbed the Indians, but subsequently enslaved them and put them to work digging out precious metals. It was easier for white men to mine the natives than to mine the mines.

Cortés and Pizarro, curiously enough, were indirect founding fathers of the United States. Their phenomenal success excited the envy of Englishmen, and helped spur some of the early attempts at colonization. Moreover, the dumping of the enormous Indian treasure chest upon Europe inflated the currency and drove prices upward. The pinch further distressed underpaid English toilers, many of whom in turn were later driven to the New World. There, ironically, they challenged Spanish supremacy.

The plunderings of the Spaniards unfortunately obscured their substantial colonial achievements, and helped give birth to the "Black Legend." This false concept meant that the conquerors merely butchered the Indians, stole their gold, and left little behind—except a half-caste brood of misbegotten offspring. There can be no doubt that the conquering Spaniard killed thousands of natives and exploited the rest, but he intermarried with them as well. He erected a tremendous empire, sprawling from California and the Floridas on the north to the southern tip of South America. He transplanted and engrafted his culture, laws, religion, and language, and laid the foundation stones in the Americas of eighteen Spanish-speaking republics.

The bare statistics of Spain's colonial empire are impressive. By 1574, thirty-three years before the first primitive English shelters in Virginia, there were about two hundred Spanish cities and towns in North and South America. A total of 160,000 Spanish inhabitants, mostly men, had brought some 5,000,000 Indians under their yoke. Majestic cathedrals dotted the land, printing presses were turning out books, and literary prizes were being awarded. Two distinguished universities were chartered in 1551, one at Mexico City and the other at Lima, Peru. Both of them antedated Harvard, the first college established in the English colonies, by eighty-five years.

It is clear that the Spaniards, who had more than a century's head start over the English, were genuine empire builders. As compared with their Anglo-Saxon rivals, their colonial establishment was larger and richer, and as an entity lasted a quarter of a century longer. The English settlers, disagreeable though the thought may be, were more successful than the Spaniards in killing off the Indians.

English Failures

Feeble indeed were the efforts of England in the 1500's to compete with the far-flung Spanish empire. Sir Humphrey Gilbert undertook to plant a colony on the bleak coast of Newfoundland, but lost his gamble and his life in 1583, when his ship sank in a storm. As legend has it:

He sat upon the deck,
    The Book [Bible] was in his hand;
"Do not fear! Heaven is as near,"
    He said, "by water as by land!" *

Sir Walter Raleigh, Gilbert's gallant half-brother, attempted in the 1580's to establish a colony in warmer climes. The settlers chose North Carolina's Roanoke Island, which lay off the then coast of Virginia—a vague region named by the Virgin Queen Elizabeth in honor of herself. With Raleigh busy at home, the ill-starred Roanoke colony mysteriously vanished, swallowed up by the wilderness. Most probably disease and hostile Indians wiped out the colonists. Among them was Virginia Dare, the first of many millions of babies of English blood born in the New World. Her known life lasted nine days.

The Anglo-Saxon was plainly losing out. When the reign of "Good Queen Bess" ended in 1603, England did not have a single permanent habitation in all the Americas. Her backwardness contrasted strikingly with the imperial achievements of both Spain and Portugal.

Huge empires cannot be erected on shoestrings. The failures of Gilbert and Raleigh merely proved that the risky business of colony building was beyond the resources of a single private purse. But the child must creep before he can walk, and these discouraging setbacks taught badly needed lessons.

England on the Eve of Empire

By the early 1600's the English were ready to enter the colonial scramble in dead earnest. Why?

Economic motivations were strong. A vigorous middle class had risen, challenging the social position of the nobles, and providing an active group of merchants who could furnish business leadership and wealth for colonial enterprises. Moreover, the joint-stock company—forerunner of the modern corporation—was now perfected. It had the virtue of enabling a considerable number of investors ("adventurers") to pool their capital— an advantage that the luckless Gilbert and Raleigh had not enjoyed.

England was also burdened with a surplus population. At least she thought she was, even though her 4,000,000 inhabitants totaled only about half those of London in the mid-20th Century. The woolen industry was experiencing boom days, and farms were being turned into grazing lands, with the sheep displacing many soil tillers. The Catholic monasteries and nunneries, which had formerly cared for the poor, had been seized by the anti-papal Crown. Penniless souls, in a period of increasingly hard times, were being turned loose on the country. In the late 1500's the land swarmed with "sturdy beggars and paupers," who engaged in "lewd and naughty practices" and who might well be dumped on America.

* Henry Wadsworth Longfellow, "Sir Humphrey Gilbert."

English colonization was also profoundly influenced by the Protestant Reformation. The German Martin Luther, who dramatically launched his reformist attack on the Church of Rome in 1517, was also one of the indirect founding fathers of the United States. The many-wived Henry VIII of England, using the Reformation for his own purposes, broke with Rome and made himself head of the Church of England. Many unhappy Protestants, especially those who felt that their king had not broken completely with the Roman Church, came to look upon America as a more desirable dwelling place for people of their faith. Many persecuted Catholics, who believed that their sovereign had gone too far, likewise began to regard America as a possible haven.

The Tudor Rulers of England

[SEE PAGE 31 FOR CONTINUATION OF TABLE.]

Name	Relation to America
Henry VII, 1485–1509	Cabot voyages, 1497, 1498
Henry VIII, 1509–1547	English Reformation begun
Edward VI, 1547–1553	Strong Protestant tendencies
Mary, 1553–1558	Catholic reaction
Elizabeth, 1558–1603	Break with Rome final; Drake; Spanish Armada defeated

International religious rivalry likewise spurred English colonization. The King of England ruled the leading Protestant nation; the King of Spain ruled the leading Catholic nation. The bitter contest between these two powers for the spoils of North America was, curiously, to take on some of the features of a religious crusade extended to the New World. English America was in some degree a child of Catholic-Protestant strife.

Elizabethan Sea Dogs

Hardy English freebooters swarmed out upon the shipping lanes in the mid-1500's. They sought to promote the twin goals of Protestantism and plunder by seizing Spanish treasure ships, even though England and Spain were technically at peace. The most famous of these semi-piratical "sea dogs" was the courtly Francis Drake. He plundered his way around the planet, and returned in 1580 with his ship ballasted with Spanish silver and gold. The venture netted profits of about 4600% to his financial backers, among whom, in secret, was Queen Elizabeth. Defying the protests of Spain, she brazenly knighted Drake on the deck of his barnacled ship. Seldom has piracy been so handsomely rewarded. Elizabeth further outraged the Spanish Crown by sending English troops to the Netherlands, where they helped the partly Protestant Dutch to wrest their independence from Catholic Spain.

The showdown came in 1588, when Philip II of Spain, self-anointed champion of Catholicism, amassed his "Invincible Armada" of some 130 ships laden with troops for an invasion of England. The English sea dogs, with craft that were swifter, more maneuverable, more numerous, and better armed, inflicted considerable damage in four running engagements. Then devastating storms took over, inflicting even heavier damage. About half of the crippled Spanish fleet finally crept back into port. But Spanish prestige, and with it the Catholic cause, had suffered a humiliating blow.

The defeat of the Spanish Armada was a red-letter event in American history. It dampened the fighting spirit of Spain, and gave further proof of the decline in her power, though by no means its end. The triumph also insured England naval dominance in the North Atlantic. It started her well on her way to becoming Mistress of the Seas—a fact of enormous importance to the American people. Control of the watery highways enabled England, with relative ease, not only to plant her colonies but to supply and protect them as well. Specifically, the victory helped clear the way for the English to settle on the Atlantic coast as far south as Virginia. This area was regarded by Spain as her own private preserve, and there she had already planted a missionary outpost which had quickly died.

The rocky road to English settlements in America was further smoothed in 1603, when Queen Elizabeth died. She carried her personal feud with Spain to her grave, and the next year the two rivals signed an uneasy peace.

A wondrous flowering of the English national spirit also followed the crippling of the Spanish Armada. The golden age of English literature dawned in this exhilarating atmosphere, with Shakespeare, who was at the forefront, making occasional poetical reference to England's American colonies. Englishmen were seized with a restlessness, with a thirst for adventure, and with a curiosity regarding the unknown. Everywhere there blossomed a new spirit of self-confidence, of vibrant patriotism, and of boundless faith in the future of the English nation.

The Jamestown Seedling

In 1606, two years after peace with Spain, the finger of destiny pointed to Virginia. A joint-stock company, known as the Virginia Company of London, received a charter from King James I of England for a settlement in the New World. The main attraction was hoped-for gold, although there was some desire to convert the heathen Indians to Christianity and to find a passage through America to the Indies. Apparently no one even faintly suspected that the seeds of a mighty nation were being planted.

The charter of the Virginia Company is a significant document in American history. It guaranteed to the overseas settlers the same rights of Englishmen that they would have enjoyed if they had stayed at home. This precious boon was gradually extended to the other English colonies, and soon became a foundation stone of American liberties.

The site selected in 1607 for the tiny colony of Englishmen was Jamestown, on the wooded and malarial banks of the James River, both named in honor of James I. Although mosquito-infested and unhealthful, the spot was easy to defend against Indians and particularly the Spaniards, who were eager to root out the heretical intruder. They actually organized several expeditions for that purpose, but lacked the courage and enterprise to launch an attack.

The early years at Jamestown proved to be a nightmare for all concerned—except the buzzards. Hundreds of wretched souls perished from disease, from actual starvation ("the starving time," 1609–1610), and later from Indian massacres. Ironically, the woods rustled with game and the rivers flopped with fish. Soft-handed English gentlemen and deported criminals wasted valuable time seeking gold when they should have been hoeing corn. They were spurred to their frantic search by edicts from the directors of the company, who threatened to abandon the colonists if they did not strike it rich.

Virginia was saved from going under at the start largely by the leadership and resourcefulness of an incredible young adventurer, Captain John Smith. Taking over in 1608, he whipped the gold-hungry colonists into line with the rule, "He who will not work shall not eat." The dusky Indian maiden Pocahontas may not have saved the captured Smith's life, as he dramatically relates, by suddenly interposing her head between his and

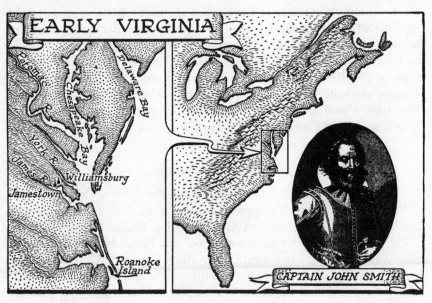

EARLY VIRGINIA

Potomac R.
Delaware Bay
Chesapeake Bay
York R.
James R.
Williamsburg
Jamestown
Roanoke Island

CAPTAIN JOHN SMITH

the Indian war clubs. But there can be little doubt that Pocahontas, who married John Rolfe in 1613, helped save the colony by enlisting the aid of the Indians and by helping to preserve the peace during these critical years.

John Rolfe, father of the tobacco industry, was likewise an economic savior of the colony. By 1616 he perfected methods of raising and curing the pungent weed—a gift of the Indians to the Old World—which eliminated much of the bitter tang. Tobacco-rush days began, as crops were planted even in the streets of Jamestown and between the numerous graves. So heavy was the concentration on the yellow leaf that foodstuffs were at first imported.

The prosperity of Virginia was built on tobacco smoke. The domesticated weed played a vital role in putting the colony on firm foundations, and in setting an example for other successful colonizing experiments. Tobacco thus helped the English settlers, threatened as they were by Catholic Spanish and French rivals, to win most of North America for Protestantism.

But tobacco—King Nicotine—was not an unalloyed blessing. It was ruinous to the soil when greedily planted in successive years. It enchained the prosperity of Virginia to the fluctuating price of a single crop. Finally, tobacco promoted the broad-acred plantation system, and with it a brisk demand for slave labor.

In 1619—a fateful date in American history—what was probably a Dutch warship appeared off Jamestown and sold some twenty Africans. Negro slavery probably would have been introduced within a few years anyhow, but this was the ill-omened beginning. At first African bondsmen were imported only in driblets, and by the end of the century there were still many more white laborers than Negroes in Virginia.

Representative self-government was also born in Virginia, ironically in the same cradle with slavery and in the same year—1619. The London Company authorized the settlers to summon an assembly, known as the House of Burgesses. It met for five days, and then adjourned on account of the heat. A momentous precedent was thus feebly established, for this assemblage was the first of many miniature parliaments to mushroom from the soil of America.

"Cavalier" Virginia

As time passed, James I grew increasingly hostile to Virginia. He hated tobacco; in fact he wrote a scorching pamphlet against the "stinking smoke." He distrusted the representative House of Burgesses, which he branded a "seminary of sedition." In 1624 he arbitrarily revoked the charter of the bankrupt Virginia Company, making Virginia a royal colony directly under his control. He likewise planned to abolish the House of Burgesses; but he died the next year, and in the subsequent change-over the newborn assembly was allowed to continue.

To add to the confusion, civil wars convulsed England in the 1640's. The personal rule of King Charles I, supported by his loyal "Cavaliers," was openly challenged by the Parliamentarians ("Roundheads"), who ultimately found their great leader in Oliver Cromwell. The Virginians showed surprising loyalty to the distant Crown, and when the Parliamentarians triumphed and Charles I was beheaded, a sprinkling of the vanquished "Cavaliers" fled to hospitable Virginia. Only a handful of them were of noble birth; most of them were Cavaliers only by sentiment or political attachment. But the tradition of aristocratic origins spread rapidly in Virginia—later "the Cavalier State"—and the belief that many of its founders were exiled noblemen came to have a profound impact on the Southern mind.

Cavalier or not, class and sectional tensions quickly developed in colonial Virginia. The lace-bedecked gentry monopolized the rich tidewater lands of the coastal areas; the Byrd family alone eventually amassed 179,000 acres. The poorer folk were forced into the wild and dangerous back country. There, though unrepresented or underrepresented in the House of Burgesses, they were compelled to bear the full brunt of the Indian massacres.

Rebellion was clearly in the making. Autocratic old Governor Berkeley, who was personally involved in fur trade with the Indians, was unwilling to antagonize the redskins by fighting back. About a thousand angry back-country men, under the leadership of a twenty-nine-year-old planter, Nathaniel Bacon, whose overseer had been tomahawked, broke out of control in 1676. They chastised the Indians, defeated Governor Berkeley, and burned Jamestown. In the hour of victory Bacon suddenly died, amid rumors that he had been poisoned by the Berkeleyites. The governor thereupon crushed the uprising with needless cruelty, hanging in all more than twenty victims.

The ill-fated Bacon's Rebellion was symptomatic of much that was to be American. It highlighted the cleavage between the old order of aristocracy and special privilege, on the one hand, and the emerging new order of free enterprise and equal opportunity, on the other. It arrayed the despised commoners against the lordly governing class, and the back-country frontier against the tidewater aristocracy. It showed at this early date that aroused colonists would unite and die for what they regarded as their rights as free men.

Maryland: Catholic Haven

Maryland—the second plantation colony but the fourth English colony to be planted—was founded in 1634 by the second Lord Baltimore, of a prominent English Catholic family. He embarked upon the venture partly to reap financial profits, and partly to create a refuge for his coreligionists. Protestant England was still persecuting Roman Catholics;

The Thirteen Original Colonies

Name	Founded by	When	Charter	Made Royal	1775 Status
1. Virginia	London Co.	1607	1606 1609 1612	1624	Royal
Plymouth	Separatists	1620	None		(Merged with Mass., 1691)
Maine	F. Gorges	1623	1639		(Bought by Mass., 1677)
2. New Hampshire	John Mason and others	1623	1679	1679	Royal (absorbed by Mass., 1641–1679)
3. Massachusetts	Puritans	c.1628	1629	1691	Royal
4. Maryland	Lord Baltimore	1634	1632	——	Proprietary
5. Connecticut	Mass. emigrants	1635	1662	——	Self-governing
6. Rhode Island	R. Williams	1636	1644 1663	——	Self-governing
New Haven	Mass. emigrants	1638	None		(Merged with Conn., 1662)
7. N. Carolina	Virginians	1653	1663	1729	Royal (separated informally from S.C., 1691)
8. New York	Dutch Duke of York	c.1613 1664	1664	1685	Royal
9. New Jersey	Berkeley and Carteret	1664	None	1702	Royal
10. S. Carolina	Eight nobles	1670	1663	1729	Royal (separated formally from N.C., 1712)
11. Pennsylvania	William Penn	1681	1681	——	Proprietary
12. Delaware	Swedes	1638	None	——	Proprietary (merged with Penn., 1682; same governor, but separate assembly, granted 1703)
13. Georgia	Oglethorpe and others	1733	1732	1752	Royal

and, among numerous discriminations, a couple seeking wedlock could not be legally married by a Catholic priest.

Fertile Maryland, planted at St. Marys with Lord Baltimore as proprietor, was the first enduring proprietorship in the New World. The King permitted the reins of executive authority to leave his own hands for those of a proprietor, but not for those of the people.

The infant colony, though it experienced some pioneering difficulties, prospered almost from the start. It benefited richly from the experience and help of neighboring Virginia, whose climate and soil were similar. Tobacco growing quickly became profitable, as lush acres were put under the plow. The back-straining labor was largely performed by Negro slaves and white indentured servants—penniless persons who had bound themselves to work for a term of years to pay off their passage.

Lord Baltimore, a canny soul, permitted unusual freedom of worship at the outset. He hoped that he would thus purchase toleration for his own fellow worshipers. But a heavy influx of Protestants threatened to submerge the Catholics and place severe restrictions on them, as in England. Faced with disaster, the Catholics of Maryland threw their support behind the famed Act of Toleration, which was passed in 1649 by the local representative assembly.

Limit of original grant to Lord Baltimore
Present boundary of Md.
MARYLAND
Susquehanna R.
Delaware R.
Potomac R.
VIRGINIA
St. Marys
Chesapeake Bay
James R.
Jamestown
EARLY MARYLAND AND VIRGINIA

The new religious statute guaranteed toleration to all Christians. But it decreed the death penalty for those, like Jews and atheists, who denied the divinity of Jesus. The law thus sanctioned less toleration than had previously existed in the settlement, but it did extend a cloak of protection to the uneasy Catholic minority. One result was that when the colonial era ended, Maryland probably sheltered more Roman Catholics than any other English-speaking colony in the New World.

Colonizing the Carolinas

The Carolinas were formally launched in 1670, after Charles II had granted to eight of his court favorites—Lords Proprietors—an expanse of wilderness ribboning across the continent to the Pacific. The noble founders hoped to make their fortunes in this warm climate by producing non-English products, such as silk, wine, and olive oil.

South Carolina started auspiciously. There was no "starving time," as in Virginia, though the first fleet was on short rations when it arrived. Moss-festooned Charles Town—named after King Charles II—rapidly became the most important seaport of the South. Many high-spirited younger sons of English noble families, deprived of an inheritance, came to the Charleston area and lent it a rich aristocratic flavor. The village also became a melting-pot community, to which French Protestant refugees and others were attracted by religious toleration.

South Carolina prospered, and gradually developed close economic and cultural ties with the flourishing British West Indies. In a broad sense, the mainland colony was but the most northwesterly of these islands. Rice and the indigo plant, which then provided the most important blue dyestuff, were grown profitably on large plantations. The hot sun and swampy land combined to create a strong demand for Negro slaves.

The Catholic Spaniards in nearby Florida bitterly resented the intrusion of the English heretics. The frontier of South Carolina was often aflame. Spanish-incited Indians brandished their bloody tomahawks, and armor-clad warriors of Spain attacked or were attacked during the successive Anglo-Spanish wars. But by 1700 South Carolina was too strong to be wiped out.

The wild northern part of the huge Carolina grant bordered on Virginia. From the older colony there drifted down a motley group of poverty-stricken outcasts and religious dissenters. Many of them had been repelled by the rarefied atmosphere of Virginia, dominated as it was by big-plantation aristocrats belonging to the Church of England. The North Carolinians, as a result, have been called "the quintessence of Virginia's discontent." The newcomers, who frequently were "squatters" without legal right to the soil, raised their tobacco and other crops on small farms, with little need for Negro slaves.

Distinctive traits developed rapidly in North Carolina. The poor but sturdy inhabitants, regarded as riffraff by their snobbish neighbors, earned a reputation for being irreligious and hospitable to pirates. Isolated from neighbors by the unaxed wilderness and by stormy Cape Hatteras, "graveyard of the Atlantic," the North Carolinians developed a strong spirit of resistance to authority. Their location between aristocratic Virginia and aristocratic South Carolina caused the area to be dubbed "a vale of humility between two mountains of conceit." Following much friction with governors, North Carolina was officially

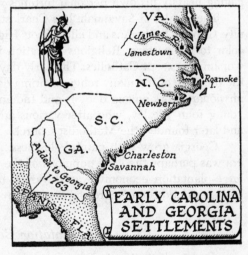

EARLY CAROLINA AND GEORGIA SETTLEMENTS

separated from South Carolina in 1712, and subsequently each segment became a royal colony.

North Carolina shares with tiny Rhode Island several distinctions. These two outposts were the most democratic, the most independent-minded, and the least aristocratic of the original thirteen English colonies.

Buffers and Debtors

Pine-forested Georgia, with the harbor of Savannah nourishing its chief settlement, was formally founded in 1733. It was the last of the thirteen colonies to be planted—by a margin of fifty-two years. Chronologically it belongs elsewhere, but geographically it may be grouped with its Southern neighbors.

Georgia was valued by the English Crown chiefly as a buffer. It would serve to protect the more valuable Carolinas from inroads by vengeful Spaniards from Florida, and by hostile Frenchmen from Louisiana. Georgia in truth suffered much buffeting, especially when wars broke out between Spain and England in the European cockpit. As a vital link in imperial defense, the exposed colony received monetary subsidies from the British government at the outset—the only one of the thirteen to enjoy this boon in its founding stage.

Georgia—named in honor of George II of England—was launched by a high-minded group of philanthropists. Aside from producing silk and wine, they were determined to create a haven for wretched souls imprisoned for debt. The ablest of the founders was the soldier-statesman James Oglethorpe, who became keenly interested in prison reform after one of his friends had died in a debtors' jail. As an able military leader, Oglethorpe repelled savage Spanish attacks. As an imperialist and a philanthropist, he saved the colony by his energetic leadership and by mortgaging heavily his own personal fortunes.

The hamlet of Savannah, like Charleston, was a melting-pot community. German Lutherans and kilted Scots Highlanders, among others, added color to the pattern. Religious toleration was extended to all Christian worshipers except Catholics. The early days of the colony were vexed by the presence of too many religious prima donnas, some of whom came for missionary work among debtors and Indians. Prominent among them was young John Wesley, who after various adventures returned to England and later founded the Methodist Church.

Georgia grew with painful slowness, and at the end of the colonial era was perhaps the least populous of the colonies. Prosperity through a large-plantation economy was thwarted by an unhealthful climate, by early restrictions on Negro slavery, and by demoralizing Spanish attacks.

The Plantation Colonies

Certain distinctive features were shared by England's Southern mainland colonies: Maryland, Virginia, North Carolina, South Carolina, and Georgia—the so-called "Charity Colony."

Broad-acred, these outposts of empire were all in some degree dominated by a plantation economy. Profitable staple crops were the rule, notably tobacco, rice, and indigo, though to a lesser extent in small-farm North

Carolina. Immense tracts in the hands of a favored few fostered a strong aristocratic atmosphere, except in North Carolina and to some extent in debtor-settled Georgia. The wide scattering of plantations and farms, often along stately rivers, made the establishment of churches and schools both difficult and expensive. In 1671 testy Governor Berkeley, who had become something of a tyrant, thanked God that no free schools existed in Virginia, though there were then actually two.

All the plantation colonies were agitated by an underprivileged back-country element, which was seeking a larger voice in government. This was less true of North Carolina, which from the beginning had embraced a poorer class of people.

All the plantation colonies were in some degree expansive. "Soil butchery" by excessive growing of tobacco drove men westward, and the long, lazy rivers facilitated their penetration of the continent.

All the plantation colonies permitted some religious toleration. The tax-supported Church of England became the dominant faith, though weakest of all in non-conformist North Carolina. The Calvinistic Puritanism of New England, with its rather grim-faced outlook on life, did not flourish in the sunny South. Many of the people, especially the wealthy landowners, were much more interested in racing horses and chasing foxes than in fighting the Devil and listening to hell-fire sermons.

SELECT READINGS *

A perceptive survey is C. L. VER STEEG, *The Formative Years: 1607–1763* (1964) [paperback]. S. E. MORISON's Pulitzer-prize *Admiral of the Ocean Sea* (1942) is a classic life of Columbus. GARRETT MATTINGLY, *The Armada* (1959) is a scholarly best seller. Social development in the non-English colonies is described in H. I. PRIESTLY, *The Coming of the White Man* (1929); in the English colonies in T. J. WERTENBAKER, *The First Americans* (1927). Old World backgrounds are developed in WALLACE NOTESTEIN, *The English People on the Eve of Colonization, 1603–1630* (1954) [paperback], and in A. L. ROWSE, *The Elizabethans and America* (1959). John Smith is racily rehabilitated in P. L. BARBOUR, *The Three Worlds of Captain John Smith* (1964), while Nathaniel Bacon is somewhat downgraded in W. E. WASHBURN, *The Governor and the Rebel* (1957). The Virginia story is detailed in R. L. MORTON, *Colonial Virginia* (2 vols., 1960). See also T. O. HANLEY, *Their Rights and Liberties: The Beginnings of Religious and Political Freedom in Maryland* (1959) and T. R. REESE, *Colonial Georgia* (1963). Detailed references: *Harvard Guide to American History*, Pt. III.

* A SUPPLEMENTARY BIBLIOGRAPHY appears in the APPENDIX of this book.

2

The Completion of English Colonization

God sifted a whole Nation that he might send Choice Grain over into this Wilderness.

REVEREND WILLIAM STOUGHTON [of Massachusetts Bay], 1668

Reforming the Reformers

LITTLE did the religious reformer John Calvin know, when he fled his native France in 1534, that he was to shape the destinies of a yet unheralded nation. Arriving in Switzerland, this radical young zealot gave the Protestant Reformation a twist which profoundly affected the thinking and character of generations of Americans yet unborn. Calvinism, ultimately somewhat watered down, became the basic theology of the dominant Puritan group in New England. It was also the creed of the Scottish Presbyterians, the French Huguenots, and the members of the Dutch Reformed Church. All these sects, as immigrants, played an influential role in American moral and spiritual life.

The awesome doctrine of predestination was a distinguishing feature of Calvinism. God in His infinite wisdom had predestined a mass of sinners, including babes in the womb, to be tortured in hell for an eternity. The Almighty had also chosen a selected few—the "elect"—to enjoy eternal bliss. Nothing that the damned could do would save them, whether faith, repentance, or good deeds. The complexities of Calvinism were later summed up by a rhymester:

> You can and you can't,
> You will and you won't.
> You'll be damned if you do,
> You'll be damned if you don't.

The Calvinists were a peculiar lot, partly because no believer could be completely sure that he was of the "elect." A gnawing doubt led to much soul searching and Scripture reading. It also led to a denial of the pleasures of this earth in a preoccupation with the satisfactions of a future life. Even though a Calvinist might be convinced that he was of the

22

"elect," he could not be certain that his neighbors were, and this curiosity led to much Puritanical prying into the lives of other people. In addition, toleration was not tolerated by the extreme Calvinists: anyone who denied the truth of Calvinism was clearly a heretic.

The Puritans of Old England, even before 1620, were unhappy over the slow progress of the Reformation. They were especially eager to de-Catholicize further the Church of England. To them it was still "popish" and "idolatrous," with its creed and ritual, and with its long black robes and other vestments.

The Puritan reformers fell into two general groups. The first consisted of the Non-conformists, who sought to change the Church of England by boring from within. Devoted and sincere though they were, they constituted a difficult and militant minority. The second type of Puritan was the Separatist. He wished to separate entirely from the Church of England and its "Romish" practices, in order that he might worship God and combat the Devil in his own way.

King James I, a shrewd Scotsman, was head of both the state and the church. He quickly perceived that if his subjects could defy him as their spiritual leader, they might one day defy him as their political leader, as in fact they later defied his son, Charles I. He therefore undertook to "harry" the more bothersome Separatists out of the land.

Pilgrims at Plymouth

The most famous congregation of Separatists, fleeing the royal wrath, departed for Holland in 1608. During the ensuing twelve years of toil and poverty, they were increasingly distressed by the "Dutchification" of their children. They longed to find a haven where they could live and die as Englishmen. America was the logical refuge, despite the early ordeals of Jamestown, and despite tales of Indian cannibals roasting steaks from their white victims before open fires.

The Separatists in Holland, after negotiating with the Virginia Company, at length secured rights to settle under its jurisdiction. But their crowded *Mayflower,* sixty-five days at sea, missed its destination and arrived off the rocky coast of New England in 1620, with a total of 102 persons. One had died en route—an unusually short casualty list—and one had been born and appropriately named Oceanus. Fewer than half of the entire party were Separatists. Prominent among the non-belongers was a peppery and stocky soldier of fortune, Captain Myles Standish, dubbed by one of his critics "Captain Shrimp." He rendered indispensable service as an Indian fighter and negotiator.

The Pilgrims did not make their initial landing at Plymouth Rock, as commonly supposed, but engaged in a number of preliminary surveys. They finally chose for their site the shore of inhospitable Plymouth Bay. This area was outside the domain of the Virginia Company, and consequently the settlers became squatters. They were without legal right to the land, and without specific authority to establish a government.

Before disembarking, the Pilgrim Fathers drew up and signed the seven-line Mayflower Compact. Though setting an invaluable precedent for later written constitutions, this document was not a constitution at all. It was a simple agreement to form a body politic, and to submit to the will of the majority under the regulations agreed upon. The Compact was signed by forty-one adult males, eleven of them with the exalted rank of "mister," though not by the servants and two seamen. It was a promising step toward genuine self-government, for soon the adult male settlers were assembling to make their own laws in open-discussion town meetings.

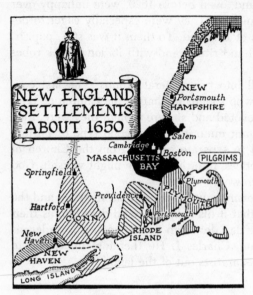

NEW ENGLAND SETTLEMENTS ABOUT 1650

The winter of 1620–1621 was a terrible one, with cold and disease taking a grisly toll. Only 44 out of the 102 survived. At one time only seven were well enough to lay the dead in their frosty graves. Yet when the *Mayflower* sailed back to England in the spring, not a single one of the courageous band left. As one of them wrote, "It is not with us as with other men, whom small things can discourage."

God prospered His children. The next autumn, that of 1621, brought bountiful harvests, and with them the first Thanksgiving Day in New England. The frail colony soon found sound economic legs in fur, fish, and lumber. But the beaver and the Bible were the early mainstays: the one for the sustenance of the body, the other for the sustenance of the soul. Plymouth proved that Englishmen could sustain themselves in this uninviting region.

The Pilgrims were extremely fortunate in their leaders. Prominent among them was the cultured William Bradford, a self-taught scholar who read Hebrew, Greek, Latin, French, and Dutch. He was chosen governor thirty times in the annual elections. His descendants are now numbered by the thousands, and the descendants of Priscilla and John Alden, who were immortalized by Longfellow's "Courtship of Myles Standish," by the tens of thousands.

The quiet and quaint little colony of Plymouth was never important economically or numerically. It claimed only seven thousand souls in 1691,

when, still charterless, it merged with its giant neighbor, the Massachusetts Bay Colony. But the tiny settlement of Pilgrims was big both morally
and spiritually.

> Aye, call it holy ground,
>   The soil where first they trod!
> They have left unstained what there they found—
>   Freedom to worship God! *

The Bay Colony Bible Commonwealth

Bustling fishing villages and other settlements gradually sprouted to
the north, on the storm-lashed shores of Massachusetts Bay. In 1629 an
energetic group of non-Separatist Puritans in England, organizing the
Massachusetts Bay Company, secured a charter from the Crown. Prompted
by both economic and religious motives, they proposed to plant a settlement in the infertile Massachusetts area, with Boston soon becoming its
hub. Stealing a march on both King and Church, the newcomers brought
their charter with them. For many years they used it as a kind of constitution, out of immediate reach of royal authority. They steadfastly denied
that they wanted to separate from the Church of England, only from its
impurities. But back in the Mother Country the highly orthodox Archbishop Laud snorted that the Bay Colony Puritans were "swine which
rooted in God's vineyard."

The Massachusetts Bay enterprise was singularly blessed. The massive expedition of 1630, with eleven vessels and hundreds of colonists,
started the establishment off on a larger scale than any of the other English
colonies. Another distinctive feature was the large proportion of fairly
prosperous members of the middle class, including an unusual number of
university graduates. "Dukes don't emigrate," the saying goes, for if men
enjoy wealth and security they do not ordinarily expose their scalps in the
wilderness. The power of deep religious convictions is further attested
by the presence in Massachusetts of well-to-do pillars of society, notably
the outspoken Richard Saltonstall and the refined John Winthrop, a
leader of genuine distinction.

The Puritan settlers on Massachusetts Bay, despite their preoccupation with things of the spirit, gave conscientious attention to earning a
livelihood. Their settlements grew marvelously, as fishing, fur trading,
and shipbuilding blossomed into important industries. The Massachusetts
Bay Colony rapidly shot to the fore as not only the biggest but the most
influential of the New England outposts.

Additional and enriching waves of Puritans were tossed upon the
shores of Massachusetts in the 1630's. The persecutions of the Puritans
by Archbishop Laud, the arbitrary rule of Charles I, and the economic
insecurity in England resulted in the "Great Puritan Migration" of 1629–

* Felicia D. Hemans, "The Landing of the Pilgrim Fathers."

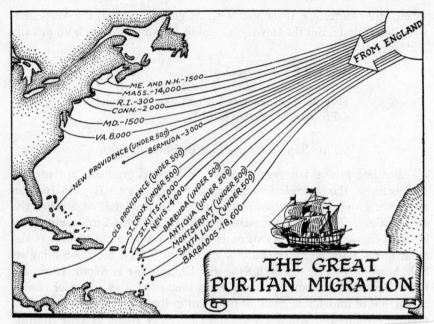

ME. AND N.H. -1500
MASS. -14,000
R.I. -300
CONN. -2,000
MD. -1500
VA. 8,000
NEW PROVIDENCE (UNDER 500)
BERMUDA -3000
OLD PROVIDENCE (UNDER 500)
ST. CROIX -12,000
ST. KITTS -12,000
NEVIS -4,000
BARBUDA (UNDER 500)
ANTIGUA (UNDER 500)
MONTSERRAT (UNDER 500)
SANTA LUCIA (UNDER 500)
BARBADOS -18,600
FROM ENGLAND

THE GREAT PURITAN MIGRATION

1640. Altogether, about 75,000 refugees left the Motherland. But not all of them were Puritans, and only about one-third came to the English mainland of North America. Many were attracted by the warm West Indies, especially by the sugar-rich island of Barbados. More Puritans came to this Caribbean islet, in fact, than to all Massachusetts.

The Bay Colony at first was a "Bible Commonwealth." Even though it enjoyed an elected assembly, much unofficial authority was wielded by a distinguished group of religious leaders or theocrats. Prominent among the "Saints" was fiery John Cotton, whose zeal sometimes led him to preach and supplicate for a total of six hours in a single day. Such men exercised great influence through their spiritual leadership, as well as through their prestige as ministers of a church closely associated with the government.

Separation of church and state was unknown in colonial Massachusetts. For more than fifty years no resident of the Bay Colony could vote in provincial elections unless he belonged to the Puritan Church, which in time was generally called the Congregational Church. On this basis, only about one-fifth of the adult white males enjoyed the ballot. The others, as non-church members, were voteless. They were nevertheless taxed—an early instance of "taxation without representation."

The Persecuted Become Persecutors

The age was not tolerant, whether in Europe or America, and the early religious leaders of Massachusetts Bay were not tolerant. Newcomers either conformed to the established Puritan Church, kept quiet, or departed—sometimes in haste. As custodians of the "true light," the Puritan emigrants from England, themselves the victims of intolerance, had little sympathy for other dissenters. The Quakers, who flouted the authority of the Massachusetts rulers, were persecuted with fines, floggings, and banishment. Four Quakers who defied expulsion, one of them a woman, were hanged on the Boston Common. But this was an extreme case.

The age was not democratic—and the Massachusetts leaders were not democrats. Holding unusual power in their own hands, they strove, like aristocrats in the other colonies, to keep it from falling into the hands of the rabble. "If the people be governors," queried the Reverend John Cotton, "who shall be governed?" The able John Winthrop feared and distrusted the "commons" as the "meaner sort," and thought that democracy was the "meanest and worst" of all forms of government.

Yet the religious and political leaders of the Bay Colony, try as they would, could not completely choke the rising voice of the masses. The beginnings of popular rule may be discerned in the charter of the colony; in the self-governing and hence democratic congregations of the Congregational Church; and above all in the "direct" or "pure" democracy of the town meeting. There the qualified voters enjoyed the priceless boon of publicly discussing local issues, often with much heat, and of voting on them by a majority-rule show of hands.

A sharp challenge to the authority of the bigwigs of Massachusetts came from Mistress Anne Hutchinson. She was an intelligent, strong-willed, and talkative woman, ultimately the mother of fourteen children. Boasting a more intimate contact with God than even the Puritan clergy could claim, she committed the sin of interpreting their sermons to others. Banished as a "leper" after a farcical trial in 1638, she set out on foot for Rhode Island, though pregnant. She finally moved to New York, where she and all but one of her household were butchered by the Indians. Back in the Bay Colony, the pious John Winthrop saw "God's hand" in her fate.

More dangerous to the Puritan leaders was a fellow clergyman, Roger Williams, a young man with radical ideas and an unrestrained tongue. Among various alarming proposals, he defended Indian claims to the soil, and he agitated—horrifying thought to the ruling caste!—for a complete separation of church and state. He argued that religious groups should be supported by voluntary contributions of members, rather than by taxes imposed upon the population at large. He was accused of inciting others to cut the cross out of an English flag, and he branded the state-connected sects as "ulcered and gangrened."

Their patience exhausted by 1635, the Bay Colony authorities found Williams guilty of disseminating "newe & dangerous opinions," and ordered him banished. He was permitted to remain several months longer because of illness, but he kept up his criticisms. The outraged magistrates, fearing that he might organize a rival colony of malcontents, then planned to exile him to England.

The Outcast Colony

Aided by friendly Indians, Roger Williams fled to the Rhode Island area in 1636, in the midst of a bitter winter. But he found, as he wrote, that

> God makes a path, provides a guide,
> And feeds in wilderness!

At Providence, the courageous and far-visioned Williams built a Baptist church, probably the first in America. He established complete freedom of religion, even for Jews and Catholics. In this respect he was not only far ahead of his age, but ahead of any of the other English settlements in the New World. He demanded no oaths regarding a person's religious beliefs, no compulsory attendance at worship, no taxes to support a state church. He even welcomed the abused Quakers, although disagreeing sharply with their views.

The outcasts who gathered about Roger Williams enjoyed additional blessings. They exercised simple manhood suffrage from the start, though this boon was later modified by a property qualification. Displaying ingrained opposition to special privilege of any sort, the doughty Rhode Islanders managed to achieve remarkable freedom of opportunity.

Other scattered settlements soon dotted Rhode Island. They consisted largely of malcontents and exiles, some of whom could not bear the stifling theological atmosphere of the Bay Colony. Many of these restless souls in "Rogues' Island" were neither democratic nor tolerant, including Anne Hutchinson, who had little in common with Roger Williams—except banishment. The Puritan clergy back in Boston sneered at Rhode Island as "that sewer" in which the "Lord's debris" had collected and rotted.

Planted by dissenters and exiles, Rhode Island became strongly individualistic and stubbornly independent. With good reason "Little Rhody" was later known as "the traditional home of the otherwise minded." Begun as a squatter colony in 1636 without legal standing, it finally established legal rights to the soil when it secured a charter from Parliament in 1644. A huge bronze statue of the "Independent Man" appropriately stands today on the dome of the state house in Providence.

The Expansion of New England

The smiling valley of the Connecticut River, one of the few fertile expanses of any size in all New England, had meanwhile attracted a sprinkling of Dutch and English settlers. Hartford was founded in 1635. The next year, 1636, saw a spectacular beginning of the centuries-long westward movement across the continent. An energetic group of Boston Puritans, led by the Reverend Thomas Hooker, swarmed as a body into the Hartford area, with Mrs. Hooker riding a horse litter.

Three years later, in 1639, the settlers of the new Connecticut River colony drafted in open meeting a trail-blazing document known as the Fundamental Orders. It was in effect a modern constitution, which established a regime democratically controlled by the substantial citizens. The essential features of the Fundamental Orders were later borrowed by Connecticut for her colonial charter, and ultimately for her state constitution.

Another flourishing Connecticut settlement began to sprout at New Haven in 1638. It was a prosperous group, containing many souls who could not endure the overbearing Puritan rulers of the Bay Colony. Themselves overbearing, they contrived to set up an iron-clad regime which was even more autocratic than that of Boston. Although only squatters without a charter, the colonists dreamed of making New Haven a flourishing seaport. But they fell into disfavor with Charles II, as a result of having sheltered two of the judges who had condemned to death his father, Charles I. In 1662, to the acute distress of the colonists, the Crown granted a charter to Connecticut which merged New Haven with the more democratic settlements in the Connecticut Valley.

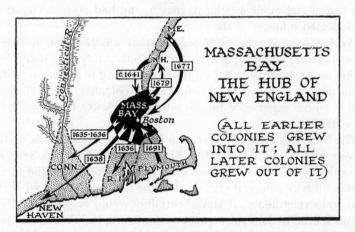

MASSACHUSETTS BAY
THE HUB OF NEW ENGLAND

(ALL EARLIER COLONIES GREW INTO IT; ALL LATER COLONIES GREW OUT OF IT)

Far to the north, enterprising fishermen and fur traders had been active on the coast of Maine for a dozen or so years before the founding of Plymouth. After disheartening attempts at colonization in 1623 by Sir Ferdinando Gorges, this land of lakes and forests was absorbed by Massachusetts Bay after a formal purchase in 1677 from the Gorges heirs. It remained a part of Massachusetts for nearly a century and a half, and then became a separate state.

New Hampshire also sprang from the fishing and trading activities along her coast. She was absorbed in 1641 by the grasping Bay Colony, under a strained interpretation of the Massachusetts charter. The King, annoyed by this display of greed, arbitrarily separated New Hampshire from Massachusetts in 1679, and made her a royal colony.

Seeds of Colonial Unity

A path-breaking experiment in union was launched in 1643, when four colonies banded together to form the New England Confederation. Old England was deeply involved in civil wars, and hence the colonials were thrown upon their own resources. The primary purpose of the Confederation was defense against foes or potential foes, notably the Indians, the French, and the Dutch. Purely intercolonial problems, such as runaway servants and criminals who fled from their own colony to another, also came within the jurisdiction of the Confederation. Each member colony, regardless of size, wielded two votes—an arrangement highly displeasing to the most populous one, Massachusetts Bay.

The Confederation was essentially an exclusive Puritan club. It consisted of the two Massachusetts colonies (the Bay Colony and bantam-sized Plymouth) and the two Connecticut colonies (New Haven and the scattered Valley settlements). The Puritan leaders blackballed Rhode Island, as well as the Maine outposts. These places, it was charged, harbored too many heretical or otherwise undesirable characters. One of the Maine towns had in fact made a tailor its mayor, and had even sheltered an excommunicated minister of the gospel.

Weak though it was, the Confederation was the first notable milestone on the long and rocky road toward colonial unity. The delegates took tottering but urgently needed steps toward acting together on matters of intercolonial importance. The rank-and-file colonists, for their part, received valuable experience in delegating their votes to properly chosen representatives.

The New England Confederation functioned usefully during the terrible war with the Indian chieftain King Philip in 1675–1676. Several hundred settlers were killed and dozens of towns were put to the torch, but the whites finally emerged victorious. If the Confederation had been continued and strengthened, it almost certainly would have spared the colonials much grief in their subsequent conflicts with the French and Indians.

Back home in England, the King paid little attention to the American colonies during the early years of their planting. They were allowed, in effect, to become semi-independent republics. This era of "salutary neglect" was further prolonged when the Crown, struggling to retain its power, became involved during the 1640's in civil wars with the Parliamentarians. Like children neglected by their parents, the American colonists grew increasingly impatient of overseas restraints.

Following the restoration of the Crown in 1660, the royalists and the Church of England element were once more firmly in the saddle. Hopes of purifying the established church fled. A renewed stream of embittered Puritans departed for America, where they added to the group of malcontents already there and to the potential sources of friction with the King.

The Stuart Dynasty in England

[SEE PAGE 12 FOR PREDECESSORS; PAGE 49 FOR SUCCESSORS.]

Name	Relation to America
James I, 1603–1625	Va., Plymouth founded; Separatists persecuted
Charles I, 1625–1649	Civil Wars, 1642–1649; Cavalier tradition
(Interregnum, 1649–1660)	Commonwealth; Protectorate (the Cromwells)
Charles II, 1660–1685	The Restoration; Carolinas founded
James II, 1685–1688	Catholic trend; Glorious Revolution, 1688
William & Mary, 1689–1702 (Mary died 1694)	King William's War, 1689–1697

The spreading American attitude of defiance was nowhere more glaringly revealed than in Massachusetts. One of the King's agents in Boston was mortified to find that royal orders were of no more effect than old issues of the London *Gazette*. Punishment was soon forthcoming. As a slap at Massachusetts, Charles II granted to rival Connecticut in 1662 a sea-to-sea charter grant, which legalized the squatter settlements. The very next year the outcasts in Rhode Island received a new charter, giving kingly sanction to the most democratic government yet devised in America. A final and crushing blow fell on the Bay Colony in 1684, when her precious charter was revoked by the London authorities.

The First American Revolution

Massachusetts suffered further humiliation in 1686, when the Dominion of New England was created by royal authority. Unlike the home-grown New England Confederation, it was imposed from London. Embracing at first all New England, it was expanded two years later to include New York and East and West Jersey. It was specifically designed to increase urgently needed efficiency in the administration of the English Navigation Laws, especially the customs regulations that were so openly flouted by American smugglers. It was also aimed at bolstering colonial defense in the event of war with the Indians, and hence from the imperial viewpoint of London was a statesmanlike move.

The head of the new Dominion was the autocratic Sir Edmund Andros, an able military man, conscientious but tactless. Establishing headquarters in Puritanical Boston, he generated much hostility by his open affiliation with the despised Church of England. The colonials were also outraged by his noisy and Sabbath-profaning soldiers, who were accused of teaching the people "to drink, blaspheme, curse, and damn."

Andros was prompt to use the mailed fist. He ruthlessly curbed the cherished town meetings, and laid heavy restrictions on the courts, the press, and the schools. Dispensing with the popular assemblies, he taxed the people without the consent of their duly elected representatives. He likewise strove to enforce the unpopular Navigation Laws and cut down smuggling. Liberty-loving colonials, accustomed to unusual privileges during long decades of neglect, were goaded to the verge of revolt.

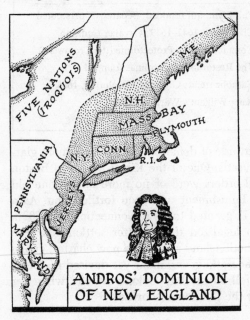

ANDROS' DOMINION OF NEW ENGLAND

The people of Old England, likewise resisting oppression, stole a march on the people of New England. In 1688–1689 they engineered the memorable Glorious (or Bloodless) Revolution. Dethroning the despotic and unpopular Catholic James II, they enthroned the Protestant rulers of the Netherlands, the Dutch-born William III and his English wife, Mary, daughter of James II.

When the news of the Glorious Revolution reached America, the ramshackle Dominion of New England collapsed in ruins. A Boston mob, catching the fever, rose against the existing regime. Sir Edmund Andros attempted to flee in woman's clothing, but was betrayed by boots protruding beneath his dress. He was then shipped off to England.

Massachusetts, though rid of the despotic Andros, did not gain as much from the crash as she had hoped. In 1691 she was arbitrarily made a royal colony, with a new charter and a royal governor. The permanent loss of the ancient charter was a staggering blow to the proud Puritans, and one from which they never fully recovered. Worst of all, the privilege of voting, once a monopoly of church members, was now to be enjoyed by all qualified property holders.

The Glorious Revolution had a widespread impact, for unrest flared forth from New England to the Carolinas. The upheaval resulted in a permanent abandonment of many of the objectionable features of the Andros system, and a temporary breakdown of the new imperial policy of enforcing the Navigation Laws.

The New England Conscience

The story of early New England was largely written by rocks. The heavily glaciated soil was strewn with countless stones, many of which were forced to the surface after the winter freeze. The Puritan fathers, in a sense, did not possess the soil; the soil possessed them by reshaping their character. Scratching a living from the protesting earth was an early American success story. Back-bending toil put a premium on industry and penny-pinching frugality, as in Scotland. Traditionally sharp Yankee traders, some of them palming off wooden nutmegs, made their mark. Connecticut in time came to be called good-humoredly "the Nutmeg State."

The grudging land also left colonial New England less racially mixed than its southern neighbors. European immigrants were not attracted in great numbers to a place where the soil was so stony—and the religion so sulphurous.

Climate likewise molded character. New England summers were often uncomfortably hot, and the winters were cruelly cold. The combination of soil, climate, and Calvinism made for energy, purposefulness, sternness, stubbornness, self-reliance, and resourcefulness.

> New England says, "Make do, or go without,"
> So they make do.*

Connecticut, not surprisingly, came to be known as "the Land of Steady Habits." Nevertheless there were a great many Puritans—legend to the contrary—who enjoyed simple pleasures: they ate plentifully, drank heartily, sang songs on occasion, and made love.

Yet life was serious business, and hell-fire was real—a hell where men shriveled and shrieked for the glory of God. An immensely popular poem in New England, where one copy for every twenty persons was sold, was clergyman Michael Wigglesworth's "Day of Doom" (1662). Especially horrifying were his descriptions of the fate of the damned:

> They cry, they roar for anguish sore,
>   and gnaw their tongues for horrour.
> But get away without delay,
>   Christ pitties not your cry:
> Depart to Hell, there may you yell,
>   and roar Eternally.

Religious tolerance was generally slow to appear. The Puritan oligarchy tried to prod sinful people into saintliness by famous "blue laws." These regulations, among other restraints, required rigid observance of the Sabbath and the repression of certain harmless human instincts. All other colonies passed similar laws, but those of New England were the most severe. In New Haven, for example, a young unmarried couple was fined twenty shillings for the crime of kissing, and in later years Connecticut came to be known as "the Blue Law State." Yet many of these restrictions were unenforceable or were greatly exaggerated by later generations.

The tense and repressive atmosphere of New England ultimately found a terrible outlet. In Salem, Massachusetts, a hysterical witchcraft

* Bianca Bradbury, "Rule of Thumb."

delusion brought about the legal lynching in 1692 of twenty persons, nineteen of whom were hanged and one of whom was pressed to death. Larger-scale witchcraft persecutions were not uncommon in Europe, and some outbreaks had already flared forth in the colonies. But the reign of horror in Salem reached an all-time peak in American experience, and seriously weakened the prestige of the Puritan clergy that had supported it.

THE TWELVE GOOD RULES

Profane no Divine ordinance.
Touch no state matters.
Urge no healths.
Pick no quarrels.
Encourage no vice.
Repeat no grievances.
Reveal no secrets.
Maintain no ill opinions.
Make no comparisons.
Keep no bad company.
Make no long meals.
Lay no wagers.

PURITAN RULES OF BEHAVIOR

The soil and climate of New England encouraged a diversified agriculture and industry. Staple products like tobacco did not flourish, as in the South. Negro slavery, although tried, could not exist profitably on small farms, especially where the surest crop was stones. No broad, fertile hinterland, comparable to that in the South, beckoned men inland. The mountains ran fairly close to the shore, and the rivers were generally short and rapid.

Repelled by the rocks, the hardy New Englanders turned instinctively to their fine natural harbors. Chopping timber from their dense forests, they became proficient in shipbuilding and commerce. They were also ceaselessly active in exploiting the inexhaustible and self-perpetuating codfish lode off the coast of Newfoundland—the "gold mines of New England," which yielded more wealth than the treasure chests of the Aztecs. During colonial days the wayfarer seldom got far from the sound of the ax and hammer, or the swift rush of the ship down the ways to the sea, or the smell of codfish. As a reminder of the importance of fishing, a handsome replica of the "sacred cod" is proudly displayed to this day in the Massachusetts State House in Boston.

Outcroppings of Plymouth Rock

The sturdy New Englanders evolved a compact social structure, the basis of which was small farms and villages. This development was but natural in a people who were partially anchored by geography, and hemmed in by Indians, French, and Dutch. Calvinism, combined with the intimacy of a closely knit community life, likewise made for unity of purpose, and also for nosiness regarding the affairs of one's neighbors. It was no accident that the later crusade for abolishing Negro slavery—with Massachusetts agitators in the forefront—sprang in some degree from the New England conscience, with its Puritanical and Calvinistic coloration.

The compactness of New England also stimulated the growth of self-government. Democracy in Congregational Church government carried over into political government. The town meeting, where the freemen met together and voted personally—and still do in many places—revealed democracy in its purest form. It was, remarked Thomas Jefferson, "the best school of political liberty the world ever saw."

Compactness also made for community responsibility and better schools. The Puritans were eager to have their children learn to read, in order to search the "sacred Book" for God's will. The famous *New England Primer*, some five million copies of which were sold, warned lisping beginners:

> Heaven to find,
> The Bible mind.

Puritan Massachusetts, not surprisingly, established the first public schools in America, and created the best educational facilities in the colonies. Harvard College, the first of a long line of colonial colleges and today the oldest corporation in America, was founded in 1636, partly to train local boys for the ministry. The Reverend Increase Mather, one of the early presidents of Harvard, published 130 books and pamphlets, and his son, Cotton, who had entered Harvard at age twelve, outdid his sire with 450.

The New England Puritans rested secure in the belief that they were God's chosen people. Prim and self-satisfied, they long boasted that

A   In *Adam's* Fall
     We Sinned all.

B   Thy Life to Mend
     This *Book* Attend.

C   The *Cat* doth play
     And after flay.

D   A *Dog* will bite
     A Thief at night.

E   An *Eagles* flight
     Is out of fight.

F   The Idle Fool
     Is whipt at School.

A page from the *New England Primer;* and the hornbook for children, so called because the printing was protected by transparent horn.

Boston was "the Hub of the Universe"—at least spiritually and intellectually. A famous jingle of later days ran:

> I come from the city of Boston,
> The home of the bean and the cod,
> Where the Cabots speak only to Lowells,
> And the Lowells speak only to God.

With the possible exception of Virginia, Massachusetts before the Civil War produced more front-rank statesmen in proportion to her population than any other state.

The impact of New England on the rest of the nation has been incalculable. Countless tens of thousands of New Englanders, ousted by their sterile soil, were destined to pull up stakes and recreate New England towns all the way to Oregon and Hawaii. A people courageous, conscientious, and willing to sacrifice for beliefs, they made the idealism of Plymouth Rock a national symbol. As flinty as their stones, as stiff as their cuffs and collars, they cross-fertilized innumerable other communities with their ideals and democratic practices. The New England conscience added something indispensable to the fiber and backbone of the American people.

The Day of the Dutch

Late in the 16th Century, the oppressed people of the Netherlands unfurled the standard of rebellion against Catholic Spain. After bloody and protracted fighting, they finally succeeded, with the aid of Protestant England, in winning their independence.

The 17th Century—the era of Rembrandt and other famous artists—was a golden age in Dutch history. The vigorous little lowland nation finally emerged as a major commercial and naval power, and then openly challenged the supremacy of her former benefactor, England. Three great Anglo-Dutch naval wars were fought in the 17th Century, with as many as a hundred ships on each side. The sturdy Dutchmen dealt out as heavy blows as they received.

Holland also became a leading colonial power, with by far her greatest activity in the East Indies. There she maintained an enormous and profitable empire for over three hundred years. The Dutch East India Company was virtually a state within a state, and at one time supported an army of 10,000 men and a fleet of 190 ships, forty of them men-of-war.

The company, seeking a passage through America to the East Indies, sent out an English explorer, Henry Hudson. He ventured into New York Bay in 1609, and then ascended the silvery Hudson River, thinking that at last he had stumbled upon the coveted short cut. But, as the event proved, he merely filed a Dutch claim to a magnificently wooded and watered area.

Much less powerful than the mighty Dutch East India Company was the Dutch West India Company, which maintained profitable enterprises in the Caribbean. At times it was less interested in trading than in raiding, and at one fell swoop in 1628 captured a fleet of Spanish treasure ships laden with loot worth $15,000,000. The company also established outposts in Africa and a flourishing sugar industry in Brazil, which for several decades was its principal activity.

New Netherland, in the beautiful Hudson River area, was planted in 1623–24 on a permanent basis. Established by the Dutch West India Company for its quick-profit fur trade, it was never more than a secondary interest of the founders. The most brilliant stroke of the company was to buy Manhattan Island from the Indians for trinkets worth about $24— twenty-two thousand acres of what is now perhaps the most valuable real estate in the world for one-tenth of a cent an acre.

New Amsterdam—later New York City—was a company town. It was run by and for the Dutch company, in the interests of the stockholders. The investors had no enthusiasm for religious toleration, free speech, or democratic practices; and the governors appointed by the company as directors-general were usually harsh and despotic. In response to repeated protests by the people, a semi-representative body was at length reluctantly granted. Religious dissenters who opposed the official Dutch Reformed Church were looked upon with suspicion, and for a while Quakers were savagely abused.

The picturesque Dutch colony took on a strongly aristocratic tinge, and retained it for generations. Vast feudal estates on the Hudson River, known as patroonships, were granted to promoters who would settle fifty persons on them. One of the largest in the Albany area was slightly larger than the later state of Rhode Island.

Quaint little New Amsterdam attracted a cosmopolitan population, as is common in seaport towns. A French Jesuit missionary, vis-

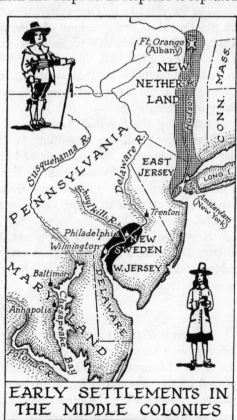

EARLY SETTLEMENTS IN
THE MIDDLE COLONIES

iting in the 1640's, noted that eighteen different languages were being spoken in the hamlet. Thus was foreshadowed the later babel of tongues.

New Woes for New Netherland

Vexations of various sorts beset the Dutch company-colony from the beginning. The directors-general were generally incompetent, though Washington Irving's later characterization of one of them as "a beer barrel on skids" is unfair. The company shareholders demanded their dividends, even at the expense of the colony's welfare. The Indians, infuriated by Dutch cruelties, retaliated with horrible massacres. As a defense measure, the hard-pressed settlers on Manhattan Island erected a stout wall, from which Wall Street derived its name.

New England was hostile to the growth of its Dutch neighbor, and the people of Connecticut finally ejected intruding Hollanders from their verdant valley. Three of the four member colonies of the New England Confederation were eager to wipe out New Netherland with military force. But Massachusetts, which would have had to provide most of the troops, vetoed the proposed foray.

The Swedes in turn trespassed on Dutch preserves, from 1638 to 1655, by planting the anemic colony of New Sweden on the Delaware River. This was the golden age of Sweden, during and following the Thirty Years' War of 1618–1648, in which her brilliant King Gustavus Adolphus had carried the torch for Protestantism. The outburst of energy in Sweden caused her to enter the costly colonial game in America, albeit on something of a shoestring.

Resenting the Swedish intrusion on the Delaware, the Dutch dispatched a small military expedition in 1655. It was led by the ablest of the directors-general, the energetic and hotheaded Peter Stuyvesant, who was dubbed "Father Wooden Leg" by the Indians. The main fort fell after a bloodless siege—later mercilessly satirized by Washington Irving—and Swedish rule came to an abrupt end. The colonists were absorbed by New Netherland.

New Sweden was never important. It passed away, leaving behind in later Delaware a sprinkling of Swedish place names and Swedish log cabins, and an admixture of Swedish blood.

Dutch Residues

The days of the Dutch on the Hudson were numbered, for the English regarded them as trespassers. In 1664, after Charles II had granted the area to his brother, the Duke of York, a strong English squadron appeared off the decrepit defenses of New Amsterdam. The fuming Peter Stuyvesant, short of all munitions except courage, was forced to surrender without firing a shot. New Amsterdam was thereupon renamed New York, in honor of the Duke of York. The English won a splendid harbor, strategically located in the middle of the mainland colonies, and a stately Hudson River penetrating the interior. The English banner now waved triumphantly, with the removal of this foreign wedge, over a solid stretch of territory from Maine to the Carolinas.

New Netherland, as the neglected stepchild of a trading company, was destined from the beginning to be English. Lacking vitality, and representing only a secondary commercial interest of the Dutch, it lay under the shadow of the vigorous English colonies to the north. In addition, it was honeycombed with New England immigrants. Numbering about one-half of New Netherland's 10,000 souls in 1664, they might in time have seized control from within.

The conquered Dutch province tenaciously retained many of the illiberal features of earlier days. An autocratic spirit was carried over, and the aristocratic element was bolstered when certain corrupt English governors granted immense acreage to their favorites. The influential land-owning families—such as the Livingstons and the De Lanceys—wielded preponderant power in the affairs of colonial New York. These monopolistic land policies, combined with the lordly atmosphere, discouraged European immigrants from coming. The physical growth of New York was correspondingly retarded.

The short-lived Dutch colony contributed little of real significance, whether to democracy, government, education, toleration, or literature. A possible exception would be the Knickerbocker themes that Washington Irving developed in the 19th Century with such charm. The Dutchmen peppered place names over the land, including Harlem (Haarlem), Brooklyn (Breuckelen), and Hell Gate (Hellegat). They likewise left their imprint on the gambrel-roofed architecture. As for social customs and folkways, no other foreign group of comparable size has made so colorful a contribution. Noteworthy are Easter eggs, Santa Claus, waffles, sauerkraut, bowling, sleighing, skating, and kolf (golf)—a dangerous game played with heavy clubs and forbidden in settled areas.

Diluted Dutch blood from New Netherland runs through the veins of many of America's "best families," including a host of "vans" and "velts." Three Presidents of the United States traced their ancestry back to the precarious colony: Martin Van Buren, Theodore Roosevelt, and Franklin D. Roosevelt. The last of the trio, when inclined to be stubborn, would speak of getting his "Dutch up."

Penn's Holy Experiment

A remarkable group of dissenters, known as Quakers, arose in England during the mid-1600's. They were supposed to have "quaked" when under deep religious emotion.

The Quakers were especially offensive to the authorities, both religious and civil. They refused to support the established Church of England with taxes. They built simple meetinghouses, without a paid clergy, and "spoke up" in meeting themselves when moved. Believing that they were all children in the sight of God, they kept their broad-brimmed hats on in the presence of their "betters," and addressed others with simple "thees" and "thous," rather than with conventional titles. They would take no oaths, because Jesus had said, "Swear not at all." This peculiarity often embroiled them with government officials, for "test oaths" were still required to establish the fact that a person was not a Roman Catholic.

The Quakers, beyond a doubt, were a people of conviction. They abhorred strife and warfare, and refused military service. Advocates of passive resistance, they would turn the other cheek and rebuild their meetinghouse on the site where their enemies had torn it down. Their courage and devotion to principle finally triumphed. Though at times they seemed stubborn and unreasonable, they were a simple, devoted, democratic people, contending in their own peculiar way for religious and civic freedom.

William Penn, a well-born and athletic young Englishman, was attracted to the Quaker faith in 1660, when only sixteen years old. His father, disapproving, administered a sound flogging. After various adventures in the army (the best portrait of the peaceful Quaker has him in armor), the youth firmly embraced the despised faith and suffered much persecution. The courts branded him a "saucy" and "impertinent" fellow. Several hundred of his less fortunate co-religionists died of cruel usage, and thousands more were fined, flogged, or cast into "nasty stinking prisons."

Penn's thoughts naturally turned to the New World, where a sprinkling of Quakers had already fled, notably to Rhode Island, North Carolina, and New Jersey. Eager to found an asylum for his people, he also hoped to experiment with liberal ideas in government, and at the same time to make a profit. Finally, in 1681, he managed to secure from the King an immense grant of fertile land, in consideration of a monetary debt owed to his deceased father by the Crown. The King called the area Pennsylvania ("Penn's Woodland") in honor of the sire. The modest son, fearing that critics would accuse him of naming it after himself, sought unsuccessfully to change the name.

Pennsylvania was by far the best advertised of all the colonies. Its founder—the "first American advertising man"—sent out paid agents and distributed countless pamphlets printed in English, Dutch, French, and German. Unlike the lures of many another American real estate promoter, then and later, Penn's inducements were generally truthful. He especially welcomed forward-looking spirits and substantial citizens, including industrious carpenters, masons, shoemakers, and other manual workers. His liberal land policy, which encouraged larger holdings of land, was instrumental in attracting a heavy inflow of immigrants.

Quaker Commonwealths

Not until 1681 did Penn launch his colony. His task was simplified by the presence of several thousand squatters—Dutch, Swedes, English, Welsh—who were already scattered along the banks of the Delaware River. Philadelphia, meaning "city of brotherly love" in Greek, was more carefully planned than most colonial cities, and consequently enjoyed wide and attractive streets. Penn farsightedly bought land from the Indians, including Chief Tammany, later patron saint of New York's Tammany Hall. His treatment of the red men was so fair that the Quaker "Broad Brims" went among them unarmed, and even employed them as baby tenders.

Penn's new proprietary regime was unusually liberal, and included a representative assembly elected by the landowners. There was no tax-supported state church. Freedom of worship was guaranteed to all residents, although Penn, under pressure from London, was forced to deny Catholics and Jews the privilege of voting or holding office. The death penalty was imposed only for treason and murder, as compared with some two hundred capital crimes in England.

Among other noteworthy features, no provision was made by the peace-loving Quakers of Pennsylvania for military defense. No restrictions were placed on immigration, and naturalization was made easy. The humane Quakers early developed a strong dislike of Negro slavery, and in the genial glow of Pennsylvania promising progress was made toward social reform.

Pennsylvania, with its many liberal attractions, drew a richly mixed racial group. The lot included numerous religious misfits who were repelled by the harsh practices of neighboring colonies. The Quaker haven boasted a surprisingly modern atmosphere in an unmodern age, and to an unusual degree afforded economic opportunity, civil liberty, and religious freedom. Even so, there were some "blue laws" aimed at "ungodly revelers," stage plays, playing cards, dice, May games, and excessive hilarity.

Under such generally happy auspices, Pennsylvania shot forth a lush growth. The Quakers were shrewd businessmen, and in a short time the settlers were exporting foodstuffs. Within two years Philadelphia claimed 300 houses and 2500 people. Within nineteen years—by 1700—the colony was surpassed in population and wealth only by long-established Virginia and Massachusetts.

William Penn, who altogether spent about four years in Pennsylvania, was never fully appreciated by his colonists. His governors, some of them incompetent and tactless, quarreled bitterly with the people, who were constantly demanding greater political control. Penn himself became too friendly with James II, the deposed Catholic King. Thrice arrested for treason, thrust for a time into a debtors' prison, and racked by apoplectic fits, he died full of sorrows. His enduring monument was not only a noble experiment in government but also a new commonwealth. Based on civil and religious liberty, and dedicated to freedom of conscience and worship, it held aloft a hopeful torch in a world of semi-darkness.

Smaller Quaker settlements flourished next door to Pennsylvania. New Jersey was started in 1664, when two noble proprietors received the area from the Duke of York. A substantial number of New Englanders, including many whose weary soil had petered out, flocked to the new colony. One of the proprietors sold West New Jersey in 1674 to a group of Quakers, who here set up a sanctuary even before Pennsylvania was launched. East New Jersey was also acquired in later years by the Quakers, whose wings were clipped in 1702 when the Crown united the two Jerseys into a royal colony.

Swedish-colored Delaware consisted of only three counties—two at high tide, the witticism goes—and was named after Lord de la Warr. Harboring some Quakers, and closely associated with Penn's flourishing colony, Delaware was granted its own assembly in 1703. But until the American Revolution it remained under the governor of Pennsylvania.

The Middle Way in the Middle Colonies

The Middle Colonies—New York, New Jersey, Delaware, and Pennsylvania—enjoyed certain features in common.

The soil was fertile and the expanse of land was broad, unlike boulder-bestrewn New England. Pennsylvania, New York, and New Jersey came to be known as the "Bread Colonies," by virtue of their heavy exports of grain.

Rivers also played a vital role. Broad, languid streams—notably the Susquehanna, the Delaware, and the Hudson—tapped the fur trade of the interior and beckoned adventuresome spirits into the back country. The rivers had few cascading waterfalls, unlike New England's, and hence presented little inducement to manufacturing by water power.

A surprising amount of industry, nonetheless, was carried on in the Middle Colonies. Virginal forests abounded for lumbering and shipbuilding. The presence of deep river estuaries and landlocked harbors stimulated commerce and the growth of seaports, like New York and Philadelphia. Even Albany, more than a hundred miles up the Hudson, was a port of some consequence in colonial days.

The Middle Colonies were in many respects midway between New England and the Southern plantation group. Except in aristocratic New York, the land holdings were generally intermediate in size—smaller than in the big-acreage South but larger than in small-farm New England. The local government was somewhere between the personalized town meeting of New England and the diffused county government of the South. There were fewer industries than in New England, more than in the South.

Yet the Middle Colonies, which in some ways were the most American part of America, could claim certain distinctions in their own right. Generally speaking, the population was more racially mixed than that of other settlements. The people were blessed with an unusual degree of religious toleration and democratic control. The earnest and devout Quakers, in particular, made a contribution to human freedom out of all proportion to their numbers. Desirable land was more easily acquired in the Middle Colonies than in New England or in the tidewater South. One result was that a considerable amount of economic and social democracy prevailed, though not conspicuously in aristocratic New York.

Modern-minded Benjamin Franklin, entering Philadelphia as a seventeen-year-old youth with a loaf of bread under each arm, found a congenial home in the urbane atmosphere of the city. It is true that he was born a Yankee in Puritanical Boston, but, as one Pennsylvanian later boasted, "he came to life at seventeen, in Philadelphia."

* * * * *

Long before 1760 the thirteen colonies as a group revealed striking similarities, even though they had developed wide differences. They were all basically English. They all exercised certain priceless Anglo-Saxon freedoms. They all possessed some measure of self-government, though by no means complete democracy. They all enjoyed some degree of religious toleration and educational opportunity. They all afforded unusual advantages for economic and social self-development. Finally—and perhaps most significantly—they were all separated from home authority by a billowing ocean moat three thousand miles wide.

SELECT READINGS*

See the books by VER STEEG [paperback] and WERTENBAKER cited at the end of the last chapter. J. T. ADAMS, *The Founding of New England* (1921) [paperback] is critical of the Puritans; S. E. MORISON provides an absorbing antidote in his *Builders of the Bay Colony* (1930) [paperback]. William Bradford's fascinating journal, *Of Plymouth Plantation, 1620–1647*, has appeared in many editions. Leading Puritan worthies are treated in T. J. WERTENBAKER, *The Puritan Oligarchy* (1947) [paperback]; in E. S. MORGAN, *The Puritan Dilemma: The Story of John Winthrop* (1958) [paperback]; in R. S. DUNN, *Puritans and Yankees* (1962); and in LARZER ZIFF, *The Career of John Cotton* (1962). Heavy intellectual fare is in PERRY MILLER, *The New England Mind* (2 vols., 1939, 1953) [paperback]. The best lives of Roger Williams are those by S. H. BROCKUNIER (1940) and O. E. WINSLOW (1957). Useful special studies are MARION STARKEY, *The Devil in Massachusetts* (1949) [paperback], on witchcraft; M. G. HALL, *Edward Randolph and the American Colonies, 1676–1703* (1960); R. E. BROWN, *Middle-Class Democracy and the Revolution in Massachusetts, 1691–1780* (1955) [democracy is upgraded]; and E. B. BRONNER, *William Penn's "Holy Experiment"* (1962). Also *Harvard Guide to American History*, Pt. III.

* A SUPPLEMENTARY BIBLIOGRAPHY appears in the APPENDIX of this book.

3

The Duel for North America

*A torch lighted in the forests of America set
all Europe in conflagration.*

VOLTAIRE

The Curtain Rises on Canada

FRANCE was another latecomer in the scramble for overseas real estate,
like England and Holland, and for basically the same reasons. She was
convulsed during the 1500's by foreign wars and domestic strife, including
the frightful clashes between the Roman Catholics and the Protestant
Huguenots. On St. Bartholomew's Day, 1572, over 10,000 Huguenots—
men, women, and children—were butchered in cold blood.

A new era dawned in 1598, when the Edict of Nantes, issued by the
French Crown, granted limited toleration to the French Protestants. The
religious wars ceased, and in the 1600's France blossomed into the mightiest and most-feared nation in Europe. Leadership of a high order was
provided by a series of brilliant ministers, and by the vainglorious King
Louis XIV. *Le Grand Monarque* reigned majestically, beginning as a five-
year-old boy, for an incredible seventy-two years (1643–1715). Though
involved with a glittering court and numerous mistresses, he was deeply
interested in overseas colonies, and bestirred himself to promote their
welfare.

Even earlier, while the religious wars were still raging in the mid-
1500's, the French had planted a few colonial seedlings. Noteworthy were
the short-lived Catholic settlements on the St. Lawrence River, and the
havens which the harassed Huguenots strove to create in Brazil, Florida,
and South Carolina. But all these feeble experiments collapsed, either of
their own weight or under the sword of Catholic enemies, whether Portuguese or Spaniards.

Success finally rewarded the exertions of France in the New World.
In 1608, the year after Jamestown, the permanent beginnings of a vast
empire were established at Quebec, the rocky sentinel commanding the
St. Lawrence River. The leading figure was Samuel de Champlain, a sol-

44

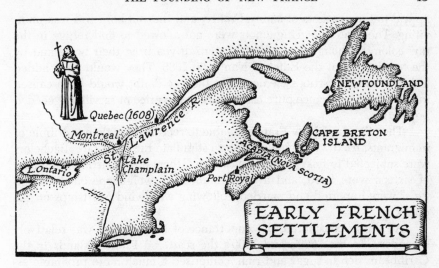

dier and explorer whose energy and leadership fairly earned for him the title "Father of New France."

Champlain entered into friendly relations—a fateful friendship—with the Algonquin Indians. Yielding to their pleas, he joined them in battle against their foes, the federated tribes of the upper New York area, better known as the Iroquois. Two shots from the "lightning sticks" of the whites routed the terrified red men, who left behind three dead and one wounded. France, to her sorrow, thus earned the lasting enmity of the Iroquois tribes. These painted warriors hampered French penetration of the Ohio Valley, ravaged French settlements, and served as allies of the British in the prolonged struggle for supremacy on the continent.

Transplanted Feudalism

The government of New France (Canada) finally came under the direct control of the King, after various commercial companies had faltered or failed. The royal regime was almost completely autocratic. There were no popularly elected assemblies, as in the English colonies; there was no trial by jury—merely the decision of the magistrate.

Feudalism was dying out in Europe, but some of its picturesque trappings were transplanted to New France. Noteworthy were the huge feudal estates, fronting the river highways, and the medieval customs, including the annual dues to the lord in chickens and other produce. The peasants (habitants) were little more than serfs. The autocracy thus established in the wilderness, unlike the regime in the English colonies, was ideal for military defense. It insured unity of purpose, speed of action, precision of movement, and a maximum concentration of meager resources.

The population of Catholic New France grew with painful slowness: as late as 1750 there were only 60,000 or so whites. The wintry blasts did not

appeal to the peasants of sunny France, and the stubborn soil was uninviting. The Protestant Huguenots were not allowed to find refuge in the
raw colony, although some 400,000 were driven from their homeland by
the termination of the Edict of Nantes in 1685. They would have added
a thrifty and industrious element, but they no doubt would have caused
internal friction. France purchased unity at the price of sacrificing needed
population.

The officials of New France, unable to recruit more than a dribble of
immigrants, tried with some success to stimulate the birth rate. Bachelors
were subjected to heavy restrictions. The fathers of unmarried daughters
of sixteen were fined, and a small number of well-chaperoned "King's
girls" were imported and married, following whirlwind courtships on the
docks.

All things considered, the importance of New France was relatively
secondary. In the 1600's and 1700's the scattered French islands in the
Caribbean, rich in sugar and rum, comprised a much more profitable establishment than the vastnesses of the snow-clad northern colony.

Red Men and Black Robes

Fur was the big "money crop" of New France. Lush pelts, notably
beaver, were popular in Europe for their warmth, adornment, and proof
of social position. More than 100,000 beaver skins were trapped in the best
years, and the Indian fur flotilla which reached Montreal in 1693 contained four hundred canoes.

But the fur-trapping business had fatal drawbacks. It was cannibal-
istic, for it ate up its own capital. The retreating animals had to be followed into the interior, and the lure of the beaver thinned out dangerously
the already scanty vanguard of French inhabitants. The English settlers,
on the other hand, were dammed up east of the Allegheny barrier, and
did not finally flow over the mountains in numbers until they had first
been pressed together into a compact social structure.

The Indians who trapped the furs were jerked from the stone age to
the iron age almost overnight. Bows and arrows gave way to firearms. The
red men became different creatures as they were debauched by the white
man's diseases and alcohol—"bottled suicide" sometimes adulterated with
pepper. The French Catholic missionaries tried desperately to block the
sale of "firewater." But they were met with the crushing argument that a
denial of French brandy would force the Indian to exchange his furs for
the rum of the English and Dutch traders, who were Protestant heretics.

The French Catholic missionaries, notably the Jesuits, labored zealously to save both the bodies and souls of the heathen Indians. The Black
Robes were at odds with the fur traders, whose chief purpose was to get
the red man drunk and rob him of his peltries for a few strings of beads.
Some of the Jesuit missionaries, their efforts unappreciated, suffered un-

speakable tortures at the hands of the Indians. Conspicuous among the martyrs was the giant Jean de Bréboeuf, who is said to have kissed the stake at which he was burned, and whose skull is still preserved as a relic in Quebec.

The role of the Jesuits was vital to New France. It is true that they made few permanent converts, despite their heroic sacrifices in establishing missions. But in the capacity of explorers, geographers, and teachers they did much to publicize New France in Old France, and thus helped save the colony.

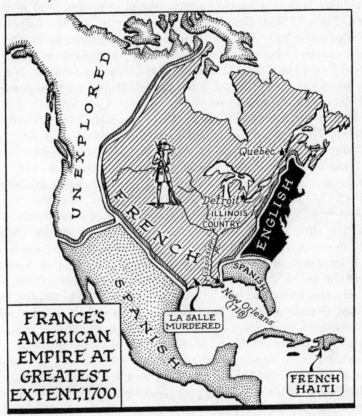

New France Fans Out

Daring French explorers and traders were inevitably drawn deeper and deeper into the heart of the continent. They walked, rode, snow-shoed, sailed, or paddled amazing distances. They were eager to find a shorter waterway to the Indies; to discover fabulous mines like those uncovered by the Spaniards in Mexico; to check Spanish penetration into the region of the Gulf of Mexico; and to thwart English traders pushing into the Ohio Valley. Partly for this last purpose Antoine Cadillac founded Detroit, "The City of Straits," in 1701.

The most famous of all the French explorers was the haughty but far-visioned La Salle. In 1682 he floated down the silent Mississippi to the point where it mingles with the Gulf, and named the interior basin "Louisiana," in honor of his sovereign, Louis XIV. Dreaming dreams of empire, La Salle proceeded to fit out a colonizing expedition of four ships in France. But he landed in Texas, after missing the delta of the Mississippi, and in 1687 was murdered by his men.

Undismayed, French officials persisted in their efforts to forestall Spain on the Gulf of Mexico. They established several fortified posts in present-day Mississippi and Louisiana, the most important of which was New Orleans (1718). Commanding the outlet of the Mississippi River, this outpost also tapped the fur trade of the great interior basin. The fertile Illinois country, where missions and trading-post forts were firmly established, became the garden of France's North American empire. Surprising amounts of grain were floated down the Mississippi for transshipment to the West Indies and to Europe.

French explorers were lured still farther inland by the call of the unknown. They ranged in a gigantic arc from the border of Texas northward through the valleys of the Arkansas, Missouri, and Platte Rivers, into Saskatchewan and Manitoba of present-day Canada. In 1743 a party of Frenchmen, though preceded some years earlier by Spaniards, glimpsed the Rocky Mountains.

But French influence was buttered too thin over a vast continent, and its lasting effect, except in Canada, was not great. French Canadians served as explorers and traders, and, in the role of backwoods engineers, as trail blazers and city founders. The far-ranging *coureurs de bois* ("runners of the woods") were also runners of risks—two-fisted drinkers, free spenders, free livers, and free lovers ("squaw men"). The singing, paddle-swinging French *voyageurs* left behind a brood of half-breeds, and peppered the land with scores of place names, including Baton Rouge (red stick), Terre Haute (high land), and Des Moines (the monks).

Other French impacts were significant, if less direct. The character of the English colonists to the south and east was toughened by a series of bitter wars with the French, prolonged throughout three-fourths of a century. New France also diverted a considerable stream of Huguenots to English America by barring her own gates to them. Among these refugees were the ancestors of such distinguished Americans as the diplomat John Jay, the poet John Greenleaf Whittier, and the silversmith-horseman Paul Revere, originally Revoire.

The Clash of Empires

As the 17th Century neared its sunset, a gigantic struggle was shaping up among three civilizations to determine the mastery of the North American continent: the English, the French, and the Spanish.

Large-scale armed conflict was avoided until 1689. Why? At first there was elbowroom enough for all. Hundreds of miles of trackless forest separated the English from the French in the north and west, and from the Spaniards in the west and south. Rivalry for the furs of the Indians could be kept within bounds.

International politics and intrigue also promoted peace. The Stuart kings of England who reigned from 1660 to 1688, Charles II and James II, not only had strong Catholic leanings toward France but were striving to build up a despotism at home. Finding Parliament stingy, they secured secret monetary subsidies from Louis XIV of France. And who bites the hand that feeds him? But the picture changed sharply in 1689, when the Catholic Louis XIV backed the exiled Catholic King of England, James II, against the two imported Protestants from Holland, William and Mary. War erupted in that year—the first of a series in a duel unto death.

Later English Kings

[SEE PAGES 12, 31 FOR EARLIER ONES.]

Name	Relation to America
William III, 1694–1702	War of Spanish Succession begun
Anne, 1702–1714	Queen Anne's War, 1702–1713
George I, 1714–1727	Navigation Laws laxly enforced
George II, 1727–1760	Ga. founded; King George's War; French and Indian War
George III, 1760–1820	American Revolution, 1775–1783

In Europe, the two antagonists were fairly well matched. England maintained the stronger navy, France the stronger army. The French boasted some 20,000,000 inhabitants, as compared with only 5,500,000 for the English.

But in America, when the final showdown came in 1754, the English settlers enjoyed an overwhelming population advantage of about 1,500,000 to 60,000. The colonists under the British flag, though of mixed racial and national origins, were predominantly English. They were also relatively compact, confined to the Eastern seaboard by the ramparts of the Alleghenies, and by unfriendly Frenchmen, Spaniards, and Indians.

Yet the population of New France, though sparse and diffuse, was far stronger than mere numbers would indicate. Being French Catholic, it was less racially mixed than that of its southern neighbors. New France also contained a higher proportion of arms-bearing men than the English colonies, especially Pennsylvania, where the Quakers opposed war.

The government of Catholic French Canada was likewise well designed for warmaking. It was tightly unified, highly centralized, heavily paternalistic, and sternly autocratic. The full might of the French Canadians could be mobilized and manipulated by one mind.

In contrast, the numerical superiority of the English colonies was largely offset by loose governmental control, both at home and from London. As a result of the numerous religious sects in the colonies and extensive popular rule, authority was widely decentralized. Andros' limited Dominion of New England, which would have provided some unity, had collapsed. Squabbling between the locally elected assemblies and the London-appointed governors was incessant. At times the colonials seemed more interested in quarreling with their royal governors than in fighting their French and Indian foes. There was also much intercolonial friction over boundaries and other local disputes. All these discords contributed to a high degree of disunity, and to a general unwillingness to assist neighbors in a common cause.

Yet elements of strength flowed from these apparent weaknesses in the English colonies. The existence of popular government and extensive democratic control encouraged individualism, self-reliance, and resourcefulness. These qualities were invaluable assets to the English settlers in the long series of Anglo-French clashes.

The English colonies, moreover, possessed an overwhelming economic advantage. They enjoyed a wide diversification of industry, with all that this meant in self-sufficiency. But French Canada was weak economically. It rested uneasily on the back of the westward-retreating beaver and, except for furs, lacked a profitable overseas commerce. The frigid Canadian colony never produced enough grain for its own use, and was forced to import large quantities of foodstuffs for its military and civilian personnel.

Other military advantages were unevenly distributed. The English colonies enjoyed the direct shield of the strong British navy, and the indirect shield of the formidable Iroquois Confederacy. The French, who also enlisted savage allies, were blessed with front-rank military leaders. Towering among them were the Comte de Frontenac and the Marquis de Montcalm, who were able to work wonders with scanty tools. The English at first were cursed with inept generals, but finally secured able ones by costly methods of trial and error—chiefly error.

Pawns on the European Chessboard

The four Anglo-French intercolonial wars, from 1689 to 1763, were in a sense American backwashes of European conflicts. The first three started in Europe and spread to America, where there was an open season on Frenchmen and Englishmen. The bulk of the English settlers, especially in these early frays, were not eager to start butchering their neighbors when dynastic rivalry in Europe led to shooting. But the colonials, as vanguards of empire, were caught in a squeeze. To a large extent the New

World colonies were regarded by Europeans as puppets whose strings could be pulled by overseas monarchs.

The four Anglo-French conflicts, which involved groupings of the powers, were all world wars. They resulted in a death struggle for the mastery of the seas, and were fought in the waters and on the soil of two hemispheres. Counting these first four clashes, there have been nine world wars since 1688. The American people, whether as British subjects or American citizens, were unable to stay out of a single one of them. Isolation from the broils of Europe was often a hope rather than a reality.

The Nine World Wars

In Europe	In America
1688–1697 War of League of Augsburg	King William's War, 1689–1697
1701–1713 War of Spanish Succession	Queen Anne's War, 1702–1713
1740–1748 War of Austrian Succession	King George's War, 1744–1748
1756–1763 Seven Years' War	French and Indian War, 1754–1763
1778–1783 War of the American Revolution	American Revolution, 1775–1783
1793–1802 Wars of the French Revolution	Undeclared French War, 1798–1800
1803–1815 Napoleonic Wars	War of 1812, 1812–1814
1914–1918 World War I	World War I, 1917–1918
1939–1945 World War II	World War II, 1941–1945

The first of the Anglo-French collisions was known in America as King William's War, and grew in part, as already noted, from the opposition of the French monarch to the expulsion of James II. The fighting was waged mainly in the various theaters of Europe, as well as in India, North and South America, and the Caribbean.

The fortunes of battle in America seesawed. Indians, led by Frenchmen, ravaged with torch and tomahawk the frontiers of New England, and wiped out the village of Schenectady, New York. The English colonials, after failing miserably in attempts to seize Quebec and Montreal, temporarily captured the stronghold of Port Royal in Nova Scotia. But the shooting abroad ended in a virtual draw, and by the terms of the treaty of peace in 1697 all captured territory was returned.

The uneasy truce ending King William's War lasted a scant four years. In 1701 hostilities broke out anew, following the brazen attempt of Louis XIV to abolish the Pyrenees Mountains by seating his grandson on the throne of Spain. England could not and would not tolerate this dangerous unbalancing of the balance of power.

The subsequent struggle, known as the War of Spanish Succession, was the most far-flung yet fought in Europe: England and her European allies were banded together against France, Spain, and their allies. Though

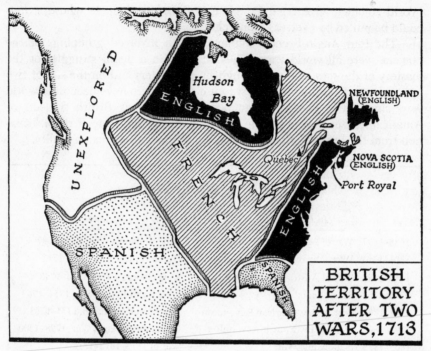

UNEXPLORED

Hudson Bay

ENGLISH

NEWFOUNDLAND (ENGLISH)

FRENCH

Québec

NOVA SCOTIA (ENGLISH)

Port Royal

ENGLISH

SPANISH

SPANISH

BRITISH
TERRITORY
AFTER TWO
WARS, 1713

extending to the Caribbean, the fighting occurred mainly in Europe, where England captured and retained the defiant Rock of Gibraltar.

The conflagration spread rapidly to America. Spain was now on the side of France, so the South Carolinians engaged in bloody but inconclusive skirmishes with the Spaniards in Florida. The war whoops of the French-led Indians, as before, split the night air along the northern frontier, notably at Deerfield, Massachusetts. The ill-trained colonials, happily combining pluck with luck, again captured the French fortress of Port Royal in Nova Scotia.

The peace terms, signed in 1713, revealed how definitely France and her Spanish ally had been worsted. England was rewarded with Nova Scotia, Newfoundland, and the bleak Hudson Bay region. These immense areas applied the pincers to the St. Lawrence settlements of France, and foreshadowed their ultimate doom. Except for Nova Scotia, the English colonials had not captured any of these spoils. The final New World transfers were actually determined by the successes of British arms in the Old World. The Duke of Marlborough, for example, scored a notable victory against the French at Blenheim in Germany (1704).

Side Shows and Stalemates

By the treaty of 1713 the British had won limited trade rights in Spanish America, but these involved much friction over smuggling. The ill feeling flared up when an English Captain Jenkins, seized by the

Spanish revenue authorities, had one ear sliced off. The Spanish commander reportedly sneered, "Carry this home to the King, your master, whom, if he were present, I would serve in like fashion." The victim, with a tale of woe on his tongue and a shriveled ear in his hand, aroused furious resentment when he reached England.

The War of Jenkins' Ear, curiously named, broke out in 1739 between the English and the Spaniards. It was confined to the Caribbean Sea and to the buffer colony of Georgia, where the philanthropist-soldier James Oglethorpe fought his Spanish foes to a standstill.

The small-scale scuffle with Spain in America soon merged with the large-scale War of Austrian Succession in Europe. It exploded with full fury in 1740, when Frederick the Great of Prussia treacherously seized the province of Silesia from his Austrian neighbor, the young and beautiful Maria Theresa. The talented empress fought back with masculine determination, and when Spain and France joined the Prussians, England entered the fray on the side of Austria.

The War of Austrian Succession was waged mainly in Europe, although side-show skirmishes also occurred in the Caribbean and along the thinly manned English colonial frontier in North America. The French had built a seemingly impregnable fortress, Louisbourg, on Cape Breton Island, commanding the Gulf of St. Lawrence and serving as a pistol pointed at the heart of New England. An expedition of rustic New Englanders was organized to seize it. With the support of a British fleet, and with incredibly good luck, the raw and sometimes drunken recruits blundered into victory and captured the prize in 1745.

But the peace terms of 1748 were determined by the global picture. In Europe, the fighting had been inconclusive, except that Frederick of Prussia retained the rich province he had faithlessly wrested from his queenly neighbor. The British had lost Madras in India to France, and

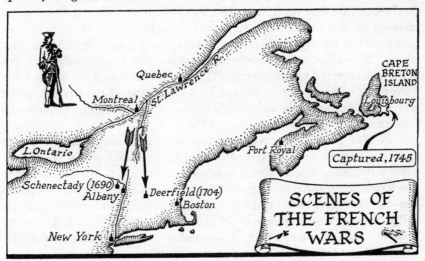

while regaining this valuable foothold in the general restoration, they handed back Louisbourg to their foe. The victorious New Englanders were outraged. Taking a provincial stand, they felt that their interests had been sacrificed to the selfishness of Old Englanders. Although they were finally reimbursed for the expenses of their expedition, money did not completely salve their pride or quiet their fears.

The American Volcano Erupts

As the drama unfolded in the New World, the Ohio Valley became the chief bone of contention between the French and British. The Ohio country was the critical area into which the westward-driving English would inevitably penetrate. It was the key to the continent which the French had to retain, particularly if they were going to link their Canadian holdings with those of the lower Mississippi Valley. By the mid-1700's the English colonials, painfully aware of these basic truths, were no longer so reluctant to shoulder the responsibilities of empire. Alarmed by French land grabbing and cutthroat fur-trade rivalry in the Ohio Valley, they were determined to fight for their economic security and for the supremacy of their way of life in North America.

Rivalry for the rich lands of the upper Ohio Valley brought tensions to the snapping point. In 1749 a group of English colonial speculators, chiefly influential Virginians who included the Washington family, had secured rights to a grant of 500,000 acres in this region. In the same disputed area the French had erected, or were about to erect, a chain of forts commanding the strategic Ohio River.

In 1753 the governor of Virginia ushered George Washington, a twenty-one-year-old surveyor and fellow Virginian, onto the stage of history. The tall and well-proportioned youth was commissioned to warn the French that they must leave the Ohio Valley, and while delivering the message he was to spy out their armed strength. Young Washington, already marked out as an able and ambitious young man of promise, accomplished this difficult and dangerous mission. But the French were not going to be ejected by mere words. They tightened their hold on the Ohio Valley by building a strong outpost, Fort Duquesne, at the strategic point where the Monongahela and Allegheny Rivers join to form the Ohio—the later site of Pittsburgh.

In 1754, shortly after his hazardous errand, Washington was sent to the Ohio country as a lieutenant colonel in command of about 150 Virginia militiamen. Encountering a small detachment of French troops in the forest about forty miles from Fort Duquesne, the Virginians opened fire—the first shots of the globe-girdling new war. The French leader was killed and his forces retreated. Washington wrote: "I heard the bullets whistle, and, believe me, there is something charming in the sound." He later changed his views.

The French promptly returned with reinforcements, and surrounded Washington behind his hastily constructed breastwork, Fort Necessity. After a ten-hour siege, he was forced to surrender his entire command in July, 1754—ironically the Fourth of July. But he was permitted to march his men away with the full honors of war.

With the shooting already started and in danger of spreading, the British authorities in Nova Scotia took vigorous action. Understandably fearing a stab in the back from the French Acadians, whom England had acquired in 1713, the British officials uprooted some four thousand

THE OHIO COUNTRY
1753 – 1754

of them in 1755. The unhappy French deportees were scattered as far south as Louisiana, where the descendants of the Acadians are now called "Cajuns."

Girding for Global War

The first three Anglo-French colonial wars had all started in Europe, but the picture was now reversed. The fourth struggle, known as the French and Indian War, began in America. Touched off by George Washington in the wilds of the Ohio Valley in 1754, it continued on an undeclared basis for two years, and then widened into the most titanic conflict the world had yet seen—the Seven Years' War. It was fought not only in America but in Europe, in the West Indies, in the Philippines, in Africa, and on the ocean. The Seven Years' War was a seven seas war.

The principal adversaries in Europe were England and Prussia on one side, arrayed against France, Spain, Austria, and Russia on the other. The bloodiest theater was in Germany, where Frederick the Great deservedly won the title of "Great" by repelling French, Austrian, and Russian armies, often with the manpower odds three to one against him. The British government, unable to send him troop reinforcements, liberally subsidized him with gold. Luckily for the English colonials, the French wasted so much of their strength in this blood-draining European contest that they were unable to throw an adequate force into the New

World. "America was conquered in Germany" was the shrewd observation of Britain's William Pitt.

In previous intercolonial clashes, the Americans had revealed a lamentable lack of unity. The colonists who were nearest the shooting had responded much more generously with volunteers and money than those who had enjoyed the safety of greater distances. Even the Indians had laughed at the inability of the colonials to pull together. With bullets already whining in the Ohio country, the crisis called for concerted action.

In 1754 the British government summoned an intercolonial Congress at Albany, New York, near the Iroquois country. Travel-weary delegates from only seven of the thirteen colonies put in an appearance. The immediate purpose was to keep the scalping knives of the Iroquois tribes on the side of the British in the spreading war, and this objective was gained when the chiefs were harangued and presented with gifts.

JOIN, or DIE.

The longer-range purpose at Albany was to achieve a higher degree of colonial unity, and thus bolster the common defense against France. The month before the Congress assembled, ingenious Benjamin Franklin published in his *Pennsylvania Gazette* the most famous cartoon of the colonial era. Showing the separate colonies as parts of a disjointed snake, it broadcast the slogan, "Join or Die."

Franklin himself, a wise and witty counselor, was the leading spirit of the Albany Congress. His outstanding contribution was a well-devised scheme for colonial home rule. It was unanimously adopted by the Albany Congress, but was rejected by the individual colonies and by the London government. To the colonials, it did not seem to give enough independence; to the British officials, it seemed to give too much. The disappointing result confirmed one of Franklin's sage observations. All people agreed on the necessity of union, he noted, but their "weak noddles" were "perfectly distracted" when they attempted to agree on details.

Years of Defeat

The opening battles of the French and Indian War went badly for the English colonials. Haughty and bull-headed General Braddock, a sixty-year-old officer experienced in European warfare, was sent to Virginia with a strong detachment of British regulars. After gathering supplies, he set out briskly in 1755 with some 2000 men to capture Fort Duquesne at the forks of the Ohio. A considerable part of his force consisted of ill-disciplined colonial militiamen ("buckskins"), whose behind-the-tree methods of fighting Indians won "Bulldog" Braddock's contempt.

Braddock's expedition moved slowly. Axmen laboriously hacked a path through the dense forest, thus opening a road that was later to be an important artery to the West. A few miles from Fort Duquesne, Braddock encountered a much smaller French and Indian vanguard. At first the enemy force was repulsed, but it quickly melted into the thickets and poured a murderous fire into the ranks of the Redcoats. George Washington, an energetic and fearless aide to Braddock, had two horses shot under him, and Braddock himself was mortally wounded. The entire force was routed but not wiped out.

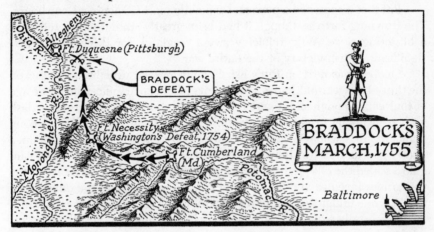

The Indians, inflamed by this easy victory, took to a wider warpath. The whole frontier from Pennsylvania to North Carolina, left virtually naked by Braddock's defeat, felt their fury. Scalping forays occurred within eighty miles of Philadelphia, and in desperation the local authorities offered bounties for Indian scalps: $50 for a squaw and $130 for a brave. George Washington, with only 300 men, did heroic work in helping to defend the scorched frontier.

The British undertook a full-scale invasion of Canada in 1756, now that the undeclared war in America had at last merged into a world conflict. But they foolishly tried to attack a number of exposed wilderness posts simultaneously, instead of throwing all their strength at Quebec and Montreal. If these strongholds had fallen, all the outposts to the west would have withered on the vine for lack of supplies. But such sound strategy was not followed, and defeat after defeat tarnished British arms, both in America and in Europe.

Years of Victory

In the hour of crisis Britain brought forth, as she so often has, a superlative leader—William Pitt. A tall and imposing figure, whose flashing eyes were set in a hawk-like face, he was popularly known as the "Great Commoner." He drew much of his strength from the common people, who admired him so greatly that they kissed his horses. A splendid orator endowed with a majestic voice, he believed passionately in his cause, in his country, and in himself.

Pitt became head of the London government in 1757. Throwing himself headlong into his task, he soon earned the title "Organizer of Victory." He wisely decided to soft-pedal assaults against the French West Indies, which had been bleeding away much British strength, and concentrate on the vitals of Canada—the Quebec-Montreal area. He also picked young and energetic leaders, bypassing incompetent and cautious old generals.

Pitt first dispatched a powerful expedition in 1758 against Louisbourg. The frowning fortress, though it had been greatly strengthened, fell after a blistering siege. Wild rejoicing swept England, for this was the first significant British victory of the entire war.

Quebec was next on Pitt's list. For this crucial expedition he picked the thirty-two-year-old James Wolfe, who had been an officer since the age of fourteen. Though slight and sickly, Wolfe combined a mixture of dash with painstaking attention to detail. The British attackers were making scant progress when Wolfe, in a daring move, sent a detachment up a poorly guarded part of the rocky eminence protecting Quebec. This vanguard scaled the cliff, pulling itself upward by bushes. In the morning the two armies faced each other on the Plains of Abraham on the outskirts of Quebec, one under Wolfe and the other under Montcalm. Both commanders fell mortally wounded, but the French were defeated and the city surrendered.

The battle of Quebec ranks as one of the most significant engagements in British and American history. Yet it was only one of the bumper crop of victories in 1759, known in British history as "the wonderful year." The English writer Horace Walpole noted, "We were forced to ask every morning what victory there is, for fear of missing one."

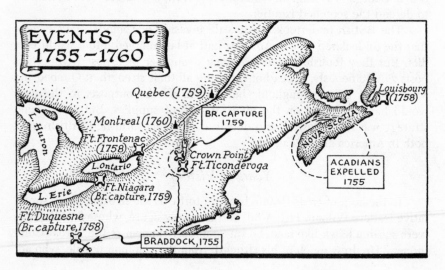

EVENTS OF
1755 – 1760

Quebec (1759)

Montreal (1760)

BR. CAPTURE
1759

Louisbourg
(1758)

L. Huron

Ft. Frontenac
(1758)

L. Ontario

Crown Point
Ft. Ticonderoga

NOVA SCOTIA

ACADIANS
EXPELLED
1755

L. Erie

Ft. Niagara
(Br. capture, 1759)

Ft. Duquesne
(Br. capture, 1758)

BRADDOCK, 1755

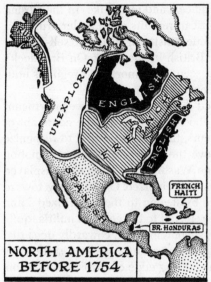

NORTH AMERICA
BEFORE 1754

NORTH AMERICA
AFTER 1763

Yet the triumph at Quebec was not completely decisive. Winter descended, ice-locking the St. Lawrence River, and leaving the scurvy-ridden and outnumbered British army facing heavy attacks from Montreal. But with spring, the ice broke and reinforcements came. Montreal fell in 1760, and the French flag waved in Canada for the last time. The war continued savagely in other theaters for three more years. France and Spain were lucky to escape as well as they did, but the beating that they received was reflected in the severe peace terms.

By the Treaty of Paris (1763), the French were thrown completely off the continent of North America. The bitter pill was sweetened somewhat when they were allowed to retain several small but valuable sugar islands in the West Indies, and two never-to-be-fortified islets in the Gulf of St. Lawrence for fishing stations. The final blow came when the French, to compensate their luckless Spanish ally for her losses, ceded to Spain all trans-Mississippi Louisiana, plus the outlet of New Orleans. Spain, for her part, turned Florida over to England in return for Cuba, where Havana had fallen to British arms.

Great Britain thus emerged as the predominant power in North America, while taking her place as the leading naval and colonial power of the world.

Mother-and-Daughter Friction

The American colonials, baptized by fire, emerged with increased confidence in their military strength. They had borne the brunt of battle at first; they had fought bravely beside the vaunted British regulars; and they had gained valuable experience, officers and men alike. In the closing days of the struggle some 20,000 American recruits were under arms.

The French and Indian War, while bolstering colonial self-esteem, simultaneously shattered the myth of British invincibility. On Braddock's bloody field the "buckskin" militia had seen the demoralized regulars huddling helplessly together, or fleeing their unseen enemy.

Ominously, friction had developed during the war between arrogant English officers and the raw colonial "boors." Displaying the contempt of the professional soldier for rank amateurs, the British refused to recognize any American militia commission above the rank of captain—a demotion highly displeasing to "Colonel" George Washington. They also displayed the usual condescension of snobs from the civilized Old Country toward the "scum" who had confessed failure by fleeing to the uncivilized Land of the Second Chance. General Wolfe referred to the colonial militia, quite unfairly, as "in general the dirtiest, most contemptible, cowardly dogs that you can conceive." The energetic and hard-working American settlers, on the other hand, felt that they were the cutting edge of British civilization. They believed that they deserved credit rather than contempt for risking their lives to build up a New World empire.

British officials were even more distressed by the reluctance of the colonials to support the war effort wholeheartedly. American shippers and smugglers, using fraudulent papers, developed a golden traffic with the enemy ports of the Spanish and French West Indies. This wholesale trade in foodstuffs kept some of the hostile islands from starving at the very time when the British navy was trying to subdue them. In the last year of the war, the British authorities, deeply angered, forbade the export of all supplies from New England and the Middle Colonies.

Nor had the conduct of other colonials been praiseworthy. Self-centered and regarding the war as remote, large numbers of them had been loath to provide men and money for the conflict. They demanded the rights and privileges of Englishmen, without the duties and responsibilities of Englishmen. It was not until Pitt had offered to reimburse the colonies for a substantial part of their expenditures—some £900,000— that they plunged in with some enthusiasm. If the Americans had to be bribed to defend themselves against a relentless and savage foe, was it possible that they would ever unite to strike the Mother Country?

The curse of intercolonial disunity, present from the beginning, had continued throughout the recent hostilities. It had been caused mainly by enormous distances; by geographical barriers like rivers; by conflicting religions, from Catholic to Quaker; by varied national backgrounds, from German to Irish; by differing types of colonial governments; by numerous boundary disputes; and by the resentment of the crude back-country democracy against the aristocratic bigwigs. Many of the colonials felt much more kindly toward Englishmen at home than they did toward their English-speaking neighbors in the New World.

Non-combatant Pennsylvania Quakers traded with the French, and in this cartoon (c. 1760) Franklin points out that the Quaker (with fox's head) will flourish, regardless of who wins. The Historical Society of Pennsylvania

But disunity received some heavy blows during the French and Indian War. When soldiers and statesmen from widely separated colonies met around common campfires and council tables, they were often agreeably surprised by what they found. Despite deep-seated jealousy and suspicion, they discovered that they were all fellow Americans who generally spoke the same language and shared common ideals. Barriers of disunity began to melt, although a long and rugged road had to be traveled before a nation could emerge.

Men of Destiny

The removal of the French menace in Canada profoundly affected American attitudes. While the French hawk had been hovering in the north and west, the colonial chicks had been forced to cling close to the wings of the mother hen. Now that the hawk was killed, they could range far afield with a new spirit of independence.

The French, humiliated by the British and saddened by the fate of Canada, consoled themselves with one wishful thought. Perhaps the loss of their American empire would one day result in Britain's loss of her American empire. The history of the United States in a sense began with the fall of Quebec and Montreal; the infant republic was cradled on the Plains of Abraham.

The Spanish and Indian menaces, as well as the French menace, were removed by the recent war. Spain was eliminated from Florida, although now entrenched in Louisiana and New Orleans. And the Indian allies of France were left in the lurch. A violent post-war flare-up against the white men occurred in the Ohio Valley and Great Lakes region in 1763, with the vengeful chieftain Pontiac as one of the leaders. Catching the British napping, the Indians wiped out a number of their posts. But the whites, rallying in superior numbers, crushed the uprising and rendered the frontier more secure.

The land-hungry American colonials were now free to burst over the dam of the Appalachian Mountains, and flood out over the grassy western

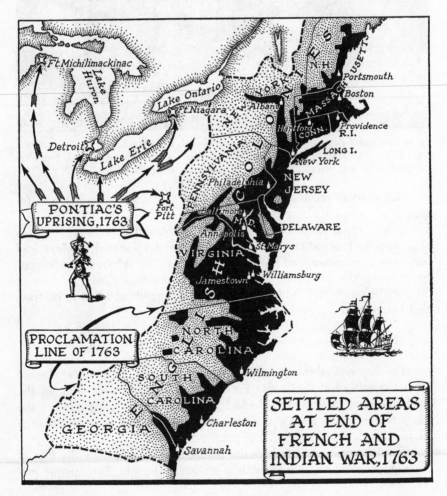

SETTLED AREAS
AT END OF
FRENCH AND
INDIAN WAR, 1763

lands. A tiny rivulet of Daniel Boones had already trickled into Tennessee and Kentucky; other courageous pioneers were preparing for the long trek over the mountains.

Then, out of a clear sky, the British government issued its Proclamation of 1763. It flatly prohibited settlement in the area beyond the Appalachian Mountains, pending further adjustments. The truth is that this hastily drawn document was not designed to oppress the colonials at all, but to work out the Indian problem fairly in the interests of the fur traders and others concerned.

But countless Americans, particularly land speculators, were dismayed and angered. Was not the land beyond the mountains their birthright? Had they not, in addition, purchased it with their blood in the recent war? With complete defiance of surveyors' lines, they darkened the westward trails. In 1765 scores of wagons creaked through the town of Salisbury, North Carolina, on their way "up west." This wholesale flouting of royal authority boded ill for the longevity of British rule in America.

The French and Indian War also caused the colonials to catch a new vision of their ultimate destiny. With the path cleared for the conquest of a continent, with their birth rate high and their energy boundless, they sensed that they were a potent people on the march. And they were in no mood to be hobbled.

The British, whose suddenly swollen empire had tended to produce a swollen head, were in no mood for back talk. Puffed up over their recent victories, they were already annoyed with their unruly colonials. The stage was set for a violent family quarrel.

SELECT READINGS*

Broad outlines appear in H. H. PECKHAM, *The Colonial Wars, 1689–1762* (1964). On the backgrounds of New France consult G. M. WRONG, *The Rise and Fall of New France* (2 vols., 1928), and the older but classic volumes of FRANCIS PARKMAN, notably *Montcalm and Wolfe* (2 vols., 1884). The voluminous Parkman accounts are streamlined, without loss of flavor, in *The Battle for North America* (ed. JOHN TEBBEL, 1948) and *The Parkman Reader* (ed. S. E. MORISON, 1955) [paperback]. P. C. PHILLIPS, *The Fur Trade* (2 vols., 1961) deals largely with New France. An impressive biographical contribution is D. S. FREEMAN'S exhaustive and sympathetic *Young Washington* (2 vols., 1948). See also BERNHARD KNOLLENBERG'S revealing *George Washington: The Virginia Period* (1965) and LEE MC CARDELL, *Ill-Starred General: Braddock of the Coldstream Guards* (1958), which is sympathetic. The story is fully told in CHRISTOPHER HIBBERT, *Wolfe at Quebec* (1959) and C. P. STACEY, *Quebec, 1759: The Siege and the Battle* (1959). Also *Harvard Guide*, Pt. III.

* A SUPPLEMENTARY BIBLIOGRAPHY appears in the APPENDIX of this book.

4

Colonial Life on the Eve of Revolt

Driven from every other corner of the earth, freedom of thought and the right of private judgment in matters of conscience direct their course to this happy country as their last asylum.

SAMUEL ADAMS, 1776

Conquest by the Cradle

THE TERM "thirteen original colonies" is misleading. There were more than twenty colonies under British control in North America by 1775, including Canada, Florida, and the various islands of the West Indies. But only thirteen of them unfurled the standard of revolt. A few of the non-rebels, such as Canada and Jamaica, were larger, wealthier, or more populous than some of the thirteen.

The white inhabitants of the thirteen colonies by 1760 numbered about 1,600,000; by 1775 they had pulled themselves up, largely by their birth-rate bootstraps, to about 2,500,000. With remarkable fertility, they were doubling their population approximately every twenty-three years. The unfriendly Dr. Samuel Johnson, back in England, growled that the Americans were multiplying like their own rattlesnakes. Energetic and well-fed pioneer peoples tend to be extraordinarily fertile, and in those frontier days a large family was regarded as an economic asset. There were many more trees to chop down and more fabrics to weave than there were hands for the tasks.

Marriage—especially early marriage—was encouraged. An unwed girl of twenty-one could be referred to as "an antique virgin." Widows often remarried promptly; one of them used the leftover refreshments of her first husband's funeral for her second wedding. Babies arrived with almost frightening frequency. Benjamin Franklin was one of fifteen by two mothers; William Phips, a Massachusetts governor, was one of twenty-seven—all by the same mother. Excessive child-bearing drained the vitality of many pioneer women, as the weather-eroded colonial tombstones eloquently reveal, and a number of the largest families were borne by several mothers.

64

The net results of the baby-boom were startling, despite the terrifying death rate among infants and children. (One mother lost twenty in early childhood.) Imaginative Americans of the colonial era found satisfaction in computing how many generations must pass before the population would number 600,000,000 or so. Such calculations in turn engendered a feeling of confidence and independence—a spirit that boded ill for a long-continued attachment to the apron strings of the Mother Country.

Immigrants likewise swelled the total, as tens of thousands poured in from the British Isles and Europe. They, too, were an unusually fertile lot, for adults who have enough energy to emigrate are ordinarily of a child-begetting and child-bearing age.

The bulk of the population was cooped up east of the Alleghenies, although by 1775 a vanguard of pioneers had settled in the stump-studded clearings of Tennessee and Kentucky. The most populous colonies in 1775 were Virginia, Massachusetts, Pennsylvania, North Carolina, and Maryland—in that order. There were only four communities that might properly be termed cities: Philadelphia, including suburbs, was first with about 34,000, while New York, Boston, and Charleston were strung out behind. About 90% of the people lived in rural areas.

The Mingling of the Races

Colonial America was a melting pot, and had been from the outset. The population, although basically English in stock and language, was picturesquely mottled with sizable foreign groups.

Heavy-accented Germans constituted about 6% of the total population, or 150,000 by 1775. Fleeing religious persecution, economic oppression, and the ravages of war, they had flocked to America in the early 1700's, and had settled chiefly in Pennsylvania. Known popularly but erroneously as the Pennsylvania Dutch, they totaled about one-third of the colony's population. In Philadelphia the street signs were painted in both German and English.

The German newcomers moved into the back country of Pennsylvania, where their splendid stone barns gave mute evidence of their industry and prosperity. Not having been brought up as Englishmen, they had no deep-rooted loyalty to the British Crown, and they clung tenaciously to their German language and customs. But as permanent settlers they became the forebears of many distinguished Americans, including President Dwight D. Eisenhower.

The Scotch-Irish, who in 1775 numbered about 175,000, or 7% of the population, were an important non-English group, although English-speaking. They were not Irish at all, but turbulent Scots Lowlanders who, over a period of many decades, had first been transplanted to northern Ireland. Their experiences on the Emerald Isle had been harrowing. The

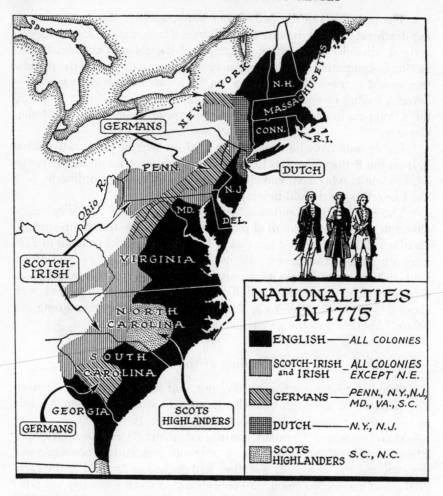

NATIONALITIES IN 1775

ENGLISH——*ALL COLONIES*

SCOTCH-IRISH and IRISH——*ALL COLONIES EXCEPT N.E.*

GERMANS——*PENN., N.Y., N.J., MD., VA., S.C.*

DUTCH——*N.Y., N.J.*

SCOTS HIGHLANDERS——*S.C., N.C.*

Irish Catholics already there, hating Scotch Presbyterianism, resented the intruders. The economic life of the Scotch-Irish was severely hampered, especially when the English government placed burdensome restrictions on their production of linens and woolens.

Early in the 1700's tens of thousands of embittered Scotch-Irish finally pulled up stakes and came to America, chiefly to tolerant and deep-soiled Pennsylvania. Finding the best acres already taken by Germans and Quakers, they pushed out onto the frontier. There many of them illegally but defiantly squatted on the unoccupied land, and quarreled with both red and white owners. It was said, somewhat unfairly, that the Scotch-Irish kept the Sabbath—and all else they could lay their hands on. Pugnacious, lawless, and individualistic, they brought with them the Scottish secrets of whiskey distilling and proceeded to set up their own stills. Already experienced colonizers and agitators in Ireland, they proved to be superb frontiersmen and Indian fighters. They cherished no love for the

British government which had uprooted them, and many of them—including the youthful Andrew Jackson—joined the embattled American revolutionists.

About 5% of the piebald colonial population consisted of other foreign groups. These embraced French Huguenots, Welsh, Dutch, Swedes, Hebrews, Irish, Swiss, and Scots Highlanders—as distinguished from the Scotch-Irish. Except for the Scots Highlanders, these hodge-podge elements were also markedly deficient in a sense of loyalty to the British Crown.

The largest single non-English group was African, predominantly Negro slaves, constituting in all about 20% of the total population, or about 500,000 in 1775. Excluding Negroes, 90% of the colonials spoke English.

Estimated Population Elements, 1790*

[BASED ON FAMILY NAMES]

English and Welsh	2,605,699	82.1%
Scotch (including Scotch-Irish)	221,562	7.0%
German	176,407	5.6%
Dutch	78,959	2.5%
Irish	61,534	1.9%
French	17,619	0.6%
All other whites	10,664	0.3%
	3,172,444	100.0%
Negro	757,181	19.2% of total
GRAND TOTAL	3,929,625	

* Rossiter, *A Century of Population Growth* (1909). Later estimates by Barker and Hansen (1931) are not here used because they are confused by the inclusion of Spanish and French elements *later* a part of the United States.

The population of the thirteen colonies, though basically Anglo-Saxon, was perhaps the most mixed that could be found anywhere in the world. Counting Negroes, nearly 40% was of non-English origin, although New England boasted more native born and persons of English blood than the other sections. Of the fifty-six signers of the Declaration of Independence in 1776, eighteen were non-English, and eight of these had been born outside the colonies.

Men of Quality

Social inequalities existed in all the colonies, despite the leveling tendencies of a crude frontier life. Cleavages were sharpest in the South, with its planter aristocracy, and perhaps least sharp in small-farm New England. The transplanted settlers were merely recreating on a modified scale the social structure they had known at home. But yeasty democratic forces were working significant changes. The most remarkable feature of the social ladder was the rags-to-riches ease with which an ambitious person might rise from a lower rung to a higher one.

At the top of the social ladder towered the aristocrats. They were the merchant princes (like John Hancock), the landed gentry (like George Washington), the wealthier professional men, and the clergy of the established churches. In addition, there were the well-dressed British officials, including the governors and other "ruffle-shirted Anglicans."

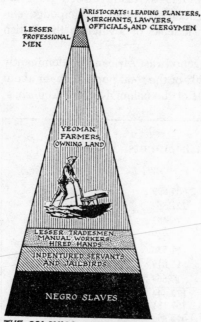

THE COLONIAL SOCIAL PYRAMID, 1775
(AN APPROXIMATION)

The English law of primogeniture encouraged social barriers. By permitting the eldest son to inherit all or most of his father's estate, this ancient restriction helped perpetuate a landed aristocracy of wealth, especially in the South. The Southern gentry—with their charm, culture, and leisure for both fox hunting and statecraft—contributed richly to American social and political life.

The aristocrats were proud of their superior status, and often dressed flashily to show it off, displaying brocades, satins, and laces. Early colonial laws expressly forbade persons of the "meaner sort" to dress above their station. In the 18th-Century South a tailor was fined and jailed for racing his horse—"a sport only for gentlemen."

The colonials were often seated in churches and schools according to their social rank. John Adams, later second President of the United States, was placed fourteenth in a class of twenty-four at Harvard, where ability also affected one's standing. Only a fraction of those settlers coming to early New England were entitled to be addressed by the exalted title of "mister."

The Lower Rungs

Below the aristocracy was the middle class—the backbone of the colonies. It consisted chiefly of the small farmers, often clad in buckskin breeches, who owned modest holdings and tilled them with their own hands. Closely associated with this group were the skilled artisans, with their well-greased leather aprons, and the smaller tradesmen. America's most famous printer, Benjamin Franklin, was never fully accepted by the snobs of his adopted Philadelphia. The son of a Boston candlemaker, he was looked down upon as a social climber—a person "in trade."

Below the prosperous middle class were "hired hands" and other propertyless poor whites. Happily, the ne'er-do-wells were not numerous. Extreme poverty and extreme wealth were both rather rare.

Even lower on the social ladder were the indentured servants, of whom perhaps 250,000 had come by 1775. These "white slaves" were mainly persons who could not afford to pay their passage across the Atlantic. In return for transportation, they voluntarily agreed to mortgage the sweat of their bodies for a period of years, usually five or more. Their lot was often harsh, and runaways were common.

Indentured servants, upon redeeming themselves, frequently secured land, and the more enterprising souls often became prosperous. Nor did any serious social stigma attach to them. Some even broke up into the ranks of the aristocracy, and two became signers of the Declaration of Independence. The indentured-servant system admittedly inflicted much hardship, but it did give tens of thousands of impoverished people a chance to start anew in the Land of Opportunity.

Far less desirable than the voluntary indentured servants were the paupers and convicts who were involuntarily shipped over as indentured servants. Altogether, about 50,000 jailbirds were dumped on the American colonies by the London authorities. This riffraff crowd was generally sullen and undesirable, and not bubbling over with good will for the King's government. But many convicts were the unfortunate victims of circumstances and of a viciously unfair penal code. Some of them, in fact, came to be highly respected citizens.

Negro slaves were the mudsills of society. Enchained in all the colonies, they were concentrated in the warm plantation South. In South Carolina, for example, they outnumbered the whites two to one. Some of the colonial legislatures, foreseeing the dangers resulting from a large population of slaves, attempted to restrict or halt their importation. But all such efforts were vetoed by the London authorities. This action, though taken in the interests of imperial policy and of the British and New England slave traders, was looked upon by many colonials as a callous disregard of their welfare. It was assailed by Thomas Jefferson in an early draft of the Declaration of Independence, but the proposed clause was finally dropped, out of regard for Southern feelings.

Professional People

The leading profession was the Christian ministry. In 1775 clergymen wielded less influence than in the early days of Massachusetts, when fanaticism had burned more fiercely. But they still occupied a position of high prestige.

Most physicians were poorly trained and not highly esteemed. Not until 1765 was the first medical school established, although European centers attracted some students. Aspiring young doctors served for a while as apprentices to older practitioners, and were then turned loose on their "victims." Bleeding was a favorite remedy; when the physician was not available, a barber was often summoned.

Plagues were a constant nightmare. Especially dreaded was smallpox, which about one out of five persons caught, including the heavily pockmarked George Washington. A crude form of inoculation was introduced in 1721, despite the objections of many physicians and some of the clergy, who opposed tampering with the will of God. Powdered dried toad was a favorite prescription for smallpox. With sanitation and other safeguards in a primitive state, the death rate was appallingly high and life expectancy was tragically short.

The profession of law had come into some prominence by the mid-1700's. In a pioneering society, where much honest manual labor remained to be done, the parties to a dispute often presented their own cases in court. Lawyers were at first regarded as noisy windbags or trouble-making rogues. An early Connecticut law classed them with drunkards and brothel keepers; and as a young law student future President John Adams was frowned upon as a suitor by the father of the girl whom he finally married.

But by about 1750, seaboard society had passed the pioneering stage, and trained attorneys were generally recognized as serving a useful purpose. Able to defend colonial rights against the Crown on legal grounds, lawyers like the eloquent James Otis and the flaming Patrick Henry took a lead in the agitation that led to revolt. Other lawyer-orators played hardly less important roles in fashioning new constitutions and in serving in representative bodies.

Workaday America

Agriculture was the leading industry, occupying about 90% of the people. Tobacco continued to be the staple crop in Maryland and Virginia. The Middle ("Bread") Colonies were growing huge quantities of grain, and by 1759 New York alone was exporting 80,000 barrels of flour a year. Seemingly the farmer had only to tickle the soil with a hoe and it would laugh with a harvest.

Fishing (including whaling), although ranking far below agriculture, was still profitable. Pursued in all the colonies, it was a major industry in New England, which exported smelly shiploads of dried cod to the Catholic countries of Europe. The fishing fleet also stimulated shipbuilding and served as a nursery for seamen.

A bustling commerce, both coastwise and overseas, enriched all the colonies, especially the New England group, New York, and Pennsylvania.

Commercial ventures and land speculation, in the absence of later get-rich-quick schemes, were the surest avenues to speedy wealth. Yankee seamen were famous in many climes not only as skilled mariners but as tight-fisted traders.

The so-called triangular trade was infamously profitable, though small in relation to total colonial commerce. A skipper, for example, would leave a New England port with a cargo of rum and sail to the coast of Africa. Bartering the fiery liquor for slaves, he would proceed to the West Indies with his screaming and dying cargo sardined below deck. There he would exchange the survivors for molasses, which he would then carry to New England, where it was distilled into rum. The Yankee captain would then repeat the trip, making a profit at each angle of the triangle.

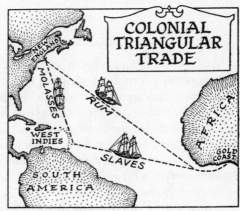

Manufacturing in the colonies was of only secondary importance, although there was a surprising variety of small establishments. As a rule, people could get ahead faster in soil-rich America by tilling the land. Huge quantities of "kill devil" rum were distilled in Rhode Island and Massachusetts, and even some of the "elect of the Lord" developed an overfondness for it. Handsome beaver hats were manufactured in quantity, despite British restrictions. Smoking iron forges, including Pennsylvania's Valley Forge, likewise dotted the land, and in fact were more numerous in 1775 than those of England. In addition, household manufacturing, including the spinning and weaving of the womenfolk, added up to an impressive output.

Lumbering was perhaps the most important single manufacturing industry. Countless cartloads of virgin timber were consumed by shipbuilders, at first chiefly in New England, and then elsewhere in the colonies. By 1770 about four hundred vessels of assorted sizes were splashing down the ways each year, and about one-third of the British merchant marine was American-built.

American naval stores—such as tar, pitch, rosin, and turpentine—were highly valued, for Britannia was anxious to insure her mastery of the seas. The London government offered generous bounties to stimulate production of these vitally needed products; otherwise they would have had to come from uncertain and possibly hostile Baltic areas. Towering trees, ideal as masts for His Majesty's Navy, were marked with the King's broad arrow for future use. The luckless colonial who was caught cutting down reserved timber was subject to fine. Even though there were countless unreserved trees and the ones selected were for the common defense, this shackle on free enterprise engendered some bitterness in the well-timbered localities.

As in all pioneering countries, skilled craftsmen and hard-muscled laborers were scarce and highly prized. The workingman consequently commanded more respect than in Europe, and partly for reasons of convenience often ate with the family of his employer. The colonial dining table was another cradle of democracy.

Horsepower and Sailpower

All sprawling and sparsely populated pioneer communities are cursed with oppressive problems of transportation. America, with a scarcity of both money and manpower, was no exception.

Not until the 1700's were there roads connecting even the major cities, and these dirt thoroughfares were treacherously poor. A wayfarer could have rumbled along more rapidly over the Roman highways in the days of Caesar Augustus, nearly two thousand years earlier. It actually took twenty-nine days for news of the Declaration of Independence—the story of the year—to reach Charleston from Philadelphia.

Roads were often clouds of dust in the summer, and quagmires of mud in the winter. The stagecoach traveler faced such additional dangers as tree-strewn roads, rickety bridges, carriage overturns, and runaway horses. A man venturesome enough to journey from Philadelphia to New York, for example, would not think it amiss to make his will and assemble his family for prayers before departing.

Where man-made roads were wretched, heavy reliance was placed on God-grooved waterways. Population tended to cluster along the banks of navigable rivers. There was also much coastwise traffic, and although it was slow and undependable, it was relatively cheap and pleasant.

Taverns sprang up along the main routes of travel, as well as in the cities. Their facilities customarily included such items as bowling alleys, pool tables, bars, and gambling equipment. Before a cheerful, roaring fire all social classes would mingle, including the village loafers. The tavern was yet another cradle of democracy.

Gossips also gathered at the taverns, which were clearinghouses of information, misinformation, and rumor—frequently stimulated by alcoholic refreshment. A successful politician, like the wirepulling Samuel Adams, was often a man who had a large alehouse acquaintance in places like Boston's Green Dragon Tavern. The taverns were important in the crystallizing of public opinion, and proved to be hotbeds of agitation as the revolutionary movement gathered momentum.

An intercolonial postal system was established by the mid-1700's, although private couriers continued to be used. The service was slow and infrequent, and secrecy was difficult to maintain. Mail carriers, serving long routes, would sometimes pass the time by reading the letters entrusted to their care.

Children of God

Religion still had a powerful grip on the people. The Sabbath was observed with rigidity, church attendance was faithful, and long-winded sermons were followed with rapt attention. The Bible was almost universally read as the infallible word of God, supplemented by such religious books as Bunyan's *Pilgrim's Progress* and Baxter's *Call to the Unconverted*. The famed *New England Primer* hammered home such precepts as:

> Christ crucify'd,
> For Sinners dy'd.

Yet things of the spirit were not the all-absorbing preoccupation in 1775 that they had been in the heyday of the Puritan oligarchs. Life in the 1600's had been harsh and grinding, and religion had taken on the stern character of its pioneer surroundings. But as men attained more ease and luxury, the appeal of a fire-and-brimstone religion became less attractive, and fanaticism faded. Somewhat more liberal doctrines were sharply challenging Calvinism. They proclaimed that human beings were not necessarily predestined to damnation, but might save themselves by repentance and good works. Many of the unorthodox worshipers even argued that a spiritual conversion was not necessary for church membership, and some of the orthodox churches grudgingly made concessions to these views.

The trend away from a wrathful God was temporarily checked by the Great Awakening—a rousing series of mass revivals which began in Europe and swept through America in the 1730's and 1740's. The leading Great Awakener in America was a tall, delicate, and intellectual Massachusetts theologian and preacher, Jonathan Edwards ("the Artist of Damnation"). He proclaimed with burning conviction the need for a thoroughgoing conversion from sin to righteousness. Warming to his subject, he would paint in lurid detail the landscape of hell and the eternal torments of the damned. "Sinners in the Hands of an Angry God" was the title of one of his famous sermons.

George Whitefield was a less intellectual but more emotional English pulpit-thumper. His magnificent voice could be heard by many thousands of enthralled listeners in an open field, and his eloquence caused the thrifty Benjamin Franklin to empty his pockets into the collection plate. During these roaring revival meetings, countless sinners professed conversion, while hundreds of the "saved" groaned, shrieked, or rolled in the snow from religious excitation.

The Great Awakening touched off the first significant battle in Amer-

Estimated Religious Census, 1775

Name	Number	Chief Locale
Congregationalists	575,000	New England
Anglicans	500,000	N.Y., South
Presbyterians	410,000	Frontier
German Churches (incl. Lutheran)	200,000	Penn.
Dutch Reformed	75,000	N.Y., N.J.
Quakers	40,000	Penn., N.J., Del.
Baptists	25,000	R.I., Penn., N.J., Del.
Roman Catholics	25,000	Md., Penn.
Methodists	5,000	Scattered
Jews	2,000	N.Y., R.I.
Estimated Total Membership	1,857,000	
Estimated Total Population	2,493,000	
Percentage Church Members	74%	

ica between conservatism and liberalism in religion. The Congregationalists and Presbyterians split over this issue, and many of the believers in religious conversion went over to the Baptists and other more emotional sects. The multiplying of denominations, which weakened the hold of the old-line clergy, also made for more tolerance and democratic control.

The Great Awakening was the first spontaneous mass movement of the American people. As such, it tended to break down sectional boundaries, as well as denominational lines. It foreshadowed revolutionary new departures elsewhere, even in the field of governmental control. The King would do well to look to his colonies.

Temples of the Lord

Two "established" or tax-supported churches were conspicuous in 1775: the Anglican and the Congregational. A large segment of the population, surprisingly enough, did not worship in any church. And in the colonies where there was an "established" faith, only a minority of the people belonged to it.

The Church of England, whose members were commonly called Anglicans, was formally established in Georgia, North and South Carolina, Virginia, Maryland, and a part of New York. Established also in England, it served in America as a major prop of kingly authority. The British officials naturally made vigorous efforts to impose it on additional colonies, but they ran into a stone wall of opposition.

THE DOMINANCE OF ESTABLISHED CHURCHES

The Anglican Church in America fell somewhat short of its promise. Secure and self-satisfied, like the parent establishment in England, it clung to a faith that was less fierce and more worldly than the religion of Puritanical New England. Sermons were shorter; hell was less scorching; and amusements, like Virginia fox hunting, were less frowned upon. Most of the Anglican clergy were earnest and devout men, but some were indolent and worldly, and occasionally a scoundrel would appear who was more interested in winning at cards than in winning souls for the Lord.

The influential Congregational Church, which had grown out of the Puritan Church, was formally established in all the New England colonies, except Rhode Island. At first Massachusetts taxed all residents to support Congregationalism, but later relented and exempted members of other well-known denominations. Presbyterianism, though closely associated with Congregationalism, was never made official in any of the colonies.

Ministers of the gospel, looking to this sinful world, increasingly grappled with burning political issues. As the early rumbling of revolution against the British Crown could be heard, sedition flowed freely from pulpits. Presbyterianism, Congregationalism, and Rebellion were triplets. Many of the leading Anglican clergymen, not wholly unaware of what side their bread was buttered on, naturally supported their King.

Established (Tax-Supported) Churches in the Colonies, 1775

		When Disestablished
Mass. (incl. Me.) ⎫ Connecticut ⎬ CONGREGATIONAL New Hampshire ⎭		1833 1818 1819
Rhode Island	NONE	
New York	ANGLICAN (in N.Y. City and three neighboring counties)	1777
New Jersey ⎫ Delaware ⎬ NONE Pennsylvania ⎭		
Maryland ⎫ Virginia ⎪ North Carolina ⎬ ANGLICAN South Carolina ⎪ Georgia ⎭		1777 1786 1776 1778 1777

(Note persistence of the Congregational establishment in New England.)

The Anglicans in America were seriously handicapped by not having a resident bishop, whose presence would be convenient for the ordination of young ministers. American students of Anglican theology had to travel to England to be ordained. On the eve of the Revolution there was serious talk of creating an American bishopric, but the scheme was violently opposed by non-Anglicans, who feared a tightening of the royal reins. The controversy poured oil on the glowing embers.

Religious toleration had indeed made enormous strides in America, at least when compared with halting steps abroad. Roman Catholics were still generally discriminated against, as in England. But there were fewer Catholics in America, and hence the anti-papist laws were less severe and less strictly enforced. In general, a man could worship—or not worship—as he pleased.

Lamps of Learning

The time-honored English ideal regarded education as a boon reserved for the aristocratic few, not for the unwashed many. Education should be for leadership, not citizenship, and primarily for the male sex. Only slowly and painfully did the colonials break away from the chains of these ancient concepts.

Puritan New England, largely for religious reasons, was more zealously interested in education than any other section. Dominated by the Congregational Church, it stressed the need for Bible reading by the individual worshiper. The primary goal of the clergy was to make good Christians rather than good citizens.

Education flourished almost from the outset in New England. The population was compact, and contained an impressive number of graduates from the English universities, especially Cambridge, the intellectual center of Puritanism. The New Englanders, at a relatively early date, established primary and secondary schools, which varied widely in the quality of instruction and in the length of time that their doors remained open each year. Back-straining farm labor drained much of the youth's time and energy. A memorable Massachusetts law of 1647 thrust squarely on each township the responsibility for providing schools, and hence did much to lay the foundation stones of the American public school system.

Fairly adequate primary and secondary schools were also pounding knowledge into the heads of reluctant "scholars" in the Middle Colonies and in the South. Some of these places were tax-supported; others were privately operated. The South, with its white and Negro population diffused over wide areas, was severely handicapped in attempting to establish an effective school system. Wealthy families leaned heavily on private tutors.

The general atmosphere in the colonial schools and colleges was grim and gloomy. The emphasis was on religion and on the classical languages, notably Latin and Greek. The stress was not on experiment and reason, but on doctrine and dogma. The age was one of orthodoxy, and independence of thinking was discouraged. Discipline was severe, with many a mettlesome lad being "birched" with a birch switch. Sometimes punishment was inflicted by an indentured-servant teacher, who could himself be whipped and who therefore was not inclined to spare the rod.

College education was regarded—at least at first in New England—as more important than instruction in the ABC's. The church would wither if a new crop of ministers was not trained to lead the spiritual flocks. Harvard College was founded in 1636, primarily to advance learning but partly as a ministerial training school. Many well-to-do families, especially in the South, sent their boys abroad to English institutions.

Colonial Colleges				
Name	Original Name (if different)	Location	Opened or Founded	Denomination
1. Harvard		Cambridge, Mass.	1636	Congregational
2. William and Mary		Williamsburg, Va.	1693	Anglican
3. Yale		New Haven, Conn.	1701	Congregational
4. Princeton	College of New Jersey	Princeton, N.J.	1746	Presbyterian
5. Pennsylvania	The Academy	Philadelphia	1751	Non-sectarian
6. Columbia	King's College	New York City	1754	Anglican
7. Brown	Rhode Island	Providence, R.I.	1764	Baptist
8. Rutgers	Queen's College	New Brunswick, N.J.	1766	Dutch Reformed
9. Dartmouth *		Hanover, N.H.	1769	Congregational

* Begun as an Indian missionary school

For purposes of convenience and economy, nine local colleges were planted during the colonial era. Student bodies were small, numbering about two hundred boys at the most; and at one time lads as young as eleven were admitted to Harvard. The caliber of instruction was poor by present-day standards. The curriculum was still heavily loaded with theology and the "dead" languages, although by 1750 there was a distinct trend toward "live" languages and other modern subjects. A significant contribution was made by the practical-minded and skeptical Benjamin Franklin, who had a large hand in launching what became the University of Pennsylvania. As the first American college free from denominational control, it sharply reduced the overemphasis on religion.

Culture in the Backwoods

The rupturing toil of pioneer life left little energy or inclination for artistic effort. The American was too busy chopping down trees to sit around painting landscapes, especially when a hostile Indian might burst from a nearby thicket. There was no esthetic tradition; and many clergy-men regarded art an an invention of the Devil.

As the colonists gradually acquired some wealth and leisure, their surplus energy went into religious and political leadership, not art. The materialistic atmosphere was not favorable to artistic endeavor. One fa-mous painter, John Trumbull of Connecticut (1756–1843), was discour-aged in his youth by his father with the chilling remark, "Connecticut is not Athens." Charles W. Peale (1741–1827), best known for his portraits of George Washington, ran a museum, stuffed birds, and practiced den-tistry. Benjamin West (1738–1820) and John S. Copley (1738–1815) suc-ceeded in their ambition to become famous painters, but they had to go to England to complete their training. Only there could they find subjects who had the leisure to sit for their portraits, and the money to pay hand-somely for them.

American architecture was largely imported from the Old World, and modified to meet the peculiar climatic and religious conditions of the New World. Even the lowly log cabin was apparently borrowed from Sweden. The red-bricked Georgian style, so common in the pre-Revolution dec-ades, was introduced about 1720, and is best exemplified by the beauty of now-restored Williamsburg, Virginia.

Colonial literature, like art, was generally undistinguished, and for about the same reasons. Among numerous handicaps, it was dominated by theology, although many sermons had literary quality. What little writ-ing emerged is known only to specialists, with two noteworthy exceptions.

The "Great Awakener" Jonathan Edwards, who customarily arose at four o'clock to put in a fourteen-hour day, wielded a busy pen. His re-ligious writings were as numerous as they were hairsplitting, and estab-lished him as the finest theological mind ever produced in America. Some of his treatises, rivaling those of John Calvin in explaining Calvinism, were widely read in Presbyterian Scotland. His most famous work, *On the Freedom of the Will*, was perhaps the first American book of world importance. It was translated into many languages, including Arabic.

The amazingly versatile Benjamin Franklin, often called "the first civilized American," also shone as an important literary light. Although his incomplete autobiography is a classic, he was best known to his con-temporaries for *Poor Richard's Almanack*, which he edited from 1732 to 1758. This famous publication, containing many pithy sayings culled from the thinkers of the ages, emphasized such homespun virtues as thrift, in-dustry, morality, and common sense. Examples are: "What maintains one vice would bring up two children"; "Plough deep while sluggards sleep"; and "Honesty is the best policy." "Poor Richard" was well known in Eu-rope and was more widely read in America than anything else, except the Bible. As a teacher of both old and young, Franklin's influence in shaping American character was incalculable. His down-to-earth approach to life did much to offset the influence of clergymen like Jonathan Edwards. Franklin was more eager to save money than souls.

Science, rising above the shackles of theology and superstition, was making some progress, though lagging behind the Old World. A few botanists, mathematicians, and astronomers had won some repute, but genial Benjamin Franklin was perhaps the only first-rank scientist produced in the American colonies. His spectacular experiments with electricity, including the kite-flying episode, won him numerous honors in Europe. But his mind had a practical turn, and among his numerous inventions were bifocal spectacles and the highly efficient Franklin stove. His lightning rod, not surprisingly, was condemned by the less liberal clergy as "presuming on God" by attempting to control the "artillery of the heavens."

Pioneer Presses

Stump-grubbing Americans were too poor to buy quantities of books, and too busy to read them. One South Carolina merchant in 1744 advertised the arrival of a shipment of "printed books, Pictures, Maps, and Pickles." A few private libraries of fair size were to be found, especially among the clergy. The Byrd family of Virginia had perhaps the largest collection in the colonies, consisting of about four thousand volumes. Bustling Benjamin Franklin established in Philadelphia the first privately supported circulating library in America; and by 1776 there were about fifty public libraries and collections supported by subscription.

Hand-operated colonial printing presses were active in running off pamphlets, leaflets, and journals. On the eve of the Revolution there were about forty colonial newspapers, chiefly weeklies which consisted of a single large sheet folded once. The columns ran heavily to dull essays, frequently signed by Cicero, Philosophicus, and Pro Bono Publico. The news often lagged many weeks behind the event, especially in the case of overseas happenings, in which the colonials were deeply interested. Newspapers proved to be a powerful agency for airing colonial grievances and building up opposition to British control.

A celebrated legal case, in 1734–1735, involved John Peter Zenger of New York, whose newspaper had severely criticized the corrupt royal governor. Charged with seditious libel, the accused was haled into court, where he was defended by a distinguished Philadelphia lawyer, Andrew Hamilton, then nearly eighty. Zenger argued that he had printed the truth, while the bewigged royal Chief Justice ruled that the mere fact of printing, irrespective of the truth, was enough to convict. The jury, swayed by the eloquence of Hamilton, defied the red-robed judges and returned a verdict of "Not guilty." The spectators burst into cheers.

The Zenger decision was epochal. Though not accepted by other royal judges, in time it helped set a precedent against judicial tyranny in libel suits. Newspaper editors had something of a burden lifted from their backs, even though complete freedom of the press was unknown during the pre-Revolutionary era.

The Political Animal

The colonials may have been backward in natural or physical science, but they were making noteworthy contributions to political science.

The thirteen colonial governments presented a varied structure. By 1775, eight of the colonies had royal governors, who were appointed by the King. Three were under proprietors who themselves chose the governors—Maryland, Pennsylvania, and Delaware. And two—Connecticut and Rhode Island—elected their own governors under self-governing charters.

Practically every colony utilized a two-house legislative body. The upper house, or council, was normally appointed by the Crown in the royal colonies, and by the proprietor in the proprietary colonies. It was chosen by the voters in the self-governing colonies. The lower house, as the popular branch, was elected by the people—or rather by those persons who owned enough property to qualify as voters. In several of the colonies, the back-country elements were seriously underrepresented, and they

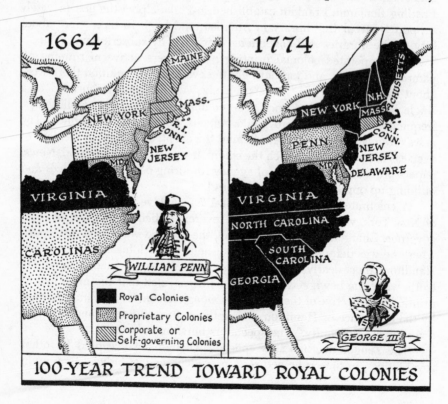

1664

MAINE
MASS.
NEW YORK
R.I.
CONN.
NEW JERSEY
MD.
VIRGINIA
CAROLINAS

WILLIAM PENN

Royal Colonies
Proprietary Colonies
Corporate or Self-governing Colonies

1774

MASSACHUSETTS
N.H.
NEW YORK
MASS.
R.I.
CONN.
PENN
NEW JERSEY
MD.
DELAWARE
VIRGINIA
NORTH CAROLINA
SOUTH CAROLINA
GEORGIA

GEORGE III

100-YEAR TREND TOWARD ROYAL COLONIES

hated the ruling colonial clique perhaps more than they did kingly authority. The legislatures, in which the people were directly represented,
voted such taxes as they chose for the necessary expenses of colonial government. Self-taxation through representation was a precious privilege
which Americans had come to cherish above most others.

The governors appointed by the King were generally able men, sometimes outstanding figures, and their households were an important segment of Europe's cultural frontier. But the appointees were sometimes
incompetent or corrupt, and included broken-down politicians badly in
need of a job. The worst of the group was impoverished Lord Cornbury,
first cousin of Queen Anne, who was made governor of New York and
New Jersey in 1702. He proved to be a drunkard, a spendthrift, a grafter,
an embezzler, a religious bigot, and a vain fool, especially when he appeared in public dressed like a woman. Even the best of the King's appointees had trouble with the colonial legislatures, basically because the
royal governor represented a bothersome trans-Atlantic authority some
three thousand miles away.

But the colonial assemblies were by no means defenseless. Some of
them employed the trick of withholding the governor's salary unless he
yielded to their wishes. He was normally in need of money—otherwise he
would not have come over to this God-forsaken country—so he was usually forced to terms. But one stubborn governor of North Carolina died
with his salary eleven years in arrears.

The British government, in leaving the colonial governor to the tender
mercies of the legislature, was guilty of poor administration. In the interests of simple efficiency the London authorities should have arranged to
pay him from independent sources. As it was, control over the purse by
the colonial legislatures led to prolonged bickering, which proved to be
one of the persistent irritants that generated a spirit of revolt.

Administration at the local level was also varied. County government
was the rule in the plantation South; town-meeting government predomi-
nated in New England; and a modification of the two developed in the
Middle Colonies. In the town meeting, with its open discussion and open
voting, direct democracy was at its best. In this unrivaled cradle of democracy, sturdy Americans learned to cherish their privileges and exercise
their duties as citizens of the New World commonwealths.

Yet the ballot was by no means a birthright. Religious or property
qualifications for voting existed in all the colonies in 1775, and even stiffer
qualifications for holding office. The privileged upper classes, fearful of
democratic excesses, were unwilling to grant the ballot to every "biped of
the forest." Perhaps half of the adult white males were thus disfranchised.
But because of the ease of acquiring land and thus satisfying property requirements, the right to vote was not beyond the reach of most industrious
and enterprising colonials.

By 1775 America was not yet a true democracy—socially, economically, or politically. But it was far more democratic than England and Europe. Colonial institutions were giving freer rein to the democratic ideals of tolerance, opportunity for education, equality of economic opportunity, freedom of speech, freedom of the press, freedom of assembly, and representative government. And these democratic seeds, planted in rich soil, were to bring forth a lush harvest in later years.

Colonial Folkways

Everyday life in the colonies may now seem glamorous, especially as reflected in antique shops. But judged by modern standards, it was drab and tedious. For the mass of the people, the labor was heavy and constant —from daybreak to backbreak.

Food was plentiful, though the diet was coarse and monotonous. Americans probably ate more bountifully, especially of meat, than any people in the Old World. Lazy or sickly was the man who could not manage to fill his stomach.

Basic comforts now taken for granted were lacking. The churches were not heated at all, except for charcoal foot-warmers which the women-folk carried. During the frigid New England winters, the preaching of hell-fire may not have seemed altogether unattractive. Drafty homes were poorly heated, chiefly by inefficient fireplaces. There was no running water in the houses, no plumbing, and probably not a single bathtub in all colonial America. The flickering lights were inadequate, for illumination was provided by candles and whale-oil lamps. Garbage disposal was primitive. Long-snouted hogs customarily ranged the streets to consume refuse, while buzzards, protected by law, flapped greedily over tidbits of waste.

Amusement was eagerly pursued where time and custom permitted. The militia assembled periodically for musters, which consisted of several days of drilling, liberally interspersed with merrymaking and eyeing the girls. On the frontier, pleasure was often combined with work at house-raisings, quilting bees, husking bees, and apple parings. Funerals and weddings everywhere afforded opportunities for social gatherings, which customarily involved the swilling of much strong liquor.

Winter sports were common in the North, while in the South card playing, horse racing, cockfighting, and fox hunting were favorite pastimes. George Washington was a superb rider. In the non-Puritanical South, dancing was the rage—jigs, square dances, the Virginia reel—and the athletic Washington could swing his fair partner with the best of them.

Other diversions beckoned. Lotteries were universally approved, even by the clergy, and were used to raise money for churches and colleges. Stage plays were popular in the South, but they were frowned upon in the Quaker and Puritan colonies, and were even forbidden by law. Many New

England clergymen regarded play-acting as time-consuming and immoral; their flocks derived much real satisfaction from religious lectures instead.

Holidays were everywhere celebrated, but Christmas was frowned upon in New England as an offensive reminder of Roman Catholicism. "Yuletide is fooltide" was a common Puritan sneer. Thanksgiving Day came to be a truly American festival, for it combined thanks to God with an opportunity for jollification and gorging.

* * * * *

The American colonials in 1775 were a remarkable people: restless, energetic, ambitious, resourceful, ingenious, and independent-minded. With every passing year they were less willing to bow their necks to the yoke of overseas authority. They were like a fast-growing and well-muscled farm boy who is coming of age, and who expects to be treated as an adult and not as a lackey. With a boundless continent before them, with amazing pioneer achievements behind them, and with an astonishing fertility within them, they had caught a vision of their destiny and were preparing to grasp it. Woe unto him who should try to thwart them!

SELECT READINGS

Social history is absorbingly treated in L. B. WRIGHT, *The Cultural Life of the American Colonies, 1607–1763* (1957) [paperback]. Challenging insights may be found in D. J. BOORSTIN, *The Americans: The Colonial Experience* (1958) and H. M. JONES, *O Strange New World: American Culture: The Formative Years* (1964). A lively collection of contemporary readings is *The Colonial Image* (J. C. MILLER, ed., 1962). Classic cultural studies are CARL BRIDENBAUGH, *Cities in the Wilderness* (1938) and *Cities in Revolt: Urban Life in America, 1743–1776* (1955), [both paperback]. Broad concepts are handled in MAX SAVELLE, *Seeds of Liberty* (1948); MICHAEL KRAUS, *The Atlantic Civilization: Eighteenth-Century Origins* (1949); and T. J. WERTENBAKER, *The Golden Age of Colonial Culture* (1942) [paperback]. Special topics are revealingly presented in E. S. GAUSTAD, *The Great Awakening in New England* (1957); in J. S. EZELL, *Fortune's Merry Wheel: The Lottery in America* (1960); and in BERNARD BAILYN, *The New England Merchants in the Seventeenth Century* (1955) [paperback]. BENJAMIN FRANKLIN's classic *Autobiography* [paperback] is still indispensable. Standard lives of Franklin are the detailed treatment by CARL VAN DOREN (1938) [a Pulitzer-prize winner] and V. W. CRANE (1954). See also F. B. TOLLES, *Quakers and the Atlantic Culture* (1960); L. W. LEVY, *Legacy of Suppression: Freedom of Speech and Press in Early American History* (1960) [paperback]; R. E. and B. K. BROWN, *Virginia, 1705–1786: Democracy or Aristocracy?* (1964) [democracy is upgraded]; E. S. MORGAN, *Visible Saints: The History of a Puritan Idea* [halfway covenant] (1963); R. B. PERRY, *Puritanism and Democracy* (1944). Also *Harvard Guide*, Pt. III.

5

The Road to Revolution

---

*The Revolution was effected before the war commenced. The
Revolution was in the minds and hearts of the people. . . .*

JOHN ADAMS, 1818

The Roots of Revolution

THE AMERICAN REVOLUTION, in a broad sense, was not the same thing as
the American War of Independence. The war itself lasted only eight years.
But the revolution lasted over a century and a half, and began when the
first permanent English settlers landed on the shores of America. Insurrection of thought always precedes insurrection of deed. And over the years
such a change occurred in the thinking of the colonists that the revolution
was nearly completed in their minds before the bullets began to fly. America was a revolutionary force from the day of its discovery.

The colonies were settled largely by emigrants who were discontented or rebellious in spirit—by people who had failed to adjust themselves to their harsh lot in the Old World. Most of them had not been able
to get along, whether socially, politically, economically, or religiously.
Some of them were tired of taking off their hats and standing bareheaded
in the presence of their "betters." Others wanted a larger share in government, or a richer portion of this world's goods, or an opportunity to worship God as they chose.

The nightmare of crossing the Atlantic normally lasted about six to
eight weeks, often much longer. The ships were frequently turned into
"floating coffins" by food shortages or epidemics of disease; in one extreme
case 350 out of 400 passengers and crew perished. Cannibalism was not
unknown, and starving men fought over the bodies of vermin. As a sailor's
song ran:

> We ate the mice, we ate the rats,
> And through the hold we ran like cats.

The perilous crossing left many emotional scars. The survivors who
staggered ashore on the Promised Land were, as a rule, isolated spiritually
from the faraway Old World. They were more than ever aware that the

arm of the London government, weakened by three thousand miles of ocean, could not reach them nearly so effectively as at home.

The lonely American wilderness likewise stimulated ideas of independence. Back in England the villagers had lived near graveyards that contained the bones of their ancestors for a thousand years past. Born into such conservative surroundings, the poor plowman did not question the social rut in which he found himself. But in the New World he was not held down by the scowl of his overlords.

In America all was strange, crude, different. The dense forests and the rugged pioneering conditions changed patterns of living, and consequently habits of thought. Those wretched settlers perished who could not adapt themselves to their raw surroundings, and hundreds of the early Virginia colonists paid the supreme penalty. Before long, men were eating Indian corn, wearing Indian moccasins and buckskin, and in extreme instances on the frontier uttering the war whoop as they scalped their fallen red foe. Hacking a home out of the wilderness with an ax developed strength, self-confidence, individualism, and a spirit of independence.

As the Americans matured, they acquired privileges of self-government enjoyed by no other colonial peoples. They set up thirteen parliaments of their own, and aped the parliamentary methods of the Mother Country. Ultimately they came to regard their own legislative bodies as more or less on a footing with the great Mother of Parliaments in London. One governor of Rhode Island would wear no wig unless it had been made in England and was exactly like that worn by the Speaker of the British House of Commons.

The Mercantile Theory

The British Empire was acquired in "a fit of absent-mindedness," as the old saying goes, and there is much truth in it. Not one of the original thirteen colonies, except Georgia, was formally planted by the British government. The actual founding was done haphazardly by trading companies, religious groups, land speculators, and others. The London authorities did not even dream that a new nation was being born. And the colonials themselves, busily chopping down trees, were no less shortvisioned.

The governmental machinery in London for controlling the colonies was relatively simple. As it had evolved by 1696, the principal agency was the Board of Trade, which consisted of eight salaried members, joined in an advisory capacity by certain other prominent officials. With the passage of time, interest in the Board flagged, and membership on it became something of a joke. Yet the recommendations of the Board regarding the colonies were often made into law, either by act of Parliament or in regulations adopted by the Privy Council.

The basic philosophy under which the English settlements were ultimately exploited was mercantilism—commonly called the mercantile theory. This meant roughly that the colonies existed for the benefit of the Mother Country—that they should add to its wealth, prosperity, and self-sufficiency. Otherwise why go to all the trouble and expense of governing and protecting them? The settlers were regarded more or less as tenants. They were expected to produce tobacco and other products needed in England, and not to bother their heads with dangerous experiments in self-government.

Specifically, how were the American colonies to benefit the Mother Country? First of all, they were to insure Britain's naval supremacy by furnishing ships, ships' stores, seamen, and trade. In addition, they were to provide a profitable consumer's market for the English manufacturers at home. Finally, they were to keep gold and silver money within the Empire by growing products, such as sugar, that otherwise would have to be bought from foreigners. The ideal of "Buy British" would thus be promoted in a manner that foreshadowed later protective tariff systems.

Trammels on Trade

Numerous measures were passed by Parliament to enforce the mercantile system. Most famous were the Navigation Laws. The first of these, enacted in 1651, was aimed at rival Dutch shippers who were elbowing their way into the American carrying trade. The Navigation Laws, as finally perfected, restricted commerce to and from the colonies to English vessels. This regulation not only kept money within the Empire but bolstered the British—and colonial—merchant marine, which was an indispensable auxiliary to the Royal Navy.

An alert Parliament from time to time enacted additional laws favorable to the Motherland. European goods consigned to America had to be landed first in England, where customs duties could be collected and where the British middleman would get his cut of the profit. Still other curbs required certain "enumerated" products, notably tobacco, to be sent to England and not to a foreign market, though prices in the latter might be higher.

The colonials, in the interests of the Empire, were even restricted in what they might produce at home. They were forbidden to manufacture for export certain products, such as woolen cloth and beaver hats, because the colonies were supposed to complement and not compete with English industry.

The Americans also felt the pinch in the field of currency. No banks existed in the colonies, and the money problem on the eve of the Revolution was acute. The industrious colonials were now buying more goods from England than they were selling to her, so the difference had to be made up in hard cash. Every year gold and silver money, much of it in quaint Spanish coins from the West Indies, was drained out of the colonies. The colonials simply did not have enough left for the convenience of everyday purchases. Barter became necessary, and even butter, nails, pitch, and feathers were used for purposes of exchange.

The currency problem came to a boil when dire need finally forced many of the colonies to issue paper money. Unfortunately, it proved to be of depreciating value. British merchants and creditors, understandably worried, squawked so loudly that Parliament was forced to act. It restrained the colonial legislatures from printing paper currency and from passing lax bankruptcy laws—practices that might result in defrauding British merchants. The Americans, who felt that their welfare was again being sacrificed, reacted angrily. Another burning grievance was thus heaped upon the pile of combustibles already smoldering.

The officials in London naturally kept a watchful eye on the legislation passed by the colonial assemblies. If such laws conflicted with British regulations or policy, they were declared null and void by the Privy Council—just as the Supreme Court of the United States today declares laws unconstitutional.

This so-called royal veto was necessary for efficient government, and it was used rather sparingly—469 times in connection with 8,563 laws. But the colonies understandably took a narrower view. Some of them were aggrieved when, in the interests of the Mother Country, they were forbidden to take steps that they deemed desirable, such as curbing the degrading trade in Negro slaves.

The Merits of Mercantilism

The British mercantile system has long been regarded by red-blooded Americans as thoroughly selfish and deliberately oppressive, if not downright malicious.

The truth is that until 1763 the Navigation Laws imposed no intolerable burden, partly because they were laxly enforced. Ingenious colonial merchants early learned to disregard or evade restrictions that they found vexatious. In fact, some of the early American fortunes were amassed by wholesale smuggling. The wealthy and vain John Hancock of Massachusetts came to be known, not altogether fairly, as the "King of Smugglers."

The Americans, in addition, were fortunate enough to reap direct benefits from the mercantile system. The British government paid liberal bounties to those colonials who produced ships and ships' stores, even though English competitors complained heatedly. When independence came, the bounties dried up and many of these American producers were forced to the wall.

Virginia tobacco planters, in particular, enjoyed valuable privileges. While forbidden to ship their yellow leaf to any place other than England, they were guaranteed a monopoly of the British market. Moreover, tobacco growing was outlawed in England and Ireland, although the plant had already been raised in England with some success.

The colonials, furthermore, fared well in other fields. They enjoyed the undiluted rights of Englishmen, as well as unusual opportunities for self-government. They were not compelled to tax themselves to support a professional army and navy for protection against French, Dutch, Spaniards, Indians, and pirates. Although the colonists went to some little expense in "training" militiamen, they enjoyed the shield of a strong army of British Redcoats and the mightiest navy in the world—without a penny of cost. After independence, the Americans were required to tax themselves to maintain a tiny army and navy, both of which afforded inadequate protection.

In manufacturing and trade the colonials were not badly off. They were denied the privilege of fabricating specified articles for export, but this regulation worked no serious hardships, because it was laxly enforced and because other pursuits were usually more profitable. The Americans were forced to deal with the British middleman, but they would have done so anyhow, owing to a common language, liberal credit arrangements, and familiar business methods.

"Prosperity trickles down" is a common saying; and the Americans enjoyed a generous share of Britain's profits under the mercantile system. The average American was probably better off economically than the average Englishman at home. If the colonies existed for the benefit of the Mother Country, it was hardly less true that the Mother Country existed for the benefit of the colonies. The well-meaning officials in London were working for the welfare of the Empire as a whole, and they gave over-all unity to its policies. A wise man does not behead or starve the goose that lays the golden eggs. Mistakes were made by the British authorities, but they were not, until revolt was precipitated, the mistakes of malice.

Mercantilism had sufficient merit to be widely adopted and long perpetuated. All other colonial nations of that age, including Spain and France, embraced mercantilistic principles completely and enforced them ironhandedly. Mercantilism has endured to the present century, even in the United States. Interested groups of Americans seek to insure prosperity for manufacturers and wage earners by protective tariffs, and to bolster the national defense by subsidies to shipbuilders. American Navigation Laws—shades of the 17th Century!—are still designed to prevent foreign shippers from encroaching on our coastwise trade, even that between Hawaii and the mainland.

The Menace of Mercantilism

The mercantile system, even when painted in its rosiest colors, burdened the colonials with annoying liabilities. Economic initiative was thwarted, because Americans were not at complete liberty to buy, sell, ship, or manufacture under conditions that they found most profitable. The Southern colonies were generally favored over the Northern ones, chiefly because they grew non-English products like tobacco, sugar, and rice. Revolution was one seed that sprouted vigorously from the stony soil of New England, for the proud sons of the Puritans resented being treated like unwanted relatives.

The one-crop Virginians, despite London's preference for Southern colonies, nursed rankling grievances. Forced to sell all their tobacco in England, they were at the mercy of British merchants, who often gouged them. Many of the fashionable Virginia planters were plunged into debt by the declining price of tobacco, and were forced to buy their necessities in England by mortgaging future crops. Some debts, becoming hereditary, were bequeathed by father to son. Impoverished Virginia vied for leadership in agitating for revolt against England; and unfriendly critics sneered that her cry, "Liberty or Death," might better have been "Liberty or Debt." While this charge was unfair in many cases, countless Virginians welcomed the opportunity to end their economic bondage to the Mother Country.

Finally—and of overshadowing importance— mercantilism was debasing from the standpoint of the Americans. The colonies, many of them felt, were being milked, as cows are milked. They were to be kept in a state of perpetual economic adolescence, and were never to come of age. As Benjamin Franklin wrote in 1775:

> We have an old mother that peevish is grown;
> She snubs us like children that scarce walk alone;
> She forgets we're grown up and have sense of our own.

Revolution broke out, as Theodore Roosevelt later remarked, because England failed to recognize an emerging nation when she saw one.

Taxation without Representation

The titanic Seven Years' War, which ended in 1763, marked a new relationship between Britain and her trans-Atlantic colonies. A revolution in British colonial policy precipitated the American Revolution.

Victory-flushed Britain emerged from the conflict with one of the biggest empires in the world—and also, less happily, with the biggest debt. It amounted to £140,000,000, about half of which had been incurred in defending the American colonies. The British officials wisely had no intention of asking the colonials to help pay off this crushing burden. But London felt that the Americans, presumably for their own protection, should be asked to defray one-third the cost of maintaining a garrison of some 10,000 Redcoats.

Prime Minister George Grenville, an honest and able financier not noted for tact, moved vigorously. Dedicated to efficiency, he first aroused the resentment of the colonials in 1763 by ordering the British navy to enforce the Navigation Laws. Then he proposed to raise the revenue for the military force by a stamp tax, after first vainly asking the Americans for suggestions. The act that passed Parliament in 1765 imposed a levy on about fifty items, all of which were to use stamped paper or have stamps affixed to them. The list included bills of lading, diplomas, playing cards, dice, pamphlets, and marriage licenses and other legal documents.

Grenville, like many Britishers on both sides of the Atlantic, did not regard this new tax as intolerable. Englishmen for two generations had endured a stamp tax, and the current one was far heavier than that passed for the colonies. Grenville also believed that the colonials were technically represented in the Parliament that had passed this measure. Under the existing theory of "virtual representation," every member of Parliament represented all British subjects everywhere, even those in Boston and Charleston. Actually, Parliament had for many years levied customs duties at American seaports, and the colonials had raised no strong objection to them.

Yet the Americans, striving to wrest a living from the wilderness, were deeply alarmed. They were already paying substantial local taxes, voted by their own assemblies, and they were aroused by the prospect of double taxation. It is true that they had not protested against the customs duties long levied by Parliament, but these were indirect taxes, paid at the customs house and passed on indirectly to the consumer in higher prices. Such imposts were intended primarily to regulate trade, not to raise revenue. But the Stamp Act tax was a direct tax, levied directly on the consumer, primarily for revenue and not regulation. It was admittedly a light tax, but once it was accepted it might be the entering wedge for ruinous taxes. Many Americans feared that if they were forced to pay one penny, they might one day have to pay their last penny.

"Taxation without representation is tyranny" was the cry that burst from the throats of thousands of Americans. There was some inconsistency in the slogan, for in America taxation without representation had long been the lot of religious dissenters, of small farmers, and of the back-country pioneers. Nor did the colonials really want direct representation in Parliament. If they had obtained it, any gouty member of the House of Commons could have proposed an oppressive tax bill for the colonies, and the American representatives could have been overwhelmingly out-voted.

What the colonials really wanted was a return to the "good old days" before the French and Indian War. Then the Navigation Laws had been only laxly enforced, and the Americans had suffered no taxation, except by their own regularly elected assemblies. Betraying a quite human preference for benefits without burdens, the colonists were unwilling to shoulder the new responsibilities that went with being part of a great empire.

Parliament Capitulates

The colonial outcry against the hated tax took various forms. The most conspicuous in some ways was the Stamp Act Congress of 1765, which brought together in New York City twenty-seven distinguished delegates from nine colonies. After dignified debate, the members drew up a statement of their rights and grievances, and besought the King and Parliament to repeal the odious legislation.

The Stamp Act Congress, which was largely ignored in England, made little splash at the time in America. But it did do something to break down sectional suspicions, for it brought together around the same table leading men from the different colonies. The Stamp Act Congress was one more halting but significant step toward intercolonial unity.

More effective than the Congress was the widespread adoption of non-importation agreements against British goods. Garments of homespun became fashionable, and the eating of lamb chops was discouraged lest wool-bearing sheep not be allowed to mature. The non-importation agreements were in fact a promising stride toward union; they united the American people for the first time in common action.

Violence also attended colonial protests. Groups of ardent spirits, known as Sons of Liberty, took the law into their own hands. Crying "Liberty, Property, and No Stamps," they enforced the non-importation agreements against violators, often with a coat of tar and feathers. The houses of unpopular officials were wrecked, their money was stolen, and stamp agents were hanged in effigy.

Shaken by violence, the machinery for collecting the tax broke down. On that day in 1765 when the new act was to go into effect, the stamp agents had all been forced to resign, and there was no one to sell the stamps. While flags flapped at half-mast, the law was openly and flagrantly defied—or rather, nullified.

England was hard hit. Merchants and manufacturers suffered from the colonial non-importation agreements, and hundreds of laborers were thrown out of work. Loud demands converged on Parliament for repeal of the Stamp Act. But many of the members could not understand why 7,500,000 Britons had to pay heavy taxes to protect the colonies, while nearly 2,000,000 colonials refused to pay for only one-third of the cost of their own defense.

After a stormy debate, and as a matter of expediency and not of right, Parliament in 1766 reluctantly repealed the unpopular Stamp Act. At the same time, and by an overwhelming vote, it saved face by passing the Declaratory Act. This futile measure proclaimed that Parliament had the right "to bind" the colonies "in all cases whatsoever." The bare assertion of this right was but a feeble victory for parental authority, for the unruly colonials had proved that the London government could be forced to yield to boycotts and mob action.

America forthwith burst into an uproar of rejoicing. The grateful residents of New York erected a leaden statue to King George III—a tribute which was later melted into thousands of bullets to be fired at his own troops.

Tax Turmoil Again

Control of the British ministry was now seized by the gifted but erratic "Champagne Charley" Townshend, who could deliver brilliant speeches in Parliament while drunk. Rashly promising to pluck feathers from the colonial goose with a minimum of squawking, he persuaded Parliament in 1767 to pass the Townshend Acts. The most important of these new regulations was a light import duty on glass, white lead, paper, and tea. Townshend deferred to the sensitive colonials by making this tax, unlike the Stamp Act, an indirect customs duty payable at American ports.

The colonists, flushed as they were with their recent victory over the Stamp Tax, were in a rebellious mood. The impost on tea was especially irksome, for an estimated one million persons drank "the cup that cheers" twice a day, and even the Indians used it when firewater was not available.

The new Townshend revenues, worse yet, would be used to pay the salaries of the royal governors and judges in America. From the standpoint of efficient administration by London, this was a reform long overdue. But the ultra-suspicious Americans, who had beaten the royal governors into line by control of the purse, regarded Townshend's move as another attempt to enchain them.

The old non-importation agreements, previously potent, were now revived against the Townshend Acts. But they proved less effective than those devised against the Stamp Act. The colonials, again enjoying prosperity, took the new tax less seriously than might have been expected, partly because it was light and indirect. They found, moreover, that they could secure smuggled tea at a cheap price, and consequently smugglers increased their activities, especially in Massachusetts.

The British officials, faced with a breakdown of law and order, landed two regiments of troops in Boston in 1768. Many of the soldiers, unfortunately, were drunken and profane characters. The liberty-loving colonials, resenting the presence of the red-coated ruffians, taunted the "lobster backs" unmercifully.

A clash was inevitable. On the evening of March 5, 1770, a crowd of some sixty townspeople set upon a squad of ten soldiers, one of whom was hit by a club and another of whom was knocked down. Acting apparently without orders but under extreme provocation, the troops fired a volley which killed or wounded eleven citizens. Both sides were in some degree to blame, and in the subsequent trial only two of the soldiers could be found guilty of manslaughter. They were released after being branded on the hand.

The so-called Boston Massacre—a skirmish rather than a "massacre"—further aroused the colonials against the British, especially after the con-

The Bloody Massacre perpetrated in King—ı-Street *BOSTON* on March 5.th 1770 by a party of the 29.th REG^t.

THE BOSTON MASSACRE
After Paul Revere's somewhat fanciful engraving

viction spread that the Americans had been wholly unoffending. Paul Revere wrote:

Unhappy Boston! see thy sons deplore
Thy hallowed walks besmear'd with guiltless gore.

Massacre Day was observed as a patriotic holiday until 1776, when the more glorious Fourth of July eclipsed it.

Cells of Sedition

By 1770 King George III, then only thirty-two years old, was definitely seeking to restore the declining power of the British monarchy. He was a good man in his private morals, but he proved to be a bad ruler. Earnest, industrious, stubborn, lustful for power, and cursed with periodic fits of insanity, he surrounded himself with cooperative spirits, notably his corpulent Prime Minister, Lord North.

The ill-timed Townshend Acts had failed to produce revenue, though producing near rebellion. The net proceeds from the tax in one year were £295, and during that time the annual military costs to Britain in the colonies had mounted to £170,000. The non-importation agreements, though feebly enforced, were pinching British manufacturers. The government of Lord North, bowing to various pressures, finally persuaded Parliament to repeal the Townshend revenue duties. But the three-pence tax on tea was retained to keep alive the principle of Parliamentary taxation.

The flames of discontent in America continued to be fanned by numerous acts, including the redoubled efforts of the British officials to enforce the existing Navigation Laws. Resistance was further whipped up by a master propagandist and engineer of rebellion, Samuel Adams of Boston, a cousin of John Adams. Unimpressive in appearance (his hands trembled), he had failed miserably in private life. His friends had to buy him a suit of clothes when he left Massachusetts on intercolonial busi-

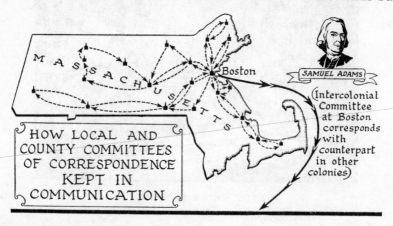

HOW LOCAL AND COUNTY COMMITTEES OF CORRESPONDENCE KEPT IN COMMUNICATION

SAMUEL ADAMS

(Intercolonial Committee at Boston corresponds with counterpart in other colonies)

ness. But zealous, tenacious, and courageous, he was ultra-sensitive to infractions of colonial rights. Cherishing a deep faith in the common man, he appealed effectively to what was called his "trained mob." Skillful also as a pamphleteer, he soon became known as the "Penman of the Revolution."

The signal contribution of Samuel Adams was to organize in Massachusetts the local committees of correspondence. After he had formed the first one in Boston during 1772, some eighty towns in the colony speedily set up similar organizations. Their chief function was to spread propaganda and information by interchanging letters, and thus to keep alive opposition to British policy. One critic referred to the committees as "the foulest, subtlest, and most venomous serpent ever issued from the egg of sedition." No more effective device for stimulating resistance could have been contrived, and later revolutionists have adopted some of its underground techniques in establishing "cells."

Intercolonial committees of correspondence were the next logical step. Virginia led the way in 1773 by creating such a body as a standing committee of the House of Burgesses. Within a short time every colony had established a central committee through which it could exchange ideas and information with other colonies. These intercolonial groups, which were supremely significant in stimulating and disseminating sentiment in favor of united action, evolved directly into the first American Congresses.

Tea Parties Brew a Revolution

Thus far—that is, by 1773—nothing had happened to make rebellion inevitable. Non-importation was weakening. Increasing numbers of colonials were reluctantly paying the tea tax, because the legal tea was now cheaper than the smuggled tea, and cheaper than tea in England. Even John Adams on one occasion hoped that the tea he was drinking was smuggled Dutch tea, but he could not be sure.

A new ogre entered the picture in 1773. The powerful British East India Company, overburdened with 17,000,000 pounds of unsold tea, was facing bankruptcy. If it collapsed, the London government would lose heavily in tax revenue. The ministry therefore decided to assist the company by giving it a complete monopoly of the American tea business. The terms thus granted would enable the giant corporation to sell the leaves more cheaply than ever before, even with the three-pence tax added. But to many American consumers, principle was more important than price.

Violence was inevitable, for the new tea monopoly had many aspects that were hateful to the colonials. Above all, it seemed like a shabby at-

Boston customs official, John Malcolm, paraded after being tarred and feathered, January 25, 1774. Detail from an English cartoon. Harvard College Library

tempt to trick the Americans, with the bait of cheaper tea, into acceptance
of the detested tax. Once more the colonials rose in their wrath. Not a
single one of the several thousand chests of tea shipped by the company
was landed in the hands of the consignees. At Annapolis, the Marylanders
burned both the cargo and the vessel. At Boston, which was host to the
most famous tea party of all, a band of white townsfolk, disguised as Indians, boarded the three tea ships on December 16, 1773. They smashed
open 342 chests and dumped the "cursed weed" into the harbor, while a
silent crowd watched approvingly from the wharves.

Reactions varied. Extremists in America rejoiced; conservatives shuddered. This wanton destruction of private property was going too far. The
British at home were outraged, while even friends of America in England
hung their heads. Punishment and coercion were the only possible responses of the London authorities, as long as the mercantilist philosophy
prevailed and the colonials refused to accept responsibility. The granting
of some kind of home rule to the Americans might have prevented rebellion, but the Britons of that age were not blessed with such vision.

Parliament Legislates a Rebellion

An outraged Parliament responded speedily to the Boston Tea Party.
By huge majorities in 1774 it passed a series of "Repressive Acts," which
were designed to chastise Boston in particular, Massachusetts in general.

The most drastic of all was the Boston Port Act. It closed the tea-
stained harbor until damages were paid and order could be assured. By
other "Intolerable Acts"—so they were called in America—many of the
chartered rights of Massachusetts were swept away. Restrictions were likewise placed on the precious town meetings. Contrary to previous practice,
enforcing officials who killed colonials in line of duty could now be sent
to England for trial. There, suspicious Americans assumed, they would
be likely to get off scot-free.

By a fateful coincidence, the "Intolerable Acts" were accompanied in
1774 by the Quebec Act. Passed at the same time, it was erroneously regarded in English-speaking America as one of the "repressive" measures.
Actually, the Quebec Act was a good law in bad company. For fourteen
years the British government had debated how it should administer the
60,000 or so conquered French subjects in Canada, and it had finally
framed this farsighted and statesmanlike measure. The French were guaranteed their Catholic religion. They were also permitted to retain many
of their old customs and institutions, which did not include a representative assembly or trial by jury in civil cases. In addition, the old boundaries
of the Province of Quebec were now extended southward all the way to
the Ohio River.

The Quebec Act, from the viewpoint of the French Canadians, was
a shrewd and conciliatory measure. If England had only shown as much

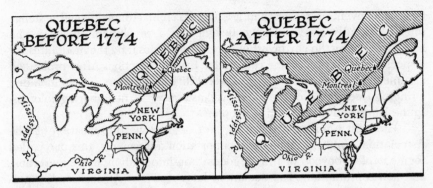

foresight in dealing with her English-speaking colonies, she might not have lost them.

But from the viewpoint of the American colonials as a whole, the Quebec Act was the most intolerable of the "Intolerable Acts." All the other "repressive" laws slapped directly at Massachusetts, but this one had much wider application. It seemed to set a dangerous precedent in America against jury trials and popular assemblies. It alarmed land speculators, who were distressed to see the huge trans-Allegheny area snatched from their grasp. It aroused the host of anti-Catholics, who were shocked by the extension of Roman Catholic jurisdiction southward into a huge region that had once been earmarked for Protestantism—a region about as large as the thirteen original colonies. One angry Protestant cried that there ought to be a "jubilee in hell" over this enormous gain for "popery."

Readying for Revolt

The American colonials, rasped by the Quebec Act, responded sympathetically to the plight of Massachusetts. She had put herself in the wrong by the wanton destruction of the tea cargoes; now the Mother Country had put herself in the wrong by savage punishment that did not seem to fit the crime. Flags were flown at half-mast throughout the colonies on the day that the Boston Port Act went into effect, and sister colonies rallied to send food to the stricken city. Rice was shipped even from faraway South Carolina.

The most memorable response to the "Intolerable Acts" was the summoning of a Continental Congress in 1774. It was to meet in Philadelphia to consider ways of redressing colonial grievances. Twelve of the thirteen colonies, with Georgia alone missing, sent fifty-five distinguished men, among them Samuel Adams, John Adams, George Washington, and Patrick Henry. Intercolonial frictions were partially melted away by social activity after working hours; in fifty-four days George Washington dined at his own lodgings only nine times.

The First Continental Congress deliberated for seven weeks, September 5 to October 26, 1774. It was not a legislative but a consultative body;

it was a convention rather than a Congress. John Adams played a stellar role. Eloquently swaying his colleagues to a revolutionary course, he helped defeat by the narrowest of margins a proposal by the moderates for a species of American home rule under British direction. After prolonged argument, the Congress drew up several dignified papers. These included a ringing Declaration of Rights, as well as appeals to neighboring colonies, to the King, and to the British people.

The most significant action of the Congress was the creation of The Association. Unlike previous non-importation agreements, this one called for a *complete* boycott of British goods: non-importation, non-exportation, and non-consumption. The document known as The Association, by providing for concerted action, was the closest approach to a written constitution that the colonies as a unit had yet devised. But still there was no genuine move toward independence—merely an effort to bring about a repeal of the offensive legislation and a return to the happy days before Parliamentary taxation. If colonial grievances were redressed, well and good; if not, the Congress was to meet again in May, 1775.

But the deadly drift toward war continued. The petitions of the Continental Congress were rejected, after considerable debate, by strong majorities in Parliament. Chickens squawked and tar kettles bubbled as violators of The Association were tarred and feathered. Muskets were being collected, men were openly drilling, and a clash seemed imminent.

In April, 1775, the British commander in Boston sent a detachment of troops to nearby Lexington and Concord. They were to seize stores of colonial gunpowder, and also to bag the "rebel" ringleaders, Samuel Adams and John Hancock. At Lexington, the colonial "Minute Men" refused to disperse, and shots were fired which killed eight Americans and wounded several more. The British Redcoats pushed on to Concord, whence they were forced to retreat by the homespun Americans.

> By the rude bridge that arched the flood,
>   Their flag to April's breeze unfurled,
>   Here once the embattled farmers stood,
>   And fired the shot heard round the world.*

The bewildered British, enduring a murderous fire from militiamen crouched behind thick stone walls, finally gained the sanctuary of Boston. England now had a war on her hands.

Imperial Strength and Weakness

The Americans had brashly rebelled against the mightiest empire in the world. The population odds were about three to one against them—some 7,500,000 Britons to 2,500,000 colonials. The odds in monetary wealth and naval power were overwhelmingly in favor of the Mother Country.

* Ralph Waldo Emerson, "Concord Hymn."

The British maintained a professional army of some 50,000 men, which was later increased, as compared with the more numerous but wretchedly trained American militia. George III, in addition, had the money with which to hire foreign soldiers, and some 30,000 Germans—so-called Hessians—were ultimately employed. The British also enrolled about 50,000 American Loyalists, and enlisted the services of many Indians, who, though unreliable fair-weather fighters, ravaged long stretches of the frontier. One British officer boasted that the American war would offer no problems that could not be solved by an "experienced sheep herder."

Yet the Mother Country was weaker than she seemed at first glance. Oppressed Ireland was a latent volcano, and British troops had to be de-

ALL LOCALITIES SHOWN IN BLACK OR LISTED WERE BRITISH-HELD. NOTE HOW SMALL THE EMPIRE WAS IN RELATION TO ITS LATER SIZE (AUSTRALIA, S.AFRICA, ETC.). THE RELATIVELY POOR CANADIAN AREA IS DECEPTIVELY LARGE; THE RICH WEST INDIAN AREA DECEPTIVELY SMALL.

tached to watch her. The French, rankling from their recent defeat, were awaiting an opportunity to stab Britain in the back. The London government was confused and inept. There was no William Pitt, "organizer of victory," only the stubborn George III and his pliant Lord North.

Many earnest and God-fearing Britons had no desire whatever to kill their American cousins. William Pitt withdrew his son from the army rather than see him thrust his sword into fellow Anglo-Saxons struggling for liberty. The English Whig party, opposed to Lord North's Tory party, openly cheered American victories—at least at the outset. Aside from trying to embarrass the Tories politically, many Whigs believed that the battle for English freedom was being fought in America. If George III triumphed overseas, his rule at home might become completely tyrannical. This outspoken sympathy in England, though plainly that of a minority, greatly encouraged the Americans. If they continued their resistance long enough, the Whigs might come into power and deal generously with them.

The British army in America had to operate under discouraging difficulties. The generals were second-rate. The soldiers, though generally first-rate, embraced some scum and were brutally treated. There was one extreme case of eight hundred lashes on the bare back for striking an officer. Provisions were often rancid, wormy, and scarce. The British army in New York at one time had flour for only fourteen days; and a supply of biscuits, captured some fifteen years earlier from the French, was softened by dropping cannon balls on them.

Other handicaps loomed. The Redcoats had to conquer the Americans; a draw would be a victory for the colonials. The British were operating some three thousand miles from their English base, and distance added greatly to the delays and uncertainties arising from storms and other mishaps. Military orders were issued in London which, when received in America many weeks later, would not fit the changing situation.

The geographical expanse in America was enormous: roughly 1000 by 600 miles. The United States had no urban nerve center, like France's Paris. The British armies captured every city of any size, yet they made little more than a dent in the entire country. The Americans wisely traded space for time. Benjamin Franklin calculated that during the prolonged campaign in which the Redcoats captured Bunker Hill and killed some 150 Yankees, about 60,000 American babies were born.

American Advantages and Disadvantages

The revolutionists were blessed with outstanding leadership. George Washington was a giant among men; Benjamin Franklin was a master among diplomats. Open foreign aid, theoretically possible from the start, was eventually secured from France. Numerous European officers, many of them unemployed and out at the elbows, volunteered their swords for pay. In a class by himself was a wealthy young French nobleman, the Marquis de Lafayette. Fleeing from boredom, loving glory and ultimately liberty, at age nineteen the "French gamecock" was made a major general in the colonial army. His commission was largely a recognition of his family influence and political connections, and the services of this teenage general in securing further aid from France were invaluable.

Other circumstances aided the Americans. They were fighting defensively, with the odds, other things being equal, favoring the defender. In agriculture, the colonies were mainly self-sustaining, like a kind of Robinson Crusoe's island. The colonial "buckskins," moreover, were a tough, self-reliant people. As marksmen, they far outshone the British, who often pointed rather than aimed their weapons. A competent American rifleman at two hundred yards could hit a man's head.

The Americans, in addition, enjoyed the moral advantage that came from what they regarded as a just cause. The historical odds were not impossible, for other peoples had triumphed in the face of greater obstacles: the Greeks against Persians, the Swiss against Austrians, the Dutch against Spaniards.

Yet the American rebels were badly organized for war. From earliest days they had been almost fatally lacking in unity. The Continental Congress, which directed the conflict, was hardly more than a debating society, and it grew weaker as the struggle dragged on. The disorganized colonials fought almost the entire war before they were able to adopt a written constitution—the Articles of Confederation.

Jealousy everywhere raised its disruptive head. The individual states, proudly regarding themselves as sovereign, resented the attempts of Congress to exercise its weak powers. Intense sectional jealousy boiled up over the appointment of military leaders; and there were even distrustful New Englanders who almost preferred British officers to Americans from other sections.

Economic difficulties were well-nigh insuperable. For one thing, metallic money had already been heavily drained away. A cautious Continental Congress, moreover, was unwilling to raise anew the explosive issue of taxation. The rebel government was forced to print "Continental" paper money profusely, and as this currency poured from the presses, it depreciated until it was "not worth a Continental." One barber contemptuously papered his shop with the almost worthless dollars. The confusion was thickened when the individual states were compelled to issue depreciated paper money of their own.

Inflation of the currency inevitably skyrocketed prices. The families of the soldiers at the fighting front were hard hit, and hundreds of anxious husbands and fathers deserted. Debtors easily acquired handfuls of the semi-worthless money and gleefully paid their debts "without mercy"—sometimes with the weapons of the authorities to back them up.

A Rabble in Arms

Basic military supplies in the colonies were dangerously scanty, especially firearms and powder. Benjamin Franklin seriously proposed going back to the bow and arrow. Even where food was accumulated, wagons were often not available to haul it. At Valley Forge, in the winter of 1777–1778, the shivering American soldiers were without bread for three successive days. In one Southern campaign they fainted for lack of food.

Manufactured goods were generally in short supply in agricultural America, and clothing and shoes were appallingly scarce. The path of the patriot fighting men was often marked by bloody snow. At frigid Valley Forge, during one anxious period, 2800 men were barefooted or nearly naked. Woolens were desperately needed against the wintry blasts; and in general the only real uniform of the colonial army was uniform raggedness. During a grand parade at Valley Forge some of the officers appeared wrapped in woolen bed covers. One Rhode Island detachment was known as the "Ragged, Lousy, Naked Regiment."

American militiamen were numerous but highly unreliable. Able-bodied American males—perhaps several hundred thousand of them—had received rudimentary training, and some 90,000 of these recruits served for short terms in the rebel armies. But poorly trained plowboys, though better shots, could not stand up in the open field against professional British troops advancing with bare bayonets. Many of these undisciplined warriors would, in the words of Washington, "fly from their own shadows."

A few thousand regulars—perhaps 7000 or 8000 at the end of the war—were finally whipped into shape by stern drillmasters. Notable among these officers was an organizational genius, the picturesque German "Baron" von Steuben. He spoke no English when he reached America, but he soon taught his men that bayonets were not for broiling beefsteaks over open fires. These soldiers of the Continental Line, as they gained experience, were able to hold their own in open battle against crack British troops.

The morale of the Revolutionary army was badly undermined by American profiteers. These grasping gentry, putting profits above patriotism, sold to the British because the invader could pay in gold. Speculators forced prices sky-high; and some Bostonians made profits of 50% to 200% on army clothing when the American army was freezing at Valley Forge. Washington never had as many as 20,000 effective troops in one place at one time, despite bounties of land and other inducements dangled before prospective volunteers. Yet if the rebels had thrown themselves into the struggle as one man, they could easily have raised many times that number.

The brutal truth is that only a select minority of the American colonials attached themselves to the cause of independence with a spirit of selfless devotion. These were the dedicated souls who bore the burden of battle and the risks of defeat; these were the freedom-loving patriots who deserved the gratitude and approbation of generations yet unborn. Seldom have so few done so much for so many.

SELECT READINGS

E. S. MORGAN, *The Birth of the Republic, 1763–1789* (1956) [paperback] is brief and incisive. Recent scholarship is compressed into L. H. GIPSON, *The Coming of the Revolution, 1763–1775* (1954) [paperback]. Old but still challenging is C. M. ANDREWS, *The Colonial Background of the American Revolution* (1924) [paperback]. Comprehensive and charmingly written is J. C. MILLER, *Origins of the American Revolution* (1943), a Book-of-the-Month-Club choice. CARL BRIDEN-BAUGH, *Mitre and Sceptre* (1962) is the fullest treatment of colonial fears of a British-created Anglican episcopate. A critical reexamination is BERNHARD KNOLLEN-BERG, *Origin of the American Revolution, 1759–1766* (1960) [paperback]. The role of the Vice-Admiralty Courts in stirring up trouble is elaborated in CARL UBBELOHDE, *The Vice-Admiralty Courts and the American Revolution* (1960), and in O. M. DICKERSON, *The Navigation Acts and the American Revolution* (1951) [paperback]. A scholarly treatment may be found in E. S. and H. M. MORGAN, *The Stamp Act Crisis* (1953) [paperback] and in B. W. LABAREE, *The Boston Tea Party* (1964). The role of the press receives extended coverage in A. M. SCHLESINGER, SR., *Prelude to Independence: The Newspaper War on Britain, 1764–1776* (1958) and B. I. GRANGER, *Political Satire in the American Revolution, 1763–1783* (1960). Useful biographical studies are W. HANNA, *Benjamin Franklin and Pennsylvania Politics* (1964); J. C. MILLER, *Sam Adams* (1936); R. D. MEADE, *Patrick Henry: Patriot in the Making* (1957); and DUMAS MALONE, *Jefferson the Virginian* (1948), the first volume of an authoritative multi-volume biography. Also *Harvard Guide,* Pt. III.

6

America Secedes from the Empire

---

*These are the times that try men's souls. The summer soldier
and the sunshine patriot will, in this crisis, shrink from the
service of their country; but he that stands it* now, *deserves
the love and thanks of man and woman. . . .*

THOMAS PAINE, December, 1776

Congress Chooses a Commander

THE BLOODSHED at Lexington and Concord in April, 1775, was a clarion call
to arms. About 20,000 musket-bearing "Minute Men" swarmed around
Boston, there to coop up the bewildered British.

The Second Continental Congress met in Philadelphia the next month,
on May 10, 1775; and this time the full slate of thirteen colonies was represented. The conservative element in Congress was still strong, despite the
shooting in Massachusetts. There was no real sentiment for independence
—merely a desire to continue fighting in the hope that King and Parliament would consent to a redress of grievances. The Congress hopefully
drafted new appeals to the British people and King—appeals that in due
course were flatly rejected. Anticipating a possible rebuff, the delegates
also adopted measures to create an army and navy, and to raise money
for the war.

Perhaps the most important single action of the Congress was to select
George Washington, one of its members already in officer's uniform, to
head the hastily improvised army besieging Boston. The choice was made
with considerable misgivings. The tall, dignified, blue-eyed Virginia
planter, then forty-three, had never risen above the rank of a colonel in
the militia. His largest command had numbered only 1200 men, and that
had been some twenty years earlier. Falling short of true military genius,
he was actually destined to lose more pitched battles than he won.

But the distinguished Virginian was gifted with outstanding powers
of leadership and immense strength of character. He radiated patience,
courage, self-discipline, and a sense of justice. He was a great moral force
rather than a great military mind—a symbol and a rallying point. Men
instinctively trusted him; they sensed that when he put himself at the head

of a cause, he was prepared, if necessary, to go down with the ship. He insisted on serving without pay, though he kept a careful expense account. Later he sternly reprimanded his steward at Mount Vernon for providing the British, under duress, with supplies. Washington would have preferred to let the enemy put the torch to his mansion.

The Continental Congress, though dimly perceiving Washington's qualities of leadership, chose more wisely than it knew. His selection, in truth, was largely political. Americans in other sections, already jealous, were beginning to distrust the large New England army that was being collected around Boston. Prudence suggested a general from Virginia, the largest and most populous of the colonies. As a man of wealth, both by inheritance and by marriage, Washington could not be accused of being a fortune seeker. As an aristocrat, he could be counted on to check the excesses of the masses.

Loyal Rebels

The clash of arms continued on a strangely inconsistent basis. On the one hand, the Americans were vehemently protesting their loyalty to the King, and earnestly voicing their desire to patch up existing difficulties. On the other hand, they were raising armies and shooting down His Majesty's soldiers. This curious war of inconsistency was fought for fourteen long months—from April, 1775, to July, 1776—before the fateful plunge into independence was taken.

The tempo of warfare gradually increased. In May, 1775, a tiny American force surprised and captured the British garrisons at Ticonderoga and Crown Point, on the scenic lakes of upper New York. A priceless store of powder and artillery for the siege of Boston was thus secured. In June, 1775, the colonials seized a hill, now known as Bunker Hill, from which they menaced the enemy in Boston. The British, instead of cutting off the retreat of their foes by flanking them, blundered bloodily when they launched a frontal attack with 3000 men under General William Howe. The sharpshooting Americans, numbering 1500 and strongly entrenched, mowed down the advancing foe with frightful slaughter. But their scanty store of powder finally gave out, and they were forced to abandon the hill. With two more such victories, remarked the French Foreign Minister, the British would have no army left in America.

Following Bunker Hill, the King slammed the door on all hope of reconciliation. In August, 1775, he formally proclaimed the colonies in rebellion, with all that this implied in the way of future hangings. The next month he further widened the chasm when he completed arrangements for hiring thousands of German troops (so-called Hessians) to help crush his rebellious subjects. The six German princes involved in the transaction needed the money (one reputedly had seventy-four children); George III needed the men.

The news of the Hessian deal was shocking to the colonials. The quarrel, they felt, was within the family. Why bring in outside mercenaries, especially these fiercely mustached foreigners, who had an exaggerated reputation for bestiality?

The Hessians proved to be good soldiers in a mechanical sense, but many of them were more interested in plundering than in fighting. For good reason they were dubbed "Hessian flies." Seduced by American promises of land, hundreds of them finally deserted and remained in the United States to become respected citizens.

War in the Name of Peace

The unsheathed sword continued to take its toll. In October, 1775, on the eve of a cruel winter, the British burned Falmouth (Portland), Maine. In that same autumn the rebels daringly undertook a two-pronged invasion of Canada. The American leaders believed, erroneously, that the conquered French were restive under the British yoke. A successful assault on Canada would add a fourteenth colony, and at the same time deprive Britain of a valuable base for striking at the colonies in revolt. This large-scale attack, involving some 2000 American troops, contradicted the claim of the colonials that they were merely fighting defensively for a redress of grievances. The invasion northward was offensive warfare with a vengeance.

The bold stroke for Canada narrowly missed success. One invading column under the Irish-born General Richard Montgomery, late of the British army, pushed up the Lake Champlain route and captured Montreal. It was joined at Quebec by the bedraggled army of General Benedict Arnold, whose men had been reduced to eating dogs and shoe leather during their grueling march through the Maine woods. The assault on Quebec, launched on the last day of 1775, was beaten off. The able Montgomery was killed; the dashing Arnold was wounded in one leg. The vanquished remnants under his command retreated up the St. Lawrence River, the way Montgomery had come. The French-Canadian leaders, who had been generously treated by the British in the Quebec Act of 1774, showed no real desire to welcome the anti-Catholic invaders.

Bitter fighting continued in the colonies, though the Americans disclaimed all desire for independence. In January, 1776, the British set fire to the Virginia town of Norfolk. In March they were finally forced to evacuate Boston, taking with them the leading friends of the King. (Evacuation Day is still celebrated annually in Boston.) In the South the rebellious colonials won two victories in 1776: one in February against some 1500 defenders of the Crown at Moore's Creek Bridge, in North Carolina; and the other in June against an invading British fleet at Charleston harbor.

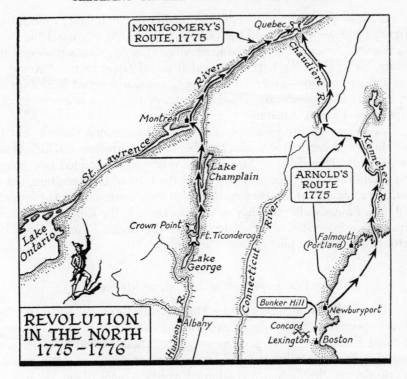

MONTGOMERY'S ROUTE, 1775

ARNOLD'S ROUTE 1775

REVOLUTION IN THE NORTH 1775-1776

Common Sense vs. Inconsistency

Why did American spokesmen continue to deny any intention of independence? Loyalty to the Empire was deeply ingrained; colonial unity was poor; and open rebellion was highly dangerous, especially against a nation as formidable as Britain. Irish rebels of that day were customarily hanged, drawn, and quartered. American rebels might have fared no better. As late as January, 1776—five months before independence was declared—the King's health was being toasted by the officers of Washington's mess near Boston.

Gradually the Americans were shocked into a realization of their inconsistency. Their eyes were opened by harsh British acts like the burning of Falmouth and Norfolk, and especially by the hiring of the Hessians. Then, in January, 1776, came the publication of *Common Sense*, one of the most potent pamphlets ever written. Its author was Thomas Paine, in his youth an impoverished corset-maker's apprentice, who as a flaming liberal had come over from England a year earlier. His tract became a whirlwind best seller, and within a few months reached the astonishing total of 120,000 copies.

Paine flatly branded the shilly-shallying of the colonials as contrary to "common sense." Why not throw off the cloak of inconsistency? Nowhere in the physical universe did the smaller heavenly body control the larger one. Then why should the tiny island of England control the vast continent of America? As for the King, whom the Americans professed to revere, he was nothing but "the Royal Brute of Great Britain." America had a sacred mission—a moral obligation to the world—to set herself up as an independent, democratic republic, untainted by association with corrupt and monarchical Britain.

Paine's passionate protest was simple and somewhat shallow, but it was direct and persuasive. It was both high-class journalism and high-class propaganda. Thousands of American waverers were prodded into going the whole way. They not only perceived the folly of their position, but—perhaps most important—they realized that they could not hope for open aid from France as long as they swore allegiance to the King. The French Crown was interested in the destruction of the British Empire, not in its reformation under a plan of reconciliation.

The Explanation of Independence

Gradually the members of the Philadelphia Congress, instructed by their respective colonies, edged toward a clean break. On June 7, 1776, fiery Richard Henry Lee of Virginia moved that "These United Colonies are, and of right ought to be, free and independent states. . . ." After considerable debate, the motion was adopted nearly a month later, on July 2, 1776.

The passing of Lee's resolution was the formal "declaration" of independence by the American colonies, and technically this was all that was needed to sever the British tie. John Adams wrote confidently that ever thereafter July 2 would be celebrated annually with fireworks. But something more was required. An epochal rupture of this kind called for some formal explanation to "a candid world." An inspirational appeal was also needed to enlist other English colonies in America, to invite assistance from foreign nations, and to rally resistance at home.

Shortly after Lee made his memorable motion on June 7, a committee was appointed by Congress to prepare an appropriate statement. The task of drafting it fell to Thomas Jefferson, a tall, freckled, sandy-haired Virginia lawyer of thirty-three. Despite his youth, he was already recognized as a brilliant writer, and he measured up splendidly to his opportunity. After some debate and amendment, the Declaration of Independence was formally approved by the Congress on July 4, 1776. It might better have been called "The Explanation of Independence" or, as one contemporary described it, "Mr. Jefferson's advertisement of Mr. Lee's resolution."

Jefferson's pronouncement, couched in a lofty style, was magnificent. He gave his appeal universality by invoking the "natural rights" of mankind—not just British rights. He argued persuasively that since the King had flouted these rights, the colonials were justified in cutting their connection. He then set forth a long list of the presumably tyrannous misdeeds of George III. The bill of indictment included imposing taxes without consent, dispensing with trial by jury, abolishing valued laws, establishing a military dictatorship, maintaining standing armies in peacetime, cutting off trade, burning towns, hiring mercenaries, and inciting savage Indians.*

This withering blast was admittedly one-sided. But Jefferson was in effect the prosecuting attorney, and he took certain liberties with strict historical truth. He was not writing history; he was making it through what has been called "the world's greatest editorial."

The formal declaration of independence cleared the air like a thunder shower on a muggy day. Foreign aid could be solicited with greater hope of success. Those patriots who defied the King were now rebels, not loving subjects shooting their way into reconciliation. They must all hang together, Franklin is said to have grimly remarked, or they would all hang separately. Or, in the sublime language of the Great Declaration, "We mutually pledge to each other our lives, our fortunes and our sacred honor." It was in truth "a shout heard round the world."

The defiant Declaration of Independence had a universal impact like that of no other American document. It has been a source of inspiration to countless revolutionary movements against arbitrary authority. Lafayette hung a copy on a wall in his home, leaving beside it room for a future French Declaration of the Rights of Man—a declaration that was officially born thirteen years later.

Patriots and Loyalists

The War of Independence, strictly speaking, was a war within a war. Colonials loyal to the King (Loyalists) fought the American rebels (patriots), while the rebels fought both Loyalists and British Redcoats. The Loyalists were derisively called "Tories" after the dominant political party in England, while the patriots were called Whigs after the opposition party in England.

The American Revolution, like many revolutions, was a minority movement. About one-third of the people were apathetic or neutral, including those Byrds of Virginia who sat on the fence. Perhaps somewhat more than one-third were in varying degrees rebellious; probably somewhat fewer than one-third were Loyalists who remained true to their king. Families were often split over the issue of independence: Benjamin Franklin was on the patriot side, while his distinguished son was on the Loyalist side.

The Loyalists were tragic figures. For generations Englishmen in the New World had been taught fidelity to their king. Loyalty is ordinarily regarded as a major virtue—loyalty to one's family, one's friends, one's country. If the King had triumphed, as he seemed likely to do, the Loyal-

* For an annotated text of the Declaration of Independence, see Appendix.

ists would have been acclaimed patriots, and defeated rebels like Washington would have been disgraced, severely punished, and probably forgotten.

Conservative Americans generally remained loyal—the men of education and wealth, of culture and caution. Whigs like John Dickinson sneered at them with a misquotation from Shakespeare:

> This word, Rebellion, hath froze them up,
> Like fish in a pond.

But these moderate souls were satisfied with their lot, and believed that any violent change would be for the worse. They feared that the "dirty rabble," inflamed by violence, might break out of control. "If I must be devoured," moaned one aristocrat, "let me be devoured by the jaws of a lion, and not gnawed to death by rats and vermin." The Loyalists were also more numerous among the older generation. Young men make revolutions; and from the outset relatively young men like the impassioned Patrick Henry and the sleepless Samuel Adams were energetic, purposeful, militant.

The Loyalists also included in their ranks the King's officers and other beneficiaries of the Crown—men who knew which side their daily bread came from. The same was generally true of the Anglican clergy and a large portion of their flocks, all of whom had long been taught obedience to the King.

The Loyalists were usually most numerous where the Anglican Church was strongest. A notable exception was Virginia, where the debt-burdened Anglican aristocrats flocked into the rebel camp. The King's followers were well entrenched in aristocratic New York City and Charleston, and also in Quaker Pennsylvania and New Jersey, where General Washington felt that he was fighting in "the enemy's country." While his men were starving at Valley Forge, the Pennsylvania farmers were selling their produce to the British for gold.

The Loyalists were least numerous in the New England colonies, where self-government was especially strong and mercantilism especially weak. The rebels were the most numerous where Presbyterianism and Congregationalism were entrenched, notably in New England. Invading British armies expressed their contempt and anger by using Yankee churches for pigsties.

The Loyalist Exodus

Before the Declaration of Independence in 1776, persecutions of the Loyalists by the patriots were relatively mild. Adherents of the King were subjected to some brutality, including tarring and feathering and riding on fence rails.

But after the Declaration of Independence, which drew a sharp distinction between Loyalists and patriots, harsh methods prevailed. The rebels naturally desired a united front. Putting loyalty to America first, they regarded their opponents, not themselves, as traitors. Loyalists were roughly handled; hundreds were imprisoned; and a few non-combatants were hanged. But there was no wholesale reign of terror comparable to that which later bloodied both France and Russia. For one thing, the colonials reflected Anglo-Saxon reverence for order; for another, the leading Loyalists were prudent enough to flee to the British lines.

About 80,000 loyal supporters of George III were driven out of the land, but several hundred thousand or so of the mild Loyalists were permitted to stay. The estates of many of the fugitives were confiscated and sold—a relatively painless way of helping to finance the war. Confiscation often worked great hardship, as, for example, when two aristocratic old ladies were forced to live in their former chicken house.

Some 50,000 Loyalists at one time or another bore arms for the British. They also helped the King's cause by serving as spies, by inciting the Indians, and by keeping patriot soldiers at home to protect their families. The ardent Loyalists had their hearts in their cause, and one of the grave mistakes made by the British was not to make full use of them in their armies.

Defeat and Retreat

With Boston evacuated in March, 1776, the British concentrated their attention on New York as a base of operations. Here was a splendid seaport, centrally located, where the King could count on cooperation from the numerous Loyalists. An awe-inspiring British fleet stood off New York in July, 1776. It consisted of some 500 ships and 35,000 men—the largest armed force to be seen in America until the Civil War. General Washington, dangerously outnumbered, could muster only 18,000 ill-trained troops with which to meet the crack army of the invader.

Disaster befell the Americans in the summer and fall of 1776. Outgeneraled and outmaneuvered, they were routed at the Battle of Long Island, where panic seized the raw recruits. By the narrowest of margins, and thanks to a favoring wind and fog, Washington almost miraculously escaped to Manhattan Island. Retreating northward, he crossed the Hudson River to New Jersey, and finally reached the Delaware River with the British close at his heels. Tauntingly, the enemy buglers sounded the foxhunting call, so familiar to Virginians of Washington's day. The patriot cause was at low ebb when the rebel remnants fled across the river, after collecting available boats to forestall pursuit.

The wonder is that Washington's adversary, General William Howe, did not speedily crush the demoralized American force. He was no military genius, and he well remembered the horrible slaughter at Bunker Hill, where he had commanded. The country was rough, supplies were slow in coming, and as a professional soldier Howe did not relish the rigors of winter campaigning. He evidently found more agreeable the company of his mistress, the wife of one of his subordinates—a scandal with which American satirists had a good deal of ribald fun.

WASHINGTON'S RETREAT 1776

Delaware R.

New York LONG I.

Princeton

Trenton

Philadelphia

NEW YORK AND NEW JERSEY 1776-1777

Washington, now almost counted out, stealthily recrossed the ice-clogged Delaware River. At Trenton, on December 26, 1776, he surprised and captured a thousand Hessians who were sleeping off the effects of their Christmas celebration. A week later, leaving his campfires burning as a ruse, he slipped away and inflicted a sharp defeat on a smaller British detachment at Princeton. The brilliant New Jersey campaign, crowned by these two timely victories, revealed Washington at his best.

Burgoyne's Blunderings

The authorities in London adopted an intricate scheme for capturing the vital Hudson River Valley in 1777. If successful, the British would sever New England from the rest of the states and paralyze the American cause. The main invading force, under an actor-playwright-soldier, General ("Gentleman Johnny") Burgoyne, would push down the Lake Champlain route from Canada. General Howe's troops in New York, if needed, could advance up the Hudson River to meet Burgoyne near Albany. A third and much smaller British force, commanded by Colonel St. Leger, would come in from the west by way of Lake Ontario and the Mohawk Valley.

The British planners did not reckon with General Benedict Arnold. After his repulse at Quebec in 1775, he had retreated slowly along the St. Lawrence River back to the Lake Champlain area, by heroic efforts keeping an army in the field. The British had pursued his tattered force to Lake Champlain in 1776. But they could not move farther south until they had won control of the lake, which, in the absence of roads, was indispensable for carrying their supplies.

The tireless Arnold assembled a small fleet, and the British had to stop to construct a larger one. The tiny American flotilla was finally destroyed after desperate fighting, but winter was descending and the British were forced to retire to Canada. General Burgoyne had to start anew from this base the following year. If Arnold had not contributed his daring and skill, the British invaders of 1776 almost certainly would have penetrated as far south as Fort Ticonderoga. If Burgoyne had started from this springboard in 1777, instead of Canada, he almost certainly would have succeeded in his venture. Thus the apparently futile American invasion of Canada in 1775 finally paid rich dividends.

General Burgoyne began his ill-starred invasion with 7000 regular troops. He was encumbered by a heavy baggage train and a considerable number of women, many of whom were wives of the officers. Progress was painfully slow, for sweaty axmen had to chop a path through the forest, while American militiamen began to gather like hornets on Burgoyne's flanks.

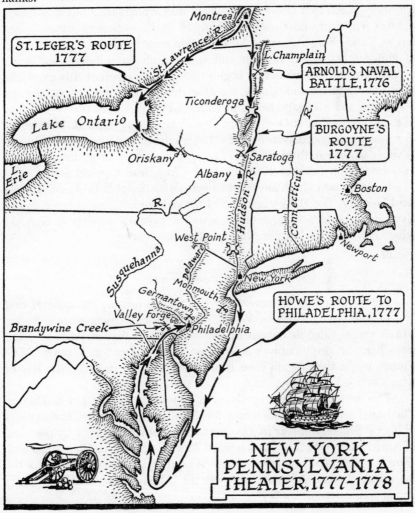

General Howe, meanwhile, was causing astonished eyebrows to rise. At a time when it seemed obvious that he should be starting up the Hudson River from New York to join his slowly advancing colleague, he deliberately embarked with the main British army for an attack on Philadelphia, the rebel capital. As scholars now know, he wanted to force a general engagement with Washington's army, destroy it, and leave the path wide open for Burgoyne's thrust. Howe apparently assumed that he had ample time to assist Burgoyne directly, should he be needed.

General Washington, keeping a wary eye on the British in New York, hastily transferred his army to the vicinity of Philadelphia. There he was defeated in two pitched battles, at Brandywine Creek and Germantown. The pleasure-loving Howe then settled down comfortably in the gay capital, while Burgoyne was floundering through the wilds of upper New York. Benjamin Franklin, recently sent to Paris as an American envoy, truthfully jested that Howe had not captured Philadelphia but that Philadelphia had captured Howe. Washington finally retired to winter quarters at Valley Forge, a strong hilly position some twenty miles northwest of Philadelphia, where his men suffered severely from hunger and cold.

Burgoyne meanwhile had begun to bog down north of Albany, while a host of American militiamen, scenting the kill, swarmed about him. In a series of sharp engagements, in which General Arnold was again shot in the leg wounded at Quebec, the British army was trapped. Meanwhile the Americans had driven back St. Leger's force at Oriskany. Unable to advance or retreat, Burgoyne was forced to surrender his entire command at Saratoga, on October 17, 1777, to the American General Gates.

Saratoga ranks high among the decisive battles of both American and world history. The victory immensely revived the faltering colonial cause. Even more important, it made possible the urgently needed foreign aid which in turn helped insure American independence.

Strange Bedfellows

France, thirsting for revenge, was eager to inflame the quarrel that had broken out in the New World. The American colonies were by far Britain's most valuable overseas possessions, and if they could be wrested from her, she presumably would cease to be a front-rank power. The French might then regain their former position and prestige, the loss of which rankled so deeply.

The American cause rapidly became something of a fad in France. The bored aristocracy, which had developed some interest in the writings of liberal French thinkers like Rousseau, was rather intrigued by the ideal of American liberty. The hard-headed French officials, on the other hand, were not prompted by a love for America but by a realistic concern for the interests of France. Any marriage with the United States would be strictly one of convenience.

After the shooting at Lexington, in April, 1775, the French officials undertook to blow on the embers. They secretly provided the Americans with life-saving amounts of powder and other munitions, chiefly through a dummy company rigged up for that purpose. About 90% of all the gunpowder used by the Americans in the first two and a half years of the war came from French arsenals.

Secrecy or semi-secrecy enshrouded all these French schemes. Open aid to the American rebels might bring a declaration of war by England; and France, still weakened by her recent defeat, was not ready to fight. She feared that the American rebellion was not yet a going concern, for the colonies were insistently proclaiming their desire to patch up differences. But the Declaration of Independence in 1776 showed that the Americans really meant business; and the smashing victory at Saratoga seemed to indicate that they had an excellent chance of winning their freedom.

THE HORSE AMERICA, *throwing his Master.*

The rider is Lord North, British Prime Minister, represented with a whip of swords. Note the Frenchman in the background. A British cartoon in the New York Public Library

After the humiliation at Saratoga in 1777, the British Parliament belatedly passed a measure which in effect offered the Americans home rule within the Empire. This was essentially everything that the colonials had ever asked for—except independence. If the French were going to break up the British Empire, they would have to bestir themselves. Wily old Benjamin Franklin, whose simple fur cap and witty sayings had taken the French public by storm, played skillfully on France's fears of reconciliation.

The French King, Louis XVI, was reluctant to intervene. Although somewhat stupid, he was alert enough to see grave dangers in aiding the Americans openly and incurring war with Britain. But his ministers at length won him over. They argued that hostilities were inevitable, sooner or later, to undo the victor's peace of 1763. If England should regain her colonies, she might well join with them to seize the sugar-rich French West Indies, and thereby secure compensation for the cost of the recent rebellion. It seemed best for the French to fight while they could have an American ally, rather than to wait and fight both Britain and her reunited colonials.

So France, in 1778, offered the Americans a treaty of alliance. It seemed to guarantee everything that Britain was offering—plus independence. Both allies bound themselves to wage war until the United States had won its freedom, and until both agreed on terms with the common foe.

This was the first entangling military alliance in the experience of the United States, and one that later caused infinite trouble. The American people, with ingrained isolationist tendencies, accepted the French entanglement with reluctance. They were painfully aware that it involved a hereditary foe which was also a Roman Catholic power. But when one's house is on fire, one does not inquire too closely into the background of those who carry the water buckets.

The Colonial War Becomes a World War

England and France thus came to blows in 1778, and the conflict begun at Lexington rapidly widened into a global conflagration. Spain entered the fray against Britain in 1779, and Holland in 1780. The combined Spanish and French navies outnumbered the warships of England, and on two occasions the British Isles seemed to be at the mercy of hostile fleets.

The weak maritime neutrals of Europe, who had suffered from Britain's dominance over the seas, now began to demand more respect for their rights. In 1780 the imperious Catherine the Great of Russia took the lead in organizing the Armed Neutrality, which she later sneeringly called the "Armed Nullity." It lined up almost all the remaining European neutrals in an attitude of passive hostility toward England. The war was now being fought not only in Europe and North America, but also in South America, the Caribbean, and Asia.

To say that America, with some European aid, defeated England, is like saying, "Daddy and I killed the bear." To the Mother Country, struggling for her very life, the scuffle in the New World seemed secondary. The Americans deserve much credit for having kept the war going until

Britain against the World

Britain and Allies		*Enemy or Unfriendly Powers*
Great Britain Some Loyalists and Indians (Total population on Britain's side: c. 8,000,000)	Belligerents (Total population: c. 39,500,000)	United States, 1775–1783 France, 1778–1783 Spain, 1779–1783 Holland, 1780–1783
		Ireland (restive)
	Members of the Armed Neutrality (with dates of joining)	Russia, 1780 Denmark–Norway, 1780 Sweden, 1780 Holy Roman Empire, 1781 Prussia, 1782 Portugal, 1782 Two Sicilies, 1783 (after peace signed)

1778, with semi-secret French aid. But they did not achieve their independence until the conflict erupted into a multi-power world war that was too big for Britain to handle. From 1778 to 1783, the French provided America with large sums of money, immense amounts of equipment, about one-half of her regular armed forces, and practically all of her naval strength.

The entrance of France into the conflict forced the British to change their basic strategy in America. Hitherto they had been able to count on blockading the colonial coast and commanding the seas. Now the French had powerful fleets in American waters, chiefly to protect their own valuable West Indian islands, but in a position to jeopardize Britain's blockade and lines of supply. The British therefore decided to evacuate Philadelphia and concentrate their strength in New York City.

In June, 1778, the withdrawing Redcoats were attacked by General Washington at Monmouth, New Jersey, on a blisteringly hot day. Scores of men collapsed or died from sunstroke. The battle was indecisive, and the British made good their escape to New York, although about one-third of their Hessian hirelings deserted. Henceforth, except for the Yorktown interlude of 1781, Washington remained in the New York area hemming in the British.

Blow and Counter-Blow

In the summer of 1780 a powerful French army of 6000 regular troops, commanded by the Comte de Rochambeau, arrived in Newport, Rhode Island. The Americans were somewhat suspicious of their former enemies; in fact, several ugly flare-ups had already occurred between the new allies.

But French gold and good will melted restraints. Dancing parties were arranged with the prim Puritan maidens; and one French officer related, doubtless with exaggeration, that "The simple innocence of the Garden of Eden prevailed." No real military advantage came immediately from the French reinforcement, although preparations were made for a Franco-American attack on New York.

The improving morale of the Americans was staggered later in 1780, when General Benedict Arnold turned traitor. A leader of undoubted dash and brilliance, he was ambitious, greedy, unscrupulous, and suffering from a well-grounded but petulant feeling that his valuable services were improperly appreciated. He plotted with the British to sell out the stronghold of West Point, which commanded the Hudson River, for £6300 and an officer's commission. By the sheerest accident the plot was detected in the nick of time, and Arnold fled to the British. "Whom can we trust now?" cried General Washington in anguish.

The British meanwhile had devised a plan to roll up the colonies, beginning with the South, where the Loyalists were numerous. Georgia was

WAR IN THE SOUTH, 1780-1781

ruthlessly overrun in 1778–1779; Charleston, South Carolina, fell in 1780. The surrender of the city to the British involved the capture of 5000 men and 400 cannon, and was a heavier loss to the Americans, in relation to existing strength, than that of Burgoyne to the British.

Warfare was now intensified in the Carolinas, where patriots bitterly fought their Loyalist neighbors. It was not uncommon for prisoners to be butchered in cold blood after they had thrown down their arms. The turn of the tide came late in 1780 and early in 1781, when American riflemen wiped out a British detachment at King's Mountain, and then defeated a smaller force at Cowpens. In the Carolina campaign of 1781, General Nathanael Greene, a Quaker-reared tactician, distinguished himself by his strategy of delay. Standing and then retreating, he exhausted his foe, General Cornwallis, in vain pursuit. The "Fighting Quaker" finally succeeded in clearing most of Georgia and South Carolina of the enemy.

The Land Frontier and the Sea Frontier

The West was ablaze during much of the war. The Indian allies of George III were busy with torch and tomahawk, egged on by British agents branded as "hair buyers," because they allegedly paid bounties for American scalps. The year 1777 was known as "the Bloody Year" on the frontier. Yet the human tide of westward-moving pioneers was not halted in its march. Eloquent testimony is provided by place names in Kentucky, such as Lexington (named after the battle) and Louisville (named after America's new ally, Louis XVI).

In the wild Illinois country the British were vulnerable to attack, for they held certain posts which they had captured from the French. An audacious frontiersman, George Rogers Clark, conceived the idea of seizing these forts by surprise. With the blessing of Virginia and £1200 in depreciated currency, he floated down the Ohio River with some 175 men and captured in quick succession Kaskaskia, Cahokia, and Vincennes. This

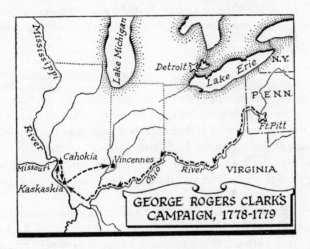

daring foray no doubt helped quiet the Indians. Clark's admirers have also assumed, without positive proof, that his occupation of the southwest corner of the great area north of the Ohio forced the British to cede the whole region to the United States at the peace table in Paris.

The infant American navy had meanwhile been laying the foundations of a brilliant tradition. It consisted of only a handful of nondescript ships, commanded by daring officers, the most distinguished of whom was a hard-fighting young Scotsman, John Paul Jones. But this tiny naval force as such never made a real dent in Britain's potent fleets. Its chief contribution was in destroying British merchant shipping, and thus carrying the war into the waters around the British Isles. An English song of the time, critical of the Royal Navy, began:

> The tradesmen stand still, and the merchant bemoans
> The losses he meets with from such as Paul Jones.

More numerous and damaging than ships of the regular American navy were swift privateers. These craft were privately owned armed ships —legalized pirates in a sense—specifically authorized by Congress to prey on enemy shipping. Altogether over 1000 American privateers, responding to the call of patriotism and profit, sallied forth with about 70,000 men. They captured some 600 British prizes, while British warships captured about as many American merchantmen and privateers.

Privateering was not an unalloyed asset. It had the unfortunate effect of diverting manpower from the main war effort and involving Americans, including Benedict Arnold, in speculation and graft. But the privateers brought in urgently needed gold, harassed the enemy, and raised American morale by providing victories at a time when victories were few. British shipping was so badly riddled by privateers and by the regular American navy that insurance rates were forced sky-high. Merchantmen were compelled to sail in convoy, and British shippers and manufacturers brought increasing pressure on Parliament to end the war on honorable terms.

Yorktown and the Final Curtain

One of the darkest periods of the American Revolution was 1780–1781, before the last decisive victory was won. Runaway inflation of the currency was continuing at full gallop. Not only was the government virtually bankrupt but Congress had been forced to repudiate its financial obligations on a forty-to-one basis. Despair was prevalent; disunion was increasing among the states; and mutiny over back pay was spreading in the army.

Meanwhile the British General Cornwallis was blundering into a fatal trap. After futile operations in Virginia, he had fallen back to Chesapeake Bay at Yorktown, there to await supplies and reinforcements. He assumed that Britain would continue to control the sea, as she long had. But these few fateful weeks just happened to be one of the two brief periods during the war in America when British naval superiority slipped away.

The French were now prepared to cooperate energetically in a brilliant stroke. Admiral de Grasse, operating with a formidable fleet in the West Indies, advised the Americans that he was free to join with them in an assault on Cornwallis at Yorktown. Quick to seize this opportunity, General Washington made a swift march of more than three hundred miles to the Chesapeake from the New York area. Accompanied by Rochambeau's French army, he succeeded in hemming the British in by land, while De Grasse blockaded them by sea. Completely cornered, Cornwallis surrendered his entire force of 7000 men, on October 19, 1781, as his band appropriately played "The World Turn'd Upside Down." The triumph was no less a French victory than an American one: the French provided essentially all the seapower and about half of the regular troops in the besieging army of some 16,000 men.

Stunned by the news of the disaster, Prime Minister Lord North cried, "Oh God! It's all over! It's all over!" But it was not. George III stubbornly planned to continue the struggle, for England was far from being crushed. She still had 54,000 troops in North America, including 32,000 in the United States. Washington returned with his army to New York, there to continue keeping a vigilant eye on the British force of 10,000 men.

Fighting actually continued for more than a year after Yorktown, with patriot-Loyalist warfare in the South especially savage. "No quarter for Tories" was the common battle cry. One of Washington's most valuable contributions was to keep the languishing cause alive, the army in the field, and the states together during these critical months. Otherwise, a satisfactory peace treaty might not have been signed.

The Dawn of Peace

After Yorktown, the war-weary British were increasingly ready to come to terms. They had suffered heavy reverses in India and in the West Indies. The Island of Minorca in the Mediterranean had fallen; the Rock of Gibraltar was tottering. Lord North's ministry collapsed in March, 1782, temporarily ending the personal rule of George III. A Whig ministry, rather favorably disposed to the Americans, replaced the Tory regime of Lord North.

Three American peace negotiators had meanwhile gathered at Paris: Benjamin Franklin, aging but acute; the flinty John Adams, vigilant for New England interests; and the impulsive John Jay of New York, deeply suspicious of Old World intrigue. The three envoys had explicit written instructions from Congress to make no separate peace, and to consult with their French allies at all stages of the negotiations. But the American representatives chafed under this directive. They well knew that it had been written by a subservient Congress, with the French Foreign Office indirectly guiding the pen.

France was in a painful position. She had induced Spain to enter the war on her side, in part by promising to deliver British-held Gibraltar. Yet the impregnable rock was defying frantic joint assaults by both Frenchmen and Spaniards. Spain also coveted the immense trans-Allegheny area, on which a vanguard of restless American pioneers was already settling.

France, ever eager to smash Britain's empire, desired an independent United States, but one feebly independent. She therefore schemed to keep the new republic cooped up east of the Allegheny Mountains. A weak America—like a horse docile enough to plow but not vigorous enough to kick—would be the easier to manage in promoting French interests and policy. France was paying a heavy price in men and treasure to win America's independence, and she wanted to get her money's worth.

But John Jay was unwilling to play France's game. Suspiciously alert, he perceived that the French could not satisfy the conflicting ambitions of both Americans and Spaniards. He saw signs—or thought he did—which seemed to indicate that the Paris Foreign Office was about to betray America's trans-Allegheny interests to satisfy those of Spain. Jay therefore secretly made separate overtures to London, contrary to his instructions from Congress. The hard-pressed British, delighted with the prospect of detaching one of their enemies from the alliance, speedily came to terms with the Americans. The preliminary treaty of peace was signed in 1782, and was made final the next year.

By the terms of the Treaty of Paris of 1783, the British formally recognized the independence of the United States. In addition, they granted generous boundaries, reaching majestically to the Mississippi on the west, to the Great Lakes on the north, and to Spanish Florida on the south. (Spain had recently captured Florida from Britain.) The Americans,

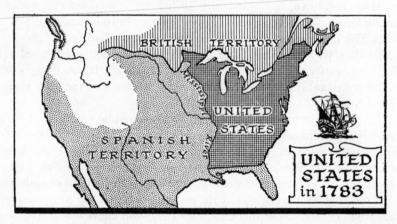

though now divorced from the Empire, were to retain a share in the coveted fisheries of Newfoundland. The Canadians, of course, were profoundly displeased.

The Americans, on their part, had to yield important concessions. The abused Loyalists were not to be further persecuted, and Congress was to make an earnest recommendation to the state legislatures that confiscated Loyalist property be restored. As for the debts long owed to British creditors, the American states were bound to put no lawful obstacles in the way of their collection. Unhappily for future harmony, the assurances regarding both debts and Loyalists were not carried out in the manner hoped for by London.

A New Nation

The British terms were generous almost beyond belief. The enormous trans-Allegheny area was thrown in as a virtual gift, for George Rogers Clark had captured only a small segment of it. Why the generosity? Had the United States beaten the Mother Country to her knees?

The key to the riddle may be found in the Old World. At the time the peace terms were drafted, England was trying to seduce America from her French alliance. She therefore made the terms as alluring as possible. The shaky Whig ministry, hanging on by its fingernails for only a few months, was more friendly to the Americans than were the Tories. It was determined, by a policy of liberality, to salve recent wounds, reopen old trade channels, and prevent future wars with the Americans over the coveted trans-Allegheny region. This far-visioned policy was regrettably not followed by the successors of the Whigs.

In spirit, the Americans made a separate peace—contrary to the French alliance. But in fact, they did not. The Paris Foreign Office for-

THE RECONCILIATION BETWEEN BRITANNIA AND HER DAUGHTER AMERICA

America (represented by an Indian) is invited to buss (kiss) her mother. Detail from an English cartoon. New York Public Library

mally approved the terms of peace, though disturbed by the lone-wolf course of its American ally. The French were immensely relieved by the prospect of bringing the costly conflict to an end, and of freeing themselves from their embarrassing promises to the Spanish Crown.

The Americans alone gained from the world-girdling war. The British, though soon to stage a comeback, were battered and beaten. The French gained sweet revenge, but plunged headlong down the slippery road to bankruptcy and revolution. In truth, Dame Fortune smiled broadly on the Americans. Snatching their independence from the furnace of world conflict, they began their national career with a splendid territorial birthright and a priceless heritage of freedom. Seldom, if ever, has any people been so favored.

SELECT READINGS

The war is sketched briefly in H. H. PECKHAM, *The War for Independence* (1958) [paperback]; more fully in J. R. ALDEN, *The American Revolution, 1775–1783* (1954) [paperback]. Attractively written is J. C. MILLER, *Triumph of Freedom, 1775–1783* (1948). The conflict is considered in its European setting in PIERS MACKESY, *The War for America, 1775–1783* (1964). On the Declaration of Independence consult DAVID HAWKE, *A Transaction of Free Men* (1964) and CARL BECKER's classic *The Declaration of Independence* (1922) [paperback]. Propaganda is developed in CARL BERGER, *Broadsides and Bayonets* (1961). The role of the Loyalists is treated in W. H. NELSON, *The American Tory* (1961); LEWIS EINSTEIN, *Divided Loyalties* (1933); P. H. SMITH, *Loyalists and Redcoats* (1964). The most revealing book on the subject is BENJAMIN QUARLES, *The Negro in the American Revolution* (1961). Political and diplomatic repercussions in Europe are developed masterfully in R. R. PALMER, *The Age of the Democratic Revolution* (2 vols., 1959, 1964) and in S. F. BEMIS, *The Diplomacy of the American Revolution* (3rd ed., 1957) [paperback]. See also R. W. VAN ALSTYNE, *Empire or Independence* (1965) [paperback]. Social aspects are covered in E. B. GREENE, *The Revolutionary Generation, 1763–1790* (1943) and in J. F. JAMESON's incisive *The American Revolution Considered as a Social Movement* (1926) [paperback]. Interesting biographies are S. E. MORISON's swashbuckling *John Paul Jones* (1959) [Pulitzer Prize] and O. A. ALDRIDGE's life of Thomas Paine entitled *Man of Reason* (1959). British troubles are laid bare in G. S. BROWN, *The American Secretary: The Colonial Policy of Lord George Germain, 1775–1778* (1963) and in W. B. WILLCOX, *Portrait of a General: Sir Henry Clinton in the War of Independence* (1964). Also *Harvard Guide*, Pt. III.

7

The Confederation and the Constitution

This example of changing the constitution by assembling the wise men of the state, instead of assembling armies, will be worth as much to the world as the former examples we have given it.

THOMAS JEFFERSON, 1787

The Residue of Revolution

THE AMERICAN REVOLUTION was not a revolution in the sense of a radical or total change. It was not a sudden and violent overturning of the political and social framework, such as later occurred in France and Russia. Significant changes were ushered in, but they were not breath-taking. What happened was accelerated evolution rather than outright revolution. During the conflict itself the mass of people went on working and praying, marrying and playing. Most of them were not seriously disturbed by the actual fighting, and many of the more isolated communities scarcely knew that a war was on.

The War of Independence heralded the birth of three modern nations. One was Canada, which received its first large influx of English-speaking population from the thousands of Loyalists who fled there from the United States. Another was Australia, which became a convict-dumping ground, now that America was no longer available for jailbirds. The third new-comer—and incomparably the most important—was the United States of America, which took its stand foursquare on republican principles and time-tested freedoms.

Yet even the political overturn was not so revolutionary as one might suppose. In some of the states, notably Connecticut and Rhode Island, the war largely ratified a colonial self-rule which already existed. The hated British officials, everywhere ousted, were replaced by a home-grown governing class, which promptly sought a local substitute for King and Parliament.

After the shooting started, the thirteen independent states were forced to devise new constitutions. For a time the manufacturing of governments was more important than the manufacturing of gunpowder. In the cases of Connecticut and Rhode Island, the yellowing charters were kept essentially intact but were retouched a bit to conform to new conditions. Significantly, none of the state constitutions was a radical departure from what the people had been accustomed to in the older colonial charters.

The newly forged state constitutions, fortunately, enjoyed many features in common. Their similarity, as it turned out, made easier the drafting of a workable federal constitution when the time was ripe. Many of the state constitutions included bills of rights, specifically guaranteeing long-prized liberties. Most of them required the annual election of legislators, who were thus forced to toe the mark. All of them had weak executive and judicial branches, at least by present-day standards. The explanation is that the legislatures, now granted sweeping powers, were more directly representative of the people and hence more responsive to popular control. A generation of quarreling with His Majesty's officials had implanted a deep distrust of strong governors and arbitrary judges.

At the end of the shooting, as before, none of the states enjoyed universal manhood suffrage. In all of them a voter or officeholder was required to own property or pay taxes. During the war the restrictions on voting were lightened in about half the states, but were increased in a few others.

Yet encouraging gains were registered for political democracy. More people—probably many more—could vote after the Revolution than before. This was especially true of the scorned back-country folk, notably the Germans and Scotch-Irish of Pennsylvania. The Tories, quite understandably, had sneered:

> Down at night a bricklayer or carpenter lies,
> Next sun a Lycurgus, a Solon doth rise.

New Social Fabrics

Social changes were striking but not bewildering. The expulsion of some 80,000 wealthy Loyalists robbed the new ship of state of valuable leadership, as well as needed conservative ballast. The loss also resulted in weakening the aristocratic upper crust, with all its culture and charm, and in a consequent gain for democratic "leveling."

War inevitably breeds a loosening of moral standards, often manifested in a spirit of "eat, drink, and be merry, for tomorrow we die." Sixty distilleries operated in Massachusetts during the war. Alarmists pointed to the sharp increase of juvenile delinquency, of Sabbath breaking, of absenteeism from churches, and of the spread of French radical ideas, notably those of the free-thinking Voltaire.

Church buildings suffered severely from the conflict. Many of them were destroyed or damaged by invading armies, which thus vented their wrath against Whiggish preachers of sedition. Old South Church in Boston, for example, was made into a riding school for British cavalry.

The Anglican Church, tainted by association with the British Crown, was ruined. A new, de-Anglicized American church had to be built on the ashes of the old one. The Protestant Episcopal Church was therefore formally launched shortly after the guns fell silent. The blow to the Anglican Church, combined with the feverish democratic spirit growing out of the war, encouraged the spread of other denominations, especially on the frontier. Conspicuous among them were the more zestful Baptists and Methodists, whose popularity resulted in part from their more democratic organization.

The protracted fight for separation of church and state resulted in spectacular gains. Although the well-entrenched Congregational Church continued to be legally established in some New England states, the Anglican Church was everywhere disestablished. The struggle for a complete divorce between religion and government proved to be bitterest in Virginia. It was prolonged to 1786, when the militant Thomas Jefferson and his co-reformers, including the lowly Baptists, won a complete victory. (See table of established churches, p. 75.)

Social democracy was further stimulated by the discarding of certain medieval heritages. Forward-looking citizens in the states, during and immediately after the war, succeeded in chiseling off the remaining shackles of entail and primogeniture. These restrictions were specifically designed to perpetuate the influence of an aristocratic family by keeping its estate intact, and in the hands of the eldest son. The struggle in Virginia proved to be a last-ditch affair. It was led by the ultra-liberal Thomas Jefferson, who remarked that the oldest son should have twice as much as the younger when he could eat twice as much and do twice as much work.

The war likewise encouraged a few humanitarian advances, notably in connection with Negro slavery. The nefarious trade in "black ivory" had been shut off during hostilities, and most of the new state constitutions forbade its renewal. The inhumanity of Negro slavery was magnified by the ringing phrases of the Declaration of Independence, which in the words of the slaveowning Jefferson proclaimed that "all men are created equal."

Education was temporarily blighted by the war, as schools were damaged, put on a part-time basis, or completely closed. Yet a refreshing spirit of liberalism began to suffuse the college curricula, partly as a result of the French alliance and the presence of French officers and troops in America. In 1782 Harvard College, one of the last diehards, finally permitted the substitution of French for Hebrew.

Economic Ferment

Economic changes begotten by the war were likewise noteworthy, but not sensational. The states seized control of former Crown lands, and although rich speculators had their day, many of the large Loyalist holdings were confiscated and cut up into small farms. The huge estate of Roger Morris in New York, for example, was sliced into 250 parcels—a development which accelerated the spread of economic democracy. The frightful excesses of the French Revolution were avoided, partly because cheap land was easily available. Men do not chop off heads so readily when they can chop down trees. It is highly significant that in the United States economic democracy, broadly speaking, preceded political democracy.

A sharp stimulus was given to manufacturing by the pre-war non-importation agreements, and later by the war itself. Goods that had formerly been imported from England were mostly cut off, and the ingenious Yankee was forced to make his own. Ten years after the Revolution the busy Brandywine Creek, near Philadelphia, was turning the water wheels of sixty mills along a seven- or eight-mile stretch. Yet America remained overwhelmingly a nation of soil-tillers.

Economically speaking, independence had its drawbacks. The coveted commerce of the Mother Country was still reserved for the loyal parts of the Empire; and now that the Americans were aliens, they were forced to find new customers. The fisheries were disrupted, and the bounties for ships and ships' stores had abruptly ended. In some respects, the hated British Navigation Laws were more disagreeable after independence than before.

New commercial channels, fortunately, compensated partially for the loss of old ones. The Americans could now trade freely with foreign nations, subject to local restrictions—a boon they had not enjoyed in the old days of mercantilism. Enterprising Yankee shippers ventured boldly—and profitably—into the Baltic and China seas. In 1784 the *Empress of China,* carrying a valuable weed (ginseng) that was highly prized by Chinese herb doctors for impotence, led the way into the Far Eastern mart.

Yet the general economic picture was far from being roseate. The war had spawned demoralizing extravagance, speculation, and profiteering, with profits as indecently high as 300%. Runaway inflation had been ruinous to middle-class citizens on fixed incomes, and Congress had failed in its feeble attempts to curb economic laws by fixing prices. The average citizen was probably worse off financially at the end of the shooting than he had been at the beginning.

The whole economic and social atmosphere was unhealthy. A newly rich class was noisily conspicuous, while once-wealthy people were left destitute. The controversy leading to the war had bred a keen distaste for taxes; and the wholesale seizure of Loyalist estates had encouraged disrespect for private property. John Adams had been shocked when gleefully told by one of his neighbors that the courts of justice were all closed—a plight that proved to be only temporary

Storm Warnings

What would the Americans do with the independence they had so dearly won? The responsibility of creating and operating a new central government had been dumped squarely into their laps.

The prospects for erecting a lasting regime were far from bright. It is always difficult to set up a new government; doubly difficult to set up a new type of government. The picture was further confused in America by men preaching "natural rights," and looking suspiciously at all persons clothed with authority. The United States was more a name than a nation.

Disruptive forces were abroad in the land. The stabilizing Tory element had been tossed overboard. The patriots had fought the war with a high degree of disunity, but they had at least enjoyed the unifying cement of a common cause. Now even that was gone. It would have been almost a miracle if any government fashioned in all this confusion had long endured.

Hard times, the bane of all regimes, set in shortly after the war, and hit bottom in 1786. As if other troubles were not enough, British manufacturers, with dammed-up surpluses, were flooding the American market with cheap goods. War-baby American industries, in particular, suffered industrial colic from such ruthless competition. One Philadelphia newspaper in 1783 urged the use of homespun cloth:

> Of foreign gewgaws let's be free,
> And wear the webs of liberty.

Yet hopeful signs could be discerned. The thirteen sovereign states were basically alike in governmental structure, and functioned under similar constitutions. The American people enjoyed a priceless political inheritance, derived partly from England and partly from their own homespun devices for self-government. Finally, they were blessed with political leaders of a high order in men like George Washington, James Madison, John Adams, Thomas Jefferson, and Alexander Hamilton.

Creating a Confederation

The Second Continental Congress of Revolution days was little more than a conference of ambassadors from the thirteen states. It was totally without constitutional authority, and in general did only what it dared to do. The states were in all respects sovereign, for they coined money, raised armies and navies, and erected tariff barriers. The legislature of Virginia even ratified separately the treaty of alliance of 1778 with France.

Shortly before declaring independence in 1776, the Congress appointed a committee to draft a written constitution for the United States.

The finished product was the Articles of Confederation. It was adopted by Congress in 1777, and was translated into French after the battle of Saratoga so as to convince France that we had a genuine government in the making. This new constitution was then sent out to the states for their approval. But final action was delayed four years, until 1781, less than eight months before the final decisive victory at Yorktown.

The chief apple of discord was western lands. Six of the jealous states, including Pennsylvania and Maryland, had no holdings beyond the Allegheny Mountains. Seven, notably New York and Virginia, were favored with enormous acreage, on the basis of earlier sea-to-sea charter grants. The six landless states argued that their more fortunate sisters would not have retained possession of this splendid prize if all the other states had not fought for it also. A major complaint was that the land-blessed states could sell their trans-Allegheny tracts, and thus pay off pensions and other debts incurred in the common cause. The states without such holdings would have to tax themselves heavily to defray these obligations. Why not turn the whole western area over to the central government?

Unanimous approval of the Articles of Confederation by the thirteen states was required, and landless Maryland stubbornly held out until March 1, 1781. She finally gave in when New York surrendered her western claims, and Virginia seemed about to do so. To sweeten the pill, Congress pledged itself to dispose of these vast areas for the "common benefit." It further agreed to carve from the new public domain a number of "republican" states, which in time would be admitted to the Union on terms of complete equality with all the others. This pledge was later redeemed in the famed Northwest Ordinance of 1787.

The priceless public lands thus transferred to the central government proved to be an invaluable bond of union. The states that had thrown their heritage into the common pot had to remain in the Union if they were to reap their share of the advantages to be derived from the land sales. An army of westward-moving pioneers purchased their farms from the federal government, and they learned to look to the national capital, rather than to the state capitals—with a consequent weakening of local influence. Finally, a uniform national land policy was made possible.

The First American Constitution

The Articles of Confederation provided for a loose confederation or "firm league of friendship." Thirteen independent states were thus linked together for joint action in dealing with common problems, such as foreign affairs. An unwieldy Congress was to be the chief agency of government. There was no executive branch—George III had left a bad taste—and the vital judicial arm was left almost exclusively to the states, which remained sovereign.

Congress, though dominant, was closely hobbled. All bills dealing

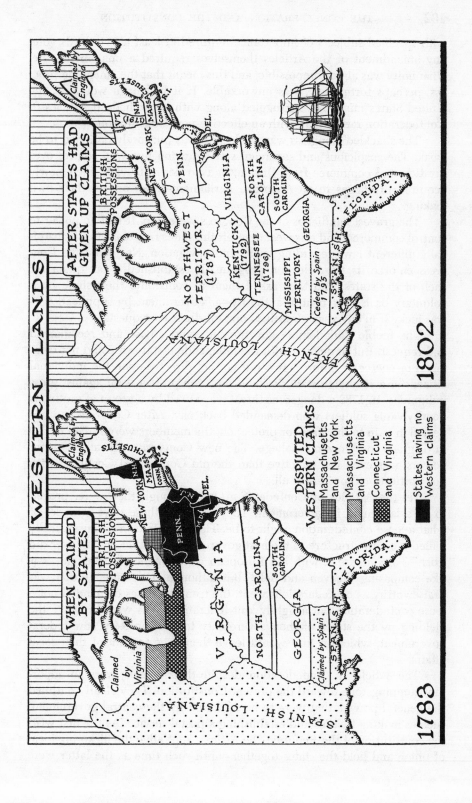

WESTERN LANDS

AFTER STATES HAD GIVEN UP CLAIMS

Claimed by England

BRITISH POSSESSIONS

NEW YORK

VT. (1791) N.H. MASS. CONN. R.I.
PENN.
N.J.
MD. DEL.

NORTHWEST TERRITORY (1787)

KENTUCKY (1792)

VIRGINIA

TENNESSEE (1796)

NORTH CAROLINA

SOUTH CAROLINA

MISSISSIPPI TERRITORY

GEORGIA

Ceded by Spain 1795

SPANISH FLORIDA

FRENCH LOUISIANA

1802

WHEN CLAIMED BY STATES

Claimed by England

BRITISH POSSESSIONS

Claimed by Virginia

NEW YORK N.H. MASS. CONN. R.I.
PENN.
N.J.
MD. DEL.

VIRGINIA

NORTH CAROLINA

SOUTH CAROLINA

GEORGIA

Claimed by Spain

SPANISH FLORIDA

SPANISH LOUISIANA

DISPUTED WESTERN CLAIMS

Massachusetts and New York

Massachusetts and Virginia

Connecticut and Virginia

States having no Western claims

1783

with specified subjects of importance required at least a two-thirds vote; any amendment of the Articles themselves required a unanimous vote. Unanimity was almost impossible, and this meant that the amending process, perhaps fortunately, was unworkable. If it had been workable, the United States might have struggled along with a patched-up Articles of Confederation rather than with an effective new Constitution.

The shackled Congress was weak—and was purposely designed to be weak. The suspicious and sovereign states, having just won control over taxation and commerce from Britain, had no desire to yield their newly acquired privileges to an American Parliament—even one of their own making.

The gravest handicaps of the Congress were two. It had no power to control commerce, and this weakness left the states free to establish chaotically different laws regarding tariffs and navigation. Nor could the Congress enforce its tax-collection program. It established a tax quota for each of the states, and then asked them to contribute their share on a voluntary basis. The central authority—a "government by supplication"—was lucky if in any year it received one-fourth of its requests.

The feeble Philadelphia government could advise and recommend and request. But in dealing with the independent states it could not command or coerce or enforce. It could not act directly upon the individual citizens of a sovereign state. It could not even protect itself against gross indignities. In 1783 a dangerous threat was raised by a group of mutinous Pennsylvania soldiers who demanded back pay. After Congress had appealed in vain to the state for protection, the members were forced to flee in disgrace to Princeton College. The new Congress, with all its paper powers, was even less effective than the old Continental Congress, with no constitutional powers at all.

Yet the Articles of Confederation, weak though they were, proved to be a landmark in government. They were for those days a model of what a loose confederation ought to be. Thomas Jefferson enthusiastically hailed the new structure as the best government "existing or that ever did exist." To compare it with the European governments, he thought, was like comparing "heaven and hell." But although the Confederation was praiseworthy as confederations went, the troubled times demanded not a loose confederation but a tightly knit federation. This would involve the yielding by the states of their sovereignty to a completely new federal government, which in turn would leave them free to control their local affairs.

The Articles of Confederation, despite their defects, were an important steppingstone toward the present Constitution. They clearly outlined the general powers that were to be exercised by the central government, such as making treaties and establishing a postal service. As the first written constitution of the Republic, the Articles kept alive the flickering ideal of union and held the states together—until such time as the latter were ripe for a strong constitution by peaceful, evolutionary methods. The anemic Articles represented what the states regarded as an alarming surrender of their power. Without this intermediary jump, they probably would never have consented to the breath-taking leap from the old Continental Congress to the present Constitution of the United States.

Landmarks in Land Laws

Handcuffed though the Congress of the Confederation was, it managed to pass two supremely farsighted pieces of legislation. These related to an immense part of the public domain recently acquired from the states, and commonly known as the Old Northwest. This area lay northwest of the Ohio River, east of the Mississippi River, and south of the Great Lakes.

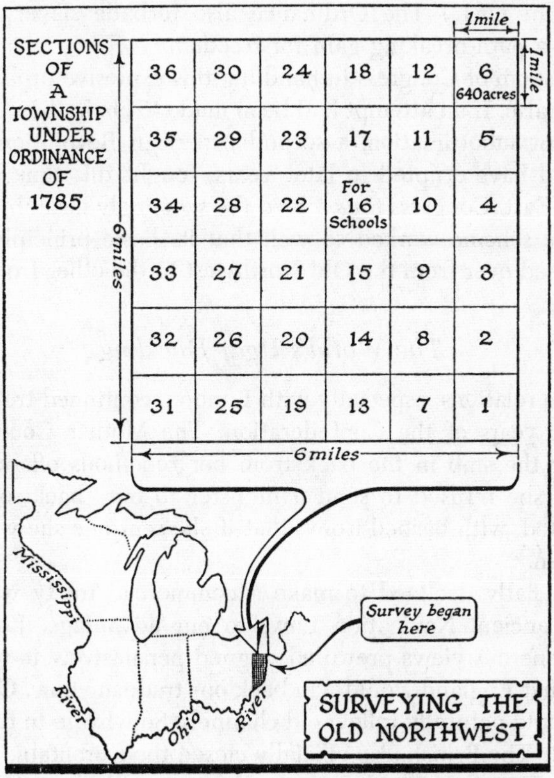

SECTIONS OF A TOWNSHIP UNDER ORDINANCE OF 1785

36	30	24	18	12	6 640acres
35	29	23	17	11	5
34	28	22	For 16 Schools	10	4
33	27	21	15	9	3
32	26	20	14	8	2
31	25	19	13	7	1

1 mile

6 miles

6 miles

Survey began here

SURVEYING THE OLD NORTHWEST

The first of these memorable laws was the Land Ordinance of 1785. It provided that the acreage of the Old Northwest should be sold, and that the proceeds should be used to help pay off the national debt. The vast area was to be surveyed before sale and settlement, thus forestalling endless confusion and lawsuits. It was to be divided into townships six miles square, each of which in turn was to be split into thirty-six sections of one square mile each. The sixteenth section of each township was set aside for the benefit of the public schools—a priceless gift to education in the Northwest.

Even more noteworthy was the Northwest Ordinance of 1787, which related to the government of the Old Northwest. This law came to grips with the problem of how a nation should deal with its colonial peoples— the same problem that had bedeviled the King and Parliament in London. The solution provided by the Northwest Ordinance was a judicious compromise: temporary tutelage, then permanent equality. First, there would be two evolutionary territorial stages, during which the area would be subordinate to the federal government. Then, when the territory could claim 60,000 inhabitants, it might be admitted by Congress as a state, with all the privileges of the thirteen charter members. (This is precisely what the Continental Congress had promised the states when they surrendered their lands in 1781.) The Ordinance also forbade slavery in the Old Northwest—a path-breaking gain for freedom.

The wisdom of Congress in handling this explosive problem deserves unstinted praise. If an attempt had been made to chain the new territories in permanent subordination, a second American Revolution almost certainly would have erupted in later years, fought this time by the West against the East. Congress thus solved the seemingly insoluble problem of empire. The scheme worked so well that its basic principles were ultimately carried over from the Old Northwest to the other frontier areas of the nation.

The World's Ugly Duckling

Foreign relations, especially with London, continued troubled during the anxious years of the Confederation. The Mother Country was not happy over the stab in the back from her rebellious offspring, and for eight years she refused to send a minister to our "backwoods" capital. She suggested, with barbed irony, that if she sent one she would have to send thirteen.

Britain flatly declined to make a commercial treaty with us, or to repeal her ancient Navigation Laws to our advantage. Lord Sheffield, whose ungenerous views prevailed, argued persuasively in a widely sold pamphlet that England would win back our trade anyhow. Commerce, he insisted, would naturally follow old channels. So why go to the Americans hat in hand? The British also officially closed their profitable West Indian trade to the United States, though the Yankees, with their time-tested skill in smuggling, illegally shared a good part of it nonetheless.

Scheming British agents were also sleeplessly active along our far-flung northern frontier. They intrigued with the disgruntled Allen brothers of Vermont, and sought to annex that troubled area to Britain. Along our northern border the Redcoats continued to hold a chain of trading posts on United States soil, and there maintained their profitable fur trade with the

Indians. One plausible excuse for staying was the failure of the American states to carry out the treaty of peace in regard to debts and Loyalists. But probably the main purpose of Britain in hanging on was to curry favor with the red men and keep their tomahawks lined up on the side of the King as a barrier against future attacks on Canada.

Area Disputed by Spain and U.S.

MAIN CENTERS of SPANISH and BRITISH INFLUENCE after 1783

All these grievances against England were maddening to patriotic Americans. Some of them demanded, with more heat than wisdom, that the United States force the British into line by imposing restrictions on their imports to America. But Congress did not control commerce, and the states could not be persuaded to adopt a uniform tariff policy. Some "easy states" deliberately kept their tariffs low in order to attract an unfair share of trade.

Spain, though the enemy of England in the recent war, was openly unfriendly to the new republic. She controlled the mouth of the all-important Mississippi, down which the pioneers of Tennessee and Kentucky were forced to float their produce. The West was thus threatened with economic strangulation. Spain likewise claimed a large area north of the Gulf of Mexico granted to the United States by the British in 1783, and at Natchez, on disputed soil, she held an important fort. She intrigued with the neighboring red men to hem the Americans in east of the Alleghenies. In fact, both Spain and England, radiating their influence out among war-like Indian tribes, prevented us from exercising effective control over about half of our total territory.

Even our French ally, now that she had humbled Britain, was cooling off. She insistently demanded the repayment of money advanced to us during the war; she restricted freedom of trade with her bustling West Indies and other ports.

The pirates of the North African states, including the arrogant Dey of Algiers, were ravaging our Mediterranean commerce and enslaving our seamen. The British purchased protection for their own subjects, and as colonials we had enjoyed this welcome shield. But as an independent nation we were too weak to fight and too poor to bribe. A few Yankee shippers engaged in the Mediterranean trade with forged British protection papers, but not all were so bold or so lucky.

John Jay, in charge of American foreign affairs during Confederation days, derived some hollow satisfaction from all these insults. He hoped that they would at least humiliate the American people into framing a new government at home that would be strong enough to command respect abroad.

The Specter of Anarchy

Economic storm clouds continued to hang low in the mid-1780's. The requisition system of raising money was breaking down; some of the states refused to pay anything, while complaining bitterly about the tyranny of "King Congress." The interest on the public debt was piling up at home, while the nation's credit was evaporating abroad.

The individual states were getting out of hand. Several of them were quarreling over boundary disputes, one of which involved minor pitched battles. Some of the states were levying duties on goods from their neighbors; New York, for example, taxed firewood from Connecticut and cabbage from New Jersey. A number of the states were again starting to grind out depreciated paper currency, and a few of them had passed laws legalizing the semi-worthless "rag money." As a contemporary rhymester put it:

> Bankrupts their creditors with rage pursue;
> No stop, no mercy from the debtor crew.

An alarming uprising, known as Shays' Rebellion, flared up in western Massachusetts in 1786. The impoverished back-country farmers, many of them Revolutionary War veterans, were losing their farms through mortgage foreclosures and tax delinquencies. Led by Captain Daniel Shays, who had fought gallantly in the Revolution, they demanded cheap paper money, lighter taxes, and a suspension of mortgage foreclosures. Hundreds of angry men, again seizing their muskets, sought to intimidate the courts into acting favorably to the debtors.

The Massachusetts authorities responded with drastic action. They raised an army of several thousand men under General Lincoln, supported partly by contributions from wealthy citizens. Several skirmishes occurred —at Springfield three Shaysites were killed and one was wounded—and the movement collapsed. Daniel Shays, who believed that he was struggling anew for the freedoms of 1776, was condemned to death but was later pardoned.

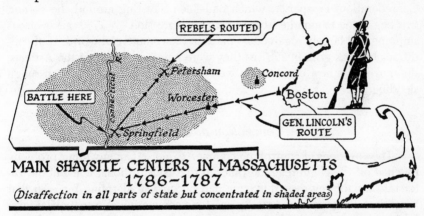

REBELS ROUTED

BATTLE HERE

Petersham

Worcester

Springfield

Concord

Boston

GEN. LINCOLN'S ROUTE

MAIN SHAYSITE CENTERS IN MASSACHUSETTS
1786–1787
(Disaffection in all parts of state but concentrated in shaded areas)

The Shaysites were crushed—but the nightmarish memory lingered on. The outburst of these distressed debtors struck fear in the hearts of the aristocrats, who began to suspect that the Revolution had raised up a Frankenstein's monster of "mobocracy." There was obviously a crying need for a stronger central government—one that could curb anarchy and the conditions leading to it. A few panicky citizens even talked of importing a European monarch to carry on where George III had failed.

How critical were conditions under the Confederation? The conservative groups, who were anxious to safeguard their wealth and position, naturally exaggerated the seriousness of the nation's plight. They were eager to persuade their countrymen to scrap the Articles of Confederation, under which the states were sovereign, in favor of a muscular central government, in which the federal authorities would be sovereign. But the poorer states'-rights people, who favored at most a simple amending of the Articles, pooh-poohed the talk of possible anarchy. Many of them were debtors who feared that a powerful federal government would force them to pay their creditors.

Yet both friends and critics of the Confederation generally agreed that it needed strengthening. Popular toasts were "Cement to the Union" and

"A hoop to the barrel." The chief differences of opinion arose over how this goal should be attained, and how a maximum amount of states' rights could be reconciled with a strong central government. The United States probably could have muddled through somehow with an amended Articles of Confederation. But the adoption of a completely new constitution certainly spared the Republic much costly indecision, uncertainty, and turmoil.

The nationwide picture was actually brightening before the Constitution was drafted. Nearly half the states had not issued semi-worthless paper currency; and some of the monetary black sheep showed signs of returning to the sound-money fold. Congressional control of commerce was in sight, specifically by means of an amendment to the Articles of Confederation. Prosperity, which had been hovering around the corner, was beginning to emerge from the fog of depression. By 1789 our overseas shipping had largely regained its place in the commercial world. Had conditions been as grim in 1787 as they were painted by foes of the Articles, the move for a new constitution would hardly have met with such rough sledding.

A Convention of Lawgivers

The vexations of controlling commerce, more than any other problem, touched off the chain reaction that led to a constitutional convention. Interstate squabbling over this issue had become so alarming by 1786 that Virginia, taking the lead, issued a call for a convention at Annapolis, Maryland. Nine states appointed delegates, but representatives from only five put in an appearance. With so feeble a showing, nothing could be done about the ticklish question of commerce. A classic-featured New Yorker, thirty-one-year-old Alexander Hamilton, brilliantly saved the convention from complete failure by engineering the adoption of his report. It called upon Congress to summon a convention to meet in Philadelphia the next year, not to deal with commerce alone but to bolster the Articles of Confederation as a whole.

The Congress, though slowly dying, was reluctant to take a step that might be the signing of its own death warrant. But after six of the states had seized the bit in their teeth and appointed delegates anyhow, Congress belatedly issued the call for a convention *"for the sole and express purpose of revising"* the Articles of Confederation.

Every state chose representatives, except independent-minded Rhode Island, a stronghold of paper-moneyites. These delegates were all appointed by the state legislatures, whose members had been elected by voters who could qualify as property holders. This double distillation inevitably brought together a select group of propertied men.

A total of fifty-five delegates from twelve states finally convened at Philadelphia on May 25, 1787, in the imposing red-brick state house. The smallness of the assemblage facilitated intimate acquaintance and hence compromise. The sessions were held in complete secrecy, with armed sentinels posted at the doors. The delegates knew that they would generate heated differences, and they did not want to advertise their own dissensions, or put crippling arguments in the mouths of the opposition.

The caliber of the delegates was extraordinarily high—"demigods," Jefferson called them. The crisis was such as to induce the ablest men to drop their personal pursuits and come to the aid of their country. Most of the members were lawyers, and most of them fortunately were old hands at constitution making in their own states.

There were giants in those days. George Washington, austere and aloof, was unanimously elected chairman; and his enormous prestige served to quiet overheated tempers. Benjamin Franklin, then eighty-one, added the urbanity of an elder statesman, though he was inclined to be indiscreetly talkative in his declining years. James Madison, then thirty-seven and a profound student of government, made contributions so notable that he has been dubbed "the Father of the Constitution." Alexander Hamilton, then only thirty-two, was present as an advocate of a superpowerful central government. His five-hour speech in behalf of his plan, though the most eloquent of the convention, netted only one favorable vote—his own.

Most of the flaming revolutionary leaders of 1776 were absent. Thomas Jefferson and Thomas Paine were in Europe; Samuel Adams and John Hancock were not elected by Massachusetts. Patrick Henry, ardent champion of states' rights, was chosen as a delegate from Virginia but declined to serve, on the ground that he "smelled a rat." It was perhaps well that these architects of revolution were absent. The time had come to yield the stage to conservative men skilled in fashioning solid political systems.

Patriots or Profiteers?

The fifty-five delegates were a conservative, well-to-do body: lawyers, merchants, shippers, land speculators, and moneylenders. Not a single spokesman was present from the poorer, debtor groups.

Some of the fifty-five members owned depreciated securities of the existing regime. These men were no doubt aware that the value of their holdings would sharply increase if they succeeded in establishing a strong new government. Unfriendly critics of a later era have charged the Founding Fathers with having deliberately set out to feather their own nests. What is the truth about these so-called "pocketbook patriots"?

Many in the Philadelphia assemblage, including the self-sacrificing Washington, were clearly prompted by patriotic motives, though some may not have been. The delegates realized that while they themselves might profit personally from a sounder government, so would the nation as a whole. If every man who stood to gain financially from a new constitution had bowed out of the picture, the country would have been robbed of its leadership, and there would have been no Constitution.

What were the Founding Fathers after? They desired above all else a firm, dignified, and respected government. In a broad sense the piratical Dey of Algiers, who drove the delegates to their work, was a Founding Father. They aimed to clothe the central authority with genuine power, especially in controlling tariffs, so that the United States could wrest satisfactory commercial treaties from foreign nations. The shortsighted hostility of the British mercantilists spurred the constitution framers to their task, and in this sense the illiberal Lord Sheffield was a Founding Father.

Other motives were present in the stately Philadelphia hall. The delegates were determined to preserve the Union, forestall anarchy, and insure security of life and property against dangerous uprisings by the "mobocracy." The specter of the recent outburst in Massachusetts held them to their labors, and in this sense Daniel Shays was a Founding Father. Grinding necessity extorted the Constitution from a reluctant nation. Fear occupied the fifty-sixth chair.

A Bundle of Compromises

Some of the travel-stained delegates, when they first reached Philadelphia, decided upon a daring step. They would completely *scrap* the old Articles of Confederation, despite explicit instructions from Congress to *revise*. Technically, these bolder spirits conspired to overthrow the existing government of the United States by peaceful means. The sovereign states were in danger of losing their sovereignty.

A scheme proposed by populous Virginia, and known as the large-state plan, was first pushed forward as the framework of the Constitution. Its essence was that representation in Congress should be based on population—an arrangement that would give the larger states their proportionate share of influence.

Tiny New Jersey, suspicious of Virginia, countered with the small-state plan. This provided for equal representation in Congress by states, regardless of size and population, as under the existing Articles of Confederation. The weaker states feared that under the Virginia plan the stronger states would band together and lord it over the rest. Angry debate, heightened by a stifling heat wave, led to deadlock. The danger loomed that the convention would break up in complete failure. Even skeptical old Benjamin Franklin proposed that the daily sessions be opened with prayer by a local clergyman.

After bitter and prolonged debate, the "Great Compromise" of the convention was fashioned and agreed upon. The cooling of tempers came coincidentally with a cooling of the temperature. The larger states were conceded representation by population in the House of Representatives

(Art. I, Sec. II, para. 3; see Appendix at end of this book), and their smaller sisters were appeased by equal representation in the Senate (see Art. I, Sec. III, para. 1). Each state, no matter how poor or small, would have two Senators. The big states, which would have to bear the major burden of taxation, obviously yielded more. As a sop to them, it was agreed that every tax bill or revenue measure must originate in the House, where population counted the more heavily (see Art. I, Sec. VII, para. 1). This critical compromise broke the log jam, and from then on success seemed within reach.

The Constitution as drafted was a bundle of compromises; they stand out in every section of it. A vital compromise was the method of electing the President indirectly through the Electoral College, rather than by direct means (see Art. II, Sec. I, para. 2). One Virginia delegate insisted that to leave the choice to the people was like asking a blind man to choose colors.

Sectional jealousy also raised its unlovely head. Should the voteless Negro slave of the Southern states count as a person in apportioning representation in the House of Representatives? The South, not wishing to be deprived of influence, said "yes." The North replied "no," arguing that the North might as logically have additional representation based on its horses. As a compromise between total representation and none at all, it was decided that a slave might count as three-fifths of a man. Hence the memorable, if somewhat illogical, "three-fifths compromise" (see Art. I, Sec. II, para. 3).

Most of the states wanted to shut off the slave trade completely. But South Carolina and Georgia, requiring slave labor in their rice paddies and malarial swamps, raised vehement protests. By way of compromise the convention stipulated that the slave trade might continue until the end of the year 1807, at which time Congress could turn off the spigot (see Art. I, Sec. IX, para. 1). It did so as soon as the prescribed interval had elapsed.

Evolution of Federal Union

1643–1684	New England Confederation	4 colonies
1686–1689	Dominion of New England	7 colonies
1754	Albany Congress	7 colonies
1765	Stamp Act Congress	9 colonies
1772–1776	Committees of Correspondence	13 colonies
1774	First Continental Congress (adopts The Association)	12 colonies
1775–1781	Second Continental Congress	13 colonies
1781–1789	Articles of Confederation	13 states
1789–1790	Federal Constitution	13 states

The Triumph of Conservatism

The heated clashes among the delegates have long been overstressed. The area of agreement was actually large; otherwise the convention would have speedily broken up. Economically, the members generally saw eye to eye; they demanded sound money and the protection of private property. Politically, they were in basic agreement; they favored a stronger government, with three branches and with checks and balances among them. Finally, the convention was virtually unanimous in agreeing that manhood-suffrage democracy—government by "democratick babblers"—was something to be feared and guarded against.

Daniel Shays, the prime bogeyman, still frightened the conservative-minded delegates. They deliberately erected safeguards against the excesses of the "mob," and they made these barriers as strong as they dared. The august federal judges were to be appointed for life. The President was to be elected *indirectly* by the Electoral College; the Senators *indirectly* by state legislatures (see Art. I, Sec. III, para. 1). Only in the case of one-half of one of the three great branches—the House of Representatives —were qualified (propertied) citizens permitted to choose their officials by *direct* vote (see Art. I, Sec. II, para. 1).

At the end of seventeen muggy weeks—May 25 to September 17, 1787 —only forty-two of the original fifty-five members remained to sign the Constitution. Three, declining to do so, had returned to their states to fight ratification. The remainder, adjourning to the City Tavern, appropriately celebrated the occasion. They little suspected that one day an 18th Amendment would be added to their handiwork forbidding the sale of alcoholic beverages.

No members of the convention were completely happy about the result. They were too near their work—too weary and discouraged. Whatever their personal desires, they had finally been forced to adopt what was acceptable to the entire body, and what presumably would be acceptable to the entire country.

Federalists vs. Anti-Federalists

The Framing Fathers early foresaw that nationwide acceptance of the Constitution would not be easy to obtain. A formidable barrier was unanimous ratification by all thirteen states, as required for amendment by the still-existent Articles of Confederation. But since absent Rhode Island was certain to veto the Constitution, the delegates boldly adopted a different scheme. They provided that when *two-thirds* of the states had registered their approval through specially elected conventions, the Constitution would become the law of the land (see Art. VII).

This was revolutionary. It was in effect an appeal over the heads of the Congress that had called the Philadelphia convention, and over the

Strengthening the Central Government

Under Articles of Confederation	Under Federal Constitution
A loose confederation of states	A firm union of people
1 vote in Congress for each state	2 votes in Senate for each state; representation by population in House (see Art. I, Secs. II, III)
⅔ vote (9 states) in Congress for all important measures	Simple majority vote in Congress, subject to presidential veto (see Art. I, Sec. VII, para. 2)
Laws executed by committees of Congress	Laws executed by powerful President (see Art. II, Secs. II, III)
No Congressional power over commerce	Congress to regulate both foreign and interstate commerce (see Art. I, Sec. VIII, para. 3)
No Congressional power to levy taxes	Extensive power in Congress to levy taxes (see Art. I, Sec. VIII, para. 1)
No federal courts	Federal courts, capped by Supreme Court (see Art. III)
Unanimity of states for amendment	Amendment less difficult (see Art. V)
No authority to act directly upon individuals, and no power to coerce states	Ample power to enforce laws by coercion of individuals and to some extent of states

heads of the legislatures that had chosen its members, to the people—or those of the people who could vote. Congress reluctantly submitted the newly framed document to the states on this basis, without recommendation of any kind.

The country was shocked by the new Constitution, so well had the secrets of the convention been kept. The public had expected the old Articles of Confederation to be patched up; now it was handed a frightening document in which, many thought, the precious jewel of state sovereignty was swallowed up. One of the hottest debates of American history was forthwith launched. The anti-federalists, who opposed the stronger federal government, were arrayed against the federalists, who naturally favored it.

A motley crowd assembled in the anti-federalist camp. It consisted primarily of the states'-rights devotees, the buckskin-clad back-country men, the one-horse farmers, the work-soiled artisans, the ill-educated and illiterate—in general, the poorer classes. They were joined by the paper-moneyites and debtors, all of whom feared that a potent central government would force them to pay off their debts at full value. Many of the lowly anti-federalists genuinely suspected that something was being put over on them by the aristocrats.

The silver-buckled federalists were more respectable; they included generally the cultured and propertied groups. Most of them lived in the settled areas along the seaboard, not in the raw back country. They were in outlook rather closely akin to the conservative Loyalist group of Revolutionary days. In fact, many of the former Loyalists gave vigorous support to the Constitution. Without them it might have failed of ratification.

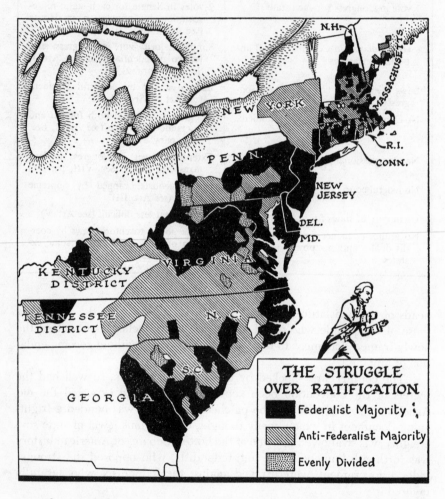

THE STRUGGLE OVER RATIFICATION

■ Federalist Majority

▨ Anti-Federalist Majority

▧ Evenly Divided

The anti-federalists, their worst fears aroused, voiced many objections to the "gilded trap" known as the Constitution. They cried with much truth that it had been drawn up by the aristocratic elements, and hence was anti-democratic. They likewise charged that the sovereignty of the states was being wiped out, and that the freedoms of the individual were jeopardized by the absence of a bill of rights. They decried the dropping of annual elections for Congressmen; the setting up of a federal stronghold ten miles square (later the District of Columbia); the presence of a standing army; the omission of any reference to God; and the highly questionable procedure of ratifying with only two-thirds of the states. For good measure the Philadelphia *Centinel* added that Franklin was a fool from age, and Washington a fool by nature.

The Battle for Ratification

Special elections, some apathetic but others hotly contested, were held in the various states for members of the ratifying conventions. Candidates—federalist or anti-federalist—were elected on the basis of their pledges for or against the Constitution.

The newly forged document was soon accepted by four small states, for they had come off much better than they could have expected. Pennsylvania, number two on the list of ratifiers, was the first large state to act, but not until high-handed irregularities had been employed by the federalists in calling a convention. These included the forcible seating of two anti-federalist members, their clothes torn and their faces white with rage, in order to complete a quorum.

Massachusetts, the second most populous state, provided an acid test. If the Constitution had failed there, the entire movement might easily have bogged down. The Boston ratifying convention at first contained an anti-federalist majority. The group included weather-beaten Shaysites and the suspicious Samuel Adams, that aging "Engineer of Revolution" who now distrusted change. The assembly buzzed with dismaying talk of summoning another constitutional convention, as though the nation had not already shot its bolt. The choice was clearly not between this Constitution and a better one, but between this Constitution and the creaking Articles of Confederation. The absence of a bill of rights was especially disturbing to the Massachusetts convention. But the federalists gave solemn assurances that the first Congress would add such a safeguard by amendment, and ratification was secured by the narrow margin of 187 to 168.

Three more states next fell into line. The last of these was New Hampshire, whose convention at first had contained a strong anti-federalist majority. The federalists cleverly engineered a prompt adjournment, and then won over enough waverers behind the scenes to secure ratification. Nine states—all but Virginia, New York, North Carolina, and Rhode Island —had now taken shelter under the "federal roof," and the new Constitution was officially adopted on June 21, 1788. Francis Hopkinson exulted in "The New Roof":

> Huzza! my brave boys, our work is complete;
> The world shall admire Columbia's fair seat.

But such rejoicing was premature so long as the four dissenters remained outside the fold.

The Laggard Four

Proud Virginia, the biggest and most populous state, provided fierce anti-federalist opposition. It was the only forum where the college-bred federalist orators encountered worthy foemen, including the fiery Patrick Henry. He professed to see in the fearsome parchment the death warrant of liberty. George Washington, James Madison, and John Marshall, on the federalist side, lent influential support. With New Hampshire about to ratify, the new Union was going to be formed anyhow, and Virginia could not very well continue as an independent state. After a close and exciting debate in the state convention, ratification carried, 89 to 79.

Ratification of the Constitution

State	Date	Vote in convention	Rank in population	1790 population
1. Delaware	Dec. 7, 1787	unanimous	13	59,096
2. Pennsylvania	Dec. 12, 1787	46 to 23	3	433,611
3. New Jersey	Dec. 18, 1787	unanimous	9	184,139
4. Georgia	Jan. 2, 1788	unanimous	11	82,548
5. Connecticut	Jan. 9, 1788	128 to 40	8	237,655
6. Massachusetts (incl. Me.)	Feb. 7, 1788	187 to 168	2	475,199
7. Maryland	Apr. 28, 1788	63 to 11	6	319,728
8. South Carolina	May 23, 1788	149 to 73	7	249,073
9. New Hampshire	June 21, 1788	57 to 46	10	141,899
10. Virginia	June 26, 1788	89 to 79	1	747,610
11. New York	July 26, 1788	30 to 27	5	340,241
12. North Carolina	Nov. 21, 1789	195 to 77	4	395,005
13. Rhode Island	May 29, 1790	34 to 32	12	69,112

New York, which also experienced an uphill struggle, was the only state that permitted a manhood-suffrage vote for the members of the ratifying convention. The result was a heavy anti-federalist majority. Hamilton at heart favored a much stronger central government than that provided by the Constitution, but contributed his sparkling personality and persuasive eloquence to whipping up support. He also collaborated with John Jay and James Madison in penning a masterly series of articles for the New York newspapers in support of the document. Though designed as propaganda, the essays remain the most penetrating commentary ever written on the Constitution, and are still widely sold in book form as *The Federalist*.

New York finally yielded. Realizing that the state could not exist apart from the Union, the convention ratified the document by the close count of 30 to 27. At the same time, it approved thirty-two proposed

REDEUNT SATURNIA REGNA.

On the erection of the Eleventh PILLAR of the great National DOME, we beg leave most sincerely to felicitate " OUR DEAR COUNTRY."

Rise it will.

☞ *The foundation good—it may yet be SAVED.*

This triumphant cartoon appeared in the *Massachusetts Centinel* on August 2, 1788. Note the two laggards, especially the sorry condition of Rhode Island.

amendments and—vain hope—issued a call for another convention to modify the Constitution.

Last-ditch dissent developed in only two states. A hostile convention met in North Carolina, then adjourned without taking a vote. Rhode Island did not even summon a ratifying convention. The two most ruggedly individualist centers of the colonial era—homes of the "otherwise minded"—thus ran true to form. They were to change their minds—unwillingly—only after the new government had been in operation for some months.

The battle for ratification, despite much apathy, was close and extremely bitter in some localities. No lives were lost, but riotous disturbances broke out in New York and Pennsylvania, involving bruises and bloodshed. There was much behind-the-scenes pressure on delegates who had solemnly promised their constituents to vote against the Constitution. The last four states ratified, not because they wanted to, but because they had to. They could not exist apart from the Union.

A Conservative Counter-Revolution

The minority had triumphed—doubly. A militant minority of American radicals had engineered the military revolution which cast off the ancient British constitution. A militant minority of conservatives—now embracing many of the earlier radicals—had engineered the peaceful revolution which overthrew the inadequate constitution known as the Articles of Confederation. Eleven states, in effect, had seceded from the Confederation, leaving two out in the cold.

The majority had not spoken. Only about one-fourth of the adult white males in the country, chiefly the propertied people, had voted for delegates to the ratifying conventions. Careful estimates indicate that if the newly forged Constitution had been submitted to a manhood-suffrage vote, it would have encountered much more opposition.

Conservatism was victorious. Safeguards had been erected against mob-rule excesses, and the democratic gains of the Revolution were conserved in the face of possible anarchy. Radicals like Patrick Henry, who had overthrown British rule, had in turn been overthrown by American conservatives. The result was a kind of peaceful counter-revolution. It restored the economic and political stability of colonial years, and set the drifting ship of state on a more promising course. The methods may have been somewhat irregular, but the fruits were highly praiseworthy.

SELECT READINGS

The most recent scholarly introduction is MERRILL JENSEN's sketchy *The Making of the American Constitution* (1964) [paperback]. It grows out of his earlier detailed studies, *The Articles of Confederation* (1940) [paperback] and *The New Nation* (1950) [paperback]. The story of the Philadelphia convention is pleasingly told in CARL VAN DOREN, *The Great Rehearsal* (1948) [paperback]. More learned is BROADUS and LOUISE P. MITCHELL, *A Biography of the Constitution of the United States* (1964) [paperback]. C. A. BEARD shocked the conservatives by his provocative and somewhat out-of-focus study of the Founding Fathers, *An Economic Interpretation of the Constitution of the United States* (1913) [paperback]. It is partially weakened by two blistering attacks: R. E. BROWN, *Charles Beard and the Constitution* (1956) [paperback] and FORREST MC DONALD, *We the People: The Economic Origins of the Constitution* (1958) [paperback]. J. T. MAIN, *The Anti-Federalists* (1961) [paperback] partially rehabilitates Beard. The discussion is continued in A. T. MASON, *The States Rights Debate: Antifederalism and the Constitution* (1964). Sectionalism is developed in J. R. ALDEN, *The First South* (1961) and W. N. CHAMBERS, *Political Parties in a New Nation* (1963) [paperback]. Finance is treated fully in E. J. FERGUSON, *The Power of the Purse: A History of American Public Finance, 1776–1790* (1961) and in C. P. NETTELS, *The Emergence of a National Economy, 1775–1815* (1962). M. L. STARKEY, *A Little Rebellion* (1955) is eminently readable on the Shays uprising. Relevant biographical studies of merit are J. C. MILLER, *Alexander Hamilton: Portrait in Paradox* (1959), now **paperbacked** as *Alexander Hamilton and the Growth of the New Nation* (1964); BROADUS MITCHELL, *Alexander Hamilton* (2 vols., 1957, 1962); IRVING BRANT, *James Madison: The Nationalist, 1780–1787* (1948) and *James Madison: Father of the Constitution, 1787–1800* (1950); CLINTON ROSSITER, *Alexander Hamilton and the Constitution* (1964). Also *Harvard Guide*, Pt. III.

8

Launching the New Ship of State

*He [Hamilton] touched the dead corpse of Public Credit,
and it sprung upon its feet.*

DANIEL WEBSTER, 1831

An Uncertain Sea

WHEN the Constitution was launched in 1789, the American republic was continuing to grow at an amazing rate. The population was still doubling about every twenty-three years, and the first official census of 1790 counted almost 4,000,000 souls. The cities had swelled proportionately: Philadelphia numbered 42,000; New York, 33,000; Boston, 18,000; Charleston, 16,000; and Baltimore, 13,000.

The population was still overwhelmingly rural, despite the flourishing cities. All but 5% of the people lived east of the mountains. The trans-Allegheny overflow was concentrated chiefly in Kentucky, Tennessee, and Ohio, all of which were welcomed as states within fourteen years. (Vermont preceded them, becoming the fourteenth state in 1791.) Foreign travelers everywhere looked down their noses at the roughness and crudity resulting from ax-and-rifle pioneering life. Yet, critical though they were, they could not fail to be impressed by evidences of energy, self-confidence, and material well-being.

The new ship of state, despite these promising signs of fair weather, did not spread its sails to the most favorable breezes. The beaten anti-federalists were disgruntled, and bitterly determined by peaceful means to weaken the Constitution. Two of the thirteen states, North Carolina and Rhode Island, were defiantly withholding ratification. In fact they did not grudgingly come aboard until 1789–1790, after the first Congress had met and threatened to club them into line with discriminatory tariff duties.

Nor was the general political outlook in 1789 auspicious. Within twelve troubled years the American people had risen up and thrown overboard their first two constitutions: the British constitution and the Articles of Confederation. A decade of constitution smashing and lawbreaking was not the best training for government making. The people had come to regard a central authority, replacing that of George III, as a necessary evil —something to be distrusted and watched.

The Men of the Western Waters, in the stump-studded clearings of Kentucky, Tennessee, and Ohio, were restive almost to the point of disloyalty. The mouth of the Mississippi, their life-giving outlet, lay in the hands of unfriendly Spaniards. Smooth-tongued Spanish and British agents, jingling gold, moved freely among them and held out seductive promises of independence.

The finances of the infant republic were likewise precarious. The revenue of the national government had declined to a trickle, while the public debt, with interest heavily in arrears, was mountainous. Worthless paper money, both state and national, was as plentiful as metallic money was scarce.

The Americans, moreover, were brashly attempting to erect a republic on an immense scale. They ignored the fact that hitherto a democratic form of government had succeeded only on a tiny scale, notably in Switzerland. The eyes of a skeptical world were on the upstart United States.

The monarchs of Europe naturally prayed for a speedy shipwreck of the American republic—and plotted to that end. They feared that if the radical new experiment prospered, their enchained peoples, pointing to the Promised Land of America, might demand the same trouble-making blessings for themselves. The most consistently dangerous "isms" of the late 18th Century, in the eyes of European royalty, were American republicanism, constitutionalism, and liberalism. The United States of America, though starting shakily, was the bane of reactionaries, the guiding star of liberals, the hope of the world.

Fair Breezes

Yet the domestic picture in 1789 had its brighter colors. The American people had achieved a high degree of political maturity; they were seasoned alumni of the self-governing town meetings, of the colonial legislatures, and of the new state governments. George Washington, so the public confidently assumed, would consent to serve as President. He was a battle-tested leader. He had voluntarily laid down dictatorial military powers once, and hence he could be trusted not to pervert his high office into a dictatorship. Philip Freneau, a contemporary poet, hailed him:

> Empires are far below thy aims,
> And scepters have no charms for thee.

The clouds of economic depression, which had reached their low point in 1786, were beginning to lift. Returning prosperity would soon be causing a spirit of buoyancy and confidence to suffuse the land.

Finally, the first elections for members of the Senate and the House of Representatives augured well. The federalists, in the face of spirited opposition, triumphed over their anti-federalist foes. The lopsided federalist majorities in Congress meant that an ambitious new program could be launched with enthusiasm, and without crippling sabotage from a potent anti-federalist opposition.

Charting a New Course

George Washington, the esteemed war hero, was unanimously chosen President by the Electoral College in 1789—the only presidential nominee ever to be honored by unanimity. Much preferring the quiet of Mount Vernon to the turmoil of politics, he was perhaps the only President who did not in some way angle for this exalted office. But his fame and prestige, which had spread throughout two hemispheres, made him an "indispensable man." Balanced rather than brilliant, he commanded men by strength of character rather than by the arts of the politician.

Washington, as President-elect, was enthusiastically acclaimed. His long journey from Mount Vernon to New York City, the temporary capital, was a triumphal procession. He was greeted by roaring cannon, pealing bells, flower-carpeted roads, and singing and shouting citizens. With appropriate ceremony, he solemnly and somewhat nervously took the oath of office on April 30, 1789, on a crowded balcony overlooking Wall Street. The cold but able New Englander John Adams was sworn in as Vice-President—an office which Benjamin Franklin thought should have carried the title "His Superfluous Excellency."

At first, there were only three full-fledged department heads under the President. They were Secretary of State Jefferson, Secretary of the Treasury Hamilton, and Secretary of War Knox, a three-hundred-pound Revolutionary general to whom were entrusted both the tiny army and the infant navy.

Thomas Jefferson, at that time minister to France, was a logical choice for Secretary of State. In this new office he was to do notable pioneering work, chiefly in laying the foundation stones of American foreign policy.

Alexander Hamilton, then only thirty-four, was eminently well qualified for the post of Secretary of the Treasury. But he regarded himself as a kind of prime minister, and on occasion thrust his hands offensively into the business of other departments. Born in the British West Indies, he never developed that passionate state loyalty which dominated so many Americans, including his archrival from Virginia, Thomas Jefferson.

The Constitution does not mention a Cabinet; it merely provides that the President "may require" written opinions of the heads of his departments (see Art. II, Sec. II, para. 1). But this system proved so cumbersome, and involved so much homework, that Cabinet meetings gradually evolved in the Washington administration. An invaluable body of special advisers was thus provided the President. Along with numerous other practices not specifically authorized, the Cabinet has become an indispensable part of the unwritten Constitution.

Evolution of the Cabinet		
Original Members	*Added 1798–1913*	*Recent Additions, 1947–1953*
Sec. of State, 1789 Sec. of Treasury, 1789 Sec. of War, 1789 (Loses Cabinet status, 1947) Attorney General, 1789 (Not head of Justice Dept. until 1870)	Sec. of Navy, 1798 (Loses Cabinet status, 1947) Postmaster General, 1829 Sec. of Interior, 1849 Sec. of Agriculture, 1889 Sec. of Commerce and Labor, 1903 (Office divided in 1913) Sec. of Commerce, 1913 Sec. of Labor, 1913	Sec. of Defense, 1947 (Subordinate to him, without Cabinet rank, are Secs. of Army, Navy, Air Force) Sec. of Health, Education, and Welfare, 1953

Other newly sawed governmental planks were nailed into place. Potent federal courts were created under the Judiciary Act passed by Congress in 1789, as authorized by the Constitution (see Art. III, Sec. 1). The first Congress likewise approved the first ten amendments to the Constitution, and these were ratified by the states in 1791. Popularly known as the Bill of Rights, the new safeguards guaranteed the most precious of American principles. Among these are the right to jury trial, assurances against unreasonable search, freedom of religion, freedom of speech, freedom of the press, freedom of assembly, and freedom of petition (see Arts. I–X).

Anti-federalists, charging that the new amendments did not go far enough, raised cries of bad faith. At the time of the struggle over ratifying the Constitution, many opponents had been informally assured that Congress would drastically amend the document so as to protect states' rights. But the first ten amendments provided no fundamental alterations. They merely guaranteed rights which the anti-federalists angrily insisted they had possessed all along.

The new government was clearly dominated by well-born and well-dressed federalists. Practically all the President's judicial and executive appointees were staunch supporters of the Constitution. Washington has been criticized, as a consequence, for not having given the opposition a fair share in the government. But he no doubt perceived that under the best of circumstances the daring experiment in republicanism might collapse, and that it would get off to a ruinous start if he filled key posts with anti-federalist obstructionists.

A strong majority of the new Congress, in addition, were men who had played an active role in framing and/or ratifying the Constitution. In a broad sense, the historic Philadelphia convention never dissolved. Its members merely went home, packed their clothes, and then moved to New York, where they secured a virtual monopoly of the leading federal offices.

Reviving the Corpse of Public Credit

Financial vexations, which had crippled the Articles of Confederation, were the most pressing. Alexander Hamilton, a financial wizard, sprang to the rescue. His plan was to shape the financial policies of the administration in such a way as to favor the wealthier groups. They, in turn, would gratefully lend the government monetary and moral support. The new federal regime would flourish, the propertied classes would grow fat, and prosperity would trickle down to the common people.

The youthful financier's first objective was to bolster the national credit. Without public confidence in the government, Hamilton could not borrow the funds with which to carry through his risky schemes. He therefore boldly urged Congress to "fund" the entire national debt at par, and to assume completely the debts incurred by the states during the Revolutionary War.

"Funding" at par meant that the federal government would pay off its debts at face value. These included outstanding securities and other obligations totaling over $54,000,000, a figure which included accumulated interest. Hamilton would raise the money by issuing new bonds and exchanging them for the depreciated bonds, which had dropped to ten or fifteen cents on the dollar. After stormy debate, Congress in 1790 passed the funding proposal, coupling with it, as will be noted, the assumption of state debts.

Scandals unfortunately attended Hamilton's audacious stroke. Greedy speculators galloped into rural areas ahead of the news, and bought for a song the depreciated paper holdings of farmers, war veterans, and widows. Hamilton has been accused of having lined his own pockets, but he was never wealthy, and died heavily in debt. Yet his Assistant Secretary of the Treasury, a less scrupulous character, profited personally from official foreknowledge.

In Hamilton's defense it may be said that discerning outsiders needed no inside tips. As soon as the Constitution neared ratification, financiers had perceived that the value of securities would rise; and an orgy of speculation began. Hamilton has also been criticized for not having sought out the original holders of the securities. But such a course would have been impossible to carry out with complete fairness. The farseeing Secretary, choosing among possible evils, decided to re-establish the public credit by one bold and dramatic move.

State Debts and Private Pocketbooks

Hamilton was willing, even eager, to have the new government take on additional obligations. While pushing the funding scheme, he urged Congress to assume the debts of the states, totaling some $21,500,000.

A convincing case was prepared by Hamilton for assumption. The state debts could be regarded as a proper national obligation, for they had been incurred in the joint war for independence. But foremost in Hamilton's thinking was the fact that assumption would chain the states more tightly to the "federal chariot," and thus strengthen the national character of the central government. The states that had dumped their load on the Federal Treasury would be properly grateful. They would work earnestly for the success of the Hamiltonian experiment, lest it collapse and throw their debts back on them.

The states that were burdened by heavy debts, like Massachusetts, were delighted by Hamilton's proposal. The states that had small debts, or had taken energetic steps to pay them off, were less happy. They saw no good reason why they should be taxed by the central government to pull their less thrifty sisters out of a fiscal hole. The battle against assumption was vigorously led by Virginia, and took on the semblance of another North-South sectional struggle, unpleasantly reminiscent of the 1787 convention. In some of the states there was even irresponsible talk of leaving the Union.

The stage was set for some old-fashioned horse trading. Virginia did not want the state debts assumed, but she did want the forthcoming federal district*—now the District of Columbia—to be located on the Potomac River. She would thus gain in commerce and prestige. Hamilton persuaded a reluctant Jefferson, who had recently come home from France, to line up enough votes in Congress for assumption. In return, Virginia would have the federal district on the Potomac. The bargain was carried through in 1790, though Jefferson later claimed that he had been outwitted. It proved to be one of the earliest instances of Congressional logrolling.†

Irregularities of a more disturbing kind accompanied assumption, or so scholars charged many years later. A number of the Congressmen, being well-to-do citizens, owned depreciated federal or state securities. Most of them voted for the Hamiltonian program, doubtless realizing that if it went into effect the value of their holdings would rise. Without their support neither funding nor assumption would have passed, and hence certain cynics have branded the Founding Fathers "Funding Fathers."

The reassuring truth is that most of the Congressmen were staunch federalists. Many of them no doubt were convinced that the success of

* Authorized by the Constitution, Art. I, Sec. VIII, para. 17

† On the frontier, heavy logs for cabins were rolled into place by enlisting the assistance of neighbors. Mutual aid in legislative bodies to pass laws for special interests came to be called logrolling—"an aye for an aye."

the new government depended on their approval of Hamilton's schemes. It would have been folly for these men to vote against what they regarded as the best interests of the nation, simply because their own pocketbooks incidentally stood to gain.

Raising Revenue

The new ship of state thus set sail dangerously overloaded. The national debt had swelled to $75,000,000, owing largely to Hamilton's insistence on honoring the outstanding federal and state obligations. A man less determined to establish a healthy public credit could have sidestepped $13,000,000 in back interest, and could easily have avoided the burden of the state debts entirely.

But Hamilton was not greatly worried. He believed that, within limits, a national debt was a "national blessing"—a kind of cement of union. The more citizens the government owed money to, the more there would be with a personal financial stake in the success of his ambitious enterprise. His unique contribution was to make of a debt—ordinarily a liability—an asset for reinvigorating the whole financial circulatory system.

HAMILTON'S FINANCIAL STRUCTURE

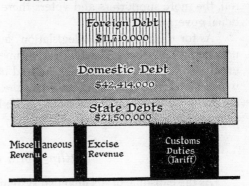

Customs duties rose from $4,399,-000 a year in 1791 to $10,751,000 a year in 1801. Excise revenue rose from $209,000 a year in 1792 to $1,582,000 in 1801. Only $18,271,-786 of the state debts was finally assumed.

Customs duties, derived from a tariff, were the fountainhead of the Hamiltonian program. They would provide the bulk of the income for payments on the huge national debt, and also for current governmental expenses. The first tariff law, a low one of about 8% on the value of dutiable imports, was speedily passed by the first Congress in 1789, even before Hamilton was sworn in. Revenue was by far the main goal, but the measure was also designed to erect a low protective wall around infant industries, which bawled noisily for more shelter than they received. Hamilton, who had the vision to see that the Industrial Revolution would soon reach America, argued in favor of more protection for the wealthy commercial and manufacturing groups. But Congress voted only two slight increases in the tariff during Washington's presidency.

Additional sources of internal revenue were urgently needed to balance the federal budget. Hamilton, with characteristic vigor, secured from Congress in 1791 an excise on whiskey. The new tax of seven cents a gallon was borne chiefly by the distillers who lived in the back country, where the wretched roads forced the farmer to reduce his bulky bushels of grain to horseback proportions. Whiskey flowed so freely on the frontier that it was used for money. A gallon of the fiery liquid passed for one shilling—or about twenty-five cents in the currency of the day.

New tensions rapidly developed over the excise. It came dangerously close to being class legislation, for it burdened the poor frontier farmers, while leaving virtually untouched the more prosperous Easterners, whose favor Hamilton was courting. It also had some of the earmarks of sectional legislation. Much of the whiskey was produced and consumed in the South and Southwest, while rum, the favorite drink of the North, was only lightly taxed.

The excise, in Hamilton's eyes, had much to commend it, even though the proceeds at first were disappointing. It would accustom the people, especially the reluctant states'-rights advocates, to a direct tax by the federal government. It would also create a small army of revenue agents, who would snoop around the stills of the defiant distillers. Hamilton no doubt perceived that the more employees there were on the federal payroll, the more supporters and voters there would be for the newborn national government.

As for the cry of "class legislation" against the excise, Hamilton was not deeply disturbed. The federal regime had to be bolstered, however unpopular his measures. Besides, he had little real sympathy for the backwoods distillers, most of whom from the outset had been unfriendly to the powerful new Constitution and to the Hamiltonian schemes with their centralizing trend.

Battling for a Bank

As the capstone of his financial system, Hamilton conceived of a Bank of the United States. An enthusiastic admirer of most things English, he took as his model the Bank of England. Specifically, he proposed a powerful private institution, of which the government would be the major stockholder, and in which the Federal Treasury would deposit its surplus monies. The central government not only would have a convenient strongbox, but federal funds would stimulate business by remaining in circulation. The Bank would also print badly needed paper money, and thus provide a sound and stable national currency.

Ardent champions of states' rights, spearheaded by Secretary of State Jefferson, cried out against a giant Bank. They predicted that their cherished state banks could not survive competition from this monopolistic monster. More alarming, the states'-righters feared that their precious liberties would be jeopardized by a grasping banking colossus, which, in fact, came to enjoy a virtual monopoly of the government's surplus funds.

Jefferson, whose written opinion was requested by President Washington, argued vigorously against the Bank. There was, he insisted, no specific authorization in the Constitution for such a financial octopus. He was convinced that all powers not categorically granted to the central government were reserved to the states, as provided in the about-to-be-ratified Bill of Rights (see Art. X). He therefore concluded that the states, not Congress, had the power to charter banks. Believing that the Constitution should be interpreted "literally" or "strictly," Jefferson and his states'-rights disciples enthusiastically embraced the theory of "strict construction."

Hamilton, also at Washington's request, prepared a well-reasoned reply to Jefferson's arguments. He boldly invoked that clause of the Constitution which stipulates that Congress may pass any laws "necessary and proper" to carry out the powers vested in the various governmental agencies (see Art. I, Sec. VIII, para. 18). The government was explicitly empowered to collect taxes and regulate trade. In carrying out these basic functions, Hamilton argued, a national bank would be not only "proper" but "necessary." By inference or implication—that is, by virtue of "implied powers"—Congress would be fully justified in establishing the Bank of the United States. In short, Hamilton contended for a "loose" or "broad" interpretation of the Constitution. He and his federalist followers thus evolved the theory of "loose construction" by invoking the "elastic clause" of the Constitution.

Hamilton's financial views prevailed. His eloquent and realistic arguments were accepted by Washington, who reluctantly signed the Bank measure into law. The explosive issue had been debated with much heat in Congress, where the old North-South cleavage again appeared ominously. The most enthusiastic support for the Bank naturally came from the commercial and financial centers of the North, while the strongest opposition formed in the agricultural South.

The Bank of the United States, as created by Congress in 1791, was chartered for twenty years. Located in Philadelphia, it was to have a capital of $10,000,000, one-fifth of it owned by the federal government. The stock was thrown open to public sale. To the agreeable surprise of Hamilton, a milling crowd oversubscribed in less than two hours, pushing aside many would-be purchasers.

The Hamiltonian Balance Sheet

Almost overnight Hamilton's fiscal feats vitalized the public credit. The Treasury was now able to secure ample funds in the Netherlands on terms more favorable than those being extended to any other borrowing nation. Honesty, as Hamilton foresaw, was the best policy.

The dynamic Secretary, with the collaboration of Washington, also strengthened the government politically while bolstering it financially. His major schemes—funding, assumption, the excise, the Bank—all encroached sharply upon states' rights. This trend, facilitated by "loose construction," was destined to continue its controversial course.

The states'-rights people naturally condemned Hamilton in savage terms. The Constitution had been ratified by a painfully narrow margin; and if the voters had foreseen how the states were going to be overshadowed by the federal colossus, they almost certainly would have voted it down. The irony is that Hamilton, in attempting to curb both the states and the masses, did perhaps as much as any other man to goad them into fighting for their interests.

The energetic financier, while achieving economic stability, somewhat incidentally furthered a concentration of monetary power. The Bank of the United States was the shining example. Actually, Hamilton's generosity toward the wealthy groups was probably unnecessary. The propertied elements, recognizing where their interests lay, were bound to support the federal experiment anyhow. Philip Freneau sneered:

> And, Sir, 'tis true
> ('Twixt me and you)
> That some have grown prodigious fat,
> And some prodigious lean.

Hamilton, though a skillful planner, was at heart a gambler—a taker of calculated risks. He was playing for enormous stakes, and the outcome might be either a resounding success or a crashing failure. The huge debt, which he had so confidently urged Congress to assume, could be paid off only if ample receipts flowed into the customs-houses. Disaster would befall the nation if our foreign trade languished, or if it were choked off by war with our best customer, Great Britain.

Luck was with Hamilton. Prosperity preceded the Constitution, and floated it over the financial reefs. Fortunately also prosperity continued, except for one brief flurry. A full-blown foreign war was avoided for more than two decades, and by that time the experimental stage had passed. Even so, the race between mounting expenditures and increasing revenues was nip and tuck for about ten years.

It was well for Hamilton's reputation that Dame Fortune smiled upon him. Otherwise the handsome young financier might have gone down in history not as the "greatest Secretary of the Treasury" but the last.

Government by the Well-Born

National political parties, in the modern sense, were unknown to America when George Washington took the inaugural oath. There had been Whigs and Tories, federalists and anti-federalists, but these groups were factions rather than parties. They had sprung into existence over hotly contested special issues; they had faded away when their cause had triumphed or had become hopelessly lost.

American political parties date their birth from the bitter clashes between Hamilton and Jefferson, chiefly over fiscal policy and foreign affairs. By 1792–1793 two well-defined groupings had crystallized: the Hamiltonian Federalists and the Jeffersonian Republicans. The two-party system has existed in the United States since that day, and has provided indispensable machinery for the functioning of democratic self-government. The party of the "outs," among other responsibilities, has traditionally played the invaluable role of both critic and brake.

The Framing Fathers, for all their wisdom, did not make due allowances for the rise of political parties. Their expectation was that the qualified voters in each presidential election would choose the members of an Electoral College. This august body would then meet in a cloistered chamber, look the entire country over, and select the ablest man for President. But political parties gradually won control of the machinery, and the Electoral College became a discretionless rubber stamp. The tendency of the parties, moreover, has been to choose not necessarily the best man but the best vote-getter.

As might be expected, most federalists of the pre-Constitution period (1787–1789) became Federalists in the Washington era. By 1793 they were welded into an effective group, largely through the magnetic leadership and organizational genius of Alexander Hamilton. Despite his dubious birth,* he had married into a prominent New York family, and had become the leader of the well-born.

The Federalists openly advocated rule by the "best people." They believed in a government by the upper classes, for the upper classes, with secondary attention to the masses. "Those who own the country," remarked Federalist John Jay, "ought to govern it." With their intellectual arrogance and Tory tastes, the Hamiltonians deplored democratic tendencies and distrusted the common man. They regarded democracy as the mother of all mischiefs, and feared the "swayability" of the crowd. Let the rich rule, insisted many Federalist leaders, for they had the leisure with which to study the problems of state. They also enjoyed all the advantages of intelligence, education, and culture. The untutored masses would only throw monkey wrenches into the machinery.

The Hamiltonians likewise advocated a powerful central government It would maintain law and order, crush democratic excesses (like Shays' Rebellion), and protect the lives and estates of the wealthy. The foreign-born Hamilton would have subordinated the sovereignty-loving states.

---

* John Adams later referred to Hamilton as the "bastard brat of a Scotch peddler." This sneer was unfair. Hamilton came of a good family, although his parents could not legally marry because of a technicality connected with his mother's divorce from her first husband.

The Hamiltonian Federalists also believed that the national government should foster business, not interfere with it. This attitude was only natural in a group in which merchants, manufacturers, and shippers were so strongly represented. Hamilton himself was somewhat inclined to put property above people. The great majority of Federalists, especially south of New England, lived in the urban areas of the seaboard, where commerce and manufacturing flourished. If a gunner could have fired cannon balls fifty miles inland, he would have hit few Hamiltonians.

The Federalists, in addition, were basically pro-British. Though Americans first of all, they felt that the nation's foreign policy should be slanted toward friendship with England, above any other outside power. Many of the Hamiltonians were merchants and shippers, and the bulk of their trade was with Britain. Most of the Loyalists of Revolution days who remained in the United States embraced the Federalist Party. They were basically conservative in their outlook, and they welcomed the Federalist bias in favor of the Mother Country, to which they retained some sentimental attachment.

Mutinous Moonshiners

The Whiskey Rebellion, which broke out in southwestern Pennsylvania in 1794, sharply challenged the authority of the new national government. The Federalist excise bore harshly on these homespun pioneer folk. They regarded it not as a tax on a luxury but as a burden on an economic necessity and a medium of exchange. Even preachers of the gospel were paid in "Old Monongahela rye." The defiant distillers finally erected Whiskey Poles, similar to the Liberty Poles of anti-Stamp Tax days in 1765, and raised the cry "Liberty and No Excise." Boldly tarring and feathering certain revenue officers, they paralyzed the collecting arm of the federal government.

President Washington, once a revolutionist, was alarmed by what he called these "self-created societies." With the enthusiastic encouragement of Hamilton, he forthwith summoned the militia of several states. Anxious moments followed the call, for there was much doubt as to whether the men in other states would march to crush a rebellion in Pennsylvania, a sister state. But despite some opposition, an army of about 13,000 men rallied to the colors, and in two widely separated columns marched briskly forth in a gorgeous, leaf-tinted Indian summer, until knee-deep mud slowed their progress. Washington accompanied the troops a part of the way; Hamilton all the way.

The federal force was overpoweringly strong—considerably larger in fact than Washington's army during much of the War of Independence. When the troops reached the hills of western Pennsylvania, they found no insurrection. The "Whiskey Boys" were overawed, dispersed, or captured. Washington, with an eye to healing old sores, pardoned the convicted

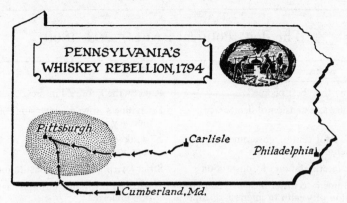

PENNSYLVANIA'S
WHISKEY REBELLION, 1794

Pittsburgh

Carlisle

Philadelphia

Cumberland, Md.

THE TWO ARMIES GATHERED AT CARLISLE AND CUMBERLAND,
AND JOINED BELOW PITTSBURGH

culprits, much to the disgust of Hamilton, who wanted to punish the real ringleaders.

The Whiskey Rebellion was small—some three rebels were killed—but its consequences were large. The federal government, now substantially strengthened, commanded a new respect. Yet the numerous foes of the Federalists condemned the administration for its extravagant and indecent display of force—for having used a sledge hammer to crush a gnat. The ranks of the Jeffersonians were consequently bolstered. The back-country men, taught a harsh lesson, now saw the wisdom of forsaking the tar kettle for the ballot box—and voting for Jefferson.

Jeffersonian Idealism

Thomas Jefferson, lanky and relaxed in appearance, emerged as the Moses of the Democratic-Republicans—known also as the Jeffersonian Republicans. Lacking personal aggressiveness, weak-voiced, and unable to deliver a rabble-rousing speech, he became a master political organizer through his ability to lead men rather than drive them. His strongest appeal was to the middle class and to the underprivileged—the "dirt" farmers, the laborers, the artisans, and the small shopkeepers.

The liberal-thinking Jefferson, with his aristocratic head set on a farmer's frame, was a bundle of inconsistencies. By one set of tests he should have been a Federalist, for he was a Virginia aristocrat and slave-owner who lived in an imposing hilltop mansion at Monticello. A so-called "traitor" to his upper class, Jefferson cherished uncommon sympathy for the common man, especially the downtrodden, the oppressed, and the persecuted. As he wrote in 1800, "I have sworn upon the altar of God eternal hostility against every form of tyranny over the mind of man."

The Jeffersonians demanded a weak central regime, for they believed that the best government was the one that governed least. The bulk of

The Two Political Parties, 1793–1800

Federalist Features	Republican (Jeffersonian) Features
Rule by the "best people"	Rule by the informed masses
Hostility to extension of democracy	Friendliness toward extension of democracy
A powerful central government at the expense of states' rights	A weak central government so as to conserve states' rights
Loose interpretation of Constitution	Strict interpretation of Constitution
Government to foster business; concentration of wealth in interests of capitalistic enterprise	No special favors for business; agriculture preferred
A protective tariff	No special favors for manufacturers
Pro-British (conservative Tory tradition)	Pro-French (radical Revolutionary tradition)
National debt a blessing, if properly funded	National debt a bane; rigid economy
An expanding bureaucracy	Reduction of federal officeholders
A powerful central bank	Encouragement to state banks
Restrictions on free speech and press	Relatively free speech and press
Concentration in seacoast area	Concentration in S. and S.W.; in agricultural areas and back country

the power, Jefferson held, should be retained by the states. There the people, in intimate contact with local affairs, could keep a more vigilant eye on their public servants. Otherwise, a monarchy might develop. Central authority—a kind of necessary evil—was to be kept at a minimum through a strict interpretation of the Constitution. The national debt, which Jefferson regarded as a burden rather than a "blessing," was to be paid off. This goal would be achieved partly by paring down the expenses of government and squeezing out unnecessary bureaucrats. Jefferson might well have said that the best government is the one that taxes least.

The Jeffersonians, themselves primarily agrarians, insisted that there should be no special privileges for special classes, particularly manufacturers. Agriculture was the favored branch of the economy. Jefferson regarded farming as essentially ennobling; it kept men away from wicked cities, out in the sunshine and close to the soil. "Let our workshops remain in Europe," he declared. Most of his followers naturally came from the agricultural South and Southwest.

The Jeffersonian Republicans, unlike the Federalist "British bootlickers," were basically pro-French. They earnestly believed that it was to America's advantage to support the liberal ideals of the French Revolution, rather than hobnob with the Tory reaction of George III.

Above all, Jefferson advocated the rule of the people. But he did not propose thrusting the ballot into the hands of every adult white male. He favored government *for* the people, but not by *all* the people—only by those men who were literate enough to inform themselves and wear the mantle of American citizenship worthily. Universal education would have to precede universal suffrage. The ignorant, he argued, were incapable of self-government. But he had profound faith in the reasonableness and teachableness of the masses, and in their collective wisdom when taught. His enduring appeal was to America's better self.

Jefferson demanded a maximum of safeguards for the masses, for he feared tyranny by the privileged groups. Daniel Shays' armed uprising in 1786 prompted him to write, "A little rebellion now and then is a good thing. . . ." It would keep the governing class from overstepping constitutional limits. The blood "of patriots and tyrants" was the "natural manure" of the tree of liberty. Jefferson also suggested that long-term laws designed to entrench aristocracy should be repealed, for there should, in his view, be no governing from the grave. In his words, "The earth belongs to the living, not to the dead."

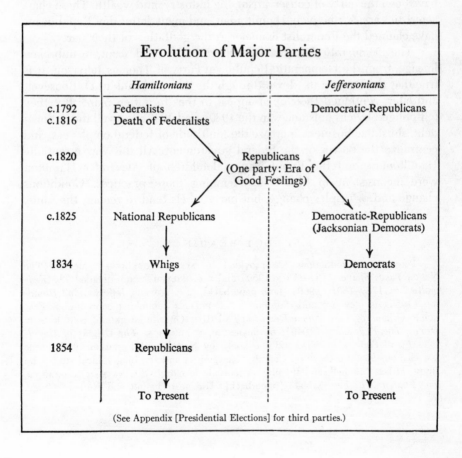

Evolution of Major Parties

	Hamiltonians		Jeffersonians
c.1792	Federalists		Democratic-Republicans
c.1816	Death of Federalists		
c.1820		Republicans (One party: Era of Good Feelings)	
c.1825	National Republicans		Democratic-Republicans (Jacksonian Democrats)
1834	Whigs		Democrats
1854	Republicans		
	To Present		To Present

(See Appendix [Presidential Elections] for third parties.)

The open-minded Virginian was a devotee of free speech, because without free speech the misdeeds of tyranny could not be exposed. He even went so far as to say that as between "a government without newspapers" and "newspapers without a government," he would choose the latter. No American statesman ever suffered more foul abuse from editorial pens; he might well have prayed for freedom *from* the Federalist press. Yet in 1801 he declared, "Error of opinion may be tolerated where reason is left free to combat it."

Stealing Each Other's Baggage

The Federalist Party expired about 1816 as a national organization, but it continued to live in spirit. Its heirs, with their conservative coloration, sought refuge with other parties, ultimately with the present-day Republicans. The Republican Party of Abraham Lincoln, to be sure, made a powerful appeal to the common people. But since the Civil War the Republicans have consistently favored a protective tariff and other profit-giving concessions to business. More than their Democratic rivals, they have been the party of conservatism, big industry, and wealth. These characteristics are distinctively Hamiltonian, and many latter-day Republicans have claimed the Federalist financier as the godfather of their party.

The Democratic Party of later times traces its descent, in unbroken lineage, from the Democratic-Republican Party of Thomas Jefferson. It is true that the Democrats, down through the days of Franklin D. Roosevelt and later, continued their open appeal to the "forgotten man." But they felt obliged by circumstances in the 1930's and 1940's to swell the national debt, subsidize business, increase the multitude of federal employees, and centralize the power of the federal government. All this was essentially Hamiltonian, and the Republican godchildren of Alexander Hamilton were inconsistent in bitterly condemning these practices. Conditions change and principles change, but party labels tend to remain the same.

SELECT READINGS

Perceptive introductions are provided by MARCUS CUNLIFFE's succinct *The Nation Takes Shape, 1789–1837* (1959) and J. C. MILLER's more detailed *The Federalist Era, 1789–1801* (1960) [both **paperback**]. C. G. BOWERS, *Jefferson and Hamilton* (1925) is racy but anti-Hamilton. C. A. BEARD's debunking continues in *Economic Origins of Jeffersonian Democracy* (1915). On administration, consult L. D. WHITE, *The Federalists* (1948); on finance, D. F. SWANSON, *The Origins of Hamilton's Fiscal Policies* (1963), and the books by Nettels and Ferguson cited in the last chapter. See also those by Chambers on politics and the biographical studies by Brant, Miller, Mitchell, and Rossiter. A journalistic narrative is NATHAN SCHACHNER, *The Founding Fathers* (1954) [**paperback**]. Also next chapter and *Harvard Guide*, Pt. IV.

9

Federalists and Foreign Friction

And ne'er shall the sons of Columbia be slaves,
While the earth bears a plant, or the sea rolls its waves.
Popular song by ROBERT TREAT PAINE
"Adams and Liberty," 1798

Liberté, Égalité, Fraternité

ONLY a few weeks after Washington's inauguration in 1789, the curtain rose on the first act of the French Revolution. Twenty-six years were to pass before the seething continent of Europe settled back into a peace of exhaustion. Few non-American events have left a deeper scar on American political and social life. In a sense, the French Revolution was misnamed: it was a *world* revolution that touched all civilized peoples.

The early stages of the upheaval were surprisingly peaceful, consisting as they did of a successful attempt to impose constitutional shackles on Louis XVI. The American people, being both liberty-loving and anti-monarchical, were pleased by this curbing of despotism. They were flattered to think that the uprising in France was but the second chapter of their own glorious revolution, as to some extent it was. Only a minority consisting of ultra-conservative Federalists—fearing change, reform, and "leveling" principles—were from the outset dubious or outspokenly hostile. The more ardent Jeffersonians were delighted.

The French Revolution entered upon a more ominous phase in 1792, when France declared war on a hostile Austria. Late in that year the glorious news reached America that the French citizen armies had hurled back the invading monarchical hosts, and that France had proclaimed herself a republic. American enthusiasm found further vent in singing "The Marseillaise" and other French revolutionary songs, and in renaming thoroughfares. King Street in New York, for example, became Liberty Street. Powerful armies and powerful ideas were on the march.

But centuries of pent-up poison could not be purged without baleful consequences. The guillotine was set up, the King was beheaded in 1793, the worship of God was abolished, and the head-rolling Reign of Terror was begun. Back in America, God-fearing Federalist aristocrats nervously

165

fingered their tender white necks and eyed the Jeffersonian masses appre-
hensively. Lukewarm Federalist approval of the early Revolution turned,
almost overnight, to bitter opposition.

Sober-minded Jeffersonians regretted the gore. But they felt, with
Jefferson, that one could not expect to be carried from "despotism to liberty in a feather bed," and that a few thousand aristocratic heads were a
cheap price to pay for human freedom. When the news came of Louis
XVI's beheading, the Pittsburgh *Gazette* brutally rejoiced, "Louis Capet
has lost his caput."

The gloating was shortsighted, for dire peril loomed ahead. The
earlier battles of the French Revolution had not hurt America directly,
but now Britain was sucked into the titanic conflict. The conflagration
speedily spread to the New World, where it vitally affected the American
people. Thus was repeated the familiar story of every great European war,
beginning with 1689, that involved a death struggle for control of the
Atlantic Ocean. (See table on p. 51.)

Bitter Fruits of Entanglement

Ominously, the Franco-American alliance of 1778 was still on the
books. By its own terms it was to last "forever." It bound the United States
to help the French defend their West Indies against future foes; and the
booming British fleets were certain to attack these strategic islands.

Many Jeffersonian Republicans insisted on honoring the alliance,
though they were less enthusiastic about defending the French island outposts at the risk of war. Aflame with the liberal ideals of the French Revolution, red-blooded Jeffersonians were eager to enter the conflict against
Britain, our recent foe, at the side of France, our recent friend. We owed
France our freedom, they argued, and now was the time to pay the debt
of gratitude.

But President Washington, level-headed as usual, was not easily
swayed by the clamor of the crowd. Enthusiastically backed by Hamilton,
he perceived that war had to be avoided at all costs. The nation in 1793
was militarily weak, economically wobbly, and politically disunited. But
solid foundations were being laid, and American cradles were continuing
to rock a bumper crop of babies. Washington sagaciously reasoned that if
we could avoid the broils of Europe for a generation or so, we would then
be populous enough and strong enough to assert our rights with vigor and
success. Otherwise, we might invite disaster.

The strategy of delay—of playing for time while our birth rate fought
our battles—was a cardinal policy of the Founding Fathers. Hamilton and
Jefferson, often poles apart on other issues, were in basic agreement on
this principle.

Accordingly, Washington boldly issued his Neutrality Proclamation
in 1793, shortly after the outbreak of war between Britain and France.

This historic document not only proclaimed the government's official neutrality in the spreading conflict, but sternly warned American citizens to be impartial toward both armed camps. The pronouncement was our first formal declaration of aloofness from Old World embroilments, and as such proved to be a major prop of the spreading isolationist tradition.

The pro-French Jeffersonians were enraged by the Neutrality Proclamation; the pro-British Federalists were overjoyed. A few days earlier an impetuous, thirty-year-old representative of the French Republic, Citizen Genêt, had landed at Charleston, South Carolina. With unrestrained zeal, he undertook to fit out privateers and otherwise take advantage of the existing Franco-American alliance. The giddy-headed envoy—all sail and no anchor—was soon swept away by his enthusiastic reception at the hands of the Jeffersonian Republicans. He foolishly came to believe that the Neutrality Proclamation did not reflect the true wishes of the American people, and he consequently embarked upon unneutral activity not authorized by the French alliance. After he had threatened to appeal over the head of "old Washington" to the sovereign voters, his recall was demanded and he was replaced by a more level-headed spokesman.

The Neutrality Proclamation clearly illustrates the fact that self-interest is the basic cement of alliances. In 1778, both France and America stood to gain; in 1793, only France. Technically, we did not flout our obligation, because France never officially called upon us to honor it. Her homeland, and especially her beleaguered West Indian islands, were urgently in need of our foodstuffs. If we had entered the war, the British fleets would have blockaded our coast and cut off those desperately needed supplies. The United States was much more useful to France as a prosperous provider than as a prostrate partner.

Embroilments with Britain

Washington's far-visioned policy of neutrality was sorely tried by the British. For ten long years—and in defiance of the peace treaty of 1783—they had been retaining the chain of northern frontier posts on United States soil. There they openly sold firearms and firewater to the Indians, who continued to butcher and scalp our westward-moving pioneers.

Angered American frontiersmen, noisily seconded by the anti-British Jeffersonians, accused Britain of deliberately egging on the Indians. Such was not the *official* policy of London. But the redskins were regarded, in certain British quarters, as potential allies in repelling a future American invasion of Canada. Unauthorized British officers at the posts, it seems clear, privately encouraged the Indians to fight for their hunting grounds until the British King—the Great White Father with the Red Coat—should return.

Other stimulants were administered to the Indians. Even if the British did not incite the red man to murder, they did sell him the firewater which emboldened him to shoot Americans with his English-manufactured gun. The pale-faced pioneers, for their part, failed to perceive that the sharpest provocation of all was their own relentless occupation of Indian lands.

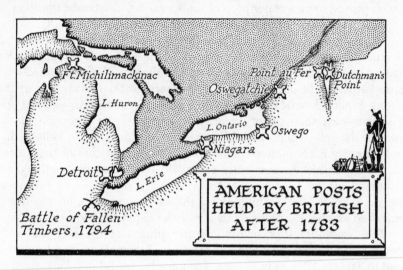

AMERICAN POSTS HELD BY BRITISH AFTER 1783

The offenses of Great Britain were no less galling on sea than on land. Embattled Britons were eager to starve out the French West Indies, and naturally expected the United States to defend them under the Franco-American alliance. Hard-boiled commanders of the Royal Navy, acting under instructions from London in 1793, struck savagely. They seized scores of American merchant ships in the West Indies, impressed scores of seamen into service on English ships, and threw hundred of others into foul dungeons.

These outrages were intolerable. A mighty outcry arose, chiefly from Jeffersonians, that America should once again fight George III in defense of her liberties. At the very least, she should cut off all supplies to her oppressor through a nationwide embargo.

But the Hamiltonians vehemently resisted all demands for drastic action. Federalist merchants, despite British seizures, were generally prospering. They believed that if we were going to fight anyone, we had better fight the "blood-drunk" Frenchmen, at the side of law-abiding Englishmen.

War with Britain, in Hamilton's eyes, would be calamitous. About 90% of the revenue supporting the nation's still-shaky financial structure flowed from customs duties, and some 75% of all customs duties came from British imports. An armed clash with England would dry up this vital revenue. The financial foundations of the government would then crumble, and financial disaster—perhaps national bankruptcy—might well be the consequence.

Jay Plays His Trumps

The Hamiltonian Federalists, in a last desperate gamble to avert war, decided to send a special envoy to London in 1794. The man finally selected was John Jay, an experienced and vigilant diplomat. The Jeffersonians were acutely unhappy over the choice, partly because they feared that so notorious a Federalist and Britain-admirer would sell out his country. Arriving in London, Jay gave the Jeffersonians further cause for alarm when, at the presentation ceremony, he kissed the Queen's hand.

Jay, truth to tell, entered the negotiations with weak cards. Britain was fighting for her very life, and she feared that if she gave up her objectionable practices of search, seizure, and impressment, she might lose the war to France. Rather than yield mastery of the seas, she was prepared to fight the "money-grubbing Yankees."

Yet Jay did hold certain trumps. Although the British did not greatly fear adolescent America, they did not want to divert critically needed strength from the war in Europe in order to chastise their "ungrateful" offspring. If England was our best customer, we were hers. And our foodstuffs and other products were hardly less important to her during the terrible conflict than her customs payments were to us. Again the wartime distresses of Europe were paving the way for a limited American diplomatic success.

After prolonged negotiations, Jay finally signed a treaty late in 1794. The British promised, as their chief concession, to evacuate the chain of posts on United States soil. Ironically, they had earlier agreed to do precisely the same thing in the Treaty of 1783, also signed by John Jay. In addition, they consented to pay damages for their recent seizures of American ships, the precise amount to be fixed by a special commission.

But Jay failed to wring any specific concessions from the British on *future* maritime seizures and impressments, or on Indian butcheries. He even yielded ground by binding the United States to pay the debts still owed to British merchants on pre-Revolutionary accounts. The precise sums, he agreed, were to be determined by other arbitral boards.

Jay's Treaty of 1794, though it was to arouse widespread indignation and anger in Jay's own country, stands out as a landmark in world history. It heralded the revival in modern times of the principle of arbitration, as provided for in the several arbitral commissions. This solution, of course, meant delay. But time was on America's side.

The Damnation of "Sir" John Jay

The United States was in no mood to gulp down the bitter parchment-pill brought home by John Jay. While the treaty was being negotiated, General ("Mad Anthony") Wayne had been making history. Belying his nickname by careful preparations, and retrieving the failures of two previous commanders, he crushed the Northwest Indians, on August 20, 1794, at the battle of Fallen Timbers in present Ohio. The fleeing foe had left on the field British-made arms, as well as the corpses of a few British-Canadian white men.

When the Jeffersonians learned of Jay's concessions, their rage was fearful to behold. The treaty seemed like an abject surrender to Britain, as well as a betrayal of the Jeffersonian South. The Southern planters would have to pay the major share of the pre-Revolutionary debts, while rich Federalist shippers were collecting damages for recent British seizures. Jeffersonian mobs hanged, burned, and guillotined in effigy that "damn'd archtraitor, Sir John Jay." His unpopular pact, more than any other issue, vitalized the newborn Democratic-Republican Party of Thomas Jefferson.

President Washington was now confronted with an agonizing decision. He realized that the treaty was highly disappointing, but he also perceived, as did Hamilton, that the choice was either this treaty or none. If it was none, war would almost certainly ensue. And war might well be ruinous, given America's financially overstrained condition. So Washington, in one of the most courageous acts of a courageous life, threw his immense prestige behind the pact.

The President's course was both condemned and condoned. "Damn George Washington," cried John Randolph of Virginia in a public toast.

**JOHN JAY
BURNED IN EFFIGY**

After a drawing by
F. O. C. Darley

Other violent Jeffersonians guillotined the President in effigy. But the Senate, after stormy debate, approved the treaty by the narrowest of margins. Thus war with Great Britain was averted for seventeen years.

A memorable pact with Spain was one of the aftermaths of Jay's Treaty, which in some ways was more important for its by-products than for its provisions. Spain feared that the Anglo-American pact foreshadowed an Anglo-American alliance—to her detriment. She therefore made haste to conclude with the United States the Pinckney Treaty of 1795. Unlike Jay's Treaty, it conceded virtually everything we demanded. At long last it granted us free navigation of the Mississippi; it yielded to us the large area north of Florida that had been in dispute for over a decade. (See map on p. 135.) America's totally unexpected diplomatic successes in this quarter were again a direct result of Spain's European distresses.

Another significant by-product of Jay's labors was the Treaty of Greenville in 1795, which involved certain Indians north of the Ohio River. Deserted by their red-coated friends at the posts, and chastised by "Mad Anthony" Wayne, they grudgingly came to terms with the "palefaces." A spacious virgin tract was thus opened to white settlement, and the bloody scalping forays virtually ceased.

Washington's Valedictory

A weary Washington had hoped to retire in 1793, at the end of his first term. He even went so far as to draft a farewell address. But his friends and advisers, including the archrivals Jefferson and Hamilton, begged him to stay. Partisanship and disunity were widespread at home; turmoil and danger loomed up abroad. This was no time to turn from a leader of international eminence to one of sectional stature, like the disagreeably stiff New Englander, John Adams. Washington was unanimously re-elected, simply because the nation could not do without him.

But two full terms were enough. Washington was not only exhausted physically, but he was weary of verbal abuse. Having lost his non-partisan standing when he became a Federalist, he was being assailed by political foes as an "American Caesar" and as the "stepfather of his country." Although he had no serious constitutional scruples against a third election, his decision to retire contributed powerfully to the foundations of the two-term tradition.

Washington's Farewell Address was not delivered orally, as commonly supposed, but was published in the newspapers of 1796. Written in close collaboration with Hamilton, it bore the stamp of the financier's incisive style. Its primary function was to announce Washington's determination to retire. But the President was prompted to add some fatherly words of advice to the people whom he had served so long and faithfully—advice growing largely out of our recent unhappy experiences with Britain and France.

The bulk of the Farewell Address, legend to the contrary, was not concerned with foreign affairs. About two-thirds of it was devoted to domestic problems, and it included a sage warning against partisan bitterness. The document has been most misunderstood in connection with alliances. Washington did not say that we should never make any alliances of any kind under any circumstances. As a military man, he favored "temporary alliances" for "extraordinary emergencies." But he strongly advised that we avoid "permanent alliances," like the still-vexatious French Treaty of 1778.

Washington added still other words of paternal wisdom. With the pro-British Federalists and the pro-French Jeffersonians clearly in mind, he urged that we avoid tying our political fortunes to the tail of a foreign kite. Subservience to overseas nations would cause us to become "in some degree a slave." With the plottings of Genêt and other French agents fresh in memory, Washington further urged that we banish foreign intrigue from both our domestic and our diplomatic affairs.

The Farewell Address was not received with undivided acclaim, partly because it bore the earmarks of a Federalist campaign document for the impending presidential election of 1796. Vociferous Jeffersonians, on fire to help our French ally, assailed Washington's impartial words as though they were a declaration of war on France. The truth is that the President, in urging no "permanent" foreign entanglements, was giving admirable advice to a weak and divided nation in the year 1796. But what is sound counsel for a growing boy may not apply to a muscular giant.

The contributions of Washington as President were enormous, even though the sparkling Hamilton at times seemed to outshine him. The central government, its fiscal feet now under it, was firmly established. The West was expanding. The merchant marine was whitening the seas. Above all, Washington had kept the nation out of both overseas entanglements and foreign wars. The experimental stage had passed, and the presidential chair could now be turned over to a less impressive figure.

Republics are notoriously ungrateful. When Washington left office in 1797, he was showered with the brickbats of partisan abuse, quite in contrast with the bouquets that had greeted his coming. Though the vast majority of his countrymen honored his name, the more venomous Jeffersonians hailed his departure as ending tyranny and graft. "This day," cried one of them, "ought to be a jubilee in the United States."

"Bonny Johnny" Adams

Who should succeed the "Father of His Country"? Alexander Hamilton was the best-known member of the Federalist Party, now that Washington had bowed out. But his financial policies, some of which had fattened the speculators, had made him so unpopular with many voters that he could not hope to be elected President. The Federalists were forced to turn to the experienced but ungracious John Adams, a rugged chip off old Plymouth Rock. The Democratic-Republicans naturally rallied behind their master-organizer and leader, Thomas Jefferson.

Political passions ran incredibly high in the presidential canvass of 1796. The presence of Washington had hitherto imposed some restraints; now the lid was off. Cultured Federalists like Fisher Ames referred to the Jeffersonians as "fire-eating salamanders, poison-sucking toads." Federalists and Democratic-Republicans even drank their liquor in separate taverns. The issues of the campaign, as it turned out, were largely personal. But the Jeffersonians again assailed the crushing of the Whiskey Rebellion, and above all the negotiation of Jay's hated treaty.

John Adams, with most of his support in New England, squeezed through by the narrow margin of 71 votes to 68 in the Electoral College. The resulting taunt, "President by three votes," was galling to his pride, which was thin-skinned. Jefferson, as runner-up, became Vice-President. The possibility of such an inharmonious combination in the future was removed by the 12th Amendment to the Constitution in 1804. (See text in Appendix.)

John Adams, one of the ablest statesmen of his day, was at sixty-two a stuffy figure. Sharp-featured, bald, and thickset ("His Rotundity"), he struck observers as being a man of stern principles who did his duty with stubborn devotion. Though learned and upright, he was a tactless and prickly intellectual aristocrat, with no appeal to the masses, and with no desire to cultivate any. Many citizens regarded him with "respectful irritation."

The crusty New Englander suffered from other handicaps as well. He had stepped into the shoes of Washington, beside whom any successor would seem pale. In addition, Adams was hated by Hamilton, who had resigned from the Treasury in 1795, and who now led the most important faction of the Federalist Party. The famed financier even secretly plotted with certain members of the Cabinet against the President. Most ominous of all, Adams inherited a violent quarrel with France—a quarrel which smelled of blazing gunpowder.

Unofficial Fighting with France

The French were deeply angered by Jay's Treaty. They condemned it as the initial step toward an alliance with England, their relentless foe. They further assailed the pact as a flagrant violation of the Franco-American Treaty of 1778. French warships, in retaliation, began to seize defenseless American merchantmen, altogether three hundred by mid-1797. Adding insult to outrage, the Paris regime haughtily refused to receive our newly appointed envoy, and even threatened him with arrest.

Though the nation was mightily aroused, President Adams kept his head. True to Washington's policy of steering clear of war at all costs, he coolly appointed a diplomatic commission of three men. It included John Marshall, the future Chief Justice of the Supreme Court.

The American envoys, reaching Paris in 1797, hoped to meet Talleyrand, the crafty French Foreign Minister. They were secretly approached by three go-betweens, later referred to as X, Y, and Z in the published dispatches. The French spokesmen, among other concessions, demanded a loan of 32,000,000 florins, plus what amounted to a bribe of $250,000 for the privilege of merely talking with Talleyrand.

These terms were intolerable. The American trio knew that bribes were standard diplomatic devices in Europe, but they gagged at paying a quarter of a million dollars for mere talk, without any assurances of a settlement. The negotiations quickly broke down, and John Marshall, on reaching New York in 1798, was hailed like a conquering hero.

War hysteria swept the United States. The slogan of the hour became "Millions for defense, but not one cent for tribute." The song of the hour was "Hail Columbia," which was sung lustily in theaters and taverns.

> Immortal patriots, rise once more!
> Defend your rights, defend your shore.

The Federalists were delighted at this unexpected turn of affairs, while all except the most rabid Jeffersonians hung their heads over the misbehavior of their fine-feathered French friends.

War preparations in America were pushed feverishly, despite considerable Jeffersonian opposition in Congress. The Navy Department was created; the three-ship navy was expanded; the Marine Corps was established. A new army of 10,000 men was authorized (but never raised), to be headed by the redoubtable but aging General Washington. He reluctantly heeded the call of duty, but stipulated that the active command be entrusted to the younger Alexander Hamilton, who became a major general. A frustrated military genius, Hamilton was intoxicated by dreams of conquest. He would lead a victorious American army, supported by the British navy, against the possessions of France's Spanish ally—specifically the Floridas, Louisiana, Mexico, and perhaps points south.

Bloodshed was confined to the sea, and principally to the West Indies. In two and one-half years of undeclared hostilities (1798–1800), American privateers and men-of-war of the new navy captured over eighty vessels flying the French colors, though a number of American merchantmen were lost to the enemy. Only a slight push seemed to be needed to plunge both nations into a full-scale war.

Adams Puts Country above Party

Embattled France, her hands full in Europe, wanted no thoroughgoing hostilities with the Americans. The outwitted Talleyrand perceived that to fight the United States would merely add one more ally to his enemies. The British, who were lending the Americans cannon and other war supplies, were actually driven closer to their wayward cousins than they were to be again for many years. The Paris Foreign Office therefore let it be known, through informal channels, that if the Americans would send a new minister, he would be received with proper respect.

The French furor brought to Adams a degree of personal acclaim that he had never known before—and was never to know again. The song "Adams and Liberty" was hardly less popular than "Hail Columbia." The President doubtless perceived that a prolongation of the war, crowned by the conquest of the Floridas and Louisiana, would bring new plaudits to the Federalist Party—and perhaps a second term to himself. But the heady wine of popularity did not sway his judgment. He realized full well, as did most other leading statesmen of the era, that war must be avoided while the country was relatively weak. The impetuous Hamilton was much less firmly wedded to this precept, especially since he was expecting an alliance with his beloved England against France and Spain.

President Adams exploded a bombshell when, early in 1799, he submitted to the Senate the name of a new minister to France. Hamilton and his war-hawk faction were enraged. But public opinion—Jeffersonian and reasonable Federalist alike—was favorable to one last try for peace. Not daring to defeat Adams outright, the Hamiltonians succeeded in expanding the one appointee into a commission of three.

The American trio found the political skies brightening when they reached Paris early in 1800. The ambitious "Little Corporal," Napoleon Bonaparte, had recently seized dictatorial power. He was eager to free his hands of the American squabble so that he might continue to redraw the map of Europe, and perhaps create a New World empire in Louisiana. The distresses and ambitions of the Old World were again working to America's advantage.

Among possible concessions, the American envoys were particularly anxious to secure a formal release from the trouble-brewing alliance of 1778. They also demanded some $20,000,000 as compensation for the recent seizures of our merchant ships. But Napoleon, a hard bargainer, flatly refused to pay anything.

After prolonged haggling, a memorable treaty known as the Convention of 1800 was signed in Paris. As finally amended later on both sides, it brought about a mutually acceptable settlement. France agreed to grant us a divorce from our twenty-two-year-old marriage of (in)convenience, but as a kind of alimony we agreed to pay the damage claims of American shippers ourselves. So ended our only peacetime military alliance for a century and a half. Its troubled history does much to explain the traditional antipathy of the American people to foreign entanglements.

Adams, flinty to the end, deserves immense credit for his unselfish and farsighted course. He not only avoided the hazards of war, but he unwittingly smoothed the path for the peaceful purchase of Louisiana three years later. He should indeed rank high among the overlooked purchasers of this vast domain. If America had drifted into a full-dress war with France in 1800, Napoleon would not have sold us Louisiana on any terms in 1803.

President Adams, the bubble of his popularity pricked by peace, was not unaware of his splendid contribution to the nation. He later suggested as the epitaph for his tombstone: "Here lies John Adams, who took upon himself the responsibility of peace with France in the year 1800."

Anti-Alienism

The Federalists meanwhile had pressed their advantage to the hilt. Capitalizing on the anti-French war hysteria, they managed to drive through Congress in 1798 a sheaf of laws designed to shackle and muzzle their Jeffersonian foes.

The first of these oppressive laws was aimed at aliens. Most European immigrants, lacking wealth, were scorned by the aristocratic Federalists. But the newcomers were welcomed as voters by the less prosperous and more democratic Jeffersonians. The Federalists in Congress, hoping to discourage the "scum" of Europe from emigrating, erected a disheartening barrier. They raised the residence requirement for aliens who desired to become citizens from a tolerable five years to an intolerable fourteen. This drastic new law did violence to the traditional American policy of open-handed hospitality and speedy assimilation.

Two additional Alien Laws struck heavily at undesirable immigrants. The President was empowered to deport dangerous foreigners in time of peace, and to deport or imprison them in time of hostilities. Though defensible as a war measure—and an officially declared war with France seemed imminent—this was an arbitrary grant of power contrary to American tradition and to the spirit of the Constitution.

But the Alien Laws were not so senseless as they may seem to a more detached generation. Hundreds of foreign agitators, fleeing the wrath of the homeland authorities, were pouring into the United States from France, England, and Ireland ("wild Irishmen"). Most of these outcasts joined the ranks of the Jeffersonians, where they naturally clamored for an anti-British policy. A few of them were French spies who should have been expelled.

The stringent Alien Laws were never enforced.* But they served their purpose by frightening out of the country certain foreign agitators, including two shiploads of Frenchmen. In addition, an undetermined number of other foreigners were discouraged from sailing to the not-so-promising land of America.

---

* The tightened naturalization requirement (which in any case was not applicable to aliens in residence before its passage) was repealed in 1802 by the Jeffersonians, who restored the former five-year rule. See below, p. 184.

Freedom Falters

The Sedition Act, the last of the harsh group sponsored by the Federalists, was a direct slap at two priceless freedoms guaranteed in the Constitution by the Bill of Rights—freedom of speech and freedom of the press (see Art. I). The law provided that anyone who impeded the policies of the government or defamed its officials, including the President, would be subject to fine and imprisonment. Severe though the measure was, the Federalists believed that it was justified. The verbal violence of the day was almost unbelievable, and foul-penned editors, some of them exiled aliens, assailed the anti-French policy of the administration in vicious terms.

Many outspoken Jeffersonian editors were indicted under the Sedition Act, but only ten were brought to trial. All of them were convicted, sometimes by packed juries swayed by prejudiced Federalist judges. A few of the victims were harmless crackpots, who should have been spared the notoriety of martyrdom. Among them was Congressman Matthew Lyon (the "Spitting Lion"), who had earlier gained fame by spitting in the face of a Federalist. He was sentenced to four months in jail for

CONGRESSIONAL PUGILISTS
Satirical representation of Matthew Lyon's fight in Congress with the Federalist Representative Roger Griswold. New York Public Library

writing of President Adams' "unbounded thirst for ridiculous pomp, foolish adulation, and selfish avarice." Another culprit was lucky to get off with a fine of $100 after he had expressed the wish that the wad of a cannon fired in honor of Adams had landed in the seat of his breeches.

The Federalists, though supported in these drastic measures by the now conservative-minded George Washington and other sane leaders, clearly overshot the mark. Hamilton, himself of foreign birth, urged his fellow partisans not to confuse violence with energy. Alarmed Jeffersonians compared the British tyranny of 1774 with the Federalist tyranny of 1798, to the advantage of the British.

The Sedition Act, at least in spirit, was in direct conflict with the Constitution. But the Supreme Court, dominated by Federalists, was of no mind to declare this Federalist law unconstitutional. (More than a century later, in 1964, it so declared.) The attempt of the Federalists to crush free speech and silence the opposition party, high-handed as it was, undoubtedly made many converts for the Jeffersonians.

Yet the Alien and Sedition Laws, despite pained outcries from the Jeffersonians, actually commanded widespread popular support. The anti-French hysteria played directly into the hands of witch-hunting conservatives. In the Congressional elections of 1798–1799 the Federalists, riding a wave of popularity, scored the most sweeping victory at the polls of their entire career.

Nascent Nullification

The Jeffersonians naturally refused to take the Alien and Sedition Laws lying down. Jefferson himself feared that if the Federalists succeeding in choking free speech and free press, they would then wipe out other precious constitutional guarantees. His own Democratic-Republican Party might even be stamped out of existence. If this had happened, the country might conceivably have drifted into a dangerous one-party dictatorship, so common abroad in later times.

As Vice-President under Adams, Jefferson was in an awkward position to protest openly against the Alien and Sedition Laws. So he secretly penned a series of resolutions, and these were officially approved by the legislature of Kentucky in 1798 and 1799. His friend and Virginia colleague, James Madison, drafted a similar but less extreme statement which was adopted by the legislature of Virginia.

Both Jefferson and Madison stressed the compact theory—a theory which had attained popularity among English political philosophers in the 17th and 18th Centuries. As applied to America by the Jeffersonians, this concept meant that the thirteen sovereign states, in creating the federal government, had entered into a "compact" or contract as to its jurisdiction. The national government was consequently the agent or creation of the states. Since water can rise no higher than its source, the individual states were the final judges of whether their agent had broken the "compact" by overstepping the authority originally granted. Invoking this logic, Jefferson's Kentucky resolutions concluded that the federal regime had exceeded its constitutional powers, and that with regard to the Alien and Sedition Acts "nullification" was the "rightful remedy."

If the Federalists had bent the bow too far in passing the Alien and Sedition Acts, Jefferson bent the bow too far in his reply. If the Federalist indiscretion had made some Jeffersonian voters, Jefferson's indiscretion made some Federalist voters. No other state legislatures, despite Jefferson's hopes, fell into line. Some of them flatly refused to endorse the Virginia and Kentucky resolutions. Others, chiefly in Federalist states, added ringing condemnations. Many Federalists argued that it was the people and not the states who had made the original compact, and that it was up to the Supreme Court—not to the states—to nullify unconstitutional legislation passed by Congress. This solution, though not specifically authorized by the Constitution, was finally adopted by the Supreme Court in 1803.

The Virginia and Kentucky resolutions were a brilliant formulation of the extreme states'-rights view regarding the Union. They were later used by Southerners to support nullification—and ultimately secession. Jefferson has been condemned, somewhat unfairly, for having started this dangerous movement. The truth is that the ideas which he set forth were in the air, and sooner or later they would have been codified by some other statesman.

Neither Jefferson nor Madison, as Founding Fathers of the Union, had any intention of breaking it up. Their resolutions were basically campaign documents designed to crystallize opposition to the Federalist Party, and to unseat it in the forthcoming presidential election of 1800. The only real nullification that Jefferson had in view was the nullification of Federalist abuses.

Federalism Fights Fire with Fire

In the heated presidential contest of 1800, Adams and Jefferson were again the standard-bearers of their respective parties. The Federalists labored under heavy handicaps. The Alien and Sedition Acts had aroused a host of enemies, although most of these critics were dyed-in-the-wool Jeffersonians anyhow. The Hamiltonian faction of the Federalist Party, robbed of its glorious war with France, split openly with President Adams. Hamilton, an unfortunate victim of arrogance, was so ill-advised as to attack the President in a privately printed pamphlet. The Jeffersonians soon got hold of it and gleefully spread it broadcast.

The most damaging blow to the Federalists was the refusal of Adams to give them a rousing fight with France. Their feverish war preparations had swelled the public debt and had required disagreeable new taxes, including a stamp tax. After all these unpopular measures, the war scare had petered out, and the country was left with an all-dressed-up-but-no-place-to-go feeling. The extensive military preparations now seemed not only unnecessary but extravagant.

Thrown on the defensive, the Federalists seized upon assorted weapons. They condemned with some success the incendiary Kentucky and Virginia resolutions. But they concentrated their fire on Jefferson himself, who became the victim of one of our earliest "whispering campaigns." He was falsely accused of having robbed a widow and her children of a trust fund, and of having fathered numerous mulatto children by his own slave women. As a liberal in religion, Jefferson had earlier incurred the wrath of the orthodox clergy, largely through his successful struggle to separate church and state in Virginia. From the New England stronghold of Federalism and Congregationalism, the preachers unfairly thundered against his atheism, although he did believe in God. Old ladies of Federalist families, fearing Jefferson's election, even buried their Bibles or hung them in wells.

The Revolution of 1800

Jefferson won by a majority of 73 electoral votes to 65. But the colorless and presumably unpopular Adams, surprisingly enough, polled more electoral strength than he had gained four years earlier—except for New York. The Empire State fell into the Jeffersonian basket, and with it the election, largely because astute Aaron Burr, a past master of wirepulling, turned New York to Jefferson by the narrowest of margins. The gifted Virginian polled the bulk of his strength in the South and West, particularly in those states where manhood suffrage had been adopted.

PRESIDENTIAL ELECTION OF 1800
(With electoral vote by state)

N.H.
VT.
N.Y. 12
MASS. 16
R.I. 4
CONN. 9
PENN. 15
N.J. 7
DEL. 3
MD. 10
VA. 21
KY. 4
N.C. 12
TENN. 3
S.C. 8
MISS. TERR.
GA. 4
INDIANA TERRITORY
NORTHWEST TERR.
FRENCH LOUISIANA
SPANISH FLORIDA

JEFFERSON

Jefferson–Republican
Adams–Federalist
Divided

ADAMS

The Jeffersonians rejoiced wildly over the end of the "Federalist Reign of Terror." Some of them, with alcoholic enthusiasm, bawled the song "Jefferson and Liberty":

Lord! how the Federalists will stare,
At Jefferson, in Adams' chair!

But Jeffersonian glee was dampened by an unexpected deadlock. Through a technicality Jefferson, the presidential candidate, and Burr, his vice-presidential running mate, received the same number of electoral votes for the Presidency. Under the Constitution the tie could be broken only by the House of Representatives (see Art. 2, Sec. I, para. 2). This body was controlled for several more months by the lame-duck Federalists, who had been swept into office during the French war scare and who were eager to elect Burr.*

The voting in the House moved slowly to a climax. As ballots were taken in wearisome succession, Congressmen snored in their seats; a sick member lay in an adjoining room. Scholars used to think that Hamilton, after bargaining with Jefferson behind the scenes, played a decisive role. But the evidence indicates that the deadlock was broken when a few Federalists, despairing of electing Burr, simply refrained from voting. The election then went to the rightful candidate.

Jefferson, with his habit of exaggeration, later claimed that the election of 1800 was a "revolution" comparable in principle to that of 1776. The truth is that the outcome was not a mass upheaval or a popular man- date from anybody for anything. If some 250 Burr-manipulated votes in New York had been turned to Adams, Jefferson would have lost. The ultra- liberal Jefferson did not—and could not—extend the suffrage. That was a privilege of the states. But he did persuade the apathetic and overawed marginal voter to go to the polls—the citizen who had just enough property to vote but who was loath to speak up against his "betters." The Federal- ists, moreover, had been in the seats of the mighty for twelve years, and the country was ripe for a change.

The election was in part a class struggle. Budding democracy was arrayed against entrenched aristocracy more openly than in any previous presidential election. The battle of the ballots resulted in a gratifying victory for the "forgotten man"—or at least the partially forgotten man.

But the election of 1800 actually was a "revolution" in a narrow party sense. The Federalists were thrown out of power, even though their sys- tem in its essentials was retained by their rivals. The Jeffersonians would have won sooner or later, because they appealed to the man behind the plow. From the beginning, they had possessed an actual or potential ma- jority of the voters. Manhood suffrage was on its way, and the rising tide of American political democracy could not be swept back by the outworn Federalist broom.

The Federalist Finale

John Adams, as fate would have it, was the last Federalist President of the United States. His party sank slowly into the mire of political ob- livion, and ultimately disappeared.

---

* A "lame duck" has been humorously defined as a politician whose political goose has been cooked at the recent elections. The possibility of another such tie was re- moved by the 12th Amendment in 1804 (for text, see Appendix).

Whatever their shortcomings, the Federalists were of the elite. They boasted a higher concentration of ability, brains, and talent than any other American party, past or present. Their brilliant political and financial leaders had built enduring foundations for the new government. Their astute diplomats, with a strong helping hand from Europe's distresses, had signed advantageous treaties with England, Spain, and France. Their statesmen had kept the peace during a crucial period when peace had to be kept.

The Federalists, though their usefulness was on the downgrade by 1800, had played an indispensable role. After all the turmoil of the American War of Independence, a conservative party was needed—conservative in the sense of conserving the democratic gains that had been won and of fending off anarchy. The Federalists provided a welcome breathing spell, a chance for the nation to get its bearings. They served, in the words of historian Henry Adams, great-grandson of John Adams, as the "half-way house between the European past and the American future."

But by 1800 the Federalists were out of place. The bustling new Republic knew instinctively where it was going. It was eager to take the high road over the mountains that would one day lead to the fulfillment of American democracy. The Federalists lost out because they were content to mark time, and would not get in step with the westward march of progress. They were unable or unwilling to unbend and appeal to the common man. They could not adapt—so they died. However distinguished their past service had been, it was no substitute for a capacity to grapple democratically with future problems. The victorious Jeffersonians were prepared to keep the Federalist edifice while ousting the aristocratic architects.

SELECT READINGS

Brief introductions are MARCUS CUNLIFFE, *The Nation Takes Shape, 1789–1837* (1959) and his *George Washington* (1958), [both **paperback**]. More detailed is J. C. MILLER, *The Federalist Era, 1789–1801* (1960) [**paperback**]. Biographical studies of Hamilton and Madison listed for Chapter VII are relevant. See also DUMAS MALONE, *Jefferson and the Rights of Man* (1951) and *Jefferson and the Ordeal of Liberty* (1962); also J. A. CARROLL and M. W. ASHWORTH, *George Washington: First in Peace* (1957). On the rise of parties consult N. E. CUNNINGHAM, *The Jeffersonian Republicans* (1958). On aspects of foreign policy, see ALEXANDER DE-CONDE, *Entangling Alliance* (1958); L. M. SEARS, *George Washington and the French Revolution* (1960); P. A. VARG, *Foreign Policies of the Founding Fathers* (1963); FELIX GILBERT, *To the Farewell Address* (1961); and JULIAN BOYD, *Number 7* (1964), on Hamilton's devious dealings with the British. On Adams, consult GILBERT CHINARD, *Honest John Adams* (1933) [**paperback**]; PAGE SMITH, *John Adams* (2 vols., 1962); S. G. KURTZ, *The Presidency of John Adams* (1957). J. C. MILLER, *Crisis in Freedom* (1951) [**paperback**] and J. M. SMITH, *Freedom's Fetters* (1956) treat the Alien and Sedition Laws. Also next chapter and *Harvard Guide*, Pt. IV.

10

The Triumph of Jeffersonian Democracy

*We can pay off his [Hamilton's] debt in fifteen years, but we
can never get rid of his financial system.*

THOMAS JEFFERSON, 1802

Responsibility Breeds Moderation

THOMAS JEFFERSON was inaugurated President on March 4, 1801, in the
swampy village of Washington, the new national capital. The loose-
jointed Virginian—"Long Tom" he was nicknamed—did not believe that
the customary planned pomp befitted his democratic ideals. Spurning
ornate horse-drawn coaches, he simply ambled over on foot to the capitol
from his boardinghouse.

The inaugural address, beautifully phrased, was a classic statement
of democratic principles. Seeking to allay Federalist fears of a bull-in-the-
china-closet overturn, Jefferson blandly stated, "We are all Republicans,
we are all Federalists." As for foreign affairs, he pledged "honest friendship with all nations, entangling alliances with none."

The rustic setting of Washington lent itself admirably to the simplicity and frugality of the Jeffersonian Republicans. In this respect, it
contrasted sharply with the elegant atmosphere of Federalist Philadelphia,
the former temporary capital. Extending democratic principles to eti-
quette, Jefferson established the rule of pell-mell at official social functions
—that is, first come, first served. The resplendently dressed British minister,
who had cut a wide swath among the pro-British Federalists, felt deeply
humiliated.

Jefferson, a widower, was shockingly unconventional. Having no
wife to police his apparel, he was wont to receive callers in sloppy attire
—on one occasion in a dressing gown and heelless slippers. He established
the precedent, not broken for 112 years, of sending messages to Congress
to be read by a clerk. Personal appearances, in the Federalist manner,
suggested too strongly a monarchical speech from the throne. Besides,
Jefferson was painfully conscious of his weak voice and unimpressive platform manner.

183

The incoming President, as if plagued by an evil spirit, was forced to reverse many of the political principles he had so vigorously championed. The basic explanation is that there were two Thomas Jeffersons. One was the private citizen, who had philosophized in his study. The other was the public official, who made the disturbing discovery that bookish theories worked out differently in the noisy arena of practical politics. The open-minded Virginian was therefore consistently inconsistent, and it is easy to quote one Jefferson to refute the other.

The triumph of Jefferson's Democratic-Republicans and the eviction of the Federalists marked the first party overthrow in our national history. The vanquished Federalists naturally feared that the victors would grab all the spoils of office for themselves. But Jefferson, in line with his conciliatory inaugural address, showed unexpected moderation. Many Federalists were retained, though in due course a considerable number of them were replaced by Jeffersonian Republicans. This process of ladling out the political gravy was agonizingly slow for expectant Republican spoilsmen, who in grim jest rephrased one of Jefferson's remarks to read, "Few die, none resign." Yet by the end of his first term, Jefferson had managed to replace about one-half of the Senate-confirmed Federalist officials.

Parceling out the spoils of office as a reward for party service is the "spoils system." Jefferson, rather than Jackson, has sometimes been referred to as the father of this vicious practice. But the force of the accusation is weakened by the small number whom the victorious Virginian appointed. Even so, he dismissed a larger percentage than Jackson.

Reform without Revolution

Jefferson, at the outset, was determined to undo the Federalist abuses begotten by the anti-French hysteria. The hated Alien and Sedition Laws had already expired. The new President speedily pardoned the "martyrs" serving sentences under the Sedition Law, and the government returned many fines. Shortly after the new Congress met, the Jeffersonians enacted the new naturalization law of 1802. It reduced the unreasonable requirement of fourteen years of residence to the former reasonable five years.

Jefferson actually kicked away only one major prop of the Hamiltonian system. Hating the excise tax, which bred bureaucrats and bore heavily on his farmer following, the Virginian early persuaded Congress to repeal it. Jefferson's devotion to principle thus cost the federal government over a million dollars a year in urgently needed revenue.

The Swiss-born and French-accented Albert Gallatin, "Watchdog of the Treasury," proved to be as able a Secretary of the Treasury as Hamilton had been. Gallatin agreed with Jefferson that a national debt was a bane rather than a blessing, and by strict economy succeeded in reducing it substantially while balancing the budget.

Except for abolishing the excise tax, the Jeffersonians left the Hamiltonian framework essentially intact. They launched no attack on the Bank of the United States, and they did not repeal the mildly protective Federalist tariff. In later years, indeed, they so far embraced Federalism as to recharter a bigger Bank and to boost the protective tariff to higher levels.

The "Revolution of 1800," so far as it was a revolution, thus turned out to be one of men rather than of measures, especially in the national government. Generally speaking, the agrarian aristocrats of the Republican South and West—men like Jefferson—elbowed aside the commercial and manufacturing aristocrats of the Federalist northern seaboard.

The "Dead Clutch" of the Judiciary

The "death-bed" Judiciary Act of 1801 was one of the last important laws passed by the expiring Federalist Congress. It created sixteen new federal judgeships and other judicial offices. President Adams, remaining at his desk until nine o'clock in the evening on his last day in office, busily signed the appointments of the so-called "midnight judges." To a man, they were Federalists.

The Federalist-sponsored Judiciary Act, though clearly a long-over-due reform, aroused bitter resentment. The packing of these lifetime posts with anti-Jeffersonian partisans was, in Republican eyes, a brazen attempt by the defeated party to entrench itself in one of the three branches of government. The Jeffersonians condemned the "midnight judges" in violent language. To them, the trickery of the Federalists was open defiance of the people's will, as recently expressed at the polls in the "Revolution of 1800."

Accordingly, the newly elected Republican Congress repealed the Judiciary Act of 1801 in the year after its passage. The Jeffersonians thus swept sixteen benches from under the recently appointed judges. The frustrated Federalists, in their turn, were bitterly critical of this "assault" on the judicial arm.

The Jeffersonians likewise had their knives whetted for the scalp of Chief Justice John Marshall, whom President John Adams had appointed to the Supreme Court in the dying days of his term. The lanky Marshall, with his rasping voice and steel-trap mind, was a distant cousin of Thomas Jefferson. As a Virginia Federalist, he was cordially disliked by the states'-rights Jeffersonians. He served for about thirty days under a Federalist administration, and thirty-four years under the administrations of the Jeffersonian Republicans and their successors. The Federalist Party died out, but Marshall went on handing down Federalist decisions imperturbably for nearly twenty years longer. He did more perhaps than Hamilton himself to engraft the Hamiltonian concept of a powerful central government upon the American political system.

MAD TOM IN A RAGE

A Federalist cartoon shows "Mad Tom" Jefferson, assisted by
brandy and the Devil, trying to pull down the Federal edifice
erected by Washington and Adams. Houghton Library, Harvard

One of the "midnight judges" of 1801 presented John Marshall with
a historic opportunity. He was obscure William Marbury, whom President
Adams had named a justice of the peace for the District of Columbia.
When Marbury found that his commission was being held up by the new
Secretary of State, James Madison, he sued for its delivery. The Supreme
Court, led by Chief Justice Marshall, somewhat incidentally slapped at
the Jeffersonians when it ruled in 1803 that Marbury had a perfect right
to his commission. Yet the black-robed tribunal retreated sharply when it
further held that it had no authority to issue a writ to enforce its opinion.
The Judiciary Act of 1789, to be sure, had tried to clothe the Supreme
Court with such power. But—most significantly—the learned justices ruled
that this part of the law, which conflicted with the Constitution, was null
and void.

The case of Marbury *vs.* Madison is epochal. For the first time in its
history the Supreme Court declared a law passed by Congress unconstitutional, and in so doing exercised the right of "judicial review." The Court

had already used this club against the states; and Marshall, emboldened by his successful defiance of Congress, repeatedly wielded his judicial veto against state legislation in subsequent years.

Judicial review was not a new concept. Some of the framers of the Constitution had favored it, but they had not included it for fear of further antagonizing the states'-rights anti-federalists. Although not specifically authorized, judicial review was implicit in the nature of the Constitution, which as the supreme law of the land could not permit legislative conflict with its own provisions. The finger of responsibility, guided in some degree by the Judiciary Act of 1789, pointed at the highest tribunal.

John Marshall had the courage and statesmanship to exercise judicial review, a doctrine which has profoundly affected our constitutional development. In doing so, he doubtless took delight in lashing out against the Kentucky resolutions of Cousin Jefferson. The latter had argued five years earlier that the states, not the Supreme Court, should exercise judicial review by nullifying acts of Congress.

The Supremacy of the Supreme Court

The decision of John Marshall regarding Marbury spurred the Jeffersonians in their desire to lay hands on the Supreme Court through impeachment. Certain Federalist judges had made themselves highly offensive, especially in Sedition Law cases, by delivering harangues from the bench against the Republican "mobocracy." Jefferson favored free speech, but not this kind of free speech. Accordingly, he urged action against the arrogant Supreme Court Justice Samuel Chase, who was so unpopular that Republicans named vicious dogs after him.

Early in 1804 impeachment charges against Chase were voted by the House of Representatives, which then passed the question of guilt or innocence on to the Senate. The indictment by the House was based on "high crimes and misdemeanors," as specified in the Constitution.* Yet the evidence was plain that the intemperate judge had not been guilty of "high crimes" but of bad manners, injudicious statements, and unrestrained partisanship. The Senate, after a determined prosecution, failed to muster enough votes to convict and remove Chase. The precedent thus established was fortunate. From that day to this, no serious attempt has been made to reshape the Supreme Bench by the impeachment tool.

John Marshall viewed the attack on Chase with deep misgivings. He suspected, with good reason, that if it succeeded he would be next—and then his other Federalist colleagues. These fears were now laid to rest. Jefferson's ill-advised attempt at "judge breaking" was a reassuring victory for the independence of the judiciary, and for the separation of powers among the three branches of the federal government.

* For impeachment, see Art. I, Sec. II, para. 5; Art. I, Sec. III, paras. 6, 7; Art. II, Sec. IV in Appendix.

The Pacifist Turns Warrior

Thomas Jefferson, the passionate champion of freedom, distrusted large standing armies as a standing invitation to dictatorship. Navies, though also suspect, were less to be feared: they could not march inland and "endanger liberties." Pinning his faith to the frail reed of an ill-trained militia, Jefferson reduced the military establishment to a mere police force of 2500 officers and men. The Jeffersonian Republicans, primarily agrarians, saw little point in protecting a few Federalist shippers with a costly navy, which all the taxpayers would have to support. Pledged as he was to rigid economy, Jefferson gladly reduced the navy to a peacetime skeleton, in accordance with the authorization already passed by the outgoing Federalist Congress.

But harsh realities forced a penny-pinching Jefferson to change his views on navies and war. The pirates of the North African states had long made a national industry of blackmailing and plundering merchantmen that ventured into the Mediterranean. The preceding Federalist administrations, in fact, had been forced to buy protection. At the time of the French crisis of 1798, when our people were shouting, "Millions for defense but not one cent for tribute," twenty-six barrels of blackmail dollars were being shipped to piratical Algiers.

At this price, war seemed cheaper than peace, and the showdown came in 1801, less than three months after Jefferson took office. The Pasha of Tripoli, dissatisfied with his share of protection money, virtually declared war on the United States by cutting down the flagstaff of the American consulate. The challenge was thrown squarely into the face of Jefferson—the non-interventionist, the pacifist, the critic of a big-ship navy, and the political foe of Federalist shippers. He reluctantly rose to the occasion by dispatching the infant navy to Tripolitan waters. After four years of intermittent fighting, marked by hair-raising exploits, Jefferson succeeded in extorting a treaty of peace from Tripoli in 1805. It was secured at the bargain price of only $60,000—a sum representing ransom payments for captured Americans.

With the pattern thus set, the punishment of the other North African corsairs continued, off and on, until after the War of 1812. The navy reaped a rich harvest of experience, while strengthening its blossoming tradition. Foreign nations in general, and the Barbary cutthroats in par-

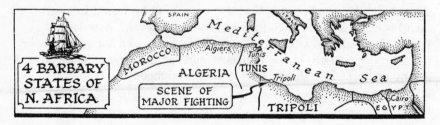

ticular, developed a wholesome respect for the United States—a United States willing and able to uphold its honor with blazing guns.

Small gunboats, which the navy had used with some success in the Tripolitan War, fascinated Jefferson. Pledged to tax reduction, he advocated a large number of tiny coastal craft—"Jeffs" or the "mosquito fleet," as they were contemptuously called. He believed that these frail vessels would prove valuable in guarding our shores, although not in defending Federalist merchantmen on the high seas.

About two hundred gunboats were constructed, democratically in small shipyards where votes could be made for Jefferson. Mounting generally one unwieldy gun, they were often more of a menace to the crew than to the prospective enemy. During a terrific hurricane and tidal wave at Savannah, Georgia, one of them was deposited eight miles inland in a cornfield, to the derisive glee of the Federalists. Jefferson's cheeseparing economy backfired badly when the War of 1812 broke out, for the whole swarm of gunboats proved virtually worthless. The money could have been much more wisely invested in a few frigates of the *Constitution* class.

The Louisiana Godsend

A secret pact, fraught with peril for America, was signed in 1800. Napoleon Bonaparte induced the King of Spain to cede to France, for certain considerations, the immense trans-Mississippi region of Louisiana, which included the New Orleans area.

Rumors of the transfer were dramatically confirmed in 1802, when the Spanish authorities at New Orleans withdrew the right of deposit guaranteed us by the treaty of 1795. Deposit privileges were vital to frontier farmers who floated their produce down the Mississippi to its mouth, there to await ocean-going vessels. A roar of anger rolled up the mighty river and into its tributary valleys. The American pioneers talked wildly of descending upon New Orleans, rifles in hand. Had they done so, the United States probably would have become embroiled in war with both Spain and France.

Thomas Jefferson, peace lover and non-interventionist, was again on the griddle. Louisiana in the senile grip of Spain posed no real threat; we could wrest the territory from her when we were ripe for it. But Louisiana in the iron fist of Napoleon, the pre-eminent military genius of his age, foreshadowed a dark and blood-drenched future. We would probably have to fight to dislodge him; and since we presumably were not strong enough to defeat his armies alone, we would have to seek allies, contrary to our fixed policy of non-entanglement.

Jefferson, hoping to quiet the clamor of the West, moved decisively. Early in 1803 he sent James Monroe to Paris to join hands with our regular minister there, Robert R. Livingston. The two envoys were instructed to buy New Orleans and as much to the east as they could get for a maximum of $10,000,000. If these proposals should fail and a crisis should develop, negotiations were to be opened with England for an alliance.

Nothing could better illustrate Jefferson's desperation. Though a passionate war hater and enemy of entangling alliances, he was proposing to make an alliance with his old foe, England, against his old friend, France, with the object of waging a defensive war.

Napoleon now suddenly decided to sell all Louisiana, and abandon his dream of a New World empire. He had failed in his efforts to reconquer the sugar-rich island of Santo Domingo, for which Louisiana was to serve as a granary. The infuriated ex-slaves, ably led by a full-blooded Negro, Toussaint L'Ouverture, had put up a stubborn resistance that was ultimately broken. Then the island's second line of defense—dreaded yellow fever—had swept away thousands of crack French troops. Santo Domingo could not be reconquered, except perhaps at a staggering cost; hence there was no need of the granary. "Damn sugar, damn coffee, damn colonies!" burst out Napoleon.

Bonaparte was about to end the twenty-month lull in his deadly conflict with Britain. Since the British controlled the seas, he feared that he might be forced to make them a gift of Louisiana. Rather than drive us into the arms of England by attempting to hold the area, he decided to sell the huge wilderness to us, and pocket the money for his schemes nearer home. He hoped that the United States, strengthened by Louisiana, would one day grow up to be a military and naval power that would thwart the ambitions of the lordly British in the New World. The distresses of France in Europe were again paving the way for America's diplomatic successes.

Events now moved dizzily. The American Minister Livingston, pending the arrival of Monroe, was busily negotiating in Paris for a window on the Gulf of Mexico at New Orleans. Suddenly, out of a clear sky, the French Foreign Minister asked him how much we would give for all Louisiana. Scarcely able to believe his ears (he was deaf anyhow), Livingston nervously entered upon the negotiations. After about a week of haggling, while the fate of America trembled in the balance, treaties were signed, under the date April 30, 1803, ceding Louisiana to the United States for $15,000,000.

Out-Federalizing the Federalists

When the news of the epochal signing reached America, Jefferson was dumfounded. He had authorized his envoys to offer not more than $10,-000,000 for New Orleans, and as much to the *east* in the Floridas as they could get. Instead, they had sent home treaties which pledged $15,000,000 for New Orleans, plus an enormous area entirely to the *west*—an area that would more than double the existing United States. We were buying an empire to get a city.

Once again the two Jeffersons wrestled with each other in the closet:

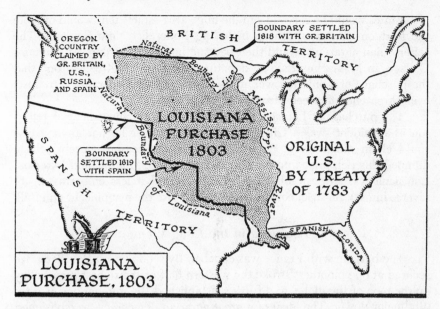

the theorist and former strict constructionist with the realist and public official. Where in his beloved Constitution was the President authorized to negotiate treaties incorporating a huge new expanse into the union—an expanse containing some 50,000 white, black, and red inhabitants? There was no such clause.

Jefferson, conscience-stricken, secretly proposed that a constitutional amendment be passed. But his friends pointed out in alarm that in the interval Napoleon, with whom thought was action, might suddenly change his mind. So Jefferson shamefacedly submitted the treaties to the Senate, while privately admitting that the purchase was unconstitutional.

The Senators were less finicky. Reflecting enthusiastic public support, they registered their prompt approval of the transaction. Land-hungry Americans were not disposed to split constitutional hairs when confronted with perhaps the most magnificent real estate bargain in history—828,000 square miles at about three cents an acre.

If Louisiana made Jefferson a loose constructionist, it made many Federalists strict constructionists. (Hamilton, to his credit, was an exception.) The Federalists argued vehemently that there was no constitutional warrant for the transfer. (Shades of the Federalists who had chartered the Bank of the United States!) Louisiana, so they claimed, was a worthless desert that would cost too much at a time when the Jeffersonians were pledged to rigid economy: $15,000,000 in one pile of silver dollars would reach three miles into the air. (Shades of the Federalists who had cheerfully assumed a debt of $75,000,000!)

What really worried the Federalists was that the signing of the Louisiana treaties was the signing of their own political death warrant.

New states would be carved from the huge area—states that would outvote the thirteen charter members, including Federalist New England. The Jeffersonian agrarians would then become hopelessly strong. At Williams College, in Massachusetts, one debating group voted fifteen to one that the purchase of Louisiana was undesirable. A few Federalist extremists even threatened to secede from the Union.

The purchase of Louisiana—the most glorious achievement of Jefferson as President—was a triumph for which neither he nor anyone else could claim much direct credit. Napoleon, for reasons purely selfish, dumped this rich prize into the laps of Livingston, Monroe, and Jefferson. Louisiana was so desirable that Jefferson found it less embarrassing to reverse himself on strict construction than to lose the magnificent windfall.

Louisiana in the Long View

The bargain with France was epochal. By scooping up Louisiana, we secured at one bloodless stroke the western half of the richest river valley on the face of the globe, and further established the foundations of a future major power. The ideal of a great agrarian democracy, as envisioned by Jefferson, would have elbowroom in the vast "Valley of Democracy." At the same time, the transfer established a precedent that was to be fol-

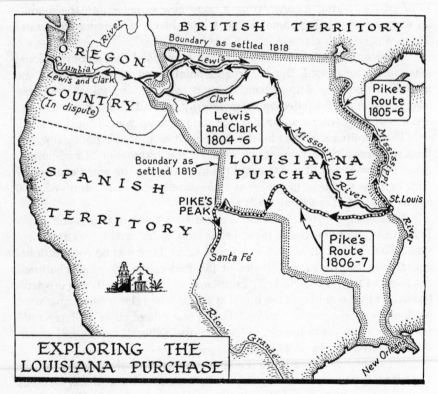

EXPLORING THE LOUISIANA PURCHASE

lowed repeatedly: namely, the acquisition of foreign territory and peoples by purchase.

The extent of the vast new area was brought home to the American people by a series of spectacular explorations. Under the direction of Jefferson, who was keenly interested in the natural treasures of his purchase, the Lewis and Clark expedition pushed up the "Great Muddy" Missouri River and over the Rockies to the mouth of the Columbia River. This dramatic venture into the unknown, from 1804 to 1806, bolstered our claim to Oregon, while further opening the West to Indian trade and exploration. Zebulon M. Pike, in 1805–1806, explored the Louisiana territory near the headwaters of the Mississippi River, and in 1806–1807 ventured into Colorado and New Mexico, sighting the peak that bears his name.

The Louisiana Purchase proved to be a landmark in American foreign policy. Overnight we avoided a possible rupture with France, and the consequent entangling alliance with England. We were thus able to continue the non-interventionist policies laid down by the Founding Fathers, though we later became involved in friction with Spain and Britain over the vague boundaries of Louisiana, north, south, and west. Not finding it necessary to throw ourselves into the arms of the Mother Country, we drifted away from her, and eventually fought her in 1812. But by that time we were bigger and stronger, and had Louisiana securely in our possession.

The Louisiana godsend likewise gave a boost to national unity, while quickening the sap of a nationalistic spirit. The once-proud Federalists, now mere sectionalists, sank ever lower in public esteem as they were reduced to complaining impotence. A few of their more extreme spokesmen attempted to plot with scheming Aaron Burr for the secession of New England and New York. But the intrigue failed, largely owing to the vigilance of Alexander Hamilton, who subsequently provoked Burr to a duel. The pistol that killed Hamilton in 1804 blew the brightest brain out of the Federalist Party—and its one remaining hope of effective leadership.

The once-restive West, which now toasted the "immortal Jefferson," was more securely riveted to the Union by the Virginian's map-changing achievement. The Men of the Western Waters were grateful to the federal government for having so fully safeguarded their interests, particularly in securing the mouth of the Mississippi. A new spirit of nationalism surged through the West.

Aaron Burr, having turned his disunionist plottings to the trans-Mississippi West, was arrested in 1806 for treason. He was tried the next year at Richmond, Virginia, but was freed after the presiding judge, Chief Justice Marshall, had infuriated the Jeffersonians by what seemed to be bias in favor of the accused. The case of the government collapsed when two witnesses to the same overt act of treason could not be found, as required by the Constitution (see Art. III, Sec. III). Burr's schemes are still somewhat shrouded in mystery, but he apparently planned to separate the western part of the United States from the eastern and unite it with conquered Spanish territory west of the Louisiana Purchase. The very fact that so dashing a figure as Burr could muster only threescore followers was significant. It indicated, among other things, that the West was developing a deeper sense of loyalty to the government in Washington.

Nutcrackered Neutrals

Jefferson was triumphantly re-elected in 1804, with 162 electoral votes for himself and only 14 for his Federalist opponent. His success was not due to Republicanizing the Federalists, as he fondly supposed, but to Federalizing the Republicans. The iron hand of circumstance gradually forced him, quite unintentionally, to kill off the opposition party by appropriating many of its principles and embracing them as his own.

But the laurels of Jefferson's first administration were withered by the new storm that broke in Europe. After unloading Louisiana in 1803, Napoleon deliberately provoked a renewal of his war with Britain—a conflict that crashed to an awesome close eleven long years later.

For two years a maritime United States—the number-one neutral carrier since 1793—enjoyed juicy commercial pickings. But a turning point came in 1805. At the battle of Trafalgar, Lord Nelson achieved immortality by smashing the combined French and Spanish fleets off the coast of Spain, thereby insuring Britain's supremacy on the waves. At the battle of Austerlitz in Austria—the Battle of the Three Emperors—Napoleon crushed the combined Austrian and Russian armies, thereby insuring his mastery of the land. Like the tiger and the shark, each power was supreme on its chosen element, and neither could come to grips with the other. The law of the jungle came to prevail.

The two antagonists, unable to hurt each other directly, were forced to strike indirect blows. In pursuance of such tactics, the London government, beginning in 1806, issued an annoying series of Orders in Council. As perfected, these edicts closed the ports under French continental control to foreign shipping, including that of America, unless the vessels first stopped at a British port. There they would pay the necessary fees and, if acceptable, secure the prescribed clearance papers. Napoleon struck back savagely in a series of decrees. In effect, they ordered the seizure of all merchantmen, including those flying the Stars and Stripes, that entered British ports.

Yankee skippers, like their predestined Calvinist ancestors, were seemingly damned if they did, damned if they did not. Even so, their carrying trade continued to prosper, because the greater the risk, the greater the profit. If only one ship in three sailed past the shoals of British Orders in Council, and over the reefs of French decrees, the owner stood to make a comfortable gain.

INTERCOURSE or *Impartial Dealings*

A cartoon by "Peter Pencil," 1809, shows Jefferson being victimized
by both England and France. Houghton Library, Harvard

British Man-Stealing

Even more galling to American pride than the seizure of wooden
ships was the seizure of flesh-and-blood American seamen. Impressment
—the forcible enlistment of able-bodied subjects—was a crude form of
conscription which the British, among others, had employed for over four
centuries. The club and stretcher were standard equipment of press gangs
from His Majesty's man-hungry ships.

The London authorities themselves set limits to this ugly practice.
They claimed the right to impress only British subjects on their own soil,
in their own harbors, or on merchantmen on the high seas. But many fair-
skinned Americans looked like Englishmen, and the benefit of the doubt
was seldom given to an experienced seaman in those short-handed days.
The result was that 6000 bona fide United States citizens, according to
the best estimates, were impressed by the "piratical man-stealers" of England during the years from 1808 to 1811 alone. A number of these luckless
souls died or were killed in the service, leaving their kinfolk and friends
deeply embittered.

The British, on their side, had counter-complaints. The United States navy and merchant marine openly encouraged the enlistment of deserters from the "floating hells" of the British navy, where discipline was taught to the tune of the cat-o'-nine-tails. The expanding American merchant marine, also short of sailors, paid seductively high wages—"dollars for shillings," the saying went. British deserters, conniving with ingenious Americans, would often secure fraudulent naturalization papers. But His Majesty's press gangs laughed aside such documents, whether genuine or not, holding to the principle "Once an Englishman, always an Englishman." The King expected every free-born Briton to do his duty in time of crisis.

England had her back to the wall, and her desperate plight colored her views. If the Yankee "dollar grubbers" had not encouraged so much desertion, the British impressers might have been willing to make fewer mistakes in manhandling our sailors. But England would not abandon her brutal practice of sailor snatching at the behest of an upstart United States. The British were making war; the Americans were making money. The British feared that they would lose the war if they gave up their hoary method of conscription—and they would fight us before they did.

Britain's determination was dramatically highlighted in 1807. A royal frigate overhauled a United States frigate, the *Chesapeake*, on the high seas about ten miles off the coast of Virginia. The British captain bluntly demanded the surrender of four alleged deserters. London had never claimed the right to seize men from a foreign warship, and the American commander, though totally unprepared for a naval duel, refused the request. The British warship thereupon fired three devastating broadsides at close range, killing three Americans and wounding eighteen. Four expostulating deserters were dragged away, and the bloody hulk called the *Chesapeake* limped back to port.

An aroused America—Federalists and Republicans alike—joined in an outburst of national wrath. Nothing like it had been seen since the French XYZ insults of 1797. Jefferson, the peace lover, could easily have had war if he had wanted it. As the event proved, if we were going to fight at all, we should have fought when the country was united.

The British were clearly in the wrong, as the London Foreign Office readily admitted. But Jefferson unwisely attempted to use the *Chesapeake* outrage as a lever to force the British to renounce impressment altogether. This they adamantly refused to do. The affair rankled for five years; and when reparation was finally made, it came too late to salve old wounds.

The Embargo Bludgeon

National honor would not permit a slavish submission to British and French mistreatment. Yet a large-scale foreign war was contrary to the settled policy of the new republic—and in addition it would be futile. The navy was weak, thanks to Jefferson's anti-navalism; and the army was even weaker. A disastrous and humiliating defeat would not improve America's plight.

The warring nations of Europe were heavily dependent upon the United States for raw materials and foodstuffs. In his eager search for an alternative to war, Jefferson seized upon this fact. He reasoned that if we voluntarily cut off our exports, the offending powers would be forced to come to us, hat in hand, and agree to respect our rights.

Congress, responding to the presidential lash, hastily passed the Embargo Act late in 1807. This rigorous law forbade the export of all goods from the United States, whether in American or in foreign ships.

Jefferson, the onetime strict constructionist, had once more flip-flopped into the camp of the loose constructionists. In the interests of the Federalist shippers, whom he disliked, he was rereading the Constitution with strange bifocals. To him, it now meant that Congress, under its authority to "regulate" commerce, could go so far as to stop foreign trade altogether.

The Federalists of New England could well have prayed for relief from their newly found Virginia friend. Forests of dead masts gradually filled once-flourishing harbors; docks that had once rumbled were deserted (except for illicit trade); and soup kitchens cared for some of the hungry unemployed. The Jeffersonian Republicans probably hurt the commerce of New England, which they avowedly were trying to protect, far more than old England and France combined were doing.

The farmers of the South and West, the strongholds of Jefferson, suffered no less disastrously than New England. They were alarmed by the mounting piles of exportable cotton, grain, and tobacco. John Randolph of Virginia remarked that the embargo was like cutting off one's toes to cure one's corns. Jefferson in truth seemed to be waging war on his fellow citizens, rather than on the offending belligerents.

The American people, from the days of the colonial Navigation Acts, have never submitted meekly to unpopular legislation. Though basically law-abiding, they have habitually flouted laws that were opposed by a majority of the population, or by a powerful minority. An enormous illicit trade mushroomed in 1808, especially along the Canadian border, where bands of armed Americans on loaded rafts overawed or overpowered federal agents. Irate citizens cynically transposed the letters of "Embargo" to read "O Grab Me," "Go Bar 'Em," and "Mobrage," and heartily denounced the "Dambargo."

Jefferson nonetheless induced Congress to pass iron-toothed enforcing legislation. The methods to be used were so inquisitorial and tyrannical as to cause some Americans to think more kindly of George III, whom Jefferson had berated in the Declaration of Independence. One indignant New Hampshire poet burst out in song:

> Our ships all in motion,
> Once whiten'd the ocean;
>   They sail'd and return'd with a Cargo;
> Now doom'd to decay
>   They are fallen a prey,
> To Jefferson, worms, and EMBARGO.

New England seethed with talk of secession; and Jefferson later admitted that he felt the foundations of government tremble under his feet.

Retreat was inevitable. An alarmed Congress, bowing to the storm of public anger, finally repealed the embargo, on March 1, 1809, three days before Jefferson's retirement. A half-loaf substitute was provided in the form of the Non-Intercourse Act. This measure formally reopened trade with all the nations of the world, except the two most important, England and France. Though thus watered down, economic coercion continued to be the policy of the Jeffersonians from 1809 to 1812, when the nation finally plunged into war.

The Embargo: A Successful Failure

Why did the embargo, Jefferson's most daring act of statesmanship, collapse so dismally? First of all, he underestimated the stubbornness of the British, as others have, and overestimated their dependence on our trade. Bumper grain crops blessed the British Isles during these anxious years; and as time wore on, the revolutionary Latin American republics unexpectedly threw open their ports for compensating commerce.

The embargo was not continued long enough or completely enough to achieve the desired results. But a statesman must know the temper of his people, and Jefferson should have foreseen that such a self-crucifying weapon could not possibly command public support. The Americans, who were notoriously men of action, did not take kindly to the passive type of heroism. They much preferred commercial activity, with all its risks, to enforced inactivity, with no chance of profit.

A crestfallen Jefferson himself admitted that the embargo was three times more costly than armed hostilities. The irony is that with only a fraction of its cost to the country, he could have built a fairly strong navy. Such a fighting force would have won more respect for American rights on the high seas, and might consequently have prevented the War of 1812 altogether.

The embargo further embroiled our relations with both Great Britain and France. It embittered the British, partly because it struck them more forcibly than it did Napoleon. The French despot naturally applauded the embargo, for it was an indirect American blockade of his enemy. He cynically helped us enforce it by seizing scores of our merchant ships in his ports; by the terms of the Embargo Act, he argued, these vessels should have been tied up at home. The mocking cooperation of Bonaparte merely rubbed salt into old sores.

The stoppage of American exports paralyzed Federalist shipping, but revived the Federalist Party. Gaining new converts, its leaders hurled their nullification of the embargo into the teeth of the "Virginia lordlings" in Washington. In 1804, the discredited Federalists had polled only 14 electoral votes out of 176; in 1808, the embargo year, the figure rose to 47 out of 175.

Curiously enough, New England plucked a new prosperity from the ugly jaws of the embargo. With shipping tied up and imported goods scarce, the resourceful Yankees reopened old factories and erected new ones. The real foundations of modern America's industrial might were laid behind the protective wall of the embargo, followed by non-intercourse and the War of 1812. It is probable that Jefferson, the avowed foe of factories, unintentionally did more for American manufacturing than did Alexander Hamilton, the outspoken friend of factories.

Jefferson's embargo, followed in modified form by non-intercourse, undeniably pinched England. Many British importers and manufacturers suffered severe losses, especially those dependent on American cotton. As thousands of factory workers were thrown out of jobs, agitation mounted in England for a repeal of the British trade restrictions that had brought on the embargo. A petition to Parliament in 1812, coming from the city of Birmingham alone, bore 20,000 names on a sheet of parchment 150 feet long. So strong was public pressure in England for relief that two days before Congress declared war, in June, 1812, the British Foreign Secretary announced that the trouble-breeding Orders in Council would be immediately suspended. The supreme irony is that Jefferson's policy of economic coercion did win in the end, but America was not patient enough to reap the reward of her sacrifices.

The Living Jefferson

Jefferson retained much of his popularity, even though it had been severely tarnished by the embargo. One public toast ran: "May he receive from his fellow citizens the reward of his merit, a halter [hangman's noose]." But his grip on his party was such that he could easily have won a third nomination and election. The international crisis was still acute; and although Jefferson was sixty-five years old, he was mentally alert and physically vigorous. He lived eighteen more years, to the age of eighty-three, glad to have escaped the "splendid misery" of the presidential penitentiary.

Jefferson, rather than Washington, was the real father of the two-term tradition. Unlike the first President, who had no serious constitutional qualms, he feared that more than two terms might open the door to dictatorship. Yet Jefferson carefully arranged for the nomination and election of a kindred spirit, his friend and fellow Virginian, the quiet, intellectual, and unassuming James Madison.

Though bitterly assailed, Jefferson left office with the consolation that he had been true to the guiding star of the other Founding Fathers. He had kept the country out of a serious foreign war. Despite numerous reversals of policy under the whiplash of practicality, he never lost his faith in democracy and in the common man. He brought a renovation rather than a revolution; the real revolution that did occur was in his own thinking. If the Federalists were the steppingstone between monarchical Europe and republican America, then the Jeffersonians were the steppingstone between aristocratic Federalism and democratic Jacksonianism.

Thomas Jefferson and John Adams died on the same day—appropriately the Fourth of July, 1826. The last words of Adams, then ninety-one, were "Thomas Jefferson still survives." He was wrong, for three hours earlier Jefferson had breathed his last. But Thomas Jefferson still survives in the democratic ideals and liberal principles of the great nation which he risked his all to found, and which he served so long and faithfully.

SELECT READINGS

A sketchy introduction by a British scholar is MARCUS CUNLIFFE, *The Nation Takes Shape, 1789–1837* (1959) [paperback]. An excellent one-volume biography by a sympathetic Frenchman is GILBERT CHINARD, *Thomas Jefferson* (1929) [paperback]. Racy but pro-Jefferson is C. G. BOWERS, *Jefferson in Power* (1936). L. W. LEVY debunks Jefferson's liberalism in *Jefferson and Civil Liberties* (1963), while M. D. PETERSON, *The Jeffersonian Image in the American Mind* (1960) [paperback] is broader and more favorable. See also C. M. WILTSE, *The Jeffersonian Tradition in American Democracy* (1935) [paperback]. The most detailed biographical treatment is IRVING BRANT, *James Madison, Secretary of State, 1800–1809* (1953). The most recent study of Jefferson's Secretary of the Treasury is F. E. EWING, *America's Forgotten Statesman: Albert Gallatin* (1959). Strong on administration is L. D. WHITE, *The Jeffersonians* (1951), while politics are handled in N. E. CUNNINGHAM, *The Jeffersonian Republicans in Power* (1963) and in his *The Jeffersonian Republicans: The Formation of Party Organization, 1789–1801* (1958). A first-class biography of the negotiator of the Louisiana Purchase is GEORGE DANGERFIELD, *Chancellor Robert R. Livingston of New York, 1746–1813* (1960). L. M. SEARS delineates the daring experiment in *Jefferson and the Embargo* (1927). Also *Harvard Guide*, Pt. IV.

11

Madison and the Second War for Independence

*The Existing War—the Child of Prostitution. May no
American Acknowledge it Legitimate.*
A FEDERALIST TOAST during the War of 1812

Madison: Dupe of Napoleon

SENSITIVE-FACED James Madison—"Little Jemmy"—took the presidential
oath on March 4, 1809, as the titanic conflict in Europe was roaring to
its climax. Small of stature, bald of head, and scholarly in appearance, he
fell tragically short of providing vigorous executive leadership. Weakened
also by factions within his Cabinet, he was unable to dominate his party,
as Jefferson had done.

The Non-Intercourse Act of 1809—that substitute for the embargo
aimed solely at Britain and France—would expire in about a year. Congress, desperately attempting to uphold American rights without resort to
war, adopted in 1810 a bargaining measure known as Macon's Bill Number 2. While permitting American trade with all the world, it dangled an
additional lure. If either England or France repealed her restrictions on
our commerce, we would restore non-importation against the non-
repealing nation. In short, we would bribe the belligerents into respecting
our rights.

This opportunity was made to order for Napoleon, a past master of
treachery. He was eager to have non-importation clamped down once
more on the British, because it would serve as a partial boycott which he
would not have to raise a finger to enforce. He was hopeful that such a
boycott would embroil us in war with Britain, for then we would be serving as his indirect ally to weaken his archenemy. He therefore blandly announced, in August, 1810, that his objectionable decrees had been repealed. At the same time, he secretly ordered the sale of confiscated
American ships.

All responsible Americans who were not the victims of wishful thinking should have examined the hollow-sounding French announcement
with extreme caution. Napoleon, prince of liars, had no intention whatever

of repealing his galling decrees. But Madison, frantically seeking to wrest a recognition of American rights from England, accepted French bad faith as good faith. He formally announced, in November, 1810, that France had complied with the terms of Macon's Bill Number 2, and that non-importation would in consequence be re-established against Britain.

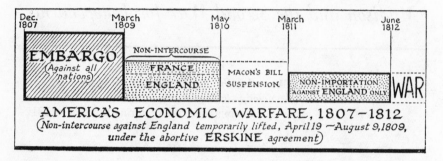

AMERICA'S ECONOMIC WARFARE, 1807–1812
(*Non-intercourse against England temporarily lifted, April 19 —August 9, 1809, under the abortive* ERSKINE *agreement*)

Madison's decision was fateful. The British were angered by America's apparent willingness to be the dupe and partner of Napoleon. The wily Bonaparte, who continued to seize our merchant ships, was delighted by the success of his transparent scheme. Once we had aligned ourselves against England commercially, we found ourselves gravitating toward France politically—and sliding rapidly down the slippery slope to war.

War Whoops Arouse War Hawks

The composition of the Twelfth Congress, which met late in 1811, was markedly different from that of its predecessor. The recent heated elections had swept away many of the older "submission men" and replaced them with young hotheads, chiefly from the South and West. The youthful newcomers—"the boys," John Randolph sneeringly called them—were on fire for a new war with the old enemy. Not having had a conflict in their own generation, these War Hawks were weary of hearing how their fathers had "whipped" the British singlehanded. They won control of the House of Representatives, and elevated to the Speakership the tall, eloquent, and magnetic Henry Clay of Kentucky, the gallant "Harry of the West," then only thirty-four years old.

The western War Hawks, first of all, were eager to wipe out the renewed Indian menace. The red men north of the Ohio River were being welded into a formidable confederacy by two remarkable twin brothers, Tecumseh and The Prophet, who were actually persuading their thirsty braves to give up firewater. The Indians, with insatiable tomahawks, were once more ravaging the frontier north of the Ohio River, using weapons purchased from the so-called British "hair buyers" of Canada.

Only a few days after the War Hawk Congress first met in Washington, news of stirring events on the frontier gave further point to the redskin menace. General William H. Harrison, advancing with a thousand men upon the Indian headquarters, repelled a night surprise attack at Tippecanoe, in present Indiana, on November 7, 1811. The so-called victory was both costly and indecisive, although it seemed more glorious the farther the American army withdrew from the danger zone.

The battle of Tippecanoe further inflamed American patriots, especially when they learned that British-made arms had been found on the bloody field. War Hawks like Representative Felix Grundy of Tennessee, three of whose brothers had been butchered by the savages, believed that there was only one way to remove the menace of the Indians, and that was to eliminate their Canadian base.

Canada, in itself, was a lush prize. The War Hawks made no bones about their determination to seize this enormous and richly wooded area, so desirable and apparently so defenseless. "On to Canada," "On to Canada," was their ominous chant. The Southern expansionists, hardly less vocal, cast a covetous eye toward Florida, then weakly held by Britain's ally, Spain.

A free sea, as well as free land, was one of the goals of the War Hawks. One of their most popular slogans ran, "Free Trade and Sailors' Rights." Yet why should the men beyond the mountains, most of whom had never seen a body of salt water larger than a salt lick, want to fight for maritime rights?

War Vote in House of Representatives, 1812

(SHOWING WESTERN AND SOUTHWESTERN WAR SENTIMENT)

		For War	Against War
N.H. Vt.	Frontier New England	3 3	2 1
Mass. R.I. Conn.	Maritime and Federalist New England; Mass. includes frontier Maine	6 0 0	8 2 7
N.Y. N.J. Del.	Commercial and Federalist Middle States	3 2 0	11 4 1
Penn. Md.	Jeffersonian Middle States	16 6	2 3
Va. N.C. S.C. Ga.	Jeffersonian Southern States	14 6 8 3	5 3 0 0
Ohio Ky. Tenn.	The trans-Allegheny West — Nest of the War Hawks	1 5 3	0 0 0
		$\overline{79}$	$\overline{49}$

The Westerners, strange as it may seem, did have a vital interest in a free sea. They were proud, patriotic, and intensely nationalistic. The manhandling of an American sailor, though far away, struck these freedom-loving pioneers as outrageous. They might not have ships to sail the ocean, but they did have dammed-up agricultural products, which, because of the hated British Orders in Council, could not be shipped to European ports. In short, the Men of the West, despite all their misleading clamor for Canada, did have a genuine emotional and financial stake in a free sea.

The high-riding War Hawks, with scattered but essential support from other sections, finally forced a declaration of war through Congress in June, 1812. The vote in the House was 79 to 49; in the Senate, 19 to 13. The closeness of the count betrayed a dangerous degree of national disunity. Members of Congress from the pro-British maritime and commercial centers of New England, as well as from the Middle Atlantic States, almost solidly opposed hostilities. Thus the West and Southwest, mostly landlocked, presented the sea-fronting East with a war for a free sea that the East vehemently resented.

A Choice of Foes

Why did the United States fight Britain and not France? Napoleonic seizures of our ships since 1803 had numbered 558, as compared with 917 for Britain. Logically, we should have fought both offenders, if we were going to fight at all.

Why single out England? The Mother Country was the hereditary enemy, and the Jeffersonian Republican party was traditionally anti-British and pro-French. This Gallic attachment partly explains why the Jeffersonians, disliking Federalist shipping, were ostensibly going to war to protect that shipping.

Nearness of offenses was also a vital factor. Napoleon, to be sure, had confiscated our ships and imprisoned our sailors, but his misdeeds were faraway and in another world. British impressments and seizures, on the other hand, often took place within sight of our shores. And on the frontier the red savages, bearing British arms, were smashing into the cabins of American pioneers.

To declare war on France would avail us nothing, for she was not vulnerable. We had no border in common with her, and hence could not come to grips with Napoleon's armies. But a victorious war with England, aside from avenging our grievances, would be profitable as well as patriotic. Her merchant marine, the richest in the world, would fall easy prey to our swarming privateers. And Canada, the choicest prize of all, looked like a sitting duck.

Costly illusions beckoned us northward. The invasion of Canada, we fondly believed, would be absurdly simple—a "frontiersmen's frolic"; a "mere matter of marching," said Jefferson. The trick could be turned, boasted Henry Clay, by the militiamen of Kentucky alone.

The population odds supported such optimism. The United States numbered over 6,000,000 whites, as compared with 500,000 for Canada. A majority of the Canadians were Frenchmen, whose loyalty was then dubious, and a considerable number of the rest were recent American emigrants, whose loyalty was even more dubious. The Mother Country, bogged down in the Napoleonic War, could spare few troops for North America. Europe's distresses were now pointing the way anew to our military successes.

The Northern mirage helped destroy our last precious stores of patience. If Canada had not been so near, so desirable, so seemingly helpless, we probably would have endured British offenses a few more months. If we had done so, we would have learned of Britain's official announcement of the forthcoming repeal of her odious Orders in Council—an announcement made ironically two days *before* Congress voted war. If there had then been an Atlantic cable, the War Hawks probably could not have forced through the Senate a formal declaration of hostilities. A change of three votes would have brought a tie. But the tempting proximity of Canada turned American heads, and President Madison plunged rashly into the conflict, contrary to the time-tested policy of the Founding Fathers.

Allies of Anti-Christ

New England, though facing the sea, condemned the declaration of war for a free sea. The disagreeable news was greeted with muffled bells, flags at half-mast, and public fasting. Congressman Turner, who had voted for war, was kicked through the streets of Plymouth, Massachusetts, by a frenzied mob.

Why the opposition? For one thing, violations of American rights were an old story; they had been continuing for about twenty years. The extent of impressment, though serious, had been exaggerated. Manufacturing in New England was mushrooming, and the luckier shippers, despite intermittent confiscations, were still raking in money. Profits dull patriotism. New England was also the traditional stronghold of pro-British Federalism, and resented the pro-French favoritism of the "Virginia Dynasty" in Washington.

Federalist New England, moreover, had long been allied in sympathy with Old England. The Mother Country—"that fast-anchored isle"—was the last real bulwark of constitutional government left in the Old World. At a time when she was straining every nerve to defeat the despotism of Napoleon, the Federalists believed that America should be helping her. Instead the United States—the presumed friend of freedom and constitutionalism—was stabbing England in the back. Cold-bloodedly and calculatingly, we had concluded that Britain's war to the death with

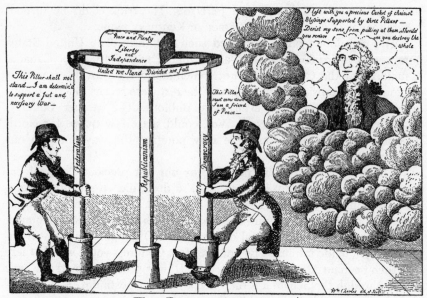

THE PRESENT State of our COUNTRY.

Partisan disunity over the War of 1812 threatens the nation's very existence.
The pro-war Jeffersonian at the left is attacking the pillar of Federalism; the
anti-war Federalist at the right is trying to pull down Democracy. The spirit
of Washington warns them that the country's welfare depends upon all
three. A cartoon by William Charles. New York Public Library

Napoleon, in indirect defense of our own liberties, would enable us to
seize her territory.

Nor did the sinfulness of the conflict, in Federalist eyes, end here.
Not only had we treacherously pushed the Mother Country into the abyss
of an unwanted war, but we had permitted ourselves to be tricked into
it by her archenemy, Napoleon. More than that, we had become virtual
allies of the "Corsican butcher"—the "anti-Christ of the age."

The Federalist charge of a quasi-alliance with France contained much
distasteful truth. As the war in Europe ground on, the Jeffersonian Republicans rejoiced over Napoleon's triumphs, while the Federalists, no less
loudly, hailed the victories of Britain and her allies over Bonaparte.

The Federalists likewise opposed the War of 1812 because they were
opposed to the acquisition of Canada. The seizure of this vast area, like
the purchase of Louisiana, would merely add more agrarian states from
the wild Northwest. These, in turn, would increase the voting strength of
the Jeffersonians. Some New England Federalists, it seemed, feared the
New West far more than they did Old England. They were determined,
wrote one versifier,

> To rule the nation if they could,
> But see it damned if others should.

The bitterness of the New England Federalists against "Mr. Madison's War" led to treason or near treason. In a sense, the government in Washington fought two enemies simultaneously: Old England and New England. The money holders of New England, possessing much of the nation's gold, probably lent more dollars to the British than to the Federal Treasury. The farmers of New England sent huge quantities of supplies north to Canada, including droves of cattle, and these foodstuffs enabled the British armies to invade New York. The governors of New England thought first of local defense. They stubbornly refused to permit their militia to serve outside the borders of their states, though men were desperately needed in the regular army.

Yet the disloyalty of New England, deplorable though it was, has perhaps been overstressed. The Jeffersonians in this section, comprising a substantial minority, vigorously opposed Federalist obstructionism. The New England states actually contributed a surprising number of volunteers to the regular army; Massachusetts alone sent as many as Virginia.

America the Unready

The War of 1812, largely because of widespread disunity, easily ranks as America's worst-fought major war. There was no burning national anger, as in 1807, following the *Chesapeake* outrage. The War Hawks in Congress were no more than a zealous minority. President Madison, who had fallen under their domination, knew that there was serious disunity. But he made the near-fatal error of sponsoring a declaration of war in the hope that it would cause the nation to rally around the flag. New England and other Federalist centers were content to let it fall into the mire.

The American manpower pool was deceptively large. There were some 6,000,000 whites in 1812, at least a million of whom were males of the arms-bearing age. But the harassed national government never mustered more than 7000 regulars and militia for any one battle. The supreme lesson of this conflict was the folly of leading a divided and apathetic people into war.

The country was dangerously unprepared, despite a warning going back nineteen years to 1793, when Britain and France had first locked horns. We were still suffering from our own embargo and non-intercourse, which we had partially enforced for the better part of four years. Congress had shortsightedly permitted the Bank of the United States to expire in 1811, at a time of all times when a powerful financial institution was needed. It was knifed largely by the jealousies of the competing state banks.

The regular army was quite inadequate, for it was ill-trained, ill-disciplined, and widely scattered. It had to be supplemented by the even more poorly trained militia, who were often distinguished by speed of foot in leaving the battlefield. Some of the ranking generals were semi-

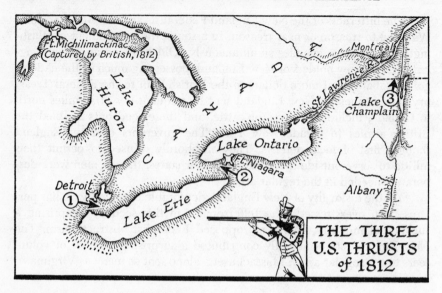

Ft.Michilimackinac (Captured by British, 1812)

Lake Huron

Montreal

St. Lawrence R.

Lake Champlain ③

C A N A D A

Lake Ontario

Ft. Niagara ②

Detroit ①

Albany

Lake Erie

THE THREE U.S. THRUSTS of 1812

senile heirlooms from the Revolutionary War, rusting on their laurels and lacking in vigor and vision. By a process of trial and error—chiefly costly error—they were gradually weeded out by 1814. But by that time the golden prize of Canada had slipped from our grasp.

The offensive strategy adopted in Washington was poorly conceived. As the roads of Canada were few and bad, the bulk of the population was scattered along the St. Lawrence, its tributary rivers, and the Great Lakes. Over these arterial waterways all essential supplies—both military and civilian—had to be transported. Once Montreal was captured, everything to the west was bound to die, just as the leaves of a tree wither when the trunk is girdled. If the United States had thrown everything it had against Montreal when the defenders were heavily outnumbered, all of Canada probably would have fallen.

But instead of laying ax to the trunk of the tree, the Americans frittered away their strength in the three-pronged invasion of 1812. One thrust started from the American wilderness outpost of Detroit, under General Hull. He quickly retired to his base, and then surrendered his entire army to a numerically inferior enemy without firing a shot. The second American invasion, launched across the Niagara River, was beaten back. The New York militia balked at crossing the Canadian line, while their countrymen on the other side were being shot down or forced to surrender. A third force marched bravely for Montreal along Lake Champlain, but turned back when the militia refused to cross the New York-Canada border.

The British and Canadians from the outset displayed energy. Early in the war they captured the American fort of Michilimackinac, commanding the upper Great Lakes and a huge Indian-inhabited area to the south. In their brilliant defensive operations, the Canadians received vital help from a small but efficient force of professional British soldiers. Above all, they were blessed with an inspired British leader, General Isaac Brock, whose most immovable ally was "General Mud."

Invasion in Reverse

In 1813 the American invasions of Canada were again hurled back in confusion. The Canadians, many of them descended from the evicted American Loyalists of 1776–1783, fought bravely for their new homes and firesides. They had not impressed our sailors or seized our ships, and they regarded the invasion as a wanton attack—"the War of Defense," they called their side of it.

Control of the Great Lakes was essential for transporting military supplies westward, and an energetic naval officer, Oliver Hazard Perry, bestirred himself on the shores of Lake Erie. He contrived to build a fleet of green-timbered ships, manned largely by even greener seamen, plus some Kentucky riflemen. In a bitter engagement on Lake Erie, he silenced and captured a less powerful British fleet. "We have met the enemy and they are ours," he reported to his superior, "two ships, two brigs, one schooner, and one sloop." His victory, combined with his slogan, infused new life into the flagging American cause.

With the control of Lake Erie firmly in American hands, the British holdings to the west, both at Malden and at captured Detroit, quickly withered. Forced to withdraw eastward into Canada, the retreating Redcoats were overtaken by General Harrison's army and beaten at the Battle of the Thames. There, in October, 1813, the gifted Indian leader Tecumseh, now a brigadier general in the British army, lost his life.

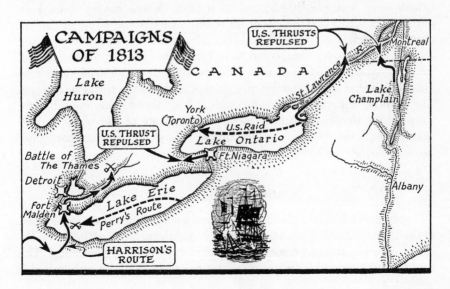

Despite these successes, the Americans by late 1814, far from invading Canada, were grimly defending their own soil against the invading British. In Europe, the diversionary power of Napoleon was destroyed in mid-1814, and the dangerous despot was marooned on the Mediterranean isle of Elba. The United States, which had so brashly provoked war behind the protective skirts of Napoleon, was now left to face the music alone. As thousands of redcoated veterans began to pour into Canada, Europe's distresses, for once, failed us.

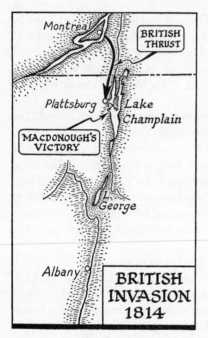

Assembling some 10,000 crack troops, the British prepared in 1814 for a crushing blow through New York, along the familiar lake-river route. In the absence of roads, the invader was forced to bring his supplies over the Lake Champlain waterway. A weaker American fleet under Thomas Macdonough challenged the British. The battle was desperately fought near Plattsburg, September 11, 1814, on floating slaughterhouses. The American flagship at one point was in grave trouble. But Macdonough, unexpectedly turning his ship about with cables, confronted the enemy with a fresh broadside, and snatched victory from the teeth of defeat.

The results of this heroic naval battle were momentous. The invading British army was speedily forced to retreat, though having gained an initial success at Plattsburg over an outnumbered force of American recruits. The defeat on the lake gravely endangered the supply lines of the invader. Macdonough thus saved New York from conquest, New England from detachment, and the Union from possible dissolution. He also profoundly affected the concurrent negotiation of the peace treaty in Europe. The victories of Perry and Macdonough, though achieved on inland lakes, were by far the most decisive naval engagements of the war. That of Macdonough, though the more important, is largely forgotten, partly because he devised no blood-tingling slogan.

Beating Off the British

A second formidable British force, containing about 4000 men, landed in the Chesapeake Bay area in August, 1814. Advancing rapidly on Washington, it easily dispersed some 6000 panicky militia at Bladensburg. The invader then entered the capital and set fire to most of the public buildings, including the Capitol and the White House ("the Yankee Palace"). President Madison and his aides, chased into the surrounding hills like frightened rabbits, witnessed from afar the billowing smoke. The British fleet next appeared before Baltimore, a nest for privateers, but was beaten off by the doughty defenders at Fort McHenry, despite "bombs bursting in air." At the same time the American land defenders, though they had been driven back at first, caused the attacking army to withdraw.

The wanton destruction of Washington reflected little credit on the British. They claimed that they had acted in retaliation for the unauthorized burning of certain public buildings by an American raiding party at York (Toronto) in 1813. But the deliberate application of the torch served only to inflame anti-British bitterness in the United States. The memory of the Chesapeake campaign was further kept alive when Francis Scott Key, an American anxiously watching the bombardment at Baltimore from a British ship, was inspired to write the words of "The Star-Spangled Banner." Set to the tune of an old English tavern refrain, the song very quickly attained widespread popularity.

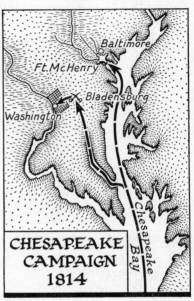

CHESAPEAKE CAMPAIGN 1814

The third British blow of 1814, aimed at New Orleans, menaced the entire Mississippi Valley. Gaunt and hawk-faced Andrew Jackson, fresh from crushing the Southwest Indians at the battle of Horseshoe Bend in what is now Alabama, was placed in command. His hodge-podge force consisted of 7000 sailors, regulars, pirates, Negroes, Frenchmen, and militiamen from Louisiana, Kentucky, and Tennessee. They threw up their entrenchment, and

> Behind it stood our little force—
> None wished it to be greater;
> For ev'ry man was half a horse,
> And half an alligator.*

The overconfident British, numbering 8000 battle-seasoned veterans, blundered badly. They made the mistake of launching a frontal assault, on January 8, 1815, on the entrenched American riflemen and cannoneers. The British attackers suffered the most devastating defeat of the entire war, losing over 2000 in killed and wounded in half an hour, as compared with some 70 for the Americans. The slaughter was as useless as it was

---

* Popular song, "The Hunters of Kentucky."

horrible, for the treaty of peace had been signed at Ghent two weeks earlier. But Jackson, who had almost been caught napping, became more than ever the hero of the West. Was he not greater than Napoleon, for had he not whipped the British, who had whipped Napoleon?

The smashing triumph at New Orleans was the only decisive American land victory that had not been set up by naval power. Yet if a nation is going to win only one rousing battle in a war, a better taste is left in the mouth if that engagement is the last one. The glorious news from New

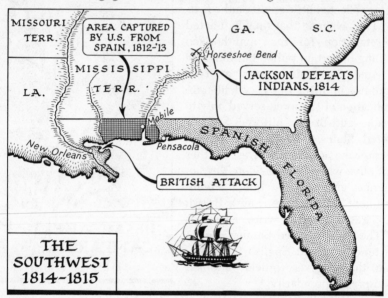

Orleans reached Washington early in February, 1815, and about two weeks later came the tidings of the treaty of peace. Naïve Americans leaped to the conclusion that the British, beaten to their knees by Jackson, had hastened to make terms while they could. More support was thus given to the legend that we soundly "thrashed" the British for a second time in the War of 1812.

Iron Men in Wooden Ships

Man for man and ship for ship the American navy did much better than the army. But the results of its heroism have been grossly exaggerated.

The British navy in 1812 boasted more than 800 men-of-war. Of these oaken craft, 219 were ships-of-the-line of the 74-gun class, and 296 were frigates of roughly the 44-gun class. Little wonder that the motto of the British *Naval Register* was:

> The winds and seas are Britain's wide domain,
> And not a sail, but by permission, spreads.

The United States, by contrast, had only sixteen ships in its entire navy, the largest of which were 44-gun frigates, unable to stand up to British ships-of-the-line. There could be no saltwater fleet engagements in the slam-bang Trafalgar tradition; the only fleet battles were fought on the interior lakes.

The American frigates and smaller sloops did engage in a series of spectacular duels with the British men-of-war. In the frigate class, the Americans won four out of five of the single-ship contests, and in the sloop class, eight out of nine. The American craft on the whole were more skillfully handled, had better gunners, and were manned by non-press-gang crews who were burning to avenge the indignity to the *Chesapeake*. Some of the American frigates were specially designed super-frigates, notably the *Constitution* ("Old Ironsides"). They had thicker sides, heavier firepower, and larger crews. They should have defeated their foes in the frigate category, and generally did, amid angry enemy charges that they were "disguised" ships-of-the-line.

The British were deeply humiliated by their naval defeats, all the more so because they had sneered at our "few fir-built frigates, manned by a handful of bastards and outlaws." In a few months they lost more warships to the Americans than the French and Spaniards together had captured from them in many years of fighting.

After three straight losses in frigate duels, the English rang the bells of London Tower in joy over one gratifying victory. The ill-omened American frigate *Chesapeake*, rashly taken into battle with an inexperienced crew, had been captured off Boston by the British frigate *Shannon* on June 1, 1813. From the dying lips of the American commander, Captain Lawrence, came the stirring slogan "Don't give up the ship. Blow her up." The British at length put an end to American single-ship frigate victories when they ordered their frigates to sail in pairs.

The loss of a dozen or so ships by the Royal Navy was negligible. But the victory-hungry Americans received from these triumphs a badly needed tonic for their morale. When the conflict ended, there were only two or three ships of the American navy at large; Britain still had over 800. The United States obviously did not win the war on the sea. But the dramatic sloop and frigate duels gave further support to the legend that we had vanquished the British.

Swift and annoying American privateers—the "militia of the sea"—numbered about 500. They were in fact much more damaging than the regular navy, and had an important bearing on the outcome of the war. Built to fly from stronger warships, rather than fight them, these speedy craft captured or destroyed some 1350 British merchantmen, even pursuing them into the English Channel and the Irish Sea. Assisted by fast-sailing sloops of the navy, Yankee privateers made things so hot that Lloyd's of London refused to insure unconvoyed British merchantmen crossing the Irish Sea.

Yet the privateers were not an unmixed blessing. They lost scores of their own number, and diverted valuable manpower from the navy and army. But they siphoned urgently needed wealth into the country, boosted sagging morale, and slowed up British operations in Canada and elsewhere by capturing arms and supplies. More than that, the privateers brought the war home to British manufacturers, merchants, and shippers, who in turn exerted strong and effective pressure on Parliament to end this purposeless and costly war.

The Royal Navy, stung to the quick, finally retaliated by throwing a ruinous naval blockade along our coast, and by landing raiding parties almost at will. American economic life, including fishing, was crippled. Urgently needed customs revenues were choked off, and near the end of the war the United States Treasury was unable to meet its outstanding obligations.

Peace Proposals and Counter-Proposals

Czar Alexander I of Russia, late in 1812, unexpectedly proposed mediation between the quarreling Anglo-Saxon cousins. He was then hard pressed by Napoleon's invading Grand Army, and did not wish to see his British ally fritter away its strength in America. Nothing came of the Czar's feeler immediately, but the machinery was set in motion which,

Bruin become MEDIATOR *or Negociation for* PEACE.

The Russian Bear attempts to mediate between America and a chastened John Bull. America expresses concern over John Bull's horns, the Orders in Council. A cartoon by William Charles. New York Public Library

in 1814, brought five American peace commissioners to the quaint city of Ghent, now in Belgium. This quarrelsome group was headed by the early-rising and Puritanical John Quincy Adams, son of John Adams, who was much annoyed by the late-hour card playing of his spirited colleague, Henry Clay.

The British envoys at the outset were prepared to make breath-taking demands. Their position was bolstered by the knowledge that His Majesty's troops occupied the eastern portion of Maine, and still held Fort Niagara. Britain, through her red allies, also loosely controlled the vast region between the Great Lakes and the Mississippi, embracing all or substantial parts of what were to be Minnesota, Wisconsin, Michigan, and Illinois. The British negotiators felt justified, therefore, in demanding a neutralized Indian buffer state. Thrust between Canada and the United States, it would deprive us of an immense area.

The British diplomats further insisted upon control of the Great Lakes, so as to forestall a future invasion of Canada. With the defense of Canada also in mind, they demanded a substantial part of conquered Maine. This territory was desired for a military road from Halifax to Quebec, to be employed during those months when the St. Lawrence River was ice-locked.

The demands from London, harsh though they seemed, were not too far out of line with British military successes, past and prospective. The American negotiators, for their part, flatly rejected the proposed terms without even waiting to hear from the Department of State.

Then, as if by magic, the atmosphere at the peace table changed. The British envoys had presented their drastic proposals with the utmost confidence; they fully expected that news would soon arrive of crushing victories by the Redcoats at both Plattsburg and Washington. But when tidings came of the repulses in upper New York and at Baltimore, the British were more willing to listen to compromise. The government in Washington, for its part, was now reluctantly prepared to keep silent on the burning issue of impressment, even though it had originally insisted on abandonment of this maddening practice.

In England, the atmosphere likewise changed. Irate Britons were impatient to chastise the "insolent" and "treacherous" Yankees. But the "Iron Duke" of Wellington, conqueror of Napoleon, warned that the United States could not be successfully invaded without British control of the Great Lakes. Such control could be achieved only at a heavy cost, if at all; and England was debt-burdened and war-weary from her twenty-year-old clash with France. American sloops and privateers were taking their deadly toll. The Congress of Vienna, designed to unscramble the map of Europe, was at a critical stage. France was restive, and Napoleon might forsake nearby Elba to meet his Waterloo (which he soon did).

Revenge was sweet—but expensive. Much as the British yearned to thrash their upstart offspring, they finally decided that this satisfaction would cost too much, and would involve them too deeply at a time when a vigilant eye had to be kept on France. The distresses of Europe, once again, were bringing us diplomatic success. The War of 1812 was largely "won" in Europe, so far as it was won at all by us. The British Lion was content to lick his wounds.

The Gains of Ghent

The Treaty of Ghent, signed the day before Christmas in 1814, was so inconclusive as to be little more than an armistice. Both sides simply agreed to stop fighting and to restore conquered territory. No mention was made of those grievances for which America had ostensibly fought: the Indian menace, search, seizures, Orders in Council, impressments, and confiscations. These omissions have often been cited as further evidence of the insincerity of the War Hawks. Rather, they are proof that the Americans did not defeat the British decisively. With neither side able to impose its will, the treaty negotiations—like the war itself—ended as a virtual draw.

Time—the great healer—solved certain problems that the negotiators could not untangle. Impressment was never thereafter a burning issue between the two nations. The British navy was reduced to a peace footing, and less brutal methods of enlistment were devised. The Peace of Ghent, like Jay's Treaty of 1794, was also a victory for arbitration, because four boundary disputes were referred to arbitral commissions.

The Treaty of Ghent, which blithely swept problems under the rug, had one great merit. It was not a victor's peace, so no territorial booty had to be won back. There were wounds—but not incurable wounds. The treaty had done nothing, so nothing had to be undone. Therein lay the secret of its longevity.

The Treaty of Ghent proved to be immensely welcome to the United States. The American people had rather expected to lose some territory at the peace table, so dark was the military outlook early in 1815. But when the treaty reached the United States, the public mood rocketed from gloom to glory. The popularity of the pact was so overwhelming that it was unanimously approved by the Senate. A slogan of the hour became "Not One Inch of Territory Ceded or Lost"—a watchword that contrasted strangely with the "On to Canada" at the outset of the war.

Hard Feelings at Hartford

Defiant New England continued to be a problem. She was by far the most prosperous section during the conflict, owing largely to illicit trade with the enemy in Canada and to the absence of a British blockade until 1814. But the embittered opposition of the Federalists to the war continued unabated. Late in 1812, when our first wartime presidential election had to be held, they combined with disaffected Republicans and almost unseated President Madison. If the state of Pennsylvania alone had been transferred to their electoral column, they would have triumphed.

As the war dragged on, New England extremists became more vocal. A small minority of them proposed secession from the Union, or at least a separate peace with England. Ugly rumors were afloat about "Blue Light" Federalists—treacherous New Englanders who supposedly flashed lanterns on the shore so that blockading British cruisers would be alerted to the movements of American ships.

The most spectacular manifestation of Federalist discontent was the ill-omened Hartford Convention. Late in 1814, when the capture of New Orleans seemed imminent, Massachusetts issued a call for a convention at Hartford, Connecticut. The states of Massachusetts, Connecticut, and Rhode Island dispatched full delegations, while

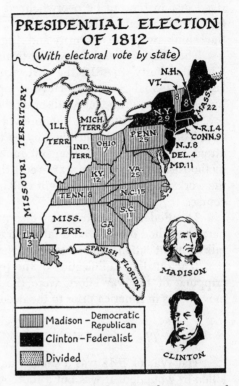

PRESIDENTIAL ELECTION OF 1812
(With electoral vote by state)

Madison – Democratic Republican
Clinton – Federalist
Divided

MADISON

CLINTON

New Hampshire and Vermont sent partial representation. This group of prominent men, twenty-six in all, met in complete secrecy for about three weeks—December 15, 1814, to January 5, 1815—to discuss their grievances and to seek redress for their wrongs.

The Hartford Convention was actually less radical than alarmists supposed. Its immediate goal was to secure financial assistance from the federal government, because the shores of New England were then being ravaged by British blockading squadrons. A minority of the delegates at Hartford gave vent to much wild talk of secession, but they were outvoted by the moderate Federalists. The report and resolutions adopted by the convention, in fact, resemble a modern political platform.

The Hartfordites, who resented the war-bent policies of the administration, were especially eager to restore New England to her leading role on the national stage. They formally recommended amendments to the Constitution aimed at hobbling Congress and restoring Federalist influence by a kind of minority veto. These would require a two-thirds vote before an embargo could be imposed, before new Western states could be admitted, and before war could be declared—except in case of actual invasion.

Three special envoys from Hartford, bearing the demands of the convention, proceeded to the burned-out capital of Washington. The trio arrived just in time to be overwhelmed by the glorious news from New Orleans, followed by that from Ghent. Pursued by the jeers of the press, they slunk away into obscurity and disgrace.

The Hartford resolutions, as it turned out, were the death song of the Federalist Party. In 1816, the next year, the Federalists nominated their last presidential candidate. He was lopsidedly defeated at the polls by James Monroe, President Madison's fellow Virginian.

The stench of treason, unhappily, has clung to the Hartford Convention. The taint was not justified by its formal resolutions, which were an attempt of moderates to iron out rankling grievances by constitutional methods—in the American way. Yet if the war had not ended when it did, the work of the Convention might well have paved the way for treasonable courses.

The Federalist doctrines of disunity, which lived on long after the party had died out, blazed a fateful trail. Until 1815, there was far more talk of nullification and secession in New England than in any other section. The outright nullification of the Jeffersonian embargo, and the later crippling of the war effort, were the two most damaging nullification movements in America prior to the events leading to the Civil War.

The Second War for American Independence

The War of 1812 was a small war, involving about 6000 Americans killed or wounded. It was but a footnote to the mighty European conflagration. In 1812, when Napoleon invaded Russia with about 500,000 men, Madison tried to invade Canada with about 5000 men. But if the American conflict was globally inconsequential, its results were highly consequential.

Formally, the Americans wrested no recognition of their rights on the high seas, but informally they did. No longer did gouty British lords sneer at the "striped bunting" over "American cockboats." We had shown that we would resent, sword in hand, what we regarded as grievous wrongs. Britain and other nations developed, though grudgingly, a new respect for our fighting men. Naval officers like Perry and Macdonough were the most effective type of negotiators; the hot breath of their broadsides spoke the most eloquent diplomatic language. America's diplomats abroad were henceforth treated with less scorn. In a diplomatic sense, if not in a military sense, the conflict could be called the Second War for American Independence.

A new nation, moreover, was welded in the fiery furnace of armed conflict. Sectionalism, now identified with the discredited New England Federalists, was given a black eye. The painful events of the war glaringly revealed, as perhaps nothing else could have done so unmistakably, the folly of sectional disunity.

The entire nation thrilled to the victories of its warriors. A brilliant naval tradition, already well launched, was strengthened by the exploits of our gallant tars. The ineptitudes of the insubordinate or fleeing militia were forgotten. The battle-singed regular army, which in the closing months of the war had fought bravely and well, had won its spurs. New war heroes emerged, men like Andrew Jackson, William Henry Harrison, and Winfield Scott. All three were to become presidential candidates, two of them successful.

The Indians of the Southwest had been crushed by Jackson at Horseshoe Bend, and the Indians of the Northwest by Harrison at the Battle of the Thames. Left in the lurch by their pale-faced British friends at Ghent, the redskins were forced to make such terms as they could. They reluctantly consented, in a series of treaties, to relinquish vast areas of forested land north of the Ohio to the energetic pioneer.

Manufacturing, with its bustle and whir, increased behind the wooden wall of the British blockade. In an economic sense, as well as in a diplomatic sense, the War of 1812 may be regarded as the Second War for American Independence. The industries that were thus stimulated by the fighting rendered America less dependent than before on the workshops of Europe.

Mutual Misgivings

Unhappily, the war revived and intensified bitterness toward the Mother Country. The uglier incidents of the conflict, notably the burning of Washington, added fuel to a century of Britain hating and Britain baiting. A contemporary American war song, "Johnny Bull," proclaimed:

> But if again he should be vain
> Or dare to be uncivil,
> We'll let him know his rebel foe
> Can thrash him like the D——.

Mutual suspicion and hate were perhaps the most enduring heritages of this frustrating little war. Few Americans could have guessed in 1815 that it was to be our last armed conflict with England.

Canadian patriotism and nationalism, no less than American patriotism and nationalism, received a powerful stimulus from the clash. The outnumbered Canadians, fighting bravely in defense of their homeland against the Yankee invader, won their full share of the laurels. Their national song, "The Maple Leaf," eloquently recalls these battles.

All future hope of our annexing Canada, at least by non-forcible means, was given a deadly blow. Peaceful Yankee penetration might have won this rich prize, but cave-man aggression had defeated its own ends. It had strengthened the arm of those Canadians, led by the sons of the

Loyalists, who would die in the last ditch before they would live under the Stars and Stripes. The irony is that the Loyalists, whom we had defeated in our first war with England, helped thwart us in our second war with England.

Many Canadians, especially western fur traders, cried that they had been betrayed by the Treaty of Ghent. They were especially aggrieved over Britain's failure to secure the defensive bulwark of an Indian buffer state, or even mastery of the Great Lakes. Fully expecting the frustrated Yankee to come again, they felt naked in the face of their former enemy.

Naval armament on the Lakes continued to be a perplexing problem. When the war ended, both the Americans and the British were engaged in building powerful and costly warships. But the economy-minded London officials, who perceived that such warships could not be used by the salt-water Royal Navy, finally became receptive to American proposals for arms limitation.

In 1817 Great Britain went so far as to negotiate with the United States the Rush-Bagot disarmament agreement. This memorable pact severely limited naval armament on the Great Lakes, despite Canadian misgivings and protests. The immediate results have been greatly overpraised, but the principle of disarmament was gradually extended to border fortifications, which disappeared in the 1870's. The happy result was that the United States and Canada ultimately came to share the longest unfortified boundary in the world—5527 miles long, including Alaska.

Larger Legacies

The obvious military lessons of the war went largely unheeded by our people, owing in part to overemphasis on the spectacular naval duels. Forgotten were the perils of unpreparedness, the dangers of disunity, the muddlings of the militia. We assumed, mistakenly, that we had won the war decisively—without preparing for it. Then why should we go to all the expense of building an adequate military establishment if, as we believed, we could defeat our enemies without one? Unpreparedness was sanctified by seeming success.

The finish-fight at Waterloo, in 1815, proved to be one of the decisive battles of American history. With Napoleon safely marooned on the island-rock of St. Helena, some 5000 miles away, Europe slumped back into a peace of exhaustion. Deposed monarchs were restored to battered thrones, as the Mother Continent prepared to take the rutted road back to conservatism, illiberalism, and reaction.

The American people now experienced all the joys of emancipation. Freed from the shin-kicking side blows of the belligerents, they no longer had to scan the Atlantic horizon for approaching sails—sails that might bring news of impending calamities. Americans thrilled to a new sense of nationality. They were like subject peoples attaining their majority, and for the first time shaking off completely the shackles of colonialism. Turning their backs on the Old World, they faced resolutely toward the West. Unlike monarchy-cursed Europe, they were ready to take the high road toward democracy, liberalism, and freedom. The steady tramp, tramp, of the westward-moving pioneers came to be the giant drumbeat of a new destiny.

SELECT READINGS

MARCUS CUNLIFFE, *The Nation Takes Shape, 1789–1837* (1959) [paperback] provides a convenient introduction. More detailed are H. L. COLES, *The War of 1812* (1965); F. F. BEIRNE, *The War of 1812* (1949); A. Z. CARR, *The Coming of War* (1960); and P. C. T. WHITE, *A Nation on Trial: America and the War of 1812* (1965) [paperback]. On causation, J. W. PRATT, *Expansionists of 1812* (1925) stresses Western pressures; BRADFORD PERKINS, *Prologue to War: England and the United States, 1805–1812* (1961) and REGINALD HORSMAN, *The Causes of the War of 1812* (1962) stress free seas; R. R. BROWN, *The Republic in Peril: 1812* (1964) stresses the need for saving the republican form of government. The relevant volumes of HENRY ADAMS' nine-volume *History of the United States* (1889–1891) still contain magnificent reading, both on the war and on the peace. A popularized account of the Peace of Ghent is F. L. ENGELMAN, *The Peace of Christmas Eve* (1962). IRVING BRANT continues his strong pro-Madison bias in the relevant volumes of his six-volume work: *James Madison: The President, 1809–1812* (1956) and *James Madison: Commander-in-Chief, 1812–1836* (1961). Other useful biographical studies are BERNARD MAYO, *Henry Clay: Spokesman of the New West* (1937); G. G. VAN DEUSEN, *The Life of Henry Clay* (1937); and MARQUIS JAMES' spirited *Andrew Jackson: The Border Captain* (1933) [paperback]. Also *Harvard Guide*, Pt. IV.

12

The Post-War Upsurge of Nationalism 1815–1824

. . . The American continents . . . are henceforth not to be considered as subjects for future colonization by any European powers.
PRESIDENT JAMES MONROE, December 2, 1823

Nascent Nationalism

THE most noteworthy by-product of the War of 1812 was a heightened nationalism—the spirit of nation-consciousness or national oneness. We may not have fought the war as one nation, but we emerged one nation. So exhilarating was the post-war era that President Madison, despite his blunders, enjoyed the unusual distinction of being more popular when he left the White House in 1817 than when he entered it in 1809.

A weak nationalism had existed since Revolution days, but the vibrant new nationalism was compounded of many additional ingredients. It sprang partly from pride in our recent victories, partly from the setback to Federalist sectionalism and states'-rightism, partly from a lessening of our economic and political dependence on Europe, and partly from an exulting confidence in the future. Swelling numbers of our citizens—although probably not yet a majority of them—were coming to regard themselves as first of all Americans, and secondarily as citizens of their respective states.

The refreshing new mood even manifested itself in the birth of a distinctively national literature. Washington Irving and James Fenimore Cooper attained international recognition in the 1820's, significantly as our first writers of importance to use American scenes and themes. School textbooks, often British in an earlier era, were now being written by Americans for Americans. In the world of magazines, the highly intellectual *North American Review* saw the light of day in 1815—the year of the triumph at New Orleans. Even American painters increasingly celebrated the glories of American landscapes on their canvases.

Evidences of the new nationalistic spirit could be seen in many other theaters. A more handsome national capital began to rise from the ashes of Washington—a capital fit to symbolize our prospective greatness. The army was expanded to 10,000 men, even though this number was hardly adequate for a serious emergency. Old fears that our liberties might be crushed by a standing army largely melted away in the warm sun of the new nationalism.

The navy, for a time at least, also received reasonably satisfactory financial support. It further covered itself with glory in 1815, when the heroes of the late war administered a thorough beating to the piratical plunderers of North Africa. These gratifying victories, encouraged by the spirit of nationalism, further inflamed the spirit of nationalism.

The rising tide of nation-consciousness also touched finance. The War of 1812 had demonstrated the folly of permitting the Bank of the United States to expire in 1811, on the very eve of hostilities. Weak state banks, responding to the vacuum, had seemingly sprung up beside every village pump. The country was flooded with depreciated banknotes, which had weakened the national Treasury and had hampered the war effort.

A new Bank of the United States, in response to these obvious needs, was voted by Congress in 1816. It was modeled on the first one but had a total capital of $35,000,000—three and one-half times that of the original institution. The Jeffersonian Republicans, taught a painful lesson during the war, supported the revived institution. In fact, they cleverly but inconsistently borrowed the same arguments for a bank that Hamilton had used against Jefferson in 1791. The Federalist minority in Congress, opposing Republican measures with its dying gasps, no less inconsistently denounced the Federalist-spawned Bank as unconstitutional.

The Second Bank of the United States unfortunately started off on a less favorable foot than the First. Badly managed in its early years, it finally settled down and contributed richly to the economic life of the country. The "moneyed monster," as it was branded by its enemies, further broadened nationalism as it thrust its numerous branches out across state boundaries.

Industrial Nationalism

Nationalism likewise manifested itself in manufacturing. Patriotic Americans took pride in the numerous factories that had recently mushroomed forth, largely as a result of the self-imposed embargoes, followed by the hostilities with Britain.

When the war ended in 1815, British competitors ruthlessly undertook to recover lost ground. They began to dump the contents of their bulging warehouses on the United States, often cutting their prices below cost in an effort to strangle the American war-baby factories in the cradle. The infant industries bawled lustily for protection. To many red-blooded Americans it seemed as though the British, having failed on the battlefield to crush our fighters, were now seeking to crush our factories.

A nationalistic Congress responded by passing the path-breaking Tariff of 1816. The legislators were impressed with the desirability of saving the new industries for the national defense, while at the same time promoting the general welfare. The Tariff of 1816, significantly, was the first in our history whose aims were primarily protective. Its rates—roughly 20% to 25% on the value of dutiable imports—were not high enough to provide completely adequate safeguards, but the law was a noteworthy beginning. A strongly protective trend was started, and simultaneously the appetites of the war-stimulated industries were whetted.

The battle in Congress over the Tariff of 1816 reflected North-South sectional crosscurrents. Thirty-four-year-old Representative John C. Calhoun of South Carolina—slender, handsome, black-haired, intense, and intellectual—played a stellar role in the debates. A recent War Hawk and an ardent nationalist, he supported the tariff bill with all his eloquence and vigor. In 1816 there was some likelihood that the destiny of his native South lay in manufacturing, as well as in the intensive cultivation of King Cotton. But within a few years Calhoun became a relentless foe of a highly protective tariff. He sadly concluded that it was being used to enrich a few Yankee manufacturers, rather than to build up the economic self-sufficiency and well-being of the entire nation.

House Vote on Tariff of 1816

	For	Against
New England	17	10
Middle States	44	10
West (Ohio)	4	0
South and Southwest	23	34
	88	54

(NOTE: Even in South Carolina, Calhoun's state, the vote in favor of the bill was 4 to 3.)

Calhoun encountered a worthy adversary in Daniel Webster of New Hampshire, also thirty-four. Stocky, beetle-browed, and dark-haired, "Black Dan" Webster eloquently opposed the highly protective duties of the Tariff of 1816. He took this stand even though he was later to be a burning nationalist and an ardent champion of high protection. The explanation is simple. Manufacturing in New England had not yet pushed shipping into a back seat, and the shippers of Webster's New Hampshire district feared that a tariff wall would interfere with their carrying trade. New England, though favoring protection, was not yet completely willing to exchange the mainsail for the loom.

The new nationalism was further highlighted by a grandiose plan of

Henry Clay for developing a profitable home market. Still radiating the nationalism of War Hawk days, he threw himself behind a kind of house-that-Jack-built scheme known by 1824 as the American System. First, there would be the protective tariff, behind which Eastern manufacturing would flourish. Revenues gushing from the tariff would provide funds for roads and canals, especially in the fast-developing Ohio Valley. Through these new arteries of transportation would flow foodstuffs and raw materials from the South and West to the North and East. In return, a stream of manufactured goods would flow from the North and East to the South and West.

The wedding of tariff revenues to internal improvements looked promising on paper. The entire country would prosper, while state boundaries would tend to become mere surveyors' lines. The nation would grow more self-sufficient, and under the warm glow of prosperity the spirit of nationalism would deepen.

Road Blocks to Internal Improvements

The eloquent demands of Henry Clay and others for internal improvements struck a responsive chord with the public. The recent attempts to invade Canada had all failed partly because of oath-provoking roads—or no roads at all. Men who have dug wagons out of hub-deep mud do not quickly forget their blisters and backaches. The outcry for better transportation, rising most noisily in the raw West, was one of the most striking aspects of the nationalism inspired by the War of 1812.

Hope for more roads and canals came from an unexpected source. The Second Bank of the United States had been required to pay the federal government a bonus of $1,500,000 for its privileges. Calhoun, seeking to divert this sum to internal improvements, induced Congress in 1817 to pass the Bonus Bill, under which the Bank money would be parceled out to the states. But President Madison sternly vetoed this hand-out measure. In his view, the spending of federal funds for internal improvements within the individual states—but not across state lines—was a direct violation of the Constitution.

This anti-improvement veto threw a wet blanket over the new spirit of nationalism. Madison's successor, President Monroe, generally followed the same line of negative reasoning—with the same disheartening results. The individual states, though lacking sufficient resources, were forced to venture ahead with building programs of their own. The most notable of these was the Erie Canal, triumphantly completed by New York in 1825. (See pp. 309 ff.)

On the transportation question, the Jeffersonian Republicans were not consistently inconsistent. On all other important problems, they were at last prepared to gulp down the Hamiltonian doctrine of loose construction. Madison and Monroe, political heirs of Jefferson, could easily have argued that roads and canals solely within the states contributed to the economic and social welfare of the country as a whole, while bolstering the common defense. But on this issue their consciences became tender, and instead they timidly recommended an appropriate constitutional amendment. It was never enacted.

The enfeebled Federalists, now strict constructionists, could grudgingly applaud the vetoes of the Jeffersonian Republican Presidents. New England, in particular, strongly opposed federally constructed roads and canals, for such outlets would further drain away its population and create competing states beyond the mountains.

The Era of Good Feelings

James Monroe—tall, courtly, and mild-mannered—was nominated in 1816 by the Republicans. They thus undertook to continue the so-called "Virginia Dynasty" of Washington, Jefferson, and Madison. The anemic Federalists ran a candidate for the last time in their checkered history, but he was crushed by 183 electoral votes to 34.

The death of the once-proud Federalist Party was due to various diseases, shortcomings, and misfortunes. The list would include its disgraceful war record; its inability to choke down the new nationalistic program; and the borrowing of its tenets by the Jeffersonians. Many former Federalists followed their stolen principles into the opposition camp; others gradually crawled away to the political graveyard. The irony is that the original Hamiltonians, while the party of the "ins," had been conspicuously nationalistic; now the party of the "outs," they opposed the nationalism of the Republicans.

In James Monroe, the man and the times most auspiciously met. As the last President to wear an old-style cocked hat, he straddled two generations: the bygone age of Washington and the Founding Fathers; the new age of nationalism and militant Americanism. Never brilliant, and probably not great, the serene Virginian with gray-blue eyes was in intellect and personal force the weakest of our first eight Presidents. But the times called for sober administration, not heroics. And Monroe was an experienced, level-headed executive, with an ear-to-the-ground talent for interpreting popular rumblings.

The newly born nationalism was further cemented by a good-will tour that Monroe undertook early in 1817, ostensibly to inspect military defenses. He pushed as far north as the New England states, and then westward to Detroit, viewing en route the Niagara Falls. Even in Federalist New England, "the enemy's country," he received a heart-warming welcome; and the Boston *Centinel* was so far carried away as to announce that an "Era of Good Feelings" had been ushered in. This pleasant phrase since then has been commonly used to describe the administration of Monroe.

The "Era of Good Feelings," unfortunately, was something of a misnomer. It is true that considerable tranquillity and prosperity smiled upon the early years of Monroe, but the period was a troubled one. The burning issues of the tariff, the bank, internal improvements, and the sale of public lands were being hotly contested. Sectionalism was crystallizing, and the conflict over slavery was beginning to raise its ugly head.

The vanquished Federalist Party was breathing its dying gasps, leaving the field to the triumphant Republicans. But where there is only one party, or where one of the parties enjoys an overwhelming majority, the tendency is for factions to develop and fight among themselves. By the early 1820's there was an Era of Inflamed Feelings. Political giants—men like Clay, Calhoun, Jackson, and John Quincy Adams—were elbowing for power and championing the clashing economic interests of their respective sections.

The Curse of Hard Times

Much of the "goodness" went out of the "good feelings" in 1819, when a devastating panic descended. It brought deflation, depression, bankruptcies, bank failures, unemployment, soup kitchens, and overcrowded pesthouses known as debtors' prisons.

This was the first of the fearsome national panics since Washington took office. It was to be followed by a succession of others every twenty or so years, in what seemed an inevitable cycle. Many factors contributed to

HARD TIMES IN OHIO
A satire on Western migration, from a pamphlet of 1819.
American Antiquarian Society, Worcester, Massachusetts

the catastrophe of 1819, but looming large among them was overspeculation in Western lands. The Bank of the United States, through its Western branches, had become deeply involved in this popular type of outdoor gambling.

The financial paralysis of the panic, which lasted in some degree for several years, was a rude setback to the nationalistic ardor. The various parts of the country tended to drift back toward the old sectionalism, as they concentrated on bailing themselves out as best they could. The West was especially hard hit. When the pinch came, the Bank of the United States forced the weak ("wildcat") western banks to the wall, and foreclosed mortgages on countless farms. All this was technically legal but politically unwise. In the eyes of the western debtor, the Bank soon became a kind of Financial Devil.

A more welcome child of the panic was new legislation for the public domain. The sorry plight of the Western farmer, combined with the evils of land speculation, had laid bare the inadequacies of the Land Act of 1800, as amended in 1804. By its terms, the pioneer could buy a minimum of 160 acres at $2.00 an acre over a period of four years, with a down payment of $80. When hard times came, whole communities would default on their installments. The new Land Act of 1820 lightened the burden somewhat, for it permitted the buyer to secure 80 virgin acres at a minimum of $1.25 an acre in cash—for a total cost of $100. There was less acreage but less outlay.

Backwashes from the Panic of 1819 were to be found also in the social and political world. Attention was directed to the inhumanity of imprisoning debtors, for in extreme cases, often overplayed, mothers were torn from their infants for owing a few dollars. Agitation for abolishing imprisonment for debt was increased in a number of states. Though ultimately helping the debtor, the panic bore especially hard on the one-suspender men, East and West, and helped cultivate the seedbed for Jacksonian democracy.

Growing Pains of the West

The West, out of which had ridden the super-patriotic War Hawks of 1812, was by far the most nationalistic of the sections. Being new, it had no long-established states'-rights tradition. It had early learned to focus its eyes on the national government, from which it had secured most of its land, directly or indirectly. It was a mixing bowl within the huge American melting pot, for on the frontier men from all the sections rubbed elbows.

Marvelous indeed had been the onward march of the West, for nine new frontier states had joined the original thirteen between 1791 and 1819. With a view to preserving the North-South sectional balance, most of these commonwealths had been admitted alternately, one free and another slave. (See Admission of States, in Appendix.)

Why this breath-taking expansion? Fundamentally, there was the generations-old westward movement, which had been going on since early colonial days. In addition, the siren call of new cheap lands—"the Ohio fever"—had a special appeal to immigrants from Europe. Quaintly garbed newcomers from abroad were beginning to shuffle down the gangplanks in impressive numbers, especially after the war of embargoes and bullets had ended. Land exhaustion in the older tobacco states, where the soil was "mined" rather than cultivated, likewise propelled men westward. Glib-tongued speculators, dangling promises of small down payments, made easier the purchase of new holdings.

The Western boom was stimulated by additional developments. The acute distress of the embargo years turned many saddened faces toward the setting sun. The crushing of the Indians in the Northwest and South, by General Harrison and General Jackson, quieted the frontier and opened up huge new tracts. The building of highways improved the land routes to the Ohio Valley. Noteworthy was the Cumberland Road, begun in 1811, which ran ultimately from western Maryland to Illinois. The employment of the first steamboat on Western waters, also in 1811, gradually heralded a new era in upstream navigation.

But the West, despite the continuous inflow of settlers, was still weak in population and influence. Not potent enough politically to make its demands heard, it was forced to ally itself with sister sections. Thus strengthened, it demanded cheap acreage, and partially achieved its goal in the Land Act of 1820. It demanded cheap transportation, and slowly got it, despite the constitutional qualms of the Presidents and the hostility of diehard Easterners. Finally, it demanded cheap money, issued by its own "wildcat" banks, and fought the powerful Bank of the United States to attain its goal.

Slavery and the Sectional Balance

Sectional tensions were glaringly revealed in 1819, when the territory of Missouri knocked on the doors of Congress for admission as a slave state. This fertile and well-watered area contained sufficient population to warrant statehood. But the House of Representatives threw a monkey wrench into the plans of the Missourians by passing an inflammatory amendment. It decreed that no more slaves should be brought into Missouri, and also provided for the gradual emancipation of children born to slave parents already there. A gradually mounting roar of anger burst from slaveholding Southerners. They were joined by many depression-cursed pioneers who favored unhampered expansion of the West, and by many Northerners, especially members of the dying Federalist Party, who were eager to play politics.

The South saw in the Missouri amendment an ominous threat to the sectional balance. When the Constitution was adopted in 1788, the North and South were running neck and neck in wealth and population. But with every passing decade the North was becoming wealthier and more thickly settled—a population advantage reflected in an increasing Northern majority in the House of Representatives. Yet in the Senate, with eleven states free and eleven slave, the Southerners had maintained equality. They were therefore in a good position to thwart any Northern effort to interfere with slavery where it existed, and they did not want to lose this advantage, twelve to eleven.

The future of the slave system also caused Southerners profound concern. Missouri was the first state entirely west of the Mississippi River to be carved out of the Louisiana Purchase, and the Missouri emancipation amendment might set a damaging precedent for all the rest of the area. Even more disquieting was another possibility. If Congress could abolish the "peculiar institution" in Missouri, might it not attempt to do likewise in the older states of the South? The wounds of the Constitutional Convention of 1787 were once more torn open.

Ugly moral questions also protruded, even though the overshadowing issue was political and economic balance. A small but growing group of anti-slavery agitators in the North, heirs of the Federalists, seized the occasion to raise an outcry against the evils of slavery. They were determined that the plague of human bondage, if they could possibly prevent it, should not spread to the virgin territories.

The Missouri Compromise

The deadlock was at length broken in 1820 by the time-honored American solution of compromise—actually a bundle of three compromises. Henry Clay of Kentucky, gifted conciliator, played a leading role. Congress agreed to admit Missouri as a slave state. But at the same time free-soil Maine, which until then had been a part of Massachusetts, was admitted as a separate state. The balance between North and South was thus kept at twelve states each, and remained there for fifteen years. Although Missouri was permitted to retain slaves, all future bondage was prohibited in the Louisiana Purchase territory north of the line of 36° 30′ —the southern boundary of Missouri.

This horse-trading adjustment was essentially a fair one, though denounced by extremists on each side as a "dirty bargain." Both North and South yielded something; both gained something. The South won the prize of Missouri as an unalloyed slave state. The North won the concession that Congress could control or forbid slavery in the remaining territories. More gratifying to many Northerners was the fact that the immense area north of 36° 30′, except Missouri, was forever closed to the blight of slavery. Yet the restriction on future slavery in the territories was not unduly offensive to the slaveowners, partly because the northern prairie land did not seem adapted to slave labor.

Neither North nor South was acutely displeased, although neither was completely happy. As evidence, the Missouri Compromise lasted thirty-four years—a vitally important formative period in the life of the youthful

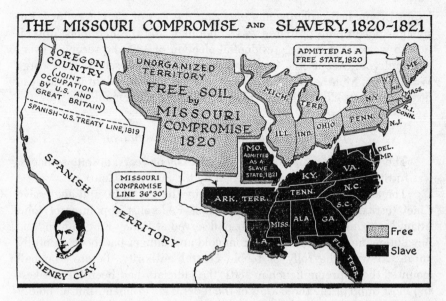

THE MISSOURI COMPROMISE AND SLAVERY, 1820–1821

republic—and during that time it preserved the shaky but sacred compact of the states. Yet the embittered dispute over slavery heralded the future breakup of the Union. It was a "fire bell in the night," wrote the aged but alert Jefferson.

The Missouri dispute proved to be another serious setback to nationalism, and a tremendous stimulus to sectionalism—in the North, South, and West. From this time forward the embattled South began to develop a nationalism of its own—a kind of sectional nationalism. Needing sectional reinforcements, it cast flirtatious eyes toward the adolescent West, which in turn was seeking allies.

Hotheads in both the North and South, numbering only a tiny minority, clamored for secession or a shooting showdown in 1820. But fortunately for the Union, hostilities were postponed. With every passing decade the North was becoming stronger in population, wealth, industry, and transportation—all of which added up to military strength.

The Missouri solution was admittedly a compromise—a partial surrender on both sides. Subsequent generations have tended to sneer at Henry Clay and the other architects of the settlement as weak men— "appeasers." Yet the fact should not be overlooked that compromise and statesmanship are often Siamese twins. In a free and peaceful association of once-sovereign states, no group of them could lord it over the others— that is, if they were all going to live together under the same roof. Without compromise there could have been no Constitution in 1787. Compromise made the Union in 1789; compromise saved the Union until 1860. When compromise broke down, the Union broke up.

The Missouri Compromise and the concurrent Panic of 1819 should have dimmed the political star of President Monroe. Certainly both unhappy events had a dampening effect on the Era of Good Feelings. But smooth-spoken James Monroe was so popular, and the Federalist opposition so weak, that in the presidential election of 1820 he received every electoral vote except one. Unanimity was an honor reserved for George Washington. Monroe, as it turned out, was the only President in American history to be re-elected after a term in which a major panic began.

John Marshall and Judicial Nationalism

The upsurging nationalism of the post-Ghent years, despite setbacks, was further reflected and strengthened by the Supreme Court.

The august tribunal was dominated by the tall, thin, and aggressive Chief Justice John Marshall, a "deathbed" Federalist appointee of John Adams' expiring administration. He had served at Valley Forge during the Revolution, and while suffering from cold and hunger had been painfully impressed with the folly of feeble central authority. Before Marshall mounted the Supreme Bench in 1801, the judiciary had been the weakest and most timid of the three arms of the federal government. But he boldly asserted the doctrine of judicial review of Congressional legislation in the case of Marbury vs. Madison (1803). And long before the end of his thirty-four years of service, he had made the judiciary perhaps the strongest branch of the national government.

Marshall, whose formal legal schooling had lasted only six weeks, was a judicial statesman rather than a strictly impartial judge. He examined a case through the colored lenses of his Federalist philosophy, and undertook to find legal precedents to support his Hamiltonian preconceptions. Sure of his ground, he wrote some of his most important decisions even before the lawyers had concluded their arguments.

In the vain hope of offsetting Marshall's Federalism, President Jefferson and his successors appointed Republicans to the Supreme Court. But by this time many Republicans had come to accept the Federalist ideal of a strong central government, and the masterful Marshall found it easy to lead his colleagues the rest of the way. The Jeffersonians raged, while Jefferson himself privately condemned the "twistifications" of his cousin, "the crafty chief judge." But Marshall pushed ahead inflexibly on his Federalist course, though bending slightly toward the end before the rising popular demands for a more democratic control of government.

For over three decades, the ghost of Alexander Hamilton spoke through the lanky, black-robed judge. As a shaper of the Constitution in the direction of a more potent central government, Marshall ranks as the foremost of the Moulding Fathers. As a wealthy businessman and land speculator, he instinctively shared Hamilton's preference for the propertied class. As a Virginia aristocrat, he likewise deplored democratic excesses, and resolutely opposed manhood suffrage and the rule of the unwashed masses.

Setbacks for States' Rights

One group of Marshall's decisions—perhaps the most famous—resulted in bolstering the power of the federal government at the expense of the states. A notable case in this category was McCulloch vs. Maryland (1819). The suit involved an attempt by the state of Maryland to destroy a branch of the Bank of the United States by imposing a heavy tax on its notes. John Marshall, speaking emphatically for the Court, declared the Bank constitutional by invoking the Hamiltonian doctrine of implied powers (see p. 157). At the same time, the Chief Justice bolstered federal authority and slapped at state infringements when he denied the right of Maryland to tax the Bank. Ringingly he declared "that the power to tax involves the power to destroy," and "that a power to create implies a power to preserve."

Two years later, in 1821, the case of Cohens vs. Virginia gave Marshall one of his greatest opportunities. The Cohens, found guilty by the Virginia courts of illegally selling lottery tickets, appealed to the Supreme Tribunal. Virginia won, in that the conviction of the Cohens was upheld. But she lost, in that Marshall resoundingly asserted the right of the Supreme Court to review the decisions of the state supreme courts in all questions involving the powers of the federal government. The states'-rights people were aghast.

Hardly less significant in Marshall's career was the celebrated "steamboat case," Gibbons vs. Ogden (1824). The suit grew out of an attempt by the state of New York to grant to a private concern a monopoly of water-borne commerce between New York and New Jersey. The Chief Justice sternly reminded the upstart state that the Constitution conferred on Congress alone the control of interstate commerce (see Art. I, Sec. VIII, para. 3). He thus struck a crushing blow at states' rights, while upholding the sovereign powers of the federal government. Interstate streams were thus cleared of judicial snags, while the departed spirit of Hamilton no doubt applauded.

Dikes against Democratic Excesses

Another group of Marshall's decisions, no less memorable, bolstered judicial barriers against democratic or demagogic attacks on property rights.

The notorious case of Fletcher vs. Peck (1810) arose when a Georgia legislature, swayed by bribery, granted 35,000,000 acres to private speculators. The next legislature, yielding to an angry public outcry, canceled the crooked transaction. But the Supreme Court, with Marshall presiding, decreed that the legislative grant was a contract (even though fraudulently secured), and that the Constitution forbids state laws "impairing" contracts (Art. I, Sec. X, para. 1; p. 983). The decision is perhaps most noteworthy as further protecting property rights against popular pressures. It is also one of the earliest clear assertions of the right of the Court to invalidate state laws conflicting with the federal Constitution.

A similar principle was upheld in the case of Dartmouth College vs. Woodward (1819), perhaps the best-remembered of Marshall's decisions. The college had been granted a charter by King George III in 1769, but the democratic New Hampshire legislature had seen fit to change it. Dartmouth appealed the case, employing as counsel its most distinguished alumnus, Daniel Webster ('01). The "Godlike Daniel" pulled out all the stops of his tear-inducing eloquence when he declaimed, "It is, sir, as I have said, a small college. And yet there are those who love it. . . ."

Marshall needed no dramatics in the Dartmouth case. He put the states firmly in their place when he ruled that the original charter must stand. It was a contract—and the Constitution protected contracts against state encroachments. The Dartmouth College decision had the fortunate effect of safeguarding business enterprise from domination by the states. But it had the unfortunate effect of creating a precedent which enabled chartered corporations, in later years, to escape the handcuffs of needed public control.

If John Marshall was a Moulding Father of the Constitution, Daniel Webster was an Expounding Father. Time and again he left his seat in the Senate, stepped downstairs, and there expounded his federalistic and nationalistic philosophy before the Supreme Bench. The cadaverous Chief Justice, so Webster reported, approvingly drank in the familiar arguments as a baby sucks in its mother's milk. The two men dovetailed with each other. Webster's classic speeches in the Senate, challenging states' rights and nullification, were largely repetitions of the arguments that he had earlier presented on numerous occasions before a sympathetic Supreme Court.

During Marshall's judicial reign, manhood suffrage was flowering and America was veering—perhaps too sharply—toward stronger popular control. The Chief Justice stoutly held the judicial dike against these upwashing democratic trends. Almost singlehanded, he shaped the Constitution along conservative, centralizing lines that ran somewhat counter to the new spirit of the century.

The decisions of John Marshall are felt even today. In this sense his nationalism was the most tenaciously enduring of the era. Even after the masses had won control under President Andrew Jackson, they could not successfully assault the highest towers of the judicial fortress. While bolstering the federal union and nascent nationalism, Marshall checked the excesses of popularly elected state legislatures, and thus stabilized business. Through him, the conservative Hamiltonians triumphed from the tomb.

Nationalism in Foreign Affairs

The burning nationalism of the years after the War of 1812 was likewise reflected in the shaping of foreign policy. To this end, the nationalistic President Monroe teamed with his nationalistic Secretary of State, John Quincy Adams, the cold and scholarly son of the cold and scholarly ex-President. The younger Adams, a statesman of the first water, happily rose above the ingrown Federalist sectionalism of his native New England.

To its credit, the Monroe administration succeeded in negotiating with England the much underrated Treaty of 1818. This multi-sided agreement disposed of some of the unfinished business left piled on the peace table at Ghent. For one thing, the Newfoundland fisheries quarrel had continued to bob up, and the new pact achieved a temporary settlement when the Americans were permitted to share coveted privileges with their Canadian cousins. In addition, the treaty makers agreed to define the vague northern limits of Louisiana. Henceforth the boundary would run along the 49th parallel to the Rocky ("Stony") Mountains.

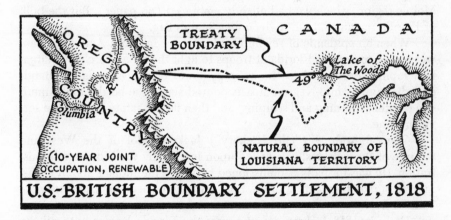

U.S.-BRITISH BOUNDARY SETTLEMENT, 1818

The British-American negotiators, at the same time, discussed the possibility of running the same dividing line on to the Pacific. But agreement was then impossible. The Treaty of 1818 consequently provided for a ten-year joint occupation of the untamed Oregon Country, without surrender of the rights or claims of either America or Britain. With time on the side of an awesomely growing United States, the postponement of the Oregon dispute foreshadowed a final decision favorable to American demands.

To the south lay semi-tropical Spanish Florida, thrust like a giant thumb into the Gulf of Mexico. This coveted peninsula, so red-blooded Americans believed, occupied a part of the map which geography and Providence had destined for the United States. Already we had nibbled

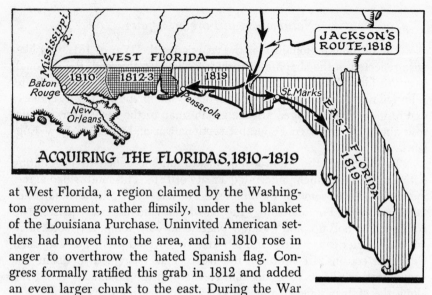

ACQUIRING THE FLORIDAS, 1810–1819

at West Florida, a region claimed by the Washington government, rather flimsily, under the blanket of the Louisiana Purchase. Uninvited American settlers had moved into the area, and in 1810 rose in anger to overthrow the hated Spanish flag. Congress formally ratified this grab in 1812 and added an even larger chunk to the east. During the War of 1812 with Britain (Spain's ally), a small American army seized the Mobile region, which we had already embraced (on paper). But the bulk of Florida remained, tauntingly, under Spain's flag.

When an epidemic of revolutions broke out in South America, Spain was forced to denude Florida of troops to fight the rebels. A chaotic situation rapidly developed in the swampy Land of the Everglades. Bands of Indians and white-Negro outcasts poured across the border into American territory, burning and scalping, and then fled to safety behind the surveyor's line.

General Andrew ("Old Hickory") Jackson, idol of the West and scourge of the redskins, was called upon in 1817 by the Monroe administration. He was formally commissioned to punish the Indians and, if necessary, to pursue them into Florida. But he was to respect all posts under the Spanish flag.

Early in 1818 Jackson swept across the Florida border with all the fury of an avenging angel. He hanged two Indian chiefs without trial, and, after hasty military trials, executed two British subjects for assisting the Indians. He also seized the two most important Spanish posts in the area, St. Marks and Pensacola, and deposed the Spanish governor, who perhaps escaped hanging only by good luck.

The Florida Swap

Jackson had clearly exceeded his instructions from Washington, unclear though they may have been. By dishonoring the Spanish flag, he had been guilty of a hostile act. By putting to death two British subjects who had a better right than he to be in Florida, he had caused a vengeful outcry for war to rise from British hotheads. With difficulty a sane London government quieted the jingoes.

President Monroe in alarm consulted his Cabinet. All members were for disavowing or disciplining the over-zealous Jackson—all except the lone wolf John Quincy Adams, who refused to howl with the pack. An ardent patriot and nationalist, the flinty New Englander finally won the others over to his point of view. Far from apologizing, he took the offensive and emphatically informed Spain that she had violated the Spanish-American Treaty of 1795 by not suppressing the outlaws of Florida. He then insisted that the alternatives were for the Spaniards to control the area (a task which they admitted was impossible) or cede it to us (a course which was galling to their pride).

Again Spain's distresses, both at home and in her rebellious Latin American colonies, operated to America's advantage. The Spaniards now perceived that they were going to lose Florida anyhow. They wisely decided to sell the alligator-infested area while they could get something for it, rather than give it away after a humiliating and costly war.

The Florida Purchase Treaty of 1819, so called, was mislabeled. It involved much more than Florida. The western boundary of the Louisiana territory, hitherto vague, was made to zigzag along the Rockies to the 42d parallel. The line then turned due west to the Pacific, to separate Oregon from Spanish holdings. Texas, although claimed by the United States under the elastic blanket of the Louisiana Purchase, was excluded by the new boundaries from American jurisdiction. The vast plains of Texas were more important to Spain than was fast-slipping Florida; Florida was more immediately important to the United States. Texas could come later—and did.

In 1819 Spain, in effect, ceded Florida to the United States in exchange for our yielding dubious pretensions to Texas. We also agreed to assume claims for damages in the sum of $5,000,000—uncollectible claims which our citizens had filed against the Spanish government. Spain lost Florida, but saved face. She also avoided losing $5,000,000, and preserved Texas—temporarily.

When the Spanish-American pact of 1819 was signed, it seemed like a fair bargain, even though Western-minded American patriots decried the surrender of Texas. By one stroke of the pen, we ended protracted friction with Spain, rounded out our continental domain, and gave another boost to swelling national pride.

The Menace of Monarchy

After the Napoleonic nightmare, the rethroned autocrats of Europe banded together in a kind of monarchical protective association. Determined to restore the good old days, they undertook to stamp out the democratic tendencies that had mushroomed from soil richly manured by the ideals of the French Revolution. The world must be made safe *from* democracy.

The crowned autocrats acted promptly. With complete ruthlessness, they smothered the embers of rebellion in Italy (1821) and in Spain (1823). According to the European rumor-factory, the despots were also gazing across the Atlantic for a new world to enchain. Russia, Austria, Prussia, and France, acting in partnership, would presumably send powerful fleets and armies to the revolted colonies of Spanish America, and there restore the thick-headed Spanish King to his ancestral domains. At any rate, this was the gossip.

Clear-thinking Americans were alarmed. Sympathetic to democratic revolutions everywhere, they had cheered when the Latin American republics rose from the ruins of monarchy. Americans feared that if the European powers intervened in the New World, the cause of republicanism would suffer irreparable harm. The physical security of the United States—the Mother Lode of democracy—would be endangered by the proximity of powerful and unfriendly forces.

The southward push of the Russian Bear, from the chill region now known as Alaska, had already publicized the menace of monarchy to North America. In 1821 the Czar of Russia issued a decree extending

THE WEST AND NORTHWEST 1819-1824

Russian jurisdiction over one hundred miles of the open sea down to the line of 51°, an area which embraced most of the coast of present-day British Columbia. The energetic Russians had already established trading posts as far south as the entrance to San Francisco Bay, and the fear prevailed in the United States that they were planning to cut us off from California, our prospective window on the Pacific Ocean.

Great Britain, Mistress of the Seas, was now beginning to play a lone-hand role on the complicated international stage. In particular, she rebelled against going along with the Continental European powers in crushing the newly won liberties of the Spanish-Americans. The revolutionists had thrown open their monopoly-bound ports to outside trade, and British shippers, as well as the Americans, had found the profits sweet.

Accordingly, in August, 1823, George Canning, the haughty British Foreign Secretary, approached our minister in London with a startling proposition. Would not the United States join with Britain in a joint declaration, specifically warning the European despots to keep their hands off the Latin American republics? The American minister, lacking instructions, referred this fateful scheme to his superiors in Washington.

Mr. Monroe and His Doctrine

Reactions in America to the Canning proposal varied. The intimate advisers of President Monroe, including the aged Jefferson and Madison, recommended that we lock arms with the hitherto distrusted Mother Country. The one notable exception was again the lone-wolf nationalist, Secretary Adams, who was hardheaded enough to beware of Britons bearing gifts. Why should the lordly British, with the mightiest navy afloat, need America as an ally—an America which had neither naval nor military strength? Such a union, argued Adams, was undignified—like a tiny "cockboat in the wake of the British man-of-war."

Adams, ever alert, thought that he detected the joker in the Canning proposal. The British feared that the aggressive Yankee would one day seize Spanish territory in the Americas—perhaps Cuba—which would jeopardize England's possessions in the Caribbean. If Canning could seduce the United States into joining with him in support of the territorial integrity of the New World, our own hands would be morally tied.

A self-denying alliance with Britain would not only hamper American expansion, concluded Adams, but it was unnecessary. He had good reason to suspect that the European powers had not agreed upon any definite plans for invading the Americas. In any event, the British navy would not permit the hostile fleets to come, because the South American markets had to be kept open at all costs for English merchants. It was presumably safe for Uncle Sam, behind the protective wooden petticoats of the British navy, to blow a defiant, nationalistic blast at all Europe. The distresses of the Old World again set the stage for another American diplomatic victory.

The Monroe Doctrine was born late in 1823, when the nationalistic Adams won the nationalistic Monroe over to his way of thinking. The President, in his regular annual message to Congress of December 2, 1823, incorporated an emphatic warning to the European powers. Its two basic features were (1) non-colonization and (2) non-intervention.

Monroe first directed his verbal blast at the lumbering Russian Bear in the Northwest. With emphatic tones he proclaimed, in effect, that the era of colonization in the Americas had ended, and that henceforth there would be a permanently closed season. What the great powers had they might keep, but neither they nor any other Old World country might seize or otherwise acquire more. This lofty declaration was later resented by those nations, notably Germany and Italy, that were ununified and hence unable to take out colonial hunting licenses until late in the century.

Monroe simultaneously sounded a blast against foreign intervention. He was clearly concerned with regions to the south, where fears were felt for the newly fledged Spanish-American republics. The President bluntly warned the crowned heads of Europe to keep their hated monarchical systems out of this hemisphere. In return, the United States would not intervene in the war that the Greeks were then fighting against the Turks for their independence.

Monroe's Dictum Abroad

The ringing declaration of Monroe quickened the patriotic pulse of nationalistic young America. We found it exhilarating, even though we had no effective army or navy, to shake our collective fists at all the European despots and loudly warn them to stay away. While gratifying our national pride and striking a blow for democratic rule, we were also striking a blow for the "Almighty Dollar," as represented by the freshly opened Latin American markets.

Reactions in England were mixed. The British press, likewise savoring the juicy Latin American markets, was generally favorable to Monroe's forceful warning. But Canning was irked, for he perceived that the Monroe Doctrine was aimed at possible land grabbing by Britain, as well as by Europe. "Hands Off" applied to all outside powers, including proud Britain. As two later poets had Monroe say to the powers:

> "With what you have, we have no quarrel.
> We only draw one simple moral
> From Labrador to Darien
> And South to Horn and back again,
> *'These gates are shut. Respect these gates.'*
> Yours truly,
>   The United States." *

---

* Rosemary and Stephen Vincent Benét, *A Book of Americans* (Rinehart and Company, copyright 1933), p. 57. Reprinted by permission.

The ermined monarchs of Europe were angered. Having resented the incendiary American experiment from the beginning, they were now deeply offended by Monroe's high-flown pronouncement—all the more so because of the gulf between our loud pretensions and our physical strength. But though offended by the upstart Yankee, the European powers found their hands tied, and their frustration increased their annoyance. Even if they had worked out definite plans for invading the Americas, they would have been helpless before the booming broadsides of the British navy.

The emphatic warning of Monroe, when issued, made little splash in the newly hatched republics to the south. It was evident that Uncle Sam was only secondarily concerned about his neighbors, because he was primarily concerned about defending himself against future invasion. Only a relatively few upper-class Latin Americans knew of the message, and these generally recognized that the oaken sides of the British navy—not the paper pronouncement of James Monroe—stood between them and a hostile Europe.

Monroe's message actually did not have much contemporary significance. Americans applauded it, and then forgot it as they turned back to the task of felling trees and Indians. Not until 1845 did President Polk revive the doctrine, and not until mid-century did it become an important national dogma.

The new doctrine of Monroe was not even necessary, in a narrow sense, when given to the world. Secretary Adams, in firm diplomatic notes, had already warned Russia against trespassing on the Northwest Coast. Even before Monroe's provocative message, the Czar had decided to retreat. This he formally did in the Russo-American Treaty of 1824, which fixed his southernmost limits at the line of 54° 40'—the present southern tip of the Alaska panhandle.

The danger of an invasion of Latin America by the European powers was actually not imminent in 1823. But this does not mean that the monarchs, if unhampered, could not in time have drawn up a blueprint for conquest. Aside from the presence of the British navy, they were dissuaded from making incursions in later years by other attractions and deterrents. Among attractions were the richer and easier pickings of Asia and Africa; among deterrents was the growing strength of the United States and its neighbors.

Monroeism in Retrospect

The Monroe Doctrine might more accurately have been called the Self-Defense Doctrine. James Monroe was concerned basically with the security of his own country—not of Latin America. The United States has never willingly permitted a powerful foreign nation to secure a foothold near its strategic Caribbean vitals. Yet in the absence of the British navy or other allies, the strength of the Monroe Doctrine has never been greater than our power to eject the trespasser. The Doctrine, as often noted, was just as big as our fleet—and no bigger. But the attaching of Monroe's name to the Self-Defense Doctrine has given it dignity, as well as the prestige that comes from a distinguished personage.

Monroe and Adams must share about equally the credit for the authorship of the so-called Monroe Doctrine. But its basic principles, in one form or another, had on the whole been earlier set forth by Washington, Jefferson, Hamilton, and others. Monroe and Adams merely collected and codified existing ideas, giving them a new emphasis and slant.

The Monroe Doctrine has had a long career of ups and downs. It was never law—domestic or international. It was not a pledge or an agreement, except with ourselves. It was merely a simple, personalized statement of the policy of President Monroe. What one President says, another may unsay. And Monroe's successors have ignored, revived, expanded, distorted, or magnified the original version, chiefly by adding interpretations. Like ivy on a tree, it has grown with our growth.

But the Monroe Doctrine in 1823 was largely an expression of the vibrant post-1812 nationalism suffusing the United States. Although directed at a specific menace in 1823, and hence a kind of period piece, the Doctrine proved to be the most famous of all the long-lived offspring of that nationalism. While giving vent to a spirit of patriotism, it simultaneously deepened the illusion of isolation. Many unthinking Americans falsely concluded, then and later, that we were in fact isolated from European dangers simply because we wanted to be, and because, in a nationalistic outburst, we had publicly proclaimed that we were going to be.

SELECT READINGS

An excellent introduction is GEORGE DANGERFIELD, *The Awakening of American Nationalism, 1815–1828* (1965) [paperback], which is related to his Pulitzer-prize *The Era of Good Feelings* (1952). Consult also M. N. ROTHBARD, *The Panic of 1819* (1962); GLOVER MOORE, *The Missouri Controversy, 1819–1821* (1953); E. S. CORWIN, *John Marshall and the Constitution* (1919); and A. J. BEVERIDGE, *The Life of John Marshall* (4 vols., 1916–1919). On the Monroe Doctrine the best single volume is DEXTER PERKINS, *A History of the Monroe Doctrine* (new ed., 1955) [paperback]. Related to the Doctrine is J. A. LOGAN, JR., *No Transfer: An American Security Principle* (1961). On Calhoun consult M. L. COIT's Pulitzer-prize *John C. Calhoun* (1950) [paperback] and C. M. WILTSE's more detailed *John C. Calhoun, Nationalist, 1782–1828* (1944). See also G. M. CAPERS, *John C. Calhoun, Opportunist* (1960); R. N. CURRENT, *John C. Calhoun* (1963); and S. F. BEMIS' Pulitzer-prize *John Quincy Adams and the Foundations of American Foreign Policy* (1949). Also *Harvard Guide*, Pt. IV.

13

The Emergence of Jacksonian Democracy

*The people's government made for the people, made by
the people, and answerable to the people.*

DANIEL WEBSTER, 1830, in reply to Hayne

The Miracle of the Ballot

DEMOCRACY had been something of a taint in the days of the Federalist
aristocrats. Mrs. George Washington, after a presidential reception, was
shocked to find a greasy mark on the wallpaper, left there, she was sure,
by an uninvited "filthy democrat."

But by the 1820's and 1830's, if not before, aristocracy was becoming
a taint, and democracy was becoming respectable. Lucky indeed was the
aspiring politician who could boast of birth in a log cabin. In 1840 Daniel
Webster publicly apologized for not being able to claim so lowly a birthplace, though quickly adding that his brother could.

The New Democracy, so called, was based on manhood suffrage
rather than on the old property qualifications. Snobbish bigwigs, unhappy
over the change, referred sneeringly to "coonskin Congressmen" and to
the enfranchised "bipeds of the forest." To them, the tyranny of King
Numbers was no less offensive than that of King George.

The frontier state of Vermont, admitted in 1791, was the first to place
the ballot in the hands of all adult white males. The trend continued,
notably in the West, where land was so easily obtained as to render almost
meaningless the old property qualification. The contagion of manhood
suffrage gradually crept back upon the more conservative East, which
already had made considerable progress in this direction.

Government *by* the *masses*—instead of government *of* them *by* the
upper classes—was finally introduced at the national level in the days of
Andrew Jackson. The Common Man was at last coming into his own: the
sturdy American who donned plain trousers rather than silver-buckled
knee breeches, who besported a plain haircut and a coonskin cap rather
than an ornate wig, and who wore no man's collar, often not even one of
his own. Instead of the old divine right of kings, America was now witness-
ing the divine right of the people.

243

The Reign of King Numbers

A debasement of the political tone was one unfortunate by-product of the New Democracy, commonly called Jacksonian democracy. A statesman was unable to elevate the unlettered masses to his own intellectual level. Rather, the masses dragged the politician down to the level of their own emotions and prejudices. Mudslinging frequently proved more effective than a sober discussion of issues. Candidates for office also made increasing use of banners, badges, parades, barbecues, free drinks, and baby-kissing. Yet cutthroat competition for public favor did have the virtue of "bringing out the vote."

Successful politicians were now forced to unbend and curry favor with the voting masses. Fatally handicapped was the candidate who appeared to be too clean, too well-dressed, too grammatical, too high-brow-ishly intellectual, too conspicuously fit. The Western belief was spreading that a man was well qualified for high office if he was a superior militia commander or a victorious Indian fighter, like Andrew Jackson, or even an outstanding hunter. The semi-literate Davy Crockett was elected to the legislature of Tennessee, mainly on the basis of his prowess with the rifle. Later he killed 105 bears in a single season, and his constituents began to talk of running him for the Presidency.

With the emergence of "nose-counting" democracy, the masses were demanding and securing a fuller measure of popular control. Jeffersonian democracy had preached that the people should be governed as little as possible; Jacksonian democracy argued that the people might govern as much as they liked. Members of the Electoral College, to an increasing degree, were being chosen directly by the people, rather than by state legislatures. Presidential nominations by a Congressional caucus, meeting secretly behind closed doors, were no longer in good odor. This procedure was now regarded as furtive, aristocratic, and subversive of good government. The delicate checks and balances among the three federal branches were weakened when the President was indirectly indebted to Congress for his exalted office.

New and more democratic methods of nominating presidential candidates would have to be found. In 1824 the voters, bawling "The People Must Be Heard" and "Down with King Caucus," turned against the candidate (Crawford) who had been selected by the Congressional clique. For a brief period nominations were made by some of the state legislatures. But these did not seem democratic either, and in 1831 the first of the circus-like national nominating conventions was held. Here the people exercised—or seemed to exercise—a higher degree of direct control, though regrettably their will has sometimes been thwarted by paunchy bosses in smoke-filled rooms.

Yet manhood suffrage, on balance, conferred incalculable benefits. The dignity of the common man was increased; and his greater personal responsibility led to a greater flowering of his talents. The national spirit was unshackled for marvelous achievements. If the masses made mistakes, they made them themselves and were not the victims of aristocratic domination. If at times they stumbled, they stumbled forward.

"Corrupt" Bargaining

The woods were full of presidential timber in 1824. Four candidates towered above the others: Andrew Jackson of Tennessee, the tall, silvermaned, and hollow-cheeked "Old Hero" of New Orleans; Henry Clay of Kentucky, the gamey and gallant "Harry of the West"; William H. Crawford of Georgia, a giant of a man, able though ailing; and John Quincy Adams of Massachusetts, highly intelligent, experienced, and aloof.

The four rivals had much in common. They were all outstanding figures; they were all strong nationalists; and they were all presumed to have roughly similar views on such burning issues as the tariff and internal improvements.

The results of the noisy campaign were interesting but confusing:

	Electoral Vote	Popular Vote
Jackson	99	153,544
Adams	84	108,740
Crawford	41	46,618
Clay	37	47,136

Jackson, the war hero, clearly had the strongest personal appeal, especially in the West. He polled almost as many popular votes as his next two rivals combined, but he failed to win a majority of the electoral vote. In such a deadlock the House of Representatives, as directed by the 12th Amendment (see Appendix), had to choose among the first three rivals. Clay was thus eliminated. But since he enjoyed all the influence of a popular Speaker of the House, he was in a position to help throw the election to the candidate of his choice.

Clay reached his fateful decision by a process of elimination. Crawford was out of the picture, having recently been prostrated by a paralytic stroke. Clay hated the "military chieftain" Jackson, who in turn bitterly resented Clay's public denunciation of his Florida foray in 1818. The only candidate left was the puritanical Adams, with whom Clay—a free-living gambler and duelist—had never established cordial personal relations. But the two men had much in common politically, because both were ardent nationalists and advocates of the American System. Shortly before the final balloting in the House, Clay met privately with Adams and assured him of his support.

The day of decision came early in 1825. The House of Representatives met amid tense excitement, with sick members being carried in on stretchers. On the first ballot, thanks largely to Clay's behind-the-scenes influence, Adams was elected President. A few days later, the victor announced that Henry Clay would be the new Secretary of State.

The Secretaryship of State was then the prize plum, even more so than today. Three of the four preceding Secretaries had reached the Presidency, and the high Cabinet office had come to be regarded as an almost certain runway to the White House. By allegedly dangling the Secretaryship as a bribe before Clay, the ungracious Adams, the second choice of the people, apparently defeated the first choice of the people.

Masses of angered Jacksonians, most of them common folk, raised a roar of protest against the "Corrupt Bargain," and the clamor continued for nearly four years. Jackson condemned Clay as the "Judas of the West," and John Randolph of Virginia publicly assailed the alliance between "the Puritan [Adams] and the black-leg [Clay]." Clay, outraged, responded with a challenge to a duel, the bloodless outcome of which proved nothing, except perhaps weak nerves and poor marksmanship.

No positive evidence has yet been unearthed to demonstrate that Adams and Clay entered into a formal bargain, corrupt or otherwise. But the outward circumstances were so damning as to render denials unconvincing. Even if a bargain had been struck, it was not necessarily corrupt, for deals of a similar nature are the stock in trade of politicians. But this "bargain," however innocent it may have been, differed from others in its apparent flouting of the popular will by both Adams and Clay. Both men erred, the one by offering the post under circumstances sure to arouse suspicion, the other by accepting it. The best that can be said of them is that neither avoided the appearance of evil.

A Puritan Misfit

John Quincy Adams was a chip off the old family glacier. Short, thick-set, and billiard-bald, he was even more frigidly austere than his distinguished father, John Adams. Shunning people, he often went for solitary swims, sometimes stark naked, in the Potomac River. Essentially a closeted thinker rather than a politician, he was irritable, sarcastic, and tactless. Yet few men have ever come to the Presidency with a more brilliant record in statecraft, especially in handling foreign affairs. John Quincy Adams ranks as one of our most successful Secretaries of State, yet one of our least successful Presidents.

A man of puritanical honor, Adams entered upon his four-year sentence in the White House smarting under charges of "bargain," "corruption," and "usurpation." Fewer than one-third of the voters had cast their ballots for him. As our first "minority President," he would have found it difficult to win popular support even under the most favorable conditions. Possessing almost none of the arts of the politician, he had achieved high office by commanding respect rather than by courting popularity. In an earlier era, an aloof Adams could win the votes of propertied men by sheer ability. But with the raw New Democracy in the driver's seat, a statesman without mass appeal could hardly hope for success at the polls.

Political spoilsmen annoyed Adams. Whether through high-mindedness or ineptitude, he resolutely declined to oust efficient officeholders in order to create vacancies for political supporters. During his entire administration he removed only twelve public servants from the federal payroll. Such stinginess caused countless Adams men to throw up their hands in despair. If the President would not reward party workers with political gravy, why should they labor to keep him in office?

Adams' nationalistic views involved him in further woes. The old Jeffersonian Republican party was breaking into fragments, most of which tended to coalesce around a common hatred of the Adams-Clay partnership. The flinty President refused to recognize that the popular tide was turning away from the post-Ghent nationalism toward states' rights and sectionalism. Confirmed nationalist that he was, Adams urged upon Congress in his first annual message the construction of roads and canals. He renewed George Washington's proposal for a national university, and went so far as to advocate federal support for an astronomical observatory, similar to Europe's more than 130 "lighthouses of the skies."

The public reaction to some of these proposals was prompt and unfavorable. To many workaday Americans grubbing out stumps, astronomical observatories seemed like a scandalous waste of public funds. The South in particular bristled up. If the federal government should take on such heavy financial burdens, it would have to continue its hated tariff duties. If it could meddle in local concerns like education and roads, it might even try to lay its lengthy hand on the "peculiar institution" of Negro slavery.

The land policy of Adams likewise antagonized the Westerners. They clamored for wide-open expansion, and were angered by the President's well-meaning attempts to curb feverish speculation in the public domain. The fate of the Cherokee Indians, who were about to be evicted from their fertile holdings in Georgia, generated additional bitterness. Ruggedly honest Adams, in attempting to deal fairly with the friendless redskins, further offended the West in general and the state of Georgia in particular. The governor of the Cracker State, threatening a resort to arms, successfully resisted the efforts of the Washington government to enforce federal authority. Another fateful chapter was thus written in the nullification of the national will.

Fumbling Foreign Affairs

If Adams was inept politically, he was deft diplomatically, and in foreign affairs he was expected to shine. But he quickly ran afoul of his old diplomatic adversary in London, George Canning. The clever Foreign

Secretary, still smarting from Secretary Adams' rebuff at the time of the Monroe Doctrine, apparently took peculiar delight in thwarting his recent antagonist at every turn.

Trade with the British West Indies continued to be a thorny issue. Ever since the United States had broken away from the Empire in 1776, this rich traffic had been officially closed, or subjected to annoying restrictions. When President Adams made a somewhat tactless attempt to induce the London government to reopen trade in 1826, Canning administered a stinging rebuff of his own.

Another bitter cup was the Panama Congress of 1826. This assemblage of the American republics was summoned by Simón Bolívar, leading hero of the South American wars for independence. Its major purpose was to discuss problems of defense and peaceful intercourse common to all the American republics. Secretary Henry Clay, a passionate pioneer in Pan-Americanism, eagerly accepted the invitation for the United States to attend. President Adams thereupon appointed two delegates. But at the same time he unnecessarily and unwisely sought confirmation by the Senate, as well as expense money from Congress.

The ensuing debate in Congress was both windy and ill-tempered. The foes of Adams and Clay united to denounce the Panama scheme, while isolationists decried the danger of foreign entrapments. The South, with an eye to its slave problem, was sensitive about sending delegates to a conference in which Negro representatives would be "putting on airs."

Adams finally won Congressional approval, but his victory was little better than a defeat. One of the delegates died en route. The other reached Panama after the high-sounding Congress, which had almost drowned in a sea of words, had adjourned without agreeing on anything of consequence. Hoots of derision were showered upon Adams' head. The tragedy is that the foes of the administration sacrificed a splendid opportunity for the United States to assume leadership of the Pan-American movement at the very outset.

Tariff Trickery

The tariff issue provided yet another hair shirt for Adams. Congress had come to grips with the problem in 1824, under President Monroe, when it increased the protective tariff of 1816. Formerly the general level had been 20% to 25% on the value of dutiable goods; now it was boosted to new heights of about 37%. But the woolen manufacturers, dissatisfied with their share of protection, clamored for higher rates.

The Jacksonites, seeking to unhorse Adams, seized this opportunity to play politics with the Tariff of 1828. They rigged up a bill that was seemingly more concerned with manufacturing a President than with protecting manufacturers. A part of their scheme was to push the duties as high as about 45% on the value of certain manufactured items. At the same time, a heavy tariff would be imposed on certain raw materials, notably wool. Such products were so urgently needed for manufacturing, especially in New England, that even this industrial section would presumably reject the entire measure. Adams, whose stronghold was New England, would thus be given another political black eye.

But the New Englanders spoiled this pretty little game. Though disliking the proposed new duties on raw materials, many of them were anxious to continue the principle of protection. As a consequence, enough of them choked down the dishonest Tariff of 1828 to force its passage. Daniel Webster, who had earlier fought the mild Tariff of 1816, and John C. Calhoun, who had sponsored it, had by this time completely reversed their positions. The future of New England clearly lay in the factory, rather than on the waves, while the destiny of the South lay in the cotton fields.

House Vote on Tariff of 1828 ("*Tariff of Abominations*")

[COMPARE 1816 TARIFF, PAGE 224.]

	For	Against	
New England	16	23	(manufacturers and shippers divided)
Middle States	57	11	(Pa., N.Y. for high protection)
West (Ohio, Ind., Ill., Mo.)	17	1	(pro-improvements and pro-tariff)
South (incl. La.)	3	50	(almost unanimously anti-tariff)
Southwest (Tenn., Ky.)	12	9	(divided)
Total	105	94	

The Southerners, as heavy consumers of manufactured goods, were shocked by the excessive rates of the Tariff of 1828. Hotheads promptly branded it the "Black Tariff" or the "Tariff of Abominations." Several Southern states adopted formal protests, and in South Carolina flags were lowered to half-mast. "Let the *New* England beware how she imitates the *Old*," cried one eloquent Carolinian who remembered 1776.

Why did the South, especially South Carolina, react so angrily against the tariff? The Old South—the seaboard area first settled—was the least flourishing of all the sections. The bustling Northeast was experiencing a boom in manufacturing; the expanding West was prospering from rising land values and a multiplying population; and the energetic Southwest was expanding into virgin cotton acreage. The overcropped lands of the Old South were petering out, and the price of cotton was falling sharply during these anxious years. John Randolph of Virginia grimly quipped that masters would soon cease to advertise for their fugitive slaves, and slaves would advertise for their fugitive masters. So the Old

South—unhappy and down at the heel—was seeking a scapegoat; and the tariff proved to be a convenient and plausible one.

The Tariff Yoke in the South

Southerners believed, not illogically, that the "Yankee tariff" discriminated against them. They sold their cotton and other farm produce in a world market completely unprotected by tariffs, and were forced to buy their manufactured goods in an American market heavily protected by tariffs.

The plight of the South may best be illustrated by a hypothetical case. Let us suppose that in 1828 an English manufacturer of footgear could sell his shoes in South Carolina at $1.25 a pair, whereas a Massachusetts factory would have to charge $1.50 for a pair of equal quality. The con-

TARIFF INEQUALITIES, NORTH AND SOUTH

The protective tariff under which the North grows fat and prosperous brings economic hardship to the South. *United States Weekly Telegram,* 1832

sumers in South Carolina would naturally buy the British footwear. But if a tariff of fifty cents a pair were levied on foreign shoes at the Charleston customhouse, the British shoes would cost $1.75 a pair. The Southerners, if economy-minded, would be forced to buy the Yankee product at $1.50. They would thus be taxed twenty-five cents on each purchase to support the shoe manufacturers of the North.

Towering tariff walls discourage imports. If a system of completely free trade had existed in 1828, the British would probably have bought more raw materials from those nations that consumed their manufactured goods. Rather than sail their ships away from American ports empty, they would have purchased more cotton, tobacco, and other products from the South. Little wonder that Southern leaders regarded the protective tariff as a foe of their economic development. On the other hand, they failed to recognize that a prosperous manufacturing Northeast contributed to their prosperity by consuming their cotton and other farm produce.

The South Carolinians took the lead in protesting against the new "Tariff of Abominations." Their legislature went so far as to publish in 1828, though without formal endorsement, a pamphlet known as "The South Carolina Exposition," which had been secretly written by John C. Calhoun, one of the few top-flight political theorists ever produced by America. As Vice-President of the United States he was forced to conceal his authorship of the document. "The Exposition" boldly denounced the recent tariff as unjust and unconstitutional. Going a stride beyond the Kentucky and Virginia resolutions of 1798, it bluntly and explicitly proposed that the states should nullify it—that is, they should declare it null and void within their borders.

Calhoun actually found himself caught in an awkward straddle. Still a Unionist and an ardent nationalist, he was also a Southern sectionalist. He therefore desperately sought a formula that would protect the minority in the South from the "tyranny of the majority" in the North and West. Seizing upon nullification, he undertook by this explosive solution to preserve the Union and prevent secession. He aimed not to destroy the Union, but to salvage it by quieting the fears of those forces that might one day destroy it.

Calhoun's "Exposition," at least in its immediate effects, was a false alarm. No other state joined South Carolina in her heated anti-tariff protest. But the disruptive theory of nullification was given further publicity, while the even more dangerous doctrine of secession was foreshadowed. South Carolina, as it turned out, was not then prepared to force the controversy to a showdown. The election of Carolina-born Andrew Jackson to the Presidency had occurred two weeks earlier, and the "Old Hero" —a fellow cotton planter and slaveowner—was expected to sympathize with the plight of the South.

"Whole Hog" for Jackson

The presidential campaign for Andrew Jackson had started early. It began on February 9, 1825, the day of John Quincy Adams' controversial election by the House, and continued noisily for nearly four years.

Even before the election of 1828, the temporarily united Republicans of the Era of Good Feelings had split into two camps. One was the National Republicans, with the ultra-nationalistic Adams as their standard-bearer. The other was the Democratic-Republicans, with the fiery Jackson heading their ticket. The rallying cries of the Jackson zealots were "Bargain and Corruption," "Huzza for Jackson," and "All Hail Old Hickory." The Jackson "hurrah boys" defiantly planted hickory poles for their elongated hero; the "Adamites" adopted the oak as the symbol of their oakenly independent candidate.

"Shall the people rule?" was the chief issue of 1828, at least in the eyes of Jacksonians. Their argument was that the will of the voters had been thwarted in 1825 by the backstairs "bargain" of Adams and Clay. The only way to right the wrong was to seat Jackson, who would then bring about "reform" by sweeping out the "dishonest" Adams gang. "Jackson and Reform" was widely mouthed as a slogan, while hickory brooms were brandished as tokens of a forthcoming clean sweep. Seldom has the public mind been so successfully poisoned against an honest and high-minded President.

Mudslinging reached a disgraceful level, partly as a result of the taste of the new mass electorate for bare-knuckle politics. Adams would not stoop to gutter tactics, but many of his adherents were less upright. They printed black-bordered handbills, shaped like coffins, recounting the numerous duels and brawls of Jackson, and trumpeting his hanging of six mutinous militiamen. "Old Hickory" was also branded an adulterer, which technically though innocently he had been. He had married an estimable woman, Rachel Robards, confident that her divorce had been granted. To the consternation of both, they discovered two years later that it had not been, and they made haste to correct the marital miscue.

Rachel Jackson was crushed by the vicious charges of adultery. She lived to see her husband win the Presidency, but she died—allegedly of a broken heart—before she could become First Lady of the Land. Jackson, devotedly attached to his wife, was convinced that his enemies had killed her. He never forgave them.

The Jackson men also hit below the belt. President Adams had purchased, with his own money and for his own use, a billiard table and a set of chessmen. In the mouths of rabid Jacksonites, these articles became "gaming tables" and "gambling furniture" for the "presidential palace." Much criticism was also unfairly directed at the large sums that Adams had received over the years in federal salaries, well earned though they had been.

The "Revolution" of 1828

General Jackson, accustomed to victory on the battlefields, was no less victorious at the ballot boxes. The popular tally was 647,286 votes for him, to 508,064 for Adams, with an electoral count of 178 to 83. Support for Jackson came mainly from the West and South, and to a considerable extent from the sweat-stained laborers of the Eastern seaboard. Generally speaking, the common people—though by no means all of them—voted for "Old Hickory." Adams won the backing of his own New England, and notably of the propertied "better elements" of the Northeast.

The election of 1828 has often been called, with exaggeration, the "Revolution of 1828." Actually, as in 1800, there was no upheaval or land-slide that swept out the incumbent. Adams, in fact, polled a respectable 44% of the popular vote. A considerable part of Jackson's support, more-over, was lined up by machine politicians, especially in New York and Pennsylvania, and not entirely among the leather-aproned artisans and other manual workers.

But the concept of a *political* revolution in 1828 is not completely farfetched. The large turnout of voters proved that the common people, es-pecially in the manhood-suf-frage states, now had the vote and the will to use it for their ends. The discontented West, with its numerous rustics and debtors, flocked enthusiasti-cally to the polls for Jackson. The results show that the po-litical center of gravity was beginning to shift away from the conservative seaboard East toward the up-and-com-ing new states across the mountains.

So in a broader sense the election was a "revolution," more so than in 1800. It was

PRESIDENTIAL ELECTION OF 1828

(With electoral vote by state)

Jackson – Democratic
Adams – National Republican
Divided

JACKSON

J.Q. ADAMS

a peaceful revolution, achieved by ballots instead of bullets, by counting heads instead of crushing them. "Shall the people rule?" cried the Jack-sonians. The answering roar seemed to say, "The people shall rule!" In the struggle between the poorer masses and the entrenched classes, the homespun folk scored a resounding triumph. Rejecting the candidate who lacked the common touch, they rejoiced as though they had been de-livered from some impending danger.

America hitherto had been ruled by an oligarchy of brains and wealth, whether aristocratic Federalist shippers or aristocratic Jeffersonian plant-ers. The victory of Jackson accelerated the transfer of national power from the countinghouse to the farmhouse, from the East to the West. If Jeffer-son had been the hero of the gentleman farmer, Jackson was the hero of the "dirt farmer." The plowholder was now ready to take over the govern-ment—*his* government.

Adams, though President-reject, still had before him an enviable public career. Ever high-minded, he did not deem it beneath his dignity to accept election to the House of Representatives from Massachusetts. There he served with conspicuous success for seventeen fruitful years. Affectionately known as the "Old Man Eloquent," he fought stalwartly for free government, free speech, free soil, and free men. A rough and savage debater, he finally was stricken in the House in 1848, at age eighty. His funeral was the greatest pageant of its kind that Washington had yet seen. Ironically, the popularity that had escaped him in life came to him in death.

The Advent of "Old Hickory"

Andrew Jackson to a considerable degree personified the New West. He reflected its individualism, its Jack-of-all-trades versatility, its opportunism, its energy, its directness, and its prejudices. He was a genuine folk hero. The backwoods preacher who cried that Jesus was "just another Andrew Jackson" reflected a not uncommon sentiment.

Jackson's upbringing was not of the best. Born a posthumous child in the Carolinas and early orphaned, "Mischievous Andy" grew up without parental restraints. As a youth, he displayed much more interest in brawling and cockfighting than in his scanty opportunities for reading and spelling. Although he ultimately learned to express himself in writing with vigor and clarity, his grammar was always rough-hewn and his spelling was unique, like that of many contemporaries. He sometimes misspelled a word two different ways in the same letter.

Jackson early had the foresight to emigrate "up West" to Tennessee, where a fighting man was more highly regarded than a writing man. There —through native intelligence, force of personality, and powers of leadership—he became a judge and a member of Congress. His passions were so terrible that on occasion he would choke into silence when he tried to speak. He won his greatest fame as a commander of militia troops, who dubbed him "Old Hickory" in honor of his toughness. Afflicted with a violent temper, he became involved in numerous duels, stabbings, and other frays. But, rough and forthright as democracy itself, he made things move.

Jackson was unique. He was the first President from the West, and the first without a college education, except Washington. He had risen from the masses, but he was not one of them, except insofar as he shared many of their prejudices. Essentially a frontier aristocrat, he owned many slaves, cultivated broad acres, and lived in one of the finest mansions in America—the Hermitage, near Nashville, Tennessee. More Westerner than Easterner, more country gentleman than common clay, he was hard to fit into a neat category.

> He's none of your old New England stock,
> Or your gentry-proud Virginians,

> But a regular Western fighting-cock
> With Tennessee opinions.*

Jackson, contrary to legend, did not create the New Democracy. Before 1828, he had not contributed a single significant idea to it. As a clever and extremely lucky opportunist, he was the beneficiary of the New Democracy, and rose into office on the crest of its wave.

While President, Jackson proved to be an unfailing storm center. As a former military man, he demanded prompt and loyal support from his subordinates. If one was not for him, one was against him. Cherishing strong ideas as to his constitutional prerogatives, he ignored the Supreme Court on several conspicuous occasions. He likewise defied or dominated Congress as few Presidents have done. His six predecessors had wielded

BORN TO COMMAND

OF VETO MEMORY

HAD I BEEN CONSULTED

KING ANDREW THE FIRST.

Jackson assailed as a tyrant who tramples underfoot the Constitution, the courts, and domestic welfare.
Houghton Library, Harvard

the veto ten times; during his two terms he employed it twelve times, including seven uses of the pocket veto—that is, retaining a bill unsigned

* Rosemary and Stephen Vincent Benét, *A Book of Americans* (Rinehart and Company, copyright 1933), p. 61. Reprinted by permission.

when the adjournment of Congress falls before the expiration of the constitutional ten-day period (see Art. I, Sec. VII, para. 2). Jackson's use of
the veto was perfectly legitimate, but his numerous enemies pilloried him
as "King Andrew the First."

The inauguration of Jackson symbolized the newly won ascendancy
of the masses. "Hickoryites" poured into Washington from far places,
sleeping on hotel floors or in hallways. They were curious to see their
hero take office, and perhaps to pick up a well-paying office for themselves. Nobodies mingled with notables as the White House, for the first
time, was thrown open to the multitude. A milling crowd of clerks, shopkeepers, Negroes, hobnailed artisans, and grimy laborers surged in, wrecking the china and furniture, and threatening the "people's champion" with
cracked ribs. Jackson was hastily spirited through a side door, and the
White House miraculously emptied itself when the word was passed that
huge bowls of punch had been placed on the lawns.

To strait-laced conservatives, the inaugural orgy in Washington
seemed like the end of the world. "King Mob" reigned triumphant as
Jacksonian vulgarity replaced Jeffersonian simplicity. Old ladies of both
sexes shuddered, drew their blinds, and recalled the opening mob scenes
of the French Revolution.

Nationalizing the Spoils System

The spoils system—that is, rewarding political supporters with public
office—was introduced into the federal government on a large scale under
President Jackson. A modest beginning had already been made under
Jefferson.

The basic idea was as old as politics. Its name came later from Senator Marcy's classic remark in 1832, "To the victor belong the spoils of the
enemy." The system had already secured a firm hold in New York and
Pennsylvania, where well-greased machines had been set up. Professional
politicians, by ladling out the "gravy" of office, had been able to make
politics a full-time business, rather than a side line.

A house cleaning of some sort in Washington was clearly needed. No
party overturn had occurred since the defeat of the Federalists in 1800,
and even that had not produced wholesale evictions. During the ensuing
twenty-eight years, festering evils had developed in the civil service. The
old colonial-system ideal of holding office during good behavior had bred
some incompetence and corruption, as well as considerable indifference
and insolence ("uncivil servants"). A few officeholders, their commissions
signed by President Washington, were lingering on into their eighties,
drawing breath and salary but doing little else.

Jackson fully shared the view of the New Democracy that "Every
man is as good as his neighbor"—perhaps "equally better." Since this was

believed to be so, and since the routine of office was also thought to be simple enough for any upstanding American to learn quickly, why encourage the development of an aristocratic, bureaucratic, officeholding class? Experience, of course, had some value. But alertness and new blood had more—at least in the eyes of Jacksonians.

The New Democracy also trumpeted the ideal of "rotation in office" —or "a turn about is fair play." Since experience was discounted, and since officeholding provided valuable training for citizenship, let as many citizens as possible feed at the public pie counter for a short time.

More Victors than Spoils

Elected as a reformer, Jackson believed that the swiftest road to reform was to sweep out the old Adams-Clay gang and bring in his own trusted henchmen. Furiously aroused against his foes, he agreed with a follower that the old Adams "barnacles" must "be scraped clean from the Ship of State."

The spoilsmen now had their inning. Office seekers hounded Jackson at every turn, and even invaded his privacy. In view of such pressures, it is remarkable that he removed so few incumbents rather than so many. During his eight years, only one-fifth of the old civil servants were dismissed, leaving more than 9000 out of the original 11,000. The "clean sweeps" were to come in later administrations.

Even so, a demoralizing practice was begun on a national scale. Insecurity replaced former security and discouraged many able citizens from entering the public service. Terrible hardships were worked on poor men with large families. One discharged employee cut his throat from ear to ear; another went raving mad. Fitness, merit, and the ideal of public service were subordinated, while the office was prostituted to political ends. The question was not "What can he do for the country?" but "What has he done for the party?" or "Is he loyal to Jackson?"

Scandal inevitably accompanied the new system. Men were appointed to high office who had openly bought their posts by campaign contributions. Illiterates, incompetents, and plain crooks were given positions of public trust. Samuel Swartwout, despite ample warnings of his untrustworthiness, was awarded the high-salaried post of Collector of the Customs of the Port of New York. Nearly nine years later he "Swartwouted out" for England, leaving his accounts more than a million dollars short.

Finally, the spoils system built up a smooth-running political machine. Its delicate gears were lubricated by contributions from expectant party members, and by percentage levies on the salaries of officeholders—a kind of political job-insurance. The system at length secured such a tenacious hold that more than half a century passed before its grip could be partially loosened.

Setbacks for Nationalism

Jackson's Cabinet was mediocre, and its members were used primarily as executive clerks. The only person of conspicuous ability was the smooth and keen-witted Secretary of State, Dutch-descended Martin Van Buren of New York, who shone as a gifted conciliator and wirepuller. A balding, sharp-featured little man, he was affectionately addressed by Jackson as "Matty." But he was known to his enemies as the "Little Magician."

The official Cabinet was privately supplemented by an extra-official cabinet. It grew out of Jackson's informal meetings with his boon companions, some of whom were newspapermen who kept him in touch with the fickle winds of public opinion. The enemies of the President branded these shirt-sleeved cronies as the Kitchen Cabinet. Subsequent generations have retained the picture of an uncouth clique gathering in the kitchen and spitting tobacco juice in the general direction of a pot-bellied stove. Actually, the group did not meet in the kitchen; its over-all influence has been grossly exaggerated; and it was not unconstitutional. The President is free to consult with such unofficial advisers as he desires.

The regular Cabinet was wrecked in 1831, as a result of the "Eaton malaria." Secretary of War Eaton had married the daughter of a Washington boardinghouse keeper, the attractive Peggy O'Neal, whom the tongue of scandal had perhaps unfairly linked with some of the male boarders. She was consequently snubbed by the ladies of Jackson's official family, conspicuous among whom was the blue-blooded wife of Vice-President John C. Calhoun. The President, whose own spouse had been done to death by scandalmongers, was chivalrously aroused against the defamers of Mrs. Eaton's chastity. With a zeal worthy of a better cause, he tried to force the social acceptance of the black-haired beauty. But the all-conquering general finally had to acknowledge defeat in the "Petticoat War" at the hands of the female phalanx.

The Eaton scandal played directly into the hands of Secretary Van Buren. An unencumbered widower, he further curried favor with Jackson by paying marked attention to Mrs. Eaton, whose physical charms lightened his self-imposed task. Jackson turned increasingly against Calhoun, and finally broke with him completely. The followers of the South Carolinian were purged from the Cabinet in 1831. Calhoun himself, resigning the Vice-Presidency the next year, entered the Senate as a champion of South Carolina.

It would be absurd to say that Peggy Eaton caused the Civil War. But up to this time Calhoun had publicly been a strong nationalist, despite his secret espousal of nullification in "The South Carolina Exposition" of 1828. As Vice-President, he thought himself in line for the Presidency after Jackson had served one term. The open break with "Old Hickory," though foreshadowed earlier, completely blighted his hopes. He gradually abandoned his weakening nationalism and became an inflexible defender of

Southern sectionalism. Seeking extreme medicines for protecting the states and preserving the Union, the "Great Nullifier" incidentally contributed to the almost fatal illness of the Union.

Jackson himself dealt nationalism a body blow by his hostility to localized roads and canals. It is true that he signed a number of measures which appropriated federal funds for ambitious internal improvements. But his states'-rights principles rebelled against spending money from the Washington Treasury for roads built entirely within individual states and unrelated to an interstate network. He headlined his antagonism in 1830, when he vigorously vetoed a bill for the projected Maysville Road, which lay completely within Henry Clay's Kentucky. This setback was incidentally a slap at the internal improvements aspect of the American System, so ardently championed by Clay, the "corrupt bargainer" whom Jackson never forgave. The veto was also a signal victory for Eastern and Southern states'-rightism in its struggle with Jackson's own West.

The Webster-Hayne Duel

Sectional jealousies found a spectacular outlet in the Senate during 1829–1830. Hidebound New England, resenting the marvelous expansion of the West, was determined to call a halt. The lavish distribution of Western acreage was draining off Eastern population, while further upsetting the political balance. Late in 1829, therefore, Senator Foot of Connecticut introduced a resolution designed to curb the sale of public lands.

Sectional passions flared forth angrily on the floor of the Senate. The Western Senators, as might have been expected, sprang furiously to the defense of their interests. The South, needing sectional allies in its controversies with the Northeast, promptly sided with the West. Its most persuasive spokesman was Senator Robert Y. Hayne, of South Carolina, one of the silver-tongued orators of his generation.

Hayne's great oratorical effort in the Senate was an impressive performance. He roundly condemned the disloyalty of New England during the War of 1812, as well as her selfish inconsistency on the protective tariff. Airing in detail the grievances of the South, he reserved his heavy fire for the "Tariff of Abominations" (1828). He then acclaimed Calhoun's dangerous doctrine of nullification as the only means of safeguarding the minority interests of his section. Hayne, like Calhoun, did not advocate a breakup of the Union; rather, he was seeking to protect Southern rights within the Union and under the Constitution. But his arguments were carefully stored up by nullifiers and secessionists for future use.

The "Godlike" Daniel Webster, spokesman for New England, now took the floor. Matchless orator and leader of the American bar, he awed people by his majestic presence. Splendidly endowed, he possessed craglike brows, flashing eyes, a sonorous voice, a nobly cast head, and a well-chested frame. His whole life up to this point, including his frequent appearances before Chief Justice Marshall, had been a preparation for this two weeks' running debate with Hayne in January of 1830.

After defending New England with vigor, if not complete candor, Webster quickly passed on to the larger issue of Union. Insisting that the *people* and not the *states* had framed the Constitution (here he was on shaky historical ground *), he decried the insidious doctrine of nullification. Either the Supreme Court would judge the constitutionality of laws, or the Republic would be torn by revolution. If each of the twenty-four states was free to go its separate way in obeying or rejecting federal laws, there would be no true bond of union but only a "rope of sand." Webster's concluding outburst, which brought tears to men's eyes, was a magnificent tribute to the Union, ending with those imperishable words: "Liberty and Union, now and forever, one and inseparable."

Cement for the Union

Webster did not overpower Hayne with his thunderous oratory; Hayne did not defeat Webster with his smooth-tongued eloquence. There were no official judges. The polished Southerner was sounder than Webster on historical and economic grounds; the impassioned New Englander was sounder on constitutional practicalities and common sense—on things as they were rather than as they had been. Each section was satisfied with its champion.

The impact of Webster's reply was spectacular. About 40,000 copies were printed in three months, and arguments for the Union were seared into the minds of countless Northerners. Among them was young Abraham Lincoln, just turning twenty-one and moving from Indiana to the Illinois frontier. Webster's inspirational conclusion found its way into the school readers, and was memorized by countless tens of thousands of impressionable schoolboys—the Boys in Blue who in 1861–1865 were willing to lay down their lives for the Union.

Webster, beyond a doubt, had a large hand in winning the Civil War for the North. He probably did more than any other person to arouse the oncoming generation of Northerners to support and fight for the ideal of Union. The nation was saved no less by the thunder of Webster's replies to Hayne than by the thunder of General Grant's replies to the cannonading of General Lee.

Meanwhile, hot-tempered "Old Hickory" had been keeping strangely silent on the question of Southern grievances. The states'-rights leaders, on the occasion of a Jefferson Day banquet in 1830, schemed to smoke him out. Their strategy was to devise a series of toasts in honor of Jefferson,

---

* The original preamble of the Constitution of 1787 had read: "We the people of the states of"—and then they were listed by name. But when it was objected that all the states might not ratify, the formula "We the people of the United States" was adopted. (For text of the Preamble, see Appendix.)

onetime foe of centralization, that would lean toward states' rights and nullification. The plotters assumed that the "Old Hero"—a fellow Southerner—would be swept along by the tenor of the toasts and speak up in favor of states' rights.

Jackson, forewarned and inwardly fuming, had carefully prepared his response. At the proper moment he rose to his full height, fixed his eyes on Calhoun, and with dramatic intensity proclaimed:

"OUR UNION: IT MUST BE PRESERVED!"

The Southerners were dumbfounded, and Calhoun haltingly replied, in part:

"THE UNION, NEXT TO OUR LIBERTY, MOST DEAR!"

Some seventy other anticlimactic toasts followed, but in effect the party was over.

Jackson's military ire had been aroused. As Commander-in-Chief, he would stand for no back talk from the states, and particularly from the hated Calhoun. But, as fate decreed, the showdown with the Palmetto State of South Carolina was postponed for over two years.

SELECT READINGS

The best general introductions are GEORGE DANGERFIELD, *The Awakening of American Nationalism, 1815–1828* (1965) and G. G. VAN DEUSEN, *The Jacksonian Era, 1828–1848* (1959), [both **paperback**]. A. M. SCHLESINGER, JR., in his pro-Jackson, Pulitzer-prize *The Age of Jackson* (1945) [**paperback**] stresses the support of Eastern labor for Jackson, a view that has come under heavy attack in LEE BENSON, *The Concept of Jacksonian Democracy: New York as a Test Case* (1961) [**paperback**]. See also WALTER HUGINS, *Jacksonian Democracy and the Working Class: A Study of the New York Workingmen's Movement, 1829–1937* (1960) and MARVIN MEYERS, *The Jacksonian Persuasion* (1957) [**paperback**]. More broadly conceived is J. W. WARD, *Andrew Jackson: Symbol for an Age* (1955) [**paperback**]. R. V. REMINI has two revealing books: *Martin Van Buren and the Making of the Democratic Party* (1959) and *The Election of Andrew Jackson* (1963) [**paperback**]. On administrative aspects consult L. D. WHITE, *The Jacksonians* (1954) and S. H. ARONSON, *Status and Kinship in the Higher Civil Service* (1964). See also CHILTON WILLIAMSON, *American Suffrage from Property to Democracy, 1760–1860* (1960). S. F. BEMIS, *John Quincy Adams and the Union* (1956) is the second and concluding volume of a distinguished biography by a Pulitzer-prize author. Even more readable is MARQUIS JAMES' Pulitzer-prize *Andrew Jackson: Portrait of a President* (1937) [**paperback**]. Also *Harvard Guide*, Pt. IV.

14

Jacksonian Democracy at Flood Tide

I met nullification at the threshold.
ANDREW JACKSON, 1833

"Nullies" in South Carolina

THE "abominable" Tariff of 1828 continued to rankle with hot-blooded South Carolinians. Some of them took to wearing ill-fitting homespun garments, untaxed by the hated Yankee tariff, while their slaves strutted about in discarded broadcloth. The nullifiers—"nullies," they were called—tried valiantly to muster the necessary two-thirds vote in the South Carolina legislature for nullification. But they were blocked by a determined minority of Unionists or "submission men."

Back in Washington, Congress touched off the fuse by passing the new Tariff of 1832, which fell far short of meeting all Southern demands. It is true that the measure pared away the worst of the "abominations," and reduced the imposts to about the level of the moderate Tariff of 1824—roughly 35%, or a reduction of 10%. Yet the new law was frankly protective, and to many Southerners it had a disquieting air of permanence.

House Vote on Tariff of 1832

	For	Against	
New England	17	17	(divided on *moderate* tariff)
Middle States	52	18	(Pa., N.Y. protectionist strongholds)
West (Ohio, Ind., Ill., Mo.)	18	0	(undeveloped West for tariff to support improvements)
South (incl. La.)	27	27	(note division on *moderate* tariff)
Southwest (Tenn., Ky.)	18	3	(West favorable to tariff)
Total	132	65	

(The vote was badly divided because the bill was really a compromise between extreme protection and free trade. Compare vote on 1828 tariff, p. 249.)

South Carolina was now nerved for drastic action. Nullifiers and Unionists clashed head on in the state election of 1832. The "nullies," defiantly wearing palmetto cockades on their hats, emerged with more than a two-thirds majority. The state legislature thereupon issued a call for a special convention. Several weeks later the delegates, meeting in Columbia, solemnly declared the existing federal tariff to be null and void within the borders of South Carolina. The hotheaded assemblage further called upon the state legislature to undertake any necessary military preparations. As a final act of defiance, the Columbia convention threatened to take South Carolina out of the Union if the Washington government attempted to collect the customs duties by force.

President-General Jackson, his military instincts rasped, reacted violently. Hating Calhoun and pledged to uphold the Union, he privately threatened to hang the nullifiers. But fortunately for compromise, he was much less pugnacious in public. He dispatched modest naval and military reinforcements to the Palmetto State, while quietly preparing a sizable army. He also issued a ringing proclamation against nullification, to which the governor of South Carolina, ex-Senator Hayne, responded with a counter-proclamation. If civil war was to be avoided, one side would have to surrender, or both would have to compromise.

Senator Henry Clay of Kentucky, master of conciliation, now stepped forward. An unforgiving foe of Jackson, he had no desire to see the "Old Hero" win new laurels by crushing the Carolinians and then returning with the scalp of Calhoun dangling from his belt. The gallant Kentuckian therefore threw his influence behind a compromise bill, which would gradually reduce the Tariff of 1832 by about 10% over a period of eight years. By 1842 the rates would be at approximately the mildly protective level of 1816—that is, 20% to 25% on the value of dutiable goods.

The compromise tariff of 1833 finally squeezed through Congress. The debate was bitter, with most of the opposition naturally coming from protectionist New England and the Middle States. Calhoun and the South favored the compromise, so it was evident that Jackson would not have to use firearms and rope. But at the same time, and partly as a face-saving device, Congress passed the Force Bill, known among Carolinians as the

House Vote on Compromise Tariff of 1833

	For	Against	
New England	10	28 ⎫	(opposition in manufacturing centers to
Middle States	24	47 ⎭	lowered tariff)
West	10	8	(divided on *moderate* tariff)
South and Southwest	75	2	(strong Southern support for compromise)
Total	119	85	

"Bloody Bill." It authorized the President to use the army and navy, if necessary, to collect federal tariff duties.

The South Carolinians welcomed this opportunity to extricate themselves without loss of face from a dangerously tight corner. To the consternation of the Calhounites, no other Southern states had sprung to their support, though Georgia and Virginia had toyed with the idea. Moreover, an appreciable Unionist minority within South Carolina was gathering guns, organizing militia, and nailing the Stars and Stripes to flagpoles. Faced with civil war within and invasion from without, the Columbia convention met again and repealed the ordinance of nullification. As a final but futile gesture of fist-shaking, this assemblage nullified the unnecessary Force Act and adjourned.

A Victory for Both Sides

Neither Jackson nor the "nullies" won a clear-cut triumph. The admirers of "Old Hickory" have insisted that he avoided an armed clash, induced the South Carolinians to repeal their ordinance of nullification, and preserved the Union. On the other hand, the danger of disunion seems to have been considerably exaggerated.

South Carolina actually emerged with untarnished laurels. Although confronted with overwhelming odds, she had forced a reduction of the tariff to as reasonable a level as she could have expected. She had not only saved face but she had surrendered no principle. Unrepentant and defiant,

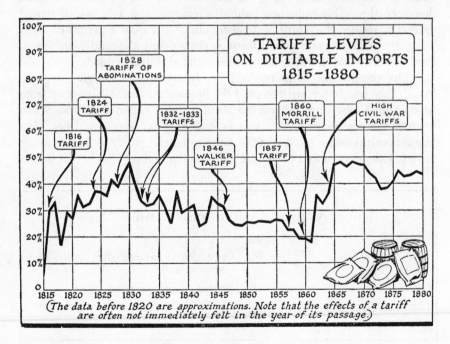

TARIFF LEVIES ON DUTIABLE IMPORTS 1815–1880

1816 TARIFF

1824 TARIFF

1828 TARIFF OF ABOMINATIONS

1832–1833 TARIFFS

1846 WALKER TARIFF

1857 TARIFF

1860 MORRILL TARIFF

HIGH CIVIL WAR TARIFFS

(The data before 1820 are approximations. Note that the effects of a tariff are often not immediately felt in the year of its passage.)

she felt that she had won; and the people of Charleston—the "Cradle of Secession"—gave a gala "victory ball" for the volunteer troops. But ominously—and no doubt in recognition of their close shave—the South Carolinians gradually abandoned nullification in favor of the more thoroughgoing concept of secession.

Later generations, looking back through the smoke of the Civil War, have branded the "appeasement" of South Carolina in 1833 as sheer folly. Unbloody and unbowed, she could have been voted the state most likely to secede. (In 1860 she was the first to go.) If Jackson had only strangled the serpent of secession in the cradle, so the argument runs, there might have been no frightful Civil War.

Yet force was the risky solution. The flare-up in South Carolina was no mere Whiskey Rebellion, and the nation was not yet ready to drink the cup of blood. Violence tends to beget violence. Armed invasion might have aroused other Southern states and touched off a civil war, at a time when the Unionists were even worse prepared for it than in 1861. Force is a confession that statesmanship has failed. Reasonable compromise was in the American tradition, and in 1833 any other course seemed unwise.

The Bank as a Political Football

Jackson, a man of violent dislikes, came to share the prejudices of his own West against the "moneyed monster" known as the Bank of the United States (B. U. S.). He might have tolerated a renewal of its charter in 1836, with adequate safeguards. But hated Henry Clay aroused his ire by throwing himself behind a premature move in the Senate to recharter the Bank in 1832—four years early. "Gallant Harry" was the leading candidate of the National Republicans for the Presidency, and with a fateful blindness he looked upon the Bank issue as a sure-fire winner.

Clay's scheme was to force a recharter bill through Congress, and then send it on to the White House. If Jackson signed it, he would alienate his worshipful Western followers. If he vetoed it, as seemed certain, he would presumably lose the Presidency in the forthcoming election by alienating the wealthy and influential groups in the East. Clay seems not to have fully realized that the "best people" were now only a minority, and that they generally condemned Jackson anyhow.

The recharter bill slid through Congress on greased skids, as planned, but was killed by a scorching veto from Jackson. The "Old Hero" assailed the plutocratic and monopolistic Bank as unconstitutional. The Supreme Court had earlier declared it constitutional in the case of McCulloch vs. Maryland (1819), but Jackson acted as though he believed that the executive branch was superior to the judicial branch. He had taken an oath to uphold the Constitution as he understood it, not as his foe, John Marshall, understood it.

Jackson's veto message went on to condemn the Bank as not only anti-Western but anti-American. A substantial minority of its stockholders were foreigners, chiefly Britons, for whom Americans still harbored a war-born hate. Thus, at one bold stroke, Jackson succeeded in appealing to the prejudices of the West against the East. He was setting the log cabin against the business office, the impoverished debtor against the steely-eyed creditor. More than that, he was arousing the "native" American against the foreigner, the states'-righter against the centralizer.

The gods continued to misguide Henry Clay. Delighted with the financial fallacies of Jackson's message, but blind to its political appeal, he arranged to have thousands of copies printed as a campaign document. The accusations of "Old Hickory" may have seemed demagogic to the moneyed men of the country, but they made good sense to the common men. The issue of the Bank was now thrown into the noisy arena of the Clay-Jackson presidential canvass of 1832.

Brickbats and Bouquets for the Bank

What of Jackson's vigorous charges? The bank was undeniably anti-Western in that it was hostile to the wobbly "wildcat banks," whereas the Westerners were not. It had foreclosed on many Western farms, and had thus drained "tribute" into its Eastern coffers. It was, for that era, a mammoth super-bank—a "monster monopoly"—and hence out of touch with the shirt-sleeved, sweaty New Democracy. It was undeniably plutocratic, run by a silk-stockinged money aristocracy, headed by the able but high-handed Nicholas Biddle (dubbed "Czar Nicholas I"). The Bank was also in some degree autocratic and tyrannical, especially when it turned the screws on the weak "rag money" banks.

The charge that the Bank was a "hydra of corruption" contained much truth. Biddle cleverly lent funds where they would make influential friends. In 1831 alone, a total of fifty-nine members of Congress borrowed sums from "Biddle's Bank" totaling about a third of a million dollars. And one does not ordinarily bite the hand that feeds him. During one period Daniel Webster was a director of the Bank, its chief paid counsel, its debtor in the sum of many thousands of dollars, and a member of the United States Senate, where he eloquently battled for his employer's interests. Judicious loans by Biddle to newspaper editors likewise insured a "good press," and led to the sneer, "Emperor Nick of the Bribery Bank." Whomever he could not corrupt, it was believed, he crushed.

Yet the Bank had much to commend it. An eminently sound organization, it was the only national financial institution of its kind in all our history. It kept the fly-by-night Western banks under some restraint—banks that often consisted of little more than a few chairs and a suitcase full of printed notes. It reduced bank failures and, at a time when the country was flooded with depreciated paper money, issued sound banknotes ("Old Nick's Money"). It helped the West expand by making credit and sound currency reasonably abundant. It was a safe depository for the funds of the Washington government, which it also served by transferring and disbursing money. It admittedly had a monopoly of surplus federal funds, but that monopoly had been specifically authorized by the people's representatives in Congress.

The Bank, in short, was a highly important and useful institution. But it had fallen into the hands of a wealthy clique. Its officers were not only arrogant, but they were not fully aware of their responsibilities to society in the management of what amounted to a public utility. Without question, the range of its beneficiaries was being unduly narrowed.

New Laurels for "Old Hickory"

Clay, as a National Republican, and Jackson, as a Democrat, were the chief gladiators in the presidential campaign of 1832. The gaunt general, who had earlier favored one term for a President and rotation in office, was easily persuaded by his cronies not to rotate himself out of office. Presidential power is a heady brew—and habit-forming.

The campaign of 1832 was colorful and noisy. The "Old Hero's" adherents again raised the hickory pole and bellowed, "Jackson Forever: Go the Whole Hog." Admirers of Clay shouted "Freedom and Clay," while his foes harped on his dueling, gambling, cockfighting, and fast living.

The campaign was memorable for several new features. The Republic witnessed for the first time nominations by national nominating conventions (three of them), which now took over from the state legislatures the function of naming candidates. The first national party platform was also published. And for the first time there was a third-party ticket in the field —the short-lived anti-Masonic group, which opposed the secrecy of the Masons. But on the whole, the "hurrah" froth of the preceding campaign was subordinated to the solid issue of the Bank.

Henry Clay and his overconfident National Republicans enjoyed impressive advantages. Ample funds flowed into their campaign chest, including $50,000 in "life insurance" from the B. U. S. Most of the newspaper editors, some of them "bought" with Bank loans, dipped their pens in acid when they wrote of Jackson. The oratorical big guns of the nation, including the incomparable Webster, were lined up on the side of Clay. The same was true of the middle and upper income groups.

Yet Jackson won easily over the sparkling Kentuckian. The popular count stood at 687,502 to 530,189; the electoral count at 219 to 49. The Jacksonian wave swept irresistibly over the West and South, washed into Pennsylvania and New York, and even broke into rock-ribbed New England.

Henry Clay, long bitten by the presidential bug, was crushed. Himself magnetically appealing, he had enlisted on his side the big money, the brilliant oratory, the "solid" citizenry, and the sound financial reasoning. But "Old Hickory," the idol of the masses, won because he had the votes. The poor always outnumber the rich—and in 1832, as in 1824 and 1828, the poor voted for Andrew Jackson.

Badgering Biddle's Bank

An aroused Jackson was not one to let the financial octopus die in peace. He was convinced that he now had a mandate from the voters, and he had good reason to fear that the slippery Biddle might manipulate the Bank so as to force its recharter. Jackson therefore decided to "remove" the federal deposits gradually, thus cushioning the final shock when the Bank expired in four years. He would accomplish his objective by depositing no more funds with Biddle, and by using existing deposits to defray the day-to-day expenses of the government.

"Removing" the deposits involved nasty complications. Jackson, his dander up, was forced to reshuffle his Cabinet before he could find a Secretary of the Treasury who would bend to his iron will. The surplus federal funds henceforth were placed in several dozen state institutions—the so-called "pet banks" or "Jackson's pets." These new depositories were selected partly because of their pro-Jackson sympathies, but in truth they were not nearly so weak as pictured by "Old Hickory's" enemies.

Biddle, for his part, was compelled to retrench after losing the federal deposits. But he called in loans with unnecessary severity, and evidently for the purpose of forcing a reconsideration of the charter by Congress. A number of the wobblier banks were driven to the wall by "Biddle's Panic," and the vengeful conduct of the dying "monster" seemed to justify the earlier accusations of its foes.

The teetering financial structure of the country received an additional shock in 1836, the year the Bank breathed its last. "Wildcat" currency had become so unreliable in the West that Jackson authorized the Treasury to issue a Specie Circular—a decree which required all public lands to be purchased with "hard" or metallic money. This drastic step was no doubt overdue, but coming at this time it gave the wild speculative bubble another sharp prick.

Inflationary pressures nevertheless continued. By 1835 the national debt was paid for the first time since Hamilton's day, but additional funds still poured into the Federal Treasury. This revenue flowed principally from the customhouses, which were benefiting from the high tariff duties and the heavy imports resulting from "flush" times. In 1836 a scheme passed Congress for distributing the surplus above $5,000,000 to the states. When this transfer began, early in 1837, the risky speculative spiral was given another boost. Later that year the panic broke, and the bothersome problem of the surplus became the even more bothersome problem of a deficit.

Transplanting the Tribes

Wondrous indeed was the continued expansion of the American population. The unflagging fertility of the people, aided by considerable immigration, brought the total figure to nearly 13,000,000 by 1830—or more than three times that of 1790.* Most of the states east of the Mississippi had been admitted, leaving islands of red men marooned on lands coveted by their white neighbors.

President Jackson, himself a veteran Indian fighter, wasted little sympathy on the paint-bedaubed "varmints." He accepted fully the brutal creed of his fellow Westerners that "the only good Indian is a dead Indian." When Georgia attempted to evict the Cherokees, and the Supreme Court upheld the rights of the Indians, Jackson viewed the continued defiance of the state with unaccustomed composure. Hating both the redskins and Chief Justice Marshall, he is supposed to have remarked, "John Marshall has made his decision; now let him enforce it."

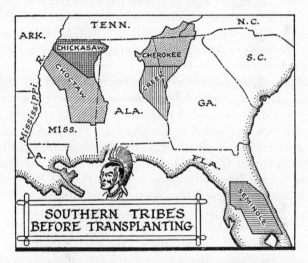

SOUTHERN TRIBES
BEFORE TRANSPLANTING

The only feasible solution of the white-red problem seemed to be a removal of the Eastern Indians, in a body, to the wide-open spaces of the Great Plains West. Jackson threw his support behind the proposed scheme. The red men were to exchange their ancestral lands for compensating tracts in the wilds beyond the Mississippi, notably in what is now Oklahoma. There they could be "permanently" assured of no further encroachments by the insatiable white men. In 1830 Congress wrote this policy into law, and in subsequent years scores of treaties were negotiated with the Indians. But as the land-hungry palefaces pushed west faster than anticipated, the pacts turned out to be mere scraps of paper. The "permanent" frontier lasted about fifteen years.

* For population figures from 1790 to 1960, see Appendix.

The uprooting of more than 100,000 Indians occurred in the 1830's. Although the victims suffered intensely from hunger and exposure on the "Trail of Tears," there were only two serious flare-ups. The redskins of Illinois and Wisconsin, ably led by Black Hawk, resisted eviction. They were bloodily crushed in 1832 by regular troops, including Lieutenant Jefferson Davis of Mississippi, and by volunteers, including Captain Abraham Lincoln of Illinois.

The Seminole Indians of Florida, joined by runaway Negro slaves, fled to the swampy Everglades. For several years they waged a costly and bloody guerrilla war. Their spirit was at last broken in 1837, when the American field commander treacherously seized their half-breed leader, Osceola, under a flag of truce.

Brass-Knuckle Diplomacy

Trigger-tempered General Jackson seemed temperamentally unfitted for diplomacy. But in this field he turned out to be much more successful than President J. Q. Adams, his diplomatically seasoned predecessor.

How would Jackson get along with the British? Sober citizens had misgivings, for the fiery general had fought them in two wars. He had also borne on his head, since age fourteen, a sword scar brutally inflicted by a British officer. The problem of reopening trade with the British West Indies provided an acid test of Jackson's views. John Quincy Adams, the astute diplomat, had demanded reopening as a right. Jackson, with surprising moderation, requested it as a privilege. The British, no doubt expecting a saber-rattling approach, were thrown off guard. Death had taken the imperious Canning from the London Foreign Office, and Great Britain was veering toward free trade, away from her ancient Navigation Laws. The British therefore agreed to reopen this once-lucrative West Indian commerce, subject to the payment of normal customs duties.

As an international bill collector, Jackson proved equally successful, though much less velvet-gloved. In 1831 the Paris government belatedly agreed to pay the United States several million dollars, as compensation for American ships illegally seized during the Napoleonic upheaval. But partly because of political tensions in France, the initial payments were not forthcoming when due. Jackson, short on patience, recommended in his annual message of 1834 that, if necessary, the federal government should seize French property in the United States and pay off the debt with the proceeds.

French pride, traditionally thin-skinned, was hurt. The Paris government closed its legation in Washington, and ordered Chargé Alfonse Pageot home. He sailed with his American wife (whose father was a friend of Jackson) and his infant son, Andrew Jackson Pageot (whose godfather was the President). The American legation in Paris was likewise closed, and the buzz of war preparations was increased on both sides.

Jackson was urged by well-wishers to apologize, but this course he sulphurously refused to follow.

War with France seemed imminent. But the British, not wishing to see their French ally squander its strength in America, successfully mediated. Europe's distresses were still coming to America's aid. The French officials, carefully rereading Jackson's messages to Congress, insisted that they now found in them a satisfactory apology—though Jackson loudly insisted that he had not apologized. At all events, arrangements were finally made to pay the debt; and Monsieur Pageot, Madame Pageot, and little Andrew Jackson Pageot sailed back to America.

Jackson had raised international blood pressures dangerously high over this relatively trifling affair. But he did get the money. He also ended a dispute that had explosive possibilities, and he created a new respect in European capitals for the robust young republic. The Henry Clayites condemned the verbal violence employed, while the President's followers elatedly retorted, "Hurrah for Jackson!" "No Explanations! No Apologies!"

The Lone Star Flickers

Spacious-minded Americans continued to covet the vast expanse of Texas, which the United States had abandoned in the Florida negotiations of 1819. The Spanish authorities were desirous of populating this virtually unpeopled area, but before they could carry through their contemplated plans, the Mexicans won their independence. The new officials in Mexico City thereupon concluded arrangements in 1823 for granting a huge tract of land to Stephen Austin, with the understanding that he would bring in 300 families. The American immigrants were to be of the established Roman Catholic faith, and in addition were to become properly Mexicanized.

These two restrictions were largely ignored. The hardy pioneers who reached Texas remained Americans at heart, resenting the trammels imposed by a "foreign" government. They were especially annoyed by the presence of Mexican soldiers, many of whom were ragged and lousy ex-convicts.

The Texas-Americans, virile and prolific, numbered about 30,000 by 1835. Most of them were law-abiding and God-fearing men, but some of them had left the "states" only one or two jumps ahead of the sheriff. "G. T." (Gone to Texas) became current explanatory slang. Among the adventurers were Davy Crockett, the fabulous rifleman, and James Bowie, the presumed inventor of the murderous knife that bears his name. It was widely known in the Southwest as the "genuwine Arkansas toothpick."

The American individualists who came to Texas were not easy to push around. Friction rapidly increased between Mexican "greasers" and Texan "gringos" over such issues as slavery, immigration, and states' rights. The explosion finally came when a dictator, Santa Anna, swept away cherished privileges guaranteed to Texas by the Mexican constitution of 1824.

Early in 1836 the liberty-loving Texans declared their independence and unfurled their Lone Star flag, and the war was on. Santa Anna, at the head of a superior force, swept ferociously into Texas. Trapping a band of nearly 200 Texans at the Alamo in San Antonio, he wiped them out to a man, including Jim Bowie, who was shot as he lay sick on his cot, and Davy Crockett, whose body was found riddled with bullets. A short time later a band of about 400 American volunteers, having thrown down their arms when surrounded at Goliad, were ruthlessly butchered as "pirates." These operations further delayed the Mexican advance.

The Texan war cries—"Remember the Alamo!" "Remember Goliad!" and "Death to Santa Anna!"—swept up into the United States. A popular American song ran:

> For every wound and every thrust
> On prisoners dealt by hand accurst
> A Mexican shall bite the dust
> Remember the Alamo!

Additional scores of vengeful Americans seized their rifles and rushed to the aid of their relatives, friends, and compatriots. But despite their efforts, the Lone Star was in danger of being dimmed forever.

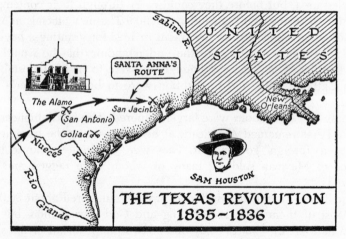

THE TEXAS REVOLUTION
1835-1836

Long-headed Sam Houston proved equal to the occasion. A commanding figure of a man and a natural leader of the Texans, he lured the pursuers northward to San Jacinto, near the site of the city that now bears his name. Suddenly he turned, on April 21, 1836. Taking full advantage of the Mexican siesta hour, he wiped out the invading force and captured Santa Anna, who was found cowering in the tall grass near the battlefield. Confronted with thirsty Bowie knives, the quaking dictator was speedily induced to sign two treaties. By their terms he agreed to withdraw Mexican troops and to recognize the Rio Grande as the southwestern boundary of Texas. When released, he repudiated the whole agreement as illegal and as extorted under duress.

Texas: An International Derelict

Mexico no doubt had a genuine grievance against the United States. The Texans, courageous though they were, could hardly have won their independence without unneutral help in the form of men and supplies from their American cousins. The Washington government, as the Mexicans emphatically pointed out, had a solemn obligation under international law to enforce its leaky neutrality statutes. But American public opinion, overwhelmingly favorable to the Texans, openly nullified the existing legislation; and the federal authorities were powerless to act.

Jackson's heart was torn over the Texas issue. He hated the Mexican "greasers" and admired the heroism of Sam Houston, his old comrade-in-arms against the Indians. But he was in no haste to recognize Texas formally as an independent republic. To do so would touch off the whole explosive issue of slavery, at a time when he was trying to engineer the election of his hand-picked successor, Martin Van Buren. But with Van Buren safely under the wire, he extended to Texas the right hand of recognition, the day before he left office in 1837.

The republic of Texas had every expectation of being joined to the United States, for what nation in its right mind would refuse so princely a dowry? The radiant Texan bride, officially petitioning for annexation in 1837, presented herself for marriage. But the expectant groom, Uncle Sam, was pulled back by the black hand of the slavery issue, and forced to reject the petition. The anti-slavery zealots of the North were opposing annexation with increasing vehemence. They argued that the whole scheme was merely a conspiracy cooked up by the Southern "slavocracy" to bring new slave pens into the Union.

At first glance, the accusations of a "slavery plot" seemed plausible. Most of the early settlers in Texas, as well as the American volunteers during the recent revolution, had come from the states of the South and Southwest. But scholars have concluded that the settlement of Texas was merely the normal and inexorable march of the westward movement. Most of the immigrants came from the South and Southwest simply because these states were closer. It was proximity rather than conspiracy.

The jilted Texan bride was left in a dangerous predicament. Fearing the return of the villain, Santa Anna, she went so far as to flirt openly with Britain and France for support. An ugly situation, involving balance-of-power politics, began to develop at the southern doorstep of the United States. It could not be allowed to go on indefinitely.

The End of King Andrew

New parties were in the making as the 1830's lengthened. By 1834, the Democratic-Republicans of Andrew Jackson had unashamedly adopted the once-tainted name of "Democrats." The National Republicans, glamorously led by Henry Clay, chose the time-honored name of Whig—a name closely associated with patriotism during the Revolutionary War. (See chart, p. 163.)

The Whig Party was a hodgepodge of malcontents—"an organized incompatibility." Their guiding star at this time was opportunism; their chief cement was hatred of Jackson and hunger for the spoils of office. Under the same political roof were gathered all kinds of Whigs: protectionists and free-traders, Southern nullifiers and Northern nationalists, rich Southern planters and poor Northern farmers.

As the presidential election of 1836 approached, the Whigs did not feel strong enough to beat the Jacksonian Democrats in a straight-out fight. Their strategy was to nominate several locally prominent "favorite sons," who would then so scatter the vote that no candidate would get a majority. The deadlock would then have to be broken by the House of Representatives, and there the Whigs would have a chance. With Henry Clay bowing out of a near-hopeless race, the leading "favorite son" was heavy-jawed General William Henry Harrison of Ohio, chastiser of Indians and hero of the battle of Tippecanoe.

Martin Van Buren of New York, a smooth-as-silk politician, was rough "Old Hickory's" choice as his successor. The hollow-cheeked Jackson, now nearing seventy, was too old and ailing to consider a third term. But he was not loath to try to serve a third term through Van Buren, who had proved himself to be something of a "yes man." Leaving nothing to chance, the General carefully rigged the nominating convention, and rammed his favorite down the throats of the delegates. Van Buren was supported by the Jacksonites without undue enthusiasm, even though he had promised to tread faithfully in the military-booted footsteps of his predecessor.

The finespun schemes of the Whigs availed nothing. Van Buren, the dapper "Little Magician," squirmed into office by the close popular vote of 762,678 to 735,651, but by the comfortable margin of 170 votes to 73 in the Electoral College. "Old Hickory" could now step out.

In retrospect, the Jackson years were fruitful ones. It is true that they were marred by noise and bluster, as well as by bull-in-the-china-closet finance and diplomacy. Yet the rough-hewn "Old Hero"—through forthrightness, energy, and strength of character—did far better than might have been expected. He demonstrated anew the value of strong executive leadership, led the common people into national politics, united them into the powerful and long-lived Democratic Party, and proved that they could be trusted with both the vote and high office. Reasserting the prestige of the Presidency, he amazed the weak-kneed politicians by showing that the courageous course often wins the most votes.

The other side of the ledger is less satisfying. Jackson cannot escape some blame for his encouragement of the spoils system and of unsound finance, with its heartbreaking hundred-year legacy of thousands of bank failures. No one can deny that the B. U. S. was a powerful and—ultimately —a corrupting monopoly, which needed to have its wings clipped. But chopping off its head instead of its wings was of dubious benefit to the entire nation.

Big Woes for the "Little Magician"

Martin Van Buren, the eighth President of the United States, was the first to be born under the American flag. Bland of face, bald of head, slender of figure, the adroit little New Yorker has been described as "a first-class second-rate man." An accomplished wirepuller and spoilsman, he was also a statesman of wide experience in both legislative and administrative life. In intelligence, education, and training, he was above the average of our Presidents since Jackson. The myth of his complete mediocrity sprang from a series of misfortunes over which he had no control.

From the outset, the new politician-President labored under severe handicaps. As a machine-made candidate, he incurred the resentment of many Democrats—the men who objected to having a "bastard politician" smuggled into office beneath the tails of "Old Hickory's" military coat. Jackson, the master showman, had been the dynamic type of executive, whose administration had resounded with furious quarrels and cracking heads. The easygoing Van Buren seemed to rattle about in the military boots of his testy predecessor. The people felt let down. Inheriting Jackson's mantle without his popularity, the polished New Yorker also inherited the "Old Hero's" numerous and vengeful enemies.

Van Buren's four years were filled with toil and trouble. The Canadian rebellion of 1837, as will be noted, stirred up ugly incidents along our northern frontier and threatened to involve us in war with Britain. The anti-slavery agitators in the North were in full cry, and among other grievances were condemning the prospective annexation of Texas.

Worst of all, Van Buren inherited a searing depression from Jackson. Much of his energy had to be devoted to the purely negative task of battling the panic, and there were not enough rabbits in the "Little Magician's" tall silk hat. Hard times ordinarily blight the reputation of a President—and Van Buren was no exception.

Depression Doldrums

The Panic of 1837 was a product of the financial sickness of the times. Its basic cause was overspeculation, prompted by a mania of get-rich-quickism. Gamblers in Western lands were doing a "land-office business" on borrowed capital, much of it in the shaky currency of the "wildcat banks." The speculative craze spread to canals, roads, railroads, new cotton lands, and slaves.

But speculation alone did not cause the crash. Jacksonian finance, including the Bank War and the Specie Circular, gave an additional shove to an already teetering structure. Failures of wheat crops, ravaged by the Hessian fly, deepened the distress. Grain prices were forced so high that mobs in New York City, three weeks before Van Buren took the oath, stormed warehouses and broke open flour barrels. The panic really began before Jackson left the White House, but its full fury burst about Van Buren's bewildered head.

Financial stringency abroad likewise left its imprint on America. Late in 1836, while Jackson was still President, the failure of two prominent British banks created uneasiness, and this in turn caused English investors to call in loans to Americans. The resulting pinch in the United States, combined with other setbacks, marked the beginning of the panic. Europe's financial distresses have often been our distresses, and every major American panic has in some degree been affected by conditions abroad.

Hardship was acute and widespread. American banks collapsed by the hundreds, including some of the "pet banks," which carried down with them several millions in government funds. Commodity prices tobogganed, the sale of public lands fell off, and customs revenues dried to a rivulet. Factories closed their doors, while unemployed workers trod the pavements.

The mass of the people simply had to wait for the economic blizzard to blow itself out. The view prevailed, unchanged until the next century, that the less governmental interference there was the better. The luckless "Little Magician," stymied by this hands-off philosophy, could cope with the crisis only indirectly.

Van Buren sought to bring partial relief through his much-debated "Divorce Bill." Convinced that some of the financial fever had come from the injection of government funds into politics, he championed the principle of divorcing the public revenue from private banks. The so-called Independent Treasury Bill is his chief claim to constructive statesmanship. The scheme was to lock the surplus federal money in government vaults and sub-treasuries, which would be located in the larger cities. The funds could be disbursed as needed, and they would not only be safe but completely divorced from politics. They would also be removed from business, which as a consequence was hampered.

Van Buren's hole-in-the-ground device was never highly popular. It was supported only lukewarmly by his fellow Democrats, many of whom longed for the uncertain but lush days of the "pet banks." It was condemned by the Whigs, primarily because it would put an end to their hopes for a revived Bank of the United States. After a prolonged struggle, the Independent Treasury Bill finally passed Congress in 1840. Repealed the next year by the victorious Whigs, the sub-treasury scheme was re-enacted by the triumphant Democrats in 1846, and then continued until merged with the Federal Reserve System in 1921.

"Tippecanoe" and "Little Van"

Van Buren, though panic-tainted, was renominated by the Democrats in 1840, albeit without unrestrained enthusiasm. They had no acceptable alternative to what the Whigs called "Martin Van Ruin." Not to have run him again would have been a damaging admission that the party had foisted an unsound choice upon the country in 1836.

The Whigs, hungering for the spoils of office, scented victory in the air. The pangs of the panic were still being felt; and voters blindly blame their woes on the party in power. The Whigs turned again not to their ablest statesmen—the Clays and Websters—but to their ablest vote-getter: William H. Harrison of Ohio, a coarse-featured military chieftain.

The aging general, nearly sixty-eight when the campaign ended, was a small-bore candidate. Despite an inflated reputation, he had been only moderately successful in civilian and military life, notably at the battles of Tippecanoe (1811) and the Thames (1813). "Old Tippecanoe" was then living quietly in a sixteen-room mansion, located on a 3000-acre farm near North Bend, Ohio. His views on current issues were only vaguely known. He was nominated primarily because he was issueless and enemy-less—and a most unfortunate precedent was thus set. John Tyler of Virginia was selected as his vice-presidential running mate.

The Whigs played the political game with their cards close to the vest. They published no platform, fearing to make plaguing commitments and unwilling to reveal the deep divisions within their own patchwork party. They hoped to sweep their hero into the White House by a frothy huzza-for-Harrison campaign.

A dull-witted Democratic editor played directly into Whig hands. Stupidly insulting the West, he sneered at Harrison as an impoverished old farmer who would be content with a pension, a log cabin, and a barrel of hard cider—the poor Westerner's champagne. The Whigs glee-fully took up the challenge and, stressing the hard cider and log cabin theme, turned the campaign into a huge political revival meeting. The Harrisonites portrayed their hero as the poor "Farmer of North Bend," who had been called from his plow and his log cabin to drive the corrupt Jackson spoilsmen from the "presidential palace."

A non-existent candidate rapidly began to take shape in the hands of the Whig myth-makers. The real Harrison was not lowborn, but one of the F. F. V.'s (First Families of Virginia). He was not poverty-stricken; he did not live in a one-room log cabin; he did not swill down gallons of hard cider; and he did not plow his fields with his own "huge paws."

Whig propagandists made merry with little Martin Van Buren, the

A HARD ROAD TO HOE!

Jackson urges Van Buren toward the White House over a road littered with log cabins and hard cider. Van Buren, handicapped also by his unpopular sub-treasury policy, would evidently prefer the smoother road back to his Kinderhook home. A campaign cartoon of 1840. Library of Congress

"Flying Dutchman." He was denounced as a supercilious aristocrat, who wore corsets and ate French food with golden teaspoons from golden plates. The rough-timbered Democratic Party of Andrew Jackson, deeply rooted in the West, was thus saddled with a simpering dandy from the aristocratic East. The aristocratic Whig Party of Webster and Biddle, no less inconsistently, had come up with a backwoods nominee from the Democratic West—a reasonably good facsimile of hatchet-faced General Jackson. As a Whig campaign song proclaimed:

> Ole Tip, he wears a homespun shirt,
> He has no ruffled shirt, wirt, wirt.
> But Matt, he has the golden plate,
> And he's a little squirt, wirt, wirt.

Log Cabins and Hard Cider

The Democrats, who had hurrahed Jackson into the White House, now discovered to their chagrin that this was a game two could play. Acres of Whig audiences and miles of Whig marchers chanted or shouted such slogans as: "Harrison, Two Dollars a Day and Roast Beef" and "With Tip and Tyler We'll Bust Van's Biler." Log cabins were dished up in every conceivable form. Bawling Whigs, stimulated by fortified cider, rolled huge inflated balls from village to village and state to state—balls that represented the snowballing majority for "Tip and Ty." As they pushed, they sang:

Tippecanoe, and Tyler too.
And with them we'll beat little Van, Van, Van,
Oh! Van is a used-up man.

Claptrap was king, as the electoral debauch reached an all-time intellectual low. There was little sober discussion of real issues. The Democrats inquired earnestly about the Bank, internal improvements, and the tariff. The replies were "log cabin," "hard cider," "Harrison is a poor man." The Van Burenites, protesting futilely, were drowned in a tidal wave of apple juice.

Harrison won by the surprisingly close margin of 1,275,016 popular votes to 1,129,102, but by the overwhelming electoral count of 234 to 60. The hard-ciderites had seemingly received a mandate to go to Washington, tear down the White House, and erect a log cabin.

Basically, the vote was a protest against hard times—a thunderous shout of "Out with the old and in with the new." But the barrage of buncombe and silly slogans set a most unfortunate example for future campaigns. Democracy calls for hard thinking, not hard cider; for dignity, not delirium. Yet an able, well-organized, and well-entrenched political party, committed to solid principles, was hooted out of office by a meaningless hoopla campaign.

The Democrats were baffled. They complained with much bitterness and no little truth that they had been shouted down, sung down, lied down, and drunk down. Yet, though outsloganed, they had kept their ranks intact. Even in defeat they were a stronger party than the Whigs. Though temporarily overdosed with hard cider, they would be heard from again.

SELECT READINGS

The best general introduction is G. G. VAN DEUSEN, *The Jacksonian Era, 1828–1848* (1959) [paperback]. Colorful detail abounds in MARQUIS JAMES' Pulitzer-prize *Andrew Jackson: Portrait of a President* (1937) [paperback] and in C. G. BOWERS' pro-Jackson *The Party Battles of the Jackson Period* (1922). A. M. SCHLESINGER, JR., stoutly supports Jackson's bank policy in his Pulitzer-prize *The Age of Jackson* (1945) [paperback]. Less favorable is BRAY HAMMOND's Pulitzer-prize *Banks and Politics in America, from the Revolution to the Civil War* (1957), Old but still useful is R. C. H. CATTERALL, *The Second Bank of the United States* (1903), which should be read in the light of T. P. GOVAN, *Nicholas Biddle: Nationalist and Public Banker, 1786–1844* (1959). The second volume of a three-volume biography, C. M. WILTSE, *John C. Calhoun, Nullifier, 1829-1839* (1951) deals with the nullification crisis. The color of the frothy presidential campaign of 1840 comes through in R. G. GUNDERSON, *The Log-Cabin Campaign* (1957). See also references for the preceding chapter and *Harvard Guide*, Pt. IV.

15

Manifest Destiny in the Forties

. . . Our manifest destiny [is] to overspread the continent allotted by Providence for the free development of our yearly multiplying millions.

JOHN L. O'SULLIVAN, 1845 *

The Accession of "Tyler Too"

A HORDE of hard-ciderites descended upon Washington early in 1841, clamoring for the spoils of office. General Harrison, bewildered by the uproar, was almost hounded to death by Whig spoilsmen.

The real leaders of the Whig Party regarded "Old Tippecanoe" as little more than an impressive figurehead. Daniel Webster, now Secretary of State, and Henry Clay, the uncrowned king of the Whigs and their ablest spokesman in the Senate, would grasp the wheel. The aging general was finally forced to rebuke the overzealous Clay and pointedly remind him that William Henry Harrison was President of the United States.

The schemes of Clay and Webster soon hit a fatal snag. Before the new term had fairly started, Harrison came down with pneumonia. Wearied by official functions and plagued by office seekers, the enfeebled old warrior died after only four weeks in the White House—the shortest administration in American history.

The "Tyler too" part of the Whig ticket, hitherto an afterthought, now claimed the spotlight. What manner of man did the nation now wake up to find in the presidential chair? Tall, slender, and blue-eyed, with classical features and a high forehead, Tyler was a Virginia gentleman of the old school—gracious and kindly, yet stubbornly attached to principle. He had earlier resigned from the United States Senate, quite unnecessarily, rather than accept distasteful instructions from the Virginia legislature. Still independent-minded, he had forsaken the Jacksonian Democratic fold for that of the Whigs, largely because he could not stomach the high-handed tactics of "Old Hickory."

Although Tyler's enemies accused him of being a Democrat in Whig clothing, this charge was only partially true. The Whig Party was some-

---

* Earliest known use of the term "manifest destiny," sometimes called "manifest desire."

thing of a catchall, and the accidental President belonged to the minority wing, which contained a number of Jeffersonian states'-righters. Tyler had in fact been put on the ticket partly to attract the vote of this influential group, many of whom were Southern gentry.

Yet Tyler, high-minded as he was, should never have consented to run on the ticket. Though the dominant Clay-Webster group had published no platform, every alert politician knew what the unpublished platform contained. And on virtually every major issue the obstinate Virginian was at odds with the majority of his Whig Party, which was pro-Bank, pro-protective tariff, and pro-internal improvements. "Tyler too" rhymed with "Tippecanoe," but there the harmony ended. As it turned out, President Harrison, the Whig, served for only four weeks, while Tyler, the ex-Democrat who was still largely a Democrat at heart, served for 204 weeks.

A President without a Party

After the hard-won, hard-cider victory, the Whigs could bring their secret platform out of Clay's waistcoat pocket. To the surprise of no one, it outlined a strongly nationalistic program.

Financial reform came first. The Whig Congress made haste to pass a law abolishing the Independent Treasury system, and President Tyler, disarmingly agreeable, signed it. Clay next drove through Congress a bill for a "Fiscal Bank," which would establish a new Bank of the United States.

Tyler's hostility to a centralized bank was notorious, and Clay—the "Great Compromiser"—would have done well to conciliate him. But the Kentuckian, robbed repeatedly of the Presidency by lesser men, was in an imperious mood and riding for a fall. When the bank bill reached the presidential desk, Tyler flatly vetoed it on both practical and constitutional grounds. A drunken mob gathered late at night near the White House and shouted insultingly, "Huzza for Clay!" "A Bank! A Bank!" "Down with the Veto!"

The crestfallen Whig leaders tried again. Striving to meet Tyler's objections to a "Fiscal Bank," they hastened to pass another bill providing for a "Fiscal Corporation." But the President, still unbending, vetoed the offensive substitute. The Democrats were jubilant, for they had been saved from another financial "monster" only by the pneumonia that had felled Harrison.

The Whig extremists, boiling with indignation, condemned Tyler as "His Accidency" and as an "Executive Ass." Widely burned in effigy, he received numerous letters threatening him with death. A wave of influenza then sweeping the country was called the "Tyler grippe." To the delight of the Democrats, the stiff-necked Virginian was formally expelled from his party by a caucus of Whig Congressmen, and a serious attempt to impeach him was made in the House of Representatives. His entire Cabinet resigned in a body, except the politically ambitious Secretary of State Webster, who was then in the midst of delicate negotiations with England.

The proposed Whig tariff also felt the prick of the President's well-inked pen. Surprisingly enough, Tyler did sign a law passed in 1841 for bringing additional revenue to the depression-drained Treasury. But he looked with frosty eye on the major tariff scheme of the Whigs. It provided, among other features, for the distribution among the states of revenue from the sale of public lands in the West. Tyler could see no point in squandering federal money when the Federal Treasury was barren, and he again wielded an emphatic veto.

The chastened Clayites redrafted their tariff bill. They chopped out the offensive dollar-distribution scheme, and pushed down the rates to about the moderately protective level of 1832, roughly 32% on dutiable goods. Tyler had no fondness for a protective tariff, but realizing the need for additional revenue, he reluctantly signed the law of 1842. In subsequent months, the pressure for higher customs duties slackened as the country gradually edged its way out of the depression.

The War of Words with England

Hatred of England during the 19th Century came to a head periodically, and had to be lanced by treaty settlement or by war. The poison had festered ominously by 1842.

Anti-British passions were compounded of many ingredients. At bottom lay the bitter, red-coated memories of the two Anglo-American wars. In addition, the genteel pro-British Federalists had been swept out, yielding to the boisterous Jacksonian democracy. British travelers, looking down their aristocratic noses at the crude scene, wrote acidly of the to-

**LIFE IN AN
AMERICAN HOTEL**

An English caricature of American rudeness and readiness with the pistol. *Punch,* 1856

bacco spitting, slave auctioneering, lynching, eye gouging, and other unsavory features of our rustic civilization. The travel books penned by these
critics, whose views were avidly read on both sides of the Atlantic, stirred
up angry outbursts in America.

But the literary fireworks did not end here. British magazines added
fuel to the flames when, enlarging on the travel books, they launched
sneering attacks on Yankee shortcomings. American journals struck back
with "you're another" arguments, thus touching off the "Third War with
England." Fortunately, it was fought with paper broadsides, and only ink
was spilled. British authors, including Charles Dickens, entered the fray
with gall-dipped pens, for they were being robbed of rich royalties by the
absence of an American copyright law.

Sprawling America, with expensive canals to dig and railroads to
build, was a borrowing nation in the 19th Century. Britain, with her overflowing coffers, was a lending nation. The coupon-clipping creditor is
never popular with the debtor, and the phrase "bloated British bondholder" rolled bitterly from many an American tongue. When the Panic of
1837 broke, and several states defaulted on their bonds, or repudiated
them openly, honest Englishmen assailed Yankee trickery. One of them
offered a new stanza for an old song:

> Yankee Doodle borrows cash,
> Yankee Doodle spends it,
>   And then he snaps his fingers at
> The jolly flat [simpleton] who lends it.

Troubles of a more dangerous sort came closer to home in 1837, when
a short-lived insurrection erupted in Canada. It was supported by such a
small minority of Canadians that it never had a real chance of success. Yet
hundreds of hot-blooded Americans, hoping to strike a blow for freedom
against the ancient enemy, furnished military supplies or volunteered for
armed service. The Washington regime tried manfully, though futilely, to
uphold its weak neutrality regulations. As was true during the Texan revolution, it simply could not enforce unpopular laws in the face of overwhelming popular opposition.

A provocative incident on the Canadian frontier brought passions
to a boil in 1837. A tiny American steamer, the *Caroline*, was engaged in
carrying supplies to the insurgents across the swift Niagara River. It was
finally attacked on the New York shore by a determined British force,
which set the vessel on fire. Lurid American illustrators showed the flaming ship, laden with shrieking souls, plunging over the Niagara Falls. The
craft actually sank short of the Falls, and only one American was killed.

This unlawful invasion of American soil—a counter-violation of neutrality—had alarming aftermaths. The Washington officials lodged vigorous
but ineffective protests. Three years later, in 1840, the incident was dramatically revived in the state of New York. A Canadian named McLeod,

after allegedly boasting in a tavern of his part in the *Caroline* raid, was arrested and indicted for murder. The London Foreign Office, which regarded the *Caroline* raiders as members of an armed force and not as criminals, made it clear that his execution would mean war. Fortunately, McLeod was freed after establishing an alibi. It must have been airtight, for it was good enough to convince a New York jury. The tension forthwith eased.

Manipulating the Maps

An explosive controversy of the early 1840's was the Maine boundary dispute. The St. Lawrence River is ice-bound several months of the year, as the British, remembering the War of 1812, well knew. They were determined, as a defensive precaution against the Yankees, to build a road westward from the seaport of Halifax to Quebec. But the proposed route ran through disputed territory—claimed also by Maine under the misleading peace treaty of 1783. Tough-knuckled lumberjacks from both Maine and New Brunswick entered the disputed no man's land. Ugly fights flared up; both sides summoned the local militia. The small-scale lumberjack war threatened to widen into a full-dress shooting war.

As the crisis deepened in 1842, the London Foreign Office took an unusual step. It sent to Washington a non-professional diplomat, the conciliatory financier Lord Ashburton, who had married a wealthy American woman. He speedily established cordial relations with Secretary Daniel Webster, who had recently been lionized during a visit to England.

The two statesmen, their nerves frayed by protracted negotiations in the heat of a Washington summer, finally agreed to compromise on the Maine boundary. On the basis of a rough, split-the-difference arrangement, the Americans were to retain some 7000 square miles of the 12,000 square miles of wilderness in dispute. The British got less land, but won the desired Halifax-Quebec route. During the negotiations the *Caroline* affair, dragged out since 1837, was patched up by an exchange of notes.

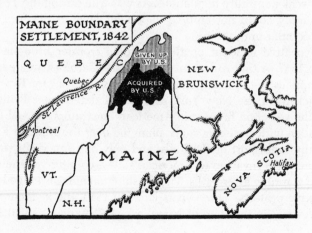

The surrender of 5000 square miles of American soil to the British proved highly unpopular, especially among loyal Maine men. One irate United States Senator branded the treaty a "solemn bamboozlement." But Webster had obtained an ancient map which indicated, ironically, that the British were entitled to the entire area in dispute. When he secretly displayed his find in Washington, the treaty slipped through the Senate on greased skids.

British imperialists roundly condemned Lord Ashburton for his "capitulation." But the opposition evaporated when the London officials turned up with another yellowing map: it proved that the Americans were entitled to the entire area in contention. Thus each party to the negotiation secretly held the other's trump card in the historic "Battle of the Maps."

Historians have since proved that the United States had a valid claim to the entire lost territory. This fact was not known at the time, perhaps fortunately, for the British were in no mood to give up the Halifax route. The yielding of 5000 square miles of pine-forested land, at least in 1842, seemed like a cheap price to pay for avoiding a senseless war.

The Lone Star Shines Alone

The jilted Texan bride, during the uncertain eight years since 1836, had been leading a precarious existence. Mexico, refusing to recognize her independence, regarded the Lone Star Republic as a province in revolt, to be reconquered at some future time—*mañana*. Mexican officials defiantly threatened war if the American eagle should gather the fledgling republic under its protective wings.

The Texans were forced to maintain a backbreaking military establishment. Vastly outnumbered by their Mexican foe, they could not tell when he would strike again. Mexico actually did make two half-hearted raids, which, though ineffectual, foreshadowed more fearsome efforts. Confronted with such perils, the Lone Star Republic was driven to flirting openly with England and France, in the hope of securing the defensive shield of a protectorate.

London and Paris were both intensely interested in an independent and powerful Texas. Such a republic would check the southward surge of the American colossus, whose bulging biceps posed a constant threat to British possessions in the New World. A strong puppet Texas, dancing to the strings pulled by Britain, could be turned upon the United States. The subsequent clashes would create a smoke-screen diversion, behind which foreign powers could move into the Americas and challenge the detested Monroe Doctrine. French schemers were likewise attracted by the hoary game of divide and conquer. It would result, they hoped, in the fragmentation, militarization, and Balkanization of America.

Dangers threatened from other foreign quarters. British abolitionists were busily intriguing to get a foothold in Texas. If successful in freeing the Negroes there, they presumably would inflame the nearby slaves of the South. In addition, British merchants regarded Texas as a potentially important free-trade area—an offset to the tariff-walled United States. English manufacturers likewise perceived that the billowing plains of the Lone Star Republic were one of the great cotton-producing areas of the future. An independent Texas would relieve British looms of their fatal dependence on American fiber, a supply which might be cut off in time of crisis by embargo or by war.

The Texan Nuptials

Partly as a result of the fears aroused by British schemers, Texas became a leading issue in the presidential campaign of 1844. The foes of expansion opposed annexation, while Southern hotheads cried, "Texas or Disunion." When the pro-expansion Democrats triumphed, President Tyler interpreted the narrow Democratic victory, with dubious accuracy, as a "mandate" to acquire Texas.

Eager to crown his troubled administration with this splendid prize, Tyler deserves much of the credit—or blame—for shepherding Texas into the Union. Despairing of a two-thirds vote for a treaty in the Senate, he now made haste to arrange for annexation by a joint resolution. This alternative required only a simple majority in both houses of Congress. After a spirited debate, the resolution passed early in 1845, and the Lone Star Republic was formally invited to become the twenty-eighth star in the American flag. After some coyness, the waiting bride unpacked her mildewing wedding dress, and was formally embraced as a full-fledged state.

Mexico angrily charged that the Americans had despoiled her of Texas. This was to some extent true in 1836, but hardly true in 1845, for Texas was no longer Mexico's to be despoiled of. As the years stretched out, it had become increasingly evident that the Mexicans would not be able to reconquer their lost province. Yet like Aesop's dog in the manger, they would not concede the right of Texas to dispose of herself as she chose.

By 1845, the Lone Star Republic had become a danger spot, inviting foreign intrigue that menaced the American people. Her continued existence as an independent nation threatened to involve the United States in a series of ruinous wars, both in America and in Europe. Americans were in a "lick all creation" mood when they sang "Uncle Sam's Song to Miss Texas":

> If Mexy back'd by secret foes,
>   Still talks of getting you, gal;
> Why we can lick 'em all you know
>   And then annex 'em too, gal.

What other power would have spurned the imperial domain of Texas? The bride was so near, so rich, so fair, so willing. Whatever the peculiar circumstances of the Texas revolution, the United States can hardly be accused of unseemly haste in achieving annexation. Nine long years were surely a decent wait between the beginning of the courtship and the consummation of the marriage.

Oregon Fever

The so-called Oregon country was an enormous wilderness. It sprawled magnificently west of the Rockies to the Pacific Ocean, and north of California to the line of 54° 40′—the present southern tip of the Alaska panhandle. All or substantial parts of this immense area were claimed at one time or another by four nations: Spain, Russia, Great Britain, and the United States.

Two claimants dropped out of the scramble. Spain, though the first to raise her banner in Oregon, bartered away her claims to us in the so-called Florida Treaty of 1819. The Russian Bear retreated to the line of 54° 40′ by the treaties of 1824 and 1825 with America and Britain. These two remaining rivals now had the field to themselves.

The British claims to Oregon were strong—at least to that portion north of the Columbia River. They were based squarely on prior discovery and exploration, on treaty rights, and on actual occupation. The most important colonizing agency was the far-flung Hudson's Bay Company, which was trading profitably with the Oregon Indians for their furs.

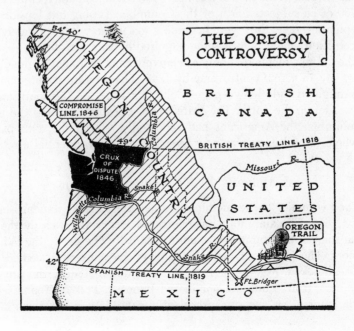

The Americans, for their part, could also point pridefully to exploration and occupation. Captain Gray in 1792 had stumbled upon the majestic Columbia River, which he named after his ship; and the famed Lewis and Clark expedition of 1804–1806 had ranged overland through the Oregon Country to the Pacific. This shaky American foothold was ultimately strengthened by the presence of missionaries and other settlers, a sprinkling of whom reached the grassy Willamette River Valley, south of the Columbia, in the 1830's. These men of God, in saving the soul of the Indian, were instrumental in saving the soil of Oregon for the United States. They stimulated interest in a faraway domain which countless Americans had earlier assumed would not be settled for centuries.

The scattered Americans and British in Oregon continued to live peacefully side by side. At the time of negotiating the Treaty of 1818, the United States had sought to divide this vast domain along the line of the 49th parallel. But the British, who regarded the Columbia River as the St. Lawrence of the West, were unwilling to yield this vital artery. A scheme for peaceful joint occupation was accordingly adopted, pending a future settlement.

The handful of Americans in the Willamette Valley was suddenly multiplied in the early 1840's, when a flush of "Oregon fever" seized hundreds of our restless pioneers. In increasing numbers their creaking covered wagons jolted over the Oregon Trail as the human rivulet widened into a stream. By 1846 there were about 5000 American settlers south of the Columbia River, some of them hardy "border ruffians," expert with the Bowie knife and the "revolving pistol."

The British, in the face of this rising torrent of humanity, could muster only 700 or so subjects north of the Columbia. Losing out lopsidedly in the population race, they were beginning to see the wisdom of arriving at a peaceful settlement before being engulfed by their neighbors.

The curious fact is that only a relatively small segment of the Oregon country was in actual controversy by 1845. The area in dispute consisted of the rough triangle between the Columbia River on the south and the 49th parallel on the north. The British had repeatedly offered the line of the Columbia; the Americans had repeatedly offered the 49th parallel. The whole fateful issue was now tossed into the presidential election of 1844.

A Mandate(?) for Manifest Destiny

The two major parties nominated their presidential standard-bearers in May, 1844. The ambitious but frustrated Henry Clay, easily the most popular man in the country, was enthusiastically chosen by the Whigs at Baltimore. The Democrats, meeting later in the same city, seemed hopelessly deadlocked. Finally the expansionists, dominated by the pro-Texas Southerners, trotted out and nominated James K. Polk of Tennessee, the first "dark horse" or "surprise" presidential candidate in American history.

Polk may have been a "dark horse," but he was not an unknown or decrepit horse. Speaker of the House of Representatives for four years and governor of Tennessee for two terms, he was a determined, industrious, and intelligent public servant. Sponsored by Andrew Jackson, his friend and neighbor, he was rather hollowly built up by the Democrats as "Young Hickory." The Whigs attempted to jeer him into oblivion with the taunt, "Who is James K. Polk?" They soon found out.

The campaign of 1844 was, in part, an expression of the mighty emotional upsurge known as Manifest Destiny. Countless Americans in the 1840's and 1850's, feeling a sense of mission, believed that Almighty God had "manifestly" destined our people for a hemispheric career. We would irresistibly spread our uplifting and ennobling democratic institutions over at least the entire North American continent, and possibly over South America as well.

The expansionist Democrats were strongly under the intoxicating spell of Manifest Destiny. They came out flat-footedly in their platform for the "Reannexation of Texas" and the "Reoccupation of Oregon," all the way to 54° 40′. Outbellowing the Whig log-cabinites in the game of slogans, they shouted, "Young Hickory, Dallas, and Victory" and "All of Oregon or None." They also condemned Clay as a "corrupt bargainer," a dissolute character, and a slaveowner. (Their own candidate, Polk, also owned slaves.)

The Whigs, as noisemakers, took no back seat. They countered with such slogans as "Hooray for Clay" and "Polk, Slavery, and Texas, or Clay, Union, and Liberty." They also spread the lie that a gang of Tennessee slaves had been seen on their way to a Southern market with the initials J.K.P. [James K. Polk] branded on them.

On the crucial issue of Texas, the acrobatic Clay tried to ride two horses at once. The "Great Compromiser" appears to have compromised away the Presidency when he wrote a series of confusing letters. They seemed to say that while he personally favored annexing slaveholding Texas (an appeal to the South), he also favored postponing action on Texas (an appeal to the North). He might have lost more ground if he had not "straddled," but he certainly alienated the more ardent anti-slavery people.

In the stretch drive, "Dark Horse" Polk nipped Henry Clay at the wire, 170 to 105 in the Electoral College and 1,337,243 to 1,299,062 in the popular column. Clay would have triumphed if he had not lost New York State by a scant 5000 votes. There the tiny anti-slavery Liberty Party absorbed nearly 16,000 votes, many of which would presumably have gone to the unlucky Kentuckian. Ironically, the anti-Texas Liberty Party, by helping to insure the election of pro-Texas Polk, hastened the annexation of the Lone Star Republic.

The expansionist Democrats, flushed with victory, proclaimed that they had received a mandate from the voters to annex Texas. But a presidential election is seldom, if ever, a clear-cut mandate on anything. The only way to secure a true indication of the voters' will is to hold a special election on the issue in question. The picture that emerges in 1844 is not one of mandate but of muddle. What else could there have been when the results were so close, the personalities so colorful, and the issues so numerous—including Oregon, Texas, the tariff, slavery, the Bank, and internal improvements? Yet this unclear "mandate" was interpreted by President Tyler as a clear mandate to annex Texas—and he acted accordingly.

Polk the Purposeful

"Young Hickory" Polk, unlike "Old Hickory" Jackson, was not an impressive figure. Of middle height, lean, long-haired, and stern-faced, he took life seriously and drove himself mercilessly into a premature grave. Methodical and hard-working rather than brilliant, he was shrewd, narrow, conscientious, tenacious, and persistent. "What he went for he fetched," wrote a contemporary. Purposeful in the highest degree, he entered office with a positive four-point program, and with unprecedented success achieved it completely in less than four years.

One of Polk's goals was a lowered tariff. His Secretary of the Treasury, wispy Robert J. Walker, devised a tariff-for-revenue bill which reduced the average rates of the Tariff of 1842 from about 32% to 25%. With the strong support of low-tariff Southerners, Walker lobbied the measure through Congress, though not without loud complaints from the Clayites, especially in New England and the Middle States, that American manufacturing would be ruined. But these prophets of doom missed the mark.

House Vote on Tariff of 1846

	For	Against
New England	9	19
Middle States	18	44
West and Northwest	29	10
South and Southwest	58	20
Total	114	93

The Walker Tariff of 1846 actually proved to be an excellent revenue producer, largely because its passage was followed by boom times and heavy imports.

A second objective of Polk was the restoration of the Independent Treasury, unceremoniously dropped by the Whigs in 1841. The pro-Bank Whigs in Congress presented vigorous opposition, but victory at last crowned the President's efforts in 1846.

The third and fourth points on Polk's "must list" were the acquisition of California and the settlement of the Oregon dispute.

The "reoccupation" of the "whole" of Oregon had been promised to the Northern Democrats in the campaign of 1844. But the Southern Democrats, once they had "reannexed" Texas, rapidly cooled off. Polk, himself a Southerner, had no intention of insisting on the 54° 40′ pledge of his own platform. Feeling bound by the three offers of his predecessors, he again proposed to John Bull the compromise line of 49°. But the British minister in Washington haughtily spurned this olive branch.

The next move on the Oregon chessboard was up to Britain. Fortunately for peace, the London ministry began to experience a change of

RIDICULOUS EXHIBITION; OR, YANKEE-NOODLE PUTTING HIS HEAD INTO THE
BRITISH LION'S MOUTH

British view of American bluster on the Oregon issue. *Punch,* 1846

heart. British anti-expansionists ("Little Englanders") were now persuaded that the Columbia River after all was not the St. Lawrence of the West, and that probably the turbulent American hordes would one day seize the Oregon country. Why fight a hazardous war over this wilderness on behalf of a hated monopoly, the Hudson's Bay Company, which had already "furred out" much of the area anyhow?

Early in 1846 the British, hat in hand, came around and themselves proposed the line of 49°. Polk, irked by his previous rebuff, threw the responsibility for a decision squarely into the lap of the Senate. The Senators speedily accepted the offer and approved the subsequent treaty, despite a few diehard shouts of "Fifty-four forty forever!" The fact that the United

States was then a month deep in the Mexican War doubtless influenced the final decision.

Satisfaction with the Oregon settlement among Americans was not unanimous. The Northwestern states, hotbed of Manifest Destiny and "fifty-four fortyism," joined the anti-slavery men in condemning what they regarded as a base betrayal by the South. Why *all* of Texas and not *all* of Oregon? Because, sneered the expansionist Senator Benton of Missouri, "Great Britain is powerful and Mexico is weak."

So Polk, despite all the campaign bluster, got neither "fifty-four forty" nor a fight with Britain. But he did get something that in the long run was better: a reasonably fair compromise without the shedding of a drop of blood.

Basic Causes of the Mexican War

Sun-drenched California was another worry of Polk's. He and other disciples of Manifest Destiny had long coveted its verdant valleys, and especially the spacious bay of San Francisco. This splendid harbor was widely regarded as America's future window on the Pacific Ocean.

The population of California in 1845 was curiously mixed. It consisted of some 7000 sun-basking Spanish-Mexicans, plus more than ten times as many dispirited Indians. There were fewer than a thousand foreigners, mostly Americans, some of whom had "left their consciences at Cape Horn." Given time, these transplanted Yankees might yet bring California into the Union by "playing the Texas game."

Polk was eager to buy California from Mexico, but relations with Mexico City were dangerously embittered. Among other friction points, the United States had claims against the Mexicans for some $3,000,000 in damages to American citizens and their property. The revolution-riddled regime in Mexico had agreed to assume this debt, but had been forced to default on its payments.

A more serious bone of contention was Texas. The Mexican government, after threatening war if the United States should acquire the Lone Star Republic, had recalled its minister from Washington following annexation. Diplomatic relations were completely severed.

The deadlock with Mexico over Texas was further tightened by a question of boundaries. During the long era of Spanish-Mexican occupation, the southwestern boundary of Texas had been the Nueces River. But the expansive Texans, on rather farfetched grounds, were claiming the more southerly Rio Grande instead. Polk, for his part, felt a strong moral obligation to defend Texas in her claim, once we had annexed her domain.

The Mexicans were much less concerned about this boundary quibble than the United States. In their eyes all of Texas was still theirs, although temporarily in revolt, and the quarrel over the two rivers seemed somewhat pointless. Yet Polk was careful to keep American troops out of the explosive no man's land between the Nueces and the Rio Grande, as long as there was any real prospect of peaceful adjustment.

The golden prize of California continued to cause Polk much anxiety. Disquieting rumors (now known to have been ill-founded) were circulating that the British Lion was about to buy or seize California—a grab that the Americans could not tolerate under the Monroe Doctrine. In a last desperate throw of the dice, Polk dispatched John Slidell to Mexico City as minister late in 1845. The new envoy, among other alternatives,

was instructed to offer a maximum of $25,000,000 for California and the intervening territory. But the proud Mexicans would not even permit Slidell to present his "insulting" proposition.

American Blood on American(?) Soil

Polk was now prepared to force a showdown. On January 13, 1846, he ordered 4000 men, under General Zachary Taylor, to march from the Nueces River to the Rio Grande, provocatively near Mexican forces. Polk's presidential diary reveals that he expected at any moment to hear of a clash. When none occurred after an anxious wait, he informed his Cabinet, on May 9, 1846, that he proposed to ask Congress to declare war on the basis of (a) unpaid claims and (b) Slidell's rejection. These, at best, were rather hollow pretexts. Two Cabinet members thereupon spoke up and said that they would feel better satisfied if Mexican troops should fire first.

That very evening, as fate would have it, news of bloodshed arrived. On April 25, 1846, Mexican troops had crossed the Rio Grande and had attacked General Taylor's command, with a loss of sixteen Americans killed or wounded.

Polk, no doubt relieved, dispatched a stirring war message to Congress. He declared that despite "all our efforts" to avoid a clash, hostilities had been forced upon us by the shedding of "American blood on the American soil." A patriotic Congress overwhelmingly voted for war, and enthusiastic volunteers cried, "Ho for the Halls of the Montezumas!" and "Mexico or Death!" Inflamed by the war fever, even anti-slavery Whig centers joined with the rest of the nation, though they later condemned "Jimmy Polk's war." As James Russell Lowell lamented,

> Massachusetts, God forgive her,
> She's akneelin' with the rest. . . .

Polk, in his message to Congress, was making history—not writing it. If he had been a historian, he would have explained that American blood had been shed on soil which the Mexicans had reason to regard as their own. A gangling, rough-featured Whig Congressman from Illinois, one Abraham Lincoln, introduced certain resolutions that requested information as to the precise "spot" on American soil where American blood had been shed. He pushed his "spot" resolutions with such persistence that he came to be known as the "spotty Lincoln." The more extreme anti-slavery agitators of the North, many of them Whigs, branded the President a liar—"Polk the Mendacious."

Did Polk provoke war? California was the fourth and remaining point on his program. Mexico would not sell it at any price. The only way to get it was to use force, or wait for an internal American revolt. But delay seemed hazardous, for the claws of the British Lion might snatch the ripening California fruit from the talons of the American Eagle. Our grievances against Mexico were annoying yet tolerable; in later years we endured even worse ones. But in the circumstances of 1846 patience had ceased to be a virtue, at least as far as Polk was concerned. So he pushed the quarrel to a bloody clash on the Rio Grande.

Both sides, in fact, were spoiling for a fight. Hotheaded Americans, especially Southern and Southwestern expansionists, were eager to teach the Mexican "greasers" a lesson. The Mexicans, in turn, were burning to chastise the "Bullies of the North." Possessing a considerable standing army, heavily overstaffed with generals, they boasted of invading the United States, freeing the Negro slaves, and lassoing whole regiments of American "gringos." They were hoping that the dispute over Oregon would blossom into a full-dress war, as it came near doing, and further pin down the hated *Yanquis*. A conquest of Mexico's vast and arid country seemed fantastic, especially in view of the bungling American invasion of Canada in 1812.

Both sides were fired by moral indignation. The Mexicans could fight with the flaming sword of righteousness, for had not the "insolent" Yankee picked a fight by polluting their soil? Many earnest Americans, on the other hand, sincerely believed that the enemy had provoked the war by invading our territory.

The Mastering of Mexico

Polk wanted California—not war. But when war came he hoped to fight it on a limited scale, and then pull out when he had won the prize. The dethroned Mexican dictator Santa Anna, who was then exiled in Cuba, let it be known that if the American blockading squadron would permit him to slip into Mexico, he would sell out his country. This discreditable intrigue was finally carried through. But the doubly treacherous Santa Anna, self-styled "Napoleon of the West," rallied the Mexicans to a desperate defense of their soil against the "gringo" invader.

American operations in the Southwest and in California were completely successful. In 1846 General Stephen W. Kearny led a detachment of about 1700 troops over the famous Santa Fe trail, from Fort Leavenworth to Santa Fe. This sun-baked outpost, its plazas drowsy with history, was easily captured. But before Kearny could reach California, the fertile province was won. When war broke out, Captain John C. Frémont, the dashing explorer, had just "happened" to be there with several dozen well-armed men. In helping to overthrow Mexican rule in 1846, he collaborated with American naval officers and with the local Americans, who had hoisted the short-lived banner of the California Bear Flag Republic.

General Zachary Taylor meanwhile had been spearheading the main thrust. Known as "Old Rough and Ready" because of his iron constitution and incredibly sloppy appearance—he sometimes wore a Mexican straw hat—he fought his way across the Rio Grande into Mexico. After several gratifying victories, he reached Buena Vista. There, on February 22–23, 1847, his weakened force of 5000 men was attacked by some 20,000 troops under Santa Anna. The Mexicans were finally repulsed with extreme difficulty, and overnight Zachary Taylor became the "Hero of Buena Vista." One Kentuckian was heard to say that "Old Zack" would be elected President in 1848 by "spontaneous combustion."

Sound American strategy now called for a crushing blow at the enemy's vitals—Mexico City. General Taylor, a good leader of modest-sized forces but no Bonaparte, could not win decisively in the semi-deserts of northern Mexico. The command of the new expedition, which pushed in-

KEARNY'S ROUTE
1846

MEXICAN CESSION
(Together with all Texas)

Platte R.

Ft. Leavenworth
Missouri R.

Bent's Fort

Colorado R.

Los Angeles

San Diego

Gila R.

Santa Fe

CLAIMED BY TEXAS

Arkansas R.

Mississippi R.

Red R.

TEXAS

M E X I C O

Rio Grande

Corpus Christi

TAYLOR'S ROUTE
1846–1847

Monterrey

Buena Vista

Matamoros

SCOTT'S ROUTE
1847

MAJOR CAMPAIGNS
of MEXICAN WAR

Mexico City   Vera Cruz

land from the coastal city of Vera Cruz early in 1847, was entrusted to General Winfield Scott. A handsome giant of a man, Scott had emerged as a hero from the War of 1812 and had subsequently earned the nickname of "Old Fuss and Feathers" because of his resplendent uniforms and strict discipline. He was severely handicapped in the Mexican campaign by inadequate numbers of troops, by expiring enlistments, by a more numerous enemy, by mountainous terrain, by disease, and by political backbiting at home. But he succeeded in battling his way up to Mexico City, by September, 1847, in one of the most brilliant campaigns in American military annals.

Fighting for Peace

Polk was anxious to end the shooting as soon as he could secure his territorial goals. Accordingly, he sent along with Scott's invading army the Chief Clerk of the State Department, Nicholas P. Trist, who among other weaknesses was afflicted with an overfluid pen. Trist and Scott arranged for an armistice with Santa Anna, at a cost of $10,000. But the wily dictator pocketed the bribe, and then used the time to bolster his defenses.

Negotiating a treaty with a sword in one hand and a pen in the other was ticklish business. Polk, disgusted with his blundering envoy, abruptly recalled Trist. The wordy diplomat thereupon dashed off a sixty-five-page letter, explaining why he was not going to come home. The President was furious. But Trist, seizing a fleeting opportunity to conclude negotiations, signed the Treaty of Guadalupe-Hidalgo on February 2, 1848, and forwarded it to Washington.

The terms of the treaty were sweeping. They confirmed the American title to Texas, and yielded the enormous area stretching westward to Oregon and the ocean and embracing coveted California. This total expanse, including Texas, was about one-half of Mexico. The United States agreed to pay $15,000,000 for the land, and to assume the claims of its citizens against Mexico in the amount of $3,250,000.

Polk promptly submitted the treaty to the Senate. Although Trist had proved highly annoying, he had generally followed his original instructions. And haste was imperative. The anti-slavery Whigs in Congress—"Mexican Whigs," they were called—were condemning this "damnable war" with increasing heat. They were even threatening to vote down supplies for the armies in the field. If they had been able to do so, Scott probably would have been forced to retreat, and the full fruits of victory might have been tossed away.

Another peril impended. A swelling group of American expansionists, intoxicated by Manifest Destiny, was clamoring for all of Mexico. If we had seized it, we would have been saddled with an intolerably costly and vexatious policing problem. Farseeing Southerners like Calhoun, disturbed by the mounting anger of the anti-slavery agitators, realized that the South would do well not to be too greedy. The treaty was finally approved by the Senate, 38 to 14. Oddly enough, it was condemned both by opponents who wanted all of Mexico and by opponents who wanted none of it.

The victor does not ordinarily pay an indemnity, especially after a costly conflict has been "forced" on him. Yet Polk, who had planned to offer $25,000,000 before the war, arranged to pay $18,250,000 after winning the war. Cynics have charged that the Americans were pricked by guilty consciences; apologists have pointed proudly to the "Anglo-Saxon spirit of fair play." A decisive consideration was the need for haste, while there was still a responsible Mexican government to carry out the treaty, and before political foes at home, notably the anti-slavery zealots, sabotaged Polk's expansionist program.

Profit and Loss

The Mexican War was a small one, as wars go. It cost only 13,000 American lives, most of them taken by disease. But the fruits of the fighting were enormous.

The total expanse of the United States, already vast, was increased by about one-third (counting Texas)—an addition greater than that of the Louisiana Purchase. A sharp stimulus was given to the spirit of Manifest Destiny, for, as the proverb has it, the appetite comes with eating.

The Mexican War, as fate ordained, was the blood-spattered school-room of the Civil War. The campaigns provided invaluable field experi-ence for most of the officers destined to become leading generals in the forthcoming conflict, including Captain Robert E. Lee and Lieutenant U. S. Grant. The Military Academy at West Point, founded in 1802, fully justified its existence through the well-trained officers it contributed. The navy likewise did valuable yet unspectacular work in throwing a crippling blockade around Mexican ports. The Marine Corps, in existence since 1798, won new laurels, and to this day sings in its stirring hymn of the Halls of Montezuma.

The United States army waged the war without defeat and without a major blunder, despite formidable obstacles and a half dozen or so re-markably long marches. Chagrined British critics, as well as other foreign skeptics, reluctantly revised upward their estimate of Yankee military prowess. The opposing armies, moreover, emerged with increased respect for each other. The Mexicans, though poorly led, fought heroically, and at Chapultepec, near Mexico City, the teen-age lads of the military acad-emy (*los niños*) perished to a boy.

The vanquished Mexicans have never forgotten, nor will they soon forget, that the northern "gringos" tore away half of their country. The argument that they were lucky not to lose all of it could scarcely be ex-pected to lessen their bitterness. The war marked an ugly turning point in the relations between the United States and Latin America as a whole. Hitherto, Uncle Sam had been regarded with some complacency, even friendliness. Henceforth, he was increasingly to be feared as the "Colossus of the North." Suspicious neighbors to the south began to condemn him as a greedy and untrustworthy bully, who might next despoil them of their heritage.

Most ominous of all, the war rearoused the snarling dog of the slavery issue, and the beast did not stop yelping until silenced by the Civil War. Abolitionists assailed the Mexican conflict as one provoked by the South-ern "slavocracy" for its own evil purposes. As James Russell Lowell had Hosea Biglow drawl in his Yankee dialect:

> They jest want this Californy
> So's to lug new slave-states in
> To abuse ye, an' to scorn ye,
> An' to plunder ye like sin.

In support of Lowell's accusation, the bulk of the American volunteer troops were admittedly from the South and Southwest. But, as in the case of the Texan revolution, the basic explanation was proximity rather than conspiracy.

The quarrel over slavery extension also erupted on the floors of Congress. In 1846, shortly after the shooting started, Polk requested an appropriation of $2,000,000 with which to buy a peace. Representative David Wilmot of Pennsylvania, fearful of the Southern "slavocracy," introduced a fateful amendment. It stipulated that slavery should never exist in any of the territory to be wrested from Mexico.

The disruptive Wilmot amendment twice passed the House, but not the Senate. The Southern members, unwilling to be robbed of prospective slave states, fought the restriction with tooth and nail. The anti-slavery men, in Congress and out, battled no less bitterly on the other side. The so-called Wilmot Proviso soon came to symbolize the burning issue of slavery in the territories.

The opening shots of the Mexican War were, in a broad sense, the opening shots of the Civil War. President Polk left the nation the splendid physical heritage of California, but unfortunately he left also the ugly moral heritage of an embittered slavery dispute. The Mexicans could later take satisfaction in knowing that the territory wrenched from them had proved to be a frightful apple of discord.

SELECT READINGS

Excellent introductions are G. G. VAN DEUSEN, *The Jacksonian Era, 1828–1848* (1959) and R. A. BILLINGTON, *The Far Western Frontier, 1830–1860* (1956), both paperback. O. P. CHITWOOD, *John Tyler* (1939) may be supplemented by ROBERT SEAGER, *And Tyler Too: A Biography of John and Julia Gardiner Tyler* (1963). FREDERICK MERK, *Manifest Destiny and Mission in American History* (1963) deals broadly with the subject, while N. A. GRAEBNER, *Empire on the Pacific* (1955) portrays Polk as an advance agent of Manifest Destiny. An older detailed study is A. K. WEINBERG, *Manifest Destiny* (1935) [paperback]. An illuminating survey is O. A. SINGLETARY, *The Mexican War* (1960) [paperback]. More detailed are A. H. BILL, *Rehearsal for Conflict* (1947) and R. S. HENRY, *The Story of the Mexican War* (1950). J. H. SMITH's older Pulitzer-prize and pro-United States classic, *The War With Mexico* (2 vols., 1919), must not be overlooked. A useful evaluation is C. A. MC COY, *Polk and the Presidency* (1960). Also *Harvard Guide*, Pt. IV.

16

The Revolution in Industry and Transportation
1790–1860

The progress of invention is really a threat [to monarchy].
Whenever I see a railroad I look for a republic.

RALPH WALDO EMERSON, 1866

The March of Mechanization

A GIFTED GROUP of British inventors, beginning about 1750, perfected a series of machines for the mass production of textiles. This enslavement of steam multiplied the power of man's muscles some ten thousandfold, and ushered in the modern factory system.

The so-called Industrial Revolution has been misnamed. It was not a revolution in the sense of an overnight change or upheaval. The machines developed in England were gradually improved over several decades, and the British people were scarcely aware that a significant shift was taking place. Nor was the Industrial Revolution solely industrial. It was accompanied by a no less spectacular transformation in the agencies of transportation and communication.

The factory system gradually spread from England—"the world's workshop"—to other lands. After a generation or more it reached western Europe, and then the United States. Why was the infant American republic, destined to be an industrial giant, so slow to embrace the machine?

There is no simple answer. For one thing, fertile soil in America was cheap. Land-starved descendants of land-starved peasants were not going to coop themselves up in smelly factories when they might till their own soil in God's fresh air and sunlight. Labor was therefore generally scarce, and enough nimble hands to operate the machines were hard to find. Money for capital investment, moreover, was not plentiful in pioneering America. Raw materials were undeveloped, undiscovered, or unsuspected. The United States was one day to become the leading coal producer of the world, but a considerable amount of coal used in colonial times was imported from England.

Additional obstacles hindered the spread of the factory system. The sparsely sprinkled population did not provide the backlog of a domestic consuming market, without which manufacturing on an immense scale was unprofitable. Even if there had been thickly settled areas, the manufactured articles could not easily have been carried to them, owing to the absence of railroads and other efficient means of transportation.

Long-established British factories, which provided cutthroat competition, posed another problem. Their superiority was attested by the fact that a few unscrupulous Yankee manufacturers, out to make a dishonest dollar, learned to stamp their own product with faked English trademarks.

The British also enjoyed a monopoly of the textile machinery, whose secrets they were anxious to keep out of the hands of foreign competitors. Parliament enacted laws, in harmony with the ancient mercantilistic system, forbidding the export of the machines, or the emigration of mechanics able to reproduce them.

Despite all these handicaps, a surprising amount of small-scale manufacturing existed in the United States when the Republic was launched. As early as 1791, Alexander Hamilton reported that the wheels of seventeen different kinds of enterprises were humming. Yet the future industrial colossus was still snoring. Not until well past the middle of the next century did the value of the output of our factories exceed that of our farms.

Ending the Fiber Famine

Samuel Slater has been called the "Father of the Factory System" in America, and seldom can the paternity of a movement more properly be pinned onto one person. As a skilled British mechanic of twenty-one, he was attracted by bounties being offered in the United States to English workmen familiar with the textile machines. Having memorized the plans of the machinery, he escaped in disguise to America and won the backing of Moses Brown, a Quaker capitalist in Rhode Island. Laboriously reconstructing the machines with the aid of a blacksmith and a carpenter, he put into operation in 1791 the first efficient American machinery for the spinning of cotton thread.

The ravenous machine was now ready, but where was the cotton fiber? Hand-picking one pound of lint from three pounds of seed was a full day's work for one slave, and this process was so expensive that cotton cloth was relatively rare. In 1785 eight bales of cotton were seized for fraudulent entry at Liverpool, England. The officials charged that so much cotton could not have been produced in America.

Another mechanical genius now entered the picture, Massachusetts-born Eli Whitney. After graduating from Yale College, he journeyed to Georgia to serve as a private tutor while preparing for the law. There he was informed that the poverty of the South would be relieved if someone could only invent a workable device for separating the seed from the short-staple cotton fiber. Within ten days, in 1793, he constructed a crude machine which was fifty times more effective than the hand-picking process. The cotton gin (short for en*gine*) was so simple that rivals infringed on Whitney's patent, and in the end he netted only relatively small profits from this particular brain child.

Few machines have ever wrought so tremendous a change. The gin affected not only the history of America but that of the world. Almost overnight the raising of cotton became highly profitable, and the South was soon tied hand and foot to the throne of King Cotton. Human bondage had been dying out, but the insatiable demand for cotton reriveted the chains on the limbs of the luckless Negro. As slavery was a major factor in bringing on the Civil War, the Yankee Eli Whitney, while briefly sojourning in the South, unintentionally had a large hand in causing the bloody clash.

The North likewise prospered, for the cotton gin poured out avalanches of snowy fiber for the spindles of the Yankee machines. The American phase of the Industrial Revolution, which first blossomed in cotton textiles, was well on its way. Yet many decades were to pass before Priscilla's spinning wheel was driven into the attic, and from there into the antique shops.

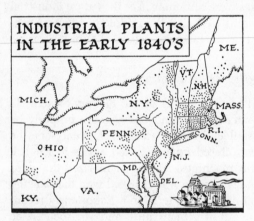

INDUSTRIAL PLANTS IN THE EARLY 1840'S

The earliest textile factories merely spun the fiber into cotton thread or woolen yarn. The actual weaving into cloth was done laboriously by hand in the home or by contract weavers. Not until 1814, at Waltham, Massachusetts, was the first dual-purpose plant established: it spun the fiber and wove the finished cloth under the same roof. Water power and steam power were gradually coming to supplant mother-and-daughter power.

The factory system at first flourished most actively in New England, though branching out into the more populous areas of New York, New Jersey, and Pennsylvania. The South, increasingly wedded to the production of cotton, could boast of comparatively little manufacturing.

New England was singularly favored for several reasons. Her narrow belt of stony soil discouraged farming and hence made manufacturing more attractive than elsewhere. A relatively dense population provided labor; shipping brought in capital; and snug seaports made easy the import of raw materials and the export of the finished products. Finally, the rapid rivers—notably the Merrimack in Massachusetts—provided abundant water power to turn the cogs of the machines.

Marvels in Manufacturing

The American factory system developed slowly until about 1807, when there began the fateful sequence of the embargo, non-intercourse, and the War of 1812. Stern necessity dictated the manufacture of substitutes for normal imports, while the stoppage of European commerce was temporarily ruinous to Yankee shipping. Both capital and labor were driven from the waves into the factory as New England, in the happy phrase of John Randolph, exchanged the trident for the distaff. Generous bounties were offered for home-grown manufacturing; "Buy American" became a popular slogan; and patriotism prompted the wearing of baggy homespun garments. President Madison donned some at his inauguration, where he was said to have been a walking argument for the better processing of native wool.

The honeymoon days of manufacturing ended abruptly with the Peace of Ghent in 1815. British competitors unloaded their dammed-up surpluses at ruinously low prices, and American newspapers were so full of British advertisements for goods on credit that little space was left for news. In one Rhode Island district, all 150 mills were forced to close their doors, except the Slater plant. Congress was prodded into giving some relief in 1816, when it passed a mildly protective tariff.

As the factory system spread, it embraced numerous other industries in addition to textiles. Prominent among them was the manufacturing of firearms, and here the wizardly Eli Whitney again appeared with a remarkable contribution. Frustrated in his earlier efforts to monopolize the cotton gin, he turned to the mass production of muskets for the United States army. Up to this time each part of a firearm had been hand-tooled, and if the trigger of one broke, the trigger of another might or might not fit. About 1798 Whitney conceived the idea of having machines make each part, so that all the triggers, for example, would be as much alike as the successive imprints of a copperplate engraving. Journeying to Washington, he dismantled ten of his new muskets in the presence of skeptical officials, scrambled the parts together, and then quickly reassembled ten different muskets.

The principle of interchangeable parts was widely adopted by 1850, and it ultimately became the basis of the modern mass-production, assembly-line methods. It gave to the North that vast industrial plant which insured military preponderance over the South. The Yankee Eli Whitney, by inventing the cotton gin, perhaps made inevitable the Civil War. The Yankee Eli Whitney, by popularizing (if not inventing) the principle of interchangeable parts, contributed heavily to the winning of that war by the Union.

The factory system of the North received another strong boost about 1850, when the sewing machine was perfected for making clothing, both in the home and in the factory. Here emerged the figure of Elias Howe, who suffered such extreme poverty that when his wife died he had to wear borrowed "Sunday" clothes to her funeral. He finally succeeded commercially where others had failed; and the royalties from his invention, patented in 1846, rapidly mounted to $4000 a week. The new stitching device was also utilized for the mass production of boots and shoes.

The sewing machine was of incalculable significance. It was the foundation of the ready-made clothing industry, which took root about the time of the Civil War. It drove the seamstress from the shelter of the private home into the factory, where as a human robot she tended the chattering mechanisms. The sewing machine likewise played a significant role in winning the Civil War for the North. It released for the armies tens of thousands of young men who, as shoemakers or tailors, would have been tied to their benches; and it put uniforms on their backs and boots on their feet.

Great inventions seem to unchain the human imagination and stimulate other inventions. The ingenuity of the American people before the Civil War is best revealed by the number of patents registered in Washington. The decade ending in 1800 saw only 306; the decade ending in 1860 saw the amazing total of 28,000. America was truly the land of the free and the home of the ingenious. Yet in 1838 the Clerk of the Patent Office had resigned in despair, complaining that all worthwhile inventions had been discovered.

Wage Slaves

One ugly offspring of the factory system was an increasingly acute labor problem. Hitherto manufacturing had been carried on in the home, or in the small shop, where the master craftsman and his apprentice, rubbing elbows at the same bench, could maintain an intimate and friendly relationship. The Industrial Revolution submerged this personal association in the impersonal ownership of the sprawling factory. Around it, like tumors, the slum-like hovels of the "wage slaves" tended to cluster.

Women and children were also sucked into the unhealthy vortex of the factory. There, six days a week, they were required to toil for a pittance during a dreary stint of twelve or thirteen hours—"from dark to dark." The plight of the women was normally bad enough, but it was worse for children of both sexes. Young folk, ranging from four to sixteen years of age, were mentally blighted, emotionally starved, physically stunted, and even brutally whipped. In Samuel Slater's mill of 1791, the first nine machine-tenders were seven boys and two girls, all under twelve.

Happily there were a few exceptions to these dismal conditions. This was notably true in Lowell, Massachusetts, among the clean and attractive factory girls. To the surprise of visitors, including Charles Dickens, they published their own newspaper. But the "Song of the Manchester Factory Girl" was no doubt overdrawn:

> She tends the loom, she watches the spindle,
>   And cheerfully talketh away;
> Mid the din of wheels, how her bright eyes kindle!
>   And her bosom is ever gay.

The laboring man himself had no bed of roses. He failed to share proportionately in the golden glow of prosperity produced by the factory system. His hours were long, his wages were low, and his meals were hastily gulped. He was forced to work in unsanitary buildings that were poorly ventilated, lighted, and heated. He was forbidden by law to form labor unions to raise his wages, for such cooperative activity was regarded as a criminal conspiracy. It is not surprising, therefore, that only twenty-four recorded strikes occurred before 1835.

Triumphs for the Toilers

The plight of the wage worker improved markedly in the 1820's and 1830's. In the full flush of Jacksonian democracy, many of the states granted the laboring man the vote. Brandishing the ballot as his weapon, he first strove to lighten his burden through workingmen's parties. Aside from the ten-hour day, higher wages, and pleasanter working conditions, he demanded public education for his children and an end to the inhuman practice of imprisonment for debt.

The employers, fearing the rise of the "rabble" in politics, fought the ten-hour day to the last ditch. They argued that reduced hours would lessen production, increase costs, and demoralize the workhand. He would have so much leisure time that the Devil would lead him into mischief. An encouraging gain was at length registered for labor in 1840, when President Van Buren established the ten-hour day for federal employees on public works. In ensuing years, a number of states gradually followed this path-breaking example by reducing the hours of workingmen.

Despite these victories, the begrimed wage earner had his ups and downs in the decades before the Civil War. He was especially hard hit by the panics of 1837 and 1857. Depressions always hurt the manual worker, because they bring unemployment and glut the labor market. The efforts of the workingman to use the ballot as a bludgeon often turned out badly, and some of the labor reformers became bogged down in crack-brained schemes.

Disillusioned, the day laborer at last learned that his most potent weapon was to lay down his tools, even at the risk of prosecution under the law. Dozens of strikes erupted in the 1830's and 1840's, most of them for higher wages, some for the ten-hour day, and a few for such unusual goals as the right to smoke on the job. The workingman usually lost more strikes than he won, for the employer could resort to such tactics as the importing of strikebreakers—often derisively called "scabs" or "rats."

Toilers the nation over won a resounding legal victory in 1842. The

Supreme Court of Massachusetts ruled in the case of Commonwealth *vs.* Hunt that labor unions were not illegal conspiracies, provided that their methods were "honorable and peaceful." This epochal decision did not legalize the strike overnight throughout the country, but it was a significant signpost of the times. Trade unions still had a rocky row to hoe, stretching ahead for nearly a century, before they could meet management on relatively even terms.

The Revolution in Reaping

Agricultural implements used by American farmers in the dawning years of the Republic were incredibly primitive—hardly better than those of the Egyptians in the days of Joseph and the Pharaohs. Some improvement came in the early 1800's, when the crude wooden plow gradually gave way to the iron-tipped plowshare. Progress was halting, partly because of superstitious objections that iron would poison the soil.

The slowness of reaping grain was a serious bottleneck. In Europe, crops were limited by the scarcity of the land; in America, by the scarcity of labor for harvesting with sickle and scythe. The answer to the American problem was the mechanical mower-reaper, patented in 1834 by the Virginia-born Cyrus Hall McCormick. Other mechanics had earlier invented graincutters, and McCormick had plenty of competition long after he began to manufacture. But he was able to outdistance his rivals by making superior machinery and by employing sound business methods, which included installment-plan selling. With more than 12,000 patents added, McCormick's first-born contraption became a smooth-working mechanical wonder.

No other American invention has cut so wide a swath. Broadly speaking, the mower-reaper was to the North what the Negro slave was to the South, only it was a mechanical slave, substituting machinery for muscles. In a certain sense, Cyrus McCormick—the transplanted Virginian—won the Civil War for the Union. His clattering cogs further widened the population advantage of the North, partly by insuring a profitable opening of new Western lands, and partly by stimulating European immigration to them. The wondrous new machine freed countless able-bodied men for the fighting front, and piled up mountains of grain for both civilian and military use.

Nor did McCormick's contribution end here. By helping to win the war, the mower-reaper helped free the Negro slaves. While doing so, it partially freed the white farm laborer. It straightened him up and set him down on the seat of his red-chariot reaper. There, behind stout horses, he could speedily and effortlessly do the work of scores of men. In a world-wide theater, McCormick's mechanical marvel helped win the age-old battle against food shortages and starvation, not only in America but wherever billowing fields of grain greet the husbandman.

Highways and Byways

A revolution in transportation and communication paralleled the revolution in industry—and was largely responsible for it. Without a solution of the oppressive American problem of distance, the United States could never have become a powerful, well-knit nation. The conquest of space was no less important than the conquest of the savages.

Cheap and efficient carriers were imperative if raw materials were to be transported to the factories, and if the finished product was to be delivered to the consumer. On December 3, 1803, a firm in Providence, Rhode Island, sent a shipment of yarn to a point sixty miles away, notifying the purchaser that the consignment could be expected to arrive in "the course of the winter." A mighty industrial nation could not emerge until more effective agencies for haulage were devised.

In 1789, when the Constitution was launched, primitive colonial methods of travel were still in use. Water-borne commerce, whether along the coast or on the rivers, was slow, uncertain, and often dangerous. Stagecoaches and wagons lurched over bone-shaking roads. Passengers would be routed out to lay nearby fence rails across muddy stretches, and occasionally horses would drown in muddy pits while wagons sank slowly out of sight.

A promising change for the better came in the 1790's, when a private company completed the Lancaster turnpike in Pennsylvania. It was a broad, hard-surfaced highway that thrust sixty-two miles westward, from Philadelphia to Lancaster. As the driver approached the toll gate, he was confronted with a barrier of sharp pikes, which were turned aside when he paid his toll. Hence the term "turnpike."

The Lancaster Pike proved to be a highly successful venture, returning at one time 15% dividends on the stock. It attracted a rich trade to Philadelphia, and touched off a turnpike-building boom that lasted about twenty years. It also stimulated Western development. The turnpikes beckoned to the canvas-covered Conestoga wagons, whose creaks heralded an advance that knew no real retreat.

Western road building, always expensive, encountered many obstacles. Looming large among them were the states'-righters, who opposed federal aid to local projects. And there were always the Easterners, who resented the draining off of their population to a rival section.

The West scored a memorable triumph when the federal government, in 1811, began to construct the great National Road or Cumberland Road. This highway ultimately stretched from Cumberland, in western Maryland, to Vandalia, in Illinois, a distance of 591 miles. The War of 1812 interrupted construction, and states'-rights shackles on internal improvements hampered federal grants. But the thoroughfare was belatedly brought to its destination, in 1852, by a combination of aid from the states and the federal government.

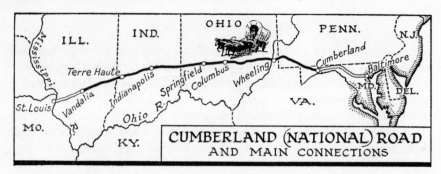

CUMBERLAND (NATIONAL) ROAD AND MAIN CONNECTIONS

The famous Cumberland Road, with branches radiating out, was a stimulant to American prosperity. As the broad highway to the West, it made freight-carrying cheaper and faster. It hastened the flow of European immigrants over the mountains; it stimulated population centers; it enhanced land values. It also wrote a colorful chapter in the history of American transportation. Brightly painted stagecoaches, named after prominent statesmen and pulled by four to six foam-flecked horses, careened down the dusty highroad at breakneck speed, often better than twenty miles an hour. The age of rapid land transportation was dawning.

Reversing the Rivers

The steamboat craze, which overlapped the turnpike craze, was touched off by an ambitious painter-engineer named Robert Fulton. Several other men had earlier built steamboats, but these craft had all been unprofitable, largely because of weak engines and even weaker financing.

Fulton, luckier than the others, won the financial backing of a wealthy New Yorker. He installed a powerful English steam engine in his *Clermont*, which was nicknamed by a dubious public "Fulton's Folly." (Spectacular inventions of a revolutionary nature were usually greeted with jeers and sneers; and America owes much to those men who courageously persisted in their "follies.") On a historic day in 1807, the quaint little ship, belching sparks from its single smokestack, churned steadily from New York City up the Hudson River toward Albany. It made the run of 150 miles in 32 hours.

The success of the steamboat was sensational. Man could now in some degree control wind, wave, tide, and downstream current. Within a few years Fulton had changed all of America's navigable streams into two-way arteries, thereby doubling their carrying capacity. Hitherto keelboats had been pushed up the Mississippi, with quivering poles and raucous profanity, at less than one mile an hour—a process that was prohibitively costly. Now the steamboats could churn rapidly against the current, ultimately attaining speeds in excess of ten miles an hour. "By golly," an old Negro was heard to exclaim, "the Mississippi has got her massa now!"

By 1820 there were some sixty steamboats on the Mississippi and its tributaries; by 1860, about one thousand, some of them luxurious river palaces. Keen rivalry among the swift and gaudy steamers sometimes led to memorable races. Excited passengers would urge the captain to pile on wood at the risk of bursting the boilers, which all too often exploded with tragic effects.

The chugging steamboats played a vital role in the opening of the West and South, both of which were richly endowed with navigable rivers. Like bunches of grapes on a vine, population clustered along the banks of the broad-flowing streams. The cotton growers and other farmers made haste to take up the now-profitable virgin soil. Not only could they float their produce to market, but, hardly less important, they could ship in at low cost their shoes, hardware, and other manufactured necessities.

Clinton's Big Ditch

The canal craze overlapped the boom in turnpikes and steamboats. A few short canals had been built around falls and elsewhere in colonial days, but ambitious projects lay in the lap of the future. The resourceful citizens of New York, cut off from federal aid by states'-righters, themselves began the Erie Canal in 1817. They were blessed with the driving leadership of Governor DeWitt Clinton, whose expensive project was scoffingly called "Clinton's Big Ditch."

The Erie Canal, which finally ribboned 363 miles, was completed by sections. Each stretch was profitably opened when finished. Finally, in 1825, a garland-bedecked canal boat glided from Buffalo, on Lake Erie, to New York harbor. There, with colorful ceremony, Governor Clinton emptied a cask of water from the lake to symbolize "the marriage of the

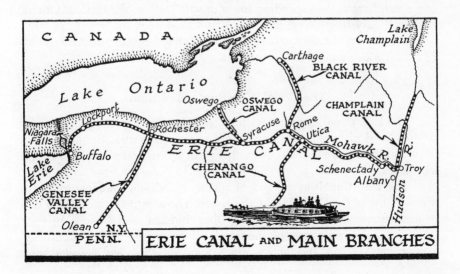

ERIE CANAL AND MAIN BRANCHES

waters." Shorter spurs were later built, including those that connected the Erie Canal with Lake Ontario.

Breath-taking success greeted the vast new enterprise. In truth, the water that Clinton poured into New York harbor baptized an Empire State. Passengers and bulky freight could now be handled with cheapness and dispatch, at the dizzy speed of five miles an hour. The cost of shipping a ton of grain from Buffalo to New York City fell from $100 to $5, and the time of transit from about twenty days to six. A popular bargeman's song ("Fifteen Years on the Erie Canal") ran:

> Low bridge! Everybody down!
> Low bridge! We're coming to a town!
> You'll always know your neighbor,
> You'll always know your pal,
> If you ever navigated the Erie Canal.

Ever-widening economic ripples followed the completion of "Clinton's Big Ditch." The value of land along the route skyrocketed, and new cities —like Rochester and Syracuse—shot forth as the population thickened. The industry of the Empire State boomed, as New York City expanded into the seaboard queen of the nation. The new profitableness of farming in the Old Northwest—notably in Ohio, Michigan, Indiana, Illinois—attracted thousands of European immigrants to the unaxed lands now available. Steamship traffic on the Great Lakes connected with the Erie Canal, and frontier villages like Cleveland, Chicago, and Detroit began to experience an amazing growth.

The Erie Canal ushered in other profound economic and political changes. The price of potatoes in New York City was cut in half, and many dispirited New England farmers, no longer able to face this ruinous competition, abandoned their rocky holdings and went elsewhere. Some became mill hands, thus speeding the industrialization of America. Others, finding it easy to go West over the Erie Canal, took up new farm lands south of the Great Lakes, where they were joined by countless thousands of New Yorkers and other Northerners.

The Canal Web Binds the Union

The Erie Canal, together with its tributaries and rivals, proved to be a vital bond of union. The Republic was immeasurably strengthened as East and West were knit more closely together by a vast network of canals and lakes.

The Erie Canal, as a bond of union, contributed immeasurably to the winning of the Civil War by the North. The keystone states of the Old Northwest were the tier formed by Ohio, Indiana, and Illinois. In their southern half dwelt tens of thousands of Southerners from Kentucky, Tennessee, Virginia, and the Carolinas, many of whom had deserted their tobacco-gutted soil. But their numbers were ultimately offset by the tens of thousands of Yankees brought by the Erie Canal to the northern part of the Old Northwest. The huge man-made waterway thus played a decisive role in holding Ohio, Indiana, and Illinois in the Union when the guns began to boom in 1861.

The Erie Canal helped win the Civil War for the North in yet another way. Hitherto the states of the upper Mississippi Valley had been fatally dependent on the Mississippi River as their major outlet to the sea. Many Southerners were convinced, as secession impended, that some of these commonwealths would have to secede with them or suffocate. But the Erie Canal, with its supporting network of canals interlocked with the east-west railroads, had robbed the Mississippi of much of its traffic. Governor Clinton and his fellow canal-builders had picked up the huge river, figuratively speaking, flung it over the Alleghenies, and forced it to empty into the sea at New York City. The gain of New York was the loss of New Orleans, and the upper Mississippi Valley could now exist without having to jump when the South cracked the whip.

The Erie Canal influenced the outcome of the Civil War in an even larger theater. It sped the rapid industrialization of the North, while contributing immensely to its wealth. Industrial sinews and riches were both to be decisive factors when the sections finally came to death grips.

The astonishing success of the Erie Canal stimulated competition, especially from the rivals of New York City. The Philadelphians, defying both geography and the law of gravity, constructed a temporarily profitable canal over the Allegheny Mountains. The boats were picked up by a

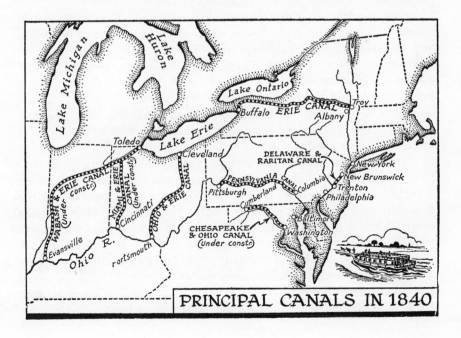

PRINCIPAL CANALS IN 1840

portage railroad and carried to an elevation of nearly 2300 feet, from which they were let down on the other side.

A web of canals was likewise dug in the Old Northwest to connect with the Great Lakes and the Mississippi River. On one of the Ohio waterways, the youthful James A. Garfield, later to become President, drove mules over the towpath. But few of these enterprises proved rewarding, and by 1838 twelve states had accumulated canal debts of $60,000,000.

The canal craze unhappily led to an orgy of speculative expansion, in which British capitalists and others were unwisely induced to invest. The boom had about reached its peak when the steam locomotive puffed in. Yet for many decades after the railroads had proved their worth, some of the canals continued to reap profits, especially in handling bulky freight. When the northern canals froze over, in those days of completely free enterprise, competing railroads promptly raised their rates—a practice later forbidden by law. It is interesting to note that an enlarged and improved Erie Canal, known as the New York Barge Canal, still handles an immense amount of freight.

When the Iron Horse Was a Colt

The railroad proved to be the most noteworthy contribution to a solution of the great American problem of distance. It was fast, reliable, cheaper than canals to construct, and not frozen over in winter. Able to go almost anywhere, the iron monster defied the map. More than that, it drew the East and West closer together, thus offsetting the north-south pull of the Alleghenies and the Mississippi.

Early experiments with railroads involved the use of various kinds of power, including wind, dogs, horses, and finally steam. The first important line was begun by the Baltimore and Ohio Company, significantly on Independence Day, 1828. At the colorful dedication ceremony, the first stone was laid at Baltimore by Charles Carroll, then aged ninety, the only surviving signer of the Declaration of Independence. The steam locomotive for railroads—truly a declaration of independence from primitive transportation—was not, as commonly supposed, a Yankee invention. It had already been used to a trifling extent in England.

The American locomotive, though soon to make the grade, encountered initial setbacks. A famous nine-mile race was staged in 1830 between a horse-drawn car and the "Tom Thumb," the crack locomotive of the Baltimore and Ohio. The noisy iron horse was winning when it broke down. The gray quadruped then clattered on to victory, amid wild cheers from the foes of mechanical progress. But dumb animals rapidly lost out, as numerous railroads began to radiate out from the main cities like spokes from the hub of a wheel. By 1860, only thirty-two years after the Baltimore and Ohio ceremony, the United States boasted 30,000 miles of railroad track, three-fourths of it in the partly industrialized North.

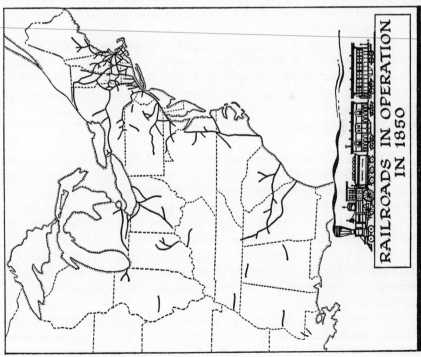

RAILROADS IN OPERATION IN 1860

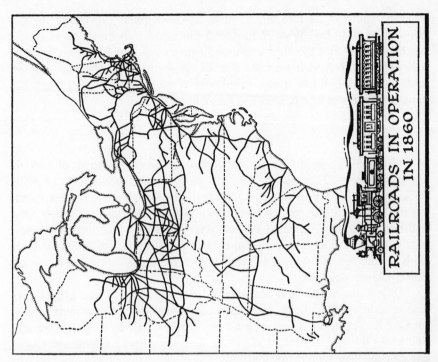

RAILROADS IN OPERATION IN 1850

The railroad, as fate would have it, contributed powerfully to the winning of the Civil War. It hastened the rapid industrialization of the North, with all that this development meant in superior resources, wealth, and population. And it played an indispensable role in the provisioning and transporting of the armies—a role that was all the more significant because the war was fought over so vast an area.

Pioneers of the Rail

The hoarse screech of the locomotive sounded the doom of various vested interests. They rallied against progress and in defense of their pocketbooks, as men so often do. The turnpike investors and tavern keepers did not relish the loss of business, and farmers feared for their hay-and-horse market. The canal backers were especially violent. Mass meetings were held along the Erie Canal, and in 1833 the legislature of New York prohibited the railroads from carrying freight—a futile restriction that could not long stand.

Objections to the Iron Monster did not end here. It was branded as undemocratic, for no ordinary citizen could own one. It was sacrilegious, for God had given men and animals legs. Finally, it was a public menace. Sparks set fire to haystacks and houses, and supposedly frightened chickens so that they would not lay eggs. Good old four-legged Dobbin was preferred. He sent out no sparks, carried his own fuel, made little noise, and would not explode.

The early railway coach was a torture chamber on wheels, and no place for weaklings or cowards. Live cinders burned holes in clothes—one woman found thirteen in her gown. The brakes were so feeble that the engineer might miss the station twice, both coming and backing up. The rails were flimsy iron strips fastened on wood; and appalling accidents all too frequently turned the wooden "miniature hells" into flaming funeral pyres.

Railroad pioneers ran into additional obstacles. Arrivals and departures were conjectural, and timetables were little better than ill-kept promissory notes. Further complications were caused by the variance in gauge, or space between the rails. When a passenger came to a different line, he would often have to change cars, after wiping cinders from his eyes. In 1840 there were seven transfers between Philadelphia and Charleston. Violence flared up in Erie, Pennsylvania, in 1853, when the hotel and trucking men sprang to arms. Fearing that the trains would go through without stopping, they unsuccessfully attempted to prevent an alteration of the gauge.

But needed railway improvements were gradually installed. Gauges became standardized, safety devices were adopted, solid iron rails were laid, and the Pullman sleeping "palace" was introduced in 1859. America at long last was being bound together with ribs of iron.

The Golden Age of Wooden Ships

A marvelous expansion of American merchant shipping on the high seas occurred in the decades before the Civil War. The Industrial Revolution not only spurred this development, but was greatly benefited by it.

Mechanical progress on the waves was not so spectacular as that on land. It is true that the American steamer *Savannah* crossed the Atlantic in 1819, though using sail power much of the time, and though pursued for a day by a British captain who thought her afire. But not until about mid-century did steam threaten the primacy of the white-sailed windjammer.

Yankee shipping experienced sharp ups and downs in the 19th Century. It had flourished during the turbulent Napoleonic era, when the United States was the leading neutral carrier. But it was badly hit by the embargo, non-intercourse, and the War of 1812. When peace came in 1815, overseas commerce gradually revived, though encountering head winds in the panics of 1819 and 1837. The golden age of the merchant marine in the 19th Century came in the 1850's, when America boldly challenged the British for the trident of maritime supremacy—the only time during the century that we were to do so.

Many influences contributed to this thrilling saga of the sea. Hordes of immigrants, fleeing Europe and famine-ravaged Ireland, clamored for space on Yankee packet boats. American agricultural surpluses, thanks partly to the McCormick mower-reaper in the 1850's, needed cargo space. The repeal in 1846 of the restrictive British corn laws put England on essentially a free-trade basis, and thus made possible the wholesale export of American grain to the British Isles. The preoccupation of the European powers with the Crimean War, from 1854 to 1856, likewise brought a sudden demand for American shipping.

Less prosaic impulses were also at work. The most sensational of all was the discovery of gold in California in 1848, and in Australia in 1851. A frantic demand developed for rapid passage to the gold fields.

The Epic of the Clipper

Saucy clipper ships, which showed their rivals a streak of foam, were America's answer to the clamor for speed. Long, narrow, and majestic, with towering masts and clouds of canvas, these fleet craft could in a fair breeze outrun any steamer.

> Stately as churches, swift as gulls,
> They trod the oceans, then—
> No man had seen such ships before
> And none will see again.*

* Rosemary and Stephen Vincent Benét, *A Book of Americans* (Rinehart and Company, copyright 1933), p. 75. Reprinted by permission.

Donald McKay, at Boston, was the most famous master builder. One of his clippers, *Champion of the Seas,* logged the all-time record of 465 nautical miles in twenty-four hours (average, 19.78 knots). On shorter stretches, several of the clippers attained speeds in excess of 21 knots— records that have never been surpassed by any kind of sailing vessels. The tea-loving English had to have their fresh leaves from the Far East, and for a time the American clippers wrested much of this trade from their slower-moving British competitors.

The graceful clipper had its brief and glorious day in the 1840's and 1850's, but on the eve of the Civil War the British were clearly winning the race for maritime supremacy. The rich gold diggings of California and

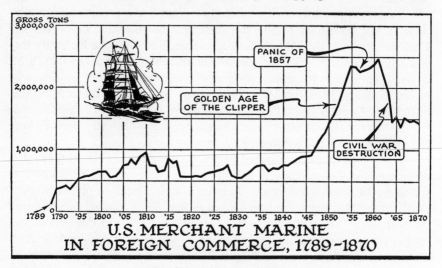

U.S. MERCHANT MARINE
IN FOREIGN COMMERCE, 1789–1870

For later years see p. 734.

Australia were petering out, and breakneck speed was no longer at a premium. The British were turning to iron tramp steamers ("teakettles"), which, though less romantic than the clippers, were steadier, more capacious, and more profitable. At the same time, American investors were finding richer returns in railroad building and other enterprises at home.

The British government generously subsidized its steamship operators, notably the Cunard line. But the Washington regime, hampered by states' rights in shipping as well as in internal improvements, provided only half-hearted support. The crack American Collins line, which at one time rivaled the Cunarders, suffered several crippling accidents and finally sold out to its British competitors.

Other setbacks followed. The disastrous Panic of 1857 dealt a heavy blow to American shipping, while from 1861 to 1865 Confederate commerce raiders caused even costlier damage. Not until some fifty years later, during the World War of 1914–1918, did the American merchant marine regain its place as a worthy challenger of the British.

Miracles in Communication

Speedier agencies of transportation, whether the railroad or the steamer, meant faster communication. Two wonder-working inventions accelerated the pace miraculously.

The perfection of the telegraph in America was achieved by the heavily bearded S. F. B. Morse, whose name is immortalized by the Morse Code. Though one of America's foremost portrait painters, he was forced by poverty to forsake his brush for the telegraph key. After prolonged disappointments and hunger, he finally secured from Congress, to the accompaniment of the usual jeers, an appropriation of $30,000 to support his experiment with "talking wires."

In 1844 Morse strung a wire from Washington to Baltimore, a distance of forty miles, and clicked out the historic message, "What hath God wrought?" The government might have controlled the telegraph, as it does the post office, but declined on the ground that the new device would not pay. Despite early mechanical imperfections, the invention was rather rapidly accepted. Morse won both fame and fortune, and the business transactions of the nation were brought around a common table.

The trans-Atlantic cable was the crowning achievement of a wealthy New York paper manufacturer, Cyrus Field. Amid much ridicule, he formed a company to lay a cable between Newfoundland and Ireland, through water two miles deep. After the cable had broken during four successive attempts, Field—"the greatest wirepuller of modern times"—spectacularly achieved his goal in 1858.

Wild rejoicing rocked the nation. New York City reveled in a two-day cable carnival, and Queen Victoria exchanged congratulatory messages with President Buchanan. After three weeks and several hundred messages, the cable failed and remained useless for eight years. Heroes became villains overnight, and skeptics falsely accused the promoter of having faked messages so as to sell his stock at a high figure.

Field, though financially pinched, did not despair. In 1866, after the Civil War and another failure, he laid a heavier cable with gratifying success. The derided dreamer once more became an honored hero, whose achievement is an epic of vision, courage, and perseverance.

No story of rapid American communication would be complete without reference to the Far West. By 1858 horse-drawn overland stages, later immortalized by Mark Twain's *Roughing It*, were running regularly all the way to California. Even more dramatic was the Pony Express, which was established in 1860 to carry mail from St. Joseph, Missouri, to Sacramento, California, a distance of about 1960 miles. The daring lightweight riders, leaping onto wiry Indian ponies saddled at stations approximately ten miles apart, could make the trip in an amazing ten days. The unarmed horsemen clattered on, summer or winter, day or night, through dust or snow, past red Indians and white bandits. In eighteen months of weekly or bi-weekly

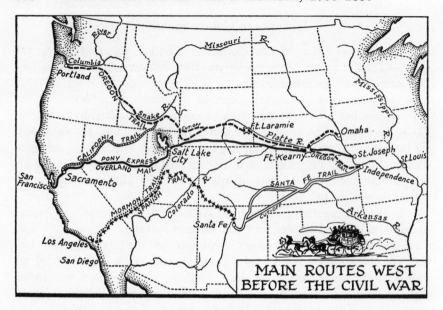

MAIN ROUTES WEST
BEFORE THE CIVIL WAR

operation, the promoters missed only one trip, though losing money heavily. When the telegraph to California was completed in 1861, the Pony Express yielded to mechanical progress. But in its brief and dramatic day it symbolized American resourcefulness, toughness, energy, speed, and boldness.

A new epoch was thus written in the first half of the 19th Century when the faithful horse was partially replaced by steam and electric current. The change highlighted a revolution in communication, transportation, and industry, while foreshadowing even more momentous changes to come.

SELECT READINGS

Solid introductions are P. W. GATES, *The Farmer's Age: Agriculture, 1815–1860* (1960) and G. R. TAYLOR, *The Transportation Revolution, 1815–1860* (1951). Engagingly written is F. R. DULLES, *Labor in America* (1949). The canal era is described in M. S. WAGGONER, *The Long Haul West* (1958) and CARTER GOODRICH, *Government Promotion of American Canals and Railroads, 1800–1890* (1960). The biographical approach is used in C. M. GREEN, *Eli Whitney and the Birth of American Technology* (1956) [paperback]. Challenging interpretations appear in L. M. HACKER, *The Triumph of American Capitalism* (1940); in T. C. COCHRAN and W. MILLER, *The Age of Enterprise* (1942) [paperback]; and in STUART BRUCHEY, *The Roots of American Economic Growth, 1607–1861* (1965). Completely fascinating are S. E. MORISON, *Maritime History of Massachusetts, 1783–1860* (1921) [paperback] and his appreciative account of the clipper ships in *By Land and By Sea* (1953). Also *Harvard Guide*, Pt. IV.

17

Population, Religion, and Education, 1790–1860

America was bred in a cabin.
MORRIS BIRKBECK, 1817

Children of Environment

THE searing impact of the wilderness left a permanent scar on the early colonists, as well as on subsequent generations. Even in colonial days a distinctively American type began to emerge, and in the 19th Century it crystallized. The people of the United States, despite noteworthy cultural gains, have never fully shaken off the effects of their centuries-long battle with the primitive. This fact goes far to explain why today the individual American—breezy and often noisy—differs markedly from his quieter and more reserved English cousin. "In the United States," wrote Gertrude Stein, "there is more space where nobody is than where anybody is. This is what makes America what it is."

The West, with its raw frontier conditions, was the most typically American part of America. George Washington, a product of tidewater Virginia, was outwardly an English aristocrat; Andrew Jackson, a product of frontier Tennessee, could not be mistaken for an Englishman. As Ralph Waldo Emerson wrote in 1844, "Europe stretches to the Alleghenies; America lies beyond."

Yet crudeness could be found on both sides of the mountains. The Eastern seaboard was scorned by many cultured Europeans as an uncouth backwoods area. The East in turn looked down upon the West as an uncouth backwoods area. The peculiar traits developed by a grinding frontier existence gradually worked back upon the East, and ultimately colored our entire national character.

The "go-aheaditive" American sprang from a restless race of men. Thanks to his invigorating climate and the challenge of tremendous tasks, he was nervous and energetic. A born hustler—always "a-doin'"—he was foot-loose and frequently on the move. A "tall tale" of the frontier described chickens that voluntarily crossed their legs every spring, waiting

319

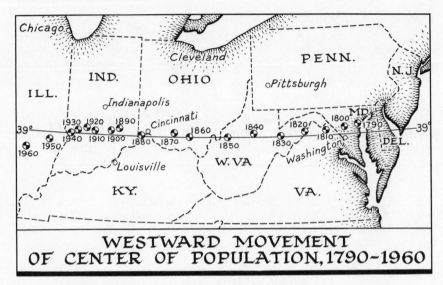

WESTWARD MOVEMENT OF CENTER OF POPULATION, 1790–1960

Note the remarkable equilibrium of the north-south pull from 1790 onward, and the strong spurt west and south in the 1940–1950 decade.

to be tied for the annual move west. Even in repose, the American was characteristically whittling, chewing, jiggling, and rocking. The rocking chair—"the chair that travels but stays at home"—was a typically American device. At the dinner table, the rule seemed to be "gobble, gulp, and go." The American had no time for four o'clock tea, as the English did. There was too much cream to be skimmed off the continent—furs, timber, wildlife—with a consequent squandering of soil and natural resources. "Git a plenty while you're agittin'," Indiana-born Edward Eggleston had his Hoosier schoolmaster say.

Men with the Bark On

The mad scramble for riches led not only to waste but to superficiality. Wooden bridges were flung across streams, until time permitted the surface-skimming American to build stone spans. The breathless pursuit of wealth inevitably led to accusations of dollar-chasing and crass materialism. John Stuart Mill, the noted English writer, scathingly remarked in the 1840's that in America the life of one sex was "devoted to dollar hunting, and of the other to the breeding of dollar hunters." Dollar grabbing was undeniably important, but the thrill of the chase was hardly less so. The accumulation of wealth was everywhere recognized as the badge of success and the symbol of power.

The rough-and-tough American—especially the Westerner—was often crude, ruthless, and even brutal. Tobacco chewing and indelicate spitting —"the salivary propensity"—became a national scandal in the decades before the Civil War. One visiting Briton suggested that the spittoon, not the eagle, should be America's national emblem; and a group of Japanese visitors in 1860 noted that the white man had brown saliva. Frontier wrestling, often of the no-holds-barred type, sanctioned such niceties as the biting off of noses or the gouging out of eyes. "Look out, or I'll measure the length of your eyestrings [eye muscles]" was an expressive frontier warning. Nor was brutality directed solely at fellow white men. The Indians stood in the way of our expansion, and when they fought back they were brushed aside or killed off, like the wild animals.

The American was ingenious, inventive, adaptable, resourceful, self-sufficient—a jack of all trades. He had to be, especially on the frontier, where there was no room for specialists. "Root, hog, or die"—the Western saying directed at hogs left to dig their own roots—might well have been the national motto.

The American was strenuous, courageous, pugnacious—over-endowed with the "lick all creation" spirit. He had sublime faith in his military prowess, untrained and amateurish though he might be. He was tough and tenacious. Learning early to laugh at adversity, he fought the elements, the wild animals ("varmints"), his Canadian and Mexican neighbors, and, above all, the Indians. The Englishman Rudyard Kipling later wrote in grudging admiration:

> He greets the embarrassed Gods, nor fears
> To shake the iron hand of Fate
> Or match with Destiny for beers.

Gamblers All

Marooned by geography, the American was self-centered, provincial, and isolationist, whether in his home community or in the world community. Individualistic and self-reliant, he depended on his own trusty ax and especially his rifle, which, in the Western phrase, made all men "equally tall." Emerson's popular lecture-essay, "Self-reliance," struck a deeply responsive chord. Yet the pioneer, in tasks clearly beyond his own strength, would call upon his neighbors for logrolling, and upon his government for help in building internal improvements.

The American was confident, buoyant, optimistic—a born booster, a teller of "tall tales," an admirer of the giant lumberjack, fabled Paul Bunyan. Pessimism was a kind of treason; "knockers" were not wanted. The ancestors of the Americans, as well as the immigrants themselves, had to be courageously optimistic to undertake the storm-lashed Atlantic crossing. "The cowards never started; the weak died on the way" ran the saying.

Those who reached the New World were all gamblers. They gambled their lives against disease and Indians, and their crops and fortunes against the elements. The people of the United States are distilled not only from a select group of brave men and women but also from a long line of risk-takers. Even those who failed had at least one satisfaction: they realized that someone had to take the first steps if the Republic was to achieve its ultimate destiny. "It's better to be a has-been," one heard, "than a never-was."

The American was boastful—a trait growing out of his easy optimism. The game of poker ("brag"), with its premium on successful bluffing, attained great popularity in the West, where it was a favorite of Henry Clay. The American was painfully aware of his nation's many physical and cultural shortcomings, and while smarting under the sneers of monocled foreigners, he would boast loudly and defensively of the splendid cities that would one day rise from his malarial swamps. Significantly, he bragged of the future, while Europeans boasted of their past. He also learned early to worship bigness, partly because America excelled in size. Above all, he had unbounded faith in the future, in progress, in the "American dream."

The Torch of Democracy

The robust American was essentially democratic. In his social democracy, especially beyond the mountains, he set no store by caste, tradition, or family trees. The first question was not "Who is he?" but "What can he do?" On the frontier, where all men were "equally better," a common expression was "I'm as good as you be." Or as a Hungarian immigrant later remarked, "The President is Mister and I am Mister too."

Democracy, especially on the frontier, also extended to the life of the spirit. All men were free to launch their own religion—and many did. State-supported churches disappeared in the decades after the Revolution, and in the West there was the elbow-rubbing equality of the camp meetings. As one camp-meeting song ran:

> Come hungry, come thirsty, come ragged, come bare,
> Come filthy, come lousy, come just as you are.

Economic democracy—free enterprise—prevailed to an unusual degree in the United States. Any thrifty and industrious citizen could hope to attain wealth, and many enterprising souls worked their way to the top rung of the economic and social ladder, in the "rags to riches" tradition.

Political democracy was one of our proudest boasts. Manhood suffrage came to be the rule. We realized that the world was skeptically watching our vast experiment in political democracy, and this awareness contributed further to our self-conscious boastfulness. Emerson once observed that the American eagle was something of a peacock.

The American, moreover, was a freedom lover. Not one to be pushed about, he had forcibly overthrown the rule of George III and set up a republic. He cherished states' rights and localism, largely because these ideals enabled him to keep a more watchful eye on his public servants. He applauded freedom abroad, as well as in America. Responding to the flattery of imitation, he enthusiastically hailed democratic revolutions whenever they occurred, and often assisted them with money and volunteers. He cheered as thrones crashed, and he openly pitied people who did not have the "gumption" to rise up and break their autocratic chains. Mark Twain caught the spirit of anti-monarchical America when he had Huck Finn remark to Nigger Jim, "Sometimes I wish we could hear of a country that's out of kings."

Yet the workaday American, despite his radical political ideas, was basically a conservative in his economic thinking. This state of mind was primarily due to the diffusion of prosperity and property—to the ease of satisfying an age-old hunger for land.

The American was intensely patriotic and nationalistic—an America lover. Instead of inheriting his land, he had subdued it himself, contending against both the elements and the Indians. And one cherishes the possessions one has to fight for. Thomas Jefferson once urged his friend James Monroe to go to France so that he might better appreciate the "precious blessings" of his own country.

The March of the Millions

The amazing multiplication of our people continued decade after decade, without serious slackening. By mid-century the population was still doubling approximately every twenty-three years, as in colonial days.

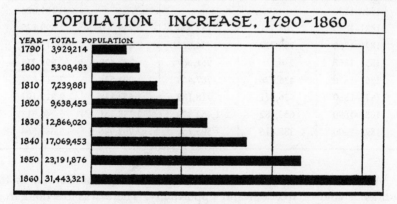

POPULATION INCREASE, 1790–1860

YEAR	TOTAL POPULATION
1790	3,929,214
1800	5,308,483
1810	7,239,881
1820	9,638,453
1830	12,866,020
1840	17,069,453
1850	23,191,876
1860	31,443,321

By 1860 the original thirteen states had more than doubled in number: thirty-three stars then graced the American flag. The United States was the fourth most populous white nation in the world, exceeded by only three European countries—Russia, France, and Austria.

Urban growth continued proportionately and explosively. In 1790 there had been only two cities that could boast 20,000 or more souls: Philadelphia and New York. By 1860 there were forty-three; and about three hundred other places claimed over 5000 inhabitants apiece. New York was the metropolis; New Orleans, the "Queen of the South." Cincinnati, which excelled in meat packing, was dubbed the "porkopolis of the West," while frontier Chicago was coming along fast.

Such overrapid urbanization unfortunately brought undesirable by-products. It intensified the problems of smelly slums, feeble street lighting, inadequate policing, impure water, foul sewage, ravenous rats, and improper garbage disposal. Hogs, as snouted scavengers, ran wild in many city streets as late as the 1840's. Boston in 1823 pioneered with a sewage system; and New York in 1842 abandoned wells and cisterns for a piped-in water supply. The city thus unknowingly eliminated the breeding place of many disease-carrying mosquitoes.

A continuing high birth rate accounted for most of the increase in population, but by the 1840's the tide of immigration was adding hundreds of thousands more. Before this decade immigrants had been flowing in at the rate of about 60,000 a year, but suddenly the influx was tripled in the 1840's, and then quadrupled in the 1850's.

During these two feverish decades over a million and a half Irish, and nearly as many Germans, poured into our ports. Why did they come?

Irish and German Immigration by Decade

Years	Irish	German	All Others	Grand Total
1820–1830				151,824
1831–1840	207,381	152,454	239,290	599,125
1841–1850	780,719	434,626	497,906	1,713,251
1851–1860	914,119	951,667	732,428	2,598,214
1861–1870	435,778	787,468	1,091,578	2,314,824
1871–1880	436,871	718,182	1,657,138	2,812,191
1881–1890	655,482	1,452,970	3,138,161	5,246,613
1891–1900	388,416	505,152	2,793,996	3,687,564

America still beckoned to the struggling masses of Europe as the traditional land of freedom and opportunity. There was freedom from aristocratic caste and state church; there was abundant opportunity to secure land and better one's condition. Letters sent home by immigrants already here—"America letters"—often described in glowing terms the richer life in the United States: low taxes, no compulsory military service, and "three meat meals a day." The introduction of transoceanic steamships also meant that the immigrant could come speedily, in a matter of ten or twelve days instead of ten or twelve weeks. He was still jammed into unsanitary quarters, with a shockingly high death rate, but the nightmare was more endurable because it was shorter.

The Emerald Isle Moves West

Ireland, already groaning under the heavy hand of British overlords, was prostrated in the mid-1840's. A terrible rot attacked the potato crop, on which the people had become dangerously dependent, and about one-fourth of the population was swept away by disease and hunger. Starved bodies were found dead by the roadsides with blades of grass in their mouths.

Tens of thousands of destitute Irish, fleeing the Land of Famine for the Land of Plenty, flocked to America in the "Black Forties." In lesser numbers they emigrated to Australia, Canada, and other lands. Ireland's great export has been population; and the Irish take their place next to the Jews as a dispersed people.

The uprooted Irish, too poor to move West and buy the necessary livestock and equipment, swarmed into the larger seaboard cities. Noteworthy were Boston and particularly New York, which rapidly became the largest Irish city in the world. Before many decades had passed, there were more people of Irish blood in America than on the "ould sod" of Erin's Isle.

The Irish received no red-carpet treatment. Forced to live in dirt and squalor, they worsened already vile slum conditions. They were looked down upon by the older "native American" stock, especially "proper" Bostonians, who regarded the impoverished newcomers as a social menace. The luckless Irish "Paddies" (Patricks) were forced to resort to pick-and-shovel drudgery on canals and railroads, and they were hated by those laborers whose jobs they took. "No Irish Need Apply" was a sign commonly hung in shop windows, and often abbreviated to NINA.

The Irish in still other ways created problems. It is true that they were traditionally agreeable, generous, witty, and lighthearted. But they loved a fight, and were inclined to seek refuge from their hardships in the bottle. A contemporary song ("Paddy Works on the Erie [Railway]") ran:

> In eighteen hundred and forty-eight,
> I learned to take my whisky straight,
> 'Tis an illygant drink and can't be bate,
> For working on the railway.

The Irish newcomers, capitalizing on their good nature and warm-handedness, revealed a flair for politics, especially at the local level. They soon began to exercise control over powerful city machines, notably Tammany Hall in New York. Stalwart Irishmen, red-faced and genially brogued, gradually came to dominate the police forces and fire departments of metropolitan areas.

American politicians made haste to cultivate the Irish vote, especially in the politically potent state of New York. Irishmen cherished long-standing grievances against the British, and their burning hatred lost nothing in the transplanting across the Atlantic. As the Irish-Americans increased in numbers—nearly two million came between 1830 and 1860—the government in Washington saw political gold in those Hibernian hills. Administration spokesmen, on the eve of elections, often found it politically profitable to fire verbal volleys at London—a process vulgarly known as "twisting the British Lion's tail."

The Flight of the Forty-Eighters

The influx of refugees from Germany between 1830 and 1860 was hardly less spectacular than that from Ireland. During these troubled years, over a million and a half thrifty Germans stepped onto American soil. The bulk of them were poor people, displaced by crop failures and by other hardships. But a strong sprinkling were German liberals. Saddened by the collapse of the revolutions of 1848, they had decided to wash their hands of the autocratic Fatherland and flee to America—the one bright hope of democracy.

The liberal German "Forty-Eighters," who came to America for free government, are not to be confused with the "Forty-Niners," who came to California for free gold. The future history of Germany—and indeed of the entire world—might well have been less war-torn if these forward-looking spirits had remained at home as a seedbed for genuine democracy in the Old Country. At all events, Germany's loss was America's gain. Zealous German liberals like the lanky and public-spirited Carl Schurz, a relentless foe of slavery and public corruption, contributed richly to the elevation of American political life.

Many of the Germanic newcomers, unlike the impoverished Irish, possessed a modest amount of this world's goods. Most of them pushed out to the rich lands of the Middle West, notably Wisconsin, where they established themselves on model farms. Like the Irish, they formed an influential body of voters whom the American politician shamelessly wooed. But the Germans were less potent politically than the Irish because their strength was more widely scattered.

The hand of the Germans in shaping American life was widely felt in still other ways. They had fled from the militarism and wars of Europe, and consequently came to be a bulwark of the isolationist sentiment of the Mississippi Valley. Better educated on the whole than the stump-grubbing American, they warmly supported public schools, including their *Kindergarten* (children's garden). They likewise did much to stimu-

late art and music. As outspoken champions of freedom, they became relentless enemies of slavery during the fevered years before the Civil War.

Yet the Germans—often dubbed "damned Dutchmen"—were not altogether welcome neighbors. Regarding themselves as culturally superior,
they looked down their noses at both the poor Irishman and the "native"
American. They were not only snobbish but clannish. Uncurbed by Puritan tradition, they made merry on the Sabbath and drank huge quantities
of an amber beverage called *Bier* (beer), which dates its real popularity
in America from their coming. Their Old World drinking habits, like
those of the Irish newcomers, gave a definite setback to the movement
for greater temperance in the use of alcohol.

Flare-ups of Anti-Foreignism

The inpouring of this immigrant "rabble" in the 1840's and 1850's inflamed the latent hates of American "nativists." The fear deepened that
these hordes of foreign "scum" would outbreed, outvote, and overwhelm
the old "native" stock. Not only did the Germans and Irish take jobs from

A bitter "nativist" cartoon charging Irish and German immigrants with
"stealing" elections. New York Public Library

"native" Americans, but the great body of the displaced Irishmen were
Roman Catholics, as were a substantial minority of the Germans. The
Church of Rome was still widely regarded by many old-line Americans as
a "foreign" church.

The Roman Catholics were now on the move. They had formed an
almost negligible minority during colonial days, and a tiny minority later.

But with the enormous influx of the Irish and Germans in the 1840's and 1850's, the Catholics became a powerful minority. In 1840 they had ranked fifth, behind the Baptists, Methodists, Presbyterians, and Congregationalists. By 1850, with some 1,800,000 communicants, they had bounded into first place—a position they have never lost.

The "native" Americans were alarmed by these swelling figures. They professed to believe that in due course the alien riffraff would "establish" the Catholic Church at the expense of Protestantism and would introduce "popish idols." The noisier American "nativists" rallied for political action. In 1849 they formed the Order of the Star-Spangled Banner, which in a few years was to develop into the formidable American or "Know-Nothing" Party—a name derived from its secretiveness. The "nativists" agitated for rigid restrictions on immigration and naturalization, and for laws authorizing the deportation of alien paupers. They also sponsored a lurid literature of exposure, much of it pure fiction. The authors, sometimes posing as escaped nuns, described sin as they imagined it behind brick convent walls. One of these books—Maria Monk's *Awful Disclosures* (1836)—sold over 300,000 copies.

Even more ugly was occasional mass violence. As early as 1834 a Catholic convent near Boston was burned by a howling mob, and in ensuing years there were a few scattered attacks on Catholic schools and churches. The most frightful outburst occurred during 1844 in Philadelphia, where Catholic Irishmen fought back against the threats of the "nativists." The City of Brotherly Love did not quiet down until two Catholic churches had been burned and some thirteen citizens had been killed and fifty wounded in several days of fighting. These wild manifestations of intolerance, though infrequent and generally localized in the larger cities, remain an unfortunate blot on the record of our treatment of minority groups.

Religious Readjustments

Religion and morality both suffered from the surgical shock of separation from the Mother Country. The setback to orthodoxy resulted partly from the Revolution-spawned demoralization earlier discussed (pp. 126–127); partly from the rapid extension of the frontier; and partly from the skepticism and infidelity stimulated by the French Revolution. French freethinking was reflected in Thomas Paine's widely circulated book *The Age of Reason* (1794), which, while affirming the existence of God, violently attacked the Bible and orthodox religion.

A sharp reaction against irreligion set in about 1800, when the Second Great Awakening aroused the nation, East and West. Roaring revivals stirred the masses, and huge camp meetings were held on the frontier. At these "religious fairs" as many as 25,000 persons would swarm into tents to drink in the hell-fire gospel. As one of their hymns recounted:

My thoughts on awful subjects roll,
Damnation and the dead;
What horrors seize a guilty soul
Upon a dying bed!

Thousands of emotionally starved souls "got religion," and in their ecstasy engaged in orgies of rolling, dancing, barking, and jerking. Many of the "saved" soon "backslid" into their former sinful ways. But on the whole the revivals improved morality, increased church membership, and encouraged urgently needed humanitarian reform. Easterners were inspired to engage in missionary work in the Indian country, in Hawaii, and in far-away Asia.

Church attendance was a fairly regular ritual for about three-fourths of the 23,000,000 Americans in 1850. The Congregationalists, Presbyterians, and Episcopalians, as the older and more conservative faiths, continued to flourish in the East. More popular in the West and South were the Methodists and the Baptists. The success of both Methodists and Baptists lay in stressing personal conversion (contrary to predestination), a relatively democratic control of church affairs, and a rousing emotionalism. As a frontier jingle ran:

The Devil hates the Methodist
Because they sing and shout the best.

The Methodists, taking a page from English experience, were prime movers in the promotion of the first Sunday Schools. The religious instruction of their youth was thus undertaken under the auspices of a church.

Bishop Francis Asbury (1745–1816), English-born and somewhat domineering, was the outstanding figure in early American Methodism. A tall, frail bachelor, he traveled an estimated 300,000 miles over wretched or non-existent roads, praying, preaching, and organizing. He rode one horse about 25,000 miles in five years.

The fabulous Peter Cartwright (1785–1872) was the best-known of the Methodist "circuit riders," as the traveling frontier preachers were called. This ill-educated but powerful servant of the Lord ranged for a half-century from Tennessee to Illinois, calling upon sinners to repent. With bellowing voice and flailing arms, he converted thousands of souls to the Lord. Not only did he lash the Devil with his tongue, but he knocked out rowdies who attempted to break up his meetings. His Christianity was definitely muscular.

The Fragmentation of Faiths

Religious denominations in the United States tended to break into new sects. This development was partly—and not surprisingly—a product of our cherished democratic freedom of worship. It was also the natural outgrowth of conditions on the frontier, where the population was widely scattered.

The newly born Unitarian faith began to gather momentum, particularly in New England, about 1800. It held that God existed only in *one* person (hence *uni*tarian), and not in the orthodox Trinity—the Father, the Son, and the Holy Ghost.

The Unitarian sect emerged from the liberal ideas set in motion by the American Revolution and other vitalizing forces. It was primarily a protest against the hell-fire doctrines of Calvinism, especially predestined damnation and total depravity. The Unitarians, although denying that Jesus was divine, stressed the essential goodness of man rather than his vileness, and proclaimed salvation through integrity and good works. Embraced by many leading thinkers, including Ralph Waldo Emerson, the Unitarian movement continued to be highly intellectual.

The Millerites or Adventists, who mustered several hundred thousand adherents, enjoyed an immense vogue in the 1830's and 1840's. Named after the eloquent and commanding William Miller, they interpreted the Bible to mean that Christ would return to earth on October 22, 1844. Donning their go-to-meeting clothes, they gathered in prayerful assemblies to greet their Redeemer. The failure of Jesus to descend on schedule dampened but did not destroy the movement.

The United States, on the eve of the Civil War, was clearly becoming more tolerant. The vicious attacks by the "nativists" on Catholics were the exception rather than the rule. By mid-century the old state laws had been abolished which denied officeholding to Catholics, Jews, and atheists. A wide variety of creeds prevented the dominance of any one.

Religious diversity was further increased by the disruption of the churches over the slavery issue. By 1844–1845 both the Southern Baptists and the Southern Methodists had split with their Northern brethren over human bondage. The Methodists came to grief over the case of a slave-owning bishop in Georgia, whose second wife added several household slaves to his estate. In 1857 the Presbyterians, North and South, parted company. The secession of the Southern churches, in fact, foreshadowed the secession of the Southern states. First the churches split, then the political parties split, and then the Union split.

A Desert Zion

An amazing development was the rise of the Church of Jesus Christ of Latter-Day Saints (the Mormons), under the leadership of Joseph Smith. The tall, blue-eyed Smith, an ill-educated and visionary spirit reared on the Vermont-New York frontier, reported that he had received some golden plates from an angel. When deciphered, they constituted the Book of Mormon, published in 1830.

After establishing a religious oligarchy, Smith encountered serious

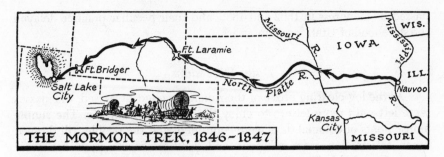

THE MORMON TREK, 1846-1847

opposition from his non-Mormon neighbors, first in Missouri and then in Illinois. His cooperative sect offended rank-and-file Americans, who were individualistic and dedicated to free enterprise. The Mormons aroused further antagonism by voting as a unit, and by openly drilling their militia for defensive purposes. Charges of polygamy likewise arose and increased in intensity, for Joseph Smith was reputed to have several wives.

Continuing hostility to the Mormons finally drove them to desperate measures. In 1844 Joseph Smith and his brother were murdered and mangled by a mob in Carthage, Illinois, and the movement seemed near collapse. But the falling torch was seized by a remarkable Mormon Moses named Brigham Young, an aggressive leader, an eloquent preacher, and a gifted administrator. Determined to escape further persecution, Young in 1847–1848 led his oppressed and despoiled followers over vast rolling plains to Utah. Overcoming various pioneer hardships, the Mormons soon made the desert bloom by means of ingenious and cooperative methods of irrigation. The crops of 1848, threatened by hordes of crickets, were saved when flocks of gulls appeared, seemingly miraculously, to gulp down the invaders. (A monument to the sea gulls stands in Salt Lake City today.)

The population of Utah grew remarkably. By the end of 1848 some 5000 settlers had arrived, and other large bands were to follow. Many devoted Mormons in the 1850's actually made the 1300-mile trek across the plains pushing two-wheeled carts. Under the rigidly disciplined management of Young, the Mormon community became a prosperous frontier theocracy and a cooperative commonwealth. Young had from nineteen to twenty-seven wives—some of them wives in name only—and fifty-six children. The population was further swelled by thousands of immigrants from Europe, where the Mormons had established a flourishing missionary movement.

Serious friction developed when the Washington government was unable to control the hierarchy of Brigham Young, who had been made territorial governor in 1850. A federal army was dispatched in 1857 against the Mormons, who harassed its lines of supply and rallied to die in their last dusty ditch. Fortunately, the quarrel was finally adjusted without serious bloodshed. The Mormons later ran afoul of the anti-polygamy laws passed by Congress in 1862 and 1882, and their peculiar practice delayed the statehood of Utah for many years.

Daily Diversions

As the log-clearing phase of the American pageant passed, the masses were left with more leisure to enjoy the good things of life. The simple amusements of colonial days were continued, and the people still derived much satisfaction from religious and political meetings, which were primly attended in "Sunday best" clothes. But a wider range of diversions gradually became established.

As the 19th Century unfolded, the stage took on greater respectability, even in Boston, where the Puritans had frowned upon the theater as "the Devil's chapel." Resourceful managers attempted to quiet ancient prejudices by stressing the moral value of their productions; for example, one of Shakespeare's famous plays was advertised as: "Hamlet: Filial Piety." The classical English dramas continued their popularity, and in the 1850's *Uncle Tom's Cabin* and *Ten Nights in a Barroom* were also playing to packed houses.

Early in the century many of the leading actors were visitors from England, but gradually local stars began to flash across the American stage. The handsome and arrogant Edwin Forrest (1806–1872) was the first top-flight American performer, and his rivalry with a visiting English artist inflamed his New York devotees to riot in 1849. This frightful affair ended with twenty-two persons killed and thirty-six wounded.

Other headliners had their day. English-born Junius Brutus Booth (1796–1852), a gifted though alcoholic tragedian, played Hamlet for a famous run of one hundred nights in New York. Two of his sons trod the boards as tragedians: Edwin T. Booth (1833–1893), who gained fame as an actor; John Wilkes Booth (1838–1865), who gained great infamy as the assassin of President Lincoln. The most talented American actress of the century was contralto-voiced Charlotte Cushman (1816–1876), who proved to be a smashing success in both male and female parts, including Romeo and Juliet.

Sports continued to relieve the monotony of everyday drudgery. Horse racing still attracted an enthusiastic and open-pursed following. Embryonic baseball had attained so much popularity by 1845 that a uniform set of rules was adopted. Flashy and inflammable showboats were churning the main rivers, bringing their variety shows to a gaping public. The traveling circus was drawing appreciative crowds, although the huge three-ring spectacles were not introduced until after the Civil War.

The most famous showman of the era was Phineas T. Barnum (1810–1891), a shrewd and cynical Connecticut Yankee. He got his start during the 1830's and 1840's in New York City, where he displayed bearded ladies and other freaks. Realizing that the American public loved to be "humbugged," he operated on the golden assumption that a "sucker" was born every minute. One of his prize hoaxes was the wizened Negro "nurse" of George Washington, alleged to be 161 years old. An autopsy later revealed her to be about 80.

Other activities were less amusing. Light-fingered gamblers were ever present to fleece the greedy and unwary, especially on the palatial river steamers. Dueling died hard in the honor-conscious South, its last stronghold. Crimes of violence still persisted in revolting numbers, partly as a result of the brutalizing influence of the frontier. Rough Western justice— often injustice—still manifested itself to an alarming degree in lynching bees, popularly known as "necktie parties."

For the upper crust, fashionable "watering places" were established at Saratoga Springs (New York) and Newport (Rhode Island). These recreational centers were frequented by the gaudily dressed elite, including many cotton-rich Southerners. Growing numbers of wealthier Americans—truly "innocents abroad"—were also making the "Grand Tour" of Europe.

Culturally, by 1860 America had traveled a long and uphill road since crude pioneering days. But a high degree of polish and sophistication, at least by European standards, lay in the lap of the future.

Free Schools for a Free People

Tax-supported primary schools were scarce in the morning years of the Republic, though private institutions were fairly common. The principle of public elementary schools, embraced by colonial Massachusetts and Connecticut, had been only imperfectly carried out. A few free institutions of a religious or charitable nature existed—the so-called "ragged schools." But poorer parents, shunning the stigma of pauperism, were loath to send their children to them.

As pressures for tax-supported public instruction rose, opponents entrenched themselves for a bitter-end fight. Operators of private schools, including church-supported institutions, naturally wanted this ripe vineyard for themselves. They argued hotly that separation of school and state was no less important than that of church and state. They further contended that public schools were anti-religious, socialistic, and contrary to free enterprise.

Childless citizens, as well as wealthy parents who favored select schools for select children, likewise voiced loud complaints. Non-parents cried "confiscation," and insisted that it was "damn foolishness to be taxed for eddicatin' other folkses brats." One irate Rhode Island farmer threatened to shoot Henry Barnard, a leading champion of free public schools, if the reformer should ever set foot on his property. A Middle Western legislator cried that he wanted only this simple epitaph when he died: "Here lies an enemy of public education."

Free public education, though lagging in the South, triumphed between 1825 and 1850. The sweaty day laborer, who now wielded increasing political influence, demanded free instruction for his children. Most important of all, the manhood suffrage of Jackson's day finally triumphed. A free vote cried aloud for compulsory free education—a union of school and state—primarily because a democracy cannot succeed without an electorate competent to inform itself. The flood of illiterate immigrants further emphasized the problem. An ignorant and voteless rabble is dangerous enough; it is trebly dangerous when the ballot has fallen into its hands. Universal suffrage could not be sanely based on universal ignorance.

Gradually the well-to-do, conservative Americans saw the light. They perceived the wisdom of strengthening the democratic processes by educating their neighbors' "brats." Otherwise, those "brats" might grow up, fall under the spell of false prophets, and vote away property rights. Taxation for education was the insurance premium that the wealthy were willing to pay for stability and democracy.

Reforming the Three R's

The famed little red grammar school—with one room, one stove, one teacher, and often eight grades—became the shrine of American democracy. Unfortunately, it was an imperfect shrine. The early free schools were open only a few months of the year, so as to allow the bigger boys to work on the farms. Classes were often taught by ill-paid, ill-trained, and ill-tempered schoolmasters, who sometimes put more stress on "lickin' " than on "larnin'." These knights of the blackboard often "boarded around" in the community, and in many instances knew scarcely more than their older pupils. Their fund of knowledge consisted of the "Three R's"—"readin', 'ritin', and 'rithmetic." To many rugged Americans, suspicious of "book larnin'," this was enough.

Reform was urgently needed. Into the breach stepped Horace Mann (1796–1859), a brilliant and idealistic graduate of Brown University, who forsook a promising career in law and politics for public service. Appointed Secretary of the Massachusetts Board of Education in 1837 at $1500 a year, he secured larger appropriations for education. These made possible more and better schoolhouses, more modern equipment, greater uniformity of instruction, longer school terms, adequately trained instructors, and higher pay for teachers—$65 a year had been common for women. The educational statesmanship of Mann included other fruitful changes, many of them inspired by European models. Looking to the future, he was largely responsible for establishing the first public teacher-training schools (normal schools) in the United States.

The dynamic influence of Horace Mann radiated out from Massachusetts to other states, and even abroad. Educators elsewhere followed his program with intense interest. Many of them, taking courage from his success, were able to win reforms modeled upon his. Mann's inspiration still endures through such sayings as: "Be ashamed to die until you have won some victory for humanity."

The improvement of the schools was paralleled by a betterment of textbooks. The early manuals were generally poor, and were often imported from England. An epochal change for the better came in 1783, when Yale-educated Noah Webster (1758–1843), a Connecticut Yankee who was a walking encyclopedia, published the first of his famous readers and spellers. His "reading lessons" were partly designed to promote patriotism. Altogether Webster's books, as the first distinctively American texts, were so popular that sales reached the amazing total of about 80,000,000 copies in one hundred years. Webster fairly earned his informal title, "Schoolmaster of the Republic." Living on his royalties, he devoted twenty years to his famous dictionary, published in 1828, which helped to unify and standardize the American language. This great work, as he intended, further knit together the union of states.

Even more influential in many ways was an Ohioan, William H. McGuffey (1800–1873), a teacher-preacher of rare power. His series of

SAD FATE OF A BOY WHO STOPPED TO PLAY IN A POND ON HIS WAY
TO SCHOOL AND WAS DROWNED
From McGuffey's *First Eclectic Reader*

grade-school readers, first published in the 1830's and enormously popular for more than half a century, sold the incredible total of 122,000,000 copies. The gems of literature that he reprinted not only elevated cultural standards but, more important, hammered home lasting object lessons

in morality, patriotism, and American idealism. A copy-exercise in the
Second Reader ran:

> Beautiful hands are they that do
> Deeds that are noble good and true;
> Beautiful feet are they that go
> Swiftly to lighten another's woe.

Probably no other person did as much as McGuffey to shape the mind and
morals of the American people in the 19th Century.

The Battle for Higher Learning

American educational objectives shifted as the 19th Century unfolded.
The ideal in colonial days had been learning for salvation and for leadership, with strong emphasis on religious leadership. The emergence of
manhood suffrage in Jackson's day caused the goal increasingly to become
education for citizenship. The belief was taking firm root that a child
should be trained to exercise intelligently his new responsibilities as a
democratic citizen.

Advocates of a broader-based education now began to demand a
tax-supported high school. Excellent private academies at the secondary
level were common, and violent opposition greeted the champions of a
tax-supported, compulsory high-school education. The old arguments
against free elementary schools were dusted off and reused. Yet the
friends of the public secondary school achieved encouraging success in
the 1840's and 1850's, and by 1860 could claim several hundred such institutions. The widespread flowering of the high school was not to come
until after the Civil War.

Higher education was likewise on the march. Colonial colleges had
weathered the Revolutionary War fairly well, and others began to multiply early in the 19th Century. The religious zeal of the Second Great
Awakening, beginning about 1800, resulted in the planting of numerous
independent liberal arts colleges, chiefly in the West and South. Largely
denominational and often wobbly, they all too frequently were established
to satisfy local pride. Yet they did furnish educational opportunities to
thousands of eager young men who otherwise would have been deprived
of a college education.

The first state-supported universities were opened in the South, beginning with North Carolina in 1795. Conspicuous among this early group
was the University of Virginia, founded in 1819. It was largely the brain
child of Thomas Jefferson, who designed its beautiful lines, and who at
times watched its construction through a telescope near his hilltop home.
True to his liberal ideals, he dedicated the university to the revolutionary
principle of education without political or religious shackles. As a partial
result, modern languages and sciences received unusual emphasis.

The state universities were designed to crown the tax-supported elementary and secondary systems, and the success of Jefferson's experiment gave the whole movement a strong push. The campaign for higher education was waged with considerable vigor in the decades just before the Civil War. It achieved gratifying gains in the South and West, where important aid was given through federal grants of land. But as in the case of the high school, the spectacular sprouting forth of state universities was not to come until after the Civil War.

Higher education for females was generally frowned upon in the early decades of the 19th Century. A woman's place was in the home, and training in needlecraft seemed more important than training in algebra. In an era when the clinging-vine type was the ideal, coeducation was regarded as wasteful and useless for the so-called weaker sex. The prejudice also prevailed that undue knowledge harmed the girlish brain, undermined health, ruined refinement, and rendered a young lady unfit for marriage. The teachers of young Susan B. Anthony, the future feminist, flatly refused to instruct her in long division.

Female schools at the secondary level began to attain some respectability in the 1820's, thanks in part to the yeoman work of Emma Willard. In 1833 Oberlin College, in Ohio, shocked the old-guard conservatives by admitting young women on a coeducational basis. A few girls' schools, some of which offered work of near-collegiate quality, were established before the Civil War, notably Mary Lyon's Mount Holyoke Seminary, at South Hadley, Massachusetts. But women's colleges did not come into their own until after the great conflict.

Adult Education

Tens of thousands of serious-minded adults craved more learning, especially those who had been starved educationally. Books were the old standbys, but often they were beyond the purse of the laboring man. The private subscription library of the colonial era continued, and tax-supported libraries, keeping pace with tax-supported education, began to emerge before the Civil War.

House-to-house peddlers enjoyed marked success in selling books. Noteworthy was Mason L. ("Parson") Weems, who also tried his hand at popularized biography. His purified life of George Washington became a best seller, and ultimately ran through more than seventy editions, including five in German. Not until the fifth edition did Weems introduce the utterly implausible tale of the cherry tree and hatchet. He did more than anyone else to create the false image of a dehumanized and priggish Washington.

Books were richly supplemented by the lyceum lecture associations, which numbered an estimated 3000 by 1835. The lyceums provided stimulating platform discussions by experts on science, literature, and morality.

Leading literary men, including Ralph Waldo Emerson, journeyed thousands of miles and delivered their messages to rapt audiences for the customary fees, ranging from about ten dollars to fifty dollars or more. Lyceum lectures continued to be popular until well into the 20th Century.

Numerous magazines were circulated during the pre-Civil War years, but most of them withered after a short life. The *North American Review*, founded in 1815, was the long-lived leader of the intellectuals. The most popular of the women's magazines was *Godey's Lady's Book* (1830–1898), which attained the enormous circulation of 150,000. It was devoured and wept over by countless millions of females.

Journalistic Giants

The newspaper—"the university of the public"—was further popularized by free, compulsory education and a consequent increase of literacy. Before 1830 a daily journal cost about six cents, a sum which the dollar-a-day manual laborer could not afford to pay. The New York *Sun*, seeking the economies of mass production, reduced its price in 1833 to one cent. It thus inaugurated the era of the "penny dreadful"—dreadful because it stressed murders, scandals, and other human-interest stories in the manner of the modern tabloid.

A leader in the new "gutter journalism" was erratic James Gordon Bennett, who in 1835 founded the New York *Herald*. His office desk consisted of two flour barrels with a plank laid across them; and he was editor, reporter, proofreader, folder, and cashier. He believed that the function of newspapers was not only to instruct but to startle, and he and other editors lowered the public taste while lowering the price of their sheets. At all events, more Americans were now reading than ever before.

The influence of journalism was immeasurably increased by the march of mechanization. The Hoe cylinder press (1846), as well as other marvelous inventions, finally enabled the flood of words to catch up with the demand.

The decades just before the Civil War marked the beginnings of the golden age of personal journalism. Newspaper publishing had not yet become a big business, and editors like Horace Greeley of the New York *Tribune* owned and published their own newspapers. The weekly edition of the *Tribune* enjoyed a wide circulation outside New York State, and since the idealistic Greeley was a leading foe of slavery, his word became law among a host of free-soilers. "Wait until the *Weekly Tribune* arrives," remarked a New York farmer when asked his opinion, "and then I can tell you what I think about it."

Passions ran incredibly high during this era of personal, hit-below-the-belt journalism. The writing-fighting editors were frequently caned, stabbed, or shot by those whom they offended with verbal volleys. The leading journalists, bespattered by inky strife, often used abusive language. "You lie, you villain," screamed Greeley at a rival editor, "you sinfully, wickedly, basely lie."

Despite all this violence and vulgarity, America was making gratifying progress in lifting the mental horizons of the masses. More people than ever before were now able to inform themselves on current issues, and with increased knowledge went an increased ability to make democracy function.

SELECT READINGS

Satisfying detail may be found in R. B. NYE, *The Cultural Life of the New Nation, 1776–1830* (1960) [paperback]. Older but rewarding social histories are J. A. KROUT and D. R. FOX, *The Completion of Independence, 1790–1830* (1944); C. R. FISH, *The Rise of the Common Man, 1830–1850* (1927); and A. C. COLE, *The Irrepressible Conflict, 1850–1865* (1934). Valuable on immigration are M. L. HANSEN's Pulitzer-prize *The Atlantic Migration, 1607–1860* (1940) [paperback]; C. F. WITTKE, *We Who Built America* (rev. ed., 1964) [paperback]; G. W. POTTER, *To the Golden Door: The Story of the Irish in Ireland and America* (1960); and C. F. WITTKE, *The Irish in America* (1956). On anti-Catholic bigotry see R. A. BILLINGTON, *The Protestant Crusade, 1800–1860* (1938) [paperback] and CARLETON BEALS' lurid *Brass-Knuckle Crusade: The Know-Nothing Conspiracy, 1820–1860* (1960). Religious stirrings are handled interestingly in B. A. WEISBERGER, *They Gathered at the River* (1958); C. A. JOHNSON, *The Frontier Camp Meeting* (1955); T. L. SMITH, *Revivalism and Social Reform in Mid-Nineteenth Century America* (1957); T. F. O'DEA, *The Mormons* (1957) [paperback]. On education consult MERLE CURTI, *Social Ideas of American Educators* (1959) [paperback] and R. M. ELSON, *Guardians of Tradition: American Schoolbooks of the Nineteenth Century* (1964). Also *Harvard Guide*, Pt. IV.

18

Social Reform and Cultural Gains, 1790–1860

---

*We [Americans] will walk on our own feet; we will work
with our own hands; we will speak our own minds.*
RALPH WALDO EMERSON, "The American Scholar," 1837

The Dawn of Scientific Achievement

THE early American, confronted with pioneering problems, was more interested in practical gadgets than in pure science. Thomas Jefferson, for example, was a gifted amateur who won a gold medal for a new type of plow. The writings of the mathematician Nathaniel Bowditch (1773–1838) on practical navigation, and of the oceanographer Matthew F. Maury (1806–1873) on ocean winds and currents, achieved international fame. They promoted safety, speed, and economy at sea. But as far as basic science was concerned, Americans were at their best in borrowing and adapting the findings of Europeans.

The youthful republic was not completely without scientific talent. The most influential scientist of the first half of the 19th Century was Professor Benjamin Silliman (1779–1864), a pioneer chemist and geologist who taught and wrote brilliantly at Yale College for more than fifty years. The distinguished French-Swiss immigrant, Professor Louis Agassiz (1807–1873), served for a quarter of a century on the faculty of Harvard College. As a path-breaking student of biology who sometimes carried snakes in his pockets, he insisted on original research and deplored the current overemphasis on memory work. Professor Asa Gray (1810–1888) of Harvard College, the Christopher Columbus of American botany, published over 350 books, monographs, and papers. His textbooks set new standards for clarity and interest.

Lovers of American bird lore owed much to the Frenchman John J. Audubon (1785–1851), who skillfully painted wild fowl in their natural habitat. His beautifully illustrated *Birds of America* attained considerable popularity. The Audubon Society for the protection of birds was named after him, although as a young man he shot much feathered game for sport.

340

Medicine in America, despite a steady growth of medical schools, was still primitive by modern standards. Bleeding remained a common practice. Plagues of smallpox were still dreaded, and the terrible yellow fever epidemic of 1793 in Philadelphia took several thousand lives. "Bring out your dead!" was the daily cry of the drivers of the death wagons.

People everywhere complained of ill health—malaria, the "rheumatics," the "miseries," and the chills. Illness often resulted from improper diet, hurried eating, perspiring and cooling off too rapidly, and ignorance of germs and sanitation. "We was sick every fall, regular," wrote the mother of President James A. Garfield. Life expectancy was still dismayingly short, and this fact accounts partly for the high proportion of young people. The suffering from decayed or ulcerated teeth was enormous; dentistry was often practiced by the muscular village blacksmith.

Patent medicines were common (one for man, two for horse), and included Robertson's Infallible Worm Destroying Lozenges. Among home remedies was the rubbing of tumors with dead toads. The use of medicine by the regular doctors was often harmful, and Dr. Oliver Wendell Holmes declared in 1860 that if the medicines, as then employed, were thrown into the sea, mankind would be better off and the fish worse off.

The victims of surgical operations were ordinarily tied down, sometimes after a stiff drink of whiskey. The surgeon then sawed or cut with breakneck speed, undeterred by the shrieks of his patient. A priceless boon for humanity came in the early 1840's when several American doctors and dentists, working independently, successfully used laughing gas and ether as anesthetics.

Humanitarian Stirrings

As the 19th Century slowly advanced, a strong reaction began to develop against the brutalities of earlier days. The crusade against slavery came to overshadow all other reforms, and to some extent it hampered them by attracting so much zeal and energy to itself. Yet gains were gradually achieved on many fronts.

Imprisonment for debt continued to be a nightmare, though its extent has been greatly exaggerated. As late as 1830 hundreds of penniless persons were languishing in filthy holes, sometimes for owing less than one dollar. The poorer working classes were especially hard hit by this merciless practice. As the embattled laborer won the ballot and asserted himself, the state legislatures gradually abolished debtors' prisons.

The criminal codes in the states were being softened at the same time, in accord with more enlightened European practices. The number of capital offenses was being reduced, and brutal punishments, such as whipping and branding, were for the most part being eliminated. The novel idea was taking hold that prisons should reform as well as punish— hence "reformatories," "houses of correction," and penitentiaries (for penance).

The victims of insanity were still being treated with incredible cruelty in the early decades of the century. The medieval concept had been that the mentally deranged were filled with unclean spirits; the 19th-Century idea was that they were willfully perverse and depraved—to be treated only as beasts. Many insane persons were chained in jails or poorhouses with sane people.

Into this dismal picture stepped a quiet New England teacher-authoress, Dorothea Dix (1802–1887). A frail spinster afflicted with persistent lung trouble, she possessed infinite compassion and will power. Never raising her voice to a screech, she traveled some 60,000 miles in eight years and assembled her damning reports on insanity from first-hand observations. Her classic petition of 1843 to the Massachusetts legislature, describing cells so foul that visitors were driven back by the stench, turned legislative stomachs and hearts. Thanks to her persistent prodding, the lot of the insane was markedly improved, and the concept began to gain acceptance that these creatures were not willfully unruly but mentally sick.

The peace movement also gained some momentum in the pre-Civil War years. In 1828 the American Peace Society was formed, to the accompaniment of a ringing declaration of war on war. A leading spirit was William Ladd, who preached when his legs were so badly ulcered that he had to sit on a stool. The ideas that he set forth were finally to bear some fruit in the international organizations for collective security of the 20th Century. The American peace crusade, linked with the European crusade, was making promising progress by mid-century, when it was set back by the bloodshed of the Crimean War in Europe and the Civil War in America.

Demon Rum

The ever-present drink problem loomed up wickedly in the early years of the century. Custom, combined with a grinding and monotonous life, led to the excessive drinking of hard liquor, even among women, clergymen, and members of Congress. Weddings and funerals all too often became disgraceful brawls, and occasionally a drunken man would fall into the open grave with the corpse. Heavy drinking decreased the efficiency of labor, and the introduction of poorly safeguarded machinery increased the danger of accident.

After earlier and feebler efforts, the American Temperance Society was formed at Boston in 1826. Within a few years about a thousand local groups sprang into existence. They implored drinkers to sign the temperance pledge, and organized children's clubs, known as the "Cold Water Army." The temperance crusaders also made effective use of pictures, pamphlets, and fervid lecturers, some of whom were reformed drunkards.

The most popular anti-alcohol writing of the era was T. S. Arthur's melodramatic novel, *Ten Nights in a Barroom and What I Saw There*

(1854). It described in lurid detail how a once-happy village was ruined by Sam Slade's tavern. The book was second only to Mrs. Stowe's *Uncle Tom's Cabin* as a best seller in the 1850's, and it enjoyed a highly successful run on the stage. Its touching theme song began:

> Father, dear father, come home with me now,
> The clock in the belfry strikes one. . . .

The early foes of Demon Drink adopted two major lines of attack. One was to stiffen the individual's will to resist the wiles of the little brown jug. The moderate reformers thus stressed "temperance" rather than "teetotalism," the total elimination of intoxicants. But less patient zealots gradually came to believe that the temptation should be removed by legislation. Prominent among this group was Neal S. Dow of Maine, a blue-nosed busybody who, as a mayor of Portland and an employer of labor, had often witnessed the debauching effect of alcohol.

Dow—the "Father of Prohibition"—was largely responsible for the passing of the so-called "Maine Law" of 1851, which supplanted the earlier effort of 1846. The drastic new statute, hailed as "the law of Heaven Americanized," prohibited the manufacture and sale of intoxicating liquor. Other states in the North followed Maine's example, and by 1857 about a dozen had passed various regulations regarding the dread traffic. But these figures are deceptive, for within a decade some of the statutes were repealed, declared unconstitutional, or openly flouted.

It was clearly impossible to legislate a thirst out of existence, especially in localities where public sentiment was hostile. Yet on the eve of

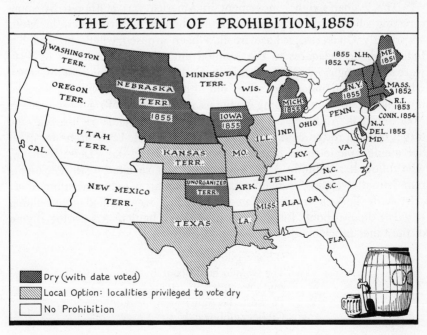

THE EXTENT OF PROHIBITION, 1855

WASHINGTON TERR.
OREGON TERR.
NEBRASKA TERR. 1855
MINNESOTA TERR.
WIS.
1855 N.H.
1852 VT.
ME. 1851
N.Y. 1855
MASS. 1852
R.I. 1853
CONN. 1854
MICH. 1855
IOWA 1855
PENN.
N.J.
DEL. 1855
MD.
UTAH TERR.
CAL.
KANSAS TERR.
MO.
ILL.
IND.
OHIO
KY.
VA.
NEW MEXICO TERR.
UNORGANIZED TERR.
ARK.
TENN.
N.C.
S.C.
MISS.
ALA.
GA.
TEXAS
LA.
FLA.

Dry (with date voted)
Local Option: localities privileged to vote dry
No Prohibition

the Civil War the prohibitionists had registered encouraging gains. There was much less drinking among women than earlier in the century, and probably much less per capita consumption of hard liquor.

Petticoats in Revolt

It was still a man's world, both in America and in Europe, when the 19th Century dawned. A wife was supposed to immerse herself in her home, and subordinate herself to her lord and master. Like Negro slaves, women could not vote; like Negro slaves, they could be legally beaten by their overlords. When they married, they could not retain title to their property.

Yet American women, though legally regarded as perpetual minors, were in a relatively good position. They were probably better treated than in any country of Europe, partly because of their scarcity in frontier communities. A Western woman could warn her spouse to be respectful, for "if you don't there's plenty will." Few American husbands were brutes; and the softer sex had quiet and time-tested ways of protecting itself, regardless of the law.

A belligerent bevy of female agitators emerged as the century neared its halfway point. Most of them had several strings to their reformist bow, and while demanding rights for women, were simultaneously battling for temperance and anti-slavery reform. American feminists received much encouragement from their sisters in Europe, where a parallel movement was gaining ground. Foul eggs and foul words could not stop them.

The woman's rights movement in America was mothered by some arresting characters. Prominent among them was Mrs. Lucretia Mott, a sprightly Quakeress, whose ire had been aroused when she and her fellow female delegates to the London anti-slavery convention of 1840 were not recognized. Mrs. Elizabeth Cady Stanton, a mother of seven who had insisted on leaving "obey" out of her marriage ceremony, shocked her fellow feminists by going so far as to advocate suffrage for women. Miss Susan B. Anthony, a militant lecturer for woman's rights, was the target of both rotten eggs and vulgar epithets. Mrs. Lucy Stone retained her maiden name upon marriage—hence the latter-day "Lucy Stoners," who follow her example. Mrs. Amelia Bloomer revolted against the current "street sweeping" female attire by donning a semi-masculine short skirt with Turkish trousers—"bloomers," they were called—amid much bawdy ridicule about "Bloomerism" and "loose habits." A sneering rhyme of the times proclaimed:

> Gibbey, gibbey gab
> The women had a confab
> And demanded the rights
> To wear the tights
> Gibbey, gibbey gab.

The fighting feminists met at Seneca Falls, New York, in a memorable Woman's Rights Convention (1848). The defiant Mrs. Stanton read a "Declaration of Sentiments," which in the spirit of the Declaration of Independence declared that "all men *and women* are created equal." One resolution formally demanded the ballot for females. The Seneca Falls meeting, which launched the modern woman's rights movement, was the object of scorn and denunciation from press and pulpit.

BLOOMERISM — AN AMERICAN CUSTOM
English satire on American feminists. *Punch,* 1851

The crusade for woman's rights was eclipsed by that against slavery in the years before the Civil War. Idiots could still vote; women could not. Yet girls were being gradually admitted to colleges, despite complaints "they'll be educating cows next." Some states, beginning with Mississippi in 1839, allowed wives to own property after marriage.

Wilderness Utopias

The leaders of the woman's rights movement often marched arm in arm with other reformers. Professional "do-gooders" popped up at every hand, giving to the 1840's the distinction of being the "hot air period" of American history. Everything was tried, from communism to socialism, through polygamy and celibacy, to rule by a prophet and guidance by spirits. Societies were formed against tobacco, profanity, and the transit of mail on the Sabbath. Various faddist diets were proclaimed, including the whole-wheat Graham bread of Sylvester Graham.

There was not "a reading man," observed Ralph Waldo Emerson, who was without some scheme for a new utopia in his "waistcoat pocket." Various reformers, ranging from the high-minded and impractical to the "lunatic fringe," labored to set up more than forty communities of a cooperative, communistic, or "communitarian" nature. Seeking human betterment, a wealthy and idealistic Scottish textile manufacturer, Robert Owen, established in 1825 a communal society of about a thousand persons at New Harmony, Indiana. Little harmony prevailed in New Harmony, which, in addition to hard-working visionaries, attracted a sprinkling of radicals, lazy theorists, and outright scoundrels. The enterprise became a sinking ship, without captain and trained crew, but with the passengers all shouting orders at once.

Brook Farm in Massachusetts, embracing two hundred acres of grudging soil, was started in 1841 with the brotherly cooperation of about twenty intellectuals. They prospered reasonably well until 1846, when they lost by fire a large new communal building shortly before its completion. The whole experiment in "plain living and high thinking" then collapsed in debt. Although a financial failure, Brook Farm was in some ways a social and educational success.

The most radical major experiment was the Oneida Colony, founded in New York in 1848. It practiced free love ("complex marriage"), birth control, and the eugenic selection of parents to produce superior offspring. The leader finally fled to Canada to escape prosecution for adultery. This curious enterprise flourished for more than thirty years, largely because its craftsmen made superior steel traps and Oneida Community (silver) Plate. But in 1879–1880 monogamy was finally adopted, and communism was abandoned.

Various communistic experiments, mostly small-scale, have been attempted in America since the days of Jamestown. But in open competition with democratic free enterprise and free land, virtually all of them sooner or later failed, passed away, or changed their methods. Perhaps the longest-lived sect has been the Shakers, who, beginning in 1778, set up the first of a score or so of religious communities. They attained a membership of about 6000 in 1840, but since they were opposed to both marriage and free love, it is not surprising that they were virtually extinct by 1940.

Artistic Achievements

Architecturally, America contributed little of note in the first half of the century. The rustic republic, still under pressure to erect shelters in haste, was continuing to imitate European models. Public buildings and other important structures followed Greek and Roman lines, which seemed curiously out of place in a wilderness setting. A remarkable Greek revival came in the years between 1820 and 1850, partly stimulated by the heroic efforts of the Greeks in the 1820's to wrest their independence from the "terrible Turk." About mid-century strong interest developed in a revival of Gothic forms, with their emphasis on pointed arches and large windows.

Many-sided Thomas Jefferson, also an architect of revolution, was probably the most distinguished American architect of his generation. He brought a classical design to his Virginia hilltop home, Monticello—perhaps the most stately residence in the nation. The quadrangle of the University of Virginia at Charlottesville, another creation of Jefferson, is by common consent one of the finest examples of classical architecture in America.

The art of painting continued to be handicapped. It still suffered from the dollar grabbing of our raw civilization; from the hustle, bustle, and absence of leisure; from the lack of a wealthy class to sit for portraits —and then pay for them. Some of our earliest painters were forced to go to England, where they found both training and patrons. America exported artists and imported art.

Painting, like the theater, had suffered from the Puritan prejudice that art was a sinful waste of time—and often obscene. John Adams once boasted that "he would not give a sixpence for a bust of Phidias or a painting by Raphael." When Edward Everett, the eminent Boston scholar and orator, placed a statue of Apollo Belvedere in his home, he had its naked limbs draped.

Competent painters nevertheless emerged. Gilbert Stuart (1755–1828), a spendthrift Rhode Islander and perhaps the most gifted of the early group, wielded his brush in England in competition with the best artists. He produced three portraits of Washington, all of them somewhat idealized and dehumanized. Truth to tell, the famous general had by then lost his teeth and some of the original shape of his face. Charles Willson Peale (1741–1827), a Marylander, painted some sixty portraits of Washington, for about fourteen of which the venerable Virginian patiently sat. John Trumbull (1756–1843), who had fought in the Revolutionary War, faithfully reproduced its scenes and spirit on about three hundred striking canvases.

During the nationalistic upsurge after the War of 1812, American painters turned increasingly from human landscapes to romantic mirrorings of local landscapes. The paint-daubers of the Hudson River School excelled in this type of art. Portrait painters gradually encountered some unwelcome competition from the invention of a crude photograph known as the daguerreotype, which was perfected about 1839 by a Frenchman, Louis Daguerre.

America Bursts into Song

Music was gradually shaking off the restraints of colonial days, when the doleful Puritans' had frowned upon non-religious singing. Melody-minded citizens received much inspiration from the emergence of European musicians—Schubert, Mendelssohn, Chopin, Wagner. Growing numbers of Americans were studying music, and the song-loving German immigrants of the 1840's and 1850's added richly to our culture. A mid-century boom in the manufacture of pianos reflected changing tastes.

BY-PRODUCT OF JENNY LIND'S TOUR
Yankee Notions, 1852

An appreciation of good music was increased by some noteworthy public performances. The New York Philharmonic Orchestra, one of our first, was organized in 1842. Ole Bull, the famous Norwegian violin virtuoso, held audiences spellbound during his five tours of the country, from 1843 to 1880. Golden-voiced Jenny Lind, the "Swedish Nightingale," who was also a talented actress and a fine Christian spirit, created a sensation in 1850–1852. She received an unprecedented $1000 for each of 150 concerts managed by showman Phineas T. Barnum, who for once did not "humbug" the public.

These visiting artists helped elevate the nation's musical taste, but Americans themselves were making solid contributions. Gifted writers of hymns were adding to American hymnology. Notable in this group was Lowell Mason (1792–1872), who is perhaps best known for "Nearer, My God, to Thee" and "From Greenland's Icy Mountains."

Rhythmic and nostalgic Negro tunes were becoming immensely popular by mid-century, especially in the uniquely American blackface minstrel shows. "Dixie," later adopted by the Confederates as their battle hymn, was written in 1859, ironically in New York City by an Ohioan. The most famous Negro songs, also ironically, were composed by a Pennsylvanian, Stephen C. Foster (1826–1864). His one excursion into the South came in 1852, after he had published "Old Folks at Home," in which an old slave laments:

> All round de little farm I wandered
> When I was young,
> Den many happy days I squandered,
> Many de songs I sung.

Foster made a valuable contribution to American folk music by capturing the plaintive spirit of the Negro slaves. An odd and pathetic figure, he finally lost both his art and his popularity, and died in a charity ward after drowning his sorrows in drink.

The nation was still too busy felling trees to write symphonies about their crashing. An eccentric Bohemian musician, A. P. Heinrich, undertook to play one of his own compositions about America at the White House. He was deeply affronted when President Tyler interrupted his piano-pounding to say, "That may all be very fine, sir, but can't you play us a good old Virginia reel?"

The Blossoming of a National Literature

"Who reads an American book?" sneered the British critic Sydney Smith in 1820. The unpalatable truth was that our rough-hewn, pioneering civilization gave little encouragement to "polite" literature. Much of our reading matter was imported or plagiarized from England.

The Americans, busy conquering half a continent, poured most of their creative efforts into practical outlets. Praiseworthy were political essays, like The Federalist of Hamilton, Jay, and Madison; pamphlets, like Tom Paine's Common Sense; and political orations, like the masterpieces of Daniel Webster. In the category of American non-religious books published before 1820, Benjamin Franklin's Autobiography (1818) is one of the very few that achieved genuine distinction. His narrative is a classic in its simplicity, clarity, and inspirational quality. At that, it records only a fragment of the Philadelphian's long and fruitful life.

A truly American literature was given a strong boost by the wave of nationalism that followed the War of Independence and especially the War of 1812. By 1820 the older seaboard areas were sufficiently removed from tree chopping so that literature could be supported as a profession. The Knickerbocker Group in New York blazed brilliantly across the literary heavens, thus enabling America for the first time to boast of a literature to match her magnificent landscapes.

Washington Irving (1783–1859), born in New York City, was the first American to win international recognition as a literary figure. Steeped in the early traditions of New Netherland, he published in 1809 his Knickerbocker's History of New York, with its amusing caricatures of the Dutch. When the family business failed, Irving was forced to turn to the goose-feather pen for a livelihood. In 1819–1820 he published The Sketch Book, which brought him immediate fame at home and abroad. Combining a pleasing style with delicate charm and quiet humor, he used English as well as American themes, and included such immortal Dutch-American tales as "Rip Van Winkle" and "The Legend of Sleepy Hollow." Europe was amazed to find at last an American with a feather in his hand, not in his hair. Later turning to Spanish locales and biography, Irving did much to interpret America to Europe and Europe to America. He was, said Thackeray, "the first ambassador whom the New World of letters sent to the Old."

James Fenimore Cooper (1789–1851) was the first American novelist, as Washington Irving was the first general writer, to gain world fame and make New World themes respectable. Marrying into a wealthy family, he settled down on what was then the frontier of New York state. Reading one day to his wife from an insipid English novel, he remarked in disgust that he could write a better one himself. She challenged him to do so —and he did.

After an initial failure, Cooper launched out upon a famous career in 1821 with his second novel, *The Spy*—an absorbing tale of the American Revolution. His stories of the sea were meritorious and popular, but his fame rests most enduringly on his Leather Stocking Tales. One of nature's noblemen, a deadeye rifleman named Natty Bumppo, cavorts with redskins in stirring adventures like *The Last of the Mohicans*. Cooper's novels had a wide vogue among Europeans, many of whom came to think of all Americans as born with tomahawk in hand.

A third member of the Knickerbocker group was the belated Puritan William Cullen Bryant (1794–1878), transplanted from Massachusetts. At age sixteen he wrote in blank verse the meditative and melancholy "Thanatopsis" (published in 1817), which was one of the first high-quality poems produced in the United States. Critics could hardly believe that it had been written on "this side of the water." Although Bryant continued with poetry as a sideline, he was forced to make his living by editing the highly influential New York *Evening Post*. Here for over fifty years he set a model for journalism that was dignified, liberal, and high-minded.

Trumpeters of Transcendentalism

The golden age of American literature came in the second quarter of the 19th Century, when an amazing outburst shook New England. One of its mainsprings was Transcendentalism.

The Transcendentalist movement of the 1830's resulted in part from a liberalizing of the old strait-jacket Puritan theology. It also owed much to foreign thinkers, including the German philosophers. The Transcendentalists believed that truth "transcends" the senses: it cannot be found by observation and reflection alone. The highest truth comes to light through inner faculties that every man possesses. It must therefore be sought by permitting the individual to follow his divine instinct.

The outward appearances of Transcendentalism are much easier to nail down than a definition of its underlying philosophy. It manifested itself in idealism, liberalism, romanticism, and mysticism; in individualism, self-reliance, and self-culture; in rebellion against the orthodox and the traditional. It led to humanitarian reform and utopian experiment; to better thoughts and better lives.

The member of the group who came to be best known was Boston-born Ralph Waldo Emerson (1803–1882). Tall, slender, and intensely blue-eyed, he mirrored inner serenity in his noble features. Trained as a Unitarian minister, he early forsook his pulpit and ultimately reached a wider audience by pen and platform. He was a never-failing favorite as a lyceum lecturer, and for twenty years took a western tour every winter. Perhaps his most thrilling public effort was a Phi Beta Kappa address, "The American Scholar," delivered at Harvard College in 1837. This brilliant appeal was an intellectual Declaration of Independence, for it urged American writers to throw off European traditions and delve into the rich mine in their own back yards.

Hailed as both a poet and a philosopher, Emerson was not of the highest rank as either. He was more influential as a practical philosopher, and through his fresh and vibrant essays enriched countless thousands of humdrum lives. Catching the individualistic mood of the Republic, he stressed self-reliance, self-improvement, self-confidence, optimism, and freedom. The secret of Emerson's popularity lay largely in the fact that his ideals reflected those of an expanding America. Among his most-quoted observations are: "Whoso would be a man, must be a non-conformist"; "A foolish consistency is the hobgoblin of little minds . . ."; "God offers to every mind its choice between truth and repose."

Henry David Thoreau (1817–1862) was Emerson's close associate—a poet, a mystic, a Transcendentalist, and a non-conformist. Condemning a government that supported slavery, he refused to pay his Massachusetts poll tax, and was jailed for a night. A gifted prose writer, he is best known for *Walden: Or Life in the Woods* (1854). The book is a record of Thoreau's two years of simple existence in a hut which he built on the edge of Walden Pond, near Concord, Massachusetts. A stiff-backed individualist, he believed that he should reduce his bodily wants so as to gain time for a pursuit of truth through study and meditation. Thoreau's *Walden* exercised a strong influence in furthering idealistic thought, both in America and abroad. It taught India's Mahatma Gandhi civil disobedience.

Transcendentalism, as well as upbringing, left its stamp on the gloomy mysticism of the Massachusetts Puritan, Nathaniel Hawthorne (1804–1864). The death of his sea-captain father on a voyage caused the impressionable youth to be brought up in an atmosphere of mourning. Gifted with a sparkling style and a powerful, if somber, imagination, he distinguished himself as a master of both the short story and the novel. His prose masterpiece is *The Scarlet Letter* (1850), a novel which deals with the effects of pride and secret sin on an adulteress and her lover, a minister of the gospel, in Puritan New England.

Poetry Comes of Age

Certain other literary figures were not actively associated with the Transcendentalist movement, though not completely immune from its influences. Professor Henry Wadsworth Longfellow (1807–1882), who for many years taught modern languages at Harvard College, was the most popular poet ever produced in America. Handsome and urbane, he lived a life of deep serenity, marred chiefly by the tragic death of two wives, the second of whom perished before his eyes when her dress caught fire. Writing for the genteel classes, he was adopted by the less cultured masses. His wide knowledge of European literature supplied him with many themes, but some of his most admired poems were based on American traditions—for example, *Evangeline, Hiawatha,* and *The Courtship of Miles Standish.* Widely quoted was his "Psalm of Life":

> Life is real! Life is earnest!
> And the grave is not its goal;
> Dust thou art, to dust returnest,
> Was not spoken of the soul.

Immensely popular in Europe, Longfellow was the only American ever to be honored with a bust in the Poets' Corner of Westminster Abbey.

The glamor of Longfellow, despite his poetic skill, has faded with time. He was too sweet, too much the conformist, too little the crusader. His most notable poetical contribution was to interpret the culture of the New World to the Old World and that of the Old World to the New.

A fighting Quaker, John Greenleaf Whittier (1807–1892), with piercing dark eyes and swarthy complexion, was the uncrowned poet laureate of the anti-slavery crusade. Less talented as a craftsman than Longfellow, he was vastly more important in influencing social action. His poems cried aloud against inhumanity, injustice, and intolerance, against

> The outworn rite, the old abuse,
> The pious fraud transparent grown.

Undeterred by insults and the stonings of mobs, Whittier helped arouse the sleeping ethical instincts of America on the slavery issue. A great conscience rather than a great poet or intellect, Whittier was one of the chief moving forces of his generation, whether moral, humanitarian, or spiritual. Gentle and lovable, he was pre-eminently the poet of human freedom. (See the examples on pp. 372, 380, 396.)

Many-talented James Russell Lowell (1819–1891), who succeeded Professor Longfellow at Harvard, ranks as one of America's better poets. He was also distinguished as essayist, literary critic, editor, and diplomat —a diffusion of talents that hampered his poetical output. He is perhaps best remembered as a political satirist in his *Biglow Papers,* especially those of 1846 dealing with the Mexican War. Written partly as poetry in the Yankee dialect, the *Papers* condemned in blistering terms the alleged slavery-expansion designs of the Polk administration. (See the example quoted on p. 298.)

Slender Dr. Oliver Wendell Holmes (1809–1894), who taught anatomy with a sparkle for many years at Harvard College, was a poet, essayist, novelist, lecturer, and wit. A non-conformist and a fascinating conversationalist, he shone among a group of literary lights who regarded Boston as "the hub of the universe." His poem "The Last Leaf," in honor of the last "white Indian" of the Boston Tea Party, came to apply to himself. Dying at age eighty-five, he was the "last leaf" among his distinguished contemporaries.

Humorous pencil sketch of Dr. Oliver Wendell Holmes. Boston Medical Library

Literary Individualists

Edgar Allan Poe (1809–1849), who spent much of his youth in Virginia, was an eccentric and morbid genius. Orphaned at an early age, cursed with ill health, and married to a child-wife of fourteen who fell fatally ill of tuberculosis, he suffered hunger, cold, poverty, and debt. Failing at suicide, he took refuge in the bottle, and died at the early age of forty. Poe was a gifted lyric poet, as *The Raven* attests. A master stylist, he also excelled in the short story, especially of the horror type. If he did not invent the modern detective novel, he at least set a new high standard in tales like *The Gold Bug*. Critics still dispute the quality of his work, but he attained considerable fame, both at home and abroad, before his untimely death in Baltimore.

The most noteworthy literary figure produced by the South before the Civil War, unless Poe is regarded as a Southerner, was novelist William Gilmore Simms (1806–1870). Quantitatively, at least, he was great, for eighty-two books flowed from his ever-moist pen, winning for him the title "The Cooper of the South." His themes dealt with the Southern frontier in colonial days, and with the South during the Revolutionary War. But he was neglected by his own section, even though he married into the socially elite and became a slaveowner. The high-toned planter aristocracy would never accept the son of a poor Charleston storekeeper.

Bold, brassy, and swaggering was the open-collared figure of Brooklyn's Walt Whitman (1819–1892). In his famous collection of poems, *Leaves of Grass* (1855), he gave free rein to his gushing genius with what he called a "barbaric yawp." Highly romantic and emotional, Whitman departed from the orthodox by dispensing with titles, stanzas, rhymes, and at times even regular meter. He handled sex with shocking frankness, although he laundered his verses in later editions, and his book was banned in Boston.

Whitman's *Leaves of Grass* was at first a financial failure. The only three enthusiastic reviews that the volume received were written by the author himself—anonymously. But in time the once-withered *Leaves of Grass*, revived and honored, won for Whitman an enormous following in both America and Europe. His fame increased immeasurably after his death.

Leaves of Grass gained for Whitman the informal title "Poet Laureate of Democracy." Singing with Transcendental abandon of his love for the masses, he caught the exuberant enthusiasm of an expanding America that had turned her back on the Old World.

> All the Past we leave behind;
> We debouch upon a newer, mightier world, varied world;
> Fresh and strong the world we seize—world of labor and the march—
> Pioneers! O Pioneers!

Here at last was the native art for which the critics had been crying. Yet no other American poet has at once been so violently damned and so extravagantly praised.

Herman Melville (1819–1891), an orphaned and ill-educated New Yorker, went to sea as a youth and served eighteen adventuresome months on a whaler. Jumping ship in the South Seas, he lived among cannibals, from whom he providentially escaped. His fresh and charming tales of the South Seas were rather popular, but his masterpiece is *Moby Dick* (1851). This epic novel is a tremendous allegory of good and evil, told in terms of the conflict between a whaling captain, Ahab, and a giant white whale, Moby Dick. Captain Ahab, who has lost a leg to the marine monster, swears to be avenged. His pursuit finally ends when Moby Dick rams and sinks Ahab's ship, leaving only one survivor.

Despite its brilliance, *Moby Dick* was virtually ignored by the public. A disheartened Melville continued to write unprofitably for some years, a part of the time eking out a living as a customs inspector, and then died in relative obscurity and poverty. Not until about thirty years after his death did scholars discover his true genius, and he is now ranked by many critics as one of America's supremely great prose writers.

Portrayers of the Past

A distinguished group of American historians was emerging, at the same time that other writers were winning distinction. Energetic George Bancroft (1800–1891), who as Secretary of the Navy helped found the Naval Academy at Annapolis in 1845, has deservedly received the title "Father of American History." He published a spirited, super-patriotic history of the United States in ten volumes (1834–1876), a work that grew out of his vast researches in dusty archives.

Two other historians are read with greater pleasure and profit today. William H. Prescott (1796–1859), who accidentally lost the sight of one eye in early childhood, conserved his remaining weak eye power and published the classic accounts of the conquest of Mexico (1843) and Peru (1847). Francis Parkman (1823–1893), whose vision was so weak that he wrote in darkness with the aid of a guiding machine, penned a brilliant series of volumes, beginning in 1851. In an epic style he chronicled the struggle between France and England in colonial times for the mastery of the North American continent.

Early American historians of prominence were almost without exception New Englanders, largely because Boston and its environs provided well-stocked libraries and a stimulating literary tradition. These chroniclers included ardent abolitionists among their relatives and friends, and hence were disposed to view unsympathetically the plight of the slave-cursed South. The writing of American history for generations to come was to suffer from an anti-Southern bias perpetuated by this early "made in New England" interpretation.

SELECT READINGS

See many of the titles for the previous chapter, especially those by Nye, Krout and Fox, Fish, and Cole. See also MERLE CURTI's Pulitzer-prize *The Growth of American Thought* (3rd ed., 1964); R. H. GABRIEL, *The Course of American Democratic Thought* (1940); also CARL BODE, *The American Lyceum* (1956) and *The Anatomy of American Popular Culture, 1840–1861* (1959). On reform, consult A. F. TYLER, *Freedom's Ferment* (1944) [paperback] and C. S. GRIFFIN, *Their Brothers' Keepers* (1960). Feminism is treated in ELEANOR FLEXNER, *Century of Struggle* (1959) and R. E. RIEGEL, *American Feminists* (1963). For literature see VAN WYCK BROOKS, *The Flowering of New England* (1936) [Pulitzer-prize, paperback]; *New England: Indian Summer* (1940); *The World of Washington Irving* (1944); *The Times of Melville and Whitman* (1947). On science consult A. H. DUPREE, *Asa Gray* (1959); EDWARD LURIE, *Louis Agassiz* (1960); F. L. WILLIAMS, *Matthew Fontaine Maury* (1963); and S. H. HOLBROOK, *The Golden Age of Quackery* (1959). On painting see J. T. FLEXNER, *That Wilder Image* (1962); on history, H. N. DOUGHTY, *Francis Parkman* (1962). Also *Harvard Guide*, Pt. IV.

19

The South and the Slavery Controversy

*If you put a chain around the neck of a slave, the
other end fastens itself around your own.*

RALPH WALDO EMERSON, 1841

"Cotton Is King!"

WHEN George Washington took the presidential oath, the economic wheels
of the South were creaking badly. They were burdened with depressed
prices, unmarketable products, overcropped lands, and the dead weight
of an unprofitable slave system. Many Southern statesmen, including
Thomas Jefferson, were talking openly of freeing their Negroes, and confidently predicting that slavery would gradually die of economic anemia.

But almost overnight the invention of the cotton gin in 1793 changed
the picture. The newly popularized short-staple cotton, which brought a
premium price, soon became the dominant Southern crop, eclipsing tobacco, rice, and sugar. The baleful institution of slavery was reinvigorated,
with the Negro being chained to the gin, and the planter to the Negro.

The Cotton Kingdom rapidly developed into a huge agricultural factory, turning out avalanches of the fluffy fiber. The magnet of quick profits
drew planters to the virgin bottom lands of the Gulf states. As long as the
soil was still vigorous, the yield was bountiful and the rewards were high.
The planters, caught up in an economic spiral, bought more slaves and
land to grow more cotton, so as to buy more slaves and land.

Cotton came to be by far the largest and most vital American export.
Not only was it valuable in establishing a balance between imports and
exports, but it held foreign nations in partial bondage. Britain was then
the leading industrial power. Her most important single manufacture in
the 1850's was cotton cloth, from which about one-fifth of her population,
directly or indirectly, drew its livelihood. About 80% of this precious supply of fiber came from the white-carpeted acres of the South.

Southern statesmen were fully aware that England was tied to them
by cotton threads, and this dependence gave them a heady sense of power.
In their eyes "Cotton was King," the gin was his throne, and the Negro

Cotton Exports Compared with Total Exports, 1800–1860

Year	Pounds of Cotton Exported	Value of Cotton Exported	Value of Total U.S. Exports	Percentage of Cotton in Relation to Total Exports
1800	17,789,803	$ 5,000,000	$ 70,971,780	7%
1810	93,261,462	15,108,000	66,757,970	22%
1820	127,860,152	22,308,667	69,691,669	32%
1830	298,459,102	29,674,883	71,670,735	41%
1840	743,941,061	63,870,307	123,668,932	51%
1850	635,381,604	71,984,616	144,375,726	49%
1860	1,767,686,338	191,806,555	333,576,057	57%

bondsmen were his henchmen. If war should ever break out between North and South, Northern warships would presumably cut off the outflow of cotton. British factories would then close their gates, starving mobs of the unemployed would force the London government to break the blockade, and the South would triumph. In truth, cotton seemed to be king.

Cavaliers All

The South before the Civil War was perhaps not so much a democracy as an oligarchy—or a government of the few, in this case dominated by a planter aristocracy. In 1850 only 1733 families owned more than one hundred slaves each, and this select group provided the cream of the political and social leadership of the section and nation. Here was the mint-julep South of the tall-columned and white-painted plantation mansion—the "big house," where dwelt the "cottonocracy."

The planter aristocrat enjoyed a lion's share of Southern wealth. He was able to educate his children in the finest schools, often in the North or abroad. His money, as was true of men like John C. Calhoun and Jefferson Davis, gave him the leisure for study, reflection, and statecraft. He felt a keen sense of obligation to serve the public. It was no accident that Virginia and her Southern sisters produced a higher proportion of front-rank statesmen before 1860 than the "dollar-grubbing" North.

But even in its best light, dominance by a favored aristocracy was basically undemocratic. It widened the gap between rich and poor. It hampered tax-supported public education, because the rich planter could and did send his children to private institutions. Yet the schools of the South, especially at the secondary level, were more numerous and efficient than is commonly supposed.

The Southern gentry were high-strung, though generally soft-spoken, courteous, hospitable, and chivalrous. Jealous of their personal honor, they clung to dueling long after it had died out in other sections. They carried on the somewhat spurious "Cavalier" tradition of early Virginia, and developed a martial spirit that is still reflected in high-quality Southern military academies.

The favorite author of Southerners was Sir Walter Scott, whose manors and castles, graced by brave Ivanhoes and fair Rowenas, roughly mirrored their own semi-feudal society. The Southern aristocrats, who on holidays would sometimes stage jousting tournaments, strove to perpetuate in the 19th Century a type of medievalism that had died out in Europe—or was rapidly dying out. Mark Twain later accused Sir Walter Scott of having had a hand in starting the Civil War. The British novelist, Twain said, aroused the Southerners to fight for a decaying social structure—"a sham civilization."

Slaves of the Slave System

The moonlight-and-magnolia tradition concealed much that was worrisome, distasteful, and sordid. The plantation economy was wasteful, largely because King Cotton and his money-hungry subjects despoiled the good earth. The urge for quick profits led to excessive cultivation or "land butchery," which incidentally caused a heavy drainage of population to the West and Northwest. The grim realities of soil exhaustion forced attention to scientific agriculture, and the pre-war South excelled in farm journals and agricultural societies. Edmund Ruffin of Virginia, who later fired one of the first shots of the Civil War at Fort Sumter, did notable pioneering work in the field of soil restoration. Yet his best efforts were less than enough to cope with the problem.

The economic structure of the South became increasingly monopolistic. As the land wore thin, many of the smaller farmers sold out their holdings to more prosperous neighbors. The big got bigger and the small smaller. When the Civil War finally broke, a large percentage of Southern farms had passed from the hands of the families that had originally cleared them.

Another cancer in the bosom of the South was the wobbliness of the plantation system. The temptation to overspeculate in land and slaves caused many a planter, including Andrew Jackson in his later years, to plunge in beyond his depth. Bankruptcy was often lurking just around the corner. Although the Negro bondsmen might in extreme cases be fed for as little as ten cents a day, there was a good deal more to the story. The slaves represented a heavy investment of capital, perhaps $1500 each in the case of prime field hands; and they might run away. The entire slave quarter might be wiped out by disease or even by lightning, as happened in one instance to twenty Negroes.

The dominance of King Cotton likewise led to a dangerous dependence on a one-crop economy, whose price level was at the mercy of world conditions. The whole hazardous system discouraged a healthy diversification of agriculture and particularly of manufacturing, for which the South was almost ideally fitted. The plantations, while concentrating on growing cotton, were forced to import huge quantities of pork and grain from the states of the upper Mississippi Valley.

The Southern planters resented having the North grow fat at their expense. They were distressed by the heavy outward flow of commissions and interest that went to Northern middlemen, bankers, agents, and shippers. All true sons of the South, especially by the 1850's, deplored the fact that when born they were wrapped in Yankee-made swaddling clothes, and that they spent the rest of their lives in servitude to Yankee manufacturing. When they died, they were laid in coffins held together with Yankee nails, and were buried in graves dug with Yankee shovels. The South furnished the corpse and the hole in the ground.

The Cotton Kingdom also repelled large-scale European immigration, which added so richly to the manpower and wealth of the North during the 1840's and 1850's. In 1860 only 4.4% of the Southern population was foreign-born, as compared with 18.7% for the North. German and Irish immigration to the South was generally discouraged by the competition of slave labor, by the high cost of fertile land, and by European ignorance of cotton growing. The diverting of non-English immigration streams to the North caused the pre-1860 South to become, except for the Negro, the most Anglo-Saxon part of the United States.

The White Man's World

Only a handful of Southern aristocrats lived in Grecian-pillared mansions. Below the 1733 families in 1850 who owned one hundred or more slaves were the less wealthy slaveowners. They totaled in 1850 some 345,000 families, representing about 1,725,000 white persons. Over two-thirds of these families—255,268 in all—owned fewer than ten slaves each.

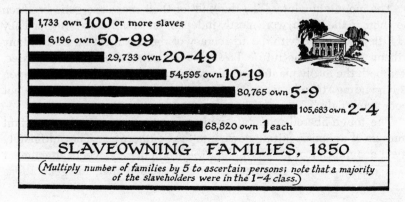

1,733 own **100** or more slaves
6,196 own **50-99**
29,733 own **20-49**
54,595 own **10-19**
80,765 own **5-9**
105,683 own **2-4**
68,820 own **1** each

SLAVEOWNING FAMILIES, 1850

(Multiply number of families by 5 to ascertain persons; note that a majority of the slaveholders were in the 1-4 class.)

Beneath the slaveowners on the social pyramid was the great body of non-slaveowning whites, who, by 1860, had swelled their numbers to 6,120,825. These rank-and-file citizens, comprising about three-fourths of the free population of the South, had no direct stake in slavery. They divided roughly into three groups: (1) the energetic lowland whites, who were by far the most numerous; (2) the listless poor whites, who were generally disease-ridden; and (3) the semi-isolated mountain whites, who were the most independent-minded.

The hundreds of thousands of energetic lowland whites included such people as mechanics, lesser tradesmen and above all small cotton farmers. Though owning no slaves themselves, they were among the stoutest defenders of the slave system. The carrot-on-the-stick ever dangling before their noses was the hope of buying a Negro or two, and of parlaying their holdings into riches—all in accord with the "American dream." They also took fierce pride in their racial superiority, which would be watered down if the slaves were freed. Many of the less prosperous lowland whites were hardly better off economically than the Negro; some, indeed, were not so well off. But they clung desperately to their one visible badge of presumed superiority.

Conspicuous among the millions of non-slaveholders was a considerable sprinkling of poor whites, who were despised by the Negroes as the "po' white trash." Known also as "hillbillies," "crackers," or "clay eaters," they were often listless, pallid, shiftless, and misshapen. Later investigations have revealed that many of them were not so much lazy as sickly, suffering from malnutrition and disease, including probably the enervating hookworm infection.

The mountain whites of the South are not to be confused with the disease-cursed poor whites of the lowland cotton belt. They were more or less marooned in the valleys of the Appalachian range, stretching all the way from western Virginia to northern Georgia and Alabama. The swirl of civilization had largely passed them by. They were a kind of living ancestry, for they retained Elizabethan folklore and speech forms that had long since died out in England.

The mountain whites, like the bulk of their more energetic brethren elsewhere in the South, were mostly independent small-crop farmers. They had little in common with the aristocracy of the broad cotton lands. Many of them, including the future President Andrew Johnson of Tennessee, hated both the lordly planter and his gangs of Negroes. They looked upon the impending strife between North and South as "a rich man's war but a poor man's fight."

The tough-fibered mountain whites constituted a vitally important peninsula of unionism jutting down into the Southern sea. They ultimately played a significant role in crippling the Confederacy. Their attachment to the Union party of Abraham Lincoln was such that, for generations after the Civil War, the only concentrated Republican strength in the Solid South was to be found in the Southern highlands.

Unchained Slaves

Below the most wretched whites in the social scale of 1860 were 251,000 free Negroes, some of whom owned a slave or two themselves. They usually had been freed by kind masters, or had purchased their freedom with earnings from labor after hours. They were a kind of "third race." Their lot was unpleasant and their "fettered freedom" was precarious, because they might be highjacked back into slavery by unscrupulous white dealers. Yet as free men they were walking examples of what might be achieved by emancipation, and hence were frowned upon by defenders of the slave system.

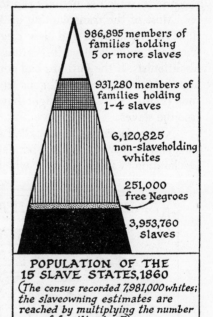

986,895 members of families holding 5 or more slaves

931,280 members of families holding 1-4 slaves

6,120,825 non-slaveholding whites

251,000 free Negroes

3,953,760 slaves

POPULATION OF THE 15 SLAVE STATES, 1860
(The census recorded 7,981,000 whites; the slaveowning estimates are reached by multiplying the number of families by 5)

Free Negroes were also unpopular in the North, where several states forbade their entrance. In 1835 New Hampshire farmers used oxen to drag into a swamp a small schoolhouse designed for colored children. The Northern freedmen were especially hated by the pick-and-shovel Irish immigrants, who feared wage-lowering competition.

Prejudice against the Negro was in fact frequently stronger in the North than in the South. The handsome and eloquent ex-slave Frederick Douglass, a self-educated orator and abolitionist of rare power, was subjected to numerous mobbings and beatings by Northern rowdies. It was observed that Southerners, who were sometimes reared by colored nurses, liked the Negro as an individual but despised him as a race. The Northerner, on the other hand, often liked him as a race but despised him as an individual.

Black Bondsmen

At the bottom of the social pyramid in the South of 1860 were nearly 4,000,000 black human chattels.

Negro slaves had existed in all the thirteen colonies before independence. Even preachers of the gospel in the North owned them, including the godly Jonathan Edwards, who kept two. The Negroes were originally snatched from darkest Africa by slave traders, who crammed them into the holds of slave ships. As a contemporary ballad ran:

> We crowded them upon the deck and stored them all below
> With eighteen inches to the man, was all they had to go.

Some of the slave ships became so filthy that, with the wind in the right direction, they could be smelled before they were sighted. The death rate on the horrible "middle passage" was incredibly high, but so were the profits, which sometimes ran to 500%.

Most of the transplanting of African slaves to English America was done by Englishmen and New Englanders. Some of these Yankee traders were descendants of early Puritans and, ironically, ancestors of the later abolitionists. If the Puritans had gone to Virginia instead of New England, and if the "Cavaliers" had gone to New England instead of Virginia, the sons of the "Cavaliers" might have fought the sons of the Puritans to free the slaves.

Negro slavery gradually died out in the North during and after the Revolutionary War. Human bondage clashed with the philosophy of the Declaration of Independence, which proclaimed that "all men are created

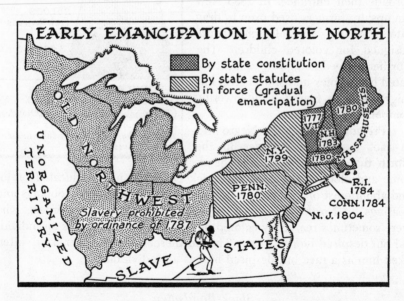

equal." But perhaps more important, slavery in the North had become economically unprofitable. Negro babies, when weaned, were sometimes given away by their owners. Financial loss often helps to create a tender conscience.

The legal importation of Negro slaves into America ended in 1808, when Congress nailed up the bars. This action was taken precisely at the end of the twenty-year period of grace prescribed in the Constitution (see Article I, Sec. IX, para. I). But the price of "Black Ivory" was so high before the Civil War that uncounted thousands of Negroes were smuggled into the South, despite the death penalty for slavers.

After the cotton gin had made slavery profitable, the planters had the wolf by the ears. It was embarrassing to hold on, dangerous to let go. To ask the owner to free his Negroes was to ask him to throw away about $2,000,000,000 in human livestock and plunge into financial ruin. Even if he were paid for his slaves at their market value, he still feared that he would go bankrupt because he could not raise cotton without a dependable labor supply. The planters believed that the Negroes, unless threatened with the lash, would not toil in the blazing sun. The slaveowners also clung to the convenient fiction that white men could not labor in the fields without ruining their health. Actually, hundreds of thousands of non-slaveholding whites hoed cotton and picked the bursting bolls without suffering ill effects.

It is true that after emancipation the ex-slave adjusted himself with considerable jarring to the wage-incentive system. But the masters doubted that this could be done—and they were unwilling to gamble. Even if the freedman should prove to be a docile and efficient wage laborer, his freedom would weaken the notion of "white supremacy" and raise the thorny issue of "keeping the Negro in his place."

In theory, the race problem could have been solved—though not the labor problem—by transporting the Negroes bodily back to Africa. But most of them did not want to return to a strange civilization after becoming partially Americanized. The republic of Liberia, on the fever-stricken West African coast, was established for ex-slaves in 1822, with its capital, Monrovia, named after President Monroe. After much expense and effort on the part of both Southerners and Northerners, some 15,000 Negroes were transplanted during the next thirty-eight years. About that many Negro babies were born in the South during a single month.

The Blessings (?) of Bondage

The ruling whites of the South, saddled with slaves, naturally came to stress more and more the advantages of their primitive system. They became even more aggressive after the Northern abolitionists began to assail both slavery and the slaveowners.

The dusky African, argued his masters, was lifted from voodooistic savagery and clothed with the blessings of western civilization, including Christianity. The Southern whites were aware of the soothing effect of religion through its promise of a better life in the hereafter, and they encouraged the slaves to attend churches of their own, or sit in the galleries of the regular churches. If the Negro were left in heathen Africa, the white owners pointed out, he would die and roast in Hell. Brought to

America, he was Christianized. Even though he was forced to hoe cotton, he was more than compensated when he finally went to Heaven for an eternity of bliss.

The "fortunate" slave—fortunate in Southern eyes—was also fed, sheltered, and clothed, from cradle to grave. On many plantations of the Old South, especially in Virginia and Maryland, he was virtually a part of the planter's family. A Southern tombstone bore this touching inscription:

JOHN:

A FAITHFUL SERVANT
AND TRUE FRIEND:
KINDLY, AND CONSIDERATE:
LOYAL, AND AFFECTIONATE:
THE FAMILY HE SERVED
HONOURS HIM IN DEATH:
BUT, IN LIFE THEY GAVE HIM LOVE:
FOR HE WAS ONE OF THEM

Southern whites were quick to contrast the "happy" lot of their bond-slaves with that of the overworked Northern wage slaves, including sweated women and stunted children. The Negro toiled in the fresh air and sunlight, not in dark and stuffy factories. He did not have to worry about slack times or unemployment, unlike the "hired hands" of the North. He was cared for in sickness and old age, unlike the Northern workers, who were turned adrift. And he was sometimes, though by no means always, spared dangerous work, like putting a roof on a house. If a neck was going to be broken, the master preferred it to be that of an Irish immigrant, rather than that of a field hand worth $1500.

The uprooted Africans, despite the harshness of their lot, often gave evidence of contentment and even happiness. Their life under the easy-going patriarchal system of Virginia and Maryland had certain attractive features. White apologists argued that the Negroes in many cases had less cause for worry than their harassed owners, who, shackled to the system, deserved no little sympathy.

The Southerners at heart were somewhat ashamed of slavery, which they delicately referred to as "the peculiar institution." If it was an evil, they felt that it was a necessary evil. But as it became more necessary, it seemed less and less evil.

Negro bondage could even be defended on moral and religious grounds. The planters remembered that they had inherited slavery from their fathers, who were not immoral men. Why trample on their graves? When attacked, the slaveholders felt bound to defend the outworn institution as a positive good. Southern editors, teachers, and preachers were at pains to justify slavery on historical and religious grounds. The Holy Scriptures refer to it repeatedly without condemning it. Abraham walked

THE NEGRO IN THE NORTH — AND IN THE SOUTH

A pro-slavery cartoon published in New York shows a chilled and rejected free Negro disconsolately passing a grogshop, while a happy Southern slave enjoys plantation life.

with God; and would God have walked with a slaveowner, asked the Southern whites, if He had disapproved of slavery?

The Dark Shadow of Slavery

The black curse of Negro slavery could not be successfully white-washed, however much Southerners might idealize the singing, dancing, and banjo-strumming of the colored "Old Folks at Home." If bondage was such a blessing, why did its victims universally pine for freedom, and why did so many take to their heels as runaways? A Negro girl, when asked if her mother was dead, replied, "Yassah, massah, she is daid, but she's free."

Slave auctions were brutal sights. The open selling of human flesh under the hammer, sometimes with four-legged cattle, was a revolting practice. Families were separated with distressing frequency, though usually not without good reason. Broken-hearted slaves were poor workers and potential runaways.

Breeding slaves, as cattle are bred, was not encouraged. But tens of thousands of Negroes from the overpopulated slave states of the Old South, notably Virginia, were "sold down the river" to the merciless field-gang labor of the lower Mississippi. Women who bore thirteen or fourteen babies were regarded as "rattlin' good breeders," and some of these fecund females were promised their freedom when they had produced ten.

Floggings were common, for the whip was the substitute for the wage-incentive system. As an abolitionist song of the 1850's lamented:

> To-night the bond man, Lord,
> Is bleeding in his chains;
> And loud the falling lash is heard
> On Carolina's plains!

But savage beatings were normally not administered without some provocation, because whipping made sullen laborers, and lash marks hurt the resale value. There are, to be sure, always some sadistic monsters in any population. But for financial as well as humane reasons, the planter did not go out and beat to death a valuable field hand before breakfast.

Slavery was undeniably degrading to the Negro. He was discouraged from developing self-discipline and initiative. He was deprived of the dignity and sense of responsibility that come from owning a home, caring for oneself, and finding labor of one's choice. He was normally denied an education, partly because reading brought ideas, and ideas brought discontent. Perhaps nine-tenths of the adult slaves at the beginning of the Civil War were totally illiterate.

Nor does the terrible indictment end here. The slave system inevitably made for loose morals, sexual and otherwise. The marriage tie was held lightly, and was sometimes solemnized simply by jumping over a broomstick. Slavery was also undemocratic because it was a denial of liberty, equality, and protection under law. It was likewise unchristian because it challenged the doctrine of universal brotherhood taught by Jesus.

The black taint also left its mark on the whites. It fostered the brutality of the whip, the bloodhound, and the branding iron. It bolstered the dangerous theory of biological race superiority. It caused the masters to struggle along under the heavy weight of world-wide disapproval. It debased the moral standards of both whites and Negroes by providing intimate association under circumstances that involved a maximum of temptation.

White blood inevitably became intermingled with black on a scandalous scale. Northern extremists charged, with self-evident exaggeration, that the South was one great "brothel," and that the Southern master commonly had a harem of colored concubines around back. Such critics also made much of lurid rumors, not altogether groundless, that beautiful and shapely girls of mixed blood were sold at New Orleans and elsewhere for fabulous prices—sometimes $5000.

The Southern whites who defended the black evil, so their critics charged, were defying the march of human progress. In doing so, they were forced to degrade themselves. As a distinguished Negro leader, Booker T. Washington, later observed, a white man cannot hold a black man in a ditch without getting down there with him.

Reasonable Abolitionism

The inhumanity of "the peculiar institution" gradually caused anti-slavery societies to sprout forth, both North and South. In 1826 there were 103 in the South, but only 40 in the North. The zeal of Northern crusaders was intensified in the 1830's and 1840's, partly as a result of the general reform movement sweeping the country. Additional support was given the anti-slavery cause by the unchaining of slaves in the British Empire during the 1830's, including the nearby British West Indies.

All shades of opinion existed in the North regarding Negro slavery. Many Northerners were surprisingly indifferent to the faraway Southern institution, or at any rate refused to take sides. Another numerous group consisted of anti-slavery men, like Abraham Lincoln, who as a practical matter did not advocate abolishing the hateful institution, but who opposed extending it into the territories. Men of this stamp, commonly called "free-soilers," grew more numerous as the Civil War impended.

Within the large anti-slavery camp was a smaller but more radical grouping known as the abolitionists. These reformers demanded that slavery be abolished outright in the South. But most of them were "moderates" who supported a kind of "gradualism"—that is, a gradual erasure

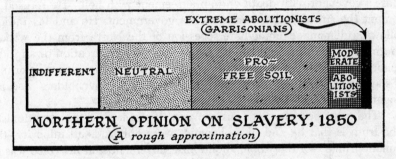

NORTHERN OPINION ON SLAVERY, 1850
(A rough approximation)

of the black blot by action of the Southern legislatures. Serious economic and social maladjustments would thus be avoided. Some of the moderate abolitionists also favored at least partial financial compensation to the owners.

Garrisonian Hotheads

The atmosphere of moderation was shattered in 1831, when a new and ominous blast came from the trumpet of William Lloyd Garrison, a mild-looking reformer of twenty-six. As James Russell Lowell put it:

> There's Garrison, his features very
> Benign for an incendiary;
> Beaming forth sunshine through his glasses
> On the surrounding lads and lasses.

The emotionally high-strung son of a drunken father who had deserted his wife, Garrison published in Boston the first issue of his militant abolitionist newspaper, *The Liberator*. This was perhaps the first paper broadside of a thirty years' verbal war, and in a sense one of the opening guns of the Civil War.

At the very outset, Garrison nailed his colors to the masthead. He proclaimed in violent tones that he would never compromise with the poisonous growth of slavery, but would stamp it out at once, root and branch. "I am in earnest—I will not equivocate—I will not excuse—I will not retreat a single inch—and I WILL BE HEARD!"

The extreme Garrison wing of the abolition movement did not understand the complex problems of the South—and evidently had no real desire to do so. Few, if any, of the abolitionist leaders had ever been near a Southern plantation. Yet, "angry for the right," they demanded immediate abolition—without compensation. Why compensate the "sinful" slaveowners, who themselves should compensate their own exploited slaves?

The accusations of the extreme abolitionists knew no restraints. The Southern "slavocrats," cried the Garrisonians, were brothel keepers and worse than criminals; they should not even be allowed seats in Congress. The Constitution upheld slavery, so Garrison publicly burned a copy of it as "a covenant with death and an agreement with hell." He refused to commit the sin of voting under such a government. He and his radical following demanded immediate secession of the North from the wicked South. Yet he did not explain, nor could he, how the creation of an independent slave republic would bring a speedy end to the "damning crime" of slavery. "All Hail Disunion" and "No Union with Slaveholders" became slogans of the Garrisonians.

The error persists that Garrison was the "voice" of the abolitionists. The truth is that he and his colleagues were only a small minority—the "lunatic fringe"—of the whole abolitionist movement. But his voice was so piercing, and his antics were so spectacular, that he overshadowed and obstructed the efforts of the more levelheaded anti-slave majority. Garrison's weekly *Liberator* was never self-supporting, and though widely known, never attained a circulation of more than 3000. This figure contrasts with the 28,000 in 1853 for the *National Era*, a journal of the moderate abolitionists, and only one of many anti-slavery papers. The moderates, who favored the Union and the ballot box, disliked Garrison—the "Massachusetts Madman." Some of them came to hate the Garrisonians even more than they hated slavery itself.

Violence Begets Violence

The abolitionists—especially the extreme Garrisonians—were unpopular in many parts of the North. The Northerners had been brought up to revere the Constitution, and to regard the clauses on slavery as a lasting bargain. The ideal of Union, hammered home by the thundering eloquence of Daniel Webster and others, had taken deep root; and Garrison's irresponsible talk of secession grated harshly on Northern ears.

The rank and file of Northerners were reasonable people. They had a deep respect for private property; and the "human cattle" of the South were no less valuable than the hooved cattle of the North. Some of the extreme abolitionists went so far as to urge the slaves to slay their masters in their beds. Decent Americans in the North, remembering the horrible uprising of the Negroes in Santo Domingo, could wish no like fate for their fellow Americans in the South.

The North also had a heavy economic stake in the South. By the late 1850's the Southern planters owed Northern bankers and other creditors about $300,000,000, and this immense sum would be lost—as, in fact, it later was—should the Union dissolve. The spindles of the New England textile mills were fed with cotton raised by the Negroes, and a disrupted labor system might cut off this vital supply and bring unemployment. The Union during these critical years was partly bound together with cotton threads, tied by "Lords of the Loom" in association with the so-called "Lords of the Lash." All these considerations taken together caused strong hostility to develop in the North against the boat-rocking tactics of the radical anti-slaveryites.

The outcries of the extreme abolitionists ultimately provoked scores of mob outbursts in the North, some of them led by respectable gentlemen in fancy attire. In 1835 Garrison, with a rope tied around him, was dragged through the streets of Boston by the so-called "Broadcloth Mob," but escaped almost miraculously. The Reverend Elijah P. Lovejoy, of Alton, Illinois, not content to attack slavery, threw mud at the chastity of Catholic women as well. His printing press was destroyed four times, and in 1837 he was killed by a mob, thus becoming "the martyr abolitionist." So unpopular were the anti-slavery zealots that politicians, if ambitious to go far in public life, usually avoided the taint of Garrisonian abolition like the plague.

The South Fights Back

The South was even less friendly than the North to the "Negro-loving" abolitionists, and there were some ugly instances of jailings, whippings, and lynchings. Shortly after Garrison fired his initial volley, the Southern anti-slavery societies, even those of a moderate stripe, withered away. The Southerners especially resented the slanders upon their statesmen, the meddling of ignorant reformers, and the appeals to the slaves to massacre their masters.

By a tragic coincidence, a slave insurrection broke out in Virginia in 1831, several months after Garrison began publishing *The Liberator*. Fanatical Nat Turner, a semi-educated Negro preacher who had visions, organized a conspiracy which resulted in the butchering of about sixty white Virginians, mostly women and children. The outburst was speedily crushed, but an understandable wave of hysteria swept over the South. Fear haunted Southern pillows, as planters in increasing numbers slept with pistols by their beds. Although Garrison had no demonstrable connection with the Nat Turner tragedy, he was bitterly blamed for it. Georgia offered $5000 for his arrest and conviction.

Regrettably, also, the controversy over abolition endangered free speech. Piles of petitions poured in upon Congress from the anti-slave reformers; and in 1836 sensitive Southerners drove through the House of Representatives the so-called "gag resolution." It required all such anti-slavery appeals to be tabled without debate. This presumed attack on the right of petition aroused the sleeping lion in the aged ex-President, Representative John Quincy Adams, and he waged a successful eight-year fight for its repeal.

The Southerners likewise resented the flooding of their mails with incendiary abolitionist literature. Even if the Negroes could not read, they could interpret the inflammatory drawings, such as those that showed masters knocking the teeth out of their slaves with clubs. In 1835 a mob in Charleston, South Carolina, looted the local post office and burned a pile of abolitionist propaganda. The authorities in Washington, though distressed by these outbursts, were powerless to force the local postmasters to deliver such hated tracts.

Ordeal by Battle

The South no doubt took the Garrisonians much too seriously, and made the mistake of regarding them as the mouthpiece of the entire North. The Southerners would have been well advised to hit the abolitionists with "a chunk of silence." But this was asking too much of human nature. The more strongly the winds of abolitionism swept down from the North, the more tightly the South wrapped the cloak of slavery about itself, and the more savagely it struck back at its tormentors. After thirty years of agitation by the abolitionists, slavery was more firmly rooted in the South than ever before.

Abolitionist violence bore a bitter harvest. For over a generation, it partially eclipsed other worthy reforms, including woman's rights. It ended all hope for the success of gradual emancipation in the northernmost of the Southern slave states, where the movement had been making promising progress. It contributed to a splitting of the parties and the churches into sectional groupings. It jeopardized fundamental American rights, both North and South, including the right to petition, freedom of speech, freedom of the press, freedom of inquiry, freedom of travel, and freedom of teaching—almost everything "free." These priceless freedoms were most severely restricted in the South, but occasionally there were disagreeable incidents in the North, as, for example, when a professor at Harvard College was dismissed for his anti-slavery views. Finally, mobbings and lynchings shook the foundations of law and order, while at the same time making more abolitionists by making more martyrs.

The radical abolitionists also helped destroy the comity between the sections—the good will that was the cement of union. Delicate social problems cannot be solved by screaming and name-calling, and the Garrisonians introduced emotion into a situation that called for light—not heat. Shouting led inexorably to shooting.

The South, angered by the holier-than-thou abuse of the Garrisonians, responded in kind. Fiery South Carolina orators like Senator R. B. Rhett and Congressman L. M. Keitt could fully hold their own. This exchange of

LIKE MEETS LIKE

Garrison (right) is here pilloried as a foe of the Union no less dangerous than the South Carolina secessionist Keitt. *Vanity Fair,* 1861

epithets, in an ever-widening circle, elicited even more violent epithets. Men spoke the same language, but no longer understood one another. Bonfires of hatred were lighted that in the end were only partially extinguished by buckets of blood. When secession finally came, many Southerners felt a sense of relief in getting away from "abolitionist nagging."

Was Bloodshed Necessary?

Short of war, the only feasible solution of America's slave problem was probably gradual emancipation, possibly with compensation. But the heat generated by the extremists on both sides helped destroy all hope of compromise. The South finally worked itself into a state of mind that would not accept compensated emancipation, and the North into a state of mind that would not offer it. If the South had been approached more sanely, it might ultimately have accepted such a reasonable solution. Yet even this assumption is questionable because of the issue of presumed race superiority.

The abolitionists, so their defenders say, helped arouse the moral conscience of the North, at a time when there was widespread apathy. Whittier's anguished cry did not go unheeded:

> What! mothers from their children riven!
> What! God's own image bought and sold!
> Americans to market driven,
> And bartered as the brute for gold!

The Garrisonians no doubt hastened the freeing of the slave by a number of years. But emancipation came at the price of a civil conflict which tore apart the social and economic fabric of the South. About a million whites were to be killed or disabled before some four million slaves could be freed, under conditions that took the lives of tens of thousands of Negro soldiers and ex-slaves. The war itself cost nearly $20,000,000,000, including interest and pensions. Compensated emancipation at full value —about $2,000,000,000—would have been far cheaper in dollars and cents.

The bewildered Negro was caught in the middle. The sudden, overnight liberation of the slaves was in many ways a calamity for them. And freedom by no means solved the race problem.

What were the prospects of peaceful emancipation in the 1850's? The slave system was based primarily upon the presumed profitableness of cotton culture, which in turn depended largely on rich new acres. The virgin lands were being ravished, and signs were multiplying that the boom days were passing. The South, staggering under the increased burden of a slave economy, and responding to the more enlightened "spirit of the age," might in time have listened to the voice of compensated emancipation. But again, with the race issue hanging over their heads, the planters might have turned a deaf ear. They were inclined to view the entire system as permanent rather than evolutionary.

Emotionalism thus slammed the door on any fair adjustment. Statesmen like Daniel Webster and Abraham Lincoln came to believe, not unreasonably, that the Garrisonians were doing more harm than good. All other western nations, including Brazil, ultimately rid themselves of the tumor of Negro slavery without the surgery of the sword, although admittedly their problems were different. Solution by civil war, even though it called forth much self-sacrifice and devotion to ideals, tragically scarred the body and soul of America.

SELECT READINGS

Brief introductions appear in J. G. RANDALL and DAVID DONALD, *The Civil War and Reconstruction* (1961), Chs. 2, 3; and in ALLAN NEVINS, *Ordeal of the Union* (2 vols., 1947), Chs. 13–15. An older classic is U. B. PHILLIPS, *Life and Labor in the Old South* (1929) [paperback]. More recent are CLEMENT EATON, *The Growth of Southern Civilization, 1790–1860* (1961) [paperback]; *A History of the Old South* (1949); *The Mind of the Old South* (1964); and *The Freedom-of-Thought Struggle in the Old South* (1964) [paperback]. See also W. R. TAYLOR's treatment of the myth in *Cavalier and Yankee* (1961) [paperback] and J. H. FRANKLIN, *The Militant South, 1800–1861* (1956) [paperback], which stresses the tradition of violence. On treatment of the Negro in the North see L. F. LITWACK, *North of Slavery* (1961) [paperback].

On slavery itself see K. M. STAMPP, *The Peculiar Institution* (1956), which takes a much less favorable view of slavery than does U. B. PHILLIPS' classic *American Negro Slavery* (1918). See also S. M. ELKINS, *Slavery: A Problem in American Institutional and Intellectual Life* (1959). On the Atlantic slave trade consult D. P. MANNIX and MALCOLM COWLEY, *Black Cargoes* (1962) [paperback]. Also useful are P. J. STAUDENRAUS, *The African Colonization Movement, 1816–1865* (1961) and W. S. HOWARD, *American Slavers and the Federal Law, 1837–1862* (1963).

Balanced treatments of abolitionism are LOUIS FILLER, *The Crusade against Slavery, 1830–1860* (1960) [paperback] and G. H. BARNES, *The Anti-Slavery Impulse* (1933). Markedly unsympathetic toward the white South is D. L. DUMOND, *Antislavery: The Crusade for Freedom in America* (1961). J. H. FRANKLIN, *From Slavery to Freedom* (1948) sets forth the view of a prominent Negro historian. The semi-mythical Underground Railway is examined in WILLIAM BREYFOGLE, *Make Free* (1958), LARRY GARA, *The Liberty Line* (1961), and HENRIETTA BUCKMASTER, *Let My People Go* (1959) [paperback]. See also H. R. MUELDER, *Fighters for Freedom* (1959) and H. R. FLOAN, *The South in Northern Eyes, 1831–1861* (1958) [paperback].

The most recent biographies of Garrison are R. B. NYE (1955), J. L. THOMAS (1963), and W. M. MERRILL (1963). Other recent biographies of abolitionists are BETTY L. FLADELAND's of Birney (1955), M. L. DILLON's of Lovejoy (1961), and OSCAR SHERWIN's and also I. H. BARTLETT's of Phillips (1958, 1961). Also *Harvard Guide*, Pt. IV.

20

Renewing the Sectional Struggle, 1848–1854

Secession! Peaceable secession! Sir, your eyes and mine are never destined to see that miracle.

SENATOR DANIEL WEBSTER, 1850
[Seventh of March speech]

The Popular Sovereignty Panacea

THE year 1848, signalized by an outburst of revolutions in Europe, was filled with unrest in America. The booty recently wrested from Mexico proved to be a bone of contention, for it raised anew the issue of extending slavery into the territories. The danger was ever present that the whole explosive question might disrupt the solid ranks of both Whigs and Democrats.

Each of the two great political parties was a vital bond of national unity, for each had powerful support both North and South. If they should be replaced by two purely sectional groupings, the days of the Union would be numbered. To politicians, the wisest strategy seemed to be to sit on the lid of the slavery-issue cauldron and try to ignore the boiling within. Even so, the lid bobbled up and down ominously in response to the agitation of fanatical Northern abolitionists and hotheaded Southern "fire-eaters."

The Democrats in 1848 were forced to seek a new standard-bearer. President Polk, broken in health by overwork and chronic diarrhea, had pledged himself to a single term. The Democratic national convention at Baltimore turned to an aging leader, General Lewis Cass, a veteran of the War of 1812. Though a statesman of wide experience and considerable ability, he was sour-visaged and somewhat pompous. His enemies dubbed him General Gass. The Democratic platform, in line with the current lid-sitting strategy, was silent on the burning issue of slavery in the territories.

But Cass himself had not been silent. His views on the extension of slavery were well known, because he was the reputed father of "popular sovereignty." This was the doctrine that the sovereign people of a territory, under the general principles of the Constitution, should themselves determine the status of slavery.

Popular sovereignty had a persuasive and widespread appeal. It was in full accord with the democratic tradition of letting the people rule. It was consistent with the Declaration of Independence and with the basic principles of self-determination. It had only one serious moral drawback: it might serve to spread the blight of Negro slavery.

New Triumphs for Taylor

The Whigs, meeting in Philadelphia, cashed in on the "Taylor fever." They nominated frank and honest Zachary Taylor, the "Hero of Buena Vista," who had never held civil office or even voted for President. Henry Clay, the living embodiment of Whiggism, should logically have been nominated. But he had made too many speeches—and too many enemies.

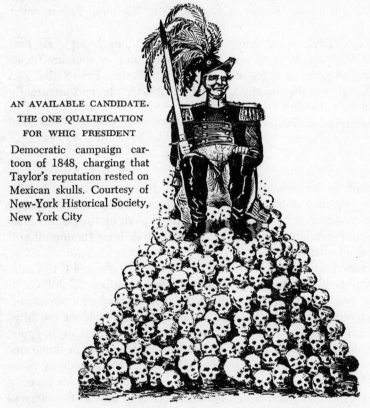

AN AVAILABLE CANDIDATE. THE ONE QUALIFICATION FOR WHIG PRESIDENT

Democratic campaign cartoon of 1848, charging that Taylor's reputation rested on Mexican skulls. Courtesy of New-York Historical Society, New York City

The Whigs, as usual, pussyfooted in their platform. Eager to win at any cost, they dodged all troublesome issues and merely extolled the homespun virtues of their candidate. The self-reliant old frontier fighter, something of a babe in the woods politically, had not committed himself on the issue of slavery extension. But as a wealthy resident of Louisiana, living on a sugar plantation, he owned scores of slaves.

Ardent anti-slavery men in the North, distrusting both Cass and Taylor, organized the Free-Soil Party. Aroused by the conspiracy of silence in the Democratic and Whig platforms, they made no bones about their own stand. They came out foursquare for the Wilmot Proviso, and against slavery in the territories. Going beyond other anti-slavery groups, they broadened their appeal by advocating federal aid for internal improvements, and by urging free government homesteads for settlers. The new party trotted out wizened old Martin Van Buren, and marched into the fray shouting, "Free soil, free speech, free labor, and free men."

With the slavery issue shoved under the rug by the two major parties, the politicians on both sides opened fire on personalities. The amateurish Taylor had to be carefully watched, lest his indiscreet pen puncture the reputation won by his sword. His admirers puffed him up as a gallant knight and an American Napoleon, and made much of his remark, allegedly uttered during the Battle of Buena Vista, "General Taylor never surrenders."

"Old Zack" Taylor's wartime popularity pulled him through. He harvested 1,360,099 popular votes and 163 electoral votes, as compared with Cass's 1,220,544 popular votes and 127 electoral votes. Free-Soiler Van Buren, although winning no state, polled 291,263 ballots, and apparently diverted enough strength from Cass in the crucial state of New York to throw the election to Taylor.

"Californy Gold"

President Taylor—stocky, rough-featured, heavy-jawed—was a military square peg in a political round hole. He would have been spared much embarrassment if he could have continued to sit on the political lid. But the discovery of gold in California, early in 1848, blew the top off and ripped open old sectional sores.

A fantastic horde of adventurers poured into the valleys of California. Singing Stephen C. Foster's "O Susannah" and shouting "Gold! Gold! Gold!" they began tearing frantically at the yellow-graveled streams and hills. A fortunate few of the bearded miners "struck it rich" at the "diggings." But the luckless many, who netted blisters instead of nuggets, probably would have been money ahead if they had stayed at home unaffected by the "gold fever." The most reliable profits were made by those who mined the miners, notably by charging exorbitant rates for laundry and other personal services. Soiled clothing was even sent as far away as the Hawaiian Islands for washing.

The overnight inpouring of tens of thousands of people—one of the great folk movements of history—completely overwhelmed the one-horse government of California. A distressingly high proportion of the newcomers were lawless men, accompanied by virtueless women. A contemporary song ran:

> Oh what was your name in the States?
> Was it Thompson or Johnson or Bates?
> Did you murder your wife,
> And fly for your life?
> Say, what was your name in the States?

The presence of so many undesirable characters led to an outburst of crime. Robbery, claim jumping, and plain murder were commonplace, and such violence was only partly discouraged by rough vigilante "justice." In San Francisco, from 1848 to 1856, there were scores of killings but only three hangings.

The great majority of Californians, who were decent and law-abiding, grappled earnestly with the problem of erecting an adequate state government. Privately encouraged by President Taylor, they drafted a constitution in 1849 which excluded slavery, and then boldly applied for admission to the Union. Southern politicians, alarmed by this "impertinent" stroke for freedom, arose in violent opposition. Would California prove to be the straw that broke the back of the Union?

Southern Sorrows

The South was especially worried, as it had been for several decades, by the ever-tipping political balance. There were then fifteen slave states and fifteen free states. The admission of California would destroy the delicate equilibrium in the Senate, perhaps irretrievably. Potential slave territory under the American flag was running short, if it had not already disappeared. Agitation had already developed in the territories of New Mexico and Utah for admission as non-slave states. The fate of California might well establish a precedent for the rest of the Mexican Cession territory—an area purchased largely with Southern blood.

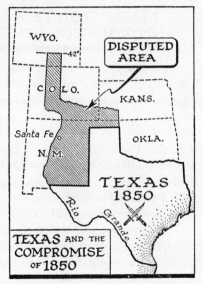

Texas nursed an additional grievance of her own. She claimed a huge area east of the Rio Grande and north to the 42nd parallel, embracing in part about half the territory of present New Mexico. The federal government was proposing to detach this prize from the Lone Star State, and hot-blooded Texans were threatening to descend upon Santa Fe and seize what they regarded as rightfully theirs. The explosive quarrel foreshadowed the firing of gunpowder.

The South was also angered by the constant agitation in the North for the abolition of slavery in the District of Columbia. The Southerners looked with horror on the prospect of a ten-mile-square oasis of free soil thrust between slaveholding Maryland and slaveholding Virginia.

Even more disagreeable to the South was the loss of runaway slaves. Many of these fugitives were assisted north by the Underground Railroad, which the anti-slaveryites were operating at full steam. It consisted of a chain of stations (anti-slavery homes), through which thousands of passengers (runaway slaves) were spirited by conductors (usually abolitionists) from the slave states to the free-soil sanctuary of Canada.

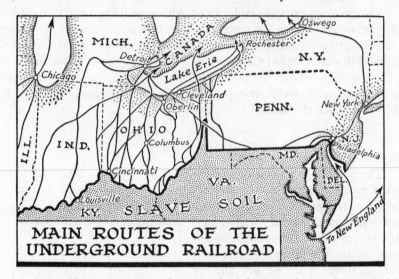

MAIN ROUTES OF THE
UNDERGROUND RAILROAD

A new and more stringent fugitive slave law was being demanded by Southerners. The old one, passed by Congress in 1793, had proved inadequate to cope with runaways, especially since unfriendly state authorities were failing to provide needed cooperation. Unlike cattle thieves, the abolitionists who ran the Underground Railroad did not gain personally from their secret activities. But from the standpoint of the slaveowners the loss was infuriating, whatever the motives. The moral judgments of the abolitionists seemed, in some ways, more galling than outright theft. They reflected not only a holier-than-thou attitude but an unwillingness to obey the laws solemnly passed by Congress.

The most careful estimates show that the South in 1860 was losing about 1000 runaways a year, out of its total of about 4,000,000 slaves. The slaveholders would have been well advised to write off these losses as negligible and unavoidable, like deaths from whooping cough. But the principle of the thing weighed heavily with them. They rested their argument on the Constitution, which protected slavery, and on the laws of Congress, which provided for slave-catching.

Yet the South of 1850, despite its complaints, was relatively well off.

It enjoyed then, as it had from the beginning, more than its share of the leadership of the national government. It had placed in the White House Zachary Taylor, a Virginia-born and Louisiana-domiciled slaveowner. It had a majority in the Cabinet and on the Supreme Bench. If outnumbered in the House, it had equality in the Senate, where it could hope to exercise a veto voice. Its cotton fields were expanding, and the price of the snowy fiber was profitably high. And few sane men, North or South, believed that slavery was seriously threatened where it already existed in the South.

Twilight of the Giants

Southern fears were such that Congress was confronted with a dire emergency in 1850. Free-soil California was banging on the door of the Union for admission, and "fire-eaters" in the South were voicing ominous threats of secession. The crisis brought into the Congressional forum the most distinguished assemblage of statesmen since the Constitutional Convention of 1787—the Old Guard of the dying generation and the young gladiators of the new. That "immortal trio"—Clay, Calhoun, and Webster —appeared together for the last time on the public stage.

Henry Clay, now seventy-three years of age, played a crucial role. The "Great Pacificator" had come to the Senate from Kentucky to engineer his third and greatest compromise. The once-glamorous statesman—though disillusioned, enfeebled, and racked by a cruel cough—was still eloquent, conciliatory, captivating. He proposed and skillfully defended a series of compromises. He was ably seconded by thirty-seven-year-old Senator Stephen A. Douglas of Illinois, the five-foot-four "Little Giant," whose role was less spectacular but hardly less important. Clay urged with all his persuasiveness that the North and South both make concessions, in a spirit of fair-mindedness, and that the North partially yield by enacting a more effective fugitive slave law.

Senator John C. Calhoun, then sixty-eight and dying of tuberculosis, upheld the South in his last formal speech. Too weak to deliver it himself, he sat bundled up in the Senate chamber, his eyes glowing within a stern and emaciated face, while a younger colleague read his fateful words. Although approving the purpose of Clay's proposed concessions, Calhoun rejected them as not providing adequate safeguards. His impassioned plea was to leave slavery alone, to return runaway slaves, to give the South its rights as a minority, and to restore the political balance. He had in view, as was later revealed, an utterly impracticable scheme of electing two Presidents, one from the North and one from the South, each wielding a veto.

Calhoun died in 1850, before the debate was over, uttering the sad words, "The South! The South! God knows what will become of her!" Appreciative fellow citizens in Charleston erected to his memory an imposing monument, which bore the inscription "Truth, Justice, and the Constitution." Calhoun had striven to preserve the Union, and had taken his stand on the Constitution, but his proposals in their behalf almost undid both.

Daniel Webster next took the Senate spotlight to uphold Clay's compromise measures in his last great speech—a reply to Calhoun that ranks with his reply to Hayne. Now sixty-eight years old, and suffering from a liver complaint aggravated by high living, he had lost some of the resonance of his magnificent voice. Speaking deliberately and before overflowing galleries, the leonine Senator urged all reasonable concessions to the South, including a new fugitive slave law with teeth.

As for slavery in the territories, asked Webster, why legislate on the subject? To do so was an act of sacrilege, for Almighty God had already passed the Wilmot Proviso. The good Lord had decreed—through climate, topography, and geography—that a plantation economy, and hence a slave economy, could not profitably exist in the Mexican Cession territory. Webster sanely concluded that compromise, concession, and sweet reasonableness would provide the only solutions. "Let us not be pygmies," he pleaded, "in a case that calls for men."

Webster's famed Seventh of March speech, 1850, was by all odds his finest, if measured by its immediate effects. It helped turn the tide of opinion in the North toward compromise. The clamor for printed copies became so great that Webster mailed out more than 100,000, remarking that 200,000 would not satisfy the demand. His tremendous effort visibly strengthened Union sentiment. It was especially pleasing to the banking and commercial centers of the North, which stood to lose millions of dollars by secession. One prominent Washington banker impetuously canceled two notes of Webster's, totaling $5000, and sent him a personal check for $1000 and a message of congratulations.

But the abolitionists, who had mistakenly regarded Webster as one of themselves, upbraided him as a traitor. The poet Whittier lamented:

> So fallen! so lost! the light withdrawn
> Which once he wore!
> The glory from his gray hairs gone
> For evermore!

But these reproaches were most unfair. Webster, who had long regarded slavery as an evil but disunion as worse, despised the abolitionists and never joined their ranks.

Deadlock and Danger

The stormy Congressional debate of 1850 was not finished, for the Young Guard from the North was yet to be heard from. This was the vigorous group of newer statesmen who, unlike the aging Old Guard, had not grown up with the Union. They were more interested in purging and purifying it than in patching and preserving it.

William H. Seward, the wiry and husky-throated freshman Senator from New York, was an able spokesman for many of the younger Northern radicals. A strong anti-slaveryite, he came out flat-footedly against concession. He evidently did not fully realize that compromise had brought the Union together and had held it together, and that when the sections could no longer compromise, they would have to part company.

Seward argued earnestly that Christian legislators must obey God's moral law as well as man's mundane law. He therefore appealed, with reference to slavery in the territories, to a "higher law" than a Constitution that sanctioned human bondage. This alarming phrase, later added to his "irrepressible conflict" speech of 1858, probably cost him the presidential nomination and the Presidency in 1860.

As the great debate in Congress ran its heated course, deadlock seemed certain. Blunt old President Taylor, who had allegedly fallen under the influence of "Higher Law" Seward, seemed bent on vetoing any compromise passed by Congress. His military ire was aroused by the threats of Texas to seize Santa Fe. He seemed doggedly determined to "Jacksonize" the dissenters, if need be, by leading an army against the Texans in person and hanging all "damned traitors." If troops had begun to march, the South probably would have rallied to the defense of her sister states, and the Civil War might have erupted in 1850.

Breaking the Log Jam

At the height of the controversy in 1850, President Taylor unknowingly helped the cause of compromise by dying suddenly of typhoid fever. Portly, round-faced Vice-President Millard Fillmore, a colorless and conciliatory New York lawyer-politician, took over the reins. As presiding officer of the Senate, he had been impressed with the arguments for compromise, and he gladly signed the series of measures that passed Congress after seven long months of stormy debate.

The balancing of interests in the so-called Compromise of 1850 was as follows:

Concessions to the North	Concessions to the South
California admitted as a free state.	The remainder of the Mexican Cession area to be formed into the territories of New Mexico and Utah, without restriction on slavery. Hence open to popular sovereignty.
Territory disputed by Texas and New Mexico to be surrendered to New Mexico.	Texas to receive $10,000,000 from the federal government as compensation.
Abolition of the slave trade (but not slavery) in the District of Columbia.	A more stringent Fugitive Slave Law, going beyond that of 1793.

The struggle to get these measures accepted by the country was hardly less heated than that on the floor of Congress. In the Northern states, "Union savers" like Senators Clay, Webster, and Douglas took the stump in behalf of the compromise. The ailing Clay himself delivered more than seventy speeches, as a powerful sentiment for acceptance gradually crystallized in the North. It was strengthened by a growing spirit of good will, which flowed partly from a feeling of relief, and partly from a wave of prosperity enriched by California gold.

But the "fire-eaters" of the South were still violently opposed to concessions. One extreme South Carolina newspaper avowed that it loathed the Union and hated the North as much as it did Hell itself. A movement in the South to boycott Northern goods gained some headway, but in the end the Southern Unionists, assisted by the warm glow of prosperity, won out over the disunionists.

The fate of the ill-starred Nashville Convention was an important straw in the wind. In mid-1850, an assemblage of Southern extremists had met in Nashville, Tennessee, ironically the burial place of the Unionist Andrew Jackson. The delegates had not only taken a strong position in favor of slavery, but had condemned the compromise measures of Henry Clay then being hammered out in Congress. Meeting again later in the year after the bills had passed, the convention proved to be a dud. By that time Southern opinion had reluctantly accepted the verdict of Congress.

Like the calm after a storm, a second "Era of Good Feelings" dawned. Disquieting talk of secession subsided. Reasonable men, both North and South, were determined that the compromises should be a "finality," and that the explosive issue of slavery should be laid to rest forever.

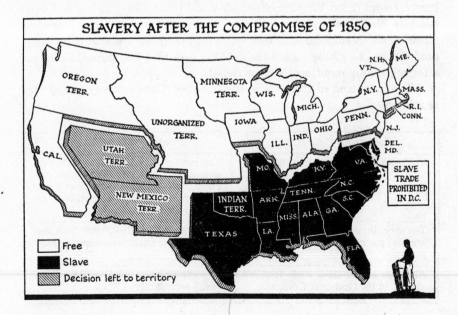

SLAVERY AFTER THE COMPROMISE OF 1850

Balancing the Scales

Who got the better of the Compromise of 1850?

The answer is clearly the North. California, admitted as a free state, tipped the Senate balance permanently against the South. The territories of New Mexico and Utah were theoretically open to slavery on the basis of popular sovereignty. But the iron law of nature—the "highest law" of all —had loaded the dice in favor of free soil. The Southerners urgently needed more slave territory to restore the "sacred balance." If they could not carve new states out of the recent conquests from Mexico, where else would they get them?

Even the apparent gains of the South rang hollow. Disgruntled Texas received $10,000,000 but in the long run this was an inconsequential sum. The immense area in dispute had been torn from the side of slaveholding Texas, and was almost certain to be free. The South had halted the drive toward abolition in the District of Columbia, at least temporarily, by permitting the outlawing of the slave traffic. But even this move was an ominous entering wedge toward complete emancipation in the nation's capital.

Most alarming of all, the drastic new Fugitive Slave Law stirred up a storm of opposition in the North. The fleeing Negro not only could not testify in his own behalf, but he was denied a jury trial. These harsh practices, from the point of view of Northerners, threatened to create dangerous precedents for the whites. For technical reasons, the federal commissioner who handled the case would receive five dollars if the runaway was freed, and ten dollars if not—an arrangement that strongly resembled a bribe. Freedom-loving Northerners who aided the slave to escape were liable to heavy fines and jail sentences. They might even be summoned to join the slave-catchers who were chasing the fugitive, and this possibility rubbed salt into old sores.

So savage was the new statute that it touched off an explosive chain reaction in the North. Many shocked moderates, hitherto passive, were driven into the swelling ranks of the abolitionists. Cried John Pierpont:

> Lashed with her hounds, must we
> Run down the poor who flee
> From Slavery's hell?

The Underground Railroad stepped up its timetable. Infuriated Northern mobs rescued Negroes from their pursuers. Massachusetts, in one of the most flagrant cases of nullification on record, made it a penal offense for any state official to enforce the new federal statute. Other states passed "personal liberty laws," which denied local jails to federal officials and otherwise hampered enforcement. The abolitionists rent the heavens with their protests against the man-stealing statute. A meeting presided over by Garrison in 1851 declared, "We execrate it, we spit upon it, we trample it under our feet."

The Fugitive Slave Law was an appalling blunder. No single irritant of the 1850's was more persistently galling to both sides, and none did more to keep alive in the North a spirit of antagonism against the South. The Southerners in turn were embittered because the Yankees would not in good faith execute the law—the one real and immediate "gain" of the South in the Great Compromise.

Should the shooting showdown have come in 1850? From the standpoint of the secessionists, yes; from the standpoint of the Unionists, no. Time was fighting for the North. With every passing decade this huge section was forging farther ahead in population and wealth—in crops, factories, foundries, ships, and railroads.

Delay also added immensely to the moral strength of the Northerners —to their will to fight for the Union. In 1850 countless thousands of moderates in the North were unwilling to pin the South to the rest of the nation with bayonets. But the inflammatory events of the 1850's did much to bolster the Northern will to resist secession, whatever the cost. This one feverish decade gave the North time to accumulate the strength that provided the margin of victory. Thus the Compromise of 1850, from one point of view, won the Civil War for the North.

The Doom of the Whigs

The Democratic nominating convention of 1852, meeting in Baltimore, surprised the nation. Hopelessly deadlocked, it finally stampeded to the second "dark horse" candidate in our history, an unrenowned New Hampshire lawyer-politician, Franklin Pierce. The Whigs tried to jeer him back into obscurity with the cry, "Who is Frank Pierce?"

Pierce, though handsome, was a weak and indecisive figure. Youngish, erect, smiling, and convivial, he had served without real distinction in the Mexican War. As a result of a painful injury he was known as the "Fainting General," though scandalmongers were quick to point to an early overfondness for alcohol. But he was enemyless because he had been inconspicuous, and as a pro-Southern Northerner he was acceptable to the slavery wing of the Democratic Party. His platform came out emphatically for the finality of the Compromise of 1850, Fugitive Slave Law and all.

The Whigs, also meeting in Baltimore, missed a splendid opportunity to capitalize on their record in statecraft. Able to boast of a praiseworthy achievement in the Compromise of 1850, they might logically have nominated either President Fillmore or Senator Daniel Webster, both of whom were closely associated with it. But having won in the past only with military heroes, they turned to another, "Old Fuss and Feathers" Winfield Scott, the ablest American general of his generation. Although he was a huge and impressive figure, his vain and imperious manner bordered on haughtiness. His personality not only repelled the masses but eclipsed his genuinely statesmanlike achievements. The Whig platform praised the Compromise of 1850 as a lasting arrangement, though less enthusiastically than the Democrats.

With slavery and sectionalism to some extent soft-pedaled, the campaign degenerated into a dull and childish attack on personalities. The Democrats ridiculed Scott's pomposity; the Whigs charged that Pierce was the hero of "many a well-fought *bottle.*" The Democrats cried exultantly, "We Polked 'em in '44; we'll Pierce 'em in '52."

Fortunately for the Democrats, the Whig Party was hopelessly split. The anti-slavery Whigs of the North swallowed Scott as their standard-bearer but deplored his platform, which endorsed the hated Fugitive Slave Law. The current phrase ran, "We accept the candidate but spit on the platform." The Southern Whigs, who doubted Scott's loyalty to the Compromise of 1850 and especially to the Fugitive Slave Law, accepted the platform but spat on the candidate. More than 5000 Georgia Whigs—"finality men"—voted for Daniel Webster, although the peerless orator had died nearly two weeks earlier.

General Scott, often victorious on the battlefield, met defeat at the ballot box. His friends remarked whimsically that he was not used to "running." Actually, he was stabbed in the back by his fellow Whigs, notably in the South. The pleasant Pierce won in a landslide, 254 electoral votes to 42, although the popular count was much closer, 1,601,274 to 1,386,580.

The election of 1852 was fraught with frightening significance, though it may have seemed spiritless at the time. It marked the end of the disorganized Whig Party as a major influence, and within a few years the complete death of this group. The Whigs were governed at times by the crassest opportunism, and they won only two presidential elections (1840, 1848) in their long and checkered career. They finally choked to death trying to gag down the Fugitive Slave Law. But their great contribution —and a magnificent one indeed—was to help implant and uphold the ideal of Union through leaders like Clay and Webster. Both of these statesmen, by unhappy coincidence, died during the campaign. But the good that they had done for the Union lived after them, and contributed powerfully to the preservation of the United States.

Pierce the Expansionist

The Pierce administration at the outset displayed vigor. The new President, standing self-confidently before some 15,000 people on inauguration day, delivered from memory a clear-voiced inaugural address. His Cabinet contained aggressive Southern elements, including as Secretary of War one Jefferson Davis, future President of the Confederacy. The

Southerners were determined to acquire more slave territory, and the compliant Pierce was prepared to be their willing tool.

The stirring events of the mid-century years, both at home and abroad, were opening American eyes to new vistas. Everywhere in the United States one could see evidences of heightened patriotism, nationalism, and devotion to the democratic ideal. We had greeted the revolutions that broke out in Europe during 1848 as new chapters in the book of human liberty begun by us in 1776. But these uprisings brought much disappointment and heartache. The crushing of the Hungarian revolution by the Austrian Emperor in 1849, with the aid of ruthless Russian Cossacks, aroused widespread bitterness in America against crowned despots. Louis Kossuth, the dynamic Hungarian leader in exile, visited the United States in 1851, and was everywhere hailed as a conquering hero—to the keen dissatisfaction of the European monarchs.

The intoxicating victories of the Mexican War further stimulated the spirit of Manifest Destiny. The conquest of a Pacific frontage, and the discovery of gold there, aroused lively interest in the Isthmian land routes of Central America, chiefly in Panama and Nicaragua. Many Americans were looking even farther ahead to potential canal routes, and to the islands flanking them, notably Spain's Cuba.

Nicaragua was of vital concern to Great Britain, the leading maritime and commercial power. Fearing that the grasping Yankees would monopo-

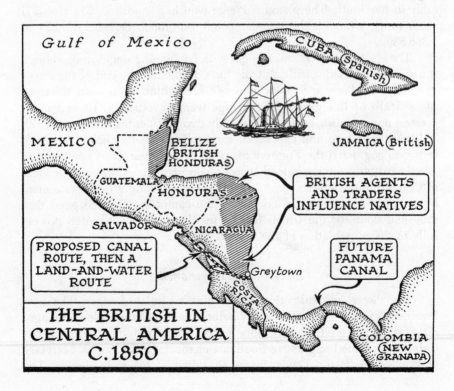

THE BRITISH IN CENTRAL AMERICA C. 1850

lize the trade arteries there, the British made haste to secure a solid foot-hold at Greytown, the eastern end of the proposed Nicaraguan canal route. This naked challenge to the Monroe Doctrine forthwith raised the ugly possibility of an armed clash. The crisis was happily surmounted in 1850 by the Clayton-Bulwer Treaty, which stipulated that neither America nor Britain would fortify or secure exclusive control over any future Isthmian waterway. This agreement, at the time, seemed necessary to halt the British, but to American canal promoters in later years it proved to be a bothersome ball and chain.

The United States had become a Pacific power with the acquisition of California and Oregon, both of which faced the Orient. The prospects of a rich trade with the Far East now seemed rosier. We had already established contacts with China, and our shippers were urging the Washington authorities to take active steps to establish commercial relations with Japan. The Mikado's kingdom, after some unfortunate experiences with the European world, had withdrawn into a cocoon of isolationism and remained there for over two hundred years. But by 1853, as events proved, Nippon was ready to emerge.

The Washington government was now prepared to pry open the bamboo gates of Japan. It dispatched a fleet of seven awesome, smoke-belching warships, commanded by Commodore Matthew C. Perry, brother of the hero of the Battle of Lake Erie in 1813. By a judicious display of force and tact, he persuaded the Japanese in 1854 to sign a memorable treaty. It provided for only a commercial foot in the door, but it was the beginning of an epochal relationship between the Land of the Rising Sun and the Western World. This achievement, though almost unheralded at the time, was to take on heightened significance in later years.

Cuba: Pearl of the Antilles

Sugar-rich Cuba, lying off our southern doorstep, was the number-one objective of Manifest Destiny in the 1850's. Supporting a large population of shackled Negroes, it was coveted by the South as the only potential slave territory of consequence then available. When carved into several slave states, it would once more restore the political balance in the Senate.

Cuba was a kind of heirloom—the most important remnant of Spain's once-mighty New World empire. Polk, the expansionist, had taken steps to offer $100,000,000 for it, but the sensitive Spaniards had replied that they would see it sunk into the ocean before they would sell it to the Yankees at any price. With purchase completely out of the question, seizure was apparently the only way to pluck the ripening bunch of bananas.

Private adventurers from the South now undertook to shake the tree of Manifest Destiny. During 1850–1851 two filibustering expeditions, each containing several hundred armed men, descended upon Cuba. Both feeble efforts were repelled, and the last one ended in tragedy when the leader and fifty followers—some of them from the best families of the South—were summarily shot or strangled. So outraged were the Southerners that an angry mob sacked Spain's consulate in New Orleans.

The Spanish officials in Cuba rashly forced a showdown in 1854, when they invoked a technicality to seize an American steamer, *Black Warrior*. Now was the time for the Pierce administration, dominated as it was by the South, to provoke a war with Spain and seize Cuba. The major powers of Europe—England, France, and Russia—were about to become deeply enmeshed in the Crimean War, and consequently were unable to come to the help of Spain.

An incredible cloak-and-dagger episode followed. The Secretary of State in Washington instructed the American ministers in Spain, England, and France to prepare confidential recommendations for the acquisition of Cuba. Meeting initially at Ostend, Belgium, the three envoys drew up a top-secret dispatch, soon known as the Ostend Manifesto. This startling document urged that the administration offer $120,000,000 for Cuba. If Spain refused, and if her continued ownership endangered American interests, the United States would "be justified in wresting" the island from her.

The so-called Ostend Manifesto quickly leaked out. Northern free-soilers, already angered by the Fugitive Slave Law and other gains for slavery, rose in an outburst of wrath against the "manifesto of brigands." Confronted with possible disruption at home, the red-faced Pierce administration was forced to drop its brazen schemes for Cuba.

The slavery issue, like a two-headed snake with the heads at cross purposes, deadlocked America's territorial expansion in the 1850's. The

MASTER JONATHAN TRIES TO SMOKE A CUBA, BUT IT DOESN'T AGREE WITH HIM!
English chortle over America's Cuban debacle. *Punch*, 1850

North, flushed with Manifest Destiny, was developing a renewed appetite for Canada. The South coveted Cuba. Neither section would permit the other to get the apple of its eye, so neither got either. The shackled black hands of Harriet Beecher Stowe's fictional Uncle Tom, who had already made such a profound impression in the North, held the South back from Cuba. The internal distresses of the United States were such that, for one of the few times in the century, the Republic could not take full advantage of Europe's distresses—in this case the Crimean War.

Pacific Railroad Promoters

Acute transportation problems were another legacy of the Mexican War. The newly acquired prizes of California and Oregon might just as well have been islands some 8000 miles west of the nation's capital. The sea routes to and from the Isthmus, to say nothing of those around South America, were too leisurely and too long. Covered-wagon travel past grinning skulls was possible, but it was too slow and too dangerous. A popular song recalled:

> They swam the wide rivers and crossed the tall peaks,
> And camped on the prairie for weeks upon weeks.
> Starvation and cholera and hard work and slaughter,
> They reached California spite of hell and high water.

Feasible land transportation was imperative—or the newly won possessions on the Pacific Coast might break away. Camels were even proposed as the answer. Several score of the temperamental beasts—"ships of the desert"—were imported from the Near East, but mule-driving Americans did not adjust to them. A far-stretching transcontinental railroad was clearly the only real solution of the problem.

Railway promoters, both North and South, had projected many drawing-board routes to the Pacific Coast. But the estimated cost in all cases was so great that for many years there could obviously be only one line. Should its terminus be in the North or in the South? The favored section would reap rich rewards in wealth, population, and influence. The South, yearly falling farther behind in the economic race with the North, was eager to extend a railroad line through adjacent Southwestern territory all the way to California.

Another chunk of Mexico now seemed desirable, for the campaigns of the recent war had shown that the most feasible railway route ran slightly south of the Mexican border. Secretary of War Jefferson Davis, a Mississippian influential with President Pierce, arranged to have James Gadsden, a prominent South Carolina railroad man, appointed minister to Mexico. Finding Santa Anna in power for the sixth and last time, and as usual in need of money, Gadsden made gratifying headway. He negotiated a treaty in 1853, which ceded to the United States the Gadsden Purchase

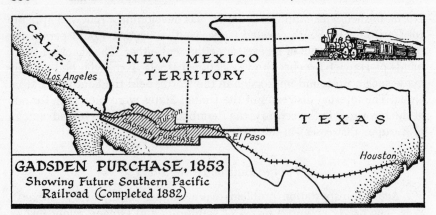

GADSDEN PURCHASE, 1853
Showing Future Southern Pacific
Railroad (Completed 1882)

area for $10,000,000. The transaction aroused much criticism among Northerners, who condemned the administration for paying a huge sum for a cactus-strewn desert nearly the size of Gadsden's own South Carolina. Undeterred, the Senate approved the pact.

The Gadsden Purchase enabled the South to claim the coveted railroad with even greater insistence. A southern track would be easier to build, because the mountains were less high and because the route, unlike the proposed northern lines, would not pass through unorganized territory. Texas was already a state, and New Mexico (with the Gadsden Purchase added) was a formally organized territory, with federal troops available to provide protection against marauding red men. Any northern or central line would have to be thrust through the unorganized territory of Nebraska, where the buffalo and Indians roamed at will.

Northern railroad boosters were quick to reply that if organized territory was the test, then Nebraska should be given an organized status. Such a move was not premature, because thousands of land-hungry pioneers were already poised on the Nebraska border. But all schemes proposed in Congress for organizing the territory were greeted with apathy or hostility by many of the Southern members. Why should the South hasten the creation of new free-soil states, and thus cut its own throat by facilitating the northern railroad route?

The Kansas-Nebraska Blunder

At this point in 1854 Senator Stephen A. Douglas of Illinois again stalked onto the stage of destiny. A squat, bull-necked, and heavy-chested figure, the "Little Giant" radiated the energy and breezy optimism of the self-made man. An ardent booster for the West, he had invested heavily in Chicago real estate and in railway stock, and was eager to have the Windy City become the eastern terminus of the proposed Pacific railroad. He would thus endear himself to the voters of Illinois, benefit his own section, and enhance the value of his private holdings.

Senator Douglas—a "steam engine in breeches"—threw himself behind a plan that would enlist the support of a reluctant South. The proposed Territory of Nebraska would be carved into two territories, Kansas and Nebraska. Their status regarding slavery would be settled by popular sovereignty—a democratic concept to which Douglas and his Western constituents were deeply attached. Kansas, which lay west of slaveholding Missouri, would presumably choose to become a slave state. But Nebraska, lying west of free-soil Iowa, would presumably become a free state.

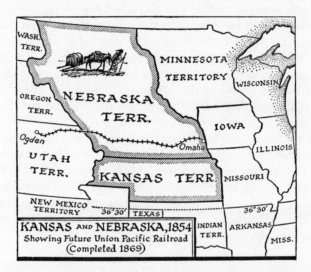

KANSAS AND NEBRASKA, 1854
Showing Future Union Pacific Railroad
(Completed 1869)

The Kansas-Nebraska scheme ran headlong into a formidable political obstacle. The Missouri Compromise of 1820 had forbidden slavery in all the Nebraska territory, which lay north of the sacred 36° 30' line, and the only way to open the region to popular sovereignty was to repeal the ancient compact outright. This bold step Douglas was prepared to take, even at the risk of shattering the Great Compromise of 1850.

A number of Southerners, who at first had not thought of Kansas as slave soil, rose to the bait. Here was a chance to get one more desperately needed slave state. The pliable President Pierce, under the thumb of his Southern advisers, threw the weight of his administration behind the Kansas-Nebraska Bill.

The Missouri Compromise, now thirty-four years old, could not be brushed aside lightly. Whatever Congress passes it can also repeal, but by this time the North had come to regard the sectional pact as something almost as sacred as the Constitution itself. The free-soil members of Congress struck back furiously. They met their match in the violently gesticulating Douglas, who was beyond doubt the ablest rough-and-tumble debater of his generation. Employing twisted logic and oratorical fireworks, he drove the bill through Congress ruthlessly, although receiving strong support from many Southerners. So great were political passions that bloodshed was barely averted. Some of the members even carried a concealed revolver or a bowie knife—or both.

The motives of Douglas in prodding anew the snarling dog of slavery have long been disputed by historians. His personal interests have already been mentioned. In addition, his foes accused him of fishing for the Presidency in 1856, even though there is considerable evidence to the contrary. His admirers have also argued plausibly in his defense that if he had not championed the ill-omened bill, someone else would have.

The truth seems to be that Douglas acted somewhat impulsively and recklessly. He did not feel keenly on the issue of slavery, and declared repeatedly that he did not care whether it was voted up or down in the territories. What he failed to perceive was that hundreds of thousands of his fellow countrymen in the North *did* feel violently on this moral issue. They regarded the repeal of the Missouri Compromise as an intolerable breach of faith, and they would henceforth resist to the last ditch all future demands of the South for slave territory.

A true statesman, like a skillful chess player, must foresee the possible effects of his moves. Douglas, to be sure, predicted a "hell of a storm," but he grossly underestimated its proportions. His political foes in the North greeted his name with frenzied boos, hisses, and "three groans for Doug." But he still enjoyed a high degree of popularity among his own loyal following in the Democratic Party, especially in Illinois, a stronghold of popular sovereignty.

Fruits of Legislative Folly

The Kansas-Nebraska Act—a curtain raiser to a terrible drama—was one of the most momentous measures ever to pass Congress. By one way of reckoning, it led directly down the slippery slope to Civil War.

The North was intensely angered by what it regarded as an act of bad faith. Henceforth all compromise with the South was rendered immeasurably more difficult, and without compromise there was bound to be conflict.

The Fugitive Slave Law of 1850, heretofore enforced in the North only halfheartedly, was now a dead letter. The Kansas-Nebraska Act fatally wrecked two compromises: that of 1820, which it repealed specifically, and that of 1850, which Northern public opinion repealed indirectly.

Northern abolitionists and Southern "fire-eaters" alike were stirred to new outbursts. The growing legion of anti-slaveryites was swelled by numerous recruits, who resented what seemed to be a grasping move by the "slavocracy" for Kansas. The Southerners, in turn, were to become inflamed when the free-soilers attempted to wrest Kansas from them, contrary to the backstage understanding.

The proud Democratic Party—now over half a century old—was temporarily wrecked by the Kansas-Nebraska Act. The Democrats managed to elect a President two years later, but he was the last one of their party for twenty-eight long years.

The most durable offspring of the Kansas-Nebraska blunder was the new Republican Party. It sprang up spontaneously in the Middle West, notably in Wisconsin and Michigan, as a mighty moral protest against the gains of slavery. Gathering together dissatisfied elements, it soon numbered disgruntled Whigs (including Abraham Lincoln), Democrats, Know-Nothings, and other foes of the Kansas-Nebraska Act. The hodge-podge party spread eastward with the rapidity of a prairie fire, and with the zeal of a religious crusade. Unheard-of and unheralded at the beginning of 1854, it elected a Republican Speaker of the House of Representatives within two years. Never really a third-party movement, it erupted with such force as to become almost overnight the second major political party.

The long-dreaded sectional rift had at last arrived. The new Republican Party would not be allowed to show its face south of the Mason and Dixon line. Countless Southerners subscribed wholeheartedly to the sentiment that it was "a nigger-stealing, stinking, putrid, abolition party." The Union was in dire peril.

SELECT READINGS

Sketchy but penetrating is R. F. NICHOLS, *The Stakes of Power, 1845–1877* (1961) [paperback], which retraces some of the ground in his Pulitzer-prize *The Disruption of American Democracy* (1948) [paperback]. Detailed treatments may be found in J. G. RANDALL and DAVID DONALD, *The Civil War and Reconstruction* (1961) and ALLAN NEVINS, *Ordeal of the Union* (2 vols., 1947). See also A. O. CRAVEN, *The Coming of the Civil War* (2d ed., 1957), his *Civil War in the Making, 1815–1860* (1959), and his *The Growth of Southern Nationalism, 1848–1861* (1953). The standard work is HOLMAN HAMILTON, *Prologue to Conflict: The Crisis and Compromise of 1850* (1964), which upgrades Douglas. Unabashedly pro-Douglas is G. F. MILTON, *The Eve of Conflict* (1934), which may be corrected by G. M. CAPERS, *Stephen A. Douglas* (1959). See also M. L. COIT's Pulitzer-prize *John C. Calhoun* (1950) [paperback] and C. M. WILTSE, *John C. Calhoun: Sectionalist, 1840–1850* (1951). The standard lives of the two Presidents are R. J. RAYBACK, *Millard Fillmore* (1959) and R. F. NICHOLS, *Franklin Pierce* (1958). Also *Harvard Guide*, Pt. IV.

21

Drifting Toward Disunion, 1854–1861

*A house divided against itself cannot stand. I believe this
government cannot endure permanently half slave and
half free.*

ABRAHAM LINCOLN, 1858

Literary Combustibles

THE clouds of sectional conflict were further darkened in 1852—and
later years—by an inky phenomenon. Mrs. Harriet Beecher Stowe, a wisp
of a woman and the mother of a half-dozen children, published her heart-
tugging novel, *Uncle Tom's Cabin.* Dismayed by the passage of the Fugitive Slave Law, she was determined to awaken the North to the wickedness of slavery by portraying its terrible inhumanity. Her book, though
lacking high literary quality, was distinguished by powerful imagery and
touching pathos. "God wrote it," she explained in later years.

The success of the novel at home and abroad was sensational. Several
hundred thousand copies were published in the first year, and the totals
soon ran into the millions as the tale was translated into more than a score
of languages. It was also put on the stage in "Tom shows" for unprecedented runs. No other novel in American history—perhaps in all history—
can be compared with it as a political force. To tens of millions of people
it made slavery appear almost as evil as it really was.

When Mrs. Stowe was introduced to President Lincoln in 1862, he
remarked with twinkling eye, "So you're the little woman who wrote the
book that made this great war." The truth is that *Uncle Tom's Cabin*
helped start the Civil War—and win it. The South condemned that "vile
wretch in petticoats" when it learned that hundreds of thousands of fellow
Americans were reading and believing her "unfair" indictment. Mrs. Stowe
had never witnessed slavery at first hand in the Deep South, but she had
seen it briefly during a visit to Kentucky, and she had lived for many years
in Ohio, a center of Underground Railway activity.

The story left a profound impression on the North. Uncounted thousands of readers swore that henceforth they would have nothing to do with

the enforcement of the Fugitive Slave Law. The tale was devoured by millions of impressionable youths in the 1850's—the later Boys in Blue who volunteered to fight the Civil War through to its grim finale. The memory of a beaten and dying Uncle Tom helped sustain them in their determination to eradicate the plague of slavery.

The novel was immensely popular abroad, especially in England and France. Countless readers wept over the kindly Tom and the angelic Eva, while deploring the brutal Simon Legree. When the guns in America finally began to boom, the common people of England sensed that the triumph of the North would spell the end of the black curse. The governments in London and Paris seriously considered intervening in behalf of the South, but they were sobered by the realization that their own people, aroused by the "Tom-mania," might not support them.

Another trouble-brewing book appeared in 1857, five years after the debut of Uncle Tom. Entitled *The Impending Crisis of the South,* it was written by Hinton R. Helper, a non-aristocratic white from North Carolina. Disliking the Negro, he attempted to prove by an array of statistics that indirectly the non-slaveholding whites were the ones who suffered most from the millstone of slavery. Unable to secure a publisher in the South, he finally managed to find one in the North.

Helper's influence was felt in unexpected quarters. It was, in fact, negligible among the poorer whites to whom he addressed his message. The book, with its so-called "dirty allusions," was banned in the South, where bonfire parties were held to keep it out of the hands of "Helperites." But in the North hundreds of thousands of copies, many in condensed form, were distributed as campaign literature by the Republicans. The Southerners were further embittered when they learned that their Northern brethren were spreading these inflammatory "lies" about them. Thus the sons of the South, reacting much as they did to *Uncle Tom's Cabin,* became increasingly unwilling to sleep under the same federal roof with their unfriendly Yankee bedfellows.

The Contest for Kansas

The rolling plains of Kansas had meanwhile been providing a horrible example of the workings of popular sovereignty, although admittedly under abnormal conditions.

The newcomers who ventured into Kansas were a motley lot. Most of the Northern settlers were just the ordinary westward-moving pioneers in search of richer lands beyond the sunset. But a small part of the inflow was financed by groups of Northern abolitionists or free-soilers. The most famous of these anti-slavery organizations was the New England Emigrant Aid Company, which sent several hundred persons to the troubled area to forestall the South—and also to make a profit. Shouting "Ho for Kansas," they carried the new breech-loading Sharps rifles, nicknamed "Beecher's

Bibles" after the prominent clergyman who had helped raise money for their purchase. Many of the Kansas-bound pioneers sang Whittier's marching song (1854):

> We cross the prairie as of old
> The pilgrims crossed the sea,
> To make the West, as they the East,
> The homestead of the free!

Southern spokesmen, now more than ordinarily touchy, raised furious cries of betrayal. They had supported the Kansas-Nebraska scheme of Douglas with the informal understanding that Kansas would become slave and Nebraska free. The Northerners, allegedly by foul means, were now apparently out to "abolitionize" *both* Kansas and Nebraska.

A few Southern hotheads, quick to respond in kind, attempted to "assist" small groups of well-armed slaveowners to Kansas. But this was a losing game. The slave was valuable and perishable property, and foolish indeed were the owners who would take him into an area where bullets were flying, and where the soil might be voted free under popular sovereignty. The census takers of 1860 found only two slaves among 107,000 souls in all the territory.

The crisis in Kansas rapidly worsened. When the day came in 1855 to elect members of the first territorial legislature, pro-slavery "border

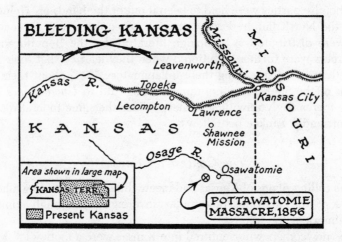

ruffians" poured in from Missouri to vote early and often. The slavery men triumphed, and then proceeded to set up their own puppet government at Shawnee Mission. The free-soilers, unable to stomach this fraudulent regime, established an extra-legal regime of their own in Topeka. The confused Kansan thus had his choice between fraudulency and extra-legality.

Tension mounted and disorders multiplied as men also feuded over conflicting land claims. The breaking point came in 1856 when a gang of pro-slavery raiders, alleging provocation, shot up and burned a part of the free-soil town of Lawrence. This outrage was but the prelude to a bloodier tragedy.

Kansas in Convulsion

The fanatical figure of John Brown now stalked upon the stage of history. Spare, gray-bearded, iron-willed, and narrowly ignorant, he was dedicated to the abolitionist cause. The power of his glittering gray eyes was such, so he claimed, that his stare could force a dog or cat to slink out of a room. Becoming involved in dubious dealings, including horse stealing, he moved to Kansas from Ohio with a part of his large family. Brooding over the recent attack on Lawrence, "Old Brown" of Osawatomie finally led a band of his followers to Pottawatomie Creek, in May, 1856, and there literally hacked to pieces five unoffending men, allegedly pro-slaveryites. This fiendish butchery, which was clearly the product of a deranged mind, besmirched the free-soil cause and brought vicious retaliation from the pro-slavery men.

Civil war, which thus flared forth in 1856, continued intermittently until it merged with the large-scale Civil War of 1861–1865. Altogether, the Kansas conflict destroyed millions of dollars' worth of property, paralyzed agriculture in certain areas, and cost scores of lives.

Yet by 1857 Kansas had enough people, chiefly free-soilers, to apply for statehood on a popular-sovereignty basis. The pro-slavery men, then in the saddle, devised a tricky document known as the Lecompton Constitution. The Kansans were not allowed to vote for or against the constitution as a whole, but for the constitution either "with slavery" or "with no slavery." If they voted against slavery, one of the remaining provisions of the constitution would protect the owners of slaves already in Kansas. So whatever the outcome of the voting, there would still be some Negro bondage in Kansas. Many free-soilers, infuriated by this transparent trick, stayed away from the polls. Left to themselves, the slaveryites approved the constitution with slavery late in 1857, with votes to spare.

The spotlight next shifted to Washington. President Pierce had been succeeded by the no less pliable James Buchanan, who was also strongly under Southern influence. Blind to future harmony within his own Democratic Party, Buchanan threw the weight of his administration behind the notorious Lecompton Constitution. But Senator Douglas, who had championed true popular sovereignty, would have none of this semi-popular fraudulency. Deliberately tossing away the strong support that he had in the South for the Presidency, he fought courageously for fair play and democratic principles. The outcome was a compromise which, in effect, submitted the *entire* Lecompton Constitution to a popular vote. The free-soil men thereupon thronged to the polls and snowed it under with their ballots. But Kansas was denied statehood until 1861, when the Southern secessionists left Congress.

President Buchanan, by antagonizing the numerous Douglas Democrats of the North, hopelessly divided the once-powerful Democratic Party. Until then, it had been the only remaining *national* party, for the Whigs were dead and the Republicans were sectional. With the disruption of the Democrats came the snapping of one of the last important strands in the rope that was precariously binding the Union together.

"Bully" Brooks

The issue of "bleeding Kansas" also brought bloodshed to the floor of the United States Senate in 1856. Senator Charles Sumner of Massachusetts, a tall and imposing figure, was a leading abolitionist—one of the few prominent in political life. Highly educated but cold, humorless, intolerant, and egotistical, he had made himself one of the most disliked men in the Senate. Brooding over the turbulent miscarriage of popular sovereignty, he delivered a blistering speech entitled "The Crime against Kansas." Sparing no epithets, he condemned the pro-slavery men as "hirelings picked from the drunken spew and vomit of an uneasy civilization." He also referred insultingly to South Carolina, and to her white-haired Senator Butler, one of the best-liked members of the Senate.

Hot-tempered Congressman Brooks, of South Carolina, now took matters into his own hands. Ordinarily gracious and gallant, he resented the insults to his state and to her Senator, who happened to be his cousin. His code of honor called for a duel, but in the South one fought only with one's social equals. And had not the coarse language of the Yankee dropped him to a lower order? To Brooks, the only alternative was to chastise the Senator as one would beat an ill-behaved dog. On May 22, 1856, he approached Sumner, then sitting at his Senate desk, and pounded the orator with a heavy cane until it broke. The victim fell bleeding and unconscious to the floor.

Sumner had been in the wrong; but this counter-outrage put Brooks in the wrong. The House of Representatives could not muster enough votes to expel the Carolinian, but he resigned and was triumphantly reelected. Southern admirers deluged Brooks with canes, some of them gold-headed, to replace the one that had been broken. The injuries to Sumner's head and nervous system were serious. The Senator was forced to leave his seat for three and a half years, and go to Europe for treatment that was both painful and costly. Meanwhile Massachusetts defiantly reelected him, and left his seat eloquently empty.

The free-soil North was mightily aroused against the "uncouth" and "cowardly" "Bully" Brooks. Copies of Sumner's abusive speech, otherwise doomed to obscurity, were sold by the tens of thousands. Every blow that struck the Senator doubtless made thousands of Republican votes. The South, although not unanimous in approving Brooks, was angered not only because Sumner had made such an intemperate speech but because it had been so extravagantly applauded in the North.

The Sumner-Brooks incident revealed how dangerously inflamed men's minds were becoming, both North and South. It was ominous that the cultured Sumner should have used the language of a barroom bully, and that the gentlemanly Brooks should have employed the tactics and tools of a thug. Emotion was displacing thought. The blows rained on Sumner's head were, broadly speaking, among the first blows of the Civil War.

"Old Buck" vs. "The Pathfinder"

With bullets whining in Kansas, the Democrats met in Cincinnati to nominate their presidential standard-bearer of 1856. They shied away from both the weak-kneed President Pierce and the dynamic Douglas. Each was too heavily blackened by the Kansas-Nebraska Act. The delegates finally chose instead James Buchanan (pronounced by many *Buck*-anan), a tall, handsome, white-haired, and well-to-do Pennsylvania lawyer, who had been minister in London during the recent Kansas-Nebraska quarrel. The suave diplomat was "Kansasless" and therefore relatively enemyless. But in a crisis that called for giants, "Old Buck" Buchanan was mediocre, irresolute, and confused.

The delegates of the fast-growing Republican Party met in Philadelphia with bubbling enthusiasm. "Higher Law" Seward was their most conspicuous leader, and he probably would have arranged to win the nomination had he been confident that this was a "Republican year." The final choice of the convention was Captain John C. Frémont, the so-called "Pathfinder of the West"—a dashing but erratic explorer-soldier-surveyor who was supposed to find the path to the White House. The black-bearded and flashy young adventurer was virtually without political experience, but like Buchanan he was not tarred with the Kansas brush. The Republican platform came out vigorously against the extension of slavery into the territories, while the Democrats declared no less emphatically for popular sovereignty.

An ugly dose of anti-foreignism was injected into the campaign, even though slavery extension was the chief concern. The recent heavy immigration from Ireland and Germany had alarmed the "nativists," as many of the old-stock Protestants were called. They organized the American Party, known also as the Know-Nothing Party because of its secretiveness, and in 1856 nominated the lackluster ex-President Fillmore. Anti-foreign and anti-Catholic, these superpatriots adopted the slogan "Americans Must Rule America." Remnants of the dying Whig Party likewise endorsed Fillmore, and they and the Know-Nothingites threatened to drain heavily from potential Republican strength.

The Republicans threw themselves behind Frémont with the zeal of crusaders. Shouting "We Follow the Pathfinder" and "We Are Buck Hunting," they organized glee clubs which sang (to the tune of the "Marseillaise"):

> Arise, arise ye brave!
> And let our war-cry be,
> Free speech, free press, free soil, free men,
> Fre-mont and victory!

"And free love," sneered the Buchanan men ("Buchaneers").

Mudslinging bespattered both candidates. "Old Fogy" Buchanan was assailed because he was a bachelor: the fiancée of his youth had died shortly after a lovers' quarrel. Frémont was attacked because of his illegitimate birth. More harmful to him was the allegation, which alienated many Know-Nothings and other "nativists," that he was a Roman Catholic.

The Fruits of '56

The bland Buchanan, although polling less than a majority of the popular vote, won handily. His tally in the Electoral College was 174 to 114 for Frémont, with Fillmore garnering 8. The popular vote was 1,838,-169 for Buchanan to 1,341,264 for Frémont, with 874,534 for Fillmore.

Why did the aroused Republicans go down to defeat? Frémont lost much ground because of grave doubts as to his capacity and sound judgment. Much more damaging were the violent threats of the Southern

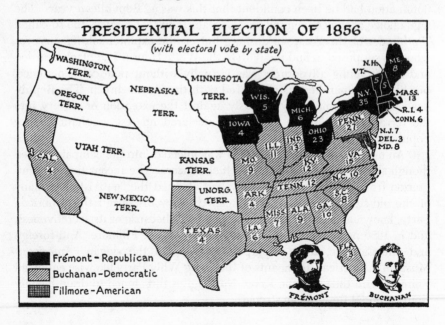

PRESIDENTIAL ELECTION OF 1856
(with electoral vote by state)

Frémont – Republican
Buchanan – Democratic
Fillmore – American

"fire-eaters" that the election of a sectional "Black Republican" would be a declaration of war on them, forcing them to secede. Many Northerners, anxious to save both the Union and their profitable business connections with the South, were thus intimidated into voting for Buchanan. Innate conservatism triumphed, aided by so-called Southern "bullyism."

It was probably fortunate for the Union that secession and civil war did not come in 1856, following a Republican victory at the polls. Frémont, an ill-balanced and second-rate figure, was no Abraham Lincoln. And in 1856 the North was more willing to let the South depart in peace than in 1860. The dramatic events of the years from 1856 to 1860 were to arouse hundreds of thousands of still-apathetic Northerners to a fighting pitch.

Yet the Republicans in 1856 could rightfully claim a "victorious defeat." The new party—a mere two-year-old infant—had made an astonishing showing against the well-oiled Democratic machine. Whittier exulted:

> Then sound again the bugles,
> Call the muster-roll anew;
> If months have well-nigh won the field,
> What may not four years do?

The election of 1856 cast a long shadow forward, and politicians, North and South, peered anxiously toward 1860.

The Dred Scott Bombshell

The Dred Scott decision, handed down by the Supreme Court on March 6, 1857, abruptly ended the two-day presidential honeymoon of the unlucky bachelor, James Buchanan. This pronouncement was one of the opening paper-gun blasts of the Civil War.

The case, basically, was simple. Dred Scott, a shiftless and illiterate Negro slave, had lived with his master for five years in Illinois and Wisconsin Territory. Sponsored by interested abolitionists, he sued for freedom on the basis of his long residence on free soil.

The Supreme Court proceeded to turn a simple legal case into a complex political issue. It ruled, quite properly, that Dred Scott was a Negro slave and not a citizen, and hence could not sue in federal courts. The tribunal could then have thrown out the case on these technical grounds alone. But a majority of the justices decided to go further, under the leadership of emaciated Chief Justice Taney from the slave state of Maryland. A sweeping judgment on the larger issue of slavery in the territories seemed desirable, particularly as a means of forestalling arguments by two free-soil members who were preparing dissenting opinions. The pro-Southern majority evidently hoped in this way to lay the vexed question completely to rest. Never were men more mistaken.

The broad decision on slavery, as handed down in the Dred Scott case, rocked the free-soilers back on their heels. A majority of the justices decreed that since a slave was private property, he could be taken into the territories and held there—regardless of what Congress or the territorial legislatures might say. The Supreme Court, to be consistent, went even further. It ruled that the now-repealed but still-venerated Missouri Compromise, which had forbidden slavery north of 36° 30', had always been unconstitutional.

A cry of delight broke from Southern throats over this unexpected victory. Slavery could not henceforth be barred in any of the territories, as long as they were territories, whatever the verdict of the people there.

Apostles of popular sovereignty, including Senator Douglas and other Northern Democrats, were appalled. Another lethal wedge was thus driven between the Northern and Southern wings of the once-united Democratic Party.

Foes of slavery extension, especially the Republicans, were infuriated by the Dred Scott setback. Their chief rallying cry had been the banishing of bondage from the territories. They now insisted that the ruling of the Court was merely an opinion, not a decision, and just as binding as the views of a Southern debating society. Republican defiance of the exalted tribunal was intensified by an awareness that a majority of its members were Southerners, and by the conviction that it had debased itself—"sullied the ermine"—by wallowing in the gutter of politics.

The Southerners in turn were inflamed by all this defiance. They began to wonder how much longer they could remain married to a section that refused to honor the Supreme Court, to say nothing of the constitutional compact which had established it.

The Panic of 1857

The bitterness caused by the Dred Scott decision was deepened by hard times, which followed a period of feverish prosperity. Late in 1857 a panic burst with disheartening force about Buchanan's harassed head. The storm was not so bad economically as the Panic of 1837, but psychologically it was probably the worst of the 19th Century.

What caused the crash? Inpouring California gold played its part by helping to inflate the currency. The demands of the Crimean War had overstimulated the growing of grain, while frenzied speculation in land and railroads had further weakened the economic fabric. When the collapse came, over 5000 businesses failed within a year. Unemployment, accompanied by hunger meetings in urban areas, was widespread.

The North, including the grain growers, was hardest hit. The South, enjoying favorable cotton prices abroad, rode out the storm with flying colors. The panic seemed to provide further proof to the South that cotton *was* king, and that his economic kingdom was stronger than that of the

North. This fatal delusion helped drive the overconfident Southerners closer to a shooting showdown.

Financial distress in the North, especially in agriculture, gave a new vigor to the demand for free farms of 160 acres from the public domain. For several decades interested groups had been urging the federal government to abandon its ancient policy of selling the land for revenue. Instead, the argument ran, acreage should be given outright to the sturdy pioneers, as a reward for their risking health and life in its development.

The proposal to make outright gifts of homesteads encountered two-fisted opposition. Eastern industrialists had long been unfriendly to free land; some of them feared that their underpaid workmen would be drained off to the West. The South was even more bitterly opposed, partly because slavery could not flourish on a mere 160 acres. Free farms would merely fill up the territories more rapidly with free-soilers, thus further tipping the political balance against the South. In 1860, after years of debate, Congress finally passed a homestead act—one that made public lands available at the nominal sum of twenty-five cents an acre. But the gift-wrapped measure was vigorously vetoed by Buchanan, near whose elbow sat leading Southern sympathizers.

The Panic of 1857 also stimulated a clamor for higher tariff rates. Several months before the crash, Congress, faced with a large Treasury surplus, had enacted the Tariff of 1857. The new law, responding to pressures from the South, reduced duties to about 20% on dutiable goods—the lowest point since the War of 1812. Hardly had the revised rates been

House Vote on Tariff of 1857

	For	Against	
New England	18	9	(manufacturing and commercial
Middle States	24	28	interests divided)
West and Northwest	14	33	(oppose reductions on wool tariff, etc.)
South and Southwest	60	2	(favor low rates)
California	2	0	
	118	72	

placed on the books when financial distress descended like a black pall. Northern manufacturers, many of whom were Republicans, noisily blamed all their misfortunes on the low tariff. As the surplus melted away in the Treasury, industrialists in the North pointed to the need for higher duties. Actually, what concerned them more was their own desire for increased protection. Thus the Panic of 1857 gave the Republicans two sure-fire issues for the election of 1860: protection for the unprotected and farms for the farmless.

A Rail Splitter Emerges

The Illinois senatorial election of 1858 now claimed the national spotlight. The term of Senator Douglas was about to expire, and the Republicans decided to run against him a rustic Springfield lawyer by the name of Abraham Lincoln. The candidate—six feet four inches in height—presented an awkward but arresting figure. His legs, arms, and neck were grotesquely long; his head was crowned by coarse and unruly hair; and his face was sad, sunken, and weather-beaten.

Lincoln was no silver-spoon child of destiny. Born in a Kentucky log cabin to impoverished Thomas Lincoln and Nancy Hanks, he began life inauspiciously. The poet has a passing horseman say:

> Well, did you hear? Tom Lincoln's wife today.
> The devil's luck for folk as poor as they!
> Poor Tom! poor Nance!
> Poor youngun born without a chance!*

Reared on the frontier, young Abe attended school for not more than a year, and being an avid reader, was mainly self-educated. All his life he said "git," "thar," "heered." Though narrow-chested and somewhat stoop-shouldered, he shone in his frontier community as a wrestler and lifter of weights, and spent some time, among other pioneering pursuits, as a splitter of logs for fence rails. A superb teller of amusing stories, he nevertheless would plunge into protracted periods of melancholy.

Lincoln's private and professional life was not particularly noteworthy. He married above himself socially, into the influential Todd family of Kentucky, and the temperamental outbursts of his high-strung wife helped to school him in patience and forbearance. After reading a little law, he gradually emerged as one of the dozen or so better-known trial lawyers in Illinois, although still accustomed to carrying important papers around in his stovepipe hat. He was widely referred to as "Honest Abe," partly because he would refuse cases that he could not conscientiously defend.

The rise of Lincoln as a political figure was less than rocket-like. After making his mark in the Illinois legislature as a Whig politician of the logrolling variety, he served one undistinguished term in Congress, 1847–1849. Until 1854, when he was forty-five years of age, he had done nothing to establish a claim to statesmanship. But the passage of the Kansas-Nebraska Act in that year lighted within him unexpected fires. After belatedly mounting the Republican band wagon, he emerged as one of the foremost politicians and orators of the Northwest. At the Philadelphia convention of 1856, where Frémont was nominated, Lincoln actually received 110 votes for the vice-presidential nomination.

* Edmund Vance Cooke, "Born without a Chance."

"Old Abe" vs. "Little Doug"

Lincoln, as the Republican nominee for Senator, boldly challenged Douglas to a series of joint debates. This was a rash act, because the "Little Giant" was probably the nation's most devastating debater. The Senator promptly accepted the challenge, and seven meetings were arranged.

At first glance, the two contestants seemed ill-matched. The well-groomed and polished Douglas, with stumpy figure and bullish voice, presented a striking contrast to the lanky Lincoln, with his baggy clothes and unshined shoes. Moreover, "Old Abe," as he was called in both affection and derision, had a piercing, high-pitched voice, and was often ill at ease when he began to speak. But as he threw himself into an argument, he seemed to grow in height, while his glowing eyes lighted up a rugged face. He relied on logic rather than on table-thumping.

The most famous of the forensic clashes came at Freeport, Illinois, where Lincoln neatly impaled his opponent on the horns of a dilemma. Suppose, he queried, the people of a territory should vote slavery down? The Supreme Court in the Dred Scott decision had decreed that they could not. Who would prevail, the Court or the people?

Legend to the contrary, Douglas and some Southerners had already publicly answered the Freeport question. The bull-necked "Little Giant" therefore had little hesitation in meeting the issue head on, honestly and consistently. He replied that no matter how the Supreme Court ruled, slavery would stay down if the people voted it down. Laws to protect the slaves would have to be passed by the territorial legislatures. These would not be forthcoming in the absence of popular approval, and bondage would soon disappear. Douglas, in truth, had American history on his side. Where public opinion does not support the federal government, as had been notably true of Jefferson's embargo, the laws and court decisions are difficult, if not impossible, to enforce.

The upshot was that Douglas defeated Lincoln for the Senate seat, whether as a result of or in spite of the debates. The "Little Giant's" loyalty to popular sovereignty, which still had a powerful appeal in Illinois, probably influenced the outcome. United States Senators were then chosen by state legislatures; and in the general election that followed the debates, more pro-Douglas members were elected than pro-Lincoln members. Yet thanks to an inequitable apportionment, the districts carried by Douglas men represented a smaller population than those carried by the Lincoln men. In these circumstances, "Honest Abe" won a clear moral victory.

Lincoln possibly was playing for larger stakes than just the Senatorship. Although defeated, he had shambled into the national limelight in company with the most conspicuous Northern politician. Newspapers in the East published detailed accounts of the debate, and Lincoln began to emerge as a potential nominee of the Republicans for President. But

Douglas, in winning Illinois, hurt his chances of winning the Presidency, while further splitting his party. After his opposition to the Lecompton Constitution and his further defiance of the Supreme Court at Freeport, Southern Democrats were determined to break up the party and the Union rather than accept him. The Lincoln-Douglas debate platform thus proved to be one of the preliminary battlefields of the Civil War.

John Brown: Murderer or Martyr?

The gaunt, grim figure of John Brown of Osawatomie now appeared again in a more terrible way. His crackbrained scheme was to invade the South secretly with his followers, call upon the slaves to rise, furnish them with arms, and establish a kind of Negro free state as a sanctuary. Brown secured several thousand dollars for firearms from extreme Northern abolitionists, and finally arrived in western Virginia with some twenty men. At Harpers Ferry, a beautifully panoramic spot, he seized the federal arsenal in October, 1859, incidentally killing seven innocent people. But the slaves failed to rise, and the wounded Brown and the remnants of his tiny band, some also wounded, were quickly captured.

"Old Brown" was convicted of murder and treason, after a hasty but legal trial. Affidavits were presented from seventeen friends and relatives as to his presumed insanity. Actually, thirteen of his near relatives

A PREMATURE MOVEMENT
"Here! Take this and follow me!"
"Please God, Mr. Brown, dat is onpossible. We ain't done
seedin' yit at our house." *Harper's Weekly*, 1859

were regarded as insane, including his mother and grandmother. Governor Wise of Virginia would have been most wise, so his critics say, if he had only clapped the culprit into a lunatic asylum.

But Brown was given every opportunity to pose, and to achieve and enjoy martyrdom. He was probably of unsound mind, but he was clever enough to see that he was worth much more to the abolitionist cause dangling from a rope than in any other way. His demeanor throughout the trial was dignified and courageous, his last words were to become a classic, and he marched up the scaffold steps without flinching. His conduct was so exemplary, his devotion to the cause of freedom so inflexible, that he seemed to take on an exalted character, however deplorable his previous record may have been. So the hangman's trap was sprung, and Brown plunged not into oblivion but into world fame. A memorable marching song of the impending Civil War ran:

> John Brown's body lies a-mould'ring in the grave,
> His soul is marching on.

The effects of the raid at Harpers Ferry were calamitous. In the eyes of the South, already embittered, "Osawatomie Brown" was a wholesale murderer and an apostle of treason. Many Southerners asked how they could possibly remain in the Union while a "murderous gang of abolitionists" were financing armed bands to wipe them out. Moderate Northerners, including the Republican leaders, openly deplored Brown's mad-brained exploit. But the South generally concluded that the violent abolitionist view was shared by the entire North.

The abolitionists and other ardent free-soilers were inexpressibly shocked by Brown's hanging. Many of them were ignorant of his bloody past and his even more bloody purposes, and they were outraged because the Virginians had hanged so earnest a reformer who was working for so righteous a cause. On the day of his execution, free-soil centers in the North tolled bells, fired guns, half-masted flags, and held mass meetings. Some spoke of "Saint John" Brown, while the serene Ralph Waldo Emerson compared the new martyr-hero with Jesus. E. C. Stedman wrote:

> And Old Brown,
> Osawatomie Brown,
> May trouble you more than ever, when you've nailed his coffin down!

Grass grows more quickly over battlefields than over scaffolds.

The Disruption of the Democrats

The presidential election of 1860 was the most fateful in American history. On it hung the issue of peace or war.

The divided Democrats met in Charleston, with Douglas the leading candidate of the Northern wing of the party. But the Southern "fire-eaters" regarded him as a traitor, as a result of his stand on the Lecompton Constitution and the Freeport Doctrine. After a bitter wrangle over the platform, the delegates from most of the cotton states walked out. When the remainder could not scrape together the necessary two-thirds vote for Douglas, the entire body dissolved in confusion. The first tragic secession was the secession of Southerners from the Democratic national convention. The practice became habit-forming.

The Democrats met again in Baltimore. This time the Douglas Democrats, chiefly from the North, were firmly in the saddle. Many of the cotton-state delegates again seceded, and the rest of the convention enthusiastically nominated their hero, the "Little Giant." The platform came out squarely for popular sovereignty and, as a sop to the South, against obstruction of the Fugitive Slave Law by the states.

The seceding Southern Democrats promptly organized a rival convention in Baltimore, in which many of the Northern states were unrepresented. They selected as their leader the stern-jawed Vice-President, John C. Breckinridge, a man of moderate views from the border state of Kentucky. The platform favored the extension of slavery into the territories and the annexation of Cuba.

A middle-of-the-road group, fearing for the Union, hastily organized the Constitutional Union Party. It consisted mainly of many former Whigs and Know-Nothings. Desperately anxious to elect a compromise candidate, they met in Baltimore and nominated for the Presidency John Bell of Tennessee. They girded for battle, ringing hand bells for Bell, and voicing the slogan, "The Union, the Constitution, and the Enforcement of the Laws."

A Rail Splitter Splits the Union

The Republicans were presented with a heaven-sent opportunity. Scenting victory in the breeze as their opponents split hopelessly, they gathered in Chicago in a huge, box-like wooden structure called the Wigwam. "Higher Law" Seward was by far the best-known of the contenders. But his radical utterances, including his "irrepressible conflict" speech of 1858, had fatally injured his prospects. His numerous enemies coined the slogan "Success Rather than Seward." Abraham Lincoln, the favorite son of Illinois, was definitely a second choice, but he was a stronger candidate because he had made fewer enemies. Overtaking Seward on the third ballot, Lincoln was nominated amid scenes of the wildest excitement.

The Republican platform had a seductive appeal for just about every important non-Southern group. For the free-soilers, non-extension of slavery; for the Northern manufacturers, a protective tariff; for the immigrants, no abridgment of rights; for the Northwest, a Pacific railroad; for the West, internal improvements at federal expense; and for the landless, free homesteads from the public domain. Persuasive slogans were "Vote Yourselves a Farm" and "Land for the Landless."

The Southern secessionists promptly served notice that the election of the "baboon" Lincoln—the "abolitionist" rail splitter—would split the Union. "Honest Abe," though hating slavery, was not an abolitionist. But he saw fit, perhaps mistakenly, to issue no statements to quiet Southern fears. He had already put himself on record; and fresh statements might create fresh antagonisms.

As the election campaign ground noisily forward, Lincoln enthusiasts staged roaring rallies and parades, complete with pitch-dripping torches

A REPUBLICAN CAMPAIGN CARICATURE
Douglas is represented as a pious character prepared
to bury Lincoln politically. *Vanity Fair*, 1860

and oilskin capes. They extolled "High Old Abe," the "Woodchopper of the West" and the "Little Giant Killer," while groaning dismally for "Poor Little Doug." Enthusiastic "Little Giants" and "Little Dougs" retorted with "We want a statesman, not a rail splitter, as President." Douglas himself waged a vigorous speaking campaign, and threatened to put the hemp with his own hands around the neck of the first secessionist.

The returns, breathlessly awaited, proclaimed a sweeping victory for Lincoln. The figures were:

	Popular Vote	Percentage of Popular Vote	Electoral Vote
Lincoln	1,866,452	40%	180 (every vote of the free states except for 3 of New Jersey's 7 votes)
Douglas	1,375,157	29%	12 (only Missouri and 3 of New Jersey's 7 votes)
Breckinridge	847,953	18%	72 (all the cotton states)
Bell	590,631	13%	39 (Virginia, Kentucky, Tennessee)

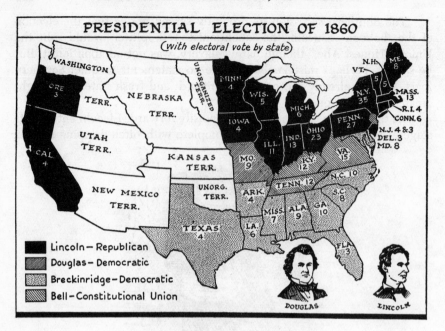

PRESIDENTIAL ELECTION OF 1860
(with electoral vote by state)

Lincoln — Republican
Douglas — Democratic
Breckinridge — Democratic
Bell — Constitutional Union

DOUGLAS   LINCOLN

The Electoral Revolution of 1860

Awkward "Abe" Lincoln had run a curious race. To a greater degree than any other President (except J. Q. Adams) he was a minority President. Sixty percent of the voters preferred some other candidate. He was also a sectional President, for in ten Southern states he polled not a single popular vote. The election of 1860 was virtually two elections: one in the North and the other in the South.

Douglas, though scraping together only twelve electoral votes, made an impressive showing. He drew important strength from all sections, and ranked a fairly close second in the popular-vote column. In fact, the Douglas Democrats and the Breckinridge Democrats together amassed 356,658 more votes than Lincoln.

The belief has gained acceptance that if the Democrats had only united behind Douglas, they would have triumphed. Yet the cold figures tell a different story. Even if the "Little Giant" had received all the votes cast for all three of Lincoln's opponents, the "Rail Splitter" would have won, 173 to 130, instead of 180 to 123. Lincoln still would have carried the populous states of the North and the Northwest. On the other hand, if the Democrats had not broken up, they could have entered the campaign with higher enthusiasm and better organization, and might have won.

The verdict of the ballot box did not, surprisingly enough, indicate a strong sentiment for secession. Breckinridge, while favoring the extension of slavery, was no disunionist. Although he was the candidate of the "fire-eaters," in the slave states he polled fewer votes than the combined

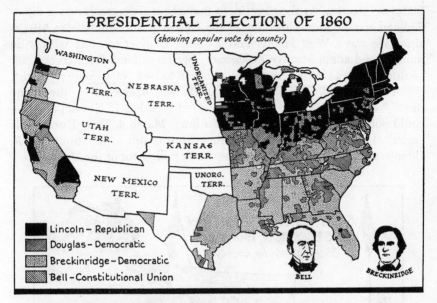

Note the strong Bell vote in the "mountain white" areas of the South and the Douglas vote in the Southerner-tinged states of the Old Northwest.

strength of his opponents, Douglas and Bell. He even failed to carry his own Kentucky.

Yet the South, despite its electoral defeat, was not badly off. It still had a five-to-four majority on the Supreme Bench. Although the Republicans had elected Lincoln, they controlled neither the Senate nor the House of Representatives. The federal government could not touch slavery in those states where it existed except by a constitutional amendment, and such an amendment could be defeated by one-fourth of the states. The fifteen slave states numbered nearly one-half of the total—a fact not fully appreciated by the Southern hotheads.

The Secessionist Exodus

The tragic chain reaction of secession now began to explode. South Carolina, which had threatened to go out if the "sectional" Lincoln came in, was as good as her word. Four days after the election of the "Rail Splitter" by "insulting" majorities, her legislature voted unanimously to summon a special convention. Meeting at Charleston in December, 1860, it unanimously voted to secede. During the next six weeks, six other states of the lower South, though somewhat less united, followed South Carolina over the precipice. Four more were to join them later, bringing the total to eleven. (See map, p. 418.)

With the eyes of destiny upon them, the seven seceders formally set up at Montgomery, Alabama, a government known as the Confederate

States of America. As their President they chose Jefferson Davis, a dignified and austere former member of the United States Senate from Mississippi. He was a West Pointer and a former Cabinet member with wide military and administrative experience; but he suffered from chronic ill-health, as well as from a frustrated ambition to be a Napoleonic strategist.

The crisis, already alarming enough, was deepened by the "lame duck" * interlude. Lincoln, although elected President in November, 1860, could not take office until four months later, March 4, 1861. During this period of protracted uncertainty, when he was still a private citizen in Illinois, seven of the eleven deserting states pulled out of the Union.

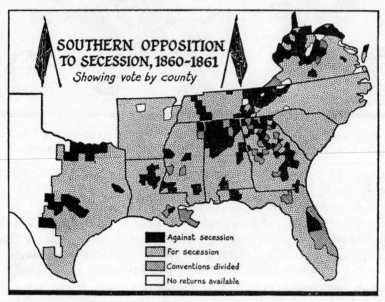

Note the concentration of opposition in the "mountain white" areas of northern Alabama and Georgia, eastern Tennessee, and northwestern Virginia (later West Virginia).

President Buchanan, the aging and sunken-cheeked incumbent, has been bitterly blamed for not holding the seceders in the Union by sheer force. Never a vigorous man and habitually conservative, he was now nearly seventy, and although devoted to the Union, he was surrounded by pro-Southern advisers. As an able lawyer wedded to the Constitution, he did not believe that the Southern states could legally secede. Yet he could find no authority in the Constitution for stopping them with guns.

"Oh for one hour of Jackson!" cried the advocates of strong-arm tactics. But "Old Buck" Buchanan was not "Old Hickory," and one important reason why he did not use force was that the tiny standing army, widely

* The "lame duck" period was shortened to ten weeks in 1933, by the 20th Amendment. See Appendix.

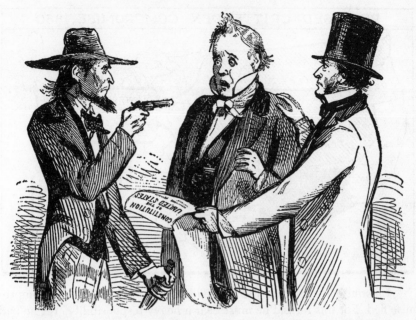

WRETCHED CONDITION OF THE OLD PARTY AT THE WHITE HOUSE

Buchanan is hard pressed between Southern threats of violence and Northern reminders of his obligation to uphold the Constitution. *Harper's Weekly*, 1861

scattered, was urgently needed to control the Indians. Public opinion in the North, at that time, was far from willing to unsheathe the sword. Fighting would merely shatter all prospects of adjustment, and until the guns began to boom there was still a flickering hope of reconciliation.

The Collapse of Compromise

The impending roar of cannon spurred final and frantic attempts at compromise—in the American tradition. The most promising of these efforts was sponsored by Senator Crittenden of Kentucky, on whose shoulders had fallen the mantle of a fellow Kentuckian, Henry Clay.

The proposed Crittenden amendments to the Constitution were designed to appease the South. Slavery in the territories was to be prohibited north of 36° 30′, but south of that line it was to be given federal protection in all territories existing or "hereafter to be acquired" (Cuba?). Future states, north or south of 36° 30′, could come into the Union with or without slavery, as they should choose. In short, the slavery men were to be guaranteed full rights in the southern territories, as long as they were territories, regardless of the wishes of the majority as previously respected under popular sovereignty. Federal protection in a territory south of 36° 30′ might even give Negro bondage a strong enough foothold to turn the entire area permanently to slavery.

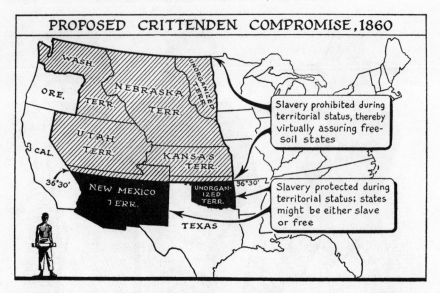

PROPOSED CRITTENDEN COMPROMISE, 1860

Slavery prohibited during territorial status, thereby virtually assuring free-soil states

Slavery protected during territorial status; states might be either slave or free

Lincoln flatly rejected the Crittenden plan, and all hope of compromise fled. For this refusal he must bear a heavy responsibility. Yet he had been elected on a platform that opposed the extension of slavery, and he felt that as a matter of principle he could not afford to yield, even though gains in the territories might be only temporary. Larger gains might come later through the acquisition of areas like Cuba and Mexico.

As for the indecisive Buchanan, how could he have prevented the Civil War by starting a civil war? No one has ever come up with a completely satisfactory answer. If he had used force on South Carolina in December, 1860, the fighting almost certainly would have erupted three months sooner than it did, and under less favorable circumstances for the federal government. The North would have appeared as the heavy-handed aggressor. And the crucial Border States, so vital to the Union, probably would have been driven into the arms of the "wayward sisters."

Farewell to Union

The seceders who parted company with their sister states left for a number of reasons. They were distressed by the inexorable tipping of the political balance against them. The crime of the North, observed James Russell Lowell, was the census returns. The Southerners were also dismayed by the triumph of the new sectional Republican Party, which seemed to threaten their rights as a minority. They were weary of free-soil criticism, abolitionist nagging, and Yankee interference, ranging from the Underground Railroad to John Brown's raid. "All we ask is to be let alone," declared President Jefferson Davis in an early message to Congress.

Many Southerners supported secession because they felt sure that their departure would be unopposed, despite "Yankee yawp" to the contrary. They were confident that the shopkeeping and codfish-catching Yankee would not or could not fight. They believed that Northern manufacturers and bankers, so heavily dependent on Southern cotton and markets, would not dare to cut their own economic throats by resorting to arms. But should war come, the immense debt owed to Northern creditors by the South—happy thought—could be promptly repudiated.

The leaders of the South regarded secession as a golden opportunity to cast aside their generations of "vassalage" to the North. An independent Dixieland could develop its own banking and shipping, and trade directly with Europe. The low tariff of 1857, which had been passed largely by Southern votes (see table on p. 403), was not in itself alarming. But who could tell when the "greedy" Republicans would win control of Congress and drive through a highly objectionable protective tariff of their own? For decades there had been this fundamental friction between the North, with its manufacturing, and the South, with its agricultural economy.

The world-wide impulse of nationalism—then stirring in Italy, Germany, Poland, and elsewhere—was active in the South. This huge area, with its distinctive civilization, was not so much a section as a sub-nation. It could not view with complacency the possibility of being lorded over, then or later, by what it regarded as a hostile nation of Northerners.

The principles of self-determination—of the Declaration of Independence—seemed to many Southerners to apply perfectly to them. Few, if any, of the seceders felt that they were doing anything wrong or immoral. The thirteen original states had voluntarily entered the Union and now seven —ultimately eleven—Southern states were voluntarily withdrawing from it.

The historical parallels ran even deeper. In 1776, thirteen American colonies, led by the rebel George Washington, had seceded from the Empire by throwing off the yoke of King George. In 1860–1861, eleven American states, led by the rebel Jefferson Davis, were seceding from the Union by throwing off the yoke of "King" Abraham Lincoln. With that yoke thrown off, the South was confident that it could work out its own peculiar destiny more happily and prosperously.

SELECT READINGS

Refer to the previous chapter for the titles by Nichols, Randall and Donald, and Craven. Richly detailed is ALLAN NEVINS, *The Emergence of Lincoln* (2 vols., 1950). DAVID DONALD, *Charles Sumner and the Coming of the Civil War* (1960) is a Pulitzer-prize biography. ALLAN NEVINS, *Frémont* (1939) is exciting fare. Lincoln's rise is developed in D. E. FEHRENBACHER, *Prelude to Greatness* (1962) [paperback] and in CARL SANDBURG, *Abraham Lincoln: The Prairie Years* (2 vols., 1926) [paperback]. On the Lincoln-Douglas debates see H. V. JAFFA, *Crisis of the House Divided* (1959). P. S. KLEIN, *President James Buchanan* (1962) does its subject full justice. See also D. M. POTTER, *Lincoln and His Party in the Secession Crisis* (1962) [paperback] and K. M. STAMPP, *And the War Came* (1950) [paperback]. Special studies are R. A. WOOSTER, *The Secession Conventions of the South* (1962) and A. D. KIRWAN, *John J. Crittenden* (1962). Also *Harvard Guide*, Pt. IV.

22

The War for Southern Independence

*My paramount object in this struggle is to save the
Union, and is not either to save or to destroy slavery.*

ABRAHAM LINCOLN, 1862

A Rail Splitter at the Helm

ABRAHAM LINCOLN solemnly took the oath of office on March 4, 1861, as
President not of the United States of America but of the disunited states
of America. Seven had departed; eight more were teetering on the edge.
The girders of the unfinished capitol dome loomed nakedly in the background, as if to symbolize the imperfect state of the Union.

Lincoln's inaugural address was firm yet conciliatory: there would
be no conflict unless the South provoked it. Secession, the President declared, was wholly impracticable, because "Physically speaking, we cannot separate."

Lincoln here put his finger on a profound geographical truth. The
North and South were Siamese twins, bound inseparably together. If they
had been divided by the Pyrenees Mountains or the Danube River, a sectional divorce would have been more feasible. But the Appalachian Mountains and the mighty Mississippi River both ran the wrong way.

Uncontested secession, moreover, would only create new controversies. What share of the national debt should the South, if successful in
seceding, be forced to take with it? What portion of the federal territories,
if any, should the Confederate states be allotted—areas so largely purchased with Southern blood? How would the fugitive slave issue be dealt
with? The Underground Railroad would certainly redouble its activity,
and it would have to transport its passengers only across the Ohio River,
not all the way to Canada. Was it conceivable that all such problems
could have been solved without recurrent armed clashes?

A united United States had hitherto been the top-dog republic in the
Western Hemisphere. If our powerful democracy were allowed to break
into two hostile parts, the European nations would be delighted. They
could gleefully transplant to America their hoary concept of the balance of

416

power. Playing the no less hoary game of divide and conquer, they could incite one snarling fragment of the United States against the other. The possessions of the European powers in the Americas, notably those of Britain, would thus be made safer against the rapacious Yankees. And the European imperialists, with no unified United States to stand across their path, could the more easily defy the Monroe Doctrine and seize territory in the Americas.

Bungling Beginnings

A horde of hungry office seekers, elbowing for the patronage pie counter, overwhelmed Lincoln at the very outset. At a time when he should have had his mind clear for pressing affairs of state, he was forced to worry about the "postmastership at Podunk."

The Cabinet was dominated by Lincoln's former rivals for the presidential nomination. Headstrong and egotistical William H. Seward, the front-running contender at Chicago in 1860, was of necessity made Secretary of State. He regarded himself as a kind of prime minister, but after some difficulty Lincoln succeeded in putting him in his place. Happily, Seward turned out to be one of our most brilliant secretaries of state.

Other Cabinet members were likewise problem children. The Secretary of the Treasury was a leading abolitionist, Salmon P. Chase of Ohio. A massive, handsome man, he was self-righteous, opinionated, and constantly goaded by the presidential bee buzzing in his bonnet. The original Secretary of War, Simon Cameron, became involved in graft, and was succeeded by the bulldog-like Edwin M. Stanton, stocky and black-haired. Though tireless and decisive, the new appointee was arrogant, irascible, vindictive, and double-dealing. A Democrat and a more distinguished lawyer than Lincoln, he had previously criticized the "imbecility" of his future chief, whom he dubbed the "original gorilla."

The Cabinet was never completely harmonious or loyal to the President. A minor civil war within his official family was but one of the many crosses that Lincoln had to bear while prosecuting the larger Civil War.

The Firing on Fort Sumter

The plight of the federal forts had meanwhile partially overshadowed political squabbles. As the seceding states left the Union, they had seized the United States arsenals, mints, and other public property within their borders. When Lincoln took office, only two forts in the South still flew the Stars and Stripes. The more important of the pair was square-walled Fort Sumter, in Charleston Harbor.

The choices presented to Lincoln by Fort Sumter were all bad. This stronghold had provisions that would last only a few weeks—until the middle of April, 1861. If no supplies were forthcoming, its commander

would have to surrender without firing a shot. Lincoln, quite understandably, did not feel that such a weak-kneed course squared with his obligation to protect federal property. But if he sent reinforcements, the South
Carolinians would undoubtedly fight back, because they could not tolerate
a powerful federal fort blocking the mouth of their most important
seaport.

After agonizing indecision, Lincoln adopted a middle-of-the-road
solution. He notified the South Carolinians that an expedition would be
sent to *provision* the garrison, though not to *reinforce* it. But in Southern
eyes "provision" spelled "reinforcement."

A Union naval force was next started on its way to Fort Sumter—a
move that was regarded by the South as an act of aggression. On April 12,
1861, the cannon of the defiant Carolinians opened fire on the fort, while
admiring crowds in Charleston applauded and waved handkerchiefs.
After a bombardment of thirty-four hours, which took no life, the stunned
garrison surrendered.

The firing on the fort wrought an electrifying change in the North.
Hitherto countless thousands of Northerners had been saying that if the
Southern states wanted to go, they should not be pinned to the rest of
the nation with bayonets. "Wayward sisters, depart in peace" was a common sentiment, expressed most emphatically by the aged commander of
the United States Army, war hero General Winfield Scott.

But the assault on Fort Sumter provoked the North to a fighting pitch.
The Southerners had wantonly fired upon the glorious Stars and Stripes,
and honor demanded that the United States fight back. Lincoln promptly

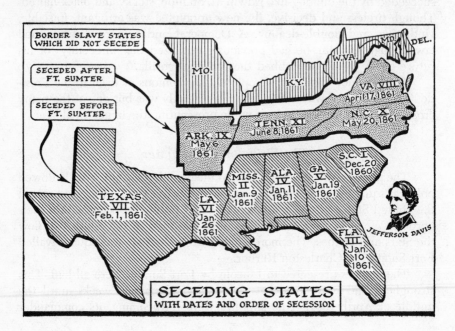

SECEDING STATES
WITH DATES AND ORDER OF SECESSION

issued a call to the states for 75,000 militiamen, and volunteers sprang to the colors in such enthusiastic numbers that many were turned away.

The call for troops, in turn, aroused the South much as the attack on Fort Sumter had aroused the North. Lincoln was now waging war—from the Southern view an aggressive war—on the Confederacy. Virginia, Arkansas, and Tennessee, all of which had earlier voted down secession, reluctantly joined their embattled sister states, as did North Carolina. Richmond, Virginia, became the new Confederate capital.

Brothers' Blood and Border Blood

The only slave states left were the crucial Border States. This group consisted of Missouri, Kentucky, Maryland, Delaware, and later West Virginia—the "mountain white" area which somewhat illegally tore itself from the side of Virginia in mid-1861. If the North had fired the first shot, some or all of these doubtful states probably would have seceded, and the South might well have won its independence. The Border group actually contained a white population that was more than half that of the entire Confederacy.

Any official statement of the North's war aims was profoundly affected by the wavering Border States. At the very outset, Lincoln was obliged to declare publicly that the North was not fighting to free the Negroes. An anti-slavery declaration would no doubt have driven the Border States into the waiting arms of the South. Lincoln deemed it necessary to insist repeatedly—even though he thereby weakened his moral cause—that his primary purpose was to preserve the Union at all costs. Thus the war was not one between slave soil and free soil, but a war for the Union with slaveholders on both sides.

The conflict between "Yanks" and "Rebs" was, unhappily, a brothers' war. There were many Northern volunteers from the Southern states, and many Southern volunteers from the Northern states. The "mountain whites" of the South sent North some 50,000 men, and the loyal slave states contributed some 300,000 soldiers to the Union army. In many a family of the Border States, one brother rode north to fight with the Blue, another south to fight with the Gray. Senator Crittenden of Kentucky, who fathered the abortive Crittenden Compromise, also fathered two sons, one of whom became a general in the Union army, the other a general in the Confederate army.

Aristocracy Sticks Together

The Confederates were buoyed up by the knowledge that they had the open sympathy of Europe's ruling classes, with the conspicuous exception of Russia. The South could reasonably hope for mediation or

armed intervention, which almost came. At the very least, it could expect
the sale of weapons, warships, and supplies, all of which did come.

Why were the upper classes of Western Europe so favorably disposed
to the Confederacy? For one thing, they had from the beginning deplored
the incendiary example of the American democratic experiment, and were
overjoyed to see the long-smoking chimney at last "take fire." Moreover,

WHAT THE TYRANTS OF THE OLD WORLD THINK OF SECESSION
"Oh, ain't we sorry!" *Harper's Weekly,* 1860

the semi-feudal aristocratic elements, especially in England, had long
cherished a fellow feeling for the semi-feudal, aristocratic society of the
South. The Foreign Offices of both Britain and France, reflecting these
pro-Southern sentiments, naturally welcomed the breakup of the fast-
growing and aggressive United States.

The leaders of British industrial and commercial life likewise hailed
the newly born Confederacy. For one thing, it would provide the long-
desired independent cotton supply. For another, it would increase the
opportunities of British shippers and manufacturers to make profits from
the South, without the hurdle of a Yankee protective tariff.

On the other hand, the working masses of England, and to some extent those of France, were praying for the North. Many of them had read
Uncle Tom's Cabin, and they sensed that a victory for the Union would
result in the freeing of the slave. The ending of human bondage anywhere
would further dignify free labor everywhere.

The common people in Britain did not yet have the ballot, but they
did have the brick—a potent weapon in the hands of rioters. Their certain

hostility to any official intervention on behalf of the South had a sobering effect on the British Cabinet. Thus the dead hands of Uncle Tom helped Uncle Sam by restraining the British and French ironclads from breaking the Union blockade.

Southern Advantages

The North and South were both unprepared for war, as Americans are wont to be. Each gained valuable experience at the expense of the other, and this fact partly explains why they contended so long on relatively even terms.

The South had only to fight defensively, behind interior lines, and consequently needed fewer troops. The North had to invade the Confederacy, conquer it, and drag it back bodily into the Union—a prodigious task involving an area roughly as large as all Western Europe south of Scandinavia. The South did not have to win the war to achieve its independence; it had merely to repulse or discourage the invader. A draw, or anything short of unconditional surrender, would be a victory. The states of the Confederacy would then be left independent—and this was all that they demanded.

Until the Emancipation Proclamation, many observers conceded to the South the superior moral cause, despite the dark stain of slavery. It was fighting for self-determination, for self-government, for its peculiar social structure, for home and hearth. Favorite slogans were "Death before Dishonor" and "For Our Altars and Our Firesides."

The South not only had splendid officers but had them from the beginning. Conspicuous among the dozen or so first-rate leaders was General Robert E. Lee, with his florid face, graying hair, and knightly bearing. In poise, magnanimity, and sense of honor he embodied all that was best in the Southern ideal. President Lincoln had unofficially offered him the command of the armies of the North, but when Virginia seceded Lee felt in honor bound to go along with his native state. His chief lieutenant was black-bearded and unpretentious young "Stonewall" Jackson, a somewhat eccentric student of theology, who with his "foot cavalry" was a master of speed and deception.

The North was much less fortunate. It was forced to use costly trial-and-error methods until it uncovered a general, in the person of U. S. Grant, who could crunch his way to victory. The Union was further handicapped by numerous political officers, including the pompously incompetent General Benjamin F. ("Beast Ben") Butler.

The Southerners were of a fighting breed. Accustomed to manage horses and bear arms from boyhood, they made excellent cavalrymen and foot soldiers. They were supremely self-confident, and their high-pitched "rebel yell" (Yeeeahhhh) was designed to strike terror into the hearts of fuzzy-chinned Yankee recruits. Yet the Northern "shopkeepers" and "clodhoppers" adjusted themselves surprisingly well to the rugged demands of military life. They may have been short on dash but they were long on determination.

Confederate Chances

The South, as primarily an immense farm, was seriously hampered by the fewness of its factories. Yet it seized the weapons stored in federal arsenals when it seceded, and managed to sneak through the Union blockade an impressive quantity of munitions. Displaying remarkable ingenuity, the Southerners developed iron works which, though limited, turned out much artillery. "Yankee ingenuity" was not confined to Yankees.

Manufacturing by Sections, 1860

Section	Number of Establishments	Capital Invested	Average Number of Laborers	Annual Value of Products	Percentage of Total Value
New England	20,671	$ 257,477,783	391,836	$ 468,599,287	24%
Middle States	53,387	435,061,964	546,243	802,338,392	42%
Western States	36,785	194,212,543	209,909	384,606,530	20%
Southern States	20,631	95,975,185	110,721	155,531,281	8%
Pacific States	8,777	23,380,334	50,204	71,229,989	3%
Territories	282	3,747,906	2,333	3,556,197	1%
	140,533	$1,009,855,715	1,311,246	$1,885,861,676	

As the war dragged on, serious shortages developed among the Southerners in such necessities as shoes, uniforms, and blankets. There were large stores of food in the South but the civilians and soldiers often went hungry. "Forward, men! They have cheese in their haversacks," was the reported cry of one Southern officer as he attacked the Yankees. Much of the hunger was caused by a breakdown of transportation, especially where the railroads were cut or destroyed by the Northern invader.

Formidable though all these handicaps were, the chances for Southern independence seemed unusually favorable. This was true even though the Confederates had to start from scratch in building a government, an army, and a navy. As one Southern general remarked, never was a major revolution undertaken with better prospects of success. Certainly the thirteen colonies in 1776 had faced more hazardous odds.

The might-have-beens are fascinating. If the Border States had seceded, if the states of the upper Mississippi Valley had turned against the Union, if a wave of Northern defeatism had demanded an armistice, and if England and/or France had broken the blockade, the South probably would have won. All of these possibilities came near happening, but none of them actually happened. Successful revolutions, including the American Revolution of 1776, have generally succeeded because of foreign intervention. The South counted on it, did not get it, and lost.

Yankee Advantages

The North was not only a huge farm but a sprawling factory as well —and wars were already being fought with both smokestacks and guns. The North boasted about three-fourths of the nation's wealth, including an overwhelming superiority in manufacturing, shipping, and banking. The Union also possessed nearly three-fourths of the 30,000 miles of railroads. Not only did it have longer and better trackage, but it had abundant facilities for repair and replacement, all of which the South sorely lacked.

The North also controlled the sea. With its vastly superior navy, it established a blockade that cut off the bulk of Southern exports and imports. This stoppage not only hampered the South economically and militarily, but finally shattered its morale. While strangling the Confederacy with one hand, the North could simultaneously keep open the sea lanes to Europe. It was thus able to exchange huge quantities of grain for munitions, and in this way it used the factories of Europe to supplement its own. During the early months of the war, the North imported many more firearms from abroad than it was able to manufacture at home.

The Union likewise enjoyed a much larger reservoir of manpower. The loyal states had a population of some 22,000,000; the seceding states, 9,000,000. This latter figure included about 3,500,000 Negroes, who were a military asset in that they could operate the farms while able-bodied whites went to the fighting front. The population advantage in favor of the North was somewhat greater than two to one, and the estimated enlistments ran 1,556,000 to 1,082,000. The manpower odds against General Lee were ordinarily about three to two, sometimes three to one. Such superior forces usually gave the North the advantage of choosing the point of attack.

A broad stream of European immigrants continued to pour into the North, thanks in part to Northern control of the seas. Though slowed down a bit by the war, especially during its first two years, the inflow totaled over 800,000 newcomers of both sexes from 1861 through 1865— or more than the total casualties in the armed services of the North. The bulk of the new arrivals were Britishers, Irish, and Germans; and large numbers of these groups were induced to enlist in the Union armies. Tens of thousands of earlier immigrants, inspired by a love of freedom and gratitude to their adopted land, likewise joined the colors. Altogether, about one-fifth of the Union forces were foreign-born. In one division, commands were given in four different languages; and some German units even had guttural-accented officers of their own nationality.

Immigration to U.S., 1860–1866

Year	Total	Britain	Ireland	Germany	All Others
1860	153,640	29,737	48,637	54,491	20,775
1861	91,918	19,675	23,797	31,661	16,785
1862	91,985	24,639	23,351	27,529	16,466
1863	176,282	66,882	55,916	33,162	20,322
1864	193,418	53,428	63,523	57,276	19,191
1865 *	248,120	82,465	29,772	83,424	52,459
1866	318,568	94,924	36,690	115,892	71,062

* Only the first three months of 1865 were war months.

About 186,000 Negro troops, mostly liberated slaves, served usefully in the Northern armies. But the proud South could not bring itself to employ slave-soldiers until 1865, when the Confederate cause was hopelessly lost. Strangely enough, the mass of the Southern slaves did not help their Northern liberators. A thousand torches in the hands of a thousand Negroes would have brought the Southern soldiers home from the front, and the war would have ended. The slaves, through the "grapevine," learned when "Massa Linkum" issued his Emancipation Proclamation. But the bulk of them—whether through personal loyalty, docility, lethargy, or lack of leadership—made no real effort to cast off the chains that bound them.

The Flag of the Union

The ideal of Union, deeply implanted, was a tremendous asset to the North. It was not a moral factor, except insofar as it involved loyalty. It was compounded largely of pride in our flag, in our accomplishments, in our future. The United States could hardly hope to shame its monarchical critics and achieve its Manifest Destiny if it split asunder. The teachings of Daniel Webster and Henry Clay had been driven home, as indicated by such popular Northern watchwords as "Union Forever" and "What God Hath Joined Let No Man Put Asunder." A rousing Northern song, widely sung since the 1850's, proclaimed:

> The union of lakes, the union of lands,
> The union of States none can sever,
> The union of hearts, the union of hands,
> And the flag of our union forever.*

The ideal of Union aroused the North with unexpected fury against the "flag of disunion," and helped hold in line the Border States. It infused

* George P. Morris, "The Flag of Our Union."

in the North the will to fight, and retained in the United States the South-erner-infiltrated states of the upper Mississippi Valley. Finally, it provided the Northerners with at least one inspiring war cry, until such time as the moral issue of slavery could be brought out into the open, as it was late in 1862.

Desceptering King Cotton

The textile factories of Britain were heavily dependent on Southern cotton, and the Confederates were unshakably confident that the British fleet would be forced to break the blockade. Why did King Cotton fail them?

English manufacturers had on hand, when the shooting started in 1861, an embarrassing oversupply of fiber. The real pinch did not come until about a year and a half later, when thousands of hungry operatives were thrown out of work. But by this time Lincoln had announced his slave-emancipation policy, and the "wage slaves" of England were not going to demand a war for the slaveowners of the South.

The direst effects of the "cotton famine" in England were relieved by several interesting developments. The hunger of the unemployed work-ers was partially satisfied when kind-hearted Americans sent over several cargoes of foodstuffs. As Union armies penetrated the South, they cap-tured considerable supplies of cotton and shipped them to England; and the Confederates also ran a limited quantity through the blockade. In addition, the cotton growers of Egypt and India, responding to high prices, increased their output. Finally, flourishing war industries in England, which supplied the needs of both North and South, took up some of the slack in unemployment.

King Wheat and King Corn—both of the Northern agricultural royalty —proved to be more potent potentates than King Cotton. During these

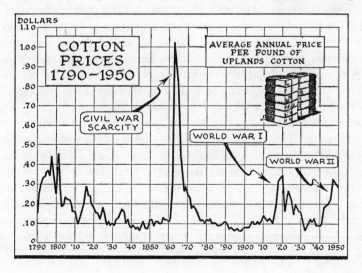

war years the North, blessed with ideal weather, produced bountiful crops of grain and harvested them with the McCormick mechanical reaper. In the same period, as luck would have it, the British suffered a series of bad harvests. They were forced to import large quantities of grain from the United States, which happened to have the cheapest and most abundant supply. If the British navy had broken the Union blockade to get out the cotton bales, it would have provoked the North to war and would have cut off this precious granary. Unemployment for some seemed better than hunger for all. Hence one Northern journal could exult:

> Wave the stars and stripes high o'er us,
> Let every freeman sing. . . .
> Old King Cotton's dead and buried: brave young Corn is King.

President Davis vs. President Lincoln

The Confederate government, like King Cotton, betrayed fatal weaknesses. Its constitution, borrowing liberally from that of the Union, had one deadly defect. Created by secession, it could not logically deny future secession to the states of the Confederacy. Jefferson Davis, while making his bow to states' rights, had in view a well-knit central government. But determined states'-rights men, unmoved by a higher loyalty, fought him bitterly. The Richmond regime even found it difficult to persuade certain state troops to serve outside their own borders. Governor Brown of Georgia, a belligerent states'-righter, at times seemed ready to secede from the secession and fight both the South and the North.

President Davis—hard, humorless, legalistic, unyielding—was repeatedly in hot water. Though an eloquent orator and an able administrator, he at no time enjoyed real personal popularity, and was often at loggerheads with Congress. At times there was serious talk of impeachment. Unlike Lincoln, Davis was somewhat imperious and inclined to defy rather than lead public opinion. Suffering acutely from neuralgia and other nervous disorders, he overworked himself with the details of both civil government and military operations. No one could doubt his courage, sincerity, and integrity, but the task proved beyond his powers. It was probably beyond the capacity of any mortal man.

Abraham Lincoln also had his troubles, but on the whole they were less prostrating. The North enjoyed the prestige of a well-organized and long-established government, financially stable and fully recognized both at home and abroad. Lincoln, the prairie politician totally without administrative seasoning, proved superior to the more experienced but less flexible Jefferson Davis. Able to relax with droll stories at critical times, "Old Abe" grew in stature as the war dragged on. Tactful, quiet, patient, yet firm, he developed a genius for interpreting and leading a fickle public opinion. Holding aloft the banner of Union through inspiring utterances, he revealed a rare charitableness toward the South and forbearance toward backbiting colleagues. "Did [Secretary] Stanton say I was a damned fool?" he replied to a talebearer. "Then I dare say I must be one, for Stanton is generally right and he always says what he means."

Strangulation by Sea

The general plan of Northern attack turned out to have four phases. First, slowly suffocate the South by blockading its coasts. Second, cut it in half by seizing control of the Mississippi River backbone. Third, chop it to pieces (a later idea) by sending troops through Georgia, and then north into the Carolinas. Fourth, strangle the Confederacy by capturing its capital (Richmond), and by pounding its remaining armies into submission.

The blockade started leakily. It was not clamped down all at once, but was extended by degrees. An airtight patrol of some 3500 miles of coast was an impossible task for the hastily improvised Northern navy, which consisted partly of converted yachts and ferryboats. But the problem of the blockading squadrons was simplified by concentrating on the principal ports and inlets. Only at such places were dock facilities available for loading bulky bales of cotton.

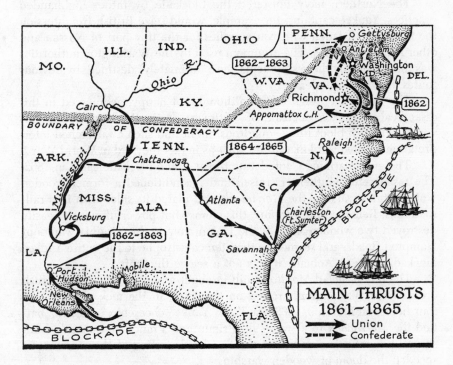

How was the blockade regarded by the mercantile powers of the world? Ordinarily, they probably would have defied it, for it was never completely effective, and was especially sieve-like at the outset. But Britain, the most important maritime nation, recognized it as binding, and warned her shippers that they ignored it at their peril. The explanation is easy. Blockade happened to be the chief offensive weapon of the British, who were still masters of the sea. They plainly did not want to tie their hands in a future war by insisting that the North maintain impossibly high blockading standards.

Blockade-running became riskily profitable, as the noose tightened around Southern necks and as the growing scarcity of goods drove prices skyward. The most successful runners were swift, gray-painted steamers, scores of which were specially built in Scotland on the Clyde River. A leading rendezvous was the West Indian port of Nassau, in the British Bahamas, where at one time thirty-five of the low-lying, speedy craft were counted. They would take on cargoes of arms brought in by tramp steamers from England, leave with fraudulent papers for "Halifax," and return a few days later with a cargo of cotton. The risks were great, but the profits would mount to 700% and more for lucky investors. Two successful voyages might well pay for capture on a third. The lush days of blockade-running finally passed as Union squadrons gradually pinched off the leading Southern ports, from New Orleans to Charleston.

The Northern navy bolstered the blockade by rather highhanded practices. Yankee captains, for example, would seize British freighters on the high seas, if laden with war supplies for the tiny port of Nassau and other halfway stations. The argument used by the Washington authorities was that obviously these shipments were "ultimately" destined, by devious routes, for the Confederacy.

The London Foreign Office, although not happy, acquiesced in this disagreeable Yankee doctrine of "ultimate destination" or "continuous voyage." British blockading squadrons might find such a farfetched interpretation highly useful in a future war—as in fact they did in World War I.

The most alarming Confederate threat to the blockade came in 1862. The resourceful Southerners raised and reconditioned a former wooden United States warship, the *Merrimack*, and plated its sides with iron railroad rails. Renamed the *Virginia*, this clumsy but powerful monster easily destroyed two wooden ships of the Union navy in the Virginia waters of Hampton Roads, and seemed to threaten catastrophe to the entire Yankee blockading fleet. (Actually it was not a seaworthy craft.)

The tiny ironclad *Monitor*, built in about a hundred days under rush orders from Washington, arrived on the scene in the nick of time. For four hours, on March 9, 1862, the little "Yankee cheesebox on a raft" battled the *Merrimack* to a standstill. Britain and France had already built several powerful ironclads, but the first battle-testing of these new craft speeded the doom of wooden warships.

The Runners of Bull Run

By the summer of 1861, a Union army of some 30,000 men was being drilled near Washington. It was ill-prepared for battle, but Northern newspaper editors, confident of ending the war in a hurry, raised the cry, "On to Richmond!" The proddings of the press and public finally forced the government to move, contrary to the better judgment of some of the generals. This is a classic example of the dangerous pressure that can be exerted by an ignorant and aroused public opinion.

The preliminaries to the disastrous defeat at Bull Run, on July 21, 1861, seemed like those of a sporting event. The raw Yankee recruits marched or straggled from the capital, accompanied by Congressmen, ladies, and others riding out to see the fun. As Herman Melville put it:

> No berrying-party, pleasure-wooed,
> No picnic party in the May,
> Ever went less loth than they
> Into that leafy neighborhood.

The ill-trained Union force encountered a smaller Confederate army at Bull Run (Manassas Junction), some thirty miles southwest of Washington. At first the battle went well for the Yankees. But "Stonewall" Jackson's gray-clad warriors stood like a stone wall (here he won his nickname), and Confederate reinforcements arrived unexpectedly. Panic suddenly seized the weary Union soldiers, and many of them fled from the field in scenes of disgraceful confusion, leaving the Confederates too exhausted or too disorganized to pursue.

The "military picnic" at Bull Run, though not decisive militarily, was significant psychologically. The defeat was better than a victory for the Union, because it dispelled all illusions of a one-punch war and caused the Northerners to buckle down to the staggering task at hand. Conversely, the victory was worse than a defeat for the South, because it inflated an already dangerous feeling of overconfidence. Many soldiers deserted from the Confederate army, some boastfully to display their trophies, others sure that the war was over. Southern enlistments fell off sharply, and preparations for a long and dreary war slackened.

"Tardy George" McClellan

Northern hopes brightened later in 1861, when General George B. McClellan was placed in command of the Army of the Potomac, as the major Union force near Washington was now called. Red-haired and red-mustached, strong and stocky, McClellan was a brilliant, thirty-four-year-old West Pointer. As a serious student of warfare who was dubbed "Young Napoleon," the energetic general had seen plenty of fighting, first in the Mexican War and then as an observer of the Crimean War in Russia.

McClellan presented a curious mixture of virtues and defects. He was a superb organizer and drillmaster, and he injected splendid morale into the Army of the Potomac. Hating to sacrifice his troops, he was idolized by his men, who affectionately called him "Little Mac." But he was a perfectionist who seems not to have realized that an army is never ready to the last button, and that wars cannot be won without running some risks. He consistently but erroneously believed that the enemy outnumbered him, partly because his reports from the Pinkerton Detective Agency were

MASTERLY INACTIVITY, OR SIX MONTHS ON THE POTOMAC
McClellan and his Confederate foe view each other cautiously, while their troops engage in visiting, marrying, and sports. *Frank Leslie's Illustrated Newspaper*, 1862

unreliable. He was overcautious—Lincoln once accused him of having "the slows"—and he addressed the President in an arrogant tone which a less forgiving person would never have tolerated.

As McClellan discreetly continued to drill his army without moving it toward Richmond, the derisive Northern watchword became "All Quiet along the Potomac." The song of the hour was "Tardy George," which began with "What are you waiting for, George, I pray?" After Lincoln had threatened to "borrow" the army if it was not going to be used, he finally gave "Tardy George" flat orders to move.

McClellan decided upon a water-borne flanking approach to Richmond. Choosing the route up the peninsula formed by the James and York Rivers, he warily advanced toward the city in the spring of 1862 with about 100,000 men. After taking a month to capture historic Yorktown, which bristled with Quaker-gun wooden cannon, he finally came within sight of the spires of Richmond. Then General Lee suddenly struck with about 70,000 troops. Brilliantly assisted by "Stonewall" Jackson, he slowly drove McClellan back to his base on Chesapeake Bay. Although the Union army was still in fighting shape, the whole Peninsular Campaign was abandoned as a costly failure.

PENINSULAR CAMPAIGN 1862

McClellan was now given a less active command, amid a storm of controversy. His enemies accused "Mac the Unready" of having moved too timorously. His defenders claimed that he would have captured Richmond if Lincoln had not withdrawn troops for the defense of Washington, which had been jeopardized by the lightning feints of "Stonewall" Jackson. It is perhaps worth noting that "Little Mac" was never decisively defeated, and that after the war Lee rated him as the ablest of his many opponents.

A Union army near Washington, strengthened by units from McClellan's command, was now entrusted to General John Pope. A handsome, dashing, soldierly figure, he boasted that in the Western theater, from which he had come, he had seen only the backs of the enemy. He quickly got a front view, for General Lee, at the Second Battle of Bull Run (August 29–30, 1862), furiously attacked him and inflicted a crushing defeat. Gloom once more enshrouded the North.

The Antietam Pivotal Point

General Lee now undertook a daring thrust into Maryland. He hoped to win a victory that would not only encourage foreign intervention, but also seduce this wavering Border State and her sisters from the Union standard. The Confederate troops sang lustily,

> Thou wilt not cower in the dust,
> Maryland! my Maryland!
> Thy gleaming sword shall never rust,
> Maryland! my Maryland!

But the Marylanders did not respond to the siren song. The presence among the invaders of so many blanketless, hatless, and shoeless soldiers dampened the state's ardor.

Events finally shaped up for a critical battle at Antietam Creek, Maryland. President Lincoln, responding to popular pressures, hastily restored "Little Mac" to active command of the main Northern army. The soldiers tossed their caps into the air and hugged his horse as they hailed his return. At Antietam, on September 17, 1862, McClellan succeeded in halting Lee in one of the bitterest and bloodiest days of the war.

Antietam was more or less a draw militarily. But Lee, finding his thrust parried, retired across the Potomac. McClellan, of whom much more had been hoped, was removed from his field command for the second and final time. His numerous critics, condemning him for not having boldly pursued the ever-dangerous Lee, finally got his scalp.

The indecisive battle of Antietam was one of the decisive battles of world history—probably the most decisive of the Civil War. The Confederacy was perhaps never again so near victory as on that fateful summer day. The British and French governments were on the verge of diplomatic mediation, a species of interference sure to be angrily resented by the North. The almost certain rebuff by Washington might well have spurred Paris and London into armed intervention. But both capitals cooled off when the Union displayed such unexpected power at Antietam, and their chill deepened with the passing months.

Antietam was also the long-awaited "victory" which Lincoln needed for launching his Emancipation Proclamation. The abolitionists and other anti-slaveryites had long been clamoring for him to take effective action. By mid-summer of 1862, with the Border States safely in the fold, Lincoln was ready to move. But he was persuaded that to issue such an edict on the heels of a series of military disasters would be folly. It would seem like a confession that the North, unable to conquer the South, was forced to call upon the slaves to murder their masters. Lincoln therefore decided to await the outcome of Lee's invasion.

Antietam served as the needed emancipation springboard. The halting of Lee's offensive was just enough of a victory to justify Lincoln's issuing, on September 23, 1862, the preliminary Emancipation Proclamation. This hope-giving document announced that on January 1, 1863, the President would issue a final proclamation. On the scheduled date he fully redeemed his promise, and the Civil War became a holy crusade.

A Proclamation without Emancipation

The Emancipation Proclamation of 1863 declared "forever free" the slaves in those Confederate states still in rebellion. The Negroes in the loyal Border States were not affected, nor were those in specific conquered areas in the South.

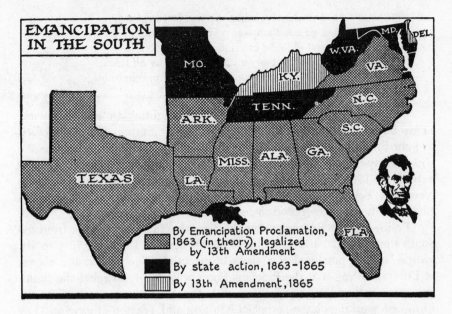

EMANCIPATION IN THE SOUTH

By Emancipation Proclamation, 1863 (in theory), legalized by 13th Amendment

By state action, 1863–1865

By 13th Amendment, 1865

Lincoln's pen, legend to the contrary, did not formally strike the shackles from a single slave, much less 3,500,000 slaves. Where the President could presumably free the slaves—that is, in the loyal Border States—he refused to do so, lest he increase the spirit of disunion. Where he could not—that is, in the Confederate states—he tried to. In short, where he *could* he would not, and where he *would* he could not.

Yet some unofficial liberation did take place at once. Thousands of jubilant slaves, learning of the proclamation, flocked to the invading Union armies, thereby hampering military operations. But many of the fugitives would have come anyhow, as they had from the war's outset. Actually, Lincoln did not go as far as legislation already passed by Congress for freeing enemy-owned Negroes. His immediate major purpose was not so much to liberate the slaves as to strengthen the moral cause of the Union at home and abroad. This he succeeded in doing. At the same time his proclamation, though of dubious constitutionality, clearly foreshadowed the ultimate doom of Negro slavery in the United States. This was legally achieved by action of the individual states and by their ratification of the 13th Amendment in 1865, eight months after the war had ended. (For text, see Appendix.)

Public reactions to the long-awaited Proclamation of 1863 were varied. "God bless Abraham Lincoln," exulted the anti-slavery editor Horace Greeley in his New York *Tribune*. But many of the more ardent abolitionists were displeased because Lincoln had not gone far enough. On the other hand, formidable numbers of Northerners, especially in the Old Northwest and the Border States, felt that he had gone too far. A Democratic rhymester sneered:

> Honest old Abe, when the war first began,
> Denied abolition was part of his plan;
> Honest old Abe has since made a decree,
> The war must go on till the slaves are all free.
> As both can't be honest, will some one tell how,
> If honest Abe then, he is honest Abe now?

Opposition mounted in the North against fighting an "abolition war." Many boys in blue, especially from the Border States, had volunteered to fight for the Union, not to fight against slavery. Desertions from the Union army increased sharply. The crucial Congressional elections in the autumn of 1862 went heavily against the administration, particularly in New York, Pennsylvania, and Ohio. The Democrats even carried Lincoln's Illinois, although they failed to secure control of Congress.

Following the Emancipation Proclamation, an outcry arose from the South that the barbaric Lincoln—"Lincoln the fiend"—was trying to stir up the "hellish passions" of a slave insurrection. The aristocratic classes of Europe, noting that the Proclamation applied only to rebel slaveholders, were inclined to sympathize with the Southern protests. But the European working classes, especially in England, reacted otherwise. They perceived that the Proclamation spelled the beginning of the end for slavery, and they were more determined than ever to oppose intervention. Gradually the diplomatic position of the Union was improved.

The North now had the stronger moral cause. In addition to preserving the Union, it had committed itself to freeing the slaves. The moral position of the South, by the same stroke of Lincoln's pen, was correspondingly weakened.

Bisecting the South

The spectacular rise of U. S. (Ulysses Simpson) Grant provided Lincoln at last with an able general—and one who did not have to be shelved after every reverse. As a mediocre student at West Point, Grant had distinguished himself only in horsemanship, although he did fairly well in mathematics. After participating with credit in the Mexican War, he was stationed at lonely frontier posts, where boredom and loneliness drove him to drink. Resigning from the army to avoid a court martial for drunkenness, he failed at various business ventures, and when war came he was working in his father's leather store in Illinois at $50 a month.

Grant did not cut much of a figure. The shy and silent shopkeeper was short, stooped, awkward, and sloppy in dress. He managed with some difficulty to secure a colonelcy in the volunteers. From then on his military experience—combined with boldness, resourcefulness, and dogged persistence—brought a meteoric rise.

Grant's first signal success came in the northern Tennessee theater. After heavy fighting, he succeeded in capturing Fort Henry and Fort

Donelson on the Tennessee and Cumberland Rivers, in February, 1862. When the Confederate commander at Fort Donelson asked for terms, Grant bluntly demanded "an unconditional and immediate surrender."

This triumph in Tennessee for Union arms was of major significance. Kentucky was riveted more securely to the Union, and the gateway was opened to the rest of Tennessee and to Georgia and the heart of the South. Grant's exploit also captured the imagination of the victory-starved North, and infused badly needed life into the Union cause.

"Unconditional Surrender" Grant was caught napping several weeks later at Shiloh, in southern Tennessee, April 6–7, 1862. But he finally managed to beat off the enemy on one of the goriest fields of the war. Lincoln resisted all demands for his removal by saying, "I can't spare this man, he fights."

Other Union thrusts were in the making. In the spring of 1862, a flotilla commanded by David G. Farragut joined with

THE MISSISSIPPI RIVER AND TENNESSEE, 1862–1863

a Northern army to strike the South a staggering blow when it seized New Orleans. With Union gunboats both ascending and descending the Mississippi, the eastern part of the Confederacy was left with a precarious back door. Through this narrowing entrance, between Vicksburg and Port Hudson, flowed herds of vitally needed cattle and quantities of other provisions from Louisiana and Texas. The fortress of Vicksburg, located on a hairpin turn of the Mississippi, was the northern sentinel protecting the lifeline to the western sources of supply.

General Grant was given command of the Union forces attacking Vicksburg, and in the face of immense difficulties displayed rare skill and daring. This was his best-fought campaign of the war. Vicksburg at length surrendered, on July 4, 1863, with the garrison reduced to eating rats. Five days later came the fall of Port Hudson, the last remaining Southern bastion on the Mississippi. The spinal cord of the Confederacy was now cut in two, and, in Lincoln's quaint phrase, the Father of Waters at last flowed "unvexed to the sea."

Marching through Georgia

General Grant, his star still rising, was now transferred to the East Tennessee theater. There, in November, 1863, he won a series of desperate engagements in the vicinity of Chattanooga, including Missionary Ridge and Lookout Mountain ("the Battle above the Clouds"). The state was thus cleared of Confederates, and the way was opened for the invasion of Georgia. Grant was rewarded by being made general-in-chief.

The conquest of Georgia was entrusted to General William Tecumseh Sherman. Red-haired and red-bearded, grim-faced and ruthless, he captured and burned Atlanta in September, 1864. He then daringly undertook to cut loose from his base of supplies, live off the country for some 250 miles, and emerge at Savannah on the sea. As a rousing Northern song ("Marching through Georgia") put it:

> "Sherman's dashing Yankee boys will never reach the coast!"
> So the saucy rebels said—and 't was a handsome boast.

But Sherman's hated "Blue Bellies," 60,000 strong, cut a sixty-mile swath of destruction through Georgia. They burned buildings, leaving only the blackened chimneys. They tore up railroad rails, heated them red-hot, and twisted them into "iron doughnuts" and "Sherman's hairpins." They bayoneted family portraits and ran off with valuable "souvenirs." "War . . . is all hell," admitted Sherman later, and he proved it by his efforts to "make Georgia howl." One of his major purposes was to destroy supplies destined for the Confederate army, and to weaken the morale of the men at the front by waging war on their homes.

Sherman was a pioneer practitioner of "total war." His success in "Shermanizing" the South was attested by increasing numbers of Confederate desertions. Although his methods were brutal, he probably shortened the struggle and hence saved lives. But there can be no doubt that the discipline of his army at times broke down, as his "bummers" and riffraff elements engaged in an orgy of pillaging. The name of "Sherman the Brute" was universally damned in the South.

SHERMAN'S
MARCH, 1864-1865

After taking Savannah, Sherman's army veered north into South Carolina, where the destruction was even more vicious. Many Union soldiers believed that this state, the "hell-hole of secession," had wantonly provoked the war. The capital city, Columbia, burst into flames, in all probability the handiwork of the Yankee invader.

Continuing northward, Sherman's conquering army had rolled deep into North Carolina by the time the war ended.

Lee's Last Lunge

After Antietam, Lincoln replaced McClellan with General A. E. Burnside, whose ornate side whiskers came to be known as "burnsides" or "sideburns." Protesting his unfitness for this heavy responsibility, Burnside proved it when he launched a frontal attack on Lee's strong position at Fredericksburg, Virginia, on December 13, 1862. A chicken could not have lived in the line of fire, remarked one Confederate officer. More than 10,000 Northern soldiers were killed or wounded in "Burnside's Slaughter Pen."

A new slaughter pen was prepared when General Burnside yielded his command to "Fighting Joe" Hooker, an able and aggressive officer but a headstrong subordinate. At Chancellorsville, Virginia, May 2–4, 1863, Lee daringly divided his numerically inferior force, and sent "Stonewall" Jackson to attack the Union flank. The strategy worked. Hooker, dazed for a time by a near hit from a cannon ball, was badly beaten but not crushed. This victory was probably Lee's most brilliant, but it was dearly bought by the South. "Stonewall" Jackson was mistakenly shot by his own men in the gathering dusk, and died a few days later. "I have lost my right arm," lamented Lee.

Lee now prepared to follow up his inspiriting victory by invading the North again, this time through Pennsylvania. A decisive blow would add strength to the peace movement in the North, while encouraging foreign intervention. Three days before the battle was joined, General George G. Meade—scholarly, unspectacular, abrupt—was aroused from his sleep at two o'clock in the morning with the unwelcome news that he would replace "Fighting Joe" Hooker. The high tide of the Confederacy was at hand.

Meade, quite by accident, took his stand on the green rolling fields near quiet little Gettysburg, Pennsylvania. There his 92,000 men in blue locked in furious combat with Lee's 76,000 gray-clad warriors. The battle seesawed throughout three days, July 1–3, 1863, and the outcome was in doubt until almost the very end. It was the failure of General Pickett's magnificent but futile charge that finally broke the back of the Confederates.

LEE'S CHIEF BATTLES
December, 1862–July, 1863

The reverse was Lee's worst defeat to date, but he took full responsibility for it, even though some of his subordinates had failed him. From now on the Southern cause was doomed, for Vicksburg had fallen on the day after the defeat at Gettysburg. Yet the men of Dixie fought on, through sweat, blood, and weariness of spirit.

Later in that dreary autumn of 1863, with the graves still fresh, Lincoln journeyed to Gettysburg to dedicate the cemetery. He read a two-minute address, following the two-hour speech of the eminent orator of the day. The President's remarks, branded by the unfriendly London *Times* as "ludicrous," were little noticed at the time. But he was speaking for the ages.

The Dawn of Peace

Grant was now brought in from the West over Meade, who was criticized for not having pursued the beaten but always dangerous Lee. Lincoln needed a general who, employing the superior resources of the North, would have the intestinal stamina to drive straight ahead, regardless of casualties. U. S. Grant, a soldier of bulldog tenacity, was the man for this meat-grinder type of warfare. His basic strategy was to strike at the enemy's armies simultaneously, so that they could not assist one another, and hence could be destroyed piecemeal. His personal motto was "When in doubt, fight."

A grimly determined Grant, with more than 100,000 men, struck for Richmond. He engaged Lee in a series of furious battles in the Wilderness of Virginia, during May and June of 1864, notably in the leaden hurricane of the "Bloody Angle" and "Hell's Half Acre." In this Wilderness Campaign Grant suffered about 50,000 casualties, or nearly as many men as Lee had at the start. But Lee lost about as heavily in proportion.

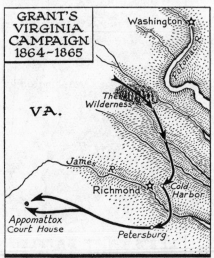

GRANT'S VIRGINIA CAMPAIGN 1864–1865

VA.

Washington

The Wilderness

James R.

Richmond

Cold Harbor

Appomattox Court House

Petersburg

In a ghastly gamble, on June 3, 1864, Grant ordered a frontal assault on the impregnable position of Cold Harbor. The Union soldiers advanced to almost certain death with papers pinned on their backs bearing their names and addresses. In a few minutes, about 7000 men were killed or wounded.

Public opinion in the North was appalled by this "blood and guts" type of fighting. Critics cried that "Grant the Butcher" had gone insane. But his basic strategy of hammering ahead seemed brutally necessary; he could trade two men for one and still beat the enemy to its knees. "I propose to fight it out on this line," he wrote, "if it takes all summer." It did—and then some.

Early in 1865 the Confederates, tasting the bitter dregs of defeat, tried desperately to negotiate for peace between the "two countries." But Lincoln could accept nothing short of Union, and the Southerners could accept nothing short of independence. So the war had to grind on—amid smoke and agony—to its terrible climax.

The end came with dramatic suddenness. Fast-advancing Northern troops captured Richmond and cornered Lee at Appomattox Court House in Virginia, in April, 1865. Grant—stubble bearded and informally dressed —met with Lee and granted generous terms of surrender. Among other concessions, the hungry Confederate troops might keep their horses for spring plowing.

The tattered and unshaven Southerners—"Lee's Ragamuffins"—wept as they took leave of their beloved commander. The elated Union soldiers cheered, but they were silenced by Grant with the stern admonition, "The war is over; the rebels are our countrymen again." Unfortunately, as the tragic sequel proved, this soldierly forgiveness was not shared by all Northern hearts.

SELECT READINGS

An able survey is J. G. RANDALL and DAVID DONALD, *The Civil War and Reconstruction* (1961); greater detail appears in J. G. RANDALL, *Lincoln the President* (4 vols., 1945–1955). The fifth and sixth volumes of ALLAN NEVINS' monumental series are *The War for the Union: The Improvised War, 1861–1862* (1959) and *The War for the Union: War Becomes Revolution, 1862–1863* (1960). R. N. CURRENT, *Lincoln and the First Shot* (1963) [paperback] partially exculpates Lincoln. See also T. H. WILLIAMS, *Lincoln and His Generals* (1952), a Book-of-the-Month-Club choice. The centennial inspired two books: F. M. DONOVAN, *Mr. Lincoln's Proclamation* (1964) and J. H. FRANKLIN, *The Emancipation Proclamation* (1963) [paperback]. BRUCE CATTON has a series of eight or so books [some paperback] on aspects of the Civil War, all readable and knowledgeable, including the Pulitzer-prize *A Stillness at Appomattox* (1953) [paperback]. D. S. FREEMAN, *R. E. Lee* (4 vols., 1934–1935) [Pulitzer prize] and *Lee's Lieutenants* (3 vols., 1942–1944) are detailed but absorbing. See also JAY LUVAAS, *The Military Legacy of the Civil War* (1959). On the Confederacy see CLEMENT EATON, *A History of the Southern Confederacy* (1954) [paperback] and CLIFFORD DOWDEY, *The Land They Fought For* (1955). HUDSON STRODE has completed his detailed three-volume biography with *Jefferson Davis, Tragic Hero* (1964). Recent biographies are W. W. HASSLER's on McClellan (1957); FREEMAN CLEAVES' on Meade (1960); and LENOIR CHAMBERS' on Jackson (2 vols., 1959). Also references for next chapter and *Harvard Guide*, Pt. IV.

23

Behind the Lines: North and South

Many are the hearts that are weary tonight,
Wishing for the war to cease. . . .

WALTER KITTREDGE,
"Tenting on the Old Camp-Ground," 1864

Diplomatic Warriors

THE diplomatic front, ordinarily active in wartime, has seldom been so critical as during the American Civil War.

The attitude of the major European countries was crucial, particularly that of France and Britain. Both nations had formidable ironclads in their navies, and if either power had decided to intervene, it could have smashed the wooden blockading fleet of the Union with terrifying ease. If this had happened, the South almost certainly would have won its independence. An infuriated North no doubt would have turned its bayonets against British Canada, there to seek vengeance and compensation.

The slippery dictator of France, Napoleon III, was openly unfriendly to the North. Behind the smoke screen of the Civil War he was attempting to prop up his puppet, the Austrian Archduke Maximilian, on the throne of Mexico. The success of this hazardous venture depended on the collapse of the Union. Napoleon had the naval strength to break the Northern blockade, but since he did not have the nerve to go it alone, he sought the support of Britain. The London government saw fit to restrain him, so intervention never came.

British officialdom, heavily tinged with aristocracy, was personally more friendly to the aristocratic South than to the "shopkeeping" North. But London proclaimed an official neutrality, and observed it rather well —at least as well as it could with its leaky neutrality laws. The North had expected the British, who were strongly anti-slavery, to sympathize warmly with its war aims. Instead, the attitude of the British officials, as they attempted to preserve a cold neutrality, seemed scarcely better than veiled hostility. James Russell Lowell sorrowfully addressed John Bull:

> We know we've gut a cause, John,
> Thet's honest, just, an' true;
> We thought 't would win applause, John,
> Ef nowheres else, from you.

The first perilous crisis with Britain came over the *Trent* affair, late in 1861. A Union warship cruising on the high seas north of Cuba stopped a British mail steamer, the *Trent,* and forcibly removed from it two Confederate diplomats who were on their way to England. The American captain was guilty of a serious error; technically he should have brought the entire ship to port for proper judicial judgment.

A wild outburst of rejoicing arose from the Northerners. They had as yet won no important military victory, and the seizure of these two eminent envoys was regarded as a brilliant stroke. Many a loyal Union man feared that if they had continued their journey, they might have persuaded Britain and France to break the blockade. Besides, patriotic Americans, remembering the impressment days of 1812, thought it great sport to give the British a dose of their own medicine. We were now dragging men from the decks of their ships for a change.

The British were outraged. Upstart Yankees could not do this sort of thing to the Mistress of the Seas. War preparations were rushed, and red-coated troops embarked for Canada, with their bands blaring, "I Wish I Was in Dixie." The London Foreign Office forthwith prepared an ultimatum, demanding a surrender of the prisoners and a proper apology.

The *Trent* crisis was surmounted, but only with grave difficulty. The Atlantic cable had gone dead, and the delays caused by steamship communication gave passions on both sides a chance to cool. Lincoln gradually perceived that the North had on its hands two "white elephants," and despite the popularity of their seizure, he reluctantly decided to release them. Secretary of State Seward was at pains to sweeten the pill for the American public. In a clever note he in effect congratulated the British on having accepted, at long last, the views for which we had futilely fought them in the War of 1812.

Confederate "Pirates"

The second dangerous Anglo-American crisis came in the autumn of 1862. The British Cabinet, yielding to the urgings of Napoleon III, was about to join France in mediating between North and South, with consequent dangers of shooting. The Union "victory" at Antietam came as a bucket of cold water to such schemes, for Canada was vulnerable to Union bayonets, and British shipping to Yankee privateers. Prime Minister Palmerston was reminded of the ancient couplet:

> Those who in quarrels interpose,
> Must often wipe a bloody nose.

The third major crisis arose over the building in England of Confederate commerce-raiders, the most famous of which was the *Alabama*. These vessels were not warships within the meaning of British law, because they left their shipyards unarmed and picked up their guns elsewhere. The *Alabama* escaped in 1862 to the Portuguese Azores, and there took on weapons and a crew from two English ships that followed her. Although flying the Confederate flag and officered by Confederates, she was manned by Britons, and she never entered a Confederate port.

The *Alabama* proceeded to light the skies from Europe to the Far East with the burning hulks of Yankee merchantmen. All told, this "British pirate" captured over sixty vessels. Competing British shippers were pleased, while an angered North had to divert naval strength from its blockade for wild-goose chases. The *Alabama* finally accepted a challenge from a Union cruiser off the coast of France, in 1864, and was quickly destroyed. A picture of the battle, widely sold in the North, bore the incendiary caption: "Built of English oak in an English yard, armed with English guns, manned by an English crew, and sunk in the English Channel."

The shortsighted officials in London began to develop twinges of conscience. They were given no peace by the American minister, Charles Francis Adams,* who persistently presented lists of sinkings and bills for damages by the British-built raider. The Foreign Office gradually perceived that it was sanctioning a dangerous precedent that might one day be used against Britain by a future foe—perhaps one without a navy (Ireland?) or even one without a seacoast. The London government, fearing that it might push the Americans too far, took drastic action in 1863. It openly violated its own inadequate laws when it seized another raider being built for the Confederates. In the subsequent trial the British government was assessed costs and damages, but its action was clear evidence of a determination to be truly neutral.

Confederate commerce-destroyers, chiefly British-built, captured in all more than 250 Yankee ships. The owners of several hundred others, fearing destruction, transferred them to a foreign flag. Under existing federal laws, these could not be transferred back. Fortunately for the North, the *Alabamas* did not cripple the war effort, because British and other neutral shipping was available. But the American merchant marine, only recently the proud challenger of England, was badly riddled. (See chart on p. 316.) Earnest citizens, deeply angered, talked quite openly of securing both revenge and recompense by seizing Canada when the war was over.

British Rams and Russian Fleets

The fourth Anglo-American crisis was touched off in 1863 by the Laird rams—two Confederate warships being constructed in Great Britain.

---

* Son of President John Quincy Adams, and grandson of President John Adams.

Specifically designed to destroy the wooden-ship Union navy with their wrought-iron rams and large-caliber guns, they were potentially far more dangerous than the swift and lightly armed *Alabamas*. If delivered to the South, these awesome craft no doubt would have sunk the blockading squadrons, and probably would have brought the Northern cities under their fire. In angry retaliation, the North doubtless would have invaded Canada, and a full-dress war with Great Britain would have broken loose.

The menace of the rams was finally removed. There were no legal grounds for detaining them, for their fraudulent papers indicated a non-Confederate purchaser. But under the persistent proddings of Minister Adams, the British government decided to pay the builder a sum in excess of the contract price, and then add the two troublesome vessels to the Royal Navy. Everyone was satisfied—except the Confederates.

The Czar of Russia, meanwhile, was watching all these events with intense interest. For purely realistic reasons he was friendly to the North, and as a result refused bluntly to participate in any Franco-British scheme for mediation or intervention. Britain was his hereditary foe, and his long-established policy was to build up a strong United States to thwart British expansion and power. He therefore favored a speedy reunion of the embattled sections, before they had bled away any more vital strength.

A BRITISH THRUST AT LINCOLN

The Russian Czar, against a background of massacred Polish rebels, joyously greets Lincoln, against a background of dead Confederate rebels. *Punch,* 1863

In the war-weary autumn of 1863, two Russian fleets, numbering about six vessels each, unexpectedly appeared at New York and San Francisco. Curious crowds, displaying friendly enthusiasm, gathered to greet the visitors. Many soft-headed Americans jumped to the conclusion that the warships had come to warn the British and French not to intervene, lest they find the Russians fighting side by side with the Americans. Several years later Oliver Wendell Holmes declared:

> Bleak are our shores with the blasts of December,
> Fettered and chill is the rivulet's flow;
> Throbbing and warm are the hearts that remember
> Who was our friend when the world was our foe.

What schemings lay behind the dramatic Russian gesture? Historians have since proved—what some critics suspected at the time—that the Czar sent his fleets to America because he was then on the verge of war with Britain and France over Poland. The Russian ships would be useless if bottled up or ice-bound in the Baltic or elsewhere. But based on friendly American ports, they could serve as *Alabamas* to ravage the vulnerable British and French shipping. The threat thus posed by the two fleets may well have helped keep the peace. The seeming friendship of the Czar was based on an understandable desire to promote his own interests, but many naïve Americans assumed that his solicitude was completely unselfish.

Volunteers and Draftees

The insatiable gods of war demanded men—lots of men. The Northern armies were at first manned solely by volunteers, with each state assigned a quota based on population. But in 1863, after volunteering had slackened off, Congress passed a federal conscription law for the first time on a nationwide scale in the United States. The provisions were grossly unfair to the poor. Rich boys could hire substitutes to go in their places, or purchase exemption outright by paying $300. "Three-hundred-dollar men" was the scornful epithet applied to these slackers.

The draft was especially detested in the Democratic strongholds of the North, and nowhere more so than in New York City. A frightful riot broke out in 1863, touched off largely by underprivileged Irish-Americans who shouted, "Down with the Draft." For several days the city was at the mercy of a burning and pillaging mob, and an estimated five hundred or so casualties were suffered. Elsewhere in the North conscription encountered resentment and an occasional minor riot.

More than 90% of the Union armies were volunteers; social and patriotic pressures to enlist were strong. As able-bodied men became scarcer, generous bounties for enlistment were offered by federal, state, and local authorities. An enterprising and money-wise volunteer might legitimately pocket more than $1000.

With money flowing so freely, an unsavory crew of "bounty brokers" and "substitute brokers" sprang up, at home and abroad. They combed the poorhouses of the British Isles and Western Europe; and on occasion an Irishman or German was befuddled with whiskey and induced to enlist. A number of the slippery "bounty boys" deserted, volunteered elsewhere, and netted another handsome haul. The records reveal that one "bounty jumper" repeated his profitable operation thirty-two times. But desertion was by no means confined to "bounty jumpers." The rolls of the Union army recorded about 200,000 deserters of all classes, and the Confederate authorities were plagued with a similar problem.

Enlistees North and South

[NUMBER OF MEN IN UNIFORM AT DATE GIVEN]

	Union	Confederate
July, 1861	186,751	112,040
Jan., 1862	575,917	351,418
Mar., 1862	637,126	401,395
Jan., 1863	918,121	446,622
Jan., 1864	860,737	481,180
Jan., 1865	959,460	445,203

The South, like the North, relied mainly on volunteers. But since the Confederacy was much less populous, it scraped the bottom of its manpower barrel more quickly. The Richmond government was forced to resort to conscription in April, 1862, nearly a year earlier than the Union.

The Confederate draft regulations, like those of the United States, worked serious injustices. As in the North, a rich man could hire a substitute or purchase exemption. Slaveowners or overseers with twenty Negroes might also claim exemption. These special privileges made for bad feeling among the less prosperous, many of whom complained that this was "a rich man's war but a poor man's fight." No large-scale draft riots broke out in the South, as in New York City. But the Confederate conscription agents often found it prudent to avoid those areas inhabited by sharpshooting mountain whites, who were dubbed "Tories," "traitors," and "Yankee-lovers."

The Dollar Goes to War

The North, with its disproportionate share of the wealth, rode through the financial breakers much more smoothly than the South. Excise taxes on tobacco and alcohol were substantially increased by Congress. An income tax was levied for the first time in our experience; and although the rates were painlessly low by later standards, they netted millions of dollars.

The tariff likewise proved to be an important revenue-raiser. Early in 1861, after enough anti-protection Southern members had walked out with their states, Congress passed the Morrill Tariff Act, superseding the low Tariff of 1857. It increased the existing customs duties some 5% to 10%, bringing them back up to about the moderate level of the Walker Tariff of 1846. But these modest rates were soon pushed sharply upward by the war. The increases were designed partly to raise additional revenue, and partly to provide more protection for the prosperous manufacturers who were being generously plucked by the new internal taxes. A protective tariff thus became identified with the Republican Party, as American industrialists, predominantly Republicans, waxed fat on these welcome benefits. (See tariff chart, p. 264.)

United States Imports and the Tariff, 1860–1866

Year	Free Goods	Dutiable Goods	Total Duties Collected	Percentage on Value of Dutiable Goods	Percentage on Value of All Goods
1860	$68,391,038	$267,891,447	$ 52,692,421	19.67%	15.67%
1861	67,421,022	207,235,303	39,038,269	18.84%	14.21%
1862	49,842,947	128,487,253	46,509,215	36.19%	26.08%
1863	30,026,756	195,348,524	63,729,203	32.62%	28.28%
1864	38,162,565	262,950,757	96,465,957	36.69%	32.03%
1865	40,097,208	169,559,317	80,635,170	47.56%	38.46%
1866	57,121,369	366,349,277	177,056,523	48.33%	41.81%

Note the sharp rise in rates in 1862, the second year of the war.

The Washington Treasury also found it desirable to issue greenbacked paper money, totaling nearly $450,000,000 at face value. This printing-press currency was inadequately supported by gold, and its value was consequently determined by the nation's credit. The greenback thus fluctuated with the fortunes of Union arms, and at one low point was worth only 39 cents on the dollar in terms of gold. The holder of the notes, victimized by this creeping inflation, was indirectly taxed as the value of the currency slowly withered in his hands.

Borrowing far outstripped both greenbacks and taxes as a money-raiser. The Federal Treasury netted in all $2,621,916,786 through the sale of bonds, which bore interest and which were payable at a later date. The modern technique of selling these issues to the people directly through "drives" had not yet been developed. Accordingly, the Treasury was forced to market its bonds through the private banking house of Jay Cooke and Company, which received a commission of three-eighths of one percent on all sales. With both profits and patriotism at stake, the bankers succeeded in making effective appeals to citizen purchasers.

Civil War Financing in the North

Fiscal Year	Customs	Internal Revenue and Income Tax	Total Taxes	Loans, Including Treasury Notes
1861–1862	$ 49,056,397		$ 50,851,729	$ 433,663,538
1862–1863	69,059,642	$ 37,640,787	108,185,534	596,203,071
1863–1864	102,316,152	109,741,134	212,532,936	719,476,032
1864–1865	84,928,260	209,464,215	295,593,048	872,574,145
Total	$305,360,451	$356,846,136	$667,163,247	$2,621,916,786

A financial landmark of the war was the National Banking System, authorized by Congress in 1863. Launched partly in response to the need for stimulating the sale of government bonds, the new scheme was also designed to establish a standard banknote currency. (The country was then flooded with depreciated "rag money" issued by unreliable bankers.) Banks that joined the National Banking System could buy government bonds and issue sound paper currency backed by them. The war-born National Banking Act thus turned out to be the first significant step taken toward a unified banking network since 1836, when the "monster" Bank of the United States was done to death by Andrew Jackson. The new system continued to function for fifty years.

Taxation by Inflation

The impoverished South was confronted with different financial problems. Customs duties were largely choked off as the strangling coils of the Union blockade tightened. Large issues of Confederate bonds were sold at home and abroad, amounting to nearly $400,000,000. The Richmond regime also increased taxes sharply, and imposed a 10% levy on farm produce. But in general the states'-rights Southerners were vigorously opposed to heavy direct taxation by the central authority.

As other sources of revenue began to dry up, the Confederate government was forced to print paper money like cigar coupons. Inflation did not ruin the South, as commonly believed. Rather, an inflation of the currency, together with the levy on farm produce, kept the Confederacy going to the end.

"Runaway inflation" occurred as the Southern presses ground out the poorly backed treasury notes, totaling in all about $1,000,000,000. The Confederate paper dollar finally sank to the point where it was worth only 1.6 cents when Lee surrendered. The extent to which the Southern currency melted away in the pockets of its holder was the extent to which that citizen·was taxed in this way by his government. Tens of millions of dollars were thus filched quietly from Confederate wallets.

"Shoddy" Millionaires

Wartime prosperity in the North seemed little short of miraculous. The marvel is that a divided nation could fight a bloody and costly conflict for four long years and then emerge more prosperous than ever before. It is true that the early months after secession, with the stoppage of cotton imports and other dislocations, brought temporary depression. But the clouds soon gave way to the sunshine of military orders and war-born civilian prosperity.

Industry boomed. New factories, sheltered by the friendly umbrella of the new protective tariffs, mushroomed forth over the face of the land. Soaring prices, resulting from inflation, unfortunately pinched the day laborer and the white-collar worker. But the manufacturers and businessmen raked in glittering profits.

The Civil War gave birth to a millionaire class for the first time in our history, though a few men of extreme wealth could have been found earlier. Many of these newly rich were noisy, gaudy, brassy, and given to

NIGHTMARE OF A WAR PROFITEER
A dead soldier forces on him the same poisonous food and drink with which he supplied the army. *Vanity Fair,* 1861

extravagant living. Their emergence merely illustrates the truth that some gluttony and greed always mar the devotion and self-sacrifice called forth by war. The story of speculators and peculators was roughly the same in both camps. But graft was more pronounced in the North than in the South, partly because there was more to steal.

Yankee "sharpness" appeared at its worst. Dishonest agents, putting profits above patriotism, palmed off aged and blind horses on government purchasers. Unscrupulous Northern manufacturers provided shoes with cardboard soles, and fast-disintegrating uniforms of reprocessed or "shoddy" wool, rather than virgin wool. Hence the reproachful term "shoddy millionaires." One profiteer reluctantly admitted that his profits were "painfully large."

Newly invented labor-saving machinery enabled the North to expand economically, even though the cream of its manpower was being drained off to the fighting front. The sewing machine wrought wonders in fabricating uniforms and military footwear. The clattering mechanical reaper, which numbered about 250,000 by 1865, proved hardly less potent than thundering guns. It not only released tens of thousands of farm boys for the army but fed them while there. It produced vast surpluses of grain which, when sent abroad, helped dethrone King Cotton. It provided profits with which the North was able to buy munitions and other mountains of supplies from England and Europe. It contributed to the bursting prosperity of the North—a prosperity that enabled the Union to weather the tempestuous war years with flying colors.

Other industries were humming at the same time. The discovery of petroleum gushers in 1859 had led to a rush of "Fifty-Niners" to Pennsylvania. The result was the birth of a new industry, with its "petroleum plutocracy" and "coal oil Johnnies." Dauntless pioneers continued to tramp westward all during the war, and altogether an estimated 300,000 souls pushed out toward the sunset. The principal magnets were gold nuggets and also free lands under the Homestead Act of 1862. Strong propellants were the federal draft agents. The only major Northern industry to suffer a crippling setback was the maritime carrying trade, which fell prey to the destructive *Alabama* and her sister raiders.

A Crushed Cotton Kingdom

Dismally different was the picture in the South, which had fought itself into complete exhaustion. The suffocation caused by the blockade, combined with the destruction inflicted by invading Yankees, took a terrible toll. Transportation collapsed. The South was even driven to the economic cannibalism of pulling up rails from the less-used lines to repair the more vital ones. Window weights were melted down into bullets; gourds replaced dishes; pins became so scarce that if a neighbor borrowed one he was urged to return it.

To the hideous end, the South revealed magnificent resourcefulness and spirit: The women buoyed up their menfolk, many of whom had seen enough of war at first hand to be heartily sick of it. A proposal was made by a number of ladies that they cut off their long hair and sell it abroad. But the scheme was not adopted, partly because of the difficulty of exporting their tresses through the blockade.

The Northern Captains of Industry had conquered the Southern Lords of the Manor. A crippled cotton South left the capitalistic North free to have its own way, with high tariffs and other benefits. Industrial giants of the North, ushering in the full-fledged Industrial Revolution, were destined to secure increasing dominance over American economic and political life. Hitherto the agrarian slavocracy of the South, by seeking sectional alliances, had acted as something of a brake on the rising industrial plutocracy of the North. Now prostrate cotton capitalism had lost out to Northern industrial capitalism. The South of 1865 was rich in little but cripples, war heroes, ruins, and memories.

Liberty in Wartime

"Honest Abe" Lincoln, when inaugurated President, laid his hand on the Bible and swore a solemn oath to uphold the Constitution. Then, driven by sheer necessity, he proceeded to tear a few holes in that hallowed document. He sagely concluded that if he did not do so, and patch the parchment later, there might not be a Constitution of a *united* United States to mend. The "Rail Splitter" was no hairsplitter.

But such infractions of the Constitution were not, in retrospect, unduly alarming. Congress, as is often true in time of crisis, generally accepted or confirmed the President's questionable acts. Lincoln, who was accused of being a "Simple Susan Tyrant," did not believe that his iron-handed authority would continue, once the nation was preserved. As he pointedly remarked in 1863, a man suffering from "temporary illness" would not persist in feeding on bitter medicines for "the remainder of his healthful life."

Congress was not in session when war erupted, so Lincoln energetically gathered the reins into his own hands. Brushing aside serious legal objections, he boldly proclaimed a blockade. His action was later upheld by the Supreme Court. He arbitrarily increased the size of the federal army—something that Congress alone is authorized to do under the Constitution (see Art. I, Sec. VIII, para. 12). Congress subsequently approved. Lincoln directed the Secretary of the Treasury to advance $2,000,-000 without appropriation or security to three private citizens for military purposes—a grave irregularity contrary to the Constitution (see Art. I, Sec. IX, para. 7). He suspended the precious writ of habeas corpus, so that anti-Unionists might be summarily arrested. In taking this drastic course, he flew in the face of a ruling by the Chief Justice of the Supreme

Court that habeas corpus could be set aside only by authorization of Congress, as provided in the Constitution (see Art. I, Sec. IX, para. 2). Nearly two years later, in 1863, Congress acquiesced in the suspension.

The Lincoln government was also guilty of many other highhanded acts. For example, it arranged for "supervised" voting in the Border States. There the intimidated citizen, holding a colored ballot indicating his party preference, was forced to march between two lines of armed troops. The federal officials also ordered the suspension of certain newspapers and the arrest of their editors on grounds of obstructing the war.

Jefferson Davis was less able than Lincoln to exercise arbitrary power, mainly because of confirmed states'-righters who revealed an intense spirit of localism. To the very end of the conflict the owners of horse-drawn vans in Petersburg, Virginia, prevented the joining of the incoming and outgoing tracks of a militarily vital railroad. The South seemed willing to lose the war before it would surrender local rights—and it did.

The Curse of Copperheadism

Hundreds of plain Northern citizens were arrested by the military authorities, chiefly on charges of hindering the Union cause by preaching defeatism or peace-at-any-price-ism. Many of the victims were seized without a formal warrant, and were held for prolonged periods without trial, as in Czarist Russia. A large percentage of the persons thus abused were so-called "Copperhead" Democrats. The Copperheads were partisans who obstructed the war effort by disloyal talk—or worse—and they were named after the poisonous copperhead snake, which strikes without warning rattle.

The most notorious case of autocratic arrest involved a prominent Copperhead, Clement L. Vallandigham. This tempestuous character was an Ohio ex-Congressman who possessed brilliant oratorical gifts and unusual trouble-making powers. A pro-Southern peace-at-any-price man, he publicly demanded an end to the "wicked and cruel" war. The civil courts in Ohio were open, and legally he should have been tried in them. But he was convicted by a military tribunal in 1863 for his allegedly treasonable utterances, and was then sentenced to prison. Lincoln decided that if Vallandigham liked the Confederates so much, he ought to be banished to their lines. This was done.

Vallandigham was not so easily silenced. Working his way to Canada, he ran for the governorship of Ohio on foreign soil, and polled a substantial but insufficient vote. He returned to his own state before the war ended, and although he defied "King Lincoln" and spat upon a military decree, he was not further prosecuted. The strange case of Vallandigham inspired Edward Everett Hale to write his moving story, *The Man without a Country* (1863), which was immensely popular in the North and which helped stimulate patriotic devotion to the Union.

THE COPPERHEAD PARTY, IN FAVOR OF A VIGOROUS
PROSECUTION OF PEACE
Harper's Weekly, 1863

Considering the hatreds aroused, civil liberties and constitutional rights emerged rather well. Some of the power usurped by the Chief Executive was retained, but most of it was gradually restored to the courts and Congress after arms were grounded. Wartime penalties on the whole were mild, and pardons were speedy. Tens of thousands of unterrified and unmolested Copperhead Democrats openly and savagely denounced Lincoln as "the Illinois Ape," demanded a cessation of the war, discouraged enlistments, and encouraged desertions. There were simply not enough jails to hold all the malcontents.

Politics as Usual

Political problems in the North added immeasurably to Lincoln's already overflowing cup of woe. Conniving factions within his own party, distrusting his ability, sought to tie his hands. Conspicuous among these critics was the group led by the overambitious Secretary of the Treasury Chase. The master stroke of the anti-Lincoln Republicans was the creation of the meddlesome Congressional Committee on the Conduct of the War, which snooped about and stirred up much more trouble than it smoothed over. The extreme abolitionists, in addition, clamored for an immediate freeing of the slaves, regardless of the political and military consequences.

Most dangerous of all were the Northern Democrats. They were badly tainted by association with the seceded Southern Democrats, who had departed with most of the brains of the party. A tragedy befell the Democrats—and the Union—when their gifted leader, Stephen A. Douglas, died of typhoid fever in the first year of the war. Inflexibly devoted to the Union, he probably could have led much of his following into the quiet paths of loyalty.

Lacking a Moses, the Democrats became badly divided. A large group of so-called War Democrats patriotically supported the Lincoln administration, but tens of thousands of Peace Democrats and regular Democrats did not. Many of the dissenters were outright Copperheads. They ranged all the way from those who wished the South Godspeed to those who favored a restored Union—but one restored by negotiation, not war.

The precarious authority of Lincoln was dependent on his retaining Republican control of Congress. His majority was menaced by the Copperheads, who were especially strong in Ohio, Indiana, and Illinois, all of which contained many Southerners. Only with extreme difficulty did the war governors of these states manage to keep them cooperating with the Union.

Keeping the Same Horse

Presidential elections in the United States come by the calendar and not by the crisis. The election of 1864 fell most inopportunely in the midst of Civil War.

The Republican Party, fearing defeat, executed a clever maneuver. Joining with the War Democrats, it proclaimed itself to be the Union Party. Thus the Republican Party passed temporarily out of existence.

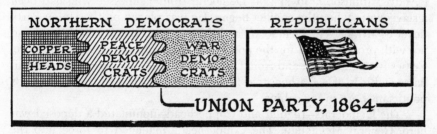

Lincoln's renomination at first encountered surprisingly strong opposition. Hostile factions whipped up considerable agitation to shelve homely "Old Abe" in favor of the handsome Secretary of the Treasury, Salmon P. Chase. Lincoln was accused of having shown a lack of force; of being overready to compromise; of not having won the war; and of having shocked many sensitive souls by his ill-timed jokes. ("Prince of Jesters," one journal called him.) But the "ditch Lincoln" move collapsed, and the President was nominated by the Union Party without serious dissent.

AN ANTI-LINCOLN CARTOON

Columbia: "Where are my 15,000 sons—murdered at Fredericksburg?"
Lincoln: "This reminds me of a little joke—"
Columbia: "Go tell your joke at Springfield!"

Lincoln cowers behind a burlesqued general. At the right is Secretary of War Stanton, whose department is represented as staging daily a theatrical performance entitled "Onward to Richmond." *Harper's Weekly,* 1863

Lincoln's vice-presidential running mate was ex-tailor Andrew ("Andy") Johnson, a loyal War Democrat from Tennessee who had been a slaveowner when the conflict began. He was placed on the Union Party ticket to attract War Democrats and the voters in the Border States, and not with proper regard for the possibility that Lincoln might die in office. Critics from the South and from Copperhead ranks condemned the candidates as birds of a feather: two ignorant, third-rate, boorish, backwoods politicians born in log cabins.

The Democrats—regular and Copperhead—nominated a deposed war hero, General McClellan. The Copperheads managed to force into the Democratic platform a plank denouncing the prosecution of the war as a failure. But "Little Mac," who could not otherwise have faced his old comrades-in-arms, repudiated this defeatist declaration.

The ensuing campaign was noisy and heated. The Democrats cried, "Old Abe removed McClellan. We'll now remove Old Abe." They also sang, "Mac Will Win the Union Back." The Union Party men shouted for "Uncle Abe and Andy," and urged, "Vote as you shot." Their most effective slogan, growing out of a homespun remark by Lincoln, was: "Don't swap horses in the middle of the stream."

Lincoln's re-election was at first gravely in doubt. The war was going badly for the administration, as "Butcher" Grant continued to be bogged down in the Wilderness of Virginia. Lincoln himself gave way to despondency, believing that political defeat was certain. The anti-Lincoln Republicans, taking heart, started a new movement to "dump" Lincoln in favor of someone else.

But the atmosphere of gloom was changed electrically, as balloting day neared, by a succession of Northern victories. General Sherman seized Atlanta. General ("Little Phil") Sheridan laid waste the Shenandoah Valley of Virginia so thoroughly that in his words "a crow could not fly over it without carrying his rations with him." Admiral Farragut captured Mobile, Alabama, after defiantly exclaiming, "Damn the torpedoes! Go ahead."

"Old Abe" pulled through, but nothing more than necessary was left to chance. At election time many Northern soldiers were furloughed home to give their support to Lincoln. One Pennsylvania veteran voted forty-nine times—once for himself and once for each absent member of his company. Other warriors were permitted to cast their ballots at the front. Lincoln, who could have won anyhow without the "bayonet vote," vanquished McClellan by 212 electoral votes to 21, with the loss of only Kentucky, Delaware, and New Jersey. But "Little Mac" ran a much closer race than the electoral count indicates. He netted a surprising 45% of the popular vote, 1,805,237 to Lincoln's 2,213,665, running up particularly large minorities in the Southerner-infiltrated states of the Old Northwest, in New York, and in his native state of Pennsylvania.

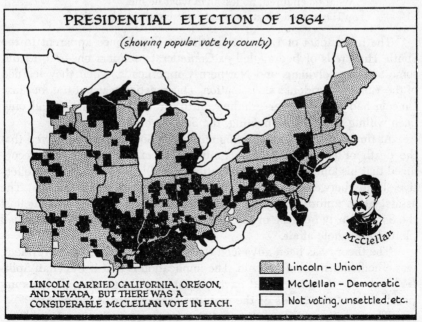

PRESIDENTIAL ELECTION OF 1864

(showing popular vote by county)

McClellan

LINCOLN CARRIED CALIFORNIA, OREGON, AND NEVADA, BUT THERE WAS A CONSIDERABLE McCLELLAN VOTE IN EACH.

Lincoln - Union
McClellan - Democratic
Not voting, unsettled, etc.

One of the most crushing defeats suffered by the South was the defeat of the Northern Democrats at the polls in 1864. The removal of Lincoln was the last real hope of a Confederate victory, and the Southern soldiers would wishfully shout, "Hurrah for McClellan!" When "Old Abe" triumphed, desertions from the sinking Southern ship increased sharply.

The Martyrdom of Lincoln

On the night of April 14, 1865 (Good Friday), only five days after Lee's surrender, Ford's Theater in Washington witnessed its most sensational drama. A half-crazed, fanatically pro-Southern actor, John Wilkes Booth, slipped behind Lincoln as he sat in his box and shot him in the head. After lying unconscious all night, the Great Emancipator died the following morning. "Now he belongs to the ages," remarked the once-critical Secretary Stanton—the finest thing he ever said.

Lincoln expired in the arms of victory, at the very peak of his fame. From the standpoint of his reputation, his death could not have been better timed if he had hired the assassin. A large number of his countrymen had not suspected his greatness, and many others had even doubted his ability. But his dramatic death helped erase the memory of his shortcomings, and caused his fine qualities to stand out in clearer relief. A contemporary, J. T. Trowbridge, lamented:

> Heroic soul, in homely garb half-hid,
>   Sincere, sagacious, melancholy, quaint;
> What he endured, no less than what he did,
>   Has reared his monument, and crowned him saint.

The full impact of Lincoln's death was not at once apparent to the South. Hundreds of bedraggled ex-Confederate soldiers cheered, as did some Southern civilians and Northern Copperheads, when they learned of the Yankee President's assassination. This reaction was natural, because Lincoln had kept the war grinding on to the bitter end. If he had only been willing to stop the shooting, the South would have won.

As time wore on, an increasing number of Southerners perceived that the death of Lincoln was a calamity for them. Belatedly, they recognized that his kindliness and moderation would have been the most effective shields between them and vindictive treatment by the victors. The assassination unfortunately increased the bitterness in the North against the South, partly because of the fantastic rumor that Jefferson Davis had plotted the whole affair.

The theory has been advanced that Andrew Johnson, now President, was crucified instead of Lincoln. The implication is that if the "Rail Splitter" had only lived he would have run into serious trouble, perhaps impeachment, at the hands of the embittered members of his party.

The crucifixion theory does not stand up under scrutiny. Lincoln no doubt would have become involved in friction with Congress; in fact, he had already found himself in some hot water. The legislative branch normally struggles to win back the power that has been wrested from it by the executive in time of crisis. But it seems unlikely that the sure-footed and experienced Lincoln would have blundered into the same quicksands that proved fatal to Johnson. Lincoln was a victorious President; and there is no arguing with victory. Enjoying battle-tested powers of leadership, he possessed in full measure tact, sweet reasonableness, and an uncommon amount of common sense. Andrew Johnson, hot-tempered and impetuous, lacked most of these qualities.

The tragic murder of Lincoln at Ford's Theater set the stage for the more terrible tragedy of reconstruction.

Ashes and Rubble

The Civil War took a grisly toll in lives. Over 600,000 men died in action or of disease, and in all over a million were killed or seriously wounded. The South, to its lasting hurt, lost the cream of its young manhood. In addition, tens of thousands of babies went unborn because potential fathers were at the front.

The monetary cost of the conflict was about $15,000,000,000. But this colossal figure does not include continuing expenses, such as pensions and interest on the national debt. The intangible costs—dislocations, disunities, wasted energies, blasted lives, bitter memories, and burning hates—cannot be calculated.

The greatest constitutional decision of the century, in a sense, was handed down at Appomattox Court House, where Lee surrendered. The champions of extreme states' rights were crushed. The national government, rewelded in the fiery furnace of war, emerged unshaken. Nullification and secession, those twin nightmares of previous decades, were laid to rest.

The Civil War was the supreme test of American democracy. It answered the question, in the words of Lincoln at Gettysburg, whether a nation dedicated to such principles "can long endure." The preservation of democratic ideals, though not an announced war aim, was subconsciously one of the major objectives of the North.

The triumph of Union arms also gave a tremendous uplift to the champions of democracy and liberalism the world over. It was not purely coincidental that the great English Reform Bill of 1867, under which Britain became a true political democracy, was passed two years after the Civil War ended. American democracy had proved itself, and this success was an additional argument used by the disfranchised British masses in securing similar blessings for themselves.

The "Lost Cause" of the South was lost, but few Americans today would argue that the end result was not for the best. America was again united physically, though for a time still divided spiritually by the passions of war. The shameful cancer of slavery was cut away, and the status of free labor was improved by the removal of servile competition. Grave dangers were averted, including constant friction and conflict between North and South, each bristling with guns. A strong and united nation was left free to fulfill its destiny as the overshadowingly powerful republic of the hemisphere—and ultimately of the world.

SELECT READINGS

See the references for the previous chapter, especially those by Randall and Nevins. The best one-volume biography is B. P. THOMAS, *Abraham Lincoln* (1952); see also R. H. LUTHIN, *The Real Abraham Lincoln* (1960). A multi-volume, anecdotal work by a famed poet is CARL SANDBURG, *Abraham Lincoln* (6 vols., 1926–1939) [paperback in 3 vols.]. For social conditions see A. C. COLE, *The Irrepressible Conflict, 1850–1865* (1934); E. D. FITE, *Social and Industrial Conditions in the North* (1910); and MARGARET LEECH, *Reveille in Washington* (1941) [paperback], a Pulitzer-prize portrait of the capital. The common soldier is described in B. I. WILEY, *The Life of Johnny Reb* (1943) and *The Life of Billy Yank* (1952) [both paperback]. See also his *The Plain People of the Confederacy* (1943) [paperback]. Lincoln's problems are analyzed in T. H. WILLIAMS, *Lincoln and the Radicals* (1941) [paperback]; R. N. CURRENT, *The Lincoln Nobody Knows* (1958) [paperback]; DAVID DONALD, *Lincoln Reconsidered* (1956) [paperback]; B. P. THOMAS and H. M. HYMAN, *Stanton* (1962); and J. G. RANDALL, *Constitutional Problems under Lincoln* (rev. ed., 1951) [paperback]. The Negro is treated in BENJAMIN QUARLES, *Lincoln and the Negro* (1962) and D. T. CORNISH, *The Sable Arm: Negro Troops in the Union Army* (1956). F. L. KLEMENT, *The Copperheads in the Middle West* (1960) is the latest book on the subject; see also WOOD GRAY, *The Hidden Civil War* (1942) [paperback]. On the Confederacy see E. M. COULTER, *The Confederate States of America* (1950); C. P. ROLAND, *The Confederacy* (1960) [paperback]. On diplomacy consult F. L. OWSLEY's revised *King Cotton Diplomacy* (1959); HENRY BLUMENTHAL, *A Reappraisal of Franco-American Relations, 1830–1871* (1959); and M. B. DUBERMAN, *Charles Francis Adams* (1961). See also DAVID DONALD, ed., *Why the North Won the Civil War* (1960) [paperback]; and EDMUND WILSON, *Patriotic Gore: Studies in the Literature of the American Civil War* (1962). Also *Harvard Guide*, Pt. IV.

24

The Ordeal of Reconstruction

With malice toward none, with charity for all, with firmness in the right as God gives us to see the right, let us strive on to finish the work we are in, to bind up the nation's wounds, to care for him who shall have borne the battle and for his widow and orphan, to do all which may achieve and cherish a just and lasting peace among ourselves and with all nations.

ABRAHAM LINCOLN, Second Inaugural, March 4, 1865

The Dawn of Peace

STAGGERING problems confronted the American people, North and South, when the guns grew cold. About a million and a half warriors in blue and gray had to be demobilized, readjusted to civilian life, and reabsorbed by the war-deranged economy. Civil government likewise had to be put back on a peacetime basis, and cleansed of encroachments by the military men.

The desperate plight of the South has eclipsed the fact that reconstruction had to be undertaken also in the North, though less spectacularly. War-inflated industries had to be deflated to a peace footing; factories had to be retooled for civilian needs.

Oppressive financial problems also loomed large in the North, now that the piper had to be paid. The national debt had shot up from a modest $65,000,000 in 1860 to nearly $3,000,000,000 in 1865—a colossal sum for those days but one not beyond the capacity of a prudent government to pay. At the same time, irksome war taxes had to be reduced to less burdensome levels.

The physical devastation inflicted by invading armies, chiefly in the South and Border States, had to be repaired. This herculean task was ultimately completed, but with discouraging slowness. The moral devastation, most evident in greed and loose living, took longer to mend because it was deeper-rooted and harder to see.

Other weighty questions clamored for answers. What was to be done with the 3,500,000 Negro slaves suddenly being plunged into the cold bath of freedom? Were the seceded states to be brought back into the Union on the old basis, and if so, with or without punishment?

459

What of the captured Confederate ringleaders? During the war a popular song had been "Hang Jeff Davis to a Sour Apple Tree," and even innocent children had lisped it. Davis was temporarily clapped into irons during the early days of his two-year imprisonment. But he and his fellow "conspirators" were finally released, partly because the chances were good that no Virginia jury would convict them. All "rebel" leaders were finally pardoned by President Johnson as a Christmas present in 1868.

Foreign Foes

Alarming disputes in the diplomatic arena likewise pressed for attention. Most immediately ominous was the presence of a strong French army in Mexico. There, behind the confusion of the American Civil War, Napoleon III had enthroned an Austrian tool, the Archduke Maximilian, on the ruins of a crushed republic—all in flagrant violation of the Monroe Doctrine.

The North, so long as it was convulsed by Civil War, pursued a walk-on-eggs policy toward France. But when the shooting stopped, Secretary of State Seward, speaking with the authority of nearly a million bayonets, turned on the pressure. By 1867 Napoleon realized that his costly gamble was doomed. He reluctantly took French leave of his ill-starred puppet, who crumpled ingloriously before a Mexican firing squad. The once-flouted Monroe Doctrine emerged with new laurels.

Poisonously embittered relations with England were less easily handled. Northerners nursed vengeful memories of British sympathy for the Confederates, as highlighted by the *Alabama* and other British-built "pirates." American anger was also directed at Canada, where, despite the vigilance of British authorities, Southern agents had been active in plotting to burn Northern cities. In one Confederate raid into Vermont, three banks were plundered and one American citizen was killed.

Hatred of England was especially venomous among the Irish-Americans, many of them Civil War veterans, who sought to help the cause of "ould Oireland" by striking north. They raised several tiny "armies," each consisting of a few hundred green-shirted men, and launched invasions of Canada, notably in 1866 and 1870. The Canadians directed harsh words at the United States government for permitting such unneutrality. But the administration was hampered by the prevalence of too much anti-British feeling, and by the presence of too many Irish voters.

American resentments toward Canada were such that, curiously enough, two great nations emerged from the fiery furnace of the American Civil War. One was a reunited United States; the other was a united Canada. The act establishing the Dominion of Canada was passed by the British Parliament in 1867, two years after Lee had surrendered. It was partly designed to bolster the Canadians, both politically and spiritually, against the prospective vengeance of the United States.

The Prostrate South

Dismal indeed was the picture presented by the war-tortured South when the rattle of musketry died. Not only had an age perished but a civilization had collapsed, in both its economic and its social structure. The moonlight-and-magnolia Old South of ante-bellum days had gone with the wind.

Handsome cities of yesteryear, like Charleston and Richmond, were gutted and weed-choked. An Atlantan returned to his once-fair home town and remarked, "Hell has laid her egg, and right here it hatched."

The skeleton hand of war had everywhere left its searing mark on social institutions. Churches were battered and dilapidated. The educational system was disrupted, with countless schools destroyed, many teachers killed in battle, and endowments wiped out. Sherman's Yankee invaders had reputedly stabled their horses in the dormitories of the University of South Carolina.

Economic life had creaked to a halt. Banks and business houses had locked their doors, ruined by galloping inflation. Factories were smokeless, silent, dismantled. The transportation system had broken down almost completely. Before the war, five different railroad lines had converged on Columbia, South Carolina; now the nearest connected track was twenty-nine miles away. Efforts to untwist the rails corkscrewed by Sherman's "bummers" were pathetically unsatisfactory.

Agriculture—the economic lifeblood of the South—was almost hopelessly crippled. Once-white cotton fields now yielded a lush harvest of green weeds. Seed was scarce, livestock had been driven off by the plundering Yankees, and the footloose Negro labor supply had taken to the highways and byways. Heart-rending instances were reported of white men hitching themselves to plows, while women or children gripped the handles. Not until 1870 did the seceded states produce as large a cotton crop as that of the fateful year 1860.

"How Are the Mighty Fallen!"

The planter aristocrats were virtually ruined by the war. Reduced to proud poverty, they were confronted with damaged or burned mansions, lost investments, and semi-worthless land. In addition, their slaves, once worth about $2,000,000,000, had been completely freed in one of the costliest confiscations of history. Some of the whites were assisted by the pitiful savings of their former slaves; a few peddled pies or took in washings. Women and children, some of them reared in the lap of luxury, were found begging from door to door.

Several thousand of the former "cotton lords" were unable to face up to their overpowering burdens. They departed for the Far West, or for such places as Mexico and Brazil, where their children gradually became

Mexicanized or Brazilianized. A few desperate Southerners sought escape in suicide, including the distinguished Virginia soil expert, Edmund Ruffin, who ironically had fired one of the first shots at Fort Sumter.

But most of the impoverished planters labored courageously to restore the glory that had once been the South. General Robert E. Lee, for example, accepted the presidency of Washington College in Virginia—later Washington and Lee—and became a highly respected educator.

THE RE-UNITED STATES
This English cartoon reflects typical
sympathy for the South. *Punch,* 1865

The loss of the aristocrats was in some degree the gain of the common folk. The poorest of the poor whites, not having had much to begin with, stood to gain from change—and some of them did. As the once-rich abandoned their broad ancestral estates, a number of small farms became available. A kind of curious economic leveling took place, with the rich leveled down and some of the poor leveled up. But many dreary years were to pass before the general economic well-being of the South equaled that of 1860.

High-spirited Southerners, especially the women, were at heart unwilling to acknowledge defeat. Having fought gallantly, they felt that they had not been beaten but had worn themselves out beating the North. Many of them, mourning the triumph of brute strength over righteousness, believed that they had won a moral victory. To them the struggle, though a "Lost Cause," was still a just war. They were conscious of no crime, and still believed that their view of secession was correct. A song widely sung in the South during the post-war years revealed no love for the Union:

> I'm glad I fought agin her, I only wish we'd won,
> And I ain't axed any pardon for anything I've done.

The continued defiance of the Southerners was disquieting. It revealed itself in references to "damyankees" and to "your government" instead of "our government." The bishop of one Southern diocese even refused to pray for President Andrew Johnson, though the latter was in sore need of divine guidance. The Southerners would have avoided much misery if they had only realized that no great rebellion has ever ended with the victors sitting down to a love feast with the vanquished.

The Year of Jubilee

The average ex-slave, freed by the war and the 13th Amendment, was to a degree childlike. Life under the lash had unfortunately left him immature—socially, politically, emotionally. To turn him loose upon the cold world was like opening the door of an orphanage and telling the children they were free to go where they liked and do as they wished. One of the cruelest calamities ever to be visited upon the much-abused Negro was jerking him overnight from bondage to freedom, without any intermediate preparation or safeguards.

Most of the Negroes were bewildered and unsettled by their new status. A goodly number of the more faithful remained on the old plantation, still addressing their former owner as "massa." But tens of thousands blithely took off to enjoy their newly found freedom; and common expressions were "free as a bird" and "free as a fool." Many freedmen no doubt were propelled by the understandable fear that they might be re-enslaved, as indeed large numbers in effect were.

The inexperience of the ex-slaves unfortunately left them exposed to the schemes of greedy whites. A "grapevine" rumor had spread among the Negroes that on a given day the Washington government would present each family with "forty acres and a mule." The freedmen sang:

> De massa run, ha! ha!
> De darky stay, ho! ho!
> It must be now dat de kingdom am a-comin'
> And de year of jubalo.

White swindlers would sell for five dollars a set of red, white, and blue pegs, with which the trusting Negro had only to stake out his acreage. He was quickly and sadly disillusioned.

The fancy-free ex-slaves were undoubtedly a problem, especially in those areas where they outnumbered the whites two to one or even ten to one. They stole food in their hunger, and got drunk, as did shiftless whites, on pilfered liquor. Other stalwart Negroes, many of whom had served in the Union armies, would jostle the whites off the sidewalks into the gutter, as whites had done to them.

The luckless Negro was in some ways a menace to himself. Once a slave to the white man, he was now a slave to hunger and cold and disease. Countless tens of thousands of friendless and rootless souls perished, especially children. The heart-rending sequel suggests that the abolitionists, in clamoring for overnight emancipation without some guidance, had conferred a dubious boon on the bondsmen.

"Black Codes" in the "Black Belt"

The Freedmen's Bureau, organized in 1865 by the War Department, was designed as a crutch to help the Negro over the rough places. Its primary functions were to feed, adjust, and educate the former slave. Many Negroes had a passion for learning, partly because they wanted to close the gap between themselves and the whites, and partly because they longed to read the Word of God. In three years the Freedmen's Bureau taught an estimated 200,000 colored folk the elements of reading. In one elementary class in North Carolina there sat four generations of the same family, ranging from a six-year-old tot to the seventy-five-year-old grandmother.

The Freedmen's Bureau, though doing much commendable work in its early career, proved to be a feeble prop indeed. It gradually became the tool of the ultra-partisan Republicans in the North, and hence fell into deep disfavor among Southern whites.

Readjusting the Negro also meant inducing him to work as a wage laborer. He was inclined, all too often, to regard freedom from bondage as freedom from work. The crushed Cotton Kingdom could not rise from its weeds until the fields were once more put under the plow and hoe. This goal could not be attained without a dependable labor supply, which the now-restless Negro was not providing. He would work a few days for wages, and then run off to squander his newly acquired "fortune." There was serious talk in the South of using large numbers of Chinese coolies, and several hundred were actually imported.

The so-called "Black Codes" were the answer of the white legislatures in the South to the problem of a stable laboring force. The pre-Civil War laws governing enslaved Negroes were no longer binding, and substitute statutes had to be enacted. The new codes were naturally more liberal than the old ones, but they were not liberal enough in the eyes of Northern anti-slaveryites and many forward-looking Southerners.

Some of the "Black Codes" were undeniably too severe. They provided that if the Negro "jumped" his labor contract, he would forfeit his back wages. Other codes stipulated that if he ran off, mileage costs would be paid the white Negro-catchers who dragged him back. In Mississippi, for example, the captured Negro would be fined and then hired out to pay off his fine—an arrangement that strongly suggested the return of pre-war slavery.

An even broader purpose lay behind the "Black Codes." They were designed to protect the Negro from his own irresponsibility, and to protect the whites from the Negroes. It is significant that the codes were generally harshest where the "black belt" was blackest—that is, where the ex-slaves outnumbered their ex-masters most heavily.

Yet any whitewashing of the "Black Codes" could not conceal one ugly fact. The sponsors of at least some of them had in mind restoring, as nearly as possible, the old slave system in a different guise. This objective was partially achieved as tens of thousands of impoverished Negroes slipped into the status of share-crop farmers, as did many of the former landowning whites. The whole luckless group gradually sank into a debtor's morass of virtual peonage, and remained there for generations to come.

The "Black Codes" naturally left a painful impression in the North. This was notably true in former anti-slavery centers, where the Southern restrictions were painted in even darker hues than they warranted. If the Negroes were being re-enslaved, men asked one another, had not the Boys in Blue spilled their blood in vain? Had the North really won the war?

The Tailor President

Few Presidents have ever been faced with a more perplexing sea of troubles than that which confronted Andrew Johnson. What manner of man was this medium-built, black-eyed, black-haired Tennessean, now Chief Executive by grace of the bullet that had killed Abraham Lincoln?

No citizen, not even Lincoln himself, had ever reached the White House from humbler beginnings. Born to impoverished parents in North Carolina, and early orphaned, Johnson never attended school for a day in his life, but was apprenticed to a tailor at age ten. Ambitious to get ahead, he taught himself to read, and later his wife taught him to write and do simple arithmetic. A self-made man, he was inclined to overpraise his maker.

"Andy" Johnson early became identified with politics in Tennessee, to which he had moved when seventeen years old. He developed into an impassioned champion of the poor whites against the well-born planter aristocrats, although he himself owned a few slaves. He excelled as a rough-and-tumble stump speaker before angry and heckling crowds, among whom on occasion he could hear a pistol being cocked. Elected to Congress, he attracted much favorable attention in the North, but not the South, when he refused to secede with his own state. After Tennessee was "redeemed" by Union armies, he was appointed war governor, and served with marked success.

The finger of destiny now pointed to Johnson for the Vice-Presidency. Lincoln's Union Party in 1864 needed to attract support from the War Democrats and other pro-Southern elements, and Johnson, a Democrat, seemed to be the ideal man. Unfortunately, he appeared on the inauguration platform the following March in a scandalous condition. He had recently been afflicted with typhoid fever, and although he was not a drinking man, he was urged by his friends to take a stiff bracer of whiskey. This he did—with disgraceful results.

"Old Andy" Johnson was unquestionably a man of parts—unpolished parts. He was intelligent, able, forceful, and gifted with homespun honesty. Steadfastly devoted to duty and to the people, he was an ardent champion of states' rights and the Constitution. He would often present copies of the hallowed document to visitors.

Yet the man who had raised himself from the tailor's bench to the President's chair was a misfit. A Southerner who did not understand the North, a Democrat who had never been accepted by the Republicans, a President who had never been elected President, he was not at home in the Republican fold. Hotheaded, contentious, and stubborn, he was a diamond in the rough. A reconstruction policy devised by the angels might well have failed in his tactless hands.

Johnsonian Justice

Johnson got off on the right foot, as far as his popularity with vengeful Northerners was concerned. Upon Lincoln's death, his hatred of the planter aristocrats again flared up, and he threatened to reconstruct the South with fire and hemp.

Loud applause burst from Republicans, especially the Radical or dominant wing of the party. These were the extremists who had condemned Lincoln's go-slow abolition policy, and they were determined to reconstruct the South radically—that is, with a rod of iron. Many Radicals had in mind safeguarding the rights of the Negro; others had been corrupted by a lust for power and punishment. Some of them had even been secretly pleased when the assassin's bullet removed Lincoln from their path, for the martyred President had shown a sweet reasonableness toward the South. The small-bore and spiteful "Andy" Johnson would presumably be a pliant tool in their hands.

But time and responsibility sobered Johnson, and within a few weeks he adopted what was essentially Lincoln's "rose-water" ten-percent plan. Lincoln had decreed in 1863 that, as a first step, a group of voters equal to one-tenth of the 1860 voting population of any Southern state must consent to take the oath of allegiance to the United States. The next step would be the organization of a new state government under a constitution which formally accepted the abolition of slavery. Lincoln would then recognize the purified new regime.

Several reconquered Southern states, taking advantage of Lincoln's lenient ten-percent plan, had reorganized their governments by 1864. But Congress flatly refused to seat their duly elected representatives, as it had a perfect right to do. The more merciless Radical Republicans, though by no means all Republicans, were determined that the South should suffer more severe penance for its sins.

The plan adopted by Johnson in 1865 closely resembled Lincoln's ten-percent plan, and in some respects was even more generous. It disfranchised certain leading Confederates, including those with taxable property worth more than $20,000, but it permitted the other whites to reorganize their own state governments. Special conventions were to be summoned in the individual states. These assemblages would repeal the ordinances of secession, repudiate all Confederate debts, and ratify the slave-freeing 13th Amendment.

Radicals in the Saddle

In the second half of 1865, the new Southern state governments were rapidly organized under the "soft" Lincoln-Johnson plan. Elections were duly held for Senators and Representatives in Congress. When that body convened in December, 1865, a considerable number of distinguished Southern members were on hand to claim their seats.

The appearance of these ex-rebels was an understandable but costly blunder. The voters of the South, seeking their ablest representatives, had turned instinctively to experienced statesmen. But, unhappily, most of the outstanding leaders of the Southern states had been "tainted" by active association with the "Lost Cause." Among the delegations elected to Congress were four former Confederate generals, five colonels, six Cabinet officers, and many members of the Richmond Congress. Worst of all, there was wispy but brainy Alexander Stephens, former Vice-President of the Confederacy, still under indictment for treason.

The presence of all these "whitewashed rebels" infuriated the Radical Republicans in Congress. The war had been fought to restore the Union, but the Radicals now saw that they could promote their own ends by postponing that restoration. During the conflict the Republicans in Congress had enjoyed a relatively free hand after the South had seceded, and they were eager to retain this advantage. Therefore, on December 4, 1865, the first day of the session, they banged shut the door in the faces of the newly elected Southern delegations.

The Republicans, looking to the future, were alarmed to note that a restored South would be stronger than ever in Congress. Before the war a Negro had counted as three-fifths of a man in apportioning Congressional representation. Now he was five-fifths of a man. Eleven Southern states had seceded; they had lost the war; and now they were entitled to twelve more votes in Congress than they had previously enjoyed. Thirty of their votes were based on Negroes who as yet could not cast a ballot. The old adage was evidently being reversed to read, "To the *vanquished* belong the spoils." Again the question was raised in the North: Who won the war?

The Radicals had good reason to fear that ultimately they would be ejected from the seats of the mighty. The Southerners might join hands with the ex-Copperheads and discontented farmers of the North and West, and then win control of Congress. If this happened, they could destroy the industrial and financial foundations of the Republican Party, which had entrenched itself deeply behind the smoke screen of the Civil War. Specifically, the Southerners might lower the high war tariffs, overthrow monopoly, repeal the Homestead Act, and curtail the lavish grants of land to the railroads. The ex-Confederates might even go so far as to repudiate the national debt and re-enslave the Negro. These last two possibilities, though remote, struck fear into the hearts of Republican bondholders and ex-abolitionists alike.

The Radical Republicans, in their efforts to avert these calamities, had one ace in the hole—the Negro vote. If they could give the ballot to the docile ex-slave and induce him to do their bidding, they would hold a powerful hand. They probably could cancel out the efforts of the Southerners to unite with the numerous Northern agrarians to destroy the Republican strangle hold in Washington.

Republican agitation for Negro suffrage was prompted by both idealistic and selfish motives. Idealists like Senator Charles Sumner were striving not only for Negro freedom but for racial equality. These ardent reformers believed that the ex-bondsman should have the ballot for protection against the whites, and for the development of his own civic responsibility as well. But less idealistic Radical Republicans—how numerous one cannot say—were plainly more interested in the welfare of the party than in that of the Negro. They would "Republicanize" the South by making the freedman their tool; they would rule or ruin.

Johnson's Clash with Congress

On what terms should the seceded states now be readmitted, if at all? Lincoln had wisely sought a union of hearts rather than a union by force. He had argued—and Johnson agreed—that the Southern states had never legally withdrawn from the Union. Their formal restoration would therefore be relatively simple. But the Radical Republicans insisted that the seceders had forfeited all their rights, and could be readmitted only on such conditions as Congress in its wisdom should lay down.

The most powerful Radical Republican was Representative Thaddeus Stevens of Pennsylvania, then seventy-four years old. He was a curious figure, with a protruding lower lip, a heavy black wig on a bald head, and a deformed foot. A devoted friend of the Negro, he had defended runaway slaves without fee and had insisted on ultimate burial in a Negro cemetery. His hatred of the South, already violent, had been further intensified when Confederate cavalry raiders pillaged and burned his Pennsylvania ironworks. He even talked wildly at times of exterminating the ex-Confederates, and of handing their estates over to the Negroes as compensation for unpaid sweat.

When Congress convened for its fateful session in December, 1865, the Radical Republicans were prepared to call the tune. Led by the zealous Stevens, a masterly parliamentarian with a razor-sharp mind and withering blasts of sarcasm, they not only denied the Southern members seats, but promptly set up the Joint (House-Senate) Committee on Reconstruction. The clubfooted Pennsylvanian, as chairman of the House contingent, was the most influential member of this inner group of fifteen. Cracking the whip relentlessly from his driver's seat, he became, as much as any one man, virtual ruler of the nation for more than a year.

A clash between the high-riding Radicals and the lenient-minded Johnson was inevitable. It came in February, 1866, when the President successfully vetoed a bill (later repassed) to extend the life of the Freedmen's Bureau. He regarded the measure, with arguable justification, as an unconstitutional invasion of the rights of the Southern states.

This Republican cartoon shows Johnson knocking Negroes out of the Freedmen's Bureau by his veto. Thomas Nast in *Harper's Weekly*, 1866

But the Radicals quickly fired back. In March, 1866, they passed the Civil Rights Bill, which conferred on the Negroes the boon of American citizenship and also struck at the "Black Codes." Johnson resolutely vetoed this objectionable measure on constitutional grounds, but in April the Radicals in Congress steam-rollered it over his veto— something that they repeatedly did henceforth. The helpless President, dubbed "Sir Veto" and "Andy Veto," was reduced to a partial figurehead as Congress assumed the dominant role in running the government. One critic called Johnson "the dead dog of the White House."

The Radicals now undertook to rivet the principles of the Civil Rights Bill into the Constitution as the 14th Amendment. They feared that the Southerners might one day win control of Congress and repeal the hated law. The proposed amendment, which was approved by Congress and sent to the states in June, 1866, was sweeping. It (1) conferred civil rights—but not the vote—on the Negro; (2) reduced proportionately the representation of a state in Congress and in the Electoral College if it denied the Negro the ballot; (3) disqualified from federal and state office ex-Confederates who as officeholders had once taken an oath "to support the Constitution of the United States"; and (4) guaranteed the federal debt, while repudiating all Confederate debts. (See text of 14th Amendment in Appendix.)

Principal Reconstruction Plans			
1864–1865	1865–1866	1866–1867	1867–1877
Lincoln's ten-percent plan	Johnson's version of ten-percent plan	Congressional plan: ten-percent plan plus 14th Amendment	Congressional plan of military reconstruction: 14th Amendment plus Negro suffrage, later established nationwide by 15th Amendment

Thus the scheme of the Radicals was roughly the broad 14th Amendment superimposed upon the lenient Lincoln-Johnson ten-percent plan. All things considered, these terms were not intolerably severe, though highly objectionable to the still-unrepentant Southerners. Negro suffrage was not yet forced on them, but they would be shorn of considerable political power if they did not adopt it voluntarily.

Swinging around the Circle

As the humid summer of 1866 slipped into autumn, the battle was squarely joined between the Radical Congress and the President. The burning issue was whether Southern reconstruction was to be carried out with the drastic 14th Amendment or without it.

The crucial Congressional elections of 1866—more important than most presidential elections—were fast approaching. Grim-visaged President Johnson was naturally eager to escape from the clutch of the Radical Congress by securing a majority favorable to his "soft" policy. Invited to be present in Chicago at the dedication of a monument to Stephen A. Douglas, he decided to speak at various cities en route in support of his views.

The famous "Swing around the Circle"—August 28 to September 15, 1866—was an oratorical comedy of errors. Johnson, his ire aroused, delivered a series of "give 'em hell" speeches, in which he accused the Radicals in Congress of having planned anti-Negro riots and murder in the South. As he spoke, hecklers would hurl insults at him. Reverting to his tree-stump speaking days in Tennessee, he would shout back angry retorts, amid cries of "You be damned" and "Don't get mad, Andy." The dignity of the presidential office sank to a new low, as the old charges of drunkenness were unfairly revived.

As a vote-getter, Johnson was eminently successful—for the opposition. His inept speechmaking heightened the cry, "Stand by Congress" against the "Tailor of the Potomac." When the ballots were all counted in the fall of 1866, the Radicals had rolled up more than a two-thirds majority in both Houses of Congress. Yet the outcome did not necessarily mean that the country favored Radical reconstruction. In many Congressional districts the voters had to choose between an ex-Copperhead and a Radical, and wry-facedly they chose the latter.

The setback at the polls merely widened the gap between the vindictive Radicals and the unrepentant Southerners. If Johnson had been farsighted, he would have urged the Southern states to accept the 14th Amendment as the best possible terms they could get. But he encouraged them not to do so. They probably needed no prompting, for all of the "sin-

THE RECONSTRUCTION DOSE

This Republican cartoon shows Johnson as a bad boy urging the South to reject the medicine with which Dr. Congress, backed up by Mrs. Columbia, is trying to restore her health. *Frank Leslie's Illustrated Newspaper*, 1867

ful eleven," except Tennessee, defiantly spurned the 14th Amendment. Their spirit was reflected in the Southern song previously quoted:

And I don't want no pardon for what I was or am,
I won't be reconstructed and I don't give a damn.

Reconstruction by the Sword

The new Radical Congress now felt fully justified in imposing on the South the Military Reconstruction Act of March 2, 1867, supplemented by three other measures. The controversial new legislation swept away the Southern state governments, which had been reorganized under Johnson's auspices. It set up five military districts, each commanded by a Union general and policed by thousands of blue-clad soldiers. More than that, the Radical restrictions, reinforced by the new state constitutions to be drawn up under federal supervision, disfranchised additional tens of thousands of Southern white leaders.

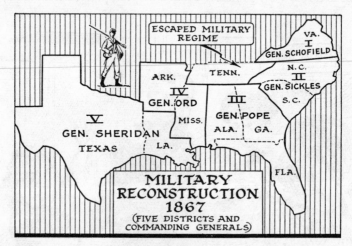

Stringent conditions were laid down for the readmission of the seceded states. The wayward sisters were required to ratify the 14th Amendment, thus giving the ex-slave full rights as a citizen. But the bitterest pill of all to white Southerners was that they were forced to guarantee in their state constitutions full suffrage for their former slaves.

The Radical Republicans were so intent on Negro suffrage that they left nothing to chance. The danger loomed that once the unrepentant states were readmitted, they would amend their constitutions so as to withdraw the ballot from the Negro. The only ironclad safeguard was to incorporate Negro suffrage in the federal Constitution. This goal was finally achieved, three years after the Military Reconstruction Act of 1867, by the 15th Amendment. Passed by Congress in 1869, it was ratified by enough states in 1870. (For text, see Appendix.)

An expression of Republican rejoicing over prospective Negro suffrage and the disfranchisement of ex-Confederates. Thomas Nast in *Harper's Weekly*, 1867

The drastic military reconstruction of the South, launched in 1867, was probably unconstitutional. The Radicals not only usurped certain functions of the President as commander-in-chief, but they set up a highly questionable martial regime. The Supreme Court had already ruled, in the case of *Ex parte Milligan* (1866), that military tribunals could not properly try civilians, even during wartime, in areas where the civil courts were open. Peacetime military rule, which involved an arbitrary suppression of newspapers, was obviously contrary to the whole spirit of our constitutional system.

The Radicals, having shackled the President, even succeeded in browbeating the Supreme Court. The learned justices, no doubt fearing that their own powers were in jeopardy, carefully avoided giving offense to the Radical Congress. They even refused, on technicalities, to assert themselves when they might have intervened. But public sentiment in the North gradually turned against the arrogant Radicals. The Supreme Court took heart from this changing atmosphere, and beginning in 1876 it stamped the brand of unconstitutionality on a number of the Congressional reconstruction laws. But by this time—nine years after the first Military Reconstruction Act—the damage had been done.

Beginning with 1867, and under the stern eye of bayonet-bearing Union soldiers, new state governments had meanwhile been set up in the South. They promptly fell under the control of "scalawags" and "carpetbaggers," who in turn used the Negroes as political tools. The "scalawags" were Southerners, sometimes able Southern Unionists, who were regarded as renegades by the ex-Confederates and who collaborated in creating the new regime. The "carpetbaggers" were mainly Northern adventurers and fortune seekers, who could supposedly pack all their worldly goods into a single carpetbag. Though many of these "damn Yankees" were offensive to the South, a kinder feeling was shown toward carpetbaggers who came down with some capital, a willingness to work, and a capacity to "mind their own business."

Prodded into line by federal officials, the Southern states got on with the distasteful task of constitution making. By 1870 all of them had reorganized their governments and had been accorded full rights. The hated "Blue Bellies" were withdrawn from a state only when the new Radical regime seemed to be firmly entrenched. Finally, in 1877, ten years after the long nightmare of military reconstruction had begun, the last federal bayonets departed.

Southern Reconstruction by State

State	Readmitted to representation in Congress	Home rule (Democratic regime) re-established	Comments
Tenn.	July 24, 1866		Ratified 14th Amendment in 1866, and hence avoided Military Reconstruction.*
Ark.	June 22, 1868	1874	
N.C.	June 25, 1868	1870	
Ala.	June 25, 1868	1874	
Fla.	June 25, 1868	1877	
La.	June 25, 1868	1877	Federal troops withdrawn in 1877, as result of Hayes-Tilden electoral bargain.
S.C.	June 25, 1868	1876	Ditto
Va.	Jan. 26, 1870	1869	
Miss.	Feb. 23, 1870	1876	
Texas	Mar. 30, 1870	1874	
Ga.	[June 25, 1868] July 15, 1870	1872	Readmitted June 25, 1868, but returned to military control after expulsion of Negroes from legislature.

* Until the 1940's, Tennessee was the only state of the secession to observe Lincoln's birthday as a legal holiday.

Enfranchised Freedmen

The sudden thrusting of the ballot into the hands of the ex-slaves, between 1867 and 1870, set the stage for stark tragedy. As might have been foreseen, it was a blunder hardly less serious than thrusting over-night freedom upon them. Wholesale liberation was probably unavoid-able, given the feverish conditions created by war. But wholesale suffrage was avoidable, except insofar as the Radicals found it necessary for their own ends, both selfish and idealistic.

The bewildered Negroes were poorly prepared for their new respon-sibilities as citizens and voters. Democracy is a delicate mechanism, which requires education and information. Yet about nine-tenths of the 700,000 adult Negro males were illiterate. When registering, many did not know their ages; and boys of sixteen signed the rolls. Some of these voters could not even give their last name, if indeed they had any. Bob, Quash, Christmas, Scipio, Nebuchadnezzar would take any surname that popped into their heads, often that of "massa." Sometimes they chose more wisely than they knew. On the voting lists of Charleston, South Carolina, there were forty-six George Washingtons and sixty-three Abraham Lincolns.

The tale would be amusing were it not so pathetic and tragic. After the Negroes were told to come in for registration, many appeared with boxes or baskets, thinking that registration was some new kind of food or drink. Others would mark their ballots and then carefully deposit them in mail boxes.

While these pitiable practices were going on, thousands of the ablest Southern whites were being denied the vote, either by act of Congress or by the new state constitutions. At one dinner in South Carolina, the com-pany consisted of a distinguished group of ex-governors, ex-Congressmen, and ex-judges. The only voter in the room was the Negro who served the meal. In some localities, about half the eligible white voters were tempo-rarily disfranchised, and at one time the Negro voters in five Southern states outnumbered the white voters, many of whom were also illiterate.

By glaring contrast most of the Northern states, before the ratification of the 15th Amendment in 1870, withheld the ballot from their tiny Ne-gro minority. Southerners naturally concluded that the Radicals were hypocritical in insisting that the Negro in the South be allowed to vote. One prominent North Carolinian jibed:

> To every Southern river shall Negro suffrage come,
> But not to fair New England, for that's too close to hum.

Gradual suffrage for qualified Negroes would have been far better for all concerned than hasty, wholesale suffrage. Presidents Lincoln and Johnson had both sagely advised such a course. They would have granted the ballot only to those ex-slaves who—through education, property ownership, or soldier-service—had indicated that they could wear the mantle of American citizenship worthily (unlike many illiterate whites).

The Republicans made haste too fast. The South might have accepted some kind of gradual Negro suffrage with fair grace. But the Radicals, seeking continued power, brushed aside the long-range welfare of the colored people. The Negro could well have prayed for deliverance from his so-called friends. The outcome was bad for the ex-slaves, for the white Southerners, and for the Republicans. Large-scale Negro voting in the South was jeopardized, once the federal troops had marched away, and within another generation it had virtually disappeared.

Enthroned Ignorance

Some of the new Southern legislatures created in 1867–1870, not unlike some Northern legislatures, presented bizarre scenes. They were dominated by newly arrived carpetbaggers, despised scalawags, and pliant Negroes. Some of the ex-bondsmen were remarkably well educated, but many others were illiterate. In a few of the states the colored legislators constituted a strong minority. In once-haughty South Carolina, the tally stood at 88 Negroes to 67 whites; and ex-slaves held offices ranging from speaker to doorkeeper. Negroes who had been raising cotton under the lash of the overseer were now raising points of order under the gavel of the speaker. As a Negro song ran:

> De bottom rail's on de top
> And we's gwine to keep it dar.

Greatly to their credit, these Negro-white legislatures passed much desirable legislation and introduced many overdue reforms. In some states a better tax system was created, state charities were established, public works were launched, property rights were guaranteed to women, and free public schools were encouraged—for Negroes as well as whites. Some of these reforms were so welcome that they were retained, along with the more enlightened state constitutions, when the Southern whites finally strong-armed their way back into control.

But the good legislation, unhappily, was often obscured by a carnival of corruption and misrule. Graft and theft ran wild, especially in states like South Carolina and Louisiana, where designing whites used naïve Negroes as catspaws. The worst black-and-tan legislatures purchased, under "legislative supplies," such items as hams, perfumes, suspenders, bonnets, corsets, champagne, and a coffin. One "thrifty" carpetbag governor in a single year "saved" $100,000 from a salary of $8000.

The public debt of the Southern states doubled and trebled, as irresponsible carpetbag legislatures voted appropriations and bond issues with lighthearted abandon. Burdensome taxes were passed in Mississippi, where some 6,000,000 acres were sold for delinquent taxes. The disfranchised and propertied whites had to stagger along under a tax burden that sometimes rose ten or fifteenfold. (This was but another glaring instance of taxation without representation.) When the whites at length regained control of these governments, they repudiated over $100,000,000 of the indebtedness that they regarded as improperly incurred. But before the war many of the Southern states were undertaxed, judged by Northern standards, and the slaves, now citizens, required education and other expensive social services.

One should also note that during this hectic era corruption was also rampant in the North, among Republicans as well as Democrats. The notorious Tweed Ring of New York City probably stole more millions, though with greater sophistication, than the worst of the carpetbag legislatures combined. And when the Southern whites regained the whip hand, graft by no means disappeared under Democratic auspices.

The Rule of Night Riders

Goaded to desperation, once-decent Southern whites resorted to savage measures against Negro-carpetbag control. A number of secret organizations blossomed forth, the most notorious of which was the Ku Klux Klan, founded in Tennessee in 1866. Besheeted night riders, their horses' hoofs muffled, would hammer on the cabin door of a politically ambitious Negro. In ghoulish tones one thirsty horseman would demand a bucket of water, pour it into a rubber attachment under pretense of drinking,

A VICTIM OF THE KU KLUX KLAN
From an anonymous pamphlet of 1872

smack his lips, and declare that this was the first water he had tasted since he was killed at the battle of Shiloh. If fright did not produce the desired effect, force was employed.

Such tomfoolery and terror proved partially effective. Many Negroes and carpetbaggers, quick to take a hint, were scared away from the polls. But those stubborn souls who persisted in their forward ways were flogged, mutilated, or even murdered. In one Louisiana parish in 1868, the whites in two days killed or wounded two hundred victims; a pile of twenty-five bodies was found half-buried in the woods. By such atrocious practices was the Negro "kept in his place." The Klan, whose original purposes were partly subverted, unfortunately became a refuge for numerous bandits and cutthroats. Any scoundrel could don a sheet.

Radicals in Congress, outraged by this night-riding lawlessness, passed the iron-toothed Force Acts of 1870 and 1871. Federal troops were able to stamp out much of the "lash law," but by this time the "Invisible Empire" had already done its work of intimidation. Many of the outlawed groups continued their tactics in the guise of "dancing clubs" or "missionary societies," though the net effect of all the hooded terrorists has probably been exaggerated. Economic reprisals were often more effective.

The shortsighted attempts of the Radicals to exploit the ex-slave as a voter backfired badly. The white South, for many decades, openly and defiantly flouted the 14th and 15th Amendments. Large-scale disfranchisement of the Negro, starting conspicuously about 1890, was achieved by intimidation, fraud, and trickery. Among various underhanded schemes were the literacy tests, unfairly administered by whites to the advantage of illiterate whites. In the eyes of otherwise honorable Southerners, the goal of White Supremacy fully justified dishonorable devices.

Johnson on Trial

The Radicals meanwhile had been sharpening their hatchets for President Johnson. Annoyed by the opposition of the "drunken tailor" in the White House, they falsely accused him of maintaining there a harem of "dissolute women." Not content with curbing his authority, they decided to remove him altogether by constitutional processes.* Under existing law the president pro tempore of the Senate, the unscrupulous and rabidly Radical "Buff Ben" Wade of Ohio, would then become President of the United States.

As an initial step, the Radicals in 1867 passed the Tenure of Office Act—as usual, over Johnson's veto. Contrary to the wholesome precedent established in Washington's day, the new law required the President to seek the consent of the Senate before he could remove his appointees, once they had been approved by that body. One purpose of the Radicals was to freeze into the Cabinet the Secretary of War, Edwin M. Stanton, a holdover from the Lincoln administration. Though outwardly loyal to Johnson, he was secretly serving as a spy and informer for the Radicals. Another purpose was to goad Johnson into breaking the law, and thus establish grounds for his impeachment.

The Tenure of Office Act ran counter to the ABC's of sound govern-

* For impeachment, see Art. I, Sec. II, para. 5; Art. I, Sec. III, paras. 6, 7; Art. II, Sec. IV, Appendix.

ment. The President is responsible to the country for the conduct of his administration; and if his appointees turn out to be inefficient, disloyal, or corrupt, he should not be saddled with them for political purposes by his foes in the Senate. Johnson, believing the Tenure of Office Act to be unconstitutional, was eager to get a test case before the Supreme Court. (That eminent tribunal finally ruled indirectly in his favor fifty-eight years later, long after the grass had been growing on his grave.) Expecting reasonable judicial speed, Johnson summarily dismissed the two-faced Stanton early in 1868. The President did not believe that the law applied to Lincoln's holdovers, even though the Radicals insisted otherwise.

The Radical-dominated House of Representatives struck back swiftly. By a count of 126 to 47, it voted to impeach Johnson for "high crimes and misdemeanors," as called for by the Constitution. Most of the specific accusations grew out of the President's so-called violation of the Tenure of Office Act, which later proved to be based on unconstitutional principles.

Justice Triumphant

The Radical-led Senate, with obvious zeal, now sat as a court to try Johnson on the trumped-up impeachment charges. The House conducted the prosecution. The trial aroused intense public interest, and with a thousand tickets printed, proved to be the biggest show of 1868. Johnson fortunately kept his dignity and sobriety, and maintained a discreet silence. His battery of attorneys was extremely able, while the House prosecutors, including oily-tongued Benjamin F. Butler and embittered Thaddeus Stevens, bungled their flimsy case.

On May 16, 1868, the day for the first voting in the Senate, the tension was electric, and heavy breathing could be heard in the galleries. By a margin of only one vote, the Radicals failed to muster the two-thirds majority for Johnson's removal. Seven independent-minded Republican Senators, courageously putting country above party, voted "not guilty." Not one of the seven was re-elected to the Senate, though this failure was not clearly related to Republican vengefulness.

The Radicals were infuriated. "The country is going to the Devil!" cried the crippled Thaddeus Stevens, as he was carried from the hall. President-to-be Wade had even sketched out his Cabinet, with the unscrupulous Benjamin F. Butler as Secretary of State. But the nation, though violently aroused, accepted the verdict with a good temper that did credit to its political maturity. In a less stable community, an armed uprising probably would have erupted against Johnson.

The outcome of the trial was a triumph for good government, and particularly for the type of government established under the Constitution. If a hostile two-thirds majority in Congress can remove the President at will, then there is a breakdown of the traditional separation of powers between the legislative and executive branches. The Radicals were evidently determined to nullify the Presidency, and possibly also the Supreme Court. Had they done so, they might have established a kind of parliamentary or Congressional dictatorship. Although they ultimately overreached themselves, their plans miscarried by the shockingly narrow margin of one vote.

Justice finally prevailed. Johnson was no doubt guilty of bad speeches, bad judgment, and bad temper. But he was hardly guilty of high crimes and misdemeanors, as envisioned by the framers of the Constitution. His only real crime was to stand stalwartly in the path of the Radicals.

The Purchase of "Walrussia"

The Johnson administration, though largely reduced to a figurehead by the Radicals, achieved its most enduring success in the field of foreign relations.

The Russians, by 1867, were in a mood to sell the vast and chilly expanse now known as Alaska. They had already overextended themselves in North America, and they saw that in the likely event of another war with England they probably would lose their defenseless province to the sea-dominant British. Alaska, moreover, had been ruthlessly "furred out" and was a growing economic liability. The Russians were therefore eager to unload their "frozen asset" on the United States, and they put out seductive feelers in Washington. They preferred us to any other purchaser, primarily because they wanted to strengthen us further as a barrier against their ancient enemy, Great Britain.

A treaty with Russia, transferring Alaska to the United States, was duly signed in Washington early in 1867. Secretary Seward, an ardent expansionist, was eager to acquire the frigid territory for the bargain price of $7,200,000. But his enthusiasm was not shared by his countrymen. The American people, still preoccupied with reconstruction and other internal problems, were economy-minded and non-expansionist.

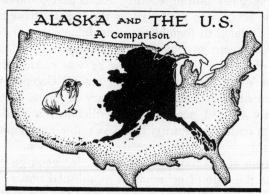

ALASKA AND THE U.S.
A comparison

Then why did Congress and the American public sanction the purchase? For one thing Russia, alone among the powers, had been conspicuously friendly to the North during the recent Civil War. We did not feel that we could offend our great and good friend, the Czar, by hurling his walrus-covered icebergs back into his face. Besides, the territory was rumored to be teeming with furs, fish, and gold, and it might yet "pan out" profitably—as it later did. So Congress and the country accepted "Seward's Polar Bear Garden," somewhat wry-facedly and derisively but nevertheless hopefully. The speculative nature of the transaction not only appealed to Yankee love of a bargain, but did something to dispel the gloom of the reconstruction era.

The Heritage of Hate

Reconstruction ranks as one of America's most tragic failures. The Republic fumbled away a splendid opportunity to close the bloody gulf between North and South. Yet such were the war-born hatreds that much of this unreason was inevitable. The nation passed through one of the most disgraceful decades of its history, as "reconstruction" took on some of the aspects of "redestruction."

The Civil War was fought openly—and on the whole honorably. When it was over, there were no wholesale blood purges. No one was executed for a purely political offense, though the foreign-born head of one Confederate prison was hanged, as were the surviving conspirators in the Lincoln assassination. Probably no large-scale and unsuccessful revolt has ever ended with so little head-rolling.

But if the victor chopped off no heads, he ground the face of his fallen foe into the dust. If the fighting was conducted cleanly, the same could not be said of the reconstructing. The noble Northern ideals of national unity and human freedom were suffocated in an orgy of hate and corruption. To many Southerners, reconstructing was a more grievous wound than the fighting itself.

The Republican Party, with its luckless Negro recruits, was indelibly blackened with the brush of reconstruction. Southern believers in White Supremacy were driven into the ranks of the Democratic Party, and the Solid South emerged—the Democratic South. The ill-prepared colored voter, duped by Radicals, had allegedly done so poorly that the South found further justification for denying him the ballot. The Negro was free, but the Negro-white problem was far from solved.

In the light of hindsight, the Radical reconstruction program was much too narrowly conceived. It could well have embraced the social and economic rehabilitation of the South, including the Negro. At a time when weed-choked Southern lands were going begging, hundreds of thousands of acres could have been made available to the ex-slave at low cost, or no cost, as Thaddeus Stevens and others had urged.

The Age of Hate—as reconstruction has been called—stirred up a vast amount of racial antagonism and intolerance. The ex-Confederate South, outraged by the Negro-carpetbag legislatures, was more determined than ever to "keep the Negro in his place," and wasted much strength in holding him there. The woes of war were bad enough, but to them were added the hates of Radical reconstruction. The result was a horrible harvest from which the nation, though tough-fibered, was long in recovering.

SELECT READINGS

Recent scholarship is richly embodied in J. G. RANDALL and DAVID DONALD, *The Civil War and Reconstruction* (1961), and also in K. M. STAMPP, *The Era of Reconstruction, 1865–1877* (1965). A popularized survey is HODDING CARTER, *The Angry Scar: The Story of Reconstruction* (1959). The plight of the Negro is stressed in J. H. FRANKLIN, *Reconstruction: After the Civil War* (1961) [paperback]. For the recent tendency to be harsh on Johnson see E. L. MC KITRICK, *Andrew Johnson and Reconstruction* (1960) [paperback]; W. R. BROCK, *An American Crisis: Congress and Reconstruction, 1865–1867* (1963); and LA WANDA and J. H. COX, *Politics, Principle, and Prejudice, 1865–1866* (1963). A still-useful older study is H. K. BEALE, *The Critical Year* [1866] (1930). Radiating pro-Southern indignation are C. G. BOWERS, *The Tragic Era* (1929) [paperback] and G. F. MILTON, *The Age of Hate* (1930). See also E. M. COULTER, *The South During Reconstruction, 1865–1877* (1947) and F. B. SIMKINS, *The South, Old and New* (1947). P. H. BUCK's Pulitzer-prize *The Road to Reunion, 1865–1900* (1937) [paperback] is comprehensive. Special studies of value are W. B. HESSELTINE, *Lincoln's Plan of Reconstruction* (1960); G. R. BENTLEY, *A History of the Freedmen's Bureau* (1955); F. W. KLINGBERG, *The Southern Claims Commission* (1955); and J. B. JAMES, *The Framing of the Fourteenth Amendment* (1956), which further challenges the theory of a big-business conspiracy. See also R. P. SHARKEY, *Money, Class and Party: An Economic Study of Civil War and Reconstruction* (1959). The Negro receives attention in J. M. MC PHERSON, *The Struggle for Equality: Abolitionists and the Negro in the Civil War and Reconstruction* (1964) and C. V. WOODWARD, *The Strange Career of Jim Crow* (1955) [paperback], which reveals Negro segregation as a late 19th-Century development. Useful biographies are FAWN M. BRODIE, *Thaddeus Stevens: Scourge of the South* (1959) and B. P. THOMAS and H. M. HYMAN, *Stanton: The Life and Times of Lincoln's Secretary of War* (1962). Also *Harvard Guide*, Pt. V.

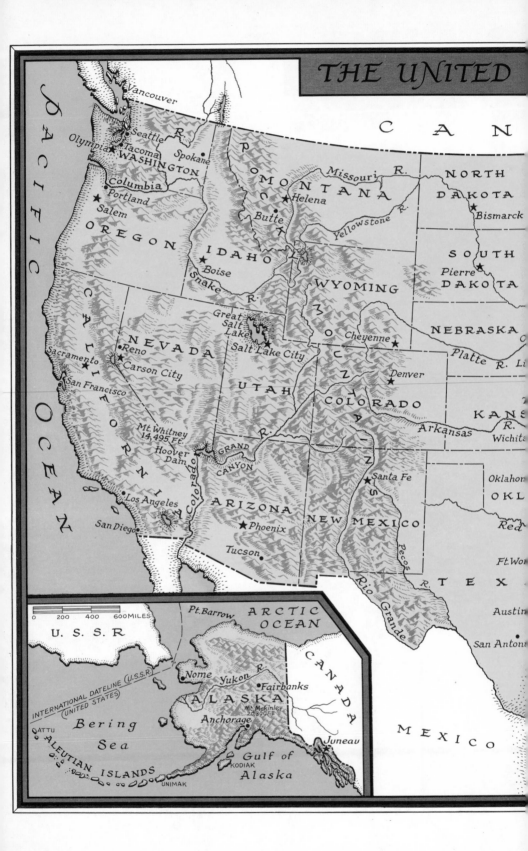

THE UNITED

C A N

PACIFIC OCEAN

Vancouver
Seattle
Olympia Tacoma
WASHINGTON
Spokane
Columbia R.
Portland
Salem
OREGON

WASHINGTON

MONTANA
Missouri R.
Helena
Butte
Yellowstone R.

NORTH DAKOTA
Bismarck

SOUTH DAKOTA
Pierre

IDAHO
Boise
Snake R.

WYOMING

NEBRASKA
Cheyenne
Platte R. Li

Great Salt Lake
Salt Lake City

NEVADA
Reno
Carson City
Sacramento
San Francisco

UTAH

COLORADO
Denver

KANSAS
Arkansas R.
Wichita

CALIFORNIA

Mt. Whitney
14,495 Ft.
Hoover Dam
GRAND CANYON

Colorado R.

Santa Fe

Oklahoma
OKL

Los Angeles
San Diego

ARIZONA
Phoenix
Tucson

NEW MEXICO

Pecos R.

Red

Ft. Wor

TEX

Rio Grande

Austin

San Anton

MEXICO

0 200 400 600 MILES

U. S. S. R.

Pt. Barrow
ARCTIC OCEAN

CANADA

INTERNATIONAL DATELINE (U.S.S.R.)
(UNITED STATES)

Nome
Yukon R.
Fairbanks
ALASKA
Mt. McKinley
20,300 FT.
Anchorage

Bering Sea

ATTU
ALEUTIAN ISLANDS
UNIMAK

Gulf of Alaska
KODIAK

Juneau

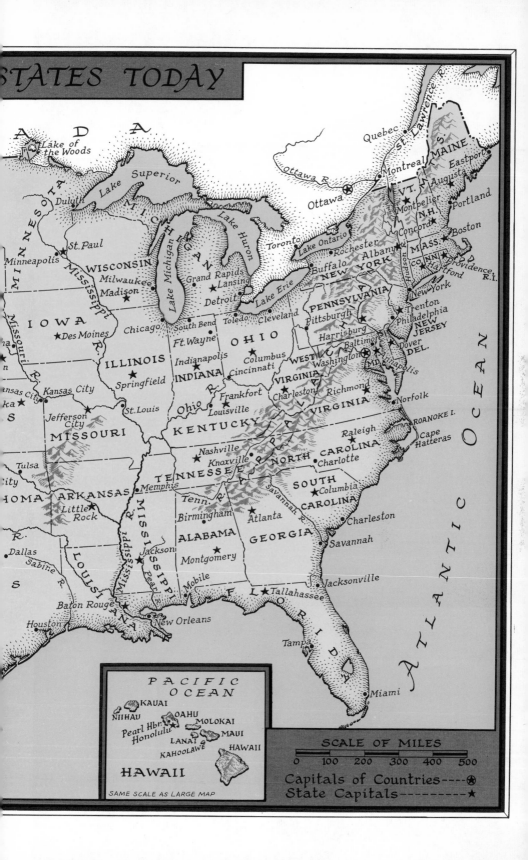

STATES TODAY

SCALE OF MILES

0   100   200   300   400   500

Capitals of Countries----⊛
State Capitals----------★

PACIFIC OCEAN

KAUAI
NIIHAU   OAHU
Pearl Hbr.   MOLOKAI
Honolulu   LANAI   MAUI
KAHOOLAWE   HAWAII

HAWAII

SAME SCALE AS LARGE MAP

Lake of the Woods
Duluth
Lake Superior
MINNESOTA
St. Paul
Minneapolis
WISCONSIN
Milwaukee
Madison
MICHIGAN
Lake Michigan
Lake Huron
Grand Rapids
Lansing
Detroit
Lake Erie
Toronto
Lake Ontario
Rochester
Buffalo
NEW YORK
Albany
Cleveland
Pittsburgh
PENNSYLVANIA
Harrisburg
Toledo
OHIO
Columbus
Cincinnati
Indianapolis
INDIANA
Ft. Wayne
South Bend
Chicago
ILLINOIS
Springfield
IOWA
Des Moines
Kansas City
Jefferson City
MISSOURI
St. Louis
Ohio R.
Frankfort
Louisville
KENTUCKY
WEST VIRGINIA
Charleston
VIRGINIA
Richmond
Norfolk
Washington
MD.
Annapolis
Baltimore
Dover DEL.
NEW JERSEY
Philadelphia
Trenton
New York
CONN. Hartford
Providence R.I.
MASS. Boston
N.H. Concord
VT. Montpelier
Portland
Augusta
MAINE
Eastport
Quebec
St. Lawrence
Montreal
Ottawa R.
Ottawa
Toronto
Nashville
Knoxville
TENNESSEE
Memphis
Tenn. R.
ARKANSAS
Little Rock
Tulsa
OKLAHOMA
Dallas
Sabine R.
LOUISIANA
Baton Rouge
New Orleans
Houston
MISSISSIPPI
Jackson
Pearl R.
Mobile
ALABAMA
Birmingham
Montgomery
GEORGIA
Atlanta
Savannah R.
Savannah
Charleston
SOUTH CAROLINA
Columbia
NORTH CAROLINA
Raleigh
Charlotte
Cape Hatteras
ROANOKE I.
FLORIDA
Tallahassee
Jacksonville
Tampa
Miami
ATLANTIC OCEAN
Missouri R.
Mississippi R.
CANADA

25

Grantism and Republican Rule, 1869–1880

The party that saved the nation must rule it.
REPUBLICAN "BLOODY SHIRT" SLOGAN, 1868

The Warrior Turns Politician

GENERAL U. S. GRANT was by far the most popular hero to emerge from the Civil War. The grateful citizens of Philadelphia, Washington, and his home town (Galena, Illinois) passed the hat around, and in each place presented him with a house. The people of New York tendered him a check for $105,000. The general, silently puffing his black cigar, accepted all these gifts with open arms, as if the Republic owed them to him for having rescued the Union. T. B. Aldrich rejoiced over

> The cloud-sent man! Was it not he
> That from the hand of adverse fate
> Snatched the white flower of victory?
> He spoke not a word, but saved the State.

Grant probably could have received the presidential nomination in 1868 from either the Democrats or the Republicans. He had not actively identified himself with any political party; his one presidential vote had been cast for the Democratic ticket in 1856. The simple-hearted soldier was totally without experience in non-military office, and he was a better judge of horseflesh than of political associates. But having skyrocketed from obscurity in the early months of the war, he was a living example of the American success story. His political naïveté was actually a point in his favor. The people were heartily weary of all the wrangling in Washington between Congress and Johnson; and the notion still prevailed that a good general was bound to make a good President. Success in civil war seemed to guarantee success in civil office.

The Republicans, now freed from the Union Party coalition of war days, were in fine fettle. Meeting in Chicago in 1868, they enthusiastically nominated Grant for the Presidency. Their anti-slavery goal, which had

483

originally brought the Republican Party into being, had been attained. But their leaders, having tasted the fleshpots of power, could find other reasons for keeping themselves in office. The Republican platform sounded a clarion call for continued reconstruction of the South with bayonets, and for honest repayment of Civil War borrowings.

Grant, who was always a man of few words, struck a highly popular note in his letter of acceptance when he said, "Let us have peace." This noble sentiment became a leading slogan of the campaign, and was later engraved on his Hudson River tomb.

The Bloody Shirt Triumphant

The Democrats, who assembled in New York City later in 1868, were torn by factions. Many of the Middle Western delegates, representing an unprosperous section, were agitated by the "money question." During the recent war thrifty citizens, both patriots and profiteers, had bought federal bonds with the depreciated paper greenbacks. Now these investors, most of them well-to-do Easterners, were clamoring to be paid back in gold. But the poorer agrarian Democrats, insisting on "the same currency for the bondholder and the plowholder," forced a "repudiation" plank into the New York platform. It baldly proclaimed "the Ohio Idea"—that is, that government obligations should be paid in greenbacks, unless otherwise stipulated. The Democrats also denounced military reconstruction of the South by the Radical Republicans.

The Middle Western Democrats got the "repudiation" platform, but the Eastern Democrats got the candidate. Deadlocked over various aspirants, they finally stampeded to the chairman of the convention, the able but reluctant Horatio Seymour. Six times governor of New York, he had become badly tarred with Copperheadism during "the late unpleasantness."

The ensuing campaign, with its parades and waving torches, was spirited. Republicans whipped up enthusiasm for Grant, "The Man Who Saved the Nation." "Waving the Bloody Shirt"—that is, reviving unpleasant memories of the Civil War—became for the first time a prominent feature of a presidential campaign.* It found expression in such slogans as "Vote As You Shot" and "Scratch a Democrat and You Will Find a Rebel." The Republicans also aimed a blast at the "rag money" greenback proposal when they shouted, "Repudiate the Repudiators."

Grant won with ease. He bagged 214 votes in the Electoral College to 80 for Seymour, and polled 3,012,833 popular votes to 2,703,249. Yet the Republicans could not take their future control "for Grant-ed," as the expression went. Even with his enormous personal popularity, the quiet

---

* The expression is said to have derived from a speech by Representative Benjamin F. Butler, who waved before the House the bloodstained nightshirt of a Klan-flogged carpetbagger.

warrior triumphed because of the many enfranchised Negroes and the many disfranchised Southerners. A majority of all whites who voted in the election appear to have supported Seymour, and three unreconstructed Southern states would almost certainly have gone for him in a completely free election.

No one could now deny the importance of the Negro voter. The simple arithmetic was that although Grant won by a majority of only 300,000 votes, an estimated 500,000 ex-slaves cast their ballots for him. This alarming evidence that the Negro vote could win an election further hardened the Radicals in their determination to continue their drastic military reconstruction. Whatever the cost, the ballot must be kept in the hands of the compliant Negroes.

The Era of Good Stealings

The population of the Republic continued to increase by giant leaps, despite the awful bloodletting of the Civil War. By 1870, the year after Grant's inauguration, the census revealed over 38,000,000 souls, a gain of 22.6% over the previous decade. We were now the third largest white nation, ranking behind Russia and France.

But the moral stature of the Republic regrettably fell far short of matching its physical stature. The war, like most wars, had bred waste, extravagance, speculation, and graft. Where so much money is thrown about with wild abandon, unscrupulous men permit a bit to stick to their fingers. A calloused public showed an appalling degree of indifference toward dishonest practices. Nothing could better illustrate the observation that a people have no better government than they deserve. The preoccupied citizenry, pursuing the gold that gushed from the new industrial age, permitted the government to fall into the hands of incompetents and crooks.

Corruption was commonplace. A scandalous number of judges and lawyers, though by no means all of them, were purchasable or otherwise untrustworthy. Foreign investors were cheated out of their savings by railroad promoters, who in one instance left the bond-buyers with only "two streaks of rust and a right of way." Unscrupulous stock-market manipulators were a cinder in the public eye. Yet in certain circles they even commanded admiration for their buccaneering tactics, which sometimes involved the hiring of armed thugs to fight pitched battles for them.

Notorious in the financial world were two millionaires, "Jubilee Jim" Fisk and Jay Gould. The corpulent Fisk—bold, impudent, unprincipled— was often seen in public with "cuddlesome women" behind a span of fast horses. He succeeded in plundering the Erie Railroad of millions. If Fisk provided the "brass," the undersized and cunning Jay Gould provided the brains of the combination. (He died leaving an estate worth $72,000,000.) One dishonest New York legislator took $75,000 from Gould's rival, and then accepted an additional $100,000 from Gould, double-crossing the low bidder. In that era a cynical but apt definition of an honest politician was one who, when bought, would stay bought.

A few skunks can pollute a large area. Although the great majority of businessmen and government officials were decent and law-abiding, the whole atmosphere was fetid. The Man in the Moon, it was said, had to hold his nose when passing over the earth. With the air so badly contaminated, it is not surprising that the gullible Grant failed to scent some of the worst evil-doing in public life.

A Novice in Politics

U. S. Grant had less training and aptitude for civilian office than perhaps any of his predecessors. A first-rate professional soldier, he turned out to be a third-rate President. Mighty economic and social changes were sweeping the country, but the newly arrived politician was blissfully unaware of their deeper currents. As a military man, he expected heel-clicking obedience to his orders. Four of his secretaries were generals; and for a time even the White House butler was a former mess sergeant.

True to his military upbringing, Grant chose his Cabinet with all the secrecy of a night assault on Richmond, not even sharing his inner thoughts with Mrs. Grant. When the choices were finally announced, the political experts were dumfounded. The Cabinet was a hodgepodge scraped together without regard for the usual political and geographical niceties. It was composed of personal acquaintances, incompetents, misfits, and money-getters, to all of whom Grant was tenaciously loyal. Having failed repeatedly in his attempts to make money, he was unduly impressed by those who had succeeded.

In naming the Cabinet, the guiding rules seem to have been three. Were you behind a house-for-Grant movement? Or a check-for-Grant movement? Or had you stood loyally behind him when he was down at the heel? Several able and high-minded men, by sheer luck, managed to land in the Cabinet, but they were soon squeezed out. The one noteworthy exception was Secretary of State Hamilton Fish, a wealthy New Yorker at whose home Grant had been wined and dined. Fish lasted almost the entire eight years, and proved, by happy accident, to be one of our ablest secretaries of state.

At the outset, Grant was mildly favorable to civil service reform. But the politicians quickly changed his feeble convictions, after plying him with expensive cigars, choice wines, and even fast horses. A congenial crowd of hangers-on frequented the White House, and these political vultures soon convinced the general that the way to virtue was through partisan Republican politics. Grant's election was a godsend to his in-laws of the Dent family, several dozen of whom ultimately attached themselves to the public payroll. A weak Civil Service Commission was authorized by Congress in 1871, but the easygoing Grant showed little energy in cooperating with it, and Congress ceased to vote it funds.

The soldier-President at first favored leniency toward the South, in the spirit of his generous terms at Appomattox. But the Radicals flocked around him; and he who had been magnanimous in war became vindictive in peace. His famous "Let us have peace" was forgotten, and the cruelest days of reconstruction ground forward under his direction.

A Carnival of Corruption

The low ethics of the Grant era are well illustrated by a fantastic scheme of "Jubilee Jim" Fisk and Jay Gould. This precious pair conceived the plot, in 1869, of cornering all the gold on the New York market and netting additional millions. Their cunning game could succeed only if the Federal Treasury would hold back its funds. The conspirators worked on Grant directly, and also through his brother-in-law, who received $25,000 for his complicity. On "Black Friday" (September 24) Fisk and Gould madly bid the price of gold skyward, while scores of honest businessmen were driven to the wall. The bubble broke when the Treasury, contrary to Grant's earlier assurances, was forced to release gold. The subsequent Congressional probe proved that the President had been stupid and indiscreet—but not crooked. Himself honest, he served as a front for much dishonesty.

Grant likewise swallowed a scheme to annex the Caribbean republic of Santo Domingo, in which American speculators were actively involved. Sincerely believing that the island would serve useful strategic purposes, he arranged in 1869 for a treaty of annexation to be submitted to the Senate. The chairman of the Senate Committee on Foreign Relations, outspoken Charles Sumner, denounced the whole plan as fraudulent and engineered its defeat. But the President, deeply angered, got revenge when he had the Senator deposed from his chairmanship.

The notorious Tweed Ring in New York City, although unrelated to Grant, mirrored his times. Burly "Boss" Tweed, 240 pounds of rascality, employed bribery, graft, and fraudulent elections to milk the metropolis of an estimated $50,000,000 to $200,000,000. He adopted the current rule: "Addition, division, and silence." The books recorded, for example, a payment of $138,000 to a plasterer for two days of labor. Honest citizens were cowed into silence. If they protested, their tax assessments were raised.

Tweed's luck finally ran out. The New York *Times* secured damning evidence in 1871 and courageously published it, though offered $5,000,000 not to do so. A gifted cartoonist, Thomas Nast, pilloried Tweed mercilessly, after spurning a heavy bribe to desist. The portly thief complained that his illiterate following could not help seeing "them damn pictures."

BOSS TWEED MANIPULATES BALLOTS
Thomas Nast in *Harper's Weekly*, 1871

A New York attorney, Samuel J. Tilden, headed the prosecution and gained fame which later paved the path to a presidential nomination. After various delays and escapes, Tweed was finally put behind bars.

Grant himself was blackened by the Crédit Mobilier scandal, even though its most nauseous aspects had developed in 1867–1868, before he took office. The Crédit Mobilier was a railroad construction company, formed by the greedy insiders of the transcontinental Union Pacific Railway. They craftily hired themselves to build the line, paying themselves, for example, $50,000 a mile for construction that cost $30,000 a mile. In one year the Crédit Mobilier paid dividends of 348%. Fearing that Congress might call a halt, the company furtively distributed some shares of its valuable stock to certain key Congressmen.

The scandal was finally exposed by a New York newspaper in 1872, and some of the worst charges were confirmed by a Congressional investigation. Two members of Congress were formally censured, and the Vice-President of the United States was shown to have accepted twenty shares of stock and some dividends. Congressman James A. Garfield, later President, was cleared after damaging but inconclusive evidence against him had been presented. The whole deplorable episode further highlighted the low moral tone of private and public life in the Reconstruction Era.

Embroilments Abroad

The exploited masses of Cuba rose in revolt against Spain in 1868, and did battle for ten smoke-filled years. Grant prematurely and blunderingly issued a proclamation recognizing their belligerency. But the level-headed Secretary Fish, striving to avoid a clash with Spain, discreetly pigeonholed the provocative document.

Serious trouble with Spain developed anyhow. In 1873 the Spaniards seized the *Virginius*, a steamer carrying arms to the rebels and flying the Stars and Stripes with dubious legality. Although the capture took place on the high seas, the Spanish officials in Cuba forthwith executed as "pirates" fifty-three of the passengers and crew, including some American citizens. A wave of anger swept the United States. Hostilities with Spain seemed unavoidable, even though our Civil War navy was decayed and worm-eaten. But Spain was finally persuaded to pay damages to the families of those executed, and a clash was averted for twenty-five years.

Friction with Britain was basically much more alarming than that with Spain. In the troubled years after the Civil War, long-standing grievances against the British continued to rankle. Nothing caused American blood pressure to mount more alarmingly than the unsettled accounts left by the *Alabama* and her sister raiders.

The Johnson administration had attempted to grapple with the prickly *Alabama* problem. In 1869 the State Department negotiated a treaty with Britain which adjusted outstanding controversies, but did so in a manner too soft-handed for American tempers. Senator Charles Sumner, by a typically violent speech, contributed to the defeat of the pact in the Senate. He not only claimed $15,000,000 in direct damages for the depredations of the *Alabamas*, but intemperately added $2,110,000,000 for certain indirect damages and for a prolongation of the war for two years —at $1,000,000,000 a year. As England would not pay this enormous sum, the plain implication was that she ought to turn Canada over to the United States.

The British were outraged by the introduction of these indirect claims, especially in such preposterous amounts. Their mood was now such that no settlement whatever was possible for more than two years.

England Eats Humble Pie

With the passage of time, the British felt increasingly troubled by their sorry role in the *Alabama* business. Fair-minded Englishmen had long been uneasy, and now even those with less tender consciences were perceiving that their government had created a reverse-twist precedent. Suppose that rebellion should again erupt in Ireland. What was to prevent the rebels, with generous gifts from Irish-Americans, from building a half-dozen swift *Alabamas* in American ports, and then wiping British merchant shipping from the seas?

After protracted negotiations, the repentant British signed the Treaty of Washington in 1871. They not only agreed to submit the *Alabama* dispute to arbitration, but they even consented to terms that would virtually forfeit their case. The five arbitrators duly appointed met in Geneva, Switzerland, and finally assessed Britain $15,500,000 for damages caused by the commerce raiders.

The Geneva Award of 1872 was a landmark in international arbitration. As such, it set a wholesome precedent. It also healed a festering sore in Anglo-American relations, which for some years thereafter continued on a happier plane. The British were particularly pleased to wipe out the dangerous precedent created by the *Alabama*. On a wall of the Foreign Office in London they hung the canceled draft for $15,500,000, as a warning to future ministries to be more careful.

The Treaty of Washington and the Geneva Award, largely the handiwork of the patient Secretary Fish, were praiseworthy accomplishments. They constituted an oasis of achievement in a desert of scandal, and they were used as persuasive arguments in behalf of Grant when he ran for a second term in 1872.

The Liberal Republican Revolt

By 1872 a powerful reformist wave was beginning to build up throughout the nation. Decent citizens were distressed by the stench of "Grantism" and by the severity of reconstruction in the South. They noted in alarm that Grant was eager to run a second time, and that the Republican spoilsmen were eager to run him again. Reform-minded citizens gradually banded together to organize the Liberal Republican Party. Voicing the slogan "Turn the Rascals Out," the reformers urged purification of the Grant administration and amnesty for the South.

The Liberal Republicans, though presented with a golden opportunity to win with a sterling candidate, muffed their chance. Their Cincinnati nominating convention, which consisted of many starry-eyed reformers and other diverse elements, fell into the hands of amateurish newspapermen and scheming politicians. This "conclave of cranks" astounded the country by nominating the querulous and erratic Horace Greeley.

Greeley was ill equipped for the Presidency, despite his tremendous reputation as editor of the New York *Tribune*. Though a fearless moral force, he was dogmatic, emotional, and notoriously unsound in his political judgments. He did not even look like a President. With a cherubic face and innocent blue eyes peering through steel-rimmed spectacles, he would amble along in a white coat and hat, clutching a green umbrella—like a character stepping from the pages of Dickens.

The Democrats, eager to beat Grant at any cost, wryly endorsed Greeley. In doing so they "ate crow" in large gulps, for the eccentric editor had long assailed them as traitors, slave whippers, saloonkeepers, horse thieves, and idiots. Yet Greeley pleased the Democrats, North and South, when he pleaded for a clasping of hands across "the bloody chasm."

GREELEY AND THE DEMOCRATS "SWALLOW" EACH OTHER
A Republican jibe at the forced alliance between these former foes.
Thomas Nast in *Harper's Weekly*, 1872

The regular Republicans, as expected, renominated Grant on a platform that made a polite bow to civil service reform. Seldom has the voter been confronted with such a devil's choice. Both candidates had made their reputations in fields other than politics, and each was eminently unqualified, by temperament and lifelong training, for high political office.

The campaign of 1872 was mud-splattered in the extreme. The Republicans, desperately waving the Bloody Shirt, demanded to know if the cause won on the battlefield should be lost at the polls. Greeley was denounced as an atheist, a communist, a free-lover, a vegetarian, a brown-bread eater, an idiot, and a co-signer of Jefferson Davis' bail bond. "Grant beat Davis—Greeley bailed him," ran the slogan. When it was all over, "Honest Old Horace," who had waged a surprisingly good campaign on the stump, wondered if he had been running for the Presidency or the penitentiary. Grant in turn was denounced as a dictator, a loafer, a swindler, an ignoramus, a drunkard, and an "utterly depraved horse jockey."

Grant's still-great personal popularity pulled him through, as the regular Republicans shouted, "Grant us another term." He was further aided by distrust of Greeley, by nationwide prosperity, by the Bloody Shirt, and by the Negro vote in the South. Greeley was so badly beaten that Grant mistakenly regarded the result as a thumping endorsement of his administration—wrongdoing and all. The count in the electoral column was 286 to 66, and in the popular column 3,597,132 to 2,834,125.

The end for Greeley was tragic. Within a month he lost his wife, the election, his job, his mind, and his life.

The Liberal Republican movement, though outwardly a failure, left enduring footprints. It frightened the Republicans into cleaning their house before they were thrown out of it. Three weeks after Greeley's nomination in 1872, the Republican Congress passed a general amnesty act, which removed political disabilities from all except five hundred ex-Confederate leaders. Many of the Liberal Republicans, though not Greeley, advocated tariff reduction, and five weeks after his nomination Congress materially reduced the high Civil War duties. The Liberal Republican clamor for civil service reform likewise helped persuade the Republicans to fumigate the Grant administration—at least partially.

American third parties have traditionally died out because their more desirable reforms have been stolen by the regular parties. This was the epitaph engraved on the tombstone of the Liberal Republicans.

Depression Doldrums

The bad repute of the Grant years was worsened by the paralyzing panic that broke in 1873, the first since 1857. The basic causes seem to have been overspeculation and overexpansion, chiefly in mining, manufacturing, railroading, and grain farming. The crash was finally precipitated in 1873 by a financial crisis in Vienna. This overseas flurry set off a disastrous chain reaction, which resulted in the recalling of loans made by Europeans to borrowers in the United States.

The economic house of cards in America collapsed with frightening rapidity. The first severe shock came with the failure of the New York banking firm of Jay Cooke & Company, headed by the fabulously rich Jay Cooke, financier of the Civil War. Boom times became gloom times as more than five thousand businesses went bankrupt; and in New York City an army of unemployed riotously battled the police.

Even before the panic descended, the greenback issue had again popped up. Strong pressure was developing in the business world to redeem in gold—"sound money"—the depreciated paper currency issued during the Civil War. On the other hand, the agrarian and debtor groups —the "cheap money" men—demanded a generous printing of more greenbacks. They argued that a sharp rise in the prices of their depressed farm products would follow an inflation of the "battle-born currency." At the same time, the debtors would be able to pay off their debts more easily, for dollars would in theory become cheaper and easier to get.

The inflationists died hard. They forced a bill through Congress in 1874 designed to expand the paper currency from $382,000,000 to a maximum of $400,000,000 in greenbacks. The "hard money" or "gold standard" advocates clamored for Grant to wield his veto. The "soft money" men insisted that he honor the will of the people as expressed in Congress. After much painful indecision, Grant vetoed the inflationary measure, thereby winning the plaudits of the gold-moneyites. Yet in the light of subsequent misfortunes it appears that some moderate inflation of the currency would have been a boon to the country. There simply was not enough to go around. From 1870 to 1880 the per capita circulation of money had actually *decreased* from $19.42 to $19.37, even though American business, on the eve of a great new industrial revolution, was beginning to require a sharp increase in the money supply. (See chart, p. 581.)

The "sound money" men also redoubled their demands for "resumption." By this they meant a resuming of the practice, abandoned early in the Civil War, of having the Treasury redeem its paper currency on demand with metallic money. In 1875 a Republican Congress finally passed a hotly debated resumption law, to become effective in 1879. Grant's name continued to be associated with sound money, though not with sound government.

Republican prospects in the Congressional elections of 1874 were not roseate. The twin burdens of panic and continued scandal proved overpowering. The electorate, in a tidal wave of resentment, swept a Democratic majority into the House of Representatives—the first since 1858.

The End of Grantism

The breath of scandal in Washington now reeked of alcohol. In 1875 the public learned that a gigantic Whiskey Ring had been robbing the Treasury of millions of dollars in internal revenue. "Let no guilty man escape," insisted the red-faced Grant. But when he discovered his private secretary among the culprits, his views speedily changed. He volunteered a written statement for the jury, with all the weight of his exalted office behind it, and the thief escaped.

The rottenness of the Grant administration was further laid bare by a half-dozen or so other sickening scandals, one of which touched the President. In 1876 the news broke that Secretary of War Belknap, married to an extravagant wife, had pocketed some $24,000 by selling the privilege of disbursing supplies—often shoddy—to the Indians. The House unanimously voted to impeach him. But Belknap went scot-free when the Senate failed to muster enough votes for conviction, largely because he had resigned and there was doubt as to senatorial jurisdiction. Grant, ever loyal to his crooked friends, saved Belknap's skin by not only accepting his resignation but doing so "with great regret."

Yet the Grant administration was not all bad. The agony of reconstruction was nearing an end, and the "bloody chasm" was being closed by amnesty. Substantial achievements were recorded in foreign affairs; the nation was expanding westward with marvelous rapidity; and industry was on the verge of experiencing a phenomenal boom. The young Republic was so big and powerful that while scandals might shame it, they could not lame it. America was like a rhinoceros bulldozing its way through a jungle, annoyed but not hampered by ticks and lice.

It is a curious fact that Grant, who put dishonest men into office, was an unconscious father of civil service reform. The scandals of his two terms goaded many citizens into action, and added to the popularity of what had once been condemned as "snivel service" reform.

The Blaine Bubble Bursts

The politicians around Grant, like fleas urging their dog to live, besought the "Old Man" to try for a third term in 1876. The general, blind to his ineptitudes, showed a disquieting willingness. But the House of Representatives, by a thumping bipartisan vote of 233 to 18, spiked the third-term boom. It passed a resolution which sternly reminded the country—and Grant—of the anti-dictator implications of the two-term tradition.

Conspicuous among the Republican hopefuls was James G. Blaine, a radiantly personable Congressman from Maine. Among other gifts, the "Magnetic Statesman" had a photographic memory for faces and names. With fine presence, flashing eyes, and a pleasing voice, he was a thrilling speaker. Strongly inclined to demagoguery, he would twist the British Lion's tail for Irish votes, and wave the Bloody Shirt for veteran votes. The fact that he himself had not heard the whine of Confederate bullets led to the jibe "Invisible in war, invincible in peace."

Blaine's candidacy was sweeping along under full sail when suddenly, in the spring of 1876, it struck a reef. The news leaked out that Blaine, as Speaker of the House in 1869, had used his influence to secure a land grant for a Southern railroad, and that he had later sought financial favors of the same company. Blaine theatrically tried to clear his skirts before the House by reading carefully selected parts of the incriminating letters. But since he would not reveal the unread portions, even at the risk of losing the presidential nomination, the conclusion seemed justified that he had been prostituting his high public office for private gain. Other damaging revelations, which bespoke an elastic conscience, came out in later years.

Few voters could doubt Blaine's energy and ability, but many did doubt his honesty and integrity. The best that can be said for him is that he had merely done what scores of other men in public life had been doing. But moral standards were now rising—and he got caught with his hand too near the cooky jar.

One of Blaine's rivals for the presidential nomination was the handsome and imperious Roscoe ("Lord Roscoe") Conkling, United States Senator from New York. He had tangled with Blaine in a Congressional debate in 1866, and Blaine had withered him into silence by referring to his "turkey gobbler strut." Cartoonists thereafter portrayed Conkling as a turkey gobbler with the curl which he affected in the middle of his forehead. But the statuesque New Yorker ultimately got sweet revenge by helping to keep Blaine out of the Presidency.

Blaine's chances for the nomination seemed excellent, despite all drawbacks, when the Republicans met in Cincinnati. The convention was swept off its feet by the orator Robert G. Ingersoll, who nominated Blaine as "the Plumed Knight." But the delegates adjourned amid rumors that it was unsafe to turn on the gas lights, and when they met the next day they were in a more sober mood. A compromise candidate was indicated.

The man finally chosen was bearded Rutherford B. Hayes, who was obscure enough to be dubbed "the Great Unknown." Though not brilliant, Hayes possessed common sense and considerable ability. As a "Grade B" war hero, he appealed to the Civil War veterans, for he had been wounded several times and had risen to the rank of major general. Thrice governor of the doubtful and electorally potent state of Ohio,* he had proved himself to be a courageous and honest administrator. To the delight of reformers, he had come out foursquare for a cleansing of the civil service. The platform on which he ran promised reform, sound money, and "permanent pacification" of the South.

Tilden's Temporary Triumph

Samuel J. Tilden, the bachelor governor of New York, received the enthusiastic nomination of the Democrats in St. Louis. Although he had made a national reputation by helping to smash the Tweed Ring, Tilden was unimpressive in appearance. Boyish-faced and smooth-shaven, he was slightly built, sickly, nervous, and weak-voiced ("Whispering Sammy"). His leadership was intellectual rather than oratorical. The Democratic platform bitterly condemned the long years of Republican scandal, and held out a glowing promise of civil service reform.

Lack of confidence in Republican honesty was offset by a keen recollection of Democratic Copperheadism during the late "rebellion." Alarmed Republicans again unfurled the frayed Bloody Shirt and shouted, "Avoid

---

* Because of its large number of electoral votes, Ohio has become "the modern mother of Presidents," supplanting Virginia. A political saying of the 1870's went:

> Some are born great,
> Some achieve greatness,
> And some are born in Ohio.

Rebel Rule," "Vote As You Shot," and "The Boys in Blue Will See It Through." They pointed with pride to Hayes' spotless record, and proclaimed, "Hurrah! For Hayes and Honest Ways!" The Democrats countered with "Turn the Rascals Out" and "Tilden and Reform."

The secretive Samuel Tilden, though hailed as a reformer, had vulnerable joints in his armor. "Slippery Sam" had formed unsavory connections with corrupt Tammany Hall; "Thrifty Sam" had allegedly dodged a large part of his income tax in 1863. In addition, he had made a fortune —he died worth $6,000,000—by working hand in glove as an attorney with Jim Fisk and other "robber barons" of the era. Yet all these accusations against Tilden were weakened by the corruption and depression of the Grant era.

As the returns poured in, Tilden apparently had swept the country. His ticket quickly picked up 184 electoral votes of the needed 185, with twenty votes in four states doubtful because of irregular returns.* Surely Tilden could pick up at least one of these, especially in view of the fact that he had polled 264,292 more popular votes than Hayes, 4,036,298 to 4,300,590.

The Republicans, though at first prepared to concede defeat, quickly rallied. They cleverly sent "visiting statesmen" to the three doubtful Southern states of Louisiana, South Carolina, and Florida, presumably "to steal the election." The Democrats, no less determined, likewise dispatched "visiting statesmen." With such skilled persuaders at work, all three of the disputed Southern states submitted two sets of returns, one

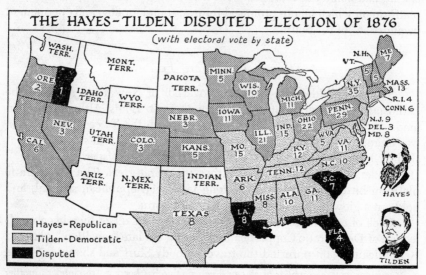

THE HAYES-TILDEN DISPUTED ELECTION OF 1876
(with electoral vote by state)

* Nineteen of these comprised the total electoral vote of Louisiana, South Carolina, and Florida. The twentieth was one of Oregon's three votes. Hayes carried Oregon, but one of its electors turned out to be ineligible because he was a federal officeholder (a postmaster), contrary to the Constitution (see Art. II, Sec. I, para. 2, Appendix).

Democratic and one Republican. The brutal truth is that both parties in these states had been guilty in some degree of irregularity, which included bribery, forgery, ballot-box stuffing, violence, and intimidation.

Dishonors Even

As the weeks drifted by, the deadlock tightened. The Constitution stipulates that the electoral returns from the states shall be sent to Congress, and in the presence of the House and Senate they shall be *opened* by the president of the Senate (see Art. XII). But who should *count* them? On this point the Constitution was silent. If counted by the president of the Senate (a Republican), the Republican returns would be selected. If counted by the Speaker of the House (a Democrat), the Democratic returns would be chosen.

Compromise or clash seemed inevitable. The danger loomed that there would be no President on March 4, 1877; and this uncertainty slowed the wheels of business. "On to Washington!" cried Democratic hotheads, and some of their armed "Minute Men" began to drill with a view to seating their "victorious" leader. Behind the scenes, the statesmen were laboring frantically, and an agreement was finally hammered out in the Henry Clay tradition—the much-underrated Compromise of 1877.

The election deadlock itself was to be broken by the Electoral Count Act, which passed Congress early in 1877. It set up an electoral commission consisting of fifteen men selected from the Senate, the House, and the Supreme Court. The fifteenth member of the commission, according to

Composition of the Electoral Commission, 1877

	Republicans	Democrats
Senate (Republican majority)	3	2
House (Democratic majority)	2	3
Supreme Court	3	2
Total	8	7

Democratic schemes, was to have been the giant-sized Justice David Davis, an independent—with Democratic leanings. But at the last moment he resigned from the Bench to go to the Senate, and the only remaining members of the Supreme Court were Republicans. A Republican rhymester chortled at the Democrats:

> They digged a pit, they digged it deep,
> They digged it for their brother;
> But through their sin they did fall in
> The pit they digged for t'other.

In February, 1877, about a month before inauguration day, the Senate and House met together in an electric atmosphere to settle the dispute. The roll of the states was tolled off alphabetically. When Florida was reached—the first of the three Southern states with two sets of returns— the disputed documents were referred to the electoral commission, which sat in a nearby chamber. After prolonged discussion the members agreed, by the strictly partisan vote of eight Republicans to seven Democrats, to accept the Republican returns. The outraged Democrats in Congress, reading the handwriting on the wall, undertook to launch a filibuster "until hell froze over."

Renewed deadlock was avoided by the rest of the Compromise of 1877, already partially concluded behind closed doors. The Democrats reluctantly agreed, in part, that Hayes might take office in return for his withdrawing federal troops from the two states in which they remained, Louisiana and South Carolina. The Republicans also promised the Democrats a substantial share of federal offices, and long-overdue federal support for internal improvements, chiefly railroads, in the impoverished South. Not all of these promises were kept in later years. But the Democrats permitted Hayes to receive the remainder of the disputed returns— all by the partisan vote of eight to seven. So close was the margin of safety that the issue was settled only three days before the new President was officially sworn in.

The outcome was a triumph for democratic government—a victory for neither candidate but for the American people. The long-exiled Democrats had been aroused almost to the point of renewed civil war. But Tilden, though regarding himself as honestly elected, acquiesced in the "steal" in order to avert an internal upheaval. Four more years of Republicanism seemed better than four more years of rebellion.

But the ugly truth is that neither party came into court with clean hands. The Republicans probably threw away enough ballots by fraud in the disputed states to rob Tilden of the election. The Southern Democrats, for their part, probably "bulldozed" enough Negroes away from the polls to deprive Hayes of the popular majority. In a sense the Democrats "stole" the election, but the Republicans "stole" it back.

Integrity on the Potomac

Rutherford B. Hayes was the only President, except possibly J. Q. Adams, to take office with a cloud on his title. He was pilloried in the press as "Old 8 to 7" and "His Fraudulency," and was cartooned with "Fraud" on his honest brow. All this cut him deeply. A man of unsullied honor and high ideals—a "Queen Victoria in breeches"—he believed himself rightfully elected. Lucy Webb Hayes, his wife and childhood sweetheart, was a kindred spirit. Family prayers were offered daily; and since both the President and Mrs. Hayes were temperance advocates, "Lemonade Lucy" served no alcohol. "The cold water administration" swept the fetid, smoke-laden atmosphere out of the White House.

Hayes began vigorously and impressively. He selected a top-flight Cabinet, and in fulfillment of his pre-election bargain, included an ex-Confederate general as Postmaster General. Several weeks after taking office, Hayes boldly withdrew the last federal troops that were supporting carpetbag governments, also in accord with the behind-the-scenes Compromise of 1877. This was an act of real courage. The President was bitterly denounced by vindictive Republicans, and especially by the carpetbaggers who craved "four more years of good stealing."

The removal of these remaining army units was epochal. It marked not only the "redemption" of the South, but the official end of political and military reconstruction. The bayonet-supported dominance of the Republicans in Louisiana and South Carolina collapsed when the last blue-clad soldiers tramped away, and the Solid Democratic South speedily solidified. If Hayes, a Union general and a Republican, could be viciously condemned for withdrawing the troops, Tilden, a non-veteran and a Democrat, probably would not have dared to take the same action at that time.

Honest Hayes—the idealist, reformer, and political purist—parted company with the blowsy spoilsmongers. He believed that public office should not be a private preserve, and that strict business principles should prevail in the conduct of governmental affairs. His inaugural address contained the refreshing declaration, "He serves his party best who serves his country best." But to his acute distress, he was unable to carry out all his noble principles. Persistent pressures finally forced him to reward with political plums a number of corrupt Southern carpetbaggers, conspicuously those who by irregular means had procured his election. He was upbraided by the reformers for having placed corruptionists in high office, and by the party hacks for not having ladled out the political gravy more generously.

Hayes enjoyed greater success in cleaning out the New York Customs House. This key agency was a hotbed of politics and a vital element in Senator Conkling's political machine. It employed some 1300 persons, who, together with blood relatives and in-laws, wielded a formidable bloc of votes. The Collector of the Port, Chester A. Arthur—later President of the United States—had become deeply involved in objectionable political activity as a henchman of Senator Conkling.

Hayes was determined to curb the spoils system in New York, while slapping at the Conkling-Grant faction. He summarily removed both Arthur and a subordinate, and forthwith nominated two replacements without consulting Conkling. The "Peacock Senator," fearing that he would lose control of the New York political machine, fought the confirmation of Hayes' nominees tooth and nail. But after a prolonged struggle, the President triumphed and was able to install his own men.

By this time Hayes was a man without a party. Denounced as "Granny" Hayes and a "Goody Two-Shoes" reformer, he was openly repudiated by the old-line politicians. He had earlier declared himself to be a single-termer, and this decision proved to be a face-saver, because he probably could not have secured renomination in any event.

The Distress of the Debtor

The Hayes era—the late 1870's—was one of alarming unrest and turbulence. The explosive atmosphere was largely a by-product of the long years of depression and deflation following the Panic of 1873. Labor disorders, flaring forth into uncontrolled violence, convulsed a number of the major Eastern cities in 1877. The paralyzing railroad strikes of that year, which verged on civil war in places like Baltimore and Pittsburgh, forced Hayes to call out the federal troops. Order was not restored until scores of rioters had been killed or injured. Neither the President nor anyone else in authority seems to have had a real appreciation of the deeper significance of changing economic currents. The new industrial age was bringing monopoly to business, injustice to labor, and depression to the farmer.

The numerous debtor groups, desperately seeking relief, grasped at the silver will-o'-the-wisp. Ably seconded by the silver producers, they were abandoning their demand for printing-press greenbacks in favor of the unlimited coinage of silver in the value ratio of sixteen ounces of silver to one of gold.

The "sacred white metal," according to its sponsors, had received a raw deal. In the early 1870's it had not been presented to the federal mints in quantity, because it commanded a higher price in the open market than the 16-to-1 ratio of the Treasury. Congress therefore had formally dropped the coinage of silver in 1873. Fate played a grim joke later in the 1870's when Western silver "strikes" shot production up and forced the price down. The miners and the debtors then belatedly began to assail the "Crime of '73," and demand a return to the "Dollar of Our Daddies," instead of the hated "rag money."

The clash over currency grew more intense. The "soft money" or "dishonest money" men indignantly demanded the free and unlimited coinage of all silver mined at the ratio of 16 to 1. The "hard money" or "sound money" advocates, for their part, scornfully demanded the coinage of none at all. A compromise was finally reached by Congress in the Bland-Allison Act of 1878, originally sponsored by Representative Richard P. ("Silver Dick") Bland of Missouri. The law provided that the Treasury, instead of coining all silver presented, would purchase from two to four million dollars' worth of bullion a month and coin it into dollars then worth only 93 cents intrinsically. Hayes, a "sound money" man, vetoed the bill. But the silverite inflationists triumphantly repassed it.

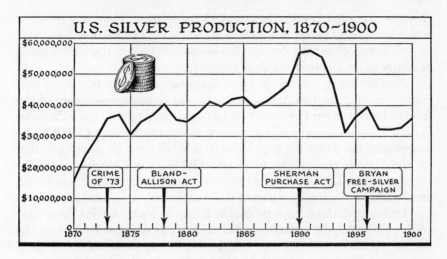

U.S. SILVER PRODUCTION, 1870–1900

$60,000,000
$50,000,000
$40,000,000
$30,000,000
$20,000,000

CRIME OF '73
BLAND–ALLISON ACT
SHERMAN PURCHASE ACT
BRYAN FREE-SILVER CAMPAIGN

$10,000,000
0
1870   1875   1880   1885   1890   1895   1900

Resumption was the other pressing financial issue of the era. The redemption of paper currency by the Treasury with metallic money was resumed on January 1, 1879, as authorized by act of Congress four years earlier. This step was finally taken despite the efforts of the "soft money" advocates to engineer a repeal. But when greenback holders found that they could get gold on demand, they kept the lighter and more convenient folding money. The credit of the government, as expected, rose sharply with this honoring of its outstanding obligations.

Foreign Friction

Economic unrest swept to California and included docile Chinese among its victims. By 1880 the Golden State could count 75,000 of these Oriental newcomers, or 9% of its entire population. In San Francisco, workingmen known as Kearneyites were violently aroused against the competition of cheap Chinese labor. Led by Denis Kearney, an Irish-born demagogue who numbered among his followers many immigrants from Erin's Isle, they cried, "Immeriky fur Immerikans, bejabers." Scores of harmless Orientals were abused in various ways, including the forcible cutting off of precious pigtails. Others were murdered outright.

Even law-abiding citizens on the Pacific Coast viewed the Chinese threat with alarm. In a catch-as-catch-can economic contest, the beef eater had no chance against the rice eater, who allegedly considered dead rats a delicacy. The present tens of thousands of coolies were regarded as a menace, the prospective millions as a calamity.

Congress finally responded to all this uproar in 1879, when it passed a bill severely restricting the influx of Chinese laborers. But Hayes, ever the man of honor, vetoed the discriminatory measure on the grounds that it flagrantly violated the existing treaty with China. Although "Missey"

Hayes was burned in effigy by outraged Californians, there was no alternative but to negotiate a new pact. This was done in 1880, and two years later Congress closed the door to Chinese coolies for a period of ten years. Subsequent laws barred the door completely.

Another hot spot developed over the prospective piercing of the isthmus connecting the two Americas. Under the dynamic leadership of the seventy-four-year-old Ferdinand de Lesseps, conqueror of the Isthmus of Suez, a French company was organized to dig the Panama Canal. Many Americans feared that the gigantic enterprise was but an entering wedge for the French government to violate the Monroe Doctrine. President Hayes, in a message to Congress in 1880, sternly warned that any future canal would be "virtually a part of the coastline of the United States."

Undaunted, the French promoters began to make the dirt fly at Panama in 1883. But the audacious undertaking was crippled by various obstacles, especially yellow fever, which swept away thousands of workers and caused de Lesseps to be dubbed "the Great Undertaker." Bankruptcy finally overwhelmed the company in 1889, amid reverberating financial scandals, and jungle vines rapidly smothered its rusting machinery. What Hayes could not prevent, nature did.

President Hayes, though not a statesman of superlative ability, has been undeservedly belittled. Opposed by his party leaders and thwarted by Democratic majorities in Congress, he was able to secure little constructive legislation. But he brought to his exalted office a high degree of patriotism, conscientiousness, and devotion to duty. He helped to make reform respectable. His signal contribution was to show that a Republican could be inflexibly honest—and also resistant to designing "friends." He not only revived faith in the integrity of his party, but restored faith—badly needed faith—in the integrity of the central government.

SELECT READINGS

The scandal-rocked Grant era is treated with brevity in J. G. RANDALL and DAVID DONALD, *The Civil War and Reconstruction* (1961) and in BRUCE CATTON, *U. S. Grant and the American Military Tradition* (1954) [paperback]. The best full-length life of Grant is W. B. HESSELTINE, *Ulysses S. Grant* (1935); see also ALLAN NEVINS' Pulitzer-prize *Hamilton Fish: The Inner History of the Grant Administration* (1936); L. D. WHITE, *The Republican Era, 1869–1901* (1958) [Pulitzer prize]; HENRY ADAMS' doleful classic *The Education of Henry Adams* (1918) [paperback]; and H. W. MORGAN, ed., *The Gilded Age* (1963) [paperback]. New light on the election of 1876 appears in C. V. WOODWARD, *Reunion and Reaction* (1951) [paperback]. Consult also HARRY BARNARD, *Rutherford B. Hayes and His America* (1954) and S. P. HIRSHON, *Farewell to the Bloody Shirt* (1962). The great strikes are described in R. V. BRUCE, *1877: Year of Violence* (1959). Also *Harvard Guide*, Pt. V.

26

Personalities, Politics, and Reform, 1880–1889

A public office is a public trust.
DEMOCRATIC CAMPAIGN SLOGAN, 1884

General Garfield vs. General Hancock

As the presidential campaign of 1880 neared, Grant's stock once more rose sharply. Republican spoilsmen, long frustrated by Hayes, pined for "four more good years of stealing." The third-term tradition, they argued, applied only to three *consecutive* terms. The "Old Man" himself had embarked upon a globe-girdling tour in 1877, during which he was royally acclaimed. But his return, wildly cheered at San Francisco in September, 1879, was prematurely timed. Enthusiasm for him had definitely waned before the conventions met in their star-spangled halls.

The stage was set for a compromise candidate when the Republicans gathered at Chicago. General Grant, quite willing to run again, was nominated by Senator Roscoe Conkling of New York. The speaker's thrilling oration began:

> And if asked what state he hails from,
> This our sole reply shall be,
> "From near Appomattox Court-house,
> With its famous apple-tree."

On the first thirty-five ballots Grant led his chief rival, the magnetic Blaine of Maine. Hopelessly deadlocked over the two aspirants, the convention finally stampeded to a dark horse, James A. Garfield of Ohio. The nominee—a tall, bearded, and broad-shouldered Congressman—had commended himself to the delegates by an eloquent speech nominating for the Presidency a fellow Ohioan, John Sherman.

Garfield enjoyed numerous assets. Born in politically potent Ohio, and in a log cabin, he had worked his way up from poverty by driving mules on the towpaths of the Ohio Canal. Later he had served brilliantly as a volunteer officer in the Civil War, and had finally risen to the rank of major general.

503

The crestfallen pro-Grant spoilsmen emerged from the convention with some slight consolation. The delegates chose for the Vice-Presidency Senator Conkling's close political henchman, Chester A. Arthur of New York, an amiable and impressively large man with ornate sideburns. The platform, generously draped in the folds of the Bloody Shirt, came out emphatically for the protective tariff, and somewhat feebly for civil service reform. One blunt Republican delegate from Texas blurted out, "What are we here for, except the offices?"

The Democrats, still wrathful over having been robbed of the Presidency in 1876, declared in their Chicago platform that the "great fraud" overshadowed all other issues. But decrepit "Old Sammy" Tilden, four years older than in 1876, declined to run again.

The cheering Democratic delegates then turned to the tall and handsome General Winfield S. Hancock—"Hancock the Superb." The nominee was a West Pointer who had served with brilliance in the Civil War, especially at Gettysburg, where he was wounded. His nomination refuted the common charge that only Republican officers had fought for the North; and he was popular in the South, where he had fair-mindedly headed one of the military reconstruction districts. The Democratic platform declared for civil service reform and a "tariff for revenue only."

The Republicans Squeeze Through

Old issues were expiring and new ones were shunned like leprosy by the politicians, who were reluctant to alienate votes. The Republicans deliberately turned their backs on deepening economic and social injustices, and strove desperately to wring another President from the Bloody Shirt by refighting the Civil War and re-emancipating the Negro. Eugene Field sneered at would-be Democratic reformers:

> Out on reformers such as these;
> By Freedom's sacred powers,
> We'll run the country as we please;
> We saved it, and it's ours.

Actually, the Southern issue was a relatively minor one for the first time since the 1840's and 1850's.

Hancock proved to be an upstanding and outspoken candidate. His character and military record were spotless, though he was absurdly accused of cowardice in battle. When asked for his views on the tariff, he candidly replied, "The tariff question is a local question." The jubilant Republicans, seizing upon this apparent stupidity, almost literally jeered Hancock out of the Presidency by proclaiming that he was "a good man, weighing 250 pounds." But the truth is that any general tariff bill is the product of pressures by many local-interest groups. They may range from Pennsylvania iron smelters to California lemon growers.

Garfield, though joyously hailed as "the Canal Boy," ran into troubled waters. He had been tainted by the Crédit Mobilier scandal, allegedly in the sum of $329, and energetic Democrats now chalked these telltale figures on buildings, walls, and fences. Undaunted, the Republicans raised a lush campaign fund by assessing officeholders a percentage of their salaries (as job insurance), and by "frying the fat" out of huge corporations (as tariff insurance). Indiana was "drenched" with Republican money ("soap"), which helped to ease it into the Garfield column.

"Boatman Jim" Garfield barely scraped across the electoral reefs. He polled only 9464 more votes than Hancock—4,454,416 to 4,444,952—but his margin in the Electoral College was the comfortable one of 214 to 155. Garfield's victory was essentially an endorsement of the status quo, including prosperity and tariffs. It was also an expression of persisting distaste for the rebellion-connected Democrats.

The Martyrdom of Garfield

James A. Garfield, who was sworn in on March 4, 1881, ranked well above the average President in ability, education, and experience. A graduate of Williams College, he had served for a time as president of what came to be Hiram College in Ohio. As one of the ablest orators in Congress, he was in wide demand as a speaker; and as a devout member of the Church of Christ, he was active as a lay preacher. He was a kindly, generous, warm-hearted Christian gentleman, and a devoted son who turned and kissed his mother after taking the inaugural oath. But he had one serious weakness: a reluctance to hurt people's feelings by saying "no."

The dividing of the spoils, which ultimately divided the party, brought Garfield no peace. For every appointment there were seemingly twenty disappointments. The overwhelming inrush of office-hungry Republicans finally wrung from Garfield the anguished exclamation, "My God! What is there in this place that a man should ever want to get into it?" At the outset, he awarded the prize plum of the Secretaryship of State to his close friend and the uncrowned king of the party, James G. Blaine. The "Plumed Knight" accepted the post as a kind of consolation prize, and with the expectation of being the "premier" of the Cabinet. Confidently planning to pursue a "spirited" foreign policy for eight years, Blaine bought an imposing house, which his ambitious wife intended to make the social center of Washington.

Trouble was meanwhile brewing with the pro-Grant Senator Conkling of New York, a colossus of conceit. As a member of the spoilsman or "Stalwart" faction of the Republican Party, he was angered by the nomination of Garfield, who belonged to Blaine's "Half-Breed" faction—half Stalwart and half reformist. Conkling was further enraged when his bitterest enemy, Blaine, was tendered the key position in the new administration. The two Half-Breeds, Blaine and Garfield, were apparently scheming to parcel out the loaves and fishes of office to the disadvantage of the Conklingites. The inevitable explosion came when Garfield, apparently hand in glove with Blaine, appointed to the coveted office of Collector of the Port of New York an archrival of Conkling.

ROSCOE CONKLING, THE CURLED
CONGRESSIONAL CAESAR

Puck, 1879

Conkling fought senatorial confirmation of the new appointment with all the weapons at his command. But when he discovered that he was not gaining ground, he spectacularly resigned and returned to Albany, where he expected to be re-elected by the legislature. The junior Senator from New York followed the lead of his senior colleague in resigning, and was thereafter dubbed "Me Too" Platt. Vice-President Arthur also journeyed to Albany, there to buttonhole legislators in behalf of his former political chief (Conkling), so as to discredit his current political chief (Garfield). Conkling's scheme finally backfired when the New York legislature failed to re-elect both him and "Me Too" Platt. Both men were thereupon retired to private life—Platt temporarily— without irreparable loss to public life.

While the Battle of Albany was thus raging, tragedy struck. A disappointed and mentally deranged office seeker, Charles J. Guiteau, shot President Garfield in a railroad station in Washington. The victim, after lingering in agony for eleven weeks, died on September 19, 1881. Guiteau, when seized, cried gleefully, "I am a Stalwart. Arthur is now President of the United States." The implication was that now the Conklingites would all get good jobs. At his trial, Guiteau went so far as to ask all those who had benefited politically by the assassination to contribute to his defense fund. He was found guilty of murder and hanged.

Statesmen are dead politicians, the saying goes, and Garfield's "martyrdom" undoubtedly enhanced his reputation. His half-year term was too short to permit a fair estimate, but he showed considerable indecision and took no vigorous steps toward civil service reform. His tragic death tended to draw the veil of charity over his shortcomings. Brutal though the thought is, Garfield's greatest single service to his country probably was to die when he did and as he did. An unwitting martyr to the evils of spoils-seeking, he departed this life in such a way as to shock the nation into taking action to correct flagrant abuses. The government had indeed come to a pretty pass when it was a case of "an office—or your life."

The Office Dignifies the Man

The blow caused by Garfield's death was rendered the more violent as men contemplated his successor. "My God! 'Chet' Arthur President of the United States!" was a frequently heard exclamation. A graduate of Union College, with Phi Beta Kappa honors, Arthur was a wealthy, handsome, and dignified widower who enjoyed a well-stocked wine cellar, an extensive library, and a wardrobe that included eighty pairs of trousers. Formerly a machine politician at the New York Customs House, he had been dismissed for purely political reasons from the only important post he had ever held before becoming Vice-President.

But the shock of new responsibilities caused "Prince" Arthur to rise to unexpected heights. He actually turned out to be a far better President than the country deserved for having elected a Vice-President of his spoils-system antecedents. Thrusting aside political ambition, he did not pull wires unduly in an effort to secure the presidential nomination in 1884. Proving to be an able administrator, he prosecuted certain post office frauds with commendable vigor, and reorganized his administration with a number of excellent appointments.

The Conklingite Stalwarts, joyously seeking to take advantage of their old crony, met a very frosty reception. It soon became evident that Arthur intended to make no clean sweep of the Half-Breeds in favor of the Stalwarts, though some officeholders were dropped. The members of the Conkling clique were so deeply disgusted that they almost regretted Garfield's death. Anxious citizens, many of whom had feared that the White House would become a loafing place for the old "customhouse crowd," were agreeably surprised.

The bullet that killed Garfield also killed Blaine's hopes. The overambitious Half-Breed, unable to get along with the Stalwart Arthur, left the Cabinet. Yet his brief term as Secretary of State had been marked by vigor and vision. "Jingo Jim" Blaine had made a somewhat bullying attempt, without success, to induce the British to give up their joint rights to a future Isthmian canal at Nicaragua or Panama, as guaranteed by the Clayton-Bulwer Treaty of 1850. (See p. 387.) Far more praiseworthy and significant was Blaine's dream of Pan-Americanism. Moving boldly, he had issued a call for the first Pan-American Conference in Washington, but his timid successor rather rudely recalled the invitations.

Civil Service Reform and Naval Reform

Agitation for cleansing the civil service meanwhile had become irresistible. The murder of Garfield, combined with noxious political scandals, increased the pressure for action. Arthur commendably threw his influence behind the movement.

The Republican Party itself began to reveal unexpected enthusiasm for reform, partly because it had lost control of the House in the mid-term elections of 1882. The lame-duck Republican legislators were fearful that their opponents would win the Presidency in 1884 and appoint only Democrats to office. To forestall such a disaster, they suddenly showed the zeal of death-bed penitents for a civil service law. The Democrats, who had clamored for reform when there was little chance of their cutting the political pie, now cooled off; they had no desire to "freeze" Republican incumbents in their jobs. Ironically, the civil service bill as finally passed was sired by the Republicans and damned by the Democrats.

The Pendleton Act of 1883—the so-called Magna Carta of civil service reform—instituted several desirable changes. It prohibited, at least on paper, financial assessments on officeholders, including lowly scrub women. It established a merit system—that is, appointment to office on the basis of aptitude rather than "pull." It set up a Civil Service Commission, which was to administer open competitive examinations to applicants for posts in the *classified service*. But offices not "classified" by the President were still the football of politics.

The success of the new anti-spoilsmen law depended largely on the cooperation of a seasoned ex-spoilsman, President Arthur. Fortunately, he cooperated with vigor. By 1884 he had classified nearly 14,000 federal offices, or about 10% of the total. Succeeding Presidents added substantially to the classified group, especially after their party had been defeated and their appointees were in danger of being swept out. This practice of snatching the plums of office from the mouths of the victors led to a cynical reversal of an old slogan: "To the *vanquished* belong the spoils."

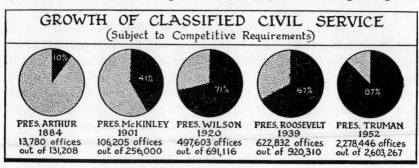

GROWTH OF CLASSIFIED CIVIL SERVICE
(Subject to Competitive Requirements)

PRES. ARTHUR	PRES. McKINLEY	PRES. WILSON	PRES. ROOSEVELT	PRES. TRUMAN
1884	1901	1920	1939	1952
13,780 offices	106,205 offices	497,603 offices	622,832 offices	2,278,446 offices
out of 131,208	out of 256,000	out of 691,116	out of 920,310	out of 2,603,267

The Pendleton Act, though widely acclaimed, fell far short of achieving a thoroughgoing reform of the civil service. But it did inscribe on the books the principle of merit, and it did halt the tide of spoilsmongering that had been rising since Jackson's day. More than that, it reversed the tide slightly, and later overwhelmingly. By the middle of the next century about 90% of the federal offices were classified or "blanketed" under civil service.

The worm-eaten navy, which still carried on its rolls the pre-1812 wooden *Constitution,* was likewise in urgent need of modernization. The Civil War fleet, a collection of "floating washtubs," had been allowed to rot away as we concentrated on internal expansion. With only two iron ships, the navy was far inferior to the iron-and-steel navies of the major European powers, and in certain categories even to that of Chile. American indifference to possible danger was almost unbelievable.

After prolonged debate, Congress in 1883 reluctantly appropriated money for four new ships—the nucleus of a modern steel navy. This was a modest beginning, but a noteworthy one. Succeeding administrations added more and stronger warships. By the time the Spanish-American War broke out in 1898, the navy ranked about fifth among world navies, and was able to give an impressive account of itself.

One good term deserves another. The achievements of Arthur were such that he fully merited a nomination "in his own right." But having angered both the Conklingites and the Blaineites, he was turned out of office in 1885, and the next year died of a cerebral hemorrhage

Private Immorality vs. Public Dishonesty

The nomination of Blaine in 1884, despite rumblings of opposition, was inescapable. The sparkling Maineite, blessed with almost every political asset except a reputation for honesty, was the clear choice of the Republicans meeting in Chicago. The reformers within the party had threatened to desert if the "Plumed Knight" were chosen, and thousands of them opposed the ticket or supported it only halfheartedly. They were sneeringly dubbed "Mugwumps"—a word of Indian derivation apparently meaning "holier than thou." Theodore Roosevelt called them "goo goos."

The victory-starved Democrats, encouraged by the nomination of a tainted Republican, believed that they could win with an outstanding reformer. At Chicago they turned enthusiastically to the stocky Grover Cleveland, whose granite jaw would not take "no" for an answer. A solid rather than a brilliant lawyer of forty-seven, Cleveland had rocketed from the mayoralty of Buffalo to the governorship of New York and the presidential nomination in three short years. The orator who placed his name before the convention lauded his courageously independent record as "reform governor," and added that the younger men also loved him "for the enemies he has made." Strong men make strong enemies; and Cleveland, "the unowned candidate," had made many enemies of the right kind, including the unsavory political bosses of Tammany Hall.

The Democrats, in high spirits, extolled their spotlessly honest candidate, "Grover the Good." At the same time they assailed the spotted Blaine, whom they represented as the "tattooed man"–tattooed with countless political dishonesties. They gleefully headlined newly unearthed letters that Blaine had penned, some of which ended with the furtive admonition "Burn this letter."

The Republicans, eager to retaliate, delved deeply into the past of bachelor Cleveland. At the outset the worst they could do was to brand him a drunkard, because as a young man he had quaffed much beer. But further probing uncovered the report that he had been involved in an affair with a Buffalo widow, to whom an illegitimate son had been born, now eight years old. Although several other men had been attentive to her at the same time, Cleveland had forthrightly assumed full responsibility and had made financial provision for the unwanted offspring.

The Democrats, who had launched the campaign on such a high moral plane, were completely crestfallen. They hurried to Cleveland and urged him to lie like a gentleman. But their ruggedly honest candidate insisted, "Tell the truth." Thereupon the Democrats, without Cleveland's sanction, desperately attempted to make something of Blaine's premarital relations with his wife. But the devoted husband explained away the charges with considerable plausibility.

The campaign of 1884 probably sank to the lowest level in American experience, as the two parties grunted and shoved for the hog trough of office. Few fundamental differences actually separated them. Even the Bloody Shirt had faded to a pale pink.[*] The tariff received considerable attention, as the Democrats contended for reduction and the Republicans tried to tar them with the brush of free trade. But personalities rather than principles claimed first attention.

The air resounded with slogans. In the great cities enormous crowds of Democrats surged through the streets, chanting—to the rhythm of left, left, left, right, left—such froth as: "Burn, burn, burn this letter!" The Republicans replied with "No, no, no free trade" and (tauntingly) "Ma, ma, where's my pa?" From the Democrats came the defiant answer, "Gone to the White House, ha, ha, ha!"

Cleveland, who swept the Solid South, squeaked through by polling 219 to 182 electoral votes, and 4,874,986 to 4,851,981 popular votes. The contest hinged on the state of New York, which Blaine lost by the paper-thin plurality of 1149 votes out of 1,167,169 cast. A change of 575 votes would have reversed the result. Basically, the issue narrowed down to a

---

[*] Neither Blaine nor Cleveland had served in the Civil War. Cleveland had hired a substitute to go in his stead while he supported his widowed mother and two sisters. Blaine was the only candidate nominated by the Republicans from Grant through McKinley (1868 to 1900) who had not been a Civil War officer.

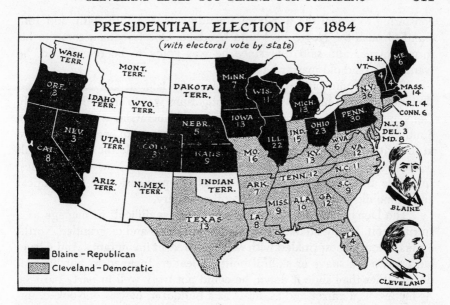

PRESIDENTIAL ELECTION OF 1884
(with electoral vote by state)

Blaine – Republican
Cleveland – Democratic

choice between public dishonesty and private immorality. Blaine's spotted record, which alienated the Mugwumps, seems to have been the deciding factor, plus a business depression, which always handicaps the party in power.

As the campaign entered its final stench, a half-dozen or so mishaps had weakened Blaine in the pivotal state of New York. Noteworthy was the blunder of an obscure Republican clergyman, who publicly proclaimed that the Democratic Party was the party of "Rum, Romanism, and Rebellion"—an accusation that was especially offensive to Roman Catholic Irishmen. Blaine, who was present at the time, did not have enough presence of mind to repudiate the statement at once. Silence seemed to give consent, and the wavering Irishmen who were driven into the Cleveland camp were probably enough to cost Blaine the election.

The Confederates Capture Washington

As Cleveland took the inaugural oath in 1885—the first Democrat to do so since Buchanan twenty-eight years before—a huge question mark hung over his portly frame. Could the party of disunion be trusted to govern the Union? A favorite Republican reminder of these years was that although not all Democrats had been rebels, all rebels had been Democrats. In fact, the Democratic Party was widely regarded in the North as "the left wing of the new Confederate army." The Republicans professed to fear economic chaos, repudiation of the Civil War debt, assumption of the defunct Confederate debts, and the awarding of federal pensions to ex-Confederates. Finally, the Republicans suspected the Democrats of conspiring to repeal the war-born amendments—the 13th, 14th, and 15th —and to push the Negro back into bondage. One freedman came to his former owner and said that since he was going to be re-enslaved, he wanted his kind old master back.

Grave responsibilities of leadership were laid on Cleveland's broad shoulders. One of his most pressing obligations was to show that not only Democrats could be trusted but Southern Democrats as well. In fact the South, for the first time in a quarter of a century, was to enjoy a real share in the national government. Cleveland's task was made the more difficult because his practical experience had been limited to New York politics. Inflexible and ingrown, he had no broad comprehension of the political and economic forces then convulsing the country.

The Democratic Party, furthermore, was as difficult to manage as a spirited colt. It consisted of frustrated Southerners and disgruntled Northerners, liberally besprinkled with relatively recent immigrants. And Cleveland was not a suave or skillful political leader. Inclined to put his foot down rather than slide it down, he could not work well in party harness. As tactless as a mirror and as direct as a bulldozer, he was outspoken, unbending, and profanely hot-tempered.

Cleveland's Cabinet was mostly composed of obscure or unknown men. The Democrats, who had been out of office since 1861, had not made the headlines. Cleveland further narrowed the North-South chasm by appointing to his Cabinet two ex-Confederates. One of them was a general, whose elevation provoked an outraged protest from the Grand Army of the Republic (G.A.R.)—a politically potent fraternal organization of several hundred thousand Civil War veterans, predominantly Republicans. The initials G.A.R. were humorously interpreted to mean "Generally All Republicans."

As for the civil service, Cleveland was a moderate reformer who had faith in the merit system. He believed that "public officials are trustees of the people"—an expression which was shortened to read, "A public office is a public trust." Yet the federal offices were packed with long-lived Republicans, and the dislodging of some of them could hardly be avoided.

The pressures from office seekers at length became overwhelming. The Democrats, who were ravenously hungry after their twenty-four years of exile, believed that the true path to reform was to turn out Republican "rascals" and put in their own people. They even recommended ex-convicts to Cleveland, who, decrying the "damned everlasting clatter for offices," retorted that "a Democratic thief is as bad as a Republican one." But in the interests of party harmony, he finally turned over the task of decapitating Republicans to the First Assistant Postmaster General, tactful Adlai E. Stevenson.* "Adlai's ax" chopped off the heads of about 40,000 incumbent postmasters.

But "Old Grover" won few friends by his grudging concessions. The

---

* Grandfather of the Democratic presidential nominee in 1952.

Mugwumps complained because he did not push reform far enough; the starving Democrats condemned his stinginess. Some of the latter even made a determined attempt to repeal the Pendleton Civil Service Act.

Pension Panhandlers

Cleveland, ever rigidly honest, believed that the pension roll should be an honor roll. The list should contain the names of men who had been crippled in the service of their country, not scheming malingerers and "bloodsuckers." Cleveland's position was made especially difficult because he was a Democrat and a non-veteran, and because the Grand Army of the Republic was remobilizing for new raids on the Treasury.

The existing pension legislation contained glaring loopholes. The original law, passed in 1862 during the Civil War, made provision for the veteran and his family in the event of disability or death. But many ex-soldiers, through neglect or ignorance, failed to file their claims for service-connected disabilities until much later. The Arrears of Pensions Act of 1879, passed under President Hayes, attempted to deal fairly with these worthy ex-soldiers by granting them arrears payments from the time of their discharge to the time of filing their claims.

Back pension payments, usually involving hundreds of dollars in lump sums, attracted grafters as honey attracts flies. Dishonest pension attorneys sprang forward to ferret out able-bodied veterans and induce them to file fraudulent claims. If the hardheaded Pensions Bureau rejected such an application, the claimant might appeal to his Congressman, who, mindful of the powerful G.A.R., would often present a special bill.

Hundreds of private pension bills were thus logrolled through Congress, and then sent to the White House. Handouts were granted to deserters, to bounty jumpers, to men who had never served, and to ex-soldiers who in later years had incurred disabilities in no way connected with war service. Cleveland, a slave to his conscience, read these bills carefully, vetoed several hundred of them, and then laboriously penned individual veto messages for Congress. On occasion he would wax sarcastic, as when he referred to one man who had experienced a "terrific encounter with the measles."

Despite his conscientious use of the veto, Cleveland signed hundreds of private pension bills. But he got little credit for his cooperation. His critics, predominantly of the G.A.R., accused him of having fallen victim to the "tyranny of the trivial." Pointing to the overflowing treasury, they insisted that this was no time for penny pinching at the expense of the veterans—even those who claimed that their eyes had been weakened by Civil War diarrhea.

A lavish Congress attempted to add several hundred thousand new pensioners to the rolls when, in 1887, it passed the Dependent Pension Bill. This overgenerous law awarded a pension to any veteran who had served ninety days and who was now unable to earn his living. Cleveland courageously vetoed the bill, for he feared that the measure would encourage fraud and put worthy veterans in an undesirable class. The bill stayed vetoed.

CLEVELAND CALLS A HALT TO LOGROLLING
Thomas Nast in *Harper's Weekly*, 1886

Cleveland heaped insult on injury when, also in 1887, he ordered certain captured Confederate flags to be returned to the South. This conciliatory gesture was greeted with an outcry of "Treason!" from Republican ex-soldiers; and the National Commander of the G.A.R. cried, "May God palsy the hand that wrote that order!" Cleveland was forced to back down when he discovered that only Congress could authorize a return of the flags. Eighteen years later, under a Republican Congress, this step was quietly taken. The passions of war had cooled, and what had once seemed disgraceful was now graceful.

Taxation without Justification Is Tyranny

During the Civil War the tariff schedules had been jacked up to new high levels, partly to raise revenue for the insatiable military machine. American industry, which was preponderantly Republican, had profited from this protection, and was loath to see the sheltering benefits reduced in peacetime. But the high duties continued to pile up revenue at the customhouses, and by 1881 the Treasury's annual income in excess of expenditures had mounted to an embarrassing $145,000,000. Most of the government's revenue, in those pre-income tax days, came from the tariff.

The Republican Congress in 1883 had, somewhat halfheartedly, attempted to reduce the tariff schedules. But the results of this first general revision since the Civil War were disappointing. The so-called "Mongrel Tariff," thanks to energetic lobbyists for industry, provided no real reduction and actually increased certain rates.

Grover Cleveland, the rustic Buffalo attorney, had known little about the tariff before entering the White House. But as he read up on the subject, he was much impressed by arguments for lowered barriers. Since tariffs are normally shouldered off onto the consumers by the manufacturers in the form of increased prices, Cleveland concluded that a high tariff taxed the many for the benefit of the few. He likewise perceived that a moderate tariff would lower prices to the consumer, principally by permitting more competition from foreign goods. As for protection, he concluded that it was often the public that needed protection from the giant corporations, and not the giant corporations—once "infant" industries—that needed protection from low-wage foreigners.

The swelling surplus was clearly an evil. It withdrew money from circulation at a time when a multiplying population and an expanding industry needed more currency rather than less. The surplus was also a standing temptation to grafters and bureaucratic vultures. The federal government is not designed as a profit-making institution, and it should not take more money from the pockets of the people than necessary for legitimate expenditures. Emphasizing the fact that a tariff is an indirect tax, Cleveland believed with the Democratic platform that "unnecessary taxation is unjust taxation."

Congress could reduce the vexatious surplus in two ways. One was to squander it on overgenerous pensions and "pork-barrel bills," and thus curry favor with veterans and other self-seeking groups. The other was to lower the tariff—something that the big industrialists vehemently opposed.

Cleveland, who did not look upon the Treasury as a grab bag, believed that the more honest course was to reduce customs duties. He repeatedly tried to prod Congress in this direction, but he encountered only Democratic apathy and Republican hostility. His irritation mounting, he decided to force a dramatic showdown on the tariff. He would bring the issue sensationally to the attention of the country by an appeal over the heads of the members of Congress.

In alarm, the Democratic politicians begged Cleveland not to stir up the hornets' nest of the tariff. The nation was prosperous, and if the President would only mark time, he was almost certain to be re-elected, with the other Democrats riding into office on his capacious coattails. But Cleveland spurned the flabby course. "What is the use," he insisted, "of being elected or re-elected unless you stand for something?"

Like a bombshell, Cleveland's low-tariff appeal burst upon Congress late in 1887. The annual message of the President had always been devoted to a review of the year's events, but Cleveland concentrated his fire solely on the tariff. Despite Republican charges, he did not advocate free trade at all—merely a reduction of the tariff to more manageable levels.

Cleveland succeeded admirably in forcing the issue out into the open. Democrats everywhere were profoundly depressed; Republicans were jubilant over the so-called "Free Trade Manifesto." Blaine gloated, "There's one more President for us in protection." The British were pleased, for they had long been on a free-trade basis and they were hampered by our high protective walls. But British approval was no asset in an anti-British America.

Exit "Old Grover"

Grover Cleveland was renominated at St. Louis in 1888 by the dismayed Democrats. They had no other outstanding leader; and even Cleveland's critics conceded that their best chance for victory at the polls lay with him.

The Republican convention at Chicago was less cut-and-dried. James G. Blaine still had enthusiastic followers, many of whom shouted, "Blaine or Bust." But the aging and ailing "Plumed Knight" bowed out when he saw that he could not get a near-unanimous nomination, and that his name would again be dragged in the gutter. He recommended as a compromise choice Benjamin Harrison of Indiana, whom the convention finally nominated.

Harrison, with his short body and long beard, was not an impressive figure or a commanding leader. A graceful orator, a spotlessly honest Presbyterian elder, and a prosperous corporation lawyer, he had served one term in the United States Senate. He hailed from the doubtful and electorally important state of Indiana; he had risen to the rank of brigadier general in the Civil War on the strength of meritorious combat service; and he sprang from one of the most distinguished families in American history. His grandfather was President ("Old Tippecanoe") Harrison. The grandson, "Little Ben," was joyously hailed as "Young Tippecanoe," and was pictured as wearing his grandfather's military hat. The Democrats maliciously cartooned him as rattling around in the oversize martial headgear.

The campaign of 1888 was waged on a fairly high level, quite in contrast with the Blaine-Cleveland brawl four years earlier. There was some feeble flapping of the Bloody Shirt, and some slight attention to the private life of Cleveland. The "Beast of Buffalo," who had married his beautiful twenty-one-year-old ward during his second year in the White House, was now absurdly accused of beating his wife during drunken fits. But the tariff was the overshadowing issue. Republican and Democratic propagandists flooded the country with some ten million pamphlets on the subject.

Yet the two parties shadow-boxed rather than tangled on the tariff issue. The Democrats advocated a tariff for needed revenue only, while their opponents extravagantly denounced "free trade." Shouting "Tippecanoe and tariff, too!" the Republicans insisted that a high tariff was needed to protect American labor, with its high wage, from the competition of "pauper Europe." They also argued with much force that "a surplus is easier to handle than a deficit."

Politicians in both camps energetically twisted the British Lion's tail. A quarrel had recently come to a head over the Canadian fisheries, and the Irish-American vote seemingly had to be cultivated by stirring up passions against England. Out in California a man claiming English birth wrote to the British minister in Washington, Sir Lionel Sackville-West, for advice on how to vote. The stupid diplomat replied, in effect, that a vote for Cleveland was a vote for England. The Republicans seized upon the indiscreet Sackville-West letter and made it a front-page sensation. The crucial Irish vote in New York, normally Democratic, began to slip away; and Cleveland was forced to bundle the "damned Englishman" off home—one of the few wobbly acts of his entire career. Crowds of gleeful Republicans surged through the streets of New York chanting:

> West, West, Sackville-West,
> He didn't want to go home,
> But Cleveland thought it best.

The accusation that the Cleveland administration favored both England and free trade proved highly embarrassing. It probably alienated enough Irish and other anti-English voters to damage the Democrats seriously. One Republican song hailed Cleveland as "England's favorite candidate."

The specter of a lowered tariff spurred the Republicans to frantic action. They raised a war chest of some three million dollars—the lushest yet—largely by "frying the fat" out of frightened industrialists. The money was widely used to line up corrupt "voting cattle" known as "repeaters" and "floaters." In Indiana, a crucial state, votes were shamefully bought for as high as $20 each.

On election day, Harrison nosed out Cleveland, 233 to 168 electoral votes. A change of 6502 votes in New York would have reversed the outcome. The popular count was 5,439,853 for Harrison to 5,540,309 for Cleveland, who, though defeated, polled 100,456 more votes than the winner. Such are the curiosities of the Electoral College. Cleveland may well have lost the Presidency by boldly arousing the sleeping dog of the tariff issue. But the election statistics indicate that if he had raised the question six months or so earlier, and had allowed time for the campaign of education to sink in, he might have won handily.

Cleveland: Man of Principle

Cleveland's first administration on the whole was a success, even with the dragging anchor of a Republican Senate. He displayed a rare degree of courage, honesty, and concern for the public welfare. Among other laudable achievements, he retrieved for the government some 81,000,000 acres of the public domain in the West—land that in many cases had been improperly acquired by the "cattle barons" or the railroad "octopus."

Cleveland's accomplishments did not end here. He pushed the construction of the new steel navy even more energetically than his predecessor had. His administration, as will be noted, could claim two legislative landmarks in 1887: the Dawes Act, designed to help the Indians, and the Interstate Commerce Act, designed to curb the railroads.

Some men grow in office; otherš swell. Cleveland grew, although it must be admitted that with his countrified background he had much room for growth. Under pressure to show that the treason-stained Democrats could be trusted to govern in the interests of the nation as a whole, he measured up to his high responsibility.

Cleveland remarked, shortly after his defeat, that he would rather have his name attached to his tariff message than be President. "Perhaps I made a mistake from the party standpoint," he said, "but damn it, it was right." He demonstrated, as Andrew Jackson had done, that doing the honest thing often wins more applause from the voters than kowtowing for votes. "Politics be damned" is often the most effective politics.

SELECT READINGS

Politics and administration are discussed in L. D. WHITE, *The Republican Era, 1869–1901* (1958). See also MATTHEW JOSEPHSON's depressingly critical *The Politicos, 1865–1896* (1938). Grover Cleveland is sketched in H. S. MERRILL, *Bourbon Leader* (1957) [paperback] and sympathetically revealed in ALLAN NEVINS' Pulitzer-prize *Grover Cleveland* (1932). The best one-volume lives are R. G. CALDWELL, *James A. Garfield* (1931) and G. F. HOWE, *Chester A. Arthur* (1934). See also D. S. MUZZEY, *James G. Blaine* (1934). Special studies of significance are ARI HOOGENBOOM, *Outlawing the Spoils: A History of the Civil Service Reform Movement* (1961) and D. M PLETCHER, *The Awkward Years: American Foreign Relations under Garfield and Arthur* (1962). The fullest treatment is H. J. CLANCY, *The Presidential Election of 1880* (1958). See also GLENN TUCKER, *Hancock the Superb* (1960). Also *Harvard Guide*, Pt. V.

27

Transportation, Industry, and Labor, 1865–1900

The railroads are not run for the benefit of the dear public. That cry is all nonsense. They are built for men who invest their money and expect to get a fair percentage on the same.

WILLIAM H. VANDERBILT, 1882

The Iron Colt Becomes an Iron Horse

THE feverish years after the Civil War witnessed an unparalleled outburst of railroad construction. When Lincoln was shot in 1865, there were only 35,000 miles of steam railways in the United States, mostly east of the Mississippi. By 1900 the figure had spurted up to 192,556, or more than that for all Europe combined.

Transcontinental railroad building was so costly and risky as to require governmental subsidies. The extension of rails into thinly peopled regions was unprofitable until the areas could be built up; and private promoters were unwilling to face initial losses. Congress, impressed by arguments relating to military and postal needs, began to advance liberal money loans to two favored companies in 1862, and added enormous donations of acreage paralleling the tracks. All told, the Washington government rewarded the railroads with 155,504,994 acres, while the western states contributed 49,000,000 more—a total area much larger than Texas.

The usual maps, showing in solid black ribbons the huge areas handed to the railroads, are misleading. The federal grants of land along the tracks were awarded, checkerboard fashion, in alternate sections. Furthermore, about one-sixth of the total acreage thus given away was taken back by the government because the recipients had violated the original agreements. Even so, in some cases the profits from the sale of lands more than paid the cost of laying the rails.

Loud criticisms, especially in later years, were leveled at the lavish disposal of so valuable a birthright to greedy corporations. But critics were prone to overlook the fact that the land was virtually worthless until the railroads could open it up to people and industry. Besides, the govern-

519

ment itself received certain valuable services from the subsidized lines, including preferential rates for military purposes.

Frontier villages touched by the magic wand of the iron rail became flourishing cities; those that were bypassed often withered away as "ghost towns." Little wonder that communities fought one another for the privilege of playing host to the railroads. Ambitious towns customarily held out monetary and other attractions to the builders, who sometimes blackmailed them into contributing more generously.

Spanning the Continent

The deadlock in the 1850's over the proposed transcontinental railroad was broken when the South seceded, leaving the field to the North. In 1862, the year after the guns first spoke at Fort Sumter, Congress made provision for starting the much-talked-about line. One weighty argument for action was the urgency of bolstering the Union, already disrupted, by binding the Pacific Coast more securely to the rest of the Republic.

The *Union* Pacific Railroad—note the word "Union"—was thus commissioned by Congress to thrust westward from Omaha, Nebraska. For each mile of track constructed, the company was granted twenty square miles of land, alternating in 640-acre sections on either side of the track. For each mile the builders were also to receive a generous federal loan, ranging from $16,000 on the flat prairie land to $48,000 for mountainous

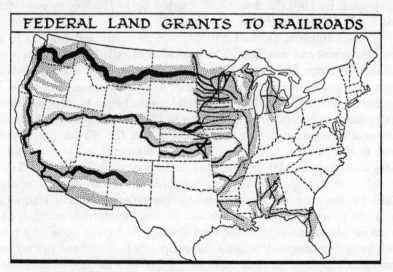

FEDERAL LAND GRANTS TO RAILROADS

The dotted portions, often misleadingly shown as wide black strips, indicate areas within which the railroads *might* be given some land. The heavy black lines are in proportion to the land finally granted to the railroads (the actual checkerboard arrangement cannot be represented in so small a map). See R. S. Henry, "The Railroad Land Grant Legend in American History Texts," *Mississippi Valley Historical Review*, xxxii (1945), 180.

country. The laying of rails began in earnest after the Civil War ended in 1865; and with juicy loans and land grants available, the "groundhog" promoters applied whip and spur.

Sweaty construction gangs, containing many Irish "Paddies" who had fought in the Union armies, worked at a frantic pace. On one record-breaking day, a sledge-and-shovel army of some 5000 men laid ten miles of track. A favorite song was:

> Then drill, my Paddies, drill;
> Drill, my heroes, drill;
> Drill all day,
> No sugar in your tay,
> Workin' on the U. P. Railway.

When hostile Indians attacked, the laborers would drop their picks and seize their rifles. Scores of men lost their lives as they built the line with one hand and fended off the whooping red men with the other. Relaxation and conviviality were provided by the tented towns, known as "hells on wheels," which sprang up at rail's end, sometimes numbering as many as 10,000 men and a sprinkling of painted prostitutes. The fabulous profits of the huge enterprise were reaped by the insiders of the Crédit Mobilier construction company. They slyly pocketed $73,000,000 for some $50,000,-000 of breakneck building, while bribing Congressmen to look the other way.

Rail laying at the California end was undertaken by the Central Pacific Railroad. This line pushed boldly eastward from boom-town Sacramento, over and through the towering, snow-clogged Sierra Nevada. Four farseeing men—the so-called Big Four—were the chief financial backers of the enterprise. The quartet included the heavy-set, enterprising ex-Governor Leland Stanford of California, who had useful political connections, and the burly, energetic Collis P. Huntington, an adept lobbyist. The Big Four cleverly operated through two construction companies, and although they pocketed tens of millions in profits, they kept their skirts relatively clean by not becoming involved in the bribery of Congressmen.

The Central Pacific, which was granted the same princely subsidies as the Union Pacific, had the same incentive to haste. Some 10,000 pigtailed Chinese coolies, with picturesque basket hats and flapping pantaloons, proved to be cheap, efficient, and docile laborers. The rocky Sierra Nevada presented a formidable barrier; and the nerves of the Big Four were strained when the coolies could chip only a few feet a day through rocky tunnels, while the Union Pacific was galloping westward across the plains.

The "wedding of the rails" was finally consummated near Ogden, Utah, in 1869, as two locomotives kissed cowcatchers. The colorful ceremony included the breaking of champagne bottles and the driving of the last ceremonial golden spike by Leland Stanford, who clumsily wielded a silver sledge. In all, the Union Pacific built 1086 miles; the Central Pacific, 689.

The completion of the transcontinental line—a magnificent engineering feat for that day—was one of America's most impressive peacetime undertakings. It spiked the West Coast more firmly to the Union, and foreshadowed a flourishing trade with the Orient. It penetrated the arid barrier of the deserts, and paved the way for the phenomenal growth of the Great West. Men compared this electrifying achievement with the Declaration of Independence and the emancipation of the slaves, while jubilant Philadelphians again rang the cracked bell of Independence Hall.

Crisscrossing the Country

With the westward trail now blazed, four other transcontinental lines were completed before century's end. None of them secured monetary loans from the federal government, as did the Union Pacific and the Central Pacific. But all of them received generous grants of land.

The Northern Pacific Railroad, stretching from Lake Superior to Puget Sound, reached its terminus in 1883. On this gala occasion Henry Villard, the German-born journalist–railroad man, dispatched over it his "Gold Spike Special," which was loaded with notables.

Two lines paralleled to some extent in New Mexico and California. One—the Atchison, Topeka, and Santa Fe—stretching through the Southwestern deserts to California, was completed in 1884. The other, the

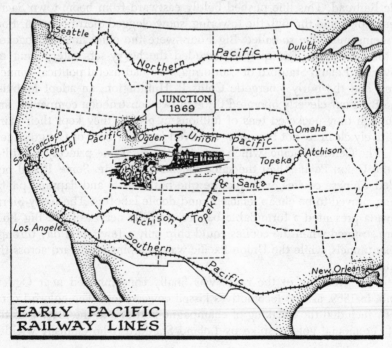

EARLY PACIFIC RAILWAY LINES

Southern Pacific, ribboned from New Orleans to San Francisco, and was consolidated in the same year. Two of the Big Four of Central Pacific fame—Huntington and Stanford—had a large hand in the construction and exploitation of the new line (with which the Central Pacific was later merged). The South had finally won its direct route to the West Coast.

The last spike of the last of the five transcontinental railroads of the 19th Century was hammered home in 1893. The Great Northern, which ran from Duluth to Seattle north of the Northern Pacific, was the creation of a long-visioned Canadian-American, James J. Hill. Endowed with a high sense of public duty, he perceived that the prosperity of his railroad depended on the prosperity of the area that it served. He ran agricultural demonstration trains through the "Hill Country," and imported from England blooded bulls, which he distributed to the farmers. His enterprise was so soundly organized that it rode through later financial storms with flying colors.

The romance of the rails was not without its sordid side. Most of the early construction was dangerously hasty and flimsy. The main object of the subsidy chasers seemed to be to throw down any kind of line so as to get the lavish federal bounties, and then go back and rebuild later. The breathless pace of rail laying also led to extravagant costs. One result was excessive overcapitalization or "stock watering"—that is, the marketing of two or three times more stock than was represented by the true physical valuation of the railroad.*

The pioneer builders were often guilty of gross overoptimism. Avidly seeking land bounties, and pushing into areas that lacked enough potential population to support a railroad, they sometimes laid down rails that led "from nowhere to nothing." When prosperity failed to smile upon their coming, they went into bankruptcy, carrying down with them the savings of trusting investors. Many of the large railroads in the post–Civil War decades passed through numerous bankruptcies, mergers, or reorganizations.

Consolidation and Mechanization

The success of the Western lines was facilitated by welding together and expanding the older Eastern networks, notably the New York Central. The moving genius in this enterprise was "Commodore" Cornelius Vanderbilt—burly, boisterous, white-whiskered. Having made his millions in steamboating, he daringly turned, in his late sixties, to a new career in railroading. Though ill-educated, ungrammatical, coarse, and ruthless, he was clear-headed and clear-visioned. Offering superior service at lower rates, he amassed a fortune of $100,000,000. His name is perhaps best re-

---

* "Stock watering" originally referred to the practice of making cattle thirsty by feeding them salt, and then having them bloat themselves with water before they were weighed in for sale.

membered through his contribution of $1,000,000 to the founding of Vanderbilt University in Tennessee.

Two significant new improvements proved a boon to the railroads. One was the steel rail, which the virile Vanderbilt helped popularize when he replaced the old iron tracks of the New York Central with the tougher metal. Steel was safer and more economical because it could bear a heavier load. A standard gauge of track width likewise came into wide use during the post-war years, thus eliminating the expense and inconvenience of numerous changes from one line to another.

Further improvements played a vital role in railroading. The Westinghouse air brake, widely adopted in the 1870's, was a marvelous contribution to efficiency and safety. The Pullman Palace Cars, advertised as "gorgeous traveling hotels," were introduced on a considerable scale in the 1860's. Alarmists condemned them as "wheeled torture chambers" and potential funeral pyres, for the wooden cars were equipped with swaying kerosene lamps. Appalling accidents continued to be an almost daily tragedy, despite safety devices like the telegraph, double-tracking, and (later) the block signal.

Revolution by Railroads

The far-flung tentacles of the railways touched intimately countless phases of American life. For the first time a sprawling United States became united in a physical sense, bound together with ribs of iron and steel.

The railroad network, more than any other single agency, spurred the amazing industrialization of the post–Civil War years. Puffing locomotives opened fresh markets for manufactured goods, and sped raw materials to the factory. The forging of the rails themselves provided the largest single backlog for the adolescent steel industry.

The screeching Iron Horse likewise stimulated mining and agriculture, especially in the West. It took the farmer out to his land, carried the fruits of his toil to market, and brought to him his manufactured necessities. Clusters of farm settlements paralleled the railroads, just as they earlier had the rivers.

The railway boomed the cities, and played a leading role in the great cityward movement of the last decades of the century. The iron monsters could feed enormous concentrations of people, and at the same time insure them a livelihood by providing raw materials and markets.

The railroad companies also broadened the mighty stream of immigration. Seeking settlers to whom their land grants might be sold at a profit, they advertised seductively in Europe, and sometimes offered to transport the newcomers free to their farms.

Finally, the railroad, more than any other single factor, was the maker of millionaires. A raw new aristocracy, consisting of "lords of the rail," replaced the old Southern "lords of the lash." The multi-webbed lines became the playthings of Wall Street; and colossal wealth was amassed by stock speculators and railroad wreckers like "Jubilee Jim" Fisk and the pious rascal "Uncle Daniel" Drew. As the Benéts have said,

> He toiled not, neither did he spin,
> But how he raked the dollars in! *

Mightier millions were made less sensationally by the Vanderbilts, the Hills, and other empire builders.

Wrongdoing in Railroading

Corruption lurks nearby when fabulous fortunes can be acquired overnight. The generous loans and bounties, whether granted by federal or local authorities, led inevitably to the bribery of legislators and other evil practices, most notoriously in the case of the Crédit Mobilier.

Some of the arrogant "railroad barons" felt no obligation whatever to the public. They regarded their railroads as purely private preserves, and they resented outside interference. "Can't I do what I want with my own?" was a common query. A heady sense of power replaced a sobering sense of responsibility. Crusty old Cornelius Vanderbilt of the New York Central, when told that the law stood in his way, burst out: "Law! What do I care about the law? Hain't I got the power?" His son, William H. Vanderbilt, when asked in 1883 about the discontinuance of a fast mail train, is said to have snorted, "The public be damned!"

Some of the railroad kings were virtually industrial monarchs. As manipulators of an unprecedented natural monopoly, they exercised more direct control over the lives of more people than did the President of the United States—and their term was not limited to four years. Yet giants like Vanderbilt did serve a useful function by bringing order out of chaos, and by otherwise improving transportation service.

As the decade of the 1880's lengthened, the long-suffering public began to rebel against railroad "robber-baronism." Many of the money-hungry railway kings would put their heads together and resort to the practice of pooling—that is, raising rates in a given area by secret agreement, and then pooling or sharing the profits. Other rail barons granted secret rebates or "kickbacks" to powerful shippers. Some lines would discriminate in rates and services against their enemies. Others would slash their rates on competing lines, and make up their losses on non-competing lines, where they might charge more for a "short haul" than for a long one.

The railroad moguls, moreover, were adept in protecting their privileged position. They would issue free passes to journalists, legislators, and other public men. They would bribe judges and legislatures, maintain

* Rosemary and Stephen Vincent Benét, *A Book of Americans* (Rinehart and Company, copyright 1933), p. 95. Reprinted by permission.

powerful lobbies, and elect their own "creatures" to high office. They would also contribute freely to the campaign funds of "friendly" politicians, who in turn would support the "railroad rascals."

Extortionate rates were the chief complaint of the public against the railroads. Charging "all that the traffic would bear," the companies had the farmer at their mercy, especially where rivers and canals did not offer alternate routes. A difference of only a few cents a bushel in production costs might spell the difference between relative prosperity and crushing indebtedness. In some communities a man did not even dare to go into private business without the "permission" of the railroad. The railway magnates, in their turn, argued that they had to pay dividends on their stock —often heavily "watered"—and consequently had to place a rate burden on the farmer.

Bridling the Iron Horse

It was not wholesome that so many should be at the mercy of so few. Impoverished farmers, especially in the Middle West, began to wonder if the nation had not escaped from the slavery power only to fall into the hands of the money power, as represented by the railroad plutocracy.

But the American people, though quick to respond to political injustice, were slow to take action against economic injustice. Dedicated to free enterprise and to the principle that competition is the soul of trade, they cherished a traditionally keen pride in progress. They remembered that Jefferson's ideals were hostile to governmental interference with business. Above all, there shimmered the "American dream": the hope that in a catch-as-catch-can economic system anyone might become a millionaire.

The depression that followed the Panic of 1873 goaded the embattled farmers into organized protest. Their efforts were especially vigorous in the Middle West, where, as will be noted, they launched the Granger movement (Patrons of Husbandry). In response to such pressures the various state legislatures attempted to regulate the railroad monopoly, and in Illinois the legislators achieved considerable initial success. The feeling was growing that either the state had to control the railroads or the railroads would one day control the government.

State railway restrictions suffered a severe setback in 1886, with the famed Wabash case. The Supreme Court in Washington held that the individual state, while free to control commerce solely within its borders, could not regulate railroad traffic moving in interstate commerce. Under the Constitution such action was reserved solely for Congress (see Art. I, Sec. VIII, para. 3). Foes of railroad monopoly had long been urging federal control, and the whole dynamite-charged issue was now tossed into the legislative mill in Washington.

After heated debate, Congress passed the Interstate Commerce Act of 1887. It specifically prohibited such vicious practices as rebates and

UNCLE SAM'S WILD WEST SHOW

The new Interstate Commerce Commission cautiously sets about lassoing refractory railroads under Uncle Sam's watchful eye. *Harper's Weekly,* 1887

the pooling of profits. It required the railroad company to publicize its rates. It decreed that there should not be a higher charge for a short haul than for a long haul, and forbade unfair discrimination against shipments or shippers. Finally, it set up the Interstate Commerce Commission (I.C.C.) to enforce and administer the new legislation.

The results were disappointing. The law designed to curb the mechanical monsters was not greatly feared by some of the operators, and was even welcomed by those who were eager to put an end to cutthroat tactics. The value of some railroad stocks actually rose after the passage of the act. Moreover, the law displayed only toothless gums, as is so often true of "first" legislation. The courts further weakened possible control by ruling that the Interstate Commerce Commission had no power to fix rates and make other regulations. All this lay in the lap of the future.

But the Interstate Commerce Act of 1887, though undeniably flabby and extravagantly overpraised, was an epochal law. It was the first large-scale attempt by the Washington government to regulate any kind of private business in the interests of society at large. It was the curtain raiser for more effective railroad legislation later, in that it inscribed on the statute books the principle of national control. It foreshadowed the doom of completely rugged individualism in industry, for it served full notice that America was no longer to be the happy hunting ground of the privileged few, at the expense of the underprivileged many.

Miracles of Mechanization

Post-war industrial expansion, partly a child of the railroad network, rapidly began to assume gigantic proportions. When Lincoln was elected in 1860, the United States ranked only fourth among the manufacturing nations of the world. By 1894 we had spurted into first place; and we have never relinquished that leadership. Why the sudden upsurge?

Liquid capital, previously scarce, was now becoming abundant. The word "millionaire" had not been coined until the 1840's, and in 1861 only a handful of men were in this class. But the Civil War, partly through profiteering, brought immense fortunes into being; and these accumulations could now be combined with the customary borrowings from foreign capitalists.

The prodigious natural resources of the United States were now about to be fully exploited, including coal, oil, and iron. For example, the Minnesota–Lake Superior region, which had yielded some iron ore by the 1850's, contributed the fantastically rich Mesabi range by the 1890's. This priceless bonanza, where the mountains of red-rusted ore could be scooped up by steam shovels, ultimately became one of the cornerstones of America's vast empire of steel.

Unskilled labor, both home-grown and imported, was now inexpensive and plentiful. Steel, the keystone industry, came to be based largely on the sweat of cheap immigrant labor, working in two twelve-hour shifts seven days a week.

American ingenuity at the same time played its vital role. Mass-production techniques, pioneered by Eli Whitney, were being perfected and utilized by the Captains of Industry. American inventive genius experienced a rich flowering in the post-war years: between 1860 and 1890 some 440,000 patents were issued. Numerous inventions hastened the so-called Second American Industrial Revolution. Business practices were facilitated by the cash register, the stock ticker, and Christopher Sholes' typewriter ("literary piano"), which brought home-confined women into industry. Urbanization was speeded by the refrigerator car, the electric dynamo, and F. J. Sprague's electric railway, which displaced animal-drawn cars. A New Orleans mass meeting proclaimed:

> Lincoln Set the Negroes Free!
> Sprague Has Set the Mule Free!
> The Long-Eared Mule No More Shall Adorn Our Streets.

In some ways the most important of the new inventions was the telephone, introduced by Alexander Graham Bell in 1876. A teacher of the deaf who was given a dead man's ear to experiment with, he remarked that if he could make the dumb talk, he could make iron speak. America was speedily turned into a nation of "telephoniacs," as a gigantic system was erected on his invention. The social impact of the invention was further revealed when an additional army of "number please" ladies was drawn from the home into industry.

The most versatile inventor of them all was Thomas A. Edison, who as a youth had been considered so dull-witted that he was taken out of school. This "Wizard of the Wires" ran a veritable invention factory in New Jersey. He is perhaps best known for his perfection in 1879 of the incandescent electric light, which he unveiled after trying some six thousand filaments. So deaf that he was not easily distracted, he displayed sleepless energy and a flair for practical money-making schemes rather than pure science. He invented, perfected, or did useful exploratory work on the phonograph, the mimeograph, the dictaphone, and the moving picture. "Genius," he said, "is one percent inspiration and ninety-nine percent perspiration."

The Trust Titan Emerges

Expanding markets and daring leadership further stimulated industrialization. The rapid growth of population provided millions of new consumers, and giants of Napoleonic stature stepped forward to exploit them. Men like Andrew Carnegie, J. Pierpont Morgan, and John D. Rockefeller, to name only three, were sensationally successful in developing important new techniques.

The breath-taking expansion of industry after the Civil War was partly sparked by the perfecting of the trust. This innocent-appearing device was designed to control a large part of the market for some one commodity—for example, petroleum. The stockholders in various smaller oil companies would assign their stock to the board of directors of the *trust*. This board, acting as *trustees* for the stockholders, would pay them dividends out of the profits of the consolidated enterprise.

The monopolistic trust enjoyed immense advantages. These were especially striking when compared with the methods of the earlier, non-monopolistic types of business organization, all of which had been individually owned or operated as small partnerships or corporations. Like ordinary corporations, the trust was not only permanent but it limited the financial liability of its stockholders. In addition, its size enabled it to take full advantage of the money-saving techniques of mass production, and hence to market cheaply, if it chose, a high-quality product. It could limit production, fix prices, and secure favorable railroad rates. So effective was the new colossus that it was often able to drive weaker competitors completely to the wall and achieve monopoly or near-monopoly. Yet the trust, despite all its ruthlessness, played a significant role in the emergence of the industrialized new America.

The Dawn of the Age of Steel

"Steel is king!" might well have been the exultant war cry of the new industrialized generation. The mighty metal ultimately held together our new steel civilization, from skyscrapers to coal scuttles, while providing it with food, shelter, and transportation.

Now taken for granted, steel was a scarce commodity in the wood-and-brick America of Abraham Lincoln. Considerable iron went into railroad rails and bridges, but steel was expensive and was used largely for products like cutlery. The Iron Horse snorted exclusively over iron rails; and when in the 1870's "Commodore" Vanderbilt of the New York Central began to use steel rails, he was forced to import them from England.

Yet within an amazing twenty years the United States had outdistanced all foreign competitors, and was pouring out more than one-third of the world's supply of steel. By 1900 the vibrant Republic was making as much as England and Germany combined. America's emergence as an industrial power was hardly less spectacular than her later emergence as a major political and military power.

What wrought the transformation? Chiefly the invention of the 1850's of a method of making cheap steel—the Bessemer process. It was named after a derided British inventor, although an American had stumbled on it a few years earlier. William Kelly, a Kentucky manufacturer of iron kettles, discovered that cold air blown on red-hot iron caused the metal to become white-hot by igniting the carbon and thus eliminating impurities. He tried to apply the new "air boiling" technique to his own product, but his customers decried "Kelly's fool steel" and his business declined. Gradually the Bessemer-Kelly process took hold, and these two "crazy men" ultimately made possible our present steel civilization.

A revolutionary steel-fabricating process was not the whole story. The United States was one of the few places in the world where one could find relatively close together abundant coal for fuel, rich iron ore for smelting, and other essential ingredients for making steel. The nation also enjoyed an abundant labor supply, guided by industrial know-how of a high order. The stage was set for miracles of production.

Men of Steel

The kingpin steelmaster, and the personification of the age of steel, was Andrew Carnegie, an undersized, charming Scotsman. As a tow-headed lad, he was brought to America by his impoverished parents in 1848, and got a job as a bobbin boy at $1.20 a week. Mounting the ladder of success so fast that he scorched the rungs, he forged ahead by working hard, doing the extra chore, cheerfully assuming responsibility, and smoothly cultivating influential people.

After accumulating some capital, Carnegie entered the steel business in the Pittsburgh area. A splendid organizer and administrator, he achieved gratifying success by picking high-class associates and by eliminating many of the middlemen. Although inclined to be tough-fisted in business, he was not a monopolist, and he disliked monopolistic trusts. His remarkable organization was a partnership which involved, at its maximum, about forty "Pittsburgh millionaires." By 1900 Carnegie was producing one-fourth of the nation's Bessemer steel, and the partners were dividing profits of $40,000,000 a year, with the "Napoleon of the Smokestacks" himself receiving a cool $25,000,000. These were the pre-income-tax days, when millionaires were rich and profits represented take-home pay.

Into the picture now stepped the financial giant of the age, J. Pierpont Morgan. "Jupiter" Morgan had made a legendary reputation for himself and his Wall Street banking house by financing the reorganization of railroads, insurance companies, and banks. An impressive figure of a man, with massive shoulders, shaggy brows, piercing eyes, and a bulbous red nose, he had established an enviable reputation for integrity. He did not believe that "money power" was dangerous, except when in dangerous hands—and he did not regard his hands as dangerous.

The force of circumstances brought Morgan and Carnegie into collision. By 1900 the little Scotsman, weary of turning steel into gold, was eager to sell his holdings. Morgan had meanwhile plunged heavily into the manufacture of steel pipe tubing. Carnegie, cleverly threatening to invade the same business, was ready to ruin his rival if he did not receive his price. The steelmaster's agents haggled with the imperious Morgan for eight agonizing hours, and the financier finally agreed to buy out his potential competitor for the equivalent of over $400,000,000 in cash. Fearing that he would die "disgraced" with so much money, Carnegie dedicated the remaining years of his life to giving it away for public libraries, pensions for professors, and other philanthropic purposes—in all disposing of about $350,000,000.

Morgan moved rapidly to expand his new industrial empire. He took the Carnegie holdings, added others, "watered" the stock liberally, and in 1901 launched the enlarged United States Steel Corporation. Capitalized at $1,400,000,000, it was America's first billion-dollar corporation—a larger sum than the total estimated wealth of the United States in 1800. The Industrial Revolution, with its hot Bessemer breath, had at last come into its own.

American Beauty Roses

The sudden emergence of the oil industry was one of the most striking developments of the years during and after the Civil War. Traces of oil found on streams had earlier been bottled for back-rub and other patent medicines, but not until 1859 did the first well in Pennsylvania—"Drake's Folly"—pour out its liquid "black gold." Almost overnight an industry was born which was to take more wealth from the earth—and more useful wealth at that—than all of the gold extracted by the Forty-Niners and their Western successors. The soaring popularity of kerosene as an illuminant for lamps struck a crippling blow at the old whale-oil business.

John D. Rockefeller—lanky, shrewd, ambitious—came to dominate the oil industry. Born to a family of precarious income, he became a successful businessman at age nineteen. One upward stride led to another, and in 1870 he organized the Standard Oil Company of Ohio, nucleus of the great trust formed in 1882. Locating his refineries in Cleveland, he sought to eliminate the middleman and squeeze out competitors.

Rockefeller flourished in an era of completely free enterprise. So-called piratical practices were employed by "corsairs of finance," and business ethics were distressingly low. Rockefeller, operating "just to the windward of the law," pursued a policy of rule or ruin. "Sell all the oil that

is sold in your district" was the hard-boiled order that went out to his local agents. Rockefeller — "Reckafellow," Carnegie once called him—was not inclined to mercy. He ironhandedly ruined competitors by cutting prices until his victim went bankrupt or sold out, whereupon higher prices would be likely to return. Rockefeller's son later said that the giant American Beauty rose could be produced "only by sacrificing the early buds that grow up around it." His father pinched off the small

ROCKEFELLER NIPS COMPETING BUDS
Literary Digest, 1905

buds with complete ruthlessness. Employing spies and extorting secret rebates from the railroads, he even forced the lines to pay him rebates on the freight bills of his competitors!

The Standard Oil Company was undeniably heartless, but its rivals were no less so in this age of dog-eat-dog competition. A kind of social-economic Darwinism seemingly prevailed in the jungle world of big business, where, in certain areas, only the fittest survived. By 1877 Rockefeller controlled 95% of all the oil refineries in the country, and could raise or lower prices at will. His profits were enormous.

On the other side of the ledger, Rockefeller's oil monopoly did turn out a superior product at a relatively cheap price. It achieved important economies, both at home and abroad, by its large-scale methods of production and distribution. This, in truth, was the tale of the other trusts as well.

The efficient use of expensive machinery called for bigness, and consolidation proved more profitable than ruinous price wars.

Other trusts blossomed along with the American Beauty of oil. They included the Sugar Trust, the Tobacco Trust, the Leather Trust, and the Harvester Trust, which amalgamated some two hundred competitors. The meat industry arose on the backs of bawling Western herds, and Meat Kings like Gustavus F. Swift and Philip Armour took their place among the new royalty. Wealth was coming to dominate commonwealth.

Tackling the Trust Evil

The trusts, with their thirst for power, had neither souls nor social consciences. Rockefeller, who believed in the Divine Right of Monopoly, wielded more influence over more people than many kings. "God gave it to me," he is said to have remarked of his princely fortune. Many an industrial tycoon, defying state control, became a kind of private state within a public state. The ideal of "social stewardship" was still a stranger.

Plutocracy, like the earlier slavocracy, took its stand firmly on the Constitution. The clause which conferred on Congress sole jurisdiction over interstate commerce was a godsend to the monopolists; their high-priced lawyers used it time and again to thwart controls by the state legislatures. The giant trusts likewise sought refuge behind the 14th Amendment, which had been originally designed to protect the rights of the ex-slaves as persons. The courts ingeniously interpreted a corporation to be a legal "person," and decreed that as such it could not be deprived of its property by a state without "due process of law" (see Art. XIV, para. 1). There is some debatable evidence that clever corporation lawyers, when the 14th Amendment was being fashioned in 1866, deliberately built in this loophole.

The great industrialists likewise sought to incorporate in "easy states," like New Jersey, where the restrictions on Big Business were mild or nonexistent. For example, the Southern Pacific Railroad, with much of its trackage in California, was incorporated in Kentucky.

The growing concentration of capital, through trusts and other combines, was astounding. By 1890 the value of all property in the United States was estimated at $65,000,000,000, of which $25,000,000,000 represented the assets of corporations. Cynics sneered that U.S.A. meant United Syndicates of America.

At long last, the masses of the people began to mobilize against monopoly. They first tried to control the trusts through state legislation, as they had earlier attempted to curb the railroads. Failing here, as before, they were forced to appeal to Congress. After prolonged pulling and hauling, the Sherman Anti-Trust Law of 1890 was finally passed.

The Sherman Act flatly forbade combinations in restraint of trade, without any distinction between "good" trusts and "bad" trusts. Bigness, not badness, was the sin. The law proved ineffective, largely because it had only baby teeth or no teeth at all, and because it contained legal loopholes through which clever corporation lawyers could wriggle. But the new act was unexpectedly effective in one respect. Contrary to its original purpose, it was used to curb labor unions or labor combinations which were deemed to be restraining trade.

The early prosecutions of the trusts by the Justice Department under the Sherman Act of 1890, as it turned out, were neither vigorous nor successful. The decisions in seven of the first eight cases fought by the Attorney General were adverse to the government. More new trusts were formed in the 1890's under President McKinley than during any other like period. Not until 1914 were the paper jaws of the Sherman Act fitted with reasonably sharp teeth. Until then, there was some question whether the government would control the trusts or the trusts the government.

But the iron clutch of monopolistic corporations was being threatened. A revolutionary new principle had been written into the law books by the Sherman Anti-Trust Act of 1890, as well as by the Interstate Commerce Act of 1887. The greed of private monopoly must henceforth be subordinated to the need of the general public.

The Birth of the New South

Agriculture in the post-war South was meanwhile having a hard struggle to get back on its maimed feet. Much of the cotton was grown by Negro and white sharecroppers, who farmed land, often with one mule, for a share of the crop. Many of these unfortunate creatures, slipping into debt, rapidly became enchained to the soil as virtual peons. The cotton industry as a whole received a welcome uplift when the by-products of cotton, notably cottonseed oil, were first marketed profitably on a wholesale basis.

The successful machine production of cigarettes, beginning in the 1880's, is associated with the colorful figure of James Buchanan Duke. Famous for his "Duke's Mixture," he operated from Durham, North Carolina, the home of roll-your-own Bull Durham, and later of Chesterfields. Such distinguished literary figures as Tennyson, Carlyle, and Lowell were all Bull Durham addicts. Duke became president of the monopolistic American Tobacco Company, and many of his millions went eventually to the endowment of Duke University, near Durham.

Cotton manufacturing in the South, earlier established on a small scale, shot ahead in the 1880's. The Southerners had long resented having to ship their fiber to New England, and their cry was "Bring the mills to the cotton." The South had the raw product, water power, cheap land, cheap labor, a mild climate, low taxes, seaports, and railroads. The two crippling drawbacks were the scarcity of capital and the lack of know-how.

Smokestacks in increasing numbers began to prick the Southern skyline. As capital was amassed—much of it from the North—new textile mills were erected, and many of the older New England factories closed up shop and moved closer to the cotton. The iron industry also secured a firm footing, particularly in besmogged Birmingham, "the Pittsburgh of the South," which enjoyed close proximity to both coal and iron ore.

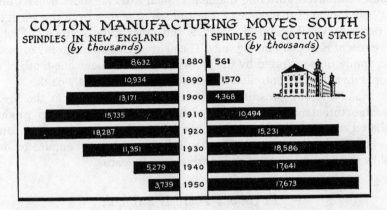

COTTON MANUFACTURING MOVES SOUTH

SPINDLES IN NEW ENGLAND (by thousands)		SPINDLES IN COTTON STATES (by thousands)
8,632	1880	561
10,934	1890	1,570
13,171	1900	4,368
15,735	1910	10,494
18,287	1920	15,231
11,351	1930	18,586
5,279	1940	17,641
3,739	1950	17,673

The diversification of industry was no doubt an economic boon to the South. The poor whites who were drawn into the sordid villages near the factories lived in no bed of roses, but most of them were probably better off than when they had eked out an existence in shacks on hookworm-ridden plots. For weal or woe, the vibration of the loom, the screech of the saw, the roar of the furnace, and the thunder of the locomotive proclaimed that the New South—the Industrialized South—had arrived.

The Impact of the Industrial Revolution

The economic transformation wrought during the decades after the Civil War enormously increased the wealth of the Republic. The standard of living rose sharply, and the well-fed American worker enjoyed more physical comforts than his co-workers in any other powerful nation. Urban centers mushroomed as the insatiable factories demanded more American labor, and as immigrants poured into the vacuums created by new jobs.

Early Jeffersonian ideals were withering before the smudgy blasts from the new smokestacks. As agriculture declined in relation to manufacturing, America could no longer aspire to be a nation of small freehold farms. Jefferson's concepts of free enterprise, with neither help nor hindrance from the Washington government, were being thrown out the factory window. Tariffs had already provided assistance; and the long arm of federal authority was now committed to decades of corporation curbing and "trust busting."

Probably no single group was more profoundly affected by the new Industrial Age than women. Sucked into industry by recent inventions, chiefly the typewriter and the telephone switchboard, millions of stenographers and "hello girls" achieved a new economic and social independence. Careers also meant delayed marriages and smaller families.

The clattering Machine Age likewise accentuated class divisions. "Industrial buccaneers" flaunted bloated fortunes, while their rags-to-riches spouses displayed glittering diamonds. Such extravagances evoked bitter criticism. Some of it was envious but much of it rose from the small and increasingly vocal group of socialists and other radicals, many of whom were recent European immigrants. The existence of an oligarchy of money was amply demonstrated by the fact that by 1900 about one-tenth of our people owned and controlled nine-tenths of the nation's wealth.

Finally, strong pressures for foreign trade developed as the tireless machine threatened to flood the domestic market. American products radiated out all over the world—notably the five-gallon kerosene can of the Standard Oil Company. The flag follows trade, and empire tends to follow the flag—a harsh lesson we were soon to learn.

In Unions There Is Strength

The sweat of the laborer lubricated the vast new industrial machine. Yet the wageworker did not share proportionately with either the employers or society the benefits of the Age of Big Business.

The workingman, suggestive of the Roman galley slave, was becoming a lever-puller in a giant mechanism. His originality and creativeness were being stifled, and less value than ever before was being placed on his old manual skills. Before the Civil War he might have toiled in a small plant, the owner of which hailed him in the morning by his first name and inquired after his wife's ailments. But now the factory hand was employed by a depersonalized, bodiless, soulless, and often conscienceless corporation. The directors knew him not; and in fairness to their stockholders they could not engage in large-scale private philanthropy.

As new machines were invented, many of the older employees were thrown out of work. In the long run more jobs were created than destroyed, but in the short run the manual worker was often hard hit. Labor is the most perishable of all commodities. A pair of shoes unsold today may be sold tomorrow, but a day's labor not sold today is lost forever.

A glutted labor market, moreover, severely handicapped the wage earners. The vast new railroad network could shuttle unemployed workers, including Negroes and immigrants, into areas where wages were high, and thus beat standards down. The inpouring Europeans further worsened conditions. During the 1880's and 1890's and later, the labor market had to absorb several hundred thousand unskilled workers a year.

Individual laborers were powerless to battle singlehandedly against giant industry. Forced in self-defense to organize and fight for their rights, they found the dice heavily loaded against them. The corporation could dispense with the individual worker much more easily than the worker could dispense with the corporation. The employer could pool vast wealth through thousands of stockholders, retain high-priced lawyers, buy up the local press, and put pressure on the politicians. He could import strikebreakers ("scabs") and hire armed thugs to beat up labor organizers.

The corporation had still other weapons in its well-stocked arsenal. It could call upon the federal courts—presided over by well-fed and conservative judges—to issue injunctions ordering the strikers to cease striking under penalty of the law. If defiance and disorders ensued, the corporation could request the state and federal authorities to bring in troops. The employer could lock his doors against rebellious workers—a process called the "lockout"—and then starve them into submission. He could compel them to sign "ironclad oaths" or "yellow dog contracts," both of which were solemn agreements not to join a labor union. He could put the names of obnoxious agitators on a "black list" and circulate it among fellow employers. The corporation might even own the "company town," with its high-priced grocery stores. Through the granting of credit for provisions, the worker was often kept in perpetual debt, and in some localities was reduced to a status that suggested medieval serfdom.

The public, annoyed by recurrent strikes, was often deaf to the outcry of the worker. American wages were perhaps the highest in the world, although a dollar a day for pick-and-shovel labor does not seem excessive. Carnegie and Rockefeller had battled their way to the top, and a common view prevailed that the laboring man could do likewise. Somehow the strike seemed like a foreign importation—socialistic and hence unpatriotic. Big Business might combine into trusts to raise prices, but the worker must not combine into unions to raise wages. Unemployment seemed to be an act of God, and a prevalent attitude in well-to-do circles was "The laborer be damned."

Labor Limps Along

Labor unions, which had been few and disorganized in 1861, were given a strong boost by the Civil War. This bloody conflict, with its drain on manpower, put more of a premium on labor; and the upward-spiraling cost of living provided an urgent incentive to unionization. By 1872 there were several hundred thousand organized workers and thirty-two national unions, which included such well-known crafts as bricklayers, typesetters, and shoemakers.

The National Labor Union, organized in 1866, represented a giant-boot stride by the workingmen. This organization lasted six years and attracted the impressive total of some 600,000 members, including skilled and unskilled and farmers. Its keynote was social reform, although its concern with the specific objectives of laborers was shown by its agitation for the eight-hour day and the arbitration of industrial disputes. It finally succeeded in winning an eight-hour day for government workers, but the devastating depression of the 1870's dealt it a knockout blow. Labor was generally rocked back on its heels during these troubled years. Wage reductions in 1877, as earlier noted in connection with the Hayes administration, touched off a series of strikes on the railroads which were so violent as to verge on civil war.

A new organization—the Knights of Labor—seized the torch dropped by the defunct National Labor Union. Officially known as The Noble Order of the Knights of Labor, it began inauspiciously in 1869 as a secret society, with a private ritual, passwords, and a grip. Secrecy, which continued until 1881, seemed essential to forestall possible reprisals by employers.

The Knights of Labor, even more zealously than the National Labor Union, sought to include all workingmen in "one big union." Their slogan was: "An injury to one is the concern of all." The welcome mat was rolled out for the skilled and unskilled, for men and women, for whites and Negroes. The Knights excluded only liquor dealers, professional gamblers, lawyers, bankers, and stockbrokers.

Setting up broad goals, the embattled Knights refused to tilt their lance in politics. Instead, they campaigned for economic and social reform, including cooperatives and codes for safety and health. Giving voice to the war cry, "Labor is the only creator of values and capital," they frowned upon industrial warfare while championing industrial arbitration. The ordinary work day was then ten hours or more, and the Knights put on a determined campaign for the eight-hour stint. A favorite song of these years ran:

> Hurrah, hurrah, for labor, it is mustering all its powers,
> And shall march along to victory with the banner of eight hours.

Under the eloquent leadership of Terence V. Powderly, an Irish-American of nimble wit and fluent tongue, the Knights won a number of strikes for the eight-hour day. By 1886, though their claim of a million members was evidently exaggerated, they were clearly a force to be reckoned with.

Evil Days for the Knights

For all their outward success, the Knights were riding for a fall. They became involved in a number of May Day strikes in 1886, about half of which failed. The focal point was Chicago, "hog butcher for the world," which contained about 80,000 Knights. The city was also honeycombed with a few hundred anarchists, many of them foreign-born, who were advocating a violent overthrow of the American government.

Tensions rapidly built up to the bloody Haymarket Square episode. Labor disorders had broken out, and on May 4, 1886, the Chicago police advanced on a meeting called to protest alleged brutalities by the authorities. Suddenly a dynamite bomb was thrown which killed or injured several dozen persons, including policemen.

Hysteria swept the Windy City. Eight anarchists were rounded up, although it was never proved that they had anything to do directly with the bomb. But the judge and jury held that since they had preached incendiary doctrines, they could be charged with conspiracy. Five were sentenced to death, one of whom committed suicide, and the other three were given stiff prison terms.

Agitation for clemency mounted. In 1892, some six years later, John P. Altgeld, a German-born Democrat of strong liberal tendencies, was elected governor of Illinois. After studying the Haymarket case exhaustively, he pardoned the three survivors. Violent abuse was showered on him by the conservatives, unstinted praise by those who thought the men innocent. He was defeated for re-election, and died a few years later in relative obscurity. Whatever the merits of the case, Altgeld displayed courage in opposing what he regarded as a gross injustice.

The Haymarket Square bomb helped blow the props from under the Knights of Labor. They were intimately associated in the public mind, though mistakenly, with the anarchists. The eight-hour movement suffered correspondingly, and subsequent strikes by the Knights met with scant success.

Another fatal handicap of the Knights was their inclusion of both skilled and unskilled workers. Unskilled labor could be easily shouldered aside by strikebreaking "scabs." The high-class craft unions, which enjoyed a semi-monopoly of skills, could not readily be replaced, and hence enjoyed a superior bargaining position. They finally tired of sacrificing this advantage in order to pull the chestnuts of the unskilled out of the fire. By 1890 the Knights had melted away to 100,000 members, and these gradually fused with other protest groups of the 1890's.

KNIGHTS OF LABOR AT ODDS WITH SKILLED CRAFT UNIONS
Capital looks on happily. Thomas Nast in *Harper's Weekly*, 1886

Federation to the Fore

The powerful American Federation of Labor, which next stole the spotlight, was largely a creation of squat, square-jawed Samuel Gompers. This colorful Jewish cigar maker, born in a London tenement and removed from school at age ten, was brought to America when thirteen. Taking his turn at reading informative literature to fellow cigar makers in New York, he was pressed into overtime service because of his strong voice. Gompers rose spectacularly in labor ranks, and was elected president of the American Federation of Labor every year from 1886 to 1924, except one.

The American *Federation* of Labor was just what it called itself—a federation. It consisted of an association of self-governing national unions, each one of which retained its independence, with the A. F. of L. unifying over-all strategy. No individual laborer as such could join the central organization.

Gompers adopted a down-to-earth approach, and soft-pedaled attempts to engineer sweeping social reform. A bitter foe of socialism, he kept the Federation squarely on the well-worn path of conservatism. He had no quarrel with capitalism as such, but he wanted labor to win its fair share. His objectives were better wages and hours, as well as other improved conditions for the worker. Another major goal of Gompers was the "trade agreement" authorizing the "closed shop"—or all-union labor. His chief weapons were the walkout and the boycott, enforced by "We don't patronize" signs. The stronger craft unions of the Federation, by pooling funds, were able to amass a war chest that would enable them to ride out prolonged strikes.

The A. F. of L. thus established itself on solid foundations. Though attempting to speak for all workers, it fell far short of being fully representative of them. Composed of skilled crafts, like the carpenters and the bricklayers, it was willing to let unskilled laborers shift for themselves. Though hard pressed by big industry, the Federation was basically nonpolitical. But it did attempt to persuade its members to reward friends and punish foes at the polls. The A. F. of L. weathered the Panic of 1893 reasonably well, and by 1900 could boast a membership of 500,000. Unfriendly critics referred quite inaccurately to Gompers' organization as "the Labor Trust."

Labor disorders continued throughout the years from 1881 to 1900, during which there was an alarming total of over 23,000 strikes. These disturbances involved 6,610,000 workers, with a total loss to both employers and employees of $450,000,000. The strikers lost about half their strikes, and won or compromised the remainder. Perhaps the gravest weakness of organized labor was that it still embraced only a small minority of all workingmen.

But attitudes toward labor had begun to change perceptibly by 1900. The public was beginning to concede the right of workingmen to organize, to bargain collectively, and to strike. As a sign of the times, Labor Day was made a legal holiday by act of Congress in 1894. A few enlightened industrialists had come to perceive the wisdom of avoiding costly economic warfare by bargaining with the unions and signing agreements. But the vast majority of employers continued to fight organized labor, which achieved its grudging gains only after recurrent strikes and frequent reverses. Nothing was handed to it on a silver platter. Management still held the whip hand, and several trouble-fraught decades were to pass before labor was to gain a position of relative equality with capital. If the Age of Big Business had dawned, the Age of Big Labor was still some distance from the horizon.

SELECT READINGS

A penetrating survey is s. p. hays, *The Response to Industrialism, 1885–1914* (1957) [paperback]. More detailed is ida m. tarbell, *The Nationalizing of Business, 1878–1898* (1936). See also e. c. kirkland, *The Coming of the Industrial Age* (1960), his *Industry Comes of Age: Business, Labor, and Public Policy, 1860–1897* (1961), and his *Dream and Thought in the Business Community, 1860–1900* (1956) [paperback]. ray ginger, *The Age of Excess: The United States from 1877 to 1914* (1965) handles colorfully both industrial and social development. matthew josephson assails the business tycoons in *The Robber Barons* (1934). On the railroads see r. e. riegel, *The Story of the Western Railroads* (1926), and oscar lewis' popularly written *The Big Four* (1938). Also popularized are s. h. holbrook, *The Story of American Railroads* (1947) and *The Age of the Moguls* (1953). More recent studies are g. r. taylor and i. d. neu, *The American Railroad Network, 1861–1890* (1956); r. w. fogel, *The Union Pacific Railroad: A Case in Premature Enterprise* (1960) and *Railroads and American Economic Growth* (1964); w. s. griswold, *A Work of Giants: Building the First Transcontinental Railroad* (1962); and james mc cague, *Moguls and Iron Men* (1964), also the story of the first transcontinental railroad. allan nevins is favorably disposed in his *Study in Power: John D. Rockefeller* (2 vols., 1953); see also h. f. williamson and a. r. daum, *The American Petroleum Industry: The Age of Illumination, 1859–1899* (1959). On steel, consult david brody, *Steelworkers in America* (1960). c. v. woodward, *Origins of the New South, 1877–1913* (1951) is an admirable analysis. Organized labor is treated in philip taft, *The A.F. of L. in the Time of Gompers* (1957) and *The A.F. of L. from the Death of Gompers to the Merger* (1959). Also useful are j. o. morris, *Conflict within the AFL: A Study of Craft versus Industrial Unionism, 1901–1938* (1958); g. n. grob, *Workers and Utopia: A Study of Ideological Conflict in the American Labor Movement, 1865–1900* (1961); and bernard mandel, *Samuel Gompers* (1963). See also s. r. spencer, *Booker T. Washington and the Negro's Place in American Life* (1955) [paperback]. Also *Harvard Guide*, Pt. V.

28

New Social and Cultural Horizons, 1865–1900

---

*So at last I was going to America! Really, really going, at last! The
boundaries burst. The arch of heaven soared. A million suns shone out
for every star. The winds rushed in from outer space, roaring in my
ears, "America! America!"*

MARY ANTIN, *The Promised Land*, 1912

Aliens within Our Gates

THE nation's upsurging population foreshadowed large-scale social and
cultural changes—changes hardly less spectacular than those occurring at
the same time in the world of industry. The census of 1870 enrolled 39,-
818,449 souls; that of 1900 almost doubled the earlier figure with a remarkable 75,994,575. Urban centers were booming marvelously, owing largely
to expanding industry and multiplying railroads. By 1890, three out of ten
Americans were city dwellers, in striking contrast to the overwhelmingly rural population of stagecoach days.

Despite the confusion of movement and change, a sturdy and honest
middle class continued to provide stability. Proud possessors of homes
and farms, these solid, industrious folk formed the backbone of America's
social structure. The gaudy new millionaires of the Gilded Age, who were
struggling to rise from the cash register to the social register, merely provided the froth.

The richly colored stream of immigration from Europe continued to
widen. In every decade from the 1850's through the 1870's, more than
2,000,000 aliens had stepped upon our shores. By the 1880's the stream
had become a rushing torrent, for in that decade a record-breaking total
of more than 5,000,000 poured in. A new high for a single year was reached
in 1882, when 788,992 arrived—or over 2100 a day. This figure was not exceeded until 1903.

Until the 1880's, the bulk of these immigrants were easy to assimilate.
Most of them had come from the British Isles and Western Europe, chiefly

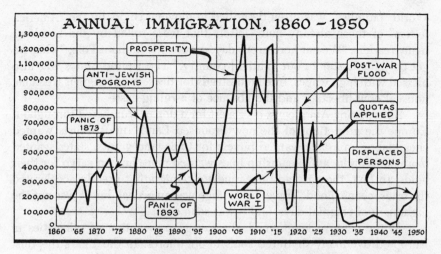

ANNUAL IMMIGRATION, 1860 – 1950

The figure for 1955 is 237,000; for 1960, 265,000.

Germany and Scandinavia. They were generally fair-skinned Anglo-Saxon and Teutonic types; and they were usually Protestants, except for the Catholic Irish and some Catholic Germans. They enjoyed a comparatively high degree of literacy, and were accustomed to some kind of constitutional government. Their native institutions were so much like ours that their Americanization was usually speedy, especially when they took up farms.

But in the 1880's a new element appeared, commonly known as the New Immigration. For the first time in American experience, a substantial proportion of the new arrivals came from Southern and Eastern Europe. Among them could be found swarthy and black-bearded Italians, Croats, Slovaks, Magyars, Greeks, and Poles. In the 1880's these picturesque new types totaled 19% of the inpouring immigrants; by the first decade of the next century they constituted a surprising 66% of the total inflow.

South Europe Uprooted

Why were these bright-shawled and quaint-jacketed strangers hammering on our gates? An unfortunate few were paupers, feeble-minded, or criminals, whose home governments were eager to assist them out of the fatherland. Some were fleeing compulsory military service. But the vast majority emigrated because America was painted as the land of opportunity, and they sought to escape the poverty and squalor of their native soil. Unfortunately, many of them merely exchanged one slum for another; and it was their children rather than themselves who profited from the transplanting.

The "America fever" proved highly contagious in Europe. The New

World "paradise" was often described in glowing colors by the "America letters" of those already here—letters that were soiled by the hands of many readers. "We eat here every day," wrote one jubilant Pole, "what we get only for Easter in our [native] country." The United States was also blessed with high wages, free homesteads for the settler, religious freedom, unusual civil liberties, and the absence of a ruling caste.

Enterprising Americans, ever alert for a dollar, trumpeted throughout Europe the attractions of the new Promised Land. Industrialists wanted cheap labor, railroads wanted buyers for their land grants, states wanted more population, and steamship lines wanted more human cargo for their holds. In fact, the ease and cheapness of emigrating greatly accelerated the transoceanic flood. Travel in steerage was an ordeal, but it was not the nightmare of colonial days, and it was soon over.

As the century lengthened, the savage persecution of minorities in Europe drove many shattered souls to our shores. In the 1880's the Russians turned violently upon their own Jews, chiefly in the Polish areas. Tens of thousands of these nerve-racked creatures, fleeing their burning homes, arrived in the seaboard cities of the Atlantic Coast, notably New York. Too poor to move farther, they huddled together in the already stinking slums, and there they found Americanization unusually difficult.

Anti-foreignism or "nativism," earlier touched off by the Irish and Germans in the 1840's and 1850's, once more flared forth. The hordes of immigrants from Eastern and Southern Europe were especially hard to digest. They were non-Teutonic and preponderantly Roman Catholic; they had been accustomed to cringe before despotism; they were generally il-

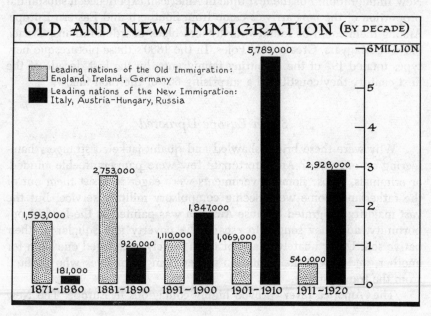

OLD AND NEW IMMIGRATION (BY DECADE)

Leading nations of the Old Immigration: England, Ireland, Germany

Leading nations of the New Immigration: Italy, Austria-Hungary, Russia

literate; they were poverty-stricken; and they tended to hive together in our jam-packed cities rather than move out to farms. The "Little Italys" and "Little Polands" of New York and Chicago were soon to claim more inhabitants than many of the largest cities of the Old Country.

The newcomers, who threatened to drown the earlier comers in a foreign sea, aroused widespread alarm. They were not only numerous but they had a high birth rate, as is common among people with a low standard of living and enough youth and vigor to pull up stakes. Old-line Americans protested that the original Anglo-Saxon Puritan stock would soon be outbred and outvoted. Still more horrifying to them was the prospect that it would be mongrelized by a mixture of "inferior" South European blood, and that the distinctively Anglo-Saxon types would disappear in a darker blend. T. B. Aldrich, a son of New England, cried out in anguish:

> O Liberty, white Goddess! is it well
> To leave the gates unguarded?

"Native" Americans voiced additional complaints. They objected to the creation of new rabbit-hutch slums, and condemned what they branded as the pauperism and bad morals of "smelly" Europeans. The alien arrivals were also assailed for a willingness to work for "starvation" wages, and for importing in their intellectual baggage such dangerous "isms" as socialism, communism, and anarchism. Many Big Business leaders, who welcomed the flood of cheap manual labor, began to fear that they had embraced a Frankenstein monster.

Narrowing the Welcome Mat

Anti-foreign organizations, common in the 1840's and 1850's, were now revived in a different guise. Notorious among them was the American Protective Association (A.P.A.), which was created in 1887 and which soon claimed a million militant members. In seeking its "nativist" goals, the A.P.A. urged voting against Roman Catholic candidates for office, and sponsored the publication of fictional tales about runaway nuns.

Organized labor was quick to throw its weight behind the move to choke off the rising tide of foreigners. The newly arrived Europeans, frequently used as strikebreakers, were hard to unionize because of the language barrier, the strangeness of their new surroundings, and the relatively high wages. Labor leaders argued, not illogically, that if American industry was entitled to protection from foreign goods, the American workingman was entitled to protection from foreign laborers.

The regulation of immigration had, from earliest days, been entrusted to the states. Those with favored ports of entry—such as New York, Boston, and Philadelphia—grappled with the problem as best they could. But there was always the loophole of the "easy states," as well as the possibility of smuggling in foreigners, often diseased or deranged offscourings, by way of Canada and Mexico. The task of regulating immigration, like that of regulating the railroads and the trusts, ultimately became so burdensome that it had to be dumped into the lap of the federal government.

Congress finally erected the first flimsy bars against the inpouring immigrants. The first restrictive law—that of 1882—banged the gate in the faces of paupers, criminals, and convicts, all of whom had to be returned at the expense of the careless or greedy shipper. Congress further responded to pained outcries from organized labor when, in 1885, it prohibited the importation of immigrant workmen under contract—invariably for sub-standard wages. In later years, supplementary federal laws lengthened the list of undesirables by adding such categories as the insane, polygamists, prostitutes, alcoholics, anarchists, and persons afflicted with contagious diseases. An ironclad literacy test, long a goal of the "nativists" because it would favor the Old Immigration over the New, encountered vigorous opposition. It was not enacted until 1917, after three Presidents had vetoed it on the ground that literacy was more a test of opportunity than of intelligence.

The year 1882, which saw the first restrictions against certain undesirable groups of every nationality, also saw a law to bar completely one racial group—the Chinese (see p. 502). Hitherto America had gathered to her mighty breast the oppressed and underprivileged of all races and climes. Hereafter the gates would be padlocked against defective undesirables—plus the Chinese. Four years later, in 1886, the Statue of Liberty was erected in New York harbor as a gift from the people of France. But the words of Emma Lazarus that were inscribed on the base rang a bit hollow:

> . . . Give me your tired, your poor,
> Your huddled masses yearning to breathe free,
> The wretched refuse of your teeming shore.

Advocates of more rigid restriction accused the New Immigrants, in particular, of exploiting America. This charge was partially true of those who came with the intention of going back to the Old Country when they had "made their pile." Of the approximately 20,000,000 immigrants who arrived from 1820 to 1900, about 5,000,000 "birds of passage" returned to their native sod. But most of the aliens who came were exploited to some extent by dollar-conscious Americans, whether in verminous city slums or in soot-stained mining slums. These displaced Europeans, unlike "nativists" cradled in America, became American citizens with their clothes on. They stepped off the boat, many of them full-grown and well muscled, ready to put their shoulders to the nation's industrial wheels. America owes much to these later comers—to their brawn, their brains, their courage, and their reforming zeal.

New Frontiers in the Cities

A vast cityward movement was gathering momentum in the 1880's and 1890's, not only in the United States but elsewhere in the world. In 1860 no American city could boast a million inhabitants; by 1890, New York, Chicago, and Philadelphia had spurted past the million mark. By 1900 New York, with some 3,500,000, was the second largest city in the world, outranked only by London.

The spectacular drift to the city is not hard to explain. It was speeded by machine-made jobs, by seductively high wages, and by the growing monotony of the farm, where there were too many cows to milk and hogs to feed. The urban centers were becoming more attractive with their net-

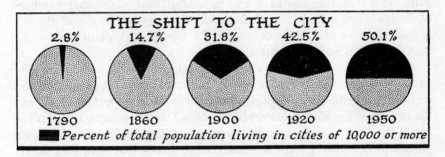

THE SHIFT TO THE CITY

2.8%   14.7%   31.8%   42.5%   50.1%

1790   1860   1900   1920   1950

■ Percent of total population living in cities of 10,000 or more

work of telephones and their bright lights, especially after the flickering gaslight era gave way to electricity. Noteworthy also were improvements in central heating, public water systems, indoor plumbing, sewage disposal, asphalt pavements, and transportation. The giant Brooklyn Bridge, dedicated in 1883, blazed the way for bigger and better spans. Electric-powered elevated cars and subways were introduced near the end of the century, inspiring the quip "The public be jammed." Congestion in the cities was markedly relieved by the cloud-brushing skyscraper in 1885; the Americans were apparently becoming modern cliff dwellers.

But the jagged skyline of America's perpendicular civilization could not conceal the ugliness of a feverish growth. Human pigsties, known as slums, became more crowded, more dirty, more unhealthful. Thousands of families were trapped in ill-ventilated and foul-smelling shacks and cellars, without plumbing. In these tumble-down tenements, conspicuously in New York's infamous "Lung Block," hundreds of immigrants coughed away their lives. "Flophouses" abounded where the half-starved and unemployed might sleep for a few cents on vermin-infested mattresses. Democracy found difficult rootage in the garbage-strewn alleyways of New York. Yet, marvelous to relate, the vast majority of these underprivileged souls grew up to be decent and law-abiding citizens.

Crime and corruption, unfortunately, flourished in the teeming cities. Criminals ranged from burly thugs with blackjacks to "city slickers" palming off "gold bricks" on "hayseeds" from the country. Crookedness in city government was most luridly exemplified by New York's notorious Tweed Ring. The boss and the machine made willing tools of the befuddled and purchasable immigrants. The American governmental system, nurtured in wide-open spaces, was least successful in the stone forests and asphalt jungles of the great cities.

Challenges to the Church

The bells tolling every Sunday morning in countless belfries were deceptive. Worshipers had vastly increased in numbers, but they had decreased in the intensity of their religious convictions. In the age-old struggle between God and the Devil, the Wicked One had registered dismaying gains. The mounting emphasis was on materialism; distressing numbers of devotees worshiped "the bitch goddess success." Money was the accepted measure of achievement, and the Gospel of Wealth proclaimed that God prospered the righteous.

Heavy blows were dealt the traditional faith of the fathers by new trends. There was an increasing sale of books on comparative religion and on historical criticism as applied to the Bible. Most important of all was the impact of the English naturalist Charles Darwin, who in 1859, on the eve of the Civil War, had published his unsettling *The Origin of Species*. He set forth in lucid form the sensational theory that man had slowly evolved from lower forms of life—a theory that was soon summarized to mean "the survival of the fittest." In American minds the struggle for the survival of the Union eclipsed for a time the struggle for the survival of the fittest, and the real impact of Darwinism was delayed until the postwar years.

The theory of evolution cast serious doubt on a literal interpretation of the Bible, which relates how God created the heaven and the earth in six days. The conservatives, or "Fundamentalists," stood firmly on the Scripture as the inspired and infallible word of God, and they condemned the "bestial hypothesis" of the Darwinians. The "Modernists" parted company with the "Fundamentalists," and defiantly refused to accept the Bible in its entirety as either history or science.

The furious battle over Darwinism created rifts in the churches and colleges of the post-Civil War era. "Modernist" clergymen were removed from their pulpits; teachers of biology who embraced evolution were dismissed from their chairs. But as time wore on, an increasing number of liberal thinkers found it possible to reconcile Darwinism with Christianity. They heralded the revolutionary theory as a newer and grander revelation of the ways of the Almighty. As W. H. Carruth observed:

> Some call it Evolution,
> And others call it God.

But Darwinism undoubtedly did much to loosen religious moorings and to promote unbelief. The most bitterly denounced skeptic of the era was a golden-tongued orator, Colonel Robert G. Ingersoll, who lectured widely on "Some Mistakes of Moses" and "Why I Am an Agnostic." He might have gone far in public life if he had stuck to politics and refrained from attacking orthodox religion and "giving hell hell," as he said.

Denominational Gains and Losses

The Protestant churches, in particular, suffered heavily from the weakening of religious ties. The larger houses of worship, with their beautiful stained-glass windows and thundering pipe organs, were tending to become a kind of sacred diversion or amusement. The churches, while growing complacent with wealth, were distressingly slow to raise their voices against social and economic abuses. John D. Rockefeller was a pillar of the Baptist Church; J. Pierpont Morgan, of the Episcopal Church. Trinity Episcopal Church in New York actually owned some of the city's worst slum property.

The Roman Catholic and Jewish faiths gained enormous strength from the New Immigration. By 1900 the Roman Catholics had increased their lead as the largest single denomination, in all numbering nearly 9,000,000 communicants. The Roman Catholic and Jewish churches kept the common touch better than many of the leading Protestant churches. Cardinal Gibbons (1834–1921), an urbane Catholic leader devoted to American unity, was immensely popular with Roman Catholics and Protestants alike. Acquainted with every President from Johnson to Harding, he employed his powerful liberal sympathies to assist the American labor movement.

By 1890 the variety-loving American could choose from one hundred and fifty religious denominations, two of them newcomers. One was the Salvation Army, which invaded America from England in 1879 and established a beachhead on the street corners. Appealing frankly to the down-and-outers, it did much practical good.

The other important new faith was the Church of Christ, Scientist (Christian Science), founded by Mrs. Mary Baker Eddy in 1879, after she had suffered much ill-health. Preaching that the true practice of Christianity heals sickness, she set forth her views in a book entitled Science and Health with Key to the Scriptures (1875), which sold an amazing 400,000 copies before her death. A fertile field for converts was found in our hurried, nerve-racked, and urbanized civilization, to which Mrs. Eddy held out the hope of relief from discords and diseases through prayer as taught by Christian Science. When she passed on in 1910, she had founded an influential church which embraced several hundred thousand devoted worshipers.

Learning for Young and Old

Public education continued its upward climb. The ideal of tax-supported elementary schools, adopted on a nationwide basis before the Civil War, was still gathering strength. Americans were accepting the proposition that a free government cannot be run successfully if the people are shackled by ignorance. Beginning about 1870, more and more states were making at least a grade-school education compulsory, and this gain, incidentally, helped check the frightful abuses of child labor. In compulsory education the South lagged behind its sister states.

Spectacular indeed was the spread of the high schools, especially by the 1880's and 1890's. Before the Civil War, private academies at the secondary level were common, and tax-supported high schools were rare, numbering only several hundred. But the concept was now gaining impressive support that a high-school education, as well as a grade-school education, was the inalienable birthright of every American. By 1900 there were some six thousand high schools. In addition, free textbooks were being provided in increasing quantities by the taxpayers of the states during the last two decades of the century.

Teacher-training schools, then called "normal schools," likewise experienced a striking expansion after the Civil War. In 1860 there were only twelve of them; in 1910, over three hundred. The kindergarten, earlier borrowed from Germany, also began to gain strong support. The New Immigration in the 1880's and 1890's brought vast new strength to the private Catholic parochial schools, which were fast becoming a major pillar of the nation's educational structure. The dominance of non-religious public education was correspondingly weakened.

The scorned Negro, regrettably, was not getting his fair share of the educational harvest. A notable leader emerged in the person of a slave-born mulatto, Booker T. Washington, who had slept under a board sidewalk in order to save pennies for his education. Called in 1881 to head a new Negro normal and industrial school at Tuskegee, Alabama, he began with forty students in a tumble-down shanty. Undaunted by adversity, he undertook to teach the Negroes useful trades so that they would merit a position of economic equality with the whites. His policies were attacked as "Uncle Tomism" by certain Negro intellectuals who feared that their race was being condemned to perpetual manual labor. But Washington stuck to his guns, and through his gifts as a speaker and organizer did much to improve Negro education and race relations.

American public education, though showering benefits liberally on children, passed by millions of adults. This deficiency was partially remedied by the Chautauqua movement, a successor to the lyceums, which was launched in 1874 on the shores of Lake Chautauqua, in New York. The organizers achieved gratifying success through nationwide public lectures, often held in tents and featuring well-known speakers, including

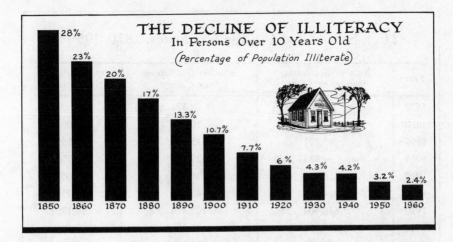

THE DECLINE OF ILLITERACY
In Persons Over 10 Years Old
(Percentage of Population Illiterate)

28% | 23% | 20% | 17% | 13.3% | 10.7% | 7.7% | 6% | 4.3% | 4.2% | 3.2% | 2.4%
1850 | 1860 | 1870 | 1880 | 1890 | 1900 | 1910 | 1920 | 1930 | 1940 | 1950 | 1960

the incomparable Mark Twain. In addition, there were extensive Chautauqua courses of home study, for which 100,000 persons enrolled in 1892 alone.

The crowded cities, with all their ulcers, provided better educational facilities than the old one-room, one-teacher red schoolhouse. The success of the public schools is attested by the falling of the illiteracy rate from 17% in 1880 to 10.7% in 1900. Americans were developing a profound faith—sometimes an excessive faith—in education as the remedy for most of their ills.

The Halls of Ivy

Colleges and universities also sprouted forth like lusty young saplings in the decades after the Civil War. Parents in multiplying numbers were eager to make sacrifices so that their children might secure a college education—something that now seemed indispensable in the scramble for the golden apple of success. The educational battle for women, only partially won before the war, now turned into a rout of the masculine diehards. Women's colleges, like Vassar, were gaining ground; and universities open to both sexes were blossoming forth all over the land, notably in the Middle West.

The almost phenomenal growth of higher education owed much to the Morrill Act of 1862. This enlightened law, passed after the South had seceded, provided a generous grant of the public lands to the states for support of education. The land-grant colleges, most of which were state universities, in turn bound themselves to perform certain services, such as providing military training. The Hatch Act of 1887, supplementing the Morrill Act, provided federal funds for the establishment of agricultural experiment stations in connection with the land-grant colleges.

Generous though the federal government was to the colleges, its benefactions were partially eclipsed by private philanthropy. Many of

High-School and College Graduates, 1870–1950

Year	Number Graduating from High School	Number Graduating from College	Interim Population Increase
1870	16,000	9,371	
1880	23,634	10,353	26.0%
1890	43,731	15,539	25.5%
1900	94,883	27,410	20.7%
1910	156,429	37,199	21.0%
1920	311,266	48,622	14.9%
1930	666,904	122,484	16.1%
1940	1,221,475	186,500	7.2%
1950	1,199,700	432,058	14.5%
1960	1,864,000	392,440	18.4%

the new industrial millionaires, developing tender social consciences, donated immense fortunes to educational enterprises. In the twenty years from 1878 to 1898 they gave away about $150,000,000. Noteworthy among the new private universities of high quality to open their doors were Cornell (1865) and Leland Stanford Junior (1891), the latter founded in memory of the deceased fifteen-year-old only child of a builder of the Central Pacific Railroad. The University of Chicago, opened in 1892, speedily forged into a front-rank position, owing largely to the lubricant of Rockefeller's oil millions. A Chicago newspaper was prompted to proclaim:

> Let us then be up and doing,
> All becoming money kings;
> Some day we may be endowing
> Universities and things.

Significant also was the sharp increase in professional and technical schools, where laboratory methods were replacing the solo experiment performed by the instructor in front of his class. Towering among the specialized institutions was the Johns Hopkins University, opened in 1876, which maintained our first high-grade graduate school. Several generations of American scholars, repelled by their English cousins and attracted by painstaking Continental methods, had attended German universities. Johns Hopkins ably carried on the Germanic tradition of heavily foot-noted volumes. Reputable scholars no longer had to go abroad for a gilt-edged graduate degree; and Dr. Woodrow Wilson, among others, received his Ph.D. at Johns Hopkins.

The March of the Mind

The old cut-and-dried classical curriculum in the colleges was on the run, as the new industrialization brought insistent demands for "practical" courses and specialized training in the sciences. The elective system, which permitted students to choose more courses in cafeteria fashion, was gaining popularity. It was given a powerful boost in the 1870's, when Dr. Charles W. Eliot, a vigorous young chemist, became president of Harvard College and embarked upon a long career of educational statesmanship. During the closing decades of the century, summer school courses and university extension work were securing a promising foothold.

The winds of dangerous doctrines—or seemingly dangerous doctrines—threatened to shipwreck freedom of teaching in the colleges. Disagreeable incidents involved the dismissal of professors who taught evolution or expressed hostility to high tariffs. For many years, some of the Big Business alumni of Yale vainly sought the bald scalp of the low-tariff economist and sociologist William Graham Sumner.

Medical schools and medical science after the Civil War were prospering. Despite the enormous sale of patent medicines and Indian remedies—"good for man or beast"—the new scientific gains were reflected in improved public health. Revolutionary discoveries abroad, such as those of the French scientist Louis Pasteur and the English physician Joseph Lister, left their imprint on America. The popularity of heavy whiskers waned as the century ended, for such hairy adornments were now coming to be regarded as germ traps. As a consequence of new health-giving precautions, including campaigns against public spitting, life expectancy at birth was measurably increased.

Many capable scientists and thinkers adorned our university faculties, but few enjoyed international reputations. American genius shone best in applying scientific knowledge to practical problems, as was notably true of the wizardly Thomas A. Edison. One of the most brilliant philosophers thus far produced in America, the slight and sickly William James (1842–1910), served for thirty-five years on the Harvard faculty. Through his numerous writings he gave wide currency to the philosophical concept known as pragmatism, which emphasized the practical side of thinking. Truth was to be tested, above all, by the practical consequences of belief. This kind of reasoning chimed in with the mood of a materialistic, cash-value America, which was already hotly in pursuit of the dollar.

The Appeal of the Press

Books continued to be a major source of edification and enjoyment, both for juveniles and adults. Best sellers of the 1880's were generally old favorites like *David Copperfield* and *Ivanhoe*.

American authors with unpublished manuscripts on their hands were greatly encouraged by new copyright arrangements. In 1891, after a half-century of intermittent debate, Congress enacted a law making possible an international copyright. Foreign writers could henceforth secure royalties from America, and American writers could hope to reap rich rewards from abroad. (Longfellow had been "honored" with some twenty unauthorized publishers in England.) Aspiring young American authors no longer had to fear the competition of cheap, royaltyless foreign reprints.

Public libraries—the poor man's university—were making encouraging progress, especially in Boston and New York. The magnificent Library of Congress building, which opened its doors in 1897, provided thirteen acres of floor space in the largest and costliest edifice of its kind in the world. A new era was inaugurated by the generous gifts of Andrew Carnegie. The open-handed Scotsman, book-starved in his youth, con-

SCOTSMAN CARNEGIE BESIEGED BY MONEY SEEKERS
Minneapolis *Tribune,* 1899

tributed $60,000,000 for the construction of public libraries all over the country. By 1900 there were about nine thousand free circulating libraries in America, each with at least three hundred books.

The roaring newspaper presses, speeded up by the invention of the linotype in 1885, more than kept pace with the demands of a word-hungry public. But the heavy investment in machinery and space was accompanied by a growing unwillingness to offend advertisers and subscribers. The old bare-knuckle editorials were, to an increasing degree, being supplanted by feature articles and non-controversial syndicated material. The day of journalistic giants like Horace Greeley was passing.

Sensationalism, at the same time, was beginning to debase the public taste. The semi-literate immigrants, combined with the urban commuters, created a profitable market for news that was simply and punchily written. Sex, scandal, and other human-interest stories were blatantly headlined, as a vulgarization of the press accompanied the growth of circulation. Critics vainly complained of "presstitutes."

Two new journalistic tycoons emerged. Joseph Pulitzer, Hungarian-born and near-blind, was a leader in the techniques of sensationalism. His use of the colored comic supplements, featuring the "Yellow Kid," gave the name of Yellow Journalism to his lurid sheets. A close and ruthless competitor was youthful William Randolph Hearst, who had been expelled from Harvard College for a crude prank. Able to draw on his California father's mining millions, he ultimately built up a powerful chain of newspapers.

Unfortunately, the over-all influence of Pulitzer and Hearst was bad. Although both championed many worthy causes, both prostituted the press in their struggle for increased circulation; both "stooped, snooped, and scooped to conquer." Their flair for scandal and sensational rumor was happily somewhat offset by the introduction of syndicated material and by the strengthening of the Associated Press, which had been founded in the 1840's.

Apostles of Reform

Magazines partially satisfied the public appetite for good reading, notably old standbys like *Harper's*, the *Atlantic Monthly*, and *Scribner's Monthly*. Possibly the most influential journal of all was the liberal and highly intellectual New York *Nation*, which was read largely by professors, preachers, and publicists. Launched in 1865 by the Irish-born Edwin L. Godkin, a merciless critic, it crusaded militantly for civil service reform, honesty in government, and a moderate tariff. The *Nation* attained only a modest circulation—about ten thousand in the 19th Century —but Godkin believed that if he could reach the right ten thousand leaders, his ideas through them might reach the ten millions.

Another journalist-author, Henry George, was an original thinker who left an enduring mark. Poor in formal schooling, he was rich in idealism and in the milk of human kindness. After seeing poverty at its worst in India, and land grabbing at its greediest in California, he dipped his pen in ink. His disquieting treatise, *Progress and Poverty*, undertook to solve "the great enigma of our times"—"the association of progress with poverty." He argued that poverty is attributable to rent, and concluded that a single tax on land was the remedy for many social and economic ills.

George soon became one of the most controversial figures of his age. His single-tax ideas were so horrifying to propertied men that his manuscript was rejected by numerous publishers. Finally published in 1879, the book gradually broke into the best-seller lists and ultimately sold some three million copies. George also lectured widely in America, where he influenced thinking about the maldistribution of wealth, and in Britain, where he left a considerable mark on English Fabian socialism.

Edward Bellamy, a quiet Massachusetts Yankee, was another journalist-reformer of remarkable power. In 1888 he published a socialistic novel, *Looking Backward*, in which the hero, falling into a hypnotic sleep, awakens in the year 2000. He looks backward and finds that the social and economic injustices of 1887 have melted away under an idyllic government. To a nation already alarmed by the trust evil, the book had an enormous appeal and sold over a million copies. Scores of Bellamy Clubs were formed to discuss this mild Utopian socialism, and they had a profound influence on American reform movements near the end of the century.

Literary Landmarks

American literature after the Civil War, unhappily, did not live up to its pre-war promise. Perhaps too many future authors, North and South, had bled to death on the battlefield; perhaps the money-grubbing goals of the new industrial era were unfavorable to artistic achievement. Perhaps New England was becoming too narrow, smug, and ingrown, as the brilliant Boston school of writers gradually burned itself out. The romantic sentimentality of a youthful era was giving way to a rugged realism that reflected more faithfully the materialism of an industrialized age.

In an era of poetical decline, Walt Whitman was one of the few luminaries of yesteryear who remained active. Although shattered in health by service as a Civil War nurse, he brought out successive—and purified—revisions of his hardy perennial, *Leaves of Grass*. The assassination of Lincoln inspired him to write two of the most moving poems in American literature, "O Captain! My Captain!" and "When Lilacs Last in the Dooryard Bloom'd."

The curious figure of Emily Dickinson, one of America's most gifted lyric poets, did not emerge until 1886. In that year she died and her poems were uncovered. A Massachusetts spinster and recluse, disappointed in love, she wrote over a thousand short lyrics on odd scraps of paper. Only two were published during her lifetime, and those without her consent.

> How dreary to be somebody!
> How public, like a frog
> To tell your name the livelong day
> To an admiring bog!

Among the lesser poetical lights was a tragic Southerner, Sidney Lanier (1842–1881). Oppressed by poverty and ill-health, he was torn between flute playing and poetry. Dying young of tuberculosis, he wrote some of his finest poems while afflicted with a temperature of 104°. He is perhaps best known for his "The Marshes of Glynn," a poem of faith inspired by the current clash between Darwinism and orthodox religion.

In novel writing, William Dean Howells (1837–1920), an Ohioan, achieved genuine distinction in his mastery of realism and his perfection of form. Perhaps the best-known of his numerous books is *The Rise of Silas Lapham* (1885), an absorbing tale of the newly rich class in the United States. Although he had never attended high school, Howells was offered professorships of literature at Harvard, Yale, and Johns Hopkins, to say nothing of honorary degrees from six universities, including Oxford.

Another distinguished novelist and master of realism was Henry James (1843–1916), a brother of the Harvard philosopher. A New Yorker who turned from the law to literature, he found his favorite theme in the contrast between Americans and Europeans of the leisure class, especially Englishmen. He finally took up residence in England, as did a number of his disillusioned literary brethren, and died a naturalized British subject.

Stephen Crane, the fourteenth child of a Methodist minister, published, at age twenty-four, *The Red Badge of Courage* (1895). This stirring novel of a young Civil War recruit under fire was a triumph of realism, though the author had never seen a battle and wrote solely from the printed records. He died of tuberculosis in 1900, when only twenty-nine years of age.

Literature for the Masses

General Lewis ("Lew") Wallace—lawyer-soldier-author—was a colorful figure. Having fought with distinction in the Civil War, he sought to battle the prevailing wave of skepticism with his novel *Ben Hur: A Tale of the Christ* (1880). A phenomenal success, the book sold an estimated two million copies in many languages, including Arabic and Chinese, and later appeared on stage and screen. It was the *Uncle Tom's Cabin* of the anti-Darwinists, who were struggling against skepticism directed at the Scriptures.

Two other writers, Bret Harte and Mark Twain, rode out of the West. Harte (1836–1902), a foppishly dressed New Yorker, had moved to California, where he found fame and temporary fortune by striking it rich with gold-rush stories. He is best known for his realistic "The Luck of Roaring Camp" and "The Outcasts of Poker Flat," and for the popular poem "Plain Language from Truthful James." It advertised a common California prejudice:

> That for ways that are dark
> And for tricks that are vain,
> The heathen Chinee is peculiar. . . .

Mark Twain, christened Samuel L. Clemens (1835–1910), was one of the few literary giants yet produced by America. Poorly schooled in frontier Missouri, the footloose "Prince of Humorists" received much of his education in the great University of Experience. For a time he served as a pilot on the Mississippi River, and later took his pen name, Mark Twain, from the boatman's cry meaning "two fathoms." Moving to California, he attracted some attention with his *The Celebrated Jumping Frog of Calaveras County and Other Sketches* (1867), and particularly with his *The Innocents Abroad* (1869), an almost instantaneous success.

MARK TWAIN ON HIS
CELEBRATED JUMPING FROG
From a poster advertising one
of his public lectures

Many other books flowed from Twain's busy pen, and his *The Adventures of Tom Sawyer* (1876) and *The Adventures of Huckleberry Finn* (1884) rank among American masterpieces. His later years were soured by bankruptcy growing out of unwise investments, and he was forced to take to the lecture platform and amuse what he called "the damned human race." It was a great tribute to his self-tutored genius—and to American letters—when England's Oxford University awarded him an honorary degree in 1907. Journalist, humorist, satirist, and foe of social injustice, he made his most enduring contribution in recapturing frontier realism and humor in the authentic American dialect.

A far less talented writer was Horatio ("Holy Horatio") Alger, a Puritan-reared New Englander, who in 1866 forsook the pulpit for the pen. Deeply interested in New York newsboys, he wrote more than a hundred volumes of juvenile fiction that sold over twenty million copies. His stock formula was that virtue, honesty, and industry are rewarded by success, wealth, and honor—a kind of survival of the purest. Although Alger's own bachelor life was criticized, he implanted morality and the conviction that there is always room at the top (especially if one marries the boss's daughter).

Cheaper and more sensational were the millions of "dime novels." Paint-bedaubed Indians and quick-triggered characters like "Deadwood Dick" shot off vast quantities of powder, as virtue invariably triumphed. The lurid "paperbacks" were frowned upon by parents, but goggle-eyed youths read them in haylofts or in schools behind the capacious covers of geography books. The king of dime novelists was Harlan F. Halsey, who made a fortune by dashing off about 650 novels, sometimes one in a day.

Women in Arms

Once the shackles were stricken from the slave, American reforming zeal turned to other goals, including woman's rights. The embattled females increased their cry for the ballot, particularly after it had been forced into the hands of the illiterate Negro. The austere fighting Quakeress, Susan B. Anthony (1820–1906), continued as a militant leader, despite showers of rotten eggs and decayed vegetables.

The persistent crusade for female suffrage—"Ballots for Both"—registered encouraging gains before the end of the century. Growing numbers of women were being permitted to vote in local elections, particularly on issues relating to the schools. The Territory of Wyoming—later called "the Equality State"—reflected the high regard of the West for the scarcer sex when it granted unrestricted suffrage to women in 1869. This important breach in the dike once made, other states followed Wyoming's example. Paralleling these triumphs, most of the states by 1890 had taken action to permit wives to own or control their property after marriage.

The "softer" sex was becoming more independent and more articulate, though American females had long enjoyed a degree of freedom

Marriages and Divorces, 1890–1960

Year	Marriages	Divorces	Ratio of Divorces to Marriages
1890	570,000	33,461	1–17
1900	709,000	55,751	1–12
1910	948,166	83,045	1–11
1920	1,274,476	170,505	1–7
1930	1,126,856	195,961	1–5
1940	1,595,879	264,000	1–6
1950	1,667,231	385,144	1–4.3
1960	1,523,381	393,000	1–3.8

unknown in Europe. Industrialization and urbanization were luring tens of thousands of women into business. A career was now an attractive alternative to early matrimony; hence marriages were being delayed and parents were having fewer children. Smaller families were also a result of crowded conditions in the cities, higher living standards, and the spread of birth control.

The gradual emancipation of females was reflected in a disquieting increase in the divorce rate. A partial explanation was that womenfolk no longer would tolerate abuse at the hands of their lords and masters. Uniformity in divorce laws, owing to the chaotic states'-rights tradition, was lamentably lacking. "Easy states," like Nevada and Wyoming, did a bustling business in dissolving marital ties.

Prohibition and Social Progress

Alarming gains by Demon Rum spurred the temperance reformers to redoubled zeal. Especially obnoxious to them was the shutter-doored corner saloon, which was misleadingly called "the poor man's club." It helped keep him, as well as his family, poor. The imbibing of liquor had increased during the nerve-racking days of the Civil War; and immigrant groups, accustomed to alcohol in the Old Country, were hostile to restraints. Whiskey-loving foreigners in Boston were wont to hiss at temperance lecturers.

The National Prohibition Party, organized in 1869, polled a sprinkling of votes in some of the ensuing presidential elections. Among the favorite songs of these earnest souls were "I'll Marry No Man If He Drinks," "Vote Down the Vile Traffic," and "The Drunkard's Doom."

> Now, all young men, a warning take,
> And shun the poisoned bowl;
> 'Twill lead you down to hell's dark gate,
> And ruin your own soul.

Militant petticoats entered the alcoholic arena, notably when the Woman's Christian Temperance Union (W.C.T.U.) was organized in 1874. The white ribbon was its symbol of purity, and the saintly Frances E. Willard—also a champion of planned parenthood—was its leading spirit. Less saintly was a muscular and mentally deranged Kansan, Mrs. Carry A. Nation, whose first husband had died of alcoholism. With her hatchet she boldly smashed saloon bottles and bars, and she brought considerable disrepute to the prohibition movement by the violence of her one-woman crusade.

But rum was now on the run. The potent Anti-Saloon League was formed in 1893, with its members singing lustily, "The Saloon Must Go" and "Vote for Cold Water, Boys." State-wide prohibition, which had

PUTTING THE BURDEN WHERE IT BELONGS

The cartoonist argues that the costs of crime and pauperism, the offspring
of alcohol, should be borne by the dealers in alcohol. *Harper's Weekly,* 1883

registered surprising gains in Maine and elsewhere before the Civil War,
was sweeping new states into the "dry" column.

The banners of other social crusaders were aloft. The much-needed
American Society for the Prevention of Cruelty to Animals was created
by Henry Bergh in 1866, after he had witnessed brutality to horses in
Russia. The American Red Cross was organized in 1881, with the dynamic
five-foot Clara Barton, an "angel" of the Civil War battlefields, as a leading spirit. Organized philanthropy, a forerunner of the Community Chest,
was becoming popular, beginning with Buffalo in the 1870's, and was
replacing the old haphazard methods of giving. More money went into
salaries and other costs, but the recipients of charity also got more, despite a poet's protest against

> The organized charity, scrimped and iced,
> In the name of a cautious, statistical Christ.

Artistic Triumphs

America still lacked artists to match her magnificent mountains. Art had been of sickly growth in the rustic years of the Republic, largely because of an absence of leisure and wealth. The nation now had both, but on the whole the results were disappointing. Perhaps the roar of our industrialized civilization repelled the delicate muses. Perhaps art itself was becoming mechanized. The roll-film camera, popularized by George Eastman in the 1880's, enabled every man to be his own artist.

Several portrait painters of high distinction nevertheless emerged, notably James A. M. Whistler (1834–1903). This eccentric and quarrelsome Massachusetts Yankee had earlier been dropped from West Point after failing in chemistry. "Had silicon been a gas," he later quipped, "I would have been a major general." Moving to Europe, he did much of his work in England, including the celebrated portrait of his mother. Another gifted portrait painter, likewise self-exiled in England, was John Singer Sargent (1856–1925). His flattering but somewhat superficial likenesses of the British nobility were much sought after.

Other brush wielders, no less talented, brightened the artistic firmament. Self-taught George Inness (1825–1894) looked like a fanatic with his long hair and piercing gaze, but he became America's leading landscapist. Thomas Eakins (1844–1916) attained a high degree of realism in his paintings, a quality not appreciated by portrait sitters who wanted their moles overlooked. Boston-born Winslow Homer (1836–1910), who as a youth had secretly drawn sketches in school, was perhaps the greatest painter of the group. Earthily American and uncontaminated by foreign influences, he revealed rugged realism and boldness of conception. His canvases of the sea and of fisherfolk are masterly, and no American artist has excelled him in portraying the sheer might and majesty of the ocean.

America's most gifted sculptor to date was probably Augustus Saint-Gaudens (1848–1907). Born in Ireland of an Irish mother and a French father, he became an adopted American. Although he sculptured many noble statues, his most striking work is the "Adams Monument" (1891), a shrouded and enigmatic female figure representing grief. It was erected in a Washington cemetery by the historian Henry Adams in memory of his beloved wife, who had died by her own hand.

Music was likewise gaining popularity. America of the 1880's and 1890's was developing high-quality symphony orchestras, notably in Boston and Chicago. The famed Metropolitan Opera House of New York was erected in 1883. In its fabled "Diamond Horseshoe" the newly rich, often under the pretense of enjoying the imported singers, would flaunt their jewels, gowns, and furs. A marvelous new development was the reproduction of music by mechanical means. The phonograph, though a squeakily imperfect instrument when invented by Edison, had by 1900 reached over 150,000 homes. The nation was rapidly being dosed with "canned music."

The most original architects of the era sought to escape the hodge-podge borrowings from Europe by stressing usefulness of design—realism in building. The most noteworthy contribution of this sort was the sky-scraper. Coming first as a ten-story building in Chicago in 1885, it was made practicable by the perfecting of the elevator. An opinionated Chicagoan, Louis H. Sullivan (1856–1924), added much to the skyscraper by his guiding principle, "Form follows function."

A revival of classical architectural forms—and a setback for realism —came with the great Columbian Exposition. Held in Chicago in 1893, it honored the four hundredth anniversary of Columbus' first voyage. This so-called "dream of loveliness," which was visited by 27,000,000 people, did much to raise American artistic standards and promote city planning, although many of the spectators were attracted primarily by the torsal contortions of the hootchy-kootchy dancer, "Little Egypt."

Fun and Frolic

The lighter side of life was not neglected by the workaday American. The pursuit of happiness, heralded in the Declaration of Independence, had by century's end become a frenzied scramble. Americans sought their pleasures fiercely, as they had overrun their continent fiercely. And now they had more time to play.

Varied diversions beckoned. As a nation of "joiners" contemptuous of royalty, we inconsistently sought to escape from democratic equality in the aristocratic hierarchies of lodges. The legitimate stage still flourished, as appreciative audiences responded to the lure of the footlights. Vaudeville, with its coarse jokes and graceful acrobats, continued to be immensely popular during the 1880's and 1890's.

The circus—high-tented and multi-ringed—finally emerged full-blown. Phineas T. Barnum, the master showman who had early discovered that "the public likes to be humbugged," joined hands with James A. Bailey in 1881 to stage the "Greatest Show on Earth."

The "Wild West" show, first exhibited in 1883, was even more distinctively American. Headed by the knightly and goateed William F. ("Buffalo Bill") Cody, the troupe included war-whooping Indians, live buffalo, and deadeye marksmen. Among them was the girlish Annie Oakley. Rifle in hand, at thirty paces she could perforate a tossed-up card half a dozen times before it fluttered to the ground. (Hence the term "Annie Oakley" for a punched ticket, later for a free pass.)

Baseball, already widely played before the Civil War, was clearly emerging as the national pastime. A league of professional players was formed in the 1870's, and in 1888 an all-star baseball team toured the world, using the pyramids as a backstop while in Egypt.

The gladiatorial trend toward spectators' sports, rather than participants' sports, was well exemplified by football. This rugged game, with its dangerous flying wedge, had become popular well before 1889, when Yaleman Walter C. Camp chose his first "All American" team. The Yale-Princeton game of 1893 drew fifty thousand rabid spectators, while foreigners complained that the nation was getting sports "on the brain."

Even pugilism, with its long background of bare-knuckle brutality, gained a new and gloved respectability in 1892. Agile "Gentleman Jim" Corbett, a scientific boxer, wrested the world championship from the aging and alcoholic John L. Sullivan, the fabulous "Boston Strong Boy."

Two crazes swept the country in the closing decades of the century. Croquet became enormously popular, though condemned by moralists of the "naughty nineties" because it exposed feminine ankles and promoted flirtation. The low-framed "safety" bicycle came to replace the high-seated model. By 1893 a million bicycles were in use, and thousands of young ladies were turning to this new "spinning wheel."

Basketball was invented in 1891 by James Naismith, a Y.M.C.A. instructor in Springfield, Massachusetts. Designed as an active indoor sport that could be played during the winter months, it spread rapidly and enjoyed enormous popularity in the next century.

The land of the skyscraper was plainly becoming more standardized, owing largely to the new industrialization. To an increasing degree, Americans were falling into the ways of lock-step living—playing, reading, thinking, and talking alike. They were eating the same canned food, wearing the same ready-made clothes. But what they had lost in variety, they were gaining in efficiency. They were still inseparably wedded to the ideal of unlimited human progress, and they still glimpsed, with invincible optimism, the unexplored vistas that stretched into the future.

SELECT READINGS

See previous chapter for titles by Hays, Tarbell, Ginger, and Spencer. Colorful social histories are ALLAN NEVINS, *The Emergence of Modern America, 1865–1878* (1927) and A. M. SCHLESINGER, *The Rise of the City, 1878–1898* (1933). On the role of immigration, see OSCAR HANDLIN's Pulitzer-prize *The Uprooted* (1951) [paperback] and JOHN HIGHAM, *Strangers in the Land* (1955) [paperback]. Useful also is BLAKE MC KELVEY, *The Urbanization of America, 1860–1915* (1963). The church for the era is treated in F. P. WEISENBURGER, *Ordeal of Faith* (1959) and *Triumph of Faith* (1964). For intellectual currents see H. S. COMMAGER, *The American Mind* (1950) [paperback]; RICHARD HOFSTADTER, *Social Darwinism in American Thought* (rev. ed., 1955) [paperback]; J. E. GOULD, *The Chautauqua Movement* (1961); and AUGUST MEIER, *Negro Thought in America* (1963). On reform, consult C. A. BARKER, *Henry George* (1955) and S. E. BOWMAN, *The Year 2000* (Bellamy) (1958); on literature, VAN WYCK BROOKS, *The Confident Years* (1952) and *Howells* (1959); on architecture, SHERMAN PAUL, *Louis Sullivan* (1962) [paperback]; on sport, F. R. DULLES, *America Learns to Play* (1940). Also *Harvard Guide*, Pt. V.

29

The Great West and the Agricultural Revolution, 1865–1890

Go west, young man, and grow up with the country.

HORACE GREELEY, 1850

The Indian Barrier

WHEN the Civil War crashed to a close, the frontier line was still wavering westward. The long fringe of settlement, bulging outward here and there, ran roughly north through central Texas and onward to the Canadian border. Between this jagged line and the settled areas on the Pacific slope, there were virtually no white men. The only exceptions worth mentioning were the islands of Mormons in Utah, occasional trading posts and gold camps, and a few scattered Spanish-Mexican settlements in the Southwest.

The sprawling expanse of the Great West was a rough square which measured about one thousand miles on each side. Embracing mountains, plateaus, deserts, and plains, it was the habitat of the Indian, the buffalo, the wild horse, the prairie dog, and the coyote. Twenty-five years later—that is, by 1890—the entire domain had been carved into states, except for four territories. Men flung themselves greedily on this enormous prize, as if to ravish it. Never before in human experience, probably, had so huge an area been reduced so rapidly to a semblance of civilization.

The Indian, to his misfortune, stood in the path of the white man. Like the blades of mighty scissors, two lines of onward moving pioneers were closing in simultaneously—one from the Pacific Coast, the other from the trans-Mississippi West. A clash was inevitable between an acquisitive civilization and a static culture, for the march of progress crushed under its feet the hunting grounds and hence the food supply of the red man.

Tens of thousands of half-naked Indians roamed the spacious Western plains in 1860. Some of them had surrendered immense portions of their ancestral lands, but not until they had received solemn promises from the Great White Father in Washington that they would be left unmolested and would receive annual gifts of food, clothing, and other supplies. Regrettably, the federal agents were sometimes corrupt, and palmed off moth-eaten blankets, spoiled beef, and similarly defective provisions on the friendless redskins. One of these cheating officials, who had

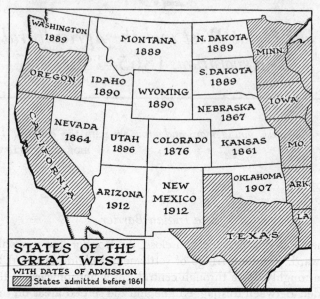

STATES OF THE
GREAT WEST
WITH DATES OF ADMISSION
////// States admitted before 1861

For exact order of admission, see table in Appendix.

drawn a salary of $1500 a year, returned home after four years with an estimated $50,000.

The grasping "palefaces" were guilty of many additional provocations. They flagrantly disregarded treaty promises, openly seized the land of the Indians, wantonly slaughtered their game, and occasionally debauched their squaws. During the Civil War the Sioux of Minnesota, facing starvation and taking advantage of the white man's quarrel, went on the warpath and murdered several hundred settlers. The uprising was finally crushed by federal troops, and nearly forty of the culprits, after a trial, were hanged at a well-attended mass execution.

From 1868 to about 1890, almost incessant warfare raged in various parts of the West between Indians and whites. A printed list of the names of the engagements alone covers over one hundred pages. The fighting was fierce and harrowing, especially the winter campaigning in sub-zero weather.

> Saddle! saddle! saddle!
> Redden spur and thong.
> Ride like the mad tornado,
> The track is lonely and long.

Generals W. T. Sherman, P. H. Sheridan, and G. A. Custer, all of whom had won their spurs in the Civil War, gathered further laurels in the West. They were matched against formidable adversaries, for the Indians of the plains, unlike those first encountered by the American colonists, were mounted on swift ponies and enjoyed baffling mobility. To the disgust of the American soldiers, "the hostiles" were often better armed than the federal troops sent against them with clumsy muzzle-loaders. Conscienceless white fur traders, seeking a profit at any price, would provide the Indians with the most modern repeating rifles.

The Receding Red Man

The savagery was not all on the side of the Indians. Where fighting is protracted and uncivilized, the standards of combat are ordinarily pulled down to the more primitive level. The whites were often the immediate aggressors, and sometimes shot peaceful red men on sight, just to make sure they would give no trouble. At Sand Creek, Colorado, in 1864, Colonel J. M. Chivington's militia massacred in cold blood some 400 Indians who apparently thought they had been promised immunity. The squaws were shot praying for mercy, the children had their brains dashed out, and the braves were tortured, scalped, and unspeakably mutilated. On several notorious occasions, innocent Indians were killed for outrages by fellow tribesmen; sometimes they were shot just for "sport."

The most spectacular of these clashes was the Sioux War of 1876–1877, touched off when a horde of gold-greedy white men rushed into the Black Hills of South Dakota during the stampede of 1875. The proud and warlike Sioux, their lands invaded despite treaty guarantees, took to the warpath. Conspicuous among their leaders was heavy-set Sitting Bull, a medicine man as wily as he was influential.

The Sioux braves were hotly pursued by the lithe and impetuous George A. Custer, the buckskin-clad "boy general." Attacking what turned out to be a superior force of some 2500 well-armed warriors near the Little Big Horn River in present Montana, the "White Chief with Yellow Hair" and his 264 officers and men were wiped out in 1876 when two supporting columns failed to come to their rescue. (Sitting Bull sat out this battle, safely "making medicine" in his tent.) But white reinforcements later arrived, and Sitting Bull and the remnants of his band were finally driven to Canada, whence hunger forced them to return and surrender.

The Nez Percé Indians of Idaho were likewise goaded into warfare in 1877, when gold-crazed white miners trespassed upon their beaver streams. Chief Joseph, a noble and unusually humane leader, established himself as a remarkable strategist when he undertook a retreat of fifteen hundred miles to Canada, only to be cornered thirty miles from safety.

The fierce Apache tribes of Arizona and New Mexico were perhaps the most difficult to subdue. Led by Geronimo, whose eyes blazed hatred of the whites, they were pursued into Mexico by federal troops using the sun-flashing heliograph, which impressed the Indians as "big medicine." The scattered remnants of the braves were persuaded to surrender after their squaws had been exiled to Florida. The Apaches ultimately became successful farmers in Oklahoma, where they raised stock instead of scalps.

The relentless fire-and-sword policy of the whites at last shattered the spirit of the Indians. The vanquished redskins were finally segregated in "human zoos," known as reservations, there to eke out a sullen existence as wards of the government. Their white masters had at last discovered that the red men were much cheaper to feed than to fight.

The downfall of the hapless Indians was engineered by a number of factors. Of cardinal importance was the railroad, which shot an iron arrow through the heart of the West. The locomotive ("bad medicine wagon") could bring out unlimited numbers of troops, farmers, cattlemen, sheepherders, and settlers. The luckless Indians were also ravaged by the diseases of the white men, to which they showed little resistance, and by his firewater, to which they showed almost no resistance. Finally, the virtual extermination of the buffalo resulted in the near-extermination of the plains Indians.

Thundering Herds

Millions of buffalo—described by early Spaniards as "hunchback cows"—darkened the Western prairies when the Americans first pushed across the Mississippi. These shaggy, lumbering beasts were the staff of life for the Indian. Their flesh provided food; their dried dung provided fuel ("buffalo chips"); their hides provided clothing, lariats, bowstrings, and harness.

When the Civil War closed, there were still some fifteen million of these meaty creatures grazing on the grasslands of the Western plains. In 1868 one of the Kansas Pacific locomotives had to wait eight hours for the herd to amble across the tracks; experience had shown that trying to smash through would produce only mangled meat and derailment. Much of the food supply of the railroad construction gangs came from buffalo steaks. William F. ("Buffalo Bill") Cody—sinewy, telescopic-eyed, and a crack shot—killed over four thousand in eighteen months while employed as a scout by the Kansas Pacific.

With the building of the railroad, the massacre of the herds began in dead earnest. Most of the stupid creatures were slain for their hides and in response to the insatiable demand for buffalo robes, which were then highly fashionable. Others were felled merely for their tongues or a few other choice cuts, while the rest of the carcass was left to be picked by the vultures. Countless buffalo were shot for sheer amusement with repeating rifles. "Sportsmen" on lurching railroad trains would lean out the windows and blaze away at the beasts to satisfy their lust for slaughter or excitement.

Such wholesale butchery could have only one end. By 1885 fewer than a thousand buffalo were left, and the once-numerous quadrupeds were in danger of complete extermination. Somewhat like the Indians, a few thousand of the clumsy animals have been kept alive on reservations, largely as living museum pieces. The whole story is a shocking example of the greed and waste that accompanied the conquest of the continent.

"Lo, the Poor Indian!"

By 1890 the Indian was an administrative problem rather than a military menace, even though occasional bands of alcoholically stimulated braves would "go off the reservation." The principal tasks of the whites were to police the red men and adjust them to a more restricted life. The national conscience, already a bit uneasy, had been pricked in 1881 when a sentimental poet-novelist, Helen Hunt Jackson, published her devastating *A Century of Dishonor*. The book was a historical account of governmental injustice in treating and cheating the Indian. Even more impressive in many ways was her supplementary novel, *Ramona* (1884), a love story of injustice to the California aborigines. This romantic tale ultimately sold some 600,000 copies.

An aroused public sentiment now demanded that something be done for the shabbily treated red men. The most significant response came in 1887, when Congress passed the Dawes Act—the first serious attempt on a national scale to civilize the Indians. The tribes hitherto had been regarded as domestic nations within the American nation, and until 1871 treaties had been made with them as with foreign governments. The Dawes Act provided for dissolving many of the tribes as legal entities,

PATIENCE UNTIL THE INDIAN IS CIVILIZED

The white victim of Indian raids gets cold comfort from Secretary of the Interior Carl Schurz, the German-American reformer. Thomas Nast in *Harper's Weekly*, 1878

and for wiping out tribal ownership of property. The land was now granted to individual Indians, with 160 acres going to the head of a family, double that amount if grazing areas were involved. But lest designing whites be tempted to get the Indians drunk and trick them into signing away their birthright for a song, the holdings were made inalienable for twenty-five years.

Further changes in Indian policy occurred in succeeding decades. In 1906 the Burke Act extended the probationary period of Uncle Sam's stepchildren before granting full citizenship. The goal was also adopted of preserving the cultural heritage of the Indians, instead of forcing them to travel completely the "white man's road."

Under the new federal policies, defective though they were, the Indian population started to mount slowly. The total number had been reduced by 1887 to about 243,000—the result of bullets, bottles, and bacteria—but the census of 1950 counted 343,410. Possibly more Indians dwell in the United States today than were here when Columbus came, even though their blood is much diluted with that of their conquerors.

The "noble red man" was partly a creation of literary imagination, especially that of James Fenimore Cooper. Rapacious and unfriendly whites, overlooking the same defects in their own kind, have referred to the Indians as dirty, lousy, cruel, treacherous, polygamous, lazy, and thieving. The truth is that the redskins were children of a more primitive culture, and one cannot fairly judge them by higher standards. Yet many of them, notably the Cherokees who were resettled in Oklahoma, have shown noteworthy adaptability to the economic ways of the whites.

The American people, despite the lengthy record of bloody clashes, owe a genuine debt to the Indian. He traded the furs which kept many of the early colonies on their economic feet. He provided corn, potatoes, tobacco, tomatoes, maple sugar, beans, squash, and other foods, while demonstrating how they could be produced. He showed the white men how to make birch canoes, snowshoes, and toboggans, and taught them the value of many medicinal plants and herbs. He added immeasurably to our pioneering difficulties, but above all he helped make us a tough and resourceful people. A substantial part of the American pageant could be written in terms of a relentless, three-hundred-year campaign against the Indians—one of the decisive campaigns of world history.

From Dishpan to Ore-Breaker

The conquest of the Indians and the coming of the railroad were life-giving boons to the mining frontier. The golden gravel of California continued to yield "pay dirt," and in 1858 an electrifying discovery convulsed Colorado. Avid "Fifty-Niners" or "Pike's Peakers" rushed west to tear at the ramparts of the Rockies. But there were more miners than minerals; and many a gold-grubber, with "Pike's Peak or Bust" inscribed on the canvas of his covered wagon, creaked wearily back with the added inscription, "Busted, by Gosh." Yet countless bearded fortune seekers stayed on, some to strip away the silver deposits, others to extract nonmetallic wealth from the earth in the form of golden grain.

The "Fifty-Niners" also poured feverishly into Nevada in 1859, after the fabulous Comstock Lode had been uncovered. A fantastic amount of gold and silver, worth more than $340,000,000, was mined by the "Kings of the Comstock" from 1860 to 1890. The state of Nevada, "child of the Comstock Lode," was prematurely railroaded into the Union in 1864 so as to provide three electoral votes for President Lincoln.

Smaller "lucky strikes" drew frantic gold-and-silver seekers into Montana, Idaho, and other Western states. Boom towns, known as "Helldorados," sprouted from the deserts like magic. Every third cabin was a saloon, where sweat-stained miners drank bad liquor ("rot gut") in the company of bad women. Lynch law and hempen vigilante justice, as in early California, preserved some semblance of order. And when the "diggings" petered out, the gold-seekers decamped, leaving picturesque "ghost towns" silhouetted in the desert, like Virginia City, Nevada.

Once the loose surface gold was gobbled up, ore-breaking machinery had to be erected to smash the gold-bearing quartz. This operation was so expensive that it could ordinarily be undertaken only by corporations pooling the wealth of stockholders. Gradually the Age of Big Business came to the mining industry. The dusty, bewhiskered miner, dishpan in hand, was replaced by the impersonal and beardless corporation, with its costly machinery and trained engineers. The once-picturesque gold-washer became just another day laborer, for it took gold to get gold.

Yet the mining frontier had played a vital role in the subduing of the continent. Magnet-like, it attracted population and wealth, while advertising to the world the wonders of the wild Western expanses. The amassing of precious metals helped finance the Civil War, facilitated the building of railroads, and forced a partial solution of the Indian problem. The outpouring of silver and gold enabled the Washington Treasury to resume specie payments in 1879, and precipitated the silver issue into American politics. The silver Senators, representing the thinly peopled "acreage states" of the West, used their disproportionate influence to promote the interests of the silver producers. Finally, the mining frontier added to American folklore and literature, as the writings of Bret Harte and Mark Twain so colorfully attest.

Beef Bonanzas

When the Civil War ended, the grassy plains of Texas supported several million tough, long-horned cattle. These scrawny beasts, whose horn spread sometimes reached eight feet, were killed primarily for their hides. There was no way of getting their meat profitably to market.

The problem of marketing was neatly solved when the transcontinental railroads thrust their iron feelers into the West. The cattle could now be shipped bodily to the stockyards, and under the leadership of "beef barons" like the Swifts and Armours, the highly industrialized meat-packing industry sprang into being as one of the main cogs of American economic life. Drawing upon the gigantic stockyards at Kansas City and Chicago, the packers could ship their products to the East Coast in the newly perfected refrigerator cars.

The most spectacular feeder of the new slaughterhouses was the "Long Drive." The Texas cattle raisers, with herds numbering from one thousand to ten thousand head, would drive their animals slowly over the unfenced and unpeopled plains until they reached a railroad terminal. The bawling beasts grazed en route on the free government grass. Favorite terminal points were "cow towns" like Dodge City—"the Bibulous Babylon of the Frontier"—and Abilene (Kansas), Ogallala (Nebraska), and Cheyenne (Wyoming). At Abilene, order was maintained by "Judge Colt" in the person of Marshal James B. ("Wild Bill") Hickok, a fabulous gunman who killed only in self-defense or in line of duty, and who was finally shot in the back while playing poker.

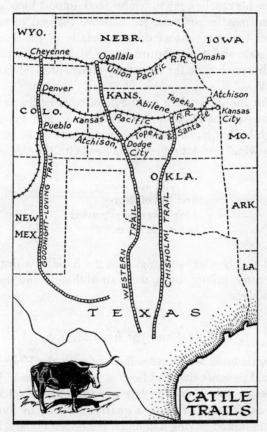

CATTLE TRAILS

While the lush grass was available, the Long Drive proved immensely profitable—that is, to the luckier cattlemen who escaped the Indians, stampedes, cattle fever, and other hazards. From 1866 to 1888 rumbling herds, which totaled over 4,000,000 steers, were driven northward from the beef bowl of Texas. In peak years the profits to some cattlemen would soar as high as 40%. The steer was king in a Cattle Kingdom richly carpeted with grass.

What the Lord giveth, the Lord also taketh away. The railroad made possible the Long Drive; the railroad ultimately ruined the Long Drive, primarily because the locomotives ran both ways. The same rails that took the cattle from the open range to the kitchen range brought out the homesteader and the sheepherder. Both of these intruders, amid flying bullets, put up barbed-wire fences that were too numerous to be cut down by the cowboys. Severe winters, with blinding blizzards that reached 68° below zero, left tens of thousands of dazed cattle starving and freezing. Overexpansion and overgrazing likewise took their toll.

The only escape for the stockman was to elevate cattle raising to the rank of a big business, and avoid the perils of overproduction. The breeder learned to fence his ranches, lay in winter feed, import blooded bulls, produce fewer and meatier animals. He likewise learned to organize. The Wyoming Stock-Growers' Association, especially in the 1880's, virtually controlled the state and its legislature. Many highhanded and illegal practices went on, but such were the more ugly phases of the overrapid taming of the "Wild West."

These were the days when cowboyhood was in flower. The equipment of the lone cowhand—from "shooting irons" and ten-gallon hat to chaps and high-heeled boots—served a useful, not an ornamental, function. The "genuwine" gun-toting cowpuncher, with the sky as his canopy, could boast:

> I'm wild and woolly
> And full of fleas;
> Ain't never been curried
> Below the knees.

These bronzed and bowlegged Knights of the Saddle, with their colorful trappings and cattle-lulling songs, were an authentic and important part of American folklore.

Free Land for Free Men

A new day dawned for Western farmers with the Homestead Act of 1862—an epochal measure that had been vigorously opposed by the South in the years before secession. The law provided that a settler could acquire as much as 160 acres of land (a quarter section) by living on it five years, improving it, and paying a nominal fee of ten dollars. Pre-emption, or first choice, was still possible for certain squatters at $1.25 an acre.

The Homestead Act marked a drastic departure from previous policy. Hitherto public land had been sold primarily for revenue; now it was to be given away in order to encourage a rapid filling of waste spaces and to provide a stimulus to the family farm—"the backbone of democracy." The act was a godsend to a host of farmers who could not afford to buy large holdings, and during the forty years from the date of its passage about half a million families carved out new homes in the vast open spaces.

But the Homestead Act often turned out to be a cruel hoax. The standard 160 acres, which had proved adequate in the well-watered Mississippi basin, often proved quite inadequate in the rain-scarce Great Plains. Countless thousands of homesteaders were forced to give up the one-sided struggle. Uncle Sam, it was said, bet 160 acres against ten dollars that the settler could not live on his homestead for five years. One of these unsuccessful gambles in Greer County, western Oklahoma, inspired a famous folk song:

> Hurrah for Greer County! The land of the free,
> The land of the bedbug, grasshopper, and flea;
> I'll sing of its praises, I'll tell of its fame,
> While starving to death on my government claim.

Naked fraud was spawned by the Homestead Act and sister laws. Much more of the public domain wound up in the clutches of land-grabbing promoters than in the hands of bona fide farmers. Unscrupulous corporations would use "dummy" homesteaders—often aliens bribed with cash or a bottle of beer—to grab off the best properties containing timber, minerals, and oil. Settlers would later swear that they had "improved" the property by erecting a "twelve by fourteen" dwelling, which turned out to measure twelve by fourteen *inches*. In later years the Washington officials were only partially successful in unraveling the tangled skein of deceit. So functioned the government's first big "giveaway" program.

Taming Western Deserts

The life-giving railways also played a major role in developing the agricultural West, primarily by making possible the profitable marketing of crops. In addition, the railroad officials sought to induce Americans and European immigrants to buy the cheap lands earlier granted to the companies by a generous government. A leader in such "induced colonization" was the Northern Pacific Railroad, which at one time had nearly a thousand paid agents in Europe distributing hundreds of thousands of roseate leaflets in various languages.

A shattering of the myth of the Great American Desert further opened the gateways to the agricultural West. The wind-swept prairies were for the most part treeless, and the tough sod had been pounded solid by millions of buffalo hoofs. Pioneer explorers and trappers had assumed that the soil must be sterile, simply because it was not heavily watered and did not support immense forests. But once the prairie sod was broken —and this was done in Kansas with special plows pulled by four powerful yoke of oxen—the earth proved to be astonishingly fruitful.

The boom in Western farming was aided by additional stimulants. Improved irrigation techniques—"the miracle of water"—caused deserts to bloom, notably in Mormon Utah. Tough strains of wheat that were resistant to cold and drought were imported from Russia, and they blos-

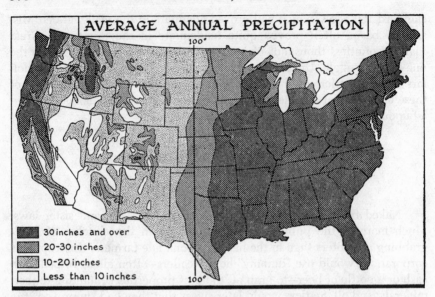

AVERAGE ANNUAL PRECIPITATION

■ 30 inches and over
▨ 20-30 inches
▩ 10-20 inches
□ Less than 10 inches

somed into billowing yellow carpets. New flour-milling processes, which brought John S. Pillsbury of Minneapolis both fame and fortune, increased the demand for grain.

The wheat growers were lured out onto the poorer marginal lands, owing to the high prices in the 1870's produced by crop failures in other parts of the world. Farmers rashly pushed beyond the 100th meridian as far west as the semi-arid regions of eastern Colorado and Montana, where they developed the special techniques of "dry" farming. To their dismay, they were to discover in the next decade that dry farming succeeds best in wet years, and that dusty farms produce dust bowls.

Barbed wire, hardly less than the railroad, bound together the Great West. Fences were necessary to contain livestock, as well as to enclose water holes. Wood was too scarce on the treeless prairies, and ordinary wire would not hold a rampaging steer. In 1874 Joseph F. Glidden invented a superior type of barbed wire, and in 1883 the company using his patent was turning out 600 miles of the new product each day. Among other contributions, barbed wire gave the farmer greater protection against trespassing cattle, and spelled the doom of the Long Drive.

The West Comes of Age

The Great West experienced a fantastic growth of population from the 1870's to the 1890's. A current quip was that one could not tell the truth about the West without lying. Confederate and Union veterans alike moved into the sunset with their families, as did tens of thousands of inpouring immigrants.

A parade of new Western states proudly joined their Eastern sisters.

Boom-town Colorado, offspring of the Pike's Peak gold rush, was greeted in 1876 as "the Centennial State." In 1889–1890 a Republican Congress, eagerly seeking more Republican electoral and Congressional votes, admitted in a wholesale lot six new states: North Dakota, South Dakota, Montana, Washington, Idaho, and Wyoming. The Mormon Church formally and belatedly banned polygamy in 1890, but not until 1896 was Utah deemed worthy to be added to the constellation of the Stars and Stripes. Only Oklahoma, New Mexico, and Arizona remained to be erected into states from contiguous territory on the mainland of North America.

In a last gaudy fling, the Washington government made available to settlers vast stretches of fertile plains formerly occupied by the Indians in the district of Oklahoma ("the Beautiful Land"). Scores of overeager and well-armed "sooners," illegally jumping the gun, had entered Oklahoma territory. They had to be evicted repeatedly by federal troops, who on occasion would shoot the horses of intruders. On April 22, 1889, all was in readiness for the legal opening, and some 50,000 "boomers" were poised expectantly on the boundary line. At high noon the bugle shrilled, and a horde of "Eighty-Niners" poured in on lathered horses or careening vehicles. That night a lonely spot on the prairie had mushroomed into the tented city of Guthrie, with over 10,000 souls. By the end of the year Oklahoma boasted 60,000 inhabitants, and Congress erected into a territory the domain that in 1907 was to be "the Sooner State."

The mad haste of the "boomers" underscored the fact that profitably productive free land was no longer easy to obtain. In 1890—a watershed date—the Superintendent of the Census in Washington announced that for the first time in America's experience a frontier line was no longer discernible. All the unsettled areas were now broken into by isolated bodies of settlement.

This momentous announcement has somehow led to a pair of misconceptions. One is that the year 1890 marked a sharp break with the past; the other is that thereafter little or no land was taken up under the Homestead Act of 1862.

Actually, few Americans in 1890 realized that the frontier line had disappeared. The Homestead Act remained on the books—and still does—and more millions of acres were taken up after 1890 than between 1862 and 1890. But in general the new lands were less desirable, and many sterile or parched farms, though well watered with sweat, had to be abandoned. To this day the federal government, which owns nearly one-fourth of all American soil, has many millions of acres which may be homesteaded. But they are mostly grazing lands and other marginal areas incapable of sustaining a decent standard of living. From time to time, considerable acreage is rendered attractive for homesteading by the completion of irrigation or reclamation projects.

As the 19th Century neared its sunset, the westward-tramping American people were disturbed to find that their fabled free land was going

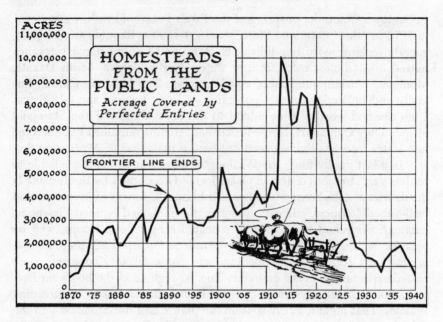

ACRES

HOMESTEADS
FROM THE
PUBLIC LANDS
*Acreage Covered by
Perfected Entries*

FRONTIER LINE ENDS

or had gone. The Secretary of War had prophesied in 1827 that it would take five hundred years to fill the West. But when the nation learned that its land, unlike its air, was not inexhaustible, the seeds were planted in the public mind for the belated conservation movement of later decades.

The Folding Frontier

The frontier was more than a place: it was also a state of mind and a symbol of opportunity. Its passing ended a romantic phase of our internal development, and created new economic and psychological problems.

The footloose American is distinguished by his mobility; the automobile trailer is a typically American device. Our farmers, unlike the European peasant, have never remained rooted to their soil. The sale of land for a profit, as settlement closed in, was often the settler's most profitable crop.

Much speculation has been voiced about the frontier as a safety valve. The theory is that when hard times came, the unemployed who were cluttering the city pavements merely moved west, took up farms, and prospered.

The truth is that relatively few city dwellers, at least in the populous Eastern centers, emigrated to the frontier. Most of them did not know how to farm; few of them possessed enough money to transport themselves west and then pay for livestock and expensive machinery. The initial outlay for equipment had become so heavy by the 1880's and 1890's that the West was decreasingly a land of opportunity for farmers, though it might be for ranchers, miners, and day laborers. A large proportion of the settlers who moved west came from farms on the older frontier, which was within striking distance of the new frontier.

But the safety-valve theory does have some validity. For one thing, free acreage lured westward a host of immigrant farmers. Many of these newcomers would have stayed in the Eastern cities to aggravate problems of unemployment and slum-festering. The frontier also drew off some restless spirits, and no doubt exercised a powerful psychological influence. It is true that the Easterner seldom pulled up stakes and moved west, yet in theory he could always flee to the frontier. This prospect often gave a lift to his drooping spirit—and perhaps also a lift to the wages paid by his employer.

Once the fertile and well-watered free lands were gone, farmers could no longer move west in significant numbers. They had to stand and fight, and consequently they voiced their grievances more and fled from them less. Some farmers actually turned their backs upon the West and moved east. In fact, the cityward movement near the end of the century partially replaced the old Westward Movement.

American history cannot be properly understood unless it is viewed in the light of this westward-moving experience—an experience that was centuries-long and soul-searing. Though raucous and raw, the frontier was the cradle of youthful and robust Americanism, and it left an enduring imprint on the older settlements. The Wild West, with its pistol-popping days, was about to disappear, but much of its distinctive flavor remained with our people. There lingered its incurable optimism, its resilient toughness, its handy-man resourcefulness, its zestful eagerness for social and economic reform. Its spirit still endures in the cowboy-worship in the ever-popular Western movies and fiction. They recapture the spirit of the sagebrush saga, when men were men and women were scarce and highly prized.

The Farm Becomes a Factory

The role of the American farmer, who had once been a jack-of-all-trades, was rapidly changing. In colonial days he had lived on a kind of Robinson Crusoe's island; he had raised his own food, and his womenfolk had woven the clothing. But diversification of crops faded with the passing decades; and after the Civil War, if not earlier, the immense grain-producing areas of the Mississippi Valley found themselves in the throes of an agricultural revolution. Prices were so favorable that the farmer was concentrating on a single money-crop, such as wheat or corn. He could use his profits to buy his foodstuffs at the country store, instead of raising them himself. He could secure his manufactured goods in town or by mail order, perhaps from the Chicago firm of Aaron Montgomery Ward, established in 1872, with its first catalog a single sheet.

The prosperous farmer was now both a specialist and a businessman. As a cog in the vast industrial machine, he was intimately tied in with banking, railroading, and manufacturing. He had to buy expensive machinery both to plant and to harvest his crops. The same powerful steam engine could drag behind it simultaneously the plow, seeder, and harrow. The speed of wheat harvesting was immensely increased in the 1870's by John F. Appleby's twine binder, and then in the 1880's by the "combine" —the combined reaper-thresher, drawn by twenty to forty horses, which both reaped and bagged the grain. The use of such costly equipment naturally called for first-class management. But the farmer, often deficient as a businessman, was inclined to blame the banks and railroads, rather than his own shortcomings, for his losses.

The amazing mechanization of agriculture in the post-war years was almost as striking as the mechanization of industry. America was rapidly becoming the world's bread basket and butcher shop. The farm was attaining the status of a factory—an outdoor grain factory. The bonanza wheat farms of the Minnesota–North Dakota area, for example, were enormous. By 1890 there were at least a half-dozen farms larger than 15,000 acres, with communication by telephone from one part to another. King Wheat was achieving an increasingly prominent position in the galaxy of agricultural potentates.

Deflation Dooms the Debtor

Once the farmer became committed to a one-crop economy—wheat or corn—he was in the same leaky boat with the cotton grower of the South. As long as prices stayed high, all went well. But when they skidded downward in the 1880's, misery and bankruptcy fell like a blight upon once-prosperous farm belts.

The one-crop farmer, once free, was no longer the master of his own destiny. He was engaged in one of the most fiercely competitive of businesses, for the price of his grain was determined in a world market by the world output. If the wheat fields of Argentina, Russia, and other foreign countries smiled, the price of his grain would fall and he would face ruin, as he did in the 1880's and 1890's.

Low prices and a deflated currency were the chief worries of the sun-bronzed farmer—North, South, and West. If he had borrowed $1000 in 1885, when wheat was worth about a dollar a bushel, he expected to pay back the equivalent of 1000 bushels, plus interest, when his mortgage fell due. But if he let his debt run to 1890, when wheat had fallen to about fifty cents a bushel, he would have to pay back the price of 2000 bushels for the $1000 he had borrowed, plus interest. This pound of flesh struck him as unjust, though his steely-eyed creditor often branded the complaining debtor a slippery and dishonest rascal.

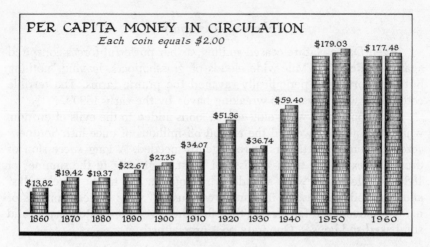

PER CAPITA MONEY IN CIRCULATION

Each coin equals $2.00

$13.82	$19.42	$19.37	$22.67	$27.35	$34.07	$51.36	$36.74	$59.40	$179.03	$177.48
1860	1870	1880	1890	1900	1910	1920	1930	1940	1950	1960

The deflationary pinch on the debtor flowed partly from the static money supply. There were simply not enough dollars to go around, and as a result prices were forced down. In 1870, the amount in circulation for each person was $19.42; in 1890 it was only $22.67. Yet in these twenty years business and industrial activity, increasing manyfold, had intensified the scramble for available currency.

The luckless farmer was caught in a treadmill. Despite unremitting toil in the blazing sun, he operated year after year at a loss, and lived off his fat as best he could. In a vicious circle, his farm machinery increased his output of grain, lowered the price, and drove him even deeper into debt. Mortgages engulfed homesteads at an alarming rate; by 1890 Nebraska alone reported more than 100,000 farms blanketed with mortgages. The repeated crash of the sheriff-auctioneer's hammer kept announcing to the world that another sturdy American husbandman had become landless in a landed nation.

Ruinous rates of interest, running from 8% to 40%, were charged on mortgages, largely by local agents of Eastern loan companies. The wind-burned sons of the sod, who felt that they deserved praise for developing the country, cried out in despair against the loan sharks and the Wall Street octopus. Laws designed to halt excessive interest charges brought little real relief.

Farm tenancy rather than farm ownership was spreading at an alarming rate. The trend was especially marked in the share-cropping South, where cotton prices sank as dismayingly as those of Northern wheat. By 1880 one-fourth of all American farms were operated by tenants. The United States was ready to feed the world, but under the new industrial feudalism the ill-fated farmers were about to sink back into a status suggesting Old World serfdom.

Unhappy Husbandmen

Even Dame Nature ceased smiling, as her powerful forces conspired against agriculture. Mile-wide clouds of grasshoppers, leaving "nothing but the mortgage," periodically ravaged the prairie farms. The terrible cotton-boll weevil was also wreaking havoc by the early 1890's.

The good earth was going sour. Floods added to the evils of erosion, which had already washed the topsoil off millions of once-lush Southern acres. Expensive fertilizers were urgently needed. A long succession of droughts seared the trans-Mississippi West, beginning in the summer of 1887. Whole towns were abandoned. "Going home to the wife's folks" and "In God we trusted, in Kansas we busted" were typical laments of many impoverished farmers, as they fled their weather-beaten shacks and sun-baked sod houses. One irate poet proclaimed:

> Fifty miles to water,
> A hundred miles to wood,
> To hell with this damned country,
> I'm going home for good.

To add to his miseries, the hard-pressed husbandman was gouged by his government—local, state, and national. His land was overassessed and he paid heavy local taxes, while wealthy Easterners concealed their stocks and bonds in safe-deposit boxes. The protective tariff of these years, while pouring profits into the pockets of the manufacturer, imposed heavy burdens on agriculture, especially in the South. The cotton producer or grain grower had to sell his low-priced unprotected product in a highly competitive world market, while buying his high-priced manufactured goods in a highly protected home market.

The unfortunate farmer was also "farmed" by the corporations and processors. He was at the mercy of the Harvester Trust, the Barbed Wire Trust, and the Fertilizer Trust, all of which could control or limit output and raise prices to extortionate levels. The middlemen took a juicy "cut" from the selling price of the goods that he bought, while storage rates for his grain at the warehouses and elevators were pushed up by the operators.

The railroad octopus, in addition, had the grain growers in its grip. Freight rates could be so high that the farmer sometimes lost less if he burned his corn for fuel than if he shipped it. If he raised his voice in protest, the vengeful railroad operators might let his grain spoil in damp places, or refuse to provide him with cars when needed.

The farmers in 1890 represented nearly one-half of the total population, but they were hopelessly disorganized. The manufacturers and railroads were well organized, and they employed persuasive lobbyists. But the farmers were by nature independent and individualistic—dead set against consolidation or regimentation. They never did organize successfully to restrict production until forced to do so by the Washington government nearly half a century later. Meanwhile they were slowly being goaded into a large-scale political uprising.

The Farmers Take Their Stand

Agrarian unrest had flared forth earlier in the Greenback movement shortly after the Civil War. Prices sagged in 1868, and a host of farmers unsuccessfully sought relief from low prices and high indebtedness by demanding an inflation of the currency with paper money.

The National Grange of the Patrons of Husbandry—better known as the Grange—was organized in 1867. Its leading spirit was Oliver H. Kelley, a shrewd and energetic Minnesota farmer then working as a clerk in Washington. A primary objective at first was to stimulate the minds of the farm folk by social, educational, and fraternal activities.

The Grange, with its picnics, music, and lecturers, had much colorful appeal. Kelley was a Mason, and he introduced a mumbo-jumbo of passwords and secrecy, as well as a four-ply hierarchy, ranging for men from Laborer to Husbandman, and for women from Maid to Matron. The movement was a godsend to the sun-bonneted and bony-handed womenfolk, who were cursed with loneliness in widely separated farmhouses. The Grange spread with the rapidity of the old-time prairie fire, and by 1875 claimed 800,000 members, chiefly in the Middle West and South. Buzzing with gossip, they often met in red schoolhouses around pot-bellied stoves.

The Grangers gradually raised their aim from self-improvement to improvement of the farmers' plight. In a determined effort to break free from the clutches of the trusts, they established cooperatives for both consumers and producers. Their most ambitious experiment in this field was an attempt to manufacture harvesting machinery, but this bold venture, partly as a result of mismanagement, ended in financial disaster.

The embattled Grangers also went into politics, and enjoyed their most gratifying success in the grain-growing regions of the upper Mississippi Valley, chiefly in Illinois, Wisconsin, Iowa, and Minnesota. There, through state legislation, they made a determined effort to regulate railway rates and the storage rates charged by railroads and by the operators of warehouses and grain elevators. Many of the state courts, notably in Illinois, were disposed to recognize the principle of public control of private business for the general welfare. But a number of the so-called Granger Laws were badly drawn, and they were bitterly fought through the high courts by the well-paid lawyers of the "interests." Following judicial reverses, notably at the hands of the Supreme Court in the famous Wabash Railroad decision of 1886 (see p. 526), the Grangers declined rapidly in influence. But their organization has lived on as a vocal champion of farm interests.

THE GRANGE AWAKENING THE SLEEPERS

The farmer tries to arouse the apathetic public to the dangers of the onrushing railroad monopoly. Culver Service

Agrarian grievances also found a vent in the Greenback Labor Party, which combined the inflationary appeal of the earlier Greenbackers with a program for improving the lot of labor. In 1878, the high-water mark of the movement, the Greenback-Laborites polled over a million votes and elected fourteen members of Congress. In the presidential election of 1880 the Greenbackers ran General James B. Weaver, an old Granger who was a favorite of the veterans and who possessed a remarkable voice and bearing. He spoke to perhaps a half-million citizens in a hundred or so speeches, but polled only 3% of the total popular vote.

The Populist Crusade

A striking manifestation of agrarian discontent, mounting in the late 1880's, came through the Farmers' Alliances, North and South, white and Negro. Like the Grangers, these groups sponsored picnics and other social gatherings; they bestirred themselves in politics; they organized cooperatives of various kinds; and they strove to break the strangling grip of the railroads and manufacturers. By about 1890 the members of the Farmers' Alliances probably numbered more than 1,000,000 so-called "calamity howlers," many of whom sang, "Toilers Unite" and "Where Will the Farmer Be?"

A new grouping—the People's Party—began to emerge spectacularly in the early 1890's. Better known as the Populists, and cynically dubbed the "Popocrats," these zealous souls attracted countless recruits from the Farmers' Alliances. The higher the foreclosure rate on mortgages, the deeper the anger of the aroused soil tillers. Numerous whiskered prophets —not to say "crackpots"—sprang forward to lead the Populists. Among these assorted characters was an eloquent red-haired "spellbinder," Ignatius Donnelly of Minnesota, who was three times elected to Congress.

The queen of the "calamity howlers" was undeniably Mary Elizabeth ("Mary Yellin'") Lease, a tall, mannish woman who was dubbed "the Kansas Pythoness." In 1890 she made an estimated 160 speeches. Upbraiding the moneyed aristocracy, and denouncing the government "of Wall Street, by Wall Street, and for Wall Street," she cried that the people of Kansas should raise "less corn and more hell." They did. The big-city New York *Evening Post* snarled, "We don't want any more states until we can civilize Kansas."

Yet the Populists, despite their peculiarities, were not to be laughed aside. In deadly earnest, they were leading an impassioned campaign to relieve the misfortunes of the farmer. The smile faded from Republicans and Democrats alike as countless thousands of Populists sang, "Goodbye, My Party, Good-bye." The yawning Eastern plutocrats would do well to heed these Western "hayseeds," for at long last the calloused and gallused sons of toil were marshaling their vast political strength.

SELECT READINGS

Vivacious chapters appear in R. A. BILLINGTON, *Westward Expansion* (2d ed., 1960). W. P. WEBB's provocative *The Great Plains* (1931) [paperback] is a landmark. The Indians are disposed of in R. K. ANDRIST, *The Long Death* (1964) and W. H. LECKIE, *The Military Conquest of the Southern Plains* (1963). On mining see RODMAN PAUL, *Mining Frontiers of the Far West, 1848–1880* (1963) and W. S. GREEVER, *The Bonanza West* (1963). For beef, see E. S. OSGOOD, *The Day of the Cattleman* (1929) [paperback] and LEWIS ATHERTON, *The Cattle Kings* (1961). EVERETT DICK has a picturesque story in *The Sod-House Frontier* (1937). Indispensable is J. D. HICKS, *The Populist Revolt* (1931) [paperback]; more sweeping is F. A. SHANNON, *The Farmers' Last Frontier: Agriculture, 1860–1897* (1945). An older work is S. J. BUCK, *The Granger Movement* (1913) [paperback]. See also MARTIN RIDGE, *Ignatius Donnelly* (1962); NORMAN POLLACK, *The Populist Response to Industrial America* (1962); W. T. K. NUGENT, *The Tolerant Populists: Kansas Populism and Nativism* (1963). Also *Harvard Guide*, Pt. V.

30

The Revolt of the Debtor, 1889–1900

> *The humblest citizen of all the land, when clad in the armor of a righteous cause, is stronger than all the hosts of error.*
>
> WILLIAM J. BRYAN, Cross of Gold speech, 1896

The Return of the Republicans

BENJAMIN HARRISON—stocky, dignified, and heavily bearded—was inaugurated President under weeping heavens on March 4, 1889. The outgoing Grover Cleveland obligingly held an umbrella over him. The new President was an honest and earnest party man, but unhappily he was brusque and abrupt. He could charm a crowd of ten thousand people with his oratory, but he would chill them individually with a clammy handshake. He came to be known, rather unfairly, as "the White House Ice Chest."

James G. Blaine, uncrowned king of the party, was awarded as a consolation prize the coveted Secretaryship of State. Still burning with ambition, the "Plumed Knight" did not get along well with his chief. Harrison, who was admittedly a lesser figure, somewhat resented his overpowering subordinate.

During the recent presidential campaign, Harrison had made his polite bow to civil service reform. But the Republicans, after their four-year fast, clamored hungrily for the fleshpots of federal office. Harrison followed the strict letter of the civil service law, but beheaded many Democrats. To his credit, he appointed to the Civil Service Commission a bespectacled and violently energetic New Yorker, Theodore Roosevelt. This eager-beaver young politician got his position as a reward for his oratory in the recent campaign, but ironically his new job was to prevent the parceling out of offices for political purposes.

The Republicans in the House of Representatives could not expect smooth sailing; they had only three votes more than the necessary quorum of 163 members. If the Democrats continued their practice of refusing to answer roll calls, the Republicans could muster a quorum only with difficulty. The Democrats were also prepared to make numerous delaying

586

motions. These included time-consuming demands for a roll call to determine the presence of a quorum, even though one was obviously present.

Into this dynamite-charged forum stepped the new Republican Speaker of the House, Thomas B. Reed of Maine. A hulking figure who towered six feet three inches and weighed about 275 pounds, he had already made his mark as a masterful debater. Cool and collected, he spoke with a harsh nasal drawl, and wielded a verbal harpoon of sarcasm. One Congressman who had declaimed that he would "rather be right than President," like Henry Clay, was silenced by Reed's rasping sneer that he would "never be either." Men cringed at "the crack of his quip."

Early in 1890 the redoubtable Reed undertook singlehandedly to change the House rules. He believed that the majority should legislate, in accord with democratic practices, and not be crippled by a filibustering minority. He therefore ignored Democratic speakers who sprang to their feet and sought to suggest the absence of a quorum. In piecing out quorums, he counted as present certain Democrats in the chamber who had not answered the roll and who, rule book in hand, furiously denied that they were legally present. For three days pandemonium rocked the House, while Reed held his ground, reputedly counting as present Congressmen who were in the barber shop or on trains headed for home.

The gavel rule of "Czar" Reed finally prevailed. The Fifty-first or "Billion Dollar" Congress—the first in peacetime to appropriate approximately this sum—gave birth to a bumper crop of bouncing legislative babies. When the Democrats won control of the House two years later, they paid Reed the compliment of reluctantly adopting some of his reforms for speedier action.

Gravy for All

President Harrison, himself a Civil War general, was disposed to deal generously with his old comrades-in-arms. He appointed as Commissioner of Pensions James Tanner, who had lost both legs at the second Battle of Bull Run. A professional pension lobbyist, Corporal Tanner threatened to drive a six-mule team through the Treasury, and to wring "from the hearts of some the prayer, 'God help the surplus.'" His spendthrift policies and ineptitude cost him his job in less than a year, but he encouraged further extravagance in ladling out pensions.

The "Billion Dollar Congress" cooperated by opening wide the federal purse strings in the Pension Act of 1890. It conferred pensions on all Civil War veterans who had served for ninety days and who were now unable to do manual labor. Between 1891 and 1895 the host of pensioners was thus raised from 676,000 to 970,000, and by the time Harrison left office in 1893 the annual bill had been increased from $81,000,000 to $135,000,000.

A policy of liberality toward old soldiers had special attractions for

Republican politicians. It helped to solve the problem of the Treasury surplus—a problem that had bedeviled President Cleveland. It helped to save the protective tariff by making plausible, even necessary, the continuance of high customs duties. It helped to secure Republican votes, for the aging veterans of the G.A.R. (Grand Army of the Republic) were grateful to the G.O.P. (Grand Old Party) for its handouts.

The gavel of "Czar" Reed, pounding imperiously, drove additional bills through the "Billion Dollar Congress." Conspicuous among them was the Sherman Anti-Trust Act of 1890. This pioneering law, though a feeble bludgeon, did something to quiet the mounting uproar against bloated corporations.

Noteworthy also was the Sherman Silver Purchase Act of 1890. The Western silver miners were acutely unhappy over the limited silver-purchase program under the Bland-Allison Law of 1878, and many of them were demanding unrestricted government buying of the "beloved white metal." At the same time, many debt-burdened Western and Southern farmers were clamoring for the unlimited coinage of silver. They were convinced that the addition of an immense amount of silver money would inflate the currency, and thus make for higher prices and easier debt payments. The "Gold Bug" East looked with conservative horror on any such tampering with the money supply, but hungered for the profits that might be reaped from a boost in the tariff schedules.

The stage was thus set for a huge logrolling operation. The Western silver agitators agreed to support a protective tariff, which they detested, if the Eastern protectionists would support a silver bill, which they distrusted. As a part of the Sherman Silver Purchase Act of 1890, the Treasury was to buy a total of 4,500,000 ounces monthly—about all that was being mined—and pay for it in notes redeemable in either silver or gold. The new law, while boosting the price for the miners, would approximately double the minimum amount of silver that could be acquired under the old Bland-Allison law.

The McKinley Tariff Bill

The high-protection Republicans, mistakenly claiming a mandate from the voters in 1888, prepared to push the tariff schedules higher. A brand-new bill was sponsored in the House by William McKinley of Ohio, who was soon to be dubbed "the high priest of high protection." The rates were boosted to the highest peacetime level yet—an average of 48.4% on dutiable goods. The once-bothersome surplus was neatly disposed of by putting raw sugar on the free list and giving a bounty of two cents a pound to the American producers of sugar.

The McKinley Bill, by raising slightly the tariff duties on certain agricultural products, made a feeble attempt to quiet the outcries of the

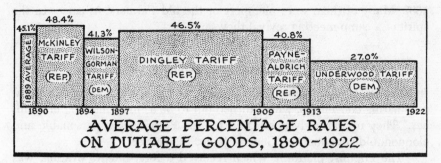

AVERAGE PERCENTAGE RATES ON DUTIABLE GOODS, 1890–1922

See p. 264 for earlier figures; p. 810 for later figures.

farmers. But the concession was a hollow one indeed. Few foreign growers of farm produce—wheat, corn, barley, potatoes—could hope to compete with the soil-rich Americans on their own ground.

The McKinley duties on manufactured goods, as ill luck would have it, actually brought new woes to the farmer. Some Eastern manufacturers raised their prices even before the law went into effect. Tin peddlers—a number of them reportedly in the pay of the Democrats—went systematically from house to house in the Middle West, displaying their wares to the housewife. They would cleverly but dishonestly say that yesterday a pie pan sold for ten cents, but today for twenty-five cents—all because of the wicked new Republican tariff.

Sweeping tariff revisions, like the McKinley Act, usually boomerang against the party in power. Since 1833 the regime in Washington has rarely survived a major tariff overhauling, except where war has intervened. Mounting discontent against the McKinley Bill, combined with other grievances, caused the voters to rise in their wrath, especially in the Middle Western farm belt. The Congressional landslide of 1890 reduced the Republican membership of the House from 166 to a scant 88 members, as compared with 235 Democrats. The Farmers' Alliance men were notably successful in the Southern and Western states, and the new Congress was to contain nine of their spokesmen. Even the highly publicized William McKinley was swept out of office, partly because of a Democratic gerrymander * of his district. But he was elected governor of Ohio the next year, and remained in the limelight.

Presidential Hopefuls

Malcontents among laborers and agrarians, aroused to new fury by the McKinley Bill, were about to fuse into the Populist Party early in

---

* To "gerrymander" is to rearrange electoral districts in such a way as to submerge some of the voting strength of the opposition. In Massachusetts in 1812 one grotesquely shaped district resembled a salamander, whence the term "gerrymander," after Elbridge Gerry, then governor of the commonwealth.

1892. Many of them were members of the old Farmers' Alliance. In the spirit of a camp-meeting revival they sang:

> Bring out the good old ballot, boys,
> We'll *right* our every *wrong*.

In July, 1892, the Populists formally met at Omaha in their presidential nominating convention, which turned out to be a "mass meeting of maniacs." They uproariously nominated for the Presidency a personable and eloquent old Greenbacker, General James B. Weaver.

The Populist platform, which received a forty-minute ovation, was a rabble-rousing summation of grievances. It horrified the Eastern conservatives by proclaiming that "tramps and millionaires" come from "the same prolific womb of governmental injustice." It demanded the free and unlimited coinage of silver at the ratio of 16 to 1, as a means of increasing the currency in circulation. It urged a graduated income tax. It insisted on government ownership of the telephone and telegraph, and particularly of the railroad. The time had come, the Populists declaimed, "when the railroad corporations will either own the people or the people must own the railroads. . . ."

Several weeks earlier, in June, 1892, the Republican delegates had gathered in Minneapolis. Renomination of the standoffish Harrison was unavoidable, even though he was cordially disliked by the party bosses. Three days before the convention met, Secretary Blaine dramatically resigned from the Cabinet, as if to focus attention on himself. But the aging "Plumed Knight's" plume was drooping badly, and Harrison was renominated without undue difficulty on a platform which vigorously upheld the protective tariff.

The Democratic Man of Destiny was the portly but energetic ex-President, Grover Cleveland. He had built up a profitable law practice in New York City, and after hobnobbing with a wealthy clientele, had become increasingly unprogressive in outlook. Yet such was his reputation that he was nominated at Chicago on the first ballot.

Unhorsing Harrison

The presidential campaign of 1892 was on the whole clean, quiet, and creditable. The Republicans cried, "Grover, Grover, all is over," while the Democrats came back with:

> Grover! Grover!
> Four years more of Grover,
> Out they go, in we go,
> Then we'll be in clover.

A few faint appeals were made to the fast-fading Bloody Shirt. Among suggestive Republican songs were "When Harrison Heard the Bugle's

Call" and "How Will the Soldier Vote?" But the tariff, as in the preceding campaign, was the overshadowing issue. The high-tariff Republicans chorused, "Hail Protection" and "Good-bye, Free Traders, Good-bye." The low-tariff Democrats countered with "Drive the High-Tariff Tinkers to the Wall" and "Free Wool to Make Our Breeches."

An epidemic of strikes then sweeping the country proved damaging to Harrison's cause. They eloquently refuted the shopworn Republican argument that high protection was necessary for high wages. The most notorious outburst flared forth at Carnegie's Homestead plant near Pittsburgh, following a pay slash for the steelworkers. The company called in three hundred armed Pinkerton detectives. The defiant strikers, armed with rifles and dynamite, forced their assailants to surrender after a pitched battle in which ten persons were killed and some sixty wounded. Troops were eventually called out, and both the strike and the union were broken. But the unsavory episode doubtless lost thousands of votes for the Republicans.

With this unexpected boost from the Pinkerton Agency, Cleveland unseated Harrison. "Old Grover" polled 277 electoral votes to his opponent's 145, and 5,556,918 popular votes to 5,176,108. Cleveland became the first man in our history to receive a popular plurality three times, though he took office only twice.

The Populists made a remarkable showing. Singing "Good-bye, Party Bosses," they rolled up 1,041,028 popular votes and 22 electoral votes for

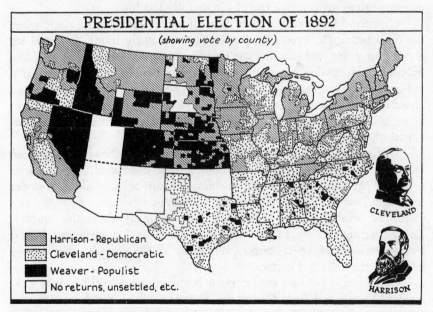

PRESIDENTIAL ELECTION OF 1892
(showing vote by county)

CLEVELAND

HARRISON

Harrison - Republican
Cleveland - Democratic
Weaver - Populist
No returns, unsettled, etc.

Note the concentration of Populist strength in the semi-arid farming regions of the western half of the country. (Compare with the annual-precipitation map on p. 576.)

General Weaver. They thus became one of the few third parties in American history to break into the electoral column. But their electoral votes came only from six Middle Western and Western states, four of which (Kansas, Colorado, Idaho, and Nevada) fell completely into the Populist basket. The new party was deprived of valuable allies when the indebted farmers of the Solid South, though sorely tempted, refused to desert the Democratic camp.

Old Grover Again

Grover Cleveland took office once more in 1893, the only President ever re-elected after defeat. He was the same old bull-necked and bull-headed Cleveland, with a little more weight, polish, conservatism, and self-assertiveness. He was still inclined to put his foot down rather than slide it down, to demand a whole loaf or none, to go his own resolute way rather than hold his nose and play ball with the politicians. But if it was the same old Grover Cleveland, it was not the same old country. The debtors were up in arms.

Cleveland's Attorney General, Richard Olney, was a stocky and conservative Yankee, cut from the same piece of cloth as his stubborn and pugnacious chief. As a wealthy corporation lawyer associated with the railroads, he had no stomach for a vigorous prosecution of big business under the Interstate Commerce Act and the Sherman Anti-Trust Act. His record was generally one of weakness and deliberate failure, for he was not a man to "betray a trust." He joyfully lost his cases.

Cleveland had hardly seated himself in the presidential chair when the devastating Panic of 1893 burst about his burly frame. It lasted for about four years, and was in some respects the worst of the century. Contributing causes were no doubt the splurge of overspeculation, labor disorders, and the current agricultural depression. Free-silver agitation had also damaged American credit abroad, and the usual pinch on American finances had come when European banking houses, after earlier failures, began to call in loans from the United States.

Distress was acute and widespread. About eight thousand American business houses collapsed in six months, and dozens of railroad lines went into the hands of receivers. Business executives "died like flies under the strain," wrote Henry Adams. Soup kitchens were set up for the unemployed, while gangs of hoboes tramped aimlessly about the country. Local charities did what they could, but the federal government, bound by the let-nature-take-its-course philosophy of the century, was unable to relieve the suffering masses.

Cleveland, who had earlier been bothered by a surplus, was now burdened with a deficit. Under the Sherman Silver Purchase Act, the Treasury was required to issue legal tender notes for the silver bullion that it bought. The bearers of the paper currency would then present it for gold, and by law the notes had to be reissued. The new holders would repeat the process, thus draining out the precious yellow metal in an "endless chain" operation.

A reluctant Cleveland was finally forced to call upon Congress for help. Alarmingly, the gold reserve in the Treasury had dropped below $100,000,000, which was popularly regarded as the safe minimum for supporting about $350,000,000 in outstanding greenbacks. Cleveland saw no alternative but to halt the bleeding away of gold by engineering a repeal of the Sherman Silver Purchase Act of 1890. For this purpose he summoned Congress in an extra session in the summer of 1893.

Unknown to the country, complications threatened from another quarter. A malignant growth had developed in the roof of Cleveland's mouth, and it had to be removed on a private yacht with extreme secrecy. If the President had died under the knife, his place would have been taken by the "soft money" Vice-President, Adlai E. Stevenson—an eventuality that would have deepened the crisis.

The debate in Congress over the repeal of the silver act was meanwhile running its heated course. An eloquent young Congressman from Nebraska, the thirty-three-year-old William Jennings Bryan, held the galleries spellbound for three hours as he championed the cause of free silver. The friends of silver announced that "hell would freeze over" before Congress passed the repeal measure. But an angered Cleveland used his office-giving power to break the filibuster in the Senate. He thus alienated the Democratic silverites and disrupted the ranks of his party at the very outset of his administration.

Gold Shortages and Job Shortages

The hemorrhaging of gold from the Treasury was only partially stopped by the repeal of the Sherman Silver Purchase Act. Other currency was still being presented for redemption, and in February, 1894, the gold reserve sank to a dismaying $41,000,000. The nation was in grave danger of going off the gold standard.

Again Cleveland was forced to act vigorously. As a champion of sound money, he could see no alternative but to sell government bonds for gold and deposit the proceeds in the Treasury. Two bond issues were floated in 1894, totaling over $100,000,000, but the "endless chain" operations continued relentlessly.

Early in 1895, Cleveland turned in desperation to J. P. Morgan and a Wall Street syndicate. After tense negotiations at the White House, the bankers agreed to lend the government $65,000,000 in gold. They were obviously in business for profit, so they charged a commission amounting to about $7,000,000. But they did make a significant concession when they agreed to obtain one-half of the gold abroad and take the necessary steps to dam it up in the leaky Treasury. The loan, at least temporarily,

WEST AND SOUTH FEED THE COUNTRY WHILE WALL STREET MILKS IT

A cartoon of the 1890's highly popular with Democrats and Populists

helped restore confidence in the nation's finances. Following one more public bond sale and a business upswing, the crisis was surmounted.

But the bond deal stirred up a storm of controversy. The Wall Street ogre, especially in the eyes of the silverites and other debtors, was a symbol of all that was wicked and grasping. Cleveland's secretive dealings with mighty "Jupiter" Morgan were savagely condemned as a "sell-out" of the national government. But Cleveland was certain that he had done no wrong. Sarcastically denying that he was "Morgan's errand boy," he asserted: "Without shame and without repentance I confess my share of the guilt."

Meanwhile several ragged armies of unemployed, victims of the depression, were staging demonstrations. The most famous of these marches was that of "General" Jacob S. Coxey, a wealthy Ohio quarry owner, who started for Washington in 1894 with several score of men, accompanied by a score or so of newspaper reporters. His platform included a demand that the government relieve unemployment by an inflationary public works program, supported by some $500,000,000 in legal tender notes to be issued by the Treasury. Coxey himself rode in a carriage with his wife and infant son, appropriately named Legal Tender Coxey, while his "army" tramped along behind, singing with obvious exaggeration:

We're coming, Grover Cleveland, 500,000 strong,
We're marching on to Washington to right the nation's wrong.

The "Commonweal Army" of Coxeyites finally straggled into the nation's capital. But the "invasion" took on the aspects of a comic opera when "General" Coxey and his "lieutenants" were arrested for walking on the grass. Other armies—"petitions in boots"—were less well behaved, and accounted for considerable disorder and pillage.

Government by Injunction

Violent flare-ups occurred elsewhere in connection with current labor outbursts, notably in Chicago. The most frightening was the crippling Pullman strike of 1894. Eugene V. Debs, an impetuous but personally lovable labor leader, had helped organize the American Railway Union of about 150,000 members. The Pullman Palace Car Company, which maintained a model town near Chicago for its employees, was hit hard by the depression and cut wages about one-third. But it did not reduce rent for the company houses. The workers finally struck—in some places overturning Pullman cars—and paralyzed railway traffic from Chicago to the Pacific Coast.

The terrorism in Chicago was serious but not completely out of hand. At least this was the judgment of Governor Altgeld of Illinois, a friend of the downtrodden who had pardoned the Haymarket Square anarchists the year before. But Attorney General Olney, an archconservative and an ex-railroad attorney, prevailed upon Cleveland to dispatch federal troops. His legal grounds were that the strikers were interfering with the transit of the United States mail. Cleveland supported Olney with the ringing declaration, "If it takes the entire army and navy to deliver a postal card in Chicago, that card will be delivered."

To the delight of conservatives, the Pullman strike was crushed by this bayonet-supported intervention from Washington. Debs and his leading associates, who had defied a federal court order (injunction) to cease striking, were sentenced to six months' imprisonment for contempt of court. Ironically, the lean labor agitator spent much of his enforced leisure reading radical literature, which ultimately influenced him to assume leadership of the Socialist movement in America.

Embittered cries of "government by injunction" now burst from organized labor. This was the first time that such a weapon had been used conspicuously by Washington to break a strike, and it was all the more distasteful because defiant laborites who were held in contempt could be imprisoned without jury trial. Signs multiplied that employers were striving to smash labor unions by court action. Non-labor elements of the country, including the Populists and other debtors, were likewise incensed. They saw in this brutal Pullman episode further proof of an unholy alliance between Big Business and the courts.

Tariff Tinkering

The McKinley Tariff of 1890 had been designed to keep protection high and the surplus low. It succeeded admirably in achieving both goals. By 1894 the Treasury was faced with an alarming deficit of $61,000,000.

The Democrats undertook to frame a tariff that would provide adequate revenue with moderate protection, as they had promised in the

Cleveland-Harrison campaign of 1892. The Wilson Bill, aimed at these objectives, was introduced in the House by an ex-college president, William L. Wilson of West Virginia. As a concession to the Populists and other foes of plutocracy, the measure included a tax of 2% on incomes over $4000. Wealthy Joseph H. Choate growled, "Communistic, socialistic."

When the new tariff bill reached the Senate, it was pounced upon by a swarm of lobbyists in the pay of Big Industry. After much button-holing and vote trading, the Wilson-Gorman Bill was drastically revamped by the addition of over 630 amendments. The Sugar Trust stirred up a scandal when it inserted benefits to itself worth a sweet $20,000,000 a year. As a result of such backstairs pressures, the Wilson-Gorman law of 1894 fell scandalously short of establishing a low tariff, even though it did reduce the existing McKinley rates from 48.4% to 41.3% on dutiable goods. (See chart, p. 589.)

Cleveland was outraged by what he regarded as a gross betrayal of Democratic campaign pledges. In an angry outburst he publicly denounced the bill as "party perfidy and party dishonor"—to the raucous glee of the Republicans. But to veto the patchwork affair would leave the even higher McKinley Tariff on the books, so Cleveland grudgingly let the bill become law without his signature. The Wilson-Gorman hodgepodge at least had the redeeming feature of the income tax, which was highly popular among the mass of the people.

But the income tax lasted less than a year. In 1895 the Supreme Court, by a close five-to-four decision, struck down this part of the Wilson-Gorman Act.* The only popular feature of the unpopular tariff law thus perished under the judicial tomahawk. A chorus of denunciation rose from the Populists and other impoverished groups, who were more than ever convinced that the courts were only the tools of the plutocrats.

Democratic political fortunes naturally suffered. The tariff dynamite which had blasted the Republicans out of the House in 1890 now dislodged the Democrats, with a strong helping hand from the depression. The revitalized Republicans, singing "The Soup House" and "Times Are Mighty Hard," won the Congressional elections of 1894 in a landslide, and now had 244 votes to 105 for the Democrats. The prospects of the Republicans for 1896 seemed roseate. They were openly boasting that they had only to nominate a "rag baby" or a "yaller dog," and they could put it in the White House. Such optimism misread the signs of the times.

The discontented debtors, including the Populists, were turning in throngs to free silver as a cure-all. An enormously popular pamphlet, entitled *Coin's Financial School* (1894), was being distributed by the hundreds of thousands of copies. Written by William Hope Harvey, it was illustrated by clever woodcuts, one of which depicted the gold ogre beheading the beautiful silver maiden. In fiction parading as fact, the

* It violated the "direct tax" clause. See Art. I, Sec. IX, para. 4, Appendix.

booklet showed how the "little professor"—"Coin" Harvey—overwhelmed the bankers and professors of economics with his brilliant sallies in behalf of free silver. The belief was gaining momentum among silverites and debtors that there was a foul conspiracy on foot, both nationally and internationally, to elevate gold above silver.

Mark Hanna's Fair-Haired Boy

The leading candidate for the Republican presidential nomination in 1896 was ex-Congressman William McKinley of Ohio, sponsor of the ill-starred tariff bill of 1890. He had established a creditable Civil War record, having risen to the rank of major; he hailed from the electorally potent state of Ohio; and he could point to long years of honorable service in Congress, where he had made many friends by his kindly and conciliatory manner. Rather small in stature, he added to his inches by his dignity and by his resemblance to Napoleon—a characteristic seized upon by the cartoonists. He was widely hailed as "the Napoleon of Protection" and "the Advance Agent of Prosperity."

As a presidential candidate, McKinley was peculiarly the creation of a fellow Ohioan. Marcus Alonzo Hanna had made his fortune in the iron business, and he now coveted the role of President-maker. He was personally attracted to McKinley; "I love McKinley," he once said. When the overgenerous Ohio Congressman faced bankruptcy after unwisely endorsing a friend's notes for about $100,000, Hanna and his rich associates paid off the obligation.

Hanna, as a wholehearted Hamiltonian, believed that a prime function of government was to aid business. Honest, earnest, rough, and direct, he became the personification of Big Industry in politics. He was often cartooned, quite unfairly, as a bloated bully in a loud checkered suit with a dollar sign on each checker. As a conservative in business, he was a confirmed "standpatter,"

HANNA RAISES "HONEST" MONEY
IN WALL STREET
New York Journal, 1896

content to let conditions stand as they were. He believed that in some measure prosperity "trickled down" to the laborer, whose dinner pail was full when business flourished.

The hard-fisted Hanna, although something of a novice in politics, organized his pre-convention campaign for McKinley with consummate skill and with a liberal outpouring of his own money. "Czar" Reed was a leading challenger. But his sarcastic tongue had made too many enemies, and he was too uncompromisingly opposed to silver. The convention steam roller, well lubricated with Hanna's dollars, nominated McKinley on the first ballot at St. Louis in June, 1896.

The Republican platform cleverly straddled the monetary question. It declared for the gold standard, even though McKinley's voting record in Congress had been embarrassingly friendly to silver. But the platform made a gesture toward the silverites when it came out for international bimetallism, or a world-wide gold-silver standard. The joker was that all the leading nations of the world would have had to agree to such a scheme, and this obviously they would not do. The platform also condemned hard times and Democratic incapacity, while pouring praise upon the protective tariff.

Bryan: Silverite Messiah

The Democratic camp was riddled with dissension. Cleveland was no longer the leader of his party; dubbed "the Stuffed Prophet," he was undeniably the most unpopular man in the country. The labor-debtor groups remembered too vividly the silver-purchase repeal, the Pullman strike, the unpopular Morgan bond deal. Ultra-conservative in finance, Cleveland was now more a Republican than a Democrat on the silver issue.

The rudderless Democratic convention met in Chicago in July, 1896, with the silverites in command. Shouting insults, they refused, by a vote of 564 to 357, to endorse their own Cleveland administration. They had the enthusiasm and the numbers; all they lacked was a leader.

The new Moses suddenly appeared in the person of William Jennings Bryan of Nebraska. Then only thirty-six years of age and known as "the Boy Orator of the Platte," * he stepped confidently onto the platform before 15,000 people. A masterful presence was set off by his handsome features, his smooth-shaven jaw, and his raven-black hair. He radiated honesty, sincerity, and energy. Bryan had a good mind but not a brilliant one; he was less a student of books than of human nature; and he possessed broad human sympathies. But he was a great heart rather than a great head; a great voice rather than a great brain.

The setting at Chicago was made to order for a magnificent oratorical

* One contemporary commented brutally that the Platte River was "six inches deep and six miles wide at the mouth."

outburst. Bryan could be sure of a sympathetic hearing, for as a Congressman and a nationwide lecturer he had already emerged as one of the leading champions of free silver. A hush fell over the convention as he stood before it. With an organ-like voice that rolled into the outer corners of the huge hall, he delivered a fervent plea for silver. Rising to heights of eloquence, he thundered, "We will answer their demands for a gold standard by saying to them: 'You shall not press down upon the brow of labor this crown of thorns, you shall not crucify mankind upon a cross of gold.'"

The Cross of Gold speech was a sensation. Swept off its feet in a tumultuous scene, the convention nominated Bryan the next day on the fifth ballot. The platform declared for the unlimited coinage of silver at the ratio of sixteen ounces of silver to one of gold, though the market ratio was about thirty-two to one.

The Democratic "Gold Bugs," unable to swallow Bryan, bolted their party over the silver issue. The conservative Senator Hill of New York, when asked if he was a Democrat still, replied, "Yes, I am a Democrat still—*very* still." The Democratic minority, including Cleveland, charged that the Populist-silverites had stolen both the name and the clothing of their party, and refused to support Bryan. They nominated a lost-cause ticket of their own, and many of them, including Cleveland, hoped for a McKinley victory.

The Populists were left out in the cold, for the Democratic majority had appropriated their main plank—"sixteen to one." The bulk of the confused "Popocrats," rather than submit to a hard-money McKinley victory, endorsed Bryan in their convention. Singing "The Jolly Silver Dollar of the Dads," they became in effect the "Demo-Pop" party. But the faithful middle-of-the-road Populists refused to support Bryan, and went down with their colors nailed to the mast.

The Pied Piper of the Platte

Mark Hanna smugly but mistakenly assumed that he could make the tariff the chief issue of the campaign. Bryan, a dynamo of energy, forced the free-trade issue into a back seat when he took to the stump in behalf of free silver. Sweeping through twenty-seven states and traveling 18,000 miles, he made between five and six hundred speeches—thirty-six in one day—and even invaded the East, "the enemy's country." Vachel Lindsay caught the spirit of his leadership:

> Prairie avenger, mountain lion,
> Bryan, Bryan, Bryan, Bryan,
> Gigantic troubadour, speaking like a siege gun,
> Smashing Plymouth Rock with his boulders from the West.*

* Vachel Lindsay, *Collected Poems* (The Macmillan Company, copyright 1925), p. 99 ("Bryan, Bryan, Bryan, Bryan").

Free silver became almost as much a religious as a financial issue. Hordes of fanatical free-silverites hailed Bryan as the Moses to lead them out of the wilderness of debt. Lusty-throated followers sang, "We'll All Have Our Pockets Lined with Silver" and "No Crown of Thorns, No Cross of Gold."

Bryan aroused panic among Eastern conservatives with his threat of converting their holdings overnight into fifty-cent dollars. Their pocket nerve rasped, the "Gold Bugs" vented their fear in abusive epithets, which ranged all the way from "fanatic" and "madman" to "traitor" and "murderer." "In God We Trust, with Bryan We Bust," the Republicans sneered, while one prominent Eastern clergyman shouted, "That platform was made in Hell."

A REPUBLICAN VIEW OF BRYAN
New York *Press*, 1896

Widespread fear of Bryan and the "silver lunacy" caused "Dollar Mark" Hanna, now chairman of the Republican National Committee, to enjoy huge success as a money raiser. He "shook down" the trusts and plutocrats, and piled up an enormous "slush fund" for a "campaign of education"—or of propaganda—depending on one's point of view. The Republicans amassed the most formidable campaign chest thus far in American history. At all levels—national, state, and local—it amounted to about $16,000,000, as contrasted with about $1,000,000 for the poorer Democrats—roughly "sixteen to one." With some justification, the Bryan-ites accused Mark Hanna of "buying" the election, and of floating Mc-Kinley into the White House on a tidal wave of greenbacks.

The Pocketbook Vote

With a golden stream gushing into his coffers, Hanna waged a high-pressure campaign against silver. He distributed tens of millions of pamphlets, tracts, leaflets, and posters, many of them in the native languages of immigrant groups. He sent out hundreds of "spellbinders" onto the stump, where they engaged in the free and unlimited coinage of speeches. There was a maximum of shouting and a minimum of thinking, primarily because only a few trained economists were able to grasp fully the implications of silver and gold bimetallism—and even they disagreed. "The whole currency question," wrote the humorist "Mr. Dooley" (F. P. Dunne), "is a matter of lungs."

The Republicans harped constantly on their promise of prosperity. Reminding the voters of Cleveland's "Democratic panic," they appealed to the "belly vote" with their prize slogan: "McKinley and the Full Dinner Pail." Their candidate, though an effective orator, was no match for Bryan in the rough-and-tumble of stump speaking. He remained at his Ohio home, conducting a quiet and dignified "front porch" campaign. Stressing prosperity, he read calm and confident little speeches to delegations of visiting Republicans.

Bryan's cyclonic campaign, launched with irresistible enthusiasm, began to lose momentum as the weeks passed. If the election had been held in August, instead of November, the "Peerless Leader" might well have won. But Hanna's splendid organization and far-flung campaign of "education" gradually began to tip the scales. Also, during the weeks just before the election, the price of wheat rose sharply, owing largely to crop failures abroad. Hostility to the Republican Party in the vast wheat belt began to wane, even though agriculture generally remained depressed.

Fear probably was the strongest ally of Hanna, the worst enemy of Bryan. Republican businessmen placed contracts with manufacturers, contingent on the election of McKinley. A few factory owners, with thinly veiled intimidation, paid off their workers and told them not to come to work on Wednesday morning if Bryan won. Such were some of the refinements of the "Stop Bryan, Save America" crusade.

Plowholders vs. Bondholders

Hanna's campaign methods paid off, for on election day McKinley triumphed decisively. The vote was 271 to 176 in the Electoral College, and 7,104,779 to 6,502,925 in the popular column. Responding to fear, hope, and excitement, an unprecedented outpouring of voters tramped to the polls. McKinley ran strongly in the populous East, where he carried every county of New England, and in the upper Mississippi Valley. Bryan's states, concentrated in the debt-burdened South and the trans-

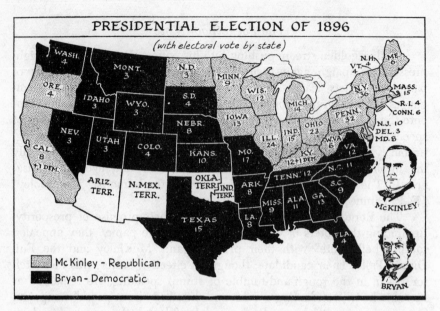

PRESIDENTIAL ELECTION OF 1896
(with electoral vote by state)

☐ McKinley - Republican
■ Bryan - Democratic

Mississippi West, involved more acreage than McKinley's but less population—only the South and the desert, cynics said.

The free-silver election of 1896—the most significant since Lincoln's victories in 1860 and 1864—highlighted serious sectional cleavages. One basic reason for Bryan's defeat, despite his strength in the South and West, was his lack of appeal to the urban laborer. Many an Eastern wage earner voted for his job and his full dinner pail, threatened as they were by free silver, free trade, and closed factories.

The Bryan-McKinley battle likewise produced an ugly mass-class conflict, probably the most serious since the election of Jefferson in 1800. The debtors, the farmers, the poorer folk, and other malcontents were for the most part pitted against the more prosperous pillars of society. It was the age-old story of the underprivileged many against the privileged few, of the indebted back country against the rich seaboard, of the city against the country, of the agrarians against the industrialists and businessmen, of the nobodies against the somebodies.

As a matter of simple humanitarianism, the mortgage-crushed agrarians deserved some relief from social and economic ills not of their own making. They did not look upon themselves as "dishonest," especially when they cried out against having to pay back dearer dollars than those they had borrowed. Silver was a symbol—a misleading symbol—of their plight. Bryan believed that the basic issue was not free silver but free people—a free people seeking escape from the trammels of entrenched wealth.

The outcome was a smashing victory for the apostles of Big Business; Alexander Hamilton again triumphed from the grave. McKinley's election no doubt upheld the nation's financial honor and averted serious economic strains. But the gravity of these dangers was grossly exaggerated by Mark Hanna's propaganda mill.

Standpattism Enthroned

The eminently "safe" McKinley took the inaugural oath in 1897. Though a man of considerable ability, he was an ear-to-the-ground politician who seldom got far out of line with majority opinion. His cautious, conservative nature caused him to shy away from the flaming banner of reform—or even of progressivism. Business was given a free rein, and the trusts, which had supported him in 1896, were allowed to develop mighty muscles without serious hindrance.

McKinley, unlike Cleveland, worked smoothly in party harness. Able to get along well with Congress—he had served there for many years—he shone best at reconciling conflicting interests. Conciliatory and warm-handed, he would send an angry-faced man away beaming, sometimes wearing a carnation from the presidential desk. He continued to maintain close relations with Mark Hanna. But he was by no means under the thumb of his mentor, despite Vachel Lindsay's cruel query:

Where is McKinley, Mark Hanna's McKinley,
His slave, his echo, his suit of clothes?

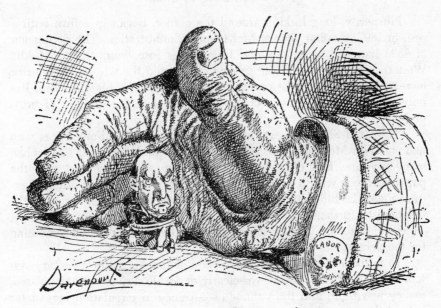

McKINLEY IN THE PALM OF HANNA'S HAND
New York *Journal*, 1896

The new "standpat" Cabinet was both conservative and aged. The venerable Senator John Sherman of Ohio, now seventy-four years old and suffering from a serious loss of memory, was "kicked upstairs" into the post of Secretary of State. Mark Hanna coveted his Senate seat, and the old man was induced to resign so that the governor of Ohio could reward McKinley's benefactor with the vacated place.

The tariff issue, which had played second fiddle to silver in the "Battle of '96," quickly forced itself to the front. The Republicans were reluctant to tackle legislation that would firmly establish the gold standard; there were still too many silverites left in Congress. But action on the tariff was both possible and pressing. The current Wilson-Gorman law was not raising enough revenue to cover the annual Treasury deficits, and the Republican trusts had purchased additional protection by their generous contributions to Hanna's "slush fund."

The Dingley Tariff Bill was jammed through the House in 1897, under the tattooing gavel of the rethroned "Czar" Reed. The proposed new rates were high, but not high enough to satisfy the paunchy lobbyists, who once again descended upon the Senate. Over 850 amendments were tacked onto the overburdened bill. The resulting piece of patchwork finally established the average rates at 46.5%, substantially higher than the Democratic Wilson-Gorman Act of 1894, and in some categories even higher than the McKinley Act of 1890. (See chart, p. 589.)

The Swan Song of Silver

Prosperity, long lurking around the corner, began to return with a rush in 1897, the first year of McKinley's administration. The depression of 1893 had run its course, and farm prices rose. Paint-thirsty Middle Western barns blossomed out in new colors, and the wheels of industry increased their hum. Like crowing roosters causing the sun to rise, Republican politicians claimed credit for bringing in the sunlight of prosperity.

The Gold Standard Act, loudly demanded by hard-moneyites who had voted for McKinley, was not passed by Republicans until 1900, when many silverites had disappeared from Congress. It provided that the paper currency was to be redeemed freely in gold. The last-ditch silverites fought the bill with bitterness but without success. The cries of the inflationists, further stifled by returning prosperity, gradually died away. Thus ended some twenty years of paternalistic attempts to do something for the debtor.

In retrospect, a controlled expansion of the American monetary system in the 1880's and 1890's was clearly desirable. Prices were depressed, money was tight, and the volume of currency in circulation lagged far behind the increasing volume of business. (See chart, p. 581.) The agrarian debtors had a good cause: relief from social and economic hardship through the inflation of the dollar supply. But free silver, which aroused unreasoning and exaggerated fears, was a poor sword. By brandishing this tinseled weapon, Bryan actually defeated his own ends. The free-silver will-o'-the-wisp not only discredited the case for needed currency expansion, but seriously set back the agrarian reform movement.

Nature and science gradually provided an inflation of the money supply that the "Gold Bug" East had fought so frantically to prevent. The electrifying discovery of new gold deposits in Canada, South Africa, and Australia eased the pressure, as did the perfecting of the cheap cyanide process for extracting gold from low-grade ore. Moderate inflation thus took care of the per capita currency needs of an explosively expanding America. The tide of "silver heresy" rapidly receded, and the "popocratic" fish were left gasping high and dry on a golden-sanded beach.

SELECT READINGS

Consult the books by Hicks and Shannon cited for the previous chapter. A comprehensive survey is H. U. FAULKNER, *Politics, Reform, and Expansion, 1890–1900* (1959) [paperback]. On Cleveland, see ALLAN NEVINS' Pulitzer-prize *Grover Cleveland* (1932) and J. R. HOLLINGSWORTH, *The Whirligig of Politics* (1963). The Harrison-Cleveland campaign of 1888 is portrayed in H. J. SIEVERS, *Benjamin Harrison, Hoosier Statesman: From the Civil War to the White House, 1865–1888* (vol. II, 1959). The most recent scholarly treatment is P. E. COLETTA, *William Jennings Bryan: Political Evangelist, 1860–1908* (1964). On the 1896 campaign consult S. L. JONES, *The Presidential Election of 1896* (1964); R. F. DURDEN, *The Climax of Populism: The Election of 1896* (1965); and P. W. GLAD, *The Trumpet Soundeth: William Jennings Bryan and His Democracy, 1896–1912* (1960) and *McKinley, Bryan, and the People* (1964) [paperback]. Consult also IRWIN UNGER, *The Greenback Era* (1964) and THEODORE SALOUTOS, *Farmer Movements in the South, 1865–1933* (1960). McKinley is belatedly done justice in MARGARET LEECH's Pulitzer-prize *In the Days of McKinley* (1959) and in H. W. MORGAN, *William McKinley and His America* (1963). Also *Harvard Guide*, Pt. V.

31

The Path of Empire

*We assert that no nation can long endure half republic
and half empire, and we warn the American people
that imperialism abroad will lead quickly and inevitably
to despotism at home.*

DEMOCRATIC NATIONAL PLATFORM, 1900

Stirrings of Imperialism

A SHARP REORIENTATION of American foreign policy occurred in the sunset decades of the 19th Century. It roughly paralleled the far-reaching changes which were taking place in manufacturing, agriculture, and the social structure.

Before the Civil War, the United States had adopted two basic foreign policies regarding Europe. One was the isolationist creed of non-involvement and non-entanglement in foreign broils. It meant in brief, "We'll keep out." The other was the Monroe Doctrine, which meant basically, "You keep out." We had warned the non-American powers to stay away, partly because we valued our freedom from European despots, and partly because we wanted to continue our expansive Manifest Destiny without hindrance. In addition to our two basic policies, we had made some halting progress toward the arbitration of international disputes, especially those with the powerful European nations whom it would not pay us to fight.

The Civil War, with its violent dislocations, left a marked imprint on our foreign policy. The spirit of isolation continued more deeply rooted than ever, while the Monroe Doctrine emerged with new laurels after the ejection of the French intruders from Mexico in 1867. But the once-surging spirit of Manifest Destiny was dead. Too much blood and treasure had been drained away by the Civil War; too much energy and enterprise were being channeled into Reconstruction, Indian fighting, railroad building, and other feverish preoccupations. From the end of the Civil War to the 1880's, the indifference of most Americans to the outside world was almost unbelievable.

In 1881 James G. Blaine, the "spirited" Secretary of State, brought a refreshing new outlook to American foreign policy. He had visions of expanding our economic and diplomatic interests into the Far East, the Pacific, and especially Latin America. As a warm admirer of the pioneer Pan-Americanist Henry Clay, Blaine issued invitations to the Latin American republics for the first great Pan-American conclave, to be held at Washington. But the bullet that killed President Garfield blasted Blaine's plans, and his stodgy successor in the State Department rather rudely recalled the invitations.

Blaine's burning interest in Latin America also extended to the proposed Isthmian canal. But there was one insurmountable legal obstacle. By the terms of the yellowing Clayton-Bulwer Treaty of 1850, the United States had agreed with Britain on joint control and protection of the prospective waterway. In a resolute attempt to shake off this shackle, Blaine dispatched a series of blustering notes to London. Even though the British Lion stood annoyingly firm, the "Plumed Knight's" resounding phrases stirred American sensitivity and pride.

As far as a Pan-American conference was concerned, Blaine had happily cast his seeds on fertile ground. One of his successors in the State Department gradually began to see the light regarding the "Big Sister" policy. The United States again issued invitations for the first general meeting of its kind, and eighteen American republics sent delegates to Washington in 1889. By a curious turn of the wheel of chance, Blaine returned as Secretary of State under Harrison, just in time to shine in the congenial role of host.

If achievement could be measured by flowery words, the First Pan-American Conference would have been a sensational success. But the concrete results were meager. The frock-coated delegates did little more than open a crack in the door for economic cooperation, as was later seen in reciprocal tariff reduction. They also set up a clearinghouse for information, ultimately known as the Pan-American Union, which was later housed in a Carnegie-given marble palace in Washington. But the Washington Conference itself was a trail-blazing beginning—the first of a long and increasingly important series of inter-American assemblages.

Chip-on-the-Shoulder Diplomacy

The rising new spirit in America manifested itself in a series of diplomatic crises or near-wars in the late 1880's and early 1890's.

Seals were the bone of contention with Britain. The United States had acquired with Alaska the two tiny Pribilof Islands, the breeding place of some four million fur seals. Sealskin coats were then fashionable, and Canadian seal poachers found it profitable to range off our islands outside the three-mile limit. There they reddened the water with the indiscriminate slaughter of the sleek mammals, without regard to sex.

Drastic action was needed to save the seals from going the way of the buffalo. In the late 1880's, American revenue vessels boldly seized several Canadian sealing craft on the high seas. The Canadians and British reacted angrily against this violation of freedom of the seas—ironically, a time-honored American principle.

Secretary Blaine, who inherited the quarrel, had a good ethical case but a poor legal one. Yet he strove energetically to convince London that since we owned the breeding ground of the seals, we had some jurisdiction over the furry creatures outside the three-mile line. The unrestrained slaughter, he argued, was contrary to good public morals.

The dispute over seals was finally referred to an arbitral tribunal sitting at Paris in 1893. After due deliberation, the arbitrators decided every major legal point against the United States. But to safeguard the seals they set up a closed zone, which happened to be too small, and a closed season, which happened to be the wrong time of the year. The result was a resounding defeat for both the Americans and their seals, but something of a victory for international arbitration. The salvation of the herd was to come in 1911 by a different type of international agreement.

PROTECTING THE SEALS

SIBERIA

RUSSIA / U.S.

ALASKA

CANADA

PRIBILOF ISLANDS Open-sea sealing within 60 miles forbidden British and Americans by 1893 award

Bering Sea

Open-sea sealing north and east of this line May1–July31 forbidden British and Americans by 1893 award

Open-sea sealing north of this line forbidden by convention of 1911 between U.S., Great Britain, Russia, and Japan

Other diplomatic controversies quickened the patriotic pulse. We skirted close to the brink of bloodshed with Germany in 1889, as will be noted later, over the palm-shaded islands of Samoa. We almost clashed with Italy in 1891, when eleven Italians were lynched in New Orleans, following a series of murders that pointed to the stiletto of the Sicilian Blackhanders. Diplomatic relations were severed; war impended. Ominously, the Italian navy, on paper at least, was much stronger than ours. But hostilities were happily averted when the United States, as a friendly act, agreed to pay $25,000 to Italy.

An even uglier clash in 1892 involved Chile. That elongated republic had recently been convulsed by civil war, and the Washington government had seemingly shown undue sympathy toward the faction that eventually lost. In an atmosphere crackling with hostility, a party of sailors from an American warship, the *Baltimore,* was allowed shore leave at Valparaiso. A fight broke out in the True Blue saloon, and when order was finally restored, two American sailors were dead and nearly a score of others were injured. An aroused President Harrison made stern demands on Chile, and hostilities seemed inevitable. Alarm spread to the Pacific Coast of the United States, for Chile, as a Pacific naval power, boasted some formidable modern warships.

So enormous was the power of the United States, actual and potential, that Chile was finally forced to knuckle under and pay an indemnity of $75,000. The Chileans have never completely forgotten what to them was undue severity—using a sledgehammer to crush a butterfly. Although the ordinarily aggressive Blaine in this instance tried to restrain the anger of his chief, much of the good will he had so laboriously created at the recent Pan-American Conference was tossed away.

The Venezuelan Squall

American dislike of the Britishers, which periodically came to a head, flared forth ominously in 1895–1896 over Venezuela. For more than a half-century the jungle boundary between British Guiana and Venezuela had been in dispute. The Venezuelans, whose claims on the whole were extravagant, had repeatedly urged arbitration. But the prospect of a peaceful settlement faded when gold was discovered in the disputed area.

President Cleveland, a champion of righteousness and no lover of Britain, finally decided upon a strong protest. His no less pugnacious Secretary of State Olney was authorized to present to London a smashing note, which Cleveland later dubbed a "twenty-inch gun" blast. Olney declared in effect that the British, by attempting to dominate Venezuela in this quarrel and acquire more territory, were flouting the Monroe Doctrine. London should therefore submit the dispute to arbitration. Not content to stop here, Olney haughtily informed the number-one naval power that the United States was now calling the tune in the Western Hemisphere.

The British officials, unimpressed, took four months to prepare their reply. Preoccu-

THE VENEZUELA-BR. GUIANA
BOUNDARY DISPUTE

pied elsewhere, they were inclined to shrug off Olney's lengthy blast as just another twist of the Lion's tail designed to elicit cheers from Irish-American voters. When London's answer finally came, it flatly denied the relevance of the Monroe Doctrine, and no less emphatically spurned arbitration. In short, the affair was none of our business.

President Cleveland—"mad clear through," as he put it—sent a bristling special message to Congress. He urged an appropriation for a commission of experts, who would run the line where it ought to go. Then, he implied, if the British would not accept this rightful boundary, the United States would fight them.

"THE REAL BRITISH LION"
A widespread American concept in the 1890's. New York *Evening World*, 1895

The entire country, irrespective of political party, was swept off its feet in an outburst of mass insanity. War seemed inevitable, despite the fact that Britain had thirty-two warships of the battleship class to only five for the United States.

Fortunately, sober second thoughts prevailed on both sides of the Atlantic. The British, though vastly annoyed by their upstart cousins, had no real urge to fight. Canada was vulnerable to invading American armies, and Britain's rich merchant marine was vulnerable to American commerce raiders. The European atmosphere was menacing, for Britain's traditional policy of "splendid isolation" was leaving her dangerously isolated. Russia and France were unfriendly; and Germany, under the saber-rattling Kaiser Wilhelm II, was about to challenge British naval supremacy.

The Venezuelan crisis had evidently passed its peak when the German Kaiser, blunderingly and unwittingly, increased chances of a peaceful solution. An unauthorized British raiding party of six hundred armed men was captured by the Dutch-descended Boers in South Africa, and the Kaiser forthwith cabled his congratulations to the victors. Overnight, British anger against America was largely deflected to Germany. After further negotiations, London consented to arbitrate the Venezuelan dispute. The final decision, ironically, awarded the British the bulk of what they had claimed from the beginning.

America had skated close to the thin ice of a terrible war, but the results on the whole were favorable. The prestige of the Monroe Doctrine was immensely enhanced. Europe was irked by our claim to domination in this hemisphere, and both Latin America and Canada were somewhat alarmed. But we had made our claim stick. Many citizens of the smaller Latin American republics were pleased by the determination of the United States to protect them, and when Cleveland died in 1908, some of our southern neighbors lowered their flags to half-mast.

The chastened British, their eyes fully opened to the European peril, were now determined to cultivate the friendship of the United States. They inaugurated an era of "patting the Eagle's head," which replaced a century or so of our "twisting the Lion's tail." Growing numbers of Englishmen were willing to heed Tennyson's earlier injunction:

> Be proud of those strong sons of thine
> Who wrench'd their rights from thee!

The New Manifest Destiny

A heady new spirit of Manifest Destiny had begun to surge through American veins by the early 1890's. The reconstructed South was rising again; and the closing of the frontier indicated that old energies would have to be diverted into different channels. America was bursting with a sense of power generated by the vast increase in her population, wealth, and industrial productiveness. "Expand or explode" was accepted as an elemental law, and many manufacturers were seeking new overseas markets for the contents of their bulging warehouses.

Other forces were stimulating international-mindedness. The lurid yellow press of Pulitzer and Hearst was whetting the popular taste for excitement. The missionary-conscious churches were on the lookout for new overseas vineyards to till. Outward-looking advocates of a "large policy" were interpreting Darwinism to mean that the earth belonged to the energetic, the strong, the fit—that is, to the virile Americans. Jingoes, including the fight-thirsty young Theodore Roosevelt and the scholarly Congressman Henry Cabot Lodge, were whooping it up for expansion and, if need be, war.

The new steel navy was being pushed with vigor. It found a potent ally in the pen of Captain Alfred T. Mahan, who in 1890 published his *Influence of Sea Power upon History, 1660–1783.* His basic theme was that the prizes of victory and world dominion went to those nations that won and retained control of the sea. These findings were avidly read by Englishmen, Germans, and Japanese; and Mahan unwittingly stimulated the fateful naval race that gained momentum in the early years of the next century.

In the United States, the gospel according to Mahan eventually shaped the thinking of many large-minded Americans. They came to believe that naval power and world power were Siamese twins. Red-blooded citizens redoubled their agitation for a mightier navy, while demanding an American-built Isthmian canal that would shuttle the warships from the Atlantic to the Pacific and back.

New great-power alignments were in the making. Germany was emerging as the colossus of Europe, and as the latecomer in the colonial scramble was scooping up leavings from the banquet table of earlier diners. Japan's debut as a world power came when she gave anemic China a bad beating during 1894–1895, thereby exposing the weakness of the Chinese Empire to a predatory world. In 1898 the Germans, responding to the world-wide spirit of grab, extorted a valuable leasehold from China at Shantung; and in the same year the Russians followed suit at Port Arthur.

A dangerous spirit of bellicosity was abroad in the United States by 1898. Our people craved new sensations, for many were bored with threadbare issues like the tariff and free silver. America had not fought a rousing war for over thirty years. The restless younger generation was jealous of the Civil War veterans, with their idealized tales of "tenting on the old camp ground."

War scares with Germany, Italy, Chile, and Britain had whetted the national appetite, while leaving it frustrated. If we were going to show the world that we were "some pumpkins," we might have to fight somebody. If we were going to "keep up with the Joneses," we would have to acquire overseas real estate, as the other powers were doing. The upsurge of the new Manifest Destiny became hardly less irresistible than that of the old Manifest Destiny in the 1840's and 1850's.

Schemings in Samoa

The broad-bosomed Pacific Ocean witnessed some of the first manifestations of the new Manifest Destiny. As early as 1878, we had secured rights to a naval base in Samoa, at the harbor of Pago Pago, where our sailors and whalers had found refreshment of various kinds. Britain and Germany likewise became covetously interested in this idyllic archipelago,

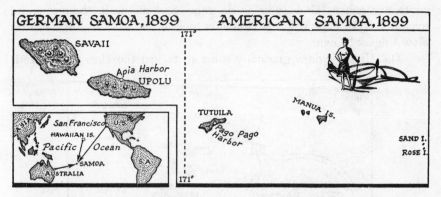

and Britons, Germans, and Americans frantically intrigued with the natives for commercial and strategic control. Robert Louis Stevenson, who had gone to Samoa in an attempt to shake off tuberculosis, has left us a graphic picture of the rivalries in his book *A Footnote to History* (1892).

Tension mounted to the breaking point between the Germans and Americans in Samoa. On a memorable day in 1889, the crews of three German and three American men-of-war were glowering at each other over loaded guns. Hostilities might well have started then and there, had not a frightful hurricane wrecked all six warships in Apia harbor.

The diplomats meanwhile had taken over at the Berlin Conference, meeting in the spring of 1889. The discussions went forward under the direction of the imperious Prince Bismarck, with the no less imperious Secretary Blaine cabling instructions from Washington to the American delegates. The solution finally adopted was a three-way protectorate, operated jointly by the Americans, Germans, and British. This awkward arrangement, inherently unworkable, was widely criticized in America as a reckless departure from the non-entanglement warnings of the Founding Fathers.

The Samoan sequel was the familiar story of too many cooks overheating the broth. In 1899, ten years later, the islands were divided outright between Germany and America, with Britain granted compensation elsewhere. A new mood was evidently coming over the American people when they were prepared to risk entanglement—even war—for these faraway island flyspecks.

The Hawaiian Pear

The Hawaiian archipelago had early attracted the attention of Americans. In the morning years of the 19th Century, the breeze-brushed islands became a halfway station and provisioning point for Yankee shippers, sailors, and whalers. In 1820 came the first New England missionaries, who preached the twin blessings of Protestant Christianity and protective calico. They came to do good—and did well; their sons did even better. In some respects Honolulu took on the earmarks of a typical New England town.

The United States gradually came to regard the Hawaiian Islands

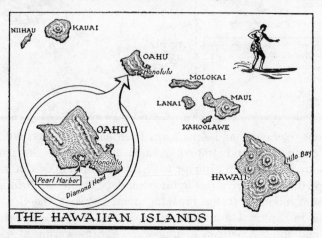

THE HAWAIIAN ISLANDS

as a virtual extension of its own coastline. The State Department, beginning with the 1840's, sternly warned other powers to keep their hands off. The American grip was further tightened in 1875 by a commercial reciprocity agreement, and in 1887 by a treaty with the native government guaranteeing to the United States naval-base rights at spacious Pearl Harbor.

But trouble, both economic and political, was brewing in the languid insular paradise. Sugar culture, which had become immensely profitable, was dealt a crushing blow in 1890, when the McKinley Tariff erected barriers unfavorable to the Hawaiian product. The white planters, mostly Americans, were further alarmed by the increasingly autocratic tendencies of dusky Queen Liliuokalani, who insisted that native Hawaiians should control Hawaii. The desperate whites, though only a tiny minority, organized a successful revolt early in 1893. It was openly assisted by American troops, who landed under the unauthorized orders of the expansionist American minister in Honolulu. "The Hawaiian pear is now fully ripe," he wrote exultantly to his superiors in Washington, "and this is the golden hour for the United States to pluck it."

Hawaii, like Texas of earlier years, seemed ready for annexation to the United States—at least in the eyes of the ruling American whites. An appropriate treaty was forthwith rushed to Washington. But before it could be railroaded through the Senate, the Republican President Harrison went out and the Democratic President Cleveland came in. To the chivalrous Grover Cleveland, who set great store by "national honesty," it seemed as though our powerful republic had gravely wronged the deposed Queen Liliuokalani.

Cleveland abruptly withdrew the treaty from the Senate, and then sent to Hawaii a special investigator. The subsequent probe revealed the damning fact that a majority of the Hawaiian natives did not favor annexation at all. But the white revolutionists were firmly in the saddle, and Cleveland could not unhorse them without using armed force—a step which American public opinion would never have tolerated. Stalemate consequently ensued. Although the Queen could not be reinstated, the move for annexation had to be abandoned temporarily.

The question of annexing Hawaii touched off the first full-fledged imperialistic debate in American experience. Cleveland was bitterly criticized for trying to stem the New Manifest Destiny, and a popular jingle ran:

> . . . Liliuokalani,
> Give us your little brown hannie.

But Cleveland's motives, in a day of international land grabbing, were honorable both to himself and to his country.

The Cuban Pesthouse

The Cuban people, frightfully misgoverned, rose again against their Spanish oppressor in 1895. The roots of their revolt were partly economic. The sugar industry—the backbone of the island's prosperity—was crippled when the American tariff of 1894 restored high duties on the toothsome Cuban product.

Driven to desperation, the insurgents adopted a scorched-earth policy. They reasoned that if they did enough damage, Spain might be willing to move out. Or the United States might move in, and help the Cubans win their independence. In pursuance of this destructive strategy, the *insurrectos* put the torch to cane fields and sugar mills, and even dynamited passenger trains.

American sympathies, ever on the side of patriots fighting for freedom, went out to the Cuban underdogs. Aside from pure sentiment, we had an investment stake of about $50,000,000 in Cuba, and an annual trade stake of about $100,000,000. Moreover, Spanish misrule in Cuba menaced the shipping routes of the West Indies and the Gulf, and less directly the future Isthmian canal.

Fuel was added to the Cuban conflagration in 1896 with the coming of General Valeriano ("Butcher") Weyler. He undertook to crush the rebellion by herding many civilians into barbed-wire concentration camps, where they could not give assistance to the armed *insurrectos*. Lacking proper sanitation, these enclosures turned into deadly pestholes, in which the victims died like flies.

An outraged American public demanded action. Congress in 1896 overwhelmingly passed a resolution which called upon President Cleveland to recognize the belligerency of the revolted Cubans. But as the government of the insurgents consisted of hardly more than a few fugitive leaders under palm trees, Cleveland—an anti-jingoist and anti-imperialist—refused to budge. He defiantly remarked that if Congress declared war he would not, as Commander-in-Chief, issue the necessary order to mobilize the army.

The Mystery of the Maine

The atrocities in Cuba were made to order for the sensational new "yellow journalism." William R. Hearst and Joseph Pulitzer, then engaged in a titanic duel for circulation, attempted to outdo each other with screeching headlines and hair-raising "scoops," and lesser competitors zestfully followed suit.

Where atrocity stories did not exist, they were invented. Hearst sent the gifted artist Frederic Remington to Cuba to draw sketches, and when the latter reported that conditions were not bad enough to warrant hostilities, Hearst is alleged to have replied, "You furnish the pictures and I'll furnish the war." Among other things, Remington depicted Spanish

REMINGTON'S DISROBING PROPAGANDA
New York *Journal*, 1897

customs officials brutally disrobing and searching an American woman. Most readers of Hearst's *Journal*, their indignation soaring, had no way of knowing that this task was performed by female attendants.

"Butcher" Weyler was removed in 1897, yet affairs steadily worsened. There was some talk in Spain of granting the restive island a type of self-government, but such a surrender was so bitterly opposed by many Spaniards in Cuba that they engaged in furious riots. Early in 1898 the United States sent the second-class battleship *Maine* to Cuba, ostensibly for a "friendly visit" but actually to protect and evacuate Americans if a dangerous flare-up should again occur.

The already explosive situation suddenly grew acute, on February 9, 1898, when Hearst luridly headlined a private letter written by the Spanish minister in Washington, Dupuy de Lôme. This indiscreet epistle, which had been stolen from the mails, described President McKinley as an ear-to-the-ground politician who lacked good faith. The resulting uproar was so violent that De Lôme was forced to resign.

The tragic climax came a few days later, on February 15, 1898, when the *Maine* mysteriously blew up in Havana harbor, with a loss of 260 officers and men. Two investigations were undertaken, one by United States naval officers, the other by Spanish officials, whom the Americans would not trust near the wreck. The Spanish commission announced that the explosion had been internal and presumably accidental; the American commission reported that the blast had been caused by a submarine mine. The Washington government, not unmindful of popular indignation, spurned Spanish proposals of arbitration.

The riddle of how the *Maine* was blown up, and by whom, has never been solved. Internal accidental explosions have occurred in warships with distressing frequency. Cuban insurgents may have sunk the vessel in order to force America into the war on their side; irresponsible and unauthorized Spanish officials may have done so. Spanish authorities in Cuba, acting under orders from home, may have engineered the blowup. But this is the least plausible theory of all, for the Madrid government was actually doing everything it honorably could to avert hostilities.

The Americans, now war-mad, blindly accepted the least likely explanation. Lashed to fury by the yellow press, they leaped to the conclusion that the Spanish government had been guilty of intolerable treachery. The battle cry of the hour became:

> Remember the Maine!
> To hell with Spain!

Nothing would do but to hurl the "dirty" Bourbon flag out of this hemisphere.

Unloosing the Dogs of War

The common belief that professional diplomats cause wars is not borne out by the events of 1898. American negotiators, by patient persuasion, had induced the Madrid authorities to yield substantially to Washington's basic demands, including an armistice in Cuba.

But the American public was on fire for war. The cautious President was condemned by jingoes as "Wobbly Willie" McKinley, while fight-hungry Theodore Roosevelt snarled that the "white-livered" occupant of the White House did not have "the backbone of a chocolate éclair." The President, whose shaken nerves required sleeping pills, was even being hanged in effigy.

The private desires of McKinley clashed sharply with the public demands of the people. He did not want hostilities, for he had seen enough bloodshed as an army officer in the Civil War. Mark Hanna and Wall Street did not want war, for business might be unsettled. But a frenzied public, lashed by the yellow press, clamored for war to free the abused Cubans. Overborne, the President finally yielded and gave the people what they wanted.

But public pressures did not fully explain McKinley's course. He had no faith in Spain's promises regarding Cuba; she had made and broken them before. He was certain that there would have to be a showdown sooner or later. He believed in the democratic principle that the people should rule, and he was loath to deny the American masses what they demanded—even if it was not good for them. He also perceived that if he stood out against war, the Democrats would make political capital out of his stubbornness. Bryan might sweep into the Presidency two years later under a banner inscribed, "Free Cuba and Free Silver." The gold-standard McKinley was a staunch party man, and to him it seemed better to break up the remnants of Spain's once-glorious empire than to break up the Grand Old Party.

On April 11, 1898, McKinley sent his war message to Congress, urging armed intervention to free the oppressed Cubans. The legislators responded uproariously with what was essentially a declaration of war. In a burst of self-righteousness, they likewise adopted the Teller Amendment. This proviso proclaimed to the world that when we had overthrown Spanish misrule, we would give the Cubans their freedom—a declaration that caused imperialistic Europeans to smile skeptically.

May Day at Manila

The American people plunged into the war lightheartedly, in the spirit of school boys off to a picnic. Bands blared incessantly "There'll Be a Hot Time in the Old Town Tonight" and "Hail, Hail, the Gang's All Here."

But American jubilation seemed premature to Old World observers. The regular United States army, commanded by corpulent Civil War oldsters, was totally unprepared for a war under tropical skies. It numbered only 2100 officers and 28,000 men, as compared with some 200,000 Spanish troops in Cuba. The American navy, at least to trans-Atlantic experts, seemed slightly less powerful than that of Spain. The European powers, moreover, were generally friendly to their Old World associate. The only conspicuous exception was the British, who were ardently wooing their giant offspring.

Yet in one important respect Spain's apparent superiority was illusory. Her navy, though formidable on paper, was in wretched condition. It labored under the added handicap of having to operate thousands of miles from its home base. But the new American navy, now fifteen years old and ranking fifth among the fleets of the world, was in fairly good trim, though the war was to lay bare certain defects.

The readiness of the navy owed much to two men: the easygoing Secretary Long and his pugnacious subordinate Assistant Secretary Theodore Roosevelt. The Secretary hardly dared leave his desk for fear that his overzealous underling would stir up a hornets' nest. On February 25, 1898, while Long was away for a week end, Roosevelt had cabled Commodore George Dewey, commanding the American Far Eastern Fleet at Hong Kong, to descend upon Spain's Philippines in the event of war. McKinley subsequently confirmed these orders, even though an attack in the Far East seemed like a strange way to free nearby Cuba.

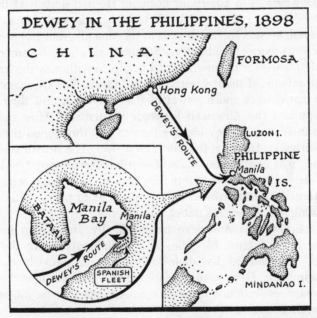

DEWEY IN THE PHILIPPINES, 1898

Dewey carried out his orders magnificently on May 1, 1898. Sailing boldly with his six warships at night into the fortified harbor of Manila, he trained his guns the next morning on the ten-ship Spanish fleet, one of whose craft was only a moored hulk without functioning engines. The entire collection of antiquated and overmatched vessels was quickly destroyed, with a loss of nearly four hundred Spaniards killed and wounded, and without the loss of a single life in Dewey's fleet. An American consul who was there wrote that all the American sailors needed was cough drops for throats made raw by cheers of victory.

Imperialistic Plums

George Dewey, quiet and taciturn, became a national hero overnight. He was promptly promoted to the rank of admiral, as the price of flags rose sharply. An amateur poet blossomed forth with:

> Oh, dewy was the morning
> Upon the first of May,
> And Dewey was the Admiral,
> Down in Manila Bay.
> And dewy were the Spaniards' eyes,
> Them orbs of black and blue;
> And dew we feel discouraged?
> I dew not think we dew!

Yet Dewey was in a perilous position. He had destroyed the enemy fleet, but he could not storm the forts of Manila with his sailors. His nerves frayed, he was forced to wait in the steaming-hot bay while troop reinforcements were assembled, with painful slowness, in America.

Foreign warships meanwhile had begun to gather in the harbor, ostensibly to safeguard their countrymen in Manila. The Germans sent five vessels, a naval force more powerful than Dewey's, and their haughty admiral spurned the American blockade regulations. After several disagreeable incidents, Dewey lost his temper and threatened the arrogant German with war. Happily, the storm blew over. The British commander, by contrast, was conspicuously successful in carrying out London's new policy of friendliness. The groundless legend thus took root that the British dramatically interposed their ships so as to prevent the Germans from blowing the Americans out of the water.

The long-awaited American troops, finally arriving in force, captured Manila on August 13, 1898. They collaborated with the Filipino insurgents, commanded by their well-educated, part-Chinese leader, Emilio Aguinaldo. Dewey, to his later regret, had brought this shrewd and magnetic revolutionist from exile in Asia, so that he might weaken Spanish resistance.

The thrilling events in the Philippines had meanwhile focused attention on Hawaii. The impression spread throughout America that we needed the mid-Pacific archipelago as a coaling and provisioning halfway station, in order to send supplies and reinforcements to Dewey. The truth is that we could have used the islands without annexing them, so eager was the Honolulu government to compromise itself. But an appreciative American public would not leave Dewey in the lurch. A joint resolution of annexation was rushed through Congress and approved by McKinley on July 7, 1898.

The residents of Hawaii, granted American citizenship with annexation, received full territorial status in 1900. These events in the Pacific paradise, though seemingly sudden, were but the culmination of nearly a century of Americanization by sailors, whalers, traders, and missionaries.

Confusion in Cuba

Shortly after the outbreak of war, the Spanish government dispatched a fleet of warships to Cuba. It was commanded by Admiral Cervera, who protested that his wretchedly prepared craft would court suicide. Four armored cruisers finally set forth (one without its main battery), accompanied by six torpedo boats, three of which had to be abandoned en route.

Panic seized the Eastern seaboard of the United States, even though it was obvious to experts that Cervera would have to stop at a West Indian port to replenish his coal supply. American vacationers abandoned their seashore cottages, while nervous investors moved their securities to inland depositories. Demands for protection poured in on Washington from nervous citizens, and the Navy Department was forced to detach some useless old Civil War ships to useless places for morale purposes. The power of a panicky and ignorant public opinion is a fearsome thing, and if Spain had been a stronger foe the results might have been disastrous. As fate would have it, Cervera found refuge on May 19, 1898, in bottle-shaped Santiago harbor, Cuba, where he was blockaded by the more potent American fleet.

Sound strategy seemed to dictate that an American army be sent in from the rear to drive out Cervera. The command of the invading force was entrusted to three-hundred-pound General William R. Shafter, who was so blubbery and gout-stricken that he had to be carried about on a door. The ill-prepared American conquerors were unequipped for war in the tropics, though amply provided with heavy woolen underwear and uniforms designed for sub-zero operations against the Indians.

The "Rough Riders," a part of the invading army, now charged onto the stage of history. This colorful regiment of volunteers, short on discipline but long on dash, consisted largely of Western cowboys and other hardy characters, with a sprinkling of ex-polo players and ex-convicts. Nominally commanded by Colonel Leonard Wood, the group was organized principally by glory-hungry Theodore Roosevelt, who had resigned from the Navy Department to serve as lieutenant colonel. Though totally without military experience, he used his strong political "pull" to secure his commission and to by-pass physical standards. He was so nearsighted that as a safeguard he took along a dozen pairs of spectacles, cached in handy spots.

About the middle of June a bewildered American army of 17,000 men finally embarked at one-track Tampa, Florida, amid scenes of indescribable congestion and confusion. The "Rough Riders" ("Teddy's Terrors"), fearing that they would be robbed of action and glory, rushed one of the transports, and courageously held their place for almost a week in the broiling sun. About half of them finally got to Cuba without their horses, and the bowlegged regiment then came to be known as "Wood's Weary Walkers."

The landing near Santiago, Cuba, was made without serious opposition. The Spaniards, even more disorganized than the Americans, were unable to put into the field at this spot more than two thousand men.

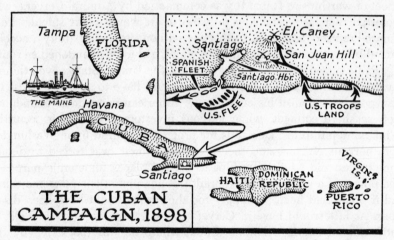

Brisk fighting broke out on July 1 at El Caney and San Juan Hill, up which Colonel Roosevelt and his horseless "Rough Riders" charged. They suffered heavy casualties, but the colorful colonel, having the time of his life, shot a Spaniard with his revolver, and rejoiced to see his victim double up like a jack rabbit. He later wrote a book on his "Rough Riding" exploits which, "Mr. Dooley" remarked, ought to have been entitled *Alone in Cubia.*

Curtains for Spain in America

The American army, fast closing in on Santiago, spelled doom for the Spanish fleet. Admiral Cervera, again protesting against a suicidal move, was flatly ordered to fight for the honor of the flag. The odds against him were heavy: the guns of the U.S.S. *Oregon* alone threw more metal than his four armored cruisers combined. After a running chase, on July 3, the foul-bottomed Spanish fleet was entirely destroyed, as the wooden decks caught fire and the blazing infernos were beached. About five hundred Spaniards were killed, as compared with one for the Americans. "Don't cheer, men," admonished Captain Philip of the *Texas;* "the poor devils are dying." Shortly thereafter Santiago surrendered.

Hasty preparations were now made for a descent upon Puerto Rico before the war should end. The American army, commanded by Indian-fighter General Nelson A. Miles, met little resistance, as most of the population greeted the invaders as conquering heroes. "Mr. Dooley" was led to refer to "Gin'ral Miles' Gran' Picnic an' Moonlight Excursion." By this time Spain had satisfied her honor, and on August 12, 1898, she signed the terms of an armistice.

Had the Spaniards held out a few months longer in Cuba, the American army might have melted away. The inroads of malaria, typhoid, dysentery, and yellow fever became so severe that the bulk of the troops were incapacitated—"an army of convalescents." Others suffered from odorous canned meat, some of which was dubbed "embalmed beef." The fiery and insubordinate Colonel Roosevelt, who had no regular military career to jeopardize, was a ringleader in making demands on Washington that the army be moved before it perished. About 25,000 men, 80% of them ill, were transferred to chilly Long Island, where the light summer clothing finally arrived.

One of the worst scandals of the war was the high death rate from sickness, especially typhoid fever. This disease was rampant in the unsanitary training camps located in the United States. All told, nearly 400 men lost their lives to bullets; over 5000 to bacteria and other causes.

A "goat" had to be found, even though the American people themselves were basically to blame for many of the ineptitudes and blunders. They had insisted on plunging into war without adequate preparations. The victim of their wrath proved to be Secretary of War Russell A. Alger, a silver-tongued orator and wealthy lumberman, whom McKinley was forced to dismiss. He might have ranked as a competent Secretary of War —if there had been no war.

Duty, Destiny, and Dollars

Late in 1898 the Spanish and American negotiators met in Paris, there to begin heated discussions. McKinley had sent five commissioners, including three Senators, who would have a final vote on their own handiwork. War-racked Cuba, as expected, was freed from her Spanish overlords. The Americans experienced little difficulty in securing the isolated island of Guam, which had been captured early in the conflict from Spaniards who had not known that a war was on. The United States also obtained Puerto Rico, the last crumb of Spain's once magnificent American empire.

The knottiest problem of all was the Philippines. These lush islands not only embraced a land area larger than the British Isles but contained a completely alien population of some seven million souls. McKinley, who admitted that before the war he could not have told where the islands were by two thousand miles, was confronted with a devil's dilemma. He did not feel that we could honorably give them back to Spanish misrule, especially after we had fought a war to free Cuba. And we would be turning our backs upon our responsibilities in a cowardly fashion, he believed, if we simply pulled up anchor and sailed away.

Other alternatives for the Philippines were trouble-fraught. The ill-prepared native Filipinos, if left to govern themselves, might fall into anarchy. One of the major powers might then try to seize them, possibly aggressive Germany, and a world war might be touched off into which

UNCLE SAM'S WHITE ELEPHANT
New York *Herald*, 1898

the United States would be sucked. The least of the evils consistent with national honor and safety seemed to be to acquire all the Philippines, and then perhaps give them their freedom later.

President McKinley, ever sensitive to public opinion, kept a carefully attuned ear to the ground. The rumble that he heard seemed to call insistently for the entire group of islands. Zealous missionaries were eager for new converts; and the invalid Mrs. McKinley, to whom her husband was devoted, expressed deep concern about the half-naked natives. Wall Street had opposed the war; but awakened by the booming of Dewey's guns, it was clamoring for profit-making opportunities in the Philippines.

"If this be commercialism," cried Mark Hanna, then "for God's sake let us have commercialism."

The troubled McKinley, impaled on this multi-horned dilemma, finally went down on his knees beseeching divine guidance. An inner voice seemed to tell him, so he later reported, to take all the Philippines and Christianize and civilize them. This course of action apparently coincided with the demands of the American people, and with the McKinley-Hanna outlook. The mixture of things spiritual and material in McKinley's reasoning was later slyly summarized by an historian: "God directs us—perhaps it will pay." Profits thus joined hands with piety.

Fresh disputes broke out with the Spanish negotiators in Paris, once McKinley had reached the momentous decision to keep the Philippines. Manila had been captured the day *after* the armistice was signed, and the islands could not properly be listed among the spoils of war. The deadlock was broken when we finally agreed to pay Spain $20,000,000 for this Philippine liability—one of the best bargains the Spaniards ever drove. Ex-Speaker "Czar" Reed sneered at our having acquired a lot of Malays, at three dollars a head, "in the bush."

The Course (Curse?) of Empire

The ratification of the pact of Paris, which was to set the Republic on a strange and troubled course, touched off one of the most impassioned debates of American history. Except for frigid Alaska and coral-reefed Hawaii, we had hitherto acquired only contiguous territory on this continent. All of our previous acquisitions had been thinly peopled and capable of ultimate statehood. But in the Philippines we had a distant tropical area, thickly populated by Asiatics of alien race, tongue, religion, and governmental institutions.

The foes of annexation—anti-imperialists—had other arrows in their quiver. The Filipinos panted for freedom; and to annex them would violate our own "consent of the governed" philosophy in the Declaration of Independence. Despotism abroad might well beget despotism at home. Finally, annexation would precipitate the United States into the political and military cauldron of the Far East.

The expansionists or imperialists, on the other hand, could sing a more seductive siren song. They pointed to patriotism and to the glory of annexation—"don't dishonor the flag by hauling it down." They stressed the opportunities for exploiting the islands, and played up possible trade profits. Manila, in fact, might become the Hong Kong of the Far East. The richer the natural resources of the islands appeared to be, the less capable of self-government the Filipinos seemed to be. Rudyard Kipling, the British poet laureate of imperialism, urged us down the slippery path:

Take up the White Man's burden—
Ye dare not stoop to less—
Nor call too loud on Freedom
To cloak your weariness.

In short, the wealthy Americans must share the responsibility of uplifting the underprivileged, underfed, and underclad of the world.

In the Senate the Spanish treaty encountered such heated opposition that it seemed doomed to certain defeat. But at this juncture William J. Bryan unexpectedly sallied forth as its champion. As a Democratic volunteer colonel whom the Republicans had been careful to keep out of Cuba, he apparently had no reason to help the McKinley administration out of a hole. But free silver was dead as a political issue. Bryan's foes assumed that he was preparing to fasten the stigma of imperialism on the Republicans, and then to sweep into the Presidency in 1900 under the flaming banner of anti-imperialism.

Bryan could support the treaty on plausible grounds. He argued that the war would not officially end until we had ratified the pact. We already had the islands on our hands, and the sooner we accepted the document, the sooner we could give the Filipinos their independence. After Bryan had used his strong personal influence with certain Democratic Senators, the treaty was approved, on February 6, 1899, with only one vote to spare. But the responsibility, as Bryan had foreseen, rested primarily on the Republicans.

The White Man's Headaches

Puerto Rico was a poverty-stricken island, the fertility of whose million inhabitants, including many Negroes, outran that of their soil. By the Foraker Act of 1900 Congress accorded the Puerto Ricans a limited degree of popular government, and in 1917 granted them United States citizenship. Although the American regime worked wonders in education, sanitation, good roads, and other physical improvements, many of the inhabitants continued to agitate for independence.

A complex legal problem was posed by the question: Does the Constitution follow the flag? Did American laws, including tariff laws, apply with full force to the newly acquired possessions, chiefly the Philippines and Puerto Rico? Beginning in 1901 with the Insular Cases, a badly divided Supreme Court decreed in effect that the flag outran the Constitution, and that the outdistanced document did not necessarily extend with full force to the new acquisitions. Congress was thus left with a free hand to determine the degree of applicability. The Court apparently modified its views somewhat under the pressure of public opinion as expressed in the presidential election of 1900. This shift led "Mr. Dooley" to remark that whether the Constitution followed the flag or not, the Supreme Court followed the "iliction returns."

Cuba, scorched and disorganized, presented another vexatious problem. An American military government was set up under the administrative genius of General Leonard Wood, who wrought miracles in government, finance, education, agriculture, and public health. Under his leadership a frontal attack was launched on yellow fever. Spectacular experiments were performed by Dr. Walter Reed and others upon American soldiers, who volunteered as human guinea pigs; and the stegomyia mosquito was proved to be the lethal carrier. A cleanup of breeding places for mosquitoes wiped out yellow fever in Havana, while at the same time removing the recurrent fear of epidemics in cities of the South and the Atlantic seaboard.

The United States, honoring its word as pledged in the self-denying Teller Amendment of 1898, withdrew from Cuba in 1902. The Old World imperialists could scarcely believe their eyes. But the Washington government could not turn this rich and strategic island completely loose on the international sea; a grasping power like Germany might secure dangerous lodgment near our soft underbelly. The Cubans were therefore forced, despite their protests, to write into their constitution of 1901 the so-called Platt Amendment.

The hated amendment placed a severe hobble on the Cubans. They bound themselves not to impair their independence by treaty, or by contracting a debt beyond their resources. They further agreed that the United States might intervene to restore order and to provide mutual protection. Finally, they promised to sell or lease needed coaling or naval stations, ultimately two, to their powerful northern neighbor.

New Horizons

The Spanish-American War was in reality a kind of gigantic coming-out party. Despite a common misconception, the conflict did not cause the United States to become a great power. Dewey's thundering guns merely advertised the fact that we were already a great power.

The war itself was short (113 days), spectacular, low in casualties, and uninterruptedly successful—despite the disorganization. American prestige rose sharply, and European powers grudgingly accorded us more respect. In Germany, Prince Bismarck growled that there was a special Providence which looked after drunkards, fools, and the United States of America. At times it seemed as though not only Providence but the Spaniards were fighting on our side. So great in fact was our good fortune that rejoicing citizens found in our victories further support—misleading support—for their aversion to adequate preparedness.

An exhilarating new spirit suffused America. Our national pride was touched and our cockiness was increased by what John Hay called a "splendid little war." The enthusiasm over our triumphs made it easier for us to rush down the thorny path of empire. We did not start the war with avowed imperialistic motives, but after falling through the cellar door of imperialism in a drunken fit of idealism, we wound up with imperialistic and colonial fruits in our grasp. The harassed British imperialists were pleased, partly because of the new-found friendship, partly because misery loves company. But our German rivals were envious, and our Latin American neighbors were suspicious of our southward push.

By taking over the Philippine liability, the United States became a full-fledged Far Eastern power. Hereafter these distant islands were to be our "heel of Achilles"—a kind of indefensible hostage given to Japan. With singular shortsightedness, we assumed dangerous commitments that we were unwilling to defend by proper naval and military outlays.

But the lessons of unpreparedness were not altogether lost. Captain Mahan's preaching of big navyism seemed vindicated, and our pride in the exploits of the navy brought popular support for more and better battleships. The inept Secretary Alger was succeeded in the War Department by a masterly organizer, Elihu Root, who established for the first time a general staff and founded the War College in Washington. His genius later paid rich dividends when we found ourselves involved with Germany in World War I.

One of the happiest results of the conflict was the further closing of the bloody chasm between North and South. Thousands of patriotic Southerners had flocked to the Stars and Stripes, and the gray-bearded General Joseph ("Fighting Joe") Wheeler—a Confederate cavalry hero of about a thousand Civil War skirmishes and battles—was given a command in Cuba. He was reported to have cried, in the heat of battle, "To hell with the Yankees! Dammit, I mean the Spaniards."

A no less gratifying result was the victory over disease. Without the conquest of yellow fever, which had helped ruin the French in Panama, there might have been no Isthmian canal. The splendid pioneering work of Dr. Jesse W. Lazear, who lost his life, and Dr. James Carroll, who suffered a severe heart ailment, deserve unstinted praise. These unsung heroes of the test tube merit a no less glorious place in our annals than war heroes like Admiral George Dewey and Colonel Theodore Roosevelt.

SELECT READINGS

Refer to Leech and Morgan (on McKinley) and Nevins (on Cleveland) for the previous chapter. Main outlines are sketched in F. R. DULLES, *America's Rise to World Power, 1898–1954* (1955) [paperback]. See also E. R. MAY, *Imperial Democracy* (1961) on America's emergence; WALTER LA FEBER, *The New Empire* (1963), on trends from 1860–1898; H. W. MORGAN, *America's Road to Empire* (1965) [paperback], on the fruits of the Spanish War; J. W. PRATT, *Expansionists of 1898* (1936) [paperback]; and W. A. RUSS, *The Hawaiian Revolution* (1959) and *The Hawaiian Republic* (1961). W. A. SWANBERG, *Citizen Hearst* (1961) is colorful. On the war itself see FRANK FREIDEL, *The Splendid Little War* (1958) [paperback] and WALTER MILLIS, *The Martial Spirit* (1931). Also *Harvard Guide*, Pt. V.

32

America on the World Stage, 1899–1909

Little Brown Brothers

THE liberty-loving Filipinos were tragically misled. They had assumed
that they, like the Cubans, would be granted their freedom after the war.
A clear-cut pledge by Congress to this effect probably would have averted
the sorry sequel, but the Senate by the narrowest of margins refused to
pass such a resolution. Filipino bitterness toward the American troops
continued to mount, and finally erupted into open insurrection on February 4, 1899.

The war with the Filipinos, unlike the "splendid" little set-to with
Spain, was sordid and prolonged. It involved more savage fighting, more
soldiers killed in action, and far more scandal. The anti-imperialists redoubled their protests. In their view the United States, having plunged
into war with Spain to free Cuba, was now fighting ten thousand miles
away to rivet shackles on a people who asked for nothing but liberty.

As the ill-equipped Filipino armies were defeated, they melted into
the jungle and began waging a vicious guerrilla warfare. Many of the
primitive natives used barbarous methods, and inevitably the infuriated
American troops were dragged down to their level. A brutal soldier song
betrayed inner feelings:

> Damn, damn, damn the Filipinos!
> Cross-eyed kakiak ladrones!
> Underneath the starry flag
> Civilize 'em with a Krag [rifle],
> And return us to our own beloved homes.

Atrocity tales rocked and shocked the United States, for such methods were not representative of America's better self. Uncle Sam's soldiers

629

LIBERTY HALTS AMERICAN BUTCHERY IN THE PHILIPPINES
Life, 1899

were goaded to such extremes as to use the painful "water cure," which consisted of forcing water down the victim's throat until he yielded information or died. Reconcentration camps were even established which strongly suggested those of "Butcher" Weyler in Cuba. America, having begun the Spanish war with noble ideals, now dirtied her hands. One New York newspaper published a reply to Rudyard Kipling's famous poem:

> We've taken up the white man's burden
>   Of ebony and brown;
> Now will you kindly tell us, Rudyard,
>   How we may put it down?

The backbone of the Filipino insurrection was finally broken in 1901, when Emilio Aguinaldo was captured by a clever if unsporting ruse. But sporadic fighting dragged on for many dreary months.

The problem of a government for the conquered islanders worried President McKinley, who in 1899 appointed a Philippine Commission to survey the debris and make appropriate recommendations. In its second year this body was headed by William H. Taft, an able and amiable lawyer-judge from Ohio who weighed about 350 pounds. Forming a strong attachment for the Filipinos, he called them his "little brown brothers" and danced light-footedly with their tiny women. But among the American soldiers, who were sweatily combing the jungles, a different view of the insurgent prevailed:

> He may be a brother of Big Bill Taft,
> But he ain't no brother of mine.

"Benevolent assimilation" of the Philippines proceeded with painful slowness. Millions of American dollars were poured into the islands to improve roads, sanitation, and public health. Important economic ties, including trade in sugar, developed between the two peoples. American teachers—"pioneers of the blackboard"—set up an unusually good school system, and helped make English a second language. But all this vast expenditure, which brought little to America in substantial return, was ill appreciated. The Filipinos, who hated compulsory civilization, preferred less sanitation and more liberty. Like caged eagles, they beat against their gilded bars until they got their freedom.

Breaking a Lance for China

Uncle Sam waded farther into the chilly waters of international affairs in 1899, when American delegates participated in the world disarmament conference at The Hague, in the Netherlands. Summoned at the invitation of the Russian Czar, the parley completely disappointed high hopes of reducing arms. But it did succeed in further codifying international law. It also set up the Permanent Court of Arbitration at The Hague, housed in the magnificent "Temple of Peace" donated by steelman Andrew Carnegie.

Much more exciting events had meanwhile been brewing in the Far East, notably in enfeebled China. Following her defeat by Japan in 1894–1895, the imperialistic European powers, notably Russia and Germany, moved in. Like vultures descending upon a stranded whale, they began to tear away valuable leaseholds and economic spheres of influence from the Manchu government.

A growing group of Americans viewed the vivisection of China with alarm. Churches were worried about their spiritual vineyards; manufacturers and exporters feared that Chinese markets would be monopolized by Europeans. An alarmed American public, openly prodded by the newspapers and privately prodded by certain free-trade British, demanded that the Washington government do something. Secretary of State John Hay, a quiet but witty poet-novelist-diplomat with a flair for capturing the popular imagination, finally decided upon a dramatic move.

In the summer of 1899 Hay dispatched to all the great powers a communication which soon came to be called the Open Door note. He urged them to announce that in their leaseholds or spheres of influence they would respect certain Chinese rights and the ideal of fair competition. In short, in their dealings with foreign traders the intruding powers would observe the Open Door. The principle was not new, for we had tried repeatedly to make it the basis of our commercial dealings with China in the 19th Century. But the phrase "Open Door" quickly caught the public fancy and gained wide acceptance.

Hay's proposal of this self-denying policy caused much squirming in the leading capitals of the world. It was like asking all men who do not have thieving designs to stand up and be counted. Italy alone accepted the Open Door unconditionally; she was the only major power that had no leasehold or sphere of influence in China. Britain, Germany, France, and Japan all accepted, but subject to the condition that the others acquiesce unconditionally. Russia, with covetous designs on China's Manchuria, in effect politely declined. But John Hay, rather than run the risk of a flat rejection, cleverly interpreted the Russian refusal as an acceptance, and proclaimed that the Open Door was in effect. Under such dubious midwifery was the infant born, and no one should have been surprised when the child proved to be sickly and relatively short-lived.

Hinging the Open Door

Open Door or not, patriotic Chinese were angered by being used as a mat by the Europeans. In 1900 a super-nationalistic group known as the Boxers broke loose with the cry "Kill Foreign Devils." Over two hundred luckless whites were murdered, and a number of foreign diplomats were besieged in the capital, Peking.

A rescue force of some 18,000 soldiers, hastily assembled, arrived in the nick of time. This multi-nation contingent consisted of Japanese, Russian, British, French, German, and American troops, with the American contribution some 2500 men. Such participation in a joint military operation, especially on the other side of the world, was plainly contrary to our time-honored principles of non-entanglement and non-involvement. But we had not been a Far Eastern power in the days of George Washington.

The victorious allied invaders acted angrily and vindictively. They assessed prostrate China an excessive indemnity of $333,000,000, of which our share was to be $24,500,000. When we discovered that this sum was much more than enough to pay damages and expenses, we remitted about $18,000,000 of it. The Peking government, appreciating this gesture of good will, set aside the money to educate a selected group of Chinese students in the United States. These bright young men later played a significant role in the Westernization of the Orient.

Secretary Hay now let fly another paper broadside, for he feared that the triumphant powers might use the Boxer outrages as a pretext for carving up China outright. His new circular note to the powers in 1900 announced that henceforth the Open Door would embrace the territorial integrity of China, as well as her commercial integrity. Remembering his previous Russian rebuff, he did not this time ask for replies.

Defenseless China, as it turned out, was spared partition during these troubled years. But her salvation was probably not due to Hay's fine phrases, which the American people were loath to back up with fighting men. China owed her preservation far more to the fact that the other powers were strong; none of them could trust the others to gain an advantage.

Kicking "Teddy" Upstairs

The renomination of President McKinley by the Republicans in 1900 was a foregone conclusion. He had piloted the country through a victorious war; he had acquired rich though burdensome overseas real estate; he had established the gold standard; and he had brought the promised prosperity of the full dinner pail. "We'll stand pat!" was the poker-playing counsel of Mark Hanna. McKinley was renominated at Philadelphia on a platform that smugly endorsed prosperity, the gold standard, and overseas expansion.

An irresistible vice-presidential boom had developed for "Teddy" Roosevelt, the cowboy-hero of San Juan Hill. Capitalizing on his war-

TWO VIEWS OF THE ROUGH RIDER AS VICE-PRESIDENT
Left, Washington *Times;* right, Washington *Post*

born popularity, he had been elected governor of New York, where Thomas C. ("Easy Boss") Platt had found him headstrong and difficult to manage. Platt and his cronies therefore devised a scheme to kick the colorful colonel upstairs into the Vice-Presidency.

The plot to railroad Roosevelt worked beautifully. The Rough Rider, gesticulating wildly, attended the nominating convention, where his Western-style cowboy hat made him stand out like a white crow. He had no desire to die of slow rot in the vice-presidential burying ground, but he was eager to prove that he could get the nomination if he wanted it. He finally gave in when, to the accompaniment of cries of "We Want Teddy," he received a unanimous vote. Mark Hanna was apoplectically profane. He went about moaning that there would be only one heartbeat between that wild-eyed "madman"—"that damned cowboy"—and the Presidency of the United States.

William Jennings Bryan, now a colonel also, was the overwhelming choice of the Democrats meeting at Kansas City. He was not a shooting-war hero, but he had run the risks of typhoid fever and "embalmed beef" in army camps. The free-silver issue was now defunct, but Bryan, a slave to consistency, forced a silver plank down the throats of his protesting associates. He thus helped crucify himself on a cross of silver. The Democratic platform proclaimed, as did Bryan, that the "paramount" issue was Republican overseas imperialism.

Imperialism or Bryanism?

Campaign history repeated itself. McKinley, the soul of dignity, sat safely on his front porch, as before. Bryan, also as before, took to the stump in a cyclonic campaign, assailing both imperialism and Republican-fostered trusts.

The super-energetic Rough Rider, Theodore Roosevelt, out-Bryaned Bryan. He toured the country with revolver-shooting cowboys, and his popularity cut heavily into Bryan's support in the Middle West. Flashing his magnificent teeth and pounding his fist fiercely into his palm, Roosevelt denounced all dastards who would haul down Old Glory.

The Bryanites loudly pursued their "paramount" issue of imperialism. Lincoln, they charged, had abolished slavery for 3,500,000 Africans; McKinley had re-established it for 7,000,000 Malays. But the question of imperialism was actually growing stale, for it had been before the novelty-loving American people for more than two years. We had the Philippines on our hands anyhow, and the real question was not "Shall we keep them?" but "What shall we do with them in the future?"

The Republicans countered, with evident success, by charging that "Bryanism," not imperialism, was the paramount issue. By this accusation they meant that Bryan would rock the boat of prosperity, once he got into office with his free-silver lunacy and other dangerous ideas. The voters were much less concerned about imperialism than about "Four Years More of the Full Dinner Pail" and "Let Well Enough Alone." Prosperity at home was more important than freedom abroad. When the smoke cleared off, McKinley had triumphed by a much wider margin than in 1896: 7,207,923 to 6,358,133 popular votes, and 292 to 155 electoral votes.

The victory of 1900 was not a mandate for or against imperialism, legend to the contrary. The confused voters were not asked to decide this issue but, basically, to select either McKinley or Bryan. Many citizens who favored Bryan's anti-imperialism feared his free silver; many who favored McKinley's "sound money" hated his imperialism. If there was any mandate at all it was for the two "P's": prosperity and protection. The country, content with good times, anticipated four more years of a full dinner pail crammed with fried chicken. And "Boss" Platt of New York gleefully prepared to go to Washington on inauguration day to see Vice-President Roosevelt "take the veil."

Brandisher of the Big Stick

The kindly McKinley had scarcely been in office another six months when, in September, 1901, he was murdered by an obscure and deranged anarchist. Roosevelt thus became President at age forty-two, the youngest thus far in our history. Knowing that he had a reputation for impulsiveness and radicalism, he sought to reassure the country by announcing that he would carry out the policies of his distinguished predecessor. Cynics sneered that he would indeed carry out McKinley's program— to the garbage heap.

What manner of man was Theodore Roosevelt? Born into a wealthy and distinguished New York family, he had built up his spindly, asthmatic body by a stern and self-imposed routine of exercise. Graduating from Harvard with Phi Beta Kappa honors, he published at the age of twenty-four the first of some thirty volumes of muscular prose. Then came busy years, which involved duties as a ranch owner and bespectacled cowboy in the Dakotas, followed by various political posts.

The Rough Rider's high-voltage energy was unquenchable. Believing that it was better to wear out than to rust out, he would shake the hands of some 6000 persons at one stretch, or ride horseback a hundred miles in a day, as an example for portly cavalry officers. It is not surprising that this human volcano gathered about him a group of athletic, tennis-playing cronies, who were popularly dubbed "the Tennis Cabinet."

Incurably boyish and bellicose, Roosevelt loved a fight—"an elegant row." He never ceased to preach the virile virtues and to denounce civilized softness, with its pacifists and other "flubdubs" and "mollycoddles." An ardent champion of military and naval preparedness, he adopted as his pet proverb, "Speak softly and carry a big stick, [and] you will go far." If a statesman had the Big Stick, he could work his will among foreign nations without shouting; if he lacked it, shouting would do no good. The Rough Rider had both a big stick and a big voice.

Wherever Roosevelt went, there was a great stir. Shockingly unconventional, he loved to break hoary precedents—the hoarier the better.

TEDDY AND THE BIG STICK
New York *Globe*

He was a colossal egoist, and his self-confidence bordered on self-righteousness. So sure was he of the correctness of his convictions that he impetuously branded people liars who disagreed with him. As a true cosmopolite, he loved people and mingled with all ranks of men, from Catholic cardinals to professional prize fighters.

As an outspoken moralizer and reformer, Roosevelt preached dogmatic platitudes from the White House pulpit. John Morley, a British author, found him an interesting combination of St. Paul and St. Vitus. Yet the Rough Rider was an opportunist who would compromise rather than butt his head against a stone wall. He was, in reality, much less radical than his violent and blustery actions would indicate. A violent middle-of-the-roader, he stood just a little left of center, and bared his mule-like teeth at liberals and reactionaries alike.

Roosevelt rapidly developed into a master politician with an idolatrous personal following. T.R.—as he was called—had an enormous popular appeal, partly because the common man saw in him a fiery champion. A magnificent showman, he was always front-page copy; and his cowboyism, his bear shooting, his outsize teeth, and his pince-nez glasses were ever the delight of the cartoonist. Though a staunch party man, he detested many of the dirty-handed bosses; but he learned, as Cleveland never did, to hold his nose and work with them.

Above all, the Rough Rider was a direct-actionist. He believed that the President should lead; and although he made mistakes, he kept things noisily moving—generally forward. Never having been a lawyer, he condemned the law and the courts as too slow. He had no real respect for the delicate checks and balances among the three branches of the government. Finding the Constitution too rigid, he would on occasion ignore it; finding the Senate too windy, he would often circumvent it; finding Congress too rebellious, he tried a mixture of coercion and compromise on it.

Roosevelt finally developed his extraordinary "stewardship theory," which must have made Jefferson and others writhe in their graves. The President, so the Rough Rider felt, may take any action in the general interest that is not specifically forbidden by the laws and the Constitution. Wallace Irwin noted:

> The Constitution rides behind
> And the Big Stick rides before,
> (Which is the rule of precedent
> In the reign of Theodore.) *

The Canal and Colombia

Foreign affairs absorbed much of Roosevelt's bullish energy. Having traveled extensively in Europe, he enjoyed a far more intimate knowledge of the outside world than most of his predecessors.

The Spanish-American War had focused interest on the Central American isthmus. The Caribbean and Pacific windfalls of the United States further emphasized the need of constructing the long-talked-about canal, through which only ink had flowed for centuries. The American people had witnessed a dramatic object lesson when the battleship *Oregon*, stationed on the Pacific Coast at the outbreak of hostilities, made a forced-draft dash around South America to join the fleet in Cuban waters. Alarmists speculated on what might have happened if this warship had not arrived in time for the battle of Santiago, and if the Spanish fleet had been stronger. An Isthmian canal would plainly augment the strength of the navy by increasing its mobility. Such a waterway would also make easier the defense of Hawaii and the Philippines, and facilitate the operations of the American merchant marine.

* From "The Ballad of Grizzly Gulch," in *At the Sign of the Dollar* (1903). Reprinted by permission of the author.

The initial obstacles in the path of the canal builders were legal rather than geographical. By the terms of the ancient Clayton-Bulwer Treaty, concluded with Britain in 1850, the United States could not secure exclusive control over such a route. But by 1901 our British cousins were willing to yield ground. Confronted with an unfriendly Europe and bogged down in the South African Boer War, they signed with us in 1901 the Hay-Pauncefote Treaty. It not only gave us a free hand to build the canal, but conceded the right to fortify it as well.

The legal barriers now removed, the next question was: Where should the canal be dug? Many American experts favored the Nicaraguan route, but the agents of the old French Canal Company were eager to salvage something from the costly failure at Panama. Represented by a young, energetic, and unscrupulous engineer, Philippe Bunau-Varilla, the New Panama Canal Company suddenly dropped the price of its holdings from $109,000,000 to the fire-sale price of $40,000,000.

The Nicaragua-versus-Panama issue was hotly debated in Congress, where one of the chief objections raised against Nicaragua was its volcanic activity. Providentially for Bunau-Varilla, Mount Pelée, on the West Indian island of Martinique, blew its top in May, 1902, and wiped out thirty thousand souls. The clever Frenchman hastily secured ninety Nicaraguan postage stamps, each bearing a picture of the country's most fearsome volcano, and sent them to the Senators. Senator Mark Hanna delivered a logical and persuasive speech, in which he stressed the sub-

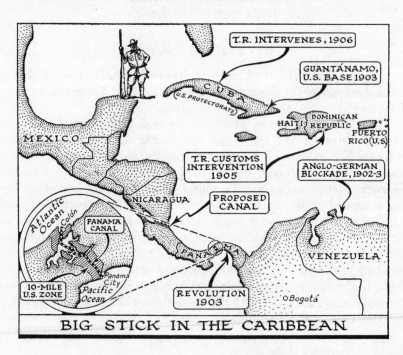

BIG STICK IN THE CARIBBEAN

stantial engineering advantages of the Panama route. In June, 1902, Congress finally accepted his views.

The scene now shifted to Colombia, of which Panama was an unwilling part. A treaty highly favorable to the United States was negotiated with the Colombian government in Bogotá. It granted the lease of a six-mile-wide zone in perpetuity, in return for $10,000,000 and an annual payment of $250,000. But when the pact was submitted to the Bogotá Senate, it was unanimously rejected. The Isthmian strip was regarded as one of Colombia's most valuable natural assets, and many Colombians felt that they were not getting enough money. Evidence later unearthed indicates that if the United States had been willing to pay an additional $15,000,000, the treaty would have been approved.

Roosevelt was angered by his setback at the hands of what he called these "dagoes." Frantically eager to be elected President "in his own right" in 1904, he was anxious to "make the dirt fly" so as to impress the voters. "Damn the law," he cried privately, "I want the canal built!" He likewise assailed "the blackmailers of Bogotá," who, like armed bandits, were blocking the onward march of civilization. He failed to point out, in his understandable chagrin, that the Senate of the United States also rejects treaties.

Puppet Panama

The disgruntled Panamanians, who had rebelled numerous times in previous years, were ripe for another revolt. They had counted on a wave of prosperity to follow construction of the canal, and they feared that the United States would now turn to the Nicaraguan route. Bunau-Varilla was no less disturbed by the prospect of losing the company's $40,000,000. Working hand in glove with the Panama revolutionists, he raised a tiny "patriot" army consisting of members of the Panamanian fire department, plus five hundred "bought" Colombian troops—price $100,000.

The Panama revolution occurred on November 3, 1903, with the incidental killing of a Chinese bystander. Colombian troops were gathered to crush the uprising, but American naval forces would not let them cross the isthmus. Roosevelt justified this highly questionable interference by a strained interpretation of the treaty of 1846 with Colombia.

Roosevelt moved rapidly to make Panama a virtual outpost of the United States. Three days after the uprising, he hastily extended the right hand of recognition to the newly hatched republic. Fifteen days later, Bunau-Varilla, who was now the Panamanian minister despite his French citizenship, signed the Hay–Bunau-Varilla treaty in Washington. The price of the canal strip was left the same, but the zone was widened from six to ten miles. And the French company gleefully pocketed its $40,000,-000 from the United States Treasury.

Roosevelt, it seems clear, did not actively plot to tear Panama from the side of Colombia. But the conspirators knew of his angrily expressed views, and they counted on his using the Big Stick to prevent Colombia from intervening. The Rough Rider, as chance would have it, became so indiscreetly involved in the affair as to create the impression that he had been a secret party to the intrigue.

The United States unfortunately suffered a black eye as a result of Roosevelt's "cowboy diplomacy." The European imperialists, who were old hands at this sort of thing, could now raise their eyebrows sneeringly at our superior moral pretensions—and they did.

Completing the Canal

The so-called rape of Panama marks an ugly downward lurch in our relations with Latin America. Much fear had already been aroused by our seizure of Puerto Rico and by our stranglehold on Cuba. The fate of Colombia, when she dared defy the Colossus of the North, indicated that the weak sister republics were not safe. Even though the government of infant Panama was recognized in Latin America, the era of the bullying "Big Brother" policy was definitely launched.

Roosevelt vehemently defended himself against all charges of evil-doing. He claimed that he had received a "mandate from civilization" to start the canal, and that Colombia had wronged the United States by not permitting herself to be benefited. To deal with these "blackmailers," he insisted, was like "nailing currant jelly to the wall."

But Roosevelt was not completely candid. He failed to point out that the Nicaragua route was just about as feasible, and that it was available without having to start a revolution. Yet this alternative would have involved some delay, and the presidential election of 1904 was fast approaching.

Active work was begun on "making the dirt fly" in 1904, but serious difficulties were encountered, ranging from labor troubles to landslides. The organization was finally perfected under an energetic but autocratic West Point engineer, Colonel George Washington Goethals. At the outset, sanitation proved to be more important than excavation. Colonel William C. Gorgas, the quiet and determined exterminator of yellow fever in Havana, ultimately made the Canal Zone "as safe as a health resort."

Americans finally succeeded where Frenchmen had failed. The colossal canal project was completed in 1914, just as World War I was breaking out, at an initial cost of about $400,000,000. The whole enterprise, in the words of the English writer James Bryce, was "the greatest liberty Man has ever taken with Nature."

Roosevelt as ex-President continued to exult over this geographical surgery. He was at pains to point out that even though the debate went

ROOSEVELT MAKES THE DIRT FLY AT PANAMA
New York *Herald*, 1903; reprinted by permission of the New York *Sun*, Inc.

on over his "rape" of Panama, ships went through the canal. Colombia had offered to arbitrate her grievance, but the United States, though often an advocate of such methods, declined to risk a decision at the hands of foreigners. Subsequent Democratic Congresses, quite willing to do penance for the Republican sins of Roosevelt, attempted to apologize to Colombia and to indemnify her for her loss. But the still-violent Rough Rider cried that this would be done over his dead body, and his friends in the Senate defeated the proposed treaty.

Oil provided an unexpected lubricant. Gushers of liquid "black gold" were discovered in Colombia, and would-be exploiters from Yankeeland were getting the cold shoulder. Roosevelt was now dead. In 1921 the United States Senate, suddenly troubled by a tender conscience, approved a heart-balm treaty, which granted Colombia $25,000,000 without an apology. But such a sum is in itself an apology. The tragedy is that in 1903 about half this so-called "canalimony," in addition to the original $10,000,000, would probably have averted the scandal.

Venezuelan Vexations

The republic of Venezuela lay in the iron grip of dictator Cipriano Castro, whom Roosevelt branded "an unspeakably villainous little monkey." Castro had defaulted on his nation's indebtedness to certain European powers, and late in 1902 Great Britain took the lead in inducing Germany to join in collecting the debts by force. Roosevelt had no serious objections: he believed that misbehaving republics might properly be "spanked."

The spanking proved effective. The Germans sank two Venezuelan gunboats, and with unnecessary ruthlessness bombarded a Venezuelan town early in 1903. Dictator Castro hastened to accept an arbitration proposal that he had earlier spurned, and the Washington officials were glad to transmit his acceptance to the European powers.

The people of the United States, less acquiescent, were now angrily aroused against this iron-fisted intervention. The British ringleaders, fearful of ruining the newly won American friendship, pulled in their horns, leaving Germany to bear the full brunt of our disapproval. The European powers finally accepted arbitration of their monetary claims in 1903, and the unhappy affair was patched up.

Roosevelt released the "inside" story thirteen years later, when he was aroused against a Germany that had brutally invaded Belgium. Describing a threatening ten-day ultimatum which he had presented to the Kaiser, he indicated that he had big-sticked the Germans out of Venezuela. Although historians have cast serious doubt on his tale, he probably did exert some behind-the-scenes influence on the German Emperor. Among other pressures, Admiral Dewey was stationed menacingly in the Caribbean with a powerful naval force.

The famous doctrine of Monroe was no doubt strengthened as a result of the Venezuela episode, whatever question may exist as to Roosevelt's exaggerated tale. A resentful American public had served warning that it would frown upon European powers which, with mailed fist, set out to "spank" our weak Latin American neighbors.

T.R.'s Perversion of Monroe's Doctrine

Defaulted debts were involved also in the revolution-rent Dominican Republic, whose "chronic wrongdoing" Roosevelt deplored. He feared that the Germans or other Europeans might come as bill collectors. If they came, they might stay; if they stayed, they would violate the Monroe Doctrine; if they violated the Monroe Doctrine, we might have to fight them.

The Rough Rider therefore evolved a curious policy of "preventive intervention," better known as the Roosevelt corollary of the Monroe Doctrine. Under it we would intervene ourselves, take over the customhouses, pay off the debts, and keep the troublesome powers on the other side of the Atlantic. We had a moral obligation to do so, Roosevelt argued, because we would not permit the European nations themselves to intervene in the bankrupt banana republics.

This new application of the Big Stick in the Caribbean was put into operation in 1905. It was formalized by a Dominican treaty two years later, after the Rough Rider had engaged in a "glorious" quarrel with the Senate. Crooked Dominican officials, who had enjoyed much juicy graft, were not happy over our interference, and they acquiesced only after some judicious arm-twisting from Washington. But from a debt-collecting point of view, the customhouse intervention was unquestionably a success.

The Roosevelt corollary, though tacked onto the Monroe Doctrine, bore only a strained relation to the original dictum of 1823. Monroe had in effect said to the European powers, "Thou shalt not intervene." The Rough Rider changed this warning to mean, "We shall intervene to prevent European intervention." The Roosevelt doctrine was actually so radical as to be a completely new policy, but it gained readier acceptance by being associated with the honored name of Monroe. Yet in its own right, the corollary had considerable merit as a defensive stroke.

Roosevelt's reinterpretation of Monroe's doctrine had its dark side. It probably did more than any other one step to promote the "Bad Neighbor" policy begun in these years. As time wore on, the new corollary was used to justify wholesale interventions and repeated landings of the marines, all of which helped turn the Caribbean into a "Yankee lake." Latin Americans mistakenly cursed the unoffending Monroe, when they should have directed their ire at the offending Roosevelt. To them it seemed as though the Monroe Doctrine, far from providing a shield, was a cloak behind which the United States sought to throttle them. Wallace Irwin poked fun at the new interventionism:

> Here's a bumper to the doctrine of Monroe, roe, roe,
> And the neighbors whom we cannot let alone;
> Through the thirst for diagnosis we're inserting our proboscis
> Into everybody's business but our own.*

The shadow of the Big Stick likewise fell on Cuba in 1906. Revolutionary disorders brought an appeal from the Cuban president, and, "necessity being the mother of intervention," United States marines were landed. These police forces were withdrawn temporarily in 1909, but in Latin American eyes this episode was but another example of the creeping power of the Colossus of the North.

The Big Stick in Two Hemispheres

The Rough Rider, booted and spurred, had meanwhile been charging into the Canada-Alaska boundary controversy. Our vast northern neighbor had, for several years, seriously disputed with us the line between herself and the Alaska panhandle. We contended that under the

* From "Monroe Doctrinings," in *Random Rhymes and Odd Numbers* (The Macmillan Company, copyright 1906). Reprinted by permission of the publisher.

original Russo-American treaty of 1824, the boundary should follow the snake-like windings of the coast. The Canadians argued that the line should be run straighter, leaving the heads of the deeper inlets in their hands. Finally, in 1903 a treaty was concluded between London and Washington. It referred the controversy to six "impartial justices of repute," three Americans appointed by President Roosevelt and three British subjects—two Canadians and one Briton—named by Edward VII.

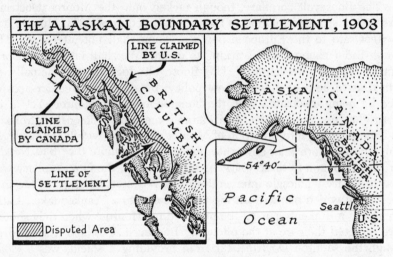

THE ALASKAN BOUNDARY SETTLEMENT, 1903

The so-called Alaska boundary arbitration actually created more disputes than it solved. Roosevelt, cocksure as usual, convinced himself that the Canadian claims were "an outrage pure and simple." Behind the scenes, he brandished his Big Stick, threatening that if America lost he would seize what was properly ours with our own troops. The key British arbitrator, faced with the awful responsibility of starting a war, may have been unduly swayed. The tribunal finally voted four to two—the two being Canadians—in favor of the basic American contention, although narrowing somewhat the coastal strip. The Canadians were deeply angered, perhaps more so by the British, who had sacrificed them, than by Roosevelt, who had browbeaten them.

A bigger storm had meanwhile been brewing in North Africa over French-protected Morocco, at which the imperial-minded Germans were casting covetous looks. In 1905 the Kaiser landed there and made a saber-rattling speech. Overnight an international crisis developed, involving France and Britain as the chief adversaries of Germany. At the prompting of the Kaiser, Roosevelt consented to help arrange for an international conference at Algeciras, Spain, in 1906.

Two American delegates were sent to the parley on Morocco, despite the non-entanglement warnings of the Founding Fathers. Roosevelt privately took the side of France, partly because he distrusted the Kaiser, whom he dubbed "that autocratic zigzag." When deadlock developed at

Algeciras, the Rough Rider flourished his Big Stick at the erratic German ruler and, in his own words, gently "stood him on his head." As the German army was not ready to march, the Kaiser backed down and suffered something of a diplomatic defeat.

But why should the United States be embroiling itself in Morocco? Our trade and investment stake—the Open Door—was negligible. Roosevelt in effect was developing a further new interpretation of the Monroe Doctrine. He evidently believed that we were justified in intervening in overseas crises that might touch off globe-girdling hostilities, because such a conflagration probably would suck us in. It is possible that his timely intervention prevented world-wide war from breaking out in 1906 rather than in 1914.

The Second Hague Disarmament Conference met in 1907. Although officially called by the Czar, as before, it was actually initiated by Roosevelt, who responded to the proddings of American public opinion. Nothing was accomplished in the way of arms reduction, owing largely to the opposition of the militaristic Germans to disarmament and arbitration. But the Conference did adopt some useful regulations on such subjects as international debt collection, humane warfare, and the rights and obligations of neutrals. Although the United States was represented at The Hague—another step away from the time-honored isolation—the war-loving Roosevelt, deep in the Japanese crisis, was rather indifferent to the sessions.

The Bear That Walks Like a Man

The Russian bear, having lumbered across Asia, was seeking to bathe his frostbitten paws in the ice-free ports of China's Manchuria, notably Port Arthur. To Japan, Manchuria in Czarist hands was a springboard pointed at her strategic heart. Russian troops had invaded Manchuria during the Boxer outburst of 1900, and despite solemn promises were showing a disquieting reluctance to withdraw. The Czar was obviously stalling until his trans-Siberian railroad could be finished, as it would be in a few months. The Japanese, with the clock ticking against them, suddenly precipitated war in 1904 by a sneak attack on the Russian fleet at Port Arthur.

On paper, American sympathies should have gone out to Russia, for she was a traditional friend of long standing. During the 19th Century we had managed to get along unusually well with her, primarily because of our common bitterness against Britain, and also because we had little to do with the Russians. But by the sunset of the century our ancient grudge against Mother England was evaporating, and we were coming into direct contact with Russia as she menaced our Open Door interests in China. We were also repelled by her naked imperialism, and especially by Czarist despotism, which was highlighted by shocking descriptions of Siberian prison camps in American magazines of the 1880's and 1890's. Worst of all were the terrible massacres of Russian Jews, which broke out anew with frightful fury at the time of the Russo-Japanese War.

Tiny Japan had a sentimental claim to our sympathy, for she was peculiarly the protégé of America. We had forced open her gates to Western civilization, and we had taken great pride in the speed with which she had acquired a veneer of Occidental culture. As between Russia and Japan, Russia seemed to be the big bully and Japan the underdog—and our hearts went out to the Japanese. The Russians resentfully reminded us how they had stood by us during the dark days of our Civil War—though for selfish reasons, as is now known.

Unblessed Are the Peacemakers

The Japanese, undersized but efficient, administered a humiliating series of beatings to the inept Russians, in Manchuria and on the sea. But as the war dragged on, Japan began to run short of men and yen—a weakness that she did not want to betray to the enemy. The Tokyo officials therefore approached Roosevelt in the deepest secrecy, and asked him to take steps that would bring the negotiators together in a peace conference.

The Rough Rider, though he did not relish the unpopular role of umpire, felt that a speedy end of the war was to America's interests. Either Japan or Russia might collapse completely, and thus upset the balance of power in the Far East. The surviving combatant would then become dominant, to the jeopardy of our commercial, missionary, and other interests.

Under Roosevelt's vigorous shepherding, the Japanese and Russian peace delegates gathered near Portsmouth, New Hampshire, in 1905. The politely bowing Orientals, on the basis of their victories, presented stern demands. They asked for a huge indemnity and for all of the island of Sakhalin, which commands the Amur River—the Mississippi of Siberia.

Agreement at Portsmouth was not easy. Roosevelt encountered stubbornness in both the Japanese and Russians; in disgust he branded the Czar "a preposterous little creature." After the Rough Rider had blustered fearsomely behind the scenes, the Japanese reluctantly gave ground. They abandoned their claims for an indemnity, and agreed to accept half of Sakhalin. But they strengthened their pre-eminent position in Korea, and displaced Russia as the dominant foreign power in Manchuria.

Brickbats rained upon Roosevelt, the honest broker, from both sides. He was condemned by the Russians, who unconvincingly boasted that they could still whip the "Japanese monkeys," and by the Nipponese, who felt robbed of their indemnity. Throughout Japan, Roosevelt's portrait was turned to the wall. But he found some solace in the Nobel Peace Prize of 1906, which he probably deserved, despite his earlier glorification of war.

Two historic friendships were blighted on the wind-swept plains of Manchuria. That between Russia and America, already strained, fell upon more evil days. That between Japan and America entered upon a new and more troubled phase. The United States had emerged in 1898 as a great power, with crucial interests in the Far East. During 1904–1905 Japan likewise emerged as a great power, with ambitions that conflicted directly with ours. We could no longer pat our bright little protégé on the head and show him off. Japan and America were now rivals; and feelings of suspicion, fear, and jealousy were bound to supplant the one-time happy relationship.

Coolies in California

The population of America's Pacific Coast was directly affected by the Russo-Japanese War. A new restlessness came to the rice paddies of Japan, largely as a result of the dislocations and tax burdens wrought by the recent conflict. Large numbers of Japanese laborers, with their wives and numerous offspring, began to pour into the spacious valleys of California. By 1906, there were approximately 70,000 Japanese on the Pacific Coast.

The people of the Golden State, confronted by another "yellow peril," were fearful of being drowned in an Oriental sea. Seizing upon a new variant of the old anti-Chinese slogan, they cried, "The Japanese must go." The eastern part of the United States, indifferent to the problem of the prolific Japanese, did not share the alarm of the Pacific Coast.

A showdown on the Japanese question came in 1906. Following the frightful earthquake and fire of that year in San Francisco, the local school authorities, pressed for space, decreed that Oriental children would have to attend a school specially set aside for them. This edict, though aimed at overage Japanese "boys," was designed basically to advertise to the rest of the nation the alarm of California over the influx of cheap coolie labor.

The Japanese school incident forthwith precipitated an international crisis. The people of Japan, highly sensitive on questions of race, regarded the discrimination as an insult to them and their beloved children. On both sides of the Pacific, irresponsible war talk sizzled in the yellow press—the real "yellow peril." Roosevelt, who in his Rough Rider days had welcomed shooting, was less happy over the prospect of California's stirring up a war which all the other states would have to fight. He therefore invited the entire San Francisco Board of Education, headed by a bassoon-playing mayor under indictment for graft, to come to the White House.

The President finally broke the deadlock, but not until he had waved his Big Stick and bared his big teeth. The Californians were persuaded to repeal the offensive school order and to accept what came to be known as "the Gentlemen's Agreement." This secret understanding was worked out, during 1907–1908, by an exchange of diplomatic notes between Washington and Tokyo. The Japanese, on their part, agreed to stop the flow of coolies to the mainland of the United States by refusing to issue passports. The Californians, their fears largely allayed, henceforth slept easier.

Battleship Diplomacy

Roosevelt, who loved grand flourishes, dreamed up a fantastic one for the benefit of Japan. Though not a coward, he was afraid that the Japanese thought him afraid. He suspected that his intercession between California and Japan was being interpreted in Tokyo as prompted by fear of the Nipponese. The American navy was then second among the navies of the world, thanks to the Rough Rider's unremitting efforts in behalf of preparedness, and that of Japan was fifth. Partly to impress the Japanese with the potency of the Big Stick, Roosevelt decided to send the entire battleship fleet out to the Pacific Coast, and subsequently from there all the rest of the way around the world.

Pained protests arose from numerous American critics. They charged that the mad scheme would provoke war; that the fleet would break down trying to make the trip; and that the Eastern seaboard would be stripped of its defenders. But Roosevelt resolutely issued the final orders, and late in 1907 the sixteen smoke-belching battleships started from Virginia waters. Their commander pointedly declared that he was ready for "a feast, a frolic, or a fight."

The globe-girdling fleet—to the accompaniment of cannonading champagne corks—received a series of tumultuous receptions. At South American ports the Yankee warships were greeted with heart-warming rejoicing, for they were the effective teeth of the Monroe Doctrine as it applied to European intervention. The entire flotilla finally reached the Pacific Coast in fighting trim, and then steamed on to Hawaii, New Zealand, and Australia. After the customary cheers had died away, the prows of the ships were headed for Japanese waters, where alarmists claimed that secret mines were planted.

The overwhelming reception in Japan was by all odds the high point of the trip. Tens of thousands of kimonoed school children had been trained to wave tiny American flags and sing "The Star-Spangled Banner"—in English. In the happy diplomatic atmosphere created by the visit of the fleet, the Root-Takahira agreement of 1908 was reached with Japan. Both powers solemnly pledged themselves to respect each other's territorial possessions in the Pacific, and to uphold the Open Door in China. The ordinarily bellicose Roosevelt, who thus went out of his way to avoid a fight with Japan, not unreasonably regarded the battleship cruise as his most important contribution to peace.

The returning fleet, after visiting the Mediterranean, steamed into home waters early in 1909, just in time to usher out the Roosevelt regime in a blaze of glory. The spectacular exhibition of the Great White Fleet— the Big Stick in action—undoubtedly popularized and accelerated American naval preparedness. The Monroe Doctrine was correspondingly strengthened against European intervention. Finally, this breath-taking demonstration wrote another chapter in our emergence as a great power, and in the development of international-mindedness in our people.

SELECT READINGS

Broad outlines appear in F. R. DULLES, *America's Rise to World Power* (1955) [paperback]. More detailed is H. K. BEALE, *Theodore Roosevelt and the Rise of America to World Power* (1956) [paperback]. Standard lives of Theodore Roosevelt are H. F. PRINGLE's barbed, Pulitzer-prize *Theodore Roosevelt* (1931) [paperback] and W. H. HARBAUGH, *Power and Responsibility* (1961). On the Open Door see TYLER DENNETT's Pulitzer-prize *John Hay* (1933) and A. W. GRISWOLD, *The Far Eastern Policy of the United States* (1938) [paperback]. On the Japanese problem consult T. A. BAILEY, *Theodore Roosevelt and the Japanese-American Crises* (1934); ROGER DANIELS, *The Politics of Prejudice* (1962); and W. R. BRAISTED, *The United States Navy in the Pacific, 1897–1909* (1958). Also *Harvard Guide*, Pt. VI.

33

Theodore Roosevelt and the Square Deal

If elected, I shall see to it that every man has a square deal, no less and no more.

THEODORE ROOSEVELT, 1904

A Square Deal for Labor

THEODORE ROOSEVELT, though something of an imperialistic busybody abroad, was a liberal at home. His sportsman's instincts prompted him to demand a "square deal" for capital, labor, and society at large. He was especially concerned about the public, caught in the middle.

The "square deal" for labor received its acid test in 1902, when a crippling strike broke out in the anthracite coal mines of Pennsylvania. Some 140,000 besooted workers, many of them illiterate immigrants, had long been frightfully exploited and accident-riddled. They demanded, among other improvements, a 20% increase in pay and a reduction of the working day from ten to nine hours.

The mine owners, confident that a chilled public would react against the miners, refused to arbitrate or even negotiate. One of their spokesmen, the multimillionaire George F. Baer, reflected the high-and-mighty attitude of certain ungenerous employers. The workers, he wrote, would be cared for "not by the labor agitators, but by the Christian men to whom God in His infinite wisdom has given the control of the property interests of this country. . . ." Thus closed minds meant closed mines.

As coal supplies dwindled, factories and schools were forced to close, and even hospitals felt the icy grip of winter. Desperately seeking a solution, Roosevelt summoned representatives of the striking miners and the stubborn owners to the White House. He was vastly annoyed by the "extraordinary stupidity and bad temper" of the "wooden-headed gentry" who operated the mines. As he later confessed, if it had not been for the dignity of his high office, he would have taken one of them "by the seat of the breeches" and "chucked him out of the window."

The Rough Rider finally resorted to his trusty Big Stick when he threatened to seize the mines and operate them with federal troops. Even though coal cannot be extracted with bayonets, the owners grudgingly consented to arbitration. A compromise decision ultimately gave the miners a 10% pay boost and a working day of nine hours. But their union was not officially recognized as a bargaining agent.

Keenly aware of the mounting antagonisms between capital and labor, Roosevelt urged Congress to create a new Department of Commerce and Labor. This goal was achieved in 1903. (Ten years later the agency was split into two.) An important arm of the newly born Department of Commerce and Labor was the Bureau of Corporations, which was authorized to probe businesses engaged in interstate commerce. The Bureau was highly useful in helping to break the stranglehold of monopoly, and in clearing the road for the era of "trust busting."

New Railroad Restrictions

The American people love bigness but hate monopoly, and Roosevelt shared their prejudices. The bite of the much-ballyhooed Sherman Anti-Trust Act of 1890 had proved almost completely toothless, and "trustification" was spreading at an alarming rate. The Rough Rider, who habitually hurled harsh words at the "predatory rich," was distressed by the sinister power and wealth of the trusts. Especially disheartening to thoughtful observers was the contrast between marble-halled Fifth Avenue and the tumble-down slum areas.

"Trusts" rapidly came to be a fighting word. Roosevelt believed that these gigantic organizations, with their efficient tools of production, were here to stay. In his eyes, bigness did not necessarily spell badness. He concluded that there were "good" trusts, with public consciences, and "bad" trusts, with unbridled greed and lust for power. Yet the less discriminating public began to cry with increasing vigor, "Smash the trusts." Thrown on the defensive, the monopolists countered by insisting that success in business was not a crime, and that prosecution under antitrust laws was often persecution. But there was clearly a crying need for judicious regulation.

The many-webbed railroads, having grown arrogant like the trusts, were also badly in need of restraint. The Interstate Commerce Act of 1887, tossed as a feeble sop to the public, had proved almost completely illusory. The railroads could endlessly appeal all decisions on rates to the federal courts—a process that might take as long as ten years.

Under the spurs of the Rough Rider, Congress passed effective railroad legislation, beginning with the Elkins Act of 1903. This curb was aimed primarily at the rebate evil, which had now become so rampant that some of the operators actually welcomed regulation. Heavy fines could henceforth be imposed, not only on the railroads that gave rebates but also on the shippers who accepted them. Within a few years a number of railroads and manufacturers were convicted under the new law and suffered painful penalties. The most spectacular case broke in 1907, when Judge Kenesaw Mountain Landis found the Standard Oil Company guilty on 1462 counts of accepting rebates. He thereupon fined the offending corporation an unprecedented $29,240,000. But a higher court set aside this judgment, which seemed more like vengeance than justice.

Much more effective than the Elkins Act in restraining the railroads was the Hepburn Act of 1906. Free passes, with their hint of bribery, were severely restricted. The once-infantile Interstate Commerce Commission was expanded, and its reach was extended to include express companies, sleeping-car companies, and pipelines. The Commission for the first time was given real molars when it was authorized, on complaint of shippers, to nullify existing rates and establish maximum rates.

The Hepburn Bill, though backed by an exasperated public, lost some of its teeth in the Congressional machinery. The House passed it by the overwhelming margin of 346 to 7, but in the more conservative Senate the railroad lobby rallied for a last-ditch stand. The lobbyists finally secured a compromise proviso to the effect that rate decisions might be appealed to the federal courts. But the burden of initiating action rested squarely on the railroads and other carriers.

Trust Busting with a Padded Stick

Roosevelt, as a trust buster, first burst into the headlines in 1902 with an attack on certain railroads. In a spectacular move he authorized his Attorney General to file suit under the Sherman Anti-Trust Act against the Northern Securities Company. This gigantic corporation was a holding company, of which J. P. Morgan was the chief financier, and "Empire Builder" James J. Hill the leading organizational genius. These Napoleonic planners sought to achieve a virtual monopoly of the railroads of the Northwest, and potentially of an even vaster area.

The railway promoters appealed their case to the highest tribunal. Early in 1904, by a five-to-four decision, the Supreme Court held that the Northern Securities Company violated the Sherman Anti-Trust Act and must be dissolved. The decision jolted the financial world and angered Big Business, but enormously puffed up the reputation of Roosevelt as a trust smasher.

The Big Stick crashed down on other giant monopolies, as Roosevelt initiated over forty legal proceedings against them. The Supreme Court in 1905 declared the Beef Trust illegal, and the heavy hand of justice fell upon monopolists handling sugar, fertilizer, harvesters, and other key commodities.

But the dissolution of a trust did not necessarily mean its destruction. Many of the so-called victories for the public were sensational rather than substantial. The biggest trusts were too brawny and too deeply entrenched; and after setbacks in the courts they would cleverly assume, quicksilver-like, other and sometimes more monopolistic forms. Shortly after the sensational dissolution of the Standard Oil Company in 1911, the stock of the much-condemned corporation doubled in value and the price of gasoline and kerosene rose.

Roosevelt did not swing his Big Stick with maximum force, despite his exaggerated prestige as a crusher of trusts. Unwilling to throw overboard completely the time-honored traditions of free enterprise, he felt that the solution of the trust problem lay in regulation rather than in strangulation. "Mr. Dooley" thus summarized T.R.'s views: "On wan hand I wud stamp thim undher fut; on th' other hand not so fast."

The harsh truth is that more trusts were formed under Roosevelt than under the combined administrations of his predecessor (McKinley) and his successor (Taft). To be sure, the Rough Rider could point with pride to the Bureau of Corporations and to new regulatory railway legislation. But he is best known for having reactivated the Sherman Anti-Trust Act rather than for having secured sweeping anti-trust laws. The huge industrial combines were actually mightier when Roosevelt left the White House than they had been when he entered it. His allegedly wishy-washy successor, William Howard Taft, "busted" more trusts than he did. But some of these prosecutions had been launched under Roosevelt, and certainly the task of succeeding Presidents would have been made more difficult if he had not flourished his Big Stick at bloated monopoly.

The War against Waste

The American people, who confidently assumed that their natural resources were inexhaustible, had ravaged their vast domain with unparalleled speed and greed. The West was eager to accelerate the process, for it believed that rapid expansion "built up the country" and increased prosperity by pushing up land values. As for being worried about the future, a common frontier query was, "What has posterity ever done for us?" But long before the end of the 19th Century, far-visioned men could see that such a squandering of our birthright would have to be halted or we would sink into the poverty of backward European areas.

A feeble step in the right direction had come under President Hayes in 1877, when Congress passed the Desert Land Act. The federal government agreed to sell up to 640 acres at $1.25 an acre, provided that the purchaser would reclaim the thirsty soil in three years. This pioneering law led to some irrigation and much fraud. Witnesses would swear that they had seen the land being irrigated—which often meant that a bucket of water had been poured on the place.

An aroused Congress, confronted with the end of the frontier, had finally made a major move toward conservation. In the law of 1891 it

authorized the President to set aside public forest lands for national reserves. Under Presidents Harrison, Cleveland, and McKinley some 46,-
000,000 acres of magnificent trees were rescued from the lumberman's
saw and preserved for a grateful posterity.

Congress had further grappled with the reclamation problem in 1894,
when it approved the Carey Act. Arid federal lands in the West would
be ceded to individual states, provided that the state in each instance
would cause the land to be irrigated and settled upon. This forward-
looking measure, through the happy marriage of desert and water, led to
the cultivation of about a million barren acres.

A new day in the history of conservation dawned with the advent
of Roosevelt. He looked upon the crusade, though still in the creeping
stage, as one phase of the fight against predatory corporations. Hunts-
man, rancher, lover of the great out-of-doors, he was appalled by the
pillaging of timber and mineral resources. By 1900 only about a quarter
of our virgin forests remained erect, three-fourths of them in private
hands. Roosevelt proceeded to set aside in federal reserves some 125,-
000,000 acres, or about three times the acreage saved in the same way by
his three predecessors. He similarly earmarked millions of acres of coal
deposits, as well as water resources useful for irrigation and power.

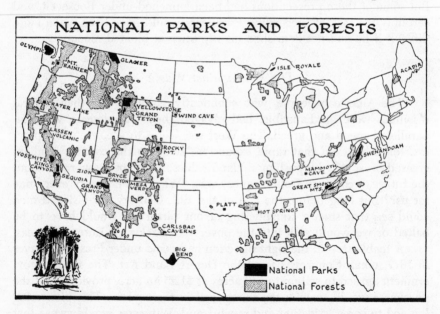

NATIONAL PARKS AND FORESTS

■ National Parks
▒ National Forests

But the Rough Rider's concept of conservation went far beyond
these immediate goals. In his mind the whole question was tied up with
the destruction of wildlife, with forest fires, and with dust storms in treeless areas. He was deeply concerned about floods caused by the indis-

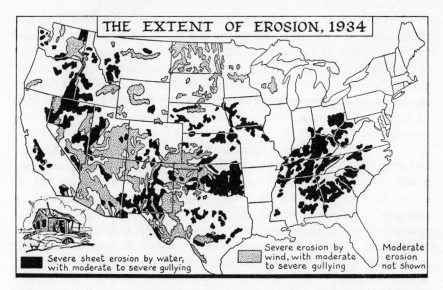

THE EXTENT OF EROSION, 1934

Severe sheet erosion by water, with moderate to severe gullying

Severe erosion by wind, with moderate to severe gullying

Moderate erosion not shown

criminate cutting of timber, and about the erosion of gutted lands that cried aloud for expensive fertilizers. He was eager to do something about the silting up of rivers by turbulent floods, and about improving the navigation of streams, lakes, and canals through an intelligent program of flood control. He repeatedly made vigorous recommendations to Congress designed to improve these conditions, although remedial action in some areas was like locking the barn door after the horse was stolen.

Conservation at Flood Tide

Roosevelt was not the originator of the conservation movement. Other zealots before him had broken important ground, notably Gifford Pinchot, head of the federal Division of Forestry and a red-blooded member of T.R.'s Tennis Cabinet. But Roosevelt seized the banner of leadership, and charged into the fray with all the weight of his prestige, his energy, his firsthand knowledge, and his invective.

The thirst of the desert still unslaked, Congress responded to the spurs of the Rough Rider by passing the Newlands Act of 1902. The federal government was authorized to collect money from the sale of public lands in the sun-baked Western states, and then use these funds for the development of irrigation projects. The settlers repaid the cost of reclamation from their now-productive soil, and the money was put into a revolving fund to finance more such enterprises. The giant Roosevelt Dam, constructed in Arizona on the Salt River, was appropriately dedicated by ex-President Roosevelt in 1911. The sum total of these engineering projects actually approximated the magnitude of the Panama Canal.

The most dramatic single move that Roosevelt made toward conservation came in 1908, when he summoned the Conference of Governors to Washington. The group consisted of prominent governors, justices of the Supreme Court, selected members of Congress, and celebrities like Bryan, Cleveland, and Carnegie. One encouraging result of these deliberations was to inspire the governors to carry on the good work at home. Eighteen months later, forty-one states had set up active conservation commissions.

Conservation, including reclamation, was probably Roosevelt's most enduring tangible contribution to his countrymen. The Isthmian canal would have been dug sooner or later, but lands that are eroded and resources that are gutted do not readily come back. The Rough Rider took conservation out of the conversation stage, threw the force of his colorful personality behind it, dramatized it, and aroused public opinion to a constructive crusade. Conservation under Roosevelt became almost a religion; the more truly scientific stages of the movement were to come in later decades.

President "In His Own Right"

The "Cowboy President" looked forward to the election of 1904 with keen concern. Resenting the sneering title "His Accidency," he was frantically eager to secure popular endorsement by election under his own colors. He was undeniably the idol of the masses—the children's "Teddy Bear" honored his bear-shooting exploits—but the conservative Republican bosses regarded him as an unmanageable maverick. They pined for a standpatter like Mark Hanna, his only possible rival, who, as "Roosevelt luck" would have it, died early in 1904.

The Rough Rider was nominated at Chicago in 1904 by acclamation. As an antidote to his presumed radicalism, the delegates chose for Vice-President a frigid standpatter from Indiana, Charles W. Fairbanks— dubbed "Icebanks." The platform likewise offset Roosevelt's wild tendencies by upholding tariff protection and the gold standard, while letting the trusts off with a verbal slap on the wrist.

The radical Bryan Democrats, twice led down to defeat by the "Peerless Leader," were unhorsed at the St. Louis convention. The hard-bitten conservative wing, now back in the saddle, loudly demanded a "safe and sane" candidate. The Eastern "safe-and-saners" managed to push forward the colorless Judge Alton B. Parker, an impeccably respectable New York lawyer of high character. As a vote getter of considerable power in his home state, "Parker the Silent" was actually more liberal than his reactionary followers represented him to be.

The Democratic platform reflected the unhappiness of the Democrats over Roosevelt's usurpations of legislative and judicial functions. It flayed his administration as "spasmodic, erratic, sensational, spectacular, and arbitrary." No reference was made to the silver issue, though Parker angered the Bryanites by sending a telegram to the convention in which he came out irrevocably for the gold standard.

The ensuing canvass was tame. Judge Parker, hitting at Rough Riderism, demanded a "government of law, not of men." He finally injected some fireworks when he charged that the Republicans were collecting campaign funds from corporations which expected substantial favors in return. Roosevelt promptly let go a pained cry of "liar," but a subsequent Congressional investigation proved that the accusation had some validity. The Standard Oil Company contributed a lubricant of $125,000.

Full dinner pails added luster to the Republican cause, but the overshadowing issue was T.R.'s personality—"Theodore Roosevelt, one and

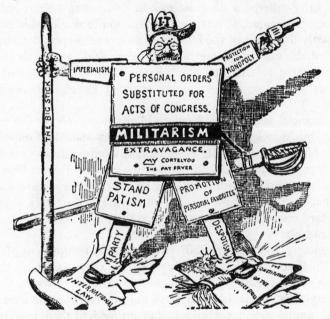

ANTI-T.R. ELECTION CARTOON
New York *World*, 1904

indivisible." His popularity was not dimmed by loose charges that while in Cuba he had shot a Spaniard in the back; and his worshipful following sang lustily, "Three Cheers for the Rough Rider" and "We Want Teddy for Four Years More."

The colorful cowboy won in a canter, and proved to be the first "accidental" President to succeed himself. The electoral count was 336 to 140; the popular count, 7,623,486 to 5,077,911. The Roosevelt avalanche even swept down into the border state of Missouri. The painfully pedestrian Parker proved to be the worst-beaten major candidate since

Horace Greeley was snowed under in 1872. Many Bryanites, protesting Parker's stand on gold, deliberately stayed away from the polls.

The victory was a glorious personal triumph for the Rough Rider and "my policies." The voters clearly preferred Roosevelt, the impetuous candidate of the conservative party, to Parker, the conservative candidate of the impetuous party. In his hour of elation the "dee-lighted" winner announced that he regarded his partial first term of three and one-half years as a full term, and that under no circumstances would he be a candidate for a third term. This was a tactical blunder, for the power of the king wanes when the people know that he will be dead in four years.

The Financial "Reign of Terror"

Prosperity suffered a sharp setback in 1907, when a short but devastating panic descended. It was partly a reaction to world-wide economic trends, partly the result of the billions of dollars in corporation stock that had glutted the market. Centering heavily in Wall Street, the financial flurry was known as "the Rich Man's Panic," and was featured by frightened "runs" on banks. Suicides and criminal indictments were commonplace.

The financial world made haste to blame Roosevelt for the panic. It cried that this "quack," "demagogue," and "crazy man" had unsettled industry by his boat-rocking Big Stick tactics. Conservatives damned him as "Theodore the Meddler," and dubbed the current distress "the Roosevelt Panic." The Rough Rider lashed back at his critics when he accused "certain malefactors of great wealth" of having deliberately engineered the monetary crisis so as to force the government to relax its assaults on the corporations.

Fortunately, the Panic of 1907 paved the way for long-overdue fiscal reforms. Precipitating a currency shortage, the flurry laid bare the need for a more elastic medium of exchange. In a crisis of this sort, the hard-pressed banks were unable to increase the volume of their money, and those with ample supplies were reluctant to lend to their less fortunate sisters. Congress in 1908 responded to existing pressures by passing the Aldrich-Vreeland Act, which authorized National Banks to issue emergency currency backed by various kinds of collateral. The path was thus being smoothed for the epochal Federal Reserve Act of Wilson's administration.

Roots of Reformism

Hardly had the 20th Century dawned when the nation was convulsed by a reform movement, the like of which we had not seen since the 1840's. Roosevelt's name is inevitably connected with this feature of his presidential years, and hasty observers have assumed that he was one of the moving forces behind it. The truth is that he was not so much a reformer as the beneficiary of a tidal wave of reform that caught him up and carried him along with itself.

The ground swell of the new reformist wave went far back—to the Greenback Labor Party of the 1870's, the Farmers' Alliance of the 1880's, and the Populists of the 1890's. As the turn of the century approached, critics of political, economic, and social evils became steadily more numerous and more noisy. The gist of their complaints was that the problems of government had become too complex for the machinery of government. The old philosophy of hands-off individualism seemed increasingly out of place in the new machine age. The United States, so angry reformers charged, now had a government of, by, and for the crooked corporations. The nation was admittedly better off than many foreign lands, but not nearly so well off as its natural resources should have made it. The Promise of American Life had plainly not been fulfilled.

Well before 1900 various individual crusaders had made noteworthy contributions to the literature of reform. The group included Henry George, with his *Progress and Poverty* (1879), and Edward Bellamy, with his *Looking Backward* (1888), the most famous of fifty or so Utopian novels.* The keen-eyed and keen-nosed Danish immigrant Jacob A. Riis, working as a reporter for the New York *Sun,* published in 1890 *How the Other Half Lives.* His account was a damning indictment of the dirt, disease, vice, and misery of the New York slums. Riis deeply influenced Theodore Roosevelt, who several years later headed the New York Police Commission.

"Bloated trusts" and "dirty-handed millionaires" had already been under heavy fire from Bryan, Altgeld, and the Populist leaders. Gifted knights of the pen also entered the fray. In 1894 Henry Demarest Lloyd charged headlong into the Standard Oil Company with his book entitled *Wealth versus Commonwealth.* Embittered and lonely Dr. Thorstein Veblen published in 1899 *The Theory of the Leisure Class,* a violent assault on such evils as "predatory wealth," the idle rich, and absentee landlordism. A brilliant young novelist-reformer, Frank Norris, portrayed the deadly grip of the California railroads on the wheat farmers in *The Octopus* (1901); and in its posthumously published sequel, *The Pit* (1903), he mercilessly exposed Chicago wheat speculators.

The Socialists, now growing in numbers, must take high rank among the ardent critics of existing injustices. Many of them were European immigrants who decried "bloody capitalism," and they began to register appreciable strength at the ballot boxes as the century turned. They received much of their inspiration from abroad, where countries like Germany were launching daring experiments in state socialism. In faraway Australia and New Zealand, too, socialist reforms were being undertaken which attracted much notice in America.

The Socialists found a welcome ally in young Jack (John Griffith)

* George and Bellamy are discussed earlier, on pp. 555–556.

London, the illegitimate-born, ill-educated "oyster pirate" of San Francisco Bay, who became a prolific writer of novels. Steeped in Darwin and in Marx and other German thinkers, London was deeply concerned with the class struggle and with the clash between the civilized brain and primitive force. His stirring tales, such as *The Call of the Wild* (1903) and *The Sea Wolf* (1904), owed their popularity chiefly to their exciting plots, but on a higher level they were closely related to the current reformist agitation.

Men with Muckrakes

By 1902–1903 a group of "Muckrakers"—flaming young reformers with prickly pens—had embarked on a determined campaign to lay bare the muck of iniquity in American society. They sought not to overthrow capitalism but to cleanse it. They had deep faith in the democratic processes, and earnestly believed that the evils afflicting the country flowed not from democracy but from the absence of enough democracy.

The Muckrakers, who became a front-page sensation, were given their nickname in 1906 by President Roosevelt. Annoyed by their excess of zeal, he compared them to the man in Bunyan's *Pilgrim's Progress* who was so intent on raking up muck that he could not see the celestial crown being held above him. The Muckrakers were aided by the rise of ten- or fifteen-cent popular magazines, like *McClure's, Cosmopolitan, Collier's,* and *Everybody's,* all of which catered to the public taste for sensational articles. These revelations boomed circulation, and some of the most scandalous were published in book form.

The muckraking movement began in dead earnest in 1902. A crack New York reporter, Lincoln Steffens, launched a series of articles in *McClure's* entitled "The Shame of the Cities." He fearlessly unmasked the corrupt alliance between Big Business and municipal government. Steffens was followed in the same magazine by Miss Ida M. Tarbell, who published a devastating exposé of the Standard Oil Company. Fearing legal reprisals, the muckraking magazines went to great pains and expense to check their material—paying as much as $3000 to verify a single Tarbell article. R. S. Baker was successfully sued for $15,000 and costs, but his case was a noteworthy exception.

The Muckrakers tilted their pen-lances at varied targets. They assailed the malpractices of life insurance companies and the tariff lobbies. They roasted the Beef Trust, the "Money Trust," the railroad barons, and the corrupt amassing of American fortunes. Thomas W. Lawson, an erratic speculator who had himself made $50,000,000 on the stock market, exposed the practices of his accomplices in "Frenzied Finance." This series of articles, appearing in 1905–1906, rocketed the circulation of *Everybody's.* Lawson, by fouling his own nest, made many enemies among his rich associates, and he died a poor man.

David G. Phillips shocked an already startled nation by his series in *Cosmopolitan* entitled "The Treason of the Senate" (1906). The author boldly charged that seventy-five of the ninety Senators did not represent the people at all but the railroads and trusts. This withering indictment aroused President Roosevelt. Phillips continued his slashing attacks through novels, and was fatally shot in 1911 by a deranged young man whose family he had allegedly maligned.

Some of the most effective fire of the Muckrakers was directed at social evils. The ugly list included the immoral "white slave" traffic in women, the rickety slums, the appalling number of industrial accidents, and the exploitation of Negroes. The abuse of child labor was brought luridly to light by John Spargo's *The Bitter Cry of the Children* (1906).

Patent-medicine vendors likewise came in for savage criticism. These conscienceless vultures sold incredible quantities of adulterated or habit-

THE PATENT MEDICINE FRAUD
Kemble in *Collier's*, 1905; copyright 1905 by
The Crowell-Collier Publishing Company

forming drugs, while "doping" the press with lavish advertising. The muckraking attacks in *Collier's* were ably reinforced by Dr. H. W. Wiley, chief chemist of the Department of Agriculture, who with his famous "Poison Squad" performed experiments on himself.

The pure-food advocates received unexpected support from Upton

Sinclair's socialistic novel *The Jungle*. Published in 1906, this best-selling assault on the meat industry was ultimately translated into seventeen languages. It described in stomach-turning detail the filth, disease, and putrefaction in Chicago's damp, ill-ventilated stockyards. Many readers, including Roosevelt, were so sickened that for a time they found meat unpalatable. The President was moved by the loathsome mess in Chicago to appoint a special investigating commission, whose cold-blooded report almost outdid Upton Sinclair's novel. It related how piles of poisoned rats, rope ends, splinters, and other debris were scooped up and canned as potted ham. A cynical jingle ran:

> Mary had a little lamb,
> And when she saw it sicken,
> She shipped it off to Packingtown,
> And now it's labeled chicken.

The Golden Age of Reformers

Roosevelt at first was not hostile to the so-called literature of exposure. But when in 1906 he saw that a debased public taste was beginning to demand dirt for dirt's sake, he spoke out against the excesses of the muckrakers. Yet these flaming souls, whatever their motives, added to the popularity of T.R.'s trust-busting activities, and helped build up popular pressure behind Congress.

A basketful of badly needed reform legislation was the result of all this agitation. The Meat Inspection Act, passed by Congress in 1906, decreed that the preparation of meat shipped over state lines would be subject to federal inspection. The Pure Food and Drug Act of 1906 was designed to prevent the adulteration and mislabeling of foods and drugs. Like many "firsts," this long-overdue law was riddled with loopholes that had to be plugged later. Both these pieces of legislation encountered bitter resistance, particularly from those special interests or quacks who found it profitable to cheat or poison the public. The White Slave Act (Mann Act), aimed at preventing the interstate transportation of women for immoral purposes, received Congressional approval in 1910.

The reformers actually achieved their most sweeping gains at the state and local levels, for Congress was too much under the influence of lobbyists paid by "the interests." Public-spirited city dwellers were making promising headway in halting the corrupt sale of franchises for street cars and other public utilities. The "invisible government" of trusts and bosses received a damaging blow when the city-manager type of municipal self-rule was devised. Until then, government by experts, sneered at as contrary to the Jacksonian ideal, had gained little ground.

The embattled urban reformers launched house-cleaning assaults on additional evils. These included the smelly tenements, the unhealthful sweatshops, juvenile delinquency, and notorious vice-at-a-price, which flourished in red-light districts unchallenged by the bribed police. Substantial gains were chalked up among the cities in public health, housing, and sanitation. Civil service reform was likewise making encouraging strides, and the confusing "long ballot," overloaded with lists of candidates, was being shortened. A determined campaign was also under way in many localities to achieve equality before the law for both the rich and the poor, the powerful and the friendless.

Pioneer Progressives

The Muckrakers were the godfathers of a widespread pressure for reform called Progressivism, which gathered tremendous momentum in the early 1900's. The crusade was part of a world-wide movement, for there were similar cross-currents in many foreign countries at the same time. In America, progressives were to be found in both major parties, and at all levels of government. Conspicuous among them were the long-suffering white-collar workers, who at long last were joining the farmers in demands for relief from abuses.

Progressivism first bubbled up in individual states like Wisconsin, which became a yeasty laboratory of reform. The governor of the Badger State, pompadoured Robert M. ("Fighting Bob") La Follette, was an undersized but overengined crusader who emerged as the most militant of the Progressive Republican leaders. After a desperate fight with entrenched monopoly, he reached the governor's chair in 1901. Routing the lumber and railroad "interests," he wrested a gratifying measure of control from the crooked corporations and returned it to the people. He also perfected a scheme for regulating public utilities, and labored in close association with experts on the faculty of the state university at Madison.

Other states moved steadily toward the Progressive camp, as they undertook to regulate railroads and trusts, chiefly through public utilities commissions. Oregon was not far behind Wisconsin, and California made giant-boot strides under the stocky Hiram W. Johnson. Elected Republican governor in 1910, this dynamic prosecutor of grafters helped break the dominant grip of the Southern Pacific Railroad on California politics, and then set up a well-oiled machine of his own. Heavily whiskered Charles Evans Hughes, the able and fearless Progressive Republican governor of New York, had earlier gained national fame as a remorseless investigator of malpractices by gas and insurance companies and by the coal trust.

Political Progressivism

Various schemes to insure popular control of the government were being seized upon. They were most numerous in the states of the more liberal West, which had inherited the Populist tradition. Newfangled devices—notably the initiative, the referendum, and the recall—were invented to regain the power that had slipped from the hands of the people into those of the "interests." The "initiative" permitted the voters to initiate needful legislation themselves, especially that which the trust-dominated state legislatures had refused to enact. The "referendum" placed laws on the ballot for approval or veto by the people—laws that in many instances had been lobbied through by glib-tongued spokesmen for Big Business. The "recall" enabled the voters in special elections to remove undesirable elected officials, particularly those who had become tainted by bosses or lobbyists.

The rooting out of graft also became a prime objective of earnest progressives. A number of the state legislatures passed corrupt-practices acts, which limited the amount of money that a candidate might spend for his election. Such legislation also restricted huge gifts from corporations, for which the donors would expect compensating favors. The secret Australian ballot was likewise being introduced more widely in the states to counteract boss rule. Bribery was less feasible when the briber could not tell if he was getting his money's worth from the bribed.

The widespread demand for popular control of government extended to the "quadrennial madhouses" known as national nominating conventions. The voters realized that they had no real hand in selecting the presidential candidate, who all too often was chosen in a smoke-filled and boss-ruled hotel room. The presidential preferential primary, adopted by some of the states, was designed to give the mass of the people an effective voice in making nominations. But in actual practice the party wire-pullers managed to retain a large measure of dominance.

Direct election of United States Senators also became a favorite goal of progressives, especially after the Muckrakers had exposed the scandalous tie-in between greedy corporations and Congress. By 1900 the Senate contained so many rich men that it was sometimes referred to as "the Millionaires' Club." Too many of the prosperous-appearing solons, elected as they were by trust-dominated legislatures, heeded the voice of their "masters" rather than that of the voters.

A constitutional amendment to bring about the popular election of Senators had rough sledding in Congress, for the plutocratic members of the Senate were satisfied with existing methods. But a number of states established primary elections in which the voters expressed their preferences for the Senate. The local legislatures, when choosing Senators, found it politically wise to heed the voice of the people. Partly as a result of such pressures, the 17th Amendment to the Constitution, approved in 1913, established the direct election of United States Senators. (See text, Appendix.) But the expected improvement in caliber did not fully materialize.

Woman suffrage, the goal of feminists for many decades, likewise received powerful new support from the progressives early in the 1900's.

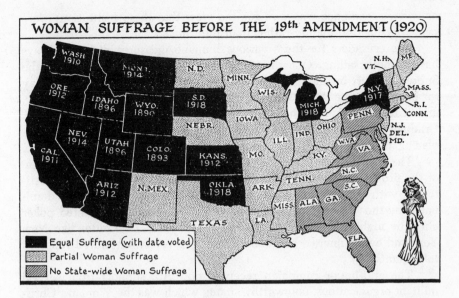

WOMAN SUFFRAGE BEFORE THE 19th AMENDMENT (1920)

Equal Suffrage (with date voted)
Partial Woman Suffrage
No State-wide Woman Suffrage

Reformers believed that the petticoat vote would elevate the political tone, and foes of the saloon felt that they could count on the support of enfranchised females. The "suffragists," crying "Votes for Women" and "Equal Suffrage for Men and Women," protested bitterly against "Taxation without Representation." Many of the states, especially the more liberal ones in the West, gradually extended the vote to women. But by 1910 nationwide female suffrage was still a decade away; and a suffragist could still be sneeringly defined as "One who has ceased to be a lady and has not yet become a gentleman."

Landmarks in Social Progress

The fired-up progressives, working through their state legislatures, tackled head-on a series of social problems. Noteworthy were safety and sanitation codes, which, among other improvements, closed dangerous trades to minors. The enacting of brand-new workingmen's compensation laws, or the bolstering of existing laws, provided the toiler with reasonably adequate protection. Heretofore he had often been forced into costly and futile lawsuits to prove negligence on the part of his employer. In addition, some of the forward-looking states adopted eight-hour laws; and Roosevelt himself inaugurated the eight-hour day on government jobs.

Other social evils clamored for attention. The steaming and unsanitary sweatshops were a public scandal in the urban areas. Some of the states, lashed by public outcries, passed laws regulating the hours of labor by women in such places, as well as the conditions under which they toiled. Prisons and reform schools likewise came under sharp scrutiny, as wider acceptance was won for the view that these institutions were primarily for reformation rather than punishment.

The crusaders for these various humane measures did not always have smooth sailing. One dismaying setback came in 1905, when the Supreme Court invalidated a New York law establishing a ten-hour day for bakers. Yet the Progressive wave finally washed up into the judiciary, and in 1917 the Court upheld a ten-hour Oregon law for factory workers. Gradually the concept of the employer's responsibility to society was replacing the old dog-eat-dog philosophy of unregulated free enterprise.

The shutter-doored corner saloon likewise attracted the ire and fire of the progressives. Alcohol was closely associated with legalized prostitution, with the drunken voter, with crooked city administrations dominated by the "booze" interests, and with the "boss," who counted poker chips by night and miscounted ballots by day. By 1900 cities like New York and San Francisco had one saloon for every two hundred reported inhabitants.

The anti-liquor campaign received powerful support from several militant organizations, noteworthy among which was the Woman's Christian Temperance Union (W.C.T.U.). The saintly Frances E. Willard, one of its founders, would fall on her knees in prayer on saloon floors. She found a vigorous ally in the Anti-Saloon League, which was aggressive, well organized, and well financed. The Prohibition Party, which had put a presidential ticket in the field as early as 1872, was likewise snowballing strength.

Caught up in the prohibition crusade, some states and numerous counties passed "dry" laws, which controlled, restricted, or abolished alcohol. The major cities were generally "wet," for they had a large immigrant vote accustomed in the Old Country to the free flow of wine and beer. When the World War erupted in 1914, nearly one-half of our population lived in "dry" territory, and nearly three-fourths of our total area had outlawed the saloon. (See map on p. 746.) Demon Rum was groggy, and he was to be floored—but not for the ten-count—by the 18th Amendment in 1919.

The Taft-Bryan Presidential Sweepstakes

Roosevelt was still so immensely popular in 1908 that he could easily have won a second presidential nomination, and almost certainly the election. Although at loggerheads with Congress and hated by Big Business, he almost hypnotized the masses. The Benéts have captured his appeal:

> T.R. is spanking a Senator,
> T.R. is chasing a bear,
> T.R. is busting an Awful Trust
> And dragging it from its lair.

They're calling T.R. a lot of things
—The men in the private car—
But the day-coach likes exciting folks
And the day-coach likes T.R.*

Roosevelt did not really want to leave the White House; he had enjoyed a "bully time" in the presidential goldfish bowl. But he felt bound by his impulsive post-election promise after his victory in 1904.

The departing Rough Rider naturally sought a successor who would carry out "my policies"—that is, the forward-looking Roosevelt program. The man of his final choice was his amiable and ample-girthed Secretary of War, William Howard Taft, a moderate progressive. Taft had made an admirable record under T.R. as an administrator in subordinate capacities. As an heir apparent, he had often been called upon by the President to "sit on the lid"—all 350 pounds of him—when Roosevelt was away from Washington.

T.R. ENGINEERS TAFT'S NOMINATION AT CHICAGO
Harding in the Brooklyn *Eagle*, 1904

Big-stick methods were in evidence at the Republican convention of 1908 in Chicago. The Rough Rider, wielding his enormous influence backstage, had lined up enough delegates behind his handwritten platform and hand-picked candidate. He also employed the convention ma-

* Rosemary and Stephen Vincent Benét, *A Book of Americans* (Rinehart and Company, copyright 1933), p. 111. Reprinted by permission.

chinery at Chicago—the "steam roller"—to push Taft's nomination through on the first ballot. The Republican (Roosevelt) platform, pointing with pride in all directions and praising T.R.'s policies, declared against monopoly, and promised both tariff revision and currency reform.

Three weeks later, in July, 1908, the Democrats met at mile-high Denver, in the heart of the silver country. The Bryanites had returned to the driver's seat of the party, and they had no stomach for another drubbing under a stodgy candidate like Judge Parker. Twice-beaten Bryan, the hardy quadrennial, was nominated with high enthusiasm on the first ballot. The platform condemned the flighty personal rule of Roosevelt, as well as the alleged stranglehold of the trusts on American life.

The campaign of 1908 was even duller in some ways than that of 1904, though both the portly Taft and the balding "Boy Orator" took to the stump. Taft, who read cut-and-dried speeches to large crowds, made a strenuous effort to present himself as a progressive in the West and a conservative in the East. Four "P's" helped the Republican ticket: prosperity, Progressivism, prosecution of the trusts, and personalities—Taft and Roosevelt, largely Roosevelt. The progressive Bryan, attempting to capitalize on the Rough Rider's popularity, endorsed many Rooseveltian policies. Alleging that they had been stolen from him, he represented himself as the logical man to carry them out.

A prosperous country was quite content to accept the stable leadership of Taft—the man so emphatically endorsed by Roosevelt, who in a sense was running again. "Shall the people rule?" cried the silver voice of Bryan. They decided to do so with solid Judge Taft, who polled 321 electoral votes to 162 for the "Peerless Leader." The popular count was 7,678,908 to 6,409,104. Bryan garnered fewer votes than in 1896, despite the increase in population, though he fared much better than the colorless Parker. The Socialists amassed a surprising tally of 420,793 for Eugene V. Debs, the "hero" of the Pullman strike of 1894.

Bryan, champion of lost causes, was through as a presidential possibility. Yet a number of the ideas that he sponsored were seized upon and put into operation by the Republicans. He once quipped that he was the only man in America who could rule the nation by losing the Presidency.

The King Is Dead

Roosevelt, ever in the limelight, left early in 1909 for a long-deferred lion hunt in Africa. His numerous enemies clinked glasses to the toast "Health to the Lions." But the savage beasts failed to "do their duty." To an ex-President all the rest of life is an anticlimax, and the tragedy of Roosevelt is that he left his exalted office too young, at the age of fifty, when still bursting with energy. Ex-Presidents are always something of a problem, and here was one who did not take kindly to the role of a private citizen.

In retrospect, the red-blooded Roosevelt was clearly a progressive with the brakes on, and his reputation as a reformer was inflated. "My spear knows no brother!" he cried. But actually he fought many a sham battle. Willing to compromise and settle for half a loaf, he would often fail to drive a reform through to its logical conclusion. The number of laws that he inspired was certainly not in proportion to the amount of noise that he emitted. But in his defense one must note that he was confronted by a conservative, unsympathetic, and often hostile Congress.

What was Roosevelt's great contribution? It was probably not in laws like the Hepburn railway act or in deeds like the digging of the Panama Canal, but in helping to give the people a renewed faith in themselves and their democracy in a troubled time. His enthusiasm and perpetual youthfulness, like an overgrown Boy Scout's, appealed to the young of all ages. As a kind of umpire, he served as a political lightning rod to protect the conservatives against popular indignation. He strenuously sought the middle road between unbridled individualism and paternalistic socialism.

Two other contributions carried over beyond Roosevelt's presidency. First, he helped to direct and make respectable the Progressive movement. His Square Deal, in a sense, was the grandfather of the New Deal later launched by his fifth cousin, Franklin D. Roosevelt. Second, to a greater degree than any of his predecessors, he opened the eyes of the American people to the fact that they lived in the same world with other nations, and that as a great power they had fallen heir to responsibilities from which there was no escape.

SELECT READINGS

Consult lives of Roosevelt by Pringle and Harbaugh, for previous chapter. Incisive introductions are G. E. MOWRY, The Era of Theodore Roosevelt, 1900–1912 (1958) [paperback]; H. U. FAULKNER, The Quest for Social Justice, 1898–1914 (1931); and J. M. BLUM, The Republican Roosevelt (1954) [paperback]. See also H. U. FAULKNER, The Decline of Laissez Faire (1951). On conservation consult S. P. HAYS, Conservation and the Gospel of Efficiency, 1890–1920 (1959) and ELMO RICHARDSON, The Politics of Conservation (1962). Recent lives of Gifford Pinchot are by M. N. MC GEARY (1960) and M. L. FAUSOLD (1961). On pure food and drugs, see O. E. ANDERSON, The Health of a Nation (1958) and J. H. YOUNG, Toadstool Millionaires (1961). For reformism in general consult E. F. GOLDMAN's racy Rendezvous with Destiny (1952) [paperback] and JOHN CHAMBERLAIN's ironical Farewell to Reform (1932) [paperback]. The Progressive movement is treated in G. E. MOWRY, Theodore Roosevelt and the Progressive Movement (1946) [paperback]; R. S. MAXWELL, La Follette and the Rise of the Progressives in Wisconsin (1956); and R. H. WIEBE, Businessmen and Reform (1962). Classic contemporary accounts are J. A. RIIS, The Making of an American (1901); LINCOLN STEFFENS, Autobiography (1931) and his The Shame of the Cities (1904) [paperback]; and La Follette's Autobiography (1913) [paperback]. Also Harvard Guide, Pt. VI.

34

Taft and the Progressive Revolt

The conscience of the people, in a time of grave national problems, has called into being a new party, born of the nation's sense of justice.

PROGRESSIVE PARTY PLATFORM, 1912

A Round Peg in a Square Hole

WILLIAM HOWARD TAFT, who was inaugurated in 1909 during one of the worst sleet storms of the century, inspired widespread confidence. "Everybody loves a fat man," the saying goes; and the jovial Taft, with mirthquakes of laughter bubbling up from his abundant abdomen, was personally popular. He had graduated second in his class at Yale, and had established an admirable reputation as a lawyer and judge, though he was widely regarded as hostile to labor unions. He had been a trusted administrator under Roosevelt—in the Philippines, at home, and in Cuba, where he had served capably as a "trouble shooter." A bit of popular doggerel ran:

> Pattern for all beneath the sun,
> To Taft award the palm and bun!
> They told him what they wanted done—
> He done it.

But "good old Will" suffered from fatal political handicaps. First of all, he followed the noise, bluster, and showmanship of Roosevelt; and any successor was bound to seem a pale anticlimax. Taft could not rush into situations with gnashing teeth; he could not brand men liars, and then dash off to shoot bears. Instead, he played a little golf, at a time when this pastime was a "dude's game," and his bulging figure looked ridiculous in a golfing outfit.

Roosevelt believed in a government by men—at least by one man (T.R.). Taft was an ingrained legalist who believed in a government by laws rather than by men. With his careful legal training, he cringed at the offhand Rooseveltian dictum: "Damn the law!" He searched the statute books to see if he could find any authority for his proposed actions; Roosevelt had scanned them to see if there was anything to stop his actions.

Roosevelt had led the discordant elements of the Republican Party by the sheer force of his personality. Taft, though talented in other ways, had none of the arts of a dashing political leader, and none of Roosevelt's zest for the fray. "Politics make me sick" is the refrain that runs through his private letters. He had permitted himself to be pushed into the presidential prison by his ambitious wife and brothers; his own ambition was for membership on the Supreme Court. Recoiling from the clatter of controversy, he generally adopted an attitude of passivity toward Congress. He was a poor judge of public opinion; and his candor made him a chronic sufferer from the "foot-in-mouth" disease.

Taft was no doubt a mild progressive, but at heart he was more wedded to the status quo than to change. Carried along on the coattails of Roosevelt's vigorous progressivism, he at first seemed to be more progressive than he actually was. The heavy responsibilities of the Presidency further sobered him, so that at times he appeared to be downright reactionary.

Taft's administration at the outset was packed with standpatters, including some who suffered from hardening of the intellectual arteries. The Cabinet—an ultra-conservative body—was dominated by six prosperous lawyers. It unhappily contained no representative of the party's "insurgent" wing, which was on fire for reform of current abuses. The leading Cabinet member was an able corporation lawyer, Secretary of State Philander C. Knox, otherwise known as "Sleepy Phil" because of his weak-kneed prosecution of the trusts as Attorney General under McKinley.

The Payne-Aldrich Betrayal

Agitation for a sharp reduction of the high Dingley Tariff of 1897 had gained momentum during the "reign" of Roosevelt. But the Rough Rider had been much too adroit, despite his apparent rashness, to tackle this dynamite-laden issue. The outcry for reform finally became so overwhelming that the Republican platform of 1908 definitely pledged a tariff revision, without saying whether the revision would be up or down. Taft interpreted this promise to mean a substantial reduction, and forthrightly announced that he would strive toward that goal.

The clamor for tariff revision was but one aspect of the current Progressive crusade. The existing Dingley Act was thought to be contributing to the high cost of living, and to the much-feared expansion of the trusts. Impassioned spokesmen for the agricultural Middle West argued further that tariff walls hampered the importation of cheap manufactured goods, and at the same time hurt the sale of American farm surpluses abroad. But the hidebound Old Guard Republicans, many of them well-fed beneficiaries of protection, were content to let the high Dingley Tariff stand. "Aren't all our fellows happy?" asked one of their leaders, the shrewd, cynical, cigar-chewing Speaker of the House, Joseph G. ("Uncle Joe") Cannon.

But tariff revision could not be sidestepped. The transparently honest Taft, true to his promises, called Congress into special session in March, 1909. The so-called Payne Bill, as approved by the House, provided for modest reductions. But these proved distasteful to the Senate, then dominated by a coterie of Old Guard reactionaries. The group was brilliantly led by multimillionaire Senator Aldrich of Rhode Island, who, though personally charming, was dictatorial. With an arrogant display of power, the senatorial Old Guard engineered 847 changes in the Payne Bill, some 600 of which were revisions upward. As a feeble sop to the public, hides and a few other items, including sea moss and canary-bird seed, were put on the free list. "Mr. Dooley" was prompted to remark that "Practically ivrything nicissry to existence comes in free." Actually, the duties were reduced from 46.5% to 40.8%. (See chart on p. 589.)

When it became evident that the Payne-Aldrich Bill would bring no substantial downward revision, alarm and anger swept through the grain-growing Middle West. The frustrated farmers increased their cries for a high tariff on Western agricultural produce and a lowered one on Eastern manufactured articles. A group of a half-dozen or so Middle Western Senators, led by stumpy and grim-faced "Battling Bob" La Follette of Wisconsin, fought the Payne-Aldrich Bill tooth and nail. Unable to prevent its passage, they at least advertised its fraud to the entire country. But the senatorial insurgents did not emerge empty-handed. They did force into the measure a pioneering 1% tax on corporation profits, and they did give added impetus to the move for adding an income-tax amendment to the federal Constitution.

The Payne-Aldrich hodgepodge put Taft on an awkward spot. It is true that he could point to some slight reductions, and that the bill contained other redeeming features, including provision for a fact-finding Tariff Commission. But the measure seemed like a flagrant betrayal of Taft's promise to reduce the tariff substantially. If he signed the Payne-Aldrich Bill, he would solemnize that betrayal. If he vetoed it, he would disrupt a party that was showing dangerous signs of breaking into insurgent and conservative factions. After much hand wringing, Taft signed.

Taft's subsequent apologies for the new tariff were most ill-advised. He might well have said that while the law was bad, it was the best he could wheedle from Congress. But instead he went out on a speaking tour and vigorously defended the Payne-Aldrich monstrosity. At Winona, Minnesota, he was so far carried away as to insist that the measure was "the best bill that the Republican Party ever passed." In the midst of the

TAFT PLEADS VAINLY FOR A LOWER TARIFF
T.R. glares from the wall, and the Big Stick gathers cobwebs.
Johnson in the Philadelphia *North American*, 1909

resulting uproar, he floundered into hotter water by explaining lamely that he had dictated the speech hurriedly between stations.

Conservation Controversies

Taft was a genuine friend of conservation, and his aid to the cause compares rather favorably with his predecessor's. He set up the Bureau of Mines to conserve mineral resources and to safeguard human resources. He secured authority from Congress to rescue from private exploitation millions of acres of coal lands in Wyoming and Montana—a withdrawal authority that Roosevelt had rather questionably exercised on his own responsibility. Taft also resolutely withdrew water-power sites from private exploitation, in pursuance of legislation passed by Congress in 1910.

Taft's praiseworthy steps toward conservation were largely erased in the public mind by the violent Ballinger-Pinchot quarrel, which erupted in 1909. The storm center was Secretary of the Interior Ballinger, a well-known expert on land law from the state of Washington. Roosevelt, who was prone to be contemptuous of statutes, had achieved much of his success in conservation by stretching existing laws to the limit—and even beyond. Ballinger, a lawyer troubled by legal scruples, reversed this process when he threw open to private development certain water-power sites in Wyoming and Montana that had been arbitrarily withdrawn under Roosevelt. Valuable coal lands in Alaska were likewise made available to giant corporations, also in accordance with the letter of the law.

Ardent Rooseveltian conservationists were scandalized by Ballinger's retreat. The Rough Rider would have burst out, "Damn the law—these natural resources must be preserved for the people!" Spearheading the criticism was a former member of Roosevelt's Tennis Cabinet, Gifford Pinchot, Chief of the Division of Forestry of the Department of Agriculture. In the resulting free-for-all, Taft, who was a stickler for administrative efficiency, felt compelled to uphold Secretary Ballinger and dismiss Pinchot for insubordination. A subsequent Congressional investigation cleared Ballinger, amid angry cries of "whitewash" from the Roosevelt men. A minority report, dictated partly by Republican insurgents, condemned Secretary Ballinger.

The bad taste left by the Ballinger uproar lingered. Taft was much too loyal to desert a subordinate under fire, so he kept the Secretary on for a year and a half after the storm broke. Later research indicates that the berated Ballinger was on sounder legal ground than many contemporaries believed. But at the time Taft appeared to be handing over to marauding interests those natural resources that Roosevelt had so spectacularly rescued. The whole unsavory episode widened the growing rift between the President and the ex-President, the one-time bosom friends.

The Insurgent Uprising

The reformist wing of the Republican Party was now up in arms. It had been aroused particularly by the unpopular Payne-Aldrich Tariff and by White House support for the presumably anti-conservationist Ballinger. Taft was being pushed increasingly into the company of the standpat Old Guard. Its leading mouthpiece in the House of Representatives was the coarse and profane "Uncle Joe" Cannon, who occupied the driver's seat of the well-oiled House machinery. He was becoming insufferably dictatorial, and even denied places on important committees to members who were so bold as to grumble against his practices.

The Republican insurgents in the House, many of them Roosevelt worshipers, were all set to stage a spectacular uprising. Led by George W. Norris of Nebraska, they made the exciting discovery that by joining hands with the Democrats they could outvote the standpat Republicans and curb the rough-tongued Cannon. Accordingly, in March, 1910, they engineered a memorable revolt against "Cannonism." After tense sessions, one of which lasted about thirty hours, they gained the whip hand. Specifically, they took away Cannon's privilege of appointing the all-important Rules Committee, made that body elective by the House, and excluded the Speaker from membership on it. Cannon, who had blocked reform legislation, now lost his arbitrary authority to decide what bills should be presented.

By the spring of 1910 the Grand Old Party was split wide open, owing in part to the clumsiness of Taft. A popular jingle voiced the longing of many Rooseveltians for their hero's return from Africa:

> Teddy, come home and blow your horn,
> The sheep's in the meadow, the cow's in the corn.
> The boy you left to 'tend the sheep
> Is under the haystack fast asleep.

THE COMMON PEOPLE AWAIT TEDDY'S RETURN
Herbert Johnson's Scrapbook

The incomparable "Teddy" returned triumphantly to New York in June, 1910, and shortly thereafter stirred up a tempest. He had already heard enough from talebearers to suspect that Taft was carrying out "my policies" on a stretcher. Unable to keep silent, he took to the stump and at Osawatomie, Kansas, shocked the Old Guard with a flaming speech. The doctrine that he proclaimed—popularly known as "the New Nationalism"—urged the national government to increase its power in order to correct crying social and political abuses. In short, Hamiltonian centralization for social betterment.

Mounting dissension within Republican ranks was further exposed by the Congressional elections in November, 1910. In a victory of land-slide proportions, the Democrats emerged with 228 seats, leaving the once-haughty Republicans with only 161. Symptomatic of the radical trend of the times was the election of a Socialist Representative, Austrian-born Victor L. Berger of Milwaukee (who was finally denied his seat in 1919). The Republicans, by virtue of holdovers, retained the Senate, 51 to 41, but the insurgents in their midst were numerous enough to make that hold precarious.

Taft the Trust Buster

The floundering President had meanwhile been gaining some fame as a smasher of monopoly. The ironical truth is that the colorless Taft caused ninety legal proceedings to be brought against the trusts during his four years, as compared with forty-four for Roosevelt in seven and one-half years. But the statistics are somewhat misleading, for Roosevelt had generated anti-trust momentum, and many of his cases were more important than Taft's.

The most sensational judicial victories of the Taft regime came in 1911, in two cases that had been initiated under Roosevelt. The Supreme Court ordered the dissolution of the mighty Standard Oil Company, which was adjudged a combination in restraint of trade under the Sherman Anti-Trust Act of 1890. At the same time the Court handed down its famous "rule of reason," namely that the government should prosecute only those combinations suspected of an "unreasonable" restraint of trade. Two weeks later, in May, 1911, the Supreme Court no less dramatically ordered the dissolution of the gigantic American Tobacco Company. But in neither case did the militant progressives feel that the breakup was as effective as it ought to be.

The Wall Street "interests" received another rude jolt in 1912–1913. The Pujo Committee, appointed by the now-Democratic House of Representatives, undertook a prolonged probe of the so-called "Money Trust." The investigators found that banking houses dominated by the Morgan and Rockefeller interests held 341 directorships in corporations worth well over twenty-two billion dollars. "The greatest monopoly in this country is the money monopoly," asserted Dr. Woodrow Wilson, a fast-rising political star in New Jersey.

Stillborn Canadian Reciprocity

Bad luck pursued Taft into foreign affairs, especially those involving Canada. For many decades our big but weak northern sister had been seeking a reciprocal tariff arrangement with the United States. Her aim was to lower duties on goods coming from the Yankees, in return for

corresponding concessions by her wealthy neighbor. With uncharacter-
istic zeal, Taft threw himself squarely behind this scheme. Reciprocal
tariff reductions might quiet the critics who were condemning the distasteful Payne-Aldrich Tariff, and perhaps restore some of his lost popularity.

In 1911 a formal agreement was signed with Canada, and the President summoned Congress in special session to approve it. But far from
gaining the hoped-for popularity, he merely stirred up a hornets' nest.
The lumbermen and grain farmers of the Middle West, where the Republican insurgents were entrenched, cried out against the loss of their
tariff protection. They accused Taft of having "sold out" to the trusts.
Many industrialists in truth welcomed free raw materials from Canada,
as well as tariff-free new markets for their finished products. But Taft,
at last aroused to the point of applying whip and spur, drove the trade
agreement through Congress. He left behind a long trail of bruised and
bitter feelings.

The champions of reciprocity in Canada, who at first had hailed the
agreement with delight, now began to cool off. The new Democratic
Speaker of the House, Champ Clark of Missouri, particularly alarmed
the Canadians, for he suggested in a highly publicized speech that reciprocity would be a step toward the inevitable annexation of our thinly
peopled northern neighbor. Taft himself rather clumsily revealed the
imperialistic claws of the measure by remarking that under it Canada
would become a mere economic satellite of the United States.

The suspicious Canadians had no desire to be a backdoor lumber
camp, or, worse yet, to be annexed to their powerful neighbor. Many of
them cried in alarm, "No truck or trade with the Yankees." A heated
special election in Canada, in which the basic issue was the British Union
Jack versus Old Glory, was won by the anti-reciprocity party. The agreement with Washington was thereupon repudiated. The ill-starred Taft,
after all his perspiring exertions, had nothing to show but failure.

The Dollar Becomes a Diplomat

The brand of "Dollar Diplomacy" was stamped, somewhat unfairly,
on the foreign affairs of the Taft administration. The concept was two-
sided: (a) using foreign policy to protect Wall Street dollars invested
abroad, and (b) using Wall Street dollars to uphold foreign policy. The
first aspect was grossly overplayed by Taft's critics; the second aspect
was widely misunderstood.

Taft, though ordinarily lethargic, bestirred himself to use the lever
of American investments to boost American diplomacy. Wall Street
bankers were warmly encouraged by Washington to pump their surplus
dollars into foreign areas of strategic concern to the United States, espe-

cially in the Far East and in the regions that might menace the Panama Canal. Otherwise investors from rival powers, say Germany, might take advantage of financial chaos and secure a lodgment inimical to our interests, both physical and commercial. The bankers would thus strengthen American defenses and foreign policies, while bringing further prosperity to their homeland and to themselves.

The Almighty Dollar thus came to supplant the Big Stick. The peace-loving Taft was not nearly so enthusiastic for military preparedness as his pugnacious predecessor, and did not push battleship construction with Rooseveltian vigor. The navy, unable to keep up with Britain and Germany in their frantic race, dropped from second to third place, just ahead of France.

Manchuria was the object of Taft's most spectacular effort to push the reluctant dollar into the Far Eastern theater. Ambitious little Japan and imperialistic Russia, recent foes, controlled the railroads of China's vital province. Taft saw in this Manchurian railway monopoly a possible strangulation of Chinese economic interests, and a consequent slamming of the Open Door in the faces of American merchants. In 1909 Secretary of State Knox blunderingly proposed that a group of American and foreign bankers buy the Manchurian railroads, and then turn them over to China under a self-liquidating arrangement. Both Japan and Russia, unwilling to be jockeyed out of their dominant position, bluntly rejected Knox's overtures. Again Taft was showered with ridicule by his bitterly partisan critics.

The revolution-cursed Caribbean—now virtually an American lake—continued to be another potentially dangerous trouble spot. Washington therefore urged Wall Street bankers to force dollars into the financial vacuums in Honduras and Haiti so as to keep out foreign funds. Under the Monroe Doctrine we would not permit foreign nations to intervene, and consequently we had some moral obligation to intervene financially to prevent economic and political disorder.

Again necessity was the mother of armed Caribbean intervention. Sporadic disorders in palm-fronded Cuba, Honduras, and Santo Domingo brought American forces in the days of Taft. A revolutionary upheaval in Nicaragua, perilously close to our nearly completed canal, resulted in the landing of 2500 marines in 1912. (See map on p. 698.)

The hapless Taft could point to a few diplomatic triumphs, even though the Big Stick did gather cobwebs. The age-old dispute over the smelly Newfoundland fisheries was finally settled in 1912, when an Anglo-American pact set up a permanent arbitral board. In the previous year an agreement signed by four nations—the United States, Britain, Japan, and Russia—rescued our North Pacific seal herd. These furry creatures had dwindled from about 4,000,000 to 123,600, but within thirty-five years the new multi-power safeguards raised the figure beyond the 3,000,000 mark. (See map on p. 608.)

The Taft-Roosevelt Rupture

The insurgent uprising in Republican ranks had meanwhile been blossoming into a full-fledged revolt. Early in 1911 the National Progressive Republican League was formed, with the fiery, white-maned Senator La Follette of Wisconsin its leading candidate for the Republican presidential nomination. The assumption was that Roosevelt, an anti-third termer, would not permit himself to be "drafted."

But the restless Rough Rider began to change his views about third terms as he saw Taft, hand in glove with the hated Old Guard, discard "my policies." In February, 1912, Roosevelt formally wrote to seven state governors that he was willing to accept the Republican nomination. His

"WHERE WILL HE LAND?"
Steele in the Denver *Post*, February, 1912

reasoning was that the third-term tradition applied to three *consecutive elective* terms. Informally he cried, "My hat is in the ring!" "The fight is on and I am stripped to the buff!"

Roosevelt forthwith seized the banner of Progressive leadership, while La Follette, who had served as a convenient pathbreaker, was protestingly thrust aside. Booted and spurred, the Rough Rider clattered into the presidential primaries then being held in many states. He shouted through half-clenched teeth that the President had fallen under the thumb of the reactionary bosses, and that although Taft meant well, he meant well feebly. The once-genial Taft, now in a fighting mood, retorted by branding the overheated supporters of Roosevelt as "political emotionalists or neurotics."

As the fight thickened, Roosevelt allowed himself to be carried away by his Progressive zeal for increased popular control of government. He strenuously advocated the "recall," or removal, of judges who might be anti-reformist or "interest-controlled." What was more shocking, he came out flatly for the recall of judicial decisions. This scheme, though not as radical as pictured, was a first-class blunder. It alienated many mild progressives who now feared that they had a wild man on their hands.

Yet Roosevelt, on the surface, seemed to be sweeping all before him. Still the popular idol, he carried most of the presidential primaries in the states that held them. He even captured Taft's Ohio. But the portly President, who had the smooth-running party machinery behind him, was successful in lining up delegates from the Solid South—an area where the Republican ticket had not won an electoral vote for decades.

A Taft-Roosevelt explosion was near in June, 1912, when the Republican convention met in Chicago. The Rooseveltites, who were about 100 delegates short of winning the nomination, challenged the right of some 250 Taft delegates to be seated. Most of these contests were arbitrarily settled in favor of Taft, whose supporters held the throttle of the convention steam roller. The Roosevelt adherents, crying "fraud" and "naked theft," finally refused to vote.

Taft triumphed, though ironically he won his renomination by the same dictatorial tactics that Roosevelt had used in his behalf four years earlier. But the Republican platform, bending to the breeze of Progressive doctrine, included declarations in favor of reforming the trusts and the currency. Roosevelt, the good sportsman, proved to be a poor loser. Having tasted for once the bitter cup of defeat, he was in a mood to lead a third-party crusade.

A Princetonian for President

The office-famished Democrats—the "outs" since 1897—were jubilant over the disruptive Republican brawl at Chicago. The party in power, so the adage runs, is seldom defeated; it splits into factions and defeats itself.

If the Democrats were to keep abreast of the times, they would have to come up with an outstanding reformist leader. Fortunately for them, one emerged in the person of Dr. Woodrow Wilson, once a mild conservative but now a militant progressive. Beginning professional life as a brilliant academic lecturer on government, he had risen in 1902 to the presidency of Princeton University, and there he had achieved some sweeping educational reforms. In the interests of promoting higher education, he had also battled to abolish the snobbish eating clubs and fuse their members with the rest of the student body. But here he had suffered defeat at the hands of the wealthy alumni.

Wilson's final struggle at Princeton involved the proposed graduate school. He was eager to build it in the physical center of the university, and thus elevate the intellectual life of the undergraduates. But the no less stubborn Dean West insisted on locating the structure on the outskirts, where the serious graduates would not be debased by undergraduate frivolity. Dean West finally secured a handsome bequest, with authority to build the school where he chose. From then on Princeton was not quite big enough for both the President and the Dean.

By 1910 Wilson had emerged as the potential governor of New Jersey. His name was nationally known, largely because his spirited campaign for educational reform chimed in with current progressive thinking. The Democrats of boss-ridden New Jersey were in need of a respectable candidate for the governorship, and they offered the nomination to Dr. Wilson. They reasoned that if they should have the good luck to win, they could privately lead the bespectacled professor around by his long academic nose, while using him as a show-window "front."

Wilson accepted the New Jersey nomination in 1910, and then put on a tremendous fighting campaign. "God! Look at that man's jaw," exclaimed one observer. In a series of eloquent speeches, Wilson boldly assailed the trusts in a state that was known as "the Mother of Trusts." He passionately advocated political and social reforms that would return the state government to the people, and thus break the iron grip of selfish minorities and "predatory" interests.

The "Schoolmaster in Politics," riding the crest of the progressive wave, was swept into the governorship. Demanding "pitiless publicity" for wrongdoing, he turned against the bewildered bosses and routed them. He then drove through the legislature a sheaf of forward-looking measures—reforms that were tailored to make reactionary New Jersey one of the more liberal states. Filled with righteous indignation, Wilson was at his best. He revealed irresistible reforming zeal, burning eloquence, superb powers of leadership, and a refreshing habit of appealing over the heads of the scheming bosses to the sovereign people. Now a figure of national eminence, Wilson was being widely mentioned for the Presidency.

When the Democrats met at Baltimore in 1912, Wilson enjoyed impressive support, though lacking a majority of the delegates. The front-running contender was the Speaker of the House, Champ Clark of Missouri. An experienced legislator and a popular orator of the old-fashioned school, he had displayed only moderately progressive tendencies. The intellectual level of some of his followers is indicated by their popular song: "They Gotta Quit Kickin' My Dawg Aroun'." Clark polled a majority of the votes on the early ballots, though falling short of the required two-thirds, while Wilson ran a strong second.

Wilson's cause was unexpectedly supported by the old war horse, William J. Bryan. Presumably willing to have lightning strike him a fourth time, he was present as a delegate from Nebraska pledged to vote for Champ Clark. But when the formidable New York delegation, with its Wall Street connections, suddenly turned to Clark, Bryan no less dramatically switched to Wilson. He proclaimed that he could not support a candidate of the moneyed interests. This spectacular shift possibly helped Wilson. But by then Clark had shot his bolt, and the Princetonian received the nomination on the forty-sixth ballot. The Democratic platform pointed up Wilson's liberalism by coming out emphatically for current progressive reforms, including anti-trust legislation, monetary changes, and tariff reduction.

The "Bull Moose" Campaign

The surge of events had meanwhile been pushing Roosevelt to the fore as a candidate for the Presidency on a third-party Progressive Republican ticket. The fighting Rough Rider, angered by his recent rebuff, was eager to lead the charge. A pro-Roosevelt Progressive convention, with about two thousand delegates from forty states, assembled in Chicago during August, 1912. Roosevelt was applauded tumultuously as he cried in a vehement speech, "We stand at Armageddon, and we battle for the Lord!" The hosanna spirit of a revival meeting suffused the convention, while the hoarse delegates sang "Onward, Christian Soldiers" and "Battle Hymn of the Republic." William Allen White, the salty Kansas journalist, later wrote, "Roosevelt bit me and I went mad."

The Progressives entered the campaign with both righteousness and high enthusiasm. Their platform—a "Covenant with the People"—endorsed thoroughgoing reforms and struck at "invisible" government. Roosevelt boasted that he felt "as strong as a bull moose," and hence the bull moose took its place with the donkey and the elephant in the American political zoo. As one poet whimsically put it:

> I want to be a Bull Moose,
> And with the Bull Moose stand
> With antlers on my forehead
> And a Big Stick in my hand.

Roosevelt and Taft were bound to slit each other's political throats; by dividing the Republican vote they guaranteed a Democratic victory. The only question, said one cynic, was which corpse would get the more flowers in the form of ballots. The two antagonists tore into each other as only former friends can. "Death alone can take me out now," cried the once-genial Taft, as he branded Roosevelt a demagogue. Roosevelt, fighting mad, assailed Taft as a "wobbler."

Despite the fur flying from clashing personalities, the basic emphasis was on Progressivism. All three candidates and all three platforms professed to favor reform in some degree; the chief difference was often over degree. Roosevelt's presumed radicalism, notably his advocacy of the recall of judicial decisions, came in for heavy fire; at the other end of the

G.O.P. DIVIDED BY BULL MOOSE EQUALS DEMOCRATIC VICTORY
Puck, 1912

scale, Taft was denounced as a reactionary. Wilson, who campaigned widely and persuasively, was inclined to ignore his two flushed-faced opponents. Cool, collected, and gentlemanly, he expounded to attentive audiences the forward-looking principles of his New Freedom. In his view the New Freedom meant new opportunities, under government regulation, for free enterprise. He especially stressed the need for fostering the spirit of competition by reducing tariffs, and also by curbing the power-hungry trusts—"that invisible empire of special interests."

The campaign of 1912 provided abundant color and drama. Political vocalizers hailed Roosevelt with such songs as "We're Ready for Teddy Again" and "The Moose Is Loose," and sang with soulful dedication:

> We will follow Roosevelt,
> Follow! Follow!
> Anywhere! Everywhere,
> We will follow on.

The Taft adherents denounced Roosevelt's dictatorial ambitions in songs like "Teddy Must Be King," while gleeful Democrats sang "Row, Row, Woodrow" and "Wilson—That's All." The heat of the campaign cooled a bit when, in Milwaukee, Roosevelt was shot in the chest by a fanatic. The Rough Rider ceased active campaigning after delivering, with Bull Moose gameness, his scheduled speech.

A Minority President

Ex-Professor Wilson won handily, with 435 electoral votes and 6,293,454 popular votes. Back in Princeton, Dean West is said to have groaned, "My God, I've made Wilson President of the United States."

"Bull Moose" Roosevelt was the lively corpse that got the more ballot-box flowers. The totals for him stood at 88 electoral votes and

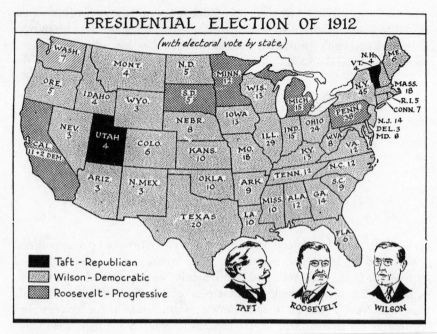

PRESIDENTIAL ELECTION OF 1912
(with electoral vote by state)

Taft - Republican
Wilson - Democratic
Roosevelt - Progressive

TAFT   ROOSEVELT   WILSON

4,119,538 popular votes. Taft carried only two states, Utah and Vermont, with 8 paltry electoral votes, while gleaning 3,484,980 popular votes.

The election figures are fascinating. Wilson, with only 41% of the popular vote, was clearly a minority President, though he had a Democratic majority in Congress. His popular total was actually smaller, despite the increase in population, than Bryan had amassed in any of his three defeats. Taft and Roosevelt together polled over a million and a quarter more votes than the Democrats. Progressivism rather than Wilson was the runaway winner. Though the Democratic total obviously included the votes of many conservatives in the Solid South, still the combined progressive vote for Wilson and Roosevelt clearly exceeded by far the tally of the more conservative Taft. To the progressive strength must be

The Presidential Vote, 1912

Candidate	Party	Electoral Vote	Popular Vote	Approximate Percentage
Woodrow Wilson	Democratic	435	6,293,454	41%
Theodore Roosevelt	Progressive	88	4,119,538	27%
William H. Taft	Republican	8	3,484,980	23%
Eugene V. Debs	Socialist	—	900,672	6%
E. W. Chafin	Prohibition	—	206,275	1%
A. E. Reimer	Socialist-Labor	—	28,750	.2%

added some of the vote of the Socialist candidate, hardy Eugene V. Debs, who rolled up 900,672 votes, or more than twice as many as he had netted four years earlier. Starry-eyed Socialists saw themselves in the White House within eight years.

The Republicans were now free to engage in some sorrowful second-guessing. If they had only united behind the progressive Roosevelt, they might well have won; if they had tried to unite behind the conservative Taft, they probably would have lost. Assuming that defeat was inevitable, they would have been well advised had they kept their ranks intact and looked forward to winning in 1916.

Roosevelt's lone-wolf course was tragic both for himself and for his former Republican associates. Until 1912 he had set great store by party loyalty; now he had brought untold woes upon himself and his party. Perhaps, to rephrase William Allen White, he had bitten himself and gone mad. The Progressive Party, which was primarily a one-man show, had no future because it had elected few candidates to state and local offices. Without patronage plums to hand out to the faithful workers, death by slow starvation was inevitable. Yet the Progressives made a tremendous showing for a hastily organized third party, and helped spur the enactment of many of their pet reforms by the Wilsonian Democrats.

Taft in Retrospect

A tormented Taft left the White House in 1913, smarting from the worst defeat yet suffered by an incumbent President. His personal humiliation, combined with the disruption of his party, caused many critics to regard him as a worse failure than Grant.

This bitter indictment of Taft is grossly unfair. His achievements in conservation and trust busting were substantial, if lacking in fireworks. In addition, the Mann-Elkins Act of 1910 brought the railroads under a tighter governmental rein, and rather belatedly extended the authority of the Interstate Commerce Commission to the telegraph and cable companies.

Gratifying strides toward better government were made under Taft. Civil service reform received a strong boost, particularly as more postmasters were added to the classified service. Congress, for its part, enacted significant reform legislation in 1910 and 1911. The new laws were specifically designed to give publicity to the campaign funds of Congressmen and to set limits to their political expenditures. Finally, a higher degree of administrative efficiency came to Washington in 1913, when Congress separated the Department of Commerce and Labor into two departments.

The West continued to march on. A needed stimulus to its development came when Congress revised the Homestead Act, in 1909 and again in 1912, to square with the realities of farming in arid regions. The

Sunshine State of New Mexico and the Grand Canyon State of Arizona were welcomed in 1912 as the forty-seventh and forty-eighth stars. Taft showed his judicial bent when he held up the admission of Arizona until an offensive provision for the recall of judges was removed from her constitution. Once in the Union, Arizona reinstated this radical provision; and there was nothing that the President or Congress could do about it.

Additional legislative landmarks dotted the Taft years. The Postal Savings Bank Act of 1910, in the teeth of bitter opposition from the bankers, belatedly provided facilities like those found in many European countries. A parcel-post system, similar to foreign models, was likewise approved in 1912, but not until the express companies had fought it hammer and tongs. An impressive total of some 700,000,000 parcels flooded through the post office during 1913, the first year of operation. Finally, the 16th Amendment, making lawful a federal income tax, was formally riveted to the federal Constitution in February, 1913. (See Appendix.)

All these measures add up to a commendable record of cautious progress, even though some of them were routine or were enacted primarily by Democratic votes. Taft, the amiable misfit, was not only unlucky but a victim of his times. Despite his mildly reformist tendencies, progressive sentiment was sweeping so rapidly past his rotund frame that he seemed to be standing still.

Taft's remaining life was fruitful. He taught law for eight pleasant years at Yale University, and in 1921 became Chief Justice of the Supreme Court. This exalted post, which he had long coveted, was one for which he was admirably fitted by training and temperament, and in which he was conspicuously successful. His eight years on the Supreme Bench were among the happiest of his life, just as the four years of his sentence in the Big White Jail had proved to be the most unhappy.

SELECT READINGS

An able introduction is G. E. MOWRY, *The Era of Theodore Roosevelt, 1900–1912* (1958) [paperback]; see also his *Theodore Roosevelt and the Progressive Movement* (1946). Sympathetic biographical coverage is H. F. PRINGLE, *The Life and Times of William Howard Taft* (2 vols., 1939); also C. G. BOWERS, *Beveridge and the Progressive Era* (1932). The rise of Wilson is described in A. S. LINK, *Wilson: The Road to the White House* (1947). A penetrating interpretation is RICHARD HOFSTADTER, *The Age of Reform* (1955) [paperback]; also E. F. GOLDMAN, *Rendezvous with Destiny* (1952) [paperback]. Many titles for the previous chapter are relevant, including those by Faulkner (two), McGeary, Fausold, Chamberlain, Wiebe, Riis, Steffens, and La Follette. Consult also AMOS PINCHOT, *A History of the Progressive Party, 1912–1916* (1958) and RICHARD LOWITT, *George W. Norris* (1963). Also *Harvard Guide*, Pt. VI.

35

Woodrow Wilson and the New Freedom

---

*This is not a day of triumph; it is a day of dedication. Here muster
not the forces of party, but the forces of humanity. . . . I summon
all honest men, all patriotic, all forward-looking men, to my side. God
helping me, I will not fail them, if they will but counsel and sustain me!*

WOODROW WILSON, Inaugural Address, 1913

An Idealist in Politics

(THOMAS) WOODROW WILSON, the second Democratic President since
1861, was a Southerner. Born in Virginia shortly before the Civil War,
and reared in Georgia and the Carolinas, the slender professor-politician
was the first man from one of the seceded Southern states to reach the
White House since Zachary Taylor, sixty-four years earlier.

The impact of Dixieland on young "Tommy" Wilson was profound.
His upbringing in the burned-out South caused him to sympathize with
the gallant attempt of the Confederacy to win its independence in 1861–
1865. His later ideal of self-determination for minority peoples, the world
over, was no doubt partly inspired by these youthful impressions. Wilson
was not only born a Southern Democrat, but he developed into a Democrat steeped in the ultra-liberal Jeffersonian tradition. Like Jefferson, a
fellow Virginian, he had strong faith in the judgment of the masses—if
they were properly informed.

The son of a Presbyterian minister, Wilson was reared in an atmosphere of extreme piety. He believed devoutly in the power of prayer and
in the presence of a personal God. At heart a clergyman, he later used the
presidential pulpit to preach his inspirational political sermons.

Wilson was not only a born reformer but an idealist who could radiate righteous indignation. Moved by a stern sense of duty when he saw
wrongdoing, he would become "angry for the right." As an earnest Christian who habitually read his Bible and prayed in the bosom of his family,
he hated war so intensely that he became at heart a pacifist. Such tendencies were reinforced by his boyhood years in Yankee-gutted Georgia.

687

Wilson was a moving orator who could rise on the wings of spiritual power to soaring eloquence. Yet he was inclined, professor-like, to be more in touch with his subject than with his audience. Skillfully using a persuasive voice, he relied not on arm waving but on sincerity and moral appeal. As a lifelong student of finely chiseled words, he turned out to be a "phraseocrat" who coined many noble epigrams. Someone has remarked that he was born halfway between the Bible and the dictionary, and never got away from either.

A penetrating student of government, Wilson believed that the Chief Executive should play a dynamic role. He was convinced that Congress could not function effectively unless the President, like a kind of prime minister, got out in front and provided leadership. Somewhat paradoxically, this reserved professor of theoretical politics became an astute practical politician. He was often dramatically effective, both as governor and as President, in appealing over the heads of legislative bodies to the sovereign people.

Splendid though Wilson's intellectual equipment was, he suffered from serious defects of personality. Though jovial and witty in private, he was cold and standoffish in public. Incapable of unbending and acting the showman, like Theodore Roosevelt, he lacked the common touch. He loved humanity in the mass rather than the individual in person. His academic background caused him to feel most at home with scholars, although he had to work wry-facedly with politicians. An austere and somewhat arrogant intellectual, he looked down his nose through pince-nez glasses upon lesser minds, including journalists. He was especially intolerant of stupid Senators, whose "bungalow" minds made him "sick."

Wilson's burning idealism—and especially his desire to reform everpresent wickedness—drove him forward faster than lesser spirits were willing to go. When concentrating on one problem, he would neglect others, for he had what he described as "a single-track mind." His sense of moral righteousness was such that he found compromise difficult: black was black, wrong was wrong, and one should never compromise with wrong. His Scotch Presbyterian ancestors had passed on to him an inflexible stubbornness. When convinced that he was right, he would break before he would bend, unlike Theodore Roosevelt. He tended to make personal enemies of his political foemen; and if he was forced to choose between principle and friend, the friend had to go.

The Day of Deserving Democrats

Wilson's inaugural address, delivered before a vast crowd on March 4, 1913, reflected his high idealism and deep moral dedication. It sketched out a program of reform designed to achieve the New Freedom for the average man—freedom from exploitation by Big Business and high finance. Wilson forthwith proceeded to push his proposals with unflagging zeal. No President since Polk the Purposeful had come to the White House with a clearer program or one destined to be more completely achieved.

Wilson's Cabinet inspired no great confidence. It was composed largely of "unknowns," principally because the Democrats had been wandering in the political wilderness for sixteen long years. The sons of the Confederacy had again captured Washington. Five members were Southern-born, including the North Carolina newspaperman-politician Josephus Daniels, who became "managing editor of the Navy." He gained considerable publicity by banning alcoholic beverages from American warships. The handsome, thirty-one-year-old Franklin D. Roosevelt of New York, who had a passion for ships, was made Assistant Secretary of the Navy.

William Jennings Bryan fell heir to the Secretaryship of State—the highest appointive post available. He was totally without experience as a diplomat, as were most of our Secretaries during those years, and he knew little international law. The New York *Sun* thought that he was about as well suited for his exalted position as a "merman to play football." But he was a liberal leader of the strongest element in the Democratic Party. The new President, though distrusting Bryan's intellectual furnishings, simply could not leave him out of the Cabinet. As "Mr. Dooley" said, it would be better for Wilson to have Bryan "in his bosom than on his back."

Bryan proved to be something of a problem child, even though he helped to give a strong liberal tinge to the administration. His reformist zeal even ran to the abolition of spirituous liquors at official functions— "grape juice diplomacy." His activities as a political spoilsman unfortunately hampered Wilson's earnest efforts to promote the merit system. Bryan had incurred many political debts over the years, for millions of Democrats had voted for him in three elections. He now eagerly sought to find gravy jobs for "deserving Democrats"—as he called them. This unhappy phrase rasped "resolute Republicans," who responded with hypocritical jeers.

Yet Bryan turned out to be a more useful Secretary of State than cynics had predicted. Buttonholing his Democratic friends in Congress, he used his immense personal influence to speed on its way Wilson's bulging portfolio of reform legislation. An ardent lover of peace, like Wilson, he bestirred himself energetically to negotiate some thirty conciliation treaties. These pacts bound the signatory nations not to begin hostilities for a year after a dispute broke out, by which time their anger presumably would have evaporated. The so-called "cooling-off" or "wait-a-bit" treaties embodied the ancient axiom, "When angry count fifty, when very angry count a hundred." The pacts might have amounted to more if World War I had not wrapped the world in flames in 1914.

More influential than any regular member of the Cabinet was another Southerner, Colonel (honorary) Edward M. House. This medium-sized, self-effacing Texan, who had helped elect Wilson, was a skilled politician and wirepuller. With a judicious rather than a profound mind, he aspired to no formal office but enjoyed the anonymous thrill that came from being the power behind the throne. For nearly seven years he was Wilson's most intimate adviser—a one-man Kitchen Cabinet.

Tackling the Tariff

Seeking the New Freedoms that would come from freeing the people from monopoly, Wilson promptly girded his loins for an all-out assault on what he called "the triple wall of privilege." He meant, of course, the tariff, the trusts, and the archaic system of banking and currency. The first barrier was the unpopular Payne-Aldrich Tariff, which badly needed overhauling.

Wilson met the tariff issue head-on, early in 1913, with refreshing decisiveness. First he summoned Congress into special session. Then he prepared an eloquent message against special privilege. But he did not send it over to the Capitol to be read by the loud-larynxed clerk, as had been the invariable rule since Jefferson's day in 1801. Instead, he appeared before a joint session of the two houses of Congress and presented

SCHOOLMASTER WILSON LAYS DOWN THE LAW TO CONGRESS
New York *Tribune*, 1913

the appeal himself with characteristic poise and effectiveness. This precedent-shattering episode further underscored Wilson's determination to provide aggressive leadership, and to achieve closer cooperation between the President and Congress. It is curious that Theodore Roosevelt, the precedent smasher, had not revived the personal appearances of George Washington and John Adams. Wilson remarked smilingly as he rode away from Capitol Hill, "I think we put one over on Teddy that time."

The new Underwood Tariff Bill ran the familiar gantlet. Providing for a substantial reduction of existing rates, it passed the House without a serious hitch. But progress was stormy when it reached the Senate, which contained many "tools" of the "special interests." A swarm of lobbyists—"the third house of Congress"—threatened to disembowel the brain child of the House, as they had done on every occasion for twenty years.

The tariff crisis was a challenge to Wilson's powers of leadership. He promptly issued a fighting appeal to the American people, with the objective of building up a backfire against the scheming lobbyists. The masses, he insisted, had no agents in Washington to look after their welfare, but the predatory interests did have. Public opinion, aroused by Wilson's eloquence, forced the lobbyists to run for cover. The Senate finally approved the new tariff bill late in 1913, after six months of windy debate.

Fruits of Freer Trade

The Underwood-Simmons Tariff was not a free-trade measure; nor was it really a low-tariff law. Wilson favored not free trade but freer opportunity. The average annual rates were chopped down from 40.8% to 27%. All told, the law reduced the duties on more than nine hundred items, and enlarged the free list by including such basic products as raw wool and steel rails. Increases were tacked on to more than eighty commodities, principally luxuries, and chiefly for revenue. The Underwood Act, though still definitely protective, achieved the first genuine tariff reduction since the Civil War, and thus honestly redeemed Democratic pledges of revision downward. (See chart on p. 589.)

The Underwood Act was also a landmark in tax legislation. Under authority granted by the 16th Amendment seven months earlier, Congress included a graduated levy, beginning with incomes of $3000 for single persons and $4000 for married couples. A married man earning $5000 would pay about $10. Such painlessly low rates were raised in 1916, owing to the World War emergency, and the next year revenue from the income tax shot ahead of that from the customs duties. The gap since then has been vastly widened.

The Underwood Tariff, though acidly criticized, was a long step toward correcting inequities. It decreased the indirect burden on the poor by lowering the customs duties, and increased the direct burden on the rich by enacting an income tax. The Southern Democrats were delighted to shift a part of the tax load onto the broad backs of their wealthy Yankee brethren, many of whom were Big Business Republicans. Northern capitalists, suspecting that they had now lost the Civil War, complained that they were the victims of class legislation and sectional discrimination.

Experts have long regarded the Underwood Act as one of the best-balanced tariff measures ever to pass Congress. But how well it would have worked in normal times will never be known. The titanic World War erupted in 1914, before the new law had been on the books a year. One unhappy result was a sharp reduction of anticipated customs revenue.

Battling the Bankers

The second bastion of the "triple wall of privilege" was the banking and currency system, now antique and outgrown. The nation's financial structure, still creaking along under the Civil War National Banking Act, revealed glaring defects. The most serious, as laid bare by the Panic of 1907, was the inelasticity of the currency. The amount of money in circulation was heavily concentrated in Wall Street, and could not be speedily expanded in times of financial stress into areas that were badly pinched.

Taft, for his part, had attempted to grapple with the banking problem. In 1908 he appointed the National Monetary Commission, headed by a reactionary banker, Senator Aldrich. After four years of study, it recommended a gigantic central bank, with numerous branches. This institution would in effect be the Third Bank of the United States. The Wall Street financiers would assume the role of long-departed Nicholas Biddle, who in phantom form struck terror into the hearts of the Bryanites. They feared that through such a monster bank the "Money Trust" would concentrate even more power in the hands of a favored few.

The Democrats, with Wilson leading the attack, prepared to battle the bankers. In June, 1913, in a second dramatic appearance before both houses of Congress, the President delivered a stirring plea for genuine banking reform. The legislative machinery then began to grind. Standpat Republicans fought vigorously for a huge private bank of fifteen branches, close to the "Money Trust." But the liberal Democrats, with Bryan bustling behind the scenes, demanded a decentralized bank, in government hands, not in those of private money-changers.

A paralyzing deadlock rapidly developed in Congress. Representative Carter Glass of Virginia, chief sponsor of the administration's banking bill, spoke dejectedly to Wilson of resignation. "Damn it, don't resign, old fellow," rejoined the President in one of his rare outbursts of profanity; "outvote them." The embattled Bryan Democrats finally triumphed over the entrenched bankers, and the epochal Federal Reserve Act was signed late in 1913.

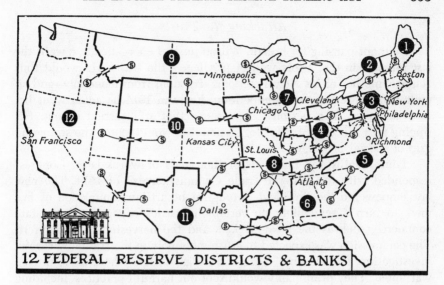

12 FEDERAL RESERVE DISTRICTS & BANKS

The Federal Reserve System, though complex, was efficient. At its head in Washington stood the Federal Reserve Board, appointed by the President. The vesting of such arbitrary power in an inner group alarmed the moneyed men, who naturally distrusted the "politicians." To achieve a compromise between centralization and decentralization, the country was divided into twelve districts, each with a centralized bank owned by the member banks. The result was centralization within decentralization. A network of interconnecting pipe lines radiated out from each of the twelve Federal Reserve reservoirs, and these speeded the flow of currency and credit to the areas in most serious financial distress. Congress thus met the long-felt need for a free-flowing currency.

The Federal Reserve Act also tightened the rein on existing institutions. All National Banks were required to join the new system, and others were at liberty to do so, once they had complied with its regulations. The twelve Federal Reserve Banks, which could be used as depositories for government funds, were actually bankers' banks. They dealt not with private individuals but with banking institutions.

An ingenious arrangement provided for expanding the paper money in time of emergency. The Federal Reserve Board was empowered to issue Federal Reserve currency backed by commercial paper—such as the promissory notes of businessmen—held by the member banks in various localities. The amount of money in circulation could thus be quickly increased to meet the legitimate needs of the business community.

The Federal Reserve Act, which absorbed and ultimately ended the hoary sub-treasury system of Van Buren, was a red-letter achievement. It carried the nation with flying banners through the financial crises of the World War of 1914–1918. The bankers who at first had viewed the Federal Reserve System with alarm were finally won over completely.

Attacking the Trusts

Without pausing for breath, Wilson pushed energetically toward the last rampart in the "triple wall of privilege"—the trusts. He would thus achieve another of his New Freedoms—freedom from monopoly—and simultaneously restore free competition. Early in 1914 he again went before Congress, in a personal appearance that still carried drama. His ringing plea this time was for legislation that would loosen the strangling grip of special privilege.

Nine months and hundreds of thousands of words later, Congress responded with the Federal Trade Commission Act of 1914. The new law empowered the President, through a bipartisan commission of five men, to turn a searchlight on certain industries engaged in interstate commerce, such as the meat packers and the harvester manufacturers. The commission was expected to crush monopoly in the cradle by careful investigation, followed by "cease and desist" orders where these proved warranted. They presumably would root out harmful practices, including price discrimination, unfair competition, false advertising, misbranding, adulteration, and bribery and threats.

Other monopolistic industries, which urgently needed tighter restraints, presented a knottier problem. They had further entrenched themselves through interlocking directorates, which involved the same person serving on different boards of directors. Astute industrialists were now resorting more and more to the device known as holding company,

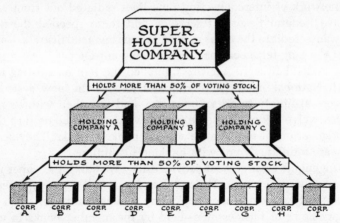

It should be borne in mind that the voting stock of a corporation is often only a fraction of the total stock.

whose chief business was to hold the stocks or securities of other companies and derive income from them. A corporation produced a useful commodity like harvesters; a holding company produced profits.

The Clayton Anti-Trust Act of 1914 attempted to come to grips with some of these evils. It forbade practices that lessened competition, created monopoly, or resulted in objectionable kinds of price discrimination. It also restricted various types of interlocking directorates and holding companies, provided that they involved monopoly. All this sounded impressive on paper, but actually the Clayton Act suffered from loopholes and other weak spots. While a definite improvement on the old Sherman Anti-Trust Act of 1890, it disappointed the more zealous foes of monopoly.

The Clayton Act also conferred certain benefits, long overdue, on organized labor. The outworn Sherman Anti-Trust Act, wishy-washy though it was in restraining trusts, had been unusually effective in crushing labor organizations. The courts had unexpectedly held that monopolistic unions, like monopolistic corporations, fell under the restraints of the Sherman Act. A classic case involved the striking hatters of Danbury, Connecticut. In 1912 they were assessed triple damages in the sum of more than $250,000, which resulted in the attachment of their savings and homes. The new Clayton Act presumably exempted labor and agricultural organizations from anti-trust prosecution, while specifically sanctioning such frowned-upon weapons as strikes and peaceful picketing. The law also prohibited the use of court injunctions in labor disputes, except in cases which could be shown to involve "irreparable injury" to property.

But the gains of labor were somewhat illusory. True, workingmen greeted the new law with enthusiasm, partly because it piously lifted human labor from the category of "a commodity or article of commerce." Samuel Gompers, with unjustified ardor, even hailed the act as the Magna Charta of labor. But conservative courts in later years, invoking restrictive clauses in the law, often clipped the wings of organized labor.

The trust issue, thus tackled by the regulatory Wilsonian legislation, gradually faded from the headlines. Corporations on the whole were inclined to obey the restraining "cease and desist" orders issued by the Federal Trade Commission. The courts, for their part, were disposed to follow the "rule of reason," and punish only those combines guilty of unreasonable restraints on trade. The coming of the Great War with Germany in 1917 caused big industry to seem less wicked. With full-scale production desperately needed, the government was disposed to relax prosecutions and wink at technical violations of the anti-trust laws.

Democratic Doldrums

President Wilson, as he drove an impressive sheaf of bills through Congress, was almost irresistible during his first eighteen months in the White House. For once, the creed of a political party was matched by deed. The "Schoolmaster President" achieved these legislative victories largely by sheer powers of leadership, with a strong assist from the Democratic party machinery and the still-vibrant spirit of progressivism. Displaying an unbending backbone, he held Congress in session for over seventy-two weeks. Critics sneered that Professor Wilson was like the teacher, ruler in hand, who keeps the students after school until they have completed their assignments.

But after the initial brilliant successes the Wilsonian spell began to wear off. Ever the idealist, the Princetonian was eager to spur the country into self-improvement more speedily than it wanted to go.

Economic depression further dampened the reformist mood. During the latter part of 1913 and much of 1914, a business recession laid a blighting hand on American industrial life. The dread specter of unemployment again stalked through the land. "Generals" Coxey and Kelly, with a down-at-the-heels assortment of hoboes and other malcontents, again mobilized "armies" for a descent upon Washington. The high-protection Republicans bitterly blamed the depression on the Underwood Tariff, which was admitting the handiwork of "cheap foreign labor."

The World War, erupting in the summer of 1914, first deepened and then dispelled the depression. The shock resulting from the European blowup, which caused the New York Stock Exchange to close, threatened financial disaster. But gradually orders began to pour in from Europe for American bread and bullets. Business perked up, and before long the nation was basking in the sunlight of unprecedented prosperity.

But before war-boom days fully arrived, the voters had expressed some discontent at the polls. As a result of the mid-term Congressional elections, held in November, 1914, the margin of the Democratic majority in the House was drastically reduced from 147 to 25. But this setback cannot correctly be interpreted as a repudiation of Wilson's record. His election in 1912 had been a triangular, three-party affair. The Congressional canvass of 1914 was the first straight-out two-party contest under Wilson; and as he won a clear majority in the House, the result could be properly hailed as a victory for the Democrats.

Triumphs for the Toilers

The unhappy farmers had been generally neglected by pro-business Republican regimes, and the Democratic Congress had enough momentum left to provide them with some much-needed relief. The Federal Farm Loan Act of 1916 made credit available to farmers at low rates of interest—a reform that had been demanded long before by the Populists. Notable among the several other attempts at rural relief was the Warehouse Act of 1916, which authorized loans on the security of staple crops. This was also a Populistic scheme. Other laws provided for aid in constructing highways and in establishing agricultural extension work in the colleges.

The laboring man, already benefited by the Clayton Act, received additional aid as the wave of progressive reform continued to foam forward. The common sailor, who had been treated with extreme brutality from cat-o'-nine-tail days onward, was now given welcome relief. The La Follette Seaman's Act of 1915, sponsored by "Fighting Bob" La Follette of Wisconsin, required decent wages, treatment, and food. But while helping mariners, the law hurt the merchant marine. The standards were pushed so high that American shipping suffered from a disadvantage in competition with the low-paying tramp steamers of the world.

Other enlightened social reforms were signed by Wilson's busily scratching pen. Notable among them was the Workingmen's Compensation Act of 1916, which granted assistance to federal civil service employees during periods of disability. In the same year Wilson approved an act restricting child labor on products flowing into interstate commerce. But this badly needed safeguard, as well as another child-labor law enacted in 1919, was struck down by the Supreme Court as an invasion of states' rights.

Railroad workers, numbering about 1,700,000, were not overlooked. An imminent strike on the railways threatened a crippling nationwide tie-up in 1916, with a consequent blow at the administration's belated attempts to get a defense program rolling. The organized Railroad Brotherhoods, pinched by the mounting cost of living, refused mediation. Wilson then moved. In another surprise appearance before Congress, he urged sweeping concessions to the workers. The response was the Adamson Act of 1916, which established an eight-hour day for all employees on trains in interstate commerce, with extra pay for overtime. Ex-Professor Wilson, though earning the gratitude of the Brotherhoods, was savagely condemned in business circles for his abject "surrender" to extortionate union officials.

Undoing Dollar Diplomacy

The quiet scholar-President, dedicated as he was to New Freedoms, recoiled from the aggressive foreign policies of his predecessors. As a lover of peace and a hater of imperialism, he was distressed by the Big Stickism of Roosevelt. As an implacable foe of the big-money interests, he detested the so-called Dollar Diplomacy of Taft. He was convinced that little good could come out of Wall Street.

Wilson had been in office only a week when, in sensational fashion, he declared war on Dollar Diplomacy in Latin America. He announced that his administration would not support American bankers and other "interests" in that area, even though some of them had invested funds there as a result of Taft's promptings.

Shifting his attack from Latin America to the Far East, Wilson further shocked the financial world just a week later, in mid-March, 1913. He proclaimed that he would give no special assistance to American bankers who, under the proddings of Taft, had rather reluctantly embarked upon a six-nation loan in China. Wilson believed that this scheme, which was designed to finance a strategic Chinese railroad, encroached objectionably on the sovereignty of China. Worse yet, it might entangle the United States. The bankers, shivering from this Wilsonian bucket of cold water, pulled out of the enterprise the next day. One of the President's capitalistic critics snarled, "Dollar Diplomacy was at least better than none at all."

But Wilson soon found, notably in Nicaragua, that his noble ideals clashed head-on with political realities. An incomplete treaty with this banana republic, negotiated in the days of Taft's Dollar Diplomacy, offered splendid strategic opportunities. The State Department therefore proceeded to complete a more favorable new one in 1916. The pact placed Nicaragua even more securely within the orbit of the United States, for it granted us a perpetual option on a Nicaraguan canal route, together with a ninety-nine-year lease on sites for bases near both ends. The treaty was so sweeping as to make Taft's Dollar Diplomacy, in the words of one critic, look like mere "ten-cent diplomacy."

Anti-Imperialism Becomes Imperialism

Revolution-rent Haiti likewise forced Wilson to eat his anti-imperialistic words. The climax of disorders came in 1914–1915, when an outraged populace literally tore to pieces the brutal Haitian president. In both years Wilson was reluctantly forced to dispatch marines to protect American lives and property. In 1916 Washington concluded a treaty with Haiti

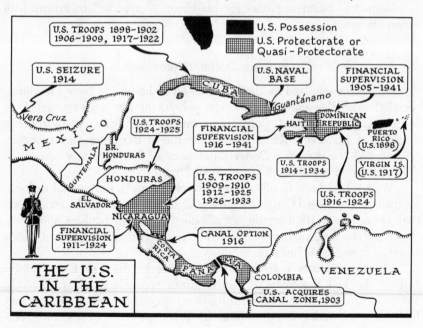

THE U.S. IN THE CARIBBEAN

which provided for United States supervision of finances and the police, and which made the mulatto republic a protectorate of its giant neighbor. Sovereignty-loving Haitians resented the presence of the Yankees; and various uprisings occurred, in which hundreds of the natives were killed by American weapons.

To Wilson's distress, the story of Santo Domingo seemed like a carbon copy of the Haitian intervention. Serious outbursts in the island republic brought the leathernecked marines in 1916, and this debt-cursed land likewise came under the protecting wings of the American eagle. Increasingly the Caribbean Sea, with its vital approaches to the now-completed Panama Canal, was taking on the earmarks of an American preserve.

The purchase of the Danish West Indies (the Virgin Islands), formally concluded in 1917, tightened the grip of the *Yanqui* in these shark-infested waters. We were forced to pay the war-inflated price of $25,-000,000, the highest in American experience. This fancy figure reflected our fear that these palm-shaded isles might be occupied by the Germans for submarine bases, with disastrous results to American shipping. We thus acquired an expensive Caribbean "poorhouse"—three main islands and some fifty islets and protruding rocks, peopled by some 20,000 impoverished Negroes.

An embarrassed Wilson, now a prisoner of circumstances, had meanwhile changed his 1913 views on the six-power loan to China. Impelled by American self-interest and the stern realities of international politics after the outbreak of World War I, he suddenly did an about-face in 1917. The bewildered Wall Street bankers were now strongly encouraged to go back into the dubious enterprise. Thus the idealist-President, instead of reversing Taft's Dollar Diplomacy, succeeded in reversing himself.

In the midst of these flip-flops, Wilson and his Democratic following did succeed in steering their traditional course in regard to the Philippines. Ever since Bryan's heyday, the Democrats had favored cutting loose from this burdensome overseas liability. The Filipinos, who panted for complete freedom, were immensely heartened in 1916, when the Democratic Congress passed the Jones Act. It granted the boon of virtual territorial status, and declared emphatically that the United States was prepared to grant independence as soon as a "stable government" could be established.

Fair Play for Japan and Britain

The menacing clouds of a grave international crisis with Japan had meanwhile appeared in 1913. The legislature of California, seeking to discourage the rapidly multiplying and acquisitive Japanese, was drafting legislation to debar them from owning land in the Golden State. Tokyo, ever sensitive to slights, lodged vigorous protests in Washington, and there was nasty talk of war. At Corregidor, in the Philippines, American gunners were kept on an around-the-clock alert for six weeks.

Wilson was deeply concerned. As a good Christian, he did not believe that the Japanese in California should suffer from discrimination. As a peace lover, he deplored action by one state that might involve all of the other forty-seven in a bloody conflict. Desperately seeking to avert a clash, he dispatched Secretary Bryan to California to plead with the legislature. The law that finally passed softened the slap somewhat by not mentioning the Japanese by name, but it prevented Oriental ownership of land by discriminating against "aliens ineligible to citizenship." Nevertheless Wilson's intercession and Bryan's friendliness helped mollify Tokyo, and the explosive crisis was surmounted.

The Japanese, already imperialistic-minded, took advantage of the European conflagration to present to the Chinese, in 1915, the so-called Twenty-one Demands. These, if accepted, would impinge severely upon the sovereignty of China and slam shut the Open Door. Under vigorous protests from Washington, Tokyo finally toned down some of its more offensive demands.

Nearer home, the disputed Panama Canal Tolls Act of 1912 caused Wilson sleepless nights. This measure, which had passed Congress in the dying months of the Taft regime, specifically exempted American coastwise ships from paying tolls. The Hay-Pauncefote Treaty with Britain in 1901 had granted us a free hand to build and fortify the canal —provided that we would open it to *all* nations on the same tolls-paying terms. We interpreted this pact to mean all *other* nations; the British interpreted it to mean *all* nations, including the United States. Downing Street therefore lodged emphatic protests.

Wilson was thus squeezed between international morality and political expediency. The exemption for American ships was popular, especially among the Irish-Americans, who cheered any twisting of the Lion's tail. But the more Wilson read the treaty, the more convinced he was that we were breaking our promise to Britain, no matter what our government's hairsplitting lawyers argued. As a Southern gentleman, he believed that a nation of honor, like a man of honor, should keep its promise —all the more so if that nation was powerful enough to enforce its own interpretation.

Appearing before Congress in March, 1914, Wilson made a moving plea for a repeal of the exemption. The House and Senate, after a stormy debate, grudgingly granted his request. The grateful British, presumably as a result of a tacit understanding, thereafter gave support to Wilson's faltering Mexican policy. So it was that less than two weeks before the firing of the shot that touched off World War I, the last serious dispute with London was settled. The absence of friction had an important bearing on the pro-British attitude that was prevalent in the United States during the conflict.

Revolution below the Rio Grande

The whine of rifle bullets across our southern border served as a constant reminder that all was not well in Mexico. Under the three-decade dictatorship of Porfirio Díaz—"Díazpotism"—the natural resources of Mexico had been exploited by foreign investors in oil, railroads, and mines. By 1913 American capitalists had optimistically sunk about a billion dollars into this backward yet richly endowed country, and some 50,000 American citizens had taken up residence south of the Rio Grande.

The surface calm of our southern neighbor merely concealed the combustibles of revolution. For if Mexico was rich, the Mexicans were poor. Most of the 15,000,000 inhabitants—predominantly peons—were landless, while a handful of wealthy landowners and foreign capitalists monopolized the wealth. The masses began to agitate irresistibly for reform, under the leadership of men like Francisco Madero, a California-educated visionary.

The blowup began in 1910, and the next year the aging Díaz fled the country to escape revolutionary vengeance. President Madero, his successor, proved utterly incapable of controlling the swirling forces thus unleashed. The revolution took an ugly turn in February, 1913, less than two weeks before Wilson entered the White House, when Madero was murdered by a conscienceless clique. It included General Huerta, a full-blooded Indian, who a few days earlier had made himself ruler.

President Wilson, to whom Taft gladly passed on the Mexican muddle, was at the outset presented with a giant-sized headache. The turmoil in Mexico inevitably led to the destruction of American lives and property there, and to an angry outcry in the United States for armed intervention. Prominent among those beating the tom-toms for war was the influential chain-newspaper publisher, William R. Hearst, whose views presumably were colored by his owning a Mexican ranch larger than all Rhode Island.

But Wilson stood firm against intervention. As a peace lover, he was opposed to violent methods, especially in behalf of the greedy "interests" that he distrusted. He persuasively justified his refusal to intervene in a speech at Mobile, Alabama, in October, 1913, when he declared that it was "perilous" to determine foreign policy "in the terms of material interest." For good measure, he went on to proclaim that the United States would never take "one additional foot of territory by conquest." This reassuring promise was widely heralded as a retreat from the interventionist twist given the Monroe Doctrine by Theodore Roosevelt.

President Huerta, though bloody-handed, brought a semblance of order to Mexico. His government was gradually recognized by a number of foreign powers, especially after he had shown a tolerant attitude toward their investors. Recognition would normally have been granted by the United States also, for our traditional policy had been to recognize firmly entrenched (*de facto*) governments, whether established by bullets or ballots.

But Wilson, who could not bring himself to recognize "government by murder," put idealism above traditionalism. Committed to the New Freedom at home, he would not be a party to crushing freedom abroad. He steadfastly refused to extend the right hand of fellowship to that "desperate brute" Huerta, who seemingly did not have the support of the Mexican masses. "I am going to teach the South American republics to elect good men," the ex-schoolmaster emphatically told a visiting Briton.

UNCLE SAM REFUSES HUERTA'S BLOOD-DRENCHED HAND
New York *Daily Tribune*, 1913

Not content with merely holding the line, Wilson next embarked upon a policy of trying to drive "the unspeakable Huerta" from office. In 1914 he lifted an earlier embargo on arms so that munitions could flow to Huerta's principal rivals, white-bearded Venustiano Carranza and swarthy Francisco Villa. Drawing a sharp distinction between the poor peons and their ruthless rulers, Wilson insisted that he was trying to help the Mexican people shake off their tyrants. Over in Germany, Emperor Wilhelm II sneered, "Morality [is] all right, but what about the dividends?"

Wilson's policy of "watchful waiting," as he called it, was intensely unpopular among Big Business Republicans and other American investors. "Wrathfully waiting," they preferred the brass-knuckled order that would come with a "strong man" like Huerta. Pressure upon Wilson for forcible intervention mounted, especially when dozens of Americans were killed during the current disorders. The President's course was branded as "deadly drifting," and Theodore Roosevelt jeered, "He kissed the blood-stained hand that slapped his face."

Meddling and Muddling in Mexico

The Mexican volcano erupted at the seaport of Tampico, in April, 1914, when a small party was arrested and taken from a United States navy launch plainly displaying the Stars and Stripes. Although the captives were promptly released with expressions of regret, the hotheaded American admiral demanded a formal apology and a salute of twenty-one guns. Huerta defiantly refused to salute the flag of a nation that did not even recognize him as the ruler of Mexico.

Wilson, heavy-hearted but stubbornly determined to eliminate Huerta, went before Congress to ask for authority to use force in Mexico. After two days of heated debate, permission was granted, on April 22, 1914. But one day earlier, Wilson had ordered the American naval units in Mexican waters, seeking to intercept a German merchantman laden with arms for Huerta, to capture the city of Vera Cruz. American marines and sailors gained their objective, which cost the lives of 19 Americans and some 200 Mexicans, to say nothing of the wounded. War hysteria swept the United States, and a full-dress shooting war seemed inevitable.

At this critical juncture Wilson was rescued from a point of no return. The ABC Powers—Argentina, Brazil, and Chile—fearful of another Mexican War, tendered their good offices. Washington promptly and gratefully accepted. The upshot was a meeting at Niagara Falls, in mid-1914, at which the five nations concerned were represented. Although the immediate results were inconclusive, the United States was able to show to the world its determination not to crush Mexico.

Huerta at length broke under the pressures from within and without. Resigning in July, 1914, and fleeing to Spain, he was soon succeeded by his arch rival, strong-willed Carranza. Wilson's "watchful waiting," though bitterly condemned, was successful at least to this extent.

The sinister figure of Francisco Villa had meanwhile stolen the center of the Mexican stage. A bloodthirsty combination of bandit and Robin Hood, he emerged as the chief rival of President Carranza, whom Wilson reluctantly supported with shipments of arms. Villa showed his anger and contempt for the hated American "gringos" in January, 1916, when his followers killed eighteen United States citizens in cold blood at Santa Ysabel, Mexico. The culminating outrage occurred in March, 1916, when Villistas shot up the town of Columbus, New Mexico, leaving behind seventeen dead Americans and many others injured.

General John J. ("Black Jack") Pershing, a grim-faced and ramrod-erect veteran of Philippine campaigns, was ordered to pursue the Mexican marauders. His hastily organized force of several thousand cavalry penetrated deep into Mexico with astonishing speed, and narrowly missed capturing Villa. President Carranza permitted the incursion with reluctance, and only after drawing up a face-saving agreement that would allow Mexico to invade the United States under reversed conditions.

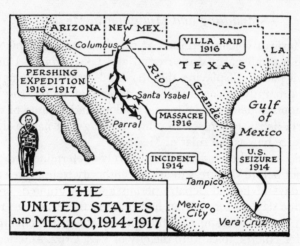

The Pershing expedition—"the perishing expedition," it was dubbed —at length ran into a blind alley. In the face of clashes with the Carranzista forces and imminent war with Germany, the American army was withdrawn early in January, 1917.

But the seemingly fruitless foray into Mexico was not without consequence. The incredibly confused mobilization of American troops, including the National Guard, advertised our military weaknesses and helped spur the preparedness movement. The Germans were not impressed with our armed strength, and the spectacle of the frustrated Pershing expedition was before them when they decided to push us into war with their all-out submarine attacks.

Wilsonian Winnings

Wilson's Mexican policy, despite charges of spinelessness, had much to commend it. Elevating human rights above property rights, in the spirit of the New Freedom, the idealist-moralist in the White House strove to leave the masses of Mexico free to reap the fruits of their own revolution. And this they did in the troubled decades that lay ahead.

In dealing with Mexico, Wilson proved to be a man of vision rather than a visionary. He kept his hands free for more pressing crises elsewhere, especially those involving the German submarines. He avoided the vexations and bloodshed of a full-fledged war—a conflict that would have absorbed vast amounts of blood and money. He resisted the clamor for taking over all Mexico—an operation that would have resembled the Philippine snarl, only many times multiplied.

Wilsonian righteousness, despite serious blunders, emerged triumphant from the Mexican muddle. "We can afford," the President had told Congress in 1913, "to exercise the self-restraint of a really great nation which realizes its own strength and scorns to misuse it." Even though the continuing self-interest of the United States elsewhere required a modified use of Dollar Diplomacy, Wilson still tried to steer his stormy course by the far-off stars of idealism.

SELECT READINGS

Ripe scholarship is compressed into A. S. LINK, *Woodrow Wilson and the Progressive Era, 1910–1917* (1954) [paperback]. A sketchy overview is W. E. LEUCHTENBURG, *The Perils of Prosperity, 1914–1932* (1958) [paperback]. Social and intellectual currents are described in H. F. MAY, *The End of American Innocence: A Study of the First Years of Our Own Time, 1912–1917* (1959) [paperback]. A brief biography of Wilson is J. A. GARRATY, *Woodrow Wilson* (1956); more detailed is ARTHUR WALWORTH's Pulitzer-prize *Woodrow Wilson* (2 vols., 1958). See also J. M. BLUM, *Woodrow Wilson and the Politics of Morality* (1956) [paperback]. The earlier presidential years are examined in depth by A. S. LINK, *Wilson: The New Freedom* (1956). Aspects of Wilson's Mexican policy are interestingly presented in R. E. QUIRK, *An Affair of Honor: Woodrow Wilson and the Occupation of Vera Cruz* (1962) [paperback] and C. C. CLENDENEN, *The United States and Pancho Villa* (1961). Also *Harvard Guide*, Pt. VI.

36

The Road to World War I

*Property can be paid for; the lives of peaceful and inno-
cent people cannot be. The present German submarine
warfare against commerce is a warfare against mankind.*

WOODROW WILSON, War Message, April 2, 1917

Thunder across the Sea

THE long-smoldering European powder magazine blew up in the summer
of 1914, when the flaming pistol of a Serb patriot killed the heir to the
throne of Austria-Hungary. An outraged Vienna government forthwith
presented a stern ultimatum to neighboring Serbia, and war seemed
inevitable. Austria-Hungary hoped to localize the conflict between herself and Serbia, but Germany most ill-advisedly gave her Austro-Hungarian ally a blank-check promise of support.

An explosive chain reaction soon followed. Tiny Serbia, backed by
her powerful Slav neighbor, Russia, refused to bend the knee sufficiently.
The Russian Czar began to mobilize his ponderous war machine, menacing Germany on the east. At the same time his ally, France, was hemming
Germany in on the west. The Germans in alarm suddenly struck at
France through unoffending Belgium; their objective was to knock their
ancient enemy out of the war so that they would have a free hand to
deal with Russia. Great Britain, her coastline jeopardized by the assault
on Belgium, was sucked into the conflagration on the side of France.

Almost overnight most of Europe was involved in a fight to the death.
On one side were arrayed the Central Powers: Germany and Austria-
Hungary—and later Turkey and Bulgaria. On the other side were the
Allied Powers, principally France, Britain, and Russia—and later Italy.
The network of alliances on which the peace of Europe had been pre-
cariously balanced seemed to be pulling the nations into the slippery
abyss, much like falling mountain climbers tied to the same rope.

Americans were stunned and bewildered, though not completely surprised. For something like two decades alarmists had been predicting a
European upheaval, but previous crises had all been surmounted. The

cry of "wolf, wolf" had been raised prematurely so many times that our people could hardly believe that the dread beast was at last on the loose. We instinctively thanked God for our billowing ocean moats, and self-righteously congratulated ourselves on having had ancestors wise enough to emigrate from the hell pits of Europe. We felt strong, smug, secure.

President Wilson promptly issued the routine proclamation of neutrality, and later warned his countrymen to be neutral in both thought and deed. At heart he was pro-Ally, for he was a lifelong admirer of British civilization and a rather frequent summer visitor to the British Isles. But outwardly he kept his sympathies in check, at least during the early stages of the conflict.

The American people, though earnestly desiring to stay out of the blood bath, on the whole sympathized strongly with the Allies. Perhaps half of our people, who now numbered about 100,000,000, traced their lineage back to British or Canadian sources. A hundred different cultural and economic ties bound us to Great Britain, and Anglo-American diplomatic relations had recently risen to a new level of friendliness.

But enthusiasm for the Allies would have been much less warm if bleeding France had not been in their ranks. The hearts of many Americans went out to our traditional friend, and a few enthusiastic volunteers entered her armed services, notably the aviation unit known as the Lafayette Escadrille. France had helped us win our independence, and we felt that we owed her an unrepayable debt. Robert Underwood Johnson prayed:

> Forget us, God, if we forget
> The sacred sword of Lafayette!

The fate of Belgium further deepened pro-Ally sentiment in America. This tiny nation, by an act of unprovoked aggression, had been largely flattened by the German steam roller. The Belgians were facing starvation when boyish-faced Herbert Hoover, a spectacularly successful mining engineer who then happened to be in London, was chosen to form a relief organization. The young master-organizer, then only forty years of age, did a magnificent job of feeding the Belgians. He was aided by generous gifts from fellow Americans, whose hearts naturally went with their donations.

Germanic Miscues

When war flamed across Europe, the German-Americans comprised our largest single foreign-born group. Counting persons with at least one foreign-born parent, transplanted peoples from the Central Powers numbered about 12,000,000. Countless thousands of German-Americans and other pro-German "hyphenated" Americans, many of whom had emigrated only physically, expressed unrestrained sympathy for the Fatherland.

Principal Foreign Elements in the United States
Census of 1910
[TOTAL U. S. POPULATION: 91,972,266]

Country of Origin		Foreign-born	Natives with Two Foreign-born Parents	Natives with One Foreign-born Parent	Total
Central Powers	Germany	2,501,181	3,911,847	1,869,590	8,282,618
	Austria-Hungary	1,670,524	900,129	131,133	2,701,786
Allied Powers	United Kingdom	1,219,968	852,610	1,158,474	3,231,052
	Ireland	1,352,155	2,141,577	1,010,628	4,504,360
	Russia	1,732,421	949,316	70,938	2,752,675
	Italy	1,343,070	695,187	60,103	2,098,360
Total for all foreign countries (including those not listed)		13,345,545	12,916,311	5,981,526	32,243,282

They were enthusiastically abetted by numerous Irish-Americans, who naturally cheered any foe of their ancient enemy, Great Britain.

But the American people as a whole were anti-German at heart even before the World War blazed forth. Germany, as a chip-on-the-shoulder newcomer among the great powers, had discriminated against our allegedly diseased pork, and had collided with our expansionist ambitions in Samoa and at Manila Bay. Elbowing for "a place in the sun," the Germans had joined the imperialistic scramble in China, the East Indies, the Pacific, and Africa. Their low-priced goods, bearing the trademark "Made in Germany," had displaced those of many foreign competitors, including Americans.

The Germans, moreover, seemed born to the sword. They had recently overtaken the United States in the current naval race, and their magnificent army of goose-steppers was reputed to be the most formidable in Europe. In short, the Germans were identified in the American mind with navalism, militarism, and saber-rattling jingoism. And their Emperor, Kaiser Wilhelm II, seemed to Americans the living embodiment of the dangers of German aggression, arrogant autocracy, and decadent monarchism. With villainous upturned mustaches, and a sinister withered arm which suggested degeneracy, he antagonized an America that was traditionally anti-monarchical.

Germany sank even lower in American esteem in 1914, when she seemingly provoked the war with calculated malice. It mattered not that the other major powers, as historians were later to prove, deserved a substantial share of the blame. Germany's guilt seemed beyond dispute when she began the conflict with a brutal assault on "poor little Belgium," whose neutrality she and the other powers had solemnly guaranteed by treaty as far back as 1839. The misdeed took on a more evil aspect when the German Chancellor blunderingly dismissed the neutrality pact as a mere "scrap of paper."

Atrocities always occur in large-scale wars—and on both sides. Most of this conflict was fought on non-German soil, and the inevitable clashes with civilians dyed the German villains a deeper black. Many Americans even came to believe that the green-clad German warriors thundered through Belgium with babies impaled on their bayonets. The Allies, for their part, were careful not to publicize the rapes and other barbarities committed by their own soldiers.

THE KAISER RAVISHES BELGIUM
New York *World*, 1914

The execution of Miss Edith Cavell by the Germans in Belgium was one of the worst blunders of the war. The victim, an English nurse behind German lines, had helped scores of convalescent Allied soldiers to escape so that they might fight another day. Her death before a firing squad was legally defensible, but it was incredibly stupid, for she was a woman and a nurse. The shock to the civilized world was reinforced by such effective propaganda as the American motion picture entitled "Edith Cavell, the Woman the Germans Shot."

Paper Bullets

America was the richest and most powerful of the neutrals. Her open aid, or at least her sympathy, was well worth cultivating.

Allied propagandists, especially the British, enjoyed unusual success in the United States. They were careful to use the tactics of the gentle wooer, partly because they could be sure of a sympathetic hearing. Moreover, most of the stories coming to America were filtered through British cables, and the scissors of the censors sheared away stories harmful to the Allied cause.

Allied agents drenched the United States with tales of German savagery—tales that stressed the inhuman submarine warfare and the abuse of Belgium. Charges of Hunnish barbarity were strengthened by atrocity stories, many of which later proved false. Among these fabrications were a "crucified Canadian," a "corpse factory" where Germans supposedly converted human bodies into soap, Belgian babies with their hands amputated, and Belgian maidens with their breasts slashed off.

German propaganda in America fell on much less fertile ground. A hostile reception was almost certain, owing to the long background of Teutonic friction and blundering. German suitors for America's favor, moreover, were inclined to use the crude embrace of the cave man, without sufficient finesse. And what little they did accomplish was largely undone by the indiscretions and ineptitudes of the militarists in the Fatherland.

A dispute still persists among scholars as to the effectiveness of Allied propaganda. No one can deny that there was a vast amount of it, but no one can measure its effects with precision. Most Americans were undoubtedly pro-Ally from the beginning, and atrocity tales from overseas merely confirmed their existing prejudices. Allied propaganda, though partly fictional, was generally based on undisputed facts, notably the invasion of Belgium, the shooting of Edith Cavell, and the sinking of the *Lusitania*.

Pro-Ally sentiment in America deepened as the anxious neutrality period lengthened. Ardent sympathizers with the Allies declared that only a "moral eunuch" could be neutral in thought, as Wilson had urged. The feeling took root that Britain was "fighting our fight," and that a person was not "100% American" unless he was pro-Ally. But the great majority of our people still fervently hoped that we could stay out of the terrible war.

Blood Money

When the European powder keg exploded in 1914, the United States was still floundering in the business recession of 1913–1914. The British and French hastened to place enormous orders for war materials, and soon American industry pulled itself out of the morass of hard times onto the peak of wartime prosperity.

U. S. Exports to Belligerents, 1914–1916

	1914	1915	1916	Percentage Relation of 1916 Figure to 1914 Figure
Britain	$594,271,863	$911,794,954	$1,526,685,102	257%
France	159,818,924	369,397,170	628,851,988	393%
Italy *	74,235,012	184,819,688	269,246,105	364%
Germany	344,794,276	28,863,354	288,899	0.08%

* Italy joined the Allies in April, 1915.

As the ravenous war machine in Europe chewed up munitions, the Allies began to exhaust their available credits in the United States. If we were not to be plunged back into the dreary days of depression, so the argument ran, American bankers would have to lend huge sums of money to the Allied governments. The Wilson administration at first frowned upon these loans, for they seemed like a flagrant act of unneutrality. But such objections rapidly faded before the prospect of renewed economic distress.

Private enterprise, notably the Wall Street firm of J. P. Morgan and Company, came to the rescue. Largely through bond sales in the United States, American agencies were able to advance to the Allies during our period of neutrality the enormous sum of $2,300,000,000. At the same time, Wall Street lent only $27,000,000 to the Germans, who were regarded as a less desirable risk. Thus the Americans were not only selling munitions to the Allied camp—munitions that were making thousands of German widows and orphans—but were providing the necessary money.

Germany and Austria-Hungary protested bitterly against the huge blood-trade in munitions, for America was fast becoming the chief arsenal of the Allies. But this profitable if disagreeable business was undoubtedly legal. The Germans themselves, as neutrals, had earlier sold military hardware for a profit. The State Department made it clear to Germany and Austria-Hungary that we were showing no favoritism whatever: we would be delighted to make money out of them also, if they would only come and get the munitions. The catch was that the British blockade prevented deliveries.

Embargoes and Briefcases

German-American groups, raising loud but futile protests, demanded that Washington forbid all shipments of arms abroad. Such a stoppage would have been entirely lawful. But by the time Congress came to grips with the explosive issue, the so-called "merchants of death" were reaping lush profits—and the new-found prosperity was too precious to be cast aside.

An American embargo on munitions would have been a heaven-sent boon to the Germans. They had built up their vast war machine with adequate stockpiles of military supplies, knowing well that, in the face of a British blockade, they probably could not import armaments from abroad. The sea-controlling Allies had amassed no such formidable stockpiles, partly because they knew that they could count on supplementary arms from neutrals, including the United States.

A stoppage of American munitions would have been a signal victory for the Germans, a stunning defeat for the Allies. Whether we did something or nothing about halting arms shipments, we would appear to be unneutral. So we followed the profitable path of doing nothing—a course that was all the easier because our hearts were with the Allies. Economically we were thus bound closer and closer to the Allied war chariot by the golden chains of trade.

German and Austrian secret agents, under orders to interrupt the lethal flow of munitions, turned to violent methods. They fomented strikes in the arms factories, and plotted fires, explosions, and other acts of sabotage. Their sinister hand was believed to be seen in the wrecking of the New Jersey Black Tom munitions plant, which blew up in 1916 with a loss of $22,000,000. Two German attachés in Washington, as well as the Austro-Hungarian Ambassador, were implicated in such undercover schemes and were forced to leave the country in 1915.

In the end German plottings backfired badly. In August, 1915, Dr. Albert, a key German agent, absent-mindedly left his briefcase on a New York elevated car. It was promptly picked up by an American Secret Service agent, and some of the documents were published in the newspapers. The American imagination was further filled with images of German spies—men with short-cropped square heads and rolls of fat on the backs of their bull necks. Thus American opinion, already ill-disposed, was further turned against the Kaiser and his Fatherland. The net result was that German propaganda achieved effects the very opposite of those intended.

The Strangulation of Germany

Formal diplomatic relations with Britain, despite America's pro-Ally bias, were not all sweetness and light. The vast global struggle, as during the Napoleonic Wars, involved a contest for sea power. And the United States, as earlier, was the most flourishing neutral carrier. The naval blockade, which was still Britain's most potent offensive weapon, was bound to apply the pincers to American shippers.

Early in the war, the British inaugurated their slow-strangulation blockade of Germany. Among other steps, they proclaimed the North Sea a military zone and proceeded to mine it heavily. Neutral ships approaching the European coast were forced to stop at the neck of the British bottle for inspection and—if approved—for their sailing directions through the deadly mined area. They would not be approved, naturally, if they carried contraband of war. The British, arbitrarily redefining contraband, included foodstuffs and other items not hitherto regarded as directly useful in waging war. American farmers and manufacturers, feeling the pinch, raised loud and long-familiar cries of protest.

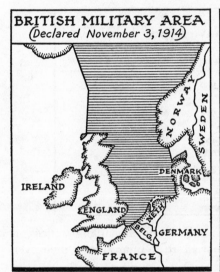

The British likewise redefined blockade. A close-in blockade of the German coasts by warships, in the old-fashioned style, was rendered risky by modern long-range guns and by lurking submarines. Alleging "unusual" or "peculiar" conditions in this conflict, the British would force American ships off the high seas into their ports. There a leisurely search could be undertaken, sometimes with X-ray photographs, to inspect cotton bales and other cargo for concealed contraband. This highly irregular procedure, quite different from the offshore blockade sanctioned by international law, evoked emphatic protests from Washington. But since the British paid for many of the cargoes thus confiscated, the edge was taken off the complaints of our shippers.

The British also arbitrarily expanded the doctrine of continuous voyage, as interpreted by the United States during the Civil War. (See p. 428.) The neutral neighbors of Germany, like Holland and Denmark, suddenly began to purchase from the United States enormous quantities of hitherto little-used goods. The imports of American lard into Denmark during the first few months of the war, for example, rose from zero to 22,000,000 pounds. Obviously, some of these commodities were slipping into Germany through the neutral "conduit pipes." The British therefore

limited such imports to their pre-war proportions, and confiscated or diverted the rest. A loud squawk arose from American merchants, but again
such complaints were partially quieted when London ultimately provided
monetary compensation.

These disagreeable British practices did violence to American traditions, and especially to the precious principle of freedom of the seas.
The United States in 1914–1915 had a powerful navy—the third strongest
in the world. If we had used it to escort our merchant ships, the British

Principal World Navies, July 1, 1914

	Total Tonnage	Number of Battleships
Britain	2,157,850	60
Germany	951,713	33
U. S.	765,133	30
France	688,840	22
Japan	519,640	15

would have been forced to abandon their objectionable practices, at
least against us. They simply could not afford to quarrel with their overseas munitions depot.

Why did the United States fail to take a stronger stand? Our sympathies, including those of the Wilson administration, were with the Allies,
and we did not want to drive our friends into a corner. The American
Ambassador in London, the editor-writer Walter Hines Page, was swept
away by admiration for the British—the one race that had "guts." He
therefore deliberately removed the sting from some of the official protests
that he presented from Washington. In addition, American shippers
could file claims and collect damages later, even though they might not
make as juicy profits as they would have harvested if left alone. Finally, German tactics, especially in using the submarine, were so much
more inhumane than those of the Allies as to eclipse British offenses.

The Periscope Emerges

The Germans did not tamely consent to being starved out by an illegal blockade—or what they regarded as one. Attempting to retaliate
against the British for mining the North Sea, they announced a submarine
war area around the British Isles. The Germans were markedly inferior
to Britain in their surface navy, but they had developed the murderous
new submarine to a high pitch of efficiency. They therefore proclaimed,

in February, 1915, that they would use their cigar-shaped marauders to sink all enemy merchant ships within the proscribed submarine zone.

German U-boat attacks posed a clear threat to the United States. Although the Berlin officials made it clear that they would try not to sink *neutral* shipping, they conceded that mistakes probably would occur. Their aim was partly to frighten away neutral merchant ships, and thus tighten the counter-blockade of Britain. But President Wilson, outraged by the submarine menace, ringingly warned Germany that she would be held to "strict accountability" for any attacks on the American flag.

The submarine, as a commerce destroyer, was a weapon so new that the ancient provisions of international law could not be made to fit it. In the days of the sailing vessel, the rule had been that a warship, upon stopping a merchantman, must first of all send a boarding party to it to ascertain its nationality and the nature of its cargo. If the victim was an enemy vessel—or a neutral vessel carrying contraband of war to the enemy—it might be captured or, if need be, sunk. But destruction could not rightfully take place until the passengers and crew had been put in a position of safety—and this did not mean in small boats hundreds of miles from land.

But the old sailing-ship practices were dangerous in the new machine age. If the fragile submarine emerged to give the customary warning, it might be rammed by the sharp prow of the merchantman or sunk by one well-directed shot from a six-inch gun. After some unhappy experiences of this sort, the Germans became allergic to giving warning. They concluded that if they were going to use their potent new weapon at all, they would have to launch their torpedoes first and write diplomatic notes later. They argued that if the antique rules of international law did not fit their modern weapons, the "unusual" or "peculiar" conditions of the conflict justified changing the rules.

The beleaguered British, who had done some rule changing of their own in regard to blockades, heatedly replied that the rules could not be changed in the middle of the game. They insisted that if the submarine could not be used according to the rules, then the submarine, not the rules, ought to be scrapped. In short, the Germans were being invited to withdraw their terrible new weapon—and to lose the war.

The Lusitania's Last Trip

The German U-boats began their deadly work on schedule. From February to early May, 1915, they sank about ninety ships of various kinds in the war zone. The grisly toll included one British passenger steamer, with the loss of an American life.

Then, on May 7, 1915, stark tragedy struck the England-bound *Lusitania*. This crack passenger liner, a four-funneled British Cunarder, was torpedoed without warning off the coast of Ireland and sank in eighteen minutes. The death roll numbered 1198 persons, 128 of whom were Americans. Many of the victims were women and children.

The salient facts about the *Lusitania* are clear. She was unarmed and unresisting. She was carrying 4200 cases of small-arms ammunition, as well as other munitions of war. Yet the nature of the cargo had no bearing whatever on the rule—long established in international law—that a passenger ship must be warned in advance of sinking.

The German people, quite understandably, rejoiced over the destruction of this death-dealing cargo. One unauthorized German even struck off a fanciful medal showing the *Lusitania* bristling with huge cannon. But the United States, as well as much of the rest of the civilized world, was swept by a wave of shock and anger. This act of "mass murder" was condemned as "piracy," and the New York *Nation* branded the deed as one for which "a Hun would blush, a Turk be ashamed." "Damnable! Damnable! Absolutely hellish!" cried "Billy" Sunday, the acrobatic evangelist. The eastern part of the United States, which was closer to the horrors of war, seethed with talk of fighting. But the rest of the country showed a strong distaste for armed hostilities.

Wilson, the peace lover, set his jaw against leading a disunited nation into war over the *Lusitania*. He well remembered the mistake in 1812 of his fellow Princetonian, James Madison. Instead, by a series of increasingly strong notes, he attempted to bring the German war lords sharply to book.

But the President's hand was weakened by painful signs of disunity. The pacifist Secretary Bryan dramatically resigned rather than sign his name to a protest that might spell shooting, and the Germans were highly pleased with this internal row. Theodore Roosevelt, again athirst for war, assailed the "flubdubs" and "mollycoddles" who recoiled from fighting. He angrily condemned the "weasel words" of that word-lover in the White House, who had sent toothless note "No. 11,765, Series B."

Yet Wilson, sticking to his verbal guns, made diplomatic progress. A new crisis developed in August, 1915, when another British liner, the *Arabic*, was sunk with a loss of two Americans. Berlin, responding to outraged protests from Washington, reluctantly agreed not to sink unarmed and unresisting passenger ships *without warning*. By thus partially muzzling the submarine, Wilson won a gratifying diplomatic victory—at least temporarily.

Pressures for Preparedness

Alert Americans had already recognized the crying need for strengthening the nation's military muscles, for the day might come when we would be pulled into the conflict. The navy was strong, but the army, consisting of about 100,000 regulars, was pathetically weak. It ranked about fifteenth among the armies of the world, in the same bracket with

Persia. In 1915 the Secretary of War reported with alarm that we had only a two-day supply of ammunition for our artillery, much of which was obsolete.

Conspicuous among the champions of rearming were Colonel Theodore Roosevelt and General Leonard Wood, old-time Rough Riders and now apostles of preparedness. They were largely instrumental in establishing, beginning in 1915, a number of summer training camps for officers, notably the one at Plattsburg, New York. Equipment was so short that trainees sometimes drilled with broomsticks in place of rifles. But even these feeble measures were opposed by the pro-German elements, by confirmed isolationists, and by pacifists. A song that caught the current mood was "I Didn't Raise My Boy to Be a Soldier."

President Wilson, still a pacifist at heart, revealed little enthusiasm at the outset for preparedness. His views were generally shared by Secretary Bryan, who proclaimed in 1915 with incredible naïveté that if war should come the President would issue a call and "the sun would go down on a million men in arms." But after repeated sinkings of passenger ships by German U-boats, Wilson gradually turned toward active preparedness. In December, 1915—fifteen long months after war had broken

WILSON PULLS LAGGARD CONGRESS INTO PREPAREDNESS
Kirby in the New York *World*, 1916

out in Europe—he belatedly urged Congress to roll up its sleeves for defense. Public pressures backed him up. Highlighting the popular agitation was a series of monster parades, one of which was led down Pennsylvania Avenue by a flag-holding Wilson.

The culmination of the preparedness campaign was a series of stop-gap measures passed by Congress, notably the National Defense Act of June, 1916. It was designed to beef up the regular army to 175,000 officers and men, and the National Guard to 450,000 officers and men, with provision for an officers' reserve corps. These increases were a promising step forward, but totally inadequate to meet the storm that was gathering.

Naval preparedness fared better, for the fleet had long been regarded as the first line of defense. President Wilson, speaking at St. Louis early in 1916, called for "incomparably the greatest navy in the world." Congress responded, in August, 1916, with a grant of $313,000,000 for new construction—the largest defense appropriation that it had yet passed. The emphasis was mistakenly on big battleships—"white elephants of the sea"—rather than on the smaller anti-submarine craft. The war ended in Europe before a single capital ship was completed.

The Council of National Defense, designed to coordinate industry and defense, was likewise set up. It consisted of six Cabinet officers and seven unpaid civilians, all of whom did yeoman work in helping to unsnarl the tangled skeins of the national economy as war impended.

An expanded merchant marine, which was urgently needed for naval auxiliary purposes, also came in for attention. In September, 1916, Congress created the Shipping Board and appropriated $50,000,000 for the purchase or construction of urgently needed craft. This program likewise proved to be based upon a shocking underestimate of requirements.

Muzzling the Submarine

Anti-travel legislation was meanwhile being vigorously urged, for the only sure way to prevent the killing of Americans on the high seas was to keep them off the submarine-infested waters. Early in 1916 two resolutions came before Congress, each of which was designed to prohibit American citizens from sailing on armed belligerent merchant ships or passenger liners into the danger zones. Both proposals commanded an impressive amount of support in Congress and throughout the country.

But Wilson, ever the stubborn idealist, was alarmed by these proposals to turn tail and run. He argued that if we surrendered our technical rights to sail on belligerent vessels, we would soon be forced to make other concessions. Before long the whole "fine fabric" of international law would break down, as much of it already had. Wilson earnestly believed that to yield our rights, even in the slightest degree, would be dishonorable.

The two "scuttle" resolutions in Congress were themselves scuttled, as an indignant Wilson brandished his presidential club. American citizens continued to sail into the danger zones, where they had a perfect legal right to go. But when killed, they were just as dead as if they had been traveling illegally.

An alarming new crisis developed with Germany in March, 1916, after she had observed the *Arabic* "muzzling" pledge for six months. A French cross-channel passenger steamer, the *Sussex,* was struck by a German torpedo, with some loss of life and serious injuries to several Americans. This attack, at least outwardly, seemed like a deliberate violation of earlier assurances by Berlin.

Outraged by the *Sussex* assault, Wilson went out on a limb. He informed the Germans, in angered phrases, that they must renounce the inhuman practice of sinking merchantmen without warning. Otherwise the United States would have to sever diplomatic relations—an almost certain prelude to war.

Germany grudgingly accepted Wilson's *Sussex* ultimatum, and hence agreed not to sink passenger ships and merchantmen without proper warning. But she attached a long string to her acceptance: we would have to persuade the Allies to respect international law in their blockade. This, obviously, was something that we could not or would not do. Wilson promptly accepted the German pledge, without mentioning the "string." He thus won another temporary but precarious diplomatic victory—precarious because Germany could pull the string whenever she chose to do so, and then we would have no recourse but to sever diplomatic relations.

"He Kept Us Out of War"

As the presidential year 1916 approached, the Bull Moose Progressives of 1912 rallied once again around Roosevelt. Meeting in Chicago in their "swan song" convention, they uproariously renominated the Rough Rider. But Roosevelt, who hated Wilson and all his works, had no stomach for leading another hopeless cause that would again split the Republicans and insure the re-election of the wordy professor. He therefore declined the nomination. In doing so he sounded the death knell of the Progressive Party, amid angry charges by the Bull Moosers that he had betrayed them for his own selfish purposes.

The Republican convention also met in Chicago at the same time, with the followers of the Rough Rider shouting, "Teddy, Teddy, Everybody's for Teddy." But the Old Guard Republicans detested the renegade who had ruptured the party in 1912. Instead, they drafted Charles Evans Hughes, a vigorous, outwardly cold, and highly intellectual justice of the Supreme Court who had been loftily remote from the party split of 1912. His character was unimpeachable; his liberal achievements as governor of New York appealed to the progressives; and his record as a member of the Supreme Court was not unduly offensive to the Old Guard. The Republican platform condemned the Democratic tariff, Democratic assaults on the trusts, and Wilsonian wishy-washiness in dealing with both Mexico and Germany.

Wilson, the dominant Democrat, was nominated by acclamation in St. Louis. The most popular theme of the convention was that he had refused to fight at every provocation. In this wildly cheering assemblage, further inspiration was found for the slogan "He Kept Us Out of War."

The heavily bewhiskered Hughes left the bench for the stump, and there he was not at home. In some speeches he assailed Wilson for not having stood up to the Kaiser more menacingly; in other areas, where the German-American vote was vital, he took a less bellicose line. This fence-straddling operation led to his being called "Charles Evasive Hughes."

Roosevelt, frothing for war, was a dubious asset to the Republicans. In a series of skin-'em-alive speeches against Wilson, he alienated many German-American voters, whom Hughes badly needed for victory. The Rough Rider not only flayed that "damned Presbyterian hypocrite Wilson" but privately sneered at Hughes as a "bearded iceberg" and as a "whiskered Wilson"—the only difference between the two men being "a shave."

The Democratic organizers, concentrating their fire on doubtful districts, played up the pro-Wilson slogan "He Kept Us Out of War." Orators warned the voters that by electing Hughes the nation would be electing a fight—with a certain frustrated Rough Rider leading the charge. A Democratic advertisement appealing to workingmen read:

> You Are Working;
> —*Not Fighting!*
> Alive and Happy;
> —*Not Cannon Fodder!*
> Wilson and Peace with Honor?
> or
> *Hughes with Roosevelt and War?*

The West Turns the Tide for Wilson

On election day Hughes, looking like a sure-fire winner, swept the East. This section contained a heavy concentration of voters who were anti-labor, anti-progressive, and pro-Big-Business. Wilson went to bed that night prepared to accept defeat, and New York newspapers displayed huge portraits of "THE PRESIDENT-ELECT—CHARLES EVANS HUGHES."

But the rest of the country turned the tide. The Middle Westerners and Westerners, attracted by Wilson's progressive reforms and anti-war policies, flocked to the polls for the President. War-boom prosperity also helped his cause. The final result, in doubt for several days, hinged on California, which Wilson carried by 3773 votes out of 999,781 cast. The Golden State was lost to Hughes by the blunders of his managers, notably the snub known as the "forgotten handshake." Though in the same hotel, Hughes had failed to meet California's favorite son, the fiery Progressive, Governor Hiram W. Johnson.

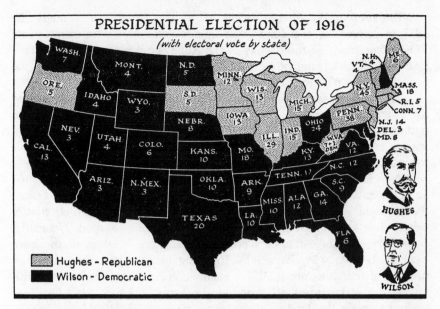

PRESIDENTIAL ELECTION OF 1916
(with electoral vote by state)

Hughes - Republican
Wilson - Democratic

HUGHES

WILSON

Wilson barely squeaked through. The final vote was 277 to 254 in the Electoral College, and 9,129,606 to 8,538,221 in the popular column. The pro-labor Wilson, who had sponsored the eight-hour law for railroad men, apparently polled strong working-class support. His liberal reform program also won the votes of many former Progressives; the defeat of the Republicans flowed largely from their failure to lure enough wayward Bull Moosers back into their camp. Wilson had not specifically promised to keep the country out of war, but probably enough people voted for him on this assumption to insure his victory. The outcome could be written largely in terms of four "P's": peace, prosperity, Progressivism, and pro-laborism.

Germany's U-Boat Challenge

Wilson, desperately seeking peace, now undertook the role of world mediator. He perceived that the surest way to keep America out of the titanic conflict was to bring it to an end before we could become involved. In the hope of securing a negotiated peace, he bluntly called upon the belligerents, in December, 1916, to state their war aims. The Allied response was fuller and franker than that of the Germans, although the Allied leaders were privately annoyed by the efforts of the President to smoke them out. Like the Germans, they cherished secret imperialistic objectives that could not stand the pitiless light of publicity.

Wilsonian mediation was foredoomed to failure. The simple truth is that by this time so much blood and treasure had been squandered that politicians could not face their people without the fruits of victory. Each side hoped for a knockout blow.

Undaunted, Wilson next went before the Senate, on January 22, 1917, to deliver one of his most moving addresses. It was an open appeal to world opinion. To the dismay of the Allies, he declared that a victor's peace would not bring peace. "It must be a peace without victory," he insisted. "Only a peace between equals can last. . . ."

The German war lords answered Wilson with a blow of the mailed fist in his face. Astounding both him and the civilized world, they announced, on January 31, 1917, that they were going to reopen their submarine campaign. This time they would sink *all* merchant ships, including ours, found within the stipulated danger zone.

American dealings with both Britain and Germany were then such as to increase the force of the U-boat bombshell. Ever since the *Sussex* pledge, some six months earlier, relations with Berlin had been outwardly calm, while those with the Allies had been friction-charged. Ironically, both Germany and America were contending for freedom of the seas, each in its own way. Especially irritating to Americans was Britain's practice of searching our mails for enemy correspondence, allegedly with an eye to our trade secrets. London also formally black-listed German-tainted firms in the United States—firms with which His Majesty's subjects were forbidden to trade. Even the pro-Ally Wilson burst out that the "poor boobs" in England "got on his nerves."

The momentous U-boat declaration from Berlin came as no sudden impulse. The war in Europe was stalemated on barbed-wire entanglements and in mud-choked trenches. Delay meant that the noose of the British blockade was drawing tighter around the necks of 65,000,000 Germans. The German naval experts were confident that an all-out submarine campaign would knock Britain out of the war in a few months—as indeed it almost did.

The Berlin officials recognized that the U-boat announcement was a virtual declaration of war. But what of it? The United States boasted a mighty fleet of battleships, yet Britain already dominated the surface of the sea. We had no formidable army, owing in part to Wilson's delay in backing an effective preparedness drive. Even if we had trained a powerful military force, we could not have transported and supplied it with the ships that we had. Seemingly we were already helping the Allies, with shipments of war materials, about all we could. The conflict would presumably be over, with Germany crowned the victor, before America the Unready could throw her full weight into the scales.

The Break with Berlin

Wilson, his high hopes for peace torpedoed by the U-boat announcement, was in the position of a poker player whose bluff has been called. In his *Sussex* ultimatum he had proclaimed in effect that if the German militarists should again open their ruthless submarine warfare, he would have to sever relations. This he reluctantly did on February 3, 1917, when the German Ambassador in Washington was handed his passports. There was no other way out—unless a proud, patriotic, and powerful United States was to be humiliated in the eyes of the world.

Yet Wilson still nursed one flickering hope for peace. Despite evidence to the contrary, he could not bring himself to believe that the Germans would carry out their threat to sink American ships. Determined as he was not to lead his people into war prematurely, he insisted that there would first have to be "overt" acts by German U-boats against American lives and property.

The issue of arming defenseless American merchantmen now forced itself unpleasantly forward. As freighters and liners continued to cling to port, piled-up surpluses clogged the docks and economic paralysis gripped the country. Mobs of irate housewives in New York demonstrated angrily for food. Wilson thereupon asked Congress for authority to arm American merchantmen against possible German assailants. But eleven peace-at-any-price Senators, mostly from the German-populated areas of the Middle West, engineered a crippling filibuster until Congress adjourned, March 3, 1917. Professor Wilson sternly lectured the "little group of willful men" who had rendered this great nation "helpless and contemptible." Then, finding the authority elsewhere in an almost forgotten law, he sent American ships to sea armed with defensive guns.

The Zimmermann note, which meanwhile had blazed across the headlines on March 1, 1917, was hardly less sensational than the U-boat announcement itself. Its author, the German Foreign Secretary, had secretly outlined a course of action pending a shooting war with America. Germany would seek to arrange a German-Mexican alliance, holding out to anti-Yankee Mexico the inducement of recovering Texas, New Mexico, and Arizona. Japan was also to be invited to join in the scheme. Hitherto the anti-Mexican Southwest and the anti-Japanese Pacific Coast had been lukewarm toward war. But this clumsy German note, intercepted by British agents, helped arouse the entire nation for action.

War by Act of Germany

The long-dreaded "overt" acts against our vessels finally came in mid-March, 1917. Three unarmed American merchantmen were sunk on the high seas by German U-boats, with a loss of thirty-six lives. As one Philadelphia newspaper observed, the "difference between war and what we have now is that now we aren't fighting back."

In the same March, 1917, the bitter prospect of war with Germany was sweetened by news from Russia. An epochal upheaval—the first Russian revolution of the era—suddenly overthrew Czarist tyranny and

"I DARE YOU TO COME OUT"
Richards in the Philadelphia *North American*, 1917

established a liberal provisional government. The American people could now look forward to fighting foursquare for democracy on the side of the Allies, without the black sheep of Russian absolutism in the Allied fold.

A reluctant Wilson, unable to escape the logic of "overt" acts, summoned Congress into special session to hear his war message. Pale and erect, he stood before the hushed joint session, on the evening of April 2, 1917, to read an inspired document. In solemn tones he declared that we had no quarrel with the German people, but only with their "military masters." By making war on all mankind they would not permit us to live in peace. Wilson then asked Congress by formal resolution to recognize the state of war "which has thus been *thrust* upon it." "It is a fearful thing," he concluded, to lead the nation into war, but "the right is more precious than peace. . . ."

On Good Friday, April 6, 1917, Congress responded with its fateful war resolution, acknowledging the fact that war had been "thrust" upon us. The debate was brief but heated, with the count 82 to 6 in the Senate, and 373 to 50 in the House. The vote indicated a gratifying degree of unity, especially in the industrial and financial East, which had developed a strong stake in the success of the Allied cause.

Practically all of the dissenters were concentrated in the Middle West—notably in Wisconsin, Illinois, Missouri, and Minnesota—where the German-Americans were numerous and vocal. One of their Senatorial spokesmen, "Fighting Bob" La Follette of Wisconsin, stirred up a storm of protest when he shouted, "I say Germany has been patient with us." Additional members of Congress probably would have voted against war if they had dared defy the whirlwind of popular indignation.

Things Men Fight For

Why were the American people finally dragged into the conflagration, despite their two and one-half years of determination to stay out?

The German U-boat was undoubtedly the precipitant. In a figurative sense, America's war declaration bore the well-known trademark "Made in Germany." Take away the submarine and we probably could have stayed out.

Choosing the right foe was not difficult. British and other Allied restrictions on our commerce were galling but endurable; claims for damages could be collected later. But the Germans resorted to the mass killing of civilians; and there was no adequate monetary recompense for taking life. One Boston newspaper luridly concluded that while the Allies were "a gang of thieves," the Germans were "a gang of murderers." Many Americans were so deeply disturbed by the U-boat, and by its threat to freedom of the seas, that at the outset they proposed to fight a limited-liability war. They would withdraw as soon as the Germans agreed to respect our rights on the high seas.

But in pointing the finger of accusation solely at the blood-spattered submarine, the American people overlooked their own share of responsibility. The fact is that the United States in some degree was to blame for inviting these ruthless reprisals. The Germans found it easier to resort to their last desperate throw of the iron dice because of our seemingly unfriendly policies. We were sending munitions in wholesale quantities to their foes; we were advancing credits for such purchases; and we were acquiescing in the "unusual" British blockade that was slowly starving the Fatherland to death. Bryan charged that the United States, whatever the justification, had failed to hold the scales of neutrality even—assuming that this was possible.

Once the "overt" acts came, the American people accepted the verdict of war with considerable enthusiasm. At heart we were pro-Ally. We were bound closely to the British and French by profitable golden threads, and these were in danger of being cut off by the cruel German tactics. Repelled by German frightfulness, we swallowed Allied propaganda the more avidly. We finally came to believe, as one American newspaper headline put it: "ENGLAND'S DEFEAT OUR DEFEAT."

Fear of the German militaristic and monarchical threat to our democracy was a clincher. Many Americans assumed that if the Kaiser won the war he would dash across the Atlantic, with millions of spike-helmeted soldiers. The Hunnish "slitters of babies' throats" would brush aside the Monroe Doctrine, and then crush precious liberties under a Prussian boot heel. Even if there should be no immediate German assault, the triumph of the Kaiser would badly upset the long-established European balance of power. The United States would then, as many long-headed Americans believed, be placed in ultimate jeopardy.

The dangers of a future attack, either directly or by way of Latin America, appear to have been more grave than those of an immediate invasion. The naval and military difficulties besetting a prompt overseas assault were immense. But countless Americans accepted such an attack as an alarming possibility. They preferred to fight in 1917, when they had European allies afloat, than to wait until they might have to face the wrath of the German militarists alone.

The American people were not duped into war by profit-seeking connivers. They were not dragged in, as was later charged, by the Wall Street bankers, the propagandists, the sloganeers, the weaponeers, the munitioneers. Although loans for the Allies were not inexhaustible, the munitions makers were reaping indecent profits, unhampered by government restrictions and wartime excess-profits taxes. Their unpublished slogan might well have been "Neutrality Forever."

As the crisis developed early in 1917, America's entrance into the war became inevitable. The desperate German militarists, with confidence in their U-boats, had concluded that they had more to gain than to lose by making the United States an open enemy. Certain defeat was too high a price for them to pay for America's continued neutrality.

SELECT READINGS

Refer to the previous chapter for the title by A. S. LINK; for full detail see his *Wilson: The Struggle for Neutrality, 1914–1915* (1960); *Wilson: Confusions and Crises, 1915–1916* (1964); for outlines, his *Wilson the Diplomatist* (1956) [paperback]. A first-rate analysis is E. R. MAY, *The World War and American Isolationism, 1914–1917* (1959). Sympathetic toward the Allies is CHARLES SEYMOUR, *American Diplomacy during the World War* (1934); unsympathetic is C. C. TANSILL, *America Goes to War* (1938). See also D. M. SMITH, *Robert Lansing and American Neutrality* (1958) and his *The Great Departure: The United States and World War I, 1914–1920* (1965) [paperback]. Racy reading is found in H. C. PETERSON, *Propaganda for War* (1939) and BARBARA W. TUCHMAN, *The Zimmermann Telegram* (1958) [paperback]. Also *Harvard Guide*, Pt. VI.

37

The War to End War, 1917–1918

The world must be made safe for democracy.
WOODROW WILSON, War Message, April 2, 1917

Idealism Enthroned

IN WOODROW WILSON, the man and the hour providentially met. The lover of peace, as fate would have it, emerged as a magnificent leader of war. Flourishing the sword of righteousness, he aroused—almost hypnotized—the nation with his inspirational ideals.

What should be the keynote of the great crusade? It is true that the German U-boats had shoved a reluctant America into the abyss. But Wilson could whip up no enthusiasm, especially in the landlocked Middle West, by insisting that we fight to make the world safe against the submarine. He would have to proclaim less localized objectives and more glorified war aims.

Wilson's burning idealism led him instinctively to the right course. Radiating the spiritual fervor of his Presbyterian forebears, he proclaimed the twin goals of "a war to end war" and a crusade "to make the world safe for democracy." He did not believe that we should fight to force our democratic way of life on other peoples. Rather, he sought to create an international atmosphere in which our democracy—any democracy— could flourish without fear of power-crazed autocrats and militarists.

This war, unlike most of its predecessors, was fought with a high degree of unity and enthusiasm. At the outset there existed considerable apathy, confusion, and even downright opposition, especially among the influential German immigrant community in the Middle West. But Wilson, holding aloft the torch of idealism, mobilized public emotion into an almost frenzied outburst. "Force, force to the utmost," he cried, while the country responded less elegantly with "Hang the Kaiser."

Selfishness and partisanship took a back seat. Highly paid business executives volunteered their services in Washington as "dollar-a-year men." Many Republicans in Congress, loyally subordinating party politics, voted for Democratic measures. In fact, at times Republicans supported Wilsonian proposals more wholeheartedly than the Democrats themselves.

The entire nation, catching the spirit of a religious revival, burst into song. It was perhaps America's singingest war. Popular on the serious side were "Keep the Home Fires Burning," "The Long, Long Trail," and above all George M. Cohan's spine-tingling "Over There":

> Over there, over there.
> > Send the word, send the word over there,
> > That the Yanks are coming, the Yanks are coming,
> > > The drums rum-tumming ev'rywhere.*

Fourteen Potent Points

Wilson soon came to be recognized as both the moral leader of the Allied cause and the spokesman for it. His early speeches, though eloquent, were rather vague and overlong. Advisers urged him to boil down his main objectives into inspirational, placard-like paragraphs that would be effective for propaganda purposes. This he did admirably in his Fourteen Points Address, delivered on January 8, 1918, before an enthusiastic Congress. A primary purpose was to keep reeling Russia in the war. The general effect was to inspire the drooping Allies to mightier efforts, while demoralizing the war-weary enemy nations by holding out alluring promises to their dissatisfied minority peoples.

The first five of the Fourteen Points were general in scope. A proposal to abolish secret treaties was pleasing to the liberals of all countries. Freedom of the seas appealed to the Germans, as well as to Americans who distrusted British sea power. The removal of economic barriers among nations was comforting to the Germans, who feared post-war vengeance. Reduction of armament burdens was gratifying to taxpayers everywhere. An adjustment of colonial claims in the interests of both natives and the great powers concerned was reassuring, especially to those people who hated both imperialism and colonialism.

Other points among the Fourteen were no less seductive. They held out the promise of partial or full independence to oppressed minority groups, such as the Poles, millions of whom lay prostrate under the heel of Germany and Austria-Hungary. The capstone point, Number Fourteen, foreshadowed the League of Nations. This hope-fraught international organization was to provide a system of collective security. Wilson earnestly hoped that the new League would effectively guarantee the political independence and territorial integrity of all countries, whether large or small.

In subsequent addresses, hardly less lofty, Wilson clarified and supplemented his original Fourteen Points. The list finally came to number

---

* "Over There" by George M. Cohan; copyright 1917; copyright renewal 1945, Leo Feist, Inc. Used by special permission of copyright proprietor.

about twenty-three. With flaming phrases Wilson declared for a just, permanent, open peace, and stressed the desirability of consulting subject peoples in the forthcoming treaty settlements. This last point—the self-determination "dynamite"—stirred anew many unrealizable hopes.

The so-called Fourteen Points proved to be a mighty engine of propaganda, for they undoubtedly undermined the enemy's "will to victory." In China, a translated volume of Wilson's speeches became a best seller. In lonely huts in the mountains of Italy, candles burned before poster-portraits of the revered American prophet. In Poland, starry-eyed university men would meet on the streets, clasp hands, and utter only one word, "Wilson."

Yet Wilson's appealing points, though raising up messianic hopes the world over, were not everywhere applauded. Certain leaders of the Allied nations, with an eye to territorial booty, were less than enthusiastic. Dyed-in-the-wool Republicans at home grumbled a bit, and some of them openly sneered at the "fourteen commandments" of "God Almighty Wilson."

Factories Go to War

The war began for America with disheartening days. On land the Allies definitely were not winning, and on sea the silent submarines took a frightful toll in April and May of 1917. During the most dismaying weeks, merchant ships were being sunk at the rate of nine a day, and at one time England had grain supplies for only six weeks. The tide was turned only when the British reluctantly adopted the convoy system and the Allies managed to perfect other anti-sub devices.

Victory was no foregone conclusion, and at best would involve a

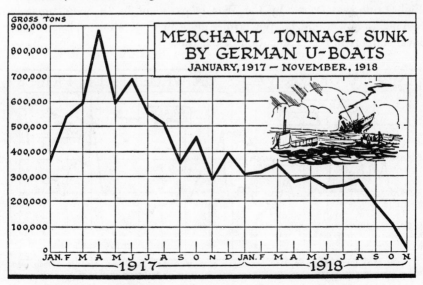

MERCHANT TONNAGE SUNK
BY GERMAN U-BOATS
JANUARY, 1917 — NOVEMBER, 1918

herculean effort. It would be achieved only if the United States could unsnarl its red tape, reorganize its giant industrial plant, and retool itself for fighting—while time still permitted. The struggle was a global conflict, which had to be fought as much with big smokestacks as with big guns. "It is not an army that we must train for war," proclaimed Wilson; "it is a nation."

An alarmed Congress conferred virtually dictatorial powers on President Wilson, much of which he delegated to subordinates. Conspicuous among them were the members of the War Cabinet, which came to consist of the heads of the six key war boards.

A dictatorship over industry was established by the War Industries Board. This powerful agency was finally headed by silver-thatched Bernard M. ("Barney") Baruch, who had shrewdly made his millions in stock-market speculation, and who was to become the famed "park-bench philosopher." The Baruch board fixed prices, established priorities, and reduced waste. It also achieved increased production through standardization. Eight thousand tons of steel were cut each year from women's corsets, and 232 kinds of buggy wheels were reduced to four. Anti-trust legislation was relaxed in the interests of increased output. Women were encouraged to enter industry and also agriculture, where they were called "farmerettes." The old saying took a new twist: "A Woman's Place Is in the War."

Brawny-armed workers were urged to put forth their best efforts, spurred by the slogan "Labor Will Win the War." Tens of thousands of Southern Negroes were drawn to the North by the magnet of war industries—the large-scale beginnings of a movement of immense sociological significance. A New Jersey anti-loafing law required all able-bodied males to be regularly employed in some useful occupation, and a "Work or Fight" rule was issued by the War Department in 1918. Fortunately, Samuel Gompers and his powerful American Federation of Labor gave loyal support to the prosecution of the war.

IMPACT OF U.S. WARS ON WHOLESALE PRICES

Yet labor harbored gnawing grievances. It is true that the wages of 1914 had nearly doubled by 1918, and that many manual laborers could sport gaudy silk shirts. But inflationary prices, spiraled upward by the war, more than kept pace with the wage scale. The pinch of H.C.L.—high cost of living—was felt in every modest American home. Not even the call of patriotism and Wilsonian idealism could stifle all labor disputes; and during the conflict there were some six thousand strikes, most of them happily brief. The National War Labor Board, with ex-President Taft as co-chairman, was finally established as the supreme court for labor disputes. More than one thousand cases came before it.

Some of the most crippling labor sabotage was engineered by the left-wing Industrial Workers of the World (I.W.W.'s), popularly known as the "I Won't Works" or "Wobblies." Advocating "one big industrial union," they chanted:

> The hours are long, the pay is small,
> So take your time and buck them all.

As transient workers in such industries as fruit and lumber, the "Wobblies" stirred up much trouble. Many of them were arrested, beaten up, or run out of town.

Hooverizing on Food and Fuel

The members of the War Trade Board became the leading "economic warriors" of the United States. By issuing the proper licenses to shippers, they controlled both the export and the import of commodities. They also continued the Allied practice of rationing imports to the neutral countries adjacent to Germany, and published a "black list" of enemy-tainted firms in neutral countries with which American citizens were forbidden to trade. Ironically, Washington had vigorously condemned both rationing and black-listing in its protests to London during our years of neutrality. But these devices, though disagreeable, could be employed within the framework of international law.

"Fuel Will Win the War" was another popular slogan. The Fuel Administration was created, headed by Harry A. Garfield, president of Williams College and a son of the murdered President. Spurred by the slogan "Mine More Coal," production was ultimately increased by about two-fifths. Despite these heroic efforts, the chilled public schools of New York had to close during one critical period for lack of coal, and certain factories were temporarily shut down.

Significant economies in fuel were achieved by voluntary self-sacrifice. There were "heatless Mondays" and "lightless nights," the latter produced by turning off electrical displays. Daylight saving time was also introduced to conserve power. Similar efforts were made to economize on petroleum, including the voluntary "gasless Sundays."

Food was an even more pressing problem. As the larder of democracy, we not only had to feed ourselves but produce enough surplus for the needs of our allies. By a happy inspiration, the man chosen to head the Food Administration was the Quaker-humanitarian Herbert C. Hoover, already world-famous for his success in feeding the destitute Belgians. A letter was promptly delivered to him which bore the sole address: "Miracle Man, Washington, D.C."

A superb organizer, Hoover mobilized the American people for less waste and more production. "Food Will Win the War—Don't Waste It" became a favorite slogan, as the Food Administration waged a whirlwind propaganda campaign through posters, billboards, newspapers, pulpits, and movies. Loyal citizens were urged to "use all leftovers," to observe "the gospel of the clean plate," and to practice "the patriotism of the lean garbage can." "Full Garbage Pails," the slogan ran, "Mean Empty Dinner Pails." Even children, when eating apples, were urged to be "patriotic to the core."

An incredible spirit of self-sacrifice aided Hoover's program. So inspiring was the spell of Wilsonian idealism that people voluntarily restricted themselves; no ration cards were issued to consumers, as was done in Europe. "To Hooverize" became a patriotic household synonym

FOOD ADMINISTRATOR HOOVER MOBILIZES HIS ARMY
Darling in the Des Moines *Register*, 1917

for "to economize." In order to save food for export, Hoover proclaimed wheatless Mondays and Wednesdays, meatless Tuesdays, and porkless Thursdays and Saturdays—all on a voluntary basis. Curious and unappetizing substitutes were found in wheatless bread ("Victory bread"), sugarless candy, and vegetarian lamb chops.

Food surpluses were piled up in still other ways. The country soon broke out in a rash of vegetable "Victory gardens," as perspiring patriots hoed their way to victory in back yards or on vacant lots. Congress severely restricted the use of foodstuffs for manufacturing alcoholic beverages, and the war-born spirit of economy and self-denial helped accelerate the wave of prohibition that was sweeping the country. Many leading brewers were German or German-descended, and this circumstance made the drive against alcohol all the more popular.

Hoover's work was sensationally successful. Farm products were increased one-fourth, and food shipments to the hard-pressed Allied countries mounted to three times our pre-war exports.

The Bridge of Boats

The Atlantic Ocean was in some respects Germany's most effective ally. The burning question was: Could we transport enough troops and supplies, in view of scanty shipping and grievous losses to submarines, to turn the tide of battle? "Ships, Ships, and More Ships" was the desperate call of the Allies.

The Shipping Board, farsightedly created in 1916, was supplemented in 1917 by the Emergency Fleet Corporation. These two agencies bestirred themselves mightily to increase available tonnage. Among other steps, enemy merchantmen in our harbors were seized and put into operation, despite efforts by their crews to wreck the machinery. Conspicuous among these vessels was the gigantic German *Vaterland*, which, renamed the *Leviathan*, served as a trans-Atlantic troop carrier. Neutral ships tied up in American harbors were at length requisitioned, with due compensation to the owners. In this haul were eighty-seven Dutch merchantmen.

A gigantic program was begun to construct new tonnage. A few concrete vessels were launched, including one appropriately named *Faith*. A wooden-ship program was undertaken, although birds were still nesting in the trees from which they were to be hammered. Prefabricated steel ships were built for the first time on a large scale, with much of the construction undertaken in shipyards on the Great Lakes, far distant from the sea. The accent was on speed, and the staccato of the riveters ("Rivets Are Bayonets—Drive Them Home") announced that "The Ships Are Coming." One frantically built vessel was launched in twenty-seven days.

Although the huge ships-for-victory program was painfully slow in

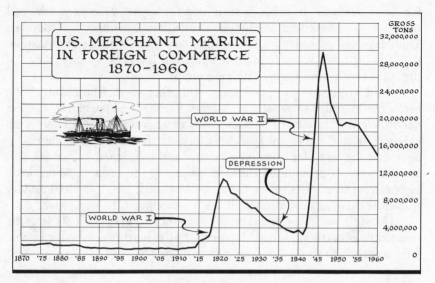

For earlier years see p. 316.

gathering momentum, ship construction finally far outran tonnage destruction by the U-boats. Long before the war ended we were laying down two keels for every one lost. On a glorious July 4, 1918, ninety-five vessels were launched in the various American yards. All told, the Shipping Board built and delivered in 1918 a total of 533 craft, many of which splashed into the water after the Armistice. The largest shipyard, the Hog Island plant near Philadelphia, alone had some eighty miles of railroads. When the war ended there were 350,000 workers in 341 shipyards —a combined establishment that represented two times the shipbuilding capacity of the rest of the world.

The railroads, which fed the trans-Atlantic "bridge of ships," creaked badly. No two lines were organized quite alike, and the thirty-odd systems were soon working at cross-purposes. The snarl became so serious that, in December, 1917, Wilson placed the entire network under government control and operation. The Director General of Railroads was the tall and hawk-nosed Secretary of the Treasury, William G. McAdoo, who had married Wilson's daughter Eleanor in the White House. He was appropriately dubbed "the Crown Prince."

The government ran the railroads at a loss, partly because it kept the rates low and the financial guarantee to the owners high. Economy was no object. Speed and the winning of the war were the major aims, and here McAdoo succeeded, even though he incurred a deficit of $862,-000,000. But the charge that he had "McAdoodled" the railroads was thereafter used as a strong argument against government ownership. The war regime in Washington likewise took over the telephones, the telegraphs, and the cables.

"Over the Top" with Dollars

Tax burdens added to the other unpleasant war burdens. The conflict was fantastically expensive, judged by previous American experience, and in the closing stages cost us $44,000,000 a day. About one-third of this total outlay was handled by a pay-as-you-go policy. Increased taxes brought increased revenue through the income tax, the corporation tax, the excess profits tax, and luxury taxes—the so-called "nuisance taxes" on theater tickets and similar items.

The bulk of the money for financing the conflict was borrowed directly from the citizen in huge bond "drives." The Treasury, in line with its policy of making the war a personal effort, abandoned the Civil War practice of marketing bonds through profit-taking banking houses. The bonds were issued in denominations as low as $50, and Thrift Stamps could be purchased by children for as little as twenty-five cents. The appeal was to both profit and patriotism. The interest rate was attractive, and the bond purchaser could proudly display a button on his lapel to prove that he was neither un-American nor pro-German.

Four great Liberty Loan drives, followed by a Victory Loan drive in 1919, netted the impressive total of $21,448,120,300. About 65,000,000 persons contributed from their savings to make "silver bullets." The drives involved much emotional appeal through monster parades and slogans like "Halt the Hun" and "Remember: It's Cheaper to Win Than to Lose." All five of the huge loans were oversubscribed—"went over the top," in the current trench-warfare phrase. Cities and regions vied with one another in competitive outbursts of patriotism.

Pressures of various kinds, patriotic and otherwise, were used to sell bonds. The unfortunate German-American who could not display a Liberty Bond button might find his house bedaubed with yellow paint. A number of luckless persons, suspected of being pro-Germans, were roughly handled, and there was at least one instance of a man who signed for a bond with a rope around his neck.

The Red Cross and other private agencies of benevolence simultaneously staged smaller drives of their own. Slogans that they used with great effectiveness were "Give Until It Hurts" and "Think What You Can Afford to Give—Then Double It."

Manipulating Minds

Mobilizing the mind for war, both in America and abroad, was an urgent task facing the Washington authorities. For this purpose, the Committee on Public Information was created. It was headed by a youngish journalist, George Creel, who, though outspoken and tactless, was gifted with zeal and imagination. His job was to "sell" America on the war, and the world on Wilsonian war aims.

The Creel organization, employing 150,000 workers at home and overseas, proved that words were weapons. It sent out an army of 75,000 "Four-Minute Men"—often longer-winded than that—who delivered over 7,500,000 speeches containing much "patriotic pep."

Creel's propaganda took varied forms. Posters were splashed on billboards in the "Battle of the Fences," as artists "rallied to the colors." Millions of leaflets and pamphlets, which contained the most pungent Wilsonisms, were showered like confetti upon the world. Special propaganda booklets with red-white-and-blue covers were distributed by the

HANGING THE KAISER—A FAVORITE SPORT

Life, 1918

millions, some of them attempting to prove that Germany had started the war with diabolical intent. Hang-the-Kaiser "movies," with such titles as "The Kaiser the Beast of Berlin" and "To Hell with the Kaiser," revealed the "Hun" in his bloodiest colors. Arm-waving song leaders by the thousands led huge audiences in songs that poured scorn on the enemy and glorified our "boys" in uniform.

Creel was unsurpassed as a mobilizer of emotion. Unlike most propagandists, he had merely to tell the truth about America's tremendous war effort—the truth was incredible enough. But he rather oversold the ideals of Wilson, and led the world to expect too much. When the President proved to be a man and not a god, the resulting disillusionment at home and abroad was disastrous. Paper bullets can be overdone.

America's most noteworthy contribution to the "science" of warfare was in "mobilizing the mind of the world." Regrettably, some of Creel's techniques were later copied by the master propagandists serving Adolf Hitler and other dictators.

Enforced Loyalty

A potential source of internal danger was the formidable group of German-Americans. They numbered over 8,000,000, counting those with at least one parent foreign-born, out of a total population of 100,000,000. Before America entered the war, an official in the German Foreign Office had boasted that there were 500,000 German army reservists in the United States. The American Ambassador proudly replied that there were 500,001 lamp posts on which they could be hanged.

The German-Americans, on the whole, proved to be gratifyingly loyal. Hundreds of thousands of them not only bought Liberty Bonds but fought bravely under the Stars and Stripes. Yet rumormongers were quick to spread tales of spying and sabotage. Even trifling epidemics of diarrhea were blamed on German agents. A few German-Americans were tarred, feathered, and beaten; and in one extreme case a German Socialist in Illinois was lynched by a drunken mob.

As emotion mounted, a frightening wave of hate-hysteria swept the nation against Germans and things Germanic in origin. Orchestras found it unsafe to present German-composed music, like that of Wagner or Beethoven; and the brilliant Austro-Hungarian violinist, Fritz Kreisler, was forbidden to play in New Jersey. The teaching of the German language was stupidly discontinued in many high schools and colleges. Sauerkraut became "Liberty cabbage," Hamburg steak became "Liberty steak," German measles became "Liberty measles," and dachshunds became "Liberty pups."

Both the Espionage Act of 1917 and the Sedition Act of 1918 reflected current fears. These twin measures were inspired partly by hysteria against the Germans, partly by a desire to prevent obstruction of the war effort. Over 1900 prosecutions were undertaken under both laws.

Socialists fell under strong suspicion of pro-Germanism, for a majority of them went on record as opposing our entrance into this "capitalistic war." A minority, stirred by patriotic impulses, thereupon seceded from the party. Eugene V. Debs, kingpin Socialist, continued to speak out violently against American participation. Convicted in 1918 under the Espionage Act, he was sentenced to ten years in a federal penitentiary. After two years, President Harding granted him a Christmas-present pardon.

A number of I.W.W.'s were likewise prosecuted during the war under the Espionage Act. In 1918 William D. ("Big Bill") Haywood and ninety-nine associates were convicted, and Haywood himself was sentenced to twenty years at Leavenworth. In all, there were 1532 arrests under the Sedition Act for disloyal utterances, 65 for threats against Wilson, and 10 for sabotage.

Censorship of a mild sort was occasionally imposed on the press. A Socialist newspaper, *The Masses* (New York), was denied second-class mailing privileges, and at one time an issue of the New York *Nation* was held up.

These prosecutions form an ugly chapter in the history of American liberty. Though doing violence to traditional freedoms, they seemed justified at the time by the grave national emergency. With the dawn of peace, presidential pardons were rather freely granted, and the nation gradually got back on even keel. Yet a few culprits lingered behind bars into the 1930's.

The Navy Brought Them Over

The navy, already cleared for action, got into the war first—though belatedly. Early in May, 1917, an initial flotilla of six destroyers arrived in Ireland for urgently needed anti-submarine operations.

All in all, the American sailors had their hands full. They helped the British battleships hem in the German high-seas fleet. They played a leading role in laying down a 230-mile mine barrage from Scotland to Norway, designed to bottle the deadly U-boats in the North Sea. This gigantic operation, involving 70,000 contact mines, was a pet scheme of young Assistant Secretary of the Navy Franklin D. Roosevelt.

The navy also assisted in tightening the British blockade noose around Germany. We did not violate international law flagrantly, but we did cooperate with the British in enforcing practices against the neutrals to which we had strongly objected while a neutral.

The muscles of the navy, though strong, bulged in the wrong places. The naval preparedness act of 1916 had authorized the building of huge battleships—a type of craft that was almost useless for anti-submarine operations. After America's entry into the conflict the construction of capital ships was halted, and in the first nine months of 1918 no fewer than eighty-three destroyers were launched. The popular cry was "Help Muzzle the Mad Dogs of the Sea." Responding to the call, the navy did yeoman work by destroying German U-boats with depth bombs and other devices.

The most spectacular achievement of the navy was to escort to France scores of troop transports, American and Allied. More than 2,000,-000 soldiers were taken "over there," but only one Europe-bound transport was torpedoed. Six vessels were lost on their way home.

"Yanks" to the Rescue

The army, long regarded as quickly expandable, was more of a problem than the navy. The United States, in every one of its major conflicts, had been confronted with two tasks: first to raise an army, and second to fight the war. This emergency was no exception.

The American people, at the outset, did not dream of sending a mighty force to France. As far as fighting went, we would use our navy to uphold freedom of the seas. We would continue to ship war material to the Allies, and supply them with Treasury loans, which finally totaled nearly ten billion dollars. But in April and May of 1917, our European associates laid their cards on the table. They confessed that they were not only scraping the bottom of their money chest, but, even more ominously, of their manpower barrel. An immense American army would have to be raised, trained, and transported, or the whole front in Western Europe would collapse.

Some kind of token force was necessary at once for European morale. The command of the American Expeditionary Forces (A.E.F.) was entrusted to efficient and stubborn General John J. ("Black Jack") Pershing, who had fruitlessly chased Villa into Mexico. On the Fourth of July, 1917, he led a tiny force of khaki-clad Americans through the streets of Paris, amid frenzied cries of "Vive l'Amérique." One of Pershing's subordinates, touching on the debt-to-France theme, appropriately remarked, "Lafayette, we are here."

The "Yanks" were coming—slowly. Not until October 23, 1917, nearly seven months after Congress had formally declared hostilities, did the first small detachments of American troops see battle action. "We are at war but not in it," ran a current quip.

The bellicose Theodore Roosevelt, still dreaming of Rough Rider days despite his sixty years, was eager to raise a volunteer division and take it to France. Such a unit no doubt would have bolstered Allied morale, but it would also have drawn off the cream of American military leadership. This conflict was a world-girdling struggle, with no place for Rough Rider heroics, and Wilson coldly rebuffed Roosevelt's offer. It was probably the bitterest disappointment of the ex-President's eventful life.

Making Plowboys into Doughboys

Conscription on a nationwide scale was the only answer to the need for raising an immense army with all possible speed. Wilson disliked a draft, as did many other Americans with Civil War memories, for such forcible methods were alien to our basic traditions. What would be gained, many citizens asked, if we militarized ourselves in order to defeat a militaristic Germany? But Wilson finally accepted and eloquently supported conscription as a disagreeable necessity.

The draft bill immediately encountered a barrage of criticism in Congress. Champ Clark of Missouri, deploring compulsion, cried out that there was "precious little difference between a conscript and a convict." Prophets of doom predicted that on draft-registration day the streets would run red with blood. At length Congress—six weeks after its declaration of war—grudgingly got around to passing the conscription bill.

The draft act, as later amended, was a true "selective service" law. It required the registration of all males between the ages of eighteen and forty-five. No "draft dodger" could purchase his exemption or hire a substitute, as in the easygoing days of the Civil War. The "selective" idea was that the government would "select" the draftee for duty in those places where he would be most useful. As a result, there were many exemptions for men in key industries, such as shipbuilding.

A UNIVERSAL DRAFT
Chopin in the San Francisco *Examiner*, 1917

The draft machinery, on the whole, worked effectively. Registration day proved to be a day of patriotic pilgrimages to flag-draped registration centers, and there was no shedding of blood. Despite all precautions, some 160,000 "slackers" escaped the draft dragnet. Notorious among them was Grover Cleveland Bergdoll, a Philadelphian who, after being given a five-year sentence, escaped to Germany.

New wrinkles were added to the old services. Provision was made for training army and navy officers in the colleges, but in general this program creaked badly. For the first time women were admitted to the armed forces: some 11,000 to the navy ("Yeomanettes") and 269 to the marine corps ("Marinettes").

The draft slipped promptly into high gear, as the singing of "Johnny, Get Your Gun" became the inspiration of the hour. Within a few frantic months the army was increased from about 200,000 men to over 4,000,000. The green draftees ("rookies") were herded into hastily built wooden camps, where they were given heavy doses of high-pressure training. As the popular song ran:

> They marched me twenty miles a day to fit me for the war—
> I didn't mind the first nineteen but the last one made me sore.

Yet morale was excellent, thanks largely to playing up the ideals of safeguarding democracy and ending war. The hastily trained men, eager to "lick" the Kaiser, were on fire to get "across the pond." After six months of concentrated effort, the "doughboys" might be shipped overseas, singing "Good-bye Broadway, Hello France." Upon arrival, they were normally given about two additional months of training before seeing front-line action.

Over There

The collapse of Russia underscored the need for haste. The communistic Bolsheviks, having seized power in Moscow, removed Russia from the "capitalistic" war early in 1918. This sudden defection released hundreds of thousands of battle-singed German veterans for the front in France. In the western theater, for the first time in the war, the Germans were developing a dangerous superiority in manpower.

German calculations as to American tardiness were not far from the mark. The High Command in Berlin had counted on knocking Britain out of the war in six months, long before America could get into the struggle. No really effective American fighting force reached France until about a year after we had been plunged into the conflict. Berlin had also reckoned on the inability of the Americans to transport their army, assuming that they were able to raise one. Here again the German predictions were not too far from the mark. Over half of the tonnage for transports was diverted by Britain and her European allies from other pressing tasks, although the United States scraped together about 46% of the needed shipping.

France gradually began to bustle with American "doughboys." The first trainees to reach the front were used as replacements in the Allied armies, and were generally employed in quiet sectors with the British and French. Enormous supply depots, as well as quarters for officers and men, were constructed in France. Here sprawled an amazing 225 miles of American barracks and 127 miles of hospital wards. The "Yanks" soon made friends with the French girls—or tried to—and one of the most sung-about women in history was the fabled "Mademoiselle from Armentières." One of the printable stanzas ran:

> She was true to me, she was true to you,
> She was true to the whole damn army, too.

Much of America's military equipment—in certain categories all of it —was borrowed from the Allies. The list included a large proportion of light artillery, howitzers, tanks, airplanes, and rifles. One basic explanation is that the American war-production program had lagged dangerously in spots. In addition the Allies, with their depleted manpower, preferred to use the available shipping space for troops and provide the equipment themselves.

Haste made waste. The hundreds of millions of dollars spent on American artillery were largely thrown away. The Browning machine gun was an excellent weapon, but it was developed too late in the war to be of significant use. The aircraft program was wastefully ineffective to the point of scandal, although the whole prodigious effort involved little outright graft. Among other bottlenecks, strikes by the I.W.W. interrupted processing of the lightweight spruce wood, although the day was saved by the L.L.L.L. (Loyal Legion of Loggers and Lumbermen). Altogether, the United States produced only 12,000 aircraft, not all of which were combat planes.

American airmen—"Cavaliers of the Clouds"—hung up an enviable record in France. In the end the United States could boast twenty-two "aces," or men who had netted five or more of the enemy craft. The leading air hero was the indestructible Captain Edward V. ("Eddie") Rickenbacker, later prominent in commercial aviation, whose bag was twenty-two airplanes and three balloons.

Hammering the Hun

The long-dreaded German drive on the Western Front exploded in the spring of 1918. Spearheaded by about half a million splendidly trained troops, the enemy war machine rolled forward with terrifying momentum. So dire was the peril that the Allied nations for the first time united under a Supreme Commander, the quiet French Marshal Foch, whose axiom was: "To make war is to attack." Until then the Allies had been fighting imperfectly coordinated actions.

The "Yanks" were finally coming—and not a moment too soon. Late in May, 1918, the forward-rolling Germans, smashing to within forty

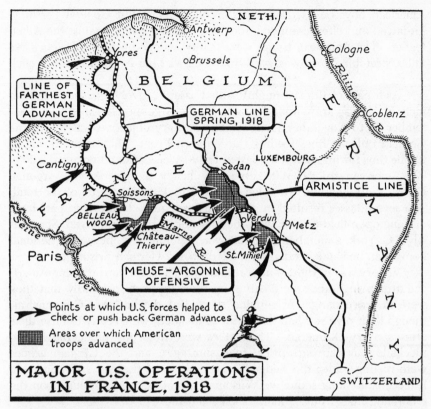

MAJOR U.S. OPERATIONS IN FRANCE, 1918

miles of Paris, threatened to knock France out of the war. Newly arrived American troops, numbering fewer than 30,000, were thrown into the breach at Château-Thierry, where they played a dramatic role in helping to stem the tide. In June the United States marines cleared the Germans from Belleau Wood. The victory was so heroic that appreciative Frenchmen renamed the place "Bois de Marins" (Marine Woods).

American weight in the scales was now being felt. By July, 1918, the tremendous German drive had spent its force, and keyed-up American boys participated in a Foch counter-offensive in the Second Battle of the Marne. This engagement marked the beginning of a German withdrawal movement that was never effectively reversed. As proof of mounting strength, seven American divisions (about 140,000 men) fought in the Second Battle of the Marne, as compared with sixty Allied divisions. In September, 1918, nine American divisions (about 180,000 men) joined with four French divisions to dislodge the Germans from the St. Mihiel sector of France.

The Americans, dissatisfied with merely bolstering the British and French, had meanwhile been demanding a separate army. Pride, patriotism, and morale all required that we have our own command, assigned to a specific fighting front. The French, on the contrary, insisted that the

American boys be used merely as replacements. But General Pershing, jut-jawed and offense-minded, fought a winning battle against the Allied leaders. The American troops were finally assigned a front of eighty-five miles, stretching northwestward from the Swiss border to meet the French lines.

As a part of the last mighty Allied assault, involving several million men, Pershing's army undertook the Meuse-Argonne offensive, from September 26 to November 11, 1918. The military objective was to cut the German railroad lines feeding the Western Front. This battle, the most titanic thus far in our history, lasted forty-seven days and engaged 1,200,-000 American troops. With especially heavy fighting in the Argonne Forest, the killed and wounded mounted to 120,000, or 10% of the total. The severe losses resulted in part from inadequate training, in part from dashing open-field tactics, with the bayonet liberally employed. Sergeant Alvin C. York, a member of an anti-war religious sect, became a national hero when he singlehandedly rounded up 132 German prisoners.

Victory was in sight—and fortunately so. The forward-dashing American armies in France were eating up their supplies so rapidly that they were in grave danger of running short. But the battered Germans, although their own soil had not yet been invaded, were ready to raise their arms and cry "Kamerad." Their allies were deserting them; the British blockade was causing critical food shortages; and the German armies were reeling under the sledge-hammer blows of the Allies. Propaganda leaflets, containing seductive Wilsonian promises, were raining upon the crumbling lines from balloons, shells, and rockets.

The Fourteen Points Disarm Germany

The Berlin government was now ready to hoist the white flag. Warned of imminent defeat by the generals, it turned to the presumably softhearted Wilson in October, 1918, seeking a peace based on the Fourteen Points. The President, in stern responses, made it clear that the Kaiser and his warlords would have to be thrown overboard before an armistice could be negotiated. The war-weary German people, whom Wilson had been trying to turn against their "military masters," took the hint. The Kaiser was forced to flee to Holland, where he lived out his remaining twenty-three years, "unwept, unhonored, and unhung."

The Fourteen Points, as it developed, proved better for propaganda purposes than for peacemaking. The Allied leaders, whose territorial ambitions were embodied in secret treaties, feared that Wilson's finespun ideals would tie their hands. But they urgently needed the support of rich Uncle Sam for post-war reconstruction. Mystery-man Colonel House, speaking for Wilson, hinted at a separate German-American treaty if the Allies were not reasonable. They finally agreed, with feet-dragging reluctance, to negotiate a peace based on the Fourteen Points. But they insisted on two reservations: one on freedom of the seas that would safe-guard British naval power, and one on reparations that would assure France of collecting compensation for damage wrought by the Kaiser's invading armies.

The exhausted Germans were through. They laid down their arms after the Allies had solemnly assured them that the peace treaty would be based on the Fourteen Points—with the two exceptions noted. The Armistice was formally signed at eleven o'clock on the eleventh day of the eleventh month of 1918, and an eerie, numbing silence fell over the Western Front. War-taut Americans burst into a delirium of around-the-clock rejoicing, as streets were jammed with laughing, whooping, milling masses. The war to end war had ended.

Vindication through Victory

The war effort of the aroused Western giant had been prodigious. We got into the fray, belatedly and awkwardly but full of dash and en-thusiasm, just in time to turn the tide to victory. More than 4,000,000 citizen-soldiers were put into uniform. The total casualties were 333,734, of which 130,274 represented deaths. Yet these gory losses were minor when bracketed with those suffered by Britain, France, and Russia. As compared with other American wars, death from disease was generally reduced. An exception was the terrible influenza epidemic of 1918, which took a world-wide toll of some 10,000,000 lives, mostly civilians. The direct cost of the war to the United States was staggering, roughly $41,755,-000,000, including some of the later pension and "bonus" charges.

American operations were not confined solely to France, for small detachments fought in Belgium, Italy, and notably Russia. The United

Comparative Losses in World War I

Men Killed in Battle		Cost in Money
1,700,000	Russia	$18,000,000,000
1,600,000	Germany	$39,000,000,000
1,385,000	France	$26,000,000,000
900,000	British Empire	$38,000,000,000
800,000	Austria	$21,000,000,000
462,000	Italy	$13,000,000,000
49,000	United States	$22,000,000,000

States, hoping to keep stores of munitions from falling into German hands when Bolshevik Russia quit fighting, contributed some 5000 troops to an Allied invasion of North Russia at Archangel. Wilson likewise sent nearly 10,000 troops to Siberia as a part of an Allied expedition, which included also more than 70,000 Japanese. The major American purposes there were to prevent Japan from getting a strangle hold on Siberia, to rescue some 45,000 marooned Czechoslovak troops, and to snatch military supplies from Red Bolshevik control. Sharp fighting at Archangel and in Siberia involved casualties on both sides, including several hundred suffered by American troops. The rulers of Soviet Russia have never allowed their people to forget these "capitalistic" interventions.

The War of 1917–1918 was our best-fought war up to that time. The few failures stemmed from haste and inexperience; the smashing success sprang from enthusiasm and unity. Every citizen was enlisted "for the duration," whether in fighting, buying bonds, increasing production, or saving fuel and food.

No lasting war heroes emerged. Stern-faced General Pershing did not have the glamor that one associates with presidential timber. The traditional glory of arms had been overshadowed by barbed wire, mechanical monsters called tanks, lethal poison gas, dirt, and lice ("cooties"). Master organizer Herbert Hoover, the so-called "Knight of the Lean Garbage Can," became the outstanding hero—and he was a civilian.

Prohibition was one of two major constitutional amendments floated through by the war emergency. The need for conserving grain and other foodstuffs, combined with an idealistic spirit of self-sacrifice, achieved ratification of the 18th Amendment in 1919. (See Appendix.) Most of America had already been voted dry by state action, but the constitutional amendment achieved—on paper—the dream of a saloonless nation.

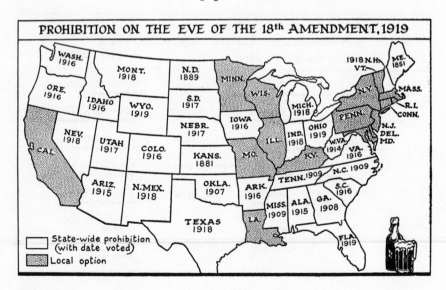

PROHIBITION ON THE EVE OF THE 18th AMENDMENT, 1919

State-wide prohibition (with date voted)

Local option

Woman suffrage, regarded as essential to national unity, was likewise stimulated by the conflict. President Wilson, hitherto reluctant, came out for this concession to the softer sex as "a vitally necessary war measure." "Votes for women" achieved a final triumph when, in 1920, the 19th Amendment was written into the Constitution. (See Appendix.) In politics, so the witticism went, the rolling pin now replaced the steam roller. But a sharp elevation of moral tone, so confidently predicted, did not follow the new amendment. Women tended to vote the same way as men.

Constitutional changes were overshadowed by economic dislocations. Swollen war industries brought bulging pay envelopes, but the invisible hand of inflation reached heavily into them. Despite burdensome war taxes, a new crop of profiteers emerged, and the select American millionaire group shot up from 16,000 to 20,000.

But the conflict, above all, was a vindication of American democracy. The German militarists had sneered at our ability to gird ourselves for battle while there was yet time. We astonished them—and to some extent ourselves—when we joined as one people in a mighty crusade for victory. Democracy, after all, did not seem so spineless.

SELECT READINGS

FRANK FREIDEL captures the spirit in *Over There* (1964), stressing photographs and contemporary reactions. MARK SULLIVAN, *Our Times*, volume V (1933) achieves the same effect in greater detail. Solid scholarship is F. L. PAXSON, *America at War* (1939). Behind-the-scenes activities are handled with gusto in the early chapters of P. W. SLOSSON, *The Great Crusade and After, 1914–1928* (1930). American propaganda efforts are colorfully portrayed in J. R. MOCK and C. LARSON, *Words That Won the War* (1939). The abuse of civil liberties is luridly described in H. C. PETERSON and G. C. FITE, *Opponents of War, 1917–1918* (1957); more briefly and soberly in H. N. SCHEIBER, *The Wilson Administration and Civil Liberties, 1917–1921* (1960). B. M. BARUCH, chairman of the War Industries Board, reminisces in *Baruch: The Public Years* (1960) [paperback]. An excellent biography is MARGARET COIT, *Mr. Baruch* (1957). A distinguished ex-foreign service officer, GEORGE F. KENNAN, has given us a perceptive study in *Soviet-American Relations, 1917–1920* (2 vols., 1956, 1958). A useful monograph is BETTY M. UNTERBERGER, *America's Siberian Expedition, 1918–1920* (1956). Also *Harvard Guide*, Pt. VI.

38

Making and Breaking the Peace

Dare we reject it [the League of Nations] and break the heart of the world?

WOODROW WILSON, 1919

Jove Steps Down from Olympus

As THE WAR in Europe crashed to a close, Woodrow Wilson towered at the peak of his popularity and power. No other man has ever occupied so dizzy a pinnacle as moral leader of the world; no other man has ever been presented with his breath-taking opportunity as a peacemaker.

Success seemed assured. Superb as a war leader, Wilson now had behind him the prestige of victory and the economic resources of the mightiest nation in the world. But regrettably his sureness of touch gradually deserted him, and he began to make a series of tragic fumbles.

The first error was the so-called "October Appeal." The war crisis had brought an enforced political unity, and the popular slogan had been "Politics Is Adjourned." The Republicans had generally supported the Democratic program for victory, although a few diehards had protested against the dictatorial powers of "Kaiser" Wilson. The Congressional election of November, 1918, was imminent, and the President believed that his hands would be strengthened at the Paris peace table if the voters should return a Democratic majority. Urged by certain politicians, he reverted to his "appeal habit" by publicly calling upon the people to elect a Democratic Congress.

The Republicans responded with the anguished accusation that the political truce had been broken. Politics, as a matter of fact, had never been "adjourned"; partisanship had merely simmered below the surface, with Theodore Roosevelt more than simmering.

On election day the voters tramped to the polls and, by a rather narrow margin, returned a Republican Congress. Whether the result was materially influenced by Wilson's unorthodox appeal cannot be determined with certainty. But he had openly staked his prestige on the outcome, and he suffered a grievous loss of face. At the Paris peace table, he was the only one of the leading statesmen not entitled to be present—that is, on the basis of a legislative majority.

Wilson next infuriated the Republicans by announcing that he was going to Paris in person to help make the peace. At that time no President had ever journeyed to Europe, though Theodore Roosevelt had visited Panama in 1906 to see "the dirt fly." Wilson's critics charged that he was showing signs of a God-complex—of a desire, as ex-President Taft put it, "to hog the whole show." The egoist-idealist in the White House was needed at home, so the Republicans argued, to grapple with the vexatious problems of reconstruction. In the hurly-burly of the Paris Peace Conference, this "mushy sentimentalist" would be overwhelmed and "bamboozled." But in Washington, at one end of a wire, he presumably could make his decisions quietly, calmly, and effectively.

Snubbing the Senate

Renewed outcries burst from Republican lips when Wilson announced the personnel of the five-man American peace commission. It consisted of himself; the quiet and faithful Colonel House, his second self; Secretary of State Lansing; a military adviser, General T. H. Bliss; and a little-known Republican, ex-career diplomat Henry White. In addition, there were scores of technical advisers, chiefly scholars from quiet campuses whom ex-Professor Wilson regarded as "his kind."

The Republicans, now the majority party on the basis of the recent Congressional election, insisted that they were not represented at all. Henry White, though a Republican, was so inconspicuous a one as to be negligible. Republicans had been good enough to fight in the war, they

THE PEACE DELEGATION—A REPUBLICAN VIEW
Left to right: Wilson, House, Lansing, White, Bliss, Baruch, Hoover, Creel.
Harvey's Weekly, 1919

complained; then why should they not have a real place at the peace table?

Wilson also snubbed the Senate in making up the peace commission, even though the jealous solons would have to approve the treaty. He did not ask their advice, partly because he had little respect for the "pygmy-minded" Senators. He did not put a single one of them on the peace commission, although there was ample precedent for doing so.

Wilson, to be sure, would have found it awkward to take along a Republican Senator, for the logical one was slender and aristocratic Henry Cabot Lodge of Massachusetts, Ph.D., Harvard. His mind, quipped one critic, was like the soil of his native New England, "naturally barren but highly cultivated." As the author of many books, Lodge had been known as "the scholar in politics" until Wilson appeared on the scene. The two men came to hate each other passionately.

But Wilson, in ignoring the Senate, seems to have been primarily preoccupied with global problems. He was like the baseball player, as someone has said, who knocked the ball into the left-field bleachers and then forgot to touch home plate.

The brutal truth is that certain Republican leaders were out to knife Wilson—that "drum major of civilization." He had trampled heavily on the corns of business tycoons with his New Freedom reforms, and the Republican Masters of Capital wanted to turn back the clock to the golden days of McKinley standpattism. The hated Wilson must not be permitted to conclude a triumphant peace. If he did, he might—unspeakable thought!—feel that he had to be re-elected for a third term to carry out its provisions.

Battling the Imperialists

Woodrow Wilson, the great prophet arisen in the West, received tumultuous receptions from the masses of France, Italy, and England late in 1918 and early in 1919. They saw in his idealism the rich promise of a better world. "Vive l'Amérique!" "Vive le Président," cried the French, while the Italians no less enthusiastically hailed "Voovro Veelson." But the statesmen of France and Italy were careful to keep the new messiah at arm's length from worshipful crowds. He might so arouse the people as to engineer an overthrow of their leaders and upset finespun imperialistic plans.

Almost from the outset, the Paris Conference of great and small nations fell into the hands of an inner clique, known as the Big Four. Such inner-sanctum diplomacy was inevitable, because the confused multi-power gathering was too unwieldy. But behind-the-scenes secrecy seemed to violate the first—and one of the most popular—of the Fourteen Points: "Open Covenants Openly Arrived At." The frustrated journalists were particularly bitter.

The Big Four proved to be both a powerful and a colorful body. Wilson, representing the richest and freshest great power, more or less occupied the driver's seat. He was joined by the genial Premier Vittorio Orlando of Italy and by the brilliant Prime Minister David Lloyd George of Britain. Perhaps the most realistic of the quartet was cynical, hard-bitten Premier Georges Clemenceau of France, the seventy-eight-year-old "organizer of victory" known as "the Tiger."

Speed was urgent when the Conference formally opened on January 18, 1919. Europe seemed to be slipping into anarchy; the red tide of International Communism was licking westward from Bolshevist Russia. A current saying in Paris was "Better a bad treaty today than a good treaty four months hence."

What problem should be tackled first? Wilson had come to Paris with his primary long-run goal the League of Nations, designed to avert future wars. The other members of the Big Four—all Old World realists —were only lukewarm about the visionary Wilsonian scheme. They were far more eager to carve up the territorial spoils of victory, as prearranged in secret treaties.

Wilson, thoroughly aroused, opposed with all his Scotch Presbyterian stubbornness an imperialistic parceling out of the booty. Such a division would have been an outrageous violation of Point Five, relating to colonies. He finally forced the acceptance of a compromise between naked imperialism and lofty idealism. The victorious powers would not receive the conquered territory outright, but only as trustees or "mandatories" of the League of Nations. Strategic Syria, for example, was awarded to France, and oil-rich Mesopotamia to Britain. This half-loaf solution, as worked out in certain backward areas, proved to be little more than the old pre-war imperialism, thinly disguised.

Wilson meanwhile had been serving as midwife for the League of Nations. The idea was not original with him; other planners in America had been working on it, as had certain far-visioned British and French thinkers. But Wilson, embracing the scheme with characteristic enthusiasm, had made it peculiarly his own. Chosen chairman of the committee that drafted the League Covenant, he labored valiantly on it after conference hours. In ten high-pressure sessions, he drove the document through in reasonably complete form, though it still needed polishing.

Wilson's next task was to get the League accepted by the entire Conference. Many members, eager to grapple with immediate problems, argued that the League of Nations should be dealt with last. Then, some intriguers hoped, it would be sidetracked, lest it interfere with imperialistic ambitions. But Wilson gained a signal victory in mid-February, 1919, when he not only won acceptance of the League Covenant but persuaded the Conference to make it an integral part of the final peace treaty. At one time he spoke so eloquently for his adopted brain child that even the hard-boiled newspaper reporters forgot to take notes.

The Senate Shows Its Teeth

Wilson, who had done amazingly well for an amateur diplomat, now had to leave the Paris battlefield for a time. It became necessary for him to make a quick trip back to America, in order to sign bills passed by Congress and attend to other pressing business.

An ugly storm was brewing in the Senate. Certain Republican solons were sharpening their knives for Wilson; they distrusted the "League of Denationalized Nations" and the "League of Nations Claptrap." To them the new scheme was either a useless "sewing circle" or an overpotent "super-state." Senator Lodge, jealous and embittered, was active in rallying his Republican following. His ranks were joined by a dozen or so

"SEEIN' THINGS"
Brooklyn *Eagle*, 1919

deep-dyed isolationists, mostly Republicans, who were known as "the Battalion of Death." This small group of "irreconcilables" or "bitter-enders" was headed by rabble-rousing orators, notably Senator William E. Borah of Idaho and Senator Hiram W. Johnson of California.

The bitterness against Wilson flared forth ominously in early March, 1919, when the Senate Republicans published a Round Robin. This was a sensational manifesto signed by thirty-nine Republican Senators or Senators-elect—enough to defeat the treaty. The signers proclaimed, for all the world to know, that the Senate would not approve the League of Nations in its existing imperfect form.

Fighting mad, Wilson struck back. On the eve of his return to Paris, he defiantly announced in a New York speech that the League would be inseparably tied into the treaty. The Senate could not cut it out without killing the whole thing—and they dared not, he was confident, break the heart of the world.

The Round Robin, a virtual stab in the back for Wilson, delighted his Allied adversaries at Paris. They were now in a stronger bargaining position, for the President would be forced to come back hat in hand. He would have to beg—as he subsequently did—for changes in the Covenant that would safeguard the sacred Monroe Doctrine and other heritages so precious to the Senators.

Frustrated France

The next grim battle was with the French, who above all things sought security against another periodic German invasion. The hardheaded Premier Clemenceau, who remembered that steel bayonets and not paper ideals had repelled the enemy, sneered at the Fourteen Points. "God gave us His Ten Commandments," he quipped, "and we broke them. Wilson gave us his Fourteen Points—we shall see."

Clemenceau demanded the German Rhineland as a buffer area, even though the acquisition of several million Germans by France would be a flagrant violation of self-determination. The heated dispute was complicated by French demands for the coal-rich Saar Valley, inhabited almost solidly by Germans.

At the peak of the French crisis, in early April, 1919, Wilson was prostrated with influenza. Burning with a temperature of 103°, he lay in his bedroom racked by fits of coughing. To every demand of Clemenceau, seated with the rest of the Big Four in the outer chamber, he returned a defiant "no." His patience exhausted, he finally took steps to order the presidential liner, the *George Washington,* to be readied for taking him back to America. The French press jeered that he was going home to mother.

The Conference was saved when the French deadlock was broken by compromise. The coveted Saar Basin would remain under the authority of the League of Nations for fifteen years, and then a vote of the population would determine its fate. France yielded her demands for the Rhineland buffer state in return for a Security Treaty, signed by Wilson and Lloyd George. By its terms both America and Britain agreed to come to the defense of the French in the event of a future attack by the German invader. The treaty was quickly pigeonholed by the United States Senate, which shied away from all entangling alliances, and it was never acted upon.

The outcome for France, which still bore the tooth marks of the Hunnish invader, was supremely disillusioning. Deprived of both the Rhineland and a feeling of security, she was forced to drink the bitter dregs of betrayal.

Self-Determination on the Defensive

The next crucial struggle was with Italy, which demanded the key port of Fiume, located near the head of the Adriatic Sea. Unfortunately, this landlocked harbor happened to be the most valuable seaport of the newly created nation of Yugoslavia. The city itself was inhabited predominantly by Italians, but the Yugoslavs were more numerous in the outskirts. To turn over these foreigners to Italy, like cattle in a pasture, would be a glaring violation of self-determination. Wilson, true to principle, fought valiantly for an acceptable alternative. But when the Italian delegates proved stubborn, he reverted to old political habits and on April 23, 1919, issued a spectacular appeal over their heads to the masses of Italy.

The Wilsonian maneuver fell flat, for the Italian delegates went home in a huff. Their people, at heart more interested in booty than in ideals, turned savagely against the once-worshiped "Voovro Veelson." Yet the American President, while not completely winning his point, kept the Italians from winning theirs—at least temporarily. The result was a hollow victory for self-determination.

The next tense battle was with the Japanese, who had been cleverly biding their time. When war broke out in 1914, Japan had joined the Allies and had seized the German holdings on China's Shantung peninsula, as well as the German islands in the Pacific. The overcrowded Japanese were naturally eager to keep all these spoils. Their persistence was rewarded when they were allowed to retain the strategic Pacific islands, though only as a mandate from the League of Nations.*

As for German rights in Shantung, Wilson opposed the Japanese claims with set jaw. To turn the fortunes of some 30,000,000 Chinese over to the tender mercies of Japan would be an intolerable violation of self-determination. The politely bowing little delegates from Nippon threatened to walk out, and if they had joined the absent Italians, the Peace Conference might well have dissolved.

In the end Wilson, with a wry face, was forced to accept a compromise on Shantung. Japan would keep Germany's economic holdings, and later return the strategic peninsula to China. The Chinese delegates in Paris, outraged, refused to sign the treaty. The whole solution smelled so much of old-time imperialism as to cause Clemenceau to jeer that Wilson "talked like Jesus Christ but acted like Lloyd George."

Victory without Peace

The completed Treaty of Versailles, after more weeks of wrangling, was handed to the Germans in June, 1919—almost literally on the point

---

* In due time the Japanese illegally fortified these islands—the Marshalls, Marianas, and Carolines—and used them as bases against the United States in World War II.

of a bayonet. They had laid down their arms on the strength of assurances that they would be granted a peace based on the Fourteen Points, with two reservations. A careful analysis of the treaty shows that only about four of the twenty-three original Wilsonian points and subsequent principles were left unmutilated. Loud and guttural cries of betrayal burst from German throats—charges that Adolf Hitler vehemently reiterated during his meteoric rise to power.

Wilson, of course, was guilty of no conscious betrayal. But the Allied powers were torn by conflicting aims, many of them sanctioned by secret treaties. There had to be compromise at Paris—or there would be no agreement. Faced with harsh political realities, Wilson was forced to compromise away some of his less-cherished Fourteen Points in order to salvage the more precious League of Nations. He was much like the mother who has to throw her sickly younger children to the pursuing wolves in order to save her sturdy first-born son.

Wilson was acutely dissatisfied with the results. Greeted a few months earlier with frenzied acclaim in Europe, he was now a fallen idol, condemned alike by disillusioned liberals and frustrated imperialists. He was keenly aware of some of the injustices that had been forced into the treaty. But he was hoping that the League of Nations—a potent League with America as a leader—would iron out the inequities.

The Treaty of Versailles, hammered out in a madhouse of conflicting ambitions, was clearly vulnerable to criticism. One of its chief weaknesses was that it fell between two stools. It tried to establish a lasting peace, while at the same time punishing the fallen foe. It was too harsh for a peace of accommodation, and too "soft"—thanks in part to Wilson—for a peace of vengeance. The victor may have peace, and he may have vengeance, but he can hardly hope to get both in the same treaty.

Yet the richly condemned Peace of Versailles had much to commend it. Not the least among its merits was its liberation of millions of minority peoples, such as Poles and Czechs, from the yoke of alien dynasties. All chaotic circumstances considered, the marvel is that any kind of an acceptable pact was signed.

Much—almost everything—depended on the good faith of the men and nations that carried out the treaty. Had they acted in the spirit intended, the results might well have been less tragic. Disappointing though Wilson's handiwork was, he saved the pact from being an old-time peace of imperialism. His critics to the contrary, the settlement was almost certainly a fairer one because he had gone to Paris in person.

The Parade of Prejudice

At home in America, breakers loomed. Wilson returned, early in July, 1919, in an uncompromising mood; privately he vowed that he would give no "nosegays" to the Senators whom he scorned. But the temper of America had been changing while the wheels of the Peace Conference were grinding. The people had been emotionally aroused to march on to Berlin and hang the Kaiser—or perhaps boil him in oil. Wilson had brought a deep feeling of frustration by negotiating a cease-fire before our patriots could enjoy their fun. Rough-Riding Colonel Theodore Roosevelt, still full of fight at the time of the Armistice, had bitterly condemned all the "peace twaddle."

"PILGRIM LANDING IN AMERICA, 1919"
Harding in the Brooklyn *Eagle*, 1919

Victory had also brought an emotional letdown. The citizenry, keyed up overlong to a spirit of self-sacrifice, were suffering the inevitable "slump in idealism." It was deepened by a disheartening feeling of dis-illusionment. The world was not "safe for democracy," and following the costly "war to end war" there were over twenty wars of varying dimensions raging all over the world. We had asked for nothing at the Paris Conference except peace. Instead of that, we were getting brickbats of ingratitude from the Allies whom we had strained ourselves to help—while of course defeating a common enemy.

Disillusion kept pace with demobilization. Homesick "Yanks," pouring back by the hundreds of thousands, added to the national discontent. Sailing to France with the unquestioned assumption that the French wore wings and the Germans horns, they had been disgusted by the ever-present manure piles and by the "gouging" of French shopkeepers. The Germans of the Rhineland—especially the blonde girls—seemed so much cleaner and nicer than the French. Perhaps, some of the "doughboys" thought, the United States had fought the wrong foe. Prolonged delays in getting back to "God's country" had likewise bred nasty tempers among American soldiers. Common complaints were "Lafayette, we are still here" and "Let Europe stew in her own juice."

Super-patriots in America, with their strong isolationist convictions, raised a furious outcry against entanglement. Revering the memory of Washington, Jefferson, and Monroe, they were hostile to a newfangled League of Nations. Why fly the glorious Stars and Stripes below the flag of some internationalized super-state? One rhymester wrote sneeringly:

> Our foreign countries, thee,
> Lands of the chimpanzee,
> Thy names we love. . . .

The Treaty of Versailles itself was assailed from all sides. Many rabid Hun-haters, regarding the pact as not harsh enough, voiced their discontent. Professional liberals, like the editors of the New York *Nation*, thought that it was too harsh—and a gross betrayal to boot. German-Americans, Italian-Americans, and other "hyphenated Americans" were aroused because the pact was not sufficiently favorable to their native lands.

Irish-Americans, traditional twisters of the British Lion's tail, denounced the League. They felt that with the votes of the five Dominions it gave Britain undue influence; and they feared that it could be used to force the United States to crush Irish independence. Huge crowds of Irish-American zealots hissed and booed the name of Woodrow Wilson.

The Martyrdom of Wilson

The President, despite mounting discontent, had reason to feel optimistic. When he brought home the treaty, with the "Wilson League" firmly riveted in as Part I, a substantial majority of the people still seemed favorable. At this time—early July, 1919—Senator Lodge had no real hope of defeating the pact. His strategy was merely to amend it in such a way as to "Americanize" or "Republicanize" it. The Republican Party, still seriously divided, could then get some political credit for the changes.

One potent weapon that Lodge could wield was delay, for delay would confuse and divide public opinion. As chairman of the powerful

Senate Committee on Foreign Relations, he formally read the entire 264-page treaty aloud, even though it had been printed. At one time only the cultured Senator and a clerk were present in the committee room. Protracted hearings were also held by the Committee, and dozens of people of various nationalities aired their grievances. The treaty was in grave danger of being drowned in a sea of words.

Wilson fretted increasingly as the hot summer of 1919 wore on. The bulky pact was bogged down in the Senate, and the nation was drifting into confusion and apathy. He therefore decided to go to the country in a spectacular speechmaking tour. He would appeal over the heads of the Senate to the sovereign people—the same people to whom he had so often appealed effectually in the past.

"GOING TO TALK TO THE BOSS"
Chicago *News,* 1919

This strenuous barnstorming campaign was undertaken in the face of protests by physicians and friends. Wilson had never been robust; he had entered the White House nearly seven years before with a stomach pump and with headache pills for his neuritis. His frail body had begun to sag under the strain of domestic partisan strife, a global war, and a hectic peace conference. But he declared that he was willing to die, like the "doughboys" whom he had sent into battle, for the sake of the new world order.

The presidential tour, begun in September, 1919, got off to a rather poor start. The Middle West received Wilson lukewarmly, partly because of the strong German-American influence in this section. Trailing after him like bloodhounds came two "irreconcilable" Senators, Borah and Johnson, who used their rabble-rousing talents in the same cities the next day or so. Hat-tossing crowds responded to the attacks on Wilson by crying, "Impeach him, impeach him."

But the story was different in the Rocky Mountain region and on the Pacific Coast. These areas, which had elected Wilson in 1916, received him with heart-warming outbursts of enthusiasm. The high point—and the breaking point—of the return trip was at Pueblo, Colorado, September 25, 1919. Wilson, with tears coursing down his cheeks, pleaded for the League of Nations as the only real hope of preventing future wars. That night he collapsed from physical and nervous exhaustion, and the rest of his speeches had to be canceled.

Wilson was whisked back to Washington, where several days later he suffered a stroke which paralyzed one side of his body. During the next few weeks he lay in a darkened room in the White House, as much a victim of the war as the unknown soldier buried at Arlington. For seven and one-half months the enfeebled President did not meet his Cabinet. Who ran the government is still something of a mystery, although it is known that Mrs. Wilson sorted and sifted the few papers that were brought to his attention. As the tragedy unfolded, many second-guessers were prone to point out that Wilson should never have left Washington. Instead, they argued, he should have tried to work out a compromise with the headstrong Senators, difficult though that course might have been.

The Great Rejection

Senator Lodge, coldly calculating, was now at the helm. After unsuccessfully attempting to amend the treaty outright, he finally came forth with fourteen formal reservations to it—a sardonic slap at Wilson's Fourteen Points. These safeguards specifically reserved the rights of the United States under the Monroe Doctrine and the Constitution, and otherwise sought to protect American sovereignty. Generally speaking, they merely restated the obvious. If the Treaty of Versailles had been approved with them attached, they probably would have been largely forgotten, as so often happens with reservations.

But Wilson, who hated Lodge, saw red at the mere suggestion of the *Lodge* reservations. He was quite willing to accept somewhat similar reservations sponsored by his faithful Democratic followers, but he insisted that the Lodge reservations "emasculated" the entire pact. The truth is that ten of them applied to the League, and only four rather harmlessly to the main body of the treaty.

Public sentiment with regard to the League had meanwhile been shifting. By late November, 1919—two months after Wilson's collapse—popular opinion apparently favored some kind of reservations, whether of the Democratic or of the Lodge stripe. But Wilson, lying in his secluded and darkened sickroom, still had faith that he could get the treaty accepted without reservations. His bedside attendants, fearful of shocking him into a relapse, dared not tell him the disagreeable truth.

Though too feeble to lead, Wilson was still strong enough to obstruct. When the day finally came for the voting in the Senate, he sent word to all true Democrats to vote *against* the treaty with the hated Lodge reservations attached. He hoped that when these were cleared away, the path would be open for ratification without reservations, or with only mild Democratic reservations.

Loyal Democrats in the Senate, on November 19, 1919, blindly did Wilson's bidding. Combining with the "irreconcilables," mostly Republicans, they rejected the treaty with the Lodge reservations appended, 55 to 39. Then the Democrats tried to ram through the pact without any reservations, but mustered only 38 votes to 53. The irreconcilable "Battalion of Death," delighted with the turn of events, had now joined hands with the regular Republicans.

Defeat through Deadlock

The nation was too deeply shocked to accept the verdict as final. Four-fifths of the Senators professed to favor the treaty, with or without reservations, yet a simple majority could not agree on a single proposition. So strong was the public indignation that the Senate was forced to exhume the defeated pact and act a second time. In March, 1920, the treaty was brought up again, with the Lodge reservations tacked on.

There was only one possible path to success. Unless the Senate approved the pact with the Lodge reservations, the entire document would be rejected. But the sickly Wilson, still sheltered behind drawn curtains and blind to disagreeable realities, again sent word to all loyal Democrats to vote down the treaty with the obnoxious Lodge reservations.

The count was closer this time. A total of twenty-one realistic Democrats, seeing that the choice was now the reserved pact or none at all, joined forces with the Lodge Republicans. A total of twenty-three loyal Democrats sided with the "Battalion of Death" to cast negative votes. On a fateful March 19, 1920, the treaty won a simple majority but failed of the necessary two-thirds majority by a count of 49 yeas to 35 nays.

Who defeated the treaty? The Lodge-Wilson personal feud, traditionalism, isolationism, Southern sectionalism, disillusionment, and politics all entered the confused picture. Lodge maneuvered astutely to prevent another rupture in the party ranks like the Taft-Roosevelt rift of 1912. But Wilson himself must bear a substantial share of the responsibility. As stubborn as when fighting Dean West at Princeton over the graduate school, he refused to accept a half-loaf. He asked for all or nothing—and got nothing. One Democratic Senator angrily charged that the President had strangled his own brain child with his own palsied hands rather than let the Senate straighten its crooked limbs. Isolationist Republicans jeeringly rewrote the 1916 slogan to read: "He Kept Us Out of Peace." One cynic said he was left "without a League to stand on."

Preparing the Solemn Referendum

Wilson had his own pet solution for the deadlock, and this partly explains why he refused to compromise on Lodge's terms. He proposed to settle the treaty issue in the forthcoming presidential campaign of 1920 by appealing to the people—the old appeal habit again—for a "solemn referendum." This course was folly, for a true mandate on the League in the noisy arena of politics was a clear impossibility.

The Republican delegates were jubilant when they met in Chicago in June, 1920. Wilson was broken and discredited; the wayward Bull Moosers had wandered back into camp. The Old Guard, spearheaded by the Senate clique, was back in the saddle. Again the saying was current, as in 1896, that all the Republicans had to do was nominate a rag baby or a yellow dog. The platform that the party bosses devised was a masterpiece of ambiguity—a teeter-totter rather than a platform. It appealed to Republicans who favored the League, like ex-President Taft, and to Republicans who derided it, like Senators Borah and Johnson.

The political woods were full of presidential hopefuls. Colorful General Leonard Wood, who had been snubbed by Wilson during the war, was the front-running candidate for the nomination. He was opposed, among others, by Senator Johnson of California, who had gained much notoriety by his unbridled assaults on the League.

As the leading contestants killed one another off, the political weather vane began to veer toward genial Senator Warren G. Harding of Ohio. A group of Senate bosses, meeting in the historic "smoke-filled" Room 404 of the Hotel Blackstone, informally decided on the affable and malleable Ohioan. Their fair-haired boy was a prosperous, back-slapping, small-town newspaper editor of the "folksy" type, quite the opposite of Wilson, who had earlier noted the Senator's "disturbingly dull" mind. Harding had further increased his acceptability by urging a return to "normalcy"—something that the country ardently desired. Despite grave doubts as to his mentality and morality, the cigar-chomping bosses helped to engineer his nomination.

When it came to the Vice-Presidency, the perspiring delegates finally rebelled against domination by the senatorial clique. Taking the bit in their teeth, they nominated a frugal, grim-faced native of Vermont, Governor Calvin ("Silent Cal") Coolidge of Massachusetts. He had commended himself to the conservative delegates by his recent role, much overrated, in breaking a policemen's strike in Boston.

The Democrats, for the first time in the history of presidential conventions, met in breeze-swept San Francisco. Wilson, ill though he was, secretly angled for a third nomination. But all such maneuvers fell flat. The President's son-in-law, lanky "Crown Prince" McAdoo, was a leading contender who suffered from the increasing public distaste for both Wilson and his in-laws. The convention at length turned to a wealthy

Ohio newspaper editor, the earnest and energetic Governor James M. Cox. The Democratic platform came out strongly for the League of Nations, as did the nominee. The vice-presidential nomination went to young Franklin D. Roosevelt, a tall, handsome, vibrant, thirty-eight-year-old New Yorker who had gained some fame as Assistant Secretary of the Navy.

The Solemn Muddlement of 1920

The ensuing campaign was rather listless, for the threadbare League issue had been under constant debate for over a year. The Socialist New York *Call* thought that the League of Nations was as "vital as a dead cat in a gutter." The confused Harding, usually kept on his front porch by the party bosses, issued a number of contradictory statements about the League. His most consistent theme was that if elected he would work for a vague Association of Nations—*a* league but not *the* League.

Harding's following was badly divided. A group of thirty-one celebrities, mostly Republicans and including Hoover, Root, and Hughes, signed a statement declaring that the election of Harding was the surest way to get us into a reserved League. Bitter-end isolationists like Borah and Johnson insisted, on the contrary, that his election was the surest way to keep us out. Republican slogans were "Let's Have Done with Wiggle and Wobble" and "Back to Normalcy."

When the sloganeering and the shouting ended, Harding was swept into the Presidency by a tremendous tidal wave of ballots. The long-frustrated women, given the vote several months earlier by the 19th Amendment, enormously swelled the totals. Harding polled 16,152,200 votes to 9,147,353 for Cox, thus amassing a prodigious plurality of 7,004,-847. The electoral count was 404 to 127. Eugene V. Debs, federal prisoner

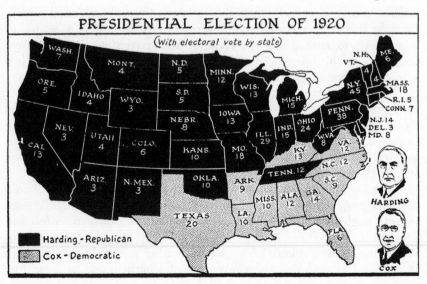

PRESIDENTIAL ELECTION OF 1920
(With electoral vote by state)

Harding - Republican
Cox - Democratic

Number 2253 at the Atlanta Penitentiary, rolled up the largest Socialist vote in our history, 919,799. Much of this left-wing support was doubtless a protest against the ineffective, second-rate Cox and the befuddled, stuffed-shirt Harding. "Thank God only one of them can be elected" was a cynical saying.

Was Harding's smashing victory a popular mandate against the League of Nations? The isolationist Republican wing gloatingly insisted that Wilson had asked for a "solemn referendum"—and now he had it. But there were so many issues that the outcome could not be a clear endorsement of any one thing. If the American people had been asked to vote for the League with reservations, they probably would have approved it. But they were never given such an opportunity.

The election of 1920 had deeper meanings. The pendulum had swung back, and the Republican Party, normally the majority since the Civil War, was returned to power. The crippled Wilson, rather than the energetic Cox, had been running. The public desire for a change found vent in a smashing repudiation of "high and mighty" Wilsonism; in fact, "Down with Wilson" was a common slogan of the period. The people were tired of professional highbrowism, star-reaching idealism, bothersome do-goodism, moral overstrain, and constant self-sacrifice. Eager to lapse back into "normalcy," they were willing to accept a second-rate President—and they got a third-rate one.

Harding's victory was the death sentence of the League of Nations in America. Republican isolationists continued to insist that the election returns were a sweeping mandate against this "superstate," and the people increasingly shunned the League as they would have shunned a leper. Among weak-kneed politicians, there is simply no arguing with a plurality of 7,000,000 votes.

Wilson, a living legend, died three years later, with admirers kneeling in the snow outside his Washington home. One unsparing critic, the newspaperman William Allen White, wrote:

> God gave him a great vision.
> The devil gave him an imperious heart.
> The proud heart is still.
> The vision lives.

The Great Betrayal

America's spurning of the League was tragically shortsighted. We had won a costly war, but we blindly kicked the fruits of victory under the table. Whether a strong international organization would have averted World War II will always be a matter of dispute. But there can be no doubt that the orphaned League of Nations was seriously crippled at the start by the refusal of the mightiest power on the globe to join it. The Allies themselves were largely to blame for the new world conflagration that broke out in 1939, but they found a convenient justification for their own timorous shortcomings by pointing an accusing finger at Uncle Sam.

The ultimate collapse of the whole Treaty of Versailles must be laid, at least in some degree, at our doorstep. This complicated pact, tied in with the four other peace treaties through the League Covenant, was a top-heavy structure designed to rest on a four-legged table. The fourth leg, the United States, was never put into place. The rickety structure teetered crazily for over a decade, and then crashed in ruins—a debacle which played into the hands of the German demagogue Adolf Hitler.

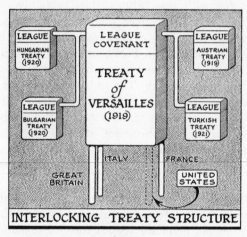

INTERLOCKING TREATY STRUCTURE

The United States lost moral face by its preach-and-run policy. We claimed advantages and opportunities without duties or responsibilities; we wanted peace—without having to pay for it. Our desertion of our war partners, even granting their imperialistic aims, marked the first serious break in the ranks of the Allies. This fatal secession indirectly facilitated the sinister ascent of Hitler and his brown-shirted bullies.

The Reparations Commission is a case in point. It had been created under the Treaty of Versailles with the understanding that we would exercise an important moderating influence. When we abdicated, the French secured a dominant voice. The result was an astronomical, trouble-breeding reparations bill of thirty-two billion dollars, presented to the Germans at pistol point. Although most of it was never paid, it contributed richly to the continuing economic chaos in Germany and elsewhere in Europe. These dangerous dislocations in turn were fuel for the propaganda machine of Adolf Hitler.

No less ominous events were set in motion when the Senate spurned the Security Treaty with France. The French, fearing that a new generation of Germans would follow in its fathers' goose-steps, undertook to build up a powerful military force. Germany, resenting the presence of strong French armies, began illegally to rearm. This witches' cauldron of uncertainty and suspicion brewed an intoxicant which helped inflame the fanatical following of dictator Hitler.

The United States, as the tragic sequel proved, hurt its own cause when it buried its head in the sands. Granted that the conduct of our Allies had been disillusioning, we had our own ends to serve by carrying through the Wilsonian program. We would have been well advised if we had resolutely assumed our war-born responsibilities, and had manfully played the role of global leadership into which we had been thrust by the iron hand of destiny. In the interests of our own security, if for no better reason, we should have used our enormous strength to shape world-shaking events. Instead, we permitted ourselves to drift along aimlessly and dangerously toward the abyss of international disaster.

SELECT READINGS

The problems are treated sketchily in A. S. LINK, *Wilson the Diplomatist* (1956) [paperback]; in detail in T. A. BAILEY, *Woodrow Wilson and the Lost Peace* (1944) [paperback] and *Woodrow Wilson and the Great Betrayal* (1945) [paperback]. The ablest pro-Wilson account is D. F. FLEMING, *The United States and the League of Nations* (1932). HERBERT HOOVER, *The Ordeal of Woodrow Wilson* (1958) [paperback] is a somewhat personalized account which is also revealing of ex-President Hoover. Detailed studies are FERDINAND CZERNIN, *Versailles, 1919* (1964); HAROLD NICOLSON, *Peacemaking 1919* (1933) [paperback]; S. P. TILLMAN, *Anglo-American Relations at the Paris Peace Conference of 1919* (1961); L. E. GELFAND, *The Inquiry: American Preparations for Peace, 1917–1919* (1963); R. N. STROMBERG, *Collective Security and American Foreign Policy* (1963). GENE SMITH, *When the Cheering Stopped* (1964) [paperback] is a rather lurid journalistic account of the tragedy following Wilson's collapse. Lodge is somewhat rehabilitated in J. A. GARRATY, *Henry Cabot Lodge* (1953). Useful monographs are R. K. MURRAY, *Red Scare: A Study in National Hysteria, 1919–1920* (1955) [paperback] and W. M. BAGBY, *The Road to Normalcy: The Presidential Campaign and Election of 1920* (1962). A new and highly favorable life of Harding is ANDREW SINCLAIR, *The Available Man* (1965). Also *Harvard Guide*, Pt. VI.

39

Harding and the Mirage of Normalcy

*America's present need is not heroics but healing; not
nostrums but normalcy; not revolution but restoration;
. . . not surgery but serenity.*

SENATOR WARREN G. HARDING, 1920

The Old Guard Returns

PRESIDENT HARDING, handsome and broad-shouldered, was one of the
best-liked men of his generation. An easygoing, glad-handed first-namer,
he exuded graciousness and love of people. So kindly was his nature that
he would brush off ants rather than crush them.

Yet the warm, smiling exterior concealed a weak, flabby interior.
With a mediocre mind, Harding quickly found himself beyond his depth
in the Presidency. "God! What a job!" was his anguished cry on one
early occasion even though he gradually developed some confidence.

Harding, like Grant, was unable to detect moral halitosis in his evil
associates, and he was soon surrounded by his poker-playing, shirt-
sleeved cronies of the "Ohio Gang." "A good guy," Harding was "one of
the boys." He hated to hurt people's feelings, especially those of his
friends, by saying "no"; and designing political leeches capitalized on
this weakness. The difference between George Washington and Warren
Harding, ran a current witticism, was that while Washington could not
tell a lie, Harding could not tell a liar.

A darling of the reactionaries, the good-fellow Harding had been
put up as a "stooge" by the Big Business Republicans. The members of
the senatorial clique were tired of a domineering figure in the White
House. They wanted a regular party man—a "putty" man—and they
thought they had found him in the amiable Ohioan.

Candidate Harding, who admitted his scanty mental furnishings, had
promised during the campaign to gather about him some of the "best
minds" of the party. Charles Evans Hughes—masterful, imperious, incisive, brilliant—brought to the Secretaryship of State a dominating if somewhat conservative leadership. The new Secretary of the Treasury was a

766

lean and elderly Pittsburgh aluminum king, Andrew W. Mellon, the multi-millionaire collector of the magnificent paintings that are now displayed in Washington as his gift to the nation. Chubby-faced Herbert Hoover, famed feeder of the Belgians and "Hooverizer," became Secretary of Commerce. An energetic businessman and engineer, he raised his second-rate Cabinet post to first-rate importance, especially in drumming up foreign trade for American manufacturers.

But the three "best minds" of the Cabinet were unfortunately offset by two of the worst. Ex-Senator Albert B. Fall of New Mexico, a scheming anti-conservationist, was appointed Secretary of the Interior. As guardian of the nation's natural resources, he was like the wolf that was hired to protect the sheep. Harry M. Daugherty, a small-town lawyer but a big-time crook in the "Ohio Gang," was assigned the duty of prosecuting wrongdoers as Attorney General.

Reaction at the Throttle

President Harding, well-intentioned but weak-willed, was a perfect "front" for the enterprising manufacturers and industrialists. The rigor mortis of reaction slowly set in, and critics raised feeble voices to lament, "You can't teach an Old Guard new tricks." The Democrats came to insist that the twelve reactionary Republican years, begun so inauspiciously by Harding, were essentially one administration as far as basic economic philosophy was concerned. Certainly the burning progressivism and reformism of the pre-war Wilson era were swept from the White House. A blowsy, nest-feathering crowd moved in and proceeded to hoodwink Harding.

The new Old Guard went the old Old Guard of Mark Hanna one better. Their plea was not for government simply to keep hands off business, but for government to act as an advance agent of business. In short, let Washington assist and protect industry but not regulate or hobble it.

The Harding conservatives, though friendly to monopoly, did not try openly to turn back the hands of the clock. They made no real attempt to repeal the Clayton Anti-Trust Act or to abolish the Federal Trade Commission, both Wilsonian reforms. They subtly and effectively achieved their ends by putting the courts and the administrative bureaus in the hands of fellow standpatters.

The Supreme Court was a striking example of this trend. Harding lived less than three years as President, but to him fell the task of appointing four of the nine justices of that august tribunal. Several of his choices were or became deep-dyed reactionaries, and they held the dike against popular currents for nearly two decades. Harding's fortunate choice for Chief Justice was ex-President Taft, who not only performed his duties ably but was more liberal than some of his associates.

The corporations, under Harding, could once more relax and expand.

The anti-trust laws were often ignored, circumvented, or feebly upheld by friendly prosecutors in the Attorney General's office. On paper, the prosecutions under Harding compared not unfavorably in number with those under Taft, Roosevelt, and Wilson. But a zeal to smash monopoly was lacking. The Interstate Commerce Commission, to single out one agency, came to be dominated by men who were personally sympathetic to the managers of the railroads. The Harding reactionaries might well have boasted, "We care not what laws the Democrats pass as long as we are permitted to administer them."

Big industrialists, striving to lessen competition, now had a free hand to set up trade associations. Cement manufacturers, for example, would use these agencies to agree upon standardization of product, publicity campaigns, and a united front in dealing with the railroads and labor. Although many of these associations ran counter to the spirit of existing anti-trust legislation, their formation was encouraged by Secretary Hoover. His sense of engineering efficiency was shocked by the waste resulting from cutthroat competition.

Advantages without Obligations

Making peace with the fallen foe was the most pressing problem left on Harding's doorstep. The United States, having rejected the Treaty of Versailles, was still technically at war with Germany, Austria, and Hungary nearly three years after the Armistice.

Peace was finally achieved by lone-wolf tactics, for the Senate "irreconcilables" would accept no other. In July, 1921, Congress passed a simple joint resolution which declared that the war was officially ended. This declaration, at the same time, formally reserved to the United States all the rights and privileges conferred upon it by the yet unratified treaty settlements. In August, 1921, Washington negotiated separate peace pacts with Germany, Austria, and Hungary. These also specifically conferred on America all the advantages of the unratified treaties—without their obligations and responsibilities. Thus was Wilsonian idealism declared bankrupt.

Isolationism was enthroned in Washington. The dominant wing of the Republican Party of McKinley and Hay, though traditionally devoted to mild imperialism and embryonic internationalism, turned its back sharply on the past. "Wobbly Warren" Harding, awed by his immense plurality, dropped his vaguely promised Association of Nations. The more unfriendly Republican newspapers sneered at the successes of the infant League of Nations, and jeered at its failures.

Official Washington continued to regard the League as a thing unclean. The Harding administration, with the Senate "irreconcilables" holding a hatchet over its head, at first refused even to support the League's world health program, though later taking halting steps toward non-political international cooperation under the new super-body. At one

"HARDING'S WAY OUT OF THE WAR"
Fitzpatrick in the St. Louis *Post-Dispatch*, 1921

time, partly through inadvertence, the State Department neglected to answer a batch of fourteen official communications from the League. The replies, when finally forthcoming, were noncommittal. The mighty American republic, in company with the other non-joiners like Ecuador, Mexico, and Hejaz, was content to till its garden alone. But the League was much too important to be completely ignored, so "unofficial observers" were sent to its seat in Geneva, Switzerland, to hang around like detectives shadowing a criminal.

The Harding administration could not completely turn its back on the outside world, notably the Middle East. The eagerness of our recent British ally to secure the lion's share of the oil reserves located there had brought strong remonstrances from Washington. The Allies had floated to victory on a flood of oil, and experts recognized that liquid "black gold" was as necessary as blood in the battles of tomorrow. Secretary Hughes, dynamically continuing the strong policy of the Wilson regime, at length secured arrangements acceptable to the American oil companies.

Bolshevist Russia, from the outset, had been getting the cold-shoulder treatment from Washington. The Wilson administration had bluntly refused to recognize the new Communist dictatorship of Moscow. The State Department charged, with complete truth, that the bloody-handed Bolsheviks had repudiated their lawful debts; that they had been guilty of bad faith; and that they were propagandizing actively in friendly countries for Communist world revolution.

The Harding regime, with its strong conservative coloration, naturally adopted this non-recognition gospel. Viewing the Russian Communists as moral lepers and economic outcasts, succeeding Republican administrations clung tenaciously to their policy for a total of twelve years.

But our distaste for the Bolsheviks did not stifle our humanitarian impulses. When a calamitous famine struck Russia in 1921, the Republican Congress, seconded by private benefactors, voted $20,000,000 for relief. The huge mission of mercy was administered under the experienced hand of the Great Humanitarian, Herbert Hoover, who received scant appreciation from the suspicious Russian leaders.

Ship-Scrapping on the Potomac

Many Republicans suffered from a disquieting awareness that America's rejection of the League had struck a heavy blow at world peace. Once elevated to power, they cast about for some kind of soul-satisfying substitute.

Disarmament was a problem that cried desperately for attention. The earnest attempts of the League in this direction were being hampered by the lone-hand course of the United States, which boasted the second mightiest navy in the world, just behind Britain's. Not only that, but when the huge building program projected in 1916 was completed, America would enjoy unquestioned primacy of the waves—provided that rival programs remained unaltered.

The naval race in which Uncle Sam found himself bore all the earmarks of deadly rivalry with Britain and Japan, our late allies. The competition with Japan was especially dangerous. Tensions had mounted to such a point in the unpacific Pacific as to confront the American people with the grim specter of war.

The aggressiveness of the Nipponese alarmed many Americans, especially the editors of the "yellow press." We had been disturbed by Japan's notorious Twenty-one Demands on China in 1915, and by her additional demands at the Paris Peace Conference regarding Shantung and the German Pacific islands. Friction had also developed with Japan during the Allied intervention in Russia's Siberia. When the American troops departed in 1920, the Japanese band struck up Stephen Foster's "Hard Times, Come Again No More."

The Anglo-Japanese alliance, first launched in 1902, was a further source of anxiety in America. If an armed clash should break out between us and Japan, we feared that our blood brothers, the British, would have to shoot white Americans on behalf of yellow Asiatics. Actually, Britain was not so bound, but many Americans thought otherwise.

Public agitation in America, fed by these perils, brought about the headline-making Washington "Disarmament" Conference in 1921–1922. President Harding, a walking mass of indecisions, was almost literally pushed into calling the multi-power parley. The imperialistic-minded Japanese were reluctant to come, for they feared that they might be forced to disgorge their recent spoils. Bolshevik Russia, blackballed by the "capitalist" nations, defiantly refused to be bound by any of the prospective agreements.

Winnings at Washington

Disarmament on land, though contemplated at Washington, proved to be impossible. Shell-shocked France, rendered insecure by our spurning the Security Treaty of 1919, was maintaining the finest army in Europe, and insisted on keeping it. She also vetoed restrictions on submarines—the poor nation's prime naval weapon.

In the negotiations for naval disarmament, the spotlight was on big battleships. Although Britain then had the largest navy, the clatter of American riveters proclaimed that we would catch up with her. Secretary Hughes dramatically proposed at Washington a holiday in building battleships, and the outright scrapping by the three major powers of dozens built or building. The scaled-down navies of America and Britain were to enjoy parity in battleships and aircraft carriers, with Japan on the small end of a 5–5–3 ratio. This arrangement sounded to the sensitive Japanese ambassador like "Rolls-Royce, Rolls-Royce, Ford."

Limits Imposed by Washington Conference

	Battle-ships	Battleship Tonnage	Aircraft Carrier Tonnage
U. S.	18	525,000	135,000
Britain	22	525,000	135,000
Japan	10	315,000	81,000
France	7	175,000	60,000
Italy	6	175,000	60,000

The Five Power Naval Treaty of 1922 embodied these terms. But it was not concluded until discussions had been deadlocked, and until face-saving compensation was offered to the insecure Japanese. The British and Americans both agreed, as an important concession, not to build additional fortifications in certain of their Far Eastern outposts, including the Philippines.

The Washington Conference likewise sought to soothe jangled American nerves by scrapping the Anglo-Japanese alliance. The pact was finally thrown into the waste basket, and the Japanese reluctantly accepted the Four Power Treaty—involving America, Britain, France, Japan—for preserving the status quo in the Pacific. In some respects, this new makeshift was more of an entanglement than the much-feared League of Nations. But because it was sponsored by the reigning Republicans, Senator Lodge gave it his powerful support. One unhappy Japanese diplomat, distressed by this weak substitute for a firm alliance, complained, "We have discarded whiskey and accepted water." Japan got a four-power agreement to talk in place of a two-power agreement to fight.

The Washington Conference also gave vulnerable China—"the Sick Man of the Far East"—something of a shot in the arm. In the Nine Power Treaty of 1922, the principal nations concerned with the Far East unanimously agreed to nail wide the Open Door. This pact was the only formal agreement ever entered into by all the major powers, except Russia and Germany, to uphold the principles proclaimed by Secretary John Hay nearly a quarter of a century earlier.

Delusive Disarmament

When the final gavel banged, the Hardingites boasted with much fanfare of their globe-shaking achievement in disarmament. But the results at Washington were, at best, somewhat illusory. Since no restrictions whatever were placed on smaller warcraft, the costly naval race was free to go merrily on in cruisers, destroyers, and submarines. In this race a penny-pinching Uncle Sam was soon lagging dangerously behind. But it is true that the American taxpayer secured substantial relief—temporarily.

To obtain parity the United States was forced to scrap more than two dozen splendid warships, built or nearing completion. A common sneer was revived: Uncle Sam, the gullible greenhorn at the poker table, wins all his wars but loses all his conferences. In this case he was accused of having "scuttled the navy"—of having scrapped fine big battleships while the other powers scrapped fine big blueprints. Actually, Britain and Japan scrapped both blueprints and battleships.

The basic truth is that at Washington we yielded *potential* naval superiority. We did so partly because our taxpayers did not want to dig down into their pockets for the money with which to achieve supremacy. American naval experts, of course, were irked by the bar against further fortifications in the Far East. One of them moaned, "Anybody can spit on the Philippines and you can't stop them."

But the Washington treaties were a compromise—and no compromise is ever completely satisfactory to any party concerned. All three major powers had to give up ships in order to get a paring down of navies. The Japanese delegates, in their view, sacrificed the most, and their people were acutely distressed by the outcome. Without our concession to them regarding future non-fortification of Far Eastern outposts, there probably would have been no final agreement.

The major achievement of the Conference was in scrapping distrust. The Pacific was pacified—temporarily. In the new and less menacing atmosphere, the Japanese grudgingly consented to retire from Siberia and Shantung, and to abandon some of their Twenty-one Demands on China.

But though it afforded short-run relief, the Conference probably hurt long-run arms limitation. It was not, despite boastful Republican claims, a "peace conference" or an adequate substitute for the League of Nations. The arms-scrapping agreement itself presented dangerous loopholes. It also hampered the earnest efforts of the League to achieve disarmament, partly because it lulled men into a false sense of security. The complete collapse of arms limitation came in the 1930's, thanks partly to the anti-League policy of the United States. The breakdown of disarmament, which resulted in piling up arms while denying them to Germany, was one more rung in the ladder by which Adolf Hitler scrambled to power.

Red-Baiting

A hysterical fear of Red Russia continued to color American thinking for several years after the Communist coup of 1917. Many nervous souls suspected that the Washington government was in imminent danger of being overthrown by the sinister tactics of bomb-and-whisker Bolsheviks. The tension was heightened by an epidemic of violent strikes that convulsed the Republic shortly after the war, many of them a result of the high cost of living. But upstanding Americans were prone to view these disorders as Red-inspired and Red-led, as indeed a few of them were.

The "Big Red Scare" of 1919–1920 resulted in a nationwide crusade against left-wingers whose Americanism was suspect. The Attorney General, A. Mitchell Palmer, who perhaps "saw Red" too easily, earned the title of "the Fighting Quaker" by his zeal in rounding up suspects. They ultimately totaled about six thousand. The drive to root out radicals was redoubled in June, 1919, when a bomb shattered both the nerves and the Washington home of Palmer. "The Fighting Quaker" was thereupon humorously dubbed "the Quaking Fighter."

Two other events highlighted the Red Scare. Late in December, 1919, a shipload of 249 alien radicals was deported on the *Buford* ("Soviet Ark") to the "workers' paradise" of Russia. One zealot cried, "My motto for the Reds is S.O.S.—ship or shoot." Hysteria was redoubled in September, 1920, when a still-unexplained bomb blast in Wall Street killed thirty-eight persons and wounded several hundred others.

Various states joined the pack in the outcry against radicals. In 1919–1920 a number of legislatures, reflecting the anxiety of "solid" citi-

BOLSHEVIKS HIDE UNDER THE STARS AND STRIPES
Philadelphia *Inquirer*, 1919

zens, passed criminal syndicalism laws. These anti-Red statutes, some of which were born of the war, made unlawful the *advocacy* of violence to secure social change. Liberals protested that mere words were not criminal deeds, and that there was a great gulf between throwing fits and throwing bombs. At all events, violence was done to traditional American concepts of free speech as I.W.W.'s and other radicals were vigorously prosecuted. The hysteria went so far that in 1920 five members of the New York legislature, all lawfully elected, were denied their seats simply because they were Socialists.

Anti-Redism and anti-foreignism were reflected in a notorious case regarded by liberals as a "judicial lynching." Nicola Sacco, a lowly shoe-factory worker, and Bartolomeo Vanzetti, a fish peddler, were convicted in 1921 of the murder of a Massachusetts paymaster and his guard. The jury and judge were probably prejudiced in some degree against the defendants because they were unnaturalized Italians, atheists, anarchists, and draft dodgers.

Liberals and radicals the world over rallied to the defense of the two aliens doomed to die. The case dragged on for six years until 1927, when the condemned men were electrocuted. Communists and other radicals were thus presented with two martyrs in the "class struggle," and many American liberals hung their heads. The evidence against the accused, though damaging, contained serious weaknesses. If the trial had been held in an atmosphere less surcharged with anti-Redism, the outcome, at worst, might well have been only a prison term.

Industrial Demobilization

The federal government ended its emergency operation of the railroad business in 1920, when the lines were returned to private control. Generous, not to say overgenerous, compensation was paid the owners.

The wartime overuse of the railroads, combined with subsequent labor difficulties, had left the lines in so hopeless a snarl that Congress was forced to step in. The Esch-Cummins Transportation Act of 1920 was designed to improve their financial health and provide arbitration of labor disputes. This law differed markedly from previous railroad legislation in that it sought to promote and encourage consolidation, rather than to thwart monopoly and enforce competition. The new philosophy was not to save the country from the railroads, as in the days of the Populists, but to save the railroads for the country.

The federal government likewise tried to pull up anchor and get out of the shipping business. When the war ended, superfluous ships were sliding down the ways in endless profusion. The Merchant Marine Act of 1920 authorized the Shipping Board, which controlled about fifteen hundred vessels, to dispose of much of the hastily built wartime fleet at bargain-basement prices. In one instance, two hundred unprofitable wooden ships brought only a little more than the initial cost of building one of them. The Board was also authorized to operate the remaining vessels, and it did so without conspicuous success.

America's sickly merchant marine faced rough seas in the 1920's. It was an important factor in the national economy and, as an auxiliary of the navy, an indispensable prop of the national defense. Yet under the La Follette Seaman's Act our shipping could not thrive in competition with certain foreigners, who all too often provided wretched food and paid starvation wages.

During the 1920's, successive Republican Congresses attempted to bail out the waterlogged merchant marine. The most noteworthy of these efforts was the Jones-White Act of 1928. Under its provisions shipping was to be encouraged by attractive subsidies, thinly disguised as mail-carrying contracts. Federal loans up to three-fourths of building costs were to be made available at low rates of interest. These arrangements worked reasonably well until the New Deal days of 1936, when Congress abandoned concealed aid in favor of outright subsidies.

Meanwhile, the return of American business to "normalcy" after the Armistice of 1918 had been seriously hampered by inflation and depression. The newly rich were far outnumbered by the newly poor, for the upward-spiraling cost of living pinched wage earners, white-collar workers, and others on fixed incomes. A major post-war recession, from 1920 to 1922, further aggravated economic conditions. In 1921 alone, about 20,000 business houses went to the wall.

Labor, caught in the middle, on the whole fared badly. A bitter strike in the steel industry against the twelve-hour, two-shift day was completely crushed in 1921. A favorite anti-labor device was to accuse the Reds of inspiring these disorders against industrial peace, as in some cases they no doubt did. Violence all too frequently flared forth, and altogether several score persons were killed or wounded by factory guards. The use of the federal injunction to crush strikes, so bitterly condemned by labor, was conspicuously revived by Attorney General Daugherty, who fully shared the Big Business bias of the Harding regime.

The Big Bull Market

The Golden Twenties began in 1922, with the end of the post-war depression and the nation's entrance upon the fantastic Long Boom. The theme song of the period might well have been the current tune:

> My sister she works in the laundry,
> My father sells bootlegger gin,
> My mother she takes in the washing,
> My God! how the money rolls in!

Yet there was something feverishly unhealthy about the inflationary joy ride; even in the best years of the 1920's several hundred banks failed annually. The something-for-nothing craze is well illustrated by real estate speculation, notably the fantastic Florida boom which culminated in 1925. Numerous underwater lots were sold to eager purchasers for preposterous sums. The whole wildcat scheme collapsed in 1926, when the peninsula was devastated by a West Indian hurricane—previously advertised as a "soothing tropical wind."

The stock exchange provided even greater sensations. Speculation ran wild, and an orgy of boom-or-bust trading pushed the bull markets up to dizzy peaks. "Never sell America short" and "Be a bull on America" were favorite catchwords, as Wall Street sharks gouged one another and fleeced greedy lambs. The stock market became a gambling den.

As the 1920's lurched forward, everybody and his brother seemed to be buying stocks "on margin"—that is, with a small down payment. Barbers, stenographers, and elevator boys cashed in on "hot tips" picked up while on duty. One valet was reported to have parlayed his wages into a quarter of a million dollars. The newly rich zoomed down the highways in shiny automobiles. "The cash register crashed the Social Register," as rags-to-riches Americans eagerly worshiped at the altar of the ticker-tape machine. So powerful was the intoxicant of fast profits that few heeded the voices raised in certain quarters to warn that this kind of prosperity, lifting itself by its own bootstraps, could not last forever.

"JUST LIKE WATER OFF A DUCK'S BACK"
Columbus *Dispatch,* 1929

Little was done by the federal government to put the brakes on money-mad speculators. In the wartime days of Wilson, the national debt had skyrocketed from the 1914 figure of $1,188,235,400 to the 1921 peak of $23,976,250,608. Conservative financing would have suggested a diversion of surplus funds for the purpose of reducing this financial burden.

A businesslike move in the direction of economic sanity was made in 1921, when a Republican Congress created the Bureau of the Budget. Its Director was to assist the President in preparing careful estimates of receipts and expenditures for submission to Congress as the annual budget. This reform, long overdue, was designed in part to prevent haphazardly extravagant appropriations.

The burdensome taxes inherited from the war were especially distasteful to Secretary of the Treasury Mellon, as well as to his fellow millionaires. Their theory was that such high levies forced the rich to invest in tax-exempt securities, rather than in the factories that provided prosperity-begetting payrolls. The Mellonites also argued, with considerable persuasiveness, that high taxes not only discouraged business but also brought a smaller net return to the Treasury than moderate taxes.

Seeking to succor the poor rich man, Mellon helped engineer a series of tax reductions from 1921 to 1926. Congress followed his leadership in repealing the excess profits tax, in abolishing the gift tax, and in reducing excise taxes, the surtax, the income tax, and estate taxes. In 1921 a wealthy man with an income of $1,000,000 had paid $663,000 in income taxes; in 1926 he paid about $200,000. Mellon's spare-the-rich policies thus shifted a substantial part of the tax burden from the backs of the wealthy to those of the middle income groups.

Mellon, the so-called "greatest Secretary of the Treasury since Hamilton," remains a controversial figure. It is true that he reduced the national debt by ten billion dollars—from about $26,000,000,000 to $16,000,000,000. But foes of the emaciated multimillionaire charged that he should have bitten a larger chunk out of the debt, especially while the country was pulsating with prosperity. He was also accused of indirectly encouraging the bull market. If he had absorbed more of the national income in taxes, his critics charged, there would have been less money left for frenzied speculation.

The Bonus Boys

Needy disabled veterans, no less than greedy millionaires, received generous treatment from the Big Business administrations of the 1920's. The Republican Congress dealt lavishly with the incapacitated ex-soldier when it set up the Veterans' Administration in 1921. The new program made openhanded provision for the building of hospitals and the beginnings of vocational rehabilitation.

But the non-disabled veterans, who had no intention of being slighted, quickly organized into pressure groups. Notable among them was the American Legion. Founded in Paris in 1919 by Colonel Theodore Roosevelt, Jr., it met periodically to renew old hardships and let off steam in good-natured horseplay. The Legion soon became distinguished for its militant patriotism, its rock-ribbed conservatism, and its uncompromising anti-Redism.

The chief grievance of the ex-"doughboys" was monetary. Drafted into the army to save their country, they had not only lost their jobs but had got along on the niggardly pay of "buck privates." When arms were grounded, many of them had had trouble getting back old jobs or securing new ones. In any event, they had lost several costly years in the ruthless economic race. Men exempt from the draft, as well as draft dodgers, had meanwhile stayed safely at home and waxed fat on war-boom wages. The ex-"doughboys" wanted their "dough"—some kind of additional payment to provide partial compensation for what they had sacrificed. Critics called this demand a holdup "bonus"; the ex-servicemen called it "adjusted compensation."

The agitation of the organized veterans, manifested notably in giant parades, finally impressed a vote-conscious Congress. In 1922 the legislators passed the first bonus bill, which was designed to grant the veteran

$50 for each month of service. President Harding, disturbed by what he regarded as a group-interest raid on the Treasury, wielded an emphatic veto. This was one of the occasions when he displayed backbone.

Re-forming their lines, the repulsed veterans gathered for a final successful attack. In 1924 a beleaguered Congress, again hoisting the white flag, passed the Adjusted Compensation Act. Each ex-soldier was to receive a paid-up insurance policy due in twenty years. It would represent $1.25 for every day overseas and $1.00 for each day of home service—altogether a sum that would add about three and a half billion dollars to the total cost of the war. Penny-pinching Calvin Coolidge, who meanwhile had come to the White House, ringingly vetoed the measure. But Congress this time overrode him, and the veterans had their bonus,

Hiking the Tariff Higher

The businessmen, not to be snubbed, had their hands outstretched—for a higher protective tariff. They were spurred into action by the prospect of an avalanche of goods from a recovering Europe, and by the blighting post-war depression.

In 1921, less than three months after Harding's inauguration, Congress passed the hastily formulated Emergency Tariff Act. It raised duties on certain agricultural products, including wool and sugar, and clamped an embargo on German dyestuffs.

This emergency legislation was followed the next year by the more comprehensive Fordney-McCumber Tariff Law of 1922. Smooth-talking lobbyists once more descended upon Congress and helped boost schedules from the average of 27% under Wilson's Underwood Tariff of 1913 to an average of 38.5%, which was almost as high as Taft's Payne-Aldrich Tariff of 1909. (See graph on p. 810.) The level of the schedules was not as important as the fact that the trend toward high protection was heavily accelerated. Duties on farm produce were increased, and the principle was set forth that the general rates were designed to equalize the cost of American and foreign production. A promising degree of flexibility was introduced for the first time when the President was authorized, with the advice of the fact-finding Tariff Commission, to reduce or increase the established duties by as much as 50%.

Presidents Harding and Coolidge, true to their big-industry sympathies, were far more friendly to tariff increases than to reductions. In six years they authorized thirty-two upward changes, including on their list vital commodities like dairy products, chemicals, and pig iron. During the same period the White House ordered only five reductions. These included mill feed and such trifling items as bobwhite quail, paintbrush handles, phenol, and cresylic acid.

The high-tariff course thus charted by the Republican regimes set off a momentous chain reaction. European producers felt the squeeze, for the American tariff walls prolonged the post-war chaos. An impoverished Europe needed to sell its manufactured goods to America, particularly if it hoped to achieve economic recovery and to pay its huge war debt to us. We needed the low-cost exports of foreign countries in order to reduce our current high cost of living. We also needed to give foreign nations a chance to make a profit from us so that they could buy our manufactured articles. International trade, we were slow to learn, is a two-way street. In general, we could not sell to others in quantity unless we bought from them in quantity—or lent them more American dollars.

The erection of towering tariff walls was a game that two could play. The two-edged American example spurred the European nations, throughout the feverish 1920's, to pile up higher barriers themselves. These artificial obstacles were doubly pernicious: they hurt not only American-made goods but the products of neighboring European countries as well. The whole vicious circle further deepened the post-war economic distress, and further disposed the Germans to welcome Hitler as a latter-day messiah.

Rationing Foreigners

Isolationist America of the 1920's, ingrown and provincial, was hostile to the influx of foreigners, as well as to the influx of foreign goods. Hordes of destitute Europeans, uprooted by the gods of war, were again flocking to the Promised Land of America. In the one year ending June 30, 1921, some 800,000 stepped upon our shores, about two-thirds of them from Southern and Eastern Europe. "Refuse the refuse" was a popular outcry of "one-hundred-percent Americans."

Congress temporarily plugged the breach in the immigration dike with the Emergency Quota Act of 1921. Newcomers from Europe were restricted in any given year to a definite quota, which was set at 3% of the persons of their nationality who had been living in the United States in 1910. This national-origins system was relatively favorable to the immigrants from Southern and Eastern Europe, for by 1910 immense numbers of them had already arrived.

The stopgap legislation of 1921 was replaced, after more mature reflection, by the Immigration Act of 1924. The quota for foreigners was cut down from 3% to 2%. The national-origins base was shifted from the census of 1910 to that of 1890, when relatively few South Europeans had arrived.* Great Britain and Northern Ireland, for example, could send 65,721 a year as against 5802 for Italy. South Europeans bitterly condemned the scheme as unfair and discriminatory—a triumph for the "nativist" belief that blue-eyed and fair-haired North Europeans were of better blood. The purpose of Congress was clearly to freeze the existing

---

* Five years later the Act of 1929, using 1920 as the quota base, virtually cut immigration in half by limiting the total to 152,574 a year.

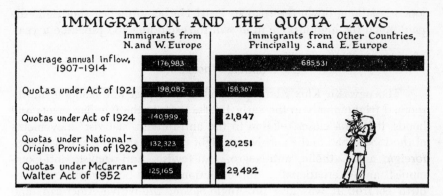

IMMIGRATION AND THE QUOTA LAWS		
	Immigrants from N. and W. Europe	Immigrants from Other Countries, Principally S. and E. Europe
Average annual inflow, 1907–1914	176,983	685,531
Quotas under Act of 1921	198,082	158,367
Quotas under Act of 1924	140,999	21,847
Quotas under National-Origins Provision of 1929	132,323	20,251
Quotas under McCarran-Walter Act of 1952	125,165	29,492

racial composition of the United States, which of course was largely North European.

The quota system proclaimed an epochal departure in American practice. It was a striking recognition of the fact that our nation was filling up, and that a "No Vacancy" sign was being hung out. Immigration henceforth died down to a comparative trickle; the famed melting pot henceforth would operate on the foreigners already here. By 1931, probably for the first time in our experience, more foreigners left than arrived. The quota restriction thus caused America to sacrifice something of her tradition of freedom and opportunity, as well as much of her color and variety. But the nation gained in racial uniformity.

The most ominous aspect of the Immigration Act of 1924 related to Japan. Relations with the Land of the Cherry Blossoms, following the air-clearing Washington Conference, had been tolerably good. They had markedly improved as a result of the outpouring of American aid to the sufferers from the frightful Tokyo earthquake of 1923, which killed more than 90,000 victims. But now everything was changed.

On paper, the Japanese were not much of a problem, for on a quota basis they would have been able to send only 185 immigrants a year. This number certainly did not constitute a "yellow horde." Yet insistent outcries from the Pacific Coast demanded that Orientals be completely excluded. The Japanese Ambassador in Washington, hoping to avert this affront, wrote to Secretary Hughes that "grave consequences" would follow the proposed action. No truer words were ever penned, but certain American politicians professed to see in them a threat of war. A spiteful Congress thereupon barred the door against Asiatics, including Japanese.

The sensitive people of Nippon were grievously offended by this resounding slap in the face, which constituted an intolerable loss of face. A Japanese super-patriot committed suicide near the American Embassy in Tokyo, and "hate-everything-American" mass meetings were widely held. The hands of the liberal friends of America in Japan were weakened, while those of the anti-American militarists and imperialists were strengthened. The military clique ultimately got into the saddle and galloped headlong down the road to Pearl Harbor. America shortsightedly paid much too high a price in ill will for excluding 185 Japanese a year.

Hooded Hoodlums

The new Ku Klux Klan, spawned by the post-war reaction, mushroomed frighteningly in the early 1920's. Despite the familiar sheets and hoods, it bore a closer relation to the anti-foreign "nativist" movements of the 1850's than to the anti-Negro night riders of the 1860's. It was anti-foreign, anti-Catholic, anti-Negro, anti-Jewish, anti-pacifist, anti-Communist, anti-internationalist, anti-evolutionist, anti-bootlegger, and anti-birth control. It was also pro-Anglo-Saxon, pro-native American, and pro-Protestant.

The reconstituted Klan spread with astonishing rapidity, especially in the Middle West and the "Bible Belt" South. At its peak in the mid-1920's, it enrolled about five million dues-paying members and wielded potent political influence. It capitalized on the typically American love of excitement, adventure, and joining, to say nothing of the adolescent love for secret ritual. The "Knights of the Invisible Empire" embraced among their officials Imperial Wizards, Grand Goblins, King Kleagles, and other horrendous "kreatures." The chief displays were "konclaves" and huge besheeted parades. The chief warning was the burning of the fiery cross. The chief weapon was the lash, supplemented by tar and feathers. Relevant songs were "The Fiery Cross on High," "One Hundred Percent American," and "The Ku Klux Klan and the Pope" (against kissing the Pope's toe).

The reign of hooded horror, so repulsive to American ideals, collapsed rather suddenly in the late 1920's. Decent-thinking people recoiled from the orgy of ribboned flesh and terrorism. Scandalous grafting by the Klan officials brought down a Congressional investigation. The bubble was punctured when the movement was exposed, not as a crusade, but as a vicious racket based on a ten-dollar initiation fee. The K.K.K. was an alarming manifestation of the intolerance and prejudice so common in the diseased minds of the 1920's. Americanism needed no such cowardly apostles, whose white sheets concealed black purposes.

Sons of Wild Jackasses

The sweat-stained farmers, more conspicuously than any other large group, were excluded from the prosperity of the fabulous 1920's. They were the stepchildren of the post-war economic order.

The farmer was caught squarely in the boom-and-bust cycle. During the war he had raked in money hand over gnarled fist; by the spring of 1920 the price of wheat had shot up to an incredible three dollars a bushel. Shortly thereafter the government guarantees were withdrawn,

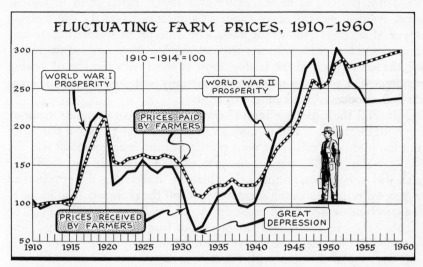

FLUCTUATING FARM PRICES, 1910-1960

a decline set in, and for about two decades dismayingly low agricultural prices prevailed.

What ailed the hard-pressed farmer? For one thing, his grain market abroad was hurt by increasingly efficient foreign production. For another, the American tariff walls, by shutting out the manufactured goods of foreigners, cut down the purchasing power of foreigners. But above all, the farmer was raising far more produce than the available market could absorb; he was in danger of being suffocated by his own golden avalanches.

The basic causes of overproduction were not hard to find. Improved seeds and livestock played an important role, but the introduction of the tractor heralded a new epoch. This steel mule was to cultivation and sowing what the McCormick mower-reaper was to harvesting. The blue-denimed husbandman no longer had to plod after the plow with high-footed gait. He could sit erect on his roaring mechanical chariot and turn under and harrow many acres in a single day. He was thus able to reduce the number of his horses and hired hands, and to grow bigger and better crops on larger areas. But such improved efficiency merely piled up more discouraging surpluses.

Overproduction inevitably meant the misery of unprofitable prices. The agricultural depression of the 1920's and 1930's turned out to be the most protracted and withering in our history. In the period from 1920 to 1932 one American farm in every four was sold for debt or taxes. The rental of farms replaced ownership at an alarming rate, and the farmers voiced their complaints with increasing vigor. As a plaintive folk song of the period ran:

No use talkin', any man's beat,
With 'leven-cent cotton and forty-cent meat.

Farm protest, as in the 1880's and 1890's, flared forth in various ways. Political movements of varying significance swept the states of the upper Mississippi Valley, and socialistic enterprises were daringly and desperately launched. Schemes without number were devised 'for relieving the sorry plight of the farmer, most of them with the aim of jacking up depressed prices. This goal was partially achieved in certain areas through producers' marketing cooperatives.

In 1921 the bipartisan farm bloc was organized in Congress, embracing both Republicans and Democrats from the farming areas of the South and the Middle West. Their most persistent farm-relief proposal was the McNary-Haugen Bill, pushed energetically between 1924 and 1928. The plan was to keep agricultural prices high by authorizing the government to buy up price-depressing surpluses and sell them abroad. The losses to the government were to be made up by a special tax on the farmers. The McNary-Haugen Bill passed Congress, but frugal Calvin Coolidge, who regarded the scheme as expensive, wasteful, and impractical, vetoed it in 1927 and again—this time with finality—in 1928.

The truth is that the industrial East, as in the days of the "Popocrats," showed a distressing lack of sympathy for the plight of the "hicks" who produced its food. Senator Moses of New Hampshire branded the Southern and Western progressive Senators as "Sons of the Wild Jackass." The Big Business forces in the East were a good deal more determined to protect American factories than to protect American farmers.

The Smell of Scandal

The loose morality and get-rich-quickism of the Harding era flared forth spectacularly in a series of scandals.

Early in 1923 Colonel Charles R. Forbes, one-time deserter from the army, was caught with his hand in the till and resigned as head of the Veterans' Bureau. As appointee of gullible Warren G. Harding, he and his accomplices looted the government to the tune of about $250,000,000, chiefly in connection with the building of veterans' hospitals. He was sentenced to two years in a federal penitentiary.

Most shocking of all was the Teapot Dome scandal, an affair which involved priceless naval oil reserves at Teapot Dome (Wyoming) and Elk Hills (California). In 1921 the slippery Secretary of the Interior, Albert B. Fall, induced his rather stupid colleague, Secretary of the Navy Denby, to transfer these valuable properties to the Interior Department. President Harding indiscreetly signed the secret order. Fall then quietly leased the lands to oilmen Harry F. Sinclair and Edward L. Doheny, but not until he had received a bribe ("loan") of $100,000 from Doheny and a large sum from Sinclair.

Teapot Dome finally came to a whistling boil. Details of the crooked transaction gradually began to leak out in March, 1923, two years after

Harding took office. Fall, Sinclair, and Doheny were indicted the next year, but the case dragged through the courts until 1929. Fall was found guilty of taking a bribe and was sentenced to one year in jail. By a curious quirk of justice, the two bribegivers were acquitted while the bribe-taker was convicted, although Sinclair served several months in jail for refusing to testify before a Senate committee.

The stench bubbling out of Teapot Dome polluted the prestige of the Washington government. Right-thinking citizens wondered what was going on when public officials could sell out the nation's resources, especially those reserved for the United States Navy. The acquittal of Sinclair and Doheny undermined faith in the courts, and gave further currency to the saying, "You can't put a million dollars in jail."

Other scandals erupted, two of them involving suicides. Persistent reports as to the underhand doings of Attorney General Daugherty brought a Senate investigation in 1924 of the illegal sale of pardons and liquor permits. Forced to resign, the accused official was tried in 1927 but was released after a jury twice failed to agree. During the trial, Daugherty hid behind the trousers of the now-dead Harding by implying that persistent probing might uncover crookedness in the White House.

Harding was mercifully spared the full revelation of this nest of iniquity, though his worst suspicions were aroused. While the scandals were beginning to break, he undertook a speechmaking tour across the country all the way to Alaska. On the return trip he died in San Francisco, on August 2, 1923, of pneumonia and thrombosis. His death may have been hastened by a broken heart resulting from the disloyalty of designing friends. Mourning millions, not yet fully aware of the graft in Washington, expressed genuine sorrow. But when all the tributes are gathered, the fact cannot be denied that Harding was not a big enough man for the Presidency—as he himself privately admitted. Such was his weakness that he tolerated persons and conditions which subjected the Republic to its worst disgrace since the days of President Grant.

SELECT READINGS

An excellent introduction is J. D. HICKS, *Republican Ascendancy, 1921–1933* (1960) [paperback]. See also H. U. FAULKNER, *From Versailles to the New Deal* (1950). F. L. ALLEN, *Only Yesterday* (1931) [paperback] reads like a novel; likewise Volume VI of MARK SULLIVAN, *Our Times* (1937) and P. W. SLOSSON, *The Great Crusade and After, 1914–1928* (1930). On economics see G. H. SOULE, *Prosperity Decade, 1917–1929* (1947); on scandals, S. H. ADAMS, *Incredible Era* (1939) [paperback] and the books on Teapot Dome by BURL NOGGLE (1962) [paperback] and J. L. BATES (1963). A favorable new life of Harding is ANDREW SINCLAIR, *The Available Man* (1965). See also A. S. RICE, *The Ku Klux Klan in American Politics* (1962). Also *Harvard Guide*, Pt. VI.

40

Calvin Coolidge and the Jazz Age

The business of America is business.

CALVIN COOLIDGE, 1925

A Yankee in the White House

THE NEWS of Harding's death, in August, 1923, was sped to Vice-President Calvin Coolidge, then visiting at the New England farmhouse of his father. By the light of two kerosene lamps the elder Coolidge, a justice of the peace, used the old family Bible to administer the presidential oath to his son.

The homespun setting was symbolic of Coolidge. As the complete opposite of Harding personally, the stern-faced Vermonter embodied the New England virtues of honesty, morality, industry, and frugality. As a youth, his father reported, he seemed to get more sap out of a maple tree than any of the other boys. Practicing a rigid economy in both money and words, "Silent Cal" came to be known in Washington conversational circles for his brilliant flashes of silence. His dour, serious visage prompted Alice Roosevelt Longworth to remark that he had been "weaned on a pickle."

Coolidge was a crystallization of the commonplace. A painfully shy individual, he was blessed with only mediocre powers of leadership. It is true that he would occasionally flash a dry wit in private; but his speeches, delivered in a nasal New England twang, were invariably boring. A staunch apostle of the status quo, he was no knight in armor riding forth to tilt at wrongs. His only horse, in fact, was an electric-powered steed on which he took his exercise. True to the Harding Big Industry philosophy, he became the "high priest of the great god Business." He believed that "the man who builds a factory builds a temple."

The hands-off temperament of "Cautious Cal" Coolidge suited the times perfectly. His thrifty, cheeseparing nature caused him to sympathize fully with Secretary of the Treasury Mellon's efforts to reduce both taxes and debts. No foe of industrial bigness, he let business have its head. "Coolidge luck" held during his five and a half prosperity-blessed years, and there were no noteworthy clouds in the American industrial sky, except those caused by factory smokestacks and the perennial farm problem.

Coolidge gave the Harding regime a badly needed moral fumigation. Yet he did not expel shady characters with undue haste, nor did he strain himself in tracking down crooks. Teapot Dome scalded the Republican Party badly, but so transparently honest was Calvin Coolidge that the scandalous oil did not rub off on him.

In his easygoing prosecution of offenders, Coolidge chimed in with the relaxed moral standards of the time. The public, though at first shocked by scandal, quickly simmered down; and an alarming tendency developed in certain quarters to excuse some of the wrongdoers on the ground that "they had gotten away with it." Some critics even condemned the government prosecutors for continuing to rock the boat. The nation's moral sense was evidently being dulled by prosperity.

The Jazz-Mad Twenties

The Harding-Coolidge era spanned the craziest years of the so-called "Jazz Age" of the "Roaring Twenties."

A moral sag normally accompanies and follows every great war. The years after 1918 were more demoralizing than usual, partly because they were shot through with a spirit of disillusionment. The nation had aroused itself to support the far-visioned idealism of Wilson—to end war and to end the threat to democracy. But our heroic sacrifices had yielded only disappointments. An atmosphere of cynicism and intolerance spread like the poison gas recently released on the battlefields of France. "Oh, yeah?" became a typically popular slang retort. Disillusionment was deepened by the "revisionist" historians of the 1920's, who published impressive documentary studies to prove that Germany had not been solely responsible for unleashing the dogs of war in 1914. Other great powers were given a generous share of the blame.

Materialism was an unlovely offspring of cynicism. Men bowed down and worshiped at the altar of the goddess Success, while seeking quick something-for-nothing riches. "Only suckers work" was a common sneer, while the horse-and-buggy virtues of earnest labor and cautious saving were often greeted with jeers.

An obsession with sex likewise accompanied the materialistic urge. The eminent Viennese physician, Dr. Sigmund Freud, had recently brought out English translations of his earlier findings. Their upshot seemed to be that sex repressions were responsible for various nervous and emotional ills of mankind. Many taboos went out the window as sex-starved Americans of the turbulent twenties let themselves go. Skirts rose higher and higher, until they hovered shockingly above the knee. Semi-nudity became fashionable as non-swimming bathing beauties besported themselves in the new one-piece bathing suits.

Syncopated jazz, up from the Negro quarter of New Orleans, elbowed classical music to one side. The blaring saxophone became the trumpet of the new machine era, while an inane popular song, "Yes, We Have No Bananas," provided a fitting theme for the lighthearted and lightheaded.

The nation more than ever became sports-mad. Baseball heroes like George H. ("Babe") Ruth, who hammered out a record-making sixty home runs in 1927, were far better known than most of our statesmen. Sports were becoming a big business. In 1921 the slugging heavyweight champion, Jack Dempsey, knocked out the dapper French light heavyweight, Georges Carpentier, before a crowd that had paid more than a million dollars—the first in a series of million-dollar "gates" in the golden 1920's.

Spiritual life seemed to be retreating before materialism in this "Era of Wonderful Nonsense." The Fundamentalist champions of the old-time religion were losing ground to the Modernists. Some of the churches were even forced to fight the Devil with worldly weapons. Faced with competition from Sunday joy-riding automobiles, to say nothing of golf links and "movie palaces," a few denominations were providing wholesome moving pictures and other attractions for their young people. One uptown house of the Lord in New York even advertised on a billboard: "Come to Church: Christian Worship Increases Your Efficiency."

"Flaming youth" spectacularly reflected the changed standards of the new age of cynicism. The once modest and long-haired maiden blossomed forth shockingly as a "flapper" in bobbed tresses and bobbed dresses. Feminists saw the further emancipation of their sex in the low-cut gown, the painted lips, the rouged cheeks, the dangling cigarette—all of which had previously been associated with fallen women. The cosmetics industry rapidly blossomed into a billion-dollar business.

The teen-agers of the frenzied 1920's, with their gin-filled hip-flasks, cut a wide swath. Glued together in syncopated embrace, they danced to jazz music squeaking from phonographs. In an earlier day a kiss had been the equivalent of a proposal of marriage. But in the new era reckless youth took to the highways and byways in automobiles, there to poach upon the forbidden land of sex as "neckers" and "petters." Alarmed guardians of the public morals decried the careening automobiles as "houses of prostitution on wheels." The ultimate in moral degeneracy was reached in 1924, when two brilliant young college graduates in Chicago, named Loeb and Leopold, kidnapped and killed a boy just for the thrill of it.

Cultural Materialism

The spirit of the flask-and-flapper age was partially reflected in the printed word. Cheap, sexy "confession" magazines were now being sold by the hundreds of thousands. The "terrible tabloids," tailored small for the convenience of subway straphangers, luridly improved on the crime stories of the 19th-Century "penny dreadfuls."

The cynical atmosphere of the jazz-and-gin era lent itself to "debunking"—a word appropriately coined in 1923. The noisiest and most influential of the debunkers was Henry L. Mencken, "the Bad Boy of Baltimore." In the green-covered monthly *American Mercury,* which he launched in 1924 and which attained great popularity among young intellectuals, he wielded a meat ax instead of a pen. Sparing nothing, he jibed at marriage, patriotism, prohibition, Rotarians, and the "booboisie" of the Southern "Bible Belt." To him, all idealism was "bilge."

Popular also with college undergraduates was F. Scott Fitzgerald's brilliant and witty novel *This Side of Paradise* (1920). The Minnesota-born author, an alcoholic Princetonian only twenty-four years old, was a sensation with his tale of uninhibited, bewildered youth in the Jazz Age. Catching the spirit of the hour (usually about 4 A.M.), he found "All gods dead, all wars fought, all faiths in man shaken."

Other literary contributions partially mirrored the restlessness and uncertainty of the times. Noteworthy among writers struggling to find a philosophy to fit the new age was Theodore Dreiser, an Indiana-bred journalist and novelist. His grim realism is perhaps best seen in a novel, *An American Tragedy* (1925), which describes the murder of a pregnant girl by her fickle young lover. Fortunately for sales, the tale was banned in Boston.

American novelists were carrying on the more conventional tradition earlier established by distinguished writers like the well-to-do New Yorker Edith Wharton and Virginia-born Willa Cather, who achieved fame through her delineation of Middle Western prairie life. Notable among the new crop of novelists was spindly Sinclair Lewis, a journalistic product of Sauk Center, Minnesota. As a master of satire, he sprang into prominence in 1920 with his *Main Street,* an attack on the small-town Middle Western life that he knew so well. His next novel, *Babbitt* (1922), pilloried George F. Babbitt, a prosperous, vulgar, middle-class real estate broker who under social pressures conformed to the respectable materialism of his group. The word "Babbittry" was quickly coined to describe his type.

Despite the moan of saxophones, high-quality poetry was still being written. Noteworthy were the poems of skilled craftsmen like Edwin A. Robinson, a reserved New Englander; Ezra Pound, an Idahoan who deserted America for Europe; T. S. Eliot, a Missourian who became a British subject; and Robert Frost, an adopted son of New England. Better known to many contemporaries were less distinguished figures like Chicago's embittered Edgar Lee Masters; Vachel Lindsay, who mixed unconventional poetry with hoboing; and Carl Sandburg, later famed as a folklorist and biographer of Lincoln. These lesser lights were perhaps better known because, like some of the novelists, they were critical of both the social and the economic structure. Edna St. Vincent Millay, a disillusioned Maine poet, described the devil-may-care spirit of rebellious youth.

> My candle burns at both ends;
> It will not last the night;
> But ah, my foes, and oh, my friends—
> It gives a lovely light!*

The theater too reflected current modes. Although losing out to the motion picture, it was, as if by compensation, attracting playwrights of genuine distinction. Perhaps the best-known play of the era was *What Price Glory* (1924), written by Maxwell Anderson and Laurence Stallings. Free-living, free-loving marines like Sergeant Quirt and Captain Flagg shocked old-timers by bringing to the stage unrestrained outbursts of profanity. Eugene O'Neill, a New York dramatist of globe-trotting experience, laid bare Freudian concepts of sex in his plays, notably *Strange Interlude*. He won a Nobel Prize in 1936.

Even architecture married itself to the new materialism and functionalism. The era of machinery continued to lure droves of people to the cities; by 1930 over one-half of our population lived in urban areas. Long-range city planning was being intelligently projected, and architects like Frank Lloyd Wright were advancing the theory that buildings should grow from their sites and not slavishly imitate Greek and Roman importations. The Machine Age outdid itself in New York City when it thrust upward the cloud-brushing Empire State Building, 102 stories high. Erected in the 1920's, it was dedicated in 1931.

The Prohibition Era

The moral decay of the 1920's was vastly accelerated by prohibition. The arid new order was authorized in 1919 by the 18th Amendment (see Appendix), as implemented by the Volstead Act passed by Congress later that year. Together they made the world "safe for hypocrisy."

The legal abolition of alcohol was fairly popular in the Middle West, and especially so in the South. Southern whites were eager to keep stimulants out of the hands of the Negro, lest he burst out of "his place." But despite the overwhelming ratification of the "dry" amendment, strong opposition was registered in the larger Eastern cities. Concentrated colonies of "wet" foreign-born peoples were loath to abandon their Old World drinking habits. Yet most Americans assumed that prohibition had come to stay. Everywhere there were last wild flings, as the nation prepared to enter upon a permanent "alcoholiday."

But the victory-flushed advocates of prohibition were naïve in the

---

* "First Fig" from *A Few Figs from Thistles* (Harper and Brothers, 1918; copyright, 1918, by Edna St. Vincent Millay). Reprinted by permission.

extreme. They overlooked the deep-rooted American tradition of strong drink and of weak control by the central government, especially over private lives. They forgot that in American experience the federal authorities had never satisfactorily enforced a law where the majority of the people—or a strong minority—were hostile to it. The high-riding drys ignored the fact that one cannot make a crime overnight out of something that millions of people have never regarded as a crime. Legislative bodies cannot legislate away a thirst.

"WHATCHA GOT IN THAT BAG?"

This slap at the drys as snooping killjoys reflected widespread popular sentiment. Weed in the New York *World*

Peculiar conditions hampered the enforcement of prohibition. Profound disillusionment over the aftermath of the war raised serious questions as to the wisdom of further self-denial. Slaking thirst became a cherished personal liberty, and many ardent wets believed that the way to bring about repeal was to violate the law on a large enough scale. Frustrated soldiers, returning from France, complained that prohibition had been "put over" on them while they were "over there." Grimy workingmen bemoaned the loss of their cheap beer, while pointing out that the idle rich could buy all the illicit alcohol they wanted. Flaming youth of the Jazz Age thought that it was "smart" to swill bootleg liquor—"liquid tonsillectomies." Millions of older citizens likewise found forbidden fruit fascinating, especially when they engaged in "bar hunts."

Prohibition might have started off on a more promising foot if there had been a larger army of enforcement officials. But the state and federal

agencies were understaffed, and their snoopers, often susceptible to bribery, were underpaid. The public was increasingly distressed as scores of
persons, many of them innocent bystanders, were killed by quick-triggered dry agents.

Prohibition simply did not prohibit. The old-time "men only" corner
saloons were replaced by thousands of "speakeasies," with their tiny
grilled window through which one spoke softly before the barred door
was swung open. Women frequented such dives. Hard liquor, especially
the cocktail, was drunk in swelling volume by both sexes. Largely because of the difficulties of transporting and concealing bottles, beverages
of high alcoholic content were popular. Foreign rumrunners, including
those from the West Indies, had their profitable inning, and countless
cases of liquor leaked down from Canada. The zeal of American prohibition agents on occasion seriously strained diplomatic relations with our
northern neighbor.

"Home brew" and "bathtub gin" became popular, as law-evading
adults engaged in "alky cooking" with toy stills. The worst of the home-
made "rot gut" produced permanent blindness and even death. The
affable bootlegger worked in silent partnership with the friendly undertaker.

The Golden Age of Gangsterism

Prohibition also spawned various shocking crimes. The lush profits
of illegal alcohol often led to bribery of the police, many of whom were
induced to see and smell no evil. Violent gang wars broke out in the big
cities between rivals seeking to corner the rich market in booze. Rival
triggermen used their sawed-off shotguns and chattering "typewriters"
(machine guns) to "erase" bootlegging competitors who were trying to
"muscle in" on their "racket." In the gang wars of the 1920's in Chicago,
about five hundred low characters were murdered. Arrests were few and
convictions were even fewer, as the button-lipped gangsters "covered"
for one another with the underworld's code of silence.

Chicago was by far the most spectacular example of lawlessness. In
1925 "Scarface" Al Capone, a greasy and loathsome character, began
six years of gang warfare which netted him millions of blood-spattered
dollars. He zoomed through the streets in an armor-plated car with
bullet-proof windows. A Brooklyn newspaper quipped:

> And the pistols' red glare,
> Bombs bursting in air
> Give proof through the night
> That Chicago's still there.

Capone could not be convicted of the cold-blooded massacre, on St.
Valentine's Day in 1929, of seven disarmed members of the rival

O'Banion gang. But he was finally sentenced to a long term in a federal penitentiary for income-tax evasion.

Gangsters rapidly moved into other profitable and illicit activities: prostitution, gambling, and narcotics. Honest merchants were forced to pay "protection money" to the organized thugs; otherwise their windows would be smashed, their trucks overturned, or their employees or themselves beaten up. Racketeers even invaded the ranks of local labor unions as organizers and promoters. Organized crime had come to be one of the nation's most gigantic businesses. By 1930 the annual "take" of the underworld was estimated to be from twelve to eighteen billion dollars— several times the income of the Washington government.

Aside from stimulating gangsterism, prohibition was criticized on other counts. Millions of dollars were spent in semi-enforcement; hundreds of millions of dollars were lost in taxes. The jails were crowded and the courts were clogged, as the result of more than half a million arrests from 1920 to 1930. Hypocrisy flourished. Hip-flasked legislators spoke or voted dry while privately drinking wet. Europeans were both amused and disgusted by the "silliness" of the Americans. Yet, on the whole, probably less liquor was drunk than in the days before prohibition. As the legendary Irishman remarked, prohibition was "a darn sight better than no liquor at all."

Stern-faced drys decried the lawless traffic in alcohol, as well as the gangsterism that it bred. Voicing alarm lest such widespread flouting of the Constitution and the federal statutes should widen into contempt for all law and order, they loudly demanded an enforcement of the seemingly unenforceable law. In defense of prohibition, they pointed to increased bank savings and decreased absenteeism in industry. They argued that personal liberty to drink was one thing in the oxcart days of Thomas Jefferson, but another in the new machine age. Drunkenness was too high-priced a luxury when the tipsy worker or automobile driver endangered not only himself but the lives of innocent people as well.

Expanding Schoolrooms

Education in the 1920's continued to make giant-boot strides. More and more states were requiring their children to remain in school until age sixteen or eighteen, or until graduation from high school. The introduction of the automobile bus made possible the consolidation of one-room bedlams into splendid union schools with excellent facilities for instruction, both mental and manual.

The most revolutionary contribution to educational theory during these yeasty years was made by mild-mannered Professor John Dewey, who served on the faculty of Columbia University from 1904 to 1930. By common consent one of America's few front-rank philosophers, he set forth the principles of "learning by doing" that formed the foundation of so-called "progressive education." He believed that the workbench was as essential as the blackboard, and that "education for life" should be a primary goal of the teacher.

The new emphasis on creating socially useful adults rendered many schools more attractive. No longer was the schoolhouse a kind of educational jail, from which the pupils burst at the end of the year chanting, as had young Dewey when a youngster in Vermont, "Good-bye school, good-bye teacher, damned old fool."

Other educational landmarks were posted. Vocational education was being stressed, at both the juvenile and adult levels. Junior colleges, which provided the first two years of higher education locally, were making it possible for hundreds of thousands of youths from poorer families to aspire to college training. University enrollments, appropriations, and endowments continued to soar.

Monkey Business

Science was one of the greatest beneficiaries of modernized university laboratories. New drugs, vitamins, and other wonders were being uncovered. X rays were now used for cancer treatment and other health-giving purposes, and hospitals were expanding. The great epsom-salts program of the Rockefeller Foundation, launched in 1909, had virtually wiped out hookworm in the South. Amazing progress was being made in improving the nation's health and in widening the life span of the average citizen. Between 1901 and 1929 the life expectancy of an infant at birth was increased from approximately fifty to fifty-nine years.

Yet science in the universities and schools was still handicapped by a nagging fire from the Fundamentalists. These old-time religionists charged that the teaching of Darwinian evolution was destroying faith in God and the Bible, while contributing to the moral breakdown of youth in the Jazz Age. Numerous attempts were made to secure laws prohibiting the teaching of evolution in the public schools, and three Southern states adopted such shackling measures. The trio included Tennessee, in the heart of the so-called "Bible Belt" South, which, curiously enough, was the last refuge of Puritanism.

The stage was set for the memorable "Monkey Trial" at the hamlet of Dayton, eastern Tennessee, in 1925. A likable young high school biology teacher of twenty-four, John T. Scopes, was indicted for teaching evolution. Batteries of newspapermen, armed with notebooks and cameras, descended upon the quiet town to witness the spectacle, as did hundreds of gaping "yokels" from the nearby hills. Scopes was defended by nationally known lawyers, while William Jennings Bryan, an ardent Presbyterian Fundamentalist, joined the prosecution. Taking the stand as an expert on the Bible, he was badly tripped up by the clever defense attorneys. Five days after the trial was over, Bryan died of apoplexy, no doubt brought on by the heat and strain.

The outcome was inconclusive. Scopes, the forgotten man of the drama, was found guilty and fined $100. But the Supreme Court of Tennessee, while upholding the law, freed him on a technicality. The Fundamentalists at best won only a hollow victory, for the absurdities of the trial cast ridicule on their cause. Increasing numbers of Christians found it possible to reconcile the realities of religion with the findings of modern science, and the membership of the churches continued to mount.

A Three-Way Race to the White House

Calvin Coolidge was the overwhelming choice of the Republicans when they met at Cleveland in June, 1924. Although he had been in the White House less than a year, he had brought respectability to his scandal-besmirched party. He had also proved to be the ideal business-man's candidate. The platform paid lip service to prohibition, and boasted that the nation's jingling cash registers resulted from Republican policies.

The Democrats were much less harmonious. Meeting in Madison Square Garden, New York, they staged one of the most dramatic brawls ever held in that pugilistic amphitheater. Liberal Governor Alfred E. Smith of New York, a Roman Catholic and a wet, locked horns with Woodrow Wilson's son-in-law, "Crown Prince" William G. McAdoo, a Protestant and a dry. After 102 indecisive ballots—the most protracted balloting marathon in our presidential history—the convention wearily, sweatily, and unenthusiastically turned to white-haired John W. Davis. A wealthy New York corporation lawyer connected with the Wall Street firm of J. P. Morgan and Company, the polished nominee was no less a conservative than the impeccable Calvin Coolidge.

The Democratic platform attacked the corruption of the Harding era, and attempted to wave the oil-stained linen of the Republicans in public. Championing Wilson's pro-League ideals, the assembled Democrats condemned what they regarded as the cowardly isolation, vacillation, and indecision of the Washington regime. Favorite Democratic slogans were "Honesty at Home—Honor Abroad" and "Remember the Teapot Dome."

The field was now wide open for a liberal candidate. White-pompadoured "Fighting Bob" La Follette of Wisconsin, perennial aspirant to the Presidency and now sixty-nine years of age, sprang forward to lead a new Progressive grouping. Its appeal to farm-labor elements was strong. La Follette's platform advocated government ownership of railroads and relief for farmers, lashed out against both monopoly and anti-labor injunctions, and urged a Constitutional amendment to limit the Supreme Court's power to invalidate laws passed by Congress. In his fight against "entrenched greed" La Follette gained support from the Socialist Party, and even from elements of the American Federation of Labor. Yet he lacked money, organization, and newspaper backing.

Prosperity Overpowers Progressivism

The campaign of 1924 was of the "ho-hum" variety. The voters were prosperity-drugged, and the experts regarded a Republican triumph as inevitable. Popular G.O.P. slogans were "Keep Cool with Coolidge" and "Keep Cool and Keep Coolidge." La Follette, ever the crusader, provided some fireworks by his attacks on the Supreme Court. The Republicans assailed his alleged socialism, and played upon the fear that he might win enough electoral votes to throw the decision into the House of Representatives, with attendant uncertainties. "Coolidge or Chaos" cried Coolidgeites in alarm—or pretended alarm.

The Democrats noisily hammered on Teapot Dome and other scandals, which ordinarily would have been enough to sink the party in power. They sardonically sang a parody of a popular song:

> But how 'n the 'ell kin the country tell,
> "You ain' gwine steal no mo'?"

"Cautious Cal" and the oil-bespattered Republicans rode into office on the crest of a landslide—a landslide which overwhelmed Davis, 15,-725,016 votes to 8,386,503. The electoral count stood at 382 for Coolidge,

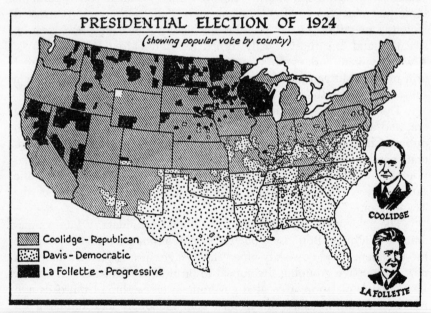

PRESIDENTIAL ELECTION OF 1924
(showing popular vote by county)

Coolidge - Republican
Davis - Democratic
La Follette - Progressive

COOLIDGE

LA FOLLETTE

Compare the pro-La Follette Western farm areas with the Populist protest areas in 1892 (p. 591). Note the persisting "mountain white" Republican vote in the South.

136 for Davis, and 13 for La Follette. "Battling Bob" carried only his own Wisconsin, though polling 4,822,856 popular votes.

Yet La Follette's fight was not altogether in vain. Though badly beaten, his Progressive organization was one of the few third-party groupings ever to break into the electoral column. As the so-called conscience of the calloused 1920's, La Follette injected a badly needed liberal tonic into a materialistic America.

Good times are hard to beat. The slogan of the Coolidge Republicans might well have been "Why swap horses in the middle of prosperity?" "Silent Cal's" triumph was basically an endorsement of prosperity, though disgruntled Democrats sneered that it was a mandate to go on stealing.

Uncle Sam: World Banker

Almost overnight the World War of 1914–1918 had reversed the international economic position of the United States. In 1914 we had been a debtor nation in the sum of three billion dollars; by 1922 we had become a creditor nation in the sum of sixteen billion dollars. The Almighty Dollar had displaced the pound sterling as the financial giant of the world.

Well-to-do Americans in the 1920's looked hungrily abroad for high-interest investment opportunities. Wall Street bankers, with the blessing of the Washington government, invested huge sums of money in Europe, Asia, and Latin America. The total outflow of private investments in the 1920's mounted to more than ten billion dollars, much of which was lost in the 1930's, when the world-wide Great Depression descended. As a perverse fate would have it, a substantial portion of this sum was used by Germany to rebuild and expand her industrial machine—the very machine that Hitler later used to crush the victims of his fury.

But the real debt problem of the 1920's—the one that overshadowed all others—was what foreign governments owed the Treasury of the United States. The so-called Allied war debts totaled $10,350,479,074.70, about 90% of which had been incurred by our wartime Allies—Britain, France, and Italy. Uncle Sam held their I.O.U.'s—and he wanted to be paid.

The war debts, to make matters worse, were closely tied up with reparations. The Allied nations, notably ravaged France and Belgium, argued that the Germans had forced a terrible conflict upon peaceful neighbors, and should therefore be held liable for full damages. The reparations bill, as finally presented to Berlin, reached the staggering figure of thirty-two billion dollars. The German masses, traditionally industrious, might have been willing to buckle down and pay a more reasonable sum, say ten billion dollars. But they recoiled from the crushing burden they were asked to shoulder, and especially from the implication that they alone had been responsible for starting the frightful conflagration.

Allied insistence on backbreaking reparations contributed markedly to Europe's post-war chaos and depression. New hatreds were aroused, especially when the reparations-collecting French in 1923 sent troops into Germany to seize the industrialized Ruhr Valley. They forgot that one cannot extract both milk and beefsteak from the same cow. The Berlin officials responded to French intervention by permitting inflation of the currency to reach runaway proportions. The wholesale printing of near-worthless paper money not only wiped out the sturdy German middle class, but also helped pave the path for Hitler and his Nazi gangsters. Altogether the Germans, with tooth-pulling reluctance, paid about four and a half billion dollars on their huge reparations bill. Yet American investors during these post-war years sank about half this amount in Germany.

Reparations were also intimately bound up with the war debts owed by former Allies to the United States. British spokesmen, hoping to avert a Pandora's box of troubles, had early suggested an around-the-board cancellation. France owed both Britain and the United States huge sums. The British were willing to forgive the French their debt, provided the United States would forgive both the French and the British their debts. If Uncle Sam had fallen in with this scheme, the French would not have been justified in presenting such a paralyzing reparations bill, and presumably the Germans would have paid a more reasonable amount with some degree of willingness. If all this had happened, endless friction would have been avoided.

But Woodrow Wilson and his successors in the White House all turned deaf ears to the plaintive pleas of the foreign debtors. The American people, badly disillusioned by the imperialistic aims of the Allies, were determined not to be the sackholders in the pretty little game of ring-around-a-rosy cancellation. Any thought of wiping the slate clean was highly unpopular with American taxpayers, who perceived that they would have to reach down into their pockets and reimburse the Treasury if the Allies did not pay. Official Washington therefore persisted in its stand that there was no connection whatever between reparations and debts.

Uncle Sam Becomes Uncle Shylock

What was the nature of the Allied war debts? The money, totaling more than ten billion dollars, had been advanced by the Treasury as credits to our Allies after we entered the conflict in 1917. These sums had been used to buy mountains of military supplies in the United States. About one-third of the so-called Allied *war* debt had been incurred after the shooting war had stopped, and a large part of this "reconstruction debt" had gone to needy nations formed out of ex-Ally or ex-enemy states.

Relatively little gold had left the United States during the war for the debtors. Yet the American taxpayer, knowing nothing of international finance, imagined that countless hogsheads filled with gold dollars had been rolled up the gangplanks for Europe. Now that the shooting was over, Uncle Sam demanded his gold "back."

The true debt picture was drastically different. The hard-pressed Allies had not wanted gold as such: they could not fire gold bullets at their German foe. They had needed credits for the purchase of war materials in the United States. Incidentally, these heavy purchases had further boomed our war-born prosperity, and had poured additional tax revenue into the Treasury. We counted our profits; the Allies counted their dead.

The French in particular felt that they had a strong moral case for debt cancellation. America the Unready had entered the war in 1917 without an army. While she was raising one, the Hun had to be held back. The French, at frightful cost, maintained a wall of flesh and blood against the German attackers until America could get into the common fray. Each nation, argued France, contributed what it had: the Allies gave lives, the Americans gave dollars. Now that the war was over, the French were not asking for the lives of their boys back. Nor should Uncle Sam, in the eyes of France, ask for his dollars back.

The war-shattered Allies employed even more practical arguments. There were only three possible ways to pay their debt to us: in gold, in goods, and, to a relatively minor degree, in services such as shipping. The European debtors either did not have enough gold or needed what they had to back

"OUR COLLECTIONS FROM FRANCE"
Fitzpatrick, St. Louis *Post-Dispatch*

their own currencies. The ex-Allies would have been glad to ship goods to the United States. But they were seriously hampered by the towering post-war tariff walls, erected in response to the alarmed outcries of American manufacturers.

"Pay anyhow" was the hard-boiled dictum of the Washington regimes in the 1920's. Calvin Coolidge, tight-lipped and tight-fisted, gave voice to a classic statement, "Well, they hired the money, didn't they?" Other American critics argued that the debtors should pay with the money they were squandering in arming themselves to the teeth. This argument completely ignored the facts that France was rearming because she felt insecure, and that she felt insecure largely because the United States had walked out on the League of Nations and the French Security Treaty of 1919.

The bill-collecting Americans made a strong point of simple honesty. A loan was a loan, they insisted, and faith in international borrowing would be destroyed if the Allies "welshed." "We went across, but they won't come across," cried a prominent Ohio politician in the 1930's.

Dunning the Debtors

The reluctant Allied debtors were finally beaten into line, but not until Washington began to exert painful economic pressures on them. The war loans had originally been made with the understanding that they would be repaid at 5% interest. This was clearly too heavy a burden, so Congress created the World War Foreign Debt Commission in 1922 to negotiate more favorable terms.

Uncle Sam, from his point of view, showed unexampled generosity toward the debtors. None of them was forgiven the principal of the obligation. But all of them, on the basis of ability to pay, received reduced interest rates over a protracted repayment period—for example, sixty-two years for Britain. The final interest figure ranged from 3.3% for the Brit-

Principal Allied Debtors		
	Debt	Interest Rate in Repayment Period
Britain	$4,277,000,000	3.3%
France	$3,404,818,945	1.6%
Italy	$1,648,034,050	0.4%
Belgium	$379,087,200	1.8%
Russia	$192,601,297	Repayment never arranged

The figures show both pre-Armistice and post-Armistice loans of credit and supplies. There were twenty debtor countries.

ish to 0.4% for the impoverished Italians. The reductions in interest for all the debtors resulted in about a 50% cancellation of the entire indebtedness, counting both principal and interest spread over many years.

By May, 1930, seventeen of the reluctant debtor nations had signed agreements with the United States. The pact with France, concluded in 1926, was violently unpopular in the land of Lafayette. Irate French crowds on occasion would attack American tourists. In the eyes of patriotic Frenchmen, Uncle Sam the Savior had now become Uncle Shylock, greedily whetting his knife for the last pound of French flesh.

In a class by herself was "brave little Finland," formerly a part of Czarist Russia. For purposes of rebuilding after the war, she had secured from the United States a relatively tiny post-Armistice commercial loan of $8,281,926. Although not a former Ally, her industry and honesty in making her payments on time won for her wide acclaim in America. She invited misleading comparisons with the reluctant Allies, who had incurred far heavier obligations.

Uncle Sam collected in all about two and three-fourths billion dollars on the debt of ten billion. Yet he harbored bitter resentment toward the European "ingrates" because they were resentful. Many Americans, in a strange reversal of sympathies, felt more kindly toward our fallen German foe than toward our late comrades-in-arms, whom we had "saved"—while saving ourselves. This unhealthy state of mind in America contributed powerfully to the storm-cellar neutrality legislation passed by Congress in the 1930's.

The debt controversy likewise left a bad aftertaste in Europe. American stevedores may not have rolled hogsheads of gold dollars up the gangplanks, but the American people did collect hogsheads of ill will. Our insistence on the repayment of the war-spawned debts further snarled the reparations tangle, and contributed richly to the post-war economic dislocations of Europe, including Germany. These ominous trends all provided abundant fuel for the propaganda mill of the fast-emerging demagogue, Adolf Hitler.

Edging toward World Responsibilities

America's look-under-the-bed fear of the League gradually began to wear off as the 1920's advanced. President Harding had stoutly asserted in 1923 that America would not enter "by the side door, or the back door, or the cellar door." But the League was much too significant to be dismissed, and American unofficial observers continued to hang around Geneva, as scarcely befitted a great power.

Gradually, under Presidents Coolidge and Hoover, the United States began to sidle toward the back door. To an increasing degree, we participated as consultants in the non-political functions of the League, such as conferences to control opium and prostitution. By March, 1930, we had sent official delegates to more than forty such parleys; and in some respects we were a member of the League in all but name. Yet unfriendly critics in America, chiefly isolationists, continued to sneer at the successes and jeer at the failures of the "League of Hallucinations."

The World Court—the judicial arm of the League—inspired much less fear in the United States. All Presidents from Wilson through Franklin D. Roosevelt urged that we join it. Despite outcries from the isolationists against the "League Court" or the "League Trap," the Senate approved our adherence to the World Court in 1926, though only after

PEACE MOURNS DEFEAT OF WORLD COURT
Kirby in the New York *World*, 1935

adding five life-preserver reservations. One of these proved unacceptable
to the League, so negotiations ended. After another futile effort in the
Senate to secure ratification in 1935, the United States washed its hands
of the World Court.

Naval disarmament meanwhile urgently needed attention, for a race
in smaller craft not limited by the Washington Conference was going
merrily on—while Uncle Sam lagged far behind. Calvin Coolidge,
economy-minded, was eager to repeat the presumed success of Harding
at Washington. Hasty plans were finally completed for a three-power
conclave at Geneva, Switzerland, in 1927. But inadequate groundwork
was laid, and the conference broke up in complete futility after an unseemly quarrel between the Americans and the British over the size of
cruisers. Isolationists in the United States, embittered by all this bickering, were more determined than ever to plow a lonely furrow.

An irresistible tidal wave of public opinion had meanwhile been
welling up in America for what was known as "outlawry of war." The
conviction spread that if the quarreling nations would solemnly take the
pledge to forswear war as an instrument of national policy, swords could
be beaten into plowshares. Coolidge's Secretary of State, Frank B. Kel-

logg, who later won the Nobel Peace Prize for his role, was lukewarm about the whole idea. After petitions bearing more than two million sig- natures had poured in on Washington, he signed with the French foreign minister in 1928 the famed Kellogg-Briand Pact. Better known as the Pact of Paris, it was ultimately ratified by sixty-two nations, including all the major powers.

The new piece of parchment was misleading in the extreme. Al- though outlawing war as an instrument of national policy, it permitted defensive war. And what scheming aggressor could not rig up the excuse of self-defense? Lacking both muscles and teeth, the pact was branded by one critic "an international kiss." The Senate nevertheless approved it by an overwhelming margin. One unfortunate effect was to lull the American people into a false sense of security—a state of mind that found an outlet in the ostrich-like isolationism and neutralism of the 1930's. As events turned out, the new pact did not abolish war. It merely abolished, in some instances, formal declarations of war.

First Blushes of Good Neighborism

The United States, despite the current anti-war sentiment, was reluc- tantly forced to adopt warlike measures in Latin America. Disorders in Nicaragua, perilously close to the Panama Canal jugular vein, had jeop- ardized American lives and property, and in 1927 President Coolidge felt compelled to dispatch over 5000 troops to this troubled banana land. His political foes, decrying mailed-fist tactics, accused him of waging a "private war," while critics south of the Rio Grande loudly assailed *Yanqui* imperialism.

Mexican friction, a persistent heritage from the days of Woodrow Wilson, continued over oil. The government in Mexico City was attempt- ing to wrest from American petroleum companies the private properties which, by the new constitution of 1917, were now legally vested in the Mexican nation. Relations between the two neighbor republics deterio- rated to an alarming degree.

Then the dark clouds rather suddenly began to lift. In 1927, Coolidge had the happy inspiration to send down to Mexico as an amateur am- bassador his old Amherst College classmate, Dwight W. Morrow, a Wall Street banker. By a combination of tact and charm, Morrow succeeded where others had failed. He was conspicuously aided by the good-will tour of aviator Charles A. Lindbergh, hero-conqueror of the Atlantic, who on this trip met his future bride, Morrow's daughter. So successful was Lindbergh as "Ambassador of the Air" that one American newspaper suggested as a new variant of an old floral theme: "Say it with fliers."

Under such happy auspices, Morrow finally worked out a temporarily acceptable compromise. The American oil companies were permitted to retain the rights they had secured prior to the constitution of 1917, but not those obtained later. Thus the Coolidge years ended with a bright new day dawning in relations with Latin America.

Farm Boy vs. City Slicker

Poker-faced Calvin Coolidge, the popular prosperity President, could probably have won renomination and re-election in 1928 with relative ease. But the close-mouthed "Sphinx of the Potomac" bowed himself out of the race—or apparently did—when he tersely stated: "I do not choose to run for President in 1928."

The logical successor to Coolidge was Secretary of Commerce Herbert C. Hoover, an orphan from an Iowa farm. Already a living legend as a result of his spectacular work in Belgian relief and wartime food conservation, the "Boy Wonder" had done wonders with the Department of Commerce. Never yet elected to a public office, he was not popular with the professional politicians, to whom he was an interloping "Herbie come lately." But he was immensely popular with the masses, who asked, "Who but Hoover?" The object of their devotion was nominated by the Republican convention in Kansas City on the first ballot. The platform clucked contentedly over prosperity and the tariff, and promised enforcement of the unenforceable prohibition amendment.

The most conspicuous Democratic contender was Alfred E. Smith, four-time governor of New York. An engaging, smiling, wisecracking personality, he had proved himself to be both an outstanding liberal leader and a phenomenal vote-getter, especially with the working classes.

But Smith suffered from fatal political handicaps. He was wet—outspokenly and drippingly wet—at a time when the country was not yet ready to abandon the "noble experiment." He seemed not quite "one hundred percent American," for though both parents were native New Yorkers, his mother's parents had been born in Ireland. He was a Roman Catholic—and no Catholic had yet been elected President. His formal education had ended with a Catholic parochial school. Sprung from the sidewalks of New York City, "Newsboy Al" was also an alumnus of the Fulton Fish Market, with an informal F.F.M. degree. He was also a political protege, though personally honest, of unsavory Tammany Hall.

Governor Smith was the top-heavy favorite when the Democrats met in Houston, Texas, late in June, 1928. Franklin D. Roosevelt of New York, now polio-crippled, eloquently nominated his good friend "Al," whom he hailed as "the Happy Warrior." The Southern wing of the Democratic party—dry, rural, and Protestant—struggled vainly against the wet, urban, Catholic contender. But Smith ran away with the nomination on the first ballot.

The Democrats at Houston awkwardly presented their wet candidate with a dry platform. Smith, undaunted, made a valiant attempt to carry alcohol on both shoulders. He sent a telegram to the convention promising to enforce the dry Volstead Act, but declaring that he would work for its moistening in accord with states' rights.

Mudslingers of 1928

Radio had now come to be an important vote-getting device, but it helped Hoover more than Smith. The ex-fish-peddler, jauntily sporting a brown derby and a long cigar, had more personal sparkle, but he could not project it through the microphone. Many voters were repelled by his East-side pronunciation ("rahdeeo" for "radio"), by his free-and-easy manner, and by his breezy, off-the-cuff speeches.

Iowa-born Herbert Hoover, with his double-breasted dignity, inspired solid confidence. He came out of the microphone better than he went in. Though rather dull and monotonous, he sounded grass-rootish and statesmanlike. Decrying un-American "socialism" and preaching "rugged individualism," he played up the benefits of Republican prosperity. His speech of acceptance smugly proclaimed, "The poorhouse is vanishing from among us." Republican campaigners echoed this sentiment, and their sloganeers, recalling the full dinner pail, proclaimed that a victory for Hoover would bring "A Chicken in Every Pot, a Car in Every Garage." (This later became "Two families in every garage.")

As bands blared Smith's theme song, "The Sidewalks of New York," the campaign sank into the sewers below the sidewalks. Despite the best efforts of Hoover and Smith, below-the-belt tactics were employed to a disgusting degree by lower-level campaigners. Religious bigotry raised its hideous head over Smith's Catholicism. An irresponsible whispering campaign claimed that "A Vote for Al Smith Is a Vote for the Pope," and

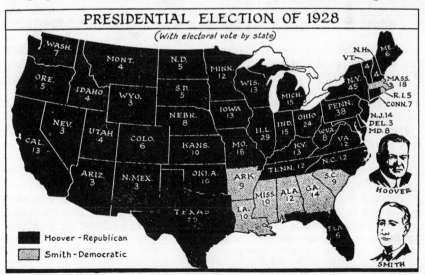

PRESIDENTIAL ELECTION OF 1928
(With electoral vote by state)

Hoover – Republican
Smith – Democratic

that the White House, under Smith, would become a branch of the Vatican. Hoover's attempts to quash such "smears" were in vain.

The proverbially Solid South—"one hundred percent American" and a stronghold of Protestant Ku Klux Klanism—shied away from Al Smith. It might have accepted a Catholic, or a wet, or the descendant of Irish grandparents, or an urbanite. But a mixture of Catholicism, wettism, and foreignism brewed on the sidewalks of New York was too bitter a dose for Southern stomachs. Smith's theme song was a constant and rasping reminder that his upbringing had not been convincingly American.

Hoover triumphed in a landslide. He bagged 21,391,381 popular votes to 15,016,443 for his embittered opponent, while rolling up an electoral count of 444 to 87. A huge Republican majority was returned to the House of Representatives. Tens of thousands of dry Southern Democrats —"Hoovercrats"—rebelled against Smith, and Hoover proved to be the first Republican candidate in forty-eight years, except for Harding's Tennessee victory in 1920, to carry a state that had seceded. He swept five states of the former Confederacy, as well as all the Border States.

Four "P's" presumably accounted mainly for Hoover's victory: personal prestige, prosperity, prohibition, and Protestantism. The satisfaction of the country with prosperity was reflected in the dwindling of the third-party protest vote. The strength of all such groups combined dropped from 4,978,689 in 1924, to a mere 337,125 in 1928.

It so happened that 1928 was a "Republican year." The Democrats probably would have lost with any nominee—even a polished Protestant of English stock, college-bred, farm-domiciled, bone-dry, Boston-accented, and descended from old Plymouth Rock.

SELECT READINGS

A lucid overview is J. D. HICKS, *Republican Ascendancy, 1921–1933* (1960) [paperback]. See also books by Faulkner, Sullivan, Allen, Slosson, and Soule for the previous chapter. Biographies of Coolidge are C. M. FUESS, *Calvin Coolidge* (1940) and W. A. WHITE's cynical *A Puritan in Babylon* (1938). See also MARVIN BARRETT, *The Jazz Age* (1959) and G. H. KNOLES, *The Jazz Age Revisited* (1955) [paperback]. On culture, consult R. S. and H. M. LYND's classic *Middletown* (1929) and *Middletown in Transition* (1937), [both paperback] Prohibition is handled in ANDREW SINCLAIR, *Prohibition* (1962) [paperback] and CHARLES MERZ, *The Dry Decade* (1931); see also J. H. LYLE, *The Dry and Lawless Years* (1960). Revealing on the Scopes trial are RAY GINGER, *Six Days or Forever?* (1958) [paperback] and L. W. LEVINE, *Defender of the Faith* [Bryan] (1965). Foreign policy is treated in L. E. ELLIS, *Frank B. Kellogg and American Foreign Relations, 1925–1929* (1961); R. H. FERRELL, *Peace in Their Time: The Origins of the Kellogg-Briand Pact* (1952); and J. C. VINSON, *William E. Borah and the Outlawry of War* (1957). On the 1928 election consult E. A. MOORE, *A Catholic Runs for President* (1956); OSCAR HANDLIN, *Al Smith and His America* (1958) [paperback]; and Smith's colorful autobiography, *Up to Now* (1929). Also *Harvard Guide*, Pt. VI.

41

Hoover and the Onset of the Depression

---

*Any party which takes credit for the rain must not be surprised
if its opponents blame it for the drought.*

DWIGHT W. MORROW, 1930

The Great Engineer in Politics

ROUND-FACED Herbert C. Hoover, a living example of the American
success-story tradition, was an intriguing mixture of two centuries. As a
poor boy who had worked his way through Stanford University, he had
absorbed the 19th-Century copybook maxims of industry, thrift, and self-
reliance. As a fabulously successful mining engineer, he had adopted to
the nth degree the efficiency-expertism of the 20th Century. Yet in his
thinking, as well as in his dignified reserve and painfully high starched
collar, he reminded one of William McKinley.

Even before entering the White House, Hoover had become world-
famous as "the Great Humanitarian." No President had yet entered office
with more international renown; certainly none had ever traveled abroad
more extensively. "Sir Herbert Hoover" he was called by those who
sneered at his protracted residence as an engineer under the British flag.
Yet long years of self-imposed exile had not weakened his grass-roots
Americanism or his determination, abundantly supported by national
tradition, to avoid foreign entanglements.

Hoover was a far cry from the ordinary back-slapping politician.
Though a citizen of the world and loaded down with international honors, he was shy, standoffish, and stiff. Personally colorless, he had been
accustomed during much of his life to giving orders to subordinates and
not to soliciting votes. Never before elected to public office, he was thin-
skinned in the face of criticism, and he did not adapt himself readily to
the necessary give-and-take of political accommodation. His real power
lay in his integrity, his humanitarianism, his passion for assembling the
facts, his efficiency, his talents for administration, and his ability to inspire loyalty in his close associates.

As befitted our newly mechanized civilization, Hoover was the ideal businessman's President. A wealthy man in his own right, he found that his conservative instincts recoiled from anything suggesting socialism, paternalism, or "planned economy."

The Cabinet, which reflected Hoover's innate conservatism, carried on unbroken the Big Industry tradition of Harding and Coolidge. Aging Andrew W. Mellon was kept on in the Treasury Department, partly to

"FINE OPPORTUNITY FOR A MODERN ENGINEER"
Darling in the Des Moines *Register*, 1929

retain the confidence of the business world. The regular Cabinet was supplemented by a group of Hoover's more vigorous intimates, who would occasionally meet and toss around a medicine ball—hence "the Medicine Ball Cabinet."

Bootleggers and Kidnappers

President Hoover was a darling of the drys. He had referred to prohibition in 1928 as a "far-reaching" "experiment, noble in motive"—hence the misleadingly telescoped "noble experiment." Yet noble though its purposes might be, prohibition was sinking to the ignoble level of lawlessness and gangsterism.

Early in his administration Hoover attempted to grapple with the liquor problem by appointing the Wickersham investigating commission. This group of eleven prominent citizens, after two years of probing, submitted a report in 1931 that was a masterpiece of contradiction. A majority of the members reported that all was not going well, but the commission as a whole recommended that the experiment be continued, with modifications. A writer in a New York newspaper poked fun at the inability of this group to liquidate the liquor problem:

> Prohibition is an awful flop.
>   We like it.
> It can't stop what it's meant to stop.
>   We like it.
> It's left a trail of graft and slime,
> It's filled our land with vice and crime,
> It don't prohibit worth a dime,
>   Nevertheless we're for it.

The lawlessness spawned by prohibition and bootlegging manifested itself further in the "snatch racket"—or kidnapping for ransom. In the early 1930's alone there were several hundred notorious cases. The entire nation was inexpressibly shocked in 1932, when the infant son of aviator-hero Colonel Charles A. Lindbergh was kidnapped and killed in New Jersey. An aroused public opinion caused Congress in 1932 to pass the so-called Lindbergh Law (modified in 1934), making interstate abduction in certain circumstances a death-penalty offense. Gradually "snatching" tapered off, owing largely to the vigilance of the Federal Bureau of Investigation (F.B.I.), under J. Edgar Hoover.

Favors for Farmers

The prosperity of the late 1920's smiled broadly as the Hoover years began. Soaring stocks on the bull market continued to defy the laws of financial gravitation. But two immense groups of citizens were not sharing proportionately in the riches flowing from the national horn of plenty: the unorganized wage earners and especially the disorganized farmers.

The Hoover administration, somewhat contrary to its philosophy of hands-off individualism, was forced to respond to the outcry of the farmers with legislative aspirin. The Agricultural Marketing Act, passed by Congress in June, 1929, was designed to help the farmers help themselves, largely through producers' cooperatives. This law set up a Federal Farm Board, with a revolving fund of half a billion dollars at its disposal. The money was lent generously to farm organizations seeking to buy, sell, and store agricultural surpluses. Four years later, in 1933, the Farm Board closed its books with the red figures showing a loss of $345,000,000, and with farm prices still dismayingly low.

In 1930 the Farm Board itself created both the Grain Stabilization Corporation and the Cotton Stabilization Corporation. The prime goal was to bolster sagging prices by buying up surpluses. But the two agencies were soon suffocated by an outpouring of farm produce, as wheat dropped to fifty-seven cents a bushel and cotton to five cents a pound.

The farmers had meanwhile clutched at the tariff as a possible straw to help keep their heads above the morass of starvation prices. During the recent presidential campaign, Hoover, the amateur in politics, had been stampeded into a politically unwise pledge. He had promised to call Congress into special session to consider agricultural relief and, specifically, to bring about "limited" changes in the tariff. These hope-giving assurances no doubt won many votes for Hoover in the Middle Western farm belt.

Tariff Tribulations

The Hawley-Smoot Tariff of 1930 followed the familiar pattern of legislative horse trading. It started out in the House as a fairly reasonable protective measure, designed to assist the farmers. But by the time the high-pressure lobbyists had pushed it through the Senate, about a thousand amendments had been added. The bill thus turned out to be the highest protective tariff in our peacetime history. The average duty on non-free goods was raised from 38.5%, as established by the Fordney-McCumber Act of 1922, to a towering 55.3%.

Countless protests against the Hawley-Smoot monstrosity poured in on Congress and the White House. The snowstorm of telegrams included

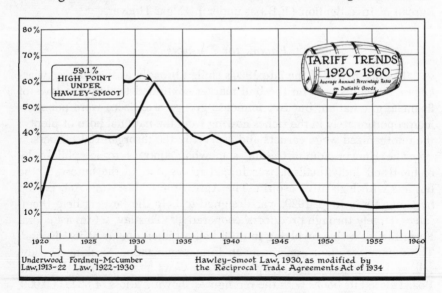

See pp. 264, 589 for earlier figures.

frantic pleas from American exporters worried about overseas markets and from bankers concerned about international payments. More than one thousand economists, mostly college professors, signed a manifesto urging Hoover to veto the bill. But the ultra-protectionist industrialists and many agricultural groups supported it.

Hoover was placed in an awkward spot. If he wielded the veto, he would disrupt his party and throw away the few desirable features of the bill. These included one for which he had resolutely fought: the 50% flexible tariff provision, to be administered by him upon recommendation of the Tariff Commission. He therefore signed the controversial bill, and defended it then and later with considerable vigor.

Critics of the new tariff marshaled formidable arguments. They charged that it would prove of no real benefit to the farmer, who, as an exporter of surpluses, did not really need protection. It would raise commodity prices at home and hurt export business abroad. Foreigners could not buy our goods unless they piled up dollars, and they could not amass dollars unless they could boost their goods over our frowning tariff walls. Hawley-Smootism, the argument further ran, would make even more difficult the payment of Allied war debts and further retard Europe's post-war recovery. Finally, the law would invite reprisals from those countries that suffered from our shortsighted selfishness.

To angered foreigners, the Hawley-Smoot Tariff was a blow below the trade belt. It seemed like a declaration of economic warfare on the entire outside world. It reversed a promising world-wide trend toward reasonable tariffs. It plunged both the United States and other nations deeper into the terrible depression which had already begun. It increased international financial chaos, and forced the United States further into the bog of economic isolationism. And economic isolationism, both at home and abroad, was playing directly into the hands of a wild-eyed, loud-shouting German demagogue, Adolf Hitler.

The threatened reprisals came quickly. Canada, our next-door neighbor and best two-way customer, pushed up her customs duties on many articles from the United States. Scores of American factories moved into Canada to escape the new barriers. By the end of 1931, twenty-five foreign countries had taken active steps to retaliate against the Hawley-Smoot Tariff. American import and export trade, already languishing under the depression, suffered further losses.

Putting America on Tires

The Great Depression, which descended like a suffocating economic smog, was the overpowering perplexity of the 1930's. It grew basically out of the malfunctioning of America's enormous industrial and agricultural machine.

The vast New Industrial Revolution had slipped into high gear in the United States during the first two decades of the 20th Century. Putting out steel tentacles in every direction, it had changed the daily life of the people as that of no other generation had been changed. Machinery was the new messiah.

The automobile, of all the inventions of the era, left the deepest mark on the individual American. It became the nucleus of an amazing industrial mechanism, with its assembly-line methods and other mass-production techniques.

Americans adapted rather than invented the gasoline engine; Europeans can claim the original honor. By the 1890's a few daring American inventors and promoters, including Henry Ford and Ransom E. Olds (Oldsmobile), were developing the infant automotive industry. By 1910 there were sixty-nine companies, with a total annual production of 181,000 horseless vehicles. The early contraptions were neither speedy nor reliable. Many a stalled motorist, profanely cranking his balky car, had to endure the jeer "Get a horse" from the occupants of a Dobbin-drawn carriage.

An enormous industry sprang into being, as Detroit became the motor-car capital of America. The mechanized colossus owed much to the stop-watch efficiency techniques of Frederick W. Taylor, a prominent inventor, engineer, and tennis player, who sought to eliminate waste motion. His epitaph reads: "Father of Scientific Management."

The best-known of the new crop of industrial statesmen was Henry Ford, who more than any other man put America on rubber tires. His high and hideous Model T ("Tin Lizzie") was cheap, rugged, and reasonably reliable, though rough and clattering. The parts of Ford's "flivver" were highly standardized, but its behavior was so individualized that it became the butt of numberless jokes.

Lean and silent Henry Ford, who was said to have wheels in his head, erected an immense personal empire on the cornerstone of his mechanical genius, though his associates provided much of the organizational talent. Ill-educated, this multimillionaire mechanic was socially and culturally narrow; "History is bunk," he once testified. But he de-

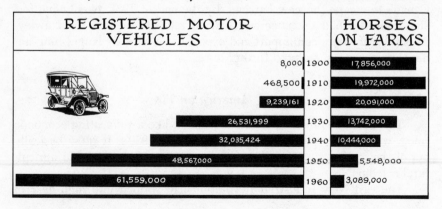

REGISTERED MOTOR VEHICLES		HORSES ON FARMS
8,000	1900	17,856,000
468,500	1910	19,972,000
9,239,161	1920	20,091,000
26,531,999	1930	13,742,000
32,035,424	1940	10,444,000
48,567,000	1950	5,548,000
61,559,000	1960	3,089,000

voted himself with one-track devotion to the gospel of standardization. After two early failures, he grasped and applied fully the techniques of assembly-line production—"Fordism." He is supposed to have remarked that the purchaser could have his automobile any color he desired—just as long as it was black. So economical were his methods that in the mid-1920's he was selling the Ford roadster for $260—well within the purse of a thrifty workingman.

The flood of Fords was phenomenal. In 1914 the "Automobile Wizard" turned out his five hundred thousandth Model T; in 1925 he was completing one gasoline buggy every ten seconds of the day. By 1930 his total had risen to 20,000,000, or, on a bumper-to-bumper basis, more than enough to encircle the globe. Long before this time Ford had become an American folk hero. A national newspaper and magazine poll conducted in 1923 revealed him to be the people's choice for the presidential nomination in 1924.

By 1929, when the Great Bull Market collapsed, there were 26,000,-000 motor vehicles registered in the United States. This figure, averaging one for every 4.9 Americans, represented far more than that for all the rest of the world put together.

The Gasoline Age

The impact of the self-propelled carriage on various aspects of American life was tremendous. A gigantic new industry emerged, dependent on steel, but displacing steel from its kingpin role. Employing directly or indirectly about six million men by 1930, it was a major prop of our national prosperity. Thousands of new jobs, moreover, were created by supporting industries. The lengthening list would include rubber, glass, and fabrics, to say nothing of thousands of service stations and garages. The American standard of living, responding to this infectious prosperity, rose to an enviable level.

New industries sprouted forth; older ones grew sickly. The oil business experienced a phenomenal development. Hundreds of new oil derricks mushroomed forth in California, Texas, and Oklahoma, as these states expanded wondrously and the new frontier became an industrial frontier. The once-feared railroad octopus, on the other hand, was hard hit by the competition of passenger cars, buses, and trucks. The age-old story was repeated: one industry's gains were another industry's pains.

Other impacts were widely felt. The speedy marketing of perishable foodstuffs, such as fresh fruits, was accelerated. The new prosperity enriched outlying farms, as city dwellers were provided with produce at attractive prices. Countless new roads ribboned out to meet the demand of the American motorist for smoother and faster highways, often paid for by taxes on gasoline. The Era of Mud ended as the nation made haste to construct the finest network of hard-surfaced roadways in the world.

Lured by new seductiveness in advertising, and encouraged by the perfecting of installment-plan buying, countless Americans with short purses acquired the habit of riding as they paid.

The zooming motor car was an agent of social change. At first a luxury, it rapidly became a necessity. Essentially a device for needed transportation, it soon developed into a badge of freedom and equality—a necessary prop for self-respect. Leisure hours could now be spent more pleasurably, and tens of thousands of cooped-up souls responded to the call of the open road on joyriding vacations. Women were further freed

A FAREWELL TO THE HORSE AS EARLY AS 1899
Davenport in the New York *Journal*

from clinging-vine dependence on males. Isolation among the sections was likewise broken down, and the less attractive states lost population at an alarming rate. We were becoming a nation of nomads.

Other social consequences of the automobile left a deep imprint. The auto bus made possible the consolidation of schools, and to some extent of churches. The trend toward hive-like urbanization was partially slowed. City workers could now live in the suburbs and commute by motor car or bus to railroad stations, there to catch the 7:52 for work.

The demon machine, on the other hand, exacted a terrible toll by catering to the American mania for speed. Citizens were becoming statistics. Not counting the hundreds of thousands of injured and crippled, the one millionth American had died in a motor accident by 1951—a figure representing more than all those killed on all the battlefields of all our wars to date. "The public be rammed" seemed to be the motto of the new age.

The virtuous old home life partially broke down as joyriders of all ages forsook the ancestral hearth for the wide open spaces. The morals of flaming youth sagged correspondingly—at least in the judgment of their elders. Even the disgraceful crime waves of the 1920's and 1930's were partly stimulated by the motor car, for gangsters could now make quick getaways.

Yet no sane American would plead for a return of the old horse and buggy. Life might be cut short on the highways, but the automobile brought its satisfactions and telescoped more pleasure and excitement into a shorter period than ever before.

Man Takes to the Air

The gasoline engine also provided the power which enabled man to fulfill his age-old dream of sprouting wings. After near-successful experiments by others with heavier-than-air craft, the Wright brothers, Orville and Wilbur, performed "the Miracle at Kitty Hawk," North Carolina. On a historic day—December 17, 1903—Orville Wright took aloft a feebly engined plane that stayed air-borne for 12 seconds and 120 feet. The fateful air age was thus launched by two obscure bicycle repairmen.

The world slowly shrank as aviation got off the ground. The public was made increasingly air-minded by unsung heroes—often martyrs—who appeared as stunt flyers at fairs and other public gatherings. Airplanes —"flying coffins"—were used with marked success for various purposes during the Great War of 1914–1918. Shortly thereafter private companies began to operate passenger lines with air-mail contracts, which were in effect a subsidy from Washington. The first transcontinental air-mail route was established from New York to San Francisco in 1920.

In 1927 modest Charles A. Lindbergh, the so-called "Flyin' Fool," electrified the world by the first solo west-to-east conquest of the Atlantic. Seeking a prize of $25,000, the lanky stunt flyer courageously piloted his single-engined plane, "The Spirit of St. Louis," from New York to Paris in a grueling 33 hours and 39 minutes.

The American people were swept off their feet. Fed up with the cynicism and debunking of the Jazz Age, they found in this wholesome and handsome youth a genuine hero. They clasped the fluttering "Lone Eagle" to their hearts much more eagerly than the bashful young man desired. In the words of Angela Morgan:

Lad, you took the soul of me
That long had lain despairing,
Sent me Heaven-faring,
Gave me wings again.°

"Lucky Lindy" received an uproarious welcome in the "hero canyon" of lower Broadway, as 1800 tons of ticker tape, shredded telephone directories, and other improvised confetti showered upon him. Lindbergh's signal achievement—it was more than a "stunt"—did much to dramatize and popularize flying, while giving a strong boost to the infant aviation industry.

The impact of the airship was tremendous. It provided the soaring American spirit with yet another dimension. At the same time, it gave birth to a huge new industry. Unfortunately, the accident rate in the early stages of aviation was frighteningly high, though hardly more so than on the early railroads. But by the 1930's and 1940's, travel by air on regularly scheduled air lines was markedly safer than on our overcrowded highways.

The tempo of our already breathless civilization was increased by man's new wings. The floundering railroad received another sharp setback through the loss of passengers and mail. A lethal new weapon was given to the gods of war, and with the coming of city-busting aerial bombs men could well debate whether the conquest of air was a blessing or a curse. The wide Atlantic was shriveling to about the size of the Aegean Sea in the days of Socrates, and isolation behind ocean moats was becoming a bygone dream.

A Nation of Dial-Turners

The speed of the airplane was far eclipsed by the speed of radio waves. Guglielmo Marconi, an Italian, invented wireless telegraphy in the 1890's, and his brain child was used for long-range communication during World War I.

The next spectacular step was the voice-carrying radio, a triumph of many minds. A red-letter day was posted in November, 1920, when the infant Pittsburgh station KDKA broadcast the news of the Harding landslide. Later miracles were achieved in trans-Atlantic wireless photographs, radio telephones, and television. In harmony with American free enterprise, radio programs were generally sustained by bothersome "commercials," as contrasted with the drabber government-owned systems of countries like Great Britain.

The radio, like other marvelous inventions, not only created a new industry, but added deeper richness to the fabric of American life. More joy was given to leisure hours, and many children who had been lured

° "Lindbergh," in *The Spirit of St. Louis,* ed. Charles Vale, (George H. Doran Company, 1927).

from the fireside by the automobile were brought back by the radio. The nation was better knit together. Various sections heard Americans with standardized accents, and countless millions "tuned in" on perennial comedy favorites like "Amos 'n' Andy." Advertising was further perfected as an art.

Educationally and culturally, the radio made an impressive contribution. Sports were further stimulated. Politicians had to adjust their speaking techniques to the new medium, and millions rather than thousands of voters heard their pleas. A host of listeners swallowed the gospel of their favorite newscaster, or were even ringside participants in world-shaking events. Finally, the musical taste of our people was distinctly elevated, as the strains of famous artists and symphony orchestras were beamed into their homes.

Filmland Fantasies

The flickering movie was the contrivance of numerous geniuses, including Thomas A. Edison. As early as the 1890's this novel contraption, though still in crude form, had attained some popularity in the naughty peep-show penny arcades. The real birth of the moving picture came in 1903, when the first story sequence reached the screen. This breathless melodrama—"The Great Train Robbery"—was featured in the five-cents-admission theaters, popularly called "nickelodeons."

A fascinating industry was thus inaugurated. Hollywood, in southern California, quickly became the movie capital of the world, for it enjoyed a maximum of sunshine and other advantages. Early producers went in heavily for nudity and heavy-lidded female vampires ("vamps"), and an outraged public forced the screen magnates to set up their own rigorous code of censorship. The motion picture really came into its own during the World War of 1917–1918, when it was used as an engine of anti-German propaganda. Specially prepared "hang the Kaiser" films aided powerfully in selling war bonds and in boosting morale.

A new era began in 1927 with the success of the first "talkie"—"The Jazz Singer," starring Al Jolson in blackface. The age of the "silents" was ushered out as theaters everywhere were "wired for sound." By 1926 reasonably satisfactory colored films were being produced.

The movies eclipsed all other new forms of amusement in the phenomenal growth of their popularity. Tens of thousands of actors and "extras" were employed in the cardboard cities behind Hollywood's high wooden fences, to say nothing of additional thousands engaged in exhibiting the films and selling popcorn. Movie "stars" of the first pulchritude commanded much larger salaries than the President of the United States, in some cases as much as $100,000 for a single picture. Many actors and actresses were far more widely known than most of our statesmen.

The "movie habit" rapidly created a nation of "cinemaniacs." By

1930 weekly admissions totaled 100,000,000—a large number of them representing "repeaters"—in a population of 122,775,000. Many of the movie-goers were openmouthed children, much of whose education, not all of it wholesome, was derived from this new type of textbook.

Other social impacts of the silver screen were incalculable. Attendance at movie "palaces" provided an escape from drab reality, and filmland became the standard for taste, styles, songs, and morals. Newsreels, travelogues, and other informative "shorts" offered infinite possibilities for education, but they constituted only a tiny part of the total offering. Two by-products of the industry were the cheap movie magazine and the no less cheap keyhole commentator, both unduly concerned with the foibles and "sex-capades" of the "stars."

Nor did the influence of the moving picture end here. It almost exterminated vaudeville, and robbed the footlighted theater of much of its patronage. It no doubt hurt attendance at religious services. Like the radio and the motor car, it contributed to the further standardization of America, for the mass of the people idolized the same actors and heard the same "hit" tunes. Hollywood dominated not only the domestic but the foreign movie market, and regrettably provided potent anti-American propaganda. There was an unwholesome overemphasis on the idle rich, the plush boudoir, the glowering gangster, and the quick-shooting cattle rustler.

Riches to Rags

When Herbert Hoover confidently took the presidential oath, on March 4, 1929, there were few black spots in the economic picture. One notable exception was the debt-blanketed farm belt. The American productive colossus—stimulated by the automobile, radio, movie, and other new industries—was roaring along at a dizzy speed. Few men sensed that it might smother its own fires by pouring out too much.

The speculative bubble was actually near the bursting point. The stock market continued to spiral upward and create a fool's paradise of paper profits, despite Hoover's early but fruitless efforts to curb speculation through the Federal Reserve Board. A few prophets of disaster were bold enough to raise warning voices, but they were drowned out by the mad chatter of the ticker-tape machine.

The catastrophic crash came in October, 1929. It was partially triggered by the British, who raised their interest rates in an effort to bring back capital that had been lured abroad by American investments. Foreign investors and wary domestic speculators began to unload their stocks, and an orgy of desperate selling followed. Tensions built up to the panicky "Black Tuesday" of October 29, 1929, when 16,410,030 shares of stocks were sold in a save-who-may scramble. Wall Street became a wailing wall.

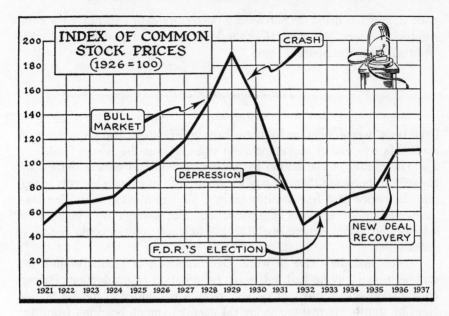

The losses, even in blue-chip securities, were fantastic. By the end of 1929—two months after the initial crash—stockholders had lost forty billion dollars in paper values, or more than the total cost of World War I to the United States. Typical prices of stocks per share were:

	Adjusted High Price Sept. 3, 1929	Low Price Nov. 13, 1929
American Can	$181⅞	$ 86
General Electric	396¼	168⅛
Montgomery Ward	137⅞	49¼

The stock-market collapse heralded a business depression, at home and abroad, which was the most prolonged and devastating in American or world experience. By the end of 1930 about six or seven million workers in the United States were jobless; two years later the figure had doubled. Unnumbered hungry and despairing men wearily walked pavements in search of non-existent jobs. Where employees were not discharged, wages and salaries were slashed.

The misery and gloom were incalculable, as forests of dead chimneys were silhouetted against the sky. Over five thousand banks collapsed in the first three years of the depression, carrying down with them the life savings of tens of thousands of widows and retired citizens. Countless thousands of honest, hard-working people lost their homes and farms to the forecloser's hammer. Bread lines formed, soup kitchens dispensed food, and at one time apple sellers stood shivering on street corners trying to peddle their wares. Foreign trade withered away, for the world-wide depression dried up purchasing power. As cash registers grew cob-webbed, the song "My God, How the Money Rolls In" was replaced with "Brother, Can You Spare a Dime?"

The Plague of Plenty

What caused the Great Depression? The basic explanation seems to have been overproduction by both farm and factory. The depression of the 1930's was one of abundance, not want. It was the "Great Glut."

The ability of the nation to produce goods had clearly outrun its capacity to consume them or pay for them. Too much income was going into the hands of a few wealthy people, who reinvested it in new fac-tories and other agencies of production. Not enough was going into salaries and wages, where revitalizing purchasing power could be more quickly felt.

Other maladies were at work. Overexpansion of credit through in-stallment-plan buying had led to overstimulation of production. Paying on so-called easy terms had caused many a consumer to plunge in be-yond his depth. Normal technological unemployment, resulting from the introduction of new labor-saving machines, had also added its burden to the abnormal unemployment of the Great Depression.

The already bleak picture was further darkened by economic anemia abroad. Britain and the Continent had never fully recovered from the upheaval of World War I. The depression in America was given a fur-ther downward push by a chain-reaction financial collapse in Europe, following the failure in 1931 of a prominent Vienna banking house. The drying up of international trade, moreover, had been hastened by the shortsighted Hawley-Smoot Tariff of 1930. European uncertainties over reparations, war debts, and defaults on loans owed to us caused tensions that reacted unfavorably on the United States. Many of these conditions had been created or worsened by our own narrow-visioned policies, but it was now too late to unscramble the omelet.

As if man-made disasters were not enough, a terrible drought scorched the Mississippi Valley in 1930. Thousands of farms were sold at auction for taxes, though in many cases kind neighbors would intimi-date prospective buyers, bid one cent, and return the property to its original owner. Farm tenancy or rental—a species of peonage—was spread-ing at an alarming rate.

By 1930 the depression had become a national calamity. Through no fault of their own, a host of industrious citizens had lost everything. They wanted to work—but there was no work. The blighting effect of all this despair on the American spirit was incalculable and long-lasting. It did things to our souls. Hitherto we had grappled with Indians, trees, stones, and other physical obstacles. But the depression was a baffling ghost that we could not grasp. Initiative and self-respect were stifled, as

SPREAD OF FARM TENANCY, 1910-1930

1910

Counties in which at least half
the land in farms was rented

1930

Counties in which at least half
the land in farms was rented

panhandlers begged for food. In extreme cases "ragged individualists" fought over the contents of garbage cans, or cooked their findings in old oil drums in shantytowns cynically named "Hoovervilles." The very foundations of America's social structure trembled.

Rugged Times for Rugged Individualists

Hoover's exalted reputation as a wonder-worker crashed hardly less dismally than the stock market. He doubtless would have shone in the prosperity-drenched Coolidge years, when he had foreseen the abolition of poverty and poorhouses. But damming the Great Depression was a task beyond his engineering talents.

The perplexed President was impaled on the horns of a cruel dilemma. As a humanitarian of philanthropic impulses, he was profoundly distressed by the widespread misery about him. Yet as a staunch individualist, deeply rooted in an earlier era of free enterprise, he shrank from the heresy of government handouts. Convinced that industry, thrift, and self-reliance were the virtues that had made America great, he feared that a government "dole" would weaken, perhaps destroy, the national fiber.

Hoover had deep faith in the efficiency of the industrial machine, which itself was undamaged by depression. He urged business to share some of the unemployment burden by not laying off men, and by reducing wages and hours in an effort to spread the available work among more people. From time to time he would attempt to encourage the public by issuing optimistic statements, which often were followed by a fresh decline. He was accused of saying, although he did not use these precise words, that prosperity was hovering—"Hoovering," critics jibed— just around the corner.

The President at length conceded that the deserving unemployed and hungry should be given a boost during the grave national emergency, but he insisted that such aid should come from local governmental agencies, and not from Washington. He would thus remain true to the American tradition of home responsibility and local self-rule. He would likewise reduce misrepresentation and graft, for the funds would be handed out by neighbors who knew intimately the needs of the recipients. And, with good reason, he sought to avoid the danger of having "pork barrel" politicians build up in Washington a huge, self-perpetuating bureaucracy, ultimately to become a tentacle of what was later cynically called "givernment."

But as the depression nightmare grew steadily worse, relief by local government agencies broke down. For one thing, the burden was overwhelming; for another, taxes could not be squeezed from moneyless people. The President was finally forced to turn reluctantly from his doctrine of log-cabin individualism and accept the new proposition that the welfare of the people in a nationwide depression is a direct concern of the national government.

Hoover at last worked out a compromise between the old hands-off policy and the direct dole then being used in England. He would assist the hard-pressed railroads, banks, and rural credit corporations, in the hope that if financial health were restored at the top of the economic pyramid, unemployment would be relieved at the bottom.

Partisan critics sneered at the "Great Humanitarian"—he who had fed the faraway Belgians but would not use federal funds to feed needy

"IT SEEMS THERE WASN'T ANY DEPRESSION AT ALL!"
Fitzpatrick in the St. Louis *Post-Dispatch*

Americans. Hostile commentators remarked that he was willing to lend government money to the big bankers, who allegedly had plunged the country into the mess. He would likewise lend money to agricultural organizations to feed pigs—but not people. Pigs, cynics noted, had no character to undermine.

Much of this condemnation was unfair. Though the continuance of widespread suffering seemed to belie the effectiveness of Hoover's measures, his efforts no doubt prevented a much more serious collapse than actually did occur. And his expenditures for relief, revolutionary for that day, paved the path for the enormous federal disbursements of his successor, Franklin D. Roosevelt.

Pioneering for the New Deal

President Hoover, in line with his "trickle down" philosophy, finally recommended that Congress grant immense sums for useful public works. Though at heart an anti-spender, he secured from Congress appropriations totaling two and one-quarter billion dollars for such projects. To alarmists, the Washington ship of state seemed in danger of sinking in a red-ink sea of unbalanced budgets and mounting debts.

The most imposing public enterprise was the gigantic Hoover Dam —originally called Boulder Dam—on the upper Colorado River. Voted by Congress in the days of Coolidge, it was begun in 1930 under Hoover and completed in 1936 under Roosevelt. It succeeded in creating a huge man-made lake for purposes of irrigation, flood control, and electric power.

But Hoover bitterly fought all schemes that he regarded as "socialistic." Notable among them was the Norris Muscle Shoals Bill, which foreshadowed the New Deal Tennessee Valley Authority. Hoover stoutly vetoed this measure, primarily because he was opposed to having the government sell electric power in competition with its own citizens in private companies.

Early in 1932 Congress, responding to Hoover's belated appeal, established the Reconstruction Finance Corporation (R.F.C.). With an initial working capital of half a billion dollars, this agency became a government lending bank. It was specifically designed to provide indirect relief by assisting insurance companies, banks, agricultural organizations, railroads, and even hard-pressed state and local governments. To preserve individualism, there would be no loans to individuals.

The "pump-priming" loans of the R.F.C. were no doubt of widespread benefit, though the organization was established many months too late for maximum usefulness. The projects that it supported were largely self-liquidating, and the government as a banker actually profited to the tune of many millions of dollars. Giant corporations so obviously benefited from this assistance that the R.F.C. was dubbed—rather unfairly— "the millionaires' dole." The irony is that the thrifty and individualistic Hoover had sponsored the project, though with reluctance, and that it actually had a strong New-Dealish flavor.

The Hoover administration also provided some indirect benefits for labor. After heated debate, Congress passed the Norris-La Guardia Anti-Injunction Act in 1932, and Hoover signed it. The measure outlawed "yellow dog" (anti-union) contracts, and expressly forbade the federal courts to issue injunctions to restrain strikes, boycotts, and peaceful picketing.

The truth is that Herbert Hoover, despite the storm of criticism directed against his "heartlessness," actually did inaugurate a significant new policy. In previous panics the masses had been forced to "sweat it out." Slow though Hoover was to abandon this 19th-Century philosophy, by the end of his term he had traveled a long way toward government assistance for masses of needy citizens—a road that Franklin D. Roosevelt was to take all the way.

Any commentator on Hoover's anti-depression measures should note that his woes were frequently increased by a hostile Congress. At critical times during his first two years, the Republican majority proved highly uncooperative. Friction worsened during his last two years. A depression-ridden electorate, rebelling in the Congressional elections of 1930, had so reduced the Republican majority that Democrats controlled the new House and almost controlled the Senate. Insurgent Republicans could—and did—combine with the opposition Democrats to harass Hoover. Some of the President's troubles were deliberately manufactured by Congressmen who, in his words, "played politics with human misery."

Routing the Bonus Army

Many veterans of World War I were numbered among the hard-hit victims of the depression. Industry had secured a "bonus"—though a dubious one—in the Hawley-Smoot Tariff. So the thoughts of the ex-"doughboys" naturally turned to what the government owed them for their services in 1917–1918, when they had been the "saviors" of democracy. A strong drive developed for the premature payment of the deferred bonus voted by Congress in 1924.

Hoover was icily unsympathetic to a bonus. As a sound-money man, he vigorously opposed all suggestions from pressure groups for further unbalancing the budget and inflating the currency. But a vote-conscious Congress, less worried about demands on the Treasury, proved more responsive. It passed a bill in 1931 enabling veterans to borrow up to 50% on their bonus (adjusted compensation) certificates, instead of 22%. This concession imposed an additional burden of cash payments on the Treasury, already in the red, of from one to two billion dollars. Hoover's emphatic veto was so much wasted ink.

Thousands of impoverished veterans were now prepared to move on to Washington, there to demand of Congress the immediate payment of their entire bonus. The "Bonus Expeditionary Forces," which mustered about twenty thousand souls, converged on the capital in the summer of 1932. The resourceful supplicants promptly set up unsanitary public camps and erected shacks on vacant lots. They thus created a menace to the public health, while attempting to intimidate Congress by their presence in force. After the pending bonus bill had failed in Congress by a narrow margin, Hoover arranged to pay the return fare of about six thousand bonus marchers. The rest refused to decamp, though ordered to do so.

Following riots that cost two lives, Hoover responded to the demands of the Washington authorities by ordering the army to evacuate the unwanted guests. A few of them were ex-convicts and Communist agitators. The eviction was carried out by General Douglas MacArthur with bayonets and tear gas, and with far more severity than Hoover had contemplated. A number of the ex-soldiers were injured as the torch was put to their pathetic shanties in the inglorious "Battle of Anacostia Flat."

This unfortunate episode brought additional condemnation to the once-popular Hoover, who by now was the most loudly booed man in the country. The Democrats, not content with his vulnerable record, used professional "smear" experts to drive him from office. Sneering remarks were heard to the effect that the "Great Engineer" had in a few months "ditched, drained, and damned the country." The existing panic was unfairly branded "the Hoover Depression." The truth is that Hoover had been oversold as a super-man—and the public reacted unfavorably when his magician's wand failed to produce rabbits.

The Diplomacy of Disarmament

As a Quaker and a world-famed humanitarian, Hoover embraced peace as the keynote of his foreign policy. He cooperated with the non-political activities of the League of Nations as fully as American public opinion would tolerate. Peace and disarmament were unusually popular themes in those depression days, partly because costly war preparations would further unbalance national budgets.

Arms limitation had a strong appeal to Hoover, whose efficient nature recoiled from the waste of war preparations. Much remained to be done. The Washington Conference of 1921–1922 had tabooed more big battleships and aircraft carriers, but the race was wide open in cruisers, destroyers, submarines, and other smaller craft. The American people, economy-minded and depression-ridden, were falling dismayingly behind in construction.

The multi-power Naval Conference of 1930, meeting with much fanfare in London, was hailed as one of the signal achievements of the Hoover years. Upper limits were placed not only on battleships and carriers but on the construction of smaller vessels. The United States was formally conceded parity with Britain in all categories of ships. The Japanese

The Naval Race 1922–1929

Warships Laid Down or Appropriated For

Japan	125
France	119
Italy	82
Britain	74
U. S.	11

were left with the small end of a 10–10–6 ratio in capital ships and heavy
cruisers. But they succeeded in raising the formula to 10–10–7 in light
cruisers and other auxiliary craft, while attaining parity in submarines.

Despite all the ballyhoo, the London Conference was only a paper
victory for disarmament. We did win naval parity with the British, but
to achieve it we would have to construct about a billion dollars' worth of
additional warships. Such a program could hardly be regarded as either
disarmament or economy, but the London Conference at least established
a ceiling. A tax-conscious America, during the apathetic 1930's, fell far
short of building the tonnage to which it was entitled.

The Debtors Default

The debt-reparations snarl, even more than armaments, felt the pressure of the global depression. American investors no longer had millions
to invest in European countries. Private loans from the United States to
Germany dried up; German reparations payments to the Allies consequently dried up. Allied debt payments to America were about to dry
up—thus ending the fantastic cycle of borrowing from America to pay
America. If Europe went completely to pot financially, the billions of
dollars in private American investments might be lost forever.

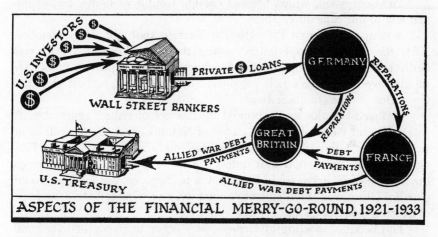

ASPECTS OF THE FINANCIAL MERRY-GO-ROUND, 1921-1933

In this critical hour—June, 1931—Hoover proposed a financial blood
transfusion in the form of a moratorium. It would provide a one-year suspension of war-debt payments, both principal and interest, to the United
States. The "Hoover holiday" was naturally acclaimed in the debt-cursed
European countries, but Hoover had some difficulty in "selling" the idea
to Congress. The feeling was general that once the one-year period of
grace had ended, the emphasis would be on the "more" in "more-
atorium." Finally, however, Congress gave its approval.

The debt crisis now came rapidly to a boil. In 1932 representatives of
the ex-Allied European powers met at Lausanne, in Switzerland, and

agreed to scale down Germany's reparations bill from the original $32,-000,000,000 to $714,000,000. The catch was that there would have to be a satisfactory Allied debt readjustment with Washington, and this in turn meant cancellation. But the American public—and Hoover—still strongly opposed cancellation; and Washington promptly rejected the scheme. To the bitter end we persistently argued that there was no connection between Allied debts and German reparations. But our saying so did not make it so.

The breathing-spell moratorium ended in 1932, but only six of the debtors put their cash on the counter. Five nations defaulted outright, including France, and by mid-1934 all the others had followed, except "honest little Finland." By this time we had our choice between cancellation and just not getting the money—and Washington chose the second course. Within a few years, as interest mounted, the original debt was larger than it had been when the payments started. In less than ten years the financial burdens of a new world war caused us to forget the defunct debt of the former one.

Warlords on the Loose

The depression, which brewed enough trouble at home, added immensely to our difficulties abroad.

A rampaging Japan stole the Far Eastern spotlight. In September, 1931, the Japanese imperialists, noting that the Western World was badly mired down, lunged into Manchuria. Alleging provocation, they rapidly overran China's rich province, and proceeded to bolt shut the Open Door in the conquered area.

Civilized peoples were stunned by this act of naked aggression. It was a flagrant violation of the League of Nations covenant, as well as of various other international agreements solemnly signed by Tokyo. Far-visioned observers feared that unless the major powers, acting through the League of Nations, could force Japan to disgorge, the League would perish. Failure would kill collective security, and wipe out the best hope of averting another global conflagration.

The League, meeting at Geneva, was eager to strengthen its hand by luring Uncle Sam into its camp. In response to an urgent invitation, an American representative for the first time sat, though unofficially, with the Council of the League during its discussions of the Manchurian crisis. An American also served on the firsthand investigating commission appointed by the League.

The intervention of the League availed nothing. Its commission of probers reported in 1932 that the Japanese incursion was unjustified. But this condemnation, instead of driving Japan out of Manchuria, merely drove Japan out of the League. Another nail was thus hammered into the coffin of collective security.

A large body of Americans, though by no means a majority, urged strong measures, ranging from boycotts to blockades. Undoubtedly a tight embargo by the League, backed by the United States, would have brought Japan sharply to book. But Hoover reflected the isolationist sentiments of most Americans, who wanted no part of the Far Eastern mess. One newspaper remarked that we did not "give a hoot in a rain barrel" about who controlled Manchuria.

The League was handicapped in taking two-fisted action by the non-membership of the United States. Washington flatly rebuffed initial attempts in 1931 to invite our cooperation in applying economic pressures. But Secretary of State Stimson, who was much more international-ist-minded than Hoover, indicated that we probably would not interfere with a League embargo. The next year Stimson was more eager to take vigorous steps, but Hoover cautiously restrained him.

Washington in the end decided to fire only paper bullets at the Japanese aggressors. The so-called Hoover-Stimson doctrine, proclaimed in 1932, declared that the United States would not recognize any territorial acquisitions achieved by force.

This verbal slap on the wrist from America did not deter the onward march of the Japanese militarists. Smarting under a Chinese boycott, they bombed Shanghai in 1932, with shocking losses to the civilians. Outraged Americans launched informal boycotts of Japanese goods, chiefly dime-store knickknacks. But there was no real sentiment for armed intervention among our depression-ridden people, the great majority of whom were isolation-inclined during the 1930's. President Hoover, who fully shared their views, believed that boycotts and embargoes spelled bayonets and bombs.

In a broad sense, collective security died and World War II was born in 1931 on the wind-swept plains of Manchuria. The League members had the economic and naval power to halt Japan, but lacked the courage to act. One reason—though not the only one—was that they could not count on our support. Even so, we came closer to stepping into the chill waters of internationalism than American prophets would have dared to predict in the early 1920's.

Bad Neighborism Becomes Good Neighborism

The coming of Hoover to the White House brought a more hopeful turn to relations with our southern neighbors. The new President was deeply interested in the colorful lands below the Rio Grande, and shortly after his election in 1928 he undertook a good-will tour of Latin America on an American battleship.

The world depression gave birth to a less aggressive attitude toward our weaker Latin neighbors. Following the stock-market collapse of 1929, our people had less money to invest abroad. As millions of dollars' worth of investments in Latin America went sour, many Yankees felt that they were more preyed upon than preying. Economic imperialism—so called—became much less popular in the United States than it had been in the Golden Twenties.

As an advocate of international good will, Hoover strove to abandon the interventionist twist given to the Monroe Doctrine by Theodore Roosevelt. In 1932 he negotiated a new treaty with the mulatto republic of Haiti, and this pact, later supplanted by an executive agreement, provided for the complete withdrawal of American bayonets by 1934. Further pleasing omens came early in 1933, when the last marines sailed away from Nicaragua after an almost continuous stay of twenty years.

Herbert Hoover, the Engineer in Politics, thus happily engineered the foundation stones of the "Good Neighbor" policy. Upon them rose an imposing edifice in the days of his successor, Franklin D. Roosevelt.

SELECT READINGS

Clear-cut introductions are J. D. HICKS, *Republican Ascendancy, 1921–1933* (1960) [paperback] and W. E. LEUCHTENBURG, *The Perils of Prosperity, 1914–1932* (1958) [paperback]. See also F. L. ALLEN's colorful *Since Yesterday* (1939) [paperback]; and the titles by Faulkner, Sullivan, and Soule for Chapter 39. Social and economic conditions are developed in DIXON WECTER, *The Age of the Great Depression, 1929–1941* (1948); G. V. SELDES, *The Years of the Locust* (1933) and BROADUS MITCHELL, *Depression Decade* (1947). A colorful account is ANDREW SINCLAIR, *Prohibition* (1962) [paperback]. A. M. SCHLESINGER, JR., *The Age of Roosevelt: The Crisis of the Old Order, 1919–1933* (1957) [paperback] is brilliantly unsympathetic toward Hoover. More favorable is H. G. WARREN, *Herbert Hoover and the Great Depression* (1959). Hoover's own memoirs are marred by excessive self-justification: *The Cabinet and the Presidency, 1920–1933* (1952) and *The Great Depression, 1929–1941* (1952).

On foreign affairs consult R. H. FERRELL, *American Diplomacy in the Great Depression* (1957); E. E. MORISON, *Turmoil and Tradition: A Study of the Life and Times of Henry L. Stimson* (1960) [paperback]; ARMIN RAPPAPORT, *Henry L. Stimson and Japan, 1931–1933* (1963); and DONALD M. DOZER, *Are We Good Neighbors? Three Decades of Inter-American Relations, 1930–1960* (1959). Also *Harvard Guide,* Pt. VI.

42

Franklin D. Roosevelt and the New Deal

This generation of Americans has a rendezvous with destiny.
FRANKLIN D. ROOSEVELT, 1936

A Politician in a Wheel Chair

THE VOTERS were in an ugly mood as the presidential campaign of 1932 neared. Countless factory chimneys remained ominously cold, while more than eleven million unemployed workers and their families sank ever deeper into the mire of poverty. The "chicken in every pot" of 1928 was seemingly being replaced by a discharge slip in every pay envelope.

Herbert Hoover, sick at heart, was renominated by the Republican convention in Chicago without undue enthusiasm. Not to run him again would be a suicidal confession of failure. The platform indulged in extravagant praise of Republican anti-depression policies, while half-heartedly promising to repeal national prohibition and return control of liquor to the states.

The rising star in the Democratic firmament was Governor Franklin Delano Roosevelt of New York, a fifth cousin of Theodore Roosevelt. Like the Rough Rider, he had been born to a wealthy New York family, had graduated from Harvard, had been elected as a kid-glove politician to the New York legislature, had served as governor of the Empire State, had been nominated for the Vice-Presidency (though not elected), and had served capably as Assistant Secretary of the Navy. Though both men were master politicians, adept with the colorful phrase, F.D.R. was suave and conciliatory, while T.R. was pugnacious and denunciatory.

Infantile paralysis, while putting steel braces on Franklin Roosevelt's legs, seemingly put steel into his soul. Until 1921, when the dread disease struck, young Roosevelt—tall, athletic, and as handsome as a Greek god—impressed observers as charming and witty yet at times supercilious and arrogant. But suffering humbled him and brought him down to the level of common clay. In courageously fighting his way back from complete helplessness to a hobbling mobility, he schooled himself in patience, tolerance, compassion, and strength of will.

Roosevelt's political appeal was amazing. His commanding presence and his golden speaking voice, despite a sophisticated accent, combined to make him the premier American orator of his generation. He could turn on charm in private conversations as one would turn on a water faucet. As a popular depression governor of New York, he had sponsored heavy state spending to relieve human suffering. Though favoring economy, he believed that money, rather than humanity, was expendable. He revealed a deep concern for the plight of the "forgotten man"—a phrase he used in a 1932 speech—although he was condemned by men of wealth as a "traitor to his class."

Roosevelt's extraordinary qualities of leadership were more apparent later than they were when the exuberant Democrats met in Chicago in June, 1932. Al Smith felt entitled to a second chance; and a beautiful friendship between the two men perished when he was pushed aside for Franklin Roosevelt, the choice of the convention on the fourth ballot. The Democratic platform came out more flat-footedly than the Republican for repeal of prohibition, assailed the so-called "Hoover depression," and promised not only a balanced budget but sweeping social and economic reforms.

The Gladiators of 1932

In the campaign that followed, Roosevelt assumed the offensive with a slashing attack on the Republican Old Dealers. In all, he traveled about 25,000 miles. He was especially eager to prove that he was not an invalid ("Roosevelt Is Robust"), and to display his magnificent torso and radiant personality to as many voters as possible.

Roosevelt consistently preached a New Deal for the "forgotten man," but he was annoyingly vague and somewhat contradictory. Many of his speeches were "ghost-written" by the so-called "Brains Trust," a small group of reform-minded intellectuals, predominantly young college professors, who, as a kind of Kitchen Cabinet, later authored much of the New Deal legislation. Roosevelt rashly promised a balanced budget and berated heavy Hooverian deficits, amid cries of "Throw the Spenders Out!" All this made ironical reading in later months.

The high spirits of the Democrats found vent in the rallying cry "Everything Will Be Rosy with Roosevelt," and in the catchy air "Happy Days Are Here Again." This theme song fitted F.D.R.'s indestructible smile, his jauntily angled cigarette holder, his breezy optimism, and his promises to do something even at the risk of bold experimentation.

Grim-faced Herbert Hoover remained at his desk in the White House, conscientiously battling the depression through short lunch hours and long working days and nights. Out on the firing line his supporters halfheartedly cried, "The Worst Is Past," "It Might Have Been Worse," "Prosperity Is Just around the Corner." Faint blushes of returning prosperity were plainly visible in the early months of the campaign, but these gradually faded as election day neared. Hoover never ceased to insist that the uncertainty and fear produced by Roosevelt's impending victory plunged the nation back into the morass of depression.

With the campaign going badly for the Republicans, a weary and despondent Hoover was persuaded to take to the stump. He stoutly reaffirmed his faith in the American system of free enterprise and individual initiative, and he gloomily predicted that if the Hawley-Smoot Tariff were repealed, the grass would grow "in the streets of a hundred cities." Such down-at-the-mouthism contrasted sharply with Roosevelt's tooth-flashing optimism.

The Humiliation of Hoover

Hoover had been swept into office on a landslide; he was swept out on one. The avalanche of votes totaled 22,821,857 for Roosevelt and 15,761,841 for Hoover; the electoral count stood at 472 to 59. The discredited President carried only six rock-ribbed Republican states.

The Great Depression unquestionably ruined the Republicans, for the electoral upheaval in 1932 seems to have been more anti-Hoover than pro-Roosevelt. The Democrats had only to harness the national grudge and let it pull them to victory over the much-booed incumbent. "A Vote for Roosevelt Is a Vote against Hoover," ran the saying. The overwhelming majority indicated an irresistible demand for a change: *a* new deal rather than *the* New Deal, for the latter was only a gleam in the eyes of its sponsors. Any upstanding Democratic candidate probably could have won.

The pre-inauguration "lame duck" period now ground slowly to an end. Hoover, though defeated and repudiated, continued to be President for four long months, until March 4, 1933. But he was helpless to embark upon any long-range policies without the cooperation of Roosevelt—and the victorious President-elect was curiously uncooperative. Hoover at length succeeded in arranging two meetings with him to discuss the war-debt muddle. But Roosevelt, who airily remarked to the press, "It's not my baby," was loath to assume responsibility without legal authority. Hoover, in fact, seems to have been trying to bind him to an anti-inflationary policy that would have made impossible some of the later New Deal experiments.

With Washington deadlocked, the vast and vaunted American economic machine clanked to a virtual halt. Banks were locking their doors all over the nation, as people nervously stuffed paper money under their mattresses. The Hooverites, then and later, accused Roosevelt of deliberately permitting the depression to worsen, so that he could emerge the more spectacularly as a savior.

F.D.R. and the Three R's

Great crises often call forth gifted leaders; and the hand of destiny tapped Roosevelt on the shoulder. On a dreary inauguration day, March 4, 1933, his resonant voice, broadcast nationally from a bulletproof stand, provided the American people with electrifying new hope. He denounced the "money changers" who had brought on the calamity, and declared that the government must wage war on the Great Depression as it would wage war on an armed foe. His clarion note was: "Let me assert my firm belief that the only thing we have to fear is fear itself."

"IT'S BEEN IN THE FAMILY FOR A LONG TIME"
Gale in the Los Angeles *Times,* 1933

Roosevelt moved decisively. Now that he had full responsibility, he boldly declared a nationwide banking holiday, March 6–10, 1933, preliminary to opening most of the banks on a sounder basis. He then summoned the overwhelmingly Democratic Congress into special session to cope with the national emergency. The members stayed at their task for the so-called "Hundred Days" (March 9–June 16, 1933), grinding out an unprecedented basketful of remedial legislation.

Roosevelt's New Deal program was sparked by three R's—relief, recovery, and reform. The short-range goals were relief and immediate recovery, especially in the first two years. The long-range goals were permanent recovery and reform of current abuses, particularly those that had produced the boom-and-bust catastrophe. The three-front objectives often overlapped and got in one another's way. But amid all the haste and topsy-turvyism, the gigantic New Deal program lurched forward.

Principal New Deal Acts During Hundred Days Congress, 1933

[ITEMS IN PARENTHESES INDICATE SECONDARY PURPOSES.]

Recovery	Relief	Reform
F.D.R. closes banks, March 6, 1933		
Emergency Banking Relief Act, March 9, 1933		
(Beer Act)	(Beer Act)	Beer and Wine Revenue Act, March 22, 1933
(CCC)	Unemployment Relief Act, March 31, 1933, creates Civilian Conservation Corps (CCC)	
F.D.R. orders gold surrender, April 5, 1933		
F.D.R. abandons gold standard, April 19, 1933		
(FERA)	Federal Emergency Relief Act, May 12, 1933, creates Federal Emergency Relief Administration (FERA)	
(AAA)	Agricultural Adjustment Act (AAA), May 12, 1933	
(TVA)	(TVA)	Tennessee Valley Authority Act (TVA), May 18, 1933
		Federal Securities Act, May 27, 1933
Gold-payment clause repealed, June 5, 1933		
(HOLC)	Home Owners' Refinancing Act, June 13, 1933, creates Home Owners' Loan Corporation (HOLC)	
National Industrial Recovery Act, June 16, 1933, creates National Recovery Administration (NRA), Public Works Administration (PWA)	(NRA; PWA)	(NRA)
(Glass-Steagall Act)	(Glass-Steagall Act)	Glass-Steagall Banking Reform Act, June 16, 1933, creates Federal Deposit Insurance Corporation

(For later New Deal measures, see p. 838.)

Firmly ensconced in the driver's seat, Roosevelt cracked the whip. Congress so fully shared the panicky feeling of the country that it was prepared to rubber-stamp bills drafted by White House advisers—measures that Roosevelt called "must legislation." More than that, Congress gave the President extraordinary blank-check powers: some of the laws that it passed expressly delegated legislative authority to the Chief Executive. One Senator remarked that if F.D.R. asked Congress "to commit suicide tomorrow, they'd do it."

Roosevelt was delighted to accept executive leadership, and Congress responded to it, although he did not always know precisely where he was going. He was inclined to do things by intuition—off the cuff. He was like the quarterback, as he put it, whose next play depends on the success of the previous play. The desperate mood of the action-starved public was such that movement, even in the wrong direction, seemed better than no movement at all.

The frantic Hundred Days Congress passed many essentials of the New Deal "three R's," though important long-range measures were added in later sessions. These reforms, already foreshadowed by the Democratic platform of 1932, were generally in keeping with the earlier Progressive–New Freedom tradition. Many of them were long overdue, sidetracked as they had been by World War I and the Old Guard reaction of the 1920's. The New Dealers, sooner or later, embraced such schemes as unemployment insurance, old-age insurance, minimum-wage regulations, and restrictions on child labor. Most of these forward-looking measures had already been adopted a generation or so earlier by the more enlightened nations of Western Europe. A few of them had been accepted on a limited basis by a sprinkling of the states, chiefly during the era of the Progressives.

Money and Banking

The banking collapse cried aloud for immediate action. Congress pulled itself together, and in an incredible eight hours had the Emergency Banking Relief Act of 1933 ready for Roosevelt's pen. The new law clothed the President with power to regulate banking transactions and foreign exchange, and to reopen solvent banks.

Roosevelt, the master showman, next turned to the radio to deliver the first of his famous "Fireside Chats." As some 35,000,000 people hung on his words, he gave assurances that it was now safer to keep money in a reopened bank than "under the mattress." Confidence returned with a gush, and the banks began to unlock their doors.

The Emergency or Hundred Days Congress buttressed public reliance on the banking system by enacting the memorable Glass-Steagall Banking Reform Act. This measure provided for the Federal Deposit Insurance Corporation, which insured individual deposits up to $5000

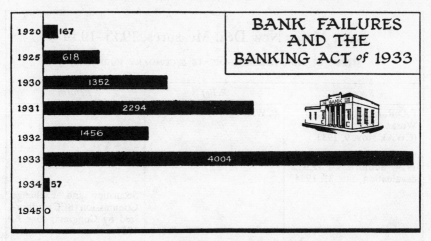

BANK FAILURES
AND THE
BANKING ACT of 1933

1920	167
1925	618
1930	1352
1931	2294
1932	1456
1933	4004
1934	57
1945	0

(later $10,000). Thus ended the disgraceful epidemic of bank failures, which dated back to the "wildcat" days of Andrew Jackson.

Roosevelt moved swiftly elsewhere on the financial front, seeking to protect the melting gold reserve and to prevent panicky hoarding. He ordered all private holdings of gold to be surrendered to the Treasury in exchange for paper currency, and then took the nation off the gold standard. The Emergency Congress responded to his recommendation by canceling the gold-payment clause in all contracts and authorizing repayment in paper money. A "managed currency" was well on its way.

Early in 1934 Roosevelt reduced the value of the gold content of the dollar to 59.06 cents, in accordance with authority granted by Congress. His theory was that this tinkering with the currency would stimulate business through controlled inflation. Prices did rise somewhat, but not in proportion to the change in the value of the currency. Alarmed conservatives, like the now "unhappy warrior" Al Smith, decried "the baloney dollar" and accused the government of robbing the people of forty cents on every dollar they owned. Actually, the purchasing power of the newly shrunken dollar was not substantially inferior to that of the old.

Jobs for the Jobless

The overwhelming unemployment problem, perhaps even more than banking, clamored for prompt remedial action. Roosevelt had no hesitancy about using federal money to assist the unemployed, and at the same time to "prime the pump" of industrial recovery. One has to pour a little water into a dry pump to start the flow.

The Hundred Days Congress responded to Roosevelt's spurs when it created the Civilian Conservation Corps (CCC)—an organization that proved to be perhaps the most popular of all the New Deal "alphabetical agencies." The law provided employment in fresh-air government camps for a total of about three million uniformed young men, many of whom

Later Major New Deal Measures, 1933–1939

[ITEMS IN PARENTHESES INDICATE SECONDARY PURPOSES.]

Recovery	Relief	Reform
F.D.R. establishes Civil Works Administration (CWA), Nov. 9, 1933	(CWA)	
Gold Reserve Act, Jan. 30, 1934, authorizes F.D.R.'s devaluation, Jan. 31, 1934		
		Securities and Exchange Commission (SEC) authorized by Congress, June 6, 1934
(Reciprocal Trade Agreements)	(Reciprocal Trade Agreements)	Reciprocal Trade Agreements Act, June 12, 1934
(FHA)	National Housing Act, June 28, 1934, authorizes Federal Housing Administration (FHA)	(FHA)
(Frazier-Lemke Act)	Frazier-Lemke Farm Bankruptcy Act, June 28, 1934	
(Resettlement Administration)	F.D.R. creates Resettlement Administration, April 30, 1935	
(WPA)	F.D.R. creates Works Progress Administration (WPA), May 6, 1935, under act of April 8, 1935	
(Wagner Act)	(Wagner Act)	(Wagner) National Labor Relations Act, July 5, 1935
		Social Security Act, August 14, 1935
		Public Utility Holding Co. Act, Aug. 26, 1935
(Soil Conservation Act)	Soil Conservation and Domestic Allotment Act, Feb. 29, 1936	
(USHA)	(USHA)	U.S. Housing Authority (USHA) established by Congress, Sept. 1, 1937
(Second AAA)	Second Agricultural Adjustment Act, Feb. 16, 1938	
(Fair Labor Standards)	(Fair Labor Standards)	Fair Labor Standards Act, June 25, 1938
		Reorganization Act, April 3, 1939
		Hatch Act, Aug. 2, 1939

might otherwise have been driven by unemployment into criminal habits. The work was useful—including reforestation, flood control, and swamp drainage—and the recruits were required to help the old folks by sending home most of their pay. Both human resources and natural resources were thus conserved, though there were minor complaints of "militarizing" "bums" and "loafers."

The first major effort of the new Congress to grapple with the millions of adult unemployed was the Federal Emergency Relief Act. Its chief aim was immediate relief rather than long-range recovery. The resulting Federal Emergency Relief Administration (FERA) was handed over to zealous Harry L. Hopkins, a spindly, shabbily dressed, chain-smoking New York social worker who had earlier won Roosevelt's friendship and who became one of his most influential advisers. Hopkins' agency finally granted about three billion dollars to the states for direct dole payments or for wages on work projects.

Immediate relief was also given two large and hard-pressed groups by the Hundred Days Congress. One section of the Agricultural Adjustment Act made available many millions of dollars to help farmers meet their mortgages. Another law created the Home Owners' Loan Corporation (HOLC). Designed to refinance mortgages on non-farm homes, it ultimately assisted about a million badly pinched households.

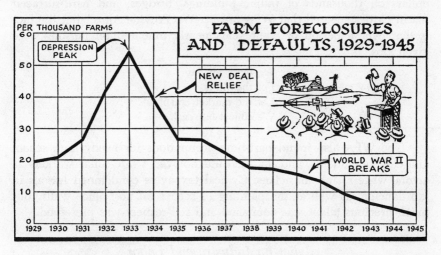

In the face of continuing unemployment, the President himself established the Civil Works Administration (CWA) late in 1933. As a branch of the Federal Emergency Relief Administration, it also fell under the direction of Hopkins. Designed to provide purely temporary jobs during the cruel winter emergency, it served a useful purpose. Tens of thousands of jobless men were employed at leaf raking and other make-work tasks, which soon came to be dubbed "boondoggling." But since this kind of labor put a premium on slow motion, the scheme was widely criticized.

Direct relief from Washington to needy families helped pull the nation through the ghastly winter of 1933–1934. But the disheartening persistence of widespread unemployment and suffering made it clear that emergency relief measures must be not only continued but supplemented. One danger signal was the appearance of numerous demagogues, who strutted forth to capitalize on popular discontent and to make pie-in-the-sky promises.

Notorious among this brood of agitators was a United States Senator, Huey P. ("Kingfish") Long of Louisiana, whose brassy, rabble-rousing talents publicized his "Share Our Wealth" program. Every family was to receive $5000, supposedly at the expense of the more prosperous citizens. Another Pied Piper was gaunt Dr. Francis E. Townsend of California, a retired physician whose savings had recently been wiped out. He attracted the pathetic support of perhaps five million "senior citizens" with his fantastic plan. Each oldster sixty years of age or over was to receive $200 a month, provided that he spent it within the month.

Partly to quiet the groundswell of unrest produced by such irresponsible proposals, Congress authorized the Works Progress Administration (WPA) in 1935. The objective was employment on useful projects. Launched under the supervision of the ailing but energetic Harry L. Hopkins, this remarkable agency ultimately spent about eleven billion dollars on thousands of public buildings, bridges, and hard-surfaced roads. Critics sneered that WPA meant "We Provide Alms," but the fact is that over a period of eight years nearly nine million persons were given jobs.

> We work all day
> For the WPA.
> Let the market crash,
> We collect our cash.

The WPA also found part-time occupations for needy high school and college students, and for such unemployed white-collar workers as actors, writers, and musicians. Cynical taxpayers condemned lessons in tap dancing, as well as the painting of scenes on post-office walls. But much precious talent was nourished and self-respect was preserved.

Relief for Industry and Labor

A daring attempt to stimulate a nationwide comeback was undertaken when the Emergency Congress authorized the National Recovery Administration (NRA). This ingenious scheme was by far the most complex and far-reaching effort by the New Dealers to combine immediate relief with long-range recovery and reform. Triple-barreled, it was designed to assist industry, labor, and the unemployed.

Individual industries—over two hundred in all—were to work out codes of "fair competition," under which hours of labor would be reduced so that employment could be spread over more men. A ceiling was placed on the maximum hours of labor; a floor was placed under wages so as to establish minimum levels.

Labor, under the NRA, was given additional benefits. Workingmen were formally guaranteed the right to organize and bargain collectively through representatives *of their own choosing*—not through hand-picked agents of the company's choosing. The hated "yellow dog" or anti-union contract was expressly forbidden, and certain safeguarding restrictions were placed on the use of child labor.

Industrial recovery through the NRA fair codes would at best be painful, for they called for self-denial by both management and labor. The patriotism of the people was appealed to by mass meetings and monster parades, which included 200,000 marchers on Fifth Avenue. A handsome Blue Eagle was designed as the symbol of the NRA, and merchants subscribing to a code displayed it on their windows with the slogan "We Do Our Part." Such was the enthusiasm with which the NRA was launched that for a brief period there was a marked upswing of business activity.

But the high-flying Blue Eagle gradually fluttered to earth. Too much self-sacrifice was expected of labor, industry, and the public for such a scheme to work. The Age of Chiselry dawned as certain unscrupulous businessmen ("chiselers") publicly displayed the indigo bird on their windows and secretly violated the codes. Complete collapse was imminent when, in 1935, the Supreme Court shot down the dying eagle in the famed Schechter "sick chicken" decision. The learned justices *unanimously* held that Congress could not "delegate legislative powers" to the Executive. They further declared that Congressional control of interstate commerce could not properly apply to a local poultry business, like that of the Schechter brothers in Brooklyn and New York. Roosevelt was in-

BIG BUSINESS HOLDS LINE AGAINST NRA
Knott in the Dallas *News*, 1933

censed by this "horse and buggy" interpretation of the Constitution, but actually the Court helped him out of a bad jam.

The same act of Congress that hatched the blue-eagled NRA also authorized the Public Works Administration (PWA), likewise intended both for industrial recovery and for unemployment relief. The agency was headed by the Secretary of the Interior, acid-tongued Harold L. Ickes, a free-swinging ex-Bull Mooser. Long-range recovery was the primary purpose of the new agency, and in time over four billion dollars was spent on some 34,000 projects, which included public buildings, highways, and parkways. One notable achievement was the Grand Coulee Dam on the Columbia River—the largest structure erected by man since the Great Wall of China. Speed was essential if the jobless were to be put back to work, but "Honest Harold" Ickes was so determined to prevent waste and extravagance that his delaying hand blocked maximum unemployment relief.

Special circumstances stimulated the recovery of one segment of business—the liquor industry. The imminent repeal of the prohibition amendment provided an opportunity to raise needed federal revenue and at the same time to provide some employment. Prodded by Roosevelt, the Hundred Days Congress in one of its earliest acts legalized light wine and beer with an alcoholic content (presumably non-intoxicating) not exceeding 3.2% by weight, and levied a tax of five dollars on every barrel so manufactured. Disgruntled drys, unwilling to acknowledge the breakdown of law and order begotten by prohibition, damned Roosevelt as "a 3.2% American." But their cause was lost. Prohibition was officially repealed by the 21st Amendment late in 1933 (see Appendix).

Relief for Farmers

A radical new approach to farm recovery was adopted when the Emergency Congress established the Agricultural Adjustment Administration (AAA). Through "artificial scarcity" this agency was to establish "parity prices" for basic commodities. "Parity" was the price set for a product that gave it the same real value, in terms of purchasing power, which it had enjoyed during the favorable period from 1909 to 1914. The AAA would eliminate price-depressing surpluses by paying the growers to cut down their crop acreage. The millions of dollars needed for these payments were to be raised by taxing the processors of farm products, such as the flour millers, who in turn would shift the burden to the consumer.

The AAA got off to a wobbly start. It was launched after much of the cotton crop for 1933 had been planted, and balky mules, trained otherwise, were forced to plow under countless young plants. Several million squealing pigs were purchased and slaughtered. Much of their meat was distributed to persons on relief, but some of it was used for fertilizer. This "sinful" destruction of food, at a time when thousands of our citizens were hungry, invited violent condemnation of the American economic system by Communists and other left-wingers.

"Planned scarcity" did have the effect of raising farm income, but the whole confused enterprise met with violent criticism. Farmers, food processors, consumers, and taxpayers were all in some degree unhappy. Paying the farmers not to farm actually increased unemployment, at a time when other New Deal agencies were striving to decrease it. When the Supreme Court finally killed the AAA in 1936, by declaring its regulatory taxation provisions unconstitutional, loud rejoicing was heard among critics of the plow-under program.

Quickly recovering from this blow, the New Deal Congress made haste to pass the Soil Conservation and Domestic Allotment Act of 1936. The withdrawal of acreage from production was now achieved by paying the farmer to plant soil-conserving crops, like soya beans, or to let his land lie fallow. With the emphasis thus on conservation, the Supreme Court placed the stamp of its approval on the revamped scheme.

The Second Agricultural Adjustment Act of 1938, passed two years later, was a more comprehensive substitute, although it continued conservation payments. If the grower observed acreage restrictions on specified commodities like cotton and wheat, he would be eligible for parity payments. Other provisions of the new AAA were designed to give the farmer not only a fairer price but a more substantial share of the national income. Both goals were achieved.

Black Blizzards

Dame Nature meanwhile had been providing some unplanned scarcity. Late in 1933 a prolonged drought struck the states of the trans-Mississippi Great Plains. Rainless weeks were followed by furious, whining winds, while the sun was darkened by millions of tons of powdery topsoil torn from once-fertile areas. Despondent citizens sat with dust masks on their faces, watching the farms swirl by.

Blown and fried out of the Dust Bowl, tens of thousands of refugees fled their ruined acres. In five years about 350,000 Oklahomans and Arkansans—"Okies" and "Arkies"—trekked to southern California in rattletrap automobiles. Their dismal story was realistically portrayed in John Steinbeck's best-selling novel, The Grapes of Wrath (1939), which proved to be the Uncle Tom's Cabin of the Dust Bowl.

The New Dealers, sympathetic toward the soil tillers, made various efforts to relieve their burdens. The Frazier-Lemke Farm Bankruptcy Act, passed in 1934, made possible a suspension of mortgage foreclosures for five years, but it was voided the next year by the Supreme Court. A revised law, limiting the grace period to three years, was unanimously upheld. In 1935 the President set up the Resettlement Administration, charged with the task of removing near-farmless farmers to better land. And millions of young trees were planted as windbreaks by the young men of the Civilian Conservation Corps.

Battling Bankers and Big Business

The reform-minded New Dealers were determined from the outset to beat into line the "money changers" who had played fast and loose with the funds of gullible investors before the Wall Street crash of 1929. The Hundred Days Congress passed the "Truth in Securities Act" (Federal Securities Act), which required promoters to transmit to the investor the fullest sworn information regarding the soundness of their stocks and bonds. The New Dealers thus reversed the old adage to read: "Let the seller beware."

In 1934 Congress undertook to protect the public further against fraud, deception, and inside manipulation. It authorized the Securities and Exchange Commission (SEC), which was designed as a watchdog administrative agency. Stock markets henceforth were to operate more as trading marts and less as gambling casinos.

The New Dealers likewise directed their fire at public-utility holding companies, those super-super-corporations. The country had been given an object lesson in the scandalous crash, during the spring of 1932, of Chicagoan Samuel Insull's multi-billion-dollar financial empire. The possibility of controlling, with a minimum of capital, a half-dozen or so pyramided layers of Big Business suggested to Roosevelt "a ninety-six-inch dog being wagged by a four-inch tail." The Public Utility Holding Company Act of 1935 finally delivered the so-called "death sentence" to this type of fatty growth, except in those cases where it might be deemed economically needful.

Harnessing the Tennessee River

The mushrooming electric-power industry, no less than the holding companies, attracted the fire of the New Deal reformers. Within a few decades it had risen from nothingness to a colossus which represented an investment of thirteen billion dollars. As a public utility, it reached directly and regularly into the pocketbooks of millions of citizens for a vitally needed service. Ardent New Dealers accused it of gouging the public with excessive rates, especially in view of the fact that it owed its success to having secured, often for a song, priceless water-power sites from the public domain.

The tempestuous Tennessee River provided the New Deal with a rare opportunity. With its tributaries, the river drained a badly eroded area about the size of England, and one containing some 2,500,000 of the most poverty-stricken people in America. The government already owned valuable properties at Muscle Shoals, where it had erected plants for the manufacture of needed nitrates in World War I. By developing the hydroelectric potential of the entire area, Washington could combine the immediate advantage of putting thousands of men to work with a long-term project for reforming the power monopoly.

The act creating the Tennessee Valley Authority (TVA) was passed by the Hundred Days Congress. This far-ranging enterprise was largely a result of the steadfast vision and unflagging zeal of Senator George W. Norris of Nebraska, after whom one of the mighty dams was named. From the standpoint of social reform and "planned economy," the TVA was by far the most revolutionary of all the New Deal schemes.

The new agency was determined to discover precisely how much the production and distribution of electricity cost, so that a "yardstick" could be set up to test the fairness of rates charged by private companies. The utility corporations fought back bitterly against this entering wedge of governmental control, and charged that the low cost of TVA power was due to dishonest bookkeeping and the absence of taxes.

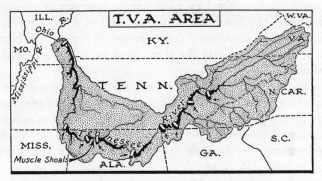

Only the nine dams on the Tennessee River are shown here.
There are more than twenty on the tributaries.

The whole scheme, they complained, was "creeping socialism in concrete."

But the New Dealers shrugged off such outcries, and pointed a prideful finger at the amazing achievements of the TVA. The gigantic project had brought to the area not only full employment and the blessings of cheap electric power, but low-cost housing, abundant cheap nitrates, the restoration of eroded soil, reforestation, improved navigation, and flood control. The rivers ran blue instead of brown; and a once poverty-cursed area was being transformed into one of the most flourishing regions in the country. Foreigners were greatly impressed with the possibilities of similar schemes in their own lands, and zealous New Dealers agitated for parallel enterprises in the valleys of the Columbia and Missouri Rivers. But the conservatives in Congress, growing bolder, confined this type of socialism to the Tennessee Valley.

Housing Reform and Social Security

A gratifying beginning had meanwhile been made by the New Deal in the field of slum clearance. With a view to speeding both recovery and better housing, Roosevelt set up the Federal Housing Administration (FHA) as early as 1934, under authority granted by Congress. The building industry was to be stimulated by small loans to householders for improving their homes or completing new ones. The FHA proved so popular that it was one of the few alphabetical agencies to outlast the Age of Roosevelt.

Congress bolstered this program in 1937 by authorizing the United States Housing Authority (USHA)—an agency designed to lend money to states or communities for low-cost construction. Though units for about 650,000 persons were launched, new building fell pathetically short of needs. New Deal efforts to expand the project ran into foul weather. Bitter opposition was raised by such special interests as real-estate promoters, builders, and landlords, to say nothing of anti-New Dealers who deplored what they considered down-the-rathole spending. Nonetheless, for the first time in a century the slum areas in America ceased growing and even shrank.

Incomparably more important than their achievements in housing was the success of the New Dealers in the field of unemployment insurance and old-age pensions. Their greatest victory was the epochal Social Security Act of 1935—one of the most complicated and far-reaching laws ever to pass Congress. To cushion future depressions, the measure provided for federal-state unemployment insurance. To provide security for old age, specified categories of retired workers were to receive regular payments from Washington, ranging from $10 to $85 a month, and financed by a payroll tax on both employers and employees. Provision was also made for the blind, cripples, delinquent children, and other dependents.

The Social Security Act was largely inspired by the example of some of the more highly industrialized nations of Europe. In the agricultural America of an earlier day, there had always been farm chores for all ages, and the large family had cared for its own dependents. But in an urbanized America, at the mercy of boom-and-bust cycles, the government was now recognizing its responsibility for the welfare of its citizens. By 1939 over 45,000,000 persons were eligible for social-security benefits, and in subsequent years further categories of workers were added and the payments to them were increased.

A New Deal for Unskilled Labor

The NRA, with its go-ahead signal for collective bargaining, had been a godsend to organized labor. As New Deal expenditures brought some slackening of unemployment, labor began to feel more secure and hence more self-assertive. A rash of walkouts occurred in the summer of 1934, including a paralyzing general strike in San Francisco which was broken only when outraged citizens resorted to strong-arm vigilante tactics.

When the Supreme Court ax beheaded the Blue Eagle, a Congress sympathetic to labor unions undertook to fill the vacuum thus created. The fruit of its deliberations was the Wagner or National Labor Relations Act of 1935. This trail-blazing law created a powerful new National Labor Relations Board for administrative purposes, and reasserted the right of labor to engage in self-organization and to bargain collectively through representatives of its own choice. The Wagner Act proved to be one of the outstanding milestones on the rocky road of the American labor movement.

Under the encouragement of a highly sympathetic National Labor Relations Board, a host of unskilled workers in the basic industries began to organize themselves into effective unions. The leader of this drive was beetle-browed, domineering, and melodramatic John L. Lewis, boss of the United Mine Workers. In 1935 he succeeded in forming the Committee for Industrial Organization (C.I.O.) within the ranks of the skilled-craft American Federation of Labor. But skilled workers, ever since the days of the ill-fated Knights of Labor in the 1880's, had shown only lukewarm sympathy for the cause of unskilled labor. In 1936, following inevitable friction with the C.I.O., the older federation suspended the upstart unions associated with the newer organization.

Nothing daunted, the rebellious C.I.O. moved on a concerted scale into the huge automobile industry. Late in 1936 the workers resorted to a new technique known as the sit-down strike; that is, they refused to leave the factory buildings of General Motors, at Flint, Michigan, and thus prevented the importation of strikebreakers. The C.I.O. finally won a resounding victory when its union, after heated negotiation, was recognized by General Motors as the sole bargaining agency for its employees.

The "Coddling" of Labor

Unskilled workers now pressed their advantage. The United States Steel Company, hitherto an impossible nut for labor to crack, averted a costly strike when it voluntarily granted rights of unionization to its C.I.O.-organized employees. But the Little Steel Companies fought back savagely. The nation was shocked in 1937 by the Memorial Day massacre at the plant of the Republic Steel Company in South Chicago. There, in a bloody fracas, the police fired upon pickets and workers, leaving the area strewn with several score dead and wounded.

The new deal for labor continued when Congress, in 1938, passed the memorable Fair Labor Standards Act (Wages and Hours Bill). Industries involved in interstate commerce were to set up minimum-wage and maximum-hour levels. Though not immediately established, the specific goals were forty cents an hour (later raised) and a forty-hour week. Labor by children under sixteen was forbidden; under eighteen, if the occupation was dangerous. The new measure was bitterly though futilely opposed by many industrialists, notably by those Southern textile manufacturers who had profited from low-wage labor.

In later New Deal days, labor unionization flourished like the proverbial green bay tree. "Roosevelt wants you to join a union" was the rallying cry of professional organizers. The Champion of the Forgotten Man received valuable support at ballot-box time from labor leaders and many appreciative workingmen. One mill worker remarked that Roosevelt was "the only man we ever had in the White House who would know that my boss is a skunk." F.D.R. was the Forgotten Man's man.

The C.I.O. surged forward, breaking completely with the A.F. of L. in 1938. On that occasion the Committee for Industrial Organization was formally reconstituted as the Congress of Industrial Organizations (the new C.I.O.), under the highhanded presidency of John L. Lewis. By

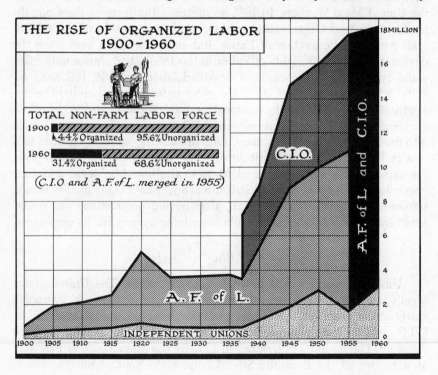

THE RISE OF ORGANIZED LABOR
1900-1960

TOTAL NON-FARM LABOR FORCE
1900
4.4% Organized   95.6% Unorganized
1960
31.4% Organized   68.6% Unorganized

(C.I.O and A.F.of L. merged in 1955)

C.I.O.

A.F. of L and C.I.O.

A. F. of L.

INDEPENDENT UNIONS

1900 1905 1910 1915 1920 1925 1930 1935 1940 1945 1950 1955 1960

18 MILLION
16
14
12
10
8
6
4
2
0

1940 the C.I.O. could claim about four million members in its constituent unions, even though bitter and annoying jurisdictional feuding, involving strikes, continued with the A.F. of L. At times labor seemed more bent on costly civil war than on its age-old war with management.

Landon Challenges "The Champ"

As the presidential campaign of 1936 impended, the New Dealers were on top of the world. They had achieved considerable progress, and millions of "reliefers" were grateful to their bountiful government. The exultant Democrats, meeting in Philadelphia, pushed through the renomination of Roosevelt, idol of the "forgotten man," in a brief rubber-stamp ceremony. The platform stood squarely on the record of the Roosevelt years.

The Republicans, assembling in Cleveland, were hard pressed to find someone to feed to "the Champ." They finally settled on colorless Governor Alfred M. Landon of Kansas, a wealthy oil man, whose chief claim to distinction was that he had balanced the budget of his state in an era of unbalanced budgets. The Republican platform, though promising relief benefits that would cost many millions, condemned the New Deal of Franklin "Deficit" Roosevelt—its radicalism, experimentation, confusion, and "frightful waste." Popular watchwords were "Defeat the New Deal and Its Reckless Spending," "Let's Get Another Deck," and "Life, Liberty, and Landon."

Landon—"the Kansas Coolidge"—was honest, sincere, homespun, "common-sensical," and as American as apple pie. But he had a poor radio voice and seemed schoolboyish on the stump. Surrounded by imitation Kansas sunflowers, he stressed "deeds, not deficits," and condemned New Deal highhandedness. Though opposing the popular Social Security Act, he advocated just enough reform to cause the Democrats to retort that he would continue the New Deal—a second-hand New Deal—in his own way. He was, they sneered, "the poor man's Hoover."

The Democrats denounced the G.O.P. as the party of the Big Moneyed Interests and the Big Depression, and amid loud choruses of boos cried, "Remember Hoover!" The embittered ex-President called for "a holy crusade for liberty." A group of wealthy Republicans and conservative Democrats had in 1934 formed the Liberty League, and they vented their reactionary spleen against "that man Roosevelt." But they hurt their own cause by erecting a made-to-order target for Roosevelt. His dander aroused, he took to the stump and denounced the "economic royalists" who sought to "hide behind the flag and the Constitution." "I welcome their hatred," he proclaimed.

A tremendous landslide overwhelmed Landon, as the demoralized Republicans carried only two states, Maine and Vermont. This dismal showing caused political wiseacres to make the old adage read: "As

Maine goes, so goes Vermont."* The popular vote was 27,751,597 to 16,-679,583; the electoral count was 523 to 8—the most lopsided in 116 years. Swollen Democratic majorities, riding in on Roosevelt's magic coattails, were again returned to Congress. The Democrats could now boast more than two-thirds of the seats in the House, and a like proportion in the Senate.

The campaign of 1936, perhaps the most bitter since Bryan's in 1896, partially bore out Republican charges of class warfare. Even more than in 1932, the needy economic groups were lined up against the so-called greedy economic groups ("Tories"). C.I.O. units contributed generously to F.D.R.'s campaign chest. Many left-wingers turned to Roosevelt, as the customary third-party protest vote sharply declined. The Negroes, who had enjoyed welcome relief handouts under the New Deal, had by now largely shaken off their traditional allegiance to the Republican Party.

Roosevelt won primarily because he appealed to the "forgotten men," who now felt that they had a champion in the White House. But much of the President's support was only pocketbook-deep. "Reliefers" were not going to bite the hand that doled out the government checks. No one, as Al Smith once remarked, wanted to "shoot Santa Claus."

Nine Old Men

Bowing his head to the sleety blasts, Roosevelt took the presidential oath on January 20, 1937, instead of the traditional March 4. The 20th Amendment to the Constitution, sponsored by Senator Norris of TVA fame, had been ratified in 1933. (See Appendix.) It swept away the post-election "lame duck" session of Congress, and shortened by six weeks the awkward period before inauguration.

Flushed with the wine of victory, Roosevelt interpreted the election as a mandate to continue New Deal reforms. But in his eyes the cloistered old men on the Supreme Bench, like fossilized stumbling blocks, stood stubbornly in the pathway of progress. To New Dealers the potent tribunal had become a kind of third legislative chamber. In nine major cases involving the New Deal, the Roosevelt administration had been defeated seven times. The Court was ultra-conservative, for six of the nine oldsters in black were over seventy. And as luck would have it, not a single member had been appointed by F.D.R. in his four years.

Roosevelt—his "Dutch up"—viewed with mounting impatience what he regarded as the obstructive conservatism of the court. Some of these Old Guard appointees were hanging on with a senile grip, partly because they felt it their patriotic duty to curb the "socialistic" tendencies of that

* Maine, which traditionally holds its state elections in September, was long regarded as a political weather vane. Hence the expression "As Maine goes, so goes the nation."

radical in the White House. Roosevelt believed that the voters in three successive elections—the presidential elections of 1932 and 1936 and the mid-term Congressional election of 1934—had returned a smashing verdict for *a* new deal—though perhaps not *the* New Deal. Democracy, in his view, meant rule by the people. If the American way of life was to be preserved, Roosevelt argued, the Supreme Court ought to get in line with the supreme court of public opinion.

Roosevelt finally hit upon a Court scheme that he regarded as "the answer to a maiden's prayer." When he sprang it on a shocked nation, early in 1937, he caught the country and the leaders of Congress completely by surprise. One basic reason was that the Court issue had not figured prominently in the recent campaign. Roosevelt bluntly asked Congress for legislation to permit him to add a new justice to the Supreme Court for every member over seventy who would not retire. The maximum membership could then be fifteen. Roosevelt pointed to the neces-

Seibel in the Richmond *Times-Dispatch*, 1937

sity of injecting vigorous new blood, for the Court, he alleged, was far behind in its work. This charge, which turned out to be false, brought heated accusations of dishonesty. At best, Roosevelt was headstrong and not fully aware of the fact that the Court, in popular thinking, had become something of a Sacred Cow.

The Court Capitulates

Congress and the nation were promptly convulsed over the scheme to "pack" the Supreme Court. Franklin "Double-crossing" Roosevelt was savagely condemned for attempting to break down the delicate checks and balances among the three branches of the government. He was accused of grooming himself as a dictator by trying to browbeat the judiciary. In the eyes of countless citizens, mostly Republicans but including many Democrats, basic liberties seemed to be in jeopardy. "God Bless the Supreme Court" was a fervent prayer.

The Court had meanwhile not been unaware of the ax hanging over its head. Whatever his motives, Mr. Justice Roberts, formerly regarded as a conservative, began to vote on the side of his liberal colleagues. "A switch in time saves nine" was the classic witticism inspired by this change. By a five-to-four decision the Court, in March, 1937, upheld the principle of a state minimum wage for women, thereby reversing its stand on a different case a year earlier. In succeeding decisions, a Court more sympathetic to the New Deal upheld the National Labor Relations Act (Wagner Act) and the Social Security Act. The case for Roosevelt's "court packing" scheme was further undermined when one of the oldest conservative members retired, to be replaced by a New Dealer.

Congress finally passed a court reform bill, but this watered-down version applied only to the lower courts. Roosevelt, the master politician, thus suffered his first major legislative defeat at the hands of his own party in Congress. The American people have never viewed lightly a tampering with the Supreme Court by the President, no matter how popular he may be. Yet in losing this battle, Roosevelt incidentally won his campaign. The Court, as he had hoped, became markedly more friendly to the New Deal. Furthermore, a succession of deaths and resignations enabled him to make nine appointments to the tribunal—more than any of his predecessors since George Washington.

Twilight of the New Deal

From 1933 to 1937 the country had been gradually inching its way out of the depression. This painful progress was no doubt largely due to the billions of dollars injected by Congress into the economic bloodstream. Although millions of disheartened souls remained unemployed, gratifying gains had been registered. "We planned it that way," remarked Roosevelt cheerily.

But in 1937 a sharp business recession set in which hit bottom in 1938. The President's numerous critics, branding this setback "the Roosevelt Depression," asserted that if F.D.R. could plan upward spirals he must also have planned the downward dip. The recession was probably

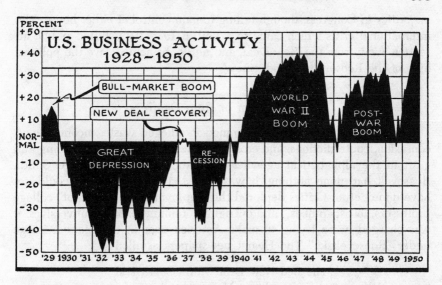

PERCENT

U.S. BUSINESS ACTIVITY 1928–1950

BULL-MARKET BOOM

NEW DEAL RECOVERY

WORLD WAR II BOOM

POST-WAR BOOM

NORMAL

GREAT DEPRESSION

RE-CESSION

'29 1930 '31 '32 '33 '34 '35 '36 '37 '38 '39 1940 '41 '42 '43 '44 '45 '46 '47 '48 '49 1950

due basically to an overrapid cutting back of "pump-priming" spending by Washington.

Undiscouraged, Roosevelt had meanwhile been pushing the remaining major reforms of the New Deal. It was not all clear sailing. Early in 1937 he urged Congress—a Congress growing more conservative—to authorize a sweeping reorganization of the national administration in the interests of streamlined efficiency. But the issue became tangled up with his presumed dictatorial ambitions in regard to the Supreme Court, and he suffered another stinging defeat. Two years later, in 1939, Congress partially relented and in the Reorganization Act gave him limited powers for administrative reforms.

The New Dealers were accused of having the richest campaign chest in history; and in truth government relief checks had a curious habit of coming in bunches just before balloting time. To remedy such practices, which tended to make a farce of free elections, Congress adopted the much-heralded Hatch Act of 1939. It prohibited federal administrative officials, except the highest policy-making officers, from active political campaigning and soliciting. It also forbade the use of government funds for political purposes, as well as the collection of campaign contributions from persons receiving relief payments. The Hatch Act was broadened in 1940 to place limits on campaign contributions and expenditures, but such clever ways of getting around it were found that on the whole the new legislation proved disappointing.

By 1938 the New Deal had clearly lost much of its early momentum. Magician Roosevelt could find few spectacular new reform rabbits to pull out of his tall silk hat. In the Congressional elections of 1938 the Republicans, for the first time, cut heavily into the unwieldy New Deal majorities in Congress, though failing to gain control of either house. The international crisis which came to a boil in 1938–1939 shifted public attention away from the New Deal, and no doubt helped save the political hide of the Roosevelt "spendocracy."

New Deal or Raw Deal?

Foes of the New Deal condemned its alleged waste, incompetence, confusion, contradictions, and cross-purposes, as well as the chiseling and graft in the alphabetical agencies—"alphabet soup," sneered Al Smith. Roosevelt had done nothing, it was said, that an earthquake could not have done better. Critics deplored the employment of "crackpot" college professors, leftist "pinkos," and outright Communists. Such subversives, it was charged, were trying to make America over in the Marxist image under "Rooseveltski." The Hearst newspapers assailed

> The Red New Deal with a Soviet seal
> Endorsed by a Moscow hand,
> The strange result of an alien cult
> In a liberty-loving land.

Hardheaded businessmen were shocked by the leap-before-you-look, try-anything-once spirit of Roosevelt. They accused him of confusing movement with progress. Will Rogers, the rope-twirling "poet lariat" of the era, remarked that if Roosevelt were to burn down the capitol, people would say, "Well, we at least got a fire started, anyhow."

"Bureaucratic meddling" and "regimentation" were also bitter complaints of anti-New Dealers; and in truth bureaucracy did blossom. The federal government, with its hundreds of thousands of employees, became incomparably the largest single business on earth. Unhappily, many of the ill-trained newcomers to the political payroll represented a setback for the merit system. (See chart on p. 508.)

Promises of budget balancing, to say nothing of other promises, had gone out the window—so foes of the New Deal pointed out. The national debt had mounted from the already enormous figure of $19,487,000,000 in 1932 to $40,440,000,000 by 1939. The government was becoming, its critics charged, a "handout state" trying to squander itself into prosperity. Such lavish spending was undermining the old virtues of thrift and initiative. The American people, once self-reliant citizens, were getting a bad case of the "gimmies." In the 19th Century, the hard-pressed American went West; now he went on relief.

The business world was bitter. Accusing the New Deal of fomenting class strife, it insisted that the laboring man and the farmer—especially the big operator—were being pampered. Countless businessmen, especially Republicans, declared that they could pull themselves out of the depression if they could only get the federal government off their backs.

Private enterprise, they charged, was being stifled by "planned economy," "creeping socialism," and the philosophy "Washington can do it better." States' rights were being ignored, and the government was competing in business with its own citizens.

The aggressive leadership of Roosevelt—"one-man super-government"—also came in for denunciation. Heavy fire was especially directed at his attempts to browbeat the Supreme Court and to create a "dummy Congress." He had even tried in the 1938 elections, with backfiring results, to "purge" members of Congress who would not lock-step with his policies.

The most damning indictment of the New Deal was that it had failed to cure the depression. It had merely administered sedatives. Despite some twenty billion dollars poured out in six years of spending and lending, of leaf raking and pump priming, the gap was not closed between production and consumption. There were even more mountainous farm surpluses under Roosevelt than under Hoover. Millions of dispirited men were still unemployed in 1939, after six years of drain and strain. Not until World War II blazed forth in Europe—the greatest pump primer of all—was the unemployment puzzle solved.

The New Deal Balance Sheet

New Dealers, on the other hand, staunchly defended their record. Admitting that there had been some waste, they pointed out that relief— not economy—had been the primary object of their multi-front war on the depression. Conceding also that there had been some graft, they argued that there had been very little in view of the immense sums spent.

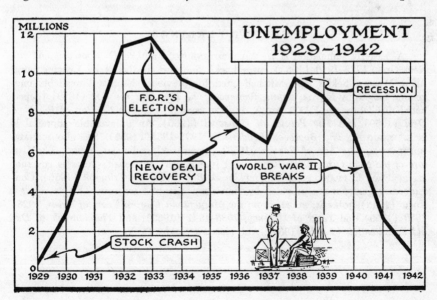

Apologists for Roosevelt further declared that the New Deal had relieved the worst of the crisis in 1933. It promoted the philosophy of "balancing the human budget," and accepted the principle that the federal government was bound to prevent mass hunger and starvation. The Washington regime was to be used, not feared. The economic system was kept from collapse; a fairer distribution of the national income was achieved; and the citizens were enabled to retain their self-respect. "Nobody is going to starve" was Roosevelt's promise.

Though hated by Big Business, Roosevelt should have been the patron saint of business, so his admirers claimed. He deflected popular resentments against business, and may have saved the American system of free enterprise. Roosevelt's quarrel was not with capitalism but with capitalists; he purged American capitalism of some of its worst abuses so that it might be saved from itself. He may have headed off socialism by a mild dose of what was condemned as "socialism." He did not hate rich men; he merely wanted "to skin them," it was said.

Roosevelt, like Jefferson, provided reform without revolution. He was upbraided by the left-wing radicals for not going far enough; by the right-wing conservatives for going too far. Choosing the middle road, he has been called the greatest American conservative since Hamilton. He demonstrated anew the value of powerful presidential leadership. He exercised that power to relieve the erosion of our greatest physical resource—the American people. He helped preserve democracy in America at a time when democracies abroad were disappearing down the dictatorial drain. And in playing this role he unwittingly girded the nation for its part in the titanic war that hung on the horizon—a war in which democracy the world over would be at stake.

SELECT READINGS

A masterly summation is w. e. leuchtenburg, *Franklin D. Roosevelt and the New Deal, 1932–1940* (1963) [paperback]. See also the books by Leuchtenburg, Allen, Wecter, Seldes, and Mitchell cited for previous chapter. A readable one-volume biography is j. m. burns, *Roosevelt: The Lion and the Fox* (1956) [paperback]. Brilliantly pro-F.D.R. are a. m. schlesinger, jr., *The Coming of the New Deal* (1959) and *The Politics of Upheaval* (1960). An unfavorable appraisal is e. e. robinson, *The Roosevelt Leadership, 1933–1935* (1955). See also richard hofstadter, *The Age of Reform* (1955) [paperback] and basil rauch, *The History of the New Deal, 1933–1938* (1944) [paperback]. Roosevelt's years as governor are analyzed in frank freidel, *Franklin D. Roosevelt: The Triumph* (1956). Contemporary glimpses are provided by madame (frances) perkins, *The Roosevelt I Knew* (1946); john m. blum, *From the Morgenthau Diaries: Years of Crisis, 1928–1938* (1959) and *Years of Urgency, 1938–1941* (1965); and *The Journals of David E. Lilienthal* (2 vols., 1964). Also *Harvard Guide*, Pt. VI.

43

Franklin D. Roosevelt and Foreign Affairs

We must be the great arsenal of democracy.
PRESIDENT ROOSEVELT, 1940

The New Deal in Diplomacy

THE 54-nation London Economic Conference, meeting in the summer of 1933, revealed how intimately Roosevelt's early foreign policy was entwined with his schemes for domestic recovery. This distinguished assemblage, in which the United States was represented, had as a major purpose a frontal attack on the globe-girdling depression. It was particularly eager to stabilize national currencies on a world-wide front; and to such a course Washington had apparently committed itself in advance.

But Roosevelt began to experience a change of heart. He evidently believed that his gold-juggling policies were stimulating faint blushes of returning prosperity. An international agreement on currency might tie his hands; and, as an astute politician, he was unwilling to sacrifice probable recovery at home for possible recovery abroad. While vacationing on a United States cruiser in the North Atlantic, he dashed off a radio message to London, scolding the Conference for trying to stabilize currencies, and urging it to turn to more basic economic ills.

Roosevelt's bombshell message blew the rug from under the London Conference. It adjourned virtually empty-handed, amid angry cries of American bad faith. The delegates, in any event, probably would have failed to produce a wonder drug for the world's economic maladies. But the devil-take-the-hindmost attitude of Roosevelt plunged the world even deeper into the morass of narrow isolationism and extreme nationalism. This unfortunate trend, as ill fortune would have it, played directly into the hands of the power-grasping dictators.

Less spectacular than Roosevelt's "torpedoing" of the London Conference was his formal recognition of the Soviet Union, late in 1933. Disagreeable though the thought might be to conservative Americans,

857

the Bolshevik government had fastened itself securely on the backs of
the Russian masses, and had won recognition from the other great powers.
There was a certain unreality in our refusing to recognize, after sixteen
long years, the official existence of the Moscow government—a regime
representing 160,000,000 people and holding sway over one-sixth of the
earth's land surface. The prolonged cold-shoulder treatment of Washington, moreover, had not caused the Soviet Union to collapse, or persuaded
the Moscow Communists to abandon their vicious propaganda for world
revolution.

Why did Roosevelt extend the right hand of recognition? He was first
of all an outspoken liberal, and not bound by the conservative course of
his Republican predecessors. Land-hungry Japan was on the rampage in
the Far East, and many Americans believed that the recognition of Moscow might bolster the Russians against the ambitious sons of Nippon.
Finally, a depression-ridden United States was willing to gamble that a
prosperous trade would develop with the Soviet Union.

Horse-trading negotiations with the Russians were finally concluded
in Washington during November, 1933. The Soviets formally promised,
among other assurances, to refrain from their revolutionary propaganda
in America. They promptly broke this pledge. The anticipated large-scale
trade with the U.S.S.R. did not develop, largely because a huge American loan, which the Russians had expected, was not forthcoming. The
Soviets were regarded as poor credit risks. Uncle Sam was to some extent duped by Moscow, but at least he was now on official speaking
terms—or name-calling terms—with the rulers of the largest and most
populous of the white nations.

Freedom for (from?) the Filipinos

The Great Depression, which blighted almost everything else, actually brightened hopes of Philippine independence. The imperialistic
dream-bubble of McKinley in the Far East had burst, and American
taxpayers were eager to cut loose from their expensive tropical liability.
Organized American labor clamored for the exclusion of low-wage
Filipinos, while depression-bedeviled American producers of sugar and
other products sought to restrict competition from the Philippines.

In 1934 Congress, not unmindful of its earlier promises of Philippine
independence, responded to the prodding of such self-seeking groups.
It passed a bill under which the potentially rich islands were to become
free, but only after a ten-year period of economic and political transition. American military establishments were to be relinquished, but
naval bases were to be reserved for future discussion.

Rather than freeing the Philippines, the American people tried to
free themselves *from* the Philippines. With a selfish eye to our own welfare, we imposed upon the Filipinos economic terms so ungenerous as

to threaten the islands with prostration. American isolationists, moreover, rejoiced to be rid of this Far Eastern heel of Achilles—so vulnerable to Japanese attack. Yet our turn-tail-and-run tactics, though applauded by anti-colonialist natives in Eastern Asia, cost us some "face" in the Far East. Certainly our turning the Filipinos loose did nothing to discourage the aggressions of the power-greedy Japanese militarists.

The Flowering of Good-Neighborism

A bright new era in relations with Latin America was heralded when Roosevelt ringingly proclaimed in his inaugural address, "I dedicate this nation to the policy of the Good Neighbor."

Old-fashioned intervention by bayonet in the Caribbean had not paid off, except in an evil harvest of resentment, suspicion, and fear. The Great Depression had cooled off Yankee economic aggressiveness, as thousands of our investors in Latin American "securities" became sackholders rather than stockholders. There were now fewer dollars to be protected by the rifles of the leathernecked marines.

Roosevelt has generally received almost exclusive credit for the Good Neighbor policy. Actually, the retreat from economic imperialism in Latin America had already been foreshadowed under Coolidge, and particularly under Hoover. But Roosevelt went the whole way, partly because of his liberal tendencies, and partly because the global political picture was shifting. With war-thirsty dictators seizing power in Europe and Asia, he was eager to line up the Latin Americans to help defend the Western Hemisphere. Ill-natured and embittered neighbors would be potential tools of the transoceanic aggressors.

President Roosevelt made it clear at the outset that he was going to renounce armed intervention, and particularly the trouble-breeding corollary of the Monroe Doctrine devised by his cousin, Theodore Roosevelt. Late in 1933, at the Seventh Pan-American Conference in Montevideo, the United States delegation formally accepted political non-intervention, and this doctrine was speedily adopted by Washington.

Deeds followed words. The last marines embarked from Haiti in 1934. In the same year restive Cuba was released from the hobbles of the Platt Amendment, under which Uncle Sam had been free to intervene. The tiny republic of Panama received a similar uplift in 1936, when the leading strings of Washington were partially unfastened.

The hope-inspiring Good Neighbor policy, with the accent on consultation and non-intervention, received its acid test in Mexico. The seizure of Yankee oil properties in 1938, under the constitution of 1917, brought vehement demands for armed intervention from United States investors. Roosevelt successfully resisted the clamoring, and a settlement was finally threshed out in 1941, although the oil companies lost much of their original stake.

Roosevelt's Good Neighbor policy proved to be spectacularly successful. His earnest attempts to inaugurate a new era of friendliness, though hurting some of our own bondholders, paid rich dividends in good will among the peoples to the south. No other citizen of the United States has ever been held in such high esteem in Latin America during his lifetime. Roosevelt was cheered with tumultuous enthusiasm when, as a "traveling salesman for peace," he journeyed to the special Inter-American Conference at Buenos Aires in 1936.

Trade a Two-Way Street

Closely associated with the Good Neighbor policy, and likewise popular in Latin America, was the reciprocal trade policy of the New Dealers. Its chief architect was high-domed Secretary of State Cordell Hull, a homespun Tennessean of the low-tariff school. Like Roosevelt, he believed that a nation can sell abroad only as it buys abroad; that towering tariff walls choke off foreign trade; and that trade wars beget shooting wars.

Responding to the Hull-Roosevelt leadership, Congress passed the Reciprocal Trade Agreements Act in 1934. Designed in part to lift American export trade from the depression doldrums, this far-visioned measure was aimed at both relief and recovery. The new legislation put into active operation the low-tariff policies of the New Dealers. (See chart on p. 810.)

The Trade Agreements Act avoided the dangerous uncertainties of a wholesale tariff revision, for it merely whittled down the most objectionable schedules of the Hawley-Smoot law by amending them. The President was empowered to lower existing rates by as much as 50%, provided that the other country involved was willing to reciprocate with similar reductions. The resulting pacts, moreover, were to become effective without the formal approval of the Senate. This refreshingly novel feature not only insured speedier action, but avoided all the evils of logrolling and wholesale lobbying in Congress.

Secretary Hull, whose zeal for reciprocity was unflagging, succeeded in negotiating pacts with twenty-one countries by the end of 1939. During these same years American foreign trade increased somewhat and the depression eased appreciably, all presumably in part as a result of the Hull-Roosevelt policies. The trade agreements undoubtedly bettered our economic and political relations with Latin America, and proved to be a strong force for peace in a war-bent world.

The Reciprocal Trade Agreements Act, with modifications, was renewed periodically by Congress—but invariably in the teeth of bitter protests from high-tariff Republicans. James G. Blaine, Republican Secretary of State of yesteryear, had fathered the reciprocal trade policy. But dyed-in-the-wool Republicans were loath to recognize the Blaine baby in

"ONE OF OUR QUAINT IDEAS ABOUT FOREIGN TRADE"
Fitzpatrick in the St. Louis *Post-Dispatch*

Democratic diapers. Manufacturers were not alone in their opposition; they were joined by many Middle Western farmers who were hurt by lowered duties on meat and other foreign imports. But a majority of the New Deal Congress felt that the interests of certain special groups, however important, should be sacrificed to those of the nation as a whole.

Storm-Cellar Isolationism

The post-1918 chaos in Europe, followed by the Great Depression, fostered the ominous concept of the totalitarian state. The individual was nothing; the state was everything. Communist Russia led the way, with the crafty and ruthless Stalin finally emerging as dictator. Boastful Benito Mussolini, a swaggering Fascist, seized the reins of power in Italy during 1922. And Adolf Hitler, a fanatic with a toothbrush mustache, plotted and harangued his way into control of Germany in 1933.

Hitler was the most immediately dangerous, because he combined tremendous power with impulsiveness. A frustrated Austrian painter, with hypnotic talents as an orator and a leader, he had secured control of the Nazi Party by making political capital of the Treaty of Versailles and the depression-born unemployment. He was thus an unlovely child of the shortsighted post-war policies of the victorious Allies, including the United States. The desperate German people had fallen in behind the new Pied Piper, for they saw no other hope of escape from the plague of economic chaos and national disgrace. In 1936 the Nazi Hitler and the Fascist Mussolini allied themselves in the Rome-Berlin Axis.

International gangsterism was likewise spreading in the Far East, where the Nipponese were on the make. Like both Nazi Germany and Fascist Italy, Japan was a so-called "have-not" power. Like them, she suffered from resentment over having been short-changed by the Treaty of Versailles. Like them, she demanded additional living space for her overcrowded millions.

Japanese navalists were not to be denied. Determined to find a place in the Asiatic sun, Tokyo gave notice in 1934 of the termination of the twelve-year-old Washington Naval Treaty. A year later at London, the Japanese torpedoed all hope of effective naval disarmament. Upon being denied complete parity, they walked out on the multi-power conference.

Jut-jawed Mussolini, seeking both glory and empire in Africa, brutally attacked Ethiopia in 1935. The black defenders, armed with spears and ancient firearms, were speedily crushed. The members of the League of Nations could have caused Mussolini's war machine to creak to a halt —if they had only dared to place an embargo on oil. But when the League quailed rather than risk global hostilities, it merely signed its own death warrant.

The spirit of isolationism, long rampant in America, received a strong impetus from these alarms abroad. Though disapproving of the dictators, we still believed that our encircling seas conferred a kind of mystic immunity. We were continuing to suffer deep disillusionment born of our participation in World War I, which we now regarded as a colossal blunder. We likewise cherished bitter memories of the ungrateful and defaulting debtors. As early as 1934 a spiteful Congress had passed the Johnson Debt Default Act, which prevented debt-dodging nations from borrowing further in the United States. If attacked again by aggressors, they could "stew in their own juice."

The American people, mired down as they were in the Great Depression, had no real appreciation of the revolutionary new forces being harnessed by the dictators. The "have-not" powers were out to become "have" powers. We were not so much afraid that the totalitarian aggressors would cause trouble as we were fearful that we might be drawn into it. Strong nationwide agitation welled up for a constitutional amendment to forbid a declaration of war by Congress—except in case of invasion— unless there was first a favorable popular referendum. With a mixture of seriousness and frivolity, a group of Princeton University students began to agitate in 1936 for a bonus to be paid to the Veterans of Future Wars (V.F.W.'s).

Legislating Ourselves into Neutrality

As the gloomy 1930's lengthened, an avalanche of lurid articles and books poured from American presses condemning the munitions manufacturers as war-fomenting "merchants of death." A Senate committee was appointed in 1934 to investigate these charges. By grossly twisting the evidence regarding our entry into World War I, the senatorial probers shifted the blame away from the German submarine and other aggressions to the American bankers and arms manufacturers. Since the munitions makers had obviously made money out of the war, many naïve souls leaped to the illogical conclusion that they had caused the war in order to make money. This kind of reasoning suggested that if the profits could only be removed from the arms business, America could keep out of any world conflict that might erupt in the future.

"THE JIG-SAW PUZZLE"
Cassel in the Brooklyn *Eagle,* 1939

Responding to overwhelming popular pressure, Congress made haste to legislate the nation out of war. The members were spurred on by the imminent danger that Mussolini's boat-rocking Ethiopian adventure would plunge the world into a new blood bath. The Neutrality Acts of 1935, 1936, and 1937, taken together, stipulated that *when the President proclaimed* the existence of a foreign war, certain restrictions would automatically go into effect. No American could legally sail on a belligerent ship, or sell or transport munitions to a belligerent, or make loans to a belligerent.

This head-in-the-sands legislation marked in effect an abandonment of our traditional policy of freedom of the seas—a policy for which we had professedly fought two full-fledged wars and several undeclared wars. The Neutrality Acts, so called, were specifically tailored to keep us out of a conflict like World War I. If they had been in effect at that time, we probably would not have been sucked in—at least not in April, 1917. We were one war too late with our legislation. What had seemed dishonorable to Wilson seemed honorable and desirable to a later disillusioned generation.

Storm-cellar neutrality proved to be a ghastly blunder. We falsely assumed that the decision for peace or war lay in our own hands, not in those of the satanic forces already unleashed in the world. Prisoners of our own fears, we failed to recognize that we should have used our enormous power to control international events in our own interest. Instead, we remained at the mercy of events controlled by the dictators.

The new neutrality policy, though of undoubted legality, was of dubious morality. We served notice that we would make no distinction whatever between the brutal aggressor and his innocent victims. By striving to hold the scales even, we actually overbalanced them in favor of the dictators who had armed themselves to the teeth. By declining to use our vast industrial strength to aid our democratic friends and defeat our totalitarian foes, we helped spur the aggressors along their blood-stained path of conquest.

Fruits of Isolationist Fears

The Spanish Civil War of 1936–1939—a proving ground and dress rehearsal for World War II—was a painful object lesson in the folly of neutrality-by-legislation. The Spanish rebels, who rose against the republican government in Madrid, were headed by dictator-minded General Francisco Franco. Generously aided by his fellow conspirators, Hitler and Mussolini, he undertook to overthrow the established Loyalist regime, which in turn was assisted on a smaller scale by the Soviet Union. This pipeline from Communist Moscow chilled the natural sympathies of many Americans, especially those of the Roman Catholic faith.

The Loyalist government was the one officially recognized by Washington. In accordance with previous American practice, this Madrid regime should have been free to purchase desperately needed munitions in the United States. But Congress, with the encouragement of Roosevelt and with only one dissenting vote, amended the existing neutrality legislation so as to apply an arms embargo to both sides in the Spanish civil conflict.

Uncle Sam thus sat on the sidelines while Franco, abundantly supplied with arms and men by his fellow dictators, strangled the republican government of Spain and set himself up as dictator. The democracies, including the United States, were so determined to stay out of war that they helped to condemn a fellow democracy to death. In so doing, they further encouraged the dictators to take the dangerous road which ended with the precipice of World War II.

American peace-at-any-price-ism was further cursed with illogic. While determined to stay out of war, we declined to build up our armed forces to a point where they could deter the aggressors. In fact, we allowed our navy to decline in relative strength. We had been led to believe that huge fleets cause huge wars; we were also trying to spare the complaining taxpayer during the grim days of the Great Depression. When President Roosevelt repeatedly called for preparedness, he was branded a warmonger. Not until 1938, the year before World War II burst, did Congress come to grips with the problem when it passed a billion-dollar naval construction act. The tragic story was repeated of too little—and that too late.

The Day of the Dictators

Sulphurous war clouds had meanwhile been gathering in the tension-taut Far East. In 1937 the Japanese militarists, at the Marco Polo bridge near Peiping, touched off the explosion that led to a full-dress invasion of China. In a sense this attack was the curtain raiser of World War II.

Roosevelt declined to invoke the recently passed neutrality legislation, on the ground that the so-called "China incident" was not an officially declared war. If he had put the existing restrictions into effect, he would have cut off the tiny trickle of munitions on which the Chinese were desperately dependent. The Japanese, of course, could continue to buy mountainous quantities of war supplies in the United States.

In Chicago—unofficial isolationist capital of America—Roosevelt delivered his sensational "Quarantine Speech" in the autumn of 1937. Profoundly disturbed by the recent aggressions of Italy and Japan, he called for "positive endeavors" to "quarantine" the aggressors—presumably by economic embargoes. The immediate result was a nationwide cyclone of protest from isolationists and other foes of involvement; they feared that a moral quarantine would lead to a shooting quarantine. Startled by this angry response, Roosevelt sought by less forthright means to curb the dictators.

America's isolationist mood deepened, especially in regard to China. In December, 1937, Japanese aviators bombed and sank an American gunboat, the *Panay*, in Chinese waters, with a loss of two killed and thirty wounded. In the days of 1898, when the *Maine* went down, this outrage might have provoked war. But after the Japanese government had hastened to make the necessary apologies and pay a proper indemnity, the American public breathed an audible sigh of relief. Japanese militarists were thus encouraged to vent their anger against the "superior" white race by subjecting American civilians in China, both male and female, to humiliating slappings and strippings.

More immediately menacing was the course of Hitler. In 1935 he had openly flouted the Treaty of Versailles by introducing compulsory military service in Germany. The next year he boldly marched into the demilitarized German Rhineland, likewise contrary to the hated treaty, while France and Britain looked on in an agony of indecision. Lashing his fanatical following to a frenzy, Hitler undertook to liquidate the Jewish population of Germany. In the end, he wiped out about six million innocent victims. Calling upon his people to sacrifice butter for guns, he whipped the new German air force and mechanized ground divisions into the most devastating military machine the world had yet seen.

Suddenly, in March, 1938, Hitler bloodlessly seized German-speaking Austria. The democratic powers, wringing their hands in despair, prayed that this last grab would satisfy his passion for conquest.

But Hitler could not stop. Later in 1938 he continued his "war of nerves" by his bullying demands for the German-inhabited Sudetenland of his neighbor, tiny Czechoslovakia. Brandishing the sword, he threatened war if he did not have his way. The leaders of Britain and France, eager to appease Hitler, sought desperately to bring the dispute to the conference table. Roosevelt, also deeply alarmed, kept the wires hot with personal messages, both to Hitler and to Mussolini, urging a peaceful settlement.

A conference was finally arranged in Munich, Germany, in September, 1938. The Western European democracies, badly unprepared for war, betrayed Czechoslovakia to Germany when they consented to the shearing away of the Sudetenland. They hoped—and these hopes were shared by the American people—that the concessions at the conference table would appease the power-lust of Hitler.

But "appeasement" of the dictators, symbolized by the ugly word "Munich," turned out to be merely surrender on the installment plan. In March, 1939, scarcely six months later, Hitler suddenly erased the rest of Czechoslovakia from the map, contrary to his solemn promise. The democratic world was again profoundly shocked.

The Armies March Again

Joseph Stalin, the Sphinx of the Kremlin, was a key to the puzzle of continued peace. In the summer of 1939 the British and French were busily negotiating with Moscow, hopeful of securing a treaty that would halt Hitler. But their bait was not sufficiently attractive. Almost overnight the Soviet Union astounded the civilized world by signing, on August 23, 1939, a non-aggression treaty with the German dictator.

The notorious Hitler-Stalin pact was epochal. It meant that the Nazi German leader now had a green light to make war on Poland and the western democracies, without fearing a stab in the back from Russia— his Communist archfoe. Consternation struck those wishful thinkers in Western Europe who had fondly hoped that Hitler might be egged upon Stalin so that the twin menaces would bleed each other to death. It was as plain as the mustache on Stalin's face that the wily Soviet dictator was plotting to turn his German accomplice against the western democracies. The two warring camps would kill each other off—and leave him bestriding Europe like a colossus.

World War II was only hours away. Hitler, intensifying his "war of nerves," demanded from neighboring Poland a return of the areas wrested from Germany after World War I. Failing to secure satisfaction, he sent his mechanized divisions crashing into Poland at dawn on September 1, 1939. He did not even bother with a declaration of hostilities.

Britain and France, honoring their commitments to Poland, promptly declared war. At long last they perceived the folly of continued "appeasement." But they were powerless to aid Poland, which succumbed in three weeks to Hitler's smashing strategy of terror. Stalin, as prearranged secretly in his fateful pact with Hitler, came in on the kill for his share of old Russian Poland. Long-dreaded World War II was now fully launched.

President Roosevelt speedily issued the routine proclamations of neutrality. The American people were overwhelmingly anti-Nazi and anti-Hitler; they fervently hoped that the democracies would win; they fondly believed that the forces of righteousness would again triumph, as in 1918. But they were desperately determined to stay out. They were not going to be "suckers" again.

The existing Neutrality Act of 1937 promptly became a burning issue in the United States. Ill-prepared Britain and France urgently needed American airplanes and other weapons, but the American law raised a sternly forbidding hand. Roosevelt summoned Congress in special session, shortly after the invasion of Poland, to consider a lifting of the arms embargo. After six hectic weeks of debate, a makeshift law emerged.

The new Neutrality Act of 1939 provided that henceforth the hardpressed European democracies might buy our war materials, but only on a "cash and carry" basis. This meant that they would have to transport the munitions in their own ships, and pay for them in cash. We would thus avoid loans, war debts, and the torpedoing of American arms-carriers. While Congress thus loosened some former restrictions in response to the clamor of interventionists, it added others in response to the clamor of isolationists. The President was now authorized to proclaim danger zones into which American merchant ships would be forbidden to enter.

The new neutrality law clearly favored the democracies against the dictators—and was so intended. Since the British and French navies controlled the Atlantic, the European aggressors could not send their ships to buy our munitions. America not only improved her moral position, but she simultaneously improved her economic position. The boom in war goods, though at first limited to the munitions industry, brought a sharp upswing from the recession of 1937–1938, and ultimately solved the decade-long unemployment crisis. (See charts, pp. 853, 855.)

The Fall of France

The months following the collapse of Poland, while France and Britain marked time, formed the period known as the "phony war." An ominous silence fell on Europe, as Hitler shifted his victorious divisions from Poland for a knockout blow at France. The inaction of this anxious period was relieved by the Soviets, who wantonly attacked neighboring Finland in an effort to secure strategic buffer territory. The debt-paying Finns, who had a host of admirers in America, were speedily granted $30,000,000 by Congress for non-military supplies. But despite heroic resistance, Finland was finally crushed by the Russian steam roller.

The "phony war" came to an abrupt end in April, 1940, when Hitler, again without warning, overran his weaker neighbors, Denmark and Norway. Hardly pausing for breath, the next month he launched an unannounced assault on Holland and Belgium, followed by a paralyzing blow at France. By late June, France was forced to surrender, but not until Mussolini had pounced on her rear for a jackal's share of the loot. Only by the so-called "miracle of Dunkirk" did the British manage to evacuate to England the bulk of their shattered and partially disarmed army. The crisis providentially brought forth an inspired leader in Winston Churchill, the bulldog-jawed orator who nerved his people to fight off the fearful air bombings of their cities.

The sudden collapse of France shocked Americans out of their daydreams. Stout-hearted Britons, singing "There'll Always Be an England," were all that stood between Hitler and the end in Europe of constitutional government. If Britain went under, Hitler would have at his disposal the workshops, shipyards, and slave labor of Western Europe. He might even have the powerful British fleet as well. This frightening possibility, which seemed to pose a dire threat to American security, steeled the American people to a tremendous effort.

Roosevelt moved with electrifying energy and dispatch. He called upon an already debt-burdened nation to build huge airfleets and a two-ocean navy, which could also check Japan. Congress, jarred out of its apathy toward preparedness, within a year appropriated the astounding sum of $37,000,000,000. This figure was more than the total cost of fighting World War I.

Congress was also shocked into passing a conscription law, approved September 6, 1940. Under this measure—the first peacetime draft in our history—provision was made for training each year 1,200,000 troops and 800,000 reserves. The act was later broadened to meet the necessities of a global war.

The Latin American bulkhead likewise needed bolstering. Holland and France, crushed under the German jackboot, both had orphaned colonies in the West Indies and South America. Would these fall into German hands? At the Havana Conference of 1940 the United States,

"JUST SO THERE'LL BE NO MISUNDERSTANDING"
Ray in the Kansas City *Star*, 1940

by implication, agreed to share with its twenty sister republics the responsibility of upholding the Monroe Doctrine. This ancient dictum, hitherto unilateral, had been a bludgeon brandished only by the hated Yankee colossus. Now multilateral, it was to be wielded by twenty-one pairs of American hands.

Bolstering Britain

Before the tragic fall of France, the Roosevelt administration had generally observed a technical neutrality. But now Americans had to choose between neutrality and unneutral assistance to Britain before she fell under the heel of the Hitlerian invader. Neutrality gradually went into the ash can.

Roosevelt at first arranged to transfer surplus federal arms to private American concerns ("dummies"), through which the weapons could be sent to bomb-blasted Britain. Thus airplanes, rifles, mortars, artillery, and ammunition were dispatched in a technically legal way across the Atlantic.

The more ardent advocates of aid to Britain formed propaganda groups, the most potent of which was the Committee to Defend America by Aiding the Allies. Its argument was double-barreled. To interventionists, it could appeal for direct succor to the British by such slogans as "Britain Is Fighting Our Fight." To the isolationists, it could appeal for assistance to the democracies by "All Methods Short of War," so that the terrible conflict would be kept in faraway Europe.

The isolationists, both numerous and sincere, were by no means silent. Determined to stay out of the bloodshed at all costs, they organized the America First Committee and proclaimed, "England Will Fight to the Last American." They contended that we should concentrate what strength we had to defend our own shores, lest a victorious Hitler, after crushing Britain, successfully assault us. Their basic philosophy was "The Yanks Are Not Coming," and their most effective speechmaker was the famed aviator, Colonel Charles A. Lindbergh.

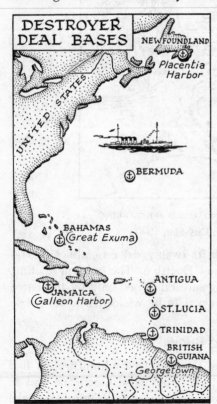

Britain was in desperate need of destroyers, for the German submarines were again threatening to starve her out with their attacks on shipping. Roosevelt moved boldly when, on September 2, 1940, he agreed to transfer to Great Britain fifty old-model, four-funnel destroyers left over from World War I. In return, the British promised to hand over to the United States eight valuable defensive base sites, stretching from Newfoundland to South America. These strategically located outposts were to be controlled by the American authorities for a period of ninety-nine years.

The transfer of fifty destroyers to a foreign navy was a highly questionable disposal of government property, despite a strained interpretation of existing legislation. The exchange was achieved by a simple presidential agreement, without so much as a "by your leave" to Congress. Noisy applause burst from the aid-to-Britain advocates and other interventionists, many of whom had long been urging such a step. But a chorus of condemnation arose from "America Firsters" and other isolationists, as well as from anti-administration Republicans. Some of them approved the transfer but decried Roosevelt's secretive and highhanded methods. Yet so grave was the crisis that the President was unwilling to submit the scheme to the uncertainties and delays of a full-dress debate in Congress.

The transfer of warships from the navy of a "neutral" United States to that of a belligerent Britain was, beyond question, a flagrant violation of neutral obligations—at least the neutral obligations that had existed before Hitler's barefaced aggressions rendered dangerous such old-fashioned concepts of fair play. Public opinion polls indicated that a majority of the American people were determined, even at the risk of armed hostilities, to provide the battered British with "all aid short of war."

Shattering the Two-Term Tradition

The distractions of a presidential election, as fate decreed, came in the midst of this grave international crisis. The two leading Republican aspirants were round-faced and flat-voiced Senator Robert A. Taft of Ohio, son of the ex-President, and an energetic lawyer-prosecutor, Thomas E. Dewey of New York. But in one of the miracles of American political history, the Philadelphia convention was swept off its feet by an interventionist latecomer, Wendell L. Willkie, a German-descended son of Hoosier Indiana. This dynamic lawyer—tousle-headed, broad-faced, and large-framed—had until recently been a Democrat and the head of a huge public-utilities corporation. A complete novice in politics, he had rocketed from political nothingness in a few short weeks. His great appeal lay in his personality, for he was magnetic, transparently sincere, and honest in a homespun, Lincolnesque way.

With the galleries in Philadelphia wildly chanting "We Want Willkie," the delegates finally accepted this political upstart as the only candidate who could possibly beat Roosevelt. The Republican platform condemned F.D.R.'s alleged dictatorship, as well as the costly and confusing zigzags of the New Deal. Willkie, an outstanding liberal, was not so much opposed to the New Deal as to its extravagances and inefficiencies. Democratic critics branded him "the rich man's Roosevelt" and "the simple barefoot Wall Street lawyer."

While the rumor-pot boiled, Roosevelt delayed to the last minute the announcement of his decision to challenge the sacred two-term tradition. Despite what he described as his personal yearning for retirement, he avowed that in so grave a crisis he owed his experienced hand to the service of his country and humanity. The Democratic delegates in Chicago, realizing that only with "the Champ" could they defeat Willkie, drafted him by a unanimous vote. "Better a Third Term than a Third-Rater" was the argument of many Democrats.

Burning with sincerity and energy, Willkie launched out upon a whirlwind, Bryanesque campaign in which he delivered over five hundred speeches. At times his voice became a hoarse croak. The country was already badly split between interventionists and isolationists, and Willkie might have widened the breach dangerously by a violent attack on Roosevelt's aid-to-Britain policies. But seeing eye to eye with F.D.R. on the necessity of bolstering the democracies, he refrained from assailing the President's interventionism, though objecting to some of his methods.

In the realm of foreign affairs, there was not much to choose between the two candidates. Both promised to stay out of the war; both promised aid to the victims of aggression; both promised to strengthen the nation's defenses. Yet Willkie, with a mop of black hair in his eyes, hit hard at Rooseveltian "dictatorship" and the third term. His enthusiastic followers cried, "Win with Willkie," "No Fourth Term Either," and "There's No Indispensable Man."

Roosevelt, busy at his desk with mounting problems, made only a few speeches. Stung by taunts that he was leading the nation by the back door into the European slaughterhouse, he repeatedly denied any such intention. One of his most specific statements was at Boston, where he emphatically declared, "Your boys are not going to be sent into any foreign wars"—a pledge that later came back to plague him. He and his

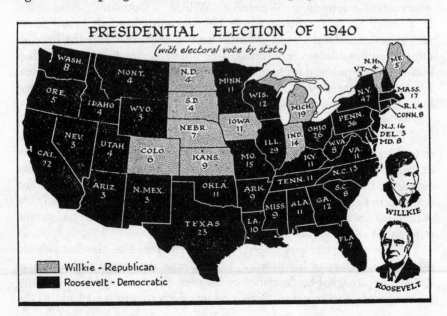

PRESIDENTIAL ELECTION OF 1940
(with electoral vote by state)

Willkie - Republican
Roosevelt - Democratic

henchmen vigorously defended the New Deal, as well as all-out preparations for the defense of America and aid to the Allies.

Roosevelt triumphed in an unprecedented turnout of the voters, although Willkie ran a strong race. The popular total was 27,244,160 to
22,305,198, and the electoral count was 449 to 82. The contest was much
less of a walkaway than in 1932 or 1936, and the Democratic majorities
in Congress were sharply reduced.

Jubilant Democrats hailed their triumph as a mandate to abolish the
two-term tradition. But the truth is that Roosevelt won in spite of the
third-term handicap. The voters generally felt that, should war come,
the experienced hand of the tried leader was needed at the helm. Less appealing was the completely inexperienced hand of the well-intentioned
Willkie, who had never held public office.

The argument that one should not change horses in the middle of a
stream was strong, especially in an era of war-spawned prosperity. Roosevelt probably would not have won if there had not been a war crisis. On
the other hand, he probably would not have run if foreign perils had not
loomed on the horizon.

Lend-Lease Largesse

By late 1940 embattled Britain was nearing the end of her financial
tether; her credits in America were being rapidly eaten up by insatiable
war orders. But Roosevelt, who had bitter memories of wrangling over
the Allied debts of World War I, was determined, as he put it, "to eliminate the dollar sign." He finally hit on the scheme of lending or leasing
American arms to the reeling democracies. When the shooting was over,
to use his comparison, the guns and tanks could be returned, just as one's
neighbor would return a length of garden hose when the fire was put out.
But isolationist Senator Taft retorted that lending arms was like lending
chewing gum: "You don't want it back."

The lend-lease bill was officially entitled "An Act Further to Promote
the Defense of the United States." Sprung on Congress and the public
after the election was safely over, it was praised by the administration
as a device that would keep America out of the war, rather than get her
into it. The United States, so Roosevelt promised, would be the "arsenal
of democracy." We would send a limitless supply of arms to the victims
of aggression, who in turn would finish the job and keep the war on their
side of the Atlantic.

Lend-lease was heatedly debated throughout the country and on the
floor of Congress. Most of the opposition came, as might be expected,
from the isolationists and from anti-Roosevelt Republicans. The scheme
was assailed as "the blank-check bill," and, in the words of isolationist
Senator Wheeler, as "the new Triple-A bill"—a measure designed to "plow
under every fourth American boy." Nevertheless lend-lease was finally

approved, in March, 1941, by sweeping majorities in both houses of Congress.

The lend-lease law was one of the most momentous bills ever to pass Congress; it was a defiant challenge hurled squarely into the teeth of the Axis dictators. The United States pledged itself, to the extent of its vast resources, to bolster those nations that were indirectly defending America by fighting aggression. When the gigantic operation ended in 1945, we had sent about fifty billion dollars' worth of arms and equipment—more than double the cost to us of World War I—to those nations fighting aggressors. The passing of lend-lease was in effect an economic declaration of war; a shooting declaration could not be very far around the corner.

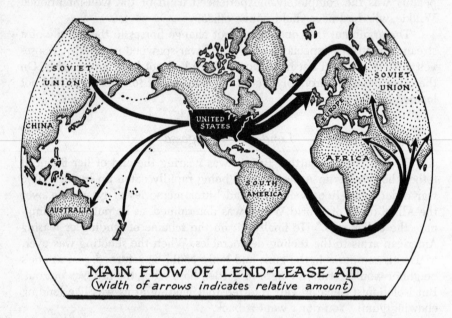

MAIN FLOW OF LEND-LEASE AID
(Width of arrows indicates relative amount)

Lend-lease, by its very nature, marked the abandonment by the American government and people of any pretense of neutrality. It was no destroyer deal signed privately by Roosevelt. It was universally debated, over drugstore counters and cracker barrels, from California to Maine; and the sovereign citizen at last spoke through convincing majorities in Congress. The bulk of the people no doubt realized that they were tossing the old concepts of neutrality out the window. But they also realized that they would play a suicidal game if they bound themselves by the oxcart rules of the 19th Century—especially while the aggressors themselves openly spurned international obligations. Lend-lease would admittedly involve a grave risk of war, but most Americans were prepared to take that chance, in preference to seeing Britain collapse and then facing the dictators alone.

Lend-lease had the somewhat incidental result of gearing our own factories for all-out war production. The enormously increased capacity thus achieved helped to save our own skins when, at long last, the shooting war exploded around our heads.

Hitler himself evidently recognized lend-lease as an unofficial declaration of war. Until then, he had scrupulously avoided attacking American ships; memories of our decisive intervention in 1917–1918 were still fresh in German minds. But after the passing of lend-lease there was little point in trying to curry favor with the United States. On May 21, 1941, the *Robin Moor,* an unarmed American merchantman, was torpedoed and destroyed by a German submarine in the South Atlantic, outside a war zone. The sinkings had started, but on a limited scale.

Strange Bedfellows Again

Two globe-shaking events marked the course of World War II before the assault on Pearl Harbor in 1941. One was the fall of France; the other was Hitler's invasion of Russia.

The two scheming dictators, Hitler and Stalin, had been uneasy yoke-fellows under the ill-begotten pact of 1939. As masters of the double-cross, neither trusted the other. They engaged in prolonged dickering in a secret attempt to divide much of the world between them, but Stalin gagged on dominant German control of the Balkans. Hitler thereupon undertook to crush his co-conspirator, seize the oil and other resources of Russia, and then have a completely free hand to snuff out Britain. He assumed that his all-conquering armies would subdue the "Mongol half-wits" of Russia in a few short weeks.

Out of a clear sky, on June 22, 1941, Hitler launched a devastating attack on his Soviet neighbor. This timely assault was an incredible stroke of good fortune for the democratic world—or so it seemed at the time. The two menaces could now slit each other's throats on the icy steppes of Russia. Or they would if the Soviets did not speedily collapse, as many of our ablest military experts predicted.

Sound American strategy seemed to dictate speedy aid to Russia while she was still afloat. Roosevelt immediately promised assistance, and backed up his words by making military supplies available. Several months later, interpreting the lend-lease law to mean that the defense of Russia was essential for the defense of the United States, he extended one billion dollars in lend-lease—the first installment on an ultimate total of eleven billions. Meanwhile the valor of the Red Army, combined with the white paralysis of an early Russian winter, had halted the Hitlerian invaders at the gates of Moscow.

With the collapse of the Soviets still a dread possibility, the drama-charged Atlantic Conference was held in August, 1941. British Prime Minister Winston Churchill, with the eternal cigar embedded in his cherubic face, secretly met with Roosevelt on a warship off the coast of

Newfoundland. This was the first of a series of history-making conferences between the two eminent leaders for the discussion of common
problems, including the menace of Japan in the Far East.

The most memorable product of the Newfoundland conversations
was the eight-point Atlantic Charter. It was formally accepted by Roosevelt and Churchill, and endorsed by the Soviet Union later that year.
Reminiscent of Wilson's Fourteen Points, the new covenant outlined the
aspirations of the democracies for a better world at the end of the war.

The Atlantic Charter was surprisingly specific. While coming out
against imperialistic acquisitions, it promised that there would be no territorial changes contrary to the wishes of the inhabitants concerned (self-
determination). The pact further affirmed the right of a people to choose
their own form of government and, in addition, to have restored to them
the governments of which they had been deprived by the dictators.
Among various other goals, the Charter declared for disarmament and a
peace of security, pending "a permanent system of general security" (a
new League of Nations).

The Atlantic Charter held out a lively hope to liberals the world
over. It was especially gratifying to subject populations, like the Poles,
who were then ground under the iron heel of the conqueror. But the
agreement was roundly condemned in the United States by isolationists
and others hostile to Roosevelt. What right, they charged, had "neutral"
America to confer with belligerent Britain on common policies? Such
critics missed the point: America was no longer neutral.

The Shooting Starts

It was inevitable that lend-lease shipments of arms to Britain on
British ships would be sunk by German wolf-pack submarines. If our
intent was to get the munitions to England, not to throw them into the
ocean, the freighters would have to be escorted by American warships.
Britain simply did not have enough destroyers. The dangerous possibility
of our being "convoyed into war" had been mentioned in Congress during
the heated debate on lend-lease, but administration spokesmen had
shunted the idea aside. Their strategy was to make only one commitment
at a time.

The fateful dice were finally cast in July, 1941. Roosevelt, by virtue
of his authority as Commander-in-Chief of the armed forces, issued orders
to the navy to escort lend-lease shipments to Iceland. The British would
then shepherd them the rest of the way.

The inevitable clashes with submarines ensued on the Iceland run.
In September, 1941, the U.S. destroyer *Greer,* provocatively trailing a
German U-boat, was attacked by the undersea craft, without damage to
either side. Roosevelt then proclaimed a shoot-on-sight policy. On October 17, the escorting destroyer *Kearny,* while engaged in a battle with

U-boats, lost eleven men when it was crippled but not sent to the bottom. Two weeks later the destroyer *Reuben James* was torpedoed and sunk off western Iceland, with the loss of about one hundred officers and men.

Neutrality was still inscribed on our statute books, but not in our hearts. Congress, responding to public pressures and confronted with a shooting war, voted in mid-November, 1941, to pull the teeth from the now-useless Neutrality Act of 1939. American merchant ships could henceforth be legally armed, and they could enter the combat zones with munitions for Britain. The American people braced themselves for wholesale attacks by Hitler's submarines.

The Foul Blow at Pearl Harbor

The final blowup came, not in the Atlantic, but in the faraway Pacific. This explosion should have surprised no close observer, for Japan, since September of 1940, had been a formal military ally of Nazi Germany—our shooting foe in the North Atlantic.

Japan's position in the Far East had grown more precarious by the hour. She was still mired down in the costly and exhausting "China incident," from which she could extract neither honor nor victory. Her war machine was fatally dependent on immense shipments from the United States of steel, scrap iron, oil, and aviation gasoline. Such assistance to the Japanese aggressor was highly unpopular in America. But Roosevelt had resolutely held off an embargo, lest he goad the Nipponese warlords into making a premature descent upon the oil-rich and weakly defended Dutch East Indies.

The Washington government, late in 1940, finally imposed the first of its embargoes on Japan-bound supplies. This blow was followed in later months by a "freezing" of Nipponese assets in the United States and a cessation of all shipments of gasoline and other sinews of war. As the oil gauge dropped, the pinch on Japan grew steadily more severe. Protracted delay was on the side of the United States. The Japanese leaders were faced with two painful alternatives. They could either knuckle under to the Americans, or break out of the embargo ring by a desperate attack on the oil supplies and other riches of Southeast Asia.

Final tense negotiations with Japan took place in Washington during November and early December of 1941. The State Department insisted that the Japanese clear out of China but, to sweeten the pill, offered to renew trade relations on a limited basis. The Japanese imperialists, after waging a bitter war against the Chinese for more than four years, were unwilling to lose face by withdrawing at the behest of the United States. As between capitulation and continued conquest, they chose the sword. They had to put up or shut up, as the American press noted. They put up.

The top officials in Washington, having "cracked" the secret code of the Japanese, knew that the decision of Tokyo was for war. But the

United States, being a democracy committed to public debate and action by Congress, could not shoot first. It had to wait for the blow to fall. Roosevelt, misled by Japanese ship movements in the Far East, evidently expected the attack to fall on British Malaya or perhaps on the Philippines. No one in high authority in Washington seems to have believed that the Japanese were either strong enough or foolhardy enough to lash out at Hawaii.

But the paralyzing blow fell on Pearl Harbor, while Tokyo was deliberately prolonging negotiations in Washington. Japanese bombers, winging in from distant aircraft carriers, attacked without warning on the "Black Sunday" morning of December 7, 1941. It was a date, as Roosevelt told Congress, "which will live in infamy." About three thousand casualties were inflicted on American personnel; many aircraft were destroyed; the battleship fleet was virtually wiped out when all eight of the craft were sunk or otherwise immobilized; and numerous small vessels were damaged or destroyed. Fortunately, three priceless aircraft carriers happened to be outside the harbor.

The next day an angered Congress officially recognized the war that had been "thrust" upon the United States. The roll call in the Senate and House lacked only one vote of unanimity. Germany and Italy, allies of Japan, spared Congress the agonizing indecision of a long debate by declaring war on December 11, 1941. This challenge was formally accepted on the same day by a unanimous vote of both Senate and House. The unofficial war, of many months' duration, was now official.

From Bystander to Belligerent

Japan's hara-kiri gamble at Pearl Harbor paid off only in the short run. It is true that our Pacific fleet was largely destroyed or immobilized, but the sneak attack aroused and united America as nothing else could have done. To the very day of Pearl Harbor, a strong majority of the American people still wanted to keep out of the war. But the isolationist group was blasted into silence by the bombs that pulverized Pearl Harbor. The only thing left to do, growled Senator Wheeler, was "to lick hell out of them."

But Pearl Harbor was far from being the full answer to the question why the United States went to war. This treacherous attack was but the last and loudest explosion in a long chain reaction. Following the fall of France, the American people were confronted with a devil's dilemma. They desired above all things to stay out of the conflict; yet they did not want Britain to be knocked out. They wished to halt the fearsome conquests by Japan in the Far East—conquests that menaced not only American trade and security but international peace as well. To keep Britain from collapsing, the Roosevelt administration felt compelled to extend the unneutral aid that invited attacks from German submarines. To keep

Japan from expanding, the Washington officials deemed it necessary to cut off vital Japanese supplies and invite possible retaliation. Rather than let democracy die and dictatorship rule supreme, a strong majority of the American people were evidently determined to support a policy that might lead to war. It did.

Clearheaded Americans had come to the conclusion that no nation was safe unless all were safe. Appeasement—the process of throwing the weaker persons out of the sleigh to the pursuing wolves—had been tried, but it had merely whetted dictatorial appetites. Power-drunk dictators had flouted international law and decency. They had turned the proverbial "scrap of paper" into heaps of torn-up pacts. Pursuing the philosophy that might makes right, they had cynically negotiated non-aggression treaties with their intended victims, so as to lull them into a false sense of security. Most Americans were determined to stand firm—and let war come if it must—because they were convinced that in an era of rapacious dictators the world could not long remain half enchained and half free.

SELECT READINGS

Useful overviews are provided by R. A. DIVINE, *The Reluctant Belligerent: American Entry into World War II* (1965) [paperback] and DEXTER PERKINS, *The New Age of Franklin Roosevelt, 1932–1945* (1957) [paperback]. More detailed are D. F. DRUMMOND's incisive *The Passing of American Neutrality, 1937–1941* (1955) and the classic volumes of W. L. LANGER and S. E. GLEASON, *The Challenge to Isolation, 1937–1940* (1952) and *The Undeclared War, 1940–1941* (1953) [both paperback]. A Pulitzer-prize interpretation by one of FDR's ghost writers is R. E. SHERWOOD, *Roosevelt and Hopkins* (1948) [paperback]. See also J. W. PRATT, *Cordell Hull, 1933–1944* (2 vols., 1964). On Good Neighborism consult BRYCE WOOD, *The Making of the Good Neighbor Policy* (1961) and D. M. DOZER, *Are We Good Neighbors?* (1959). Aspects of isolation are ably handled in R. A. DIVINE, *The Illusion of Neutrality* (1962) and W. S. COLE, *Gerald P. Nye and American Foreign Relations* (1962).

Regarding the rise of the dictators see F. J. TAYLOR, *The United States and The Spanish Civil War* (1956); ALLEN GUTTMANN, *The Wound in the Heart* [Spanish Civil War] (1962); and DOROTHY BORG, *The United States and the Far Eastern Crisis of 1933–1938* (1964). Revealing is R. H. DAWSON, *The Decision to Aid Russia, 1941* (1959). Aspects of relations with Japan are treated in W. L. NEUMANN, *America Encounters Japan* (1963); P. W. SCHROEDER, *The Axis Alliance and Japanese-American Relations, 1941* (1958); and R. J. C. BUTOW, *Tojo and the Coming of the War* (1961). The preliminaries to war with Japan are well presented in HERBERT FEIS, *The Road to Pearl Harbor* (1950) [paperback] and ROBERTA WOHLSTETTER, *Pearl Harbor: Warning and Decision* (1962). Also references for preceding chapter and *Harvard Guide*, Pt. VI.

44

America in World War II

*No matter how long it may take us to overcome this premeditated
invasion, the American people in their righteous might will win
through to absolute victory.*

FRANKLIN D. ROOSEVELT, War Message
to Congress, December 8, 1941

Trading Space for Time

THE United States was plunged into the inferno of World War II with
the most stupefying and humiliating military defeat in its history. In the
dismal months that ensued, the democratic world teetered on the raw
edge of disaster.

The Japanese fanatics forgot that when one stabs a king, one must
stab to kill. A wounded but still potent American giant pulled himself
out of the mud of Pearl Harbor, grimly determined to avenge the bloody
treachery. "Get Hirohito first" was the cry that rose from millions of infuriated Americans, especially on the Pacific Coast. These outraged souls
regarded America's share in the global conflict as a private war of vengeance in the Pacific, with the European front a kind of holding operation.

But after earlier conferences with the British, Washington wisely
adopted the grand strategy of "getting Hitler first." If we diverted our
main strength to the Pacific, Hitler might crush both Russia and Britain,
and then emerge unconquerable in Fortress Europe. But if Germany was
knocked out first, the combined Allied forces could be concentrated on
Japan, and her daring game of conquest would be up. Meanwhile enough
American strength would be sent to the Pacific to prevent the Nipponese
from digging in too deeply.

The get-Hitler-first strategy was carried through. But it encountered
much ignorant or biased criticism from two-fisted Americans who, according to the public opinion polls, at one time constituted a plurality. Aggrieved protests were also registered by shorthanded American commanders in the Pacific, and by our Chinese and Australian allies. But
Roosevelt, a competent military strategist in his own right, was able to
resist these pressures.

Given time, the Allies seemed bound to triumph. But would they be given time? It is true that they had on their side the great mass of the people of the world, but the wolf is never frightened by the number of the sheep. The United States was the mightiest military power on earth—potentially. But wars are won with weapons, not blueprints. The naked truth is that we came perilously close to losing the war to the well-armed aggressors before we could begin to throw our full weight into the scales.

Time, in a sense, was the most-needed munition. Expense was no limitation. The overpowering problem confronting America was to re-tool herself for all-out war production, while praying that the ruthless dictators would not meanwhile crush the democracies. Haste was all the more imperative because the highly skilled German scientists might turn up with unbeatable secret weapons—as they almost did.

America's task was far more complex and backbreaking than during World War I. We had to feed, clothe, and arm ourselves, as well as transport our forces to regions as far separated as Britain and Burma. More than that, we had to send a vast amount of food and munitions to our hard-pressed allies, who stretched all the way from Russia to Australia. Could the American people, reputedly "gone soft," measure up to this colossal responsibility? Was democracy "rotten" and "decadent," as the dictators sneeringly proclaimed?

One for All

National unity was no worry, thanks to the electrifying blow of the Japanese at Pearl Harbor. The cynical aggressions of the dictators had laid nakedly bare the issue of survival. This time America was not out to make the world safe for democracy, but to make the world safe—for decency. The handful of strutting pro-Hitlerites in the United States melted away, while millions of Italian-Americans and German-Americans loyally supported the nation's war program. The Communists and fellow travelers, who had decried the Anglo-French "imperialist war" before Hitler attacked Stalin in 1941, now whooped it up for an all-out assault on the Axis powers. There was no witch-hunting persecution of dissenting groups, as in World War I.

The mainland Japanese-American population of 110,000 persons, concentrated on the Pacific Coast, provided a painful exception. The Washington authorities, fearing that these people might act as saboteurs for the Mikado in case of invasion, decided to herd them together in concentration camps, though about two-thirds of the victims were American-born citizens. This brutal precaution turned out to be unnecessary, for the loyalty and combat record of the Japanese-Americans, especially those from Hawaii, proved to be admirable. Partial financial adjustment after the war did something to recompense these uprooted citizens for their sufferings and losses.

The conflict was not an idealistic crusade, as in 1917–1918. It is true that the appropriate agencies in Washington did make some effort to propagandize abroad with the Atlantic Charter, as well as with other hope-giving Rooseveltian pronouncements. But the accent was on action. We realized that we had before us a dirty job, and that the only way out was forward. We did our killing coldly, methodically, calculatingly, efficiently. It was not a singing war, as in 1917–1918. "Praise the Lord and Pass the Ammunition" enjoyed some vogue, as did "God Bless America." But the latter was a song of consecration rather than of excitation.

An unexpected degree of unity was also achieved among the Allies, thanks in part to the jolting effect of Pearl Harbor. On January 1, 1942, the representatives of twenty-six countries, including the United States, signed in Washington the Declaration of the United Nations. This group, which formed the nucleus of the yet unborn United Nations Organization, pledged itself to fight four-square, under the principles of the Atlantic Charter, and not to make a separate peace.

"THE THREE MUSKETEERS"

F.D.R., Stalin, and Churchill, drawn by Manning in the Phoenix *Arizona Republic;* reprinted by permission of the McNaught Syndicate, Inc.

The Latin American republics of the Western Hemisphere, their largest sister the victim of a treacherous attack, rallied behind the once-hated Colossus of the North. The one conspicuous exception was Fascist-inclined Argentina, with its large Italian and German population and with its burning jealousy of rich Uncle Sam, a competitor in beef and grain. Yet the Good Neighbor policy of the 1930's reaped a rich harvest during these anxious years. Pan-Americanism became more a fact than a phrase, as Washington spent billions of dollars in Latin America for tin, nitrates, and other urgently needed materials.

Aid to the ever-suspicious Soviets claimed a high priority. Dedicated to the destruction of capitalism through World Communism, the Russians accepted distrustfully the vast amount of munitions provided by their American stepbrothers-in-arms. Lend-lease materials from the United States made up only about 10% of the total military equipment of the

Soviet Union. But these contributions came in the form of desperately needed trucks, automobiles, military aircraft, and other equipment, without which the Russians probably could not have smashed their way to Berlin.

Smokestacks Go to War

America was already partially geared for a war economy when the galvanizing blow fell at Pearl Harbor. Allied orders for munitions, plus lend-lease operations and defense appropriations, had all contributed to the chassis of a mighty war-production machine. But at the outset we were only ankle-deep in the conflict.

Vital materials were in dangerously short supply, partly because we had failed to stockpile enough needed commodities. When the Japanese overran British Malaya and the Dutch East Indies, shortly after Pearl Harbor, they snapped our life line of natural rubber, and cut off most of our essential tin and quinine. Supplements or substitutes for these critical items, especially rubber, were urgently needed—and eventually were found. Most spectacular of all was the creation of a huge synthetic rubber industry, which had to be started from scratch. After much fumbling, it was brought into production just in the nick of time by "Rubber Czar" William M. Jeffers, president of the Union Pacific Railroad.

First things had to come first. A War Production Board, under genial Donald M. Nelson, vice-president of Sears, Roebuck and Company, halted non-essential building in order to conserve materials for war purposes. Priorities were set up for most industries. "Dollar-a-year men" in Washington worked at a desperate pace, and as the red tape slowly unwound they did not even have time, it was said, for a nervous breakdown.

The rationing of goods to the consumer was undertaken on a huge scale for the first time in American experience. Voluntary "Hooverizing," as in 1917–1918, was not enough. Ration tickets were issued for butter, meat, gasoline, and other necessities; and on the whole the system worked well. But a minority of selfish souls patronized illegal sellers of goods, known as "black marketeers" and "meatleggers."

The booming wartime economy boosted prices somewhat, as the quiet hand of inflation reached into every pay envelope. Among various agencies, the Office of Price Administration was set up, and it enjoyed considerable success in keeping rents and commodity prices within reasonable bounds.

Prodigies of Production

Labor, which felt the pinch of mild inflation, had to be kept happy if high production quotas were to be attained. The A.F. of L. and the C.I.O. were among the important groups that joined in no-strike pledges, with the understanding that the government would hold the lid on the cost of living. Yet prices continued to inch upward, and a rash of strikes broke out, some of them so-called "wildcat" strikes, not authorized by union leaders. Noteworthy among the troublemaking groups were the United Mine Workers, who several times were called out on strike against the coal operators by their crusty and iron-willed leader, John L. Lewis. The accident-ridden miners, who harbored genuine grievances, finally won coveted concessions after Lewis had defied the Washington authorities and had temporarily jeopardized the war effort.

The threat of lost production through strikes became so serious that Congress, in June, 1943, passed the Smith-Connally Anti-Strike Act. It authorized the seizure and operation by the federal government of tied-up industries. Strikes against any industry thus operated were made a criminal offense. Under the Smith-Connally Act, Washington seized and ran the coal mines and, for a brief period, the railroads. Yet work stoppages, dangerous though they were, actually accounted for less than 1% of the total working time of the nation's laboring force during the war. The American workingman, on the whole, was magnificently efficient.

Agricultural production was one of the miracles of these anxious years. Though shorthanded because of the demands of the armed services, the farmers rolled up their sleeves and produced bumper crops. Providentially, as in 1917–1918, weather conditions were unusually favorable. Farm income, despite the shackles of price controls, more than doubled, and countless mortgages were joyously paid off. The blue-jeaned farmers had probably never before been so prosperous, though they had to labor long and wearisome hours to provide "food for freedom." Their sweat was supplemented, as in 1917–1918, by countless thousands of volunteer green-thumbers, who optimistically planted victory gardens in back yards and vacant lots.

The Battle of Production was clearly won by 1943. Unemployment became only a bad dream, as such agencies as the Civilian Conservation Corps and the Works Progress Administration received an "honorable discharge." President Roosevelt, in fact, declared that "Dr. New Deal" had been replaced by "Dr. Win the War." But the abounding prosperity was in some degree misleading. The inflation squeeze, though fairly well controlled, was pinching white-collar workers and others on fixed incomes.

Men, Women, and Money

The armed services enrolled in all more than 15,000,000 men and women. The draft was tightened after Pearl Harbor, as millions of young men were plucked from their homes and clothed in "G.I." (government issue) outfits. Scores of training camps peppered the land, while the shaping of officer material went forward rapidly in the colleges. With an eye to the long pull, draft deferments were often granted to key workers in industry and agriculture.

Women desk-warriors came into their own. They had been used sparingly in World War I, but now some 216,000 of them were efficiently employed for non-combat duties, chiefly clerical. Best-known of these "women in arms" were the WACS (Army), WAVES (Navy), Marines, and SPARS (Coast Guard).

The War for Survival of 1941–1945, more than that of 1917–1918, was an all-out conflict. Old folks came out of retirement "for the duration" to serve in industry, or as air-raid wardens in civilian defense. Women were drawn from the home into war work, even into the heavier industries such as shipbuilding, where "Rosie the Riveter" won laurels for herself. But Rosie's unshepherded children were inclined to run wild, and an alarming wave of juvenile delinquency—or rather parental delinquency—accompanied and followed the war.

Shipbuilding, as in 1917–1918, was pressed at a frantic pace in an effort to outrace the submarine. The output of the shipyards, partly as a result of the use of prefabricated materials, was no less phenomenal than that of the industrial plants. A leading miracle-man shipbuilder was Henry J. Kaiser, who was dubbed "Sir Launchalot." In 1943 alone American shipyards produced a formidable navy. Long before the shooting stopped, the United States had incomparably the mightiest merchant fleet the world had ever seen. (See chart on p. 734.)

The war proved to be prodigiously expensive. The total bill was about $330,000,000,000—or fifteen times the cost of World War I—and this figure ran the total national debt from $48,961,000,000, in June, 1941, to $258,682,000,000 in June, 1945. When production finally got into high gear, the war was costing about a quarter of a billion dollars a day.

A strict pay-as-you-go policy was clearly too burdensome. Borrowing was the answer. About three-fifths of the total war costs were raised by selling interest-bearing bonds, redeemable by the Treasury in the future, as in 1917–1918. All told, there were eight high-pressure War Bond drives, all of them oversubscribed. An effective new wrinkle was added when regular deductions, with the consent of the worker, were taken from pay envelopes for bond purchases.

About one-third of the colossal cost of the war was paid by the government out of current revenue. This achievement was not unduly difficult, for the national income shot up to about $200,000,000,000 a year and taxes generally received a sharp boost. The list included income taxes, corporation taxes, excess profits taxes, and "nuisance" taxes on various luxuries, like diamonds and furs. Some slight but welcome relief was afforded the American taxpayer by reverse lend-lease—a process by which the Allies provided about $7,819,000,000 in goods and services against their total lend-lease bill of $50,692,000,000.

The Rising Sun in the Pacific

The initial successes of the efficiently organized Japanese militarists were breath-taking. Seldom in history has so much been conquered in so short a time with so little loss.

Simultaneously with the assault on Pearl Harbor, the Japanese launched widespread and uniformly successful attacks on various Far Eastern bastions. These included the American outposts of Guam, Wake, and the Philippines. In a dismayingly short time, the Nipponese invader seized not only the British-Chinese port of Hong Kong but also British Malaya, with its critically important supplies of rubber and tin.

The red-balled flag of Nippon did not halt. The undersized but over-ambitious soldiers of the Emperor, plunging into the snake-infested jungles of Burma, cut the famed Burma road. This was the route over which the United States had been trucking a trickle of munitions to the armies of the Chinese Generalissimo Chiang Kai-shek, who was still resisting the Japanese invader in China. Thereafter intrepid American aviators were forced to fly a handful of war supplies to Chiang "over the hump" of the towering Himalaya Mountains. Meanwhile the energetic Japanese had lunged southward against the Dutch East Indies, with their rich oil resources. The jungle-matted islands speedily fell to the assailant, after the combined British, Australian, Dutch, and American naval and air forces had been completely crushed by their numerically superior foe.

But the Philippine Islands succeeded dramatically in slowing down the Mikado's warriors. The Japanese promptly landed a small but effective army, and General Douglas MacArthur, the statuesque American commander, withdrew to a strong defensive position at Bataan, not far from Manila. There about 20,000 American troops, supported by a much larger force of ill-trained Filipinos, held off violent Japanese attacks until April 9, 1942. The defenders, reduced to eating mules and monkeys, heroically traded their lives for time in the face of hopeless odds. They grimly sang while hoping for reinforcements:

> We're the battling bastards of Bataan;
> No Mamma, no Papa, no Uncle Sam.

Before the inevitable American surrender, General MacArthur was ordered by Washington to depart secretly for Australia, there to head resistance against the Japanese. Leaving by motorboat and airplane, he proclaimed, "I shall return." After the battered remnants of his army had hoisted the white flag, they were treated with vicious cruelty in the infamous Bataan death march. The island fortress of Corregidor, in Manila Harbor, held out until May 6, 1942, when it surrendered and left Japanese forces in control of the entire archipelago.

High Tide at Midway

The aggressive little men of Nippon, making hay while the Rising Sun shone, pushed relentlessly southward. They invaded the turtle-shaped island of New Guinea, north of Australia, and landed on the Solomon Islands, from which they threatened Australia itself. Their onrush was finally checked by a crucial naval battle fought in the Coral Sea, in May, 1942. An American carrier task force, with Australian support, inflicted heavy losses on the victory-flushed Nipponese foe. For the first time in history the fighting was all done by carrier-based aircraft, and neither fleet saw or fired a shot at the other.

The relentless Japanese next undertook to seize Midway Island, more than a thousand miles northwest of Honolulu. From this strategic base, they could launch devastating assaults on Pearl Harbor, and perhaps force the weakened American Pacific fleet into destructive combat. A decisive naval battle was fought near Midway, June 3–6, 1942. Admiral Chester W. Nimitz, a high-grade naval strategist, directed a skillfully maneuvered but inferior carrier force, under Admiral Raymond A. Spruance, against the powerful invading fleet. The fighting was all done by aircraft, and the Japanese broke off action after losing four vitally important carriers.

The smashing victory at Midway, combined with the Battle of the Coral Sea, marked the turn in the tide of Japanese conquest. But the thrust of the Nipponese into the eastern Pacific did net them America's fog-girt islands of Kiska and Attu, in the Aleutian archipelago, off Alaska. This easy conquest aroused fear of an invasion of the United States from the northwest. Much American strength was consequently diverted to the defense of Alaska, including the construction of a highway through Canada.

Yet the Japanese imperialists, overextended in 1942, suffered from "victory disease." Their appetites were bigger than their stomachs. If they had only dug in and consolidated their gains, they would have been infinitely more difficult to dislodge.

Leapfrogging toward Tokyo

Following the exhilarating victory at Midway, the United States for the first time was able to seize the initiative in the Pacific. In August, 1942, American ground forces gained a toe hold on Guadalcanal Island, in the Solomons, in an effort to protect the life line from America to Australia through the Southwest Pacific. An early naval defeat inflicted by the Japanese shortened American supplies dangerously, and for weeks the United States troops held onto the malarial island only by their fingernails. After four desperate sea battles for naval control, the Japanese troops evacuated Guadalcanal in February, 1943.

American and Australian forces, under General MacArthur, meanwhile had been hanging on grimly to the southeastern tip of New Guinea, the last buffer protecting Australia. The scales of war gradually began to tip as the American navy, including submarines, inflicted lethal losses on Japanese supply ships and troop carriers. The conquest of the north coast of New Guinea was completed by August, 1944, after General MacArthur had fought his way northwestward through green jungle hells. This gratifying victory was the first leg on the long return journey to the Philippines.

The United States navy, with marines and army divisions doing the meat-grinder fighting, had meanwhile been leapfrogging the Japanese islands in the Pacific. Old-fashioned strategy required that the American forces, as they drove toward Tokyo, should reduce the fortified Japanese

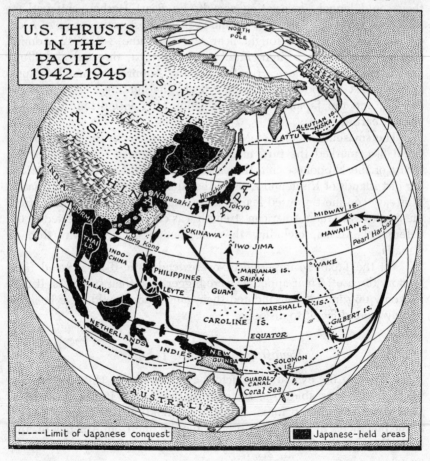

U.S. THRUSTS IN THE PACIFIC 1942–1945

------ Limit of Japanese conquest   ▓ Japanese-held areas outposts on their flank. This course would have taken many bloodstained months, for the holed-in defenders were prepared to die to the last man in their caves. The new strategy of island hopping called for bypassing some of the most heavily fortified Japanese posts, capturing nearby islands, setting up airfields on them, and then neutralizing the enemy bases through heavy bombing. Deprived of supplies from the homeland, the Mikado's outposts would slowly wither on the vine—as they did.

Brilliant success crowned the American attacks on the Japanese island strongholds in the Pacific, where Admiral Nimitz skillfully coordinated the efforts of naval, air, and ground units. In May and August of 1943, Attu and Kiska in the Aleutians were easily retaken. In November, 1943, "bloody Tarawa" and Makin, both in the Gilbert Islands, fell after suicidal resistance. In January and February, 1944, the key outposts of the Marshall group succumbed after savage fighting.

The prize islands were the Marianas, of which America's fallen Guam was one. They were spacious enough to provide abundant airfields for American super-bombers, and they were close enough to Japan to permit round-trip bombing. After bitter resistance, the major islands fell to the American attackers in July and August, 1944. With these unsinkable aircraft carriers now available, the first sustained air attacks on Japan were launched by giant bombers in November, 1944.

The Halting of Hitler

The early setbacks of the Americans in the Pacific were paralleled in the Atlantic. Hitler had entered the war with a formidable fleet of ultra-modern submarines, which operated in "wolf packs" with frightful effect, especially in the North Atlantic, the Caribbean, and the Gulf of Mexico. During ten months of 1942 more than five hundred merchantmen were reported lost—111 in June alone—as ship destruction far outran new construction.

The tide of subsea battle turned with agonizing slowness. Old techniques, such as escorting convoys of merchantmen and dropping depth bombs from destroyers, were strengthened by air patrol, radar, and the bombing of submarine bases. "Keep 'Em Sailing" was the motto of oil-begrimed merchant seamen, hundreds of whom perished as unsung heroes in icy seas.

Not until the spring of 1943 did the Allies clearly have the upper hand against the U-boats. If the Allies had not won the battle of the Atlantic, Britain would have been forced under, and a second front could not have been launched from her island springboard. The victory over the undersea raiders was nerve-rackingly narrow. When the war ended, the Germans were about to mass-produce a fearsome new submarine— one that could remain under water indefinitely and cruise at seventeen knots when submerged.

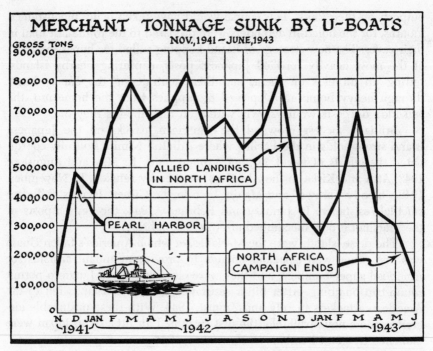

MERCHANT TONNAGE SUNK BY U-BOATS
NOV.,1941 – JUNE,1943

GROSS TONS

ALLIED LANDINGS
IN NORTH AFRICA

PEARL HARBOR

NORTH AFRICA
CAMPAIGN ENDS

Meanwhile, the turning point of the land-air war against Hitler had come late in 1942. The British, who had launched a 1000-plane raid on Cologne in May, were now cascading bombs, with American help, on pocked German cities. The Germans under Marshal Rommel—"the Desert Fox"—had driven across the hot sands of North Africa into Egypt, perilously close to the Suez Canal. A break-through would have spelled disaster for the Allies. But late in October, 1942, the British General Montgomery delivered a withering attack. With the aid of several hundred hastily shipped American Sherman tanks, he speedily drove the enemy back to Tunis, more than a thousand miles away.

On the Soviet front, the unexpected successes of the Red Army gave a new lift to the Allied cause. In September, 1942, the Russians halted the German steam roller at rubble-bestrewn Stalingrad, graveyard of Hitler's hopes. More than a score of invading divisions, caught in an icy noose, surrendered or were ultimately "mopped up." In November, 1942, the elated Russians unleashed a crushing counter-offensive, and it was never seriously reversed. A year later, Stalin had regained about two-thirds of the blood-soaked Russian motherland wrested from him by the Teutonic invader.

The North African Second Front

The Soviet leaders meanwhile had never ceased to clamor for an Anglo-American second front—a demand stridently supported by American Communists. The Red divisions were doing practically all of the mud-

and-blood fighting against Hitler's armies, and Moscow insisted that the Allies get into the war and drain off a substantial share of the invader's strength. The Russian officials did not regard the American operations in the Pacific as helpful to them, nor did they look upon the aerial assault launched by the Allies against Germany as a second front at all.

Many Americans were eager to begin a diversionary invasion of France in 1942 or in 1943, while Russia was still afloat. The fear was prevalent that the Russians, unable to hold out against Germany, might make a separate peace, as they had in 1918, and leave the western Allies to face the fury of Hitler alone. The British, remembering their fearful losses in 1914–1918, were not enthusiastic about a straight-ahead, full-fledged assault on German-held France. It might result in complete disaster. They much preferred to attack Hitler's Fortress Europe through the "soft underbelly" of the Mediterranean.

The projected invasion of French-held North Africa was a compromise second front. It seemed less risky than a possibly premature assault on the coast of France, yet it would serve as a partial answer to the demands of the Russians for a diversion. If successful, it would open the Axis-dominated Mediterranean to life-line communication with India and other parts of Asia.

The highly secret Allied attack on North Africa, launched in November, 1942, was headed by a gifted and easy-smiling American general, Dwight D. ("Ike") Eisenhower, a master of organization and conciliation. As a joint Allied operation ultimately involving some 400,000 men (British, Canadian, French, and chiefly American), the invasion was the

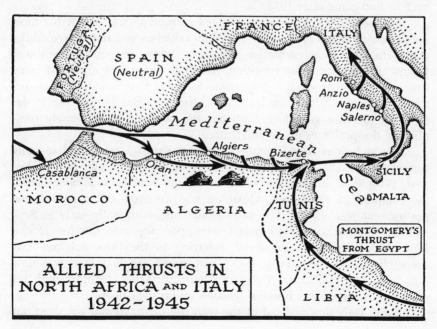

ALLIED THRUSTS IN NORTH AFRICA AND ITALY 1942–1945

mightiest water-borne effort up to that time in history. About 850 ships of various sorts were employed.

The surprise landing in North Africa was at the outset highly successful. The French, whose hearts were anti-Hitler and pro-Ally, put up only a token resistance. After bitter fighting with the Germans, who inflicted one sharp setback on the green Americans, the remnants of the German-Italian army were finally trapped in Tunis. Some 266,000 dazed survivors surrendered in May, 1943.

The North African campaign, though redeeming one continent, in itself was not conclusive. It was not the beginning of the end, but "the end of the beginning." Certain Russian spokesmen scoffed at this second-rate second front, but valuable lessons were learned for the full-fledged invasion of France.

The Road to Rome

New blows were now planned by the Allies. At Casablanca, in newly occupied French Morocco, President Roosevelt, who had boldly flown the Atlantic, met in a historic conference with Winston Churchill in January, 1943. The Big Two agreed to step up the Pacific war, invade Sicily, increase pressure on Italy, and insist upon an "unconditional surrender" of the enemy—a phrase popularized by General Grant during the Civil War. Such an unyielding policy would presumably hearten the ultra-suspicious Soviets, who professed to fear separate Allied peace negotiations. It would also forestall charges of broken armistice terms, such as had come after 1918.

The proclamation of "unconditional surrender" was one of the most controversial moves of the war. The main criticism was that it steeled the enemy to fight to a last-bunker resistance, while discouraging anti-war groups in Germany from revolting. Although there was no doubt some truth in these charges, it is impossible to prove that "unconditional surrender" either shortened or lengthened the war. But by helping to destroy the German government utterly, the new policy immensely complicated the problems of reconstruction.

The victorious Allied forces—American, British, and Canadian—now turned against the not-so-soft underbelly of Europe. Sicily fell, in August, 1943, after sporadic but sometimes bitter resistance. Shortly before the conquest of the island, Mussolini was deposed and a new Rome government was set up. Italy surrendered unconditionally early in September, 1943, while Allied troops were pouring onto the toe of the Italian boot. President Roosevelt, referring to the three original Axis accomplices—Germany, Italy, and Japan—joked grimly that it was now one down and two to go. Two years later Mussolini, together with his attractive mistress, was brutally lynched by his own people.

But if Italy dropped out of the war, the Germans did not drop out of Italy. Hitler's well-trained troops resisted the Allied invaders with methodical and infuriating stubbornness. The luckless Italians, turning their coats, declared war on Germany in October, 1943. "Sunny Italy" proceeded to belie her name, for in the snow-covered and mud-caked mountains of her elongated peninsula occurred some of the muddiest, bloodiest, and most frustrating fighting of the war.

The campaign in Italy seemed to run into a dead end. After a touch-and-go assault on the Anzio beachhead, Rome was taken on June 4, 1944. Two days later, when the tremendous cross-channel invasion of France began, Italy became a kind of sideshow. But the Allies, with limited manpower, continued to fight their way slowly and painfully into northern Italy. On May 2, 1945, only five days before the official surrender of Germany, several hundred thousand Axis troops laid down their arms.

The Italian campaign, though disappointingly slow, was by no means fruitless. It opened the Mediterranean Sea, diverted a number of German divisions from the blazing Russian and French fronts, and provided air bases for devastating bombing assaults against German Austria and southern Germany.

Hitting the Normandy Beaches

The Russians had never ceased their clamor for a two-fisted second front, and the time rapidly approached for the coordination of promised efforts. Marshal Joseph Stalin, who was keeping a careful eye on Russian military operations, was loath to leave the Soviet Union. President Roosevelt, who jauntily remarked in private, "I can handle that old buzzard," was eager to confer with him. The President seemed confident that Rooseveltian charm could woo the hardened conspirator of the Kremlin from his nasty Communist ways.

Teheran, the capital of Iran, was finally chosen as the meeting place, and to this ancient city Roosevelt daringly flew. The discussions between Stalin, Roosevelt, and Churchill—November 28 to December 1, 1943—went forward smoothly. Perhaps the most important achievement was a discussion of broad plans, particularly a synchronizing of Russian attacks on Germany from the east with the prospective grand Allied assault from the west.

The preparations for the cross-channel invasion of France were gigantic. Britain's fast-anchored isle virtually groaned with munitions, supplies, and troops, as nearly 3,000,000 fighting men were readied. The United States was to provide most of the Allied warriors, so the over-all command was entrusted to an American, General Eisenhower. He had already distinguished himself in the North African and Mediterranean campaigns, not only for his military capacity but also for his gifts as a conciliator of clashing Allied interests.

French Normandy, which was less heavily fortified than other beaches, was chosen as the area for the invasion assault. On D-Day, June 6, 1944, the enormous operation, which involved some 4600 vessels, was put into motion. Stiff resistance was encountered from the Germans, who had been misled by a feint into expecting the blow to fall farther north. The Allies quickly achieved complete mastery of the air over France. They were thus able to block reinforcements by crippling the railroads, and to increase fuel shortages by bombing gasoline manufacturing plants in Germany.

The Allied beachhead, at first clung to with finger tips, was gradually enlarged, consolidated, and reinforced. After desperate fighting, the invaders finally broke out of the German iron ring at the base of the Normandy peninsula. Most spectacular were the lunges across France by American armored divisions, brilliantly commanded by blustery and profane General George S. ("Blood 'n' Guts") Patton. The retreat of the German defenders was hastened when an American-French force landed in August, 1944, on the southern coast of France and swept northward. With the assistance of the French "underground," Paris was liberated in August, 1944, amid exuberant manifestations of joy and gratitude.

The Allied forces rolled irresistibly toward Germany, and many of the Americans encountered places, like Château-Thierry, familiar to their fathers in 1918. "Lafayette, we are here again," proclaimed some of the American soldiers jocosely. The first important German city (Aachen) fell to the Americans in October, 1944, and the days of Hitler's "Thousand-Year Empire" seemed to be numbered.

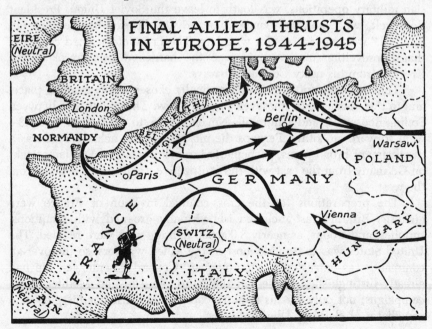

FINAL ALLIED THRUSTS IN EUROPE, 1944–1945

Fourth-Termites in '44

The heated presidential campaign of 1944, which was bound to divert energy from the war program, came most awkwardly as the titanic conflict neared its climax. But the normal electoral processes continued to function, despite some loose talk of suspending them "for the duration."

The victory-starved Republicans met in Chicago with hopeful enthusiasm. They quickly nominated the short, mustached, and dapper Thomas E. Dewey, popular vote-getting governor of New York. Regarded as a liberal, he had already made a national reputation as a prosecutor in New York City of grafting politicians, loan sharks, and other racketeers. His youth—he was only forty-two—had caused Harold Ickes to sneer that the candidate had cast his diaper into the ring. To offset Dewey's anti-isolationism, the convention nominated for the Vice-Presidency a strong isolationist, handsome and white-maned Senator John W. Bricker of Ohio. Yet the platform called for an unstinted prosecution of the war, and for the creation of a new international organization to maintain peace.

Gray-templed Franklin Roosevelt, obviously aging under the strain, was the "indispensable man" of the Democrats. No other major figure was available, and the war was apparently grinding to its grand finale. He was nominated at Chicago on the first ballot by acclamation. But in a sense he was the "forgotten man" of the convention, for, in view of his increasing age, an unusual amount of attention was focused on the Vice-Presidency.

The scramble for the vice-presidential plum turned into something of a free-for-all. Henry A. Wallace, one-time "plow 'em under" Secretary of Agriculture, had served four years as Vice-President and desired a renomination. But the conservative wing of the Democratic Party distrusted him as an ill-balanced and unpredictable liberal. The "ditch Wallace" move developed tremendous momentum, despite the popularity of Wallace with large numbers of voters and many of the delegates. With Roosevelt's blessing, the vice-presidential nomination finally went to smiling and self-assured Senator Harry S. Truman of Missouri. Hitherto inconspicuous, he had recently attained national fame as the efficient chairman of a Senate committee conducting a watchdog investigation of wasteful war expenditures.

Keeping the Winning Hurler

A dynamic Dewey took the offensive, for Roosevelt was too busily involved in directing the war to spare much time for speechmaking. The vigorous young "crime buster," with his beautiful baritone voice and polished diction, denounced the tired and quarrelsome "old men" in Washington. He cried repeatedly that after "twelve long years" of New

Dealism it was "time for a change." As for the war, Dewey would not alter the basic strategy but would fight it better—a type of "me-tooism" ridiculed by the Democrats. The fourth-term issue did not figure prominently, now that the ice had been broken by Roosevelt's third term. But "Dewey-eyed" Republicans, half-humorously, professed to fear fifth and sixth terms by the "lifer" in the White House.

In the closing weeks of the campaign, Roosevelt left his desk for the stump. He was stung by certain Republican charges, including alleged aspersions on his pet Scottie dog, Fala. He was also eager to show himself, even in chilling rains, to spike the well-founded rumors of failing health. He received substantial assistance from the new Political Action Committee of the C.I.O., which was organized to get around the law banning the direct use of union funds for political purposes. Zealous C.I.O. members, branded as Communists by the Republicans, rang countless doorbells and asked, with pointed reference to the recent depression, "What were you doing in 1932?" At times it seemed as though Roosevelt were again running against Hoover.

Roosevelt, as customary, won a sweeping victory: 432 to 99 in the Electoral College; 25,602,504 to 22,006,285 in the popular totals. Elated, he quipped that "The first twelve years are the hardest." As in every one of his previous three campaigns, he was opposed by a majority of the newspapers, which were owned chiefly by Republicans. His popular majority declined from 1940, partly because of the absence of many soldiers. Younger people tended to support Roosevelt; and consequently a Democratic Congress had passed a law making it possible for service personnel to vote. But only about one-fourth of them did so, and their absentee ballots did not affect the final result materially.

Roosevelt won, it seems clear, primarily because the war was going well. A winning pitcher is not ordinarily taken out. Foreign policy was a decisive factor with untold thousands of voters, who concluded that Roosevelt's experienced hand was needed in fashioning a future organization for world peace. Dewey spoke glibly of international cooperation, but his isolationist running mate, Bricker, implanted serious doubts. The Republican Party was still suffering from the taint of isolationism fastened on it by the Hardingites.

The Last Days of Hitler

By mid-December, 1944, the month after Roosevelt's fourth-term victory, Germany seemed to be wobbling on her last legs. The Soviet surge had penetrated eastern Germany. Allied "blockbusters," on an around-the-clock schedule, were falling like giant hailstones on cities, factories, and transportation arteries. The German western front seemed about to buckle under the sledge-hammer blows of the Americans and their allies.

Hitler then staked everything on one last throw. Secretly concentrating a powerful force, he hurled it, on December 16, 1944, against the thinly held American lines in the snow-shrouded Ardennes forest. Caught off guard, the outmanned Americans were hurled back, and the key Belgian port of Antwerp was menaced. The ten-day penetration was finally halted after the 101st Airborne Division stood firm at the vital bastion of Bastogne. The commander, Brigadier General A. C. McAuliffe, defiantly answered the premature German demand for surrender with one word, "Nuts." Reinforcements were rushed up, and the last-gasp Hitlerian offensive was at length bloodily stemmed in the Battle of the Bulge.

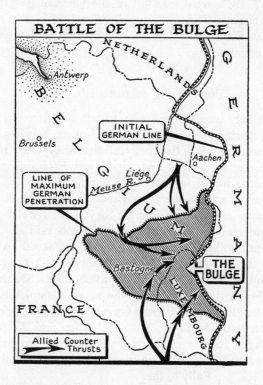

In March, 1945, forward-driving American troops reached Germany's Rhine River, where, by incredibly good luck, they found one strategic bridge undemolished. Pressing their advantage, General Eisenhower's troops reached the Elbe River in April, 1945. There, some sixty miles south of Berlin, American and Russian advance guards dramatically clasped hands, amid cries of "*Amerikanskie tovarishchi*" (American comrades). The conquering Americans were horrified to find blood-bespattered and still-stinking concentration camps, where the German Nazis had engaged in scientific mass murder. These horrors, for once, far exceeded the lurid reports of propagandists.

The vengeful Russians, clawing their way forward from the east, reached Berlin in April, 1945. After desperate house-to-house fighting, accompanied by an orgy of pillage and rape, they captured the bomb-shattered city. Adolf Hitler, after a hasty marriage to his mistress, committed suicide with her in a burned-out bunker.

Stunning tragedy had meanwhile struck the United States. President Roosevelt, while relaxing at Warm Springs, Georgia, suddenly died from a massive cerebral hemorrhage on April 12, 1945. The crushing burden of twelve years in the White House had finally taken its toll. Knots of confused and leaderless citizens gathered to discuss the future anxiously, as the bewildered and unbriefed Vice-President Truman took the helm.

On May 7, 1945, what was left of the German government surrendered unconditionally. The next day, May 8, was officially proclaimed V-E Day—Victory in Europe Day—and it was greeted with frenzied rejoicing in the Allied countries.

The Setting of the Rising Sun

Japan's rickety bamboo empire meanwhile was tottering to its fall. American submarines—"the silent service"—were sending the Japanese merchant marine to the bottom so fast that they were running out of prey. All told, our underseas craft destroyed 1042 ships, or about 50% of Nippon's entire life-giving merchant fleet.

Giant bomber attacks were even more spectacular. Launched from Guam and other captured Marianas, they were reducing the enemy's fragile cities to cinders. The massive fire-bomb raid on Tokyo, March 9–10, 1945, was annihilating. It destroyed over 250,000 buildings, gutted a quarter of the city, and killed an estimated 83,000 persons—a loss comparable to that later inflicted by atomic bombs. (See map, p. 888.)

General MacArthur was also on the move. Completing the conquest of the jungle-tangled island of New Guinea, he headed northwest for the Philippines, en route to Japan, with 600 ships and 250,000 men. In a scene well staged for the photographers, he splashed ashore at Leyte Island, October 20, 1944, with the summons: "People of the Philippines, I have returned. . . . Rally to me."

The Japanese navy—still menacing—now made one last-chance effort to destroy MacArthur by wiping out his transports and supply ships. The gigantic clash at Leyte Gulf, fought on the sea and in the air, was actually three battles (October 23–26, 1944). The Americans won all of them, though the crucial engagement was almost lost when Admiral William F. ("Bull") Halsey, was decoyed away by a feint.

The Japanese were through as a seapower: they had lost about sixty ships in the greatest naval battle of all time. The American fleets, numbering more than 4000 vessels, now commanded Asiatic seas. Several of our battleships, raised from the mud of Pearl Harbor, were finding belated but sweet revenge.

Overrunning Leyte, MacArthur next landed on the main Philippine island of Luzon, in January, 1945. Manila was his major objective. The ravaged city fell in March but the Philippines were not conquered until July. Victory was purchased only after bitter fighting against holed-in Japanese, who took a toll of over 60,000 American casualties.

The American iron ring was tightening inexorably around Nippon. The tiny island of Iwo Jima, needed as a roosting place for damaged American bombers returning from Japan, was captured by the marines in March, 1945. The desperate twenty-five-day assault cost over 4000 American dead.

The well-defended Japanese island of Okinawa was next on the list: it was needed for closer bases from which to blast and burn enemy cities and industries. The fighting dragged out from April to June of 1945. The Nipponese soldiers, fighting with cornered-rat courage from their caves, finally sold Okinawa for 80,000 American casualties. The Japanese suffered far heavier losses themselves.

The American navy, which covered the invasion of Okinawa, sustained severe damage. Japanese suicide pilots, in an exhibition of mass hara-kiri for their god-emperor, crashed their bomb-laden planes onto the decks of the invading fleet. All told, they sank over thirty ships and badly damaged scores more. The navy fortunately had developed floating repair ships and other time-saving new techniques, all of which helped it to keep up the pressure.

Atomic Awfulness

The high command in Washington was meanwhile perfecting plans for an all-out invasion of the main islands of Japan—an invasion that presumably would cost hundreds of thousands of American casualties. Tokyo, recognizing imminent defeat, had already secretly sent peace feelers to Russia, which had not yet entered the Far Eastern war. But bomb-scorched Japan still showed no outward willingness to surrender *unconditionally*.

The Potsdam conference, held near Berlin in July, 1945, sounded the death knell of the Japanese. There President Truman, still new on his job, met in a seventeen-day parley with Joseph Stalin and the British leaders. The conferees issued a stern ultimatum to Japan: surrender or be destroyed. American bombers showered the grim warning on Japan in tens of thousands of leaflets, but silence was the official response.

The Americans had a fantastic ace up their sleeves. Early in 1940, after Hitler's wanton assault on Poland, Roosevelt was persuaded by American scientists to push ahead with gigantic preparations for unlocking the secret of an atomic bomb. Congress, on Roosevelt's blank-check request, blindly made available nearly two billion dollars.

The huge atomic project was pushed feverishly forward, as American know-how and industrial power were combined with the most advanced scientific knowledge. Much technical skill was provided by British and Continental scientists, some of whom ironically had been forced to flee the torture chambers of the dictators. Finally, in the desert near Los Alamos, New Mexico, July 16, 1945, the experts detonated the first atomic bomb. It provided an awesome exhibition of unchained fury.

With Japan still refusing to surrender, the Potsdam threat was fulfilled. On August 6, 1945, a lone American bomber dropped one atomic bomb on the military-base city of Hiroshima, Japan. In a blinding flash, followed by a funnel-shaped cloud, 180,000 persons were left killed, wounded, or missing. Some 70,000 were dead or presumed dead.

Two days later, on August 8, Stalin entered the war against Japan, exactly on the deadline date previously agreed upon with his allies. The regrouped Soviet armies speedily overran the depleted Japanese defenses in Manchuria and Korea in a six-day "victory parade." Stalin was evidently determined to be in on the kill, lest he lose a voice in the final division of Japan's holdings.

The fanatically resisting Japanese, though facing atomization, did not surrender. The Americans, on August 9, dropped a second atomic bomb, on the naval-base city of Nagasaki. The explosion took a horrible toll of 80,000 persons killed or missing.

Japan could endure no more. On August 10, 1945, Tokyo sued for peace on one condition: that Hirohito, the bespectacled Son of Heaven, be allowed to remain on his ancestral throne as nominal Emperor. The Allies, despite their "unconditional surrender" policy, accepted this condition on August 14. The Japanese, though losing face, saved both their exalted ruler and their skins.

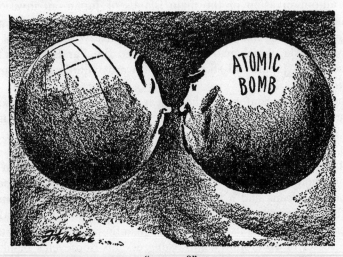

"WELL—?"

Fitzpatrick in the St. Louis *Post-Dispatch*, 1945

The formal end came, with dramatic force, on September 2, 1945. Official surrender ceremonies were conducted by General MacArthur on the battleship *Missouri* in Tokyo Bay. On the same day Americans at home hysterically celebrated V-J Day—Victory in Japan Day—as the most terrible war in history ended in a mushrooming atomic cloud.

The Allies Triumphant

World War II proved to be terribly costly. American forces suffered some one million casualties, about one-third of which were deaths. Compared with other wars, the proportion killed by wounds and disease was sharply reduced, owing in part to the use of blood plasma and of miracle drugs, notably penicillin. Yet heavy though American losses were, our Russian allies suffered casualties six times greater.

The United States was fortunate in emerging with its mainland virtually unscathed. A few shells had been lobbed onto the coast of California by a brash Japanese submarine, and a few balloons, incendiary and otherwise, had drifted rather harmlessly across the Pacific. But that was all. The rest of the world was bomb-pocked, rubble-strewn, and impoverished. Yet America's natural resources, magnificent though they were, had been seriously depleted by the ravenous jaws of the war machine.

This incredibly complex conflict was the best-fought war in American history. Though far from prepared for it at the outset, we were better prepared than for the others, partly because we had begun to buckle on our armor about a year and a half before the war officially began. We were actually fighting German submarines in the Atlantic several months before the final explosion in the Pacific at Pearl Harbor. We proved ourselves to be resourceful, tough, adaptable—able to accommodate ourselves to the tactics of an enemy who was ruthless, relentless, and at times barbarous.

Fortunately, American military leadership proved to be of the highest order. A new crop of war heroes emerged in brilliant generals like Eisenhower and MacArthur, and in imaginative admirals like Nimitz and Spruance. President Roosevelt and Prime Minister Churchill, as kindred spirits, collaborated closely in planning over-all strategy.

Industrial leaders were no less skilled, and marvels of production were performed almost daily. Assembly lines were no less important than battle lines; and victory went again to the side with the big smokestacks. The enemy was almost literally smothered in an avalanche of bayonets, bullets, bazookas, and bombs. Hitler and his Axis co-conspirators had chosen to make war with machines, and the ingenious Yankees could ask for nothing better. From 1940 to 1945, American factories rolled out an incredible 300,317 airplanes. As Winston Churchill remarked, "Nothing succeeds like excess."

The portly German Marshal Goering had sneered, "The Americans can't build planes—only electric iceboxes and razor blades." Democracy had given its answer, as the conniving dictators, despite long preparation, were overthrown and discredited. It is true that an unusual amount of direct control was exercised over the individual by the Washington authorities during the war emergency. But the American people preserved their precious liberties without serious impairment. The outcome was another vindication of the American democratic system—a system founded on faith in the power and courage of free men.

SELECT READINGS

The picture is painted with bold strokes in ALLAN NEVINS, *The New Deal and World Affairs* (1950). The United States is given due consideration in L. L. SNYDER's popularly written *The War: A Concise History, 1939–1945* (1960) [paperback]; the main outlines also appear in R. W. SHUGG and H. A. DE WEERD, *World War II, A Concise History* (1946). Abundant detail is provided by A. R. BUCHANAN, *The United States and World War II* (2 vols., 1964) [paperback]. The naval side is handled masterfully in Admiral S. E. MORISON, *The Two-Ocean War* (1963), a one-volume condensation of his monumental twelve-volume history of the United States Navy in World War II. High strategy is developed in K. R. GREENFIELD, ed., *Command Decisions* (1959) and in his *American Strategy in World War II* (1963). See also GADDIS SMITH's succinct *American Diplomacy during the Second World War, 1941–1945* (1965) [paperback]. More detailed are HERBERT FEIS' three volumes: *Churchill, Roosevelt, Stalin* (1957); *Between War and Peace: The Potsdam Conference* (1960); and *Japan Subdued: The Atomic Bomb and the End of the War in the Pacific* (1961). See also J. L. SNELL, ed., *The Meaning of Yalta* (1956); ANNE ARMSTRONG, *Unconditional Surrender* (1961).

The more important biographical or autobiographical works are H. L. STIMSON (then Secretary of War) and M. BUNDY, *On Active Service in Peace and War* (1947); E. E. MORISON, *Turmoil and Tradition* (1960) [life of Stimson] [paperback]; General D. D. EISENHOWER's best-selling *Crusade in Europe* (1948); General DOUGLAS MAC ARTHUR, *Reminiscences* (1964); General L. R. GROVES, *Now It Can be Told* (1962) [the atomic bomb project]; and ROBERT MURPHY, *Diplomat Among Warriors* (1964) [paperback]. Also *Harvard Guide*, Pt. VI.

45

Truman and the Cold War

. . . An iron curtain has descended across the Continent.
WINSTON CHURCHILL, 1946

The Man from Missouri

TRIM and bespectacled Harry S. Truman, with his graying hair and friendly, toothy grin, was called "the average man's average man." The first President since Grover Cleveland without a college education, he had farmed, served as an artillery officer in France during World War I, and failed at haberdashery. He then tried his hand at precinct-level Missouri politics, through which he rose to the United States Senate. Though a protégé of a notorious political machine in Kansas City, he had managed to keep his own skirts clean.

The roof caved in on Truman with Roosevelt's sudden death. The problems were overpowering, and the firm-mouthed new President approached his tasks with becoming humility. Gradually gaining confidence to the point of cockiness, he displayed courage, decisiveness, and a willingness to fight. Although high-schoolish as a speaker at first, he finally developed into one of the most effective rough-and-tumble speakers of his generation.

Yet by degrees the defects of Truman's common clay became distressingly apparent. A smallish man suddenly thrust into an overwhelming job, he was inclined to go off half-cocked or to stick mulishly to some wrongheaded notion. On occasion, he would dash off hot-tempered and highly indiscreet letters. Worst of all, he permitted designing old associates of the "Missouri gang" to gather around him, and, like Grant, was stubbornly loyal to them when they were caught with the cream on their whiskers. "To err is Truman" was a cynical explanation.

This was the man on whom Roosevelt's oversize mantle fell in April, 1945, when victory over Hitler was in view. Truman's most pressing task was to follow through and win both the war and the peace. Fortunately, he developed a surprising capacity to seize the tiller with bold hand in time of crisis. His motto was "The buck stops here."

903

Yalta: Bargain or Betrayal?

The Soviet Union, vast and silent, continued to be the Great Enigma. The conference at Teheran in 1943, where Roosevelt had first met Stalin on a man-to-man basis, had done something to clear the air, but much had remained unsettled.

The final fateful conference of the Big Three had taken place in February, 1945, at Yalta. At this former Czarist resort on the relatively warm shores of the Black Sea, Stalin, Churchill, and the fast-failing Roosevelt reached momentous agreements, after pledging their faith with vodka. Final plans were laid for sledge-hammering the buckling German lines and shackling the beaten Axis foe. Stalin agreed that Poland, with revised boundaries, should have a representative government based on free elections—a pledge that he soon broke. Bulgaria and Romania were likewise to have free elections—a promise also flouted. The Big Three further announced that they had decided to hold a multi-power conference, this time in San Francisco, for the purpose of fashioning a new international organization for peace.

The most controversial decisions of the Yalta conference concerned the Far East. The atomic bomb had not yet been tested, and the Washington strategists expected frightful casualties in the projected assault on Japan. From our standpoint it seemed highly desirable that Stalin should enter the Far Eastern war, pin down Japanese troops in Manchuria and Korea, and lighten American losses. Russian casualties had already been enormous, and the Soviets presumably needed inducements to bring them into the Far Eastern conflict.

Horse-trader Stalin was in a position at Yalta to exact a high price. He agreed to attack Japan within two to three months after the collapse of Germany; and he later redeemed his pledge in full. In return, the Soviets were promised the southern half of Sakhalin Island, lost by Russia to Japan in 1905, and the Japanese Kurile Islands as well. The Soviet Union was also granted joint control over the railroads of China's Manchuria, and, in a revival of Czarist imperialism, received special privileges in the two most important seaports of that area, Dairen and Port Arthur. These concessions evidently would give Stalin dominant control over the most vital industrial centers of our weakening Chinese ally, Chiang Kai-shek.

The last-minute entry of Russia into the war against Japan was hailed in America with delight. But we soon perceived that Stalin's aid had not been needed, and that in any case his desire to grab his share of the spoils would have brought him into the conflict without concessions. Critics of Roosevelt thereupon redoubled their condemnation. They charged angrily that he had sold Chiang Kai-shek down the river when he conceded control of China's Manchuria to Stalin. The consequent undermining of Chinese morale, so the accusation ran, contributed powerfully to Chiang's overthrow by the Communists four years later.

Defenders of the dead Roosevelt were not silent. They argued that if Stalin had kept his promise to support free elections in Poland and the liberated Balkans, the sorry sequel would have been different. They also contended that Stalin, with his mighty Red Army, could have secured much more of China, and that the Yalta conference definitely set limits to his ambitions. He actually pledged himself to make a treaty of friendship and alliance with Chiang's government, and he carried through his promise later in 1945.

The myth developed—especially in the Soviet Union—that Russian-American relations would not have gone sour if Roosevelt had only lived. The truth is that several weeks before his death, he was shocked to learn that the Russians had violated their free-election pledges at Yalta concerning Poland and the Balkans. He died knowing that his charm and generous treatment had failed to lure the Russian Communists away from their menacing goal of world revolution.

Birth Pangs of the United Nations

The United Nations Conference met in San Francisco, on the scheduled April 25, 1945, despite Roosevelt's dismaying death thirteen days earlier. The groundwork had been laid for the historic gathering over a period of several years. The sobered Republicans, in sharp contrast with 1919, had shown a strong disposition to go along with Democratic leadership. Roosevelt, in turn, had displayed more tact than Wilson. He had chosen both Democrats and Republicans for the American delegation, and in addition had included Senators on it. He had also avoided Wilson's mistake of riveting the new world organization to the dead weight of an unpopular peace treaty.

With a drizzling rain outside, the delegates from nearly fifty nations assembled in the classic-style San Francisco War Memorial Opera House. The United Nations Charter, as finally whipped together after nine weeks of hectic debate, bore strong resemblances to the old League of Nations Covenant. Two kingpin bodies were set up. One was the Security Council, dominated by the Big Five Powers—the United States, Russia, Britain, France, and China. The other was the Assembly, which could be controlled by the smaller countries. The new International Court of Justice was patterned after the old World Court under the League of Nations.

The response of the Senate to the United Nations Charter in 1945 contrasted strikingly with its chilly reception of the League of Nations Covenant in 1919. After a brief flurry of debate, the final vote was taken on July 28, 1945. Impressed by an overwhelmingly favorable public opinion, the Senators approved the document by a vote of 89 to 2.

Setting Up the Town Meeting of the World

The United Nations, which at length erected its permanent glass home on a Rockefeller-given site in New York City, soon disappointed the exaggerated hopes of those who had cried for One World. The Soviet bloc, a suspicious and outvoted minority, deliberately employed obstructionist tactics. As time passed, the conviction deepened that the Russians had not joined the U.N. in good faith. Evidently they had entered with the intention of snarling it up, and of using it as a megaphone for their incendiary propaganda. Particularly vicious were their wild charges of "warmongering" against the United States and its "capitalistic" associates.

"WEARIED AND GETTING NOWHERE"
Bishop in the St. Louis *Star-Times,* 1947

The big-power veto in the Security Council proved to be a near-fatal stumbling block. At San Francisco this device had been adopted in the expectation that it would be used only sparingly, but the Soviets invoked the veto-vote routinely to block any action that might thwart their unsleeping schemes for world revolution. Within a few years they had wielded this potent sickle several score times.

Despite these setbacks, the U.N. could point to success in varied theaters. It played a praiseworthy role in helping preserve the peace in Iran, in Kashmir (India), in Indonesia, and elsewhere. It was largely instrumental in creating the new Jewish state of Israel, and in allaying the subsequent hostilities that broke out between the Jews and their resentful Arab neighbors. The splendid mediatory work of Dr. Ralph J. Bunche, grandson of an American Negro slave, won for him the Nobel Peace Prize in 1950. But peace did not come to the Holy Land.

Under the Trusteeship Council, the U.N. set up trusteeships that resembled the old League of Nations mandates. In 1947 the United States insisted on—and received as a trustee—the strategic Japanese-mandated islands in the Pacific. These insular outposts, already dearly purchased with American blood, were deemed essential to our future security. (See back-cover map.)

Another significant agency of the U.N. was the Economic and Social Council. Elected by the General Assembly, it achieved substantial gains in world health and in social, cultural, and economic betterment. Prominent among its far-reaching arms was the United Nations Educational, Scientific, and Cultural Organization (UNESCO), which sought to promote a more wholesome understanding among the nations. But certain ultra-nationalistic groups in the United States condemned the experiment as internationalist and un-American.

The most disheartening failures of the U.N. came in the larger area of disarmament. The new organization was unable to create an international police force, in order to guarantee a warless world. It was likewise unable to achieve international control of the atomic bomb. The United States, feeling temporarily secure in its presumed monopoly, had established the Atomic Energy Commission to stockpile nuclear explosives, and to explore possible peacetime uses of the atom. We were quite willing to share our atomic secrets with the rest of the world, provided that there was a foolproof system of international control and inspection.

But the Soviets defiantly refused to tie their hands with any such atomic agreement. They did not want capitalistic "spies" snooping around their country, and they evidently expected to make their own city-wrecking bombs in due course. As the atomic clock ticked steadily away, the Russians came ever nearer their goal.

Retooling for Peace

After the war ended with an atomic bang, America was again confronted with the familiar pattern of demobilization. Millions of men and women in the armed forces had to be put back into civilian clothes, and this process went forward rapidly. Congress made generous financial provision for readjustment to non-military life. Several million ex-service men and women, whose schooling in most instances had been interrupted, took advantage of the educational benefits provided by Congress in the so-called "G.I. Bill of Rights." Colleges during the post-war years were crowded to the blackboards, as more than a million eager veterans entered halls of higher learning.

But the demobilization of laurel-laden warriors was conducted with indecent haste, and without proper regard for our new power position. When the enemy collapsed, the United States had the most potent striking force ever assembled—and it was relatively fresh. To wipe it out would create a power vacuum into which the aggressive men of Moscow would inevitably move. Yet tremendous pressure converged on Washington from sweethearts, parents, and children ("Bring-Daddy-Back-Home Clubs"). These earnest souls were loudly supported by homesick G.I.'s themselves, who staged incredible "I wanna go home" demonstrations all the way from Germany to India. The shortsighted views of the American people finally prevailed, and the magnificent tools of victory were tossed away. "Nothing recedes like success," ran a current quip.

The dismantling of the enormous war-production machine was a no less formidable task. In response to another insistent public clamor, wartime taxes were reduced—perhaps too rapidly in view of America's heavy financial obligations. The war had caused the national debt to shoot up to an astronomical $260,000,000,000. It was ironical indeed that the richest nation in the world, during the years after military victory, could not or would not balance its budget, at a time when high income and inflationary pressures seemed to call for balancing.

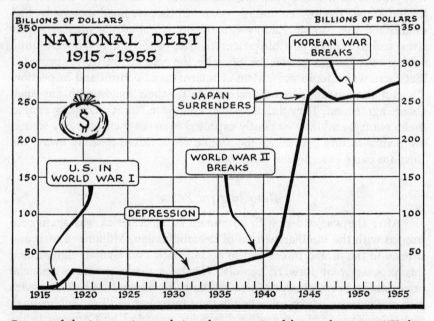

Because of the increase in population, the per capita debt was lower in 1955 than in the years immediately following World War II. See also table on page 979.

On other fronts, economic demobilization moved forward. War factories and other installations owned by the government were disposed of at closing-out prices, partly in the misplaced hope that there would never be another war. Price controls were removed, except for rents, although not until President Truman had waged a slam-bang losing fight with Congress for continued restrictions. Manufacturers and retailers were eager to get back to the old law of "supply and demand"—and they did. With rationing ended, demand outran supply; and by December, 1946, prices were about 32% higher than in the previous year.

Inflationary pressures were almost irresistible. During the war automobiles, refrigerators, stoves, and other appliances had been in desperately short supply, owing chiefly to the ravenous appetite of the munitions industries for scarce metals. When the shooting stopped, the people had amassed fat savings—an estimated $140,000,000,000—and they were starved for consumers' goods. With the purchasers bidding competitively, and with the government making heavy shipments of supplies to devastated Europe, prices were bound to soar.

Labor Tramps Ahead

The begrimed wage earner was pinched by the inflationary spiral, which had about halved the purchasing power of the Depression dollar. During the war he had been restrained from striking by high wages and high-pressure patriotism. But when the fighting ended and overtime pay was sharply reduced, he was in a rebellious mood, especially when he saw management raking in profits from the pent-up demand.

An epidemic of strikes swept the country, and during 1946 alone some 4,600,000 laborers laid down their tools for varying periods. Especially crippling were the work stoppages in such industries as steel and motor-car manufacturing. Stark drama unfolded in the bituminous coal industry when iron-willed John L. Lewis, defying a court injunction in 1946, led out his faithful miners. The strikers were forced to return to their pits, but not until a federal court had fined Lewis $10,000 and the union a whopping $3,500,000 (later reduced).

The embattled laborers were usually successful in winning wage increases, largely because the order-swamped manufacturers could pass the additional costs on to the consumer. But as prices continued to creep upward, further rounds of strikes resulted, followed by new price rises—in a dog-chasing-its-tail cycle. Yet employment continued full, and during the early post-war years attained the amazing total of 60,000,000 jobs.

Labor, on the whole, registered significant gains during these feverish post-war years. The workingman, to an increasing degree, was winning vacation allowances, old-age pensions, and other unaccustomed welfare benefits. A trail-blazing contract, signed by General Motors in 1948, included a clause to the effect that wages would rise and fall automatically with the rise and fall of the cost-of-living index.

Underprivileged Negro laborers, to an increasing degree, were sharing the new prosperity. It is true that Southern Congressmen blocked President Truman's recommendations for a national fair employment practices law and for civil rights legislation. But the plight of these "second-class citizens" was being generally improved by state legislation and changing public attitudes. Symptomatic of a new day for Negroes was the breaking of the color line in big-league baseball. Amid less controversy than predicted, the Brooklyn Dodgers led the way in 1947, when they signed a star Negro second baseman, Jack Roosevelt ("Jackie") Robinson, a former college football player.

Labor on the Defensive

The growing power of organized labor had meanwhile proved deeply disturbing to many conservatives. Asserting that Big Labor was now as much of a menace as Big Business had ever been, the diehard industrialists demanded a showdown. The Republicans gained control of Congress in 1947, for the first time in fourteen years, and proceeded to call the tune. Balding, blunt-spoken Robert A. Taft of Ohio, one of the Republican big guns of the Senate, became co-sponsor of a controversial new labor law known as the Taft-Hartley Act, which was passed in June, 1947, over President Truman's vigorous veto.

The Taft-Hartley law promptly became a storm center. Partly designed to protect the public, it contained a number of provisions that were not objectionable to open-minded workingmen. But the curbs on unions caused labor leaders to condemn the entire act as a "slave labor law." Noteworthy were the provisions outlawing the closed (all-union) shop, while making unions liable for damages resulting from jurisdictional disputes among themselves. Union leaders were required to take a non-Communist oath, though employers were not forced to do so. Despite labor's pained outcries, it is significant that Taft-Hartleyism, while annoying, did not cripple the labor movement. The A.F. of L. by 1950 could boast 8,000,000 members and the C.I.O. 6,000,000.

Wretched housing was another grievance of labor, as indeed of much of the population. New construction had been crippled or halted by the war, while at the same time the country had witnessed a bumper baby-boom. Tens of thousands of migrant workers, moreover, had hived around war industries. This trend was most conspicuous in the northern industrial areas, like Detroit, and on the Pacific Coast, notably in California, which experienced a spectacular increase of population.

Additional housing tensions were created by Negro migrants. Tens of thousands, lured to the Western states and to the North by war jobs, caused serious complications. An anti-Negro riot convulsed Detroit during June, 1943, and took a frightening toll of thirty-four lives before it was finally quelled by federal troops.

In response to Truman's persistent proddings, Congress finally tackled the housing problem. Laws were passed in 1948 and 1949 to provide federally financed construction, despite the outraged protests of real-estate promoters and other conservative groups. But these measures, though auspicious steps forward, fell far short of pressing needs. Hundreds of thousands of additional structures would have to be built if the nation was going to wipe out its disgraceful slums and provide homes to match its marvelous wealth.

Reconstruction Abroad

At the close of the war America, rich and unscarred, had a moral obligation to help her less fortunate sisters—or so many of her citizens felt. "It is now 11:59 on the clock of starvation," warned Herbert Hoover.

Aid of a non-military nature continued to flow to Europe, even though the end of the shooting brought an abrupt end to lend-lease. The United States simply could not afford to see the destitute countries of Europe fall prey to creeping Communism. Wealthy Uncle Sam carried the heavy end of the log in financing short-term relief, chiefly through the United Nations Relief and Rehabilitation Administration (UNRRA). This organization did splendid work from 1943 to 1947 in providing succor for many destitute countries of both Europe and Asia. Official relief was supplemented by personal gifts, notably the private packages of food and clothing sent by Americans to starving families in Europe under the auspices of CARE.

Displaced persons—"D.P.'s," they were called—numbered several million unfortunates uprooted by the war. Large numbers of them were anti-Communists who did not dare to return to their Communist-dominated homelands. America had room for many of these rootless souls, but Congress moved slowly in the face of possible unemployment, maladjustment, or importation of dangerous foreign doctrines. An act as finally passed in 1948—and expanded in 1950—made provision for the admission of 205,000 carefully selected persons in two years.

Two wartime associates received special attention. The prostrate Philippines, in accordance with the act of Congress in 1934, were formally awarded independence in 1946 on America's Independence Day—July 4. The United States agreed to provide substantial financial assistance, and in return received leases on more than a score of military, naval, and air-base sites.

Impoverished Britain was grudgingly voted a loan in 1946 of $3,750,-000,000. Much opposition was registered, especially on the floor of Congress, by the isolationists, the anti-British, and the economy-minded, who feared that the money would never be repaid. A cynical jingle ran:

There will always be a U.S.A.
If we don't give it away.

Germany presented especially thorny problems. Washington policy makers were determined that she should not rise in her industrial and military might, again to menace the peace of the world. Multiple goals were therefore adopted: de-Nazification, de-militarization, de-industrialization, and democratization. Some Hitler-haters in America, remembering that an industrialized Germany had been an aggressor, were determined to reduce the German Fatherland to a potato patch. But in the end less harsh courses were adopted, partly because Germany was the key to the economic recovery of Europe.

The complicated process of de-Nazification included war-crimes trials of Nazi German leaders. The Allies joined in trying the leading

"WITNESSES FOR THE PROSECUTION"
Fitzpatrick in the St. Louis *Post-Dispatch*, 1945

culprits at Nuremberg, Germany, during 1945–1946, with Associate Justice Jackson of the United States Supreme Court serving as a special prosecutor. The principal accusations were the commission of crimes against the laws of war and humanity, and the plotting of aggressions contrary to solemn treaty pledges.

The new type of justice was harsh. In 1946, nineteen of the accused Nazis were convicted: twelve were sentenced to the gallows and seven to jail terms. "Foxy Hermann" Goering, whose blubbery chest had once blazed with ribbons and medals, cheated the hangman by swallowing a hidden cyanide capsule a few hours before his scheduled execution. The trials of scores of smaller-fry Nazis continued for several years. Some legalistic critics in America condemned these proceedings as judicial lynchings, for the victims were tried for crimes that had not been clear-cut personal crimes when the war began. In any event, future aggressors were warned that they might expect the noose instead of the halo.

Russian Roadblocks to Peace

Allied efforts to make a peace treaty with Germany and Austria speedily ran onto the rocks of Soviet obstruction. Germany and Austria, as previously agreed, were arbitrarily broken into four military zones, and one of them was assigned to each of the Big Four powers: France, Britain, America, and Russia. But the ever-suspicious Russians did not work well in multi-power harness. Besides, they were eager to bleed Germany with heavy reparations, both in money and goods, and leave her so desperately impoverished that her people would fall easy prey to the seductive promises of Soviet Communism.

The ominous gulf between the Russians and the western Allies gradually widened. The Soviet Zone in eastern Germany was turned into a Communist puppet, even though the three-power Potsdam agreement of 1945 had stipulated that the German Reich was to be treated as an eco-

nomic whole. Moscow was reluctant to conclude multi-power settlements with Germany and Austria, lest these two conquered nations wriggle out from under the Soviet heel. But there were no insuperable obstacles to peace pacts with Italy, Bulgaria, Hungary, Romania, and Finland; and treaties were formally signed with these countries in 1947.

The reconstruction of Japan was much simpler than that of Germany, primarily because it was largely a one-man show. The occupying American army, under the Supreme Allied Commander, five-starred General Douglas MacArthur, was in effective control. Despite the violent protests of the Soviet officials, MacArthur went inflexibly ahead with his program for the democratization of Japan. Following the pattern in Germany, top Japanese "war criminals" were tried in Tokyo from 1946 to 1948. Eighteen of the leading offenders were sentenced to prison terms and seven were hanged.

General MacArthur, as a kind of Yankee Mikado, enjoyed phenomenal success. He made a tremendous impression on the Japanese with his aloof, Greek-god bearing; and the vanquished sons of Nippon cooperated with their conqueror to an unbelievable degree. They were clever enough to see that good behavior and the adoption of "de-mok-las-sie" would speed the end of the occupation—as it did.

The non-Communist powers, fed up with Soviet obstruction, at length concluded a separate treaty with Japan at San Francisco in 1951—six years after the surrender ceremonies. It was essentially a "soft peace," designed to help the Nipponese get back on their sandaled feet and stand as a bulwark against Communism in Eastern Asia.

The Rift with Russia

The multiplying tensions between the Soviet Union and the free world finally flared into an open quarrel. This was the overshadowingly ominous development of the post-war years.

When World War II burned itself out, a vast reservoir of good will existed in the United States for the resolute Russians. Even though they had been ultra-suspicious associates, they had helped us save our skins while saving their own. If the men in the Kremlin had sung a sweeter tune, they probably could have borrowed billions of American dollars to assist in the task of picking up the pieces left by Hitler.

Instead of milking America, the Russian rulers disdainfully kicked her in the teeth. In doing so, they all too openly revealed that they had not abandoned their zeal for Communist world revolution. They further betrayed their aggressive aims by crying "capitalist encirclement"—at the very time when we were hastily demobilizing our armed forces and they were bolstering theirs.

The Soviets forthwith proceeded to clang down the "iron curtain" over their smaller neighbors like Poland and Hungary—in flagrant violation of the Atlantic Charter and the Yalta pledges. Presumably the Kremlin wanted to bring these nations securely into its own camp as buffers against a future invasion from the capitalistic world—a capitalistic world which, in its view, was "rattling" the atomic bomb and practicing "atomic blackmail."

The iron-fisted new Soviet policy wrought a psychological Pearl Harbor. The eyes of our people were jarred wide open by the unmistakable hostility of the Kremlin to the democratic nations. Many Americans had experienced grave misgivings ever since the Bolshevik revolution in 1917, but now even the wishful thinkers were deeply disturbed. They were profoundly alarmed by Soviet sabotaging of the United Nations, and especially by the evident determination of Moscow to Communize both Italy and France and sweep to the English Channel.

Soviet aggressiveness thus aroused and forewarned our people. We were once more forced, though reluctantly, to shoulder the heavy burdens of rearmament. The supreme irony is that we not only ceased to dismantle German war-industry factories, but before long were trying to induce Germany to rearm. Her man power seemed indispensable if we were going to halt the westward surge of Soviet Communism.

Dollars to the Rescue

President Truman, backed by an aroused public opinion, finally adopted in 1947 a "get-tough-with-Russia" policy. His first dramatic move was touched off by word that Great Britain, heavily burdened, could no longer bear the financial and military load of defending Greece against Communist pressures. If Greece fell, Turkey would presumably collapse and the whole strategic Eastern Mediterranean would be lost to the free world.

In a surprise appearance, Truman stood before Congress, on March 12, 1947, and urged it to support what came to be known as the Truman Doctrine. The United States, he felt, should attempt to halt or "contain" the aggression of Communism where it threatened to jeopardize free peoples. Specifically, he asked Congress to appropriate $400,000,000 for the economic and military bolstering of both Greece and Turkey. The legislators, reflecting the changed mood of the country, responded with lopsided votes of approval. American aid was promptly rushed to the troubled spots, and Greece and Turkey were saved from the clutch of Communism.

But the Truman Doctrine proved far too limited in scope. Western Europe—notably Italy, France, and western Germany—was still suffering from the hunger and economic chaos spawned by the war. These key nations were in grave danger of being taken over by the "stomach Communists"—that is, by desperate people to whom any change would seem a change for the better.

Secretary of State George C. Marshall, a distinguished general of the recent war, stepped spectacularly into the breach. In a speech at Harvard University on June 5, 1947, he broadly hinted that the countries of Europe should get together and work out plans for their economic recovery. If they did so, the United States might help them with adequate financial assistance, pending that day when they could support themselves and consequently bolster American policy.

The democratic nations of Europe rose to the life-giving bait with enthusiasm, and in July, 1947, a conference was held in Paris to work out details. The Soviets muffed a splendid opportunity to snarl the Marshall Plan hopelessly when they stalked out of the conference. They branded the whole scheme an "imperialist" plot, cooked up by the Wall Street "Knights of the Dollar" for "the enslavement of Europe."

The next move was up to Congress, which had to vote the money. The plan as outlined by President Truman contemplated spending the enormous sum of $17,000,000,000 over a period of four years in sixteen cooperating countries. The United States was already tax-burdened and debt-ridden, and critics of the Marshall scheme, chiefly old-line isolationists, branded it "the Martial Plan," "Operation Rathole," and "the Share-the-American-Wealth Plan."

Finally, in April, 1948, Congress voted the initial appropriation—with evident reluctance. A few voices were raised to say that as good Samaritans we owed help to our distressed neighbors and recent allies. But the clincher turned out to be the naked aggression of Soviet Communism. The Marshall Plan appropriation was languishing in Congress when a

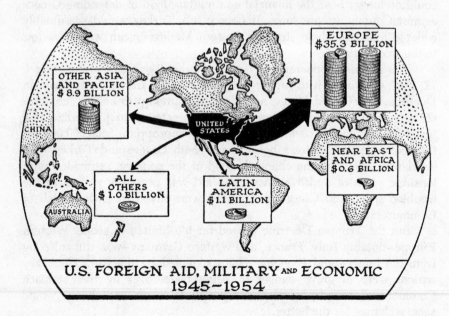

U.S. FOREIGN AID, MILITARY AND ECONOMIC
1945–1954

Communist coup in Czechoslovakia, involving the suicide (or murder?) of its Foreign Minister, provided a frightening new object lesson in how a democracy could be enchained overnight.

The Marshall Plan on the whole proved to be a gratifying success. The billions voted by Congress were administered under the Economic Cooperation Administration, headed by Paul G. Hoffman, the former president of the Studebaker automobile corporation. Life-giving American dollars pumped a needed blood transfusion into the economic veins of the anemic Western European nations, and within a few years most of them were approaching or even exceeding their pre-war production figures. The Reds in Italy and France lost some ground, and these two vital countries were saved from the creeping paralysis of Communism.

War without Shooting

The uphill struggle to stem Soviet Communism resulted in what came to be known as "the cold war." It was not war—yet it was not peace. The alarming tactics of the Kremlin completely banished the hopes of tax-weary Americans that arms could be beaten into automobiles and television sets.

Unification of the armed services, long talked about, was spurred on by the Soviet menace. In 1947 Congress passed an act which brought into being a Department of Defense, headed by a new Cabinet member called the Secretary of Defense. Under him, but without Cabinet status, were the Secretary of the Navy, the Secretary of the Army (replacing the old Secretary of War), and the Secretary of the Air Force (a recognition of air power). Unification unfortunately developed much friction in its initial stages, largely because of the persistence of the traditional service rivalries, some of which dated back to the football classics between West Point and Annapolis.

Rearmament in the United States was pushed with vigor. American military men, viewing with alarm the growing might of the Soviet colossus, warmly advocated Universal Military Training. But they had to settle in 1948 for a less sweeping new draft law, which provided for the conscription of youths from eighteen to twenty-five.

Open and official American propaganda, for the first time in our peacetime experience, was used by Washington to counter the insidious blasts from Moscow. Under the auspices of "The Voice of America," which was formally authorized by Congress in 1948, radio programs were beamed through the Iron Curtain. The management of the enterprise had serious shortcomings, and Congress half-choked "The Voice" with niggardly appropriations and a barrage of criticism. But the efforts of the Soviets to "jam" the program indicated that it was of some effect in trumpeting abroad American democratic ideals.

Red Herrings

One of the most active cold-war fronts was at home, where a new anti-Red chase was in full cry. Many nervous citizens feared that Communist spies, paid with Moscow gold, were undermining the government and treacherously misdirecting our foreign policy. In 1947 Truman ordered a loyalty investigation of federal employees, and as a result a number of possible "security risks" were dropped. The Attorney General in 1947 issued a long list of allegedly subversive organizations, membership in which would cause one's loyalty to be suspect.

The individual states likewise became intensely security-conscious. Loyalty oaths in increasing numbers were demanded of employees, educational and otherwise. Disagreeable incidents involving freedom of speech and teaching burst into the headlines. The burning question in the minds of many earnest Americans was simply put. Could we continue to enjoy to the fullest extent our old Jeffersonian freedoms in the face of a ruthless international conspiracy known as Soviet Communism?

In 1949 eleven Communists were brought before a New York jury on charges of violating the Smith Act of 1940, our first peacetime antisedition act since 1798. Seeking to hide behind the very Constitution they were attempting to destroy, the defendants were found guilty of advocating the overthrow of the government of the United States by force, and were sent to prison.

The House Committee on Un-American Activities had meanwhile thrown out a dragnet for disloyal citizens. Its most sensational catch was Alger Hiss, once a highly trusted second-flight employee of the Department of State. A New York jury in 1950 found him guilty of perjury, after he had denied under oath that he had passed State Department secrets on to Moscow agents in 1937 and 1938. He was sentenced to five years in the penitentiary.

President Truman, who had launched his own security program, jibed that the Republicans were trying to cover up their own shortcomings in Congress by dragging in "Red herrings." He regarded the findings of the inquisitors as a reflection on the vigilance and competence of the Democratic administration, as to some extent they were. But his cover-up policy merely played into the hands of avid Red-hunters like Senator Joseph R. McCarthy of Wisconsin, a Republican who irresponsibly charged in 1950 that there were scores of known Communists in the Department of State. Not a single one was found.

Airlifts and Alliances

The cold war had meanwhile come perilously close to flaring into a hot war in the rubble heap known as Berlin. Lying deep within the Soviet Zone of Germany (see map, p. 913), this democratic isle in a Red sea had been broken into four sectors, each of which was occupied by troops of one of the four great powers. Yet no provision had been made for guaranteeing joint control of the roads and railroads approaching Berlin through the Soviet-controlled zone. In 1948, following angry controversies over German currency reform and four-power control, the Russians sprang the trap. They abruptly choked off the land and water communication lines to Berlin, no doubt reasoning that the Allies would be starved out.

Rather than turn tail and run, the British and Americans, chiefly Americans, organized a gigantic airlift in the midst of the trigger-finger tension. For nearly a year the intrepid aviators, summer and winter, flew in the necessities of the Berliners, including coal—expensive coal. At its peak the airlift ("Operation Vittles") was ferrying some 4500 tons of supplies a day to more than two million people. The Berliners, once enemies, were heartened and grateful.

The Soviets were sobered by the evident determination of the Allies to stand firm. The democracies at length won an impressive moral victory when the Russians, their fingers burned by an Allied counter-blockade, formally lifted their ban on non-air shipments in May, 1949.

Two Germanies emerged from the Soviet-engineered deadlock. One was the Communist-dominated East Germany; the other was the democratically organized West Germany. The government of the West German Republic was formally and hopefully set up in 1949 at the historic Rhine city of Bonn, birthplace of Beethoven.

The Soviet menace meanwhile had been forcing the once-divided democracies of Western Europe into an unforeseen degree of unity, both economic and political. In 1948, Britain, France, Belgium, the Netherlands, and Luxembourg signed a pathbreaking defensive alliance at Brussels. A security-seeking United States, despite its deep-seated prejudice against peacetime entanglements, was drawn irresistibly toward the new grouping.

The alliance negotiations, which continued behind the scenes, reached their climax in Washington. There, on April 4, 1949, the representatives of twelve nations, with appropriate white-tie pageantry, signed the historic North Atlantic Pact. The treaty stipulated that an attack on one member by an aggressor would be an attack on all, and that the signatories would then take such action as they deemed necessary, including "armed force."

Would the United States Senate, despite a strongly favorable public opinion, reject the pact? Last-ditch isolationists pointed out that the new scheme was a dangerous involvement which would cause the Republic to become a kind of helpless tail to the European kite. But security came before tradition, and the Senate registered its approval, on July 21, 1949, by a vote of 82 to 13.

The treaty was truly epochal. The United States did not assume a hard-and-fast commitment to rush to the aid of any one of the signatories assaulted by Soviet Russia—but there was clearly a moral commitment. Due notice was served on the men of the Kremlin that they attacked at their peril, and preparations were pushed by the North Atlantic Treaty Organization (NATO) to build up an army for defensive purposes. The pact was bolstered in 1952 by the inclusion of Greece and Turkey.

It was painfully evident that the free nations of the world would have to stand together, or they might be picked off one by one—in arti-choke-eating fashion. America's willingness to enter into a peacetime military alliance, despite hoary tradition, revealed a gnawing concern over the aggressions of the Soviet Union. The cold war had forced us to face cold facts.

Democratic Divisions

Republican prospects had seldom looked rosier as the presidential campaign of 1948 neared. The G.O.P. could point happily to the Congressional elections of 1946, when the voters, responding to the slogan "Had Enough?" had elected a Republican Congress. Seemingly the country was fed up with New Deal spending, high prices, and "High-Tax Harry" Truman.

The joyous Republicans, meeting in Chicago, departed sharply from previous practice. They noisily renominated a warmed-over candidate, the once-defeated but undaunted Thomas E. Dewey of New York, still as debonair as if he had stepped out of a bandbox. The platform listed in detail the shortcomings of the New Deal, and revived the threadbare theme that it was time for a change. "Save What's Left" became a popular Republican slogan.

The Democratic politicos, gathering in Philadelphia, worked up no real enthusiasm for their hand-me-down President, Harry S. Truman. An effort was made to draft war-hero General Dwight D. Eisenhower, and when he continued to turn a deaf ear, the "dump Truman" movement collapsed. The peppery President was then chosen in the face of violent opposition from the Southern

DEMOCRATIC SPLIT RAISES G.O.P. HOPES
Bishop in the St. Louis *Star-Times*, 1948

delegates, who were alienated by his strong stand in favor of civil rights for Negroes.

Truman's nomination split the party wide open. Embittered Southern Democrats from thirteen states, like their fire-eating forebears of 1860, finally met in their own convention, in Birmingham, Alabama. Amid scenes of heated defiance, these "Dixiecrats" nominated Governor J. Strom Thurmond of South Carolina on a States' Rights Party ticket.

To add to the confusion within Democratic ranks, former Vice-President Henry A. Wallace threw his hat into the ring. Having parted he was nominated at Philadelphia by the new Progressive Party—a bizarre collection of disgruntled ex-New Dealers, pacifists, progressives, well-meaning liberals, and Communist-fronters, who chanted:

> One, two, three, four,
> We don't want another war.

Wallace, a vigorous if misguided liberal, assailed American "dollar imperialism" from the stump. Dripping rotten eggs in hostile cities, this so-called "Pied Piper of the Politburo" took a pro-Soviet line that undoubtedly weakened our diplomacy. (He later admitted his error.)

The "Miracle" of 1948

Truman's chances seemed desperate. A party is ordinarily doomed when it splits in half: this time the party had split three ways. It had been in power for sixteen long years, had made many well-publicized mistakes, and had incurred a host of enemies. It was vulnerable, moreover, to the charge of "Communist coddling."

Dewey, quite understandably, fell victim to overconfidence, especially after the public-opinion polls and the political experts had him winning in a walk. To many voters he seemed cold, smug, superior, and evasive. Non-committal in the extreme, he engaged in dispensing soothing-syrup generalities. But his strategy was basically sound: if victory is certain, why tie one's hands by making any more positive commitments than one has to?

Harry S. Truman—"the forgotten man"—was left almost alone, with little money and few active supporters. But his fighting instincts were aroused; and rolling up his sleeves, he put on a furious, free-swinging, one-man campaign. Touring the country and showing his "folksy" personality to advantage, he delivered a series of "give 'em hell" speeches at numerous whistle-stops. He condemned the Taft-Hartley "slave labor" law, and lashed out at the record of the "do nothing" Republican Eightieth Congress—the "worst in history." He airily waved aside the findings of the pollsters as "sleeping polls," designed to lull the voters to sleep.

Only a Republican genius, it was said, could lose this election; and Dewey succeeded brilliantly in snatching defeat from the jaws of victory. Truman swept to a stunning triumph, to the complete bewilderment of the politicians, pollsters, prophets, and pundits. The chagrined Chicago *Tribune* had overconfidently run off an edition with the headline "DEWEY DEFEATS TRUMAN." The statistical results are most revealing:

	Popular Vote	Electoral Vote
Truman (Democratic)	24,105,695	303 (chiefly South, Middle West, and West)
Dewey (Republican)	21,969,170	189 (chiefly New England, Middle Atlantic states)
Thurmond (States' Rights Democratic)	1,169,021	39 (Ala., Miss., La., S.C.)
Wallace (Progressive)	1,156,103	0

To make the victory all the sweeter, the Democrats regained control of Congress.

Why the sensational upset? High among the reasons must rank Republican overconfidence, fed by the poll-takers. Farmers found Truman's promises of price supports more reassuring than Dewey's; labor opposed the Republican-sponsored Taft-Hartley law; and the influential Negro vote in the large Northern cities naturally turned to Truman as a result of his pro-civil rights stand. The country was prosperous, and government checks were still flowing out from the Treasury to various voters. Finally, Truman's lone-wolf, never-say-die campaign won him the support of many Americans who admired "guts."

New Dealers Become Fair Dealers

Smilingly confident, Truman sounded a clarion note in the fourth point of his inaugural address, when he called for a "bold new program" which came to be known as Point Four. The plan was to lend American money and technical aid to backward lands, so that they might aid themselves. Truman wanted to spend millions of dollars to keep underprivileged peoples from becoming Communists, rather than to spend billions of dollars to shoot them after they had become Communists. This farseeing program was officially launched in 1950, and it brought badly needed assistance to impoverished countries, notably in Latin America, Africa, the Near East, and the Far East.

A Fair Deal, aimed at helping underprivileged peoples at home, was fully outlined in Truman's annual message to Congress, in January, 1949. The President issued an appeal for a sweeping program that would embrace badly needed housing, full employment, higher minimum wages, better price supports for farmers, new TVA's for other major river valleys, and an extension of social security. This Fair Deal program went further in some respects than the New Deal itself, and the Republicans condemned these "Fear Deal" proposals as designed to create a socialistic and spendthrift "welfare state."

The Fair Dealers, despite Truman's zeal, achieved only a small part of their program. A filibuster by Southern members of Congress blocked a federal anti-poll-tax law and a fair employment practices act. But in 1949 Congress, recognizing inflation, did boost the minimum wage to 75 cents from the 40 cents set in 1940. Progress was also made toward slum clearance and public housing in the Housing Act of 1949. Perhaps the greatest success of Truman's Fair Deal came in the Social Security Act of 1950, which broadened the old-age insurance benefits of the original law of 1935. It added some 9,700,000 beneficiaries to the 35,000,000 already covered.

Cold War Setbacks

President Truman shocked the nation by announcing, in September, 1949, that the Soviets had exploded an atomic bomb—approximately three years earlier than our experts had thought possible. American strategists since 1945 had counted on keeping the Soviets in line by the threat of a one-sided aerial attack with nuclear bombs. In fact, it is probable that the American monopoly of this lethal weapon had restrained the Russians from launching out on a sweeping course of armed aggression. But atomic bombing was now to be a game that two could play.

The unexpected success of the Soviet scientists was presumably due, at least in part, to the cleverness of Communist spies in stealing American secrets. Notorious among those Americans and Britishers who had "leaked" atomic data to Moscow were two American citizens, Julius and Ethel Rosenberg. They were convicted in 1951 of espionage, and after prolonged appeals went to the electric chair in 1953—the first peacetime American spies to be executed. The treacherous activities of such disloyal citizens, combined with fear of the A-bomb, gave strong public support to zealous Congressional Red-hunters.

Bad news of a different sort came in 1949 with the catastrophic fall of China to the Communists. Since the end of the war, and even earlier, the Washington officials had halfheartedly supported the Nationalist government of Chiang Kai-shek in his bitter civil war with the Communists. But the Generalissimo gradually began to forfeit the confidence of his people, owing to the ineptitude and corruption within his regime. Communist armies swept south overwhelmingly, and late in 1949 Chiang was forced to flee with the remnants of his once-powerful force to the last-hope island of Formosa.

The collapse of Nationalist China was a staggering defeat for the United States and its allies in the cold war—the worst to date. At one fell swoop nearly one-fourth of the world's population—some 500,000,000 souls—was swept into the Communist camp. The Republicans, seeking "goats," assailed President Truman and his suave Secretary of State, Dean

Acheson. They insisted that high-placed New Deal and Fair Deal agencies, wormy with Communists, had purposely withheld needed aid from Chiang Kai-shek so that his regime would fall. The Democrats heatedly replied that when a government has lost the support of its people, no amount of outside aid will save it—at least not any on the scale that the American people would consent to provide.

The horrifying race in "city-busting" weapons continued at a stepped-up pace. The only language that the Soviets seemed to respect was force, and weakness in the democratic world would invite disaster. Late in 1952, after tests in the South Pacific, word leaked out that an American hydrogen device, many times more lethal than the atomic bomb, had been exploded. It was assumed that the Soviets would soon have one also—and the next year they claimed that they did. If the cold war should blaze into a hot war, perhaps there would be no world left for the Communists to Communize—a sobering thought that may have given them pause. Peace through mutual terror might yet come to be the best hope of mankind.

SELECT READINGS

Overviews are HERBERT AGAR, *The Price of Power: America since 1945* (1957) [paperback]; J. W. SPANIER, *American Foreign Policy since World War II* (1960) [paperback]; and W. G. CARLETON, *The Revolution in American Foreign Policy* (1963) [paperback]. Engagingly written is E. F. GOLDMAN's analysis *The Crucial Decade: America, 1945–1955* (1956) [paperback]. HARRY TRUMAN's own story is saltily told in his *Year of Decisions* (1955) and *Years of Trial and Hope* (1956), [both paperback]. See also ALFRED STEINBERG's journalistic *The Man from Missouri* [Truman] (1962).

Various aspects of foreign policy are revealed in J. A. LUKACS, *A History of the Cold War* (1961) [paperback]; D. F. FLEMING's pro-Soviet *The Cold War and Its Origins, 1917–1960* (2 vols., 1961); N. A. GRAEBNER, *The New Isolationism* (1956); W. P. DAVISON, *The Berlin Blockade* (1958); R. E. OSGOOD, *NATO: The Entangling Alliance* (1962); HERBERT FEIS, *The China Tangle* (1953) [paperback]; F. S. DUNN, *Peace-Making and the Settlement with Japan* (1963); KAZUO KAWAI, *Japan's American Interlude* (1960); and TANG TSOU, *America's Failure in China, 1941–1950* (1963).

Aspects of Communism are developed in D. A. SHANNON, *The Decline of American Communism: A History of the Communist Party of the United States since 1945* (1959); D. J. SAPOSS, *Communism in American Politics* (1960); and K. M. SCHMIDT, *Henry A. Wallace: Quixotic Crusade, 1948* (1960). Revealing personal glimpses are found in Secretary J. F. BYRNES, *Speaking Frankly* (1947) and *All in One Lifetime* (1958); also General L. D. CLAY, *Decision in Germany* (1950). Also references for preceding chapter and *Harvard Guide*, Pt. VI.

46

Korea and the Challenge to the West

The attack upon Korea makes it plain beyond all doubt that Communism has passed beyond the use of subversion to conquer independent nations and will now use armed invasion and war.

HARRY S. TRUMAN, June 27, 1950

Korea: Crucible of Conflict

KOREA, the Land of the Morning Calm, suddenly ushered in a new and more ominous phase of the cold war—the shooting phase—in June, 1950.

Following the collapse of Japan's empire in 1945, Korea had been occupied by Russian and American troops, separated by the 38th parallel. The Soviets proceeded to Communize their northern half under a propped-up puppet regime. The Americans attempted to democratize their southern half—a vastly more difficult task—under a popularly elected government. In 1949, when order was sufficiently restored, the United States withdrew its troops.

The dam broke on June 25, 1950. The North Korean army—Russian-trained, Russian-equipped, and presumably Russian-inspired—lunged across the 38th parallel into South Korea. The weaker forces of the South Koreans crumpled before the vicious onslaught. The attack was presumably made in full confidence, both in Moscow and in North Korea, that the U.N. would do no more than express pious indignation. This view was strengthened by previous American indifference to Korea, and by an earlier statement of Secretary of State Acheson which seemed to mean, although it did not, that the United States would never fight to defend South Korea.

The life of the infant U.N. hung by a hair, for it had been brutally challenged by Soviet Communism, acting through North Korean puppets. The events of 1931, when the Japanese had plunged into Manchuria, seemed to be repeating themselves like a phonograph record with a needle stuck in one groove. The old League of Nations had faltered, and had ultimately died. If the new U.N. faltered, it almost certainly would die—and with it would perish all hope of collective security for world peace.

925

"HISTORY DOESN'T REPEAT ITSELF"

Truman and the U.N. rush to the rescue. Low in the London *Daily Herald*, 1950. Reprinted by special permission; world copyright reserved.

But the United Nations Security Council, then meeting at Lake Success, New York, rose magnificently to the challenge. (Ironically, the Soviet Union, which could have cast the usual crippling veto, was boycotting the sessions as a protest against the non-admission of Communist China to the U.N.) On the very day of the invasion, the Council unanimously branded North Korea the aggressor, and called upon all member nations "to render every assistance" to the U.N. in restoring peace.

President Truman would have to act fast, in response to this appeal, if he were to act effectively. To have asked Congress for the usual declaration of war would probably have involved enough windy debate to insure the fall of South Korea. So two days after the invasion, on June 27, 1950, Truman seized the bull by the horns. By virtue of his constitutional authority as Commander-in-Chief, he boldly issued the order for American air and naval forces to support South Korea. At the same time he instructed the navy to protect the Nationalist Chinese in Formosa against invasion from Communist China. Three days later, when it became painfully apparent that a small boy had been sent on a man's errand, Truman ordered to Korea a substantial part of the unseasoned American ground troops then occupying Japan.

The President's decisive and courageous action won vigorous applause *at the time* from the public and Congress—quite in contrast with later condemnation when the going got rougher. Weary of appeasement, the American people were evidently prepared to draw the line somewhere; and that line happened to be the 38th parallel.

The war to halt Communist aggression in South Korea was officially a United Nations action. Authorized by the U.N., President Truman chose General MacArthur, then in Japan, to head the joint forces under the blue and white United Nations flag. The United States provided the overwhelming bulk of the air units, the naval forces, the money, the supplies, and, except for the South Koreans, most of the men.

The Military Seesaw in Korea

The South Korean and American troops were relentlessly pushed back by a superior force spearheaded by Russian-made tanks. But the invader was slowed somewhat by American command of the air and sea. Reinforcements were rushed as speedily as possible from the United States, and these were ultimately joined by tiny token contingents from fifteen other members of the U.N.

The tide suddenly turned in September, 1950. General MacArthur, in a surprise move, executed a brilliant amphibious attack at Inchon, on the enemy's flank and rear. The North Koreans, their supply lines menaced, fled from South Korea in panic.

Should General MacArthur pursue the beaten foe across the 38th parallel into North Korea, as the South Koreans were already doing? If the U.N. invaded the territory of the aggressor, it would itself become—at least technically—an aggressor. Yet to halt at the boundary would simply permit the beaten Communists to rally and regroup their armies for another wanton assault at their own convenience.

The decision was a momentous one, for the Chinese Communist Premier had threatened to come into the war if North Korea were invaded. In these circumstances the U.N. Assembly rather vaguely authorized MacArthur to proceed northward, and he undertook to drive to the Yalu River, the northern border of North Korea. Late in November, 1950, he launched an all-out assault designed, in his words, to bring the boys "home by Christmas."

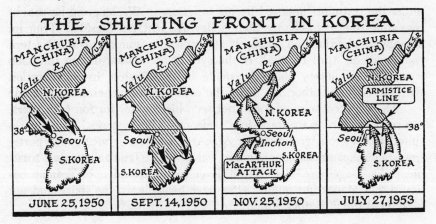

THE SHIFTING FRONT IN KOREA

The Chinese Reds made good their threat. MacArthur's forces were approaching too close to their vital hydroelectric power stations on the Manchuria-Korean border. Suddenly a horde of Chinese "volunteers"—obviously under orders from Communist Peiping—attacked in overwhelming strength. Catching the U.N. invader on the flank in sub-zero weather, they hurled back their foe in a headlong, frostbitten retreat. Complete disaster threatened; but the shattered South Korean and U.N. forces finally regrouped on the icy terrain south of the 38th parallel. There they held off the Communists, inflicted staggering losses on the "human waves" of Chinese, and retrieved some lost ground.

Five-starred General MacArthur, his military reputation partially deflated by this stunning defeat, was eager for drastic retaliation. He urged a blockade of the Chinese coast, employment of Chiang Kai-shek's Nationalist troops in Formosa, and a bombing of Red Chinese bases in Manchuria—an area which the enemy was using as a "privileged sanctuary."

General MacArthur's desire to fight with both fists, instead of one, was quite understandable. But the officials in Washington, where global policy was formulated, were more cautious. They were unwilling to risk bringing Red China formally into a full-dress conflict and touching off World War III with the Russians, who were bound to the Chinese by the thirty-year mutual aid pact of 1950. The Truman administration, strongly supported by public opinion, regarded the Soviet Union as the main foe, and shied away from pouring American money and manhood down the Chinese rathole. Such a conflict, declared General Bradley of the Joint Chiefs of Staff, would be "the wrong war, at the wrong place, at the wrong time, and with the wrong enemy."

Soldiers with Shackles

A showdown impended with General MacArthur, who naturally believed that wars should be fought through to complete victory. Restive under the restraints imposed by his superiors in Washington, he sought by various means to change their policy. An irritated President Truman, alleging insubordination, suddenly removed him from all his Far Eastern commands on April 11, 1951. In the eyes of the administration the issue was: Should military policy be made in Washington, in collaboration with the civilian authorities, or by the commanding general in the field?

The deposed hero, who had not seen his country for fourteen years, returned to receive an uproarious welcome. The hysterical reaction resulted partly from gratitude for MacArthur's past services, and partly from Republican resentment against "small-bore" Truman's tactless treatment of a "large-bore" Republican. Even many defenders of Truman believed that MacArthur might better have been shown the stairs, and not kicked out the fifth-story window.

The Korean conflict now turned into a dull, muddy, bloody affair. MacArthur was replaced by General Matthew Ridgway, who regained essentially the 38th parallel after inflicting staggering losses on the Chinese and North Koreans ("Operation Killer"). He was hammering northward when, in June, 1951, the Russian delegate to the U.N. brought new hope to a troubled world by proposing that negotiations be undertaken for a cease-fire.

The truce discussions, which began in a tent a short distance north of the firing line, provided a fantastic spectacle. Negotiations were dragged out, chiefly by Communist obstructionism, for more than two years. Amid sporadic fighting at the front, the Chinese and North Koreans strengthened their lines and dug in. It is altogether probable that at first their main purpose in seeking a battle of words was to improve their unfavorable position in the battle of weapons.

The outcry in the United States against all this shilly-shallying mounted. Americans are not a patient people; they have been accustomed to quick and heady successes. Many of our red-blooded citizens could see no point in being in a war without striving for a satisfying triumph, even though such action would be costly in lives and might wrap the world in flames.

A Business-as-Usual War

Meanwhile the home-front scenes of World War II were to some extent being re-enacted. The selective service law was extended, and many reservists were torn from their new civilian lives and sent back into action. The morale of the soldiers in Korea was sustained by rotating the men home after they had done their required stint. Although about 260,000 United States troops were bolstering the South Korean and U.N. forces at war's end, all told more than a million Americans served in Korea.

The economic pinch of the Korean War was quickly felt at home. Taxes were boosted, and buying "scares" necessitated new controls. Congress again set up agencies to impose curbs on installment buying, to establish priorities for scarce materials, and to freeze wages and prices. But such restrictions were not completely effective. The upward-thrusting inflation spiral was stimulated by war purchases, as factories hummed anew with defense orders.

The American people tried hard to maintain a normal economy while fighting the abnormal Korean War. They sought to have not only tanks but also new automobiles. Yet occasional strikes hampered the war effort, notably the crippling steel walkout of June and July, 1952.

The prolonged truce talkathon in Korea, together with upward-edging prices, reacted most unfavorably against the Truman administration. So long as the war to curb aggression and save the U.N. went well, the intervention was reasonably popular. But then came heavy reverses, mounting casualty lists, and finally a deadlock which seemed to be a farce. Increasing numbers of action-loving Americans became critical of "Truman's War."

Another unpopular aspect of the Korean intervention was the fact that only sixteen of the sixty U.N. members sent fighting contingents. The other allies were all poorer than rich Uncle Sam, who was left carrying the heavy end of the log. Some of them, notably France and Britain, offered the solid excuse of heavy military commitments elsewhere. Disturbed by the so-called willingness of the U.N. to "fight to the last American," an impressive number of our super-patriots were demanding that we go it alone. But a disruptive quarrel with our allies would have doomed collective security—the very objective for which we had intervened in the first place.

Trial by Slander

One conspicuous by-product of the war was a stepping-up of the campaign in the United States to ferret out Communists. Countless Americans, especially Republicans, believed that the China-Korea "mess" had resulted from the infiltration of Communist spies into the State Department. Republican Senator Joseph R. McCarthy of Wisconsin—"low-blow Joe," some of his foes called him—redoubled his charges, often before whirring cameras. Most of his recklessly unfair accusations were

"A-BOMB RUINS IN AMERICA"
Fitzpatrick in the St. Louis *Post-Dispatch*

later found to be without substance, but some of them proved embarrassing to a handful of suspicious characters.

All loyal Americans condemned the presence of Communists in our government—provided they were Communists and not merely non-conformists. But many earnest citizens wondered if we were not burning down the barn to get rid of a few rats. Traditional American ideals did not square with the overready assumption of guilt rather than innocence, the use of slander-and-smear tactics, and the making of great reputations by besmirching the reputations of honorable men. Such un-American methods were bringing our democracy into disrepute overseas, for they presented unpleasant parallels to the vicious anti-Communist campaigns of Hitler's Germany. Many Americans, prisoners of their suspicions, were evidently willing to yield part of their precious freedom for more security—or fancied security. Some of our citizens were actually beginning to fear one another more than they feared the Soviet Union.

The We-Like-Ike Boom

The moral tone of American public life had meanwhile been sagging to a disquieting degree. Washington swarmed with "influence peddlers," who claimed that they had special "pull" at the White House. A few persons close to the people who were close to Truman suddenly blossomed out in costly fur coats—"the Mink Dynasty." A number of Democratic income-tax collectors were found guilty of favoritism and graft. Yet the President remained stubbornly loyal to his cronies. "Turn the rascals out" was the refurbished cry of the Republicans, who branded the record of the administration as "Plunder at home, blunder abroad."

Republican prospects seemed rosy—but so they had four years earlier. The machine politicians clamored for wheel horse Senator Robert A. Taft, their ablest leader and a figure long associated with the isolationist wing of the party. But the blunt and honest Ohioan had made many enemies, notably when he attached his name to the bitterly hated Taft-Hartley labor law. The rank and file of Republicans were eager for a less vulnerable and more glamorous leader.

The most popular man in the country was war hero General Dwight D. ("Ike") Eisenhower, with his famous grin and captivating personality. Though a professional soldier, he had been temporarily demilitarized to some extent by post-war service as president of Columbia University. His familiarity with the Communist menace overseas was intimate, for in 1950 he had been made head of the army in Western Europe then being fashioned by the North Atlantic Treaty Organization. In January, 1952, he openly declared that he was a Republican (a matter previously in doubt), and that he would be available for the nomination.

Enthusiastic supporters of Eisenhower descended on Chicago in July, 1952, flashing "I Like Ike" buttons. The contest in the convention hall was close and exciting. But grass-roots sentiment for "Ike," who had polled an astonishing vote in some of the primaries, at length overcame the organization-led support of Taft. The genial general was drafted on the first ballot. The Republican platform struck hard at corruption and the Korean "mess," while stressing the threadbare theme of need for a change.

The Democratic race was wide open, since the trim Truman, though full of fight and bounce, chose not to run again. The 22nd Amendment to the Constitution, ratified in 1951 as something of a slap at the dead Roosevelt, limited future Presidents to two terms. (See Appendix.) Truman, though specifically exempted from this new restriction, preferred to pass the torch of succession on to Adlai E. Stevenson, the witty and eloquent governor of Illinois.

The Democratic delegates, assembling in Chicago in late July, 1952, were in high spirits. They sang:

> The farmer's farmin' every day,
> Makin' money, and that ain't hay!
> (Clap, clap)
> DON'T LET 'EM TAKE IT AWAY!*

Senator Estes Kefauver of Tennessee, who had run well in the primaries after heading a highly publicized Senate probe of crime, attracted a considerable coonskin-capped following. But after a tense and bitter struggle on the convention floor, Governor Stevenson was nominated on the third ballot—despite his avowed reluctance to run.

The Eisenhower Landslide

The ensuing campaign was hotly contested. Stevenson—thin, quiet, and intellectual-looking—was handicapped at the start because he was little known outside Illinois, while the sparkling Eisenhower was a five-starred household word. Television figured prominently in a presidential campaign for the first time. Both candidates appeared to good advantage —Eisenhower with his transparent sincerity, Stevenson with his touch of Wilsonian loftiness leavened by a keen sense of humor.

Eisenhower, the amateur in politics, undertook to launch a rousing "crusade" to overthrow corruptionists and clean up "the mess in Washington." He injected further fireworks when he promised to visit Korea to see what he could do to straighten out the frustrating stalemate—a hope-inspiring pledge by a distinguished general that no doubt won many votes. The Democrats replied that this was a "grandstand gesture," and that a Republican victory would bring back dreary depression days. The slogan "You Never Had It So Good" was an obvious attempt to. make political capital once more of the "Hoover Depression."

---

* "Don't Let 'Em Take It Away!" by Robert Sour and Bernie Wayne, 1952. By permission of Meridian Music Corp.

Seven "C's" hampered the Democrats. Corruption in government, which Truman pooh-poohed out of loyalty to his cronies. Corea (old spelling), with its deadlock and dead-end futility. China, which had gone down the Communist drain, allegedly as a result of the Roosevelt-Truman blunderings. Communist-coddling in government, with imprisoned Alger Hiss a chief target of attack. Cost of living, which was inching upward under the pressure of heavy spending produced by the Korean War. Controls on wages, buying, and prices, with all the consequent frustrations.

The seventh "C" was Change, which the Republicans—crying "Had Enough?"—claimed was urgently needed. The Democratic Party had been in power for nearly twenty years, and if the two-party system was to survive—so grim-faced Republicans insisted—there would have to be a thorough housecleaning. The Republicans decried the red tape, the red ink, and the Reds; the New Deal, the Fair Deal, and the Ordeal.

The war hero triumphed in a landslide so massive that the experts and pollsters were again caught off base. The tidal sweep amassed 33,824,351 votes for Eisenhower to 27,314,987 for Stevenson—an enormous plurality of more than 6,500,000 votes. The beaming military man cracked the Solid South wide open, as he rang up 442 electoral votes to 89 for his opponent. The enormous popularity of Eisenhower in large areas of the South led to the hope that a genuine two-party system could be established in Dixieland. It was now respectable to be a Southern Republican.

"Ike's" amazing personal popularity told much of the story. Even though the Democrats could point to pulsating prosperity, such was the spell cast by Eisenhower that the voters, for once, voted against their

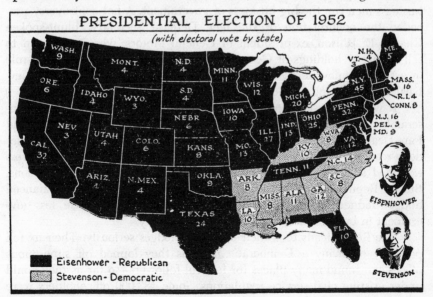

PRESIDENTIAL ELECTION OF 1952
(with electoral vote by state)

■ Eisenhower - Republican
▨ Stevenson - Democratic

own pocketbooks. "Ike" ran far ahead of his ticket, polling several million more votes than all the Republican Congressmen combined, many of whom rode into office on his military coattails. But at that, the victors won control of Congress by only a paper-thin margin.

The Republican New Deal

President-General Eisenhower was a career soldier who, in the autumn of his public life, had to adjust himself to the give-and-take of politics and the techniques of civilian government. A liberal internationalist in foreign affairs, he was a middle-of-the-road Kansas conservative in domestic affairs. He deeply respected the separation of powers among the three branches of government, and he evidently had no desire to dominate Congress in the Rooseveltian manner. Famed as a conciliator, he undertook to achieve his ends by quiet lunch-table conferences.

As a "team man," Eisenhower earnestly sought party unity. The Republicans were divided into two camps: the isolationist wing, headed by Senator Taft, and the internationalist wing, headed by men like Governor Dewey. Although Eisenhower's personal sympathies were with the Dewey group, he would have to make both wings flap together if he was to keep his party air-borne.

The Eisenhower Cabinet was noteworthy in several respects. A new post was created when the Republican Congress established the Department of Health, Education, and Welfare, under the second woman Cabinet officer in our history, the attractive and energetic Mrs. Oveta Culp Hobby of Texas. Most of the Cabinet posts were filled by big bankers or industrialists, in harmony with the Republican tradition of having big business men run the big business of government. A hot controversy preceded the confirmation of the new Defense Secretary, blunt-spoken Charles E. Wilson, ex-president of General Motors, who was forced to sell his heavy holdings of General Motors stock because of his new role in assigning juicy defense contracts. Democrats growled that the New Dealers were being replaced by Car Dealers.

It was obviously impossible for the triumphant Republicans to unscramble the eggs that had been scrambled by the New Dealers and Fair Dealers in twenty long years. The TVA, social security, and other deep-reaching changes would have to stand; in fact, the new Congress extended social security benefits to an additional ten million persons. But the Republicans were pledged to make reforms relating to a balanced budget, reduced federal outlays, lowered taxes, free enterprise, less government in business, and fewer curbs on industry.

The Republicans took their economy pledges seriously. Their ax fell painfully on many a Democratic neck as they lopped off superfluous offices and found many places for faithful followers—so far as they could under existing civil service regulations. Some 183,000 officeholders were dropped during the first year—cynically dubbed F.B.I.'s ("fired by 'Ike' "). The Republicans likewise wielded a meat ax on Truman's proposed budget, slashing more than twelve billion dollars from his estimates, and proceeded to reduce taxes sharply.

Nor did the Republicans overlook their promises to shake off governmental restrictions. Despite a temporary boost to inflation, they wiped out the price and wage controls imposed by the Truman administration during the Korean War. The Republican Congress also limited a public housing program to one year, and permitted the Hoover-sponsored Reconstruction Finance Corporation to die a natural death.

The Republican drive toward enlarged free enterprise continued in other areas. The offshore oil lands, despite a record-breaking twenty-two-hour filibustering speech by Senator Morse, were handed over to the coastal states so as to facilitate private rather than federal exploitation. The new administration naturally showed a strong preference for private as against public hydroelectric power, and shepherded through Congress an act authorizing a private atomic-energy industry to generate electricity. The traditionally high-tariff Republicans, influenced to some extent by Europe's cry of "Trade, Not Aid," reluctantly renewed for one year a limited Reciprocal Trade Agreements Act, pending a full study.

Cease-Fire in Korea

Eisenhower at the outset attempted to establish a bipartisan foreign policy—a goal which had been only partially achieved by his immediate predecessors. The Democrats in Congress, steeped in the internationalism of Franklin Roosevelt and Harry S. Truman, on the whole supported the President more effectively than his own Republicans.

Korea remained a Chinese puzzle. Eisenhower had redeemed his campaign promise by making a flying three-day visit to that war-ravaged land in December, 1952. But the stalemated truce negotiations continued on dead center. The sticking point was the demand of the Communists that the U.N. return all prisoners, willing or not, including those anti-Communists to whom we had promised asylum if they surrendered.

A new chapter of the cold war was inaugurated on March 5, 1953, when Moscow announced that Joseph Stalin—the Man of Steel—had died. Shortly thereafter the Kremlin began to adopt—for a brief period—a less snarling attitude toward the Western World in what was branded by cynics a "peace offensive." The Soviets presumably were hoping to trick the democratic nations into dropping their guard and slackening preparations for the NATO army—and in this respect they were partially successful. But while the tongues of the Russians talked peace, their hands continued to build up a menacingly powerful force on land, on sea, and in the air.

The Soviet "peace offensive" was reflected in the truce negotiations in Korea, where armistice terms were finally signed on July 27, 1953. The United Nations won a victory for human dignity when the Communists agreed that prisoners who did not want to go home would be handled by neutral countries. It was further agreed that a subsequent political conference would arrange for the evacuation of foreign troops, as well as for the peaceful settlement of the whole Korean question.

"THE PAPER CORNERSTONE"
Hesse in the St. Louis *Globe-Democrat*, 1953

    After a total of more than three years of shooting (including two of talking), the brutal and futile fighting stopped. The American people, breathing a weary sigh of relief, accepted but did not celebrate the armistice. There was no dancing in the streets. We had not lost; yet we had not won a satisfying victory, such as we had traditionally come to expect. The outcome was more like that of the frustrating War of 1812.

    The cost in Korea had been high. Though never officially declared by Congress, the conflict ranks as our third largest foreign war in outlay and losses. Over fifteen billion dollars had been spent; more than 157,000 American casualties had been suffered, over 33,000 of them deaths. The American losses amounted to about 95% of those of the sixteen participating U.N. members. The Republic of South Korea (not a U.N. member) was the most seriously hurt of all, not only at the battle front but even more grievously among civilians. Yet the casualties inflicted on the Communist armies were estimated to be far heavier than those suffered by the United Nations and South Korea combined.

Disheartening though the losses were, certain gains were evident. The United States had shown unexpected decisiveness as a global leader; no one could now say that the U.N. had died in the rice paddies of Korea in 1950 because we failed to measure up to our responsibilities. The infant organization had been saved—at least temporarily. It had halted the aggressor through joint police action—the first time in history that an international combination had thus acted collectively and effectively. The North Koreans, their fingers badly burned, had been taught the harsh lesson that aggression no longer paid. Their own land devastated, they had wound up with 1500 square miles less territory than when the war started.

Debits and Credits

At home, the "honeymoon period" of the Eisenhower administration was rapidly passing. Senator Taft died of cancer in July, 1953; and with his expert hand gone, Congress became progressively more unruly. The isolationist wing of the Republican Party began to assert itself even more vigorously. Noteworthy was the determined attempt of Senator Bricker to curb the treaty-making power of the President by constitutional amendment—a move that failed in the Senate by only the narrowest of margins.

The somewhat balky Republican Congress was slow to follow Eisenhower's leadership and carry through the "great crusade." Such issues as the tariff, revision of the Taft-Hartley labor law, health reinsurance, and the admission of Hawaii and Alaska to statehood were not acted upon at all, or were dealt with unsatisfactorily. Congress finally responded to decades-long prodding from the White House when, in May, 1954, it authorized American participation with Canada in the construction of the Great Lakes–St. Lawrence Seaway. But this favorable action did not come until our northern neighbor had threatened to go it alone.

The eagerness of Congress to encroach on Executive authority was glaringly revealed in the angry dispute between Senator McCarthy and the Army. Touched off by the Communists-in-government issue, the quarrel resulted in one of the most highly publicized television shows of 1954. Democrats, now turning the tables, were speaking cynically of the "mess in Washington."

The economic picture continued to be both feverish and spotty. A business recession, accompanied by considerable unemployment, followed the end of the heavy spending of the Korean war. Administration spokesmen referred delicately to "the slide" rather than "the slump." Farm income was sharply down, largely as a result of lower prices and extensive drought. Yet Secretary of Agriculture Benson—a hard-working, hard-praying Mormon of the old economic school—was reluctant to continue generous handouts. The vexing problem was to secure adequate parity payments for the farmer without boosting federal price supports. The latter had proved excessively costly, and had left the government knee-deep in the butter, eggs, and other produce which it had purchased to bolster prices.

The most momentous action on a domestic problem was taken not by Congress or the President but by the judiciary. The Supreme Court ruled unanimously, on May 17, 1954, that the long-established "separate but equal" school facilities granted to Negroes violated the 14th Amendment. The Court fortunately indicated that so drastic a social revolution as school desegregation would have to be worked out gradually.

Opposition in the South to the integration decision mounted with burning intensity. Just as the North had denounced the Dred Scott decision of 1857 as a political dictum by an anti-Northern court, so the South denounced the ruling of 1954 as a sociological decision by an anti-Southern court. To millions of Southerners this decree represented an unwarranted invasion of states' rights and an intolerable interference with purely local affairs. The gravest constitutional crisis since the Civil War came to a head as massive resistance to desegregation formed in the Deep South, and conspicuously also in Arkansas and Virginia. But in many other peripheral areas integration in the schools went forward slowly and without disagreeable incident.

Politics and Progress

The hotly contested Congressional elections of November, 1954, resulted in a stinging setback for the Republicans. Eisenhower, standing on his record of achievement, bluntly appealed for a Republican Congress. But the Democrats carried the Senate by a margin of one vote, and the House by a more comfortable majority. The results were widely regarded as a protest against lowered farm income and spotty unemployment, as well as a rebuke to McCarthyism and big-businessism. But—presumably as a result of Eisenhower's still-great personal popularity—the Republican losses were not so large as those ordinarily suffered by the party in power during the mid-term slump.

The conservative Republican right-wingers lost ground as a result of this reverse at the polls, and in the ensuing calmer atmosphere fairer methods were devised for dealing with "security risks." With the Democrats now in power, Red-hunting Senator McCarthy lost the chairmanship of his investigating committee; and shortly thereafter he was soundly spanked when the Senate, by a bipartisan vote of 67 to 22, agreed to "condemn" him for his abuse of fellow Senators (December 2, 1954).

The new Democratic 84th Congress cooperated unexpectedly well with President Eisenhower, especially in the area of foreign policy. It is true that the legislators shied away from the President's health reinsurance plan, a revision of the Taft-Hartley labor law, a softening of immigration restrictions, federal aid to schools, and Eisenhower's multi-billion-dollar highway improvement scheme. But Congress did pass a measure in 1955 authorizing 45,000 housing units, and a three-year extension of the reciprocal trade agreements act. A surprising development occurred when much of the newly industrialized South, reversing its historic low-tariff position, held out vainly for higher protection.

Labor chalked up significant gains, both in Washington and elsewhere. The Democratic Congress boosted the legal hourly minimum wage from seventy-five cents to one dollar. Although disappointed in a revision of the Taft-Hartley Act, labor won a resounding victory over itself early in 1955. At Miami, Florida, representatives of the feuding A.F. of L. and C.I.O. agreed to bury the hatchet and unite their total membership of some 15,000,000. When finally put into effect, the merger could only mean greater strength for organized labor. Symptomatic of a growing assertiveness among workers were the mounting demands, particularly in the automobile industry, for a "guaranteed annual wage" as a cushion against unemployment. A long stride toward this goal was taken in June, 1955, when the United Auto Workers wrested highly favorable unemployment-wage contracts from the Ford Motor Company and General Motors.

Two Worlds

The shadow of the mushroom-shaped atomic cloud continued to hang over foreign relations. President Eisenhower spectacularly proposed to the U.N., in December, 1953, that the nations pool their atomic resources for peaceful purposes. When this scheme received the usual cold shoulder from the Soviets, the United States nevertheless launched it on a limited basis. Moscow later expressed a willingness to go along.

In March, 1954, American experts detonated in the Pacific two hydrogen bombs, both of them hundreds of times more powerful than the obsolete Hiroshima model. The Soviets, it was revealed, had also devised a hydrogen bomb. Before 1945 the United States, with billowing oceans east and west, had never had reason to fear an overnight intercontinental attack. Now, with power relationships radically changing, it was vulnerable to a sudden and perhaps crippling blow.

The Eisenhower administration, faced with overpowering military costs in fending off Communism all over the world, committed itself to a "New Look" defense policy. The army and navy would be given the back seat, and the air force would be built up to deter aggressors with the threat of "massive retaliation." At the same time we would strive to beef up the armed forces being amassed by our NATO (North Atlantic Treaty Organization) allies in Europe.

Momentous progress had meantime been made toward the rearmament of West Germany and her inclusion in the camp of the western allies as a buffer against Soviet Communism. After the French had stubbornly vetoed one ambitious plan, the powers threshed out new arrangements at Paris in the autumn of 1954—arrangements designed to give West Germany her sovereignty and to admit her to NATO with a contribution of 500,000 troops. The members of NATO, including the United States, subordinated their misgivings and concluded ratification of the Paris agreements in April, 1955.

Fresh Troubles in the Far East

A crisis in the Far East had meanwhile been coming to a boil. The nineteen-nation Geneva Conference of 1954, called to deal with the Korean and Indochina problems, resulted in another stunning setback for the free world. With the French forces in northern Indochina crumbling before the Communist rebels, the conferees agreed to cut Indochina (Viet Nam) at the waist, and turn over the 13,000,000 inhabitants north of that line to the Communists. A free election, scheduled for 1956, would deter-

THE FAR EAST
1955-1956

NORTH KOREA

SOUTH KOREA

COMMUNIST CHINA

Shanghai

OKINAWA

NORTH VIETNAM

BURMA

FORMOSA

Hong Kong

DIVIDING LINE

THAILAND

INDOCHINA

PHILIPPINE ISLANDS

CAMBODIA

SOUTH VIETNAM

MALAYA

Singapore

INDONESIA

BORNEO

mine the fate of the rest of Indochina. The United States was not a party to this surrender, which was widely condemned in America as "appeasement." But late in 1954 Washington did take the lead in organizing the free nations of Southeast Asia, during a conference at Manila, into the Southeast Asia Treaty Organization (SEATO). It was designed as a weaker Far Eastern counterpart of the North Atlantic Treaty Organization (NATO).

Despite these efforts at unity, the upsurging Communists continued to show their contempt for Western weakness. The American people were bitterly aroused in 1954 when the Peiping regime, contrary to the Korean armistice, sentenced as spies eleven uniformed American airmen who had been forced down on Communist territory. Further evidence of an aggressive attitude by the Chinese Communists came with a stepping-up of preparations for attacking Chiang's refuge on Formosa, which was a vital bastion of anti-Communist strength in the Far East.

The tension became so acute that early in 1955 Eisenhower took an unparalleled step. He flatly asked Congress for advance authorization to use the armed forces of the United States to repel a Communist assault on Formosa. Such a blank check would enable him to avoid the agonizing responsibility that had fallen to Truman at the time of the North Korean invasion of 1950. Congress, impressed with the desirability of keeping Formosa afloat, approved this pre-dated war resolution by an overwhelming vote of 85 to 3 in the Senate and 409 to 3 in the House. The decision for war or peace now lay in the hands of the Communists. But there was still the flickering hope that a neutralization of Formosa might be achieved under U.N. auspices.

Soviet Smiles and Wiles

With the world braced for an explosion, the grim-faced Soviet leaders suddenly and unexpectedly put on a smiling countenance in the spring and summer of 1955. Experts could only speculate as to the motivation. Perhaps it was fear of a rearmed Germany; internal strain within the Soviet economy; friction among the successors of Stalin; fear of a terrible hydrogen-bomb war; or a desire to lull the democracies into slackening their defense preparations.

Whatever the cause, the Soviet change of front was unmistakable. After ten years of obstruction, Moscow suddenly gave way and signed a treaty, in May, 1955, to end the four-power occupation of Austria. The Moscow Communists then humbled themselves to an amazing degree when they patched up their bitter feud with Tito of Yugoslavia. In May, 1955, the Red Chinese government, presumably acting in concert with the Kremlin, released four imprisoned American airmen, preparatory to releasing the remaining seven a month later. In a striking reversal of policy, the Russians began to lift their iron curtain so as to permit a few foreign visitors to enter the U.S.S.R., and a few selected Russian tourists to leave.

Highly encouraging was the acceptance by the Soviets of a meeting at the "summit" by the heads of state of the Big Four at Geneva, in July, 1955. Eisenhower's radiant personality dominated the sessions, and he spectacularly seized the initiative in the propaganda war by proposing that the Soviets and the United States exchange their military blueprints and permit mutual "open skies" flights over their installations. A Soviet acceptance in good faith seemed highly improbable, but the sessions at Geneva adjourned in a new spirit of friendliness—at least outwardly. Soviet and Western leaders had talked freely, and apparently had convinced one another of the sincerity of their desire for peace. The groundwork was also laid for a meeting of ambassadors at Geneva to discuss the China crisis, and for a meeting of foreign ministers at Geneva, in October, 1955, to consider disarmament, German unification, and other critical issues. An atmosphere of cautious optimism began to pervade the Western World.

But a bucket of cold water suddenly descended on September 24, 1955, when President Eisenhower, then vacationing in Colorado, was stricken with a heart attack. The Republican leaders had been counting heavily on running him for a second time, for they feared that they could not win again without his immense popularity. The resulting uncertainty touched off a series of downward plunges in the stock market reminiscent of 1929.

The prospects abroad were even more disquieting. In view of Moscow's deeds, it quickly became evident that the new Soviet smile was merely a painted mask. The October meeting of foreign ministers at Geneva speedily ran into the usual deadlock, chiefly over disarmament and Soviet unwillingness to permit Germany to become both united and free. While proclaiming peace and disarmament, the Communists were brazenly shipping huge quantities of arms into the explosive Middle East, where Israel was in imminent danger of being attacked by her Arab neighbors.

Yet at home confidence returned with Eisenhower's steady recovery. An unprecedented 65,000,000 persons were gainfully employed, and the administration was soon to claim that the budget was in balance. With much justification, and with a pointed allusion to the recent Korean War, the Republicans could boast, "Only the guns are not booming."

Undaunted by the Republican slogan "Peace and Prosperity," the Democrats mapped their initial moves in the presidential campaign of 1956. Leading candidates for the Democratic nomination opened their oratorical big guns on three issues. The first was low farm income, which contrasted glaringly with the profits of business and industry. The second issue was the reputed greed of special-interest groups, some of which were faring well in the disposal of natural resources, particularly water power. The third issue was the alleged failure of foreign policy, as highlighted by the complete collapse of the conference of foreign ministers at

Geneva in November, 1955. The Republicans, who had condemned the Korean War during the campaign of 1952, now complained that politics should stop at the water's edge. But the shadow of Soviet Communism was much too menacing to permit hope that it could be ignored during a heated presidential canvass.

SELECT READINGS

The era is surveyed readably in E. F. GOLDMAN, *The Crucial Decade: America, 1945–1955* (1956) [paperback]; more sketchily in HERBERT AGAR, *The Price of Power: America since 1945* (1957) [paperback]. President D. D. EISENHOWER tells his own story (blandly) in *Mandate for Change, 1953–1956* (1963) [paperback]. Interesting insights into politics are found in WALTER JOHNSON, *1600 Pennsylvania Avenue: Presidents and the People, 1929–1959* (1960) [paperback]. Journalistic analyses of a controversial Secretary of State are J. R. BEAL, *John Foster Dulles* (1957); ROSCOE DRUMMOND and GASTON COBLENTZ, *Duel at the Brink* (1960). Also journalistic are M. J. PUSEY, *Eisenhower, the President* (1956) and R. J. DONOVAN, *Eisenhower* (1956). Less friendly are M. W. CHILDS, *Eisenhower: Captive Hero* (1958) and E. J. HUGHES' indiscreet *The Ordeal of Power* (1963) [paperback]. For a critical appraisal of McCarthyism consult R. H. ROVERE, *Senator Joe McCarthy* (1959) [paperback]. See also H. M. HYMAN, *To Try Men's Souls: Loyalty Tests in American History* (1959).

The Korean War is discussed in DAVID REES, *Korea: The Limited War* (1964). General MacArthur is criticized in HARRY TRUMAN, *Years of Trial and Hope* (1956) [paperback]; in J. W. SPANIER, *The Truman-MacArthur Controversy and the Korean War* (1959) [paperback]; in TRUMBULL HIGGINS, *Korea and the Fall of MacArthur* (1960); and in R. H. ROVERE and A. M. SCHLESINGER, JR., *The General and the President* (1951). He is defended by C. A. WILLOUGHBY and J. CHAMBERLAIN in *MacArthur, 1941–1951* (1954); by COURTNEY WHITNEY in *MacArthur* (1956); and by the General himself in *Reminiscences* (1964). See also SELECT READINGS of preceding and succeeding chapters.

47

The End of the Eisenhower Era

The Voters Still Like Ike

PRESIDENT EISENHOWER, the magnetic general, was still immensely popular, despite Democratic sneers that the only order he ever gave was to mark time. The Republicans, now a minority party, had to run him again if they hoped to win in 1956. The burning question was whether he had recovered sufficiently from his recent heart attack to run again. The doctors finally gave him a clean bill of health, despite a major abdominal operation (for ileitis) in June, 1956. He was unanimously renominated in San Francisco, as was Vice-President Nixon.

Adlai E. Stevenson, beaten by Eisenhower in 1952, wanted the nomination again, but this time he did not receive it on a silver platter. After a grueling struggle in the state primaries, he won easily on the first ballot at Chicago. The voters were thus presented with two warmed-over candidates—the first such pair since 1900—running on middle-of-the-road platforms.

The mood of the country was moderation. No one, with the notable exception of the farmers, was "mad at anybody." Jobs, wages, and profits were at all-time record levels, as indeed were inflated prices. The Republicans preened themselves on being "the party of peace." Proud of having ended the Korean deadlock in 1953, they condemned the Democrats as "the party of war" by pointing to the Democrat-led World War I, World War II, and Korean War. They conveniently overlooked the Spanish-American War and the Civil War (the bloodiest of all to America), both of them fought under Republican auspices. The Democrats, attacking President "Eisen-hoover," no less unfairly branded the Republicans as "the party of depression." A reversible salesman's "safety pin" button

944

proved popular: on one side was "I like Ike," on the other " All the Way with Adlai."

Stevenson, though still urbane, witty, and idealistic, seemed less freshly appealing than four years earlier. Eisenhower's health was a prime issue; and Stevenson bluntly warned that his opponent probably would not live out another term. In that event the country would inherit Vice-President Richard M. Nixon, whose earlier anti-Communist campaigning had raised doubts as to his statesmanship and had caused irate Democrats to dub him "Tricky Dick." Stevenson finally injected some fireworks when he urged a unilateral halting of nuclear bomb tests, in the interests of both disarmament and an unpolluted atmosphere. Eisenhower branded this scheme "incredible folly," although he adopted it himself two years later.

The explosion of the Suez crisis (see pp. 951–952) in the last week of the campaign worked in favor of Eisenhower's re-election. If World War III erupted, as seemed highly probable, the country preferred a military hero in the White House to a less experienced "egghead."

The election was a resounding endorsement of the amiable general. He had candidly told the voters that his health would permit him to be only a part-time President, but such was the "national love affair" that the people were willing to have him on his own terms. The landslide was even more awesome than that four years earlier; only Franklin Roosevelt's popular majority of 1936 exceeded it. The popular count was 35,590,472 to 26,022,752; the electoral count 457 to 73. Eisenhower was the first Republican to be re-elected since McKinley in 1900; the oldest incumbent ever to be re-elected; and probably the poorest life insurance risk to re-

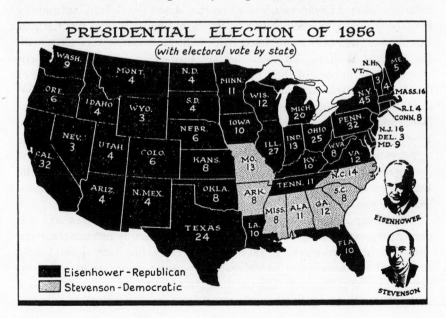

PRESIDENTIAL ELECTION OF 1956
(with electoral vote by state)

WASH. 9
ORE. 6
MONT. 4
IDAHO 4
WYO. 3
N.D. 4
S.D. 4
MINN. 11
WIS. 12
MICH. 20
N.H.
VT.
ME. 5
N.Y. 45
MASS. 16
R.I. 4
CONN. 8
NEBR. 6
IOWA 10
ILL. 27
IND. 13
OHIO 25
PENN. 32
N.J. 16
DEL. 3
MD. 9
NEV. 3
UTAH 4
COLO. 6
KANS. 8
MO. 13
KY. 10
W.VA. 8
VA. 12
CAL. 32
ARIZ. 4
N.MEX. 4
OKLA. 8
ARK. 8
TENN. 11
N.C. 14
S.C. 8
TEXAS 24
LA. 10
MISS. 8
ALA. 11
GA. 12
FLA. 10

EISENHOWER

STEVENSON

■ Eisenhower – Republican
▨ Stevenson – Democratic

enter the White House. "Any jockey would look good riding Ike," replied the Republican national chairman when congratulated on the victory. To many voters the President seemed like a kindly "father image" on whom they might lean for comfort in a troubled world.

But the President's popularity did not rub off on those politicians who had hoped to slide into office by clinging to his coattails. The Democrats retained both houses of Congress, though by relatively narrow margins. For the first time since Zachary Taylor's election in 1848—one hundred and eight years earlier—a victorious President had failed to carry with him either the House or the Senate. The vote was one of admiration for Eisenhower, not of confidence in his party.

Government by Proxy

The beginning of Eisenhower's second administration marked no sharp break with the past. Suffering a mild stroke three weeks after re-election, the President resorted more than ever to golfing and quail shooting. By now an avowed partisan, rather than a referee between parties, he got along surprisingly well with the Democratic majorities in Congress. Liberal Democrats joined with liberal Republicans to pass much of his middle-of-the-road legislation. The conservative wing of the Republican Party showed a marked distaste for Eisenhower's liberal-tinged "Modern Republicanism," so much so that the President had thought seriously of forming a new party.

Flanked by big-business advisers, Eisenhower was especially concerned about "fiscal integrity"—that is, balancing the budget and halting inflation. Liberal Democrats, reared on the "damn the deficits" attitude of the New Dealers, sneered at this "piggy-bank" concept, and insisted that Eisenhower was still more concerned with General Motors than with the General Welfare. To such "budget busters," urgent human needs seemed more important than bookkeeping needs, especially in an era of rapidly rising national income. Spurred by the demands of the Cold War, the Democratic Congresses annually appropriated for defense some forty-five billion dollars of the national budget of nearly eighty billion dollars. They would have appropriated even more but were restrained by the aging general. Fearing that we would spend ourselves into bankruptcy, he argued that he knew more about military needs than Congress. The Democrats contended that a balanced budget was out of place in an unbalanced world.

Handicapped as he was by precarious health, Eisenhower was evidently prepared to reign rather than rule. He confidently entrusted foreign affairs to his hard-working, far-flying Secretary of State, John Foster Dulles. At the same time he delegated domestic decisions to his presidential assistant, Sherman Adams, the granite-jawed ex-governor of New Hampshire who had publicly condemned Democratic corruption.

The roof caved in on Adams in 1958 when a House investigation revealed that he had accepted expensive gifts from a Boston industrialist, on whose behalf he had interceded with three federal agencies. Eisenhower, conceding that Adams had been imprudent, responded to cries for his resignation with a curt "I need him." But the need became less apparent when Adams proved to be a political liability, and Eisenhower finally accepted his resignation "with sadness" in September, 1958. With his right-hand man gone, Eisenhower did less golfing and more governing, and partly silenced demands for more vigorous leadership.

The Adams scandal highlighted an alarming moral sag throughout the nation. Congressmen were paying their relatives handsome salaries; certain members of the Eisenhower administration were being forced to resign because of their intimacy with persons or firms seeking government contracts or other favors. In 1959 the nation was shocked to learn that big-money television programs had been "rigged," and that "disc jockeys" playing records on radio had "plugged" certain recordings after receiving under-the-table payments ("payola").

Economic Cross Currents

Secretary of Agriculture Benson continued to be a highly controversial figure, but with Eisenhower's backing he resigned himself to his duty rather than resigning. The bumper crop of agricultural headaches included declining farm income (despite general prosperity), the bankruptcy of smaller farmers, the costly price-support payments by Washington (averaging over three billion dollars a year), and the fantastic farm surpluses (valued at about nine billion dollars), stored in silo-shaped containers over the land. Storage alone was costing the taxpayers about $2,000,000 a day.

There were no simple solutions. The Democrats generally advocated high and inflexible parity price supports; the Republicans favored somewhat lower and more flexible payments. Some farmers wanted to plow under price supports; others clamored for them. Congressmen feared punishment at the polls if they took away these handouts. Communist propagandists, proclaiming that half the world went to bed hungry, hammered ceaselessly at the stored (and spoiling) surpluses. The giveaway program of Washington to needy nations made only a dent in the towering pile.

The prosperity joyride suffered a severe jolt late in 1957, when a serious business "recession" set in, the third and severest since World War II. The Republicans called it a "dip"; the Democrats called it a "depression," especially when unemployment reached its peak in June, 1958, with 5,437,000 workers out of jobs. The Democrats demanded a drastic tax reduction to increase purchasing power and spur recovery. But Eisenhower refused to push the panic button. A huge highway-building program, costing some thirty-three billion dollars and financed by state-federal funds, had been authorized by Congress in 1956, and though it crept forward with disappointing slowness, it helped take up some of the slack.

Eisenhower's optimism was rewarded when boom times began to return late in 1958, and his economic advisers could warn, "Inflation is the problem." The cost of living continued to creep upward to an all-time high late in 1960, although at a much slower rate than under the preceding Democratic administrations.

For three of the eight Eisenhower fiscal years, the budget was balanced. The administration could even boast a surplus of more than one billion dollars for the fiscal year 1960. Yet American expenditures abroad were so heavy that the nation was showing an adverse balance of payments ("flight of gold"), and by 1960 was having to export about four billion dollars annually to plug the gap. Alarmed budget-parers in Congress looked with growing hostility on the yearly four billion dollars flowing to various "backward" nations as military and economic aid, primarily to keep them out of the Communist camp.

Cracking Down on Labor

Labor unrest persisted throughout the later Eisenhower years. Mechanization (automation) was throwing thousands of men out of jobs, and hundreds of thousands of young people were being pitchforked annually onto the labor market. Discontent with closed-shop union tactics led to much agitation in the states for right-to-work laws —that is, the right to take a job without having to join a union. Indiana in 1957 was the eighteenth state to adopt such legislation, although the first large industrial one.

Labor organizations were flexing their muscles awesomely, especially after the merger of the A. F. of L. and the C.I.O. in 1955. A series of strikes partially paralyzed production, notably in the steel industry, which suffered its sixth and most serious tie-up since World War II in 1959–1960. At a time when the United States was struggling to keep well ahead of the Russians, the steel stalemate lasted one-third of a year (116 days) and idled over a half million men. It finally ended early in 1960 with wage increases and other worker benefits.

Labor demanded a larger share of the unprecedented profits; management wanted to hold the line against rising costs—and inflation. The workers would strike and secure higher wages; management would raise prices correspondingly; and the workers would strike because of higher prices. This dog-chasing-its-tail cycle suggested that labor and management had entered into a conspiracy to cheat the public. In vain did President Eisenhower appeal to both management and labor to be reasonable; neither wanted to be the sacrificial goat.

The close tie-in between gangsters and certain labor leaders broke into the headlines in 1956, when an extortionist threw acid into the eyes of a journalist exposing racketeering. The next year a Senate committee began its spectacular probe of corruption in labor-management relations. The investigators were especially concerned with the use of brass knuckles and explosives to dragoon employers into accepting certain unions, and with the misuse of pension funds and other benefits. Millionaire Dave Beck, president of the gigantic Teamsters' Union (1,500,000 members), invoked the Fifth Amendment against self-incrimination 209 times to avoid telling what he had done with $320,000. He was later sentenced to prison for embezzlement. When his union defiantly elected the headstrong James R. Hoffa as his successor, the A. F. of L.–C.I.O. expelled the teamsters, and court-appointed monitors attempted to ride herd on the new teamster leader. The Senate committee finally reported that in fifteen years union officials had stolen or otherwise misused some $10,000,000.

Legislation was clearly needed to prevent collective bargaining from becoming collective bludgeoning, and to permit rank-and-file union men to have a voice in the running of their organizations without being beaten up. Teamster-boss Hoffa threatened to defeat for re-election those Congressmen who dared to vote for a "tough" labor bill. His arrogance, combined with a dramatic television appeal by President Eisenhower, spurred a drastic labor-reform bill through Congress by wide margins in September, 1959. The Landrum-Griffin Act was specifically tailored to make labor officials responsible for their financial stewardship, to prevent bully-boy tactics, to insure democratic practices within the unions, to outlaw "secondary boycotts," and to restrict picketing.

The Negro and Civil Rights

The reverberating "Black Monday" decision of the Supreme Court in 1954, ordering desegregation in the public schools, disappointed reformers. It continued to encounter "massive resistance" in the states'-rights Deep South. Resourceful Southerners devised various schemes, such as closing public schools, only to open them as private schools supported by state funds. In 1956 white rioters drove a Negro girl from the University of Alabama amid a shower of stones. A few fanatics, condemned by all decent elements in the South, dynamited schools, notably the high school in Clinton, Tennessee. But the hands raised by Northerners in horror were not completely clean, for anti-Negro discrimination in housing and jobs was still widely prevalent.

Little Rock, Arkansas, stole the spotlight in 1957. Governor Faubus summoned the state-controlled National Guard to prevent court-ordered integration at Central High School, where nine Negro students were seeking to enroll with two thousand whites. He alleged that their exclusion was necessary to avert violence. Reacting to flagrant mob defiance of federal authority, Eisenhower ordered a thousand federal paratroopers to Little Rock, and under their protection the nine Negro children attended the high school. "Military occupation," cried Governor Faubus, who accused the federal soldiers of invading the girls' rest rooms. Memories of bayonet-supported Reconstruction were revived as a new wave of states'-rights bitterness swept over the South. "Little Rock" became a catchword of Communist propaganda all over the world, even though Washington was trying to protect, not persecute, the Negro.

Massive resistance to integration in the Deep South was still continuing as the Eisenhower era ended. But considerable desegregation had occurred in the Border states and in some of the Southern states. Many Southerners, when forced to choose between integration and no education for their children, reluctantly chose integration.

Other struggles for Negro rights involved equal recreational opportunities (golf courses), unsegregated bus transportation, non-discrimination in jobs, and the elimination of the poll tax. Massive "sit-in" demonstrations by Southern Negroes at segregated lunch counters began early in 1960 as a Gandhi-like type of passive resistance. It achieved extraordinary success, especially when supported in the North by sympathetic demonstrations against Woolworth's and other chain stores.

Strenuous endeavors to safeguard the Negro in his civil rights, especially voting rights, bore fruit in two laws. The first passed Congress in 1957, after a record twenty-four-hour "filibuster" by Senator Thurmond of South Carolina. As the first civil-rights bill enacted since Reconstruction days, it set up new federal machinery to protect Southern Negroes seeking to vote. The second bill was passed in 1960, and made further progress toward guaranteeing voting rights.

Civil rights for whites were meanwhile securing more recognition. As the McCarthyite hysteria faded away, the courts were accused of leaning over backward to insure the constitutional guarantees of alleged Communists or Communist sympathizers. A determined effort by strong anti-Communist elements in Congress to clip the wings of the Supreme Court narrowly missed success in 1958.

The Butchers of Budapest

Cold-war relations with Russia continued strained at the highest levels, while more relaxed at the lower. Increasing numbers of American tourists were being allowed to enter Russia following Stalin's death in 1953. Cultural exchanges featured reciprocal exhibits in New York and Moscow, as well as tours by assorted artists. The brilliant Bolshoi ballet took America by storm in 1959; tickets were reportedly "scalped" in New York for $150 each.

Nikita S. Khrushchev, a burly, earthy ex-coalminer, continued to tighten his grip as the top Communist official in Russia. Alternately growling and grinning, he sought to defrost the Cold War and lull the free world by coos of peaceful co-existence. At a Communist party congress early in 1956 he denounced Stalin as a murderer and a blunderer, and assailed "the cult of personality."

The "softer" Khrushchev line triggered unexpected explosions among the Russian satellite nations, notably Poland and Hungary. Partly swayed by unofficial American radio propaganda featuring "liberation," the liberty-loving Hungarians revolted in 1956. After initial successes, they were treacherously overpowered by Soviet troops and tanks, which turned Budapest into a slaughterhouse.

Shocked by the unreliability of their satellites, the Soviets embarked upon a sterner policy. Khrushchev abandoned de-Stalinization for re-Stalinization, thus indicating that his recent peace offensive was only smile-deep. Soviet brutality shocked "neutralist" countries like India, and prompted many foreign Communists to tear up their party cards. But the moral black eye to Russia was largely offset by the simultaneous assault of France, Britain, and Israel upon Egypt (see below).

Both the United Nations and the United States lost face over Hungary. The Russians brazenly defied U.N. resolutions calling upon them to withdraw and to permit an on-the-spot investigation. Embittered Hungarians accused the Americans of promising liberation and then welshing when the chips were down. But armed intervention probably would have ignited World War III, and Washington reasoned that it was better for a nation to lose its liberties than for a world to die. The United States to some extent redeemed itself by dispatching medical aid and other supplies, and by lifting immigration bars so as to permit over 30,000 Hungarians to enter.

Middle East and Far East

The Suez crisis proved even more explosive. President Nasser of Egypt, an ardent Arab nationalist, was seeking funds to build an immense dam on the upper Nile for urgently needed irrigation and power. America and Britain finally offered financial help, but when Nasser began to flirt openly with the Communist camp, Secretary of State Dulles dramatically withdrew the dam offer. Thus slapped in the face, Nasser promptly regained face by nationalizing the Suez Canal, owned chiefly by British and French stockholders.

The Egyptian stroke placed a razor's edge at the jugular vein of Western Europe's oil supply. Secretary Dulles labored strenuously to ward off armed intervention, which was forbidden by the U.N. charter. But our apprehensive British and French allies, after deliberately keeping Washington in the dark, staged a joint assault on Egypt, in November,

1956. They were evidently determined to internationalize the canal and eliminate Nasser as a potential Middle Eastern Hitler.

The world teetered on the edge of the abyss. President Eisenhower, reluctantly siding against Britain and France, honored the non-aggression commitment of the U.N. charter and supported a cease-fire resolution. The Russians, who for once voted with the Americans, threatened to pour "volunteers" into Egypt. Bending to such pressures, Britain, France, and Israel resentfully withdrew their troops, and for the first time in history a U.N. police contingent was sent to restore order.

The United Nations emerged with new laurels, while the North Atlantic Treaty Organization (NATO) tottered. The British and French were angered by America's willingness to turn against old friends and join the Soviet "butchers of Budapest." The United States, irritated by the behind-the-back aggression of its NATO allies, rather grudgingly supplied them with oil during the five months when the Suez Canal was being cleared of sunken ships.

Increasing Communist pressures on the oil-saturated Middle East prompted Washington to seek a new protective parasol. The instrument seized upon was the so-called Eisenhower Doctrine, approved overwhelmingly by Congress in March, 1957. The President was formally empowered to extend economic and military aid to the nations of the Middle East, provided that they desired it and were threatened by aggression from a Communist-controlled country. But a doctrine designed to halt military operations proved ineffective in combatting Communist infiltration.

Secretary of State Dulles, who was not afraid "to go to the brink," took a strong position in the Far East as well as in the Middle East in 1958. The Chinese Communists began to shell the tiny Nationalist-held island of Quemoy, to which Chiang Kai-shek had rashly committed about one-third of his entire Formosan army. Washington, brandishing the big stick of the Seventh Fleet, backed him in his determination to hang on. At the same time, Dulles partially quieted Communist fears by flying to Formosa and inducing Chiang to renounce the use of force in regaining the Chinese mainland.

The Chinese Communists, now in a position to trigger World War III, continued to be a menace. Their brutalities in Tibet and their aggression against India's borders strengthened Washington in its determination to withhold recognition and to oppose their admission to the U.N. But the effort to keep one-fourth of the world's population out of a world organization became increasingly difficult. With the admission of fifteen new African nations to the U.N. in 1960, the balance was gradually tipping toward the Afro-Asian bloc, while the Communists turned the Assembly floor into a circus for their propaganda. The Daughters of the American Revolution and other highly nationalistic groups increased their clamor for taking the U.S. out of the U.N. and the U.N. out of the U.S.

The Race into Space

The Soviets astounded the civilized world, on October 4, 1957, by shooting into orbit around the globe a beep-beeping "baby moon" (Sputnik I), weighing 184 pounds. A month later they topped their own ace by sending aloft a mammoth satellite (Sputnik II) weighing 1120 pounds and carrying a dog.

This amazing scientific break-through was a psychological Pearl Harbor. The Soviets had long been trying to convince the uncommitted nations that the short cut to industrial production and riches lay in Communism—and the Sputniks bolstered their claim. America had seemingly taken a back seat in scientific achievement. The envious "backward" nations laughed at Uncle Sam's discomfiture, all the more so because the Soviets were occupying outer space while American troops were occupying the high school in Little Rock.

The military implications of these man-made satellites were sobering. If the Russians could fire heavy objects into outer space, they certainly could reach America with intercontinental ballistic missiles. Old-soldier Eisenhower, adopting a father-knows-best attitude toward the Soviet "gimmick," remarked that it should not cause "one iota" of concern. Others, chiefly Republicans, blamed the Truman administration for having spent more for supporting peanuts than for supporting a missile program at an early date. Agonizing soul-searching led to the conclusion that while the United States was well advanced on a broad scientific front, including color television, the Soviets had gone all-out for rocketry. Experts testified that America's bombers were still a powerful deterrent, but heroic efforts were needed if the alleged "missile gap" was not to widen.

"DIFFERENT WORLDS"

From *Herblock's Special for Today* (Simon & Schuster, 1958)

"Rocket fever" swept the nation. The government embarked upon a "crash program," amidst the confusion generated by inter-service rivalries. After humiliating and well-advertised failures (the Soviets concealed theirs), the Americans regained some prestige four months after the initial Soviet triumph. They managed to put into orbit a grapefruit-sized satellite weighing two and one half pounds. By February 5, 1961, the United States had successfully sent aloft thirty-two satellites, as compared with seven for the U.S.S.R. The American efforts in general were less spectacular but their scientific contributions were heralded (in America) as greater.

The Sputnik spur led to a critical comparison of the American educational system, already under fire as too easy-going, with that of the Soviet Union. A strong move developed to replace "frills" with solid subjects— to substitute square root for square dancing. Congress rejected demands for federal scholarships, but late in 1958 authorized $887,000,000 in loans to needy college students and in grants for the improvement of teaching the sciences and languages. Exploring space between the ears seemed necessary if we were going to "catch up with the Russians" in exploring outer space.

Cold-War Crises

The fantastic race toward nuclear annihilation continued unabated. Emboldened by his Sputniks, Khrushchev, who became Soviet premier in March, 1958, boasted openly that he would shower rockets on America. Humanity-minded scientists urged that nuclear tests be stopped before the atmosphere became so polluted as to produce generations of deformed monsters. The Soviets, after completing an intensive series of exceptionally "dirty" tests, proclaimed a suspension in March, 1958, and urged the Western world to follow. Beginning in October, 1958, Washington did halt both underground and atmospheric testing. But all attempts to regularize such suspensions by proper inspection foundered on the reef of mutual suspicions. "Bargain-basement bombs" were meanwhile in the making, with every prospect that lesser powers would soon join the exclusive nuclear club.

Thermonuclear suicide seemed nearer in July, 1958, when both Egyptian and Communist plottings threatened to engulf Western-oriented Lebanon. After its president had called for aid under the Eisenhower Doctrine, the United States boldly landed some fourteen thousand troops and helped restore order without taking a single life. This energetic action, in the teeth of Soviet condemnation and threats, served notice that Washington was unwilling to travel the well-rutted road to appeasement.

Premier Khrushchev, no doubt feeling his missile-muscles, deliberately provoked an even more ominous crisis over Berlin in November,

1958. Annoyed by this pro-Western oasis in a Communist desert, he gave the three Western powers (Britain, France, the United States) six months in which to pull their troops out of West Berlin. The Soviet East German satellite would then take over, and if the West resisted, Moscow would rush to the aid of its puppet. This could only mean World War III. But Eisenhower and Dulles, again remembering the perils of appeasement, staunchly refused to yield well-established rights. The six-month deadline passed almost unnoticed.

Summit Diplomacy

Secretary Dulles, who had traveled over 500,000 miles by air, died of a recurring cancer in 1959. His successor, Christian A. Herter, did not enjoy the President's confidence to the same degree, and Eisenhower— "the new Eisenhower"—assumed a far more active role in directing foreign policy. Taking his cue from the highly publicized tours of Khrushchev and other Russian leaders, he embarked upon a whirlwind eleven-nation good-will trip in December, 1959, all the way from India to France. Early in 1960 he staged a repeat performance in Latin America. Grinning his way through showers of confetti and shouts of "Eekay" (Ike), he scored a great personal triumph. He no doubt generated good will, but Democratic critics charged that stagecraft was no substitute for statecraft.

The burly Khrushchev, seeking new propaganda laurels, was eager to meet with Eisenhower and pave the way for a "summit conference" with Western leaders. Despite grave misgivings as to any tangible results, the President invited him to America in 1959. Arriving in New York, Khrushchev appeared before the U.N. General Assembly and dramatically resurrected the ancient Soviet proposal of complete disarmament. But he offered no practical means of achieving this end. He then journeyed out to the Pacific Coast and returned by way of Iowa, where he approvingly patted a prize pig. But the smiling, kewpie-doll exterior concealed a steely, bellicose interior, which occasionally erupted in bullying denunciations.

The most noteworthy result of the Khrushchev tour was a meeting at Camp David, the President's rustic retreat in Maryland. The premier emerged saying that his ultimatum for the evacuation of Berlin would be extended indefinitely. The world gave prayerful but premature thanks for the "spirit of Camp David."

The Paris "summit conference," scheduled for May, 1960, turned out to be an incredible fiasco. Both Moscow and Washington had publicly taken a firm stand on the burning Berlin issue, and neither could risk a public backdown. Luckily for Soviet propaganda, an American spy plane was forced down deep in Russian territory on the eve of the conference. (The Soviets, whose world-wide espionage was notorious, later admitted that Khrushchev had known at Camp David of many such flights.) After bungling bureaucratic denials in Washington, Eisenhower took the unprecedented step of assuming personal responsibility. Professing to be insulted by his "phony friend," Khrushchev stormed into Paris filling the air with invective and demanding that Eisenhower not only apologize for the spy flights but punish those responsible for them. The President obviously would not punish himself, so the conference collapsed before it could get off the ground.

Khrushchev's diplomacy by tantrum virtually ended Eisenhower's diplomacy by good-will tour. The Soviets abruptly canceled their invitation to Eisenhower to visit Russia. Communist agents, playing upon resurgent Japanese nationalism, helped engineer such violent demonstrations in Japan that the President was forced to abandon his trip to the Flowery Kingdom. The slipping prestige of the United States received another body blow.

Castroism Spells Communism

Soviet propagandists had meanwhile been making alarming inroads among our hemispheric neighbors. The Latin Americans were resentful at our lavishing billions of dollars on Europe while doling out only millions to the poor relations to the south. Liberals were outraged by our willingness to support—even decorate—bloody dictators who would insure the sanctity of dollar investments. And the American recession-depression of 1957–1958, combined with Yankee tariff barriers, further tightened the screws.

The ill-timed "good will" tour of Vice-President Nixon through South America in 1958 reaped a harvest of ill will. Communist agitators and others became increasingly violent. After being stoned, spat upon, and shouted down at Lima (Peru), Nixon narrowly escaped serious physical injury at Caracas (Venezuela). Decent Latin Americans were apologetic, but one of them explained that since the masses could not vent their anger by spitting on the United States, they spat on the Vice-President of the United States.

Most ominous of all was the Communist beachhead in Cuba. The iron-fisted dictator Batista had encouraged huge investments of American capital, and Washington in turn had given him some support. When the black-bearded Dr. Fidel Castro engineered a revolution early in 1959, he denounced the Yankee imperialists and began to expropriate valuable American properties in pursuing a land-distribution program. Washington, finally running out of cheeks to turn, released Cuba from "imperialistic slavery" by cutting off the heavy imports of Cuban sugar. Castro retaliated against this "imperialistic aggression" with further wholesale confiscations of Yankee property, and in effect made his left-wing dictatorship an economic and military satellite of Moscow. Further deliberate affronts prompted Washington to break diplomatic relations with Cuba early in 1961.

Americans talked seriously of invoking the Monroe Doctrine before the Russians set up a Communist base only ninety miles from our shores. Khrushchev angrily proclaimed that the Monroe Doctrine was dead, and indicated that he would shower missiles upon us if we attacked his good friend Castro. Soviet spokesmen later softened this threat.

"WE STAND ON OUR OWN TWO FEET"
Don Hesse in the St. Louis *Globe Democrat*

The Cuban revolution, which Castro sought to "export" to his neighbors, brought other significant responses. At San José, Costa Rica, in August, 1960, the United States induced the Organization of American States to condemn (unenthusiastically) Communist infiltration into the Americas. President Eisenhower, whom Castro dubbed "the senile White House golfer," hastily proposed a long-deferred "Marshall Plan" for Latin America. Congress responded to his recommendation with an initial authorization of $500,000,000. The Latin Americans had Castro to thank for attention which many of them regarded as too little and too late.

Nixon vs. Kennedy

The Republicans faced up to the presidential campaign of 1960 without undue optimism. They had taken a bad beating in the mid-term Congressional elections of 1958, even though both President Eisenhower and Vice-President Nixon had lashed out against the "radicals" and "high spenders." The voters had been especially disturbed by the recession, the Sherman Adams scandal, farm problems, and foreign tensions. The Democratic triumph in 1958 was the greatest partisan victory in both houses of Congress since the mid-term New Deal sweep of 1936, and the casualties were especially heavy among ultra-conservative Republican Senators. A crestfallen Eisenhower was dismayed that his "New Republicanism" had not taken root.

Vice-President Nixon was the Republican heir apparent. The ever-popular Eisenhower, nearing seventy and soon to be the oldest President in American history, was barred by the 22nd Amendment from serving a third term. Nixon had much to commend him. The "old" Nixon had been a no-holds-barred campaigner, especially in assailing left-wingers ("a white-collar McCarthy"). The "new" Nixon was represented as a mature, seasoned statesman. More in the limelight than any earlier Vice-President, he had shouldered heavy new responsibilities and had traveled globally as a "trouble shooter" in various capacities. He had vigorously defended American democracy in a famous "kitchen debate" with Khrushchev in Moscow in 1959. His supporters, flourishing a telling photograph of this finger-pointing episode, claimed that he alone knew how to "stand up to" the Russians.

Nixon's nomination in Chicago—one hundred years after Lincoln's in the same city—was in effect a coronation. Liberal and personable Governor Nelson A. Rockefeller of New York had thrown his hat into the ring, but had withdrawn it in the face of strong support by the "regulars" for the safe-and-sane Nixon. But the Rockefeller revolt did force a more liberal platform upon the Republican convention, to the acute dissatisfaction of the stand-pat wing of the party. Nixon was nominated unanimously on the first ballot. His running mate was handsome Henry Cabot Lodge, Jr., of Massachusetts (grandson of Woodrow Wilson's archfoe), who had served conspicuously for seven years as American representative to the United Nations.

By contrast, the Democratic race for the presidential nomination started as a free-for-all. The supporters of Adlai Stevenson cried "We're Madly for Adlai," and Adlai was willing. But the hard-headed politicians shied away from a two-time loser. John F. Kennedy, the wealthy, youthful, smiling Senator from Massachusetts, won impressive victories in the primaries. He then scored a first-ballot triumph in Los Angeles over his closest rival, Senator Lyndon B. Johnson, the Senate majority leader from Texas. A disappointed South was not completely appeased when Johnson accepted second place on the ticket in an eleventh-hour marriage of convenience. Kennedy's challenging acceptance speech called upon the American people for sacrifices to achieve their potential greatness, which he hailed as the New Frontier.

The Issues of 1960

Bigotry, as was inevitable, showed its ugly face. Senator Kennedy was a Roman Catholic, the first to be nominated since Al Smith's ill-starred campaign in 1928. Smear artists revived the ancient charges about the Pope's controlling the White House. Kennedy pointed to his fourteen years of service in Congress, denied that he would be swayed by Rome, and asked if some 40,000,000 Catholic Americans were to be condemned to second-class citizenship.

Kennedy's Catholicism aroused misgivings in the Protestant, Bible-belt South, which was ordinarily Democratic. "I fear Catholicism more than I fear Communism," declaimed one Baptist minister in North Carolina. But the religious issue partially canceled itself out. If many Southern Democrats supported Nixon because of Kennedy's Catholicism, many Northern Republicans supported Kennedy because of the bitter attacks on their Catholic faith.

More important probably was the international crisis, which focused attention on the "experience" of the candidates. Khrushchev made no bones about his dislike of Nixon—that "fumbler" and "grocery clerk"—although he dismissed both candidates as "lackeys of imperialism." Unable to secure a summit conference, the rotund Russian journeyed to New York, unwanted and uninvited, to head the Soviet delegation in the U.N. Assembly and woo the new Afro-Asian delegates. He violently attacked the handling of the Congo crisis by the U.N. Secretary General, demanded an unworkable revamping of the U.N. structure, denounced the Security Council as a "cuspidor," and insisted that the U.N. be moved to some other country. His purple-faced presence in New York forced all the prominent leaders of the world, including Eisenhower, to put in an appearance. His table pounding, fist shaking, shoe waving, and rocket rattling shocked many delegates, while his balcony harangues with newsmen and his clownish bear hugs with Cuba's Fidel Castro turned the star-studded assemblage into a colossal propaganda arena.

Khrushchev's bulldozing antics in New York temporarily stole the spotlight from the Presidential election, but they gave added point to the Republican slogan "Experience Counts." Republicans harped on the fact that both Nixon and Lodge were old hands at talking back to Moscow. (Slogan: "They Understand What Peace Demands.") The forty-seven-year-old Nixon emphasized the youth, immaturity, and naïveté of his forty-three-year-old opponent.

Kennedy struck back by attacking the do-nothingism of the Eisenhower administration in the face of alarming Soviet progress. He insisted that the Russians, with their nuclear bombs and Sputniks, had gained on us in prestige and power. Nixon, forced to defend the dying administration, replied that our prestige had not slipped, although Kennedy was causing it to do so by his unpatriotic talk. The aged but amazingly energetic Eisenhower, stung by these gloom-and-doom reflections on his stewardship, took to the stump in the closing days of the campaign. Democrats charged that he was trying to carry Nixon "piggyback" into the White House. But the preachments of both Nixon and Eisenhower rang a bit hollow when the State Department refused to release a secret report which allegedly proved that in foreign eyes America's prestige had slipped badly.

Kennedy's "get America moving" theme, with its call to action and sacrifice, struck a rather depressing note of self-disparagement. Ordinarily, as the politicians know, the people want tranquilizers, not challenges. But the nation has often demonstrated that when faced with the harsh realities of an international crisis it can be trusted to choose the harder road. In any case, Nixon's contention that "we never had it so good" was belied by the deepening business recession ("inventory readjustment" to the Republicans), which may well have proved decisive in the election.

A Catholic in the White House

Personalities swayed countless voters in 1960. Nixon, realizing that the Republicans were outnumbered about 60 to 40, urged the electorate to support, not the party, but the better man—that is, himself. With great energy and increasing hoarseness, he barnstormed in all fifty states. Kennedy, campaigning no less strenuously, revealed his youthful magnetism to millions of voters.

Television may well have tipped the scales. Nixon agreed to meet Kennedy in four so-called "debates"—probably a strategic error. A public figure as well known as Vice-President Nixon should never share his large following with a less well-known man. The contestants crossed words in millions of living rooms before audiences estimated at sixty million or more. Nobody "won" the debates, but Kennedy at least held his own and did not suffer by comparison with the more "experienced" Nixon.

Kennedy squeezed through by the rather comfortable margin of 303 electoral votes to 219, but with the breathtakingly close popular margin of only 113,057 votes out of nearly 69,000,000 cast. Like Franklin Roosevelt, Kennedy ran well in the large industrial centers, where he had strong support from Catholics, Negroes, and labor. But he lost several states of

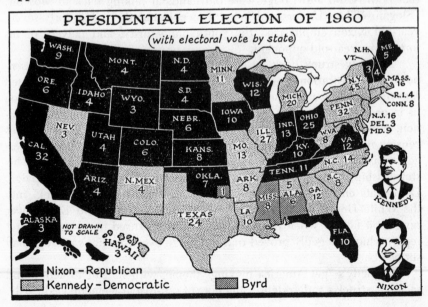

PRESIDENTIAL ELECTION OF 1960 (with electoral vote by state)

Nixon – Republican
Kennedy – Democratic   Byrd

the Bible-belt South that were presumably repelled by his Catholicism. Nixon, although not inheriting "Ike's" popularity, ran well in the less populous states of the trans-Mississippi area, especially in the Protestant farm belt. Kennedy's Catholicism both hurt and helped him, but on balance probably helped him. The Democratic Party has been traditionally the refuge of Catholics, and the passing of Eisenhower marked the return of many Republican converts to the Democratic fold.

The Democrats, although losing a few seats, swept both houses of Congress by wide margins, as was a foregone conclusion. The possibility of another Republican President handcuffed by an opposition Congress definitely hurt Nixon. Many voters were weary of government by deadlock. John Fitzgerald Kennedy—the youngest man and the first Catholic to be elected President—was free to set out for his New Frontier, provided that the die-hard conservatives in his party would join the wagon train.

Social Ferment

The heavy vote in the presidential election served as a reminder that the world-wide "population explosion" was not bypassing America. The census of 1960 revealed a remarkable increase in one decade from 150,-000,000 to nearly 180,000,000. Especially striking was the loss of population by most leading cities to the suburbs, where freeways and shopping centers provided more elbow room and less smog. With fewer farmers using more machinery to produce even larger surpluses, three of the farming states had lost inhabitants, quite in contrast with the enormous gains of Florida, Texas, and the Pacific slope. Incredible California, now in second place and soon to be in first, was experiencing a latter-day industrial gold rush.

But the multiplying millions were not an unmixed blessing. Traffic snarls, parking problems, and housing shortages clamored for attention. Even though some eight million dwelling units were constructed during the eight Eisenhower years, the demand far outran the supply. The only housing surplus was in slums. Overcrowding in the schools, some of which now ran two shifts, imposed additional burdens. The struggle to get into college, whether for education or social status or football, was becoming a nerve-racking ordeal.

The world-wide revolt of youth was fully evident in the United States. The day had passed when young folks were to be "seen and not heard." Growing numbers of teen-agers were marrying, producing offspring, and expecting the old folks to provide support and education. Juvenile delinquency was spreading, partly as a result of overcrowded slums, maladjusted minorities, and too much leisure. Pornography was infiltrating the mails. Teen-age gangs were running wild in the streets of the largest cities, knifing their rivals and beating up unoffending bystanders "just for kicks." "Adults don't understand us" was the standard complaint of youthful criminals, including murderers. Some critics blamed juvenile crime on the sadistic comic books, devoured by millions of bug-eyed youths—plus many adults. Others blamed television with its overemphasis on murder, manslaughter, and mayhem. Certainly the movies were not setting a shining example: a box-office "hit" of 1957 bore the title "I Was a Teen-age Werewolf."

The parents themselves were falling short of perfection. Drug addiction, alcoholism, and crimes of violence were on the increase. The nation in 1960 was spending far more for stimulation than for education. Millions of taut-nerved Americans, previously distinguished for energy, were gulping down tranquilizer pills, with harmful effects to their inner fiber.

The nation was revealing a curious mixture of materialism and idealism. More college youths were entering the ministry than in the years after World War I. The prospect of nuclear annihilation, combined with other tensions, was turning many Americans to the solace of religion. Church membership in 1960 embraced about 63% of the population—a marked increase over previous decades. The leading evangelist of the Western world, "Billy" (William Franklin) Graham, was attracting the greatest crowds of modern times, at home and abroad. Enormous audiences filled amphitheaters like the Yankee Stadium in New York in 1957, and thousands of sinners made public "decisions for Christ."

But there was still an unseemly emphasis on chromium-plated materialism. Rising income evidently resulted in increasing wants rather than in providing satisfactions. "Status seeking" was leading to "conspicuous consumption." With increased leisure, vast sums were being poured into swimming pools, boats, mink coats, travel, and summer homes. The lavish distribution of credit cards encouraged the wholesale expenditure of money that we did not have for luxuries that we did not need. "Charge it—and feel like a king [temporarily]" was a slogan of the era. Several million Americans were working at two jobs—"moonlighting"—in a frantic struggle to keep their heads above water.

Muses for the Masses

The artistic spirit in America, despite materialism, never had greater encouragement than in 1960. Courses in art appreciation at all levels were attracting thousands of eager learners. The great galleries were being thronged. Inexpensive painting kits were sending countless amateurs, among them President Eisenhower, out to the landscapes. The manufacturers of cheap reproductions of the master painters were doing a land-office business. Many of the unrecognized young masters, rather than starve in a garret, were being attracted to lucrative "billboard art."

The theater still commanded a large following, although Broadway shows were becoming increasingly a big business—and an infinitely risky one at that. The moving picture industry, once a foe of television, now worked hand in glove with its rival, on the ancient principle "if you can't lick 'em, jine 'em." On television screens the Western "horse opera" was partly supplanting radio's sentimental "soap opera," all to the tune of moronic and overlong singing commercials.

The music industry, once fearful of radio, was selling more recordings than ever, even though much was "rock and roll." The moaning, gyrating Elvis ("The Pelvis") Presley was receiving more money than the President of the United States. Improved techniques—such as long-playing records, high fidelity sets, and stereophonic reproduction—were adding to the popularity of recordings. The vitality and virtuosity of local musical organizations, whether operatic, orchestral, or choral, were most impressive. More people were paying to hear concerts than to watch professional football games.

American architecture, stimulated by the vast amount of new construction, was revealing extraordinary imagination, though often at the cost of convenience. Modern design, which manifested itself in structures ranging from churches to industrial buildings, tended to feature glass materials and pierced decorative screens. The death of Frank Lloyd Wright in 1959 removed one of the boldest and most controversial of the innovators. "He was more frank than right," remarked one quipster.

American literature had more to offer than critics of our materialism would concede. Beginning with the idol-smashing novelist Sinclair Lewis in 1930, five citizens of the United States have won Nobel prizes in literature. The others were the dramatist Eugene O'Neill, who attained fame with his gloom-shrouded tragedies; Pearl Buck, whose upbringing as the daughter of missionaries in China provided themes for important novels; William Faulkner, whose novels laid bare the degeneracy of the poor-white life in the South; and Ernest Hemingway, who revealed a mastery of realism in a succession of noteworthy novels. As the 1960's opened, Mrs. Buck, Faulkner, and Hemingway were still writing, but a comparable new crop of authors had failed to emerge.

Yet important new trends in literature were discernible, notably the phenomenal sales of low-priced paperbacked books. In 1939, 3,000,000 copies had been sold; in 1960, approximately 365,000,000 were sold—or a million a day. Despite the underclad females pictured on much of the trash, millions of volumes of the classics were purchased. More people were reading than ever before, and literacy was on the rise, conspicuously among Negroes. A noteworthy victory against censorship was registered in 1959, when a federal judge ruled that D. H. Lawrence's *Lady Chatterley's Lover,* long regarded as obscene, could be lawfully distributed.

An Old General Fades Away

President Eisenhower, the aging progressive-conservative, continued to enjoy extraordinary popularity to the very end. Despite Democratic jibes about "eight years of golfing and goofing," he was universally admired and respected for his dignity, sincerity, good will, and moderation.

Pessimists had predicted that Eisenhower would be a seriously crippled "lame duck" during his second term, owing to the barrier against re-election raised by the 22nd Amendment. Yet he displayed more vigor, more political know-how, and more aggressive leadership during his last two years than ever before. For an unprecedented six years, from 1955 to 1961, Congress was in the hands of the Democrats, yet he established unusual control over it. He wielded the veto 169 times, and only twice was he overridden by a two-thirds vote.

"WHAT'S SO LAME ABOUT IT?"
Alexander in the Philadelphia *Bulletin*

The country was generally prosperous, despite pockets of poverty and unemployment, recurrent recessions, and perennial farm problems. The budget was in balance, the treasury showed a surplus, and the price-up-creep was being slowed. The St. Lawrence waterway project, constructed jointly with Canada and completed in 1959, had turned the cities of the Great Lakes into bustling ocean seaports.

The flag now displayed fifty stars. Alaska attained statehood in 1959, as did Hawaii. Alaska, though gigantic, was thinly populated and non-contiguous, but these objections were overcome in a Democratic Congress that expected Alaska to vote Democratic. Hawaii had ample population (largely of Oriental descent), advanced democratic institutions, and more acreage than Rhode Island, Delaware, or Connecticut. But Democrats objected to admitting a new Republican state; Southerners wanted no more non-whites; and apprehensive citizens opposed statehood for a military base whose labor force was allegedly infiltrated by Communists. With the Alaska log jam broken, however, progress finally triumphed in 1959, and the island paradise sent three able representatives to Congress, two of them of Oriental extraction.

Eisenhower had clearly grown during his momentous eight years as President, despite political inexperience, advancing years, three major illnesses, and often lackadaisical leadership—"the bland leading the bland." He had done far better than any other professional military man in the White House, including his fellow West Pointer, General Grant, the only other Republican ever to serve two full terms. He had helped revivify the two-party system by merely getting elected. But whether or not Eisenhower's middle-of-the-roadism was enough, remained a subject for partisan debate.

SELECT READINGS

An excellent brief analysis of the Eisenhower years appears in WALTER JOHNSON, *1600 Pennsylvania Avenue: Presidents and the People, 1929–1959* (1960) [paperback]. Intimate observations may be found in Presidential Assistant SHERMAN ADAMS, *Firsthand Report* (1961) [paperback]; Vice President R. M. NIXON, *Six Crises* (1962); and speech-writer E. J. HUGHES, *The Ordeal of Power* (1963) [paperback]. A systematic study is C. A. H. THOMSON and F. M. SHATTUCK, *The 1956 Presidential Campaign* (1960). On foreign affairs consult J. W. SPANIER, *American Foreign Policy since World War II* (1960) [paperback]. A diplomatic-economic achievement of vast significance is described in W. R. WILLOUGHBY, *The St. Lawrence Waterway* (1961). On Secretary Dulles, see references for preceding chapter and also RICHARD GOOLD-ADAMS, *John Foster Dulles* (1962), an appraisal by a Britisher. Of the numerous books on the rise of Castro one may single out R. F. SMITH, *The United States and Cuba: Business and Diplomacy, 1917–1960* (1960). Among the more noteworthy books to come out of the election of 1960 are EARL MAZO, *Richard Nixon* (1959), J. M. BURNS, *John Kennedy* (1960) [paperback], and particularly T. H. WHITE, *The Making of the President, 1960* (1961) [paperback]. Also SELECT READINGS for preceding chapter.

48

New Frontiersmen on the Potomac

*And so, my fellow Americans: ask not what your country
can do for you—ask what you can do for your country.*
JOHN F. KENNEDY, Inaugural Address, 1961

The Coming of the Kennedys

A BREEZY new atmosphere swept through Washington—22° above zero—
as the New Frontiersmen rode into power, January 20, 1961. Hatless and
topcoatless, President Kennedy delivered a stirring inaugural address, in
which he called for sacrifice at home and steadfastness abroad. From the
outset of his Administration his emphasis was on energy, brains (especially Harvard-trained), and youth. As the youngest President ever
elected, he assembled one of the youngest Cabinets, including his younger
brother Robert, whom he named Attorney General despite outcries
against favoritism and inexperience.

The strong man of the Cabinet proved to be Defense Secretary
Robert S. McNamara. A human computing machine, he sacrificed a
$400,000-a-year position with the Ford Motor Company to become a pub-
lic servant at $35,000 a year. He trampled on sensitive toes as he achieved
many economies among the jealous armed services that were squabbling
for their cut of the prodigious defense pie. More important, he supervised a reversal of the grim Eisenhower–Dulles doctrine of "massive
[nuclear] retaliation." With adequate ground forces, Washington would
have more alternatives in a crisis than a global blowup or a humiliating
backdown. A balanced military arm could dampen brushfire wars before
they broke dangerously out of control.

Breakers loomed ahead in Congress, despite a lopsided Democratic
majority in both branches. Southern Democrats held a lion's share of the
all-important committee chairmanships, thanks to the operation of se-
niority ("rule by senility," critics said). Thus entrenched, these "moss-
backs" could bottle up or strangle legislation they disliked. On the floor
of Congress conservative Southern Democrats repeatedly lined up with
conservative Northern Republicans to water down or defeat bills desperately desired by President Kennedy.

After much arm-twisting, Kennedy's first Congress honored about the average number of White House requests. But the President suffered stinging rebuffs in pushing some of his pet programs, including hospital insurance for the aged under Social Security (Medicare) and large-scale federal aid for the overflowing public schools. Medicare was assailed as a foot in the door for socialized medicine by the powerful American Medical Association; aid for the public schools sank on the rock of parochial schools. Many Americans, including the ultra-cautious Catholic Kennedy, believed that support for religious schools violated the first amendment to the Constitution, which decreed separation of church and state. Yet the supporters of private schools were numerous enough to block all general aid to public schools unless they shared it.

Congress also had its butcher knife sharpened for Kennedy's foreign-aid request of $4.7 billion, which was slashed by half a billion dollars. The taxpayers were becoming increasingly critical of the more than $100 billion disbursed in assorted global grants since 1945, especially to dictators who grabbed dollars with one hand and slapped Uncle Sam with the other.

New Frontier Landmarks

Early in his administration Kennedy brought a warm heart to the Cold War when he established the Peace Corps. The peace corpsmen (and women) were dedicated Americans who volunteered to go out to about fifty backward countries and show the impoverished people how to improve their lot. At first scorned as "Kennedy's Kiddie Corps," this organization proved so useful in cultivating good will that Congress enthusiastically put it on a permanent basis, in September, 1961.

Much more costly and much less successful was the Alliance for Progress (*Alianza para el Progreso*), of which the fear-arousing Dr. Fidel Castro of Cuba was an unwitting father. With a ten-year, ten-point, twenty-billion-dollar program, it was designed to provide a kind of Marshall plan for Latin America. A primary goal was to help the Good Neighbors to decrease the ghastly gap between the indifferent rich and the wretchedly poor, and thus head off Castro-like Communism. Congress passed the initial appropriation by lopsided majorities in May, 1961, but the Alliance proved to be no alliance and, especially at the outset, progress was painfully slow. Short-sighted greed was reluctant to embrace overdue reforms, in Latin America as elsewhere in the world.

Kennedy's most spectacular legislative triumph was the Trade Expansion Act of October, 1962. One of the boldest strokes of its kind in our history, it empowered the President to slash existing tariffs at least fifty percent in the interests of promoting trade. In some cases he could eliminate them entirely.

Kennedy also induced Congress to pass the initial appropriations for his man-on-the-moon program. The estimated overall cost was some $40,000,000,000; the goal was an American on the moon by 1970. Skeptics, who saw the desperate need for such money on this planet, cried "lunar lunacy." Nevertheless, the costly space-race with the Russians continued. In April, 1961, the Soviets successfully orbited the first man. The Americans were unable to match this achievement until some ten months later, February, 1962, when Lt. Colonel John H. Glenn, Jr., circled the earth three times, and became the most idolized of a group of daring American astronauts. In October, 1964, Russians lofted three men into orbit, and revealed that, with superior booster power, they were then well ahead in the race for the moon, at least temporarily.

But American space men, more concerned with science than showmanship, managed to shoot aloft a good many more satellites than the Soviet Union. Their total scientific contribution was hailed (in America) as greater than that of the Soviets. Especially noteworthy was the Telstar communications satellite, designed for transatlantic telephone and television transmission. A fierce battle developed in Congress between anti-monopoly liberals, who wanted government ownership of Telstar, and the conservatives, who wanted private ownership. After a fiery filibuster by the liberals, a compromise bill emerged, in August, 1962, which provided for a private corporation under government regulation.

Kennedy, who was determined to check creeping inflation, ran head on into the powerful steel companies. Early in 1962 they had negotiated a wage contract, under which the workers agreed to no increase in wages, merely fringe benefits totaling about ten cents an hour. The assumption was that the companies would also hold the line on inflation. But when, some five weeks later, the leading producers suddenly announced identical increases in prices, Kennedy reacted angrily to what he deemed a "double cross." He immediately put into motion the awesome investigative and judicial machinery of the federal government, including anti-trust action and F.B.I. agents.

Overawed, the steel operators rescinded their price increases, April 13, 1962, and Kennedy chalked up a spectacular victory. But he was savagely criticized for using dictatorial tactics, and he earned the undying hostility of the free-enterprise business community, especially after he reported that his father had long regarded the steel moguls as scoundrels. In this hostile atmosphere the stock market nosedived, May 28, 1962, wiping out paper profits of some $20,000,000,000. About a year later the steel companies quietly raised their prices, without objectionable evidences of collusion. Kennedy this time did nothing, and the inflationary spiral continued to edge upward.

The Bay of Pigs Blunder

Castro's Communist Cuba continued to be a thorn in the flank of the United States, and plans for an invasion by Cuban refugees had long been brewing. With the secret encouragement of the Eisenhower administration, a group of some 1200 exiles was being trained in Guatemala with American arms and American advisers. Shortly after his election, Kennedy learned of these preparations. The invasion of a sovereign nation in peacetime was plainly a violation of both American domestic law and international obligations. Yet Castro was growing stronger by the week with Soviet arms, and his overthrow seemed urgent.

Kennedy finally decided to back the invasion attempt—with one vital reservation. He announced that in no circumstances would the United States become *directly* involved. Then followed a tragedy of errors in mid-April, 1961. Three air strikes by Cuban exiles, flying from Central America with obsolete United States planes, were to destroy Castro's air power. The first strike was only partially effective, and world opinion reacted so violently that Kennedy called off the second one. The third was ineffective. Castro retained control of the air and was thus able to destroy invading aircraft and sitting-duck supply vessels, while pressure mounted in the United States for direct help. The bullet-riddled band of exiles, who had confidently counted on American intervention, was forced to surrender.

Seldom has the Washington government bungled anything more badly. Its "indirect" involvement was so deep as to amount to futile "direct" involvement. Premier Khrushchev of Russia, denouncing American "gangsterism," pledged all necessary military assistance to his Cuban puppet. Kennedy, who might easily have found scapegoats, manfully assumed full responsibility for the failure. But his conscience troubled him, and he arranged through private contributions for the "ransoming" of the 1100 survivors in Cuba for some $62,000,000 worth of American drugs and other supplies.

Berlin and the Congo

Partly to dispel the impression of spinelessness left by the Bay of Pigs, Kennedy journeyed to Europe, in June, 1961, for conferences with leading statesmen. Crowds of West Germans turned out to cheer "Ken-ah-dee," and their enthusiasm overflowed when he proclaimed to an immense audience in trigger-tense West Berlin, "Ich bin ein Berliner." ("I am a Berliner.") A crucial meeting with Premier Khrushchev occurred in Vienna, June 3–4, 1961. Kennedy emerged grim and visibly shaken. The tough-fisted Russian adopted a belligerent attitude on Germany and West Berlin, and threatened to turn the whole city over to the Communist East Germans, with all the explosive possibilities of World War III.

But Kennedy refused to be bullied out of Berlin. He secured from Congress authority to beef up the armed forces, and he called back into active duty some 80,000 reservists and National Guardsmen. This time the Russians backed off. Their response was the Berlin Wall, hastily begun on August 13, 1961, and then extended along the entire border of East Germany. Constructed of barbed wire and concrete, it was designed to prevent the heavy drainage of population from the East German "paradise" to West Germany.

The Berlin Wall—a monument to failure—was a propaganda victory for the West. It advertised the glaring disparity between blighted East Germany and booming West Germany, and the necessity of keeping some sixteen million people in a barbed-wire jail. Kennedy was condemned by many red-blooded Republicans for not having ordered American tanks to topple the Wall of Shame before it could be completed. But naked force would probably have provoked force—and possibly the outbreak of World War III.

Meanwhile the Belgian Congo had exploded with the raping and butchering of whites, following the premature and overhasty withdrawal of Belgian colonialist overlords. The United Nations became deeply involved when, in July, 1960, the Security Council voted to send in neutral troops to avert civil war. Surprisingly, the Soviets at first supported intervention, evidently concluding that it would bolster pro-Communist elements. But when the leading left-wingers were exiled or murdered, Moscow reversed its position and tried to throw a monkey wrench into the whole "illegal" operation. Like France and numerous other nations, it flatly refused to pay its assessments for military ventures of which it disapproved. The United States kept the Congo campaign afloat by authorizing a loan of $100 million, but a shortage of funds finally forced the peace-keeping troops of the UN to withdraw prematurely, after a temporary pacification in January, 1963.

The Congo operation stirred up a hornets' nest. In the interests of unification, the United Nations forces had crushed the anti-Communist leader of the mineral-rich Katanga Province. American foes of the United Nations, chiefly extreme right-wingers, condemned this blow against freedom. Permanent financial paralysis also threatened the entire body as many members

"NEW BALANCE OF POWER" [IN THE UN]
Crawford in the *N.E.A.*

continued to default on their financial obligations, and as Uncle Sam grew increasingly weary of picking up the tab.

As these ominous cracks were developing in the glass house of the United Nations, its whole complexion was changing. When launched in 1945, it had 51 members; by 1965 it had 115. Most of the newcomers hailed from once-colonial Asia and Africa—such as Uganda, Somalia, and Rwanda. The burning anti-white memories of these peoples endured, and the United States faced the disagreeable possibility of being outvoted by tiny young nations not far removed from barbarism. All this provided further ammunition for American right-wingers, many of whom called for abandoning the leaky UN ship.

Missile Launchers in Cuba

A crowing Castro continued to annoy his powerful Yankee neighbor. Washington persisted in its partial embargo on goods to Cuba, and tried without conspicuous success to persuade other nations to follow suit. But Castro, with generous financial aid from Russia, clung to power and continued to strengthen his armed forces with made-in-Moscow muscle, presumably defensive.

Official Washington was stunned, in October, 1962, when aerial photographs revealed that Russian technicians were secretly and hastily emplacing forty-two missiles in Cuba. Armed with nuclear warheads, they could incinerate most of the major cities of the United States at a push of the button. By this sneak violation of the Monroe Doctrine the Soviets were evidently attempting to create a blackmail bludgeon that would force the United States to back down in Berlin and elsewhere in threatened hot spots.

In contrast to the Bay of Pigs, which probably had misled Moscow, Kennedy played this game of "nuclear chicken" in a masterly fashion. While quietly making large-scale preparations for an invasion of Cuba, he proclaimed, on October 22, 1962, a naval and aerial "quarantine" of all offensive weapons being shipped into the island. The seizing of Soviet ships in peacetime on the high seas would unquestionably be an act of war, but Kennedy was prepared to face up to the consequences.

In the breathless week of this eyeball-to-eyeball confrontation, Khrushchev finally flinched, on October 28, 1962. He agreed to a face-saving compromise, by which he would pull his missiles out of Cuba, and the United States in turn would pledge itself to lift the "quarantine" and not invade the island. The withdrawal of the missiles was to be certified by UN inspectors.

Neither side won a clear-cut victory, but Kennedy won the essential point—after going to the brink of global atomization. The red-faced Reds ostensibly shipped their missiles out of Cuba, but Americans feared that some were hidden in caves. A crestfallen Castro flatly refused to permit

UN verifiers to pollute his soil. (Kennedy was therefore released from his tentative pledge not to invade Cuba.) Soviet propagandists, now cooing like doves of peace, proclaimed that the Kremlin had won its objective because it had forced the Americans to keep their hands off the Cubans. But it was as plain as the beard on Castro's face that the brazen Soviet coup had backfired badly.

After the first heartfelt sigh of relief, thoughtful Americans saw that Kennedy's victory was far from complete. A resentful Castro was still there—and growing stronger militarily. In flagrant violation of the Monroe Doctrine, thousands of Russian troops and technicians lingered in Cuba. But the Soviet backdown did restore confidence among Allies who had been appalled by the Bay of Pigs. It also silenced cries that a "Castro-coddling" administration was doing nothing about the Communist arms buildup.

In the Congressional elections of November, 1962, the Democrats gained four seats in the Senate and several more in the House. As the party in power normally suffers a decline in the mid-term elections, the Democrats hailed this slight gain as a signal gain. "We were Cubanized," complained rueful Republicans.

The Test-Ban Treaty

The Cuban missile crisis focused attention anew on the terrifying race in nuclear weapons. About a year earlier, in September, 1961, the Soviets, spurning all pleas, had set off a number of mammoth, air-polluting explosions. President Kennedy in turn felt compelled to resume nuclear testing in the atmosphere lest the Russians gain an overwhelming margin of superiority.

The missile crisis in Cuba was followed by a relaxation of tensions with the Soviets, who now revealed active interest in a nuclear test-ban treaty which they had previously spurned. Prolonged negotiations were completed in Moscow, on August 5, 1963, with a pact that prohibited nuclear explosions in the atmosphere, under water, and in outer space. Only underground testing was permitted. The United States Senate, after expressing misgivings as to Moscow's motives and possible Soviet "cheating," approved the treaty with crossed fingers, 80 to 19, on September 24, 1963.

The nuclear test-ban treaty proved more important for what it promised in disarmament than for what it performed. No existing stocks of bombs were to be destroyed, and the signatories could pull out after giving three months' notice. Most of the other nations speedily subscribed to the ban. The conspicuous exceptions were France, which was developing a tiny nuclear arsenal, and China, which had not yet exploded its first nuclear device and which branded the Moscow pact a "dirty fraud." But the test-ban treaty, while reducing pollution of the atmosphere, did reduce international tensions, and to this extent created a more favorable climate for disarmament negotiations.

Two other barometers reflected a warmer atmosphere in the Cold War. In August, 1963, Moscow and Washington opened a direct "hot line" which permitted immediate communication should an accidental explosion or similar catastrophe occur. Two months later, in October, 1963, Kennedy authorized the sale of $250 million worth of surplus wheat to the Soviets, who had suffered crippling crop failures. Anti-Russian elements in the United States condemned the folly of strengthening the hand that was trying to strangle them, but most Americans apparently favored the sale. Humanitarianism pricked many consciences, and the nation was staggering under grain surpluses that were costly to store. Besides, Russian gold would partially check the alarming hemorrhaging of American gold to Europe to cover the balance of payments deficit—that is, the difference between what we expended or invested abroad and sold or earned abroad.

Balance of Payments Deficits
(in millions)

	1955	1959	1960	1961	1962	1964
Gold Stock	$ 21,753	$ 19,507	$ 17,804	$ 16,947	$ 16,057	$ 15,550
Annual Deficit	$−1,145	$−3,743	$−3,881	$−2,370	$−2,186	$−2,660

Note: The maximum gold stock of the United States had been $24 billion in 1949; there had been a net drain on it every year since 1957.

Le Grand Charles de Gaulle

If relations with Moscow were visibly thawing, those with America's fourteen NATO allies were audibly chilling. Yet the growing independence of Western Europe was in some respects a healthy sign. It indicated that these war-ravaged peoples had so far recovered, economically and psychologically, as to want to shake off the guiding hand of Big Brother in Washington.

President Kennedy nevertheless had ambitious designs for the Mother Continent. He envisioned an economically and politically united Western Europe, with Uncle Sam the dominant partner, standing as a bulwark against a westward thrust by the Communist world. But stiff-backed President de Gaulle of France, a French nationalist fanatically determined to recapture the Napoleonic *grandeur* of yesteryear, refused to permit his beloved France to play second fiddle to the dominating Yankee. He therefore undertook to build a small nuclear force ("farce," his critics said), despite pressures from Washington. He argued that in a future crisis the Americans, rather than risk the destruction of their own cities, might leave

France naked in the face of the Soviets. Instead of an interdependent partnership between Europe and the United States, he would have a France-led Europe, independent of transatlantic ties and capable of defending itself.

De Gaulle also resented efforts by the British (who had the nuclear bomb) to join hands with the Americans in providing leadership for Europe, with France in the backseat. He brusquely rejected all attempts to work out a joint nuclear force for NATO, with Uncle Sam's solo finger on the trigger. In January, 1963, with a haughty "*non*," he vetoed Britain's application for membership in the Common Market, a spectacularly successful union of the nations of Western Europe for the

PRESIDENT DE GAULLE: "WHY DO YOU AMER-ICANS STAY WHERE YOU'RE NOT WANTED?" Mauldin in the Chicago *Sun Times*

mutual lowering of tariff barriers. President Kennedy, though visibly annoyed, could only pocket his pride and await future developments.

The Chinese Dragon Breathes Fire

Red China and Red Russia were meanwhile noisily parting company. Moscow was gradually veering away from Leninism toward coexistence with the West ("creeping capitalism"), except for "wars of liberation." Peking clung to the tough old Lenin line of world revolution, even at the cost of wrapping the world in thermonuclear flames. The Chinese Reds assailed Russia's backdown in Cuba before the American "paper tiger," as well as Moscow's subsequent tendency to be "soft on capitalism." Premier Khrushchev, faced with the problem of coexistence with China, sternly reminded Peking that the American "tiger" might be "paper" but he had nuclear teeth.

As if to show their toughness, the Chinese Communists suddenly began to pour troops over the mountainous approaches to the subcontinent of India, late in October, 1962. The Indians, alarmed by what they called "yellow rats," besought American aid, ironically after having long assailed America's buildup against Communism. Washington responded by airlifting large quantities of arms. The Red assault mysteriously ceased a month after it had begun, and a troubled truce settled over the Indian border.

The alarming behavior of the Red Dragon raised anew the question of continuing the nonrecognition of Communist China and her nonseating in the UN. Many Europeans argued that the 700,000,000 or so Chinese, who were about to explode a nuclear bomb, would be easier to control within the family of nations than outside it. But most Americans, loyal to ancient policies that had repeatedly won elections, argued otherwise. They insisted that the UN by its very charter consisted of peaceloving nations, and that China should not be allowed to shoot her way in, especially after invading India. To deepen the deadlock the Red Chinese insisted that they would accept no seat in the UN unless the exiled regime of Chiang Kai-shek were unseated—and this the Americans were unwilling to do.

Falling Dominoes in Southeast Asia

In Southeast Asia the menace of Chinese Communism was less open but hardly less alarming. Fears still persisted that if Laos and South Vietnam fell to the Reds, the remainder of the area would collapse like a row of falling dominoes. The jungle kingdom of Laos, which Washington had drenched with dollars, was in grave danger of a Communist takeover; Peking was allegedly sending arms to the battling pro-Communist elements. But Kennedy was unwilling to get bogged down in a Korea-type slaughterpen in an area that adjoined the teeming manpower of China. Seeking an escape hatch, the United States participated in a fifteen-month, fourteen-power conference at Geneva which, on July 23, 1962, agreed on the neutralization and independence of Laos. But continued violations of this agreement by neighboring Reds led to repeated American aerial bombardment of supply lines, beginning late in 1964, with several planes lost.

In South Vietnam the Kennedy administration was prepared to take a firm stand. Red China's countless millions were not contiguous, and overwhelming American sea power and air power could be employed with far greater effectiveness. But the Communist warriors of South Vietnam (Viet Cong), supplied in part by Communist North Vietnam and China, used deadly guerrilla tactics to take over increasingly large agricultural areas. The Eisenhower administration had committed the United States to heavy support of the South Vietnam forces with money and military hardware, together with a few advisers. But all this did not turn the trick.

In a fateful decision President Kennedy undertook in 1961 to dispatch a few hundred military "advisers" and technicians, who were to assist the South Vietnamese but to avoid active combat. By late 1964 the American personnel had swollen to some 23,000, in addition to the 250 or so who had lost their lives in the jungle warfare. At the cost to America of about two million dollars a day, defeat was evidently coming on the installment plan, complicated by the successive overthrows of collapsible governments in South Vietnam.

An ominous new turn came to the ugly little war early in August, 1964, when North Vietnamese torpedo boats reportedly attacked two United States destroyers in international waters. President Johnson, though deep in the electoral campaign, promptly authorized a series of retaliatory bombings by American aircraft on North Vietnam naval bases. On August 7, 1964, at his request, Congress speedily and near-unanimously approved a resolution giving blank-check approval of any actions, including armed force, that he might have to take in the Southeast Asia crisis.

Johnson's new policy was tit-for-tattism. For every North Vietnam attack on American warships or land bases (or attacks presumably inspired by the North Vietnamese) the United States was prepared to respond with aerial bombings. This course posed grave dangers, but so did a do-nothing defeat or a face-losing retreat.

The Warren Court under Fire

The menace of Communism abroad seemed all the more frightening to many Americans in view of so-called "Communist coddling" by the Supreme Court at home. The "Earl Warren Court"—so named after the big, jovial, white-haired Chief Justice appointed in 1953—handed down a long series of controversial decisions which interpreted basic American freedoms so broadly as to provide loopholes through which alleged Communists escaped the clutches of the law. In the conflict between individual rights and national security, the Court upheld traditional American rights, and in so doing invalidated numerous state laws. It even decreed in 1964 that the State Department could not deny passports to known Communists who sought to travel abroad, even for subversive activity.

Nor did the Supreme Court shy away from the explosive religious issue. In two surprising decisions, in 1962 and 1963, it ruled against required prayers and Bible reading in the public schools. These decisions were based on the First Amendment, which decreed the separation of church and state, but they seemed to put the justices in the same bracket with pro-atheistic Communists. Cynics predicted that the "old goats in black coats" would soon be erasing "In God We Trust" from all coins.

Infuriating to many Southerners was the determination of the Court, following the school segregation decision of 1954, to support Negroes in civil rights cases. Five Southern state legislatures officially nullified the "sociological" Supreme Court decision, but they in turn were overruled by the high tribunal. In general, it decreed that the states could not deny to Negroes rights that were extended to white men. States'-rights Southerners complained that the "Earl Warren Court" was not interpreting the Constitution but rewriting it, at the expense of states' rights.

The Court also developed the philosophy that where the states permitted notorious evils to persist, the Court should step in. Of special concern was the over-representation in state legislatures of cow-pasture agricultural areas, especially as the urban areas were bursting their boundaries. Adopting the principle of one-man-one-vote, the Court intervened in 1962 and again more emphatically in 1964. It ruled that the state legislatures, both upper and lower houses, would have to be apportioned according to the human population, irrespective of cows. States-righters and assorted right-wingers, pointing to the non-population representation in the United States Senate, raised anew the battle cry, "Impeach Earl Warren." But a number of legislatures grudgingly went ahead with reapportionment.

From 1954 to 1964 the Court came under unremitting criticism, the bitterest since New Deal days. Its foes made numerous but unsuccessful efforts to clip its wings through bills in Congress or through Constitutional amendments. But the Court reflected perhaps not so much its own philosophy as the necessity of grappling with persistent new problems spawned by mid-century tensions. It was evidently determined to protect the rights of the individual, white or black, against the tyranny of the majority, even if the individuals in some cases were "not very nice people."

The Negro Revolution

The school desegregation decreed by the Supreme Court in 1954 continued to be slow-motion desegregation in the Deep South. No less annoying to Negroes was discrimination in voter registration, transportation, public accommodations, housing, and job opportunities ("first-class taxes, second-class jobs"). Some of these grievances were even more galling in the North than in the South.

President Kennedy, though committed to civil rights for Negroes, proceeded gingerly. Eager to steer his New Frontier schemes through Congress, he dared not incur the tomahawks of Southern members by pushing too hard on civil rights. But he did appoint a few Negroes to prominent office, and arranged for many more to be put on federally financed jobs. Somewhat belatedly, on November 20, 1962, he issued an executive order barring racial discrimination in housing constructed with federal funds.

The truth is that the Kennedy administration was suddenly caught up in a frightening revolution. Weary of waiting one hundred years for justice, and chanting "Jim Crow must go," Negroes were adopting the nonviolent tactics of civil disobedience that had been employed so effectively by Mahatma Gandhi in India. Their most distinguished leader was an eloquent Negro clergyman, the Reverend Dr. Martin Luther King, Jr., who was awarded the Nobel Peace Prize in 1964. Singing "We Shall Overcome," and resorting to sit-ins, lie-ins, wade-ins, and pray-ins, the Negroes and their white associates made substantial progress in compelling the desegregation of Southern busses, stores, restaurants, and other public accommodations, while enlarging job opportunities, North and South. On August 28, 1963, some 200,000 demonstrators, about four-fifths of them Negroes, gathered peaceably at the Lincoln Memorial in Washington to demand better jobs and a comprehensive civil rights law.

Integrating the Southern universities almost brought wholesale slaughter. Some of them desegregated without any fuss, but the University of Mississippi ("Old Miss") became a volcano. A twenty-nine year old Negro veteran of the air force, James Meredith, attempted to register in October, 1962, pursuant to a federal court order. Such violent disorders erupted that Kennedy was forced to send in some four hundred marshals and three thousand troops. Two men were killed and scores were injured in some fifteen hours of rioting, but Meredith attended class in the custody of federal marshals. He was ultimately graduated—with a sheepskin that had cost some four million dollars.

Violence begets violence, and "the long hot summer" of 1963 will long be remembered in the South. White Southern lawmen used billy clubs, high-pressure fire hoses, and electric cattle prods on Negroes who were demonstrating for their rights. In the "Battle of Birmingham," the police turned savage dogs on Negroes, and pictures of their clothing being ripped off were widely reproduced, to the delight of Communist propagandists.

As the Ku Klux Klan rode again, dozens of Negro churches were burned or bombed in Mississippi and Alabama ("Bombingham"). In September, 1963, an explosion wrecked a Baptist Church in Birmingham, killing four Negro girls who had just finished their lesson, "The Love That Forgives." Three "freedom riders" working for civil rights in Mississippi (two Negroes and one white) were brutally murdered and then buried under an earthen dam. Subsequent investigations by the F.B.I. implicated the sheriff, his deputy, and sixteen others. Mob violence also erupted in Northern cities in the summer of 1964, notably in Harlem, Rochester, and Jersey City.

Deplorable though this disorder was, the Negro was making substantial gains. The white majority was beginning to appreciate the explosiveness of the problem and the mounting impatience of Negroes who were outcasts within their own country. The rather hollow Twenty-third Amendment, effective in 1961, permitted the predominantly Negro population of Washington, D.C., to vote in presidential elections. (The ballot was still withheld from some 800,000 inhabitants in local elections—a classic example of "taxation without representation.") Also designed to help poor Southern Negroes to vote was the anti-poll-tax Twenty-fourth

Amendment, effective in 1964, and forbidding the assessment of a tax on voters in presidential or congressional elections. (See Appendix.) But the reform did not apply to state and local elections, where poll taxes still kept many poor Negroes (and whites) from voting.

A Dark Day in Dallas

The New Frontier continued to encounter hostile hatchets in Congress. Kennedy was making little or no progress with Medicare, aid to secondary education, the pending civil rights bill for Negroes, or the proposed tax cut. The latter was a daring scheme to reduce taxes, while incurring a planned deficit of $13.6 billion over a period of several years. The money that would otherwise pour into the Treasury would presumably be spent to revive the economy, avert depression, and relieve the four million or so unemployed, disproportionately Negro. Ultimately an increased national income would presumably wipe out the deficit, despite lower taxes. But conservatives, both Republicans and Democrats, cried that only a madman would slash his income when he was already deep in the red.

U. S. Public Debt

	Amount in millions	Per capita		Amount in millions	Per capita
1800	$ 83	$ 15.87	1939 (New Deal)	$ 40,440	$ 308.98
1860	65	2.06	1945 (postwar)	258,682	1,848.60
1865 (postwar)	2,678	75.01	1956 (Cold War)	276,200	1,624.71
1900	1,263	16.60	1961	296,170	1,611.65
1920 (postwar)	24,299	228.23	1962	303,470	1,625.08
1929 (post-Mellon)	16,931	139.04	1963	309,350	1,633.49

Note: Except for 1956, 1957, and 1960, there were actual or projected deficits for the years from 1956 to 1966. Owing to the increase in population, the per capita debt remained about the same.

Kennedy scheduled a fence-mending tour in the South for November, 1963. Bitterness had boiled up against him as a result of his armed intervention on behalf of civil rights: KKK stickers ("Kayo Kennedy Klan") were insultingly in evidence. Then the unbelievable happened. While riding in an open limousine in downtown Dallas, Texas, Kennedy was shot in the head by a concealed rifleman and died almost instantly. The alleged assassin, Lee H. Oswald, a left-wing malcontent, was quickly apprehended. Within hours he was shot and killed by a self-appointed avenger, Jack Ruby. Both men, an elaborate official investigation concluded (Warren Report), were acting alone and not as a part of a conspiracy. Vice President Lyndon B. Johnson, the first real Southerner and the first Johnson to attain the presidency since 1869, was promptly sworn in on a waiting airplane and flown back to Washington with Kennedy's corpse.

The murder of this young, eloquent, vibrant, and personable President, who had developed a unique "style," evoked an amazing outpouring of grief at home and abroad. Not until then did many Americans realize how fully their attractive leader and his bewitching young wife had cast a spell over them. Chopped down in his prime after only slightly more than a thousand days in the White House, he was acclaimed more for the ideals he had enunciated and the programs he had advocated than for a large sheaf of legislative reforms. Not only had he grown impressively in office but he had silenced the charge that a Catholic could not be entrusted with the presidency of the United States.

The LBJ Brand

The amazingly smooth transfer of power to President Lyndon B. Johnson impressed critical observers. A "wheeler dealer" who had become famous as a high-powered persuader and compromiser while Senate majority leader, he took hold with whirlwind vigor. Capitalizing on the shock of Kennedy's murder, he galvanized Congress into action with an impressive display of back slapping, arm twisting, "flesh pressing," and telephone pleading ("the fourth arm of government").

Congress responded with a legislative output that recalled Franklin Roosevelt's Hundred Days. Kennedy had laid the groundwork for most of these laws, and many of them no doubt would have passed in time. But the daring tax-cut scheme, applying to both personal and corporation incomes, sailed through with a minimum of difficulty. Fiscal orthodoxy flew out the window as planned deficits came in the door.

More significant in many ways was the passage of the Civil Rights Bill, strongly backed by the Southerner Johnson, after a seventy-five-day filibuster by die-hard Southern Senators. Signed on July 2, 1964, it was the most sweeping measure of its kind since Reconstruction days. Highly controversial was the public accommodations clause, which, by a strained interpretation of interstate commerce, required even isolated restaurants and hotels to admit Negroes. The Southerners insisted that this provision was unconstitutional, but the Supreme Court unanimously upheld it on the ground that it involved interstate commerce, at least indirectly.

Johnson's honeymoon period—the nine "miracle months"—was marked by other achievements. As a former New Dealer (F.D.R. was his "daddy"), he declared war on poverty and threw his weight behind a billion-dollar appropriation for the initial phase of the campaign. More than thirty million Americans were estimated to exist on the dark side of the poverty line, and he was particularly concerned with the Appalachian poverty belt, where the collapse of the soft coal industry had left tens of thousands of jobless Americans on the human slag heap. Johnson also asked for a pre-shrunk appropriation for foreign aid—a modest $3.4 billion request and the smallest in sixteen years—and Congress passed it substantially intact. He personally and energetically intervened to avert a paralyzing railroad strike over "featherbedding"—that is, the retention of some 65,000 allegedly useless jobs.

Bloody riots erupted in Panama, in January, 1964, over American occupancy of the Canal Zone under the one-sided treaty of 1903 (see p. 639). President Johnson temporarily mollified the Panamanian government. Then, in December, he announced that the United States would renegotiate the objectionable treaty and also construct a new sea-level canal, perhaps in Panama and perhaps by cheaper nuclear excavation. The old waterway was too narrow, too slow, too congested, and too vulnerable to enemy bombing.

The Great Society Versus Goldwaterism

The nomination of Lyndon Johnson by the Democrats in 1964 was a foregone conclusion: he had proved to be a stable, able, "can do" President. He was chosen by acclamation in Atlantic City, in August, 1964, by a convention which he had carefully ringmastered. The platform, which outlined what Johnson called the Great Society, stressed five P's: Peace, Prosperity (the tax cut was evidently working), anti-Poverty, Prudence, and Progress. Proclaiming unity and reasonableness, the President's program sprawled so completely over the middle of the road that it left mostly gutters for the extreme right and the extreme left.

The Republicans were bitterly divided when their delegates crowded into San Francisco's famed Cow Palace in July, 1964. Their free-for-all primaries had proved inconclusive. The moderates—a rather silent majority—had been unable to unite behind any one candidate. The leading middle-of-the-roader, Governor Nelson Rockefeller of New York, had faded, partly because of a highly-publicized divorce. Box-jawed and gray-haired Senator Barry M. Goldwater of Arizona, the leading right-winger, managed to pick up enough delegates in conservative state conventions to insure his nomination on the first ballot. The near-fanatical "Barry's Boys," riding roughshod over the moderate "Eastern Establishment," adopted a conservative platform that refused to repudiate the support of right-wing extremists, whether semi-secret John Birchers or besheeted Ku Klux Klanners. Lapel buttons proclaimed "What's Wrong with Being Right."

The Goldwater candidacy was doomed from the start. The handsome, personable and wealthy Arizonan (a "poor" millionaire), with heavy horn-rimmed glasses, radiated sincerity and charm. But his extreme "rightism" repelled millions of rank-and-file Republicans, most of whom had not favored him in the first place. While promising an aggressive and costly campaign against Communism the world over, he inconsistently urged a meat-axe slash in federal spending. By proposing that American field commanders be given discretionary authority to use tactical nuclear weapons, he had created the image of a reckless, trigger-happy Arizona cowboy who would soon "Barry us" in the debris of World War III. A Democratic slogan jeered, "Help Barry Stamp Out Peace."

The candidates never really clashed over the issues. Johnson spoke vaguely about his Great Society, and stressed the need for politicians and peoples to "reason together." Goldwater got in some telling blows when he condemned the "no-win war" in South Vietnam, wasteful spending, the excesses of big government, and "Communist coddling." ("In your heart you know he's *right*" became a Goldwater refrain.) He also assailed low ethics in government. Johnson himself, together with his wife, had become a multimillionaire while in public office, and his Senate-employed protégé, young Mr. Robert G. (Bobby) Baker, had become a mystery millionaire under highly questionable circumstances. Attempted coverups of Bobby Baker from the White House led to sneers about the "White Wash House."

But Goldwater, who habitually "shot from the lip," failed to rise above his handicaps. The impression of impulsiveness and irresponsibility would not fade. His vote against the nuclear test-ban treaty had alienated the "mother vote," just as his vote against the Civil Rights Bill had alienated the Negro vote. While "pooping around" the country (as he put it), he had earlier made many statements which were interpreted to mean, whether fairly or not, that he would be a veritable bull in the china shop. Apparently he was hostile to Social Security, labor unions, the federal income tax, the recent tax cut, the Tennessee Valley Authority (TVA), legislative reapportionment, the NATO Alliance, the Supreme Court, federally supported social welfare programs, and Johnson's anti-poverty war ("phony as a three dollar bill"). Some of these off-the-cuff views he toned down after his nomination, but he failed to erase the impression of recklessness abroad and heartlessness at home. One of his aggrieved supporters urged the newspapers to publish not what he said but what he really meant.

The Burial of Barry

On November 3, 1964, "Landslide Lyndon" Johnson swept all sections, except the South, and triumphed by the biggest popular-vote total thus far in American history, 43,121,000, or a monstrous majority of 16,000,000. He received an unprecedented 61% of the total vote, or almost precisely what the pollsters had predicted from the start. The electoral vote was 486 to 52. Goldwater carried only five states of the Deep South, plus (narrowly) his home-state Arizona, for a total of 27,-145,000 votes, or approximately 7,000,000 fewer than the losing Republican Nixon had polled in 1960. The Democrats moreover carried both houses of Congress. With better than two-to-one majorities in the Senate and House, they enjoyed the most comfortable working majority since the Franklin Roosevelt landslide of 1936—the previous all-time Presidential high. The obstructive coalition of conservative Southern Democrats and conservative Northern Republicans was smashed, and a wide-open legislative road stretched before the Great Society.

For Republicans, Goldwater had proved to be not so much a candidate as a catastrophe. Pessimists predicted that the Grand Old Party was careening down the road to the Federalist-Whig cemetery. Many able and moderate Republican candidates for lesser offices, though running far ahead of Goldwater, were "buried with Barry." The Negro vote was overwhelmingly pro-Johnson. Oddly enough, the pro-Negro party of Lincoln had found its only solid support in the anti-Negro South, once solidly Democratic.

Lyndon Johnson had won a heady triumph. But the vagueness of the Great Society was such that no one quite knew what mandate he had received: perhaps it was to move ahead—prudently. Countless voters regarded both candidates as unpalatable, and thanked God that only one of them could be elected. Probably any well known and respectable Democrat of presidential stature could have won. Millions of split-the-ticket Republicans, distrustful of Goldwater, voted for Johnson while continuing to support state and local Republican candidates. Big Business, normally Republican, was surprisingly friendly to Johnson and his

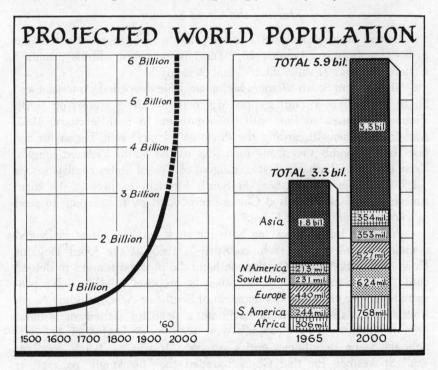

PROJECTED WORLD POPULATION

moderate approach. For the first time in memory a majority of the newspapers that endorsed a candidate supported the Democratic nominee.

Goldwater had declared that the voters, too often confronted with "me-tooism," needed a clear choice between a liberal and a conservative philosophy. "A choice and not an echo" was perhaps his most seductive slogan. But such were his contradictions that the voters had no clear-cut alternatives. His critics claimed that he was offering a choice between the 19th and the 20th Centuries in his opposition to social welfare, big government, racial equality, and concern for the poor. "Goldwater in 1864" was another satirical slogan.

The cascading world crises worked heavily to Johnson's advantage, and overshadowed a nasty scandal involving a homosexual who held an important post in the White House. (The President was evidently unaware of this black sheep.) In the earth-shaking "week that was" two weeks before the election, Premier Khrushchev of Russia was sacked and made an "unperson"; a Socialist (Labour) government attained office in Britain; and the Red Chinese exploded their first nuclear bomb. They thus became Member Five—and the only non-white member—of the exclusive Nuclear Club, with terrifying prospects for the future. These alarming events provided further ammunition for those who argued that the country needed to retain in the White House an experienced President of proven prudence.

Starting the Great Society

Behind bullet-proof glass, Lyndon Johnson took the presidential oath in his own right, on January 20, 1965. His inaugural address promised a continuing war against "misery" and "tyranny."

The crisis in South Vietnam had meanwhile deepened. American and South Vietnamese aircraft stepped up their punishing attacks on North Vietnamese bases, in line with tit-for-tattism. In mid-February, 1965, American airmen, discarding the devious "adviser" role, began for the first time to bomb Viet Cong guerrillas in the South Vietnam jungles. Early the next month, the first contingent of United States combat troops —3,500 marines—came ashore in South Vietnam to protect the main American air base. The Red Chinese responded by threatening to send in soldiers to aid the Viet Cong.

President Johnson, waving both the stick and the carrot, delivered a nationally televised speech, on April 7, 1965, at the Johns Hopkins University in Baltimore. On the one hand, he pledged himself to defend South Vietnam to the end; on the other, he proposed a billion-dollar program to aid the economic development of Southeast Asia, including North Vietnam. He also offered to negotiate a peaceful settlement without prior conditions. These proposals were warmly applauded in America, although some Republican critics sneered, "If you can't lick 'em, buy 'em." Spokesmen for Red China branded the "blackmail" package as "a big swindle," while those of North Vietnam called Johnson "a stupid pirate." Why negotiate when you are winning? By June, 1965, there were 50,000 American troops in South Vietnam, with more coming.

Criticism of Johnson's foreign policy redoubled, at home and abroad, when civil war erupted against the military regime in Santo Domingo, in April, 1965. To protect hundreds of American lives, and to prevent a possible Castro-style takeover, Johnson dispatched troops, ultimately over 20,000. This spectacular return to "gunboat diplomacy," with casualties on both sides, violated Roosevelt's Good Neighbor pledge of 1933, as well as solemn commitments to the UN and the Organization of American States (OAS). But Johnson and his advisers concluded that time did not permit extended discussions, and that it was better to be illegally safe than legally sorry. He was partially taken off the hook when the OAS voted to take over the policing operation, but the major part of the United States force remained, pending the belated arrival of a full Latin American contingent. The civil-war crisis in the unhappy banana republic remained acute.

Much more encouraging was progress on the domestic front. Aroused by the brutal murder of a white clergyman who was working for voter registration of Negroes in Alabama, President Johnson went before Congress (and a national television audience), on March 15, 1965. He urged the immediate passage of legislation that would eliminate all "illegal barriers" to the right of Negroes to vote under the Fifteenth Amendment. Public indignation was such that the voting rights bill, despite Southern protests, finally passed in August, 1965.

A milestone in the history of education was achieved in April, 1965, when Congress overwhelmingly passed an aid bill authorizing the expenditure of 1.3 billion dollars. It would provide badly needed assistance for primary and secondary schools, especially in the poverty belts. Roman Catholic opposition to the bill largely evaporated when President Johnson cleverly arranged for indirect participation by parochial and other private schools. He was thus able to bypass the church-separation clause of the First Amendment to the Constitution, pending a final judgment by the Supreme Court. Appropriately, Johnson signed the breakthrough measure in the one-room schoolhouse in Texas that he had attended as a boy.

The Democratic Congress also enacted the epochal Medicare Bill, in July, 1965. With enlarged coverage under Social Security and voluntary arrangements, it was to provide needed hospital and doctors' care for the aged, 65 and over.

Social Stirrings

Most of the social problems that had troubled the "feverish fifties" (see pp. 961–65) slopped over into the first half of the "soaring sixties"— usually in more acute form.

The nation's facilities were increasingly bedeviled by America's contribution to the worldwide population explosion, which was potentially as dangerous as an atomic explosion. The 178,000,000 Americans of 1960 had become over 190,000,000 by 1965. This disquieting growth gave a strong impetus to planned parenthood, despite opposition to birth control and legalized abortion by the Catholic Church and other groups.

Sick cities, traffic-snarled, continued to sprawl out into the suburbs. So vexatious were urban problems that President Kennedy in 1962 had sought authorization from Congress for a new Cabinet-level Department of Urban Affairs and Housing, but was rebuffed. In 1965 President Johnson managed to persuade Congress to provide heavy financial support for improved urban transportation, urban renewal (publicly financed housing), and the creation of entire "new towns."

Masses of people required mass transit, which featured earth-gobbling freeways, bumper-to-bumper crops of automobiles, and infuriating parking problems. By 1965 auto accidents, many the result of drunk driving, were taking about 45,000 lives a year, to say nothing of hundreds of thousands of injuries and millions of lost man-hours. Yet this "highway roulette," though costing more deaths a year than American battle deaths in the entire Korean conflict, was taken more or less for granted.

Urban and suburban congestion inevitably complicated the problems of smog (aerial sewage) and water pollution (chlorinated sewage), but many communities were adopting resolute remedies. The continuing flight of Negroes from the troubled South to the less troubled North and West was worsening slum conditions in the great cities. Rats gnawed unattended babies in the shabbiest tenements of Harlem.

The mounting tidal wave of students was overcrowding many schools, and contributing to an alarming number of incorrigible "punks" and high-school dropouts. Totally without saleable skills, these juveniles further glutted the labor market, and tens of thousands of them were headed for a life of degeneracy, drug addiction, and other crimes.

Adult crime, which fattened on illicit gambling, prostitution, narcotics, and racketeering, was on the increase. Law officials were being held in growing contempt by the citizenry, especially youth of the "beat" generation, who often attacked officers while they were making arrests. Other citizens refused to render needed assistance or, unlike the good Samaritan, give aid to innocent victims. "We don't want to get involved," was the commonest excuse. Volunteer vigilantes in some areas were beginning to patrol the streets, to the horror of the professional police.

Health problems still loomed large, despite a brilliant showing in the Tokyo Olympic games of 1964. Standard physical tests showed that only about half of the American children could pass tests performed by Austrians, Italians, and Swiss of the same age. Cigarettes had come under heavy fire for allegedly causing much lung cancer and other lethal diseases. The Surgeon General's report of 1964, which luridly supported such charges, did not have the dissuading effect that one might have

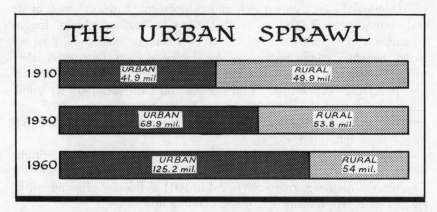

THE URBAN SPRAWL

1910 URBAN 41.9 mil. RURAL 49.9 mil.

1930 URBAN 68.9 mil. RURAL 53.8 mil.

1960 URBAN 125.2 mil. RURAL 54 mil.

supposed. President Johnson, late in 1964, urged upon Congress a massive attack on heart disease, cancer, and other leading killers. Hope persisted that breakthroughs would be achieved as spectacular as the vaccine conquest of infantile paralysis.

Church attendance continued high, but the influence of the church seemed relatively low, at least as compared with previous generations. Currents of liberalism were eddying through the Roman Catholic Church, and encouraging impetus was being given to the worldwide ecumenical movement—that is, bringing closer together the fragmented Christian faiths.

Women were slowly attaining greater recognition of their demands for equality. Increasing numbers were entering public life. Senator Margaret Chase Smith of Maine, a gray-haired, attractive matron, became a serious candidate for the Republican presidential nomination in 1964. President Johnson undertook to water down "stag government" when, early in his inherited administration, he appointed ten women to top positions.

Economic and Cultural Currents

The annual national income had zoomed to an all-time high as the nation entered 1965—over half a trillion dollars. The invigorating (and inflationary) effect of the recent tax cut was evidently being felt. President Johnson, to the amazement of seasoned observers, had achieved the near-impossible goal of enlisting the confidence and support of both business and labor.

Chronic unemployment, paralyzing about five percent of the labor force, was a perennial headache. The most serious development was the galloping mechanization of industry (automation), with the consequent elimination of jobs at the fearsome rate of some 30,000 a week. The Washington government undertook the retraining of displaced workers who had to learn new skills, but the process was an uphill one.

Organized labor, grown rich and complacent, had lost much of its early crusading zeal. The unions that clung to "featherbedding" fought automation tooth and nail, and where they had to yield they often secured monetary compensation for the displaced men. Organized labor was now seriously advocating a 35-hour week, with no reduction in total pay, plus fringe benefits like profit-sharing and paid vacations. As usual, the largest part of the nation's working force was still unorganized, and hundreds of thousands of unskilled workers were not adequately covered by a federal minimum wage law.

Labor racketeering was being partially curbed by the Landrum-Griffin Act of 1959. Iron-fisted James R. Hoffa, president of the powerful Teamsters' Union, was twice convicted in 1964 of felonies growing out of alleged graft. He remained in office pending appeals.

The nation's farmers continued to raise a lush crop of seemingly insoluble problems. Government price supports were maintained, at the multibillion-dollar level, partly for political reasons, and the bulging surpluses were still being stored in costly containers. With modern machinery and other revolutionary techniques, farms were becoming fewer, bigger, and more productive. The rich were getting richer and the poor were getting poorer or were being squeezed off their farms into the already overcrowded labor market. The census of 1960 showed that farm population had been cut in half since 1920, although the total population had increased by more than 70,000,000.

The annual federal budget in 1965, with local and state taxes rising even faster, was some $100 billion. About one-half was going to the military. At the outset of his inherited administration an economy-minded President Johnson declared war on wasteful federal expenditures, and set a good example by turning off unnecessary White House lights. The reform of tax inequities was also urgently needed, but it had been shelved in the scramble to pass the tax-cut bill of 1964. The cost of living continued to edge ever upward, and worked increasing hardships on oldsters and others on fixed incomes.

Materialistic though American society seemed to be, it had received a strong cultural boost from President Kennedy. After arranging for the aging poet Robert Frost to read a poem at his inaugural, he held a number of glamorous social affairs at the White House to which he invited the cream of the nation's cultural and intellectual elite. Early in 1965 President Johnson, following suit, proposed a National Foundation of the Arts.

But literature had seen more glorious days. Ernest Hemingway ended his life with a shotgun blast in 1961, though some of his writing continued to appear. William Faulkner died in 1962. John Steinbeck, most famous for his depression-born *Grapes of Wrath* (1939), pursued his anticlimactic career actively, and was awarded the Nobel Prize for Literature in 1962. He was the sixth American to be so honored.

The literature of the early 1960's was more distinguished for quantity than for quality, for the paperback revolution was assuming tidal-wave proportions. But meritorious work was being done in poetry, the short story, and fiction. No recognizable new giants had emerged, though some critics conceded that the novels of Louis Auchincloss and Saul Bellow were touched with greatness. Perhaps a new Golden Age was waiting in the wings.

SELECT READINGS

Sprightly and sympathetic journalistic accounts are HUGH SIDEY, *John F. Kennedy, President* (1964) and W. S. WHITE, *The Professional: Lyndon B. Johnson* (1964) [paperback]. See also PAUL BALLOT, ed., *The Thousand Days* (1964) and ANTHONY LEWIS, *et al.*, *Portrait of a Decade: The Second American Revolution* (1964). On foreign affairs consult GEORGE SULLIVAN, *The Story of the Peace Corps* (1964); A. A. BERLE, *Latin America: Diplomacy and Reality* (1962); and CLAUDE BUSS, *The Arc of Crisis* [Far East] (1961). The distressing Bay of Pigs fiasco is described in TAD SZULC and K. E. MEYER, *The Cuban Invasion* (1962) [paperback] and in HAYNES JOHNSON, *et al.*, *The Bay of Pigs* (1964). The Cuban crisis of October, 1962, is analyzed in J. DANIEL and J. G. HUBBARD, *Strike in the West* (1963) and in D. L. LARSON, ed., *The Cuban Crisis of 1962* (1963). The Kennedy assassination is described meticulously in the official Warren Report, published in 1964 in various editions. Barry Goldwater's views were perhaps best detailed in his *The Conscience of a Conservative* (1960) and in *Why Not Victory: A Fresh Look at American Foreign Policy* (1962) [both paperback]. See also R. D. NOVAK, *The Agony of the G.O.P., 1964* (1965). On aspects of the Negro revolution consult M. L. KING, JR., *Why We Can't Wait* (1964); J. W. SILVER, *Mississippi: The Closed Society* (1964); and WILLIAM BRINK and LOUIS HARRIS, *The Negro Revolution in America* (1964).

49

Widening Horizons

Men of Destiny

THE physical growth of the United States stands as a near-miracle without
parallel in human history. We started as a few struggling colonies; we
emerged as a vast empire. We conquered, cleared, cultivated, and civilized an area nearly as large as Europe in less than three centuries.

Why our amazing success?

First of all, we were blessed with a semi-isolated, near-empty continent, whose bountiful natural resources lay unscratched. Hardly less important than the discovery of America was what Americans discovered
in America.

Second, whatever our faults, we were a remarkable people: tough,
energetic, inventive, efficient, resourceful, and determined. Appropriately,
the word "American" ends in "I can." The backs and brains of our human
resources were no less important than our natural resources. The soft-
muscled descendants of the pioneers who tamed the wilderness will never
fully appreciate how much sweat lubricated the process.

Third, we developed a marvelous economic productivity. This
achievement flowed largely from the industry and efficiency of our people, who took full advantage of their fabulous natural endowment.

Fourth, we owed much to "the American way." It encouraged order
under liberty and diversity within unity. A soaring release came to the
spirit from a system of free enterprise under a representative government.
America's overshadowing contribution was not in Panama Canals and
Empire State buildings, but in demonstrating that democracy could succeed on a continental scale. And in attaining this goal we served as an
example and inspiration for liberals the world over.

Danger Signals

But the American people have no reason to grow complacent, for their "inexhaustible" natural resources are being exhausted at an alarming rate. The demands of World War II took a heavy toll of mineral deposits and oil pools. We are now being forced to tap new reserves abroad, notably the iron ore of Canada and South America. As our exploding population presses upon available resources, we are becoming a "have not" nation—on balance an importer rather than an exporter of raw materials. Nuclear reactors, whether in public or private hands, can help to regain lost ground.

We must conserve the good earth. Most of the world is hungry, and mounting birth rates are taxing tired lands. A frontier farmer of the last century could boast of wearing out three farms and three wives in one lifetime. But he was not thinking of posterity. To our shame and lasting hurt, we have permitted the topsoil—the national skin—to be eroded from an acreage roughly the size of the thirteen original states. (See map, p. 655.) Waves of concrete are now engulfing much of our fertile suburban land.

We must continue to strive for forest preservation and flood control, while seeking to preserve nature's beauty. Ax and fire have ravaged the virgin trees that once sponged up rainfall: the cream-skimming Americans have long been more interested in sawmills than in seedlings. We must change our wasteful habits and intensify our program of reforestation. Rampaging rivers every year wash away millions of dollars' worth of property. New Tennessee Valley Authorities (TVA's) in other key river valleys, with private capital playing its proper role, may hold the key to the control of erosion, flood waters, and irrigation.

We must keep our giant productive machine running at full blast. But can we do so with the tax bite—federal, state, county, and city—gouging deeper and deeper? Can we shoulder indefinitely the financial burdens imposed by arming ourselves against aggressors—with arms that are becoming crushingly costly? Can we absorb disarmament or even defense cutbacks, without ruining the nation's economy? Can we keep employment full, or must we again fall victim to the boom-and-gloom cycle of depression? Can labor and management learn to settle their quarrels without forcing a long-suffering public to impose compulsory arbitration or dictatorial controls, especially where transportation and other public utilities are involved?

We must grapple with other economic problems as well. How can we achieve a maximum of industrial efficiency with a minimum of governmental restriction? How can investors be induced to venture "risk capital" in new enterprises if taxation takes a lion's share of prospective profits? How long can a debt-cursed Treasury support the demands of pressure groups for price supports and other special handouts?

We must also take speedy steps to improve and rehabilitate our precious human resources—the people whose hands and brains shaped the Republic. American scientists have wrought miracles in the field of medicine, notably the Salk anti-polio vaccine perfected in 1955. Life expectancy at birth has increased spectacularly in recent decades. Yet the shocking fact remains that in World War I and World War II hundreds

Years of Life Expectation at Birth*

	White Males	White Females	Nonwhite Males	Nonwhite Females
1850	38.3	40.5	No records	No records
1900–02	48.23	51.08	32.54	35.04
1919–21	56.34	58.53	47.14	46.92
1939–41	62.81	67.29	52.26	55.56
1962	67.6	74.4	61.5	66.8

* The differential between whites and nonwhites was presumed to be caused largely by better food, shelter, and health care for the whites.

of thousands of young men were rejected as physically unfit for military service—despite our boasted standard of living. The soft life, automotive transportation, and the frantic pursuit of pleasure have undoubtedly weakened our fiber. The statistics point unerringly to the need for better health education, an improved diet, and cheaper hospitalization. Millions of Americans lack proper medical and dental care simply because it is unavailable or too expensive. Little wonder that strong agitation has developed for compulsory federal health insurance and other forms of government-supported medicine, including adequate medical care for the aged.

The Dilemmas of Democracy

What of our cherished political democracy? Signs multiply that our ungainly government is creaking, and cannot continue to function efficiently on such a gigantic scale. Everyone, it is said, now works for the government, either on the payroll or the tax roll. The need for streamlining and decentralizing the Washington regime is glaring. The voters can keep a more watchful eye on their government, as Thomas Jefferson observed, when as many functions as feasible are entrusted to the states and local communities.

The Washington nerve center, already confusingly complex, may break down because of poor or mediocre personnel. Essential government bureaus cannot operate without bureaucrats; hence more effective steps should be taken to recruit competent civil servants. Yet not enough high-caliber men and women are attracted to public life when we pay them poorly in money and richly in abuse. Too many young people regard a career in politics as somewhat tainted.

We never miss water until the well runs dry; and apathetic Americans need to be awakened to the boon they enjoy in democracy. They must not permit it to wither in their hands through disuse. The scandalous stay-at-home vote in national elections—often running higher than 50 percent and partly the result of restrictive voting laws—compares most unfavorably with the record of certain "backward" democratic nations. The confused voter would show more interest if a sharper cleavage could be developed between the basic philosophies of the two major political parties. In many respects, though by no means all, they represent little more than the difference between the "ins" and the "outs."

We must give redoubled attention to our schools, for if our educational system breaks down, our democracy will break down. Without proper schools, we cannot train our citizens to make democracy function. Without proper schools, we cannot protect ourselves against the wiles of demagogues and other dangerous self-seekers. Education is costly, but ignorance is more costly.

Astonishing increases in the birth rate during the 1940's and 1950's are reflected in the engulfing of our schools, colleges, and teaching staffs. The nation is like a fast-growing boy who is constantly bursting out of his trousers. Can we afford the outlays for maintaining adequate school systems in the face of the staggering defense costs imposed by the Cold War? Can we afford anything less? Must we pursue a policy of billions for bombs but pennies for progress?

The schools have done a praiseworthy job in many respects, but the educational picture has its dark shadows. We still have several million adult illiterates. Surveys have shown that an alarming percentage of able high school students are not going on to college, often because they lack money. We are threatened with a serious shortage of scientists, engineers, and medical technicians in a day when wars are won in laboratories. Nor can we afford to neglect the humanities in a day when wars are averted by statesmen.

An outsider may wonder how much the American people really value their school system—the bulwark of democracy. If they did, they would not overload and underpay the custodians of their youth. In some areas the janitors who sweep out the building are better paid than the instructors who teach in the building. Thousands of teachers are leaving their blackboards for better salaries and quieter pastures elsewhere. Countless others, who would like to teach, are being lured into more profitable professions. The pressure is mounting for the federal government, despite the danger of bureaucratic controls, to provide increasing financial support for the schools and colleges of the poorer states.

The Plight of the Minorities

American democracy—political, social, and economic—cannot fulfill its promise until its blessings reach every citizen. The plight of minority groups should be improved, especially that of the 20,000,000 or so Negroes who constitute a partially submerged one-tenth of the nation—a population as large as Canada's set down within the United States.

Yet real progress is being made, despite dissatisfaction with its slowness. North and South, more Negroes are voting, more are being elected to public office, more are enjoying fuller health, better education, larger incomes. The 20,000,000 American Negroes are driving more and better automobiles than all of the more than 200,000,000 citizens of the Soviet Union. The integration of the Negro into the Army, achieved in 1950, resulted in closer race relationships and a better utilization of manpower. The results of the school-integration decision of the Supreme Court in 1954 have disappointed the Negroes and their champions, but in many areas gradual progress toward integration is going forward, partly as a result of the Negro revolution that burst forth in the Kennedy years.

Pressure continues to mount against discrimination in job-giving because of race, color, creed, or sex. One proposed solution lies in fair-employment-practices acts, at both state and local levels, although true toleration and equality can hardly be achieved by legislation. American women—in some respects our largest minority group (though a majority) —are continuing to demand sex-equality legislation, including guarantees of equal pay for equal work. Until recent times wives were reluctant to take jobs lest they reflect shamefully on the non-support of their husbands. This stigma is fast disappearing as millions of women are leaving mechanized kitchens to seek gainful employment, either to supplement the family income or to keep busy after their children are reared.

Unfinished Business

High though our standard of living is, it reveals ugly inequalities. Vigorous efforts should be made, as President Lyndon Johnson has insisted, to improve the lot of the impoverished, and thus narrow the gap between the rich few and the poor many. A better life must be assured our millions of substandard tenant farmers, sharecroppers, migratory fruit-and-vegetable workers, and day laborers, both Negro and white. Millions of our people enjoy less than a decent standard of living, and consequently fall victim to illness, crime, and other misfortunes resulting from a low income. For all too many citizens the American way of life is squalor. A high standard of democracy and a high standard of decency go hand in hand.

The disgraceful slums, both urban and rural, cry aloud for elimination. Improper shelter contributes to disease, like tuberculosis, and to the appallingly high crime rate. Yet can new housing goals be reached without forms of socialism that will compete objectionably with private enterprise? Will construction costs continue to be so high that slum-dwellers cannot afford to pay the higher rents for substitute new dwellings?

Social security poses special problems. Millions of our citizens still do not enjoy the benefits of the existing law, and for countless others the coverage is inadequate and inflation-shrunken. Yet how far can the blanket be stretched? If it covers the individual too snugly "from womb to tomb," it may seriously undermine the time-honored virtues of thrift, initiative, and self-reliance—the very qualities that built America. The wishbone may replace the backbone. The more we strive for security, oddly enough, the less secure we seem to feel. And the mounting clamor for increased social services is coupled with a demand, quite inconsistently, for decreased taxes and a balanced budget.

The thorny problems of immigration persist. We must decide how many more immigrants—and of what kind—can be admitted without jeopardizing the welfare of Americans already here. Questions of bigotry and unfair discrimination are being raised anew against immigration quotas that spurn worthy immigrants from Southern and Eastern Europe, especially skilled workmen eager to join families already here. America is no longer the preserve of WASPS (white, Anglo-Saxon Protestants).

New problems are constantly arising in connection with leisure time. Within recent years the coffee-break has become a national institution, quite out of harmony with the nervous-breakdown spirit of the 19th Century. Hours of labor are growing shorter; old folks are retiring earlier and living much longer, thanks to the fountains of youth tapped by medical science. The era of mass leisure is upon us; we are now spending about one-seventh of the national income for pleasure. Tens of thousands of homes without indoor plumbing or running water have television aerials towering over leaky roofs. Millions of citizens are spending five hours or more a day before the square-eyed "idiot box," which, with some notable exceptions, is presenting a "vast wasteland" of rubbish if not violence. Radio programs, likewise chopped into a chatter of "commercials," are faring little better, while portable radios are piercing the quiet of hitherto secluded areas.

We must discover new frontiers in this Land of Limitless Opportunity, now that the westward-receding frontier has played out. As long as there is an open mind, there will always be an open frontier; as long as there is resourcefulness, there will be resources. There are unattained horizons in the laboratory, in industry, and in human welfare; in the brain, in the heart, and in the soul. Pioneering is still possible almost anywhere. If we are not content to strike oil or discover uranium, we can plan a rocket-ship trip to the moon or to Mars.

Americans must never confuse bigness with greatness, or judge men by what they own rather than by what they are. We no doubt have been guilty to some degree of over-emphasizing the mechanical and the material. But it will be a sad day for America if the standard of living and the conveniences of gadgetry elbow aside the spiritual values that loomed large in the morning years of the Republic. We do not need bigger television screens but better ideas—especially ideas on how to live together, nationally and globally.

The United States did vastly more than make democracy function for the first time in history on a huge scale. We emerged in the 20th Century as the undisputed leader of the democratic world. We did not seek this burdensome new responsibility. In fact, we fled from it in 1919, after World War I. But in our science-shrunken world of today, we cannot escape it: we are locked on the center of the global stage. Destiny has thrust into our hands the torch of leadership for the free world. If we fall, all the other democratic nations will presumably fall.

The World's Last Hope

The United States, once a revolutionary force in a world of conservatism, is now a conservative force in a world of revolutionism. In our day we have witnessed the Communist revolution; the revolution in Asia and Africa against colonialism, imperialism, and racism; and the Revolution of Rising Expectations everywhere. All of these pressures are hoisting

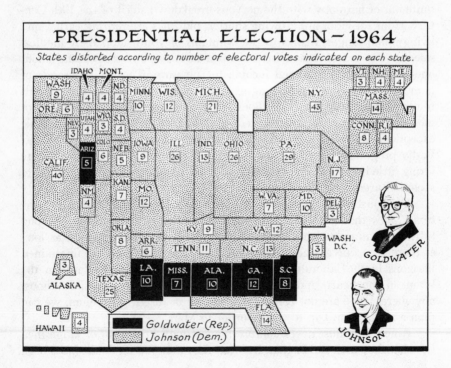

PRESIDENTIAL ELECTION – 1964

States distorted according to number of electoral votes indicated on each state.

Goldwater (Rep.)
Johnson (Dem.)

GOLDWATER

JOHNSON

storm warnings. By 1965 the American people, with 6 percent of the world's population, were enjoying about 50 percent of its wealth. A global "share the wealth movement" is gaining terrifying momentum. The submerged masses of the world are not going to be content to ride forever in oxcarts while a privileged few speed by in Cadillacs. Men are not going to live in harmony as long as two-thirds of them have to struggle to live at all.

But if the crisis is formidable, so are we. In generations past we resolutely confronted and overcame menaces as dangerous as those of today—that is, in relation to our existing strength. We need not yield to a wave of defeatism or abjectly hoist the white flag of surrender. We must exert leadership commensurate with our enormous strength. We must create events, not bow to them.

America can fulfill with flying colors her mission as foremost champion of the free world—if she will. But we must recapture much of the driving faith that we had in democracy during the early years of the Republic, when, in a monarchical world, greatly feared "isms" were American constitutionalism, republicanism, and liberalism. We should remember that we cannot fight dangerous foreign ideologies with inquisitions and bayonets, but only with better ideologies, properly communicated. We need not so much A-bombs or H-bombs as I-bombs—Idea bombs.

We must learn to live with chronic crisis. We must seek to reconcile a maximum of liberty with a maximum of security. We must strive to preserve our precious freedoms without strangling them in an effort to protect them from outside enemies. We must remember that America was founded and built by generations of nonconformists. We must not permit truth and thought to become captives in the Land of the Free. What shall it profit a nation if, to safeguard its democracy, it destroys its democracy? The best way to preserve it is to practice it.

Finally, we must keep our guard up against aggressors. Eternal vigilance is still the price to be paid for liberty. We must prepare to sacrifice—even until it hurts—to defend those priceless heritages of freedom and human dignity handed down by the Founding Fathers. To be an American is not only a rare privilege but, in these perilous times, a tremendous responsibility.

SELECT READINGS

Relevant titles of interest and value are c. n. degler, *Out of Our Past: The Forces That Shaped Modern America* (1959) [paperback]; h. b. parkes, *The American Experience* (2d ed., 1955) [paperback]; d. w. brogan, *The American Character* (1944) [paperback] and *America in the Modern World* (1960); d. m. potter, *People of Plenty* (1954) [paperback]; max lerner, *America as a Civilization* (1957) [paperback]; roger burlingame, *The American Conscience* (1957); e. m. burns, *The American Ideal of Mission* (1957); louis hartz, *The Liberal Tradition in America* (1955) [paperback]; a. a. ekirch, *The Decline of American Liberalism*

(1955); HANS KOHN, *American Nationalism* (1957) [**paperback**]; Y. ARIELI, *Individualism and Nationalism in American Ideology* (1964); R. L. BRUCKBERGER, *Image of America* (1959) [by a French Dominican, **paperback**]; L. D. BALDWIN, *The Meaning of America* (1955); MERLE CURTI, *American Paradox: The Conflict of Thought and Action* (1956); R. L. HEILBRONER, *The Future as History: The Historic Currents of Our Time and the Direction in Which They Are Taking America* (1960) [**paperback**]; CLINTON ROSSITER, *Conservatism in America* (1955) [**paperback**]; M. M. AUERBACH, *The Conservative Illusion* (1959); VANCE PACKARD, *The Status Seekers* (1959) [**paperback**] and *The Waste Makers* (1960) [**paperback**]; F. M. JOSEPH, ed., *As Others See Us: The United States Through Foreign Eyes* (1959); J. K. JESSUP, *et al., National Purpose* (1960) [**paperback**]; R. E. SPILLER and ERIC LARRABEE, *American Perspectives* (1961); D. J. BOORSTIN, *America and the Image of Europe: Reflections on American Thought* (1960) [**paperback**] and *The Image: Or, What Happened to the American Dream* (1962) [**paperback**].

DECLARATION OF INDEPENDENCE

IN CONGRESS, JULY 4, 1776

The Unanimous Declaration of the Thirteen United States of America

[Bracketed material is inserted. For background see pp. 108–109.]

WHEN, IN THE COURSE OF HUMAN EVENTS, IT BECOMES NECESSARY FOR ONE people to dissolve the political bands which have connected them with another, and to assume, among the powers of the earth, the separate and equal station to which the laws of nature and of nature's God entitle them, a decent respect to the opinions of mankind requires that they should declare the causes which impel them to the separation.

We hold these truths to be self-evident: That all men are created equal; that they are endowed by their Creator with certain unalienable rights; that among these are life, liberty, and the pursuit of happiness; that, to secure these rights, governments are instituted among men, deriving their just powers from the consent of the governed; that whenever any form of government becomes destructive of these ends, it is the right of the people to alter or to abolish it, and to institute new government, laying its foundation on such principles, and organizing its powers in such form, as to them shall seem most likely to effect their safety and happiness. Prudence, indeed, will dictate that governments long established should not be changed for light and transient causes; and accordingly all experience hath shown that mankind are more disposed to suffer, while evils are sufferable, than to right themselves by abolishing the forms to which they are accustomed. But when a long train of abuses and usurpations, pursuing invariably the same object, evinces a design to reduce them under absolute despotism, it is their right, it is their duty, to throw off such government, and to provide new guards for their future security. Such has been the patient sufferance of these colonies; and such is now the necessity which constrains them to alter their former systems of government. The history of the present King of Great Britain is a history of repeated injuries and usurpations, all having in direct object the establishment of an absolute tyranny over these states. To prove this, let facts be submitted to a candid world.

He has refused his assent to laws, the most wholesome and necessary for the public good. [See royal veto, p. 87.]

He has forbidden his governors to pass laws of immediate and pressing importance, unless suspended in their operation till his assent should be obtained; and, when so suspended, he has utterly neglected to attend to them.

He has refused to pass other laws for the accommodation of large districts of people [by establishing new counties], unless those people would relinquish the right of representation in the legislature, a right inestimable to them, and formidable to tyrants only.

He has called together legislative bodies at places unusual, uncomfortable, and distant from the depository of their public records, for the sole purpose of fatiguing them into compliance with his measures. [E.g., removal of Massachusetts Assembly to Salem, 1774.]

He has dissolved representative houses repeatedly, for opposing, with manly firmness, his invasions on the rights of the people. [E.g., Virginia Assembly, 1765.]

He has refused for a long time, after such dissolutions, to cause others to be elected; whereby the legislative powers, incapable of annihilation, have returned to the people at large for their exercise; the state remaining, in the mean time, exposed to all the dangers of invasions from without and convulsions within.

He has endeavored to prevent the population [populating] of these states; for that purpose obstructing the laws for naturalization of foreigners; refusing to pass others to encourage their migration hither, and raising the conditions of new appropriations of lands. [E.g., Proclamation of 1763, p. 63.]

He has obstructed the administration of justice, by refusing his assent to laws for establishing judiciary powers.

He has made judges dependent on his will alone, for the tenure of their offices, and the amount and payment of their salaries. [See Townshend Acts, p. 92.]

He has erected a multitude of new offices, and sent hither swarms of officers to harass our people and eat out their substance. [See enforcement of Navigation Laws, p. 92.]

He has kept among us, in times of peace, standing armies, without the consent of our legislatures. [See pp. 89, 92.]

He has affected to render the military independent of, and superior to, the civil power.

He has combined with others to subject us to a jurisdiction foreign to our constitution, and unacknowledged by our laws, giving his assent to their acts of pretended legislation:

For quartering large bodies of armed troops among us [see Boston Massacre, p. 92];

For protecting them, by a mock trial, from punishment for any murders which they should commit on the inhabitants of these states [see 1774 Act, p. 96];

For cutting off our trade with all parts of the world [see Boston Port Bill, p. 96];

For imposing taxes on us without our consent [see Stamp Act, p. 90];

For depriving us, in many cases, of the benefits of trial by jury;

For transporting us beyond seas, to be tried for pretended offenses;

For abolishing the free system of English laws in a neighboring province [Quebec], establishing therein an arbitrary government, and enlarging its boundaries, so as to render it at once an example and fit instrument for introducing the same absolute rule into these colonies [Quebec Act, p. 96];

For taking away our charters, abolishing our most valuable laws, and altering fundamentally the forms of our governments [e.g., in Massachusetts, p. 96];

For suspending our own legislatures, and declaring themselves invested with power to legislate for us in all cases whatsoever [see Stamp Act repeal, p. 91];

He has abdicated government here, by declaring us out of his protection and waging war against us. [Proclamation, p. 105.]

He has plundered our seas, ravaged our coasts, burned our towns, and destroyed the lives of our people. [E.g., the burning of Falmouth (Portland), p. 106.]

He is at this time transporting large armies of foreign mercenaries [Hessians, p. 105] to complete the works of death, desolation, and tyranny already begun with circumstances of cruelty and perfidy scarcely paralleled in the most barbarous ages, and totally unworthy the head of a civilized nation.

He has constrained our fellow-citizens, taken captive on the high seas, to bear arms against their country, to become the executioners of their friends and brethren, or to fall themselves by their hands.

He has excited domestic insurrection among us [i.e., among slaves], and has endeavored to bring on the inhabitants of our frontiers the merciless Indian savages, whose known rule of warfare is an undistinguished destruction of all ages, sexes, and conditions.

In every stage of these oppressions we have petitioned for redress in the most humble terms; our repeated petitions have been answered only by repeated injury. [E.g., pp. 98, 104.] A prince, whose character is thus marked by every act which may define a tyrant, is unfit to be the ruler of a free people.

Nor have we been wanting in our attentions to our British brethren. We have warned them, from time to time, of attempts by their legislature to extend an unwarrantable jurisdiction over us. We have reminded them of the circumstances of our emigration and settlement here. We have appealed to their native justice and magnanimity; and we have conjured them, by the ties of our common kindred, to disavow these usurpations, which would inevitably interrupt our connections and correspondence. They, too, have been deaf to the voice of justice and of consanguinity [blood relationship; see p. 104]. We must, therefore, acquiesce in the necessity which denounces [announces] our separation, and hold them, as we hold the rest of mankind, enemies in war, in peace friends.

We, therefore, the representatives of the United States of America, in General Congress assembled, appealing to the Supreme Judge of the world for the rectitude of our intentions, do, in the name and by the authority of the good people of these colonies, solemnly publish and declare, That these United Colonies are, and of right ought to be, FREE AND INDEPENDENT STATES; that they are absolved from all allegiance to the British crown, and that all political connection between them and the state of Great Britain is, and ought to be, totally dissolved; and that, as free and independent states, they have full power to levy war, conclude peace, contract alliances, establish commerce, and do all other acts and things which independent states may of right do. And for the support of this declaration, with a firm reliance on the protection of Divine Providence, we mutually pledge to each other our lives, our fortunes, and our sacred honor.

[Signed by]   JOHN HANCOCK [President]
[and fifty-five others]

CONSTITUTION OF
THE UNITED STATES OF AMERICA

[Boldface headings and bracketed explanatory matter have been inserted for the reader's convenience. Passages which are no longer operative are printed in italic type.]

PREAMBLE

On "We the people" see p. 260.   We the people of the United States, in order to form a more perfect union, establish justice, insure domestic tranquillity, provide for the common defense, promote the general welfare, and secure the blessings of liberty to ourselves and our posterity, do ordain and establish this CONSTITUTION for the United States of America.

Article I. Legislative Department

Section I. CONGRESS

Legislative power vested in a two-house Congress. All legislative powers herein granted shall be vested in a Congress of the United States, which shall consist of a Senate and a House of Representatives.

Section II. HOUSE OF REPRESENTATIVES

1. The people elect representatives biennially. The House of Representatives shall be composed of members chosen every second year by the people of the several States, and the electors [voters] in each State shall have the qualifications requisite for electors of the most numerous branch of the State Legislature.

2. Who may be representatives. No person shall be a Representative who shall not have attained to the age of twenty-five years, and been seven years a citizen of the United States, and who shall not, when elected, be an inhabitant of that State in which he shall be chosen.

3. Representation in the House based on population; census. Rep-

See 1787 compromise, p. 140.   resentatives and direct taxes [1] shall be apportioned among the several States which may be included within this Union, according to their respective numbers, *which shall be determined by adding to the whole number of free persons, including those bound to service for a term of years* [apprentices and indentured servants],

See 1787 compromise, p. 141.   *and excluding Indians not taxed, three-fifths of all other persons* [slaves].[2] The actual enumeration [census] shall be made within three years after the first meeting of the Congress of the United States, and within every subsequent term of ten years, in such manner as they shall by law direct. The number of Representatives shall not exceed one for every thirty thousand, but each State shall have at least one Representative; *and until such enumeration shall be made, the State of New Hampshire shall be entitled to choose three, Massachusetts eight, Rhode Island and Providence Plantations one, Connecticut five, New York six, New Jersey four, Pennsylvania eight, Delaware one, Maryland six, Virginia ten, North Carolina five, South Carolina five, and Georgia three.*

[1] Modified in 1913 by the 16th Amendment re income taxes (see p. 686).
[2] The word "slave" appears nowhere in the Constitution; "slavery" appears in the 13th Amendment. The three-fifths rule ceased to be in force when the 13th Amendment was adopted in 1865 (see p. 433 and Amendments below).

4. Vacancies in the House are filled by election. When vacancies happen in the representation from any State, the Executive authority [governor] thereof shall issue writs of election [call a special election] to fill such vacancies.

5. The House selects its Speaker; has sole power to vote impeach-
See Chase and ment charges (i.e., indictments). The House of Representatives
Johnson trials, shall choose their Speaker and other officers; and shall have the
pp. 187, 479. sole power of impeachment.

Section III. SENATE

1. Senators represent the states. The Senate of the United States shall be composed of two Senators from each State, *chosen by the legislature thereof*,[1] for six years; and each Senator shall have one vote.

2. One-third of Senators chosen every two years; vacancies. *Immediately after they shall be assembled in consequence of the first election, they shall be divided as equally as may be into three classes. The seats of the Senators of the first class shall be vacated at the expiration of the second year, of the second class at the expiration of the fourth year, and of the third class at the expiration of the sixth year,* so that one-third may be chosen every second year; *and if vacancies happen by resignation or otherwise, during the recess of the legislature of any State, the Executive* [governor] *thereof may make temporary appointments until the next meeting of the legislature, which shall then fill such vacancies.*[2]

3. Who may be Senators. No person shall be a Senator who shall not have attained to the age of thirty years, and been nine years a citizen of the United States, and who shall not, when elected, be an inhabitant of that State for which he shall be chosen.

4. The Vice-President presides over the Senate. The Vice-President of the United States shall be President of the Senate, but shall have no vote, unless they be equally divided [tied].

5. The Senate chooses its other officers. The Senate shall choose their other officers, and also a President *pro tempore*, in the absence of the Vice-President, or when he shall exercise the office of President of the United States.

6. The Senate has sole power to try impeachments. The Senate
See Chase and shall have the sole power to try all impeachments. When sitting
Johnson trials, for that purpose, they shall be on oath or affirmation. When the
pp. 187, 479. President of the United States is tried, the Chief Justice shall preside: [3] and no person shall be convicted without the concurrence of two-thirds of the members present.

7. Penalties for impeachment conviction. Judgment in cases of impeachment shall not extend further than to removal from office, and disqualification to hold and enjoy any office of honor, trust or profit under the United States: but the party convicted shall nevertheless be liable and subject to indictment, trial, judgment and punishment, according to law.

Section IV. ELECTION AND MEETINGS OF CONGRESS

1. Regulation of elections. The times, places and manner of holding elections for Senators and Representatives shall be prescribed in each State by the legislature thereof; but the Congress may at any time by law make or alter such regulations, except as to the places of choosing Senators.

---

[1] Repealed in favor of popular election in 1913 by the 17th Amendment (see p. 664).
[2] Changed in 1913 by the 17th Amendment (see p. 664, and Ammendments below).
[3] The Vice-President, as next in line, would be an interested party.

2. Congress must meet once a year. The Congress shall assemble at least once in every year, and such meeting *shall be on the first Monday in December, unless they shall by law appoint a different day.*[1]

Section V. ORGANIZATION AND RULES OF THE HOUSES

1. Each House may reject members; quorums. Each house shall be the judge of the elections, returns and qualifications of its own members, and a majority of each shall constitute a quorum to do business; but a smaller number may adjourn from day to day, and may be authorized to compel the attendance of absent members, in such manner, and under such penalties, as each house may provide.

See "Bully" Brooks case, p. 398.

2. Each House makes its own rules. Each house may determine the rules of its proceedings, punish its members for disorderly behavior, and with the concurrence of two-thirds, expel a member.

3. Each House must keep and publish a record of its proceedings. Each house shall keep a journal of its proceedings, and from time to time publish the same, excepting such parts as may in their judgment require secrecy; and the yeas and nays of the members of either house on any question shall, at the desire of one-fifth of those present, be entered on the journal.

4. Both Houses must agree on adjournment. Neither house, during the session of Congress, shall, without the consent of the other, adjourn for more than three days, nor to any other place than that in which the two houses shall be sitting.

Section VI. PRIVILEGES OF AND PROHIBITIONS UPON CONGRESSMEN

1. Congressional salaries; immunities. The Senators and Representatives shall receive a compensation for their services, to be ascertained by law and paid out of the treasury of the United States. They shall in all cases except treason, felony and breach of the peace, be privileged from arrest during their attendance at the session of their respective houses, and in going to and returning from the same; and for any speech or debate in either house, they shall not be questioned in any other place [i.e., they shall be immune from libel suits].

2. A Congressman may not hold any other federal civil office. No Senator or Representative shall, during the time for which he was elected, be appointed to any civil office under the authority of the United States, which shall have been created, or the emoluments whereof shall have been increased, during such time; and no person holding any office under the United States shall be a member of either house during his continuance in office.

Section VII. METHOD OF MAKING LAWS

See 1787 compromise, p. 141.

1. Money bills must originate in the House. All bills for raising revenue shall originate in the House of Representatives; but the Senate may propose or concur with amendments as on other bills.

2. The President's veto power; Congress may override. Every bill which shall have passed the House of Representatives and the Senate, shall, before it become a law, be presented to the President of the United States; if he approve he shall sign it, but if not he shall return it with his objections to that house in which it shall

---

[1] Changed in 1933 to January 3 by the 20th Amendment (see p. 850 and below).

have originated, who shall enter the objections at large on their journal, and proceed to reconsider it. If after such reconsideration two-thirds of that house shall agree to pass the bill, it shall be sent, together with the objections, to the other house, by which it shall likewise be reconsidered, and, if approved by two-thirds of that house, it shall become a law. But in all such cases the votes of both houses shall be determined by yeas and nays, and the names of the persons voting for and against the bill shall be entered on the journal of each house respectively. If any bill shall not be returned by the President within ten days (Sundays excepted) after it shall have been presented to him, the same shall be a law, in like *See Jackson's pocket* manner as if he had signed it, unless the Congress by their adjourn-*vetoes, p. 255.* ment prevent its return, in which case it shall not be a law [this is the so-called pocket veto].

3. All measures requiring the agreement of both houses go to President for approval. Every order, resolution, or vote to which the concurrence of the Senate and House of Representatives may be necessary (except on a question of adjournment) shall be presented to the President of the United States; and before the same shall take effect, shall be approved by him, or being disapproved by him, shall be repassed by two-thirds of the Senate and House of Representatives, according to the rules and limitations prescribed in the case of a bill.

Section VIII. POWERS GRANTED TO CONGRESS

Congress has certain enumerated powers:
1. It may lay and collect taxes. The Congress shall have power to lay and collect taxes, duties, imposts, and excises, to pay the debts and provide for the common defense and general welfare of the United States; but all duties, imposts and excises shall be uniform throughout the United States;

2. It may borrow money. To borrow money on the credit of the United States;

3. It may regulate foreign and interstate trade. To regulate commerce with foreign nations, and among the several States, and with the Indian tribes;

For 1798 naturaliza- **4. It may pass naturalization and bankruptcy laws.** To establish *tion see p. 176.* an uniform rule of naturalization, and uniform laws on the subject of bankruptcies throughout the United States;

5. It may coin money. To coin money, regulate the value thereof, and of foreign coin, and fix the standard of weights and measures;

6. It may punish counterfeiters. To provide for the punishment of counterfeiting the securities and current coin of the United States;

7. It may establish a postal service. To establish post offices and post roads;

8. It may issue patents and copyrights. To promote the progress of science and useful arts by securing for limited times to authors and inventors the exclusive right to their respective writings and discoveries;

See Judiciary Act **9. It may establish inferior courts.** To constitute tribunals inferior *of 1789, p. 152.* to the Supreme Court;

10. It may punish crimes committed on the high seas. To define and punish piracies and felonies committed on the high seas [i.e., outside the three-mile limit] and offenses against the law of nations [international law];

11. It may declare war; authorize privateers. To declare war,[1] grant letters of marque and reprisal,[2] and make rules concerning captures on land and water;

12. It may maintain an army. To raise and support armies, but no appropriation of money to that use shall be for a longer term than two years; [3]

13. It may maintain a navy. To provide and maintain a navy;

14. It may regulate the army and navy. To make rules for the government and regulation of the land and naval forces;

See Whiskey Rebellion, p. 160. **15. It may call out the state militia.** To provide for calling forth the militia to execute the laws of the Union, suppress insurrections, and repel invasions;

16. It shares with the states control of militia. To provide for organizing, arming, and disciplining the militia, and for governing such part of them as may be employed in the service of the United States, reserving to the States respectively the appointment of the officers, and the authority of training the militia according to the discipline prescribed by Congress;

17. It makes laws for the District of Columbia and other federal areas. To exercise exclusive legislation in all cases whatsoever, over such district (not exceeding ten miles square) as may, by cession of particular States, and the acceptance of Congress, become the seat of government of the United States,[4] and to exercise like authority over all places purchased by the consent of the legislature of the State, in which the same shall be, for the erection of forts, magazines, arsenals, dock-yards, and other needful buildings;—and

Congress has certain implied powers:

This is the famous "Elastic Clause"; see pp. 157, 233. **18. It may make laws necessary for carrying out the enumerated powers.** To make all laws which shall be necessary and proper for carrying into execution the foregoing powers, and all other powers vested by this Constitution in the government of the United States, or in any department or officer thereof.

Section IX. POWERS DENIED TO THE FEDERAL GOVERNMENT

See 1787 slave compromise, p. 141. **1. Congressional control of slave trade postponed until 1808.** *The migration or importation of such persons as any of the States now existing shall think proper to admit shall not be prohibited by the Congress prior to the year 1808; but a tax or duty may be imposed on such importation, not exceeding $10 for each person.*

See Lincoln's suspension, p. 450. **2. The writ of habeas corpus [5] may be suspended only in case of rebellion or invasion.** The privilege of the writ of habeas corpus shall not be suspended, unless when in cases of rebellion or invasion the public safety may require it.

3. Attainders [6] and ex post facto laws [7] forbidden. No bill of attainder or ex post facto law shall be passed.

---

[1] Note that the President, though he can provoke war (see the case of Polk, pp. 293–294) or wage it after it is declared, cannot declare it.

[2] Papers issued to private citizens in time of war authorizing them to capture enemy ships.

[3] A reflection of fear of standing armies earlier expressed in the Declaration of Independence.

[4] The District of Columbia, ten miles square, was established in 1791 (see p. 154).

[5] A writ of habeas corpus is a document which enables a person under arrest to obtain an immediate examination in court to ascertain whether he is being legally held.

[6] A bill of attainder is a special legislative act condemning and punishing an individual without a judicial trial.

[7] An ex post facto law is one that fixes punishments for acts committed before the law was passed.

4. Direct taxes must be apportioned according to population. No capitation [head or poll tax], or other direct, tax shall be laid, unless in proportion to the census or enumeration herein before directed to be taken.[1]

5. Export taxes forbidden. No tax or duty shall be laid on articles exported from any State.

6. Congress must not discriminate among states in regulating commerce. No preference shall be given by any regulation of commerce or revenue to the ports of one State over those of another; nor shall vessels bound to, or from, one State, be obliged to enter, clear, or pay duties in another.

See Lincoln's infraction, p. 450. **7. Public money may not be spent without Congressional appropriation; accounting.** No money shall be drawn from the treasury, but in consequence of appropriations made by law; and a regular statement and account of the receipts and expenditures of all public money shall be published from time to time.

8. Titles of nobility prohibited; foreign gifts. No title of nobility shall be granted by the United States: and no person holding any office of profit or trust under them, shall, without the consent of the Congress, accept of any present, emolument, office, or title, of any kind whatever, from any king, prince, or foreign state.

Section X. Powers Denied to the States

Absolute prohibitions on the states:

1. The states are forbidden to do certain things. No State shall enter into any treaty, alliance, or confederation; grant letters of marque and reprisal [i.e., authorize privateers]; coin money; emit bills of credit [issue paper money]; make anything but gold and silver coin a [legal] tender in payment of debts; pass any bill of *See Fletcher vs. Peck,* attainder, ex post facto law,[2] or law impairing the obligation of *p. 233.* contracts, or grant any title of nobility.

Conditional prohibitions on the states:

2. The states may not levy duties without the consent of Congress. No State shall, without the consent of the Congress, lay any *Cf. Confederation* imposts or duties on imports or exports, except what may be abso-*chaos, p. 135.* lutely necessary for executing its inspection laws: and the net produce of all duties and imposts, laid by any State on imports or exports, shall be for the use of the treasury of the United States; and all such laws shall be subject to the revision and control of the Congress.

3. Certain other federal powers are forbidden the states except with the consent of Congress. No State shall, without the consent of Congress, lay any duty of tonnage [i.e., duty on ship tonnage], keep [non-militia] troops or ships of war in time of peace, enter into any agreement or compact with another State, or with a foreign power, or engage in war, unless actually invaded, or in such imminent danger as will not admit of delay.

Article II. Executive Department

Section I. President and Vice-President

1. The President the chief executive; his term. The executive power shall be vested in a President of the United States of America. He shall hold his office during the term of four years,[3] and, together with the Vice-President, chosen for the same term, be elected as follows:

1 Modified in 1913 by the 16th Amendment (see pp. 596, 686, and Amendments below).
2 For definitions see footnotes 6 and 7 on preceding page.
3 No reference to re-election; for anti-third term 22d Amendment see p. 932 and below.

2. The President is chosen by electors. Each State shall appoint, in such manner as the legislature thereof may direct, a number of electors, equal to the whole number of Senators and Representatives to which the State may be entitled in the Congress; but no Senator or Representative, or person holding an office of trust or profit under the United States, shall be appointed an elector.

See 1787 compromise, p. 141.

See 1876 Oregon case, p. 496.

A majority of the electoral votes needed to elect a President. *The electors shall meet in their respective States, and vote by ballot for two persons, of whom one at least shall not be an inhabitant of the same State with themselves. And they shall make a list of all the persons voted for, and of the number of votes for each; which list they shall sign and certify, and transmit sealed to the seat of government of the United States, directed to the President of the Senate. The President of the Senate shall, in the presence of the Senate and House of Representatives, open all the certificates, and the votes shall then be counted. The person having the greatest number of votes shall be the President, if such number be a majority of the whole number of electors appointed; and if there be more than one who have such majority, and have an equal number of votes, then the House of Representatives shall immediately choose by ballot one of them for President; and if no person have a majority, then from the five highest on the list the said house shall in like manner choose the President. But in choosing the President the votes shall be taken by States, the representation from each State having one vote; a quorum for this purpose shall consist of a member or members from two-thirds of the States, and a majority of all the States shall be necessary to a choice. In every case, after the choice of the President, the person having the greatest number of votes of the electors shall be the Vice-President. But if there should remain two or more who have equal votes, the Senate shall choose from them by ballot the Vice-President.*[1]

See Burr-Jefferson disputed election of 1800, pp. 180–181.

See Jefferson as Vice-President in 1796, p. 173.

3. Congress decides time of meeting of Electoral College. The Congress may determine the time of choosing the electors and the day on which they shall give their votes; which day shall be the same throughout the United States.

4. Who may be President. No person except a natural-born citizen, *or a citizen of the United States at the time of the adoption of this Constitution*, shall be eligible to the office of President; neither shall any person be eligible to that office who shall not have attained to the age of thirty-five years, and been fourteen years a resident within the United States [i.e., a legal resident].

To provide for foreign-born like Hamilton

5. Replacements for President. In case of the removal of the President from office or of his death, resignation, or inability to discharge the powers and duties of the said office, the same shall devolve on the Vice-President, and the Congress may by law provide for the case of removal, death, resignation, or inability, both of the President and Vice-President, declaring what officer shall then act as President, and such officer shall act accordingly, until the disability be removed, or a President shall be elected.

6. The President's salary. The President shall, at stated times, receive for his services a compensation, which shall neither be increased nor diminished during the period for which he shall have been elected, and he shall not receive within that period any other emolument from the United States, or any of them.

7. The President's oath of office. Before he enter on the execution of his office, he shall take the following oath or affirmation:—"I do solemnly swear (or affirm) that I will faithfully execute the office

---

[1] Repealed in 1804 by the 12th Amendment (for text, see Amendments below).

of President of the United States, and will to the best of my ability preserve, protect and defend the Constitution of the United States."

Section II. POWERS OF THE PRESIDENT

See Cabinet evolution, p. 151.

1. The President has important military and civil powers. The President shall be commander in chief of the army and navy of the United States, and of the militia of the several States, when called into the actual service of the United States; he may require the opinion, in writing, of the principal officer in each of the executive departments, upon any subject relating to the duties of their respective offices, and he shall have power to grant reprieves and pardons for offenses against the United States, except in cases of impeachment.[1]

For President's removal power, see p. 478.

2. The President may negotiate treaties and nominate federal officials. He shall have power, by and with the advice and consent of the Senate, to make treaties, provided two-thirds of the Senators present concur; and he shall nominate, and by and with the advice and consent of the Senate, shall appoint ambassadors, other public ministers and consuls, judges of the Supreme Court, and all other officers of the United States, whose appointments are not herein otherwise provided for, and which shall be established by law: but the Congress may by law vest the appointment of such inferior officers, as they think proper, in the President alone, in the courts of law, or in the heads of departments.

3. The President may fill vacancies during Senate recess. The President shall have power to fill up all vacancies that may happen during the recess of the Senate, by granting commissions which shall expire at the end of their next session.

Section III. OTHER POWERS AND DUTIES OF THE PRESIDENT

For President's personal appearances, see p. 690.

Messages; extra sessions; receiving ambassadors: execution of the laws. He shall from time to time give to the Congress information of the state of the Union, and recommend to their consideration such measures as he shall judge necessary and expedient; he may, on extraordinary occasions, convene both houses, or either of them, and in case of disagreement between them, with respect to the time of adjournment, he may adjourn them to such time as he shall think proper; he shall receive ambassadors and other public ministers; he shall take care that the laws be faithfully executed, and shall commission all the officers of the United States.

Section IV. IMPEACHMENT

See Johnson's acquittal, p. 479.

Civil officers may be removed by impeachment. The President, Vice-President and all civil officers [2] of the United States shall be removed from office on impeachment for, and on conviction of, treason, bribery, or other high crimes and misdemeanors.

Article III. Judicial Department

Section I. THE FEDERAL COURTS

See Judiciary Act of 1789, p. 152.

The judicial power belongs to the federal courts. The judicial power of the United States shall be vested in one Supreme Court, and in such inferior courts as the Congress may from time to time ordain and establish. The judges, both of the Supreme and inferior courts, shall hold their offices during good behavior, and shall, at stated times, receive for their services a compensation which shall not be diminished during their continuance in office.

[1] To prevent the President's pardoning himself or his close associates.

[2] I.e., all federal executive and judicial officers, but not members of Congress or military personnel.

Section II. JURISDICTION OF FEDERAL COURTS

1. Kinds of cases that may be heard. The judicial power shall extend to all cases, in law and equity, arising under this Constitution, the laws of the United States, and treaties made, or which shall be made, under their authority;—to all cases affecting ambassadors, other public ministers and consuls;—to all cases of admiralty and maritime jurisdiction;—to controversies to which the United States shall be a party;—to controversies between two or more States;—*between a State and citizens of another State;*[1]—between citizens of different States;—between citizens of the same State claiming lands under grants of different States, and between a State, or the citizens thereof, and foreign states, citizens or subjects.

2. Jurisdiction of the Supreme Court. In all cases affecting ambassadors, other public ministers and consuls, and those in which a State shall be party, the Supreme Court shall have original jurisdiction.[2] In all the other cases before mentioned, the Supreme Court shall have appellate jurisdiction,[3] both as to law and fact, with such exceptions, and under such regulations, as the Congress shall make.

3. Trial for federal crime is by jury. The trial of all crimes, except in cases of impeachment, shall be by jury; and such trial shall be held in the State where the said crimes shall have been committed; but when not committed within any State, the trial shall be at such place or places as the Congress may by law have directed.

Section III. TREASON

1. Treason defined. Treason against the United States shall consist only in levying war against them, or in adhering to their enemies, giving them aid and comfort. No person shall be convicted of treason unless on the testimony of two witnesses to the same overt act, or on confession in open court.

See Burr trial, p. 193.

2. Congress fixes punishment for treason. The Congress shall have power to declare the punishment of treason, but no attainder of treason shall work corruption of blood, or forfeiture except during the life of the person attainted.[4]

Article IV. Relations of the States to One Another

Section I. CREDIT TO ACTS, RECORDS, AND COURT PROCEEDINGS

Each state must respect the public acts of the others. Full faith and credit shall be given in each State to the public acts, records, and judicial proceedings of every other State.[5] And the Congress may by general laws prescribe the manner in which such acts, records, and proceedings shall be proved [attested], and the effect thereof.

Section II. DUTIES OF STATES TO STATES

1. Citizenship in one state is valid in all. The citizens of each State shall be entitled to all privileges and immunities of citizens in the several States.

[1] The 11th Amendment (see Amendments below) restricts this to suits by a state against citizens of another state.

[2] I.e., such cases must originate in the Supreme Court.

[3] I.e., it hears other cases only when they are appealed to it from a lower federal court or a state court.

[4] I.e., punishment only for the offender; none for his heirs.

[5] E.g., a marriage valid in one is valid in all.

2. Fugitives from justice must be surrendered by the state to which they 'have fled. A person charged in any State with treason, felony, or other crime, who shall flee from justice, and be found in another State, shall on demand of the executive authority [governor] of the State from which he fled, be delivered up, to be removed to the State having jurisdiction of the crime.

3. Slaves and apprentices must be returned. *No person held to* *Basis of fugitive slave* *service or labor in one State, under the laws thereof, escaping into* *laws; see p. 378.* *another, shall, in consequence of any law or regulation therein, be discharged from such service or labor, but shall be delivered up on claim of the party to whom such service or labor may be due.*[1]

Section III. NEW STATES AND TERRITORIES

1. Congress may admit new states. New States may be admitted *E.g., Maine (1820);* by the Congress into this Union; but no new State shall be formed *see p. 230.* or erected within the jurisdiction of any other State; nor any State be formed by the junction of two or more States, or parts of States, without the consent of the legislatures of the States concerned as well as of the Congress.

2. Congress regulates federal territory and property. The Congress shall have power to dispose of and make all needful rules and regulations respecting the territory or other property belonging to the United States; and nothing in this Constitution shall be so construed as to prejudice any claims of the United States, or of any particular State.

Section IV. PROTECTION TO THE STATES

United States guarantees to states representative government and protection against invasion and rebellion. The United States shall guarantee to every State in this Union a republican form of government, and shall protect each of them against invasion; and *See Pullman strike,* on application of the legislature, or of the executive [governor] *p. 595.* (when the legislature cannot be convened), against domestic violence.

Article V. The Process of Amendment

The Constitution may be amended in four ways. The Congress, whenever two-thirds of both houses shall deem it necessary, shall propose amendments to this Constitution, or, on the application of the legislatures of two-thirds of the several States, shall call a convention for proposing amendments, which, in either case, shall be valid to all intents and purposes, as part of this Constitution, when ratified by the legislatures of three-fourths of the several States, or by conventions in three-fourths thereof, as the one or the other mode of ratification may be proposed by the Congress; provided *that no amendments which may be made prior to the year one thousand eight hundred and eight shall in any manner affect the first and fourth clauses in the ninth section of the first article;*[2] and that no State, without its consent, shall be deprived of its equal suffrage in the Senate.

Article VI. General Provisions

1. The debts of the Confederation are taken over. All debts con- *This pledge honored* tracted and engagements entered into, before the adoption of this *by Hamilton.* Constitution, shall be as valid against the United States under this *p. 153.* Constitution, as under the Confederation.

[1] Invalidated in 1865 by the 13th Amendment (for text see Amendments below).
[2] This clause, re slave trade and direct taxes, became inoperative in 1808.

2. The Constitution, federal laws, and treaties are the supreme law of the land. This Constitution, and the laws of the United States which shall be made in pursuance thereof; and all treaties made, or which shall be made, under the authority of the United States, shall be the supreme law of the land; and the judges in every State shall be bound thereby, anything in the Constitution or laws of any State to the contrary notwithstanding.

3. Federal and state officers bound by oath to support the Constitution. The Senators and Representatives before mentioned, and the members of the several State legislatures, and all executive and judicial officers, both of the United States and of the several States, shall be bound by oath or affirmation to support this Constitution; but no religious test shall ever be required as a qualification to any office or public trust under the United States.

Article VII. Ratification of the Constitution

See 1787 irregularity, p. 142. **The Constitution effective when ratified by conventions in nine states.** The ratification of the conventions of nine States shall be sufficient for the establishment of this Constitution between the States so ratifying the same.

Done in Convention by the unanimous consent of the States present, the seventeenth day of September in the year of our Lord one thousand seven hundred and eighty-seven and of the Independence of the United States of America the twelfth. In witness whereof we have hereunto subscribed our names.

[Signed by]   G° WASHINGTON
                                Presidt and Deputy from Virginia
                                   [and thirty-eight others]

AMENDMENTS TO THE CONSTITUTION [1]

Article I. Religious and Political Freedom

For background of Bill of Rights see p. 152. **Congress must not interfere with freedom of religion, speech or press, assembly, and petition.** Congress shall make no law respecting an establishment of religion, or prohibiting the free exercise thereof; or abridging the freedom of speech, or of the press; or the right of the people peaceably to assemble, and to petition the government for a redress of grievances.

Article II. Right to Bear Arms

The people may bear arms. A well-regulated militia being necessary to the security of a free State, the right of the people to keep and bear arms [i.e., for military purposes] shall not be infringed.

Article III. Quartering of Troops

See Declaration of Independence, above. **Soldiers may not be arbitrarily quartered on the people.** No soldier shall, in time of peace, be quartered in any house without the consent of the owner, nor in time of war, but in a manner to be prescribed by law.

Article IV. Searches and Seizures

A reflection of colonial grievances against Crown. **Unreasonable searches are forbidden.** The right of the people to be secure in their persons, houses, papers, and effects, against unreasonable searches and seizures, shall not be violated, and **no**

[1] The first ten Amendments (Bill of Rights) were adopted in 1791.

[search] warrants shall issue but upon probable cause, supported by oath or affirmation, and particularly describing the place to be searched, and the persons or things to be seized.

Article V. Right to Life, Liberty, and Property

The individual is guaranteed certain rights when on trial and the right to life, liberty, and property. No person shall be held to answer for a capital, or otherwise infamous crime, unless on a presentment [formal charge] or indictment of a grand jury, except in cases arising in the land or naval forces, or in the militia, when in actual service in time of war or public danger; nor shall any person be subject for the same offense to be twice put in jeopardy of life or limb; nor shall be compelled in any criminal case to be a witness against himself, nor be deprived of life, liberty, or property, without due process of law; nor shall private property be taken for public use [i.e., by eminent domain] without just compensation.

Article VI. Protection in Criminal Trials

See Declaration of Independence, above.

An accused person has important rights. In all criminal prosecutions, the accused shall enjoy the right to a speedy and public trial, by an impartial jury of the State and district wherein the crime shall have been committed, which district shall have been previously ascertained by law, and to be informed of the nature and cause of the accusation; to be confronted with the witnesses against him; to have compulsory process [subpoena] for obtaining witnesses in his favor, and to have the assistance of counsel for his defense.

Article VII. Suits at Common Law

The rules of common law are recognized. In suits at common law, where the value in controversy shall exceed twenty dollars, the right of trial by jury shall be preserved, and no fact tried by a jury shall be otherwise re-examined in any court of the United States, than according to the rules of the common law.

Article VIII. Bail and Punishments

Excessive fines and unusual punishments are forbidden. Excessive bail shall not be required, nor excessive fines imposed, nor cruel and unusual punishments inflicted.

Article IX. Concerning Rights Not Enumerated

The people retain rights not here enumerated. The enumeration in the Constitution, of certain rights, shall not be construed to deny or disparage others retained by the people.

Article X. Powers Reserved to the States and to the People

A concession to states' rights, p. 157.

Powers not delegated to the federal government are reserved to the states and the people. The powers not delegated to the United States by the Constitution, nor prohibited by it to the States, are reserved to the States respectively, or to the people.

Article XI. Suits against a State

The federal courts have no authority in suits by citizens against a state. The judicial power of the United States shall not be construed to extend to any suit in law or equity, commenced or prosecuted against one of the United States by citizens of another

State, or by citizens or subjects of any foreign state. [Adopted 1798.]

Article XII. Election of President and Vice-President

1. Changes in manner of electing President and Vice-President; procedure when no presidential candidate receives electoral majority. The electors shall meet in their respective States, and vote by ballot for President and Vice-President, one of whom, at least, shall not be an inhabitant of the same State with themselves; they *Forestalls repetition* shall name in their ballots the person voted for as President, and *of 1800 dispute,* in distinct ballots the person voted for as Vice-President, and they *pp. 180–181.* shall make distinct lists of all persons voted for as President, and of all persons voted for as Vice-President, and of the number of votes for each, which lists they shall sign and certify, and transmit sealed to the seat of government of the United States, directed to the *See 1876 election,* President of the Senate;—the President of the Senate shall, in the *p. 497.* presence of the Senate and House of Representatives, open all the certificates and the votes shall then be counted;—the person having the greatest number of votes for President shall be the President, if such number be a majority of the whole number of electors appointed; and if no person have such majority, then from the per- *See 1824 election,* sons having the highest numbers not exceeding three on the list *p. 245.* of those voted for as President, the House of Representatives shall choose immediately, by ballot, the President. But in choosing the President, the votes shall be taken by States, the representation from each State having one vote; a quorum for this purpose shall consist of a member or members from two-thirds of the States, and a majority of all the States shall be necessary to a choice. And if the House of Representatives shall not choose a President whenever the right of choice shall devolve upon them, before *the fourth day of March* [1] next following, then the Vice-President shall act as President, as in the case of the death or other constitutional disability of the President.

2. Procedure when no vice-presidential candidate receives electoral majority. The person having the greatest number of votes as Vice-President shall be the Vice-President, if such number be a majority of the whole number of electors appointed; and if no person have a majority, then from the two highest numbers on the list the Senate shall choose the Vice-President; a quorum for the purpose shall consist of two-thirds of the whole number of Senators, and a majority of the whole number shall be necessary to a choice. But no person constitutionally ineligible to the office of President shall be eligible to that of Vice-President of the United States. [Adopted 1804.]

Article XIII. Slavery Prohibited

Slavery forbidden. 1. Neither slavery [2] nor involuntary servi- *For background* tude, except as a punishment for crime whereof the party shall *see p. 433.* have been duly convicted, shall exist within the United States, or any place subject to their jurisdiction.

2. Congress shall have power to enforce this article by appropriate legislation. [Adopted 1865.]

Article XIV. Civil Rights for Negroes, Etc.

For background **1. Negroes made citizens; U. S. citizenship primary.** All persons *see p. 470.* born or naturalized in the United States, and subject to the juris-

---

[1] Changed to January 20 by the 20th Amendment (for text, see Amendments below).
[2] The only explicit mention of slavery in the Constitution.

diction thereof, are citizens of the United States and of the State wherein they reside. No State shall make or enforce any law which shall abridge the privileges or immunities of citizens of the United *For corporations* States; nor shall any State deprive any person of life, liberty, or *as "persons"* property, without due process of law; nor deny to any person *see p. 533.* within its jurisdiction the equal protection of the laws.

2. When a state denies Negroes the vote, its representation shall *Abolishes three-fifths* **be reduced.** Representatives shall be apportioned among the sev- *rule for Negroes,* eral States according to their respective numbers, counting the *Art. I, Sec. II,* whole number of persons in each State, excluding Indians not *para. 3, above.* taxed. But when the right to vote at any election for the choice of Electors for President and Vice-President of the United States, Representatives in Congress, the executive and judicial officers of a State, or the members of the legislature thereof, is denied to any of the male inhabitants of such State, being twenty-one years of age and citizens of the United States, or in any way abridged, ex- cept for participation in rebellion, or other crime, the basis of rep- resentation therein shall be reduced in the proportion which the number of such male citizens shall bear to the whole number of male citizens twenty-one years of age in such State.

3. Certain persons who have been in rebellion are ineligible for federal and state office. No person shall be a Senator or Represent- ative in Congress, or Elector of President and Vice-President, or hold any office, civil or military, under the United States, or under any State, who, having previously taken an oath, as a member of Congress, or as an officer of the United States, or as a member of any State legislature, or as an executive or judicial officer of any State, to support the Constitution of the United States, shall have engaged in insurrection or rebellion against the same, or given aid or comfort to the enemies thereof. But Congress may, by a vote of two-thirds of each house, remove such disability.

4. Debts incurred in aid of rebellion are void. The validity of the public debt of the United States, authorized by law, including debts incurred for payment of pensions and bounties for services in suppressing insurrection or rebellion, shall not be questioned. But neither the United States nor any State shall assume or pay any debt or obligation incurred in aid of insurrection or rebellion against the United States, or any claim for the loss or emancipation of any slave; but all such debts, obligations, and claims shall be held illegal and void.

5. Enforcement. The Congress shall have power to enforce, by appropriate legislation, the provisions of this article. [Adopted 1868.]

Article XV. Negro Suffrage

Negroes are made voters. 1. The right of citizens of the *For background* United States to vote shall not be denied or abridged by the *see p. 472.* United States or by any State on account of race, color, or previous condition of servitude.

2. The Congress shall have power to enforce this article by ap- propriate legislation. [Adopted 1870.]

Article XVI. Income Taxes

For background **Congress has power to lay and collect income taxes.** The Con- *see pp. 596, 686.* gress shall have power to lay and collect taxes on incomes, from whatever source derived, without apportionment among the several States, and without regard to any census or enumeration. [Adopted 1913.]

Article XVII. Direct Election of Senators

For background see p. 664.

Senators shall be elected by popular vote. 1. The Senate of the United States shall be composed of two Senators from each State, elected by the people thereof, for six years; and each Senator shall have one vote. The electors in each State shall have the qualifications requisite for electors of [voters for] the most numerous branch of the State legislatures.

2. When vacancies happen in the representation of any State in the Senate, the executive authority of such State shall issue writs of election to fill such vacancies: Provided, that the Legislature of any State may empower the executive thereof to make temporary appointments until the people fill the vacancies by election as the Legislature may direct.

3. This amendment shall not be so construed as to affect the election or term of any Senator chosen before it becomes valid as part of the Constitution. [Adopted 1913.]

Article XVIII. National Prohibition

For background see p. 746.

The sale or manufacture of intoxicating liquors is forbidden. *1. After one year from the ratification of this article the manufacture, sale, or transportation of intoxicating liquors within, the importation thereof into, or the exportation thereof from the United States and all territory subject to the jurisdiction thereof, for beverage purposes, is hereby prohibited.*

2. The Congress and the several States shall have concurrent power to enforce this article by appropriate legislation.

3. This article shall be inoperative unless it shall have been ratified as an amendment to the Constitution by the legislatures of the several States, as provided by the Constitution, within seven years from the date of the submission thereof to the States by the Congress. [Adopted 1919; repealed 1933 by 21st Amendment.]

Article XIX. Woman Suffrage

For background see p. 747.

Women guaranteed the right to vote. 1. The right of citizens of the United States to vote shall not be denied or abridged by the United States or by any State on account of sex.

2. The Congress shall have power to enforce this article by appropriate legislation. [Adopted 1920.]

Article XX. Presidential and Congressional Terms

Shortens lame-duck periods by modifying Art. I, Sec. IV, para. 2; see p. 850 and below.

1. Presidential, vice-presidential, and Congressional terms of office begin in January. The terms of the President and Vice-President shall end at noon on the 20th day of January, and the terms of Senators and Representatives at noon on the 3d day of January, of the years in which such terms would have ended if this article had not been ratified; and the terms of their successors shall then begin.

2. New meeting date for Congress. The Congress shall assemble at least once in every year, and such meeting shall begin at noon on the 3d day of January, unless they shall by law appoint a different day.

3. **Emergency presidential and vice-presidential succession.** If, at the time fixed for the beginning of the term of the President, the President-elect shall have died, the Vice-President-elect shall become President. If a President shall not have been chosen before the time fixed for the beginning of his term, or if the President-elect shall have failed to qualify, then the Vice-President-elect shall act as President until a President shall have qualified; and the Congress may by law provide for the case wherein neither a President-elect nor a Vice-President-elect shall have qualified, declaring who shall then act as President, or the manner in which one who is to act shall be selected, and such persons shall act accordingly until a President or Vice-President shall have qualified.

4. The Congress may by law provide for the case of the death of any of the persons from whom the House of Representatives may choose a President whenever the right of choice shall have devolved upon them, and for the case of the death of any of the persons from whom the Senate may choose a Vice-President whenever the right of choice shall have devolved upon them.

5. Sections 1 and 2 shall take effect on the 15th day of October following the ratification of this article.

6. This article shall be inoperative unless it shall have been ratified as an amendment to the Constitution by the Legislatures of three-fourths of the several States within seven years from the date of its submission. [Adopted 1933.]

Article XXI. Prohibition Repealed

For background see p. 842. 1. **18th Amendment repealed.** The eighteenth article of amendment to the Constitution of the United States is hereby repealed.

2. **Local laws honored.** The transportation or importation into any State, Territory, or Possession of the United States for delivery or use therein of intoxicating liquors, in violation of the laws thereof, is hereby prohibited.

3. This article shall be inoperative unless it shall have been ratified as an amendment to the Constitution by conventions in the several States, as provided in the Constitution, within seven years from the date of the submission thereof to the States by the Congress. [Adopted 1933.]

Article XXII. Anti-Third Term Amendment

Presidential term is limited. 1. No person shall be elected to *For background see p. 932.* the office of President more than twice, and no person who has held the office of President, or acted as President, for more than two years of a term to which some other person was elected President shall be elected to the office of President more than once. But this article shall not apply to any person holding the office of President when this article was proposed by the Congress [i.e., Truman], and shall not prevent any person who may be holding the office of President, or acting as President, during the term within which this article becomes operative [i.e., Truman] from holding the office of President or acting as President during the remainder of such term.

2. This article shall be inoperative unless it shall have been ratified as an amendment to the Constitution by the legislatures of three-fourths of the several States within seven years from the date of its submission to the States by the Congress. [Adopted 1951.]

Article XXIII. District of Columbia Vote

1. Presidential Electors for the District of Columbia. The District constituting the seat of Government of the United States shall appoint in such manner as the Congress may direct:

A number of electors of President and Vice-President equal to the whole number of Senators and Representatives in Congress to which the District would be entitled if it were a State, but in no event more than the least populous State; they shall be in addition to those appointed by the States, but they shall be considered for the purposes of the election of President and Vice-President, to be electors appointed by a State; and they shall meet in the District and perform such duties as provided by the twelfth article of amendment. [Adopted 1961.]

2. Enforcement. The Congress shall have the power to enforce this article by appropriate legislation.

Article XXIV. Poll Tax

1. Payment of poll tax or other taxes not to be prerequisite for voting in federal elections. The right of citizens of the United States to vote in any primary or other election for President or Vice-President, for electors for President or Vice-President, or for Senator or Representative in Congress, shall not be denied or abridged by the United States or any State by reason of failure to pay any poll tax or other tax.

2. Enforcement. The Congress shall have the power to enforce this article by appropriate legislation. [Adopted 1964.]

GROWTH OF U. S. POPULATION AND AREA

Census	Population of Continental U. S.	Increase over the Preceding Census		Land Area, Sq. Mi.	Pop. per Sq. Mi.
		Number	Percent		
1790	3,929,214	....	....	867,980	4.5
1800	5,308,483	1,379,269	35.1	867,980	6.1
1810	7,239,881	1,931,398	36.4	1,685,865	4.3
1820	9,638,453	2,398,572	33.1	1,753,588	5.5
1830	12,866,020	3,227,567	33.5	1,753,588	7.3
1840	17,069,453	4,203,433	32.7	1,753,588	9.7
1850	23,191,876	6,122,423	35.9	2,944,337	7.9
1860	31,443,321	8,251,445	35.6	2,973,965	10.6
1870	39,818,449	8,375,128	26.6	2,973,965	13.4
1880	50,155,783	10,337,334	26.0	2,973,965	16.9
1890	62,947,714	12,791,931	25.5	2,973,965	21.2
1900	75,994,575	13,046,861	20.7	2,974,159	25.6
1910	91,972,266	15,977,691	21.0	2,973,890	30.9
1920	105,710,620	13,738,354	14.9	2,973,776	35.5
1930	122,775,046	17,064,426	16.1	2,977,128	41.2
1940	131,669,275	8,894,229	7.2	2,977,128	44.2
1950	150,697,361	19,028,086	14.5	2,974,726*	50.7
† 1960	178,464,236	27,766,875	18.4	2,974,726	59.9

* As remeasured in 1940; shrinkage offset by increase in water area.
† Exclusive of Alaska (pop. 226,167) and Hawaii (632,772).

ADMISSION OF STATES

(See p. 146 for order in which the original thirteen entered the Union.)

Order of Admission	State	Date of Admission	Order of Admission	State	Date of Admission
14	Vermont	March 4, 1791	33	Oregon	February 14, 1859
15	Kentucky	June 1, 1792	34	Kansas	January 29, 1861
16	Tennessee	June 1, 1796	35	West Virginia	June 20, 1863
17	Ohio	March 1, 1803	36	Nevada	October 31, 1864
18	Louisiana	April 30, 1812	37	Nebraska	March 1, 1867
19	Indiana	December 11, 1816	38	Colorado	August 1, 1876
20	Mississippi	December 10, 1817	39	North Dakota	November 2, 1889
21	Illinois	December 3, 1818	40	South Dakota	November 2, 1889
22	Alabama	December 14, 1819	41	Montana	November 8, 1889
23	Maine	March 15, 1820	42	Washington	November 11, 1889
24	Missouri	August 10, 1821	43	Idaho	July 3, 1890
25	Arkansas	June 15, 1836	44	Wyoming	July 10, 1890
26	Michigan	January 26, 1837	45	Utah	January 4, 1896
27	Florida	March 3, 1845	46	Oklahoma	November 16, 1907
28	Texas	December 29, 1845	47	New Mexico	January 6, 1912
29	Iowa	December 28, 1846	48	Arizona	February 14, 1912
30	Wisconsin	May 29, 1848	49	Alaska	January 3, 1959
31	California	September 9, 1850	50	Hawaii	August 21, 1959
32	Minnesota	May 11, 1858			

PRESIDENTIAL ELECTIONS *

Election	Candidates	Parties	Popular Vote	Electoral Vote
1789	GEORGE WASHINGTON	No party designations		69
	John Adams			34
	Minor Candidates			35
1792	GEORGE WASHINGTON	No party designations		132
	John Adams			77
	George Clinton			50
	Minor Candidates			5
1796	JOHN ADAMS	Federalist		71
	Thomas Jefferson	Democratic-Republican		68
	Thomas Pinckney	Federalist		59
	Aaron Burr	Democratic-Republican		30
	Minor Candidates			48
1800	THOMAS JEFFERSON	Democratic-Republican		73
	Aaron Burr	Democratic-Republican		73
	John Adams	Federalist		65
	Charles C. Pinckney	Federalist		64
	John Jay	Federalist		1
1804	THOMAS JEFFERSON	Democratic-Republican		162
	Charles C. Pinckney	Federalist		14
1808	JAMES MADISON	Democratic-Republican		122
	Charles C. Pinckney	Federalist		47
	George Clinton	Democratic-Republican		6
1812	JAMES MADISON	Democratic-Republican		128
	DeWitt Clinton	Federalist		89
1816	JAMES MONROE	Democratic-Republican		183
	Rufus King	Federalist		34
1820	JAMES MONROE	Democratic-Republican		231
	John Q. Adams	Independent Republican		1
1824	JOHN Q. ADAMS (Min.)†	Democratic-Republican	108,740	84
	Andrew Jackson	Democratic-Republican	153,544	99
	William H. Crawford	Democratic-Republican	46,618	41
	Henry Clay	Democratic-Republican	47,136	37
1828	ANDREW JACKSON	Democratic	647,286	178
	John Q. Adams	National Republican	508,064	83
1832	ANDREW JACKSON	Democratic	687,502	219
	Henry Clay	National Republican	530,189	49
	William Wirt	Anti-Masonic	33,108	7
	John Floyd	National Republican		11
1836	MARTIN VAN BUREN	Democratic	762,678	170
	William H. Harrison	Whig		73
	Hugh L. White	Whig	736,656	26
	Daniel Webster	Whig		14
	W. P. Mangum	Whig		11
1840	WILLIAM H. HARRISON	Whig	1,275,016	234
	Martin Van Buren	Democratic	1,129,102	60

* Candidates receiving less than 1% of the popular vote are omitted. Before the 12th Amendment (1804) the Electoral College voted for two presidential candidates, and the runner-up became Vice-President. Basic figures are taken from *Historical Statistics of the United States, 1789–1945*, pp. 288–290.
† "Min." indicates minority President—one receiving less than 50% of all popular votes.

Election	Candidates	Parties	Popular Vote	Electoral Vote
1844	JAMES K. POLK (Min.) *	Democratic	1,337,243	170
	Henry Clay	Whig	1,299,062	105
	James G. Birney	Liberty	62,300	
1848	ZACHARY TAYLOR (Min.) *	Whig	1,360,099	163
	Lewis Cass	Democratic	1,220,544	127
	Martin Van Buren	Free Soil	291,263	
1852	FRANKLIN PIERCE	Democratic	1,601,274	254
	Winfield Scott	Whig	1,386,580	42
	John P. Hale	Free Soil	155,825	
1856	JAMES BUCHANAN (Min.) *	Democratic	1,838,169	174
	John C. Frémont	Republican	1,341,264	114
	Millard Fillmore	American	874,534	8
1860	ABRAHAM LINCOLN (Min.) *	Republican	1,866,452	180
	Stephen A. Douglas	Democratic	1,375,157	12
	John C. Breckinridge	Democratic	847,953	72
	John Bell	Constitutional Union	590,631	39
1864	ABRAHAM LINCOLN	Union	2,213,665	212
	George B. McClellan	Democratic	1,802,237	21
1868	ULYSSES S. GRANT	Republican	3,012,833	214
	Horatio Seymour	Democratic	2,703,249	80
1872	ULYSSES S. GRANT	Republican	3,597,132	286
	Horace Greeley	Democratic and Liberal Republican	2,834,125	66
1876	RUTHERFORD B. HAYES (Min.) *	Republican	4,036,298	185
	Samuel J. Tilden	Democratic	4,300,590	184
1880	JAMES A. GARFIELD (Min.) *	Republican	4,454,416	214
	Winfield S. Hancock	Democratic	4,444,952	155
	James B. Weaver	Greenback-Labor	308,578	
1884	GROVER CLEVELAND (Min.) *	Democratic	4,874,986	219
	James G. Blaine	Republican	4,851,981	182
	Benjamin F. Butler	Greenback-Labor	175,370	
	John P. St. John	Prohibition	150,369	
1888	BENJAMIN HARRISON (Min.) *	Republican	5,439,853	233
	Grover Cleveland	Democratic	5,540,309	168
	Clinton B. Fisk	Prohibition	249,506	
	Anson J. Streeter	Union Labor	146,935	
1892	GROVER CLEVELAND (Min.) *	Democratic	5,556,918	277
	Benjamin Harrison	Republican	5,176,108	145
	James B. Weaver	People's	1,041,028	22
	John Bidwell	Prohibition	264,133	
1896	WILLIAM McKINLEY	Republican	7,104,779	271
	William J. Bryan	Democratic	6,502,925	176
1900	WILLIAM McKINLEY	Republican	7,207,923	292
	William J. Bryan	Democratic; Populist	6,358,133	155
	John C. Woolley	Prohibition	208,914	
1904	THEODORE ROOSEVELT	Republican	7,623,486	336
	Alton B. Parker	Democratic	5,077,911	140
	Eugene V. Debs	Socialist	402,283	
	Silas C. Swallow	Prohibition	258,536	

* "Min." indicates minority President—one receiving less than 50% of all popular votes.

Election	Candidates	Parties	Popular Vote	Electoral Vote
1908	WILLIAM H. TAFT	Republican	7,678,908	321
	William J. Bryan	Democratic	6,409,104	162
	Eugene V. Debs	Socialist	420,793	
	Eugene W. Chafin	Prohibition	253,840	
1912	WOODROW WILSON (Min.)*	Democratic	6,293,454	435
	Theodore Roosevelt	Progressive	4,119,538	88
	William H. Taft	Republican	3,484,980	8
	Eugene V. Debs	Socialist	900,672	
	Eugene W. Chafin	Prohibition	206,275	
1916	WOODROW WILSON (Min.)*	Democratic	9,129,606	277
	Charles E. Hughes	Republican	8,538,221	254
	A. L Benson	Socialist	585,113	
	J. F. Hanly	Prohibition	220,506	
1920	WARREN G. HARDING	Republican	16,152,200	404
	James M. Cox	Democratic	9,147,353	127
	Eugene V. Debs	Socialist	919,799	
	P. P. Christensen	Farmer-Labor	265,411	
1924	CALVIN COOLIDGE	Republican	15,725,016	382
	John W. Davis	Democratic	8,386,503	136
	Robert M. La Follette	Progressive	4,822,856	13
1928	HERBERT C. HOOVER	Republican	21,391,381	444
	Alfred E. Smith	Democratic	15,016,443	87
1932	FRANKLIN D. ROOSEVELT	Democratic	22,821,857	472
	Herbert C. Hoover	Republican	15,761,841	59
	Norman Thomas	Socialist	881,951	
1936	FRANKLIN D. ROOSEVELT	Democratic	27,751,597	523
	Alfred M. Landon	Republican	16,679,583	8
	William Lemke	Union, etc.	882,479	
1940	FRANKLIN D. ROOSEVELT	Democratic	27,244,160	449
	Wendell L. Wilkie	Republican	22,305,198	82
1944	FRANKLIN D. ROOSEVELT	Democratic	25,602,504	432
	Thomas E. Dewey	Republican	22,006,285	99
1948	HARRY S. TRUMAN (Min.)*	Democratic	24,105,695	303
	Thomas E. Dewey	Republican	21,969,170	189
	J. Strom Thurmond	States' Rights Democratic	1,169,021	39
	Henry A. Wallace	Progressive	1,156,103	
1952	DWIGHT D. EISENHOWER	Republican	33,778,963	442
	Adlai E. Stevenson	Democratic	27,314,992	89
1956	DWIGHT D. EISENHOWER	Republican	35,590,472	457
	Adlai E. Stevenson	Democratic	26,022,752	73
1960	JOHN F. KENNEDY (Min.)*	Democratic	34,221,531	303
	Richard M. Nixon	Republican	34,108,474	219
1964	LYNDON B. JOHNSON	Democratic	43,121,085	486
	Barry M. Goldwater	Republican	27,145,161	52

* "Min." indicates minority President—one receiving less than 50% of all popular votes.

PRESIDENTS AND VICE-PRESIDENTS

Term	President	Vice-President
1789–1793	George Washington	John Adams
1793–1797	George Washington	John Adams
1797–1801	John Adams	Thomas Jefferson
1801–1805	Thomas Jefferson	Aaron Burr
1805–1809	Thomas Jefferson	George Clinton
1809–1813	James Madison	George Clinton (d. 1812)
1813–1817	James Madison	Elbridge Gerry (d. 1814)
1817–1821	James Monroe	Daniel D. Tompkins
1821–1825	James Monroe	Daniel D. Tompkins
1825–1829	John Quincy Adams	John C. Calhoun
1829–1833	Andrew Jackson	John C. Calhoun (resigned 1832)
1833–1837	Andrew Jackson	Martin Van Buren
1837–1841	Martin Van Buren	Richard M. Johnson
1841–1845	William H. Harrison (d. 1841) John Tyler	John Tyler
1845–1849	James K. Polk	George M. Dallas
1849–1853	Zachary Taylor (d. 1850) Millard Fillmore	Millard Fillmore
1853–1857	Franklin Pierce	William R. D. King (d. 1853)
1857–1861	James Buchanan	John C. Breckinridge
1861–1865	Abraham Lincoln	Hannibal Hamlin
1865–1869	Abraham Lincoln (d. 1865) Andrew Johnson	Andrew Johnson
1869–1873	Ulysses S. Grant	Schuyler Colfax
1873–1877	Ulysses S. Grant	Henry Wilson (d. 1875)
1877–1881	Rutherford B. Hayes	William A. Wheeler
1881–1885	James A. Garfield (d. 1881) Chester A. Arthur	Chester A. Arthur
1885–1889	Grover Cleveland	Thomas A. Hendricks (d. 1885)
1889–1893	Benjamin Harrison	Levi P. Morton
1893–1897	Grover Cleveland	Adlai E. Stevenson
1897–1901	William McKinley	Garret A. Hobart (d. 1899)
1901–1905	William McKinley (d. 1901) Theodore Roosevelt	Theodore Roosevelt
1905–1909	Theodore Roosevelt	Charles W. Fairbanks
1909–1913	William H. Taft	James S. Sherman (d. 1912)
1913–1917	Woodrow Wilson	Thomas R. Marshall
1917–1921	Woodrow Wilson	Thomas R. Marshall
1921–1925	Warren G. Harding (d. 1923) Calvin Coolidge	Calvin Coolidge
1925–1929	Calvin Coolidge	Charles G. Dawes
1929–1933	Herbert C. Hoover	Charles Curtis
1933–1937	Franklin D. Roosevelt	John N. Garner
1937–1941	Franklin D. Roosevelt	John N. Garner
1941–1945	Franklin D. Roosevelt	Henry A. Wallace
1945–1949	Franklin D. Roosevelt (d. 1945) Harry S. Truman	Harry S. Truman
1949–1953	Harry S. Truman	Alben W. Barkley
1953–1957	Dwight D. Eisenhower	Richard M. Nixon
1957–1961	Dwight D. Eisenhower	Richard M. Nixon
1961–1965	John F. Kennedy (d. 1963) Lyndon B. Johnson	Lyndon B. Johnson
1965–	Lyndon B. Johnson	Hubert H. Humphrey, Jr.

SUPPLEMENTARY BIBLIOGRAPHY

The brief book lists at the ends of the foregoing chapters are designed to stimulate further reading. Highly selective, they generally stress the "three R's" —reliability, recency, and readability. The publication of the invaluable *Harvard Guide to American History* (ed. Oscar Handlin, *et al.,* 1954) has made extensive book lists superfluous. The following titles supplement the end-chapter bibliographies, and should be used in connection with them.

GENERAL REFERENCE WORKS. *The Dictionary of American Biography* (ed. Allen Johnson, *et al.,* 22 vols., 1928–1958) is a magnificent set. It contains detailed sketches of prominent figures, briefer ones of lesser figures, and extensive references for further reading. (For Autobiographies and Biographies see also *Harvard Guide*, pp. 177–206.)

Projected on a smaller scale, but still useful, is the *Dictionary of American History* (ed. J. T. Adams and R. V. Coleman, 5 vols., 1940), which contains helpful entries under various topics.

Of the major cooperative sets, highest rank must be given to *The New American Nation Series* (eds. H. S. Commager and R. B. Morris, 1954–   ), planned for some fifty volumes, of which about twenty have now appeared, all in hard cover and paperback.

Brief biographies comprise *The Library of American Biography* (Oscar Handlin, ed., 1954–1959), in which nineteen volumes have appeared, most of them now paperbacked.

Brief paperbacked and hardbound surveys of the main themes of American history are included in the *Chicago History of American Civilization Series* (D. J. Boorstin, ed., 1951–   ), of which twenty-one volumes have been published.

Surveys of the six periods of American History are included in *The Making of America Series* (David Donald, ed., 1961–   ), of which five volumes have been published in hard cover and paperback.

GENERAL HISTORIES. The multi-volume histories by pioneer writers are listed in the *Harvard Guide*, pp. 209–210. Still worth reading are Henry Adams' beautifully written though highly detailed *History of the United States of America during the Administration of Jefferson and Madison* (9 vols., 1889–1891); J. B. McMaster's factual but somewhat disjointed coverage of the years from 1783 to 1865 in *A History of the People of the United States* (9 vols., 1883–1927), with emphasis on social history drawn from newspaper sources; E. P. Oberholtzer's (a pupil of McMaster) richly detailed *A History of the United States since the Civil War* (5 vols., 1917–1937), which carries the story to 1901 in the McMaster manner; and C. A. and M. R. Beard's challenging *The Rise of American Civilization* (4 vols., 1927–1942), with its strong emphasis on economic determinism. For the colonial period two remarkably thorough multi-volume works must be cited: C. M. Andrews, *The Colonial Period of American History* (4 vols., 1934–1938) [**paperback**] and L. H. Gipson, *The British Empire before the American Revolution* (9 vols., 1936–1956).

CONSERVATION. See FRONTIER AND WESTWARD MOVEMENT.

THE CONSTITUTION AND THE JUDICIARY. Two of the most recent one-volume treatises of merit are A. H. Kelly and W. A. Harbison, *The American*

Constitution (1955) and C. B. Swisher, *American Constitutional Development* (1954). More detailed coverage to 1876 may be found in H. C. Hockett, *The Constitutional History of the United States, 1776–1876* (2 vols., 1939). The most comprehensive account of its subject is Charles Warren, *The Supreme Court in United States History* (2 vols., 1947). More recent titles are Edward Dumbauld, *The Constitution of the United States* (1964); Charles Leedham, *Our Changing Constitution* (1964); Bernard Schwartz, *The Reins of Power: A Constitutional History of the United States* (1963); J. A. Garraty, ed., *Quarrels That Have Shaped the Constitution* (1964); R. G. McCloskey, *The American Supreme Court* (1960) [**paperback**]; A. T. Mason, *The Supreme Court from Taft to Warren* (1958) [**paperback**].

DIPLOMACY AND FOREIGN POLICY. T. A. Bailey, *A Diplomatic History of the American People* (7th ed., 1964) tells the story with emphasis on public opinion and with extensive bibliographies. Among other recent surveys are S. F. Bemis, *A Diplomatic History of the United States* (5th ed., 1965); Alexander DeConde, *A History of American Foreign Policy* (1963); R. W. Leopold, *The Growth of American Foreign Policy* (1962). Informative sketches appear in *The American Secretaries of State and Their Diplomacy* (ed. S. F. Bemis, 10 vols., 1927–1929), and currently being brought up to date in additional volumes by editor R. H. Ferrell. See also N. A. Graebner, ed., *An Uncertain Tradition: American Secretaries of State in the Twentieth Century* (1961) [**paperback**] and Alexander DeConde, *The American Secretary of State: An Interpretation* (1962) [**paperback**]. Regional coverage may be found in Dexter Perkins, *A History of the Monroe Doctrine* (new ed., 1955) [**paperback**]; S. F. Bemis, *The Latin American Policy of the United States* (1943); A. W. Griswold, *The Far Eastern Policy of the United States* (1938) [**paperback**]. See also Selig Adler, *The Isolationist Impulse: Its Twentieth-Century Reaction* (1957) [**paperback**].

ECONOMIC AND FINANCIAL HISTORY. See the projected ten-volume *The Economic History of the United States* edited by Henry David, *et al.* (1945–   ). Of the numerous standard textbooks on economic history the best known are perhaps H. U. Faulkner, *American Economic History* (8th ed., 1960); E. C. Kirkland, *A History of American Economic Life* (3d ed., 1951); and F. A. Shannon, *America's Economic Growth* (3d ed., 1951). A cut-and-dried guidebook is D. R. Dewey, *Financial History of the United States* (12th ed., 1936). Interpretive fare abounds in T. C. Cochran and W. Miller, *The Age of Enterprise* (1942) [**paperback**]; L. M. Hacker, *The Triumph of American Capitalism* (1940) [**paperback**]; Joseph Dorfman, *The Economic Mind in American Civilization* (5 vols., 1946–1959); C. D. North, *The Economic Growth of the United States, 1790–1860* (1961); and John Chamberlain, *The Enterprising Americans: A Business History of the United States* (1963) [**paperback**]. A classic treatment is F. W. Taussig, *The Tariff History of the United States* (8th ed., 1931). A famous muckraking exposé is Gustavus Myers, *History of the Great American Fortunes* (3 vols., 1910). Special topics are expertly handled in Clive Day, *History of Commerce of the United States* (1925); Bray Hammond, *Banks and Politics in America from the Revolution to the Civil War* (1957); Milton Friedman and Anna J. Schwartz, *A Monetary History of the United States, 1867–1960* (1963); P. B. Trescott, *Financing American Enterprise: The Story of Commercial Banking* (1963); N. S. B. Gras, *History of Agriculture in Europe and America* (1925); and J. R. Spears, *The Story of the American Merchant Marine* (new ed., 1915).

EDUCATION. Standard surveys are E. P. Cubberley, *Public Education in the United States* (rev. ed., 1934); E. W. Knight, *Education in the United States* (3rd ed., 1951); A. E. Meyer, *An Educational History of the American People* (1957); and E. W. Knight, *Fifty Years of American Education* (1952). More recent titles are M. E. Curti, *The Social Ideas of American Educators* (rev. ed., 1959) [**paperback**]; Frederick Rudolph, *The American College and University: A History* (1962); Allan Nevins, *The State Universities and Democracy* (1962); Rush Welter, *Popular Education and Democratic Thought in America* (1962); and Richard Hofstadter and Wilson Smith, eds., *American Higher Education: A Documentary History* (2 vols., 1961).

FOREIGN VISITORS. An astute analysis by a Frenchman in the 1830's is Alexis de Tocqueville, *Democracy in America* (ed. Phillips Bradley, 2 vols., 1945) [**paperback**]. No less acute are the observations of two Britishers, James Bryce, in *The American Commonwealth* (2 vols., 1888) and D. W. Brogan, *The American Character* (1944) [**paperback**]. Choice selections of foreign comments appear in Allan Nevins, *America through British Eyes* (1948); Oscar Handlin, *This Was America* (1949) [**paperback**]; and H. S. Commager, *America in Perspective* (1947) [**paperback**]. Also *Harvard Guide*, pp. 150–161.

FRONTIER AND WESTWARD MOVEMENT. Of the half-dozen general introductory treatises, R. A. Billington, *Westward Expansion* (2d ed., 1960), which contains exceptionally full bibliographies, is noteworthy for its comprehensiveness and briskness. It develops the emphasis so brilliantly pioneered by F. J. Turner, *The Frontier in American History* (1921). See also T. D. Clark, *Frontier America: The Story of the Westward Movement* (1959); R. E. Riegel, *America Moves West* (3d ed., 1956); T. S. Miyakawa, *Protestants and Pioneers* (1964); and A. K. Moore, *The Frontier Mind* (1957) [**paperback**]. Popularized is Dale Van Every, *The Frontier People of America* (4 vols., 1961–1964). Solid coverage from the legislative standpoint may be found in R. M. Robbins, *Our Landed Heritage: The Public Domain, 1776–1936* (1942) [**paperback**]. See also H. N. Smith, *Virgin Land* (1950) [**paperback**] and Marion Clawson, *Man and Land in the United States* (1965). The problems of the red man are set forth anthropologically and ethnologically in Clark Wissler, *Indians of the United States* (1940) and Paul Radin, *The Story of the American Indian* (1937). A capsuled **paperback** is W. T. Hagan, *American Indians* (1961). An able treatment of conservation is C. R. Van Hise, *The Conservation of Natural Resources in the United States* (1915). See also GEOGRAPHY AND MAPS.

GEOGRAPHY AND MAPS. The most useful study is perhaps R. H. Brown, *Historical Geography of the United States* (1948), although one must not ignore E. C. Semple's older *American History and Its Geographic Conditions* (rev. ed., 1933). A splendid collection of maps appears in C. O. Paullin, *Atlas of the Historical Geography of the United States* (1932). Less comprehensive and bulky are C. L. and E. H. Lord, *Historical Atlas of the United States* (1944) and J. T. Adams, ed., *Atlas of American History* (1943). For additional references to maps see *Harvard Guide*, pp. 70–76.

IMMIGRATION. The best general coverage is Carl Wittke, *We Who Built America* (new ed., 1964) [**paperback**]. More sketchy is M. A. Jones, *American Immigration* (1960) [**paperback**]. See also M. L. Hansen, *The Immigrant in American History* (1940) [**paperback**]; Carl Wittke, *The Irish in America* (1956); and Oscar Handlin, *The Uprooted* (1953) [Pulitzer prize, **paperback**] and *Race and Nationality in American Life* (1957) [**paperback**]. Recent trends are developed in R. A. Divine, *American Immigration Policy, 1924–1952* (1957).

INDIANS. See FRONTIER AND WESTWARD MOVEMENT.

INTELLECTUAL HISTORY. The ablest general coverage is Merle Curti's Pulitzer-prize *The Growth of American Thought* (rev. ed., 1951). Somewhat outmoded but still brilliantly provocative is V. L. Parrington, *Main Currents in American Thought* (3 vols., 1927–1930), a Pulitzer-prize classic [**paperback**] which betrays the bias of a Jeffersonian liberal. See also R. H. Gabriel, *The Course of American Democratic Thought* (2d ed., 1956) and Stow Persons, *American Minds: A History of Ideas* (1958). General coverage is found in N. M. Blake, *A History of American Life and Thought* (1963) and Harvey Wish, *Society and Thought in Early America* (1950) and *Society and Thought in Modern America* (2d ed., 1962). Special topics are handled by Richard Hofstadter's Pulitzer-prize *Anti-Intellectualism in American Life* (1963); P. C. Nagel, *One Nation Indivisible: The Union in American Thought, 1776–1861* (1964); Y. Arieli, *Individualism and Nationalism in American Ideology* (1964); Cushing Strout, *The American Image of the Old World* (1963); Loren Baritz, *City on a Hill: A History of Ideas and Myths in America* (1964); S. K. Padover, *The Genius of America* (1960).

JOURNALISM. A brief introduction is B. A. Weisberger, *The American Newspaperman* (1961) [**paperback**]; much more detailed is F. L. Mott, *American Journalism* (3d ed., 1962), a standard work. For magazines, see the same author's Pulitzer-prize *A History of American Magazines* (4 vols., 1930–1957).

LABOR. Useful surveys are J. G. Rayback, *A History of American Labor* (1959); F. R. Dulles, *Labor in America: A History* (1960); Henry Pelling, *American Labor* (1960) [**paperback**]; N. J. Ware, *The Labor Movement in the United States, 1860–1895* (1929) [**paperback**]. One should not overlook the *History of Labour in the United States* by J. R. Commons, *et al.* (4 vols., 1951–1952). Standard on the subject are Selig Perlman, *A History of Trade Unionism in the United States* (1922) and Philip Taft, *Organized Labor in American History* (1964).

LAND. See FRONTIER AND WESTWARD MOVEMENT.

LITERATURE AND THE ARTS. The most recent detailed and high-grade treatment is *Literary History of the United States* by R. E. Spiller, *et al.* (3 vols., 1948). O. W. Larkin, *Art and Life in America* (1949) is a broad-gauge approach which won a Pulitzer prize. Competent for their subjects are Lorado Taft, *The History of American Sculpture* (new ed., 1930); T. E. Tallmadge, *The Story of Architecture in America* (rev. ed., 1936); Wayne Andrews, *Architecture in America* (1960); John Burchard and A. Bush-Brown, *The Architecture of America* (1961); Virgil Barker, *American Painting* (1950); E. P. Richardson, *Painting in America* (1956); A. H. Quinn, *A History of the American Drama* (rev. ed., 1943); and J. T. Howard, *Our American Music* (3d ed., 1946).

MERCHANT MARINE. J. R. Spears, *The Story of the American Merchant Marine* (new ed., 1915).

MILITARY AND NAVAL. General accounts are O. W. Spaulding, *The United States Army in War and Peace* (1937); Walter Millis, *Arms and Men*

(1956) [paperback]; R. E. and T. N. Dupuy, *Military Heritage of America* (1956). Broadly conceived are Harold and Margaret Sprout, *The Rise of American Naval Power, 1776–1918* (1939); G. T. Davis, *A Navy Second to None* (1940); and D. W. Knox, *A History of the United States Navy* (rev. ed., 1948). More technical is E. B. Potter, *et al.*, *Sea Power: A Naval History* (1960). Monumental is V. J. Esposito, ed., *The West Point Atlas of American Wars* (2 vols., 1959). Special topics are treated in T. H. Williams, *Americans at War: The Development of the American Military System* (1960) [paperback]; R. F. Weigley, *Towards an American Army: Military Thought from Washington to Marshall* (1962); P. Y. Hammond, *Organization for Defense: The American Military Establishment in the Twentieth Century* (1961); E. R. May, ed., *The Ultimate Decision: The President as Commander in Chief* (1960).

MONEY. See ECONOMIC AND FINANCIAL HISTORY.

NEGRO. The story is set forth in J. H. Franklin's sympathetic *From Slavery to Freedom* (2d ed., 1956); sketchily in Nathaniel Weyl, *The Negro in American Civilization* (1960). See also R. W. Logan, *The Negro in the United States* (1957) [paperback] and his *The Negro in American Life and Thought* (1954) [paperback]; Lerone Bennett, *Before the Mayflower: A History of the Negro in America, 1619–1962* (1962); E. E. Thorpe, *The Mind of the Negro* (1961).

PHILANTHROPY. See R. H. Bremner, *American Philanthropy* (1960) [paperback]; Merle Curti, *American Philanthropy Overseas* (1962).

PHILOSOPHY. H. W. Schneider, *A History of American Philosophy* (1946); W. H. Werkmeister, *A History of Philosophical Ideas in America* (1949) are general.

PICTORIAL HISTORY. A veritable picture-gallery of the republic is *The Pageant of America* (ed. R. H. Gabriel, 15 vols., 1925–1929). Less exhaustive is the *Album of American History* (ed. J. T. Adams, *et al.*, 5 vols., 1944–1960). More popularized, and with historical narrative, are M. B. Davidson, *Life in America* (2 vols., 1951) and Roger Butterfield, *The American Past* (1947). See also references in *Harvard Guide*, pp. 65–68.

POLITICS, POLITICAL PARTIES, AND POLITICAL THEORY. W. E. Binkley, *American Political Parties* (3d ed., 1958) is a textbook. See also Eugene Roseboom, *A History of Presidential Elections* (1957); G. H. Mayer, *The Republican Party, 1854–1964* (1964); W. N. Chambers, *The Democrats, 1789–1964* (1964) [paperback]; H. A. Eaton, *Presidential Timber: A History of Nominating Conventions, 1868–1960* (1964). Also useful are Richard Hofstadter, *The American Political Tradition and the Men Who Made It* (1948) [paperback]; P. P. Van Riper, *History of the United States Civil Service* (1958); and R. G. Gettell, *History of American Political Thought* (1928).

RELIGION. See C. E. Olmstead, *History of Religion in the United States* (1960); W. W. Sweet, *The Story of Religions in America* (rev. ed., 1939). Useful paperbacks are J. T. Ellis, *American Catholicism* (1956); Nathan Glazer, *American Judaism* (1957); T. F. O'Dea, *The Mormons* (1957); Winthrop Hudson, *American Protestantism* (1961). See also E. S. Gaustad, *Historical Atlas of Religion in America* (1962).

SCIENCE AND INVENTION. Two of the most useful works are Bernard Jaffe, *Men of Science in America* (1944) and *A Popular History of American Inventions* (ed. W. B. Kaempffert, 2 vols., 1924). See also Roger Burlingame, *March of the Iron Men* (1938) [paperback]. A competent treatment is F. R. Packard, *History of Medicine in the United States* (2 vols., 1931). See also J. W. Oliver, *History of American Technology* (1956).

SECTIONS AND SECTIONAL HISTORIES. See also FRONTIER AND WESTWARD MOVEMENT; SOUTH. F. J. Turner's Pulitzer-prize (posthumous) *The Significance of Sections in American History* (1932) is a stimulating introduction. Somewhat unsympathetic are J. T. Adams' provocative *The Founding of New England* (1921) [paperback], *Revolutionary New England* (1923), and *New England in the Republic* (1926). Other sectional treatments of quality are J. W. Caughey, *History of the Pacific Coast* (1938) and O. O. Winther, *The Great Northwest* (1947); Earl Pomeroy, *The Pacific Slope* (1965).

SOCIAL HISTORY. See also INTELLECTUAL HISTORY; NEGRO; RELIGION. A treasure trove is *A History of American Life* (ed. A. M. Schlesinger, Sr., and D. R. Fox, 13 vols., 1929–1948). See also E. C. Rozwenc, *The Making of American Society, 1600–1877* (vol. I, 1965) and R. M. Dorson, *American Folklore* (1959) [paperback]. An absorbing narrative is F. R. Dulles, *America Learns to Play* (1940). For reformers, consult Daniel Aaron, *Men of Good Hope* (1951) [paperback]. See also N. M. Blake, *The Road to Reno: A History of Divorce in the United States* (1962); J. C. Furnas, *The Life and Times of the Late Demon Rum* (1965).

SOUTH. See also NEGRO. The fullest coverage is in the ten-volume *A History of the South* (eds. W. H. Stephenson and E. M. Coulter, 1947–   ), of which eight volumes have been published. A textbook survey is W. B. Hesseltine and D. L. Smiley, *The South in American History* (2d ed., 1960). See also C. V. Woodward, *The Burden of Southern History* (1960) [paperback]; Theodore Saloutos, *Farmer Movements in the South, 1865–1933* (1960); J. S. Ezell, *The South Since 1865* (1964).

TECHNOLOGY. See SCIENCE AND INVENTION.

TRAVEL AND TRANSPORTATION. B. H. Meyer, *et al.* offer a meaty survey in *History of Transportation in the United States before 1860* (Washington, 1917). Far more detailed and comprehensive is Seymour Dunbar, *A History of Travel in America* (4 vols., 1915). A popularized version is presented in S. H. Holbrook, *The Story of American Railroads* (1947); a paperback sketch is J. F. Stover, *American Railroads* (1961).

Additional listings of books by topics may be found in the *Harvard Guide*, pp. 211–217.

Index

1234567890

THE UNITED STATES AND ITS POSSESSION.

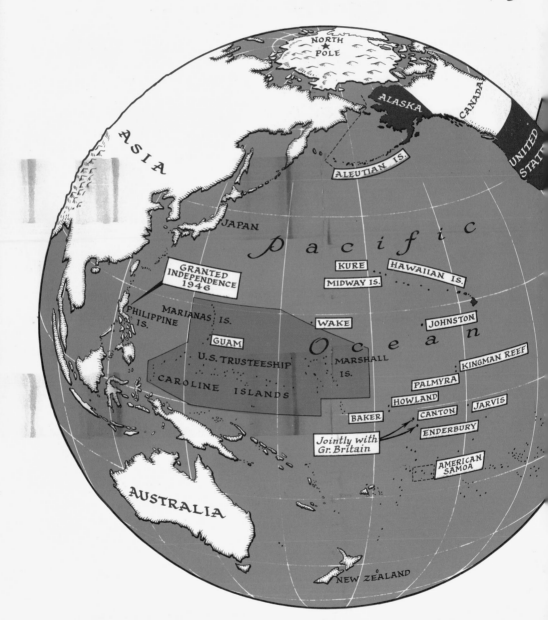

NORTH POLE

ALASKA

CANADA

ASIA

UNITED STATE

ALEUTIAN IS.

JAPAN

Pacific

KURE

HAWAIIAN IS.

MIDWAY IS.

GRANTED
INDEPENDENCE
1946

MARIANAS IS.

WAKE

JOHNSTON

PHILIPPINE
IS.

GUAM

Ocean

U.S. TRUSTEESHIP

MARSHALL
IS.

KINGMAN REEF

CAROLINE   ISLANDS

PALMYRA

HOWLAND

BAKER

CANTON

JARVIS

ENDERBURY

*Jointly with
Gr. Britain*

AMERICAN
SAMOA

AUSTRALIA

NEW ZEALAND